How Children
DEVELOP

FOURTH CANADIAN EDITION

How Children DEVELOP

Robert Siegler
Carnegie Mellon University

Nancy Eisenberg
Arizona State University

Judy DeLoache
University of Virginia

Jenny Saffran
University of Wisconsin–Madison

Susan Graham
University of Calgary

and Campbell Leaper
University of California–Santa Cruz, reviser of Chapter 15: Gender Development

WORTH PUBLISHERS
A Macmillan Higher Education Company

This is dedicated to the ones we love

Senior Vice President, Editorial and Production: Catherine Woods

Publisher: Kevin Feyen

Senior Acquisitions Editor: Daniel DeBonis

Development Editors: Peter Deane; Debbie Smith, First Folio Resource Group Inc.

Copy Editor: Arleane Ralph

Assistant Editor: Nadina Persaud

Executive Marketing Manager: Katherine Nurre

Associate Director of Market Research: Carlise Stembridge

Executive Media Editor: Rachel Comerford

Media Editor: Lauren Samuelson

Associate Media Editor: Anthony Casciano

Director of Editing, Design, and Media Production for the Sciences and Social Sciences: Tracey Kuehn

Managing Editor: Lisa Kinne

Senior Project Editor: Vivien Weiss

Production Manager: Sarah Segal

Art Director: Barbara Reingold

Senior Designer: Kevin Kall

Interior Text Designer: Lissi Sigillo

Permissions Manager: Jennifer Macmillan

Photo Researchers: Elyse Rieder; Maria DeCambra

Art Manager: Matt McAdams

Illustrations: Todd Buck Illustration; Precision Graphics; TSI Graphics, Inc.; MPS Ltd.

Composition: Tom Dart, First Folio Resource Group Inc.

Cover Image: Winter Tree, Snow Sledgers, Calke Abbey, Derby (oil on canvas), Andrew Marcara (Contemporary Artist) / Private Collection / The Bridgeman Art Library

Printing and Binding: Quad/Graphics, Versailles

ISBN-10: 1-4641-0780-7

ISBN-13: 978-1-4641-0780-1

Worth Publishers

41 Madison Avenue

New York, NY 10010

www.worthpublishers.com

about the authors:

Robert Siegler is the Teresa Heinz Professor of Cognitive Psychology at Carnegie Mellon University. He is author of the cognitive development textbook *Children's Thinking* and has written or edited several additional books on child development. His books have been translated into Japanese, Chinese, Korean, Spanish, French, Greek, Hebrew, and Portuguese. In the past few years, he has presented keynote addresses at the conventions of the Cognitive Development Society, the International Society for the Study of Behavioral Development, the Japanese Psychological Association, the Eastern Psychological Association, the American Psychological Society, and the Conference on Human Development. He also has served as Associate Editor of the journal *Developmental Psychology*, co-edited the cognitive development volume of the 2006 *Handbook of Child Psychology*, and served on the National Mathematics Advisory Panel from 2006 to 2008. Dr. Siegler received the American Psychological Association's Distinguished Scientific Contribution Award in 2005, was elected to the National Academy of Education in 2010, and was named Director of the Siegler Center for Innovative Learning at Beijing Normal University in 2012.

Nancy Eisenberg is Regents' Professor of Psychology at Arizona State University. Her research interests include social, emotional, and moral development, as well as socialization influences, especially in the areas of self-regulation and adjustment. She has published numerous empirical studies, as well as books and chapters on these topics. She has also been editor of *Psychological Bulletin* and the *Handbook of Child Psychology* and was the founding editor of the Society for Research in Child Development journal *Child Development Perspectives*. Dr. Eisenberg has been a recipient of Research Scientist Development Awards and a Research Scientist Award from the National Institutes of Health (NICHD and NIMH). She has served as President of the Western Psychological Association and of Division 7 of the American Psychological Association and is president-elect of the Association for Psychological Science. She is the 2007 recipient of the Ernest R. Hilgard Award for a Career Contribution to General Psychology, Division 1, American Psychological Association; the 2008 recipient of the International Society for the Study of Behavioral Development Distinguished Scientific Contribution Award; the 2009 recipient of the G. Stanley Hall Award for Distinguished Contribution to Developmental Psychology, Division 7, American Psychological Association; and the 2011 William James Fellow Award for Career Contributions in the Basic Science of Psychology from the Association for Psychological Science.

Judy DeLoache is the William R. Kenan Jr. Professor of Psychology at the University of Virginia. She has published extensively on aspects of cognitive development in infants and young children. Dr. DeLoache has served as President of the Developmental Division of the American Psychological Association, as President of the Cognitive Development Society, and as a member of the executive board of the International Society for the Study of Infancy. She has presented major invited addresses at professional meetings, including the Association for Psychological Science and the Society for Research in Child Development. Dr. DeLoache is the holder of a Scientific MERIT Award from the National Institutes of Health, and her research is also funded by the National Science Foundation. She has been a visiting fellow at the Center for Advanced Study in the Behavioral Sciences in Palo Alto, California, and at the Rockefeller Foundation Study Center in Bellagio, Italy. She is a Fellow of the National Academy of Arts and Sciences. In 2013, she received the Distinguished Research Contributions Award from the Society for Research in Child Development and the William James Award for Distinguished Contributions to Research from the Association for Psychological Science.

Jenny R. Saffran is the College of Letters & Science Distinguished Professor of Psychology at the University of Wisconsin–Madison, and an investigator at the Waisman Center. Her research is focused on learning in infancy and early childhood, with a particular focus on language. Dr. Saffran currently holds a MERIT award from the Eunice Kennedy Shriver National Institute of Child Health and Human Development. She has been the recipient of numerous awards for her scientific research, including the Boyd McCandless Award from the American Psychological Association for early career contributions to developmental psychology, and the Presidential Early Career Award for Scientists and Engineers from the National Science Foundation.

Susan Graham is a Professor in the Department of Psychology at the University of Calgary and holds the Tier 2 Canada Research Chair in Language and Cognitive Development. She is a fellow of the Association for Psychological Science and is an Associate Editor for the *Journal of Cognition and Development*. After completing her undergraduate degree at the University of Manitoba, she moved to Concordia University to complete her graduate studies. She received her PhD in Clinical Psychology in 1996. Her dissertation research was recognized with the International Society for Infant Studies Student Research Award. Her research focuses on language and cognitive development during the infancy and preschool years and has been funded by NSERC, SSHRC, and the Canada Research Chairs Program.

brief contents:

contents:

preface:

This is an exciting time in the field of child development. The past decade has brought new theories, new ways of thinking, new areas of research, and innumerable new findings to the field. We originally wrote *How Children Develop* to describe this ever-improving body of knowledge of children and their development and to convey our excitement about the progress that is being made in understanding the developmental process. We are pleased to continue this endeavour with the publication of the fourth Canadian edition of *How Children Develop*.

As teachers of child development courses, we appreciate the challenge that instructors face in trying to present these advances and discoveries—as well as the major older ideas and findings—in a one-semester course. Therefore, rather than aim at encyclopedic coverage, we have focused on identifying the most important developmental phenomena and describing them in sufficient depth to make them meaningful and memorable to students. In short, our goal has been to write a textbook that makes the child development course coherent and enjoyable for students and teachers alike.

Classic Themes

The basic premise of the book is that all areas of child development are unified by a small set of enduring themes. These themes can be stated in the form of questions that child development research tries to answer:

1. How do nature and nurture together shape development?
2. How do children shape their own development?
3. In what ways is development continuous and in what ways is it discontinuous?
4. How does change occur?
5. How does the sociocultural context influence development?
6. How do children become so different from one another?
7. How can research promote children's well-being?

These seven themes provide the core structure of the book. They are introduced and illustrated in Chapter 1, highlighted repeatedly, where relevant, in the subsequent fourteen content chapters, and utilized in the final chapter as a framework for integrating findings relevant to each theme from all areas of development. The continuing coverage of these themes allows us to tell a story that has a beginning (the introduction of the themes), a middle (discussion of specific findings relevant to them), and an ending (the overview of what students have learned about the themes). We believe that this thematic emphasis and structure will not only help students understand enduring questions about child development but will also leave them with a greater sense of satisfaction and completion at the end of the course.

Contemporary Perspective

The goal of providing a thoroughly contemporary perspective on how children develop has influenced the organization of our book as well as its contents. Whole new areas and perspectives have emerged that barely existed when most of today's child development textbooks were originally written. The organization of *How Children Develop* is designed to present these new topics and approaches in the context of the field as it currently stands, rather than trying to shoehorn them into organizations that once fit the field but no longer do.

Consider the case of Piaget's theory and current research relevant to it. Piaget's theory often is presented in its own chapter, most of which describes the theory in full detail and the rest of which offers contemporary research that demonstrates problems with the theory. This approach often leaves students wondering why so much time was spent on Piaget's theory if modern research shows it to be wrong in so many ways.

The fact is that the line of research that began over 40 years ago as an effort to challenge Piaget's theory has emerged since then as a vital area in its own right—the area of conceptual development. Research in conceptual development provides extensive information on such fascinating topics as children's understanding of human beings, plants and animals, and the physical universe. As with other research areas, most studies in this field are aimed primarily at uncovering evidence relevant to current claims, not those of Piaget.

We adapted to this changing intellectual landscape in two ways. First, our chapter "Theories of Cognitive Development" (Chapter 4) describes the fundamental aspects of Piaget's theory in depth and honours his legacy by focusing on the aspects of his work that have proven to be the most enduring. Second, a first-of-its-kind chapter called "Conceptual Development" (Chapter 7) addresses the types of issues that inspired Piaget's theory but concentrates on modern perspectives and findings regarding those issues. This approach allows us to tell students about the numerous intriguing proposals and observations that are being made in this field, without the artificiality of classifying the findings as "pro-Piagetian" or "anti-Piagetian."

The opportunity to create a textbook based on current understanding also led us to assign prominent positions to such rapidly emerging areas as epigenetics, behavioural genetics, brain development, prenatal learning, infant cognition, acquisition of academic skills, emotional development, prosocial behaviour, and friendship patterns. All these areas have seen major breakthroughs in recent years, and their growing prominence has led to even greater emphasis on them in this edition.

Getting Right to the Point

Our desire to offer a contemporary, streamlined approach led to other departures from the traditional organization. It is our experience that today's students take child development courses for a variety of practical reasons and are eager to learn about *children*. Traditionally, however, they have had to wait two or three or even four chapters—on the history of the field, on major theories, on research methods, on genetics—before actually getting to the study of children. We wanted to build on their initial motivation from the start.

Rather than beginning the book, then, with an extensive examination of the history of the field, we include in Chapter 1 a brief overview of the social and intellectual context in which the scientific study of children arose and provide historical background wherever it is pertinent in subsequent chapters. Rather than have an early "blockbuster" theories chapter that covers all the major cognitive and social theories at once (at a point far removed from the content chapters to which the theories apply), we present a chapter on cognitive developmental theories just before the chapters that focus on specific aspects of cognitive development, and we similarly present a chapter on social developmental theories just before the chapters that focus on specific aspects of social development. Rather than have a separate chapter on genetics, we include basic aspects of genetics as part of Chapter 3, "Biology and Behaviour," and then discuss the contributions of genetics to some of the differences among individuals throughout the book. When we originally chose this organization, we hoped that it would allow us, from the first weeks of the course, to kindle students' enthusiasm for finding out how children develop. Judging by the overwhelmingly positive response we have received from students and instructors alike, it has.

Features

The most important feature of this book is the exposition, which we have tried to make as clear, compelling, and interesting as possible. As in previous editions, we have given extra attention to making it accessible to a broad range of students.

To further enhance the appeal and accessibility of the text, we have retained three types of discussion boxes that explore topics of special interest. "Applications" boxes focus on how child development research can be used to promote children's well-being. Among the applications that are summed up in these boxes are board-game procedures for improving preschoolers' understanding of numbers; the Better Beginnings, Better Futures project and the Carolina Abecedarian Project; interventions to reduce child abuse; programs, such as PATHS, for helping rejected children gain acceptance from their peers; and Fast Track interventions, which help aggressive children learn how to manage their anger and antisocial behaviour. "Individual Differences" boxes focus on populations that differ from the norm with regard to the specific topic under consideration, or on variations among children in the general population. Some of these boxes highlight developmental problems such as autism, ADHD, dyslexia, specific language impairment, and conduct disorder, while others focus on differences in the development of children that centre on attachment status, gender, and cultural differences. "A Closer Look" boxes examine important and interesting research in greater depth than would otherwise be possible: the areas examined range from brain imaging techniques to discrepant gender identity to the developmental impact of homelessness.

We have also retained a number of other features intended to improve students' learning. These features include boldfacing key terms and supplying definitions both within the immediate text and in marginal glossaries; providing summaries at the end of each major section, as well as summaries for the overall chapter; and, at the end of each chapter, posing critical thinking questions intended to promote deeper consideration of essential topics.

The Canadian Edition

In writing the fourth Canadian edition, we retained all unique features of the original text, including the essential and updated coverage of the fourth American edition. Building on this fourth edition, our goal was to create a textbook that would engage Canadian students by situating the content in Canadian and international contexts, highlighting the remarkable scientific accomplishments of Canadian developmental scientists, drawing upon Canadian issues, and including current Canadian data and statistics whenever possible. We integrate discussion of research conducted with Canadian children and families throughout the chapters, highlighting the research conducted at universities across Canada. Finally, we have included photographs and figures that reflect the Canadian context and Canadian research.

To illustrate how we have incorporated a Canadian perspective, we highlight some of the specific information included across different chapters. Please note that this is by no means an exhaustive list of the Canadian content incorporated in each chapter!

- In our introductory chapter on child development (Chapter 1), we have included recent statistics about the prevalence of spanking in Canada and the percentage of children who live in low-income families. We also incorporate findings from the study of children who were adopted from Romanian orphanages to families in Canada.

- In the chapter on prenatal development and the newborn (Chapter 2), we incorporate Canadian statistics about maternal smoking, the use of alcohol and drugs during pregnancy, sudden infant death syndrome (SIDS), the rate of teenage pregnancies, infant mortality rates (including comparison of rates across provinces and territories, with a focus on the north), newborns with low birth weight, and multiple births.

- When discussing biology and behaviour (Chapter 3), we discuss findings from the Quebec Newborn Twin Study and information about mandated daily physical activity in schools.

- In the chapter on seeing, thinking, and doing in infancy (Chapter 5), we highlight research by Canadian researchers Kang Lee, who looked at other race effect (ORE) in children; Daphne Maurer and Catherine Mondloch, who study face perception of infants; Laurel Trainor and Sandra Trehub, who study infants' responses to music; and Diane Poulin-Dubois, who researches infants' observational learning and imitation.

- In "Development of Language and Symbol Use" (Chapter 6), we cite research from McGill University that provides insight into language and the brain, comparing brain activation in the left hemisphere for hearing speakers of English and deaf signers of American Sign Language (ASL) and Langue des Signes Québécoise (LSQ). We also describe research from Canadian researchers such as Laurel Trainor (McMaster University), Janet Werker (University of British Columbia), Diane Poulin-Dubois (Concordia University), and Geoff Hall (University of British Columbia)—whose research has shaped our understanding of language development. In addition, we discuss bilingualism from a Canadian perspective.

- In the chapter on intelligence and academic achievement (Chapter 8), we describe results of the Better Beginnings, Better Futures program in Ontario as well as Canadian studies on gifted children and the development of reading.

- In "Attachment to Others and Development of Self" (Chapter 11), we highlight Canadian research on maternal attachment, parental sensitivity, ethnic identity, sexual-minority adolescents, and bicultural integration.

- The chapter on the family (Chapter 12) has been heavily revised to represent the Canadian family, including reference to Canadian research on differences in parenting styles, the effects of economic stress on parenting, and the effects of child care on infants and young children. We include statistics on the homeless in Canada and discuss changes in families in Canada (e.g., age at marriage, age of mothers, number of working mothers, births to teens, marriage rate, divorce rate, number of lone-parent families, stepfamilies, and same-sex partners with children)

- "Peer Relationships" (Chapter 13) includes discussion of Canadian research on peer relations, including studies by researchers such as Bill Bukowski, François Poulin, and Sara Pedersen, Frank Vitaro, Tracy Vaillancourt, Shelley Hymel, Robert Coplan, and Wendy Craig. We also include statistics on time spent with friends, adolescents' use of technology, bullying, and cyberbullying

- "Moral Development" (Chapter 14) includes Canadian studies on the relationship between cultural and socioeconomic differences and morality; prosocial behaviour; aggression; and the connection between socioeconomic status and antisocial behaviour. We also highlight the Roots of Empathy program.

In addition to the Canadian focus described above, this edition has all the new and expanded coverage contained in the fourth American edition of *How Children Develop*, including areas in which there has been great progress in the past few years. Among the areas of new and expanded coverage are:

- Gene–environment relations, including methylation and the role of specific gene variants in certain behaviours

- Brain development and functioning

- Epigenetics

- Cultural influences on child development

- Positive effects of play

- Applications of research to education

- Executive functioning

- Relations among understanding of time, space, and number

- Mathematics anxiety

- Infants' understanding of other people

- Mechanisms of infants' learning

- New coverage of programs for helping children with autism spectrum disorders

- Psychological measures of emotion

- Emotional regulation

- Effects of self-esteem

- The growing role and impact of social media in children's and adolescents' lives

- Interventions to foster children's social adjustment.

Supplements

The fourth Canadian edition of *How Children Develop* features a wide array of multimedia tools designed for the individual needs of students and teachers. For more information about any of the items below, visit Worth Publishers' online catalogue at www.worthpublishers.com.

LaunchPad with LearningCurve Quizzing

A comprehensive web resource for teaching and learning psychology

LaunchPad combines Worth Publishers' awarding-winning media with an innovative platform for easy navigation. For students, it is the ultimate online study guide, with rich interactive tutorials, videos, and the LearningCurve adaptive quizzing system. For instructors, LaunchPad is a full course space where class documents can be posted, quizzes are easily assigned and graded, and students' progress can be assessed and recorded. Whether you are looking for the most effective study tools or a robust platform for an online course, LaunchPad is a powerful way to enhance your class.

> LaunchPad for *How Children Develop,* Fourth Canadian Edition, can be previewed and purchased at http://www.worthpublishers.com/launchpad/sieglercanadian4e.
>
> *How Children Develop,* Fourth Canadian Edition, and LaunchPad can be ordered together with ISBN-10: 1-4641-9213-8 / ISBN-13: 978-1-4641-9213-5.

LaunchPad for *How Children Develop,* Fourth Canadian Edition, includes the following resources:

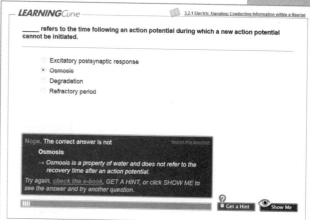

- The **LearningCurve** quizzing system was designed based on the latest findings from learning and memory research. It combines adaptive question selection, immediate and valuable feedback, and a game-like interface to engage students in a learning experience that is unique to them. Each LearningCurve quiz is fully integrated with other resources in LaunchPad through the Personalized Study Plan, so students will be able to review with Worth's extensive library of videos and activities. And state-of-the-art question analysis reports allow instructors to track the progress of individual students as well as their class as a whole.

- **Student Video Activities** include more than 50 engaging video modules that instructors can easily assign for student assessment. Videos cover classic experiments, current news footage, and cutting-edge research, all of which are sure to spark discussion and encourage critical thinking.

- **The *Scientific American* Newsfeed** delivers weekly articles, podcasts, and news briefs on the very latest developments in psychology from the first name in popular science journalism.

Additional Student Supplements

CourseSmart e-Book

The CourseSmart e-Book offers the complete text of *How Children Develop,* Fourth Canadian Edition, in an easy-to-use, flexible format. Students can choose to view the CourseSmart e-Book online or download it to a personal computer or a portable media player, such as a smart phone or iPad. The CourseSmart e-Book for *How Children Develop,* Fourth Canadian Edition, can be previewed and purchased at www.coursesmart.com.

Scientific American Reader to Accompany *How Children Develop*

The authors have compiled fifteen *Scientific American* articles relevant to key topics in the text. The selections range from classics such as Harry Harlow's "Love in Infant Monkeys" and Eleanor Gibson and Richard Walk's "The 'Visual Cliff'" to contemporary articles on such topics as the interaction of games and environment in the development of intelligence (Robert Plomin and John DeFries), the effects of child abuse on the developing brain (Martin Teicher), balancing work and family (Robert Pleck), and moral development (William Damon). These articles should enrich students' learning and help them appreciate the process by which developmental scientists gain new understanding. This premium item can be packaged with the text at no additional cost.

Take advantage of our most popular supplements!

Worth Publishers is pleased to offer cost-saving packages of *How Children Develop*, Fourth Canadian Edition, with our most popular supplements. Below is a list of some of the most popular combinations available for order through your local bookstore.

How Children Develop, 4th Ed. & LaunchPad Access Card
ISBN 10: 1-4641-9213-8 / ISBN-13: 978-1-4641-9213-5

How Children Develop, 4th Ed. & iClicker
ISBN 10: 1-4641-8283-3 / ISBN-13: 978-1-4641-8283-9

How Children Develop, 4th Ed. & *Scientific American* Reader
ISBN 10: 1-4641-8282-5 / ISBN-13: 978-1-4641-8282-2

Presentation and Faculty Support

Presentation Slides

Presentation slides are available in three formats that can be used as they are or can be customized. One set includes all the textbook's illustrations and tables. The second set consists of lecture slides that focus on key themes and terms in the book and include text illustrations and tables. A third set of PowerPoint slides provides an easy way to integrate the supplementary video clips into classroom lectures. All these pre-built PowerPoint presentations are available through http://www.worthpublishers.com/launchpad/sieglercanadian4e.

Presentation Videos

Worth's video clips for developmental psychology span the full range of topics for the child development course. With hundreds of clips to choose from, this premium collection includes research and news footage on topics ranging from prenatal development to the experience of child soldiers to empathy in adolescence. These clips are made available to instructors for lecturing in the classroom and also through LaunchPad.

Instructor's Resource Manual

Written by Lynne Baker-Ward, North Carolina State University, this innovative *Instructor's Resource Manual* includes handouts for student projects, reading lists of journal articles, course-planning suggestions, and supplementary readings, in addition to lecture guides, chapter overviews, and learning objectives. The Instructor's Resource Manual can be downloaded at http://www.worthpublishers.com/launchpad/ sieglercanadian4e.

New! Faculty Lounge

Faculty Lounge is an online forum provided by Worth Publishers where teachers can find and share favourite teaching ideas and materials, including videos, animations, images, PowerPoint slides, news stories, articles, web links, and lecture activities. Sign up to browse the site or upload your favourite materials for teaching psychology at www. worthpublishers.com/facultylounge.

Assessment

Test Bank

The Test Bank for *How Children Develop*, Fourth Canadian Edition, by Jill L. Saxon and Carolyn Ensley of Wilfrid Laurier University, features 80 multiple-choice and 20 essay questions for each chapter. Each question is keyed to the textbook by topic, type, and level of difficulty.

Test Bank on CD-ROM

The *Diploma Test Bank CD-ROM*, on a dual platform for Windows and Macintosh, guides instructors through the process of creating a test and allows them to add, edit, and scramble questions; to change formats; and to include pictures, equations, and media links. The CD-ROM is also the access point for Diploma Online Testing, which allows creating and administering examinations on paper, over a network, or over the Internet.

Course Management

Worth Publishers supports multiple Course Management Systems with enhanced cartridges for upload into Blackboard, Angel, Desire2Learn, Sakai, and Moodle (and others upon request). Cartridges are provided free upon adoption of *How Children Develop*, Fourth Canadian Edition, and can be downloaded through the catalogue page at www.worthpublishers.com.

Acknowledgments

So many people have contributed (directly and indirectly) to this textbook that it is impossible to know where to start or where to stop in thanking them. All of us have been given exceptional support by our spouses and significant others—Jerry Clore, Jerry Harris, Xiaodong Lin, Seth Pollak, and John Gerlach—and by our children—Benjamin Clore; Michael Harris; Todd, Beth, and Aaron Siegler; Avianna McGhee; Eli and Nell Pollak, and Sam and Madeline Gerlach—as well as by our parents, relatives, friends, and other loved ones. Our advisors in college and graduate school, Richard Aslin, Ann Brown, Les Cohen, Harry Hake, Robert Liebert, Jim Morgan, Paul Mussen, Ellisa Newport, Jim Pate, and Diane Poulin-Dubois, helped launch our careers and taught us how to recognize and appreciate good research. We also have all benefitted from collaborators who shared our quest for understanding child development and from a great many exceptionally helpful and generous colleagues, including Karen Adolph, Martha Alibali, Renee Baillargeon, Sharon Carver, Zhe Chen, Suzanne Curtin, Richard Fabes, Cindy Fisher, Geoff Hall, Melanie Jones, David Klahr, Patrick Lemaire, Angeline Lillard, John Opfer, Kristin Shutts, Tracy Spinrad, David Uttal, and Carlos Valiente. We owe special thanks to our assistants, Sheri Towe, Theresa Treasure, and Ena Vukatana, who helped in innumerable ways in preparing the book.

We would also like to thank the many reviewers who contributed to this and previous editions: **Daisuke Akiba,** Queens College, City University of New York; **Kimberly Alkins,** Queens College, City University of New York; **Lynne Baker-Ward,** North Carolina State University; **Hilary Barth,** Wesleyan University; **Christopher Beevers,** Texas University; **Martha Bell,** Virginia Tech; **Cynthia Berg,** University of Utah; **Rebecca Bigler,** Texas University; **Margaret Borkowski,** Saginaw Valley State University; **Eric Buhs,** University of Nebraska–Lincoln; **G. Leonard Burns,** Washington State University; **Wendy Carlson,** Shenandoah University; **Kristi Cordell-McNulty,** Angelo State University; **Myra Cox,** Harold Washington College; **Emily Davidson,** Texas A&M University–Main Campus; **Ed de St. Aubin,** Marquette University; **Marissa Diener,** University of Utah; **Sharon Eaves,** Shawnee State University; **Urminda Firlan,** Grand Rapids Community College; **Dorothy Fragaszy,** University of Georgia; **Jeffery Gagne,** University of Texas–Austin; **Jennifer Ganger,** University of Pittsburgh; **Alice Ganzel,** Cornell College; **Janet Gebelt,** Westfield State University; **Melissa Ghera,** St. John Fisher College; **Andrea Greenhoot,** University of Kansas; **Frederick Grote,** Western Washington University; **John Gruszkos,** Reynolds University; **Hanna Gustafsson,** University of North Carolina; **Alma Guyse,** Midland College; **Lauren Harris,** Michigan State University; **Karen Hartlep,** California State University–Bakersfield; **Patricia Hawley,** University of Kansas–Main; **Susan Hespos,** Northwestern University; **Doris Hiatt,** Monmouth University; **Susan Holt,** Central Connecticut State University; **Lisa Huffman,** Ball State University; **Kathryn Kipp,** University of Georgia; **Rosemary Krawczyk,** Minnesota State University; **Raymond Krukovsky,** Union County College; **Tara Kuther,** Western Connecticut State University; **Richard Lanthier,** George Washington University; **Elida Laski,** Boston College; **Kathryn Lemery,** Arizona State University; **Barbara Licht,** Florida State University; **Angeline Lillard,** University of Virginia; **Wayne McMillin,** Northwestern State University; **Martha Mendez-Baldwin,** Manhattan College; **Scott Miller,** University of Florida; **Keith Nelson,** Pennsylvania State University–Main Campus; **Paul Nicodemus,** Austin Peay State University; **Katherine O'Doherty,** Vanderbilt University; **John Opfer,** The Ohio State University; **Ann Repp,** Texas University; **Leigh Shaw,** Weber State University; **Jennifer Simonds,** Westminster College; **Rebekah Smith,** University of Texas–San Antonio; **Mark Strauss,** University of Pittsburgh–Main; **Spencer Thompson,** University of Texas–Permian Basin; **Lisa Travis,** University of Illinois Urbana–Champaign; **Roger Webb,** University of Arkansas–Little Rock; **Keri Weed,** University of South Carolina–Aiken; **Sherri Widen,** Boston College.

To the reviewers of the fourth Canadian edition, our sincere appreciation: **Alba Agostino,** Ryerson University; **Daniel Ansari,** University of Western Ontario; **Christina Besner,** Champlain College Lennoxville; **Tanya Broesch,** Simon Fraser University; **Kelly Dean Schwartz,** University of Calgary; **Jacqueline Kampman,** Thompson Rivers University; **Padmapriya Kandhadai,** University of British

Columbia; **Cheryl Kier,** Athabasca University; **Danielle Labossière,** Grenfell Campus, Memorial University of Newfoundland; **Linda Langevin,** Medicine Hat College; **Anna Matejka,** University of Toronto Mississauga; **Gene Ouellette,** Mount Allison University; **Daniel Séguin,** Mount Saint Vincent University; **Veronica Smith,** University of Alberta; **Kelly Warren,** Grenfell Campus, Memorial University of Newfoundland; **Janet F. Werker,** University of British Columbia; **Sandra Wiebe,** University of Alberta; **Lynne Zarbatany,** University of Western Ontario.

We would especially like to thank Campbell Leaper, University of California–Santa Cruz, for his major contributions to the revision of our chapter on gender development (Chapter 15). We are indebted to Campbell for bringing to the fourth edition his expertise and keen insight in this important area.

Thanks are particularly due to our friends and collaborators at Worth Publishers for their work on the fourth American edition. As acquisitions editor and publisher, respectively, Daniel DeBonis and Kevin Feyen provided exceptional support and any number of excellent suggestions. We would also like to thank Marge Byers, who nurtured our first edition from its inception and helped us realize our vision. Peter Deane, our chief development editor, is in a class by himself in both skill and dedication. Peter's creative thinking and firm understanding of the field enhanced the content of the book in innumerable ways. We are deeply grateful to him. Our thanks go also to assistant editor Nadina Persaud, senior project editor Vivien Weiss, director of editing, design, and media production for the sciences and social sciences Tracey Kuehn, art director Barbara Reingold, cover and text designer Kevin Kall, photo editor Bianca Moscatelli, photo researcher Elyse Rieder, production manager Sarah Segal, and compositor Northeastern Graphic for their excellent work. They have helped create a book that we hope you will find a pleasure to look at as well as to read. Marketing manager Katherine Nurre provided outstanding promotional materials to inform professors about the book. Anthony Casciano and Stacey Alexander managed the superb package of ancillary material.

In addition to those who so expertly crafted the American edition of the book, we would like to thank Daniel DeBonis for his enthusiasm, guidance, and outstanding support for this fourth Canadian edition. We would also like to thank our development editor, Debbie Smith, of First Folio Resource Group Inc., for her creative and keen editorial eye—her contributions have enhanced this edition in countless ways. Our thanks also go to other members of the First Folio team—compositor Tom Dart, photo researcher Maria DeCambra, and copy editor Arleane Ralph—for developing a beautiful and engaging book.

Finally, we want to thank our "book team" of sales representatives and managers. Tom Kling, Julie Hirshman, Kari Ewalt, Greg David, Tom Scotty, Cindy Rabinowitz, Glenn Russell, and Matt Dunning provided a sales perspective, valuable suggestions, and unflagging enthusiasm throughout this project. In particular, we thank the Canadian marketing and sales teams, led by Kate Nurre and Julia Jevmenova. The enthusiasm and support provided by Julia, as well as Matt Ours, Jen Cawsey, Carlo Dell'Elce, Susan Erickson, Liz Hudson, Krista Mann, and Kate Nicoll, are greatly appreciated!

DOROTHEA SHARP (1874–1955), *Young Explorers* (oil on canvas)

chapter 1:

An Introduction to Child Development

THEMES

n 1955, a group of child-development researchers began a unique study. Their goal, like that of many developmental researchers, was to find out how biological and environmental factors influence children's intellectual, social, and emotional growth. What made their study unique was that they examined these diverse aspects of development for all 698 children born that year on the Hawaiian island of Kauai and continued studying the children's development for more than 30 years.

With the parents' consent, the research team, headed by Emmy Werner, collected many types of data about the children. To learn about possible complications during the prenatal period and birth, they examined physicians' records. To learn about family interactions and the children's behaviour at home, they arranged for nurses and social workers to observe the families and to interview the children's mothers when the children were 1 year old and again when they were 10 years old. The researchers also interviewed teachers about the children's academic performance and classroom behaviour during the elementary school years, and examined police, family court, and social service records that involved the children, either as victims or perpetrators. Finally, the researchers administered standardized intelligence and personality tests to the participants when they were 10 and 18 years old and interviewed them at age 18 and again in their early 30s to find out how they saw their own development.

Results from this study illustrated some of the many ways in which biological and environmental factors combine to produce child development. For example, children who experienced prenatal or birth complications were more likely than others to develop physical disabilities, mental illness, and learning difficulties. But whether they developed such problems—and if so, to what degree—depended a great deal on their home environment. Parents' income, education, and mental health, together with the quality of the relationship between the parents, especially influenced children's development. By age 2, toddlers who had experienced severe prenatal or birth problems but who lived in harmonious middle-income families were nearly as advanced in language and motor skills as were children who had not experienced such problems. By the time the children were 10-year-olds, prenatal and birth problems were consistently related to psychological difficulties *only* if the children also grew up in poor rearing conditions.

What of children who faced both biological and environmental challenges— prenatal or birth complications *and* adverse family circumstances? The majority of these children developed serious learning or behaviour problems by age 10 years. By age 18, most had acquired a police record, had experienced mental health problems, or had become an unmarried parent. However, one-third of such at-risk children showed impressive resilience, growing up into young adults who, in the words of Werner (1989, p. 108D), "loved well, worked well, and played well."

Michael was one such resilient child. Born prematurely, with low birth weight, to teenage parents, he spent the first 3 weeks of his life in a hospital, separated from his mother. By his 8th birthday, Michael's parents were divorced, his mother had left the family, and he and his three brothers and sisters were being raised by their father, with the help of their elderly grandparents. Yet by age 18, Michael was successful in school, had high self-esteem, was popular with his peers, and was a caring young man with a positive attitude toward life. The fact that there are many children like Michael—children who show great resilience in the face of adversity—is among the most heartening findings of research on child development. Learning about the Michaels of the world inspires child development researchers to conduct further investigations aimed at answering such questions as why individual children differ so much in their response to similar environments, and how to apply research findings to help more children overcome the challenges they face.

Werner's remarkable study, like most studies of child development, raises as many questions as it answers. How, exactly, did the children's biological nature, their family environment, and the environments they encountered outside the family combine to shape their development? Can programs be designed that would allow more children from adverse backgrounds to show resilience?

Reading this chapter will increase your understanding of these and other basic questions about child development. It also will introduce you to some historical perspectives on these fundamental questions and to the perspectives and methods that modern researchers use to address them. But, first, we would like you to consider perhaps the most basic question of all: Why study child development?

Reasons to Learn About Child Development

For us, as both parents and researchers, the sheer enjoyment of watching children and trying to understand them is reason enough for studying child development. What could be more fascinating than the development of a child? But there are also practical and intellectual reasons for studying child development. Understanding how children develop can improve child-rearing, promote the adoption of wiser social policies regarding children's welfare, and answer intriguing questions about human nature. We examine each of these reasons in the following sections.

This family has lived in a one-room tent for approximately 2 years. Will these children be resilient enough to overcome their disadvantaged environment? The answer will depend in large part on how many risk factors they face, their personal characteristics, and the nature of the parenting they receive.

Raising Children

Being a good parent is not easy. Among its many challenges are the endless questions it raises over the years. Is it okay to take my infant outside in the cold weather? Should my baby stay at home, or would going to daycare be better for her social development? If my daughter starts walking and talking early, should I consider placing her in a school for gifted children? Should I try to teach my 3-year-old to read early? My son seems so lonely at preschool; how can I help him make friends? How can I help my kindergartner deal with her anger?

Child-development research can help answer such questions. For example, one problem that confronts almost all parents is how to help their children control their anger and other negative emotions. One tempting, and frequent, reaction is to spank children who express anger in inappropriate ways, such as fighting, name-calling, and talking back. In Canada, prevalence rates for spanking range from 50% to 66% (Ateah & Parkin, 2002; Gagné et al., 2007). Research shows, however, that spanking makes the problem behaviours worse and the effects are long-lasting. One large-scale study showed that the more often parents spanked their kindergartners, the more often the same children argued, fought, and acted inappropriately at school when they were 3rd graders. This relation held true for children from various backgrounds, and it held true above and beyond the effects of other relevant factors, such as parents' income and education (Gershoff et al., 2012).

Posters like this are used in the turtle technique to remind children of ways to control anger.

Fortunately, research suggests several effective alternatives to spanking (Denham, 1998, 2006). One is expressing sympathy: when parents respond to their children's distress with sympathy, the children are better able to cope with the situation causing the distress. Another effective approach is helping angry children find positive alternatives to expressing anger. For example, encouraging them to do something they enjoy helps them cope with the hostile feelings.

These strategies and similar ones, such as time outs, can also be used effectively by others who contribute to raising children, such as daycare personnel and teachers. One demonstration of this was provided by a special curriculum that was devised for helping preschoolers (3- and 4-year-olds) who were angry and out of control (Denham & Burton, 1996). With this curriculum, preschool teachers helped children recognize their own and other children's emotions, taught them techniques for controlling their anger, and guided them in resolving conflicts with other children. One approach that children were taught for coping with anger was the "turtle technique." When children felt themselves becoming angry, they were to move away from other children and retreat into their "turtle shell," where they could think through the situation until they were ready to emerge from the shell. Posters were placed around the classroom to remind children of what to do when they became angry.

The curriculum was quite successful. Children who participated in it became more skillful in recognizing and regulating anger when they experienced it and were generally less negative. For example, one boy, who had regularly gotten into fights when angry, told the teacher after a dispute with another child, "See, I used my words, not my hands" (Denham, 1998, p. 219). The benefits of this program can be long-term. In one test conducted with children in special education classrooms, positive effects were still evident 2 years after children completed the curriculum (Greenberg & Kusché, 2006). As this example suggests, knowledge of child-development research can be helpful to everyone involved in the care of children.

Choosing Social Policies

Another reason to learn about child development is to be able to make informed decisions not just about one's own children but also about a wide variety of social-policy questions that affect children in general. For example, how much trust should judges and juries place in preschoolers' testimony in child-abuse cases? Should children who do poorly in school be held back, or should they be promoted to the next grade so that they can be with children of the same age? How effective are health-education courses aimed at reducing teenage smoking, drinking, and pregnancy? Child-development research can inform discussion of all of these policy decisions and many others.

Consider the issue of how much trust to put in children's courtroom testimony. One estimate is that tens of thousands of children testify in legal cases in Canada, about crimes they either experienced or witnessed (Cunningham & Stevens, 2011). Many of these children are very young: in 2009, more than 40% of children who were victims of sexual offences in Canada were under 11 years of age (Statistics Canada, 2011c). Many of these children face the prospect of testifying in court. The stakes are extremely high in such cases. If juries believe children who falsely testify that they were abused, innocent people may spend years in jail. If juries do not believe children who accurately report abuse, the perpetrators will go free and probably abuse other children. So what can be done to promote reliable testimony from young children and to avoid leading them to report experiences that never occurred?

Psychological research has helped answer such questions. In one experiment, researchers tested whether biased questioning affects the accuracy of young children's memory for events involving touching one's own and other people's bodies. The researchers began by having 3- to 6-year-olds play a game, similar to "Simon Says," in which the children were told to touch various parts of their body and those of other children. A month later, the researchers had a social worker interview the children about their experiences during the game (Ceci & Bruck, 1998). Before the social worker conducted the interviews, she was given a description of each child's experiences. Unknown to her, the description included inaccurate as well as accurate information. For example, she might have been told that a particular child had touched her own stomach and another child's nose, when in fact the child had touched her own stomach and the other child's foot. After receiving the description, the social worker was given instructions much like those in a court case: "Find out what the child remembers."

As it turned out, the version of events that the social worker had heard often influenced her questions. If, for example, a child's account of an event was contrary to what the social worker believed to be the case, she tended to question the child repeatedly about the event ("Are you sure you touched his foot? Is it possible you touched some other part of his body?"). Faced with such repeated questioning, children fairly often changed their responses, with 34% of 3- and 4-year-olds eventually corroborating at least one of the social worker's incorrect beliefs. Children were led to "remember" not only plausible events that never happened but also unlikely ones that the social worker had been told about. For example, some children "recalled" their knee being licked and a marble being inserted in their ear.

Studies such as this have yielded a number of conclusions regarding children's testimony in legal proceedings. One important finding is that when 3- to 5-year-olds are not asked leading questions, their testimony is usually accurate, as far as it goes (Bruck et al., 2006; Howe & Courage, 1997). However, when prompted by leading questions, young children's testimony is often inaccurate, especially when the leading questions are asked repeatedly. The younger children are, the more susceptible they are to being led, and the more their recall reflects the biases of the interviewer's questions. In addition, realistic props, such as anatomically correct dolls and drawings, that are often used in judicial cases in the hopes of improving recall of sexual abuse, do not improve recall of events that occurred; they actually increase the number of inaccurate claims, perhaps by blurring the line between fantasy play and reality (M. E. Lamb et al., 2008; Poole, Bruck, & Pipe, 2011). Research on child eyewitness testimony has had a large practical impact: in various jurisdictions in Canada, multidisciplinary guidelines have been developed to assist police, child welfare workers, physicians, and other professionals in interviewing children and preparing them for court (see the Canadian Society for the Investigation of Child Abuse for examples of these guidelines). In addition to helping courts obtain more accurate testimony from young children, such research-based conclusions illustrate how, at a broader level, knowledge of child development can inform social policies.

Understanding Human Nature

A third reason to study child development is to better understand human nature. Many of the most intriguing questions regarding human nature concern children. For example, does learning start only after a child is born, or can it occur in the womb? Can later upbringing in a loving home overcome the detrimental effects of early rearing in a loveless institutional setting? Do children vary in personality and intellect from the day they are born, or are they similar at birth, with differences arising only because they have different experiences? Until recently, people could only speculate about the answers to such questions. Now, however, developmental scientists have methods that enable them to observe, describe, and explain the process of development.

A particularly poignant illustration of the way in which scientific research can increase understanding of human nature comes from studies of how children's ability to overcome the effects of early maltreatment is affected by its timing, that is, the age at which the maltreatment occurs. One such research program has examined children whose early life was spent in horribly inadequate orphanages in Romania in the late 1980s and early 1990s (Ames, 1997; McCall et al., 2011; C. A. Nelson et al., 2007; Rutter et al., 2004). Children in these orphanages had almost no contact with any caregiver. For reasons that remain unknown, the brutal Communist dictatorship of that era instructed staff workers not to interact with the children, even when giving them their bottles. Staff members provided the infants with so little physical contact that the crown of many infants' heads became flattened from the babies' lying on their backs for 18 to 20 hours per day.

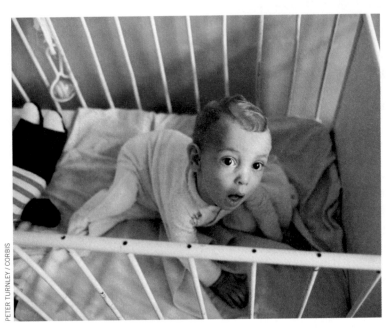

PETER TURNLEY / CORBIS

This infant is one of the children adopted from a Romanian orphanage in the 1990s. How successfully he develops will depend not only on the quality of caregiving he receives in his adoptive home but also on the amount of time he spent in the orphanage and the age at which he was adopted.

Shortly after the collapse of Communist rule in Romania, a number of these children were adopted by families around the world, including families in Canada and Great Britain. This offered the unprecedented opportunity to examine the long-term effects of early deprivation and potential for recovery. Research has shown that when these children arrived in their adoptive homes, most were severely malnourished, with more than half falling below the 5th percentile in terms of height, weight, and head circumference. Most also showed varying degrees of mental retardation and were socially immature. The parents who adopted them knew of their deprived backgrounds and were highly motivated to provide loving homes that would help the children overcome the damaging effects of their early mistreatment.

To evaluate the long-term effects of their early deprivation, the physical, intellectual, and social development of about 150 of the Romanian-born children adopted to homes in Britain was examined at age 6 years. To provide a basis of comparison, the researchers also followed the development of a group of British-born children who had been adopted into British families before they were 6 months of age. Simply put, the question was whether human nature is sufficiently flexible that the Romanian-born children could overcome the extreme deprivation of their early experience, and if so, would that flexibility decrease with the children's age and the length of the deprivation.

By age 6 years, the physical development of the Romanian-born children had improved considerably, both in absolute terms and in relation to the British-born comparison group. However, the Romanian children's early experience of deprivation continued to influence their development, with the extent of negative effects depending on how long the children had been institutionalized. Romanian-born children who were adopted by British families before age 6 months, and who had therefore spent the smallest portion of their early lives in the orphanages, weighed about the same as British-born children when both were 6-year-olds. Romanian-born children adopted between the ages of 6 and 24 months, and who therefore had spent more of their early lives in the orphanages, weighed less; and those adopted between the ages of 24 and 42 months weighed even less (Rutter et al., 2004).

Intellectual development at age 6 years showed a similar pattern. The Romanian-born children who had been adopted before age 6 months demonstrated levels of intellectual competence comparable with those of the British-born group. Those who had been adopted between ages 6 and 24 months did somewhat less well, and those adopted between ages 24 and 42 months did even more poorly (Rutter et al., 2004). The intellectual deficits of the Romanian children adopted after age 6 months were just as great when the children were retested at age 11 years, indicating that the negative effects of the early deprivation persisted over time (Beckett et al., 2006; Kreppner et al., 2007).

The early experience in the orphanages had similar damaging effects on the children's social development (Kreppner et al., 2007; T. G. O'Connor, Rutter, & English and Romanian Adoptees Study Team, 2000). Almost 20% of the Romanian-born children who were adopted after age 6 months showed extremely abnormal social behaviour at age 6 years, not looking at their parents in anxiety-provoking situations and willingly going off with strangers (versus 3% of the British-born comparison group who did so). This atypical social development was accompanied by abnormal brain activity. Brain scans obtained when the children were 8 years old showed that those adopted after living for a substantial period in the orphanages had unusually low levels of neural activity in the amygdala, a brain area involved in emotional reactions (Chugani et al., 2001). Subsequent studies have identified similar brain abnormalities among children who spent their early lives in poor-quality orphanages in Russia and East Asia (C. A. Nelson et al., 2011; Tottenham et al., 2010).

These findings reflect a basic principle of child development that is relevant to many aspects of human nature: *the timing of experiences influences their effects.* In the present case, children were sufficiently flexible to overcome the effects of living in the loveless, unstimulating institutions if the deprivation ended relatively early; living in the institutions until older ages, however, had effects that were rarely overcome, even when children spent subsequent years in loving and stimulating environments. The adoptive families clearly made a huge positive difference in their children's lives, but the later the age of adoption, the greater the long-term effects of early deprivation.

review:

There are at least three good reasons to learn about child development: to improve one's own child-rearing, to help society promote the well-being of children in general, and to better understand human nature.

Historical Foundations of the Study of Child Development

From ancient Greece to the early years of the twentieth century, a number of profound thinkers observed and wrote about children. Their goals were like those of contemporary researchers: to help people become better parents, to improve children's well-being, and to understand human nature. Unlike contemporary researchers, they usually based their conclusions on general philosophical beliefs and informal observations of a few children. Still, the issues they raised are sufficiently important, and their insights sufficiently deep, that their views continue to be of interest.

Early Philosophers' Views of Children's Development

Some of the earliest recorded ideas about children's development were those of Plato and Aristotle. These classic Greek philosophers, who lived in the fourth century B.C.E., were particularly interested in how children's development is influenced by their nature and by the nurture they receive.

Both Plato and Aristotle believed that the long-term welfare of society depended on the proper raising of children. Careful upbringing was essential because children's basic nature would otherwise lead to their becoming rebellious and unruly. Plato viewed the rearing of boys as a particularly demanding challenge for parents and teachers:

> Now of all wild things, a boy is the most difficult to handle. Just because he more than any other has a fount of intelligence in him which has not yet "run clear," he is the craftiest, most mischievous, and unruliest of brutes.
>
> (*Laws*, bk. 7, p. 808)

Consistent with this view, Plato emphasized self-control and discipline as the most important goals of education (Borstelmann, 1983).

Aristotle agreed with Plato that discipline was necessary, but he was more concerned with fitting child-rearing to the needs of the individual child. In his words,

> it would seem … that a study of individual character is the best way of making education perfect, for then each [child] has a better chance of receiving the treatment that suits him.
>
> (*Nicomachean Ethics*, bk. 10, chap. 9, p. 1180)

Plato and Aristotle differed more profoundly in their views of how children acquire knowledge. Plato believed that children have innate knowledge. For example, he believed that children are born with a concept of "animal" that, from birth onward, automatically allows them to recognize that the dogs, cats, and other creatures they encounter are animals. In contrast, Aristotle believed that all knowledge comes from experience and that the mind of an infant is like a slate on which nothing has yet been written.

Roughly 2000 years later, the English philosopher John Locke (1632–1704) and the French philosopher Jean-Jacques Rousseau (1712–1778) refocused attention on the question of how parents and society in general can best promote children's development. Locke, like Aristotle, viewed the child as a tabula rasa, or blank slate, whose development largely reflects the nurture provided by the child's parents and the broader society. He believed that the most important goal of child-rearing is the growth of character. To build children's character, parents need to set good examples of honesty, stability, and gentleness. They also need to avoid indulging the child, especially early in life. However, once discipline and reason have been instilled, Locke believed

> authority should be relaxed as fast as their age, discretion, and good behavior could allow it … The sooner you treat him as a man, the sooner he will begin to be one.
>
> (Cited in Borstelmann, 1983, p. 20)

In contrast to Locke's advocating discipline before freedom, Rousseau believed that parents and society should give children maximum freedom from the beginning. Rousseau claimed that children learn primarily from their own spontaneous interactions with objects and other people, rather than through instruction by parents or teachers. He even argued that children should not receive any formal education until about age 12, when they reach "the age of reason" and can judge for themselves the worth of what they are told. Before then, they should be allowed the freedom to explore whatever interests them.

Although formulated long ago, these and other philosophical positions continue to underlie many contemporary debates, including whether children should receive direct instruction in desired skills and knowledge or be given maximum freedom to discover the skills and knowledge for themselves, and whether parents should build their children's character through explicit instruction or through the implicit guidance provided by the parents' own behaviour.

Social Reform Movements

Another precursor of the contemporary field of child psychology was early social reform movements that were devoted to improving children's lives by changing the conditions in which they lived. During the Industrial Revolution of the eighteenth and nineteenth centuries, a great many children in Europe, Canada, and the United States worked as poorly paid labourers with no legal protections. Some were as young as 5 and 6 years; many worked up to 12 hours a day in factories or mines, often in extremely hazardous circumstances. These harsh conditions worried a number of social reformers, who began to study how such circumstances affected the children's development. For example, in a speech before the British House of Commons in 1843, the Earl of Shaftesbury noted that the narrow tunnels where children dug out coal had

© BETTMANN / CORBIS

> very insufficient drainage [and] are so low that only little boys can work in them, which they do naked, and often in mud and water, dragging sledge-tubs by the girdle and chain … Children of amiable temper and conduct, at 7 years of age, often return next season from the collieries greatly corrupted … with most hellish dispositions.
>
> (Quoted in Kessen, 1965, pp. 46–50)

The Earl of Shaftesbury's effort at social reform brought partial success—a law forbidding employment of girls and of boys younger than 10. In addition to bringing about the first child labour laws, this and other early social reform movements established a legacy of research conducted for the benefit of children and provided some of the earliest recorded descriptions of the adverse effects that harsh environments can have on children.

During the eighteenth, nineteenth, and early twentieth centuries, many young children worked in coal mines and factories. Their hours were long, and the work was often unhealthy and dangerous. Concern over the well-being of such children led to some of the earliest research on child development.

Darwin's Theory of Evolution

Later in the nineteenth century, Charles Darwin's work on evolution inspired a number of scientists to propose that intensive study of children's development might lead to important insights into human nature. Darwin himself was interested in child development and in 1877 published an article entitled "A Biographical Sketch of an Infant," which presented his careful observations of the motor, sensory, and emotional growth of his infant son, William. Darwin's "baby biography"—a systematic description of William's day-to-day development—represented one of the first methods for studying children.

Such intensive studies of individual children's growth continue to be a distinctive feature of the modern field of child development. Darwin's evolutionary theory also continues to influence the thinking of modern developmentalists on a wide range of topics: infants' attachment to their mothers (Bowlby, 1969), innate fear of natural dangers such as spiders and snakes (Rakison & Derringer, 2008), sex differences (Geary, 2009), aggression and altruism (Tooby & Cosmides, 2005), and the mechanisms underlying learning (Siegler, 1996).

The Beginnings of Research-Based Theories of Child Development

At the end of the nineteenth century and the beginning of the twentieth, the first theories of child development that incorporated research findings were formulated. One prominent theory, that of the Austrian psychiatrist Sigmund Freud, was based in large part on his patients' recollections of their dreams and childhood experiences. Freud's *psychoanalytic theory* proposed that biological drives, especially sexual ones, are a crucial influence on development.

Another prominent theory of the same era, that of American psychologist John B. Watson, was based primarily on the results of experiments that examined learning in animals and children. Watson's *behaviourist theory* argued that children's development is determined by environmental factors, especially the rewards and punishments that follow the children's actions.

By current standards, the research methods on which these theories were based were crude. Nonetheless, these early scientific theories were better grounded in research evidence than were their predecessors, and, as you will see later in the chapter, they inspired more sophisticated ideas about the processes of development and more rigorous research methods for studying how development occurs.

review:

Philosophers such as Plato, Aristotle, Locke, and Rousseau, as well as early scientific theorists such as Darwin, Freud, and Watson, raised many of the deepest issues about child development. These issues included how nature and nurture influence development, how best to raise children, and how knowledge of children's development can be used to advance their welfare.

Enduring Themes in Child Development

The modern study of child development begins with a set of fundamental questions. Everything else—theories, concepts, research methods, data, and so on—is part of the effort to answer these questions. Although experts in the field might choose different particular questions as the most important, there is widespread agreement that the seven questions in Table 1.1 are among the most important. These questions form a set of themes that we will highlight throughout the book as we examine specific aspects of child development. In this section, we introduce and briefly discuss each question and the theme that corresponds to it.

1 *Nature and Nurture*: How Do Nature and Nurture Together Shape Development?

The most basic question about child development is how nature and nurture interact to shape the developmental process. **Nature** refers to our biological endowment, in particular, the genes we receive from our parents. This genetic inheritance influences every aspect of our makeup, from broad characteristics such as physical appearance, personality, intellect, and mental health to specific preferences, such as political attitudes and propensity for thrill-seeking (Plomin, 2004; Rothbart & Bates, 2006). **Nurture** refers to the wide range of environments, both physical and social, that influence our development, including the wombs in which we spend the prenatal period, the homes in which we grow up, the schools that we attend, the broader communities in which we live, and the many people with whom we interact.

Popular depictions often present the nature–nurture question as an either/or proposition: "What determines how a person develops, heredity *or* environment?" However, this either/or phrasing is deeply misleading. All human characteristics— our intellect, our personality, our physical appearance, our emotions—are created through the *joint* workings of nature and nurture, that is, through the constant interaction of our genes and our environment. Accordingly, rather than asking whether nature or nurture is more important, developmentalists ask how nature *and* nurture work together to shape development.

That this is the right question to ask is vividly illustrated by findings on the development of schizophrenia. Schizophrenia is a serious mental illness, often characterized by hallucinations, delusions, confusion, and irrational behaviour. There is obviously a genetic component to this disease. Children who have a schizophrenic parent have a much higher probability than other children of developing the illness later in life, even when they are adopted as infants and therefore are not exposed to their parents' schizophrenic behaviour (Kety et al., 1994). Among identical twins—that is, twins whose genes are identical—if one twin has schizophrenia, the other has a roughly 50% chance of also having schizophrenia, as opposed to the roughly 1% probability for the general population (Gottesman, 1991; Cardno & Gottesman, 2000) (see Figure 1.1). At the same time, the environment is also

nature ■ Our biological endowment; the genes we receive from our parents.

nurture ■ The environments, both physical and social, that influence our development.

TABLE 1.1

Basic Questions About Child Development

1. How do nature and nurture together shape development? *(Nature and nurture)*

2. How do children shape their own development? *(The active child)*

3. In what ways is development continuous, and in what ways is it discontinuous? *(Continuity/discontinuity)*

4. How does change occur? *(Mechanisms of development)*

5. How does the sociocultural context influence development? *(The sociocultural context)*

6. How do children become so different from one another? *(Individual differences)*

7. How can research promote children's well-being? *(Research and children's welfare)*

CP IMAGES / ADRIAN WYLD

Was it nature, nurture, or a combination that led Justin Trudeau to follow in the footsteps of his father, former prime minister Pierre Trudeau?

FIGURE 1.1 Genetic relatedness and schizophrenia The closer the biological relation, the stronger the probability that relatives of a person with schizophrenia will have the same mental illness. (Adapted from Gottesman, 1991)

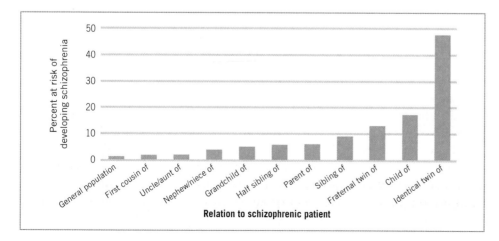

Relation to schizophrenic patient

(y-axis: Percent at risk of developing schizophrenia; x-axis categories: General population, First cousin of, Uncle/aunt of, Nephew/niece of, Grandchild of, Half sibling of, Parent of, Sibling of, Fraternal twin of, Child of, Identical twin of)

genome ■ Each person's or organism's complete set of hereditary information.

epigenetics ■ The study of stable changes in gene expression that are mediated by the environment.

methylation ■ A biochemical process that influences behaviour by suppressing gene activity and expression.

clearly influential, since roughly 50% of children who have an identical twin with schizophrenia do not become schizophrenic themselves, and children who grow up in troubled homes are more likely to become schizophrenic than are children raised in a normal household. Most important, however, is the interaction of genes and environment. A study of adopted children, some of whose biological parents were schizophrenic, indicated that the only children who had any substantial likelihood of becoming schizophrenic were those who had a schizophrenic parent *and* who also were adopted into a troubled family (Tienari, Wahlberg, & Wynne, 2006).

A remarkable recent series of studies has revealed some of the biological mechanisms through which nature and nurture interact. These studies show that just as the **genome**—each person's or organism's complete set of hereditary information—influences behaviours and experiences, behaviours and experiences influence the genome (S. W. Cole, 2009; Meaney, 2010). This might seem impossible, given the well-known fact that each person's DNA is constant throughout life. However, the genome includes not only DNA but also proteins that regulate gene expression by turning gene activity on and off. These proteins change in response to experience and, without structurally altering DNA, can result in enduring changes in cognition, emotion, and behaviour. This discovery has given rise to a new field called **epigenetics**, the study of stable changes in gene expression that are mediated by the environment. Stated simply, epigenetics examines how experience gets under the skin.

Evidence for the enduring epigenetic impact of early experiences and behaviours comes from research on **methylation**, a biochemical process that reduces expression of a variety of genes and that is involved in regulating reactions to stress (Champagne & Curley, 2009; Meaney, 2001). One recent study showed that the amount of stress that mothers reported experiencing during their children's infancy was related to the amount of methylation in the children's genomes 15 years later (Essex et al., 2013). Other studies showed increased methylation in the cord-blood DNA of newborns of depressed mothers (Oberlander et al., 2008) and in adults who were abused as children (McGowan et al., 2009), leading researchers to speculate that such children are at heightened risk for depression as adults (Rutten & Mill, 2009).

As these examples illustrate, developmental outcomes emerge from the constant bidirectional interaction of nature *and* nurture. To say that one is more important than the other, or even that the two are equally important, drastically oversimplifies the developmental process.

2 *The Active Child*: How Do Children Shape Their Own Development?

With all the attention that is paid to heredity and environment, many people overlook the ways in which children's own actions contribute to their development. Even in infancy and early childhood, this contribution can be seen in a multitude of areas, including attention, language use, and play.

Children first begin to shape their own development through their selection of what to pay attention to. Even newborns prefer to look at things that move and make sounds. This preference helps them learn about important parts of the world, such as people, other animals, and inanimate moving objects. When looking at people, infants' attention is particularly drawn to faces, especially their mother's face: given a choice of looking at a stranger's face or their mother's, even 1-month-olds choose to look at Mom (Bartrip, Morton, & de Schonen, 2001). At first, infants' attention to their mother's face is not accompanied by any visible emotion, but by the end of

One of the earliest ways children shape their own development is through their choice of where to look. From the first month of life, seeing Mom is a high priority.

the 2nd month, infants smile and coo more when focusing intently on their mother's face than at other times. This smiling and cooing by the infant elicits smiling and talking by the mother, which elicits further cooing and smiling by the infant, and so on (Lavelli & Fogel, 2005). In this way, infants' preference for attending to their mother's face leads to social interactions that can strengthen the mother–infant bond.

Once children begin to speak, usually between 9 and 15 months of age, their contribution to their own development becomes more evident. For example, toddlers (1- and 2-year-olds) often talk when they are alone in a room. Only if children were internally motivated to learn language would they practise talking when no one was present to react to what they were saying. Many parents are startled when they hear this "crib speech" and wonder if something is wrong with a baby who would engage in such odd-seeming behaviour. However, the activity is entirely normal, and the practice probably helps toddlers improve their speech.

Young children's play provides many other examples of how their internally motivated activity contributes to their development. Children play by themselves for the sheer joy of doing so, but they also learn a great deal in the process. Anyone who has seen a baby bang a spoon against the tray of a high chair or intentionally drop food on the floor would agree that, for the baby, the activity is its own reward. At the same time, the baby is learning about the noises made by colliding objects, about the speed at which objects fall, and about the limits of his or her parents' patience.

Young children's fantasy play seems to make an especially large contribution to their knowledge of themselves and other people. Starting at around age 2 years, children sometimes pretend to be different people in make-believe dramas. For example, they may pretend to be superheroes doing battle with monsters or play the role of parents taking care of babies. In addition to being inherently enjoyable, such play appears to teach children valuable lessons, including how to cope with fears and how to interact with others (Howes & Matheson, 1992; L. B. Smith, 2003). Older children's play, which typically is more organized and rulebound, teaches them additional valuable lessons, such as the self-control needed for turn-taking, adhering to rules, and controlling one's emotions in the face of setbacks (Hirsh-Pasek et al., 2009). As we discuss later in the chapter, children's contributions to their own development strengthen and broaden as they grow older and become increasingly able to choose and shape their environments.

3   *Continuity/Discontinuity*: In What Ways Is Development Continuous, and in What Ways Is It Discontinuous?

Some scientists envision children's development as a **continuous** process of small changes, like that of a pine tree growing taller and taller. Others see the process as a series of sudden, **discontinuous** changes, like the transition from caterpillar to cocoon to butterfly (Figure 1.2). The debate over which of these views is more accurate has continued for decades.

Researchers who view development as *discontinuous* start from a common observation: children of different ages seem *qualitatively different*. A 4-year-old and a 6-year-old, for example, seem to differ not only in how much they know but in the whole way they think about the world. To appreciate these differences, consider

Play contributes to children's development in many ways, including the spatial understanding and attention to detail required to complete puzzles.

Adolescents who participate in sports and other extracurricular activities are more likely to complete high school, and less likely to get into trouble, than peers who are not engaged in these activities. This is another example of how children contribute to their own development.

continuous development ■ The idea that changes with age occur gradually, in small increments, like that of a pine tree growing taller and taller.

discontinuous development ■ The idea that changes with age include occasional large shifts, like the transition from caterpillar to cocoon to butterfly.

FIGURE 1.2 Continuous and discontinuous development Some researchers see development as a continuous, gradual process, akin to a tree's growing taller with each passing year. Others see it as a discontinuous process, involving sudden dramatic changes, such as the transition from caterpillar to cocoon to butterfly. Each view fits some aspects of child development.

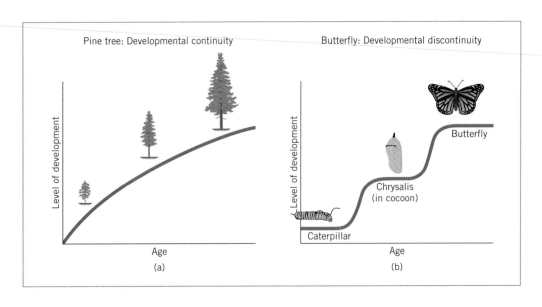

Pine tree: Developmental continuity

Level of development

Age
(a)

Butterfly: Developmental discontinuity

Level of development

Butterfly

Chrysalis (in cocoon)

Caterpillar

Age
(b)

two conversations between Beth, the daughter of one of the authors, and Beth's mother. The first conversation took place when Beth was 4 years old, the second, when she was 6. Both conversations occurred after Beth had watched her mother pour all the water from a typical drinking glass into a taller, narrower glass. Here is the conversation that occurred when Beth was 4:

Mother: Is there still the same amount of water?
Beth: No.
Mother: Was there more water before, or is there more now?
Beth: There's more now.
Mother: What makes you think so?
Beth: The water is higher; you can see it's more.
Mother: Now I'll pour the water back into the regular glass. Is there the same amount of water as when the water was in the same glass before?
Beth: Yes.
Mother: Now I'll pour all the water again into the tall thin glass. Does the amount of water stay the same?
Beth: No, I already told you, there's more water when it's in the tall glass.

Two years later, Beth responded to the same problem quite differently:

Mother: Is there still the same amount of water?
Beth: Of course!

What accounts for this change in Beth's thinking? Her everyday observations of liquids being poured cannot have been the reason for it; Beth had seen liquids

Children's behaviour on Piaget's conservation-of-liquid-quantity problem is often used to exemplify the idea that development is discontinuous. The child first sees equal amounts of liquid in similarly shaped glasses and an empty, differently shaped glass. Then, the child sees the liquid from one glass poured into the differently shaped glass. Finally, the child is asked whether the amount of liquid remains the same or whether one glass has more. Young children, like this girl, are unshakable in their belief that the glass with the taller liquid column has more liquid. A year or two later, they are equally unshakable in their belief that the amount of liquid in each glass is the same.

poured on a great number of occasions before she was 4, yet failed to develop the understanding that the volume remains constant. Experience with the specific task could not explain the change either, because Beth had no further exposure to the task between the first and second conversation. Then why, as a 4-year-old, would Beth be so confident that pouring the water into the taller, narrower glass increased the amount, and, as a 6-year-old, be so confident that it did not?

This conservation-of-liquid-quantity problem is actually a classic technique designed to test children's level of thinking. It has been used with thousands of children around the world, and virtually all the children studied, no matter what their culture, have shown the same type of change in reasoning as Beth did (though usually at somewhat older ages). Furthermore, such age-related differences in understanding pervade children's thinking. Consider two letters to Mr. Rogers, host of the children's television show *Mr. Rogers' Neighborhood*: one sent by a 4-year-old and one by a 5-year-old (Rogers, 1996, pp. 10–11):

Dear Mr. Rogers,
I would like to know how you get in the TV.

(Robby, age 4)

Dear Mr. Rogers,
I wish you accidentally stepped out of the TV into my house so I could play with you.

(Josiah, age 5)

Clearly, these are not ideas that an older child would entertain. As with Beth's case, we have to ask, "What is it about 4- and 5-year-olds that leads them to form such improbable beliefs, and what changes occur that makes such notions laughable to 6- and 7-year-olds?"

One common approach to answering these questions comes from **stage theories,** which propose that development occurs in a progression of distinct age-related stages, much like the butterfly example in Figure 1.2b. According to these theories, a child's entry into a new stage involves relatively sudden, qualitative changes that affect the child's thinking or behaviour in broadly unified ways and move the child from one coherent way of experiencing the world to a different coherent way of experiencing it. Among the best-known stage theories is Jean Piaget's theory of **cognitive development,** the development of thinking and reasoning. This theory holds that between birth and adolescence, children go through four stages of cognitive growth, each characterized by distinct intellectual abilities and ways of understanding the world. For example, according to Piaget's theory, 2- to 5-year-olds are in a stage of development in which they can focus on only one aspect of an event, or one type of information, at a time. By age 7, children enter a different stage, in which they can simultaneously focus on and coordinate two or more aspects of an event and can do so on many different tasks. According to this view, when confronted with a problem like the one that Beth's mother presented to her, most 4- and 5-year-olds focus on the single dimension of height, and therefore perceive the taller, narrower glass as having more water. In contrast, most 7- and 8-year-olds consider both relevant dimensions of the problem simultaneously. This allows them to realize that although the column of water in the taller glass is higher, the column is also narrower, and the two differences offset each other.

In the course of reading this book, you will encounter a number of other stage theories, including Sigmund Freud's theory of psychosexual development, Erik Erikson's theory of psychosocial development, and Lawrence Kohlberg's theory of moral development. Each of these stage theories proposes that children of a given age show

stage theories ■ Approaches that propose that development involves a series of discontinuous, age-related phases.

cognitive development ■ The development of thinking and reasoning.

broad similarities across many situations and that children of different ages tend to behave very differently.

Such stage theories have been very influential. In the past 20 years, however, many researchers have concluded that most developmental changes are gradual rather than sudden, and that development occurs skill by skill, task by task, rather than in a broadly unified way (Courage & Howe, 2002; Elman et al., 1996; Thelen & Smith, 2006). This view of development is less dramatic than that of stage theories, but a great deal of evidence supports it. One such piece of evidence is the fact that a child will often behave in accord with one proposed stage on some tasks but in accord with a different proposed stage on other tasks (K. W. Fischer & Bidell, 2006). This variable level of reasoning makes it difficult to view the child as being "in" either stage.

Much of the difficulty in deciding whether development is continuous or discontinuous is that the same facts can look very different, depending on one's perspective. Consider the seemingly simple question of whether children's height increases continuously or discontinuously. Figure 1.3a shows a boy's height, measured yearly from birth to age 18 (Tanner, 1961). When one looks at the boy's height at each age, development seems smooth and continuous, with growth occurring rapidly early in life and then slowing down.

However, when you look at Figure 1.3b, a different picture emerges. This graph illustrates the same boy's growth, but it depicts the amount of growth from one year to the next. The boy grew every year, but he grew

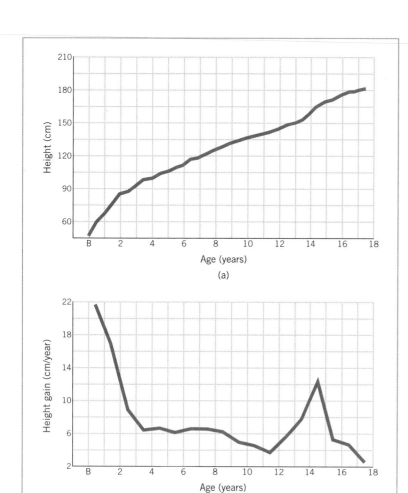

FIGURE 1.3 Continuous and discontinuous growth Changes in height can be viewed as either continuous or discontinuous. (a) Examining a boy's height in absolute terms from birth to 18 years makes the growth look gradual and continuous (from Tanner, 1961). (b) Examining the increases in the same boy's height from one year to the next over the same period shows rapid growth during the first 2½ years, then slower growth, then a growth spurt in adolescence, then a rapid decrease in growth. Viewed this way, growth seems discontinuous.

most during two periods: from birth to age 2½, and from ages 13 to 15. These are the kinds of data that lead people to talk about discontinuous growth and about a separate stage of adolescence that includes a physical growth spurt.

So, is development fundamentally continuous or fundamentally discontinuous? The most reasonable answer seems to be "It depends on how you look at it and how often you look." Imagine the difference between the perspective of an uncle who sees his niece every 2 or 3 years and that of the niece's parents, who see her every day. The uncle will almost always be struck with the huge changes in his niece since he last saw her. The niece will be so different that it will seem that she has progressed to a higher stage of development. In contrast, the parents will most often be struck by the continuity of her development; to them, she will usually just seem to grow up a bit each day. Throughout this book, we will be considering the changes, large and small, sudden and gradual, that have led some researchers to emphasize the continuities in development and others to emphasize the discontinuities.

4 Mechanisms of Development: How Does Change Occur?

Perhaps the deepest mystery about children's development is expressed by the question "How does change occur?" In other words, what are the mechanisms that produce the remarkable changes that children undergo with age and experience? A very general answer was implicit in the earlier discussion of the theme of *nature and nurture*. The interaction of genome and environment determines both what changes occur and when those changes occur. The challenge comes in specifying more precisely how any given change occurs.

One particularly interesting analysis of the mechanisms of developmental change involves the roles of brain activity, genes, and learning experiences in the development of *effortful attention* (e.g., Rothbart, Sheese, & Posner, 2007). Effortful attention involves voluntary control of one's emotions and thoughts. It includes processes such as inhibiting impulses (e.g., obeying requests to put all of one's toys away, as opposed to putting some away but then getting distracted and playing with the remaining ones); controlling emotions (e.g., not crying when failing to get one's way); and focusing attention (e.g., concentrating on one's homework despite the inviting sounds of other children playing outside). Difficulty in exerting effortful attention is associated with behavioural problems, weak math and reading skills, and mental illness (Blair & Razza, 2007; A. Diamond & Lee, 2011; Rothbart & Bates, 2006).

Studies of the brain activity of people performing tasks that require control of thoughts and emotions show that connections are especially active between the anterior cingulate, a brain structure involved in setting and attending to goals, and the limbic area, a part of the brain that plays a large role in emotional reactions (Etkin et al., 2006). Connections between brain areas such as the anterior cingulate and the limbic area develop considerably during childhood, and their development appears to be one mechanism that underlies improving effortful attention during childhood (Rothbart, Sheese, & Posner, 2007).

What role do genes and learning experiences play in influencing this mechanism of effortful attention? Specific genes influence the production of key **neurotransmitters**—chemicals involved in communication among brain cells. Variations among children in these genes are associated with variations in the quality of performance on tasks that require effortful attention (Canli et al., 2005; A. Diamond et al., 2004; Rueda et al., 2005). These genetic influences do not occur in a vacuum, however. As noted in the discussion of epigenetics, the environment plays a crucial role in the expression of genes. Infants with a particular form of one of the genes in question show differences in effortful attention related to the quality of parenting they receive, with lower-quality parenting being associated with lower ability to regulate attention (Sheese et al., 2007). Among children who do not have that form of the gene, quality of parenting has less effect on effortful attention.

Children's experiences also can change the wiring of the brain system that produces effortful attention. Rueda and colleagues (2005) presented 6-year-olds with a 5-day training program that used computerized exercises to improve capacity for effortful attention. Examination of electrical activity in the anterior cingulate indicated that those 6-year-olds who had completed the computerized exercises showed improved effortful attention. These children also showed improved performance on intelligence tests, which makes sense given the sustained effortful attention required by such tests. Thus, the experiences that children encounter influence their brain processes and gene expression, just as brain processes and genes influence children's reactions to experiences. More generally, a full understanding of the mechanisms that produce developmental change requires specifying how genes, brain structures and processes, and experiences interact.

neurotransmitters ■ Chemicals involved in communication among brain cells.

sociocultural context ■ The physical, social, cultural, economic, and historical circumstances that make up any child's environment.

5 *The Sociocultural Context*: How Does the Sociocultural Context Influence Development?

Children grow up in a particular set of physical and social environments, in a particular culture, under particular economic circumstances, at a particular time in history. Together, these physical, social, cultural, economic, and historical circumstances interact to constitute the **sociocultural context** of a child's life. This sociocultural context influences every aspect of children's development.

A classic depiction of the components of the sociocultural context is Urie Bronfenbrenner's (1979) bioecological model (discussed in depth in Chapter 9). The most obviously important component of children's sociocultural contexts is the people with whom they interact—parents, grandparents, brothers, sisters, daycare providers, teachers, friends, classmates, and so on—and the physical environment in which they live—their home, daycare centre, school, neighbourhood, and so on. Another important but less tangible component of the sociocultural context is the institutions that influence children's lives: educational systems, religious institutions, sports leagues, social organizations (such as Girl Guides, Boy Scouts, and 4-H), and so on.

Yet another important set of influences are the general characteristics of the child's society: its economic and technological advancement; its values, attitudes, beliefs, and traditions; its laws and political structure; and so on. For example, the simple fact that most toddlers and preschoolers growing up in Canada and the United States today go to child care outside their homes reflects a number of these less tangible sociocultural factors, including:

1. The historical era (50 years ago, far fewer children in Canada and the United States attended child-care centres)

2. The economic structure (there are far more opportunities today for women with young children to work outside the home)

3. Cultural beliefs (for example, that receiving child care outside the home does not harm children)

4. Cultural values (for example, that mothers of young children should be able to work outside the home if they wish).

Attendance at child-care centres, in turn, partly determines the people children meet and the activities in which they engage.

One method that developmentalists use to understand the influence of the sociocultural context is to compare the lives of children who grow up in different cultures. Such *cross-cultural comparisons* often reveal that practices that are rare or non-existent in one's own culture are common in other cultures. The following comparison of young children's sleeping arrangements in different societies illustrates the value of such cross-cultural research.

In most families in Canada and the United States, newborn infants sleep in their parents' bedroom, either in a crib or in the same bed. However, when infants are 2 to 6 months old, parents usually move them to another bedroom where they sleep alone (Greenfield, Suzuki, & Rothstein-Fisch, 2006; Mindell et al., 2010). This seems only natural to most people raised in North America, because it is how we and others whom we know were raised. From a worldwide perspective, however, such sleeping arrangements are highly unusual. In most other societies, including economically advanced nations such as Italy, Japan, and South Korea, babies almost always sleep in the same bed as their mother for the first few years, and somewhat older children also sleep in the same room as their mother, sometimes in the same bed (e.g., Nelson, Schiefenhoevel, & Haimerl, 2000; Whiting & Edwards, 1988). Where does this leave the father? In some cultures, the father sleeps in the same bed with mother and baby; in others, he sleeps in a separate bed or in a different room.

How do these differences in sleeping arrangements affect children? To find out, researchers interviewed mothers in middle-class U.S. families in Salt Lake City, Utah, and in rural Mayan families in Guatemala (Morelli et al., 1992). These interviews revealed that by age 6 months, the large majority of the U.S. children had begun sleeping in their own bedroom. As the children grew out of infancy, the nightly separation of child and parents became a complex ritual, surrounded by activities intended to comfort the child, such as telling stories, reading children's books, singing songs, and so on. About half the children were reported as taking a comfort object, such as a blanket or teddy bear, to bed with them.

In contrast, interviews with the Mayan mothers indicated that their children typically slept in the same bed with them until the age of 2 or 3 years and continued to sleep in the same room with them for years thereafter. The children usually went to sleep at the same time as their parents. None of the Mayan parents reported bedtime rituals, and almost none reported their children taking comfort objects, such as dolls or stuffed animals, to bed with them.

In many countries, including Denmark, the country in which this mother and child live, mothers and children sleep together for the first several years of the child's life. This sociocultural pattern is in sharp contrast to the North American practice of having infants sleep separately from their parents soon after birth.

Why do sleeping arrangements differ across cultures? Interviews with the Mayan and U.S. parents indicated that the crucial consideration for them in determining sleeping arrangements was cultural values. Mayan culture prizes interdependence among people. The Mayan parents expressed the belief that having a young child sleep with the mother is important for developing a good parent–child relationship, for avoiding the child's becoming distressed at being alone, and for helping parents spot any problems the child is having. They often expressed shock and pity when told that infants in the United States typically sleep separately from their parents (Greenfield et al., 2006). In contrast, U.S. culture, like Canadian culture, prizes independence and self-reliance, and the U.S. mothers expressed the belief that having babies and young children sleep alone promotes these values, as well as allowing intimacy between husbands and wives (Morelli et al., 1992). These differences illustrate both how practices that strike us as natural may differ greatly across cultures and how the simple conventions of everyday life often reflect deeper values.

Contexts of development differ not just between cultures but also within them. In modern multicultural societies, many contextual differences are related to ethnicity, race, and **socioeconomic status (SES)**—a measure of social class that is based on income and education. Virtually all aspects of children's lives—from the food they eat to the parental discipline they receive to the games they play—vary with ethnicity, race, and SES.

The socioeconomic context exerts a particularly large influence on children's lives. In economically advanced societies, including Canada, most children grow up in comfortable circumstances, but millions of other children do not. In Canada, 8.1% of children live in families whose income falls below the low income cut-off. When children live in lone-parent families headed by a woman, the rate jumps to almost 22% (Statistics Canada, 2012b).

As a recent report to the Royal Society of Canada documents, children from economically disadvantaged families tend to do less well than other children in many ways, and these effects can be long-lasting (Boivin et al., 2012). In infancy, they are

socioeconomic status (SES) ■ A measure of social class based on income and education.

more likely to have serious health problems. In childhood, they are more likely to have social/emotional and behavioural problems. Throughout childhood and adolescence, they tend to have smaller vocabularies, lower IQs, and lower math and reading scores on standardized achievement tests. In adolescence, they are more likely to have a baby or drop out of school (G. W. Evans et al., 2005; Luthar, 1999; McLoyd, 1998).

These negative outcomes are not surprising when we consider the huge array of disadvantages that poor children face. Compared with children who grow up in more affluent circumstances, they are more likely to live in dangerous neighbourhoods, to attend lower-quality child-care centres and schools, and to be exposed to high levels of air and water pollution (Dilworth-Bart & Moore, 2006; G. W. Evans, 2004). In addition, their parents read to them less, talk to them less, provide fewer books in the home, and are less involved in their schooling. Poor children also are more likely than affluent children to grow up in single-parent homes or to be raised by neither biological parent. The accumulation of these disadvantages, rather than any single one of them, seems to be the greatest obstacle to poor children's successful development (Luthar, 2006; Morales & Guerra, 2006).

And yet as we saw in Werner's study of the children of Kauai, described at the beginning of the chapter, many children do overcome the obstacles that poverty presents. Such resilient children tend to have three characteristics: (1) positive personal qualities, such as high intelligence, an easygoing personality, and an optimistic outlook on the future; (2) a close relationship with at least one parent; and (3) a close relationship with at least one adult other than their parents, such as a grandparent, teacher, coach, or family friend (E. Chen & Miller, 2012; Masten, 2007). Thus, although poverty poses serious obstacles to successful development, many children do surmount the challenges—usually with the help of adults in their lives.

6 *Individual Differences*: How Do Children Become So Different from One Another?

Anyone who has experience with children is struck by their uniqueness—their differences not only in physical appearance but in everything from activity level and temperament to intelligence, persistence, and emotionality. These differences among children emerge quickly. Some infants in their first year are shy, others outgoing. Some infants play with or look at objects for prolonged periods; others rapidly shift from activity to activity. Even children in the same family often differ substantially, as you probably already know if you have siblings.

Sandra Scarr (1992) identified four factors that can lead children from a single family (as well as children from different families) to turn out very different from one another:

1. Genetic differences
2. Differences in treatment by parents and others
3. Differences in reactions to similar experiences
4. Different choices of environments.

The most obvious reason for differences among children is that, except for identical twins, every individual is genetically unique. All other siblings (including fraternal twins) share 50% of their genes and differ in the other 50%.

A second major source of variation among children is differences in the treatment they receive from parents and other people. This differential treatment is often associated with pre-existing differences in the children's characteristics. For example, parents tend to provide more sensitive care to easygoing infants than to difficult ones; by the second year, parents of difficult children are often angry with them even when the children have done nothing wrong in the immediate situation (van den Boom & Hoeksma, 1994). Teachers, likewise, tend to provide positive attention and encouragement to pupils who are learning well and are well behaved, but with pupils who are doing poorly and are disruptive, they tend to be openly critical and to deny the pupils' requests for special help (Good & Brophy, 1996).

In addition to being shaped by objective differences in the treatment they receive, children also are influenced by their subjective interpretations of the treatment. A classic example occurs when each of a pair of siblings feels that their parents favour the other. Siblings also often react differently to events that affect the whole family. In one study, 69% of negative events, such as parents' being laid off or fired, elicited fundamentally different reactions from siblings (Beardsall & Dunn, 1992). Some children were very concerned at a parent's loss of a job; others were sure that everything would be okay.

Different children, even ones within the same family, often react to the same experience in completely different ways.

A fourth major source of differences among children relates to the previously discussed theme of the *active child:* as children grow older, they increasingly choose activities and friends for themselves and thus influence their own subsequent development. They may also accept or choose niches for themselves: within a family, one child may become "the smart one," another "the popular one," another "the bad one," and so on (Scarr & McCartney, 1983). A child labelled by family members as "the smart one" may strive to live up to the label; so, unfortunately, may a child labelled "the troublemaker."

As discussed in the section on nature and nurture and in the section on mechanisms of development, differences in biology and experience interact in complex ways to create the infinite diversity of human beings. Thus, a study of 11- to 17-year-olds found that the grades of children who were highly engaged with school changed in more positive directions than would have been predicted by their genetic background or family environments alone (W. Johnson, McGue, & Iacono, 2006). The same study revealed that children who had high intelligence were less negatively affected by adverse family environments than were other children. Thus, children's genes, their treatment by other people, their subjective reactions to their experiences, and their choice of environments interact in ways that contribute to differences among children, even ones in the same family.

7 *Research and Children's Welfare:* How Can Research Promote Children's Well-Being?

Improved understanding of child development often leads to practical benefits. Several examples have already been described, including the program for helping children deal with their anger and the recommendations for fostering valid eyewitness testimony from young children.

Another type of practical benefit arising from child-development research involves educational innovations. One fascinating example comes from studies of how children's beliefs about intelligence influence their learning. Carol Dweck and her colleagues (Dweck, 2006; Dweck & Leggett, 1988) have found that some children (and adults) believe that intelligence is a fixed entity. They see each person as having a certain amount of intelligence that is set at birth and cannot be changed by experience. Other children (and adults) believe that intelligence is a changeable characteristic that increases with learning, and that the time and effort people put into learning is the key determinant of their intelligence.

People who believe that intelligence increases with learning tend to react to failure in more effective ways (Dweck, 2006). When they fail to solve a problem, they more often persist with the task and try harder. Such persistence in the face of failure is an important quality. As the great British prime minister Winston Churchill once said, "Success is the ability to go from one failure to another with no loss of enthusiasm." In contrast, people who believe that intelligence is a fixed entity tend to give up when they fail, because they think the problem is too hard for them.

Building on this research regarding the relation between beliefs about intelligence and persistence in the face of difficulty, Blackwell, Trzesniewski, and Dweck (2007) devised an effective educational program for middle school students from low-income backgrounds. They presented randomly selected students with research findings about how learning alters the brain in ways that improve subsequent learning and thus "makes you smarter." Other randomly selected students from the same classrooms were presented with research findings about how memory works. The investigators predicted that the students who were told about the effects that learning has on the brain would change their beliefs about intelligence in ways that would help them persevere in the face of failure. In particular, the changed beliefs were expected to improve students' learning of mathematics, an area in which children often experience initial failure.

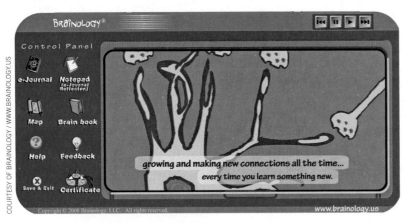

Screenshot from Brainology, a commercially available educational program based on the findings of Blackwell, Trzesniewski, and Dweck (2007). The software, like the research study, emphasizes that learning makes children smarter by building new connections within the brain.

This prediction was borne out. Children who were presented information about how learning changes the brain and enhances intelligence subsequently improved their math grades, whereas the other children did not. Children who initially believed that intelligence was an inborn, unchanging quality but who came to believe that intelligence reflected learning showed especially large improvements. Perhaps most striking, when the children's teachers, who did not know which type of information each child had received, were asked if any of their students had shown unusual improvement in motivation or performance, the teachers cited more than three times as many students who had been given information about how learning builds intelligence.

In subsequent chapters, we review many additional examples of how child-development research is being used to promote children's welfare.

review:

The modern field of child development is in large part an attempt to answer a small set of fundamental questions about children. These include:

1. How do nature and nurture jointly contribute to development?
2. How do children contribute to their own development?
3. Is development best viewed as continuous or discontinuous?
4. What mechanisms produce development?
5. How does the sociocultural context influence development?
6. Why are children so different from one another?
7. How can we use research to improve children's welfare?

Methods for Studying Child Development

As illustrated in the preceding section, modern scientific research has advanced the understanding of fundamental questions about child development well beyond that of the historical figures who first raised the questions. This progress reflects the successful application of the scientific method to the study of child development. In this section, we describe the scientific method and examine how its use has advanced understanding of child development.

The Scientific Method

The basic assumption of the **scientific method** is that all beliefs, no matter how probable they seem and no matter how many people share them, may be wrong. Therefore, until beliefs have been tested, they must be viewed as **hypotheses,** that is, as educated guesses, rather than as truth. If a hypothesis is tested, and the evidence repeatedly does not support it, the hypothesis must be abandoned no matter how reasonable it seems.

Use of the scientific method involves four basic steps:

1. Choosing a question to be answered
2. Formulating a hypothesis regarding the question
3. Developing a method for testing the hypothesis
4. Using the data yielded by the method to draw a conclusion regarding the hypothesis.

To illustrate these steps, let's make the *question to be answered* "What abilities predict which children will become good readers?" A reasonable *hypothesis* might be "Kindergartners who can identify the separate sounds within words will become better readers than those who cannot." A straightforward *method* for testing this hypothesis would be to select a group of preschoolers, test their ability to identify the separate sounds within words, and then, several years later, test the reading skills of the same children. Research has, in fact, shown that kindergartners who are aware of the component sounds within words later tend to read more skillfully than their peers who lacked this ability as kindergartners. This pattern holds true regardless of whether children are learning English, Norwegian, or Swedish (Furnes & Samuelsson, 2011). The pattern also holds whether children are learning Canadian-English as a first or second language (Chiappe & Siegel, 1999). These results support the *conclusion* that kindergartners' ability to identify sounds within words predicts their later reading skill.

The first, second, and fourth of these steps are not unique to the scientific method. As we have seen, great thinkers of the past also asked questions, formulated hypotheses, and drew conclusions that were reasonable given the evidence available to them. What distinguishes scientific research from non-scientific approaches is the third step: the methods used to test the hypotheses. When rigorously employed, these research methods yield high-quality evidence that allows investigators to progress beyond their initial hypotheses to draw firmly grounded conclusions.

The Importance of Appropriate Measurement

For the scientific method to work, researchers must use measures that are directly relevant to the hypotheses being tested. Even measures that initially seem reasonable sometimes turn out to be less informative than originally thought. For

scientific method ■ An approach to testing beliefs that involves choosing a question, formulating a hypothesis, testing the hypothesis, and drawing a conclusion.

hypotheses ■ Educated guesses.

reliability ■ The degree to which independent measurements of a given behaviour are consistent.

interrater reliability ■ The amount of agreement in the observations of different raters who witness the same behaviour.

test–retest reliability ■ The degree of similarity of a child's performance on two or more occasions.

validity ■ The degree to which a test measures what it is intended to measure.

internal validity ■ The degree to which effects observed within experiments can be attributed to the factor that the researcher is testing.

example, a researcher who hypothesized that a supplemental food program would help children suffering from malnutrition might evaluate the program on the basis of weight gain from just before the program to just after it. However, weight is an inadequate measure of nutrition: providing unlimited supplies of Cheezies would probably produce weight gain but not improve nutrition, and many people are obese yet malnourished (Sawaya et al., 1995). Better measures of nutrition would include whether more adequate levels of essential nutrients were present in the children's bloodstreams at the end of the study. (Shetty, 2006).

Regardless of the particular measure used, many of the same criteria determine whether a measure is a good one. One key criterion has already been noted—the measure must be directly relevant to the hypothesis. Two other qualities that good measures must possess are *reliability* and *validity*.

Reliability The degree to which independent measurements of a behaviour under study are consistent is referred to as **reliability.** One important type of consistency, **interrater reliability,** indicates how much agreement there is in the observations of different raters who witness the same behaviour. Sometimes the observations are qualitative, as when raters classify a baby's attachment to her mother as "secure" or "insecure." Other times the observations are quantitative, as when raters score on a scale of 1 to 10 how upset babies become when they are presented with an unfamiliar noisy toy or a boisterous stranger. In both cases, interrater reliability is attained when the raters' observations are in close agreement—as when, for example, Baby A in a group being observed for a particular behaviour gets a 6 or 7 from all the raters, Baby B gets a 3 or 4, Baby C gets an 8 or 9, and so on. Without such close agreement, one cannot have confidence in the research findings, because there is no way to tell which (if any) rating was accurate.

A second important type of consistency is **test–retest reliability.** This type of reliability is attained when measures of a child's performance on the same test, administered under the same conditions, are similar on two or more occasions. Suppose, for example, that researchers presented a vocabulary test to a group of children on two occasions one week apart. If the test is reliable, those children who scored highest on the first testing should also score highest on the second, because none of the children's vocabularies would have changed much over such a short period. As in the example of interrater reliability, a lack of test–retest reliability would make it impossible to know which result (if either) accurately reflected each child's status.

Validity The **validity** of a test or experiment refers to the degree to which it measures what it is intended to measure. Researchers strive for two types of validity: internal and external. **Internal validity** refers to whether effects observed within experiments can be attributed with confidence to the factor that the researcher is testing. For example, suppose that a researcher tests the effectiveness of a type of psychotherapy for depression by administering it to a number of depressed adolescents. If three months later many of the adolescents are no longer depressed, can it be concluded that this type of psychotherapy caused the improvement? No, because the students' recovery may have been due to the mere passage of time. Moods fluctuate, and many adolescents who are depressed at any given time will be happier at a later date even without psychotherapy. In this example, the passage of time is a source of internal invalidity, because the factor believed to cause the improvement (the psychotherapy) may have had no effect.

External validity, in contrast, refers to the ability to generalize research findings beyond the particulars of the research in question. Studies of child development are almost never intended to apply only to the particular children and research methods involved in a given study. Rather, the goal is to draw conclusions that apply to children more generally. Thus, the findings of a single experiment are only the first step in determining the external validity of the results. Additional studies with participants from different backgrounds and with different research methods are invariably needed to establish the external validity of the findings. (Table 1.2 summarizes the key properties of behavioural measures.)

external validity ■ The degree to which results can be generalized beyond the particulars of the research.

structured interview ■ A research procedure in which all participants are asked to answer the same questions.

clinical interview ■ A procedure in which questions are adjusted in accord with the answers the interviewee provides.

TABLE 1.2

Key Properties of Behavioural Measures

Property	Question of Interest
Relevance to hypotheses	Do the hypotheses predict in a straightforward way what should happen on these measures?
Interrater reliability	Do different raters who observe the same behaviour classify or score it the same way?
Test–retest reliability	Do children who score higher on a measure at one time also score higher on the measure at other times?
Internal validity	Can effects within the experiment be attributed to the variables that the researcher intentionally manipulated?
External validity	How widely can the findings be generalized to different children in different places at different times?

Contexts for Gathering Data About Children

Researchers obtain data about children in three main contexts: *interviews, naturalistic observation,* and *structured observation.* In the following sections, we consider how gathering data in each context can help answer different questions about children.

Interviews

The most obvious way to collect data about children is to go straight to the source and ask the children themselves about their lives. One type of interview, the **structured interview,** is especially useful when the goal is to collect self-reports on the same topics from everyone being studied. For example, Valeski and Stipek (2001) asked kindergartners and 1st graders questions regarding their feelings about school (How much does your teacher care about you? How do you feel when you're at school?) and also questions about their beliefs about their academic competence (How much do you know about numbers? How good are you at reading?). The children's general attitude toward school and their feelings about their relationship with their teacher proved to be positively related to their beliefs about their competence in math and reading. Asking large numbers of children identical questions about their feelings and beliefs provides a quick and straightforward way for researchers to learn about children's beliefs and attitudes.

A second type of interview, the **clinical interview,** is especially useful for obtaining in-depth information about an individual child. In this approach, the interviewer begins with a set of prepared questions, but if the child says something intriguing, the interviewer can depart from the script to follow up on the child's lead.

naturalistic observation ■ Examination of ongoing behaviour in an environment not controlled by the researcher.

The usefulness of clinical interviews can be seen in the case of Bobby, a 10-year-old child who was assessed for symptoms of depression (S. Schwartz & Johnson, 1985). When the interviewer asked him about school, Bobby said that he did not like it, because the other children disliked him and he was bad at sports. As he put it, "I'm not really very good at anything" (p. 214). To explore the source of this sad self-description, the interviewer asked Bobby what he would wish for if three wishes could be granted. Bobby replied, "I would wish that I was the type of boy my mother and father want, I would wish that I could have friends, and I would wish that I wouldn't feel sad so much" (p. 214). Such heart-rending comments provide a sense of the painful subjective experience of this depressed child, one that would be impossible to obtain from methods that were not tailored to the individual.

As with all contexts for collecting data, interviews have both strengths and weaknesses. On the positive side, they yield a great deal of data quickly and can provide in-depth information about individual children. On the negative side, answers to interview questions often are biased. Children (like adults) often avoid disclosing facts that show them in a bad light, distort the way that events happened, and fail to understand their own motivations (T. D. Wilson & Dunn, 2004). These limitations have led many researchers to use observational methods that allow them to witness the behaviour of interest for themselves.

One-on-one clinical interviews like this one can elicit unique in-depth information about a child.

Naturalistic Observation

When the primary research goal is to describe how children behave in their usual environments—homes, schools, playgrounds, and so on—**naturalistic observation** is the method of choice for gathering data. In this approach, observers try to remain unobtrusively in the background in the chosen setting, which allows them to see the relevant behaviours while minimizing the chances that their presence will influence those behaviours.

Psychologists sometimes observe family interactions around the dinner table, because mealtime comments can evoke strong emotions.

A classic example of naturalistic observation is Gerald Patterson's (1982) comparative study of family dynamics in "troubled" and "typical" families. The troubled families were defined by the presence of at least one child who had been labelled "out of control" and referred for treatment by a school, court, or mental health professional. The typical families were defined by the fact that none of the children in them showed signs of serious behavioural difficulties. Income levels and children's ages were the same for the troubled and typical families.

To observe the frequency with which children and parents engaged in negative behaviours—teasing, yelling, whining, criticizing, and so on—research assistants repeatedly observed dinnertime interactions in both troubled and typical homes. To accustom family members to

his or her presence, the research assistant for each family made several home visits before beginning to collect data.

The researchers found that the behaviours and attitudes of both parents and children in the troubled families differed strikingly from those of their counterparts in the typical families. Parents in the troubled families were more self-absorbed and less responsive to their children than were parents in the typical households. Children in the troubled families responded to parental punishment by becoming more aggressive, whereas children in the typical households responded to punishment by becoming less aggressive. In the troubled families, interactions often fell into a vicious cycle in which:

■ The child acted in a hostile or aggressive manner, for example, by defying a parent's request to clean up his or her room.

■ The parent reacted angrily, for example, by shouting at the child to obey.

■ The child escalated the level of hostility, for example, by yelling back.

■ The parent ratcheted up the aggression even further, perhaps by spanking the child.

As Patterson's study suggests, naturalistic observations are particularly useful for illuminating everyday social interactions, such as those between children and parents.

Although naturalistic observation can yield detailed information about certain aspects of children's everyday lives, it also has important limitations. One is that naturally occurring contexts vary on many dimensions, so it is often hard to know which ones influenced the behaviour of interest. For example, it was clear in the Patterson study that the interactions of troubled families differed from those of the more harmonious families, but the interactions and family histories differed in so many ways that it was impossible to specify their contributions to the current situation. A second limitation of naturalistic studies is that many behaviours of interest occur only occasionally in the everyday environment, which reduces researchers' opportunities to learn about them. A means for overcoming both limitations is the method known as structured observation.

Structured Observation

When using **structured observation,** researchers design a situation that will elicit behaviour that is relevant to a hypothesis and then observe how different children behave in that situation. The researchers then relate the observed behaviours to characteristics of the child, such as age, sex, or personality, and to the child's behaviour in other situations that are also observed.

In one such study, Kochanska, Coy, and Murray (2001) investigated the links between 2- and 3-year-olds' compliance with their mother's requests to forgo appealing activities and their compliance with her requests that they participate in unappealing ones. Mothers brought their toddlers to a laboratory room that had a number of especially attractive toys sitting on a shelf and a great many less attractive toys scattered around the room. The experimenter asked each mother to tell her child that he or she could play with any of the toys *except* the ones on the shelf. Raters observed the children through a one-way mirror over the next few minutes and classified them as complying with their mother's request wholeheartedly, grudgingly, or not at all. Then the experimenter asked the mother to leave the room and observed whether the child played with the "forbidden" toys in the mother's absence.

The researchers found that children who had complied wholeheartedly in the first instance tended to avoid playing with the forbidden toys for a longer time in

structured observation ■ A method that involves presenting an identical situation to each child and recording the child's behaviour.

Temptation is everywhere, but children who are generally compliant with their mother's requests when she is present are also more likely to resist temptation when she is absent (like this boy, the nephew of one of the authors, whose reach, despite appearances, stopped just short of the cake).

TABLE 1.3

Advantages and Disadvantages of Three Contexts for Gathering Data

Data-Gathering Situation	Features	Advantages	Disadvantages
Interview	Children answer questions asked either in person or on a questionnaire.	Can reveal children's subjective experience.	Reports are often biased to reflect favourably on interviewee.
		Structured interviews are inexpensive means for collecting in-depth data about individuals.	Memories of interviewees are often inaccurate and incomplete.
		Clinical interviews allow flexibility for following up unexpected comments.	Prediction of future behaviours is often inaccurate.
Naturalistic observation	Activities of children in everyday settings are observed.	Useful for describing behaviour in everyday settings.	Difficult to know which aspects of situation are most influential.
		Helps illuminate social interaction processes.	Limited value for studying infrequent behaviours.
Structured observation	Children are brought to a laboratory and presented pre-arranged tasks.	Ensures that all children's behaviours are observed in same context.	Context is less natural than in naturalistic observation.
		Allows controlled comparison of children's behaviour in different situations.	Reveals less about subjective experience than interviews do.

the second. Moreover, these children were also more likely to comply with their mother's request that they put away the many toys on the floor after she left the room. When retested near their 4th birthday, most children showed the same type of compliance as they had as toddlers. Overall, the results indicated that the quality of young children's compliance with their mother's requests is a somewhat stable, general property of the mother–child relationship.

This type of structured observation offers an important advantage over naturalistic observation: it ensures that all the children being studied encounter identical situations. This allows direct comparisons of different children's behaviour in a given situation and, as in the research just discussed, also makes it possible to establish the generality of each child's behaviour across different tasks. On the other hand, structured observation does not provide as extensive information about individual children's subjective experience as do interviews, nor can it provide the open-ended, everyday kind of data that naturalistic observation can yield.

As these examples suggest, which data-gathering approach is best depends on the goals of the research. (Table 1.3 summarizes the advantages and disadvantages of interviews, naturalistic observation, and structured observation as contexts for gathering data.)

Correlation and Causation

People differ along an infinite number of **variables,** that is, attributes that vary across individuals and situations, such as age, sex, activity level, socioeconomic status, particular experiences, and so on. A major goal of child-development research is to determine how these and other major variables are related to one another, both in terms of associations and in terms of cause–effect relations. In the following sections, we consider the research designs that are used to examine each type of relation.

Correlational Designs

The primary goal of studies that use **correlational designs** is to determine whether children who differ in one variable also differ in predictable ways in other variables. For example, a researcher might examine whether toddlers' aggressiveness is related

variables ■ Attributes that vary across individuals and situations, such as age, sex, and popularity.

correlational designs ■ Studies intended to indicate how variables are related to on another.

to the number of hours they spend in daycare or whether adolescents' popularity is related to their self-control.

The association between two variables is known as their **correlation.** When variables are strongly correlated, knowing a child's score on either variable allows accurate prediction of the child's score on the other. For example, the fact that the number of hours per week that children spend reading correlates highly with their reading test scores (Guthrie et al., 1999) means that a child's reading test score can be accurately predicted if one knows how much time the child spends reading. It also means that the number of hours the child spends reading can be predicted if one knows the child's reading test score.

Correlations range from 1.00, the strongest positive correlation, to −1.00, the strongest negative correlation. The direction is positive when high values of one variable are associated with high values of the other and low values of one are associated with low values of the other; the direction is negative when high values of one are associated with low values of the other. Thus, the correlation between time spent reading and reading test scores is positive, because children who spend high amounts of time reading also have high reading test scores; the correlation between obesity and running speed is negative, because the more obese the child, the slower his or her running speed.

Correlation Does Not Equal Causation

When two variables are strongly correlated and there is a plausible cause–effect relation between them, it often is tempting to infer that one causes the other. However, this inference is not justified, for two reasons. The first is the **direction-of-causation problem:** a correlation does not indicate which variable is the cause and which variable is the effect. In the above example of the correlation between time spent reading and reading achievement, greater time spent reading *might* cause increased reading achievement. On the other hand, the cause–effect relation could run in the opposite direction: greater reading skill might cause children to spend more time reading, because reading faster and with greater comprehension makes reading more enjoyable.

The second reason that correlation does not imply causation is the **third-variable problem:** the correlation between two variables may actually be the result of some third, unspecified variable. In the reading example, for instance, rather than greater reading achievement being caused by greater reading time, or vice versa, both of these aspects of reading could be caused by growing up in a family that values knowledge and intelligence.

Recognizing that correlation does not imply causation is crucial for interpreting accounts of research. Even findings published in prestigious research journals can easily be misinterpreted. For example, based on a correlation between children younger than 2 years sleeping with a night light and their later becoming nearsighted, an article in the prestigious journal *Nature* concluded that the light was harmful to visual development (G. E. Quinn et al., 1999). Not surprisingly, the claim received considerable publicity in the popular media (e.g., Torassa, 2000). Subsequent research, however, showed that the inference about causation was wrong. What actually seems to have happened is that the nearsighted infants generally had nearsighted parents, and the nearsighted parents, for unknown reasons, more often placed night lights in their infants' rooms (Gwiazda et al., 2000; Zadnik et al., 2000). As the example illustrates, even seemingly straightforward inferences of causation, based on correlational evidence, frequently prove to be wrong.

correlation ■ The association between two variables.

direction-of-causation problem ■ The concept that a correlation between two variables does not indicate which, if either, variable is the cause of the other.

third-variable problem ■ The concept that a correlation between two variables may stem from both being influenced by some third variable.

experimental designs ■ A group of approaches that allow inferences about causes and effects to be drawn.

random assignment ■ A procedure in which each child has an equal chance of being assigned to each group within an experiment.

If correlation does not imply causation, why do researchers often use correlational designs? One major reason is that the influence of many variables of great interest—age, sex, race, and social class among them—cannot be studied experimentally (see the next section) because researchers cannot manipulate them; that is, they cannot assign participants to one sex or another, to one SES or another, and so on. Consequently, these variables can only be studied through correlational methods. Correlational designs are also of great use when the goal is to describe relations among variables rather than to identify cause–effect relations among them. If, for example, the research goal is to discover how moral reasoning, empathy, anxiety, and popularity are related to one another, correlational designs would almost certainly be employed.

Experimental Designs

If correlational designs are insufficient to indicate cause–effect relations, what type of approach is sufficient? The answer is **experimental designs.** The logic of experimental designs can be summarized quite simply: if children in one group are exposed to a particular experience and subsequently behave differently from a comparable group of children who were not exposed to the experience or were exposed to a different experience, then the subsequent differences in behaviour must have resulted from the differences in experience.

Two techniques are crucial to experimental designs: *random assignment* of participants to groups and *experimental control*. **Random assignment** involves assigning the participants to one experimental group or another according to chance so that the groups are comparable at the outset. This comparability is crucial for being able to infer that it was the varying experiences to which the groups were exposed in the experiment that caused the later differences between them. Otherwise, those differences might have arisen from some pre-existing difference between the people in the groups.

Say, for example, that researchers wanted to compare the effectiveness of two interventions for helping depressed mothers improve their relationship with their infant—providing the mothers with home visits from trained therapists versus providing them with supportive phone calls from such therapists. If the researchers provided the home visits to families in one neighbourhood and the supportive phone calls to families in another neighbourhood, it would be unclear whether any differences in mother–infant relationships following the experiment were caused by differences between the effectiveness of the two types of support or by differences between the families in the two areas. Depressed mothers in one neighbourhood might suffer from less severe forms of depression than mothers in the other, or they might have greater access to other support, such as close families, mental health centres, or parenting programs.

In contrast, when groups are created through random assignment and include a reasonably large number of participants (typically 20 or more per group), initial differences between the groups tend to be minimal. For example, if 40 families with mothers who suffer from depression are divided randomly into two experimental groups, each group is likely to have roughly equal numbers of families from each neighbourhood. Similarly, each group is likely to include a few mothers who are extremely depressed, a few with mild forms of depression, and many in between, as well as a few infants who have been severely affected by their mother's depression, a few who have been minimally affected, and many in

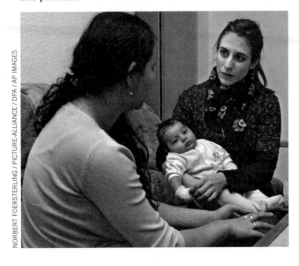

Depressed mothers often have difficulty providing sensitive parenting; home visits from trained therapists can help alleviate this problem.

NORBERT FOERSTERLING / PICTURE-ALLIANCE / DPA / AP IMAGES

between. The logic implies that groups created through random assignment should be comparable on all variables except the different treatment that people in the experimental groups encounter during the experiment. Such an experiment was in fact conducted, and it showed that home visits helped depressed mothers more than supportive phone calls did (Van Doesum et al., 2008).

The second essential characteristic of an experimental design, **experimental control,** refers to the ability of the researcher to determine the specific experiences that children in each group encounter during the study. In the simplest experimental design, one with two conditions, the groups are often referred to as the "experimental group" and the "control group." Children in the **experimental group** are presented with the experience of interest; children in the **control group** are treated identically except that they are not presented with the experience of interest or are presented with a different experience that is expected to have less effect on the variables being tested.

The experience that children in the experimental group receive, and that children in the control group do not receive, is referred to as the **independent variable.** The behaviour that is hypothesized to be affected by exposure to the independent variable is referred to as the **dependent variable.** Thus, if a researcher hypothesized that showing schoolchildren an anti-bullying film would reduce school bullying, the researcher might randomly assign some children in a school to view the film and other children in the same school to view a film about a different topic. In this case, the anti-bullying film would be the independent variable, and the amount of bullying after the children watched it would be the dependent variable. If the independent variable had the predicted effect, children who saw the anti-bullying film would show less bullying after watching it than children who saw the other film.

One illustration of how experimental designs allow researchers to draw conclusions about causes and effects is a study that tested the hypothesis that television shows running in the background lower the quality of infants' and toddlers' play (M. E. Schmidt et al., 2008). The independent variable was whether a television program was on in the room where the participants were playing; the dependent variables were a variety of measures of children's attention to the television program and of the quality of their play. The television program that was playing was *Jeopardy!*, which presumably would have been of little interest to the 1- and 2-year-olds in the study; indeed, they looked at it an average of only once per minute and only for a few seconds at a time. Nonetheless, the television show disrupted the children's play, reducing the length of play episodes and the children's focus on their play. These findings indicate that there is a causal, and negative, relation between background exposure to television shows and the quality of young children's play.

Experimental designs are the method of choice for establishing causal relations, a central goal of scientific research. However, as noted earlier, experimental designs cannot be applied to all issues of interest. For example, hypotheses about why boys tend to be more physically aggressive than girls cannot be tested experimentally because gender cannot be assigned randomly to children. In addition, many experimental studies are conducted in laboratory settings; this improves experimental control but can raise doubts about the external validity of the findings, that is, whether the findings from the lab apply to the outside world. (The advantages and disadvantages of correlational and experimental designs are summarized in Table 1.4.)

experimental control ■ The ability of researchers to determine the specific experiences that children have during the course of an experiment.

experimental group ■ A group of children in an experimental design who are presented the experience of interest.

control group ■ The group of children in an experimental design who are not presented the experience of interest but in other ways are treated similarly.

independent variable ■ The experience that children in the experimental group receive and that children in the control group do not receive.

dependent variable ■ A behaviour that is measured to determine whether it is affected by exposure to the independent variable.

The quality of infants' and toddlers' play is adversely affected by a television being on in the same room. This is true for even the most precocious children.

TABLE 1.4

Advantages and Disadvantages of Correlational and Experimental Designs

Type of Design	Features	Advantages	Disadvantages
Correlational	Comparison of existing groups of children or examination of relations among each child's scores on different variables.	Only way to compare many groups of interest (boys–girls, economically advantaged–economically disadvantaged, etc.).	Third-variable problem.
		Only way to establish relations among many variables of interest (IQ and achievement, popularity and happiness, etc.).	Direction-of-causation problem.
Experimental	Random assignment of children to groups, and experimental control of procedures presented to each group.	Allows causal inferences because design rules out direction-of-causation and third-variable problems.	Need for experimental control often leads to artificial experimental situations.
		Allows experimental control over the exact experiences that children encounter.	Cannot be used to study many differences and variables of interest, such as age, sex, and temperament.

Designs for Examining Development

A great deal of research on child development focuses on the ways in which children change, or remain the same, as they grow older and gain experience. To study development over time, investigators use three types of research designs: cross-sectional, longitudinal, and microgenetic.

Cross-Sectional Designs

The most common and easiest way to study changes and continuities with age is to use a **cross-sectional design.** This method compares children of different ages on a given behaviour, ability, or characteristic, with all the children being studied at roughly the same time—for example, within the same month. In one cross-sectional study, Evans, Xu, and Lee (2011) examined the development of lying in Chinese 3-, 4-, and 5-year-olds. The children played a game in which, to win a prize, they needed to guess the type of object hidden under an upside-down paper cup. However, before the child could guess, the experimenter left the room after telling the child not to peek while she was gone. The cup was so fully packed with candies that if the child peeked, some would spill out and it would be virtually impossible for the child to put them all back under the cup.

At all ages, many children peeked and then denied doing so. However, 5-year-olds lied more often, and their lies were cleverer. For example, many 5-year-olds explained away the presence of candies on the table by saying that they accidentally knocked over the cup with their elbow; other 5-year-olds destroyed the evidence by eating it. Three-year-olds were the least-skilled fibbers, generating implausible excuses such as that some other child had entered the room and knocked over the cup or that the candies had come out by themselves.

Cross-sectional designs are useful for revealing similarities and differences between older and younger children. However, they do not yield information about the stability of behaviour over time or about the patterns of change shown by individual children. This is where longitudinal approaches are especially valuable.

Longitudinal Designs

A **longitudinal design** involves following a group of children over a substantial period (usually at least a year) and observing changes and continuities in these children's development at regular intervals during that time. In one longitudinal study,

cross-sectional design ■ A research method in which children of different ages are compared on a given behaviour or characteristic over a short period.

longitudinal design ■ A method of study in which the same children are studied twice or more over a substantial length of time.

Brendgen and colleagues (2001) examined children's popularity with classmates each year from the time they were 7-year-olds to the time they were 12-year-olds. The popularity of most children proved to be quite stable over this period; a substantial number of children were popular in the large majority of years, and quite a few others were unpopular throughout. At the same time, some individuals showed idiosyncratic patterns of change from year to year; the same child might be popular at age 8, unpopular at age 10, and of average popularity at age 12. Such findings about the stability of individual differences over time and about individual children's patterns of change could only have been obtained in a longitudinal design.

If longitudinal designs are so useful for revealing stability and change over time, why are cross-sectional designs more common? The reasons are mainly practical. Studying the same children over long time periods involves the difficult task of locating the children for each re-examination. Inevitably, some of the children move away or stop participating for other reasons. Such loss of participants may call into question the validity of the findings, because the children who do not continue may differ from those who participate throughout. Another threat to the validity of longitudinal designs is the possible effects of the repeated testing. For example, repeatedly taking IQ tests could familiarize children with the type of items on the tests, thus improving the children's scores. For these reasons, longitudinal designs are used primarily when the main issues are stability and change in individual children over time—issues that can be studied only longitudinally. When the central developmental issue involves age-related changes in typical performance, cross-sectional studies are more commonly used.

Being excluded is no fun for anyone. Longitudinal research has been used to determine whether the same children are unpopular year after year or whether popularity changes over time.

Microgenetic Designs

An important limitation of both cross-sectional and longitudinal designs is that they provide only a broad outline of the process of change. **Microgenetic designs,** in contrast, are specifically designed to provide an in-depth depiction of the processes that produce change (P. H. Miller & Coyle, 1999; Siegler, 2006). The basic idea of this approach is to recruit children who are thought to be on the verge of an important developmental change, heighten their exposure to the type of experience that is believed to produce the change, and then intensively study the change *as it is occurring.* Microgenetic designs are like longitudinal ones in repeatedly testing the same children over time. They differ in that microgenetic studies typically include a greater number of sessions presented over a shorter time than in a longitudinal study.

Siegler and Jenkins (1989) used a microgenetic design to study how young children discover the **counting-on strategy** for adding two small numbers. This strategy involves counting up from the larger addend the number of times indicated by the smaller addend; for example, when asked the answer to 3 + 5, a child who was counting-on would start from the addend 5 and say or think "6, 7, 8" before answering "8." Prior to discovering this strategy, children usually solve addition problems by counting from 1. Counting from the larger addend rather than from 1 reduces the amount of counting, producing faster and more accurate solutions.

To observe the discovery process, the researchers selected 4- and 5-year-olds who did not yet use counting-on but who knew how to add by counting from 1. Over an 11-week period, these children received many addition problems—far

microgenetic design ■ A method of study in which the same children are studied repeatedly over a short period.

counting-on strategy ■ Counting up from the larger addend the number of times indicated by the smaller addend.

TABLE 1.5

Advantages and Disadvantages of Designs for Studying Development

Design	Features	Advantages	Disadvantages
Cross-sectional	Children of different ages are studied at a single time.	Yields useful data about differences among age groups.	Uninformative about stability of individual differences over time.
		Quick and easy to administer.	Uninformative about similarities and differences in individual children's patterns of change.
Longitudinal	Children are examined repeatedly over a prolonged period.	Indicates the degree of stability of individual differences over long periods.	Difficult to keep all participants in study.
		Reveals individual children's patterns of change over long periods.	Repeatedly testing children can threaten external validity of study.
Microgenetic	Children are observed intensively over a relatively short period while a change is occurring.	Intensive observation of changes while they are occurring can clarify process of change.	Does not provide information about typical patterns of change over long periods.
		Reveals individual change patterns over short periods in considerable detail.	Does not yield data regarding change patterns over long periods.

Discovering how to solve problems is an inherently rewarding experience. Microgenetic designs can provide insight into both the process of discovery and children's emotional response to it.

more than they would normally encounter before entering school—and each child's behaviour was videotaped for every problem. This approach allowed the researchers to identify exactly when each child discovered the counting-on strategy.

Examination of the problems immediately preceding the discovery revealed a surprising fact: necessity is not always the mother of invention. Quite a few children discovered the counting-on strategy while working on easy problems that they previously had solved correctly by counting from 1.

The microgenetic method also revealed that children's very first use of the new strategy often was accompanied by insight and excitement, like that shown by Lauren:

> *Experimenter:* How much is 6 + 3?
> *Lauren: (long pause)* 9.
> *E:* OK, how did you know that?
> *L:* I think I said … I think I said … oops, um … . 7 was 1, 8 was 2, 9 was 3.
> *E:* How did you know to do that? Why didn't you count 1, 2, 3, 4, 5, 6, 7, 8, 9?
> *L: (with excitement)* 'Cause then you have to count all those numbers.

> (Siegler & Jenkins, 1989, p. 66)

Despite her insightful explanation of counting-on and her excitement over discovering it, Lauren, and most other children, only gradually increased their use of the new strategy on subsequent problems. Many other microgenetic studies have also shown that generalization of new strategies tends to be slow (Kuhn & Franklin, 2006).

As this example illustrates, microgenetic methods provide insight into the process of change over brief periods. However, unlike standard longitudinal methods, microgenetic designs do not yield information about stability and change over long periods. They therefore are typically used when the basic pattern of age-related change has already been established and the goal becomes to understand how the changes occur. (Table 1.5 outlines the strengths and weaknesses of the three approaches to studying changes with age and experience: cross-sectional, longitudinal, and microgenetic designs.)

Ethical Issues in Child-Development Research

All research with human beings raises ethical issues, and this is especially the case when the research involves children. Researchers have a vital responsibility to anticipate potential risks that the children in their studies may encounter, to minimize such risks, and to make sure that the benefits of the research outweigh any potential harm.

In Canada, hospital- and university-based research with humans is governed by the Tri-Council Policy Statement: Ethical Conduct for Research Involving Humans (www. pre.ethics.gc.ca/eng/index/). This policy statement lays out a code of ethical conduct for investigators to follow. Some of the most important ethical principles in the policy statement are:

- Be sure that the research does not harm children physically or psychologically.

- Obtain informed consent for participating in the research, preferably in writing, from parents or other responsible adults and also from children if they are old enough that the research can be explained to them. The experimenter should inform children and relevant adults of all aspects of the research that might influence their willingness to participate and should explain that refusing to participate will not result in any adverse consequences to them.

- Preserve individual participants' anonymity, and do not use information for purposes other than that for which permission was given.

- Discuss with parents or guardians any information yielded by the investigation that is important for the child's welfare.

- Try to counteract any unforeseen negative consequences that arise during the research.

- Correct any inaccurate impressions that the child may develop in the course of the study. When the research has been completed, explain the main findings to participants at a level they can understand.

Recognizing the importance of such ethical issues, colleges and universities, as well as governmental agencies, have established institutional review boards made up of independent scientists and sometimes others from the community. These boards evaluate the proposed research to ensure that it does not violate Tri-Council ethics guidelines. However, the individual investigator is in the best position to anticipate potential problems and bears the ultimate responsibility for seeing that his or her study meets high ethical standards.

review:

The scientific method, in which all hypotheses are treated as potentially incorrect, has allowed contemporary understanding of child development to progress well beyond the understanding of even the greatest thinkers of the past. This progress has been built on a base of four types of innovations:

1. Measures that are directly relevant to the main hypotheses of the study
2. Data-gathering situations that yield useful information about children's behaviour, such as interviews, naturalistic observations, and structured observations
3. Designs that allow identification of associations and cause–effect relations among variables, notably correlational and experimental designs
4. Designs that allow analysis of the continuities and changes that occur with age and experience, notably cross-sectional, longitudinal, and microgenetic designs

Conducting scientific experiments also requires meeting high ethical standards, including not in any way harming the children who participate; obtaining informed consent for their participation in the research; preserving anonymity of all participants; and, after the study, explaining the findings to parents and, when possible, to children, at a level they can understand.

chapter summary:

Why Study Child Development?

■ Learning about child development is valuable for many reasons: it can help us become better parents, inform our views about social issues that affect children, and improve our understanding of human nature.

Historical Foundations of the Study of Child Development

■ Great thinkers such as Plato, Aristotle, Locke, and Rousseau raised basic questions about child development and proposed interesting hypotheses about them, but they lacked the scientific methods to answer them. Early scientific approaches, such as those of Freud and Watson, began the movement toward modern research-based theories of child development.

Enduring Themes in Child Development

■ The field of child development is an attempt to answer a set of fundamental questions:

1. How do nature and nurture together shape development?
2. How do children shape their own development?
3. In what ways is development continuous, and in what ways is it discontinuous?
4. How does change occur?
5. How does the sociocultural context influence development?
6. How do children become so different from one another?
7. How can research promote children's well-being?

■ Every aspect of development, from the most specific behaviour to the most general trait, reflects both people's biological endowment (their nature) and the experiences that they have had (their nurture).

■ Even infants and young children actively contribute to their own development through their attentional patterns, use of language, and choices of activities.

■ Many developments can appear either continuous or discontinuous, depending on how often and how closely we look at them.

■ The mechanisms that produce developmental changes involve a complex interplay among experiences, genes, and brain structures and activities.

■ The contexts that shape development include the people with whom children interact directly, such as family and friends; the institutions in which they participate, such as schools and religious organizations; and societal beliefs and values, such as those related to race, ethnicity, and social class.

■ Individual differences, even among siblings, reflect differences in children's genes, in their treatment by other people, in their interpretations of their own experiences, and in their choices of environments.

■ Principles, findings, and methods from child-development research are being applied to improve the quality of children's lives.

Methods for Studying Child Development

■ The scientific method has made possible great advances in understanding children. It involves choosing a question, formulating a hypothesis relevant to the question, developing a method to test the hypothesis, and using data to decide whether the hypothesis is correct.

■ For a measure to be useful, it must be directly relevant to the hypotheses being tested, reliable, and valid. Reliability means that independent observations of a given behaviour are consistent. Validity means that a measure assesses what it is intended to measure.

■ Among the main situations used to gather data about children are interviews, naturalistic observation, and structured observation. Interviews are especially useful for revealing children's subjective experience. Naturalistic observation is particularly useful when the primary goal is to describe how children behave in their everyday environments. Structured observation is most useful when the main goal is to describe how different children react to the identical situation.

■ Correlation does not imply causation. The two differ in that correlations indicate the degree to which two variables are associated, whereas causation indicates that changing the value of one variable will change the value of the other.

■ Correlational designs are especially useful when the goal is to describe relations among variables or when the variables of interest cannot be manipulated, because of technical or practical considerations.

■ Experimental designs are especially valuable for revealing the causes of children's behaviour.

■ Data about development can be obtained through cross-sectional designs (examining different children of different ages), through longitudinal designs (examining the same children at different ages), or through microgenetic designs (presenting the same children repeated relevant experiences over a relatively short period and analyzing the change process in detail).

■ It is vital for researchers to adhere to high ethical standards. Among the most important ethical principles are striving to ensure that the research does not harm children physically or psychologically; obtaining informed consent from parents and, where possible, from children; preserving participants' anonymity; and correcting any inaccurate impressions that children form during the study.

Critical Thinking Questions

1. Do children have different natures, or are differences among children purely due to differences in their experiences? What personal observations, research findings, and reasoning lead to your conclusion?

2. Why do you think that the children who spent less than 6 months in orphanages in Romania were able to catch up physically, intellectually, and socially, whereas those who spent more time there have not been able to catch up? Do you think that they will catch up in the future?

3. In what ways is it fortunate and in what ways is it unfortunate that children shape their own development to a substantial extent?

4. Did reading about sleeping arrangements in Canada, the United States, and other cultures influence what you would like to do if you have children? Explain why or why not.

5. Given what you learned in this chapter about child-development research, can you think of practical applications of the research (other than the ones described) that seem both feasible and important to you?

Key Terms

clinical interview, p. 25

cognitive development, p. 15

continuous development, p. 13

control group, p. 31

correlation, p. 29

correlational designs, p. 28

counting-on strategy, p. 33

cross-sectional design, p. 32

dependent variable, p. 31

direction-of-causation problem, p. 29

discontinuous development, p. 13

epigenetics, p. 12

experimental control, p. 31

experimental designs, p. 30

experimental group, p. 31

external validity, p. 25

genome, p. 12

hypotheses, p. 23

independent variable, p. 31

internal validity, p. 24

interrater reliability, p. 24

longitudinal design, p. 32

methylation, p. 12

microgenetic design, p. 33

naturalistic observation, p. 26

nature, p. 11

neurotransmitters, p. 17

nurture, p. 11

random assignment, p. 30

reliability, p. 24

scientific method, p. 23

sociocultural context, p. 18

socioeconomic status (SES), p. 19

stage theories, p. 15

structured interview, p. 25

structured observation, p. 27

test–retest reliability, p. 24

third-variable problem, p. 29

validity, p. 24

variables, p. 28

Mother and Child

chapter 2:

Prenatal Development and the Newborn Period

Picture the following scenario: a developmental psychologist is investigating a very young research participant's perceptual capacities and ability to learn from experience. First, she plays a loud sound near the participant's ear. She notes that the participant moves vigorously in response and concludes that the participant can hear the sound. Now she continues to play the same tone, over and over. As everyone else in the lab gets tired of repeatedly hearing the same sound, so, apparently, does the participant, who responds less and less to the repetitions of the sound and eventually does not react to it at all. Has the participant learned to recognize the sound, or just gone to sleep? To find out, the researcher next presents a different sound, to which the participant responds vigorously. The participant seems to have recognized a difference between the new sound and the old one, suggesting that the participant has experienced some simple learning. Wanting to see if the participant can learn something more complex, and in a natural setting, the researcher sends the participant home, asking the participant's mother to read aloud from a Dr. Seuss book for several minutes each day for six weeks. The idea is to see whether the participant later shows any recognition of the passages that were read. But before the researcher can test the participant again, something quite important happens: the participant is born!

This scenario is not at all fanciful. Indeed, as you will discover later in this chapter, it is an accurate description of a fascinating and informative study that helped revolutionize the scientific understanding of prenatal development (DeCasper & Spence, 1986). As you will also discover in this chapter, researchers have been asking many questions about the sensory and learning capabilities of fetuses. They have been finding that while in the womb, fetuses can detect a range of stimuli coming from the outside world, and that they can learn from these experiences and be affected by them after birth.

In this chapter, we will examine the extraordinary course of prenatal development—a time of astonishingly rapid and dramatic change. In addition to discussing the typical processes involved in prenatal development, including fetal learning, we will consider some of the ways in which these processes can be disrupted by environmental hazards. We will also examine the birth process and what the infant experiences during this dramatic turning point, as well as some of the most salient aspects of neonatal behaviour. Finally, we will outline issues associated with premature birth.

In our discussion of the earliest periods of development, most of the themes we described in Chapter 1 will play prominent roles. The most notable will be *nature and nurture,* as we emphasize how every aspect of development before birth results from the continual interplay of biological and environmental factors. The *active child* theme will also be featured, because the activity of the fetus contributes in numerous vital ways to its development. In fact, as you will see, typical prenatal development depends on certain fetal behaviours. Another theme we will highlight is the *sociocultural context* of prenatal development and birth. There is substantial cultural variation in how people think about the beginning of life and how they handle the birth process. The theme of *individual differences* comes into play at many points, starting with sex differences in survival rates from conception on. The *continuity/discontinuity* theme is also prominent: despite the dramatic contrast between prenatal and postnatal life, the behaviour of newborns shows clear connections to their behaviour and experience inside the womb. Finally, the theme of *research and children's welfare* is central to our discussion of how poverty can affect prenatal development and birth outcomes, as well as to our description of intervention programs designed to foster healthy development for preterm infants.

Prenatal Development

Hidden from view, the process of prenatal development has always been mysterious and fascinating, and beliefs about the origins of human life and development before birth have been an important part of the lore and traditions of all societies. (Box 2.1 describes one set of cultural beliefs about the beginning of life that is quite unlike those of Western societies.)

When we look back in history, we see great differences in how people have thought about prenatal development. In the fourth century B.C.E., Aristotle posed the fundamental question about prenatal development that was to underlie Western thought about it for the next 15 centuries: Does prenatal life start with the new individual already preformed, composed of a full set of tiny parts, or do the many parts of the human body develop in succession? Aristotle rejected the idea of preformation in favour of what he termed **epigenesis**—the emergence of new structures and functions during development (we will revisit this idea in its more modern form, *epigenetics*, in Chapter 3). Seeking support for his idea, he took what was then a very unorthodox step: he opened fertile chicken eggs to observe chick organs in various stages of development. Nevertheless, the idea of preformation persisted long after Aristotle, degenerating into a dispute about whether the miniature, preformed human was lodged inside the mother's egg or the father's sperm (see Figure 2.1).

epigenesis ■ The emergence of new structures and functions in the course of development.

BOX 2.1: a closer look

BENG BEGINNINGS

Few topics have generated more intense debate and dispute in Canada in recent years than the issue of when life begins—at the moment of conception, the moment of birth, or sometime in between. The irony is that few who engage in this debate recognize how complex the issue is or the degree to which societies throughout the world have different views on it.

Consider, for example, the perspective of the Beng, a people in the Ivory Coast of West Africa, who believe that every newborn is a reincarnation of an ancestor (Gottlieb, 2004). According to the Beng, in the first weeks after birth, the ancestor's spirit, its *wru*, is not fully committed to an earthly life and therefore maintains a double existence, travelling back and forth between the everyday world and *wrugbe*, or "spirit village." (The term can be roughly translated as "afterlife," but "before-life" might be just as appropriate.) It is only after the umbilical stump has dropped off that the newborn is considered to have emerged from *wrugbe* and to be a person. If the newborn dies before this point, there is no funeral, for the infant's passing is perceived as a return to the *wrugbe*.

These beliefs underlie many aspects of Beng infant-care practices. One is the frequent application of an herbal mixture to the newborn's umbilical stump to hasten its drying out and dropping off. In addition, there is the constant danger that the infant will become homesick for its life in *wrugbe* and decide to leave its earthly existence. To prevent this, parents try to make their babies comfortable and happy so they will want to stay in this life. Among the many recommended procedures is elaborately decorating the infant's face and body to elicit positive attention from others. Sometimes diviners are consulted, especially if the baby seems to be unhappy; a common diagnosis for prolonged crying is that the baby wants a different name—the one from its previous life in *wrugbe*.

So when does life begin for the Beng? In one sense, a Beng individual's life begins well before birth, since he or she is a reincarnation of an ancestor. In another sense, however, life begins sometime after birth, when the individual is considered to have become a person.

The mother of this Beng baby has spent considerable time painting the baby's face in an elaborate pattern. She does this every day in an effort to make the baby attractive so other people will help keep the baby happy in this world.

FIGURE 2.1 Preformationism A seventeenth-century drawing of a preformed being inside a sperm. This drawing was based on the claim of committed preformationists that when they looked at samples of semen under the newly invented microscope, they could actually see a tiny figure curled up inside the head of the sperm. They believed that the miniature person would enlarge after entering an egg. As this drawing illustrates, we must always take care not to let our cherished preconceptions so dominate our thinking that we see what we want to see—not what is really there. (From Moore & Persaud, 1993)

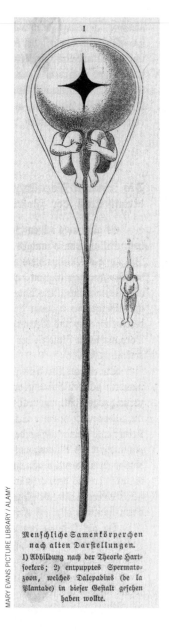

MARY EVANS PICTURE LIBRARY / ALAMY

gametes (germ cells) ■ Reproductive cells—egg and sperm—that contain only half the genetic material of all the other cells in the body.

meiosis ■ Cell division that produces gametes.

conception ■ The union of an egg from the mother and a sperm from the father.

The notion of preformation may strike you as simple-minded. Remember, however, that our ancient forebears had no way of knowing about the existence of cells and genes or about behavioural development in the womb. Many of the mysteries that perplexed our ancestors have now been solved, but as is always true in science, new mysteries have replaced them.

Conception

Each of us originated as a single cell that resulted from the union of two highly specialized cells—a sperm from our father and an egg from our mother. These **gametes,** or germ cells, are unique not only in their function but also in the fact that each one contains only half the genetic material found in other cells. Gametes are produced through **meiosis,** a special type of cell division in which the eggs and sperm receive only one member from each of the 23 chromosome pairs contained in all other cells of the body. This reduction to 23 chromosomes in each gamete is necessary for reproduction, because the union of egg and sperm must contain the normal amount of genetic material (23 *pairs* of chromosomes). A major difference in the formation of these two types of gametes is the fact that almost all the eggs a woman will ever have are formed during her own prenatal development, whereas men produce vast numbers of new sperm continuously.

The process of reproduction starts with the launching of an egg (the largest cell in the human body) from one of the woman's ovaries into the adjoining fallopian tube (see Figure 2.2). As the egg moves through the tube toward the uterus, it emits a chemical substance that acts as a sort of beacon, a "come-hither" signal that attracts sperm toward it. If an act of sexual intercourse takes place near the time the egg is released, **conception,** the union of sperm and egg, will be possible. In every ejaculation, as many as 500 million sperm are pumped into the woman's vagina. Each sperm, a streamlined vehicle for delivering the man's genes to the woman's egg, consists of little more than a pointed head packed full of genetic material (the 23 chromosomes) and a long tail that whips around to propel the sperm through the woman's reproductive system.

To be a candidate for initiating conception, a sperm must travel for about 6 hours, journeying 15 to 17 centimetres from the vagina up through the uterus to the egg-bearing fallopian tube. The rate of attrition on this journey is enormous: of the millions of sperm that enter the vagina, only about 200 ever get near the egg (see Figure 2.3). There are many causes for this high failure rate. Some failures are due to chance: many of the sperm get tangled up with other sperm milling about in the vagina; others wind up in the fallopian tube that does not currently harbour

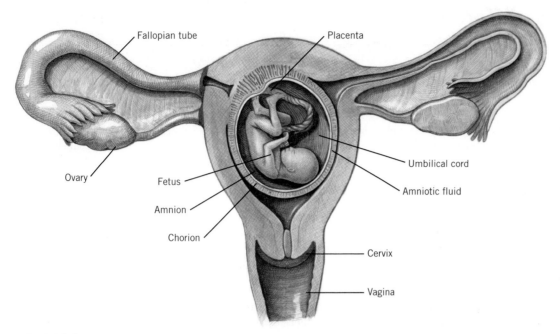

Fallopian tube

Placenta

Ovary

Fetus

Amnion

Chorion

Umbilical cord

Amniotic fluid

Cervix

Vagina

FIGURE 2.2 **Female reproductive system** A simplified illustration of the female reproductive system, with a fetus developing in the uterus (womb). The umbilical cord runs from the fetus to the placenta, which is burrowed deeply into the wall of the uterus. The fetus is floating in amniotic fluid inside the amniotic sac.

an egg. Other failures have to do with the fact that a substantial number of the sperm have serious genetic or other defects that prevent them from propelling themselves vigorously enough to reach and fertilize the egg. Thus, any sperm that do get to the egg are relatively likely to be healthy and structurally sound, revealing a Darwinian-type "survival of the fittest" process operating during fertilization. (Box 2.2 describes the consequences of this selection process for the conception of males and females.)

(a)

(b)

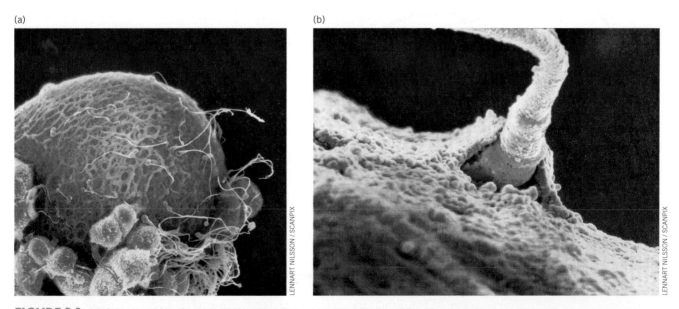

LENNART NILSSON / SCANPIX

LENNART NILSSON / SCANPIX

FIGURE 2.3 **(a) Sperm nearing the egg** Of the millions of sperm that started out together, only a few ever get near the egg. The egg is the largest human cell (the only one visible to the naked eye), but sperm are among the smallest. **(b) Sperm penetrating the egg** This sperm is whipping its tail around furiously to drill itself through the outer covering of the egg.

BOX 2.2: individual differences

THE FIRST—AND LAST—SEX DIFFERENCES

The proverbial competition between the sexes might be said to begin with millions of sperm racing to fertilize the egg. Sperm that carry a Y chromosome (the genetic basis for maleness) are lighter and swim faster than those bearing an X chromosome, so the race to the egg is won much more often by the "boys." As a result, approximately 120 to 150 males are conceived for every 100 females.

The girls win the next big competition—survival. In Canada, the ratio at birth is 105 males to 100 females. Where are the missing males? The answer is that they are miscarried at a much greater rate than females. Birth is also more challenging for boys, who, usually because of possible birth complications, are 50% more likely to need to be surgically removed from the womb by means

of a Caesarean delivery, or C-section. This heightened vulnerability is not limited to surviving the prenatal period. Boys also suffer disproportionately from most developmental disorders, including language and learning disorders, dyslexia, attention-deficit disorder, intellectual disabilities, and autism. The greater fragility of males continues throughout life, as reflected in the graph.

Differential survival is not always left in the hands of nature. In many societies, both historically and currently, male offspring are more highly valued than females, and parents resort to infanticide to avoid having daughters. For instance, Inuit families in Canada's North traditionally depended on male children to help in the hunt for food, and historically, Inuit girls were often killed at birth (E. A. Smith & Smith, 1994).

More currently, the Chinese government has strictly enforced a "one-child" policy, a measure designed to reduce population growth by forbidding couples to have more than one child. This policy resulted in many parents killing or abandoning their female babies (or giving them up for adoption to Western families) in order to make room for a male child. A more technology-intensive approach is currently practised in some countries that place a premium on male offspring: prenatal tests are used to determine the gender of the fetus, and female fetuses are selectively aborted. These cases dramatically illustrate the sociocultural model of development described in Chapter 1 (pages 18–20), showing how cultural values, government policy, and available technology all affect developmental outcomes.

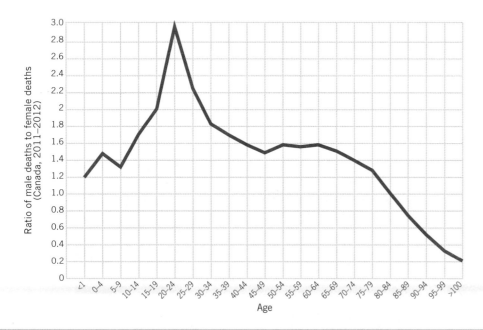

Males are more vulnerable than females across the lifespan. Beginning at birth, the Canadian male-to-female mortality ratio exceeds 1 until age 85 years. Between age 15 and 29, males are more than twice as likely as females to die. (Adapted from Statistics Canada, 2012c)

As soon as one sperm's head penetrates the outer membrane of the egg, a chemical reaction seals the membrane, preventing other sperm from entering. The tail of the sperm falls off, the contents of its head gush into the egg, and the nuclei of the two cells merge within hours. The fertilized egg, known as a **zygote,** now has a full complement of human genetic material, half from the mother and half from the father. The first of the three periods of prenatal development (see Table 2.1) has begun and, if everything proceeds normally, that development will continue for approximately 9 months (on average, 38 weeks or 266 days).

zygote ■ A fertilized egg cell.

TABLE 2.1

Periods of Prenatal Development

Conception to 2 weeks	Germinal	Begins with conception and lasts until the zygote becomes implanted in the uterine wall. Rapid cell division takes place.
3rd to 8th week	Embryonic	Following implantation, major development occurs in all the organs and systems of the body. Development takes place through the processes of cell division, cell migration, cell differentiation, and cell death, as well as hormonal influences.
9th week to birth	Fetal	Continued development of physical structures and rapid growth of the body. Increasing levels of behaviour, sensory experience, and learning.

embryo ■ The name given to the developing organism from the 3rd to 8th week of prenatal development.

fetus ■ The name given to the developing organism from the 9th week to birth.

mitosis ■ Cell division that results in two identical daughter cells.

embryonic stem cells ■ Embryonic cells that can develop into any type of body cell.

Developmental Processes

Before describing the course of prenatal development, we need to briefly outline four major developmental processes that underlie the transformation of a zygote into an **embryo** and then a **fetus.** The first is *cell division*, known as **mitosis.** Within 12 hours or so after fertilization, the zygote divides into two equal parts, each containing a full complement of genetic material. These two cells then divide into four, those four into eight, those eight into sixteen, and so on. Through continued cell division over the course of 38 weeks, the barely visible zygote becomes a newborn consisting of trillions of cells.

A second major process, which occurs during the embryonic period, is *cell migration*, the movement of newly formed cells away from their point of origin. Among the many cells that migrate are the neurons that originate deep inside the embryonic brain and then, like pioneers settling new territory, travel to the outer reaches of the developing brain.

The third process in prenatal development is *cell differentiation*. Initially, all of the embryo's cells, referred to as **embryonic stem cells,** are equivalent and interchangeable: none has any fixed fate or function. After several cell divisions, however, these cells start to specialize in terms of both structure and function. In humans, embryonic stem cells develop into roughly 350 different types of cells, which perform particular functions on behalf of the organism. (Because of their developmental flexibility, embryonic stem cells are currently the focus of a great deal of research in regenerative medicine. The hope is that when injected into a person suffering from illness or injury, embryonic stem cells will develop into healthy cells to replace the diseased or damaged ones.)

The process of differentiation is one of the major mysteries of prenatal development. Since all cells in the body have the identical set of genes, what factors determine which type of cell a given stem cell will become? One key determinant is which genes in the cell are "switched on" or expressed (see Box 2.3). Another is the cell's location, because its future development is influenced by what is going on in neighbouring cells.

The initial flexibility and subsequent inflexibility of cells, as well as the importance of location, is vividly illustrated by classic research with frog embryos. If the region of a frog embryo that would normally become an eye is grafted onto its belly area early in fetal development, the transplanted region will develop as a normal part of the belly. Thus, although the cells were initially in the right place to become an eye, they had not yet become specialized. If the transplant is performed later in fetal development, the same operation results in an eye—alone and unseeing—lodged in the frog's belly (Wolpert, 1991).

BOX 2.3: a closer look

PHYLOGENETIC CONTINUITY

Throughout this book, we will use research with non-human animals to make points about human development. In doing so, we subscribe to the principle of **phylogenetic continuity**—the idea that because of our common evolutionary history, humans share many characteristics and developmental processes with other living things. Indeed, you share most of your genes with your dog, cat, or hamster.

The assumption that animal models of behaviour and development can be useful and informative for human development underlies a great deal of research. For example, much of our knowledge about the dangers of alcohol consumption by pregnant women comes from research with non-human animals. Because scientists suspected that drinking alcohol while pregnant caused the constellation of defects now known as *fetal alcohol spectrum disorder* (page 61), they experimentally exposed fetal mice to alcohol. At birth, these mice had atypical facial features, remarkably similar to the facial anomalies of human children heavily exposed to alcohol in the womb by their mother. This fact increased researchers' confidence that the problems commonly associated with fetal alcohol syndrome are, in fact, caused by alcohol rather than by some other factor.

One of the most fascinating discoveries in recent years, discussed later in this chapter, is the existence of fetal learning. This phenomenon was first documented in one of comparative psychologists' favourite creatures—the rat. To survive after birth,

WILDLIFE GMBH / ALAMY

Scientists interested in human development have learned a great deal by studying maternal behaviour in rats.

newborns must find a milk-producing maternal nipple. How do they know where to go? The answer is that they search for something familiar to them. During the birth process, the nipples on the underside of the mother rat's belly get smeared with amniotic fluid. The scent of the amniotic fluid is familiar to the rat pups from their time in the womb, and it lures the babies to where they need to be—with their noses, and hence their mouths, near a nipple (Blass, 1990).

How was it determined that newborn rats find their mother's nipple by recognizing the scent of amniotic fluid? For one thing, when researchers washed the mother's belly clean of amniotic fluid, her pups failed to

find her nipples, and if half her nipples were washed, the pups were attracted to the unwashed ones with amniotic fluid still on them (Blass & Teicher, 1980). Even more impressive, when researchers introduced odours or flavours into the amniotic fluid, either by directly injecting them or by adding them to the mother's diet, her pups preferred those odours and tastes after birth (Hepper, 1988; Pedersen & Blass, 1982; Smotherman & Robinson, 1987). These and other demonstrations of fetal learning in rodents inspired developmental psychologists to look for similar processes in human fetuses. As you will see later, they found them.

FIGURE 2.4 Embryonic hand plate Fingers will emerge from the hand plate of this 7-week-old embryo. The fingers are formed as a result of the death of the cells between the ridges you can see in the plate. If these cells did not expire, the baby would be born with webbed rather than independent fingers.

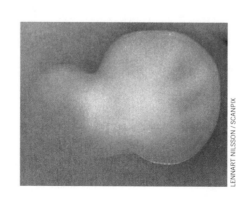

LENNART NILSSON / SCANPIX

The fourth developmental process is something you would not normally think of as developmental at all—*death*. However, the selective death of certain cells is the "almost constant companion" to the other developmental processes we have described (Wolpert, 1991). The role of this genetically programmed "cell suicide," known as **apoptosis,** is readily apparent in hand development (see Figure 2.4): the formation of fingers depends on the death of the cells in between the ridges in the hand plate.

In other words, death is preprogrammed for the cells that disappear from the hand plates.

In addition to these four developmental processes, we need to call attention to the influence of hormones on prenatal development. For instance, hormones play a crucial role in sexual differentiation. All human fetuses, regardless of the genes they carry, can develop either male or female genitalia. The presence or absence of *androgens*, a class of hormones that includes testosterone, causes development to proceed one way or the other. If androgens are present, male sex organs develop; if they are absent, female genitalia develop. The source of androgens is the male fetus itself. Around the 8th week after conception, the testes begin to produce these hormones, changing the developing organism forever. This is just one of the many ways in which the fetus influences its own development.

We now turn our attention to the general course of prenatal development that results from all the preceding influences, as well as other developmental processes.

Early Development

On its journey through the fallopian tube to the womb, the zygote doubles its number of cells roughly twice a day. By the 4th day after conception, the cells arrange themselves into a hollow sphere with a bulge of cells, called the *inner cell mass*, on one side.

This is the stage at which **identical twins** most often originate. They result from a splitting in half of the inner cell mass, and thus they both have exactly the same genetic makeup. In contrast, **fraternal twins** result when two eggs happen to be released from the ovary into the fallopian tube and both are fertilized. Because they originate from two different eggs and two different sperm, fraternal twins are no more alike genetically than non-twin siblings with the same parents.

By the end of the 1st week following fertilization, if all goes well (which it does for less than half the zygotes that are conceived), a momentous event occurs—implantation, in which the zygote embeds itself in the uterine lining and becomes dependent on the mother for sustenance. Well before the end of the 2nd week, it will be completely embedded within the uterine wall.

After implantation, the embedded ball of cells starts to differentiate. The inner cell mass becomes the embryo, and the rest of the cells become an elaborate support system—including the *amniotic sac* and *placenta*—that enables the embryo to develop. The inner cell mass is initially a single layer thick, but during the 2nd week, it folds itself into three layers, each with a different developmental destiny. The top layer becomes the nervous system, nails, teeth, the inner ear, the lens of the eyes, and the outer surface of the skin. The middle layer eventually becomes muscles, bones, the circulatory system, the inner layers of the skin, and other internal organs. The bottom layer develops into the digestive system, lungs, urinary tract, and glands. A few days after the embryo has differentiated into these three layers, a U-shaped groove forms down the centre of the top layer. The folds at the top of the groove move together and fuse, creating the **neural tube** (Figure 2.5). One end of the neural tube will swell and develop into the brain, and the rest will become the spinal cord.

The support system that is emerging along with the embryo is elaborate and essential to the embryo's development. One key

phylogenetic continuity ■ The idea that because of our common evolutionary history, humans share many characteristics, behaviours, and developmental processes with other animals, especially mammals.

apoptosis ■ Genetically programmed cell death.

identical twins ■ Twins that result from the splitting in half of the zygote, resulting in each of the two resulting zygotes having exactly the same set of genes.

fraternal twins ■ Twins that result when two eggs happen to be released into the fallopian tube at the same time and are fertilized by two different sperm; fraternal twins have only half their genes in common.

neural tube ■ A groove formed in the top layer of differentiated cells in the embryo that eventually becomes the brain and spinal cord.

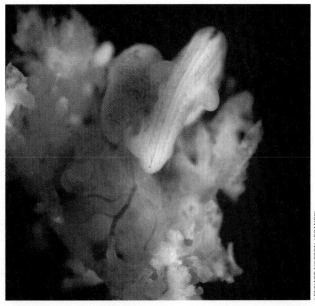

FIGURE 2.5 Neural tube In the 4th week, the neural tube begins to develop into the brain and spinal cord. In this photo, the neural groove, which fuses together first at the centre and then outward in both directions as if two zippers were being closed, has been "zipped shut" except for one part still open at the top. Spina bifida, a congenital disorder in which the skin over the spinal cord is not fully closed, can originate at this point. After closing, the top of the neural tube will develop into the brain.

LENNART NILSSON / SCANPIX

amniotic sac ■ A transparent, fluid-filled membrane that surrounds and protects the fetus.

placenta ■ A support organ for the fetus; it keeps the circulatory systems of the fetus and mother separate, but as a semi-permeable membrane permits the exchange of some materials between them (oxygen and nutrients from mother to fetus and carbon dioxide and waste products from fetus to mother).

umbilical cord ■ A tube containing the blood vessels connecting the fetus and placenta.

cephalocaudal development ■ The pattern of growth in which areas near the head develop earlier than areas farther from the head.

element of this support system is the **amniotic sac,** a membrane filled with a clear, watery fluid in which the fetus floats. The amniotic fluid operates as a protective buffer for the developing fetus, providing it with a relatively even temperature and cushioning it against jolting. As you will see shortly, because the amniotic fluid keeps the fetus afloat, the fetus can exercise its tiny, weak muscles relatively unhampered by the effects of gravity.

The second key element of the support system, the **placenta,** is a unique organ that permits the exchange of materials carried in the bloodstreams of the fetus and its mother. It is an extraordinarily rich network of blood vessels, including minute ones extending into the tissues of the mother's uterus, with a total surface area of about 8 square metres—approximately the amount of driveway covered by the family car (Vaughan, 1996). Blood vessels running from the placenta to the embryo and back again are contained in the **umbilical cord.**

At the placenta, the blood systems of the mother and fetus come extremely close to each other, but the placenta prevents their blood from actually mixing. However, the placental membrane is semi-permeable, meaning that some elements can pass through it but others cannot. Oxygen, nutrients, minerals, and some antibodies—all of which are just as vital to the fetus as they are to you—are transported to the placenta by the mother's circulating blood. They then cross the placenta and enter the fetal blood system. Waste products (e.g., carbon dioxide, urea) from the fetus cross the placenta in the opposite direction and are removed from the mother's bloodstream by her normal excretory processes.

The placental membrane also serves as a defensive barrier against a host of dangerous toxins and infectious agents that can inhabit the mother's body and could be harmful or even fatal to the fetus. Unfortunately, being semi-permeable, the placenta is not a perfect barrier, and, as you will see later, a variety of harmful elements can cross it and attack the fetus. One other function of the placenta is the production of hormones, including *estrogen*, which increases the flow of maternal blood to the uterus, and *progesterone*, which suppresses uterine contractions that could lead to premature birth (Nathanielsz, 1994).

An Illustrated Summary of Prenatal Development

The course of prenatal development from the 4th week on is illustrated in Figures 2.6 through 2.13, and significant milestones are highlighted in the accompanying text. (The fetal behaviours that are mentioned will be discussed in detail in the following section.) Notice that earlier development takes place at a more rapid pace than later development, and that the areas nearer the head develop earlier than those farther away (e.g., head before body, hands before feet)—a general tendency known as **cephalocaudal development.**

Figure 2.6: At 4 weeks after conception, the embryo is curved so tightly that the head and the tail-like structure at the other end are almost touching. Several facial features have their origin in the set of four folds in the front of the embryo's head; the face gradually emerges as a result of these tissues moving and stretching, as parts of them fuse and others separate. The round area near the top of the head is where the eye will form, and the round grey area near the back of the "neck" is the primordial inner ear. A primitive heart is visible; it is already beating and circulating blood. An arm bud can be seen in the side of the embryo; a leg bud is also present but less distinct.

FIGURE 2.6 Embryo at 4 weeks

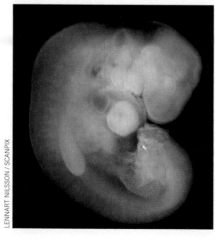

LENNART NILSSON / SCANPIX

Figure 2.7: (a) In this 5½-week-old fetus, the nose, mouth, and palate are beginning to differentiate into separate structures. (b) Just 3 weeks later, the nose and mouth are almost fully formed. Cleft palate, one of the most common birth defects worldwide, involves malformations (sometimes minor, sometimes major) of this area. This condition originates sometime between 5½ and 8 weeks prenatally—precisely when these structures are developing.

Figure 2.8: The head of this 9-week-old fetus overwhelms the rest of its body. The bulging forehead reflects the extremely rapid brain growth that has been going on for weeks. Rudimentary eyes and ears are forming. All the internal organs are present, although most must undergo further development. Sexual differentiation has started. Ribs are visible, fingers and toes have emerged, and nails are growing. You can see the umbilical cord connecting the fetus to the placenta. The fetus makes spontaneous movements, but because it is so small and is floating in amniotic fluid, the mother cannot feel them.

Figure 2.9: This image of an 11-week-old fetus clearly shows the heart, which has achieved its basic adult structure. You can also see the developing spine and ribs, as well as the major divisions of the brain.

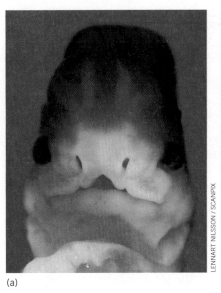
(a)

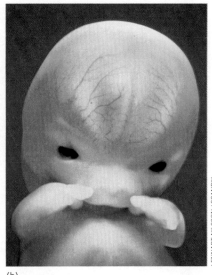
(b)

FIGURE 2.7 Face development from 5½ to 8½ weeks

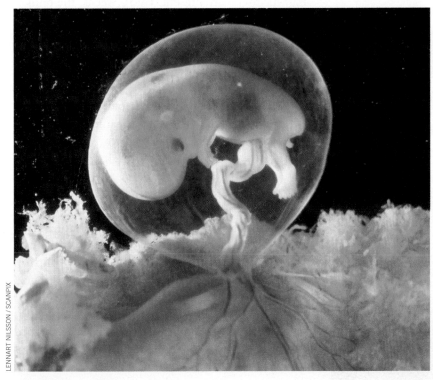
FIGURE 2.8 Fetus at 9 weeks

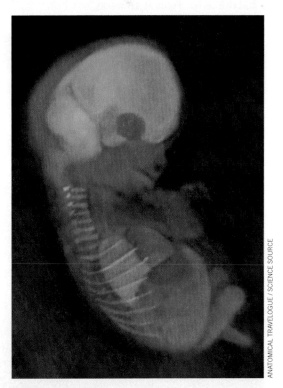
FIGURE 2.9 Fetus at 11 weeks

LENNART NILSSON / SCANPIX
ANATOMICAL TRAVELOGUE / SCIENCE SOURCE

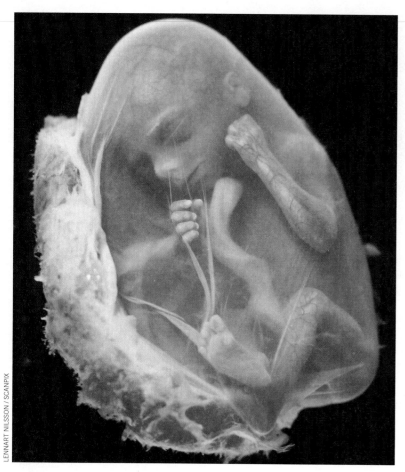

LENNART NILSSON / SCANPIX

FIGURE 2.10 Fetus at 16 weeks

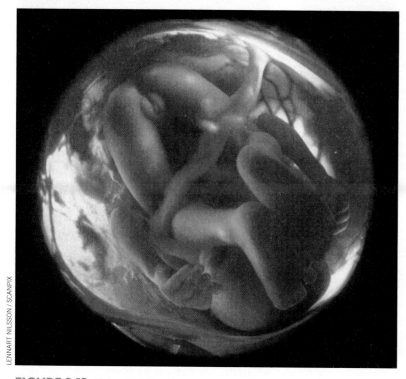

LENNART NILSSON / SCANPIX

FIGURE 2.12 Fetus at 20 weeks

LENNART NILSSON / SCANPIX

FIGURE 2.11 Fetus at 18 weeks

Figure 2.10: During the last 5 months of prenatal development, the growth of the lower part of the body accelerates. The fetus's movements have increased dramatically: its chest makes breathing movements, and some reflexes—grasping, swallowing, sucking—are present. By 16 weeks, the fetus is capable of intense kicks, although the mother feels them only as a mild "flutter." At this age, the external genitalia are substantially developed, and a different camera angle would have revealed whether this fetus is male or female.

Figure 2.11: This 18-week-old fetus is clearly sucking its thumb, in much the same way it will as a newborn. The fetus is covered with very fine hair, and a greasy coating protects its skin from its long immersion in liquid.

Figure 2.12: By the 20th week, the fetus spends increasingly more time in a head-down position. The components of facial expressions are present—the fetus can raise its eyebrows, wrinkle its forehead, and move its mouth. As the fetus rapidly puts on weight, the amniotic sac becomes more cramped, leading to a decrease in fetal movements.

Figure 2.13: The 28th week marks the point at which the brain and lungs are sufficiently developed that a fetus born at this time would have a chance of surviving on its own, without medical intervention. The eyes can open, and they move, especially during periods of rapid eye movement (REM) sleep. The

FIGURE 2.13 Fetus at 28 weeks

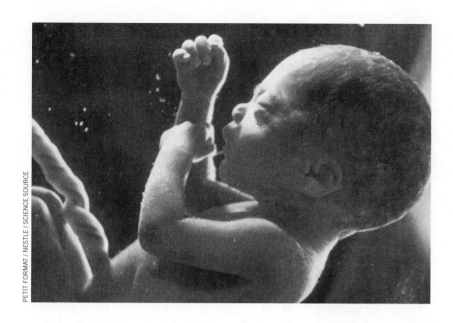

PETIT FORMAT / NESTLE / SCIENCE SOURCE

auditory system is now functioning, and the fetus hears and reacts to a variety of sounds. At this stage of development, the neural activity of the fetus is very similar to that of a newborn. During the last 3 months of prenatal development, the fetus grows dramatically in size, essentially tripling its weight.

The typical result of this 9-month period of rapid and remarkable development is a healthy newborn.

Fetal Behaviour

As we have noted, the fetus is an active participant in, and contributor to, its own physical and behavioural development. Indeed, the normal formation of organs and muscles depends on fetal activity, and the fetus rehearses the behavioural repertoire it will need at birth.

Movement

Few mothers realize how early their fetus started moving in the womb. From 5 or 6 weeks after conception, the fetus moves spontaneously, starting with a simple bending of the head and spine that is followed by the onset of increasingly complex movements over the next weeks (De Vries, Visser, & Prechtl, 1982). One of the earliest distinct patterns of movement to emerge (at around 7 weeks) is, remarkably enough, hiccups. Although the reasons for prenatal hiccups are unknown, one recent theory posits that they are essentially a burping reflex, preparing the fetus for eventual nursing by removing air from the stomach and making more room for milk (Howes, 2012).

The fetus also moves its limbs, wiggles its fingers, grasps the umbilical cord, moves its head and eyes, and yawns. Complete changes of position are achieved by a kind of backward somersault. These various movements are initially jerky and uncoordinated but gradually become more integrated. By 12 weeks, most of the movements that will be present at birth have appeared (De Vries et al., 1982), although the mother is still unaware of them.

Later on, when mothers can readily feel the movement of their fetuses, their reports reveal that how much a fetus moves is quite consistent over time: some fetuses

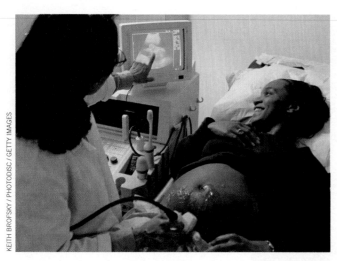

Ultrasound uses high-frequency sound waves to monitor the health and behaviour of the fetus, including patterns of movement.

are usually very active, whereas others are more sedentary (Eaton & Saudino, 1992). This prenatal *continuity* extends into the postnatal period: more active fetuses turn out to be more active infants (DiPietro et al., 1998). Furthermore, fetuses that have regular periods of sleep and waking are more likely to have regular sleep times as newborns (DiPietro, Bornstein, et al., 2002).

A particularly important form of fetal movement is *swallowing*. The fetus drinks amniotic fluid, which passes through its gastrointestinal system. Most of the fluid is then excreted back out into the amniotic sac. One benefit of this activity is that the tongue movements associated with drinking and swallowing promote the normal development of the palate (Walker & Quarles, 1976). In addition, the passage of amniotic fluid through the digestive system helps it mature properly. Thus, swallowing amniotic fluid prepares the fetus for survival outside the womb.

A second form of fetal movement anticipates the fact that at birth the newborn must start breathing. For that to happen, the lungs and the rest of the respiratory system, including the muscles that move the diaphragm in and out, must be mature and functional. Beginning as early as 10 weeks after conception, the fetus promotes its respiratory readiness by exercising its lungs through "fetal breathing," moving its chest wall in and out (Nathanielsz, 1994). No air is taken in, of course; rather, small amounts of amniotic fluid are pulled into the lungs and then expelled. Unlike real breathing, which involves an ongoing and consistent pattern of lung activity, fetal breathing is initially infrequent and irregular, but it increases in rate and stability, especially over the third trimester (Govindan et al., 2007).

Behavioural Cycles

Once the fetus begins to move at 5 to 6 weeks, it is in almost constant motion for the next month or so. Then periods of inactivity gradually begin to occur. Rest–activity cycles—bursts of high activity alternating with little or no activity for a few minutes at a time—emerge as early as 10 weeks and become very stable during the second half of pregnancy (Robertson, 1990). In the latter half of the prenatal period, the fetus moves only about 10% to 30% of the time (DiPietro et al., 1998).

Longer-term patterns, including daily (circadian) rhythms, also become apparent, with less activity in the early morning and more activity in the late evening (Arduini, Rizzo, & Romanini, 1995). This confirms the impression of most pregnant women that their fetuses wake up and start doing acrobatics just as they themselves are trying to go to sleep.

Near the end of pregnancy, the fetus spends more than three-fourths of its time in quiet and active sleep states like those of the newborn (James et al., 1995) (see page 70). The active sleep state is characterized by REM, just as it is in infants and adults.

"Well, it's a boy. And I think I can explain those sudden sharp pains in your rib cage."

Fetal Experience

There is a popular idea—promoted by everyone from scholars to cartoonists—that we spend our lives longing for the tranquil sanctuary we experienced in our mother's womb. But is the womb a haven of peace and quiet? Although the uterus and the amniotic fluid buffer the fetus from much of the stimulation impinging on the mother, research has made it clear that the fetus experiences an abundance of sensory stimulation.

Sight and Touch

Although it is not totally dark inside the womb, the visual experience of the fetus is minimal. The fetus does, however, experience tactile stimulation as a result of its own activity. In the course of moving around, its hands come into contact with other parts of its body: fetuses have been observed not only grasping their umbilical cords but also rubbing their face and sucking their thumbs (Figure 2.11). Indeed, the majority of fetal arm movements during the second half of pregnancy result in contact between their hand and mouth (Myowa-Yamakoshi & Takeshita, 2006). As the fetus grows larger, it increasingly often bumps against the walls of the uterus. By full term, fetuses respond to maternal movements (repeated rocking and swaying), suggesting that their vestibular systems—the sensory apparatus in the inner ear that provides information about movement and balance—are also functioning before birth (Lecanuet & Jacquet, 2002).

Taste

The amniotic fluid contains a variety of flavours (Maurer & Maurer, 1988). The fetus can detect these flavours, and likes some better than others. Indeed, the fetus has a sweet tooth. The first evidence of fetal taste preferences came from a medical study performed more than 60 years ago (described by Gandelman, 1992). A physician named DeSnoo devised an ingenious treatment for women with excessive amounts of amniotic fluid. He injected saccharin into their amniotic fluid, hoping that the fetus would help the mother out by ingesting increased amounts of the sweetened fluid, thereby diminishing the excess. And, in fact, tests of the mothers' urine showed that the fetuses ingested more amniotic fluid when it had been sweetened, demonstrating that taste sensitivity and flavour preferences exist before birth.

Smell

Amniotic fluid takes on odours from what the mother has eaten (Mennella, Johnson, & Beauchamp, 1995). Obstetricians have long reported that during birth they can smell scents like curry and coffee in the amniotic fluid of women who had recently consumed them. Indeed, human amniotic fluid has been shown to be rich in odorants (although many do not sound very appealing—including those described as being pungently rancid, goaty, or having a "strong fecal note") (Schaal, Orgeur, & Rognon, 1995). Smells can be transmitted through liquid, and amniotic fluid comes into contact with the fetus's odour receptors through fetal breathing, providing fetuses with the opportunity for olfactory experience. Indeed, as discussed in Box 2.3, rat pups use the familiar scent of their mother's amniotic fluid to find their mother's nipples after birth.

Hearing

Picture serious scientists hovering over a pregnant woman's bulging abdomen, ringing bells, striking a gong, clapping blocks of wood together, and even sounding an automobile horn—all to see if her fetus reacts to auditory stimulation. (Remind you of the opening to this chapter?) Such research has demonstrated that external sounds that are audible to the fetus include the voices of people talking to the woman. In addition, the prenatal environment includes many maternal sounds—the mother's heartbeat, blood pumping through her vascular system, her breathing, her swallowing, and various rude noises made by her digestive system.

The fetus of this pregnant woman may be "eavesdropping" on her conversation with her friends.

A particularly prominent and frequent source of sound stimulation is the mother's voice as she talks, with the clearest aspects being the general rhythm and pitch patterns of her speech.

The fetus responds to these various sounds from at least the 6th month of pregnancy on. During the last trimester, external noises elicit changes in fetal movements and heart rate (Kisilevsky, Fearon, & Muir, 1998; Lecanuet et al., 1995; Zimmer et al., 1993). By the time fetuses are at term, changes in heart rate patterns suggest that they can distinguish between music and speech played near the mother's abdomen (Granier-Deferre et al., 2011). The fetus's heart rate also decelerates briefly when the mother starts speaking (Fifer & Moon, 1995). (Transitory heart-rate deceleration is a sign of interest.) The fetus's extensive auditory experience with human voices has some lasting effects, as we discuss in the next section.

Fetal Learning

To this point, we have emphasized the impressive behavioural and sensory capabilities of the fetus in the early stages of development. Even more impressive is the extent to which the fetus learns from many of its experiences in the last 3 months of pregnancy, after the central nervous system is adequately developed to support learning.

Direct evidence for human fetal learning comes from studies of habituation, one of the simplest forms of learning (Thompson & Spencer, 1966). **Habituation** involves a decrease in response to repeated or continued stimulation (see Figure 2.14). If you shake a rattle beside an infant's head, the baby will likely turn toward it. At the same time, the infant's heart rate may slow momentarily, indicating interest. If you repeatedly shake the rattle, however, the head-turning and heart-rate changes will decrease and eventually stop. This decreased response is evidence of learning and memory: the stimulus loses its novelty (and becomes boring) only if the infant remembers the stimulus from one presentation to the next. When a new stimulus occurs, the habituated response recovers (increases). Shaking a bell, for example, may reinstate the head-turning and heart-rate responses.

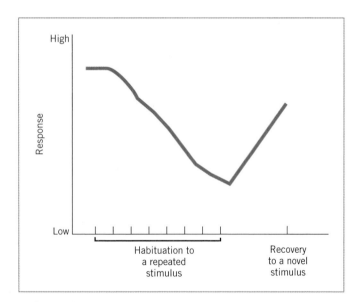

FIGURE 2.14 **Habituation** Habituation occurs in response to the repeated presentation of a stimulus. As the first stimulus is repeated and becomes familiar, the response to it gradually decreases. When a novel stimulus occurs, the response recovers. The decreased response to the repeated stimulus indicates the formation of memory for it; the increased response to the novel stimulus indicates discrimination of it from the familiar one, as well as a general preference for novelty.

habituation ■ A simple form of learning that involves a decrease in response to repeated or continued stimulation.

(Developmental psychologists have exploited habituation to study a great variety of topics that you will read about in later chapters.) The earliest time at which fetal habituation has been observed is 30 weeks, indicating that the central nervous system is sufficiently developed at this point for learning and short-term memory to occur (Dirix et al., 2009).

The mother's voice is probably the most interesting sound frequently available to fetuses. If fetuses can learn something about their mother's voice prenatally, this could provide them with a running start for learning about other aspects of speech after birth. To test this idea, Kisilevsky and colleagues (2003) tested term fetuses in one of two conditions. Half of the fetuses listened to a recording of their mother reading a poem, played through speakers placed on their mother's abdomen. The other half listened to recordings of the same poem read by another woman. The researchers found that fetal heart rate increased in response to the mother's voice, and decreased in response to the other woman's voice. These findings suggest that the fetuses recognized (and were aroused by) the sound of their own mother's voice relative to a stranger's voice. For this to be the case, fetuses must be learning and remembering the sound of their mother's voice.

After birth, do newborns remember anything about their fetal experience? The answer is a resounding yes! Like the rat pups discussed in Box 2.3, newborn humans remember the scent of the amniotic fluid in which they lived prenatally. In one set of studies, newborns were presented with two pads, one saturated with their own amniotic fluid and the other saturated with the amniotic fluid of a different baby. With the two pads located on either side of their head, the infants revealed a preference for the scent of their own amniotic fluid by keeping their head oriented longer toward that scent (Marlier, Schaal, & Soussignan, 1998; Varendi, Porter, & Winberg, 2002). These findings extend to specific flavours ingested by the mother. For instance, infants whose mothers ate anise (licorice flavour) while they were pregnant preferred the scent of anise at birth, while infants whose mothers did not eat anise showed either a neutral or negative response to its scent (Schaal, Marlier, & Soussignan, 2000).

Experiences in the womb can lead to long-lasting taste preferences. In one study, pregnant women were asked to drink carrot juice four days a week for three weeks near the end of their pregnancy (Mennella, Jagnow, & Beauchamp, 2001). When tested at around 5½ months of age, their babies reacted more positively to cereal prepared with carrot juice than to the same cereal prepared with water. Thus, the flavour preferences of these babies reflected the influence of their experience in the womb several months earlier. This finding reveals a *persistent* effect of prenatal learning. Furthermore, it may shed light on the origins and strength of cultural food preferences. A child whose mother ate a lot of chili peppers, ginger, and cumin during pregnancy, for example, might be more favourably disposed to Indian food than would a child whose mother's diet lacked those flavours.

FIGURE 2.15 **Prenatal learning** This newborn can control what he gets to listen to. His pacifier is hooked up to a computer, which is in turn connected to an audio player. If the baby sucks in one pattern (predetermined by the researchers), he will hear one recording. If he sucks in a different pattern, he will hear a different recording. Researchers have used this technique to investigate many questions about infant abilities, including the influence of fetal experience on newborn preferences.

Along with taste, newborns also remember sounds they heard in the womb. In a classic study, DeCasper and Spence (1986) asked pregnant women to read aloud twice a day from *The Cat in the Hat* (or another Dr. Seuss book) during the last 6 weeks of their pregnancy. Thus, the women's fetuses were repeatedly exposed to the same highly rhythmical pattern of speech sounds. The question was whether they would recognize the familiar story after birth. To find out, the researchers tested them as newborns. The infants were fitted with miniature headphones and given a special pacifier to suck on (see Figure 2.15). When the infants sucked in one particular pattern, they heard the familiar story through the headphones, but when they sucked in a different pattern, they heard an unfamiliar story. The babies quickly increased their sucking in the pattern that enabled them to hear the familiar story. Thus, these newborns apparently recognized and preferred the rhythmic patterns from the story they had heard in the womb.

Newborns exhibit numerous additional auditory preferences based on prenatal experience. To begin with, they prefer to listen to their own mother's voice rather than to the voice of another woman (DeCasper & Fifer, 1980). But how do researchers know that this isn't due to experience in the hours or days after birth? It turns out that newborns prefer to listen to a version of their mother's voice that has been filtered to sound the way it did in the womb (Moon & Fifer, 1990; Spence & Freeman, 1996). Finally, newborns would rather listen to the language they heard in the womb than to another language (Mehler et al., 1988; Moon, Cooper, & Fifer, 1993). Newborns whose mothers speak French prefer listening to French over Russian, for example, and this preference is maintained when the speech is filtered to sound the way it sounded in the womb.

There can be little question that the human fetus is listening and learning. Does this mean that parents-to-be should sign up for programs that promise to "educate your unborn child"? Such programs exhort the mother-to-be to talk to her fetus, read books to it, play music through speakers attached to her abdomen, and so on. Some also urge the father-to-be to speak through a megaphone aimed at the mother's bulging belly in the hope that the newborn will recognize his voice as well as the mother's. Is there any point in such exercises?

Probably not. Although it seems possible that hearing Dad's voice more clearly and more frequently might lead the newborn to prefer it over unfamiliar voices, such a preference develops very quickly after birth anyway. And it is quite clear that some of the advertised advantages of prenatal training would not occur. In the first place, the fetal brain is unlikely to be sufficiently developed to be able to process much about language meaning (after all, even newborn infants can't learn words). In addition, the liquid environment in the womb—provided by the amniotic fluid—filters out detailed speech sounds, leaving only pitch contours and rhythmic patterns. Brain development aside, this acoustic environment, along with the fetus's lack of visual access to the external world, would make it impossible for a fetus to learn the meaning of words or any kind of factual knowledge, no matter how much the mother-to-be might read aloud. In short, what the fetus learns about is the mother's voice and the general patterns of her language—not any specific content. We suspect that the current craze for prenatal education will go the way of other ill-conceived attempts to shape early development to adult desires.

Hazards to Prenatal Development

Thus far, our focus has been on the normal course of development before birth. Unfortunately, prenatal development is not always free of error or misfortune. The most dire, and by far the most common, misfortune is spontaneous abortion—commonly referred to as miscarriage. Most miscarriages occur before the woman even knows that she is pregnant. For instance, in a Chinese sample, Wang and colleagues (2003) found that approximately one-third of the fetuses did not survive to birth, and that two-thirds of those miscarriages occurred before the pregnancy was clinically detectable. The majority of embryos that are miscarried very early have severe defects, such as a missing chromosome or an extra one, that make further development impossible. About 15% of clinically recognized pregnancies end in miscarriage (Rai & Regan, 2006). Across their child-bearing years, at least 25% of women—and possibly as many as 50%—experience at least one miscarriage. Few couples realize how common this experience is, making it all the more painful if it happens to them. Yet more agonizing is the experience of the approximately 1% of couples who experience recurrent miscarriages, or the loss of three or more consecutive pregnancies (Rai & Regan, 2006).

For fetuses that survive the danger of miscarriage, there is still a range of factors that can lead to unforeseen negative consequences. Genetic factors, which are the most common, will be discussed in the next chapter. Here, we consider some of the many environmental influences that can have harmful effects on prenatal development.

Environmental Influences

In the spring of 1956, two sisters were brought to a Japanese hospital, delirious and unable to walk. Their parents and doctors were mystified by the sudden deterioration in the girls, described as having been "the brightest, most vibrant, cutest kids

MICHAEL S. YAMASHITA / CORBIS

Victims of "Minamata disease" include individuals who were exposed to methylmercury prenatally.

In the 1970s, peoples from the Grassy Narrows and White Dog First Nations, who lived near Dryden, Ontario, began experiencing the same symptoms as the residents of Minamata, Japan. A chemical and pulp mill was dumping mercury into the English–Wabigoon River System and poisoning the fish that were the First Nations' main source of food and income. Four decades after the mill stopped dumping mercury into the river system, mercury levels in fish remain above safe levels and people are still developing the symptoms of Minamata disease, including numbness in the limbs, difficulty walking a straight line, vision and hearing impairments, headaches, and exhaustion.

PETER POWER / THE GLOBE AND MAIL / CP IMAGES

you could imagine." The mystery intensified as more children and adults developed nearly identical symptoms. The discovery that all the patients were from the small coastal town of Minamata suggested a common cause for what was referred to as the "strange disease" (Newland & Rasmussen, 2003; W. E. Smith & Smith, 1975).

That cause was eventually traced to the large amounts of mercury that had been dumped into Minamata Bay by a local petrochemical and plastics factory. For years, the residents of Minamata had been catching and consuming fish that had absorbed mercury from the polluted waters of the bay. By 1993, more than 2000 children and adults had been diagnosed with what had come to be known as "Minamata disease"—methylmercury poisoning (Harada, 1995). At least 40 children had been poisoned prenatally by mercury in the fish eaten by their pregnant mothers and were born with cerebral palsy, intellectual disabilities, and a host of other neurological disorders.

The tragedy of Minamata Bay provided some of the first clear evidence of the seriously detrimental impact that environmental factors can have on prenatal development. As you will see, a vast array of environmental agents, called **teratogens,** have the potential to harm the fetus. The resulting damage ranges from relatively mild and easily corrected problems to fetal death.

A crucial factor in the severity of the effects of potential teratogens is timing (one of the basic developmental principles discussed in Chapter 1). Many teratogens cause damage only if they are present during a **sensitive period** in prenatal development. The major organ systems are most vulnerable to damage at the time when their basic structures are being formed. Because the timing is different for each system, the sensitive periods are different for each system, as shown in Figure 2.16.

There is no more dramatic or straightforward illustration of the importance of timing than the birth outcomes related to the drug thalidomide in the early 1960s. Thalidomide was prescribed to treat morning sickness (among other things), and

teratogen ■ An external agent that can cause damage or death during prenatal development.

sensitive period ■ The period of time during which a developing organism is most sensitive to the effects of external factors; prenatally, the sensitive period is when the fetus is maximally sensitive to the harmful effects of teratogens.

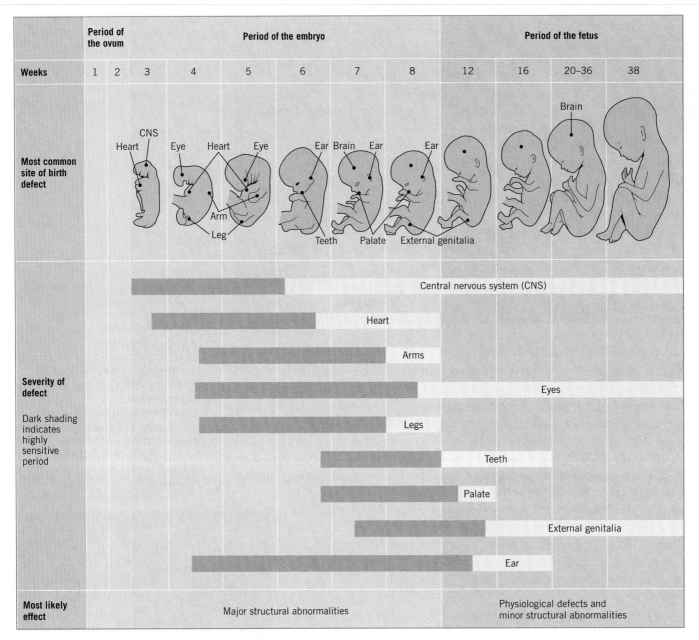

FIGURE 2.16 Sensitive periods of prenatal development The most sensitive or critical period of prenatal development is the embryonic period. During the first 2 weeks, before implantation in the uterus, the zygote is generally not susceptible to environmental factors. Every major organ system of the body undergoes all or a major part of its development between the 3rd and the 9th week. The dark green portions of the bars in the figure denote the times of most rapid development when major defects originate. The light green portions indicate periods of continued but less rapid development when minor defects may occur. (Adapted from Moore & Persaud, 1993)

was considered to be so safe that it was sold over the counter. It was sold in numerous countries, including Canada (which was the last country to withdraw thalidomide from the market). At the time, it was believed that such medications would not cross the placental barrier. However, many pregnant women who took this new, presumably safe sedative gave birth to babies with major limb deformities; some babies were born with no arms and with flipper-like hands growing out of their shoulders.

In a striking illustration of sensitive period effects, serious defects occurred only if the pregnant woman took the drug between the 4th and 6th week after conception, the time when her fetus's limbs were emerging and developing (look again at Figures 2.6 to 2.13). Taking thalidomide either before the limbs started to develop or after they were basically formed had no harmful effect.

As you can see in Figure 2.16, the sensitive periods for many organ systems—and hence the time when the most significant teratogenic damage can result from something the mother does or experiences—occur before the woman might realize she is pregnant. Because a substantial number of pregnancies are unplanned, sexually active people of child-bearing age need to be aware of behaviours that could compromise the health of a child they might conceive.

Another crucial factor influencing the severity of teratogenic effects is the amount and length of exposure. Most teratogens show a **dose–response relation:** the greater the fetus's exposure to a potential teratogen, the more likely it is that the fetus will suffer damage and the more severe any damage is likely to be.

Avoiding environmental agents that have teratogenic effects is complicated by the fact that they often cannot be readily identified. One reason is that environmental risk factors frequently occur in combination, making it difficult to separate out their effects. For families living in urban poverty, for example, it is hard to tease apart the effects of poor maternal diet, exposure to airborne pollution, inadequate prenatal care, and psychological stress resulting from underemployment, single parenthood, and living in crime-ridden neighbourhoods. Furthermore, the presence of multiple risk factors can have a *cumulative* impact. For instance, in the case of marginal prenatal nutrition, the fetus's metabolism adjusts to the level of nutritional deficiency experienced in the womb and does not reset itself after birth. In a postnatal environment with abundant opportunities for caloric intake, this sets the stage for the development of overweight and obesity. Such belated emergence of effects of prenatal experience is referred to as *fetal programming*, because experiences during the prenatal period "program the physiological set points that will govern physiology in adulthood" (Coe & Lubach, 2008).

The effects of teratogens can also vary according to *individual differences* in genetic susceptibility (probably in both the mother and the fetus). Thus, a substance that is harmless to most people may trigger problems in a minority of individuals, whose genes predispose them to be affected by it.

Finally, identifying teratogens is further complicated by the existence of *sleeper effects*, in which the impact of a given agent may not be apparent for many years. For instance, between the 1940s and 1960s, the hormone diethylstilbestrol (DES) was commonly used to prevent miscarriage and had no apparent ill effects on babies born to women who had taken it. However, in adolescence and adulthood, these offspring turned out to have elevated rates of cervical and testicular cancers.

An enormous number of potential teratogens have been identified, but we will focus only on some of the most common ones, emphasizing in particular those that are related to the *behaviour* of the pregnant woman. Table 2.2 includes the agents discussed in the text as well as several additional ones, but you should be aware that there are numerous other agents known to be, or suspected of being, hazardous to prenatal development.

PAUL FIEVEZ / BIPS / GETTY IMAGES

This young artist was damaged while in the womb because his mother took the drug thalidomide. She must have taken the drug in the second month of her pregnancy, the time when the arm buds develop—an unfortunate example providing clear evidence of the importance of timing in how environmental agents can affect the developing fetus.

dose–response relation ■ A relation in which the effect of exposure to an element increases with the extent of exposure (prenatally, the more exposure a fetus has to a potential teratogen, the more severe its effect is likely to be).

TABLE 2.2

Some Environmental Hazards to Fetus or Newborn

Drugs	Maternal Disease
Alcohol	AIDS
Accutane	Chicken pox
Birth control pills (sex hormones)	Chlamydia
Cocaine	Cytomegalovirus
Heroin	Gonorrhea
Marijuana	Herpes simplex (genital herpes)
Methadone	Influenza
Tobacco	Mumps
Environmental Pollutants	Rubella (3-day measles)
Lead	Syphilis
Mercury	Toxoplasmosis
PCBs	

Note: this list of dangerous elements is not comprehensive; there are many other agents in the environment that can have a negative impact on developing fetuses or on newborns during the birth process.

Legal drugs Although many prescription and over-the-counter drugs are perfectly safe for pregnant women, some are not. Pregnant women (and women who have reason to think they might soon become pregnant) should take drugs only under the supervision of a physician. This issue can become particularly acute in the face of public health emergencies like the 2009 H1N1 (swine flu) pandemic, during which even some physicians were confused about the appropriateness of common medications for pregnant women, including the influenza vaccine and acetaminophen (Tylenol) (Rasmussen, 2012). Other prescription drugs that are in common use by women of child-bearing age, such the acne medication isotretinoin (Accutane), are known human teratogens that cause severe birth defects or fetal death. Indeed, because of the unambiguous relationship between Accutane and birth defects, physicians require women to comply with multiple contraceptive measures and ongoing pregnancy tests before prescribing the drug.

The two legal "drugs" that wreak the most havoc on fetal development are cigarettes (nicotine) and alcohol. Because the use of these substances represents a lifestyle choice, rather than a medical remedy for a specific condition (like flu shots, antiseizure medications, or Accutane), their effects are particularly widespread.

CIGARETTE SMOKING We all know that smoking is unhealthy for the smoker, and there is abundant evidence that it is not good for the smoker's fetus, either. When a pregnant woman smokes a cigarette, she gets less oxygen, and so does her fetus. Indeed, the fetus makes fewer breathing movements while its mother is smoking. In addition, the fetuses of smokers metabolize some of the cancer-causing agents contained in tobacco. And because the mother-to-be inhales cigarette gases when someone else is smoking nearby, second-hand smoke has an indirect effect on fetal oxygen.

The main developmental consequences of maternal smoking are slowed fetal growth and low birth weight, both of which compromise the health of the newborn. In addition, evidence suggests that smoking may be linked to increased risk of sudden infant death syndrome (SIDS)

This woman is endangering the health of her fetus.

JUAN COLLADO / GETTY IMAGES

(discussed in Box 2.4) and a variety of other problems, including lower IQ, hearing deficits, and cancer.

In spite of the well-documented negative effects of maternal smoking on fetal development, it is estimated that approximately 8% of women in Canada smoke during pregnancy (Public Health Agency of Canada, 2008). For women who manage to quit smoking during pregnancy, the relapse rate is high after they give birth; roughly half begin smoking again within the first 6 months after their baby is born. Taken together, these data show that many infants are exposed to a known teratogen before birth, and numerous additional infants are exposed to a known health hazard after birth. Given that the negative effects of maternal smoking on fetal development are well publicized, you may not find it surprising that mothers who nevertheless smoke during pregnancy are less sensitive and less warm in interactions with their young infants (Schuetze, Eiden, & Dombkowski, 2006).

ALCOHOL Alcohol is currently "the most common human teratogen" (Ramadoss et al., 2008). Maternal alcohol use is the leading cause of fetal brain injury and is generally considered to be the most preventable cause. In Canada, between 5% and 8% of women report using alcohol during their pregnancies (Public Health Agency of Canada, 2008; Thanh & Jonsson, 2010). Women who are Caucasian, are between 30 and 39 years old, and have a higher income are more likely to drink during pregnancy (Tough et al., 2006). This statistic reverses the more typical pattern of maternal teratogen exposure, which tends to predominate among expectant mothers with fewer economic and social resources. Women who use alcohol before becoming pregnant (about half of women of child-bearing age) are most likely to continue using alcohol during pregnancy. In part, this may be due to the fact that many women do not realize that they are pregnant until after the fourth week of gestation, when they have missed a menstruation cycle. As we have seen, those early weeks are a crucial period in fetal development.

When a pregnant woman drinks, the alcohol in her blood crosses the placenta into both the fetus's bloodstream and the amniotic fluid. Thus, the fetus gets alcohol directly in its bloodstream, and indirectly by drinking an amniotic-fluid cocktail. Concentrations of alcohol in the blood of mother and fetus quickly equalize, but the fetus has less ability to metabolize and remove alcohol from its blood, so it remains in the fetus's system longer. Immediate behavioural effects on the fetus include altered activity levels and abnormal startle reflexes (Little, Hepper, & Dornan, 2002).

In the long run, maternal drinking can result in **fetal alcohol spectrum disorder (FASD)** (Sokol et al., 2003), which comprises a continuum of alcohol-related birth defects. Babies born to alcoholic women often exhibit a condition known as *fetal alcohol syndrome* (FAS) (Jacobson & Jacobson, 2002; Jones & Smith, 1973; Streissguth, 2001; Streissguth et al., 1993). The most obvious symptoms of FAS are facial deformities like those shown in Figure 2.17. Other forms of FAS can include varying degrees of intellectual disability, attention problems, and hyperactivity. Many children who were prenatally exposed to alcohol and show similar but fewer symptoms are diagnosed with *fetal alcohol effects* (FAE) (Mattson et al., 1998).

Even moderate drinking during pregnancy (i.e., less than one drink per day) can have both short- and long-term negative effects on development. So can occasional drinking if it involves binge drinking (more than five drinks per episode) (e.g., Hunt et al., 1995; Sokol et al., 2003). According to one study, 21% of women reported at least one incident of binge drinking before they recognized that they were pregnant (Tough et al., 2006).

fetal alcohol spectrum disorder (FASD) ■ The harmful effects of maternal alcohol consumption on a developing fetus. Fetal alcohol syndrome (FAS) involves a range of effects, including facial deformities, mental retardation, attention problems, hyperactivity, and other defects. Fetal alcohol effects (FAE) is a term used for individuals who show some, but not all, of the standard effects of FAS.

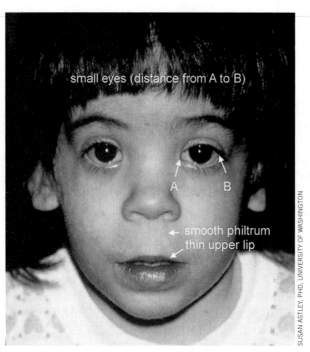

small eyes (distance from A to B)

A   B

smooth philtrum
thin upper lip

SUSAN ASTLEY, PHD, UNIVERSITY OF WASHINGTON

RICK'S PHOTOGRAPHY / SHUTTERSTOCK

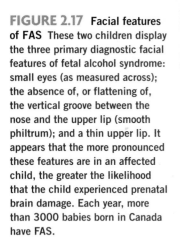

FIGURE 2.17 **Facial features of FAS** These two children display the three primary diagnostic facial features of fetal alcohol syndrome: small eyes (as measured across); the absence of, or flattening of, the vertical groove between the nose and the upper lip (smooth philtrum); and a thin upper lip. It appears that the more pronounced these features are in an affected child, the greater the likelihood that the child experienced prenatal brain damage. Each year, more than 3000 babies born in Canada have FAS.

Given the potential outcomes and the fact that no one knows whether there is a safe level of alcohol consumption for a pregnant woman, the best approach for expectant mothers is to avoid alcohol altogether.

Illegal drugs In Canada, 6.7% of women report using illegal drugs in the three months before becoming pregnant or before realizing that they are pregnant, while about 1% of women report using drugs once recognizing that they are pregnant (Public Health Agency of Canada, 2009). Almost all commonly abused illegal drugs have been shown to be, or are suspected of being, dangerous for prenatal development. It has proved difficult to pin down exactly how dangerous particular drugs are, however, because pregnant women who use one illegal substance often use others, along with smoking cigarettes and drinking alcohol (Frank et al., 2001; Lester, 1998; Smith et al., 2006).

Prenatal exposure to marijuana is suspected of affecting memory, learning, and visual skills after birth (Fried & Smith, 2001; Mereu et al., 2003). The use of cocaine in its various forms has been associated with fetal growth retardation and premature birth (Hawley & Disney, 1992; Singer et al., 2002). In addition, infants who endured prenatal exposure to cocaine have impaired ability to regulate arousal and attention (e.g., DiPietro et al., 1995; Lewkowicz, Karmel, & Gardner, 1998). Especially distressing is the case of newborns born to cocaine-addicted mothers, because they have to go through withdrawal just like a reforming addict (Kuschel, 2007).

Longitudinal studies of the development of cocaine-exposed children have revealed persistent, although sometimes subtle, cognitive and social deficits (Lester, 1998). These deficits can be ameliorated to some degree, as suggested by improved outcomes among affected children who were adopted into supportive middle-class families (Koren et al., 1998).

Environmental pollutants Most North Americans (including women of child-bearing age) come into contact with toxic metals, synthetic hormones, and various ingredients of plastics, pesticides, and herbicides that can be teratogenic (Moore,

BOX 2.4: applications

BACK TO SLEEP

For parents, nothing is more terrifying to contemplate than the death of their child. New parents are especially frightened by the spectre of **sudden infant death syndrome (SIDS).** SIDS refers to the sudden, unexpected, and unexplained death of an infant younger than 1 year. The most common SIDS scenario is that an apparently healthy baby, usually between 2 and 5 months of age, is put to bed for the night and found dead in the morning. In Canada, SIDS accounts for 17.2% of postneonatal deaths, making it the leading cause of infant mortality between 28 days and 1 year of age (Public Health Agency of Canada, 2008). Infants from socioeconomically disadvantaged and Aboriginal populations have higher incidences of SIDS than other populations (Collins et al., 2012; Luo et al., 2006).

The causes of SIDS are still not well understood. One hypothesis is that SIDS may involve an inadequate reflexive response to respiratory occlusion—that is, an inability to remove or move away from something covering the nose and mouth (Lipsitt, 2003). Infants may be particularly vulnerable to SIDS between 2 and 5 months of age because that is when they are making a transition from neonatal reflexes under the control of lower parts of the brain (the brainstem) to deliberate, learned behaviours mediated by higher brain areas (cerebral cortex). A waning respiratory occlusion reflex during this transition period may make infants less able to effectively pull their head away from a smothering pillow or to push a blanket away from their face.

In spite of the lack of certainty about the causes of SIDS, researchers have identified several steps that parents can take to decrease the risk to their baby. The

"Back to sleep." The parents of this infant are following the good advice of the foundation dedicated to lowering the incidence of SIDS worldwide. Since the inauguration of this campaign, SIDS in Canada has declined to half its previous rate (Public Health Agency of Canada, 2008).

most important one is putting infants to sleep on their back, reducing the possibility of anything obstructing their breathing. Sleeping on the stomach increases the risk of SIDS more than any other single factor (e.g., Willinger, 1995). In North America, a campaign encouraging parents to put their infants to sleep on their back—the "back to sleep" movement—has contributed to a dramatic reduction in the number of SIDS victims.

Second, to lower the risk of SIDS, parents should not smoke. If they do smoke, they should not smoke around the baby. Infants whose mothers smoke during pregnancy and/or after the baby's birth are more than 3½ times more likely to succumb to SIDS than are babies who are not exposed to smokers in their home (Anderson, Johnson, & Batal, 2005).

Third, babies should sleep on a firm mattress with no pillow or crib bumpers. Soft bedding can trap air around the infant's

face, causing the baby to breathe in his or her own carbon dioxide instead of oxygen.

Fourth, infants should not be wrapped in lots of blankets or clothes. Being overly warm is associated with SIDS.

Fifth, infants who are breastfed are less likely to succumb to SIDS (e.g., Hauck et al., 2011). Why would breastfeeding protect infants from SIDS? One possible reason is that breastfed infants are more easily aroused from sleep than formula-fed infants, and thus may more easily detect when their airflow is interrupted (Horne et al., 2004).

One unanticipated consequence of the "back to sleep" movement has been that North American infants are now beginning to crawl slightly later than those in previous generations, presumably because of reduced opportunity to strengthen their muscles by pushing up off their mattress. Parents are encouraged to give their babies supervised "tummy time" to exercise their muscles during the day.

2003). Evidence has accumulated that Inuit mothers whose diet is high in Arctic fish have infants who are exposed to lead, mercury, and polychlorinated biphenyls (PCBs), both prenatally and postnatally. This type of exposure has been associated with later difficulties in neuromotor development, particularly fine motor development (Després et al., 2005). Other studies have shown that children with high prenatal exposure to PCBs have slightly lower IQ scores than those without this exposure as long as 11 years later (Jacobson & Jacobson, 1996; Jacobson et al.,

sudden infant death syndrome (SIDS) ■ The sudden, unexpected death of an infant less than 1 year of age that has no identifiable cause.

1992). In China, the rapid modernization that has led to economic success has also taken a toll on health in general, and has led to a dramatic increase in pollution-related birth defects due to the unregulated burning of coal, water pollution, and pesticide use (e.g., Ren et al., 2011).

Occupational hazards Many women have jobs that bring them into contact with a variety of environmental elements that are potentially hazardous to prenatal development. Parking garage attendants, for example, are exposed to high levels of automobile exhaust; farmers, to pesticides; and factory workers, to numerous chemicals. As Figure 2.18 shows, even noise pollution can negatively affect fetal development. Employers and employees alike are grappling with how best to protect pregnant women from potential teratogens without subjecting them to job discrimination.

Maternal Factors

Because the mother-to-be provides the most immediate environment for her fetus, some of her characteristics can affect prenatal development. These characteristics include age, nutritional status, health, and stress level.

Age A pregnant woman's age is related to the outcome of her pregnancy. Infants born to girls 15 years or younger are three to four times more likely to die before their first birthday than are those born to mothers who are between 23 and 29 (Phipps, Blume, & DeMonner, 2002). However, the rate of teenage pregnancy has declined substantially in recent years, and in 2010, the birth rate for teenagers was only 3.9% of all live births (Statistics Canada, 2013d).

A different age-related cause for concern has to do with the increasing age of first-time mothers. In recent decades, many women have chosen to wait until their 30s or 40s to have children. At the same time, techniques to treat infertility have continued to improve, increasing the likelihood of conception for older parents. Older mothers are at greater risk for many negative outcomes for themselves and their fetus, including fetal chromosomal abnormalities (see Chapter 3) and birth complications.

Nutrition The fetus depends on its mother for all its nutritional requirements. If a pregnant woman has an inadequate diet, her unborn child may also be nutritionally deprived (Pollitt et al., 1996). An inadequate supply of specific nutrients or vitamins can have dramatic consequences. For instance, women who get too little folic acid (a form of B vitamin) are at high risk for having an infant with a neural-tube defect such as spina bifida (see Figure 2.5). General malnutrition affects the growth of the fetal brain: newborns who received inadequate nutrients while in the womb tend to have smaller brains containing fewer brain cells than do well-nourished newborns.

Because malnutrition is more common in impoverished families, it often coincides with the host of other risk factors associated with poverty, making it difficult to isolate its effects on prenatal development (Lozoff, 1989; Sigman, 1995). However, one unique study of development in very extreme circumstances made it possible to assess certain effects of malnutrition *independent of socioeconomic status* (Stein et al., 1975). In parts of Holland during World War II, people of all income and education levels suffered severe famine. Later, the health records of

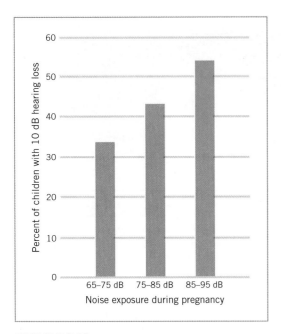

FIGURE 2.18 **Hearing loss in children whose mothers worked in a noisy factory while pregnant** The greater the noise a pregnant woman experienced, the greater the hearing impairment of her child. (Adapted from Lalande, Hétu, & Lambert, 1986)

those Dutch women who had been pregnant during this time of general malnourishment were examined. Their babies were, on average, underweight at birth, but the severity of effects depended on how early in their pregnancy the women had become malnourished. Those who became malnourished only in the last few months of pregnancy tended to have slightly underweight babies with relatively small heads. However, those whose malnutrition started early in their pregnancy often had very small babies with serious physical defects.

Disease Although most maternal illnesses that occur during a pregnancy have no impact on the fetus, some do. For example, if contracted early in pregnancy, rubella (also called the 3-day measles) can have devastating developmental effects, including major malformations, deafness, blindness, and intellectual disabilities. Any woman of child-bearing age who does not have immunities against rubella should be vaccinated before becoming pregnant.

Sexually transmitted infections (STIs) that have become increasingly common throughout the world are also quite hazardous to the fetus. Cytomegalovirus, a type of herpes virus that is present in 50% to 80% of the adult population in North America, is currently the most common cause of congenital infection (1 of every 150 infants). It can damage the fetus's central nervous system and cause a variety of other serious defects. Genital herpes can also be very dangerous: if the infant comes into contact with active herpes lesions in the birth canal, blindness or even death can result. HIV infection is sometimes passed to the fetus in the womb or during birth, but the majority of infants born to women who are HIV-positive or have AIDS do not become infected themselves. HIV can also be transmitted through breast milk after birth, but recent research suggests that breast milk contains a carbohydrate that may actually protect infants from HIV infection (Bode et al., 2012).

Evidence has been accumulating for effects of maternal illness on the development of *psychopathology* later in life. For instance, the incidence of schizophrenia is higher for individuals whose mothers had influenza (flu) during the first trimester of pregnancy (Brown et al., 2004). Maternal flu may interact with genetic or other factors to lead to mental illness.

JAVIER TENIENTE / COVER / GETTY IMAGES

These economically disadvantaged parents in Bolivia are worrying about how they are going to feed their children—a situation all too common throughout the world.

Prenatal exercise classes, as well as yoga or meditation classes, may help reduce pregnancy-related stress.

Maternal emotional state For centuries, people have believed that a woman's emotions can affect her fetus. This view is now supported by research suggesting that maternal stress can have negative consequences for development (DiPietro, 2012). For instance, the fetuses of women who reported higher levels of stress during pregnancy were more physically active throughout their gestation than were the fetuses of women who felt less stressed (DiPietro, Hilton, et al., 2002). This increased activity is likely related to hormones, including adrenaline and cortisol, that the mother secretes in response to stress (Relier, 2001). Such effects can continue after birth. In a study that involved more than 7000 pregnant women and their infants, maternal anxiety and depression during pregnancy were assessed. The higher the level of distress the pregnant women reported, the higher the incidence of behaviour problems in their children at 4 years of age— including hyperactivity and inattention in boys, conduct problems in girls, and emotional problems in both boys and girls (O'Connor et al., 2002). Findings such as these, linking prenatal maternal stress to postnatal behaviour problems, are likely to also be mediated by increased levels of maternal hormones, such as cortisol, that are elicited by stress (Susman et al., 2001; Susman, 2006).

Like other types of teratogens, it is difficult to tease apart the specific effects of maternal stress from other factors that often co-occur with stress; for example, expectant mothers who are stressed during pregnancy are likely to still be stressed after giving birth. That said, the increased popularity of prenatal yoga and meditation classes may point to ways in which pregnancy-related stress may be reduced, with potential benefits for both mother and fetus.

review:

The most rapid period of development starts at conception, with the union of egg and sperm, and continues for roughly 9 months, divided into three developmental periods: germinal, embryonic, and fetal. The processes through which prenatal development occurs include cell division, cell migration, cell differentiation, and cell death. Every major organ system undergoes all or a substantial part of its development between the 3rd and 8th week following conception, making this a sensitive period for potential damage from environmental hazards.

Scientists have learned an enormous amount about the behaviour and experience of the developing organism, which begins to move at 5 to 6 weeks after conception. Some behaviours of the fetus contribute to its development, including swallowing amniotic fluid and making breathing motions. The fetus has relatively rich sensory experience from stimulation both within and outside the womb, and this experience is the basis for fetal learning. Some effects of fetal learning after birth have been shown to be persistent.

Many environmental agents can have a negative impact on prenatal development. The most common teratogens in North America are cigarette smoking, alcohol consumption, and environmental pollution. Maternal factors (malnutrition, illness, stress, and so forth) can also cause problems for the developing fetus and child. Timing is crucial for exposure to many teratogens; the severity of effects is also related to the amount and length of exposure, as well as to the number of different negative factors with which a fetus has to contend.

The Birth Experience

Approximately 38 weeks after conception, contractions of the muscles of the uterus begin, initiating the birth of the baby. Typically, the baby has already contributed to the process by rotating itself into the normal head-down position. In addition, the maturing lungs of the fetus may release a protein that triggers the onset of labour. Uterine contractions, as well as the baby's progress through the birth canal, are painful for the mother, so women in labour are often given pain-relieving drugs. Women who self-report a great deal of fear about childbirth earlier in their pregnancies are more likely to choose pain medications, such as epidurals, during the birth process (Haines et al., 2012). Although these drugs can help the mother get through childbirth more comfortably, they may not help her baby. Indeed, many obstetric medications slow labour, and prolonged labour increases the chance of fetal oxygen deprivation, which can result in brain damage.

Is birth as painful for the newborn as for the mother? Actually, there is good reason to believe that birth is not particularly painful for the baby. Compare how much pain you feel when you pinch and pull on a piece of skin on your forearm versus when you wrap your hand around your forearm and squeeze as tightly as you can. The stretching is painful, but the squeezing is not. The mother's pain comes from her tissues being greatly stretched, but the baby experiences squeezing. Hence, the experiences of the two participants are not really comparable (Maurer & Maurer, 1988). Childbirth programs designed to prevent birth from being painful and traumatic for newborns are probably based on faulty premises.

Furthermore, the squeezing that the fetus experiences during birth serves several important functions. First, it temporarily reduces the overall size of the fetus's disproportionately large head, allowing it to pass safely through the mother's pelvic bones. This is possible because the skull is composed of separate plates that can overlap one another slightly during birth (see Figure 2.19). The squeezing of the fetus's head during birth also stimulates the production of hormones that help the fetus to withstand mild oxygen deprivation during birth and to regulate breathing after birth. The squeezing of the fetus's body also forces amniotic fluid out of the lungs, in preparation for the newborn's first, crucial gasp of air (Lagercrantz & Slotkin, 1986; Nathanielsz, 1994). This first breath usually comes by way of the birth cry, which is a very efficient mechanism for jump-starting respiration: a strong cry not only obtains some essential oxygen but also forces open the small air sacs in the lungs, making subsequent breaths easier. (An important disadvantage of Caesarean deliveries is that surgical removal from the womb deprives the fetus of the squeezing action of a normal delivery, increasing the likelihood of its experiencing respiratory problems as a newborn.)

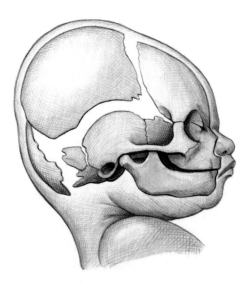 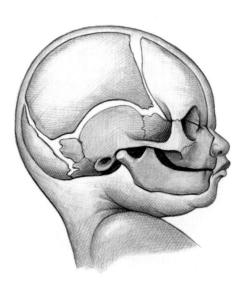

FIGURE 2.19 Head plates Pressure on the head during birth can cause the separate plates of the skull to overlap, resulting in a temporarily misshapen head. Fortunately, the condition rapidly corrects itself after birth. The "soft spot," or fontanel, is simply the temporary space between separate skull plates in the top of the baby's head.

Diversity of Childbirth Practices

Although the biological aspects of birth are pretty much the same everywhere, childbirth practices vary enormously. As with many human behaviours, what is considered a normal and desirable birth custom in one society may seem strange or deviant—or even dangerous—in another.

All cultures pursue the dual goals of safeguarding the *survival and health* of both the mother and the baby and of ensuring the *social integration* of the new person. Groups differ, however, regarding the relative importance they give to these goals. An expectant mother on the South Pacific island of Bali assumes that her husband or partner and other kin, along with any children she may already have, will all want to be present at the joyous occasion of the birth of a new child. Her female relatives, as well as a midwife, actively help her throughout the birth, which occurs in her home. Having already been present at many births, the Balinese woman knows what to expect from childbirth, even when it is her first child (Diener, 2000).

A very different scenario has been the tradition in North America, where the woman in labour usually withdraws almost totally from her everyday life. In most cases, she enters a hospital to give birth, typically attended by a small group of family or close friends. The birth is supervised by a variety of medical personnel, most of whom are strangers. Unlike her Balinese counterpart, the first-time Canadian mother has probably never witnessed a birth, so she may not have very realistic expectations about the birth process. Also, unlike her counterparts in most societies, a Canadian woman in labour has a 26% chance of having a surgical delivery by C-section—a rate that has steadily increased in Canada over the past 2 decades (Martin et al., 2012). There are a number of reasons for the ever-higher rate of surgical deliveries, including a vastly increased rate of multiple births (discussed below), changes in maternal characteristics, changes in obstetric practice, and physicians' attempts to decrease risk of lawsuits concerning medical malpractice should problems arise from a vaginal birth (e.g., Joseph et al., 2003).

Underlying the Balinese approach to childbirth is great emphasis on the social goal of immediately integrating the newborn into the family and community—hence the presence of many kin and friends to support mother and baby. In contrast, modern Western groups have elevated the physical health of the mother and newborn above all other concerns. The belief that childbirth is safer in a hospital setting outweighs the resulting social isolation of mother and baby.

The practices of both societies have changed to some degree. In Canada, the social dimensions of birth are increasingly recognized by doctors and hospitals, which often now employ certified nurse-midwives as alternative practitioners for expectant parents who prefer a less medicalized birth plan. As in Bali, various family members—sometimes even including the parents' other children—are encouraged to be present to support the labouring mother and to share a family experience. Another increasingly common practice in Canada is the use of *doulas*, individuals trained to assist women in terms of both emotional and physical comfort during labour and delivery. This shift has been accompanied by more moderate use of delivery drugs, thereby enhancing the woman's participation in childbirth and her ability to interact with her newborn. In addition, many expectant parents attend childbirth education classes, where they learn some of what their Balinese counterparts pick up through routine attendance at births. Social support is a key component of these programs; the pregnant woman's husband or partner, or some other supportive person, is trained to assist her during the birth. Such childbirth programs are generally beneficial (Lindell, 1988), and obstetricians routinely advise

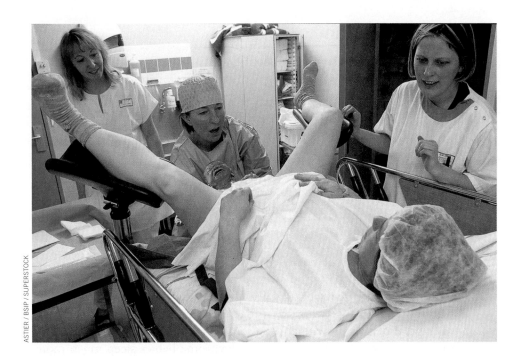

ASTIER / BSIP / SUPERSTOCK

The medical model of childbirth continues to be the most prevalent model in Canada.

COURTESY OF ROBBIE DAVIS-FLOYD

This childbirth in Brazil is quite different from the norm in Canada. The baby was born at home, welcomed by his father, older brother, and grandmother. Also present are an obstetrician and midwife who assisted with the birth.

expectant couples to enrol in them. At the same time that these changes are occurring in Canada, in traditional, nonindustrialized societies like Bali, Western medical practices are increasingly adopted in an effort to improve newborn survival rates.

review:

Research on the birth process has revealed that many aspects of the experience of being born, including squeezing in the birth canal, have adaptive value and increase the likelihood of survival for the newborn. Although cultural groups differ in their beliefs and practices related to childbirth, these differences are decreasing as expectant mothers gain access to more diverse birthing options.

state ■ Level of arousal and engagement in the environment, ranging from deep sleep to intense activity.

rapid eye movement (REM) sleep ■ An active sleep state characterized by quick, jerky eye movements under closed lids and associated with dreaming in adults.

non-REM sleep ■ A quiet or deep sleep state characterized by the absence of motor activity or eye movements and regular, slow brain waves, breathing, and heart rate.

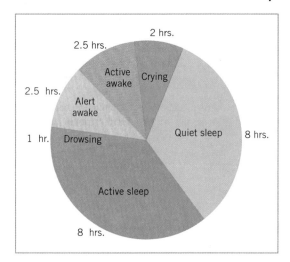

FIGURE 2.20 **Newborn states** This figure shows the average proportion of time, in a 24-hour day, that Western newborns spend in each of the six states of arousal. There are substantial individual and cultural differences in how much time babies spend in the different states.

FIGURE 2.21 **Quiet-alert state** The parents of this quiet-alert newborn have a good chance of having a pleasurable interaction with the baby.

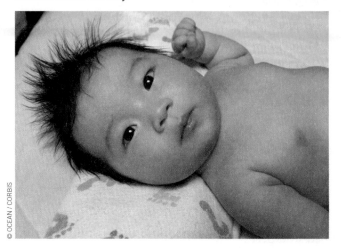

© OCEAN / CORBIS

The Newborn Infant

A healthy newborn is ready and able to continue the developmental saga in a new environment. The baby begins interacting with that environment right away, exploring and learning about newfound physical and social entities. Newborns' exploration of this uncharted territory is very much influenced by their state of arousal.

State of Arousal

State refers to a continuum of arousal, ranging from deep sleep to intense activity. As you well know, your state dramatically affects your interaction with the environment—with what you notice, do, learn, and think about. It also affects the ability of others to interact with you. State strongly mediates how young infants experience the world around them.

Figure 2.20 depicts the average amount of time in a 24-hour period that Western newborns typically spend in each of six states, ranging from quiet sleep to crying. Within this general pattern, however, there is a great deal of individual variation. Some infants cry relatively rarely, whereas others cry for hours every day; some babies sleep much more, and others much less, than the 16-hour average shown in the figure. Some infants spend more than the average of 2½ hours in the awake-alert state, in which they are fairly inactive but attentive to the environment. To appreciate how these differences might affect parent–infant interactions, imagine yourself as the parent of a newborn who cries more than the average, sleeps little, and spends less time in the awake-alert state. Now imagine yourself with a baby who cries relatively little, sleeps well, and spends an above-average amount of time quietly attending to you and the rest of his or her environment (see Figure 2.21). Clearly, you would have many more opportunities for pleasurable interactions with the second newborn.

The two newborn states that are of particular concern to parents—sleeping and crying—have both been studied extensively.

Sleep

Figure 2.22 summarizes several important facts about sleep and its development, two of which are of particular importance. First, "sleeping like a baby" means, in part, sleeping a lot; on average, newborns sleep twice as much as young adults do. Total sleep time declines regularly during childhood and continues to decrease, although more slowly, throughout life.

Second, the pattern of two different sleep states—*REM sleep* and *non-REM sleep*—changes dramatically with age. **Rapid eye movement (REM) sleep** is an active sleep state that is associated with dreaming in adults and is characterized by quick, jerky eye movements under closed lids; a distinctive pattern of brain activity; body movements; and irregular heart rate and breathing. **Non-REM sleep,** in contrast, is a quiet sleep state characterized by the absence of motor activity or eye movements and more regular, slow brain waves, breathing, and heart rate. As you can see in Figure 2.22, REM sleep constitutes fully

FIGURE 2.22 Total sleep and proportion of REM and non-REM sleep across the lifespan Newborns average a total of 16 hours of sleep, roughly half of it in REM sleep. The total amount of sleep declines sharply throughout early childhood and continues to decline much more slowly throughout life. From adolescence on, REM sleep constitutes only about 20% of total sleep time. (Adapted from Roffwarg et al., 1966, and from a later revision by these authors)

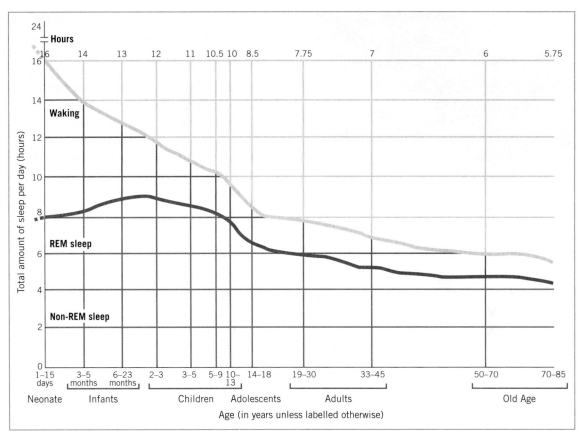

50% of a newborn's total sleep time. The proportion of REM sleep declines quite rapidly to only 20% by 3 or 4 years of age and remains low for the rest of life.

Why do infants spend so much time in REM sleep? Some researchers believe that it helps develop the infant's visual system. The normal development of the human visual system, including the visual area of the brain, depends on visual stimulation, but relatively little visual stimulation is experienced in the womb (particularly in contrast to fetal auditory stimulation, which, as you will see in the next section, is extensive). In addition, the fact that newborns spend so much time asleep means that they do not have much opportunity to amass waking visual experience. The high level of internally generated brain activity that occurs during REM sleep may help make up for the natural deprivation of visual stimulation, facilitating the early development of the visual system in both the fetus and newborn (Roffwarg, Muzio, & Dement, 1966). This theory is supported by a study showing that newborns who had been given a high level of extra visual stimulation during the day spent less of their subsequent sleep time in REM sleep than did infants exposed to lower levels of visual stimulation (Boismier, 1977).

Another distinctive feature of sleep in the newborn period is that napping newborns may actually be learning while asleep. In one study that investigated this possibility, infants were exposed to recordings of Finnish vowel sounds while they slumbered in the newborn nursery. When tested in the morning, their brain activity revealed that they recognized the sounds they had heard while asleep (Cheour et al., 2002). In a recent study, researchers trained sleeping neonates to make an eye-movement response to a puff of air toward their closed eyelids (Fifer et al., 2010). During the training phase, the newborns were repeatedly presented with a tone just before each puff of air. Given this experience, they quickly learned to expect

Most Canadian parents want to avoid the 2 a.m. fate of this young father. They regard their baby's sleeping through the night as a developmental triumph—the sooner, the better.

the air puff after the tone, as evidenced by their making an eye movement in response to the tone alone. Newborns seem able to learn in their sleep because their slumbering brains do not become disconnected from external stimulation to the same extent that the brains of older individuals do.

Another difference between the sleep of young infants and older individuals (not reflected in Figure 2.22) is in sleep–wake cycles. Newborns generally cycle between sleep and waking states several times in a 24-hour period, sleeping slightly more at night than during the day (Whitney & Thoman, 1994). Although newborns are likely to be awake during part of their parents' normal sleep time, they gradually develop the more mature pattern of sleeping through the night.

The age at which infants' sleep patterns come to match those of adults depends very much on cultural practices and pressures. For instance, many infants in North America sleep through the night by around 4 months of age—a development actively encouraged by their parents. Indeed, tired parents employ many different strategies to get their infants to sleep through the night—from adopting elaborate, often extended bedtime rituals intended to lull the baby into dreamland to gritting their teeth and letting the baby cry himself or herself to sleep. (Note: one little-known but particularly useful strategy for encouraging longer periods of nighttime sleeping is exposing the infant to bright sunlight during the day [Harrison, 2004].)

In contrast with North American parents, Kipsigis parents in rural Kenya are relatively unconcerned about their infants' sleep patterns. Kipsigis babies are almost always with their mothers. During the day, infants are often carried on their mother's back as she goes about her daily activities, and at night they sleep with her and are allowed to nurse whenever they awaken. As a consequence, these babies distribute their sleeping throughout the night and day for several months (Harkness & Super, 1995; Super & Harkness, 1986). Thus, cultures vary not only in terms of where babies sleep, as you learned in Chapter 1, but also in terms of how strongly parents attempt to influence when their babies sleep.

Crying

How do you feel when you hear a baby cry? We imagine that, like most people, you find the sound of a crying infant extremely unpleasant. Why is an infant's cry so aversive?

From an evolutionary point of view, adults' aversion to infants' crying could have adaptive value. Infants cry for many reasons—including illness, pain, and hunger—that require the attention of caregivers. Parents are likely to attempt to quiet their crying infant by taking care of the infant's needs, thereby promoting the infant's survival. This fact has led some researchers to suggest that in times of hardship, such as famine, cranky babies are more likely to survive than are placid ones, possibly because their distress elicits adult attention and they consequently get more than their share of scarce food resources (DeVries, 1984).

Parents, especially first-timers, are often puzzled and anxious about why their baby is crying. Indeed, one of the most frequent complaints pediatricians hear from parents concerns crying that the parents think is excessive but is actually common (Barr, 1998; Harkness et al., 1996). With experience, parents become better at interpreting their infants' crying, identifying characteristics of the cry itself (a sharp, piercing cry usually signals pain, for example) and considering the context (such as when the infant's last feeding was) (Green, Jones, & Gustafson, 1987).

Do all newborns' cries sound alike? Parents certainly do not think so. In fact, within the first week after birth, mothers are able to distinguish their own newborn's cries from those of other infants (e.g., Cismaresco & Montagner, 1990). Newborns' cries are also differentially shaped by the sounds of the language in their environment. A recent study that compared the crying patterns of French and German newborns found that the infants' cries followed different acoustic patterns that mimicked the pitch patterns in their home language (Mampe et al., 2009).

After the newborn period, crying behaviour typically increases, cresting at about 6 weeks of age, and then declines to about an hour a day for the rest of the first year (St James-Roberts & Halil, 1991). On a daily basis, the peak time for crying is late afternoon or evening, which can be quite disappointing to parents looking forward to interacting with their baby at the end of the workday. Increased crying late in the day may be due to an accumulation of excess stimulation during the daytime hours.

The nature of crying and the reasons for it change with development. Early on, crying reflects discomfort from pain, hunger, cold, or overstimulation, although, from the beginning, infants also cry from frustration (Lewis, Alessandri, & Sullivan, 1990; Stenberg, Campos, & Emde, 1983). Over time, crying becomes more communicative, often seeming geared to "tell" caregivers something and to get them to respond (Gustafson & Green, 1988).

Soothing What are the best ways to console a crying baby? Most of the traditional standbys—rocking, singing lullabies, holding the baby up to the shoulder, giving the baby a pacifier—work reasonably well (Campos, 1989; Korner & Thoman, 1970). Many effective soothing techniques involve moderately intense and continuous or repetitive stimulation. The combination of holding, rocking, and talking or singing relieves an infant's distress better than any one technique alone (Jahromi, Putnam, & Stifter, 2004).

One very common soothing technique is **swaddling,** which involves wrapping a young baby tightly in cloths or a blanket, thereby restricting limb movement. The tight wrapping provides a constant high level of tactile stimulation and warmth. This technique is practised in cultures as diverse and widespread as those of the Navajo and Hopi in the American Southwest (Chisholm, 1983), the Quechua in Peru (Tronick, Thomas, & Daltabuit, 1994), and rural villagers in Turkey (Delaney, 2000). Another traditional approach, distracting an upset infant with interesting objects or events, can also have a soothing effect, but the distress often resumes as soon as the interesting stimulus is removed (Harman, Rothbart, & Posner, 1997).

Touch can also have a soothing effect on infants. In interactions with an adult, infants fuss and cry less, and they smile and vocalize more, if the adult pats, rubs, or strokes them (Field et al., 1996; Peláez-Nogueras et al., 1996; Stack & Arnold, 1998; Stack & Muir, 1992). Carrying young infants, as is routinely done in many societies around the world, reduces the amount of crying that they do (Hunziker & Barr, 1986). In fact, a recent study found that crying infants showed sharper decreases in heart rate, physical movement, and crying when carried around by their mother than when held in her lap. Similar quieting responses are seen in maternal carrying in other species (think of how still lion cubs become when carried by their mother) and are conjectured to be innate cooperative mechanisms that facilitate the mother's carrying efforts (Esposito et al., 2013).

In other laboratory studies, placing a small drop of something sweet on a distressed newborn's tongue has been shown to have a dramatic calming effect (Barr et al., 1994; Blass & Camp, 2003; Smith & Blass, 1996). A taste of sucrose has an equally dramatic effect on pain sensitivity; newborn boys who are given a sweetened pacifier to suck during circumcision cry much less than babies who do not receive this simple intervention (Blass & Hoffmeyer, 1991).

swaddling ■ A soothing technique, used in many cultures, that involves wrapping a baby tightly in cloths or a blanket.

Carrying infants close to the parent's body results in less crying. Many Western parents are now emulating the traditional carrying methods of other societies around the world.

Response to distress One question that often concerns parents is how to respond to their infant's signals of distress. They wonder whether quick and consistent supportive responses will reward the infant for fussing and crying, and hence increase these behaviours, or will instead give the infant a sense of security that leads to less fussing and crying. An answer to this question comes from a longitudinal study that found that infants whose cries were ignored during the first 9 weeks actually cried less during the next 9 weeks (Hubbard & van IJzendoorn, 1991). Assessing the severity of the infant's distress *before* responding may be the key factor. If a parent responds quickly to severe distress but delays responding to minor upset, the infant may learn to cope with less serious problems on his or her own and hence end up crying less overall.

Colic No matter how or how much their parents try to soothe them, some infants are prone to excessive, inconsolable crying for no apparent reason during the first few months of life, a condition referred to as **colic.** Not only do "colicky" babies cry a lot, but they also tend to have high-pitched, particularly unpleasant cries (Stifter, Bono, & Spinrad, 2003). The causes of colic are unknown, and may include allergic responses to their mothers' diets (ingested via breast milk), formula intolerance, immature gut development, and/or excessive gassiness. Unfortunately, colic is not a rare condition: more than 1 in 10 young infants—and their parents—suffer from it. Fortunately, it typically ends by around 3 months of age and leaves no ill effects (Stifter & Braungart, 1992; St James-Roberts, Conroy, & Wilsher, 1998). One of the best things parents with a colicky infant can do is seek social support, which can provide relief from the stress, frustration, and sense of inadequacy and incompetence they may feel because they are unable to relieve their baby's distress.

Negative Outcomes at Birth

Although most recognized pregnancies in an industrialized society result in the full-term birth of a healthy baby, sometimes the outcome is less positive. The worst result, obviously, is the death of an infant. A much more common negative outcome is low birth weight, which can have long-term consequences.

Infant Mortality

Infant mortality—death during the first year after birth—is now relatively rare in the industrialized world, thanks to decades of improvements in public health and general economic levels. In Canada, the 2010 infant mortality rate was 4.9 deaths per 1000 live births (Statistics Canada, 2012c).

Although the Canadian infant mortality rate is declining over time in absolute terms, it is high compared with that of other industrialized nations. (Table 2.3 shows where Canada's infant mortality rate stood relative to the rates of a selection of developed countries in 2012.) The *relative* ranking of Canada has generally gotten worse over the past several decades, partially because the infant mortality rates in many other countries have had a higher rate of improvement and partially because of a wide variation in birth registration practices across countries (Joseph et al., 2012).

The rates of infant mortality are starkly different for different provinces and territories. For instance, infants born in Nunavut and the Northwest Territories are two to three times more likely to die before their first birthday as infants born in British Columbia and Nova Scotia. Indeed, the infant mortality rate for Nunavut and NWT is similar to the rates observed in many underdeveloped countries.

colic ■ Excessive, inconsolable crying by a young infant for no apparent reason.

infant mortality ■ Death during the first year after birth.

TABLE 2.3

Infant Mortality Rates (IMR)* for Selected Developed Nations, 2011

Country	Infant Mortality Rate	Country	Infant Mortality Rate
Iceland	0.9	Austria	3.6
Sweden	2.1	Denmark	3.6
Japan	2.3	Germany	3.6
Finland	2.4	Netherlands	3.6
Norway	2.4	Switzerland	3.6
Estonia	2.5	Australia	3.8
Czech Republic	2.7	Luxembourg	4.3
Slovenia	2.9	United Kingdom	4.3
Korea	3.0	Poland	4.7
Portugal	3.1	**Canada**	**4.9**
Spain	3.2	Hungary	4.9
Belgium	3.3	Slovak Republic	4.9
Greece	3.4	New Zealand	5.5
Italy	3.4	United States	6.1
France	3.5	Chile	7.4
Ireland	3.5	Turkey	7.7
Israel	3.5	Mexico	13.6

*Infant deaths per 1000 live births
Source: Organisation for Economic Co-operation and Development, OECD Health Data, 2013.

Why do so many babies die in the Canadian North, given that we are a highly developed country? There are many reasons, having to do with access to health care, a greater prevalence of macrosomic births (or births of very large babies), and poverty (Luo et al., 2010).

In less developed countries, especially those suffering from a breakdown in social organization due to war, famine, major epidemics, or persistent extreme poverty, the infant mortality rates can be staggering. In countries like Afghanistan, Mali, and Somalia, for example, roughly one of every 10 infants dies before age 1 year (Central Intelligence Agency, 2012).

AP PHOTO / EMILIO MORENATI

Afghanistan has one of the highest infant mortality rates in the world. Among the causes are extreme poverty, poor nutrition, and poor sanitation. The majority of the population lacks access to clean water, leading to a great many infant deaths related to dysentery, severe diarrhea, and other illnesses.

low birth weight (LBW) ■ A birth weight of less than 2500 grams.

premature ■ Any child born at 35 weeks after conception or earlier (as opposed to the normal term of 38 weeks).

small for gestational age ■ Babies that weigh substantially less than is normal for whatever their gestational age.

Low Birth Weight

Most Canadian newborns weigh between 2500 grams and 4500 grams. Infants who weigh less than 2500 grams at birth are considered to be of **low birth weight (LBW)**. Some LBW infants are **premature,** or preterm; that is, they are born at 35 weeks after conception or earlier, instead of the normal term of 38 weeks. Other LBW infants are referred to as **small for gestational age:** they may be either preterm or full-term, but they weigh substantially less than is normal for their gestational age, which is based on weeks since conception.

Slightly more than 6% of all Canadian newborns are of LBW (Statistics Canada, 2013c). As a group, LBW newborns have a heightened level of medical complications, as well as higher rates of neurosensory deficits, more frequent illness, lower IQ scores, and lower educational achievement. Very LBW babies (those weighing less than 1500 grams) are particularly vulnerable; these infants accounted for 1% of live births in Canada in 2011 (Statistics Canada, 2013c).

There are numerous causes of LBW and prematurity, including many of the infant-mortality risk factors discussed earlier. Another cause is the skyrocketing rate of twin, triplet, and other multiple births as a result of the development of increasingly successful treatments for infertility. (The use of fertility drugs typically results in multiple eggs being released during ovulation; the use of in vitro fertilization [IVF] usually involves the placement of multiple laboratory-fertilized embryos in the uterus.) Between 1995 and 2004, the rate of multiple births in Canada increased from 2.2% to 3.0% (Public Health Agency, 2008). This is a concern because the rates of LBW among multiples are quite high: 52% of multiples weigh less than 2500 grams (Statistics Canada, 2013c). (Box 2.5 discusses some of the challenges faced by parents of LBW infants.)

Of the 240 823 live births in Canada in 2009, 7564 were twins and 201 were triplets (such as these newborns) or higher-order (triplet+) multiple births (Fell & Joseph, 2012).

INSPIRESTOCK INC. / ALAMY

BOX 2.5: applications

PARENTING A LOW-BIRTH-WEIGHT BABY

Parenthood is challenging under the best of circumstances, but it is especially so for the parents of a preterm or LBW baby. First, they have to accept their disappointment over the fact that they do not have the perfect baby they had hoped for, and they may also have to cope with feelings of guilt ("What did I do wrong?"), inadequacy ("How can I possibly take care of such a tiny, fragile baby?"), and fear ("Will my baby survive?"). In addition, caring for an LBW baby can be especially time-consuming and stressful and, if the infant requires extended treatment, very expensive.

Although all new parents have a great deal to learn about caring for their infants, parents of an LBW baby face special challenges from the outset. In the hospital, they need to learn how to interact successfully with their fragile baby, who may be confined to an isolette and hooked up to life-support equipment. When their infant comes home, they may have to cope with a baby who is fairly passive and unresponsive, while being careful not to overstimulate the infant in an effort to elicit some response (Brazelton, Nugent, & Lester, 1987; Patteson & Barnard, 1990). LBW infants also tend to be fussier than the average baby and more difficult to soothe when they become upset (Greene, Fox, & Lewis, 1983). To compound matters, they often have a high-pitched cry that is particularly unpleasant (Lester et al., 1989).

Another problem for parents is the fact that LBW infants have more trouble falling asleep, waking up, and staying alert than do infants of normal birth weight, and their feeding schedules are less regular (DiVitto & Goldberg, 1979; Meisels & Plunkett, 1988). Thus, it takes longer for the baby to get on a predictable schedule, making the parents' lives more hectic.

Parents of a preterm infant also need to understand that their baby's early development will not follow the same timetable as a full-term infant's: developmental milestones will be delayed, often linked more tightly to gestational age at birth than to chronological age after birth. For instance, their infant will not begin to smile at them at around 6 weeks of age, the time when full-term infants usually reach this milestone. Instead, they may

THINKSTOCK / GETTY IMAGES

Parents of an LBW baby usually have to wait longer to experience the joy of their child's first social smile.

have to wait several more weeks for their baby to look them in the eye and break into a heart-melting smile. Thus, preterm infants are potentially more challenging to care for while being less rewarding to interact with. One consequence is that children who were born preterm are more likely to be victims of parental child abuse than are full-term infants (e.g., Spencer et al., 2006).

One step that can be helpful to parents of an LBW or preterm infant is learning more about infant development. One intervention program trained mothers—in the hospital and after returning home—to interpret their preterm babies' signals (Achenbach et al., 1990). When tested at age 7 years, their children showed significantly better cognitive skills than those of a comparison group of LBW children whose parents did not receive training. In a more recent longitudinal study, researchers randomly assigned a group of mothers of preterm infants to either receive an intervention focused on increasing parental self-confidence and responsiveness or to be in a control group that received no intervention (Nordhov et al., 2011). At age 5, a comparison of behavioural outcomes for the children in each group (as

rated by parents and preschool teachers) indicated that the children whose mothers experienced the intervention had fewer behaviour problems than did the children whose mothers did not experience the intervention. This was particularly the case in the areas of aggressive behaviour and attention deficits, which are often associated with preterm birth. This result is especially informative because the study's randomized control design means that the findings cannot be readily explained by pre-existing differences among the infants and their families.

In addition, any parent who is trying to deal with an LBW baby or an infant with other problems would do well to seek social support—from a spouse or partner, other family members, friends, or a formal support group. One of the best-documented phenomena in psychology is that we all cope better with virtually any life problem when we have support from other people. Indeed, one potentially important component of the successful intervention described in the preceding paragraph is that it included support sessions, in the hospital and during home visits, designed to encourage parents to talk about their experiences and to express their feelings.

Long-term outcomes What outcome can be expected for LBW newborns who survive? This question becomes increasingly important as newborns of ever lower birth weights—some as low as 800 grams—are kept alive by modern medical technology. The answer includes both bad news and good news.

The bad news is that, as a group, children who were LBW infants have a higher incidence of developmental problems: the lower their birth weight, the more likely they are to have persistent difficulties (e.g., Muraskas, Hasson, & Besinger, 2004). They suffer from somewhat higher levels of hearing, language, and cognitive impairments. In preschool and elementary school, they are more likely to be distractible and hyperactive and to have learning disabilities. This group is also more likely to experience a variety of social problems, including poor peer and parent–child relations (Landry et al., 1990). Finally, adolescents who were LBW babies are less likely than their siblings to complete high school (Conley & Bennett, 2002). This result holds even within twin pairs; the twin with higher birth weight is more likely to complete high school than is his or her smaller co-twin (Black et al., 2007).

The good news is that the *majority* of LBW children turn out quite well. The negative effects of their birth status gradually diminish, with children who were slightly to moderately underweight as newborns generally ending up within the normal range on most developmental measures (Kopp & Kaler, 1989; Liaw & Brooks-Gunn, 1993; Meisels & Plunkett, 1988; Vohr & Garcia-Coll, 1988). Figure 2.23 depicts a particularly striking example of this fact (Muraskas et al., 2004). Indeed, one recent follow-up study of extremely LBW infants (<1000 grams) found that by 18 to 22 months of age, 16% were unimpaired, and 22% were only mildly impaired (Gargus et al., 2009).

(a)

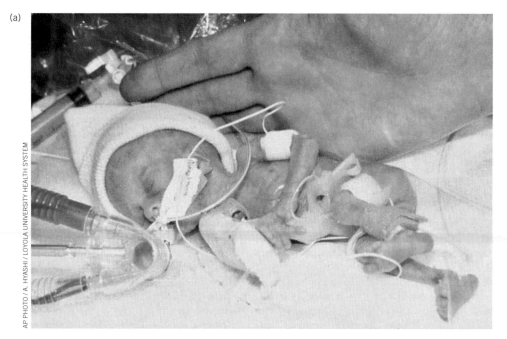

(b)

FIGURE 2.23 **Small miracles** Shown here is (a) one of the smallest newborns ever to survive and (b) the same child at 14 years of age. Born in 1989 after just 27 weeks of gestation, Madeline weighed a mere 280.7 grams—approximately the equivalent of three bars of soap. Extremely LBW infants tend to suffer serious disabilities, but Madeline is remarkably healthy, other than being a bit small for her age and having asthma. She entered high school as an honours student and enjoys playing her violin and inline skating.

AP PHOTO / A. HYASHI / LOYOLA UNIVERSITY HEALTH SYSTEM

COURTESY OF THE NEW ENGLAND JOURNAL OF MEDICINE

Intervention programs What can be done to help an LBW infant overcome his or her poor start in life? A variety of intervention programs for LBW newborns offer a prime example of our theme about the role of research in improving the welfare of children. In many intervention programs, parents are active participants, a marked change from past practice. Hospitals formerly did not allow parents to have any contact with their LBW infants, mainly because of fear of infection. Parents are now encouraged to have as much physical contact and social interaction with their hospitalized infant as the baby's condition allows.

One widely implemented intervention for hospitalized newborns is based on the idea that being touched—cuddled, caressed, and carried—is a vital part of a newborn's life. Many LBW infants experience little stimulation of this kind because of the precautions that must be taken with them, including keeping them in special isolettes, hooked up to various life-support machines. To compensate for this lack of everyday touching experience, Field and her colleagues (Field, 2001; Field, Hernandez-Reif, & Freedman, 2004) developed a special therapy that involves massaging LBW babies and flexing their arms and legs (Figure 2.24). LBW babies who receive this therapy are more active and alert and gain weight faster than those who are not massaged. As a consequence, they get to go home earlier. Recent results also suggest that having parents sing to their LBW newborns during their stay in the hospital similarly improves the newborns' health, while also calming parents' fears (Loewy et al., 2013).

Many intervention programs for LBW newborns extend beyond their hospital stay, some for several years (e.g., Ramey & Campbell, 1991). The potential of such interventions was highlighted by the Infant Health and Development Project (IHDP), which involved 985 children in eight major U.S. cities. This program was especially well designed. For one thing, the infants were randomly assigned to either the intervention group or the control group. For another, all the children were provided good health care, which ensured that this crucial factor could not affect the outcome of the research. The intervention lasted for 3 years and included an intensive early-childhood education program, as well as home visits that, among other things, encouraged the parents' continued participation in the program.

Repeated assessments of the children in this study have consistently revealed a positive effect of intervention, at least for infants who weighed more than 2000 grams. At 3 years of age, the intervention group had an advantage of 14 IQ points over the control group, although the difference was larger for the LBW children who had been relatively heavier at birth—2000 to 2500 grams versus less than 2000 grams. In follow-ups at 5 and 8 years of age, the intervention group continued to show advantages, though these were limited to those participants who had weighed more than 2000 grams at birth. In the most recent assessment, when

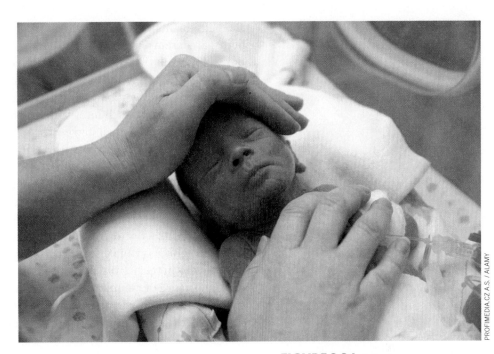

FIGURE 2.24 Infant massage
Everybody enjoys a good massage, but hospitalized newborns particularly benefit from extra touching.

PROFIMEDIA.CZ A.S. / ALAMY

the participants were 18 years old, differences favouring the intervention group—better academic performance and fewer behaviour problems—were still observed, but, again, only for those teenagers who had been the heavier LBW newborns (McCormick et al., 2006). The researchers concluded that their results provide support for early intervention to promote the development of at-risk LBW infants, but they also noted that such interventions are less likely to be successful with children who were extremely small newborns.

The IHDP story illustrates three important general points relevant to intervention efforts designed for high-risk infants. First, many intervention programs produce gains, but often those gains are relatively modest and diminish over time. Second, the success of any intervention depends on the initial health status of the infant. Like the IHDP, many programs for LBW babies have been most beneficial to those infants who are less tiny at birth. This fact is cause for concern, as modern medical technology makes it increasingly possible to save the lives of ever-smaller infants who have a high risk of permanent, serious impairment. The third point is the importance of cumulative risk: the more risks the infant endures, the lower the chances of a good outcome. Because this principle is so important for all aspects of development, we examine it in greater detail in the following section.

Multiple-Risk Model

Risk factors tend to occur together. For instance, a woman who is so addicted to alcohol, cocaine, or heroin that she continues to abuse the substance even though she is pregnant is likely to be under a great deal of stress and unlikely to eat well, take vitamins, earn a good income, seek prenatal care, have a strong social support network, or take good care of herself in other ways. Furthermore, whatever the cumulative effects of these prenatal risk factors, they will likely be compounded after birth by the mother's continuation of her unhealthy lifestyle and by her resulting inability to provide good care for her child (e.g., Weston et al., 1989).

As you will see repeatedly throughout this book, a negative developmental outcome—whether in terms of prenatal or later development—is more likely when there are multiple risk factors. In a classic demonstration of this fact, Michael Rutter (1979) reported a heightened incidence of psychiatric problems among English children growing up in families with four or more risk factors (including marital distress, low SES, paternal criminality, and maternal psychiatric disorder) (Figure 2.25). Thus, the likelihood of developing a disorder is slightly elevated for the child of parents who fight a lot; but if the child's family is also economically disadvantaged, the father engages in criminal behaviour, and the mother suffers from emotional problems, the child's risk is multiplied nearly tenfold. Similar risk patterns have been reported for IQ (Sameroff et al., 1993) and social-emotional competence (Sameroff et al., 1987).

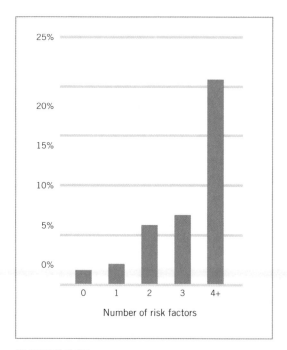

FIGURE 2.25 **Multiple risk factors** Children who grow up in families with multiple risk factors are more likely to develop psychiatric disorders than are children from families with only one or two problematic characteristics (Rutter, 1979).

Poverty as a Developmental Hazard

Because it is such an important point, we cannot emphasize enough that the existence of multiple risks is strongly related to SES. Consider some of the factors we have discussed that are known to be dangerous for fetal development: inadequate prenatal care, poor nutrition, illness, emotional stress, cigarette smoking, drug abuse, and exposure to environmental and occupational hazards. All these factors are more likely to be experienced by a woman living below the poverty line than by a middle-class woman. It is no wonder, then, that on the whole, the outcome of pregnancy is less positive for infants of lower-SES parents than for babies born to middle-class parents (Kopp, 1990; Minde, 1993; Sameroff, 1986). Nor should it be surprising that among LBW infants, the eventual developmental outcome is poorer for those in lower-SES families (Drillien, 1964; Gross et al., 1997; Kalmár, 1996; Largo et al., 1989; Lee & Barratt, 1993; McCarton et al., 1997; Meisels & Plunkett, 1988).

An equally sad fact is that in many countries, minority families are overrepresented in the lowest SES levels. In Canada, the poverty rate for racialized people ("persons, other than Aboriginal peoples, who are non-Caucasian in race or non-white in colour") was 22% compared to 9% for non-racialized persons (National Council of Welfare, 2012). Thus, their socioeconomic status places many minority fetuses, newborns, and children at increased risk for developmental difficulties.

developmental resilience ■ Successful development in spite of multiple and seemingly overwhelming developmental hazards.

Risk and Resilience

There are, of course, individuals who, faced with multiple and seemingly overwhelming developmental hazards, nevertheless do well. In studying such children, researchers employ the concept of **developmental resilience** (Garmezy, 1983; Masten, Best, & Garmezy, 1990; Sameroff, 1998). Resilient children—like those in the Kauai study discussed in Chapter 1—often have two factors in their favour: (1) certain personal characteristics, especially intelligence, responsiveness to others, and a sense of being capable of achieving their goals; and (2) responsive care from someone.

In summary, development is highly complex, from the moment of conception to the moment of birth. As you will see throughout this book, that complexity continues over the ensuing years. Although early events and experiences can profoundly affect later development, developmental outcomes are never a foregone conclusion.

review:

The experience of newborn infants is mediated by internal states of arousal, ranging from deep sleep to intense crying, with large individual differences in the amount of time spent in the different states. Newborns spend roughly half their time asleep, but after early infancy, the amount of sleep declines steadily over many years. Researchers believe that the large proportion of sleep time that newborns spend in REM sleep is important for the development of the visual system and brain. Infants' crying is a particularly salient form of behaviour for parents, and it generally elicits attention and caregiving. Effective soothing techniques involve moderately intense, continuous, or repetitive stimulation. How parents respond to their young infant's distress is related to later crying.

Negative outcomes of pregnancy are higher for minorities and for families living in poverty. Canada has higher rates of infant mortality than do many other developed nations. Just more than 6% of all infants born in Canada are LBW. Although most will suffer few lasting effects, the long-term outcome of extremely LBW babies is often problematic. Several large-scale intervention programs have successfully improved the outcome of LBW infants.

According to the multiple-risk model, the more risks that a fetus or child faces, the more likely the child is to suffer from a variety of developmental problems. Low SES is associated with many developmental hazards. Despite facing multiple risks, many children nevertheless show remarkable resiliency and thrive.

chapter summary:

Prenatal Development

- Nature and nurture combine forces in prenatal development. Much of this development is generated by the fetus itself, making the fetus an active player in its own progress. Substantial continuity exists between what goes on before and after birth in that infants demonstrate the effects of what has happened to them in the womb.

- Prenatal development begins at the cellular level with conception, the union of an egg from the mother and a sperm from the father to form a single-celled zygote. The zygote multiplies and divides on its way through a fallopian tube.

- The zygote undergoes the processes of cell division, cell migration, cell differentiation, and cell death. These processes continue throughout prenatal development.

- When the zygote becomes implanted on the uterine wall, it becomes an embryo. From that point, it is dependent on the mother to obtain nourishment and oxygen and to get rid of waste products through the placenta.

- Fetal behaviour begins 5 or 6 weeks after conception with simple movements, undetected by the mother, that become increasingly complex and organized into patterns. Later, the fetus practises behaviours vital to independent living, including swallowing and a form of intrauterine "breathing."

- The fetus experiences a wealth of stimulation both from within the womb and from the external environment. The fetus learns from this experience, as demonstrated by studies showing that both fetuses and newborns can discriminate between familiar and novel sounds, especially in speech, and exhibit persistent taste preferences developed in the womb.

- There are many hazards to prenatal development. The most common fate of a fertilized egg is spontaneous abortion (miscarriage). A wide range of environmental factors can be hazardous to prenatal development. These include teratogens from the external world and certain maternal characteristics, such as age, nutritional status, physical health, behaviour (especially the use of legal or illegal drugs), and emotional state.

The Birth Experience

- Approximately 38 weeks after conception, the baby is ready to be born. Usually, the behaviour of the fetus helps initiate the birth process.

- Being squeezed through the birth canal has several beneficial effects on the newborn, including preparing the infant to take his or her first breath.

- Cultural practices surrounding childbirth vary greatly and are in part related to the goals and values emphasized by the culture.

The Newborn Infant

- Newborns' states of arousal range from deep sleep to active crying.

- The amount of time infants spend in the different arousal states varies greatly, both across individuals and across cultures.

- REM sleep seems to compensate for the lack of visual stimulation that results from the darkness of the womb, and for the fact that newborns spend much of their time with their eyes shut, asleep.

- The sound of a baby crying can be very aversive, and adults employ many strategies to soothe distressed infants.

- The infant mortality rate in Canada is high relative to that of other developed countries. It is much higher for babies born in the Canadian North than in other parts of the country.

- Infants born weighing less than 2500 grams are referred to as being of low birth weight. LBW infants are at risk for a variety of developmental problems, and the lower the birth weight, the greater the risk of lasting difficulties.

- A variety of intervention programs have been designed to improve the course of development of LBW babies, but the success of such programs depends very much on the number of risk factors that threaten the baby.

- The multiple-risk model refers to the fact that infants with a number of risk factors have a heightened likelihood of continued developmental problems. Poverty is a particularly insidious risk to development, in part because it is associated with numerous negative factors.

- Some children display resilience even in the face of substantial challenges. Resilience seems to result from certain personal characteristics and from responsive care from someone.

Critical Thinking Questions

1. A recent cartoon showed a pregnant woman walking down a street carrying an MP3 player with a set of very large headphones clamped around her protruding abdomen. What point was the cartoon making? What research might have provided the basis for the woman's behaviour, and what assumptions is she making about what the result might be? If you or your partner were pregnant, do you think you would do something like this?

2. We hear a great deal about the terrible and tragic effects that illegal drugs like cocaine and diseases like AIDS can have on fetal development. But what two maternal behaviours associated with prenatal harm are actually the *most common* in Canada today, and what are some of the effects they can have?

3. Suppose you were in charge of a public health campaign to improve prenatal development in Canada and you could focus on only one factor. What would you target and why?

4. Describe some of the cultural differences that exist in beliefs and practices with respect to conception, pregnancy, and childbirth. Is there any practice of another culture that appeals to you more than the practices with which you are familiar?

5. Are you more encouraged or more discouraged by the results of intervention programs such as the IHDP? What would it take to make their gains larger and longer lasting?

6. Speculate on why the infant mortality rate in Canada has steadily gotten worse compared with that of other countries.

7. Explain the basic idea of the multiple-risk model and how it relates to poverty in terms of prenatal development and birth outcomes.

Key Terms

amniotic sac, p. 48

apoptosis, p. 47

cephalocaudal development, p. 48

colic, p. 74

conception, p. 42

developmental resilience, p. 81

dose–response relation, p. 59

embryo, p. 45

embryonic stem cells, p. 45

epigenesis, p. 41

fetal alcohol spectrum disorder (FASD), p. 61

fetus, p. 45

fraternal twins, p. 47

gametes (germ cells), p. 42

habituation, p. 54

identical twins, p. 47

infant mortality, p. 74

low birth weight (LBW), p. 76

meiosis, p. 42

mitosis, p. 45

neural tube, p. 47

non-REM sleep, p. 70

phylogenetic continuity, p. 46

placenta, p. 48

premature, p. 76

rapid eye movement (REM) sleep, p. 70

sensitive period, p. 57

small for gestational age, p. 76

state, p. 70

sudden infant death syndrome (SIDS), p. 63

swaddling, p. 73

teratogen, p. 57

umbilical cord, p. 48

zygote, p. 44

TILLY WILLIS (Contemporary Artist), *Waiting,* 2005 (oil on canvas)

chapter 3:

Biology and Behaviour

Several years ago, one of your authors received a call from the police. A city detective wanted to come by for a chat about some street and traffic signs that had been stolen—and also about the fact that one of the culprits was the author's 17-year-old son. In an evening of hilarious fun and poor judgment, the son, along with two friends, had stolen more than a dozen city signs and then concealed them in the family attic. His upset parents wondered how their sweet, sensitive, kind son could have failed to foresee the consequences of his actions.

Many parents have similarly wondered how their once-model children could have morphed into thoughtless, irresponsible, self-absorbed, impolite, bad-tempered individuals simply by virtue of entering adolescence. Parents are not the only ones surprised by the change in the behaviour of their offspring: teenagers themselves are often taken aback and mystified as to what has come over them. One 14-year-old girl lamented: "Sometimes, I just get overwhelmed now. … There's all this friend stuff and school and how I look and my parents. I just go in my room and shut the door. … I don't mean to be mean, but sometimes I just have to go away and calm down by myself." And a 15-year-old boy expressed similar concerns: "I get in trouble a lot more now, but it's for stuff I really didn't mean. … I forget to call home. I don't know why. I just hang out with friends, and I get involved with that and I forget. Then my parents get really mad, and then I get really mad, and it's a big mess" (Strauch, 2003).

New insights into these often abrupt developmental changes have come through research into the biological underpinnings of behavioural development. Researchers now suspect that many of the behavioural changes that are distressing both to adolescents and their parents may be related to dramatic changes in brain structure and functioning that occur during adolescence. In addition, there is growing evidence that some genetic predispositions do not emerge until adolescence and that they may contribute to these seemingly abrupt developmental changes.

Understanding the biological underpinnings of behavioural development is, of course, essential to understanding development at any point in the lifespan. The focus of this chapter is on the key biological factors that are in play from the moment of conception through adolescence, including the inheritance and influence of genes, the development and early functioning of the brain, and important aspects of physical development and maturation. Every cell in our bodies carries the genetic material that we inherited at our conception and that continues to influence our behaviour throughout life. Every behaviour we engage in is directed by our brain. Everything we do at every age is mediated by a constantly changing physical body—one that changes very rapidly and dramatically in the first few years of life and in adolescence, but more slowly and subtly at other times.

Several of the themes that were set out in Chapter 1 figure prominently in this chapter. Issues of *nature and nurture,* as well as *individual differences* among children, are central throughout this whole chapter and especially the first section, which focuses on the interaction of genetic and environmental factors in development. *Mechanisms of change* are prominent in our discussions of the developmental role of genetic factors and of the processes involved in the relationship between brain functioning and behaviour. *Continuity* in development is also highlighted throughout the chapter. We again emphasize the activity-dependent nature of developmental processes and the role of the *active child* in charting the course of his or her own development.

Nature and Nurture

Everything about you—from your physical structure, intellectual capacity, and personality characteristics to your preferences in hobbies and food—is a joint consequence of the interaction between the genetic material you inherited from your parents and the environments you have experienced from conception to the present moment. These two factors—heredity and environment—work in concert to influence both the ways in which you are like other people and the ways in which you are unique.

Long before there was any understanding of the principles of heredity, people were aware that some traits and characteristics "run in families" and that this tendency was somehow related to procreation. For as long as there have been domesticated animals, for example, farmers have practised selective breeding to improve certain characteristics of their livestock, such as the size of their horses and the milk yield of their goats, cows, or yaks. People have also long been aware that the environment plays a role in development—that a nutritious diet, for example, is necessary for livestock to produce a good milk supply or fine-quality wool. When scientists first began to investigate the contributions of heredity and environment to development, they generally emphasized one factor or the other as the prime influence—heredity *or* environment, nature *or* nurture. In nineteenth-century England, for example, Francis Galton (1869/1962), a cousin of Charles Darwin, identified men who had achieved "eminence" in a variety of fields and concluded that talent runs in families, because very close relatives of an eminent man (his father, brother, son) were more likely to be high achievers themselves than were more distant relatives.

CP IMAGES / LETHBRIDGE HERALD / IAN MARTENS

In the 1970s and 1980s, six brothers from the Sutter family reached the National Hockey League. Altogether, they played nearly 5000 games and won the Stanley Cup six times. The phenomenal athletic ability of these brothers is almost certainly due to the combination of nature—the genes they inherited from their parents—and nurture—the encouragement and support they received from their parents.

Among Galton's cases of closely related eminent men were John Stuart Mill and his father, both respected English philosophers. However, Mill himself pointed out that most of Galton's eminent men were members of well-to-do families. In his view, the relation between the achievement of these eminent men and their kinship had less to do with biological ties than with the fact that they were similar in economic well-being, social status, education, and other advantages and opportunities. In short, according to Mill, Galton's subjects rose to eminence more because of environmental factors than hereditary ones.

Our modern understanding of how characteristics are transmitted from parent to offspring originated with insights achieved by Gregor Mendel, a nineteenth-century Austrian monk who observed distinct patterns of inheritance in the pea plants that he crossbred in his monastery garden. Some aspects of these inheritance patterns were later discovered to occur in all living things (see pages 92–93). A much deeper understanding of how genetic influences operate came with James Watson and Francis Crick's 1953 identification of the structure of DNA, the basic component of hereditary transmission.

Since that landmark discovery, enormous progress has been made in deciphering the genetic code. Researchers have mapped the entire genome of myriad species of plants and animals, including chickens, mice, chimpanzees, and humans, and even several extinct species, including our closest evolutionary relative, Neanderthals (R. E. Green et al., 2010). In 2010, a consortium of geneticists began working to sequence the genomes of 10 000 vertebrate species (Lander, 2011), the expectation being that examining the genomes of such a diverse set of species will provide knowledge not only about those species but also about human evolution and the way genes function. Comparisons of the genomes of various species have already revealed much about our human genetic endowment, and they have provided numerous surprises.

"We think it has something to do with your genome."

One surprise was the number of genes that humans have: the current estimate of around 21 000 genes is far fewer than previous estimates, which ranged from 35 000 to more than 100 000 genes (Clamp et al., 2007). A second major surprise was that most of those genes are possessed by all living things. We humans share a large proportion of our genes with bears, barnacles, beans, and bacteria. Most of our genes are devoted, in decreasing order, to making us animals, vertebrates, mammals, primates, and—finally—humans. In the next section, we will look at a third surprise, one that may turn out to be a blockbuster.

As researchers have achieved better understanding of the role of hereditary factors in development, they have also come to appreciate the limits of what these factors can account for on their own. Similarly, as knowledge has grown concerning the influence of experience on development, it has become clear that experience alone rarely provides a satisfactory account. Development results from the close and continual interplay of nature *and* nurture—of genes *and* experience—and this interplay is the focus of the following section.

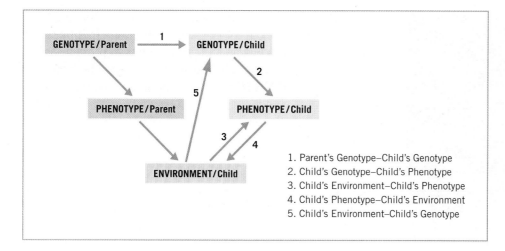

1. Parent's Genotype–Child's Genotype
2. Child's Genotype–Child's Phenotype
3. Child's Environment–Child's Phenotype
4. Child's Phenotype–Child's Environment
5. Child's Environment–Child's Genotype

FIGURE 3.1 **Development** Development is a combined function of genetic and environmental factors. The five numbered relations are discussed in detail in the text.

Genetic and Environmental Forces

The interplay of genes and experience is exceedingly complex. To simplify our discussion of interactions among genetic and environmental factors, we will organize it around the model of hereditary and environmental influences shown in Figure 3.1. Three key elements of the model are the **genotype**—the genetic material an individual inherits; the **phenotype**—the observable expression of the genotype, including both body characteristics and behaviour; and the **environment**—every aspect of the individual and his or her surroundings (including prenatal experience) other than the genes themselves.

These three elements are involved in five relations that are fundamental in the development of every child: (1) the parents' genetic contribution to the child's genotype; (2) the contribution of the child's genotype to his or her own phenotype; (3) the contribution of the child's environment to his or her phenotype; (4) the influence of the child's phenotype on his or her environment; and (5) the influence of the child's environment on his or her genotype. We will now consider each of these relations in turn.

1. Parent's Genotype–Child's Genotype

Relation 1 involves the transmission of genetic material—chromosomes and genes—from parent to offspring. You caught a glimpse of this process in Chapter 2, when we discussed the gametes (one from the mother and one from the father) that conjoin at conception to create a zygote. The nucleus of every cell in the body contains **chromosomes,** long threadlike molecules made up of two twisted strands of **DNA (deoxyribonucleic acid).** DNA carries all the biochemical instructions involved in the formation and functioning of an organism. These instructions are "packaged" in **genes,** the basic unit of heredity in all living things. Genes are sections of chromosomes. More specifically, each gene is a segment of DNA that is the code for the production of particular *proteins.* Some proteins are the building blocks of the body's cells; others regulate the cells' functioning. Genes affect development and behaviour only through the manufacture of proteins: "DNA's information translated into flesh and blood" (J. S. Levine & Suzuki, 1993, p. 19).

But here is the blockbuster surprise we mentioned earlier: researchers have discovered that genes—at least "genes" as they have been traditionally defined—make up only about 2% of the human genome (Mouse Genome Sequencing Consortium,

genotype ■ The genetic material an individual inherits.

phenotype ■ The observable expression of the genotype, including both body characteristics and behaviour.

environment ■ Every aspect of an individual and his or her surroundings other than genes.

chromosomes ■ Molecules of DNA that transmit genetic information; chromosomes are made up of DNA.

DNA (deoxyribonucleic acid) ■ Molecules that carry all the biochemical instructions involved in the formation and functioning of an organism.

genes ■ Sections of chromosomes that are the basic unit of heredity in all living things.

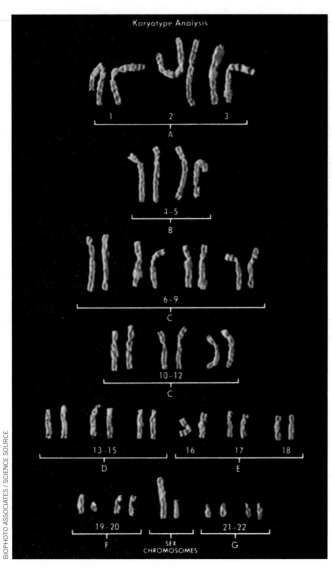

Karyotype Analysis

BIOPHOTO ASSOCIATES / SCIENCE SOURCE

FIGURE 3.2 Karyotype This colour-enhanced micrograph, called a karyotype, shows the 23 pairs of chromosomes in a healthy human male. As you can see, in nearly all cases, the chromosomes of each homologous pair are roughly the same size. The notable exception is the sex chromosomes (middle of bottom row): the Y chromosome that determines maleness is much smaller than the X chromosome. A woman's karyotype would contain two X chromosomes.

sex chromosomes ■ The chromosomes (X and Y) that determine an individual's gender.

2002). Much of the rest of our genome—once thought to be "junk" DNA—turns out to play a supporting role in influencing genetic transmission by regulating the activity of protein-coding genes (e.g., Mendes Soares & Valcárcel, 2006). Just how much of this non-coding DNA is vital to functioning, and precisely how it works, is, as of today, shrouded in mystery and controversy. Given the pace of genetic research, however, tomorrow may be a different story.

Human heredity Humans normally have a total of 46 chromosomes in the nucleus of each cell, except egg and sperm cells. (Recall from Chapter 2 that eggs and sperm each contain only 23 chromosomes, as a result of the type of cell division that produces gametes.) These 46 chromosomes are actually 23 pairs (Figure 3.2). With one exception—the sex chromosomes—the two members of each chromosome pair are of the same general size and shape (roughly the shape of the letter "X"). Furthermore, each chromosome pair carries, usually at corresponding locations, genes of the same type—that is, sequences of DNA that are relevant to the same traits. One member of each chromosome pair was inherited from each parent. Thus, every individual has two copies of each gene, one on the chromosome inherited from the father and one on the chromosome from the mother. Your biological children will each receive half of your genes, and your grandchildren will have one-quarter (just as you have half your genes in common with each of your biological parents and one-fourth with each grandparent).

Sex determination As noted, the **sex chromosomes,** which determine an individual's sex, are an exception to the general pattern of chromosome pairs being the same size and shape and carrying corresponding genes. Females have two identical, largish sex chromosomes, called X chromosomes, but males have one X chromosome and one much smaller Y chromosome (so called because it has the shape of the letter "Y"). Since a female has only X chromosomes, the division of her germ cells results in all her eggs having an X. However, because a male is XY, half his sperm contain an X chromosome and half contain a Y. For this reason, it is always the father who determines the sex of offspring: if an X-bearing sperm fertilizes an egg, a female (XX) zygote results; if an egg is fertilized by a Y-bearing sperm, the zygote is male (XY). It is the *presence* of a Y chromosome—not the fact of having only one X chromosome—that makes an individual male. A gene on the Y chromosome encodes the protein that triggers the prenatal formation of testes by activating genes on other chromosomes. Subsequently, the testes produce the hormone testosterone, which takes over the moulding of maleness (Jegalian & Lahn, 2001).

Diversity and individuality As we have noted, genes guarantee that humans will be similar to one another in certain ways, both at the species level (we are all bipedal and have opposable thumbs, for example) and at the individual level (i.e., family resemblances). Genes also guarantee differences at both levels. Several mechanisms contribute to genetic diversity among people.

One such mechanism is **mutation,** a change that occurs in a section of DNA. Some mutations are random, spontaneous errors; others are caused by environmental factors. Most are harmful. Those that occur in germ cells can be passed on to offspring; many inherited diseases and disorders originate from a mutated gene. (Box 3.1 on pages 94–95 discusses the genetic transmission of diseases and disorders.)

Occasionally, however, a mutation that occurs in a germ cell or early in prenatal development makes individuals more viable, that is, more likely to survive—perhaps by increasing their resistance to some disease or by increasing their ability to adapt to some crucial aspect of their environment. Such mutations provide the basis for evolution. This is because a person with the favourable mutated gene is more likely to survive long enough to produce offspring who, in turn, are likely to possess the mutated gene, thus heightening their own chance of surviving and reproducing. Across generations, these favourable genes proliferate in the gene pool of the species.

A second mechanism that promotes variability among individuals is the *random assortment* of chromosomes in the formation of egg and sperm. During germ-cell division, the 23 pairs of chromosomes are shuffled randomly, with chance determining which member of each pair goes into each new egg or sperm. This means that, for each germ cell, there are 2^{23}, or 8.4 million, possible combinations of chromosomes. Thus, when a sperm and an egg unite, the odds are essentially zero that any two individuals—even members of the same family—would have the same genotype (except, of course, identical twins). Further variation is introduced by the fact that when germ cells divide, the two members of a pair of chromosomes sometimes swap sections of DNA. As a result of this process, referred to as **crossing over,** some of the chromosomes that parents pass on to their offspring are constituted differently from their own.

These Elvis impersonators look like Elvis, sneer like Elvis, and even sing like Elvis (sort of). But they are not the King. The probability that any two humans (other than identical twins) have the same genotype is essentially zero.

2. Child's Genotype–Child's Phenotype

We now turn to Relation 2 in Figure 3.1, the relation between one's genotype and one's phenotype. Our examination of the genetic contribution to the phenotype begins with a key fact: although every cell in your body contains copies of all the genes you received from your parents, only some of those genes are expressed. At any given time in any cell in the body, some genes are active (turned on), while others are not. Some genes that are hard at work in neurons, for example, are totally at rest in toenail cells. As you will see, there are several reasons for this.

Gene expression: Developmental changes Genes influence development and behaviour only when they are turned on, and human development proceeds normally, from conception to death, only if genes get switched on and off in the right place, at the right time, and for the right length of time. Some genes are turned on in only a few cells and for only a few hours and then are switched off permanently. This pattern is typical during embryological development when, for example, the genes that are turned on in certain cells lead them to specialize for arm, hand, and fingerprint formation. Other genes are involved in the basic functioning of almost all cells almost all the time.

The switching on and off of genes is controlled primarily by **regulator genes.** The activation or inactivation of one gene is always part of a chain of genetic events. When one gene is switched on, it causes another gene to turn on or off, which has an impact on the status of yet other genes. Thus, genes never function

mutation ■ A change in a section of DNA.

crossing over ■ The process by which sections of DNA switch from one chromosome to the other; crossing over promotes variability among individuals.

regulator genes ■ Genes that control the activity of other genes.

alleles ■ Two or more different forms of a gene.

dominant allele ■ The allele that, if present, gets expressed.

recessive allele ■ The allele that is not expressed if a dominant allele is present.

homozygous ■ Having two of the same allele for a trait.

heterozygous ■ Having two different alleles for a trait.

in isolation. Instead, they belong to extensive networks in which the expression of one gene is a precondition for the expression of another, and so on. The continuous switching on and off of genes underlies development throughout life, from the initial prenatal differentiation of cells to the gene-induced events of puberty to many of the changes related to aging.

External factors can affect the switching on and off of genes. A dramatic example is the effect of thalidomide on limb development (described in Chapter 2), in which the sedative interferes with the functioning of genes underpinning normal growth factors (Ito et al., 2010). Another example comes from the fact that early visual experience is necessary for the normal development of the visual system, because it causes the switching on of certain genes, which, in turn, switch on other genes in the visual cortex (Maya-Vetencourt & Origlia, 2012). The ramifications of decreased visual experience are observed in cases of children with cataracts that are not removed early in life, as discussed later in this chapter.

The fact that regulator genes can repeatedly switch other genes on and off in different patterns means that a given gene can function multiple times in multiple places during development. All that is required is that the gene's expression be controlled by different regulator genes at different times. This on-again, off-again functioning of individual genes results in enormous diversity in genetic expression. By analogy, consider the fact that this book is written with only 26 letters and probably only a few thousand different words made up of combinations of those letters. The meaning comes from the order in which the letters occur, the order in which they have been "switched on and off" by the authors.

Gene expression: Dominance patterns Many of an individual's genes are never expressed; some others are only partially expressed. One reason for this is the fact that about one-third of human genes have two or more different forms, known as **alleles.** The alleles of a given gene influence the same trait or characteristic (e.g., eye colour), but they contribute to different developmental outcomes (e.g., brown, blue, hazel, grey eyes).

Let's consider the simplest pattern of gene expression—the one discovered by Mendel and referred to as the *dominant–recessive pattern*. The explanation for this pattern (unknown to Mendel) is that some genes have only two alleles, one of which is a **dominant allele** and the other a **recessive allele.** In this pattern, there are two possibilities: (1) a person can inherit either two of the same allele—two dominant or two recessive—and thus be **homozygous** for the trait in question; or (2) the person can inherit two different alleles—one dominant and the other recessive—and thus be **heterozygous** for the trait. When an individual is homozygous, with either two dominant or two recessive alleles, the corresponding trait will be expressed. When an individual is heterozygous for a trait, the instructions of the dominant allele will be expressed (see Figure 3.3).

To illustrate, let us consider two traits of no importance to human survival: the ability to roll one's tongue lengthwise and curliness of hair. If you can roll your tongue lengthwise into the shape of a tube, then at least one, but not necessarily both, of your parents must also

FIGURE 3.3 Mendelian inheritance patterns Pictured here are the Mendelian inheritance patterns for the offspring of two brown-haired parents who are both heterozygous for hair colour. The allele for brown hair (B) is dominant, and that for blond hair (b) is recessive. Note that these parents have three chances out of four of producing children with brown hair. They have two chances in four of producing brown-haired children who carry the gene for blond hair.

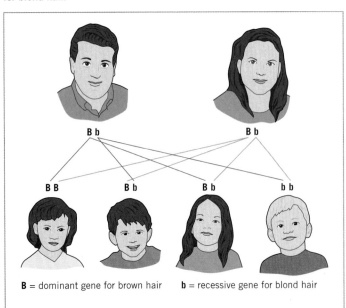

B = dominant gene for brown hair   **b** = recessive gene for blond hair

possess this remarkable but useless talent. From this statement (and Figure 3.3), you should be able to figure out that tongue-rolling is governed by a dominant allele. In contrast, if you have straight hair, then both of your parents must carry an allele for this trait, although it is possible that neither of them actually has straight hair. This is because straight hair is governed by a recessive gene, and curly hair is governed by a dominant gene.

The sex chromosomes present an interesting wrinkle in the story of dominance patterns. The X chromosome carries roughly 1500 genes, whereas the much smaller Y chromosome carries only about 200. Thus, when a female inherits a recessive allele on the X chromosome from her mother, she is likely to have a dominant allele on the chromosome from her father to suppress it, so she will not express the trait in question. In contrast, when a male inherits the same recessive allele on the X chromosome from his mother, he likely will not have a dominant allele from his father to override it, so he will express the trait. This difference in sex-linked inheritance is one reason for the greater vulnerability of males described in Chapter 2 (Box 2.2): they are more likely to suffer a variety of inherited disorders caused by recessive alleles on their X chromosome (see also Box 3.1 on pages 94–95).

Despite the traditional emphasis given to it, the dominant–recessive pattern of inheritance, in which a single gene affects a particular trait, pertains to relatively few human traits—such as hair colour, blood type, abundance of body hair, and the like—as well as to a large number of genetic disorders. Much more commonly, a single gene can affect multiple traits; both alleles can be fully expressed or blended in heterozygous individuals; and some genes are expressed differently, depending on whether they are inherited from the mother or from the father.

Inheritance patterns are vastly more complicated for most of the traits and behaviours that are of primary interest to behavioural scientists. These traits, such as shyness, aggression, thrill-seeking, and language learning, involve **polygenic inheritance,** in which several different genes contribute to any given phenotypic outcome. Gene-outcome linkages are particularly difficult to detect when many genes are involved. For this reason, you should be skeptical whenever you encounter newspaper headlines announcing the discovery of "a gene for" a complex human trait or predisposition.

3. Child's Environment–Child's Phenotype

We now come to Relation 3 in our model—the impact of the environment on the child's phenotype. (Remember, the environment includes everything not in the genetic material itself, including the variety of prenatal experiences discussed in Chapter 2.) As the model indicates, the child's observable characteristics result from the interaction between environmental factors and the child's genetic makeup.

Because of the continuous interaction of genotype and environment, a given genotype will develop differently in different environments. This idea is expressed by the concept of the **norm of reaction** (Dobzhansky, 1955), which refers to all the phenotypes that could theoretically result from a given genotype in relation to all the environments in which it could survive and develop. According to this concept, for any given genotype developing in varying environments, a range of outcomes would be possible. A child with a given genotype would probably develop quite differently in a loving, supportive family than he or she would in an alienating, abusive family. (Figure 3.4 offers a classic illustration of the norm of reaction in a genotype–environment interaction.)

polygenic inheritance ■ Inheritance in which traits are governed by more than one gene.

norm of reaction ■ All the phenotypes that can theoretically result from a given genotype in relation to all the environments in which it can survive and develop.

BOX 3.1: applications

GENETIC TRANSMISSION OF DISEASES AND DISORDERS

Thousands of human disorders—many of them extremely rare—are presently known to have genetic origins. Although our discussion here will focus on the behaviours and psychological symptoms associated with such disorders, most of them also involve a variety of physical symptoms, often including unusual physical appearance (e.g., distorted facial features), organ defects (e.g., heart problems), and atypical brain development. These and other genetically based conditions can be inherited in several different ways.

Dominant–Recessive Patterns

Many genetic disorders involve the dominant–recessive pattern of inheritance, occurring only when an individual has two recessive alleles for the condition. To date, more than 2850 such disorders have been identified (Lander, 2011). Recessive-gene disorders include PKU (discussed on page 96) and sickle-cell anemia (discussed below), as well as Tay-Sachs disease, cystic fibrosis, and many others. Disorders that are caused by a dominant gene include Huntington disease (a progressive and always fatal degenerative condition of the brain) and neurofibromatosis (a disorder in which nerve fibres develop tumours). A combination of severe speech, language, and motor difficulties that is common in a particular family in England has been traced to a mutation of a single gene (referred to as FOXP2) that acts in a dominant fashion (see S. E. Fisher & Scharff, 2009).

In some cases, a single gene can have both harmful and beneficial effects. One such case is sickle-cell disease, in which red blood cells are sickle-shaped rather than round, diminishing their capacity to transport oxygen. This disease, which can be debilitating and sometimes fatal, affects millions of people throughout the world. It is a recessive-gene disorder, so individuals who are homozygous for this trait (inheriting two sickle-cell genes, one from each parent) will suffer from the disease. Individuals who are heterozygous for this trait (carrying one normal and one sickle-cell gene) have some abnormality in their blood cells but usually experience no negative effects. In fact, if they live in regions of the world—like West Africa—where malaria is common, they benefit, because the sickle cells in their blood confer resistance against this deadly disease. In nineteenth-century Africa, malaria came to be known as the "White man's disease" because so many European explorers, lacking the sickle-cell gene, died of it.

Note that even when the root cause of a disorder is a single gene, it does not mean that that one gene is responsible for all manifestations of the disorder. The single gene simply starts a cascade of events, turning on and turning off multiple genes with effects on many different aspects of the individual's subsequent development.

Polygenic Inheritance

Many common human disorders are believed to result from interactions among multiple inherited genes, often in conjunction with environmental factors. Among the many diseases in this category are some forms of cancer and heart disease, Type 1 and Type 2 diabetes, and asthma. Psychiatric disorders, such as schizophrenia, and behaviour disorders, such as attention-deficit hyperactivity disorder, probably also involve multiple genes. More than 1100 gene loci affecting common traits and diseases have been identified to date, due largely to continually improving methods for genetic epidemiology (Lander, 2011).

Sex-Linked Inheritance

As mentioned in the text, some single-gene conditions are carried on the X chromosome and are much more common in males. (Females can inherit such conditions, but only if they inherit the culprit recessive alleles on both of their X chromosomes.) Sex-linked disorders range from relatively minor problems, like male-pattern baldness and red–green colour blindness, to very serious problems, including hemophilia and Duchenne muscular dystrophy. Another sex-linked disorder is fragile-X syndrome, which involves mutations in the X chromosome and is the most common inherited form of intellectual disability.

Chromosomal Anomalies

Some genetic disorders originate with errors in germ-cell division that result in a zygote that has either more or less than the normal complement of chromosomes. Most such zygotes cannot survive, but some do. Down syndrome most commonly originates when the mother's egg cells do not divide properly, and an egg that is fertilized contains an extra copy of chromosome 21. The probability of such errors in cell division increases with age, with the incidence of giving birth to a child with Down syndrome being markedly higher for women older than 35. (Increased paternal age has also been linked to the incidence of Down syndrome, though to a lesser extent [De Souza, Alberman, & Morris, 2009; Hurles, 2012]). The boy pictured on the next page shows some of the facial features common to individuals with Down syndrome, which is also marked by intellectual disability (ranging from mild to severe), a number of physical problems, and a sweet temperament.

Other genetic disorders arise from extra or missing sex chromosomes. For example, Klinefelter syndrome, which affects between 1 in 500 to 1000 males, involves an extra X chromosome (XXY). The physical signs of this syndrome, which can include small testes and elongated limbs, often go unnoticed, but infertility is common. Turner syndrome, which affects 1 in 2500 women, involves a missing X chromosome (XO) and is usually characterized by short stature, stunted sexual development at puberty, and infertility.

Gene Anomalies

Just as genetic disorders can originate from extra or missing chromosomes, so too can they result from extra, missing, or abnormal genes. One intriguing instance is Williams syndrome. This rare genetic disorder involves a variety of cognitive impairments, most noticeably in spatial and visual skills, but relatively less impairment in language ability (e.g., Musolino & Landau, 2012; Skwerer & Tager-Flusberg, 2011). Individuals with Williams syndrome are also typically characterized by outgoing personalities and friendliness paired with anxiety and phobias. This condition has been traced to the deletion of a small section of approximately 25 genes on chromosome 7. Some individuals, however, have a smaller deletion; in

LAUREN SHEAR / SCIENCE SOURCE

One of the most common identifiable causes of intellectual disability is Down syndrome, which occurs in about 1 of every 800 births in Canada. The risk increases dramatically with the age of the parents, especially the mother; by the age of 45, a woman has 1 chance in 32 of having a baby with Down syndrome. The degree of disability varies greatly and depends in part on the kind of care and early intervention children receive.

these cases, the degree of impairment is decreased, suggesting a clear relationship between the number of genes deleted and the resulting phenotype (Karmiloff-Smith et al., 2012). Interestingly, some individuals show a duplication of the same section of genes that is deleted in Williams syndrome. In this disorder, known as 7q11.23 duplication syndrome, the pattern of abilities and disabilities is flipped, with individuals exhibiting relatively weak speech and language abilities paired with relatively strong visuo-spatial skills (Mervis & Velleman, 2011; Osborne & Mervis, 2007).

Regulator Gene Defects

Many disorders are thought to originate from defects in regulator genes, which, as discussed on pages 91–92, control the expression of other genes. For example, a defect in the regulator gene that initiates the development of a male can interrupt the normal chain of events, occasionally resulting in a newborn who has female genitalia but is genetically male. Such cases often come to light when a young woman fails to begin menstruating or when a fertility clinic discovers that the reason a couple has failed to conceive is that the person trying to get pregnant is genetically male.

Unidentified Genetic Basis

In addition to the known gene-disorder links, there are many syndromes whose genetic origins are clear from their inheritance patterns but whose specific genetic cause has yet to be identified. For example, dyslexia is a highly heritable reading disability that probably stems from a variety of gene-based conditions. Another example is Tourette syndrome. Individuals with this disorder generally display a variety of tics, ranging from involuntary twitching and jerking to compulsively blurting out obscenities. Research suggests that Tourette syndrome probably involves a complex pattern of inheritance, making precise determination of the cause very difficult (O'Rourke et al., 2009).

The same is true for *autism spectrum disorder (ASD),* which includes both autism and Asperger syndrome and involves a wide range of deficits in social skills and communication. In Canada, it is estimated that the ASD prevalence is roughly 1 in 100 children, with boys much more likely to be diagnosed with ASD than girls (NEDSAC, 2012). The diagnosis of ASD is based on major impairments in social interaction and communication skills and a limited set of interests or repetitive behaviours. Individuals with Asperger syndrome tend to

have a milder array of symptoms and usually do not experience difficulties in language development.

ASD includes individuals with not only a range of disabilities but also, in some cases, remarkable talents in a narrowly focused area, such as mathematics or drawing. ASD is known to be highly heritable: twin studies have revealed that identical twins (who share 100% of their genes) are more than twice as likely as fraternal twins (who share 50% of their genes) to share an autism diagnosis (Ronald & Hoekstra, 2011). The difficulty in identifying the specific genetic basis for autism spectrum disorder is highlighted by the fact that, at present, there are more than 100 candidate genes associated with ASD (Geschwind, 2011; L. M. Xu et al., 2012).

The number of children diagnosed with ASD has increased dramatically in recent years. Indeed, in Canada, the *average annual increase* in prevalence of ASD between 2002 and 2008–2010 ranged from 9.7% to 14.6% (Ouellette-Kuntz et al., 2013). Part of the increase is believed to be due to greater public awareness of the syndrome, leading to a higher level of detection by parents, teachers, and doctors. In addition, current diagnostic criteria are broader than those of the past. It is thus unclear to what degree the increased level of diagnoses accurately reflects a change in the actual incidence of ASD (e.g., Gernsbacher, Dawson, & Goldsmith, 2005; Matson & Kozlowksi, 2011).

One factor that was highly publicized as a possible cause of the so-called autism epidemic—the MMR vaccine that is routinely given to young children to prevent measles, mumps, and rubella—has been *definitively* ruled out (A. W. McMahon et al., 2008; Price et al., 2010). Indeed, the original study reporting a link between the MMR vaccine and ASD (Wakefield et al., 1998) has been shown to be fraudulent and has been retracted (Godlee, Smith, & Marcovitch, 2011). Unfortunately, however, some parents continue to deny their children this important vaccine, needlessly putting them at risk for the illnesses that the vaccine prevents.

FIGURE 3.4 The norm of reaction concept This classic figure illustrates how a given genotype can develop differently in different environments. Three cuttings were made from each of seven individual plants; thus, the cuttings in each set of three had identical genes. The three cuttings from each plant were then planted at three different elevations, ranging from sea level to high mountains. The question of interest was whether the orderly differences in height that were observed at the low elevation would persist at the two higher elevations. As you can see, the order of the heights of the plants is neither orderly nor consistent across the different environments. For example, the first plant on the left, which is the tallest one at low elevation and at high elevation, is one of the shortest at medium elevation. The third plant is one of the tallest at the medium elevation and one of the shortest at the high elevation. Notice that not a single plant is always either the tallest or the shortest across the three elevations. "The phenotype is the unique consequence of a particular genotype developing in a particular environment" (Lewontin, 1982, pp. 22–23).

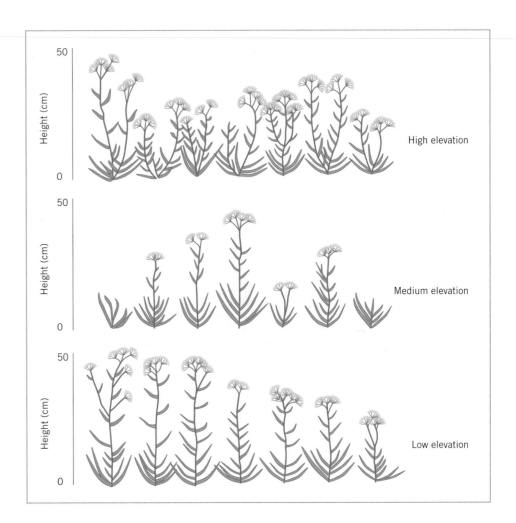

phenylketonuria (PKU) ■ A disorder related to a defective recessive gene on chromosome 12 that prevents metabolism of phenylalanine.

Examples of genotype–environment interaction Genotype–environment interactions can be studied directly by randomly assigning non-human animals with known genotypes to be raised in a wide variety of environmental conditions. If genetically identical animals develop differently in different environments, researchers can infer that environmental factors must be responsible for the different developmental outcomes. Scientists cannot, of course, randomly assign humans to different rearing conditions, but there are powerful naturally occurring examples of genotype–environment interactions for humans.

One such example is **phenylketonuria (PKU),** a disorder related to a defective recessive gene on chromosome 12. Individuals who inherit this gene from both parents cannot metabolize phenylalanine, an amino acid present in many foods (especially red meats) and in artificial sweeteners. If they eat a normal diet, phenylalanine accumulates in the bloodstream, causing impaired brain development that results in severe intellectual impairment. However, if infants with the PKU gene are identified shortly after birth and placed on a stringent diet free of phenylalanine, intellectual impairment can be avoided, as long as the diet is carefully maintained. Thus, a given genotype results in quite different phenotypes—cognitive disability or relatively normal intelligence—depending on environmental circumstances. Since early detection of this genetic disorder has such a positive effect on children's developmental outcomes, all newborn infants in Canada and the United States are routinely screened for PKU, as well as for a number of other severe and easily detected genetic disorders.

A second example of a genotype–environment interaction comes from an important study in New Zealand showing that the effects of abusive parenting vary in severity as a function of the child's genotype (Caspi et al., 2002). The researchers wanted to determine why some children who experience severe maltreatment become violent and antisocial as adults, whereas others who are exposed to the same abuse do not. The results, shown in Figure 3.5, revealed the importance of a *combination* of environmental *and* genetic factors leading to antisocial outcomes—suffering abusive treatment as a child *and* possessing a particular variant of MAOA, an X-linked gene known to inhibit brain chemicals associated with aggression. Young men who had a relatively inactive version of the MAOA gene, and who had experienced severe maltreatment, grew up to be more antisocial than other men. More concretely, 85% of the maltreated group with the relatively inactive gene developed some form of antisocial behaviour, and they were almost 10 times more likely to be convicted of a violent crime. The important point here is that neither factor by itself (possessing the inactive MAOA gene or being abused) predisposed boys to become highly aggressive; the higher incidence of antisocial behaviour was observed only for the group with both factors. As the authors of that study note, knowledge about specific genetic risk factors that make people more susceptible to particular environmental effects could strengthen multiple-risk models, such as those discussed in the previous two chapters.

Parental contributions to the child's environment Obviously, a highly salient and important part of a child's environment is the parents' relationship with the child—the manner in which they interact with him or her, the general home environment they provide, the experiences they arrange for the child, the encouragement they offer for particular behaviours, attitudes, and activities, and so on. Less obvious is the idea that the environment that parents provide for their children is due in part to the parents' own genetic makeup. Parents' behaviour toward their children (e.g., how warm or reserved they are, how patient or short-fused) is genetically influenced, as are the kinds of preferences, activities, and resources to which they expose their children (Plomin & Bergeman, 1991). For example, the child of a highly musical parent is likely to hear more music while growing up than are children whose parents are less musically inclined. Parents who are skilled readers and who enjoy and value reading are likely to read often for pleasure and information and are likely to have lots of books around the house. They are also more likely to read frequently to their children and to take them to the library. In contrast, parents for whom reading is challenging and not a source of pleasure are less likely to provide a highly literate environment for their children (Scarr, 1992).

4. Child's Phenotype–Child's Environment

Relation 4 in our model restates the *active child* theme—the child as a source of his or her own development. As noted in Chapter 1, children are not just the passive recipients of a pre-existing environment. Rather, they are active creators of the environment in which they live in two important ways. First, by virtue of their nature and behaviour, they actively evoke certain kinds of responses from others (Scarr, 1992; Scarr & McCartney, 1983). Babies who enjoy being cuddled are more likely to receive cuddling than are squirmy babies. Impulsive children hear "No," "Don't," "Stop," and "Be careful"

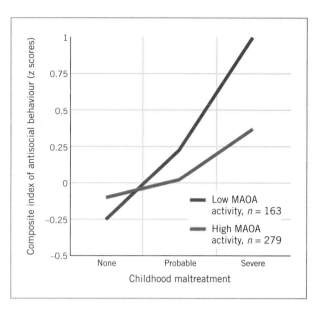

FIGURE 3.5 Genotype and environment This graph shows the level of antisocial behaviour observed in young men as a function of the degree to which they had been maltreated in childhood. As this figure shows, those young men who had experienced severe maltreatment were in general more likely to engage in antisocial behaviour than were those who had experienced none. However, the effect was much stronger for those individuals who had a relatively inactive MAOA gene. (Adapted from Caspi et al., 2002, p. 852)

This parent enjoys reading novels for **pleasure** and reads extensively for her work. She is providing a rich literary environment **for her** young child. The child may become **an avid** reader both because her mother's **genetic** makeup contributed to her enjoyment of reading and because of the physical environment (lots of books) and the social environment (encouragement of an **interest** in books) that the mother has provided.

more often than inhibited children do. Indeed, the degree to which parent–child relationships are mutually responsive is largely a function of the child's genetically influenced behavioural characteristics (Deater-Deckard & O'Connor, 2000).

The second way in which children create their own environment is by actively selecting surroundings and experiences that match their interests, talents, and personality characteristics (Scarr, 1992). As soon as infants become capable of self-locomotion, for example, they start selecting certain objects in the environment for exploration. Some very young children (especially boys) develop extremely intense interests in particular kinds of objects or activities that do not stem from parental encouragement (DeLoache, Simcock, & Macari, 2007). For example, many little boys become obsessed with vehicles and construction equipment. Other young children develop idiosyncratic and even quite peculiar interests (e.g., blenders, roadkill). For many parents, the origin of these preschool passions is totally obscure, and occasionally worrisome, because they do not realize how common these intense interests actually are.

Beginning in the preschool years, children's friendship opportunities increasingly depend on their own characteristics, as they choose playmates and pals with whom they feel compatible—the "birds of a feather flock together" phenomenon. And, as noted in Chapter 1, with age, children play an ever more active role in selecting their own environment. As they gain more autonomy, they increasingly select aspects of the environment that fit their temperament and abilities. Returning to the reading example, children who enjoy reading will read more books than will children who find reading tedious. The more they read, the more skilful readers they become, leading them to choose increasingly more challenging books, which, in turn, leads them to acquire advanced vocabulary, improve their language comprehension, and enhance their general knowledge base, resulting in greater success in school.

5. Child's Environment–Child's Genotype

The fifth relationship in our model is perhaps the most surprising. Until fairly recently, geneticists thought of the genotype as being "fixed" at birth. But as discussed in Chapter 1 (page 12), the new field of *epigenetics* has turned this conventional wisdom on its head. That is, it is now known that although the structure of DNA remains "fixed" (mutations aside), certain epigenetic mechanisms, mediated by the environment, can alter the functioning of genes and create stable changes in their expression—and some of these changes can be passed on to the next generation.

Epigenetic factors can help explain why identical twins do not have identical pathways through life: different environments can alter gene expression in subtle ways across developmental time. These stable changes in gene expression that are mediated by the environment involve processes of *methylation*, which silence gene expression. Differences in experience over the course of development are reflected in differences in methylation levels. Consider identical twin pairs at the age of 3 and at the age of 50, for example. Three-year-old co-twins have had highly overlapping life experiences, whereas many 50-year-old co-twins are likely to have had a far more divergent range of experiences. In a study that measured differences in DNA methylation levels in 3- and 50-year-old identical co-twins, researchers found that, whereas there were virtually no differences in the 3-year-olds' levels, roughly one-third of the 50-year-olds showed "remarkable" differences—and the greater the differences in the twins' lifestyle and experiences, the greater the differences in their methylation levels (Fraga et al., 2005).

How might the environment exert its effects through epigenetic mechanisms? To date, the bulk of the behavioural research on this topic has focused on non-human animal models. Research by Michael Meaney and colleagues at McGill University has provided clear evidence that low-quality maternal care has epigenetic effects, changing the animal's pattern of gene expression (for a recent review, see Zhang & Meaney, 2010). In particular, poor maternal care affects the methylation of genes involved in glucocorticoid receptors, which influence how the animal copes with stress. Interestingly, environmental enrichment can reverse these effects (T.-Y. Zhang & Meaney, 2010). As you saw in Chapter 1, there is emerging evidence suggesting similar effects of early stress on methylation in humans (e.g., Essex et al., 2013; McGowan et al., 2009). The myriad risk factors associated with growing up in poverty appear to act on developing children via epigenetic processes as well; adults who grew up in impoverished households exhibit different patterns of gene expression decades later than do adults who grew up in high-SES homes, regardless of their SES as adults (e.g., G. E. Miller et al., 2009).

Our discussion of the five kinds of gene–environment interactions has emphasized the myriad challenges in understanding how genes function in the development of individuals. Nevertheless, the conceptualization we have presented is greatly simplified. This is particularly true for the fifth relationship—epigenetics—which, when considered in full, suggests that the line between genes and environment is blurry at best. The complexity of gene–environment relationships raises both challenges and opportunities for developmental scientists. One challenge is that the genome can no longer comfortably be considered immutable irrespective of the widely varying environments in which children develop. One opportunity is that as this field continues to develop, it may become possible to determine which aspects of the environment are most likely to have a lasting impact on children's eventual health and well-being.

Behaviour Genetics

The rapidly expanding field known as **behaviour genetics** is concerned with how variation in behaviour and development results from the interaction of genetic and environmental factors. Behaviour geneticists ask the same sort of question Galton asked about eminence: "Why are people different from one another?" Why, in any group of human beings, do we vary in terms of how smart, sociable, depressed, aggressive, and religious we are? The answer given by behaviour geneticists is that all behavioural traits are **heritable;** that is, they are all influenced to some degree by hereditary factors (Bouchard, 2004; Turkheimer, 2000). As noted, the kind of traits that have been of particular interest to behaviour geneticists—intelligence, sociability, mood, aggression, and the like—are polygenic, that is, affected by the combination of many genes. They are also **multifactorial,** that is, affected by a host of environmental factors as well as genetic ones. Thus, the potential sources of variation are vast.

To fully answer Galton's question, behaviour geneticists try to tease apart genetic and environmental contributions to the differences observed among a population of people or other animals. Two premises underlie this endeavour:

1. To the extent that genetic factors are important for a given trait or behaviour, individuals who are genotypically similar should be phenotypically similar. In other words, behaviour patterns should "run in families": children should be more similar to their parents and siblings than to second- or third-degree relatives or unrelated individuals.

2. To the extent that shared environmental factors are important, individuals who were reared together should be more similar than people who were reared apart.

behaviour genetics ■ The science concerned with how variation in behaviour and development results from the combination of genetic and environmental factors.

heritable ■ Refers to any characteristics or traits that are influenced by heredity.

multifactorial ■ Refers to traits that are affected by a host of environmental factors as well as genetic ones.

"The title of my science project is 'My LIttle Brother: Nature or Nurture.'"

FIGURE 3.6 **Quebec Newborn Twin Study** The Quebec Newborn Twin Study is an ongoing study following a group of twins born between 1995 and 1998 in the Montreal area. As can be seen in the figure, the correlations for levels of physical aggression and expressive vocabulary size are higher for MZ 19-month-old twins than for DZ twins, indicating that genetic factors play a key role in these phenotypes. (Adapted from Dionne et al., 2003)

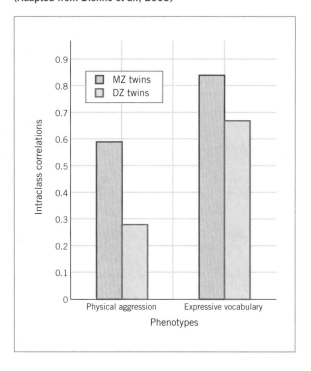

Behaviour Genetic Research Designs

As it was for Galton, the mainstay of modern behaviour-genetics research is the *family study*. In order to examine genetic and environmental contributions to a given trait or characteristic, behaviour geneticists first measure that trait in people who vary in terms of genetic relatedness—parents and their children, identical and fraternal twins, non-twin siblings, and so on. Next, they assess how highly correlated the measures of the trait are among individuals who vary in the degree to which they are genetically related. (As you may recall from Chapter 1, the strength and direction of a correlation express the extent to which two variables are related; the higher the correlation, the more precisely scores on one variable can be predicted from scores on the other.) Finally, behaviour geneticists compare the resulting correlations to see if they are (1) higher for more closely related individuals than for less closely related people, and (2) higher for individuals who share the same environment than for individuals who do not.

There are several specialized family-study designs that are particularly helpful in assessing genetic and environmental influences. One is the *twin-study* design, which compares the correlations for identical (monozygotic, or MZ) twins with those for same-sex fraternal (dizygotic, or DZ) twins. As you will recall, identical twins have 100% of their genes in common (though the expression of these genes is affected by epigenetic factors over the course of development, as discussed in the previous section), whereas fraternal twins are only 50% genetically similar (just like non-twin siblings). For twins who grow up together, the degree of similarity of the environment is generally assumed to be equal. Both types of twins shared the same womb, were born at the same time, have lived in the same family and community, and are always the same age when tested. Thus, with different levels of genetic similarity and essentially equal environmental similarity, the difference between the correlations for the two types of twins is treated as an index of the importance of genetic factors. If the correlation between identical twins on a given trait or behaviour is substantially higher than that between fraternal twins, it is assumed that genetic factors are substantially responsible for the difference. (See Figure 3.6 for an example of findings from one ongoing twin study, the Quebec Newborn Twin Study.)

Another family-study design used for assessing genetic and environmental influences is the *adoption* study. In this approach, researchers examine whether adopted children's scores on a given measure are correlated more highly with those of their biological parents and siblings or with those of their adoptive parents and siblings. Genetic influences are inferred to the extent that children resemble their biological relatives more than they do their adoptive ones.

The ideal behaviour-genetics design—the *adoptive twin* study—compares identical twins who grew up together versus identical twins who were separated shortly after birth and raised apart. If the correlations for twins reared apart are similar to those for twins reared together, it suggests that environmental factors have

BOX 3.2: individual differences

IDENTICAL TWINS REARED APART

Oskar Stohr and Jack Yufa are identical twins who were separated shortly after their birth in Trinidad. Oskar was raised by his grandmother in Germany as a Catholic and a Nazi. Jack was raised by his father, in the Caribbean, as a Jew. Despite their very different backgrounds, when the brothers first met as middle-aged men recruited for a research study in Minneapolis, they discovered a remarkable number of similarities between them:

They like spicy foods and sweet liqueurs, are absent-minded, have a habit of falling asleep in front of the television, think it's funny to sneeze in a crowd of strangers, flush the toilet before using it, store rubber bands on their wrists, read magazines back to front, dip buttered toast in their coffee. Oskar is domineering toward women and yells at his wife, which Jack did before he was separated.

(Holden, 1980, p. 1324)

Jack and Oskar are participants in the Minnesota Study of Twins Reared Apart, an extensive research project on identical twins separated early in life (Bouchard et al., 1990). More than 100 pairs of such twins have been located, recruited for the study, and brought to Minneapolis to undergo an extensive battery of physiological and psychological tests. Many twin siblings were meeting for the first time since infancy. (The reunited twins in the photo at right showed almost as many striking similarities as did Jack and Oskar, including having held several very similar jobs and being volunteer firefighters.) The motivation for this large-scale study is to examine genetic and environmental contributions to development and behaviour by comparing individuals who are genetically identical but who grew up in different environments.

The Minnesota team of investigators has been struck by the extent of the similarities they have found in the separated twins; they have identified genetic contributions to "almost every behavioural trait so far investigated, from reaction time to religiosity" (Bouchard et al., 1990).

As striking as the similarities between separated twins may be, there are several problems with automatically assuming that these similarities are attributable to genetic factors. One issue is that it would be a great oversimplification to suggest that all of the similar traits shared by separated twins are genetic. For example, it would be a stretch to argue that the men in the photograph share a set of genes that predetermined that they both would hold similar jobs and volunteer positions. As previously noted, genes code for proteins, not for anything as complex as an occupation (or choice of facial hair). An additional issue is the practice of selective placement: adoption agencies generally try to place children with families of the same general background and race, so the environments of the separated siblings are often similar in many ways. It is extremely rare for separated twins to be raised like Jack and Oskar, with different languages, religions, and cultures. In fact, the majority of the twins in most behaviour-genetics studies are from predominantly white, middle-class families in Western countries. As behaviour geneticists Levine and Suzuki (1993) commented:

Take one of those kids and put him in a really different environment, like in a family of bushmen in Africa, or in a farming village in mainland China, and then come back twenty years later and see if you find two firemen who dress the same!

(p. 241)

Identical twins Gerald Levey and Mark Newman were separated at birth and reared separately in middle-class Jewish homes in the New York area. When reunited at the age of 31, they discovered, among many other similarities, that they were both volunteer firefighters with droopy moustaches, long sideburns, and a penchant for hunting, fishing, and watching John Wayne movies. They even drank the same brand of beer, from a can, which they held with their pinkie tucked under the bottom and which they crushed when they had emptied it.

little effect. Conversely, to the extent that the correlations between identical twins who grew up in different environments are lower than those for identical twins who grew up together, environmental influence is inferred. Box 3.2 describes some of the remarkable findings that have emerged from studies of twins reared apart, as well as some of the problems with such research.

Family studies of intelligence The most common focus of behaviour-genetics family studies has been intelligence. Table 3.1 summarizes the results of more than 100 family studies of IQ through adolescence. The pattern of results reveals both genetic and environmental influences. Genetic influence is shown by generally higher correlations for higher degrees of genetic similarity. Most notable is the finding that identical (MZ) twins resemble each other in IQ more than do same-sex fraternal (DZ) twins. At the same time, environmental influences are reflected in the fact that identical twins are not identical in terms of IQ. Further evidence for an environmental role is that MZ twins who are reared together are more similar than those reared apart.

Does the relative influence that genes and environment have on intelligence change over the course of development? One might expect that as children get older and have ever more (and more varied) experiences in the world, genetic influences on IQ would decrease. Surprisingly, recent studies have revealed exactly the opposite pattern: as twins get older, the degree of variance in IQ accounted for by their genetic similarity increases. In a study of 11 000 MZ and DZ twin pairs across four countries, researchers found that the correlations in IQ between co-twins increased with age for MZ twins and decreased with age for DZ twins. These divergent patterns were observed first from childhood to adolescence, and again from adolescence to young adulthood (Haworth et al., 2010). The same pattern of results was revealed in a large longitudinal study that compared MZ and DZ twin pairs in early childhood (2- to 4-year-olds) and middle childhood (7- to 10-year-olds): for the younger children, shared environment accounted for more variance than did shared genes, with the opposite pattern observed for the older children (O. S. P. Davis, Haworth, & Plomin, 2009).

This surprising pattern of results—namely, that genetic influences increase with age—is consistent with the idea that people actively construct their own environment: the phenotype–environment correlation (Relation 3) discussed earlier (McGue et al., 1993; Scarr & McCartney, 1983). As children get older, they increasingly control their own experiences, and their parents have less influence over their activities. The effects of education may be particularly relevant to this pattern of results, given that educational experiences and achievements influence children's performance on measurements of intelligence. Younger children have little or no choice about their educational setting and opportunities, whereas older children, teens, and young adults have increasingly greater choices with regard to their educational experiences (choosing more or less challenging courses of study, more or less academically oriented peer groups, and so on). It may be that identical twins' IQs become more similar into adulthood because their common genetic predispositions lead them to select similar intellectual stimulation, whereas the IQs of fraternal twins become increasingly dissimilar because they choose divergent experiences for themselves (Scarr & McCartney, 1983).

Heritability

In their approach to the nature–nurture question, many behaviour geneticists attempt to quantify the degree to which genes contribute to various traits. To estimate how much of the variability in measures of a given trait is attributable to

TABLE 3.1

Summary of Family Studies of Intelligence

Relationship	Average Familial IQ Correlations (R)	
	Average R Reared-together biological relatives	Number of Pairs
MZ twins	0.86	4672
DZ twins	0.60	5533
Siblings	0.47	26 473
Parent–offspring	0.42	8433
Half-siblings	0.35	200
Cousins	0.15	1176
Reared-apart biological relatives		
MZ twins	0.72	65
Siblings	0.24	203
Parent–offspring	0.24	720
Reared-together non-biological relatives		
Siblings	0.32	714
Parent–offspring	0.24	720

Note: MZ = monozygotic; DZ = dizygotic.
Source: McGue et al., 1993

genetic and environmental factors, they derive heritability estimates from correlations of the type shown in Table 3.1. **Heritability** is a statistical estimate of how much of the measured variance on a trait among individuals in a given population is attributable to genetic differences among those individuals.

A crucial point to understand about heritability estimates is that they tell us nothing about the relative contributions of genetic and environmental factors to the development of an *individual.* Instead, they estimate how much of the variation among *a given population of people* is due to differences in their genes. The heritability estimate for intelligence, for example, is generally considered to be approximately 50% (Bouchard, 2004; Plomin, 1990). This means that, *for the population studied,* roughly 50% of the variation in IQ scores is due to genetic differences among the members of the population. (It does *not* mean that 50% of your IQ score is due to your genetic makeup and 50% is due to your experience.) Note that this heritability estimate indicates that the environmental contribution to the variation in IQ is also approximately 50%.

Behaviour-genetic analyses have been applied to many diverse aspects of human behaviour, several of which you will encounter in other chapters of this book. To cite just a few examples, substantial heritability has been reported for infant activity level (Saudino & Eaton, 1991), temperament (Goldsmith, Buss, & Lemery, 1997), reading disability (DeFries & Gillis, 1993), and antisocial behaviour (Gottesman & Goldsmith, 1994). Substantial heritability has even been reported for divorce (McGue & Lykken, 1992), television viewing (Plomin et al., 1990), and other factors that previously seemed more likely to be influenced by the environment than by genetics (e.g., Jaffee & Price, 2007).

The implausibility of "divorcer" or "couch potato" genes brings us back to a point we made earlier: despite the common use of the phrase, there are no genes "for" particular behaviour patterns. As we have stressed, genes do nothing more than code for proteins, so they affect behaviour only insofar as those proteins affect the sensory, neural, and other physiological processes involved in behaviour. Thus, the heritability estimate for divorce may be related to a genetic predisposition to, say, seek out novelty, and the estimate for television viewing may be related to a genetically based low activity level or short attention span.

Heritability estimates have been criticized, both from within psychology (e.g., G. Gottlieb, Wahlsten, & Lickliter, 1998; Lerner, 1995) and from outside it (e.g., J. S. Levine & Suzuki, 1993; Lewontin, 1982). Part of the criticism stems from ways that the term "heritability" is often misinterpreted or misused by the public. One very common misuse involves the application of the concept of heritability to individuals, despite the fact that, as we have emphasized, *heritability applies only to populations.*

In addition, *a heritability estimate applies only to a particular population living in a particular environment.* Consider the case of height. Research conducted almost exclusively with North Americans and Europeans—most of them white and adequately nourished—puts the heritability of height at around 90%. But what if some segment of this population had experienced a severe famine during childhood, while the rest remained well fed? Would the heritability estimate for height still be 90%? No—because the variability due to environmental factors (poor nutrition) would *increase* dramatically and, therefore, the variability that could be attributed to genetic factors would *decrease* to the same degree. The principle of variable heritability also appeared in the discussion of IQ correlations earlier in this chapter, with the heritability estimates derived from them differing for the same individuals at different points in development (O. S. P. Davis et al., 2009).

heritability ■ A statistical estimate of the proportion of the measured variance on a trait among individuals in a given population that is attributable to genetic differences among those individuals.

Furthermore, it is known that heritability estimates can differ markedly for groups of people who grow up in very different economic circumstances. In the United States, for instance, heritability estimates differ considerably as a function of socioeconomic status (SES), as shown by a large twin study that included families across the SES spectrum (Turkheimer et al., 2003). In this study, almost 60% of the variance in IQ among a sample of 7-year-olds living in poverty was accounted for by shared environment, with almost none of it attributable to genetic similarity. Affluent families follow the opposite pattern, with genetic factors contributing more than environmental ones. In a related study focused on the test scores of adolescent twins, the same pattern was observed: environmental factors trumped genetic factors for poorer teens, while genetic factors trumped environmental factors for wealthier teens (Harden, Turkheimer, & Loehlin, 2007). Although it is not fully clear what causes these differing levels of heritability, both studies suggest that qualitatively different developmental forces may be operating in poor versus affluent environments.

A related, frequently misunderstood point is that *high heritability does not imply immutability*. The fact that a trait is highly heritable does not mean that there is little point in trying to improve the course of development related to that trait. Thus, for example, the fact that the heritability estimate for IQ is relatively high does not mean that the intellectual performance of young children living in poverty cannot be improved by appropriate intervention efforts (see Chapter 8, pages 319–321).

Finally, because they are relevant only within a given population, heritability estimates tell us *nothing* about differences *between groups*. The heritability score for IQ, for example, provides little insight into the meaning of differences in the IQ scores of different groups. European-Americans, on average, score 15 points higher on IQ tests than do African-Americans. Some people mistakenly assume that because IQ is estimated to be 50% heritable, the difference between these two groups' IQ scores is genetically based. This assumption is unwarranted, given the large overall disparities between the two groups in family income and education, quality of neighbourhood schools, health care, and myriad other factors.

Environmental Effects

Every examination of genetic contributions to behaviour and development is also, necessarily, a study of environmental influences: estimating heritability automatically estimates the proportion of variance not attributable to genes. Because heritability estimates rarely exceed 50%, a large contribution from environmental factors is usually indicated.

Behaviour geneticists try to assess the extent to which aspects of an environment shared by biologically related people make them more alike and to what extent non-shared experiences make them different. The most obvious source of shared environment is growing up in the same family. Shared-environment effects can also be inferred when twins or other relatives are more similar on some trait than would be expected on the basis of their genetic relatedness. For example, substantial shared-environmental influence has been inferred for positive emotion in toddlers and young children because fraternal and identical twins who were reared together were equally similar in the degree to which they showed pleasure (Goldsmith et al., 1997). Shared-environment effects are also being discovered for disorders that have a clear genetic component. For instance, as discussed in Box 3.1, twin

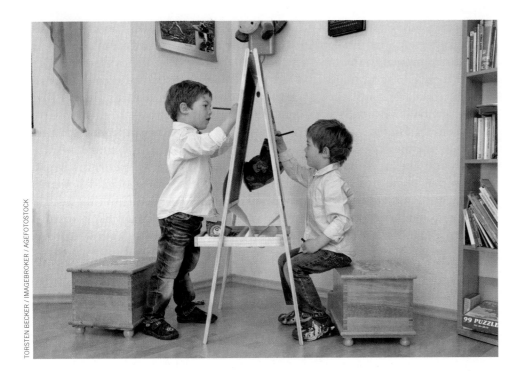

The similarity between these identical twins may be enhanced by environmental factors. Sharing similar abilities, they may enjoy similar activities and be exposed to similar environmental influences. Being of similar intelligence, they are likely to have relatively similar experiences in school. Later, they may enjoy similar success in dating and end up with spouses of similar social class.

studies of autism spectrum disorder (ASD) have consistently provided evidence for genetic effects (with heritability of the disorder being greater for MZ twins than for DZ twins). However, in a recent large-scale study of twin pairs in which at least one co-twin had an ASD diagnosis, researchers found a substantial shared-environment effect on the likelihood that the second twin also had an ASD diagnosis (Hallmayer et al., 2011).

Surprisingly, behaviour geneticists have reported little evidence of shared-environment effects for some other aspects of development. For example, with respect to personality, the correlations for adoptive siblings are often near zero (D. C. Rowe, 1994). The same is true for some types of psychopathology, including schizophrenia (Gottesman, 1991). As noted in Chapter 1, being adopted into a family with a schizophrenic sibling does not increase the risk that a child will become schizophrenic. In addition, the risk of schizophrenia is the same for the biological child of a schizophrenic parent regardless of whether the child is raised by that parent or is adopted away at birth (Kety et al., 1994).

Behaviour geneticists' investigations of the effects of non-shared environments arise from the recognition that even children who grow up in the same family do not have all their experiences in common—either inside or outside the family. Within the family, birth order may result in quite different experiences for siblings. The oldest child in a large family, for example, may have been reared by young, energetic, but inexperienced, parents, whereas that child's much younger sibling will be parented by older and more sedentary, but more knowledgeable, individuals who are likely to have more resources available than they did as first-time parents. In addition, as discussed in Chapter 1, siblings may experience their parents' behaviour toward them differently (the "Mom always loved you best" syndrome). They may also be affected quite differently by an event they experience in common, such as the divorce of their parents (Hetherington & Clingempeel, 1992). Finally, siblings may be highly motivated to differentiate themselves from one another (Sulloway, 1996). The younger sibling of a star student may strive to be a star athlete instead, and a child who observes a sibling disappearing into a self-destructive pattern of drug and alcohol abuse may become determined to follow a different path. As these examples illustrate, siblings themselves are an important part of the environment, and each provides a different constellation of experiences for the others. This is another factor that makes each child's experience within the family different.

Outside the family, siblings can also have highly divergent experiences, partly as a result of belonging to different peer groups. Highly active siblings who both like physical challenges and thrills will have very different experiences if one takes up rock climbing while the other hangs out with peers who are delinquent. Idiosyncratic life events—suffering a serious accident, having an inspiring teacher, being bullied on the playground—can contribute further to making siblings develop differently. The primary effect of non-shared environmental factors is to increase the differences among family members (Plomin & Daniels, 1987).

review:

The five relations shown in Figure 3.1 depict the complex interplay of genetic and environmental forces in development. (1) The course of children's development is influenced by the genetic heritage they receive from their mother and father, with their sex determined solely by their father's chromosomal contribution. (2) The relation between children's genotype and phenotype depends in part on dominance patterns in the expression of some genes, but most traits of primary interest to behavioural scientists are influenced by multiple genes (polygenic inheritance). (3) As the concept of norm of reaction specifies, any given genotype will develop differently in different environments. A particularly salient part of children's environment is their parents, including their parents' own genetic makeup, which influences how parents behave toward their children. (4) Children's own genetic makeup influences how they select and shape their own environment and the experiences they have in it. (5) Conversely, children's experiences can change their genetic expression through epigenetic mechanisms.

The field of behaviour genetics is concerned with how development results from the interaction of genetic and environmental factors. Using the family-study methodology, behaviour geneticists compare the correlations among individuals who vary in the degree of genetic relatedness and in similarity of their rearing environments. Heritability estimates indicate the proportion of the variance among individuals in a given population on a given trait that is attributable to genetic differences among them. Most behavioural traits that have been measured show substantial heritability; at the same time, heritability estimates reveal the close partnership of heredity and environment in development and the fallacy of considering the influences of nature and nurture as independent of each other.

Brain Development

As you will see, the collaboration between nature and nurture takes centre stage in the development of the brain and nervous system. Before discussing developmental processes in the formation of the brain, however, we need to consider the basic components of this "most complex structure in the known universe" (R. F. Thompson, 2000, p. 1).

Fundamental to all aspects of behavioural development is the development of the central nervous system and especially the brain. The brain is the font of all thought, memory, emotion, imagination, personality—in short, the behaviour, capacities, and characteristics that make us who we are.

Structures of the Brain

In our examination of the structures of the brain, we focus our discussion on two that are central to behaviour—the neuron and the cortex, as well as some of their substructures.

Neurons

The business of the brain is information. The basic units of the brain's remarkably powerful informational system are its more than 100 billion **neurons** (Figure 3.7), which constitute the grey matter of the brain. These cells are specialized for sending and receiving messages between the brain and all parts of the body, as well as within the brain itself. *Sensory neurons* transmit information from sensory receptors that detect stimuli in the external environment or within the body itself; *motor neurons* transmit information from the brain to muscles and glands; and *interneurons* act as intermediaries between sensory and motor neurons.

neurons ■ Cells that are specialized for sending and receiving messages between the brain and all parts of the body, as well as within the brain itself.

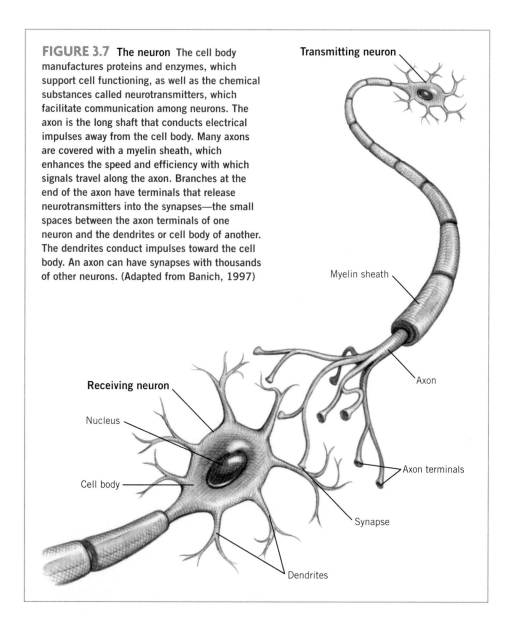

FIGURE 3.7 **The neuron** The cell body manufactures proteins and enzymes, which support cell functioning, as well as the chemical substances called neurotransmitters, which facilitate communication among neurons. The axon is the long shaft that conducts electrical impulses away from the cell body. Many axons are covered with a myelin sheath, which enhances the speed and efficiency with which signals travel along the axon. Branches at the end of the axon have terminals that release neurotransmitters into the synapses—the small spaces between the axon terminals of one neuron and the dendrites or cell body of another. The dendrites conduct impulses toward the cell body. An axon can have synapses with thousands of other neurons. (Adapted from Banich, 1997)

Transmitting neuron

Myelin sheath

Axon

Receiving neuron

Nucleus

Cell body

Axon terminals

Synapse

Dendrites

Although they vary substantially in size, shape, and function, all neurons are made up of three main components: (1) a **cell body,** which contains the basic biological material that keeps the neuron functioning; (2) **dendrites,** fibres that receive input from other cells and conduct it toward the cell body in the form of electrical impulses; and (3) an **axon,** a fibre (anywhere from a few micrometres to more than a metre in length) that conducts electrical signals away from the cell body to connections with other neurons.

Neurons communicate with one another at **synapses,** which are microscopic junctions between the axon terminal of one neuron and the dendritic branches of another. In this communication process, electrical and chemical messages cross the synapses and cause the receiving neurons either to fire, sending a signal on to other neurons, or to be inhibited from firing. The total number of synapses is staggering—hundreds of trillions—with some neurons having as many as 15 000 synaptic connections with other neurons.

Glial Cells

Glial cells, the brain's white matter, make up nearly half the human brain, outnumbering neurons 10 to 1. They perform a variety of critical functions, including the formation of a **myelin sheath** around axons, which insulates them and increases the speed and efficiency of information transmission. The importance of myelin is highlighted by the severe consequences that can arise from disorders that affect it. For example, multiple sclerosis is a disease in which the immune system attacks myelin, interfering with neuronal signalling and producing varying degrees of physical and cognitive impairment. Several psychiatric disorders, including schizophrenia and bipolar disorder, are also linked to defects in the gene that regulates production of myelin (e.g., Hakak et al., 2001; Tkachev et al., 2003).

Glial cells play a further role in communication within the brain by influencing the formation and strengthening of synapses and by communicating biochemically among themselves in a network separate from the neural network, and allowing them to efficiently regulate many aspects of brain activity (Fields, 2004).

The Cortex

The **cerebral cortex,** the surface of which is shown in Figure 3.8, is considered the "most human part of the human brain" (McEwen & Schmeck, 1994). Over the course of human evolution, the brain expanded greatly in size. According to Bryan Kolb and Ian Whishaw at the University of Lethbridge, almost all of this increase occurred in the cerebral cortex, which constitutes 80% of the brain, a much greater proportion than in other species. The folds and fissures that are apparent in Figure 3.8 form during development as the brain grows within the confined space of the skull; these convolutions make it possible to pack more cortex into the limited space.

The cortex plays a primary role in a wide variety of mental functions, from seeing and hearing to reading, writing, and doing arithmetic and to feeling compassion and communicating with others. As Figure 3.8 shows, the major areas of the cortex—the **lobes**—can be characterized in terms of the general behavioural categories with which they are associated. The **occipital lobe** is primarily involved in processing visual information. The **temporal lobe** is associated with memory, visual recognition, speech and language, and the processing of emotion and auditory information. The **parietal lobe** is important for spatial processing. It is also involved in the

cell body ■ A component of the neuron that contains the basic biological material that keeps the neuron functioning.

dendrites ■ Neural fibres that receive input from other cells and conduct it toward the cell body in the form of electrical impulses.

axons ■ Neural fibres that conduct electrical signals away from the cell body to connections with other neurons.

synapses ■ Microscopic junctions between the axon terminal of one neuron and the dendritic branches or cell body of another.

glial cells ■ Cells in the brain that provide a variety of critical supportive functions.

myelin sheath ■ A fatty sheath that forms around certain axons in the body and increases the speed and efficiency of information transmission.

cerebral cortex ■ The "grey matter" of the brain that plays a primary role in what is thought to be particularly human-like functioning, from seeing and hearing to writing to feeling emotion.

lobes ■ Major areas of the cortex associated with general categories of behaviour.

occipital lobe ■ The lobe of the cortex that is primarily involved in processing visual information.

temporal lobe ■ The lobe of the cortex that is associated with memory, visual recognition, and the processing of emotion and auditory information.

parietal lobe ■ The lobe of the cortex that governs spatial processing and integrates sensory input with information stored in memory.

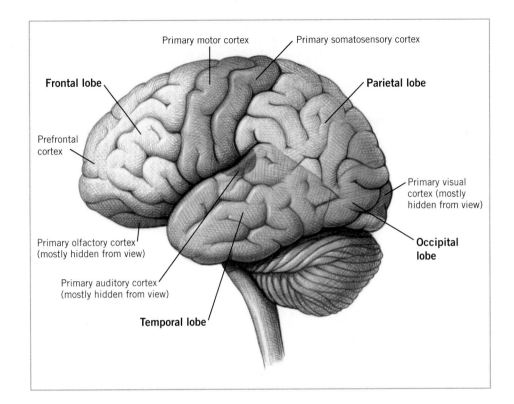

Primary motor cortex

Primary somatosensory cortex

Frontal lobe

Parietal lobe

Prefrontal cortex

Primary visual cortex (mostly hidden from view)

Primary olfactory cortex (mostly hidden from view)

Occipital lobe

Primary auditory cortex (mostly hidden from view)

Temporal lobe

FIGURE 3.8 **The human cerebral cortex** This view of the left hemisphere of an adult brain shows the four major cortical regions—known as the lobes—which are divided from one another by deep fissures. Each of the primary sensory areas receives information from a particular sensory system, and the primary motor cortex controls the body's muscles. Information from multiple sensory areas is processed in association areas.

integration of information from different sensory modalities, and it plays a role in integrating sensory input with information stored in memory and with information about internal states. The **frontal lobe,** the brain's "executive," is involved in cognitive control, including working memory, planning, decision making, and inhibitory control. Information from multiple sensory systems is processed and integrated in the **association areas** that lie in between the major sensory and motor areas.

Although it is convenient to think of different cortical areas as if they were functionally specific, they are not. It has become increasingly clear that complex mental functions are mediated by multiple areas of the brain, with an extraordinary degree of interactivity both within and across brain regions. A given area may be critical for some ability, but that does not mean that control of that ability is located in that one area. (Box 3.3 examines some of the techniques that researchers use to learn about brain functioning.)

Cerebral lateralization The cortex is divided into two separate halves, or **cerebral hemispheres.** For the most part, sensory input from one side of the body goes to the opposite side of the brain, and the motor areas of the cortex control movements of the opposite side of the body. Thus, if you pick up a hot pot with your right hand, it is the left side of the brain that receives the sensory response, registers the pain, and initiates the motor response to let go immediately.

The left and right hemispheres of the brain communicate with each other primarily by way of the **corpus callosum,** a dense tract of nerve fibres that connect them. The two hemispheres are specialized for different modes of processing, a phenomenon referred to as **cerebral lateralization.** There are notable similarities across species in hemispheric specialization. For example, most aspects of speech and language are lateralized to the left hemisphere in humans, with a similar asymmetry observed for communicative signals in non-human species, from mice to primates (Corballis, 2009).

frontal lobe ■ The lobe of the cortex that is associated with organizing behaviour; the lobe that is thought responsible for the human ability to plan ahead.

association areas ■ Parts of the brain that lie between the major sensory and motor areas and that process and integrate input from those areas.

cerebral hemispheres ■ The two halves of the cortex; for the most part, sensory input from one side of the body goes to the opposite hemisphere of the brain.

corpus callosum ■ A dense tract of nerve fibres that enable the two hemispheres of the brain to communicate.

cerebral lateralization ■ The specialization of the hemispheres of the brain for different modes of processing.

BOX 3.3: a closer look

MAPPING THE MIND

Developmental scientists employ a variety of techniques to determine what areas of the brain are associated with particular behaviours, thoughts, and feelings and how brain functions change with age. The existence of increasingly powerful techniques for investigating brain function has sparked a revolution in the understanding of the brain and its development. Here, we provide examples of some of the techniques most often used to map the mind and its workings in children.

Electrophysiological Recording

One of the techniques most often used by developmental researchers to study brain function is based on *electroencephalographic* (*EEG*) recordings of electrical activity generated by neurons. EEG is completely non-invasive (the recordings are obtained through an electrode cap that simply rests on the scalp, and can contain hundreds of electrodes), so this method can be used successfully even with infants (see photo at right). EEG recordings provide detailed information about the time course of neural events, and have provided valuable information about a variety of brain-behaviour relations.

An electrophysiological technique that is very useful for studying the relation between brain activity and specific kinds of stimulation is the recording of **event-related potentials (ERPs)**, that is, changes in the brain's electrical activity that occur in response to the presentation of a particular stimulus. One contribution these measures have made is that they reveal continuity over time. For instance, studies of infants' ERPs in response to native-speech sounds have shown that infants' ability to discriminate among these sounds predicts their language growth over the next few years (Kuhl et al.,

COURTESY CHARLES A. NELSON

EEG This EEG cap holds electrodes snugly against the baby's scalp, enabling researchers to record electrical activity generated from all over the baby's brain.

2008). A related method, called *magneto-encephalography* (*MEG*), detects magnetic fields generated by electrical currents in the brain. MEG has the added benefit of being the only non-invasive imaging method that can be used to study the fetal brain. Although the use of MEG for this purpose is in its early stages, researchers have so far been able to detect fetal neural responses to auditory stimuli and flashes of light displayed on the mother's abdomen, as well as habituation responses to repeated stimuli (Sheridan et al., 2010).

Functional Magnetic Resonance Imaging

Functional magnetic resonance imaging (fMRI) uses a powerful electromagnet to detect fluctuations in cerebral blood flow in different areas of the brain. Increased

blood flow indicates increased activity, so this technology allows researchers to determine which areas of the brain are activated by different tasks and stimuli. Since a person must be able to tolerate the noise and close confinement of an MRI machine and must also be able to remain very still, most developmental fMRI studies have been done with children 6 years of age or older, often using practice sessions in a mock scanner to help children acclimate to the MRI environment. However, recent studies have used fMRI methods to investigate neural processes in sleeping infants as young as 2 days old. One such study demonstrated that the areas of the brain that are activated by spoken language from later infancy onward are also activated by speech in neonates (Perani et al., 2011).

Other Techniques

Positron emission tomography (*PET*) measures brain activity by detecting the brain's metabolic processes and has provided important information about brain development. However, because PET scans involve injecting radioactive material into the brain, this technique is used primarily for diagnostic purposes.

One of the newest methods to be used in developmental studies is *near-infrared spectroscopy* (*NIRS*), an optical imaging technique that measures neural activity by detecting metabolic changes that lead to differential absorption of infrared light in brain tissue. The infrared light is transmitted to the brain, and its absorption is detected by means of an optical-fibre skullcap or headband. Because NIRS is silent, non-invasive, and does not require rigid stabilization of the head, it is particularly

event-related potentials (ERPs) ■ Changes in the brain's electrical activity that occur in response to the presentation of a particular stimulus.

Developmental Processes

How does the incredibly complex structure of the human brain come into being? You will not be surprised to hear that, once again, a partnership of nature and nurture is involved. Some aspects of the construction of the brain are set in motion and tightly controlled by the genes, relatively independent of experience. But, as you will see, other aspects are profoundly influenced by experience.

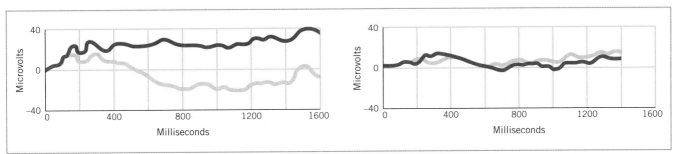

promising for research with infants and young children. Thus far, a number of attempts to pinpoint infants' brain activation in response to particular stimuli have shown mixed results, in part because the technology is still in its early stages (Aslin, 2012). One use of NIRS that has already proved successful is the monitoring of brain-oxygen levels in premature newborns. Another particularly interesting and successful application of NIRS involved a study of deaf children who had just received a cochlear implant, a surgically implanted electronic hearing device that we will discuss in Chapter 6. Because of concerns about the effects of its magnetic field, fMRI cannot be used to study brain processes in individuals with implants. NIRS was thus used to determine whether the auditory cortices of these children could respond to auditory stimulation. The NIRS showed that, rather remarkably, the auditory cortex of deaf children responded to sound within hours after the implant was activated, even though the cortex had never before been exposed to sound (Sevy et al., 2010).

ERP responses This figure shows ERP waveforms in response to novel (red line) and familiar (yellow line) stimuli. The infants who later recalled how to assemble a toy (left panel) had clearly discriminated between the familiar and novel items on an earlier recognition test. The infants who did not recall the assembly sequence (right panel) had not discriminated between the components on the earlier test. (Adapted from L. J. Carver, Bauer, & Nelson, 2000)

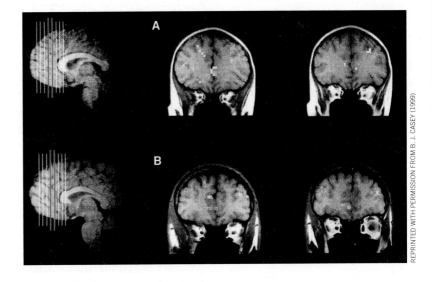

REPRINTED WITH PERMISSION FROM B. J. CASEY (1999)

fMRI images The figure shows fMRI images of the brains of a 9-year-old (panel A) and a 24-year-old (panel B) in a standard cognitive task that requires responding to some stimuli but inhibiting responding to others. (The images to the left show the "slices" of the brain averaged together in the images on the right.) The results show that the location of activation in the prefrontal cortex did not differ between children and adults, but the overall extent of activation was greater for the children (Casey, 1999).

Neurogenesis and Neuron Development

In the 3rd or 4th week of prenatal life, cells in the newly formed neural tube begin dividing at an astonishing rate—at peak production, 250 000 new cells are born every minute. **Neurogenesis,** the proliferation of neurons through cell division, is virtually complete by around 18 weeks after conception (Rakic, 1995; Stiles, 2008). Thus, most of the roughly 100 billion neurons you currently possess have been

neurogenesis ■ The proliferation of neurons through cell division.

with you since before you were born. Notably, however, we do continue to generate new neurons throughout life. During bouts of learning, for example, neurogenesis occurs in the hippocampus, a brain region important for memory processes (E. Gould et al., 1999). Neurogenesis does not always occur, however: it can be inhibited by stress (Mirescu & Gould, 2006). This pattern of results suggests that neurogenesis later in life is not fixed and predetermined but is instead adaptive, increasing under rewarding conditions and decreasing in threatening environments (e.g., Glasper, Shoenfeld, & Gould, 2012).

After their "birth," neurons begin the second developmental process, which involves migration to their ultimate destinations. Some neurons are pushed along passively by the newer cells formed after them, whereas others actively propel themselves toward their ultimate location.

Once neurons reach their destination, cell growth and differentiation occur. Neurons first grow an axon and then a "bush" of dendrites (refer to Figure 3.7). Thereafter, they take on the specific structural and functional characteristics of the different structures of the brain. Axons elongate as they grow toward specific targets, which, depending on the neuron in question, might be anything from another neuron in the brain to a bone in the big toe. The main change in dendrites is "arborization"—an enormous increase in the size and complexity of the dendritic "tree" that results from growth, branching, and the formation of **spines** on the branches. Arborization enormously increases the dendrites' capacity to form connections with other neurons. In the cortex, the period of most intense growth and differentiation comes after birth.

The process of **myelination,** the formation of the insulating myelin sheath around some axons, begins in the brain before birth and continues into early adulthood. As noted earlier, a crucial function of myelin is to increase the speed of neural conduction. Myelination begins deep in the brain, beginning with the brain stem, and moves upward and outward into the cortex at a fairly steady rate throughout childhood and adolescence and into early adulthood (Lenroot & Giedd, 2006). The various cortical areas thus become myelinated at very different rates, possibly contributing to the different rates of development for various behaviours.

This pattern diverges in interesting ways from the pattern found in our primate relative, the chimpanzee. Initially, white matter develops even more slowly in the prefrontal lobes of infant and juvenile chimpanzees than it does in young humans, suggesting one possible mechanism whereby evolutionary pressure has improved human brain function relative to that of other primates (Sakai et al., 2011). Interestingly, however, the chimpanzee shows a mature pattern of myelination at the point of sexual maturity, far earlier than that observed in humans (D. J. Miller et al., 2012). The reasons for the extended period of human myelination remain unknown, and might be both positive (facilitating improvements in executive functions after sexual maturity) and negative (making the human brain more vulnerable to disorders related to myelination discussed on page 108).

Synaptogenesis

One result of the extraordinary growth of axonal and dendritic fibres is a wildly exuberant generation of neuronal connections. In a process called **synaptogenesis,** each neuron forms synapses with thousands of others, resulting in the formation of the trillions of connections referred to earlier. Figure 3.9 shows the time course of synaptogenesis in the cortex. As you can see, it begins prenatally and proceeds very rapidly both before birth and for some time afterward. Note that both the timing

spines ■ Formations on the dendrites of neurons that increase the dendrites' capacity to form connections with other neurons.

myelination ■ The formation of myelin (a fatty sheath) around the axons of neurons that speeds and increases information-processing abilities.

synaptogenesis ■ The process by which neurons form synapses with other neurons, resulting in trillions of connections.

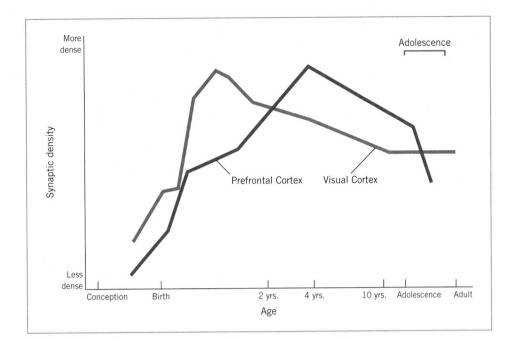

FIGURE 3.9 Synapse production and elimination Mean synaptic density (the number of synapses in a given space) first increases sharply as new synapses are overproduced and later declines gradually as excess synapses are eliminated. Note that the time scale is compressed at later stages. (Adapted from P. R. Huttenlocher & Dabholkar, 1997)

and rate of synapse production vary for different cortical areas; synapse generation is complete much earlier in the visual cortex, for example, than in the frontal area. As with myelination, the differential timing of synapse generation across areas of the brain likely contributes to the developmental timing of the onset of various abilities and behaviours.

Synapse Elimination

The explosive generation of neurons and synapses during synaptogenesis, which is largely under genetic control, results in a huge surplus—many more neural connections than any one brain can use. This overabundance of synapses includes an excess of connections between different parts of the brain: for instance, many neurons in what will become the auditory cortex are linked with those in the visual area, and both of these areas are overly connected to neurons involved in taste and smell. Canadian researchers Daphne Maurer and Cathy Mondloch (2004) have proposed that, as a consequence of this hyperconnectivity, newborns may experience synesthesia—the blending of different types of sensory input. In the case of the extra connections between the auditory and visual cortex, for example, auditory stimulation may produce a visual experience, with the infant's perceiving a sound as being of a particular colour.

We now come to what is one of the most remarkable facts about the development of the human brain. Approximately 40% of this great synaptic superfluity gets eliminated in a developmental process known as **synaptic pruning.** As you learned in the previous chapter, cell death is a normal part of development, and nowhere is that more evident than in the systematic pruning of excess synapses that continues for years after birth. This pruning occurs at different times in different areas of the brain (P. R. Huttenlocher & Dabholkar, 1997). You can see from Figure 3.9 that the elimination of synapses in the visual cortex begins near the end of the first year of life and continues until roughly 10 years of age, whereas synapse elimination in the prefrontal area shows a slower time course. During peak pruning periods, as many as 100 000 synapses may be eliminated per second (Kolb, 1995)!

synaptic pruning ▪ The normal developmental process through which synapses that are rarely activated are eliminated.

FIGURE 3.10 Brain maturation
These views of the right side and top of the brain of 5- to 20-year-olds illustrate maturation over the surface of the cortex. The averaged MRI images come from participants whose brains were scanned repeatedly at 2-year intervals. The bluer the image, the more mature that part of the cortex is (i.e., the more grey matter has been replaced with white matter). Notice that the parts of the cortex associated with more basic functions (i.e., the sensory and motor areas toward the back) mature earlier than the areas involved in higher functions (i.e., attention, executive functioning). Notice particularly that the frontal areas, involved in executive functioning, approach maturity only in early adulthood. (From Gogtay et al., 2004)

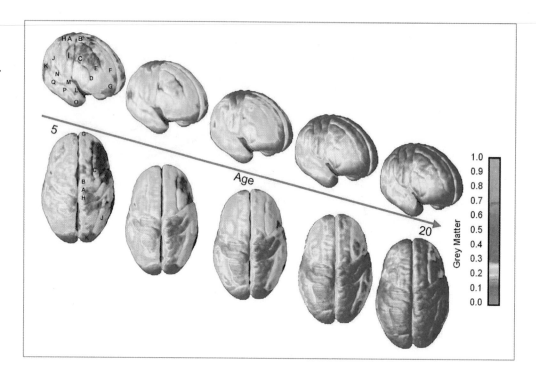

Not known until fairly recently is the fact that the brain undergoes explosive changes during adolescence, including a wave of overproduction and pruning akin to that in the first years of life (Giedd et al., 1999; Gogtay et al., 2004). Although the amount of white matter in the cortex shows a steady increase from childhood well into adulthood, the amount of grey matter increases dramatically starting around 11 or 12 years of age. The increase in grey matter proceeds rapidly, peaks around puberty, and then begins to decline as some of it is replaced by white matter (see Figure 3.10). The last area of the cortex to mature is the dorsolateral prefrontal cortex, which is vital for regulating attention, controlling impulses, foreseeing consequences, setting priorities, and other executive functions. It does not reach adult dimensions until after the age of 20.

You will notice that Figure 3.9 does not show a second proliferation and reduction of synaptic density in adolescence. One of the reasons for this is that the figure is based on cross-sectional research in which the brains of individuals of different ages were examined only at autopsy. The new data showing substantial development in the adolescent brain come from longitudinal studies in which the same individuals' brains were scanned repeatedly over several years. The dramatic changes that appear in individuals were not evident when the brains of separate groups of different ages were studied. (See the discussion of developmental research designs in Chapter 1, pages 32–34.)

The Importance of Experience

What factors determine which of the brain's excess synapses will be pruned and which maintained? Experience plays a central role in what is essentially a case of "use it or lose it." In a competitive process that has been dubbed "neural Darwinism" (Edelman, 1987), those synapses that are frequently activated are selectively preserved (Changeux & Danchin, 1976). The more often a synapse is activated, the stronger the connection becomes between the neurons involved: in short, neurons that fire together wire together (Hebb, 1949). Conversely, when a synapse is rarely active, it is likely to disappear: the axon of one neuron withdraws and the dendritic spine of the other is "pruned away."

The obvious question now is: Why does the human brain—the product of millions of years of evolution—take such a devious developmental path, producing a huge excess of synapses, only to get rid of a substantial proportion of them? The answer appears to be evolutionary economy. The capacity of the brain to be moulded or changed by experience, referred to as **plasticity,** means that less information needs to be encoded in the genes. This economizing may, in fact, be a necessity: the number of genes involved in the formation and functioning of the nervous system is enough to specify only a very small fraction of the normal complement of neurons and neural connections. In addition, if brain structures were entirely hard-wired, organisms would be unable to adapt to their postnatal environment. To complete the final wiring of the brain, nurture joins forces with nature.

The collaboration between nature and nurture in building the brain occurs differently for two kinds of plasticity. One kind involves the general experiences that almost all infants have just by virtue of being human. The second kind involves specific, idiosyncratic experiences that children have as a result of their particular life circumstances—such as growing up in Canada or in the Amazon rainforest, experiencing frequent cuddling or abuse, being an only child or one of many siblings, and so on.

Experience-Expectant Processes

William Greenough refers to the role of general human experience in shaping brain development as **experience-expectant plasticity.** According to this view, the normal wiring of the brain is in part a result of the kinds of general experiences that have been present throughout human evolution, experiences that every human with an intact sensory-motor system who inhabits a reasonably normal environment will have: patterned visual stimulation, voices and other sounds, movement and manipulation, and so forth (Greenough & Black, 1992). Consequently, the brain can "expect" input from these reliable sources to fine-tune its circuitry; synapses that are frequently activated will be strengthened and stabilized and those that are rarely activated will be "pruned." Thus, our *experience* of the external world plays a fundamental role in shaping the most basic aspects of the *structure* of our brain.

One fundamental benefit of experience-expectant plasticity is that, because experience helps shape the brain, fewer genes need to be dedicated to normal development. Another is that the brain is better able to recover from injury to certain areas, because other brain areas can take over the function that would have been performed by the damaged area. The younger the brain when damaged, the more likely recovery is.

The downside of experience-expectant plasticity is that it is accompanied by *vulnerability*. If for some reason the experience that the developing brain is "expecting" for fine-tuning its circuits does not occur, whether because of inadequate stimulation or impaired sensory receptors, development may be compromised. A good example of this vulnerability comes from children who are born with cataracts that obscure their vision. Research carried out at McMaster University in Hamilton has demonstrated that the longer a cataract remains in place after birth, the more impaired the child's visual acuity will be once it is removed. Dramatic improvement typically follows early removal, although some aspects of visual processing (especially of faces) remain affected even into adulthood (de Heering & Maurer, 2012; Maurer, Mondloch, & Lewis, 2007). Presumably, the lasting deficits of late cataract

plasticity ■ The capacity of the brain to be affected by experience.

experience-expectant plasticity ■ The process through which the normal wiring of the brain occurs in part as a result of experiences that every human who inhabits any reasonably normal environment will have.

removal occur because synapses that would normally have been activated by visual stimulation after birth were pruned because of the lack of that stimulation.

When an expected form of sensory experience is absent, what happens to areas of the brain that normally would have become specialized as a result of that experience? A wealth of data from animals indicates that such areas can become at least partially reorganized to serve some other function. Evidence of such plasticity and reorganization in humans comes from studies of adults who were congenitally deaf and who, as children, had learned American Sign Language, a full-fledged, visually based language (Bavelier, Dye, & Hauser, 2006; Bavelier & Neville, 2002). Individuals who are deaf rely heavily on peripheral vision for language processing; they typically look into the eyes of a person who is signing to them, while using their peripheral vision to monitor the hand and arm motions of the signer. ERP recordings of brain activity (see Box 3.3) showed that individuals who are deaf have responses to peripheral visual stimuli that are several times stronger than those of hearing people. In addition, their responses are distributed differently across brain regions. Thus, because of the lack of auditory experience, brain systems that would normally be involved in hearing and in spoken-language processing become organized to process visual information instead.

Similar evidence of early brain reorganization comes from research with adults who are blind. When tested for their ability to discriminate changes in musical pitch, adults who were born blind or became blind quite early performed much better than those who had become blind later in life (Gougoux et al., 2004). Presumably, connections between the visual and auditory cortex were preserved in individuals with early-onset blindness, giving them extra "brain power" to apply to the auditory task. Consistent with this idea, brain-imaging research suggests that parts of the visual cortex contribute to superior sound localization ability in adults with early-onset blindness. A related result is that individuals who are congenitally blind show activation in the "visual" cortex both when reading Braille (Sadato et al., 1998) and when processing spoken language (Bedny et al., 2011).

Sensitive periods As suggested by the foregoing examples, a key element in experience-expectant plasticity is timing. There are a few sensitive periods when the human brain is especially sensitive to particular kinds of external stimuli. It is as though a time window were temporarily opened, inviting environmental input to help organize the brain. Gradually, the window closes. The neural organization that occurs (or does not occur) during sensitive periods is typically irreversible.

As discussed in Chapter 1, the extreme deprivation that the Romanian orphans suffered early in life, when children normally experience a wealth of social and other environmental stimulation, is considered by some to be an example of a sensitive-period effect. Some investigators speculate that adolescence, during which rapid changes are occurring in the brain, may be another sensitive period for various aspects of development. Yet another sensitive period, for language learning, will be discussed in Chapter 6.

Experience-Dependent Processes

The brain is also sculpted by idiosyncratic experience through what Greenough calls **experience-dependent plasticity.** Neural connections are created and reorganized constantly, throughout life, as a function of an individual's experiences. (If you remember anything of what you have been reading in this chapter, it's because you have formed new neural connections.)

experience-dependent plasticity ■ The process through which neural connections are created and reorganized throughout life as a function of an individual's experiences.

Much of the research on experience-dependent plasticity has been focused on non-human animals, whose environments can be readily manipulated. One such method has involved comparisons between animals reared in complex environments full of objects to explore and use versus animals reared in bare laboratory cages. The brains of rats (and cats and monkeys) that grow up in a complex environment have more dendritic spines on their cortical neurons, more synapses per neuron, and more synapses overall, as well as a generally thicker cortex and more of the supportive tissues (such as blood vessels and glial cells) that maximize neuronal and synaptic function. All this extra hardware seems to have a payoff: rats (and other animals) reared in a complex environment (which is more akin to their natural environment) perform better in a variety of learning tasks than do their counterparts raised in bare cages (e.g., Sale, Berardi, & Maffei, 2009).

Highly specific effects of experience on brain structure also occur. For example, rats that are trained to use just one forelimb to get a food reward have increased dendritic material in the particular area of the motor cortex that controls the movement of the trained limb (Greenough, Larson, & Withers, 1985). In humans, research on musicians has revealed that, compared with a control group, violinists and cellists had increased cortical representation of the fingers of the left hand (Elbert et al., 1995). In other words, after years of practice, more cortical cells were devoted to receiving input from and controlling the fingers that manipulate the strings of the instruments. Similarly, in skilled Braille readers, the cortical representation of the left hand—which is used to read Braille text—is enlarged (Pascual-Leone et al., 1993).

Effects of specific experience are also evident in fMRI studies of individuals with *dyslexia*, a severe reading problem in people with normal intelligence and schooling (see Chapter 8). One example involves a remedial reading program in which 2nd and 3rd graders with dyslexia received training in recognizing the correspondence between speech sounds and letters (Blachman et al., 2004). After the training, not only did the children show marked improvement in their reading ability, but fMRI imaging revealed increased activity in their left-brain areas that was similar to the activity in the brains of good readers. The specific effects of one's reading experience also show up in the fact that reading Chinese characters recruits distinctly different brain networks than those involved in reading an alphabetic script (such as English).

As a result of growing up in a complex environment full of stimulating objects to explore and challenges to master, the brains of the rats in the top photo will contain more synapses than if they had been reared in unstimulating laboratory cages (bottom photo).

How would the cortical representations of their fingers be likely to differ for these two professional musicians?

Brain Damage and Recovery

As noted previously, because of its plasticity (especially early in life), the brain can become rewired—at least to some degree—after suffering damage. Children who suffer from brain damage thus have a better chance of recovering lost function than do adults who suffer similar damage. The strongest evidence for this comes from young children who suffer damage to the language area of the cortex and who generally recover most, if not all, of their language functions. This is because after the damage has occurred, other areas of the immature brain can take over language functions. As a result, language is largely spared, though specific linguistic impairments may remain (e.g., Zevin, Datta, & Skipper, 2012).

In contrast, adults who sustain the same type of brain damage undergo no such reorganization of language functions and may have a permanent loss in the ability to comprehend or produce speech. Greater recovery from early brain injury has also been observed for functions other than language. For example, producing appropriate facial expressions is more difficult for adults who had damage to the frontal area of the cortex during adulthood than for adults whose frontal lobe injury occurred in childhood (Kolb, 1995).

It is not always true, however, that the chance of recovery from early brain injury is greater than it is for later injury. Likelihood of recovery depends on how extensive the damage is and what aspect of brain development is occurring at the time of the damage. Consider, for example, the offspring of Japanese women who, while pregnant, were exposed to massive levels of radiation from the atomic bombs dropped on Hiroshima and Nagasaki in 1945. The rate of intellectual impairment was much higher for surviving children whose exposure had occurred very early in prenatal development, during the time of rapid neurogenesis and migration of neurons (Otake & Schull, 1984). Similarly, brain injury during early childhood generally results in more severe cognitive impairment in IQ than does later comparable injury (V. Anderson et al., 2012).

Furthermore, even when children appear to have made a full recovery from an early brain injury, deficits may emerge later. This was demonstrated in a cross-sectional study that compared cognitive performance in a group of children who had been born with cerebral damage and a control group of children with no brain damage (Banich et al., 1990). As Figure 3.11 shows, the children with brain damage did not differ from the control group in their performance on two subscales of an IQ test at 6 years of age. However, as the normal children's performance improved with age, the performance of children with brain damage fell progressively behind. The same pattern of results—decline in IQ over age for children with brain damage—was also demonstrated in a longitudinal study, in which children who had sustained early damage were tested before and after age 7 (S. C. Levine et al., 2005). These results illustrate the difficulty of predicting the development of children with cerebral injuries: behaviour that appears normal early in development may deteriorate.

On the basis of these various aspects of plasticity, we can generalize that the worst time to suffer brain damage is very early, during prenatal development and the first year after birth, when neurogenesis is occurring and basic brain structures are being formed. Damage at this point may have cascading effects on subsequent aspects of brain development, with potentially wide-ranging negative effects. In contrast, when brain damage is sustained in early childhood—that is, when synapse generation and pruning are occurring and plasticity is highest—the chances for the brain's rewiring itself and recovering lost function are best.

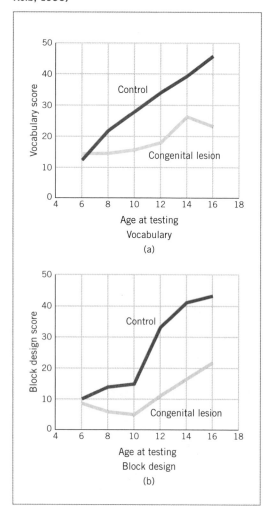

FIGURE 3.11 Emergent effects of early brain damage At 6 years of age, children with congenital brain damage scored the same as normal children on two subscales of an intelligence test. However, the children with brain damage failed to improve and fell progressively farther behind the normal children, so that by adolescence there were large differences between the two groups. (Data from Banich et al., 1990; figure from Kolb, 1995)

review:

Nature and nurture cooperate in the construction of the human brain. Some important brain structures include the neurons, which communicate with one another at synapses; the cortex, in which different functions are localized in different areas; and the cerebral hemispheres, which are specialized for different kinds of processing. The processes involved in the development of the brain include neurogenesis and synaptogenesis, followed by the systematic elimination of some synapses and the preservation of others as a function of experience.

Two forms of plasticity contribute to the development of behaviour. As a result of experience-expectant plasticity, the brain is shaped by experiences that are available to every typically developing individual in interaction with every species-typical environment. Through experience-dependent plasticity, the brain is also structured by an individual's idiosyncratic life experiences. Because of the importance of experience in brain development, sensitive periods exist during which specific experience must be present for normal development. Timing is also a crucial factor in the ultimate impact of brain damage.

The Body: Physical Growth and Development

In Chapter 1, we emphasized the multiple contexts in which development occurs. Here we focus on the most immediate context for development—the body itself. Everything we think, feel, say, and do involves our physical selves, and changes in the body lead to changes in behaviour. In this section, we present a brief overview of some aspects of physical growth, including some of the factors that can disrupt normal development. Nutritional behaviour, a vital aspect of physical development, is featured as we consider the regulation of eating. We concentrate particularly on one of the consequences of poor regulation—obesity. Finally, we focus on the opposite problem—undernutrition.

Growth and Maturation

Compared with most other species, humans undergo a prolonged period of physical growth. The body grows and develops for 20% of the human lifespan, whereas mice, for example, grow during only 2% of their lifespan. Figure 3.12 shows the most obvious aspects of physical growth: we get 3 to 4 times heavier between birth and age 10, and we get 3 times taller between birth and age 20. The figure shows averages, of course, and there are obviously huge individual differences in height and weight, as well as in the timing of physical development.

Growth is uneven over time, as you can tell from the differences in the slopes in Figure 3.12. The slopes are steepest when the most rapid growth is occurring—in the first 2 years and in early adolescence. Early on, boys and girls grow at roughly the same rate, and they are essentially equal in height and weight until around 10 to 12 years of age. Then girls experience their adolescent growth spurt, at the end of which they are somewhat taller and heavier than boys. (Remember those awkward middle-school years when the girls towered over the boys, much to the discomfort of both?) Adolescent boys experience their growth spurt about 2 years after the girls, permanently passing them in both height and weight. Full height is achieved, on average, by around the age of 15½ for girls and 17½ for boys.

Growth is also uneven across the different parts of the body. Following the principle of cephalocaudal development described in Chapter 2 (page 48), the head region is initially relatively large—fully 50% of body length at 2 months of age—but only about 10% of body length in adulthood. The gawkiness of young

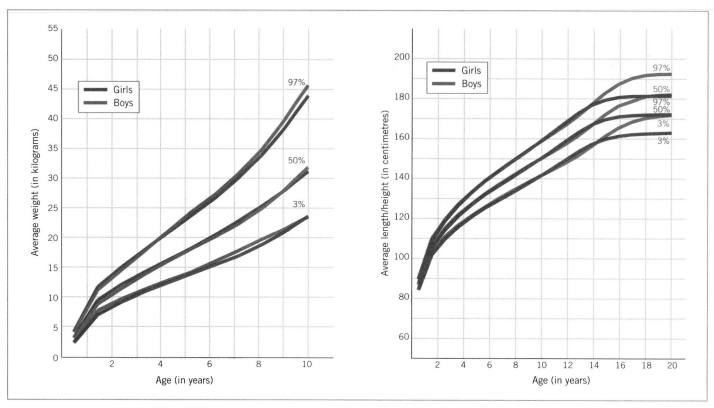

FIGURE 3.12 Growth Curves These growth curves for weight from ages 0 to 10 years and for length/height for ages 0 to 19 years are based on a World Health Organization study of children in six countries. Each curve indicates the percent of the reference population that falls below the indicated weight and height. (Data for weight are shown only for children between the ages of 0 and 10 years because, after puberty, it is recommended that BMI, rather than weight alone, be tracked because of varying ages of puberty.) (Adapted from World Health Organization, 2013)

adolescents stems in part from the fact that their growth spurt begins with dramatic increases in the size of the hands and feet; it's easy to trip over your own feet when they are disproportionately larger than the rest of you.

Body composition also changes with age. The proportion of body fat is highest in infancy, gradually declining thereafter until around 6 to 8 years of age. In adolescence, it decreases in boys but increases in girls, and that increase helps trigger the onset of menstruation. The proportion of muscle grows slowly until adolescence, when it increases dramatically, especially in boys.

Variability

There is great variability across individuals and groups in all aspects of physical development. This variability in physical development is due to both genetic and environmental factors. Genes affect growth and sexual maturation in large part by influencing the production of hormones, especially growth hormone (secreted by the pituitary gland) and thyroxine (released by the thyroid gland). The influence of environmental factors is particularly evident in **secular trends,** marked changes in physical development that have occurred over generations. In contemporary industrialized nations, adults are several centimetres taller than their same-sex great-grandparents were. This change is assumed to have resulted primarily from improvements in nutrition and general health. Another secular trend in North America today involves girls' beginning to menstruate a few years earlier than their ancestors did, a change attributed to the general improvement in nutritional status of the population.

Environmental factors can also play a role in disturbances of normal growth. For example, severe chronic stress, such as that associated with a home environment involving serious marital discord, alcoholism, or child abuse can impair growth by lowering the pituitary gland's production of growth hormone (Powell, Brasel, & Blizzard, 1967). Children raised in institutions also have a higher risk of growth

secular trends ■ Marked changes in physical development that have occurred over generations.

impairment, likely due to the combination of social stressors and poor nutrition (D. E. Johnson & Gunnar, 2011). For example, when children from Romanian orphanages arrived in their adoptive homes in Canada, their average weight was below the 4th percentile. About 8 years after adoption into their Canadian homes, there was considerable catch-up in growth. At 10½ years of age, the Romanian adoptees' average weight was around the 60th percentile and no longer differed significantly from that of Canadian-born, never-adopted children (Le Mare & Audet, 2006).

A combination of genetic and environmental factors is apparently involved in **failure to thrive,** a condition in which infants become malnourished and fail to grow or gain weight for no obvious medical reason. Because the reason for a particular infant's failure to thrive is often difficult to determine, treatment may range from hospitalization to dietary supplementation to behavioural interventions, such as rewards for positive eating behaviours (Jaffe, 2011).

Nutritional Behaviour

The health of our bodies depends on what we put into them, including the amount and kind of food we eat. Thus, the development of eating or nutritional behaviour is a crucial aspect of child development from infancy onward.

Infant Feeding

Like all mammals, human newborns obtain life-sustaining nourishment through suckling, although they require more assistance in this endeavour than do most other mammals. Throughout nearly the entire history of the human species, the only or primary source of nourishment for infants was breast milk. Mother's milk has many virtues (J. Newman, 1995). It is naturally free of bacteria, strengthens the infant's immune system, and contains the mother's antibodies against infectious agents the baby is likely to encounter after birth.

There have also been suggestions in the literature that the fatty acids in breast milk have a positive effect on cognitive development, with some studies indicating higher IQ scores for children and adults who were breastfed as infants (for review, see Nisbett et al., 2012). The challenge in this area of research in North America is that the choice to breastfeed is correlated with social class (due to factors ranging from maternal education to working conditions that make it difficult to nurse or pump breast milk on the job). However, several studies that controlled for social class still found cognitive benefits associated with breastfeeding. In one of those studies, mother–infant dyads were randomly assigned either to an intervention encouraging breastfeeding or to a control condition without intervention. The results indicated that prolonged and exclusive breastfeeding in infancy led to increased IQ scores at 6½ years of age (Kramer et al., 2008). Another study that examined genetic factors found that children who carry one of two specific alleles that regulate fatty acids showed a substantial cognitive benefit from breastfeeding, while individuals with a different allele showed a smaller benefit (Caspi et al., 2007). These results reflect the kind of genotype–environment interaction discussed earlier in this chapter, with the benefits of a particular environment (in this case, breast milk) delimited by the child's genotype.

However, in spite of the well-established nutritional superiority of breast milk, as well as the fact that it is free, many infants in Canada are exclusively or predominantly formula-fed. Recent public health efforts have begun to shift this long-time feeding trend, by educating parents about the benefits of breast milk

failure to thrive ▪ A condition in which infants become malnourished and fail to grow or gain weight for no obvious medical reason.

By breastfeeding her infant, this mother is providing her baby with many benefits that are not available in formula.

ZOUZOU / SHUTTERSTOCK

and encouraging employers to provide private space for working mothers to pump breast milk. Since these efforts were initiated, the number of newborns fed breast milk in Canada has increased to around 87%. However, this good nutritional start has been difficult for parents to maintain; by 6 months of age, only 54% of infants are still being breastfed (Statistics Canada, 2011b).

In developed countries, infant formula can support normal growth and development, although infants who are formula-fed have somewhat higher rates of infection than do those who are fed breast milk. In developing countries, however, formula feeding can exact a costly toll. Much of the developing world does not have safe water, so infant formula is often mixed with polluted water in unsanitary containers. Furthermore, economically disadvantaged, uneducated parents often dilute the formula in an effort to make the expensive powder last longer. In such circumstances, parents' attempts to promote the health of their babies end up having the opposite effect (Popkin & Doan, 1990).

Development of Food Preferences and the Regulation of Eating

Food preferences are a primary determinant of what we eat throughout life, and some of these preferences are clearly innate. Infants display some of the same reflexive facial expressions that older children and adults display in response to three basic tastes: sweet, sour, and bitter. The first produces a hint of a smile; the second, a pucker; the third, a grimace (Rosenstein & Oster, 1988; Steiner, 1979). Newborns' strong preference for sweetness is reflected both in their smiling in response to sweet flavours and in the fact that they will drink larger quantities of sweetened water than plain water. These innate preferences may have an evolutionary origin, since poisonous substances are often bitter or sour but almost never sweet. At the same time, recall from Chapter 2 (page 53) that taste preferences can also be influenced by the prenatal environment, suggesting an important role for experience even in the earliest flavour preferences.

Infants' taste sensitivity is evident in their reactions to their mother's milk, which can take on the flavour of what she eats. Babies nurse longer and take more breast milk when their mother has ingested either garlic or vanilla flavours, but they drink less breast milk after she has downed a beer (Menella & Beauchamp, 1993a, 1993b, 1996).

From infancy on, experience has a major influence on what foods children like and dislike and on what and how much they eat. For instance, preschool children's liking for particular foods increases if they observe other children enjoying them (Birch & Fisher, 1996). Children's eating is also influenced by what foods their parents encourage and discourage. This influence does not always work in the way the parents intend, however. For example, standard parental strategies of cajoling and bribing young children to eat new or healthier foods—"If you eat your spinach, you can have some ice cream"—can be doubly counterproductive. The most probable result is that the child will dislike the healthy food even more and have an even stronger preference for the sweet, fatty food used as a reward (Birch & Fisher, 1996).

Many parents become needlessly concerned with how much their young children eat. They might, however, put less effort into trying to control their children's eating behaviour if they realized that young children are actually quite good at regulating the amount of food they consume. Research has shown that preschool children adjust how much they eat at a given time based on how much they consumed earlier. For example, children were found to eat less for lunch if they had been served a snack earlier than if they had not had the snack (Birch & Fisher, 1996). (In contrast, a group of adults ate pretty much the same amount of a meal whether or not they had been served a snack earlier.)

In general, children whose parents try to control their eating habits tend to be worse at regulating their food intake themselves than are children whose parents allow them more control over what and how much they eat (S. L. Johnson & Birch, 1994). Parents' overregulation of their children's eating behaviour can have continuing effects. Adults who reported that their parents used food to control their behaviour were more likely to be struggling with their weight and with binge eating (Puhl & Schwartz, 2003).

Obesity

So many people have difficulty regulating their eating appropriately that the most common dietary problems in Canada and the United States are related to overeating and its many consequences. In Canada, around 24% of adults are considered obese (compared with 34% of adults in the United States) (Shields, Carroll, & Odgen, 2011). It is an increasing problem, not just among North Americans but also among indigenous people in many developing countries (Abelson & Kennedy, 2004). This situation exists largely because societies all over the world are increasingly adopting a "Western diet" of foods high in fat and sugar and low in fibre. Fast-food restaurants have proliferated around the globe; indeed, after Santa Claus, Ronald McDonald is the second most recognized figure worldwide (K. Brownell, 2004).

The proportion of Canadian children and adolescents between the ages of 6 and 17 years who are overweight or obese doubled between 1978 and 2004 (see Figure 3.13) (Shields, 2006). In 2011, almost one-third of all Canadian children between 5 and 17 years of age were overweight or obese (K. C. Roberts et al., 2012). The outlook for these overweight children is troubling, because they are likely to struggle with weight problems throughout their lives. Furthermore, there is a good chance they will adopt a variety of unhealthy measures to fight their weight problems—skipping meals, fasting, smoking, taking diet pills, and even undergoing liposuction—all of which can lead to further health problems.

Two important questions need to be addressed: Why do some people but not others become overweight, and why is there an epidemic of obesity? Both genetic and environmental factors play roles. Genetic factors are reflected in the findings that (1) the weight of adopted children is more strongly correlated with that of their biological parents than with that of their adoptive parents, and (2) identical twins, including those reared apart, are more similar in weight than fraternal twins are (Plomin et al., 2013). Even the *speed* of eating, which is related both to how much is eaten in a given meal and to the weight of the eater, shows substantial heritability (Llewellyn et al., 2008). Thus, genes affect individuals' susceptibility to gaining weight and how much food they eat in the first place, making it relatively difficult or easy for them to avoid becoming part of the obesity epidemic.

Environmental influences also play a major role in this epidemic, as is obvious from the fact that a much higher proportion of the population of Canada and the United States is overweight now than in previous times. Indeed, some have argued that becoming obese in North America could be considered a normal response to the contemporary taste for high-fat, high-sugar foods in ever larger portion sizes (K. D. Brownell, 2003).

A host of other factors fuel the ever-expanding waistlines of today's children. Children spend less time playing outside than their counterparts did in previous generations: fully half of today's

FIGURE 3.13 Overweight and obese
The proportion of children in Canada between the ages of 6 and 17 years who are overweight or obese has doubled in the past 26 years. (Adapted from Shields, 2006)

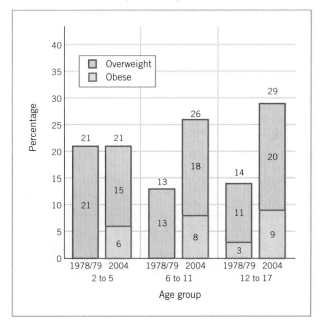

One promising way to decrease childhood obesity is through daily physical activity, which is required in most elementary schools.

preschool-age children spend less than an hour a day engaged in outdoor play (Tandon et al., 2012). One recent Canadian study demonstrated that 8- to 10-year-olds who get less than 60 minutes of physical activity a day are more likely to be overweight than children who get more than 60 minutes of physical activity a day (Chaput et al., 2012). At school, children often purchase cafeteria lunches consisting of high-fat foods (e.g., pizza, hamburgers) and high-calorie soft drinks. In addition, many families often dine out at fast-food or "all you can eat" buffet-style restaurants where they consume large portions of relatively high-calorie foods (Krishnamoorthy, Hart, & Jelalian, 2006). Finally, unhealthy foods are often less expensive and more readily available than healthier foods, making it difficult for economically disadvantaged parents to provide healthy foods to their children, even when they are motivated to do so.

Obesity puts children and adolescents at risk for a wide variety of serious health problems, including heart disease and diabetes. In addition, many obese youth suffer the consequences of negative stereotypes and discrimination in a variety of areas, even university and college admissions (M. A. Friedman & Brownell, 1995; Puhl et al., 2010). Overweight children and teenagers suffer a variety of other social problems as well. For example, overweight adolescents tend to be either socially isolated or on the fringe of their social networks (Strauss & Pollack, 2003). One large-scale study of adolescents from the Ottawa area found that overweight adolescents were more likely to be teased about their weight by peers and parents. Both normal weight and overweight girls reported more weight-based teasing than boys. Furthermore, weight-related teasing was related to depression and interpersonal problems, regardless of actual weight status (Goldfield et al., 2010). In another large-scale survey of middle school and high school students, teens who reported being teased about their weight had considered suicide more often than had their slimmer peers (M. Eisenberg, Neumark-Sztainer, & Story, 2003).

There is, unfortunately, no easy cure for obesity in children. However, some hope for the general obesity problem comes from the fact that public awareness is now focused on the severity of the problem and the variety of factors that contribute to it. Many schools have begun serving more nutritious, less caloric foods, including those available in vending machines, and fast-food chains have begun to include at least some low-calorie options on their menus. Many provinces have made daily physical activity mandatory in schools. For example, in Alberta, all students in Grades 1 to 9 must be physically active for 30 minutes a day through school activities (Alberta Education, 2006). Another helpful step comes from a recent policy statement released by a number of key Canadian health and scientific organizations that calls on the federal government to restrict the marketing of unhealthy foods targeted to young children ("Canadian Health," 2013).

By exercising together, this father and son may be taking one of the most effective steps they can toward weight control.

Undernutrition

At the same time that many people in relatively rich countries are overeating their way to poor health, the health of people in developing nations is compromised by their not getting enough to eat. Fully one-fourth of all children (and 40% of those younger than 5) living in these countries are undernourished. The nutritional deficits they experience can involve an inadequate supply of total calories, of protein, of vitamins and minerals, or any combination of these deficiencies. Severe malnutrition of infants and young children is most common in developing and/or war-torn countries. Analyses of child mortality data suggest that suboptimal nutrition (including non-exclusive breastfeeding) is an underlying cause of 35% of child deaths worldwide (R. E. Black et al., 2008).

Undernutrition and malnutrition are virtually always associated with poverty and myriad related factors, ranging from limited access to health care to warfare, famine, and natural disasters. The interaction of malnutrition with poverty and other forms of deprivation adversely affects all aspects of development. Figure 3.14 presents a model of how the complex interaction of these multiple factors impairs cognitive development (J. L. Brown & Pollitt, 1996). As you can see, malnutrition can have direct effects on the structural development of the brain, general energy level, susceptibility to infection, and physical growth. With inadequate energy, malnourished children tend to reduce their energy expenditure and withdraw from stimulation, making them quiet and passive in general, less responsive in social interactions, less attentive in school, and so on. Apathy, slowed growth, and delayed development of motor skills also retard the children's exploration of the environment, further limiting their opportunities to learn.

Can anything be done to help malnourished and undernourished youngsters? Because so many interacting factors are involved in the problem, addressing it effectively is not easy—but neither is it impossible, as shown by several large-scale intervention efforts throughout the world. For example, in one long-term project led by Ernesto Pollitt in Guatemala, a high-protein dietary supplement administered starting in infancy correlated with an increase in performance on tests of cognitive functioning in adolescence (Pollitt et al., 1993). Follow-ups on the participants in adulthood produced strong evidence for the continuing benefits of dietary supplements 25 years after the intervention (Maluccio et al., 2009). Although it is possible to improve the developmental status of malnourished children, it would be better, both for the children themselves and for society in general, to prevent the occurrence of malnutrition in the first place. As Brown and Pollitt (1996) note: "On balance, it seems clear that prevention of malnutrition among young children remains the best policy—not only on moral grounds but on economic ones as well" (p. 702).

FIGURE 3.14 Malnutrition and cognitive development Malnutrition, combined with poverty, affects many aspects of development and can lead to impaired cognitive abilities. (From J. L. Brown & Pollitt, 1996)

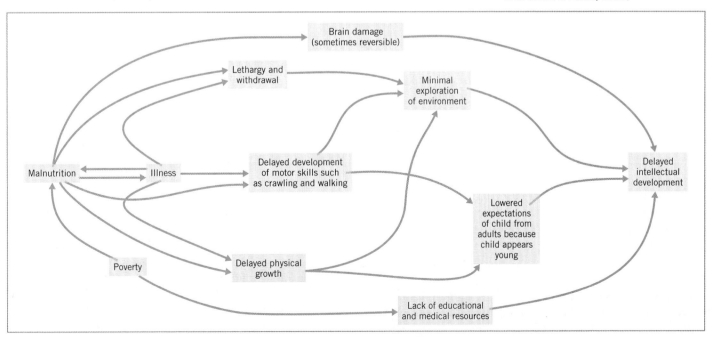

review:

Sound nutritional behaviour is vital to general health. Preferences for certain foods are evident from birth on, and, as children develop, what they choose to eat is influenced by many factors, including the preferences of their friends and their parents' attempts to influence their eating behaviour. Obesity among both adults and children has increased dramatically in Canada and much of the rest of the world in recent decades, as exposure to rich foods in large portions has increased and physical activity has decreased. However, throughout the world, the most common nutritional problem is undernutrition, which is very closely associated with poverty. The combination of malnutrition and poverty is particularly devastating to development.

chapter summary:

Nature and Nurture

■ The complex interplay of nature and nurture was the constant theme of this chapter. In the drama of development, genotype, phenotype, and environment all play starring roles, and the plot moves forward as they interact in many obvious and many not-so-obvious ways.

■ The starting point for development is the genotype—the genes inherited at conception from one's parents. Only some of those genes are expressed in the phenotype, one's observable characteristics. Whether some genes are expressed at all is a function of dominance patterns. Most traits studied by developmental scientists are influenced by multiple genes. The switching on and off of genes over time underlies many aspects of development. This process is affected by experience via methylation.

■ The eventual outcome of a given genotype is always contingent on the environment in which it develops. Parents and their behaviour toward their children are a salient part of the children's environment. Parents' behaviour toward their children is influenced by their own genotypes. Similarly, the child's development is influenced by the aspects of the environment he or she seeks out and the different responses the child's characteristics and behaviour evoke from other people.

■ The field of behaviour genetics is concerned with the joint influence of genetic and environmental factors on behaviour. Through the use of a variety of family-study designs, behaviour geneticists have discovered a wide range of behaviour patterns that "run in families." Many behaviour geneticists use heritability estimates to statistically evaluate the relative contributions of heredity and environment to behaviour.

Brain Development

■ A burgeoning area of developmental research focuses on the development of the brain—the most complex structure in the known universe. Neurons are the basic units of the brain's informational system. These cells transmit information via electrical signals. Impulses are transmitted from one neuron to another at synapses.

■ The most human part of the human brain is the cortex, because it is involved in a wide variety of higher mental functions. Different areas of the cortex are specialized for general behavioural categories. The cortex is divided into two cerebral hemispheres, each of which is specialized for certain modes of processing, a phenomenon known as cerebral lateralization.

■ Brain development involves several processes, beginning with neurogenesis and differentiation of neurons. In synaptogenesis, an enormous profusion of connections among neurons is generated, starting prenatally and continuing for the first few years after birth. Through synaptic pruning, excess connections among neurons are eliminated.

■ Experience plays a crucial role in the strengthening or elimination of synapses and hence in the normal wiring of the brain. The fine-tuning of the brain involves experience-expectant processes, in which existing synapses are preserved as a function of stimulation that virtually every human encounters, and experience-dependent processes, in which new connections are formed as a function of learning.

■ Plasticity refers to the fact that nurture is the partner of nature in the normal development of the brain. This fact makes it possible in certain circumstances for the brain to rewire itself in response to damage. It also makes the developing brain vulnerable to the absence of stimulation at sensitive periods in development.

■ The ability of the brain to recover from injury depends on the age of the child. Very early damage, during the time when neurogenesis and synaptogenesis are occurring, can have especially devastating effects. Damage during the preschool years, when synapse elimination is occurring, is less likely to have permanent harmful effects.

The Body: Physical Growth and Development

■ Humans undergo a particularly prolonged period of physical growth, during which growth is uneven, proceeding more rapidly early in life and in adolescence. Secular trends have been observed in increases in average height and weight.

■ Food preferences begin with innate responses by newborns to basic tastes, but additional preferences develop as a result of experience. Problems with the regulation of eating are evident in Canada and the United States, where an epidemic of obesity is clearly related to both environmental and genetic factors.

■ In much of the rest of the world, the dominant problem is getting enough food, and nearly half of all the children in the world suffer from undernutrition. Inadequate nutrition is closely associated with poverty, and it leads to a variety of behavioural and physical problems in virtually every aspect of the child's life. Prevention of undernutrition is needed to allow millions of children to develop normal brains and bodies.

Critical Thinking Questions

1. A major focus of this chapter was the interaction of nature and nurture. Consider yourself and your family (regardless of whether you were raised by your biological parents). Identify some aspect of who you are that illustrates each of the five relations depicted in Figure 3.1 and answer these questions: (a) How and when was your sex determined? (b) What are some alleles you are certain or relatively confident you share with other members of your family? (c) What might be an example of a gene–environment interaction in your parents' behaviour toward you? (d) What would be an example of your active selection of your own environment that might have influenced your subsequent development? (e) What aspects of your own environment might have had epigenetic effects on your gene expression?

2. People say things like "Fifty percent of a person's IQ is due to heredity and fifty percent to environment." Discuss what is wrong with this statement, describing both what heritability estimates mean and what they do not mean.

3. Relate the developmental processes of synaptogenesis and synapse elimination to the concepts of experience-expectant and experience-dependent plasticity.

4. What aspects of brain development do researchers think may be related to the traits and behaviours of adolescents?

5. Think back over your activities and observations of the past day or so. What aspects of your environment may relate to the epidemic of obesity described in this chapter?

6. Consider Figure 3.14, which addresses malnutrition and cognitive development. Imagine an undernourished 6-year-old child living in Canada. Go through the figure and generate a specific example of something that might happen to this child at each point in the diagram. Now do the same for a 6-year-old living in a developing or war-torn country.

Key Terms

alleles, p. 92
association areas, p. 109
axons, p. 108
behaviour genetics, p. 99
cell body, p. 108
cerebral cortex, p. 108
cerebral hemispheres, p. 109
cerebral lateralization, p. 109
chromosomes, p. 89
corpus callosum, p. 109
crossing over, p. 91
dendrites, p. 108
DNA (deoxyribonucleic acid), p. 89
dominant allele, p. 92
environment, p. 89
event-related potentials (ERPs), p. 110
experience-dependent plasticity, p. 116

experience-expectant plasticity, p. 115
failure to thrive, p. 121
frontal lobe, p. 109
genes, p. 89
genome, p. 88
genotype, p. 89
glial cells, p. 108
heritability, p. 103
heritable, p. 99
heterozygous, p. 92
homozygous, p. 92
lobes, p. 108
multifactorial, p. 99
mutation, p. 91
myelin sheath, p. 108
myelination, p. 112
neurogenesis, p. 111

neurons, p. 107
norm of reaction, p. 93
occipital lobe, p. 108
parietal lobe, p. 108
phenotype, p. 89
phenylketonuria (PKU), p. 96
plasticity, p. 115
polygenic inheritance, p. 93
recessive allele, p. 92
regulator genes, p. 91
secular trends, p. 120
sex chromosomes, p. 90
spines, p. 112
synapses, p. 108
synaptic pruning, p. 113
synaptogenesis, p. 112
temporal lobe, p. 108

FRENCH SCHOOL (20th century), *Learning the Alphabet of Baksheesh* (colour litho)

chapter 4:

Theories of Cognitive Development

A 7-month-old boy, sitting on his father's lap, becomes intrigued with the father's glasses, grabs one side of the frame, and yanks it. The father says, "Ow!" and his son lets go, but then reaches up and yanks the frame again. The father readjusts the glasses, but his son again grasps them and yanks. How, the father wonders, can he prevent his son from continuing this annoying routine without causing him to start screaming? Fortunately, the father, a developmental psychologist, soon realizes that Jean Piaget's theory of cognitive development suggests a simple solution: put the glasses behind his back. According to Piaget's theory, removing an object from a young infant's sight should lead the infant to act as if the object never existed. The strategy works perfectly; after the father puts the glasses behind his back, his son shows no further interest in them and turns his attention elsewhere. The father silently thanks Piaget.

This experience, which one of us actually had, illustrates in a small way how understanding theories of child development can yield practical benefits. It also illustrates three broader advantages of knowing about such theories:

1. Developmental theories provide a framework for understanding important phenomena. Theories help reveal the significance of what we observe about children, both in research studies and in everyday life. Someone who witnessed the glasses incident but who did not know about Piaget's theory might have found the experience amusing but insignificant. Seen in terms of Piaget's theory, however, this passing event exemplifies a general and profoundly important developmental phenomenon: infants younger than 8 months react to the disappearance of an object as though they do not understand that the object still exists. In this way, theories of child development place particular experiences and observations in a larger context and deepen our understanding of their meaning.

2. Developmental theories raise crucial questions about human nature. Piaget's theory about young infants' reactions to disappearing objects was based on his informal experiments with infants younger than 8 months. Piaget would cover one of their favourite objects with a cloth or otherwise put it out of sight and then wait to see whether the infants tried to retrieve the object. They rarely did, leading Piaget to conclude that before the age of 8 months, infants do not realize that hidden objects still exist. Other researchers have challenged this explanation. They argue that infants younger than 8 months do in fact understand that hidden objects continue to exist but lack the memory or problem-solving skills necessary for using that understanding to retrieve hidden objects (Baillargeon, 1993). Despite these disagreements about how best to interpret young infants' failure to retrieve hidden objects, researchers agree that Piaget's theory raises a crucial question about human nature: Do infants realize from the first days of life that objects continue to exist when out of sight, or is this something that they learn later? More significant, do young infants understand that people continue to exist when they cannot be seen? Do they fear that Mom no longer exists when she disappears from sight?

3. Developmental theories lead to a better understanding of children. Theories also stimulate new research that may support the theories' claims, fail to support them, or require refinements of them, thereby improving our understanding of children. For instance, Piaget's ideas led Munakata

The author whose son loved to grab his glasses is not the only one who has encountered this problem. If the mom in this picture was lucky enough to have read this textbook, she may have solved the problem in the same way.

ELIZABETH CREWS

and her colleagues (1997) to test whether 7-month-olds' failure to reach for hidden objects was due to their lacking the motivation or the reaching skill to retrieve them. To find out, the researchers created a situation similar to Piaget's object-permanence experiment, except that they placed the object, an attractive toy, under a transparent cover rather than under an opaque one. In this situation, infants quickly removed the cover and regained the toy. This finding seemed to support Piaget's original interpretation by showing that neither lack of motivation nor lack of ability to reach for the toy explained the infants' usual failure to retrieve it.

In contrast, an experiment conducted by Diamond (1985) indicated a need to revise Piaget's theory. Using an opaque covering, as Piaget did, Diamond varied the amount of time between when the toy was hidden and when the infant was allowed to reach for it. She found that even 6-month-olds could locate the toy if allowed to reach immediately, that 7-month-olds could wait as long as 2 seconds and still succeed, that 8-month-olds could wait as long as 4 seconds and still succeed, and so on. Diamond's finding indicated that memory for the location of hidden objects, as well as the understanding that they continue to exist, is crucial to success on the task. In sum, theories of child development are useful because they provide frameworks for understanding important phenomena, raise fundamental questions about human nature, and motivate new research that increases understanding of children.

Because child development is such a complex and varied subject, no single theory accounts for all of it. The most informative current theories focus primarily on either cognitive development or social development. Providing a good theoretical account of development in even one of these areas is an immense challenge, because each of them spans a huge range of topics. Cognitive development includes the growth of such diverse capabilities as perception, attention, language, problem solving, reasoning, memory, conceptual understanding, and intelligence. Social development includes the growth of equally diverse areas: emotions, personality, relationships with peers and family members, self-understanding, aggression, and moral behaviour. Given this immense range of developmental domains, it is easy to understand why no one theory has captured the entirety of child development.

Therefore, we present cognitive and social theories in separate chapters. We consider theories of cognitive development in this chapter, just before the chapters on specific areas of cognitive development, and consider theories of social development in Chapter 9, just before the chapters on specific areas of social development.

This chapter examines four theoretical perspectives on cognitive development that are particularly influential: the Piagetian perspective, the information-processing perspective, the sociocultural perspective, and the dynamic-systems perspective. We consider each perspective's fundamental assumptions about children's nature, the central developmental issues on which the perspective focuses, and practical examples of the perspective's usefulness for helping children learn.

These four theoretical perspectives are influential in large part because they provide important insights into the basic developmental themes described in Chapter 1. Each perspective addresses all the themes to some extent, but each emphasizes different ones. For instance, Piaget's theory focuses on *continuity/discontinuity* and the *active child*, whereas information-processing theories focus on *mechanisms of change* (Table 4.1). Together, the four perspectives allow a broader appreciation of cognitive development than any one of them does alone.

TABLE 4.1

Main Questions Addressed by Theories of Cognitive Development

Theory	Main Questions Addressed
Piagetian	Nature–nurture, continuity/discontinuity, the active child
Information-processing	Nature–nurture, how change occurs
Sociocultural	Nature–nurture, influence of the sociocultural context, how change occurs
Dynamic-systems	Nature–nurture, the active child, how change occurs

Piaget's Theory

Jean Piaget's studies of cognitive development are a testimony to how much one person can contribute to a scientific field. Before his work began to appear in the early 1920s, there was no recognizable field of cognitive development. Nearly a century later, Piaget's theory remains the best-known cognitive developmental theory in a field replete with theories. What accounts for its longevity?

One reason is that Piaget's observations and descriptions vividly convey the texture of children's thinking at different ages. Another reason is the exceptional breadth of the theory. It extends from the first days of infancy through adolescence and examines topics as diverse as conceptualization of time, space, distance, and number; language use; memory; understanding of other people's perspectives; problem solving; and scientific reasoning. Even today, it remains the most encompassing theory of cognitive development. A third source of its longevity is that it offers an intuitively plausible depiction of the interaction of nature and nurture in cognitive development, as well as of the continuities and discontinuities that characterize intellectual growth.

View of Children's Nature

Piaget's fundamental assumption about children was that they are mentally active as well as physically active from the moment of birth, and that their activity greatly contributes to their own development. His approach to understanding cognitive development is often labelled *constructivist,* because it depicts children as constructing knowledge for themselves in response to their experiences. Three of the most important of children's constructive processes, according to Piaget, are generating hypotheses, performing experiments, and drawing conclusions from their observations. If this description reminds you of scientific problem solving, you are not alone: the "child as scientist" is the dominant metaphor in Piaget's theory. Consider this description of his infant son:

> Laurent is lying on his back. … He grasps in succession a celluloid swan, a box, etc., stretches out his arm, and lets them fall. He distinctly varies the position of the fall. When the object falls in a new position (for example, on his pillow), he lets it fall two or three more times on the same place, as though to study the spatial relation.
>
> (Piaget, 1952b, pp. 268–269)

In simple activities such as Laurent's game of "drop the toy from different places and see what happens," Piaget perceived the beginning of scientific experimentation.

This example also illustrates a second basic Piagetian assumption: children learn many important lessons on their own, rather than depending on instruction from adults or older children. To further illuminate this point, Piaget cited a friend's recollection from childhood:

> He was seated on the ground in his garden and he was counting pebbles. Now to count these pebbles he put them in a row and he counted them one, two, three up to 10. Then he finished counting them and started to count them in the other direction. He began by the end and once again he found that he had 10. He found this marvelous. … So he put them in a circle and counted them that way and found 10 once again.
>
> (Piaget, 1964, p. 12)

Jean Piaget, whose work has had a profound influence on developmental psychology, is seen here interviewing a child to learn about his thinking.

SCIENCE SOURCE / GETTY IMAGES

This incident also highlights a third basic assumption of Piaget's: children are intrinsically motivated to learn and do not need rewards from other people to do so. When they acquire a new capability, they apply it as often as possible. They also reflect on the lessons of their experience, because they want to understand themselves and everything around them.

Central Developmental Issues

In addition to his view that children actively shape their own development, Piaget offered important insights regarding the roles of nature and nurture and of continuities and discontinuities in development.

Nature and Nurture

Piaget believed that nature and nurture interact to produce cognitive development. In his view, nurture includes not just the nurturing provided by parents and other caregivers but every experience children encounter. Nature includes children's maturing brain and body; their ability to perceive, act, and learn from experience; and their tendency to integrate particular observations into coherent knowledge. As this description suggests, a vital part of children's nature is to respond to their nurture.

Sources of Continuity

Piaget depicted development as involving both continuities and discontinuities. The main sources of continuity are three processes—*assimilation, accommodation, and equilibration*—that work together from birth to propel development forward.

Assimilation is the process by which people incorporate incoming information into concepts they already understand. To illustrate, when one of our children was 2 years old, he saw a man who was bald on top of his head and had long frizzy hair on the sides. To his father's great embarrassment, the toddler gleefully shouted, "Clown! Clown!" (Actually, it sounded more like "Kown! Kown!") The man apparently looked enough like a "kown" that the boy could assimilate him to his clown concept.

Accommodation is the process by which people improve their current understanding in response to new experiences. In the "kown" incident, the boy's father explained to his son that the man was not a clown and that even though his hair looked like a clown's, he was not wearing a funny costume and was not doing silly things to make people laugh. With this new information, the boy was able to accommodate his clown concept to the standard one, allowing other men with bald pates and long side hair to pass by in peace.

Equilibration is the process by which children (indeed, people of all ages) balance assimilation and accommodation to create stable understanding. Equilibration includes three phases. First, children are satisfied with their understanding of a particular phenomenon; Piaget labelled this a state of *equilibrium,* because the children do not see any discrepancies between their observations and their understanding of the phenomenon. Then, new information leads them to perceive that their understanding is inadequate. Piaget said that this realization puts children in a state of *disequilibrium;* they recognize shortcomings in their understanding of the phenomenon, but they cannot generate a superior alternative. Finally, they develop a more sophisticated understanding that eliminates the shortcomings of the old one, creating a more stable equilibrium within which a broader range of observations can be understood.

assimilation ■ The process by which people translate incoming information into a form that fits concepts they already understand.

accommodation ■ The process by which people adapt current knowledge structures in response to new experiences.

equilibration ■ The process by which children (or other people) balance assimilation and accommodation to create stable understanding.

Perhaps toddlers yelling "Kown! Kown!" set Larry, a member of The Three Stooges, on his career path.

One example of how equilibration works involves the belief—held by most 4- to 7-year-olds in a wide range of cultures (Inagaki & Hatano, 2008)—that animals are the only living things. This belief seems to stem from the assumption that only animals can move in ways that help them survive. Sooner or later, children realize that plants also move in ways that promote their survival (e.g., toward sunlight). This new information is difficult for them to assimilate to their prior thinking. The resulting disparity between their previous understanding of living things and their new knowledge about plants creates a state of disequilibrium, in which they are unsure of what it means to be alive. Later, their thinking accommodates to the new information about plants. That is, they realize that both animals and plants move in adaptive ways and that, because adaptive movement is a key characteristic of living things, plants as well as animals must be alive (Opfer & Gelman, 2001; Opfer & Siegler, 2004). This realization constitutes a more stable equilibrium, because subsequent information about plants and animals will not contradict it. Through innumerable such equilibrations, children acquire knowledge of the world around them.

Sources of Discontinuity

Although Piaget placed some emphasis on continuous aspects of cognitive development, the most famous part of his theory concerns discontinuous aspects, which he depicted as distinct *stages* of cognitive development. Piaget viewed these stages as products of the basic human tendency to organize knowledge into coherent structures. Each stage represents a coherent way of understanding one's experience, and each transition between stages represents a discontinuous intellectual leap from one coherent way of understanding the world to the next, higher one. The following are the central properties of Piaget's stage theory:

1. Qualitative change. Piaget believed that children of different ages think in qualitatively different ways. For instance, he proposed that children in the early stages of cognitive development conceive of morality in terms of the *consequences* of a person's behaviour, whereas children in later stages conceive of it in terms of the person's *intent*. Thus, a 5-year-old would judge someone who accidentally broke a whole jar of cookies as having been naughtier than someone who deliberately stole a single cookie; an 8-year-old would reach the opposite conclusion. This difference represents a *qualitative change*, because the two children are basing their moral judgments on entirely different criteria.

2. Broad applicability. The type of thinking characteristic of each stage influences children's thinking across diverse topics and contexts.

3. Brief transitions. Before entering a new stage, children pass through a brief transitional period in which they fluctuate between the type of thinking characteristic of the new, more advanced stage and the type of thinking characteristic of the old, less advanced one.

4. Invariant sequence. Everyone progresses through the stages in the same order without skipping any of them.

Piaget hypothesized four stages of cognitive development: the *sensorimotor* stage, the *preoperational* stage, the *concrete operational* stage, and the *formal operational* stage. In each stage, children exhibit new abilities that allow them to understand the world in qualitatively different ways than they had previously.

1. In the **sensorimotor stage** (birth to age 2 years), infants' intelligence is expressed through their sensory and motor abilities, which they use to perceive and explore the world around them. These abilities allow them to learn about objects and people and to construct rudimentary forms of fundamental concepts such as time, space, and causality. Throughout the sensorimotor period, infants live largely in the here and now: their intelligence is bound to their immediate perceptions and actions.

2. In the **preoperational stage** (ages 2 to 7 years), toddlers and preschoolers become able to represent their experiences in language and mental imagery. This allows them to remember the experiences for longer periods and to form more sophisticated concepts. However, as suggested by the term *preoperational,* Piaget's theory emphasizes young children's inability to perform certain *mental operations,* such as considering multiple dimensions simultaneously. This leads to children's being unable to form certain ideas, such as the idea that pouring all the water from a short, wide glass into a taller, narrower glass does not change the total amount of water, even though the column of water is higher in the second glass. In other words, they do not recognize that the increased height of the liquid column in the second glass is compensated for by its narrower width.

3. In the **concrete operational stage** (ages 7 to 12 years), children can reason logically about concrete objects and events; for example, they understand that pouring water from one glass to a taller, narrower one leaves the amount of water unchanged. However, concrete operational reasoners cannot think in purely abstract terms or generate systematic scientific experiments to test their beliefs.

4. In the final stage of cognitive development, the **formal operational stage** (age 12 years and beyond), children can think deeply not only about concrete events but also about abstractions and purely hypothetical situations. They also can perform systematic scientific experiments and draw appropriate conclusions from them, even when the conclusions differ from their prior beliefs.

With this overview of Piaget's theory, we can consider in greater depth major changes that take place in each stage.

sensorimotor stage ■ The period (birth to 2 years) within Piaget's theory in which intelligence is expressed through sensory and motor abilities.

preoperational stage ■ The period (2 to 7 years) within Piaget's theory in which children become able to represent their experiences in language, mental imagery, and symbolic thought.

concrete operational stage ■ The period (7 to 12 years) within Piaget's theory in which children become able to reason logically about concrete objects and events.

formal operational stage ■ The period (12 years and beyond) within Piaget's theory in which people become able to think about abstractions and hypothetical situations.

The Sensorimotor Stage (Birth to Age 2 Years)

One of Piaget's most profound insights was his realization that the roots of adult intelligence are present in infants' earliest behaviours, such as their seemingly aimless sucking, flailing, and grasping. He recognized that these behaviours are not random but instead reflect an early type of intelligence involving sensory and motor activity. Indeed, many of the clearest examples of the *active child* theme come from Piaget's descriptions of the development of what he called "sensorimotor intelligence."

Over the course of the first 2 years, infants' sensorimotor intelligence develops tremendously. The sheer amount of change may at first seem astonishing. However, when we consider the immense variety of new experiences that infants encounter during this period, and the tripling of brain weight between birth and age 3 (with weight being an index of brain development during this period), the huge increase in infants' cognitive abilities is more understandable. The profound developments that Piaget described as occurring during infancy call attention to a general principle: *children's thinking grows especially rapidly in the first few years.*

Infants are born with many reflexes. When objects move in front of their eyes, they visually track them; when objects are placed in their mouths, they suck them; when objects come into contact with their hands, they grasp them; when they hear noises, they turn toward them; and so on. Piaget believed that these simple reflexes and perceptual abilities are the foundation of intelligence.

Even during their first month, infants begin to modify their reflexes to make them more adaptive. At birth, for example, they suck in a similar way regardless of what they are sucking. Within a few weeks, however, they adjust their sucking according to the object in their mouth. Thus, they suck on a milk-yielding nipple in a way that enhances the efficiency of their feeding and that is different from the way they suck on a finger or even a pacifier. As this example illustrates, from the first days out of the womb, infants accommodate their actions to the parts of the environment with which they interact.

Over the course of the first few months, infants begin to organize separate reflexes into larger behaviours, most of which are centred on their own bodies. For instance, instead of being limited to exercising their grasping and sucking reflexes separately, they can integrate them: when an object touches their palm, they can grasp it, bring it to their mouth, and suck on it. Thus, their reflexes serve as building blocks for more complex behaviours.

In the middle of their first year, infants become increasingly interested in the world around them—people, animals, toys, and other objects and events beyond their own bodies. A hallmark of this shift is their repetition of actions on the environment that produce pleasurable or interesting results. Repeatedly banging a rattle and squeezing a rubber duck again and again to make it squeak are examples of favourite activities for many infants at this time.

Piaget (1954) made a striking and controversial claim about a deficiency in infants' thinking during this period—the one referred to in the chapter-opening anecdote about the father hiding his glasses. The claim was that through the age of 8 months, infants lack **object permanence,** the knowledge that objects continue to exist even when they are out of view. This claim was based largely on Piaget's observations of his own children, Laurent, Lucienne, and Jacqueline. The following account of an experiment with Laurent reflects the type of observation that inspired Piaget's belief about object permanence:

> At age 7 months, 28 days, I offer him a little bell behind a cushion. So long as he sees the little bell, however small it may be, he tries to grasp it. But if the little bell disappears completely, he stops all searching. I then resume the experiment using my hand as a screen. Laurent's arm is outstretched and about to grasp the little bell at the moment I make it disappear behind my hand, which is open and at a distance of about 15 cm from him. He immediately withdraws his arm, as though the little bell no longer existed.

> (Piaget, 1954, p. 39)

Thus, in Piaget's view, for infants younger than 8 months, the adage "out of sight, out of mind" is literally true. They are able to mentally represent (think about) only the objects that they can perceive at the moment.

By the end of the first year, infants search for hidden objects, thus indicating that they mentally represent the objects' continuing existence even when they no longer see them. These initial representations of objects are fragile, however, as reflected in the **A-not-B error.** In this error, once 8- to 12-month-olds have reached for and found a hidden object several times in one place (location A), when they see the object hidden at a different place (location B) and are prevented from immediately

ROBERT SIEGLER

Piaget proposed that when infants suck on objects, they gain not only pleasure but also knowledge about the world beyond their bodies.

object permanence ■ The knowledge that objects continue to exist even when they are out of view.

A-not-B error ■ The tendency to reach for a hidden object where it was last found rather than in the new location where it was last hidden.

FIGURE 4.1 Piaget's A-not-B task A child looks for and finds a toy under the cloth where it was hidden (left frame). After several such experiences, the toy is hidden in a different location (right frame). The child continues to look where he found the toy previously rather than where it is hidden now. The child's ignoring the visible protrusion of the toy under the cloth in the right frame illustrates the strength of the inclination to look in the previous hiding place.

searching for it, they tend to reach where they initially found the object (location A) (see Figure 4.1). Not until around their first birthday do infants consistently search first at the object's current location.

At around 1 year of age, infants begin to actively and avidly explore the potential ways in which objects can be used. The "child as scientist" example presented earlier, in which Piaget's son Laurent varied the positions from which he dropped different objects to see what would happen, provides one instance of this emerging competency. Similar examples occur in every family with an infant. Few parents forget their 12- to 18-month-old sitting in a high chair, banging various objects against the chair's tray—first a spoon, then a plate, then a cup—seemingly fascinated by the sounds made by the different objects. Nor do they forget their infant dropping bathroom articles into the toilet, or pouring a bag of flour on the kitchen floor, just to see what happens. Piaget regarded such actions as the beginnings of scientific experimentation (many parents see such behaviours in less positive terms).

In the last half-year of the sensorimotor stage (ages 18 to 24 months), according to Piaget, infants become able to form enduring mental representations. The first sign of this new capability is **deferred imitation,** that is, the repetition of other people's behaviour minutes, hours, or even days after it occurred. Consider Piaget's observation of 1-year-old Jacqueline:

> Jacqueline had a visit from a little boy … who, in the course of the afternoon, got into a terrible temper. He screamed as he tried to get out of a playpen and pushed it backward, stamping his feet. … The next day, she herself screamed in her playpen and tried to move it, stamping her foot lightly several times in succession.
>
> (Piaget, 1951, p. 63)

Piaget indicated that Jacqueline had never before thrown such a tantrum. Presumably, she had watched and remembered her playmate's behaviour, maintained a representation of it overnight, and imitated it the next day.

When we consider Piaget's account of cognitive development during infancy, several notable trends are evident.

- At first, infants' activities centre on their own bodies; later, their activities include the world around them.

This toddler's techniques for applying eye makeup may not exactly mirror those he has seen his mother use, but they are close enough to provide a compelling illustration of deferred imitation, a skill that children gain during their second year.

deferred imitation ■ The repetition of other people's behaviour a substantial time after it originally occurred.

- Early goals are concrete (shaking a rattle and listening to the sound it makes); later goals often are more abstract (varying the heights from which objects are dropped and observing how the effects vary).

- Infants become increasingly able to form mental representations, moving from "out of sight, out of mind" to remembering a playmate's actions from a full day earlier. Such enduring mental representations make possible the next stage, which Piaget called preoperational thinking.

The Preoperational Stage (Ages 2 to 7)

Piaget viewed the preoperational period as including a mix of striking cognitive acquisitions and fascinating limitations. Perhaps the foremost acquisition is the development of *symbolic representations;* among the most notable weaknesses are *egocentrism* and *centration.*

Development of Symbolic Representations

Have you ever seen preschoolers use a Popsicle stick to represent a hammer or a playing card to represent a cellphone? Forming such personal symbols is common among 3- to 5-year-olds. It is one of the ways in which they exercise their emerging capacity for **symbolic representation**—the use of one object to stand for another. Typically, these personal symbols physically resemble the objects they represent. The Popsicle stick's and playing card's shapes somewhat resemble those of a hammer and cellphone.

As children develop, they rely less on self-generated symbols and more on conventional ones. For instance, when 5-year-olds play games involving pirates, they might wear a patch over one eye and a bandana over their head because that is the way pirates are commonly depicted. Heightened symbolic capabilities during the preoperational period are also evident in the growth of drawing. Children's drawings between ages 3 and 5 make increasing use of symbolic conventions, such as representing the leaves of flowers as Vs (Figure 4.2).

Egocentrism

Although Piaget noted important growth in children's thinking during the preoperational stage, he found the limitations of this period to be as intriguing and revealing of preoperational understanding. As noted, one important limitation is **egocentrism,** that is, perceiving the world solely from one's own point of view. An example of this limitation involves preschoolers' difficulty in taking other people's spatial perspectives. Piaget and Inhelder (1956/1977) demonstrated this difficulty by having 4-year-olds sit at a table in front of a model of three mountains of different sizes (Figure 4.3). The children were asked to identify which of several photographs depicted what a doll would see if it were sitting on chairs at various locations around the table. Solving this problem required children to recognize that their own perspective was not the only one possible and to imagine what the view would be from another location. Most 4-year-olds, according to Piaget, cannot do this.

The same difficulty in taking other people's perspectives is seen in quite different contexts—for example, in communication. As illustrated in Figure 4.4, preschoolers often talk right past one another, focused only on what they themselves are saying and seemingly oblivious to their partner's comments. Preschoolers' egocentric communication is also evident when they make statements that require knowledge that they themselves possess but that their listeners couldn't be expected to have. For instance,

ILLUSTRATION BY VIVIAN HOXSEY

FIGURE 4.2 **A 4-year-old's drawing of a summer day** Note the use of simple artistic conventions, such as the V-shaped leaves on the flowers.

FIGURE 4.3 **Piaget's three-mountains task** When asked to choose the picture that shows what the doll sitting in the seat across the table would see, most children younger than 6 years choose the picture showing how the scene looks to them, illustrating their difficulty in separating their own perspective from that of others.

symbolic representation ■ The use of one object to stand for another.

egocentrism ■ The tendency to perceive the world solely from one's own point of view.

2- and 3-year-olds frequently tell daycare providers and parents things like "He took it from me," in situations where the person or object to which the child is referring is totally unclear. Egocentric thinking is also evident in preschoolers' explanations of events and behaviour. Consider the following interviews with preschoolers that occurred in the original version of the television show *Kids Say the Darndest Things:*

> *Interviewer:* Any brothers or sisters?
> *Child:* I have a brother a week old.
> *I:* What can he do?
> *C:* He can say "Mamma" and "Daddy."
> *I:* Can he walk?
> *C:* No, he's too lazy.
>
> *Interviewer:* Any brothers or sisters?
> *Child:* A 2-months-old brother.
> *I:* How does he behave?
> *C:* He cries all night.
> *I:* Why is that, do you think?
> *C:* He probably thinks he's missing something on television.

(Linkletter, 1957, p. 6)

Over the course of the preoperational period, egocentric speech becomes less common. An early sign of progress is children's verbal quarrels, which become increasingly frequent during this period. The fact that a child's statements elicit a playmate's objection indicates that the playmate is at least paying attention to the differing perspective that the other child's comment implies. Children also become better able to envision spatial perspectives other than their own during the preoperational period. We all remain somewhat egocentric throughout our lives, but most of us do improve.

Centration

A related limitation of preschoolers' thinking is **centration,** that is, focusing on a single, perceptually striking feature of an object or event to the exclusion of other relevant but less striking features. Children's approaches to balance-scale problems provide a good example of centration. If presented with a balance scale like that in Figure 4.5 and asked which side will go down, 5- and 6-year-olds centre on the amount of weight on each side, ignore the distance of the weights from the fulcrum, and say that whichever side has more weight will go down (Inhelder & Piaget, 1958).

Another good example of centration comes from Piaget's research on children's understanding of conservation. The idea of the **conservation concept** is that merely changing the appearance or arrangement of objects does not necessarily change other key properties, such as quantity of material. Three variants of the concept that are commonly studied in 5- to 8-year-olds are *conservation of liquid quantity, conservation of solid quantity,* and *conservation of number* (Piaget, 1952a). In all three cases, the tasks used to measure children's understanding employ a three-phase procedure (Figure 4.6). First, as in the figure, children are shown two objects (e.g., two glasses of orange juice, two clay sausages) that are identical in quantity, or two sets of objects (e.g., two rows of dimes) that are identical in number. Once children agree that the dimension of interest (e.g., the amount of orange juice or the number of dimes) is equal in both items, they observe a second phase in which the experimenter transforms one object or set of objects in a way that makes it look different but does not change the dimension of interest. Orange juice might be poured into a

FIGURE 4.4 Egocentrism An example of young children's egocentric conversations.

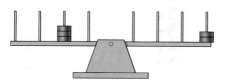

FIGURE 4.5 The balance scale When asked to predict which side of a balance scale, like the one shown above, would go down if the arm were allowed to move, 5- and 6-year-olds almost always centre their attention on the amount of weight and ignore the distances of the weights from the fulcrum. Thus, they would predict that the left side would go down, although it is the right side that would actually drop.

centration ■ The tendency to focus on a single, perceptually striking feature of an object or event.

conservation concept ■ The idea that merely changing the appearance of objects does not necessarily change other key properties.

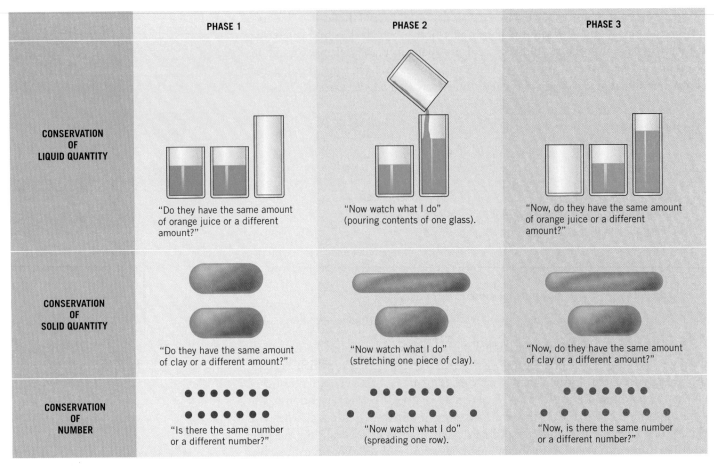

	PHASE 1	PHASE 2	PHASE 3
CONSERVATION OF LIQUID QUANTITY	"Do they have the same amount of orange juice or a different amount?"	"Now watch what I do" (pouring contents of one glass).	"Now, do they have the same amount of orange juice or a different amount?"
CONSERVATION OF SOLID QUANTITY	"Do they have the same amount of clay or a different amount?"	"Now watch what I do" (stretching one piece of clay).	"Now, do they have the same amount of clay or a different amount?"
CONSERVATION OF NUMBER	"Is there the same number or a different number?"	"Now watch what I do" (spreading one row).	"Now, is there the same number or a different number?"

FIGURE 4.6 Procedures used to test conservation of liquid quantity, solid quantity, and number Most 4- and 5-year-olds say that the taller liquid column has more liquid, the longer sausage has more clay, and the longer row has more objects.

taller, narrower, glass; a short, thick clay sausage might be moulded into a long, thin sausage; or one of the two rows of dimes might be spread out. Finally, in the third phase, children are asked whether the dimension of interest, which they earlier had said was equal for the two objects or sets of objects, is still equal.

The large majority of 4- and 5-year-olds answer "no." On conservation-of-liquid-quantity problems, they claim that the taller, narrower glass has more orange juice; on conservation-of-solid-quantity problems, they claim that the long, thin sausage has more clay than the short, thick one; and so on. Children of this age make similar errors in everyday contexts; for example, they often think that if a child has one fewer cookie than another child, a fair solution is to break one of the short-changed child's cookies into two pieces (Miller, 1984).

A variety of weaknesses that Piaget perceived in preoperational thinking contribute to these difficulties with conservation problems. Preoperational thinkers centre their attention on the single, perceptually salient dimension of height or length, ignoring other relevant dimensions. In addition, their egocentrism leads to their failing to understand that their own perspective can be misleading—that just because a tall narrow glass of orange juice or a long thin clay sausage looks as though it has more orange juice or clay than a shorter, wider one does not mean that it really does. Children's tendency to focus on static states of objects (the appearance of the objects after the transformation) and to ignore the transformation that was performed (pouring the orange juice or reshaping the clay) also contributes to their difficulty in solving conservation problems.

In the next period of cognitive development, the concrete operational stage, children largely overcome these and other related limitations.

The Concrete Operational Stage (Ages 7 to 12)

At around age 7, according to Piaget, children begin to reason logically about concrete features of the world. Development of the conservation concept exemplifies this progress. Although few 5-year-olds solve any of the three conservation tasks described in the previous section, most 7-year-olds solve all of them. The same progress in thinking also allows children in the concrete operational stage to solve many other problems that require attention to multiple dimensions. For example, on the balance-scale problem, they consider distance from the fulcrum as well as weight of objects.

However, this relatively advanced reasoning is, according to Piaget, limited to concrete situations. Thinking systematically remains very difficult, as does reasoning about hypothetical situations. These limitations are evident in the types of experiments that concrete operational children perform to solve the pendulum problem (Inhelder & Piaget, 1958) (Figure 4.7). In this problem, children are presented a pendulum frame, a set of strings of varying length with a loop at each end, and a set of metal weights of varying weight, any of which can be attached to any string. When the loop at one end of the string is attached to a weight, and the loop at the other end is attached to the frame of the pendulum, the string can be swung. The task is to perform experiments that indicate which factor or factors influence the amount of time it takes the pendulum to swing through a complete arc. Is it the length of the string, the heaviness of the weight, the height from which the weight is dropped, or some combination of these factors? Think for a minute: How would you go about solving this problem?

Most concrete operational children begin their experiments believing that the relative heaviness of the weights being dropped is the most important factor, perhaps the only important one. This belief is not unreasonable; indeed, most adolescents and adults share it. What distinguishes the children's reasoning from that of older individuals is how they test their belief. Concrete operational reasoners design biased experiments from which no valid conclusion can be drawn. For instance, they might compare the travel time of a heavy weight on a short string dropped from a high position to the travel time of a light weight on a long string dropped from a lower position. When the first string goes faster, they conclude that, just as they thought, heavy weights go faster. This premature conclusion, however, reflects their limited ability to think systematically or to imagine all possible combinations of variables. They fail to imagine that the faster motion might be related to the length of the string or the height from which the string was dropped, rather than the weight of the object.

The Formal Operational Stage (Age 12 and Beyond)

Formal operational thinking, which includes the ability to think abstractly and to reason hypothetically, is the pinnacle of the Piagetian stage progression. The difference between reasoning in this stage and in the previous one is clearly illustrated by formal operational reasoners' approach to the pendulum problem. Framing the problem more abstractly than do children in the concrete operational stage, they see that any of the variables—weight, string length, and dropping point—might influence the time it takes for the pendulum to swing through an arc, and that it is therefore necessary to test the effect of each variable systematically. To test the effect of weight, they compare times to complete an arc for a heavier weight and a lighter weight, attached to strings of equal length and dropped from the same height. To test the effect of string length, they compare the travel times of a long and a short string, with equal weight dropped from the same position. To test the influence of dropping point, they

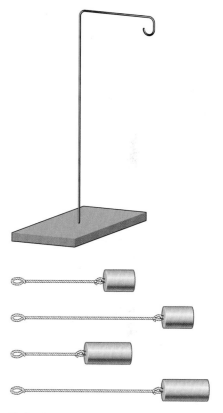

FIGURE 4.7 **Inhelder and Piaget's pendulum problem** The task is to compare the motions of longer and shorter strings, with lighter and heavier weights attached, in order to determine the influence of weight, string length, and dropping point on the time it takes for the pendulum to swing back and forth. Children younger than 12 usually perform unsystematic experiments and draw incorrect conclusions.

Teenagers' emerging ability to understand that their reality is only one of many possible realities may cause teens to develop a taste for science fiction.

vary the dropping point of a given weight attached to a given string. Such a systematic set of experiments allows the formal operational thinker to determine that the only factor that influences the pendulum's travel time is the length of the string; neither weight nor dropping point matters.

Piaget believed that unlike the previous three stages, the formal operational stage is not universal: not all adolescents (or adults) reach it. For those adolescents who do reach it, however, formal operational thinking greatly expands and enriches their intellectual universe. Such thinking makes it possible for them to see the particular reality in which they live as only one of an infinite number of possible realities. This insight leads them to think about alternative ways that the world could be and to ponder deep questions concerning truth, justice, and morality. It no doubt also helps account for the fact that many people first acquire a taste for science fiction during adolescence. The alternative worlds depicted in science-fiction stories appeal to adolescents' emerging capacity to think about the world they know as just one of many possibilities and to wonder whether a better world is possible.

The attainment of formal operational thinking does not mean that adolescents will always reason in advanced ways, but it does, according to Piaget, mark the point at which adolescents attain the reasoning powers of intelligent adults. (Some ways in which Piaget's theory can be applied to improving education are discussed in Box 4.1.)

Piaget's Legacy

Although much of Piaget's theory was formulated many years ago, it remains a very influential approach to understanding cognitive development. Some of its strengths were mentioned earlier. It provides a good overview of what children's thinking is like at different points in development (Table 4.2). It includes countless fascinating observations. It offers a plausible and appealing perspective on children's nature. It surveys a remarkably broad spectrum of developments and covers the entire age span from infancy through adolescence.

However, subsequent analyses (Flavell, 1971, 1982; Miller, 2011) have identified some crucial weaknesses in Piaget's theory. The following four are particularly important:

1. The stage model depicts children's thinking as being more consistent than it is. According to Piaget, once children enter a given stage, their thinking consistently

TABLE 4.2

Piaget's Stages of Cognitive Development

Stage	Approximate Age	New Ways of Knowing
Sensorimotor	Birth to 2 years	Infants know the world through their senses and through their actions. For example, they learn what dogs look like and what petting them feels like.
Preoperational	2–7 years	Toddlers and young children acquire the ability to internally represent the world through language and mental imagery. They also begin to be able to see the world from other people's perspectives, not just from their own.
Concrete operational	7–12 years	Children become able to think logically, not just intuitively. They now can classify objects into precisely defined categories and understand that events are often influenced by multiple factors, not just one.
Formal operational	12 years and beyond	Adolescents can think systematically and reason about what might be, as well as what is. This allows them to understand politics, ethics, and science fiction, as well as to engage in scientific reasoning.

shows the characteristics of that stage across diverse concepts. Subsequent research, however, has shown that children's thinking is far more variable than this depiction suggests. For instance, most children succeed on conservation-of-number problems by age 6, whereas most do not succeed on conservation-of-solid-quantity problems until age 8 or 9 (Field, 1987). Piaget recognized that such variability exists but underestimated its extent and failed to explain it.

2. Infants and young children are more cognitively competent than Piaget recognized. Piaget employed fairly difficult tests to assess most of the concepts he studied. This led him to miss infants' and young children's earliest knowledge of these concepts. For instance, Piaget's test of object permanence required children to reach for the hidden object after a delay; Piaget claimed that children do not do this until 8 or 9 months of age. However, alternative tests of object permanence, which analyze where infants *look* immediately after the object has disappeared from view, indicate that by 3 months of age, even these young infants at least suspect that objects continue to exist (Baillargeon, 1987, 1993).

BOX 4.1: applications

EDUCATIONAL APPLICATIONS OF PIAGET'S THEORY

Piaget's view of children's cognitive development holds a number of general implications for how children should be educated (Case, 1998; Piaget, 1972). Most generally, it suggests that children's distinctive ways of thinking at different ages need to be considered in deciding how to teach them. For instance, children in the concrete operational stage would not be expected to be ready to learn purely abstract concepts such as inertia and equilibrium state, whereas adolescents in the formal operational stage would be. Taking into account such general age-related differences in cognitive level before deciding when to teach particular concepts is often labelled a "child-centred approach."

A second implication of Piaget's approach is that children learn best by interacting with the environment, both mentally and physically. One research demonstration of this principle involved promoting children's understanding of the concept of speed (Levin, Siegler, & Druyan, 1990). The investigation focused on problems of a type beloved by physics teachers: "When a race horse travels around a circular track, do its right and left sides move at the same speed?" It appears obvious that they do, but, in fact, they do not. The side toward

The child and adult are holding onto a bar as they walk around a circle four times. On the first two trips around, the child holds the bar near the pivot; on the second two, the child holds it at its end. The much faster pace needed to keep up with the bar when holding onto its end leads the child to realize that the end was moving faster than the inner portion (Levin et al., 1990).

the outside of the track is covering a slightly greater distance in the same amount of time as the side toward the inside and therefore is moving slightly faster.

Levin and her colleagues devised a procedure that allowed children to actively experience how different parts of a single object can move at different speeds. They attached one end of a 2.1-metre-long metal

bar to a pivot that was mounted on the floor. One by one, 6th graders and an experimenter took four walks around the pivot while holding onto the bar. On two of the walks, the child held the bar near the pivot and the experimenter held it at the far end; on the other two walks, they switched positions (see figure). After each walk, children were asked whether the inner or outer part of the bar had moved faster.

The differences in the speeds required for walking while holding the inner and the outer parts of the metal bar were so dramatic that the children generalized their new understanding to other problems involving circular motion, such as cars moving around circular tracks on a computer screen. In other words, physically experiencing the concept accomplished what years of formal science instruction usually fail to do. As one boy said to the experimenter, "Before, I hadn't experienced it. I didn't think about it. Now that I have had that experience, I know that when I was on the outer circle, I had to walk faster to be at the same place as you" (Levin et al., 1990). Clearly, relevant physical activities, accompanied by questions that call attention to the lessons of the activities, can foster children's learning.

3. Piaget's theory understates the contribution of the social world to cognitive development. Piaget's theory focuses on how children come to understand the world through their own efforts. From the day that children emerge from the womb, however, they live in an environment of adults and older children who shape their cognitive development in countless ways. A child's cognitive development reflects the contributions of other people, as well as of the broader culture, to a far greater degree than Piaget's theory acknowledges.

4. Piaget's theory is vague about the cognitive processes that give rise to children's thinking and about the mechanisms that produce cognitive growth. Piaget's theory provides any number of excellent descriptions of children's thinking. It is less revealing, however, about the processes that lead children to think in a particular way and that produce changes in their thinking. Assimilation, accommodation, and equilibration have an air of plausibility, but how they operate is unclear.

These weaknesses of Piaget's theory do not negate the magnitude of his achievement: it remains one of the major intellectual accomplishments of the past century. However, appreciating the weaknesses as well as the strengths of his theory is necessary for understanding why alternative theories of cognitive development have become increasingly prominent.

In the remainder of this chapter, we consider the three most prominent alternative theories: *information-processing, sociocultural,* and *dynamic-systems.* Each type of theory can be seen as an attempt to overcome a major weakness of Piaget's approach. Information-processing theories emphasize precise characterizations of the processes that give rise to children's thinking and the mechanisms that produce cognitive growth. Sociocultural theories emphasize the ways in which children's interactions with the social world, both with other people and with the products of their culture, guide cognitive development. Dynamic-systems theories emphasize infants' and young children's developing physical and mental capabilities and how these capabilities are attained.

review:

Piaget's theory of cognitive development emphasizes the interaction of nature and nurture, continuities and discontinuities, and children's active contribution to their own development. The continuities of development are produced by assimilation, accommodation, and equilibration. Assimilation involves interpreting incoming information to fit current understanding. Accommodation involves adapting one's thinking toward being more consistent with new experiences. Equilibration involves balancing assimilation and accommodation in a way that creates stable understandings.

As depicted by Piaget, the discontinuities of cognitive development involve four discrete stages: (1) the sensorimotor stage (birth to age 2), in which infants begin to know the world through the perceptions of their senses and through their motor activities; (2) the preoperational stage (ages 2 to 7), in which children become capable of mental representations but tend to be egocentric and to focus on a single dimension of an event or problem; (3) the concrete operational stage (ages 7 to 12), in which children reason logically about concrete aspects of the environment but have difficulty thinking abstractly; and (4) the formal operational stage (age 12 and beyond), in which preadolescents and adolescents become capable of abstract thought.

Among the important strengths of Piaget's theory are its broad overview of development, its plausible and attractive perspective on children's nature, its inclusion of varied tasks and age groups, and its endlessly fascinating observations. Among the theory's important weaknesses are its overstatement of the consistency of children's thinking, its underestimation of infants' and young children's cognitive competence, its lack of attention to the contribution of the social world, and its vagueness regarding cognitive mechanisms.

Information-Processing Theories

SCENE: DAUGHTER AND FATHER IN THEIR YARD. A PLAYMATE RIDES IN ON A BIKE.

Child: Daddy, would you unlock the basement door?
Father: Why?
C: 'Cause I want to ride my bike.
F: Your bike is in the garage.
C: But my socks are in the dryer.

(Klahr, 1978, pp. 181–182)

What reasoning could have produced this 5-year-old's enigmatic comment "But my socks are in the dryer"? David Klahr, an eminent information-processing theorist, formulated the following model of the thought process that led to it:

Top goal: I want to ride my bike.
  Bias: I need shoes to ride comfortably.
  Fact: I'm barefoot.

Subgoal 1: Get my sneakers.
  Fact: The sneakers are in the yard.
  Fact: They're uncomfortable on bare feet.

Subgoal 2: Get my socks.
  Fact: The sock drawer was empty this morning.
  Inference: The socks probably are in the dryer.

Subgoal 3: Get them from the dryer.
  Fact: The dryer is in the basement.

Subgoal 4: Go to the basement.
  Fact: It's quicker to go through the yard entrance.
  Fact: The yard entrance is always locked.

Subgoal 5: Unlock the door to the basement.
  Fact: Daddies have the keys to everything.

Subgoal 6: Ask Daddy to unlock the door.

Klahr's analysis of his daughter's thinking illustrates two notable characteristics of **information-processing theories.**[1] One is the precise specification of the processes involved in children's thinking. Klahr's approach, for example, used **task analysis**— that is, the identification of goals, the obstacles that prevent their immediate realization, the prior knowledge and information in the environment relevant to them, and the potential processing strategies for overcoming the obstacles and attaining the goals.

Such task analysis helps information-processing researchers understand and predict children's behaviour and allows them to rigorously test precise hypotheses regarding how development occurs. In some cases, it also allows them to formulate computer simulations, a type of mathematical model that expresses ideas about mental processes in particularly precise ways. For example, Simon and Klahr (1995) created computer simulations of the knowledge and mental processes that led young children to fail on conservation problems and of the somewhat different knowledge and mental processes that allowed older children to succeed on them.

information-processing theories ■ A class of theories that focus on the structure of the cognitive system and the mental activities used to deploy attention and memory to solve problems.

task analysis ■ The research technique of identifying goals, relevant information in the environment, and potential processing strategies for a problem.

---

[1] Here and throughout this section, we use the plural term "information-processing *theories*" rather than the singular term "information-processing *theory*" because information-processing theories consist of a variety of related approaches rather than a single set of unified ideas. For the same reason, in subsequent sections we refer to "sociocultural theories" and "dynamic-systems theories."

problem solving ■ The process of attaining a goal by using a strategy to overcome an obstacle.

A second distinctive feature of information-processing analysis is an emphasis on thinking as an activity that occurs over time. Often, a single simple behaviour, such as the initial request of Klahr's daughter that he open the basement door, reflects an extended sequence of rapid mental operations. Information-processing analyses identify what those mental operations are, the order in which they are executed, and how increasing speed and accuracy of mental operations lead to cognitive growth.

View of Children's Nature

Information-processing theorists see children's cognitive growth as occurring continuously, in small increments that occur at different times on different tasks. This depiction differs fundamentally from Piaget's belief that children progress through qualitatively distinct, broadly applicable stages, separated only by brief transition periods.

The Child as a Limited-Capacity Processing System

In trying to understand differences in children's thinking at various ages, some information-processing theorists draw comparisons between the information processing of computers and that of humans. A computer's information processing is limited by its hardware and by its software. The hardware limitations relate to the computer's memory capacity and its efficiency in executing basic operations. The software limitations relate to the strategies and information that are available for performing particular tasks. People's thinking is limited by the same factors: memory capacity, speed of thought processes, and availability of useful strategies and knowledge. In the information-processing view, cognitive development arises from children's gradually surmounting their processing limitations through (1) expansion of the amount of information they can process at one time, (2) increases in the speed with which they execute thought processes, and (3) acquisition of new strategies and knowledge.

The Child as Problem Solver

Also central to the view of human nature held by information-processing theories is the assumption that children are active problem solvers. As suggested by Klahr's analysis of his daughter's behaviour, **problem solving** involves goals, perceived obstacles, and strategies or rules for overcoming the obstacles and attaining the goals. A description of a younger child's problem solving reveals the same combination of goal, obstacle, and strategy:

> Georgie (a 2-year-old) wants to throw rocks out the kitchen window. The lawn mower is outside. Dad says that Georgie can't throw rocks out the window, because he'll break the lawn mower with the rocks. Georgie says, "I got an idea." He goes outside, brings in some green peaches that he had been playing with, and says: "They won't break the lawn mower."
>
> (Waters, 1989, p. 7)

In addition to illustrating the typical goal–obstacle–strategy sequence, this example highlights another basic tenet of information-processing approaches: children's cognitive flexibility helps them pursue their goals. Even young children show great ingenuity in surmounting the obstacles imposed by their parents, the physical environment, and their own lack of knowledge.

Central Developmental Issues

Like all the theories described in this chapter, information-processing theories examine how *nature and nurture* work together to produce development. What makes information-processing theories unique is their emphasis on precise descriptions of *how change occurs*. The way in which information-processing theories address the issues of nature and nurture and how change occurs can be seen particularly clearly in their accounts of the development of memory and problem solving.

The Development of Memory

Memory is crucial to everything we do. The skills we use on everyday tasks, the language we employ when writing or speaking, the emotions we feel on a given occasion—all depend on our memory of past experiences and the knowledge acquired through them. Indeed, without memory of our experiences, we lose our very identity, a devastating syndrome that has been observed in patients with certain types of amnesia (Reed & Squire, 1998). Memory plays a role in all cognitive developmental theories, but it is especially central to information-processing theories. Most such theories distinguish among *working memory, long-term memory,* and *executive functions*.

Working memory **Working memory** involves actively attending to, gathering, maintaining, storing, and processing information. For instance, if after reading a story about birds, a child were asked a question about it, the child would, through working memory, bring together relevant information from the story, inferences made from that information, and prior knowledge about birds, and would then process the information to construct a reasonable answer.

Working memory is limited in both its capacity (the amount of information that it can store) and in the length of time it can retain information without updating activities. For example, a child might be able to remember a sequence of five digits but not six, and might be able to remember them for 5 or 10 seconds without repeating them but not for a longer time. The exact capacity and duration vary with the task and the type of material being processed, but for a given task and type of material, both capacity and speed increase with age and relevant experience (Schneider, 2011).

The basic organization of working-memory subsystems seems to be constant from early in childhood. However, the capacity and speed of operation of working memory increase greatly over the course of childhood and adolescence (Cowan et al., 1999; Gathercole et al., 2004). These changes are believed to occur in part because of increasing knowledge of the content on which working memory operates and in part because of maturational changes in the brain (C. A. Nelson, Thomas, & De Haan, 2006) (see Figure 4.8).

Long-term memory In contrast to the moment-to-moment nature of working memory, **long-term memory** consists of the knowledge that people accumulate over their lifetime. It includes factual knowledge (e.g., knowing the capitals of different countries or the teams that won the Stanley Cup in the past 5 years), conceptual knowledge (e.g., the concepts of justice, mercy, and equality), procedural knowledge (e.g., knowing how to tie a shoe or play a video game), attitudes (e.g., likes and dislikes regarding political parties or anchovies), reasoning strategies (e.g., knowing how to take an argument to its logical extreme to show its inadequacy), and so

working memory ■ Memory system that involves actively attending to, gathering, maintaining, storing, and processing information.

long-term memory ■ Information retained on an enduring basis.

FIGURE 4.8 Brain maturation All of the major areas of the cortex shown here continue maturing after birth. Brain maturation continues for a particularly long time in the prefrontal cortex, an area that is especially involved in planning, inhibiting inappropriate behaviour, and adopting new goals in response to changing situations.

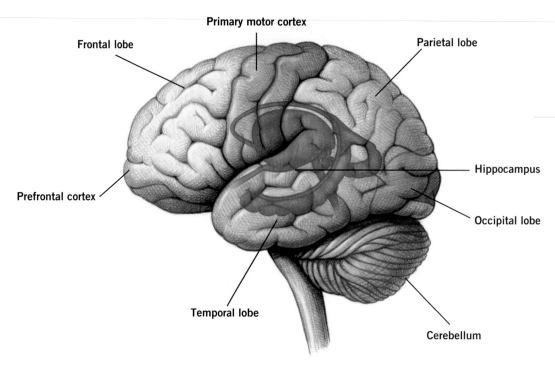

on. Long-term memory can thus be thought of as the totality of one's knowledge, whereas working memory can be regarded as the subset of that knowledge that is being processed at a given time (Cowan, 2005; Ericsson & Kintsch, 1995).

In contrast to the severe limits on the capacity and duration of working memory, long-term memory can retain an unlimited amount of information for unlimited periods. To cite one notable example, research shows that people who studied Spanish or algebra in high school often retain a substantial amount of what they learned in the subject 50 years later, despite their not having used the information in the interim and their having accumulated vast stores of other skills, concepts, and knowledge in long-term memory over that period (Bahrick, 1987).

Executive Functioning Executive functions involve the control of cognition. The prefrontal cortex (Figure 4.8) plays a particularly important role in this cognitive control. Three major types of executive functions are *inhibiting* tempting actions that would be counterproductive; *enhancing working memory* through use of strategies, such as repeating a phone number that would otherwise be forgotten; and *being cognitively flexible*, for example, taking someone else's perspective in an argument despite the fact that it differs from one's own. As these examples suggest, executive functioning integrates information from working memory and long-term memory to accomplish goals (e.g., Diamond, 2013; Miyake & Friedman, 2012; Rose, Feldman, & Jankowski, 2011).

The ability of executive functions to control thinking and action—enabling the individual to respond appropriately rather than acting impulsively or doing what he or she is used to doing—increases greatly during the preschool and early elementary school years. One aspect of this improvement is children's increased cognitive flexibility in shifting goals. For example, when they are assigned the task of sorting toys by their colour for a long period and then are asked to sort the same toys by shape, most 3-year-olds have difficulty switching goals, but 5-year-olds make the switch with ease (Baker, Friedman, & Leslie, 2010; Zelazo et al., 2003). The ability to inhibit habitual responses occurs slightly later and is evident in everyday games such as "Simon Says." Preschoolers have great difficulty inhibiting the impulse to quickly respond to commands that are not preceded by the critical phrase in such games, whereas early elementary school children are much better at inhibiting the impulse to act immediately (Dempster, 1995; Diamond, Kirkham, & Amso, 2002; Sabbagh et al., 2006). Strategies for controlling working memory tend to develop a little later, largely in the first few years of elementary school (Schneider, 2011).

As you might anticipate, the need for strong executive functioning continues to pose challenges well beyond early childhood. For instance, resisting the temptation to daydream while doing one's homework, keeping quiet while the teacher is talking, and inhibiting disrespectful replies to parents or teachers are difficult even for many adolescents (Bunge & Zelazo, 2006; Munakata, Snyder, & Chatham, 2012).

The quality of executive functioning during early childhood is highly predictive of many important life outcomes years later, including academic achievement in later grades, enrolment in university, and income and occupational status during adulthood (Blair & Razza, 2007; Duncan et al., 2007; McClelland & Cameron, 2011; Mischel & Ayduk, 2011; Moffitt et al., 2011). Fortunately, several training programs for preschoolers have shown considerable promise for improving young children's executive functioning (Diamond, 2013; Diamond et al., 2007; Raver et al., 2009).

In one such training study, disadvantaged preschoolers were randomly assigned to classrooms using a curriculum designed to improve executive functioning (Raver et al., 2011). The intervention involved instructing teachers in strategies—including stating and implementing clear rules, rewarding positive behaviours, and redirecting negative behaviours in positive directions—that would help children inhibit impulses to disrupt classroom activities. By the end of the school year, this approach had led to improvements in the children's behaviour and self-regulatory skills. Even more impressive, for the next 3 years, children who had been in the intervention classrooms continued to perform better in math and reading than did children in a control group (Raver et al., 2011).

Explanations of memory development Information-processing theorists try to explain both the processes that make memory as good as it is at each age and the limitations that prevent it from being better. These efforts have focused on three types of capabilities: *basic processes*, *strategies*, and *content knowledge*.

BASIC PROCESSES The simplest and most frequently used mental activities are known as **basic processes.** They include *associating* events with one another, *recognizing* objects as familiar, *recalling* facts and procedures, and *generalizing* from one instance to another. Another basic process, which is key to all the others, is **encoding**—the representation in memory of specific features of objects and events. With development, children execute basic processes more efficiently, enhancing their memory and learning for all kinds of materials.

Most of these basic processes are familiar, and their importance obvious. However, encoding is probably less familiar. Appreciating its significance requires some understanding of the way in which memory works. People often think of memory as something akin to an unedited video recording of our experiences. Actually, memory is far more selective. People *encode* information that draws their attention or that they consider relevant, but they fail to encode a great deal of other

basic processes ■ The simplest and most frequently used mental activities.

encoding ■ The process of representing in memory information that draws attention or is considered important.

THE FAMILY CIRCUS   **By Bil Keane**

"Mirror, mirror, on the wall, who's the fairest of the mall?"

Misencoding common sayings can lead to memorable confusions.

information. Information that is not encoded is not remembered later. This failure is probably evident in your own memory of the loonie; although you have seen this coin many times, you most likely have not encoded whether the loon faces to the right or to the left.

Studies of how children learn to solve balance-scale problems illustrate the importance of encoding for learning and memory. As discussed on page 139, most 5-year-olds predict that the side of the scale with more weight will go down, regardless of the distance of the weights from the fulcrum. Five-year-olds generally have difficulty learning more advanced approaches to solving balance-scale problems that take into account distance as well as weight because they do not encode information about distance of the weights from the fulcrum. For instance, 5-year-olds are shown a balance scale with varying arrangements of weights on pegs; the scale is then hidden behind a barrier, and the children are asked to reproduce the arrangement on an identical balance scale. Five-year-olds generally reproduce the correct number of weights on each side but rarely put them the correct distance from the fulcrum (Siegler, 1976). Teaching them to encode distance by telling them that both weight and distance are important enables them to learn more advanced balance-scale rules that peers who were not taught to encode distance have trouble learning (Siegler & Chen, 1998).

Like improved encoding, improved speed of processing plays a key role in the development of memory and learning. As shown in Figure 4.9, processing speed increases most rapidly at young ages but continues to increase in adolescence (Kail, 1991, 1997; Luna et al., 2004).

Two biological processes that contribute to faster processing are myelination and increased connectivity among brain regions (Luna et al., 2004). As discussed in Chapter 3, from the prenatal period through adolescence, increasing numbers of axons of neurons become covered with myelin, the fatty insulating substance that promotes faster and more reliable transmission of electrical impulses in the brain (Paus, 2010). Myelination enhances executive function, contributing to the ability to resist distractions (Dempster & Corkill, 1999; Wilson & Kipp, 1998). Greater connectivity among brain regions also increases processing capacity and speed by increasing the efficiency of communication among brain areas (Thatcher, 1998).

FIGURE 4.9 Increase with age in speed of processing on two tasks Note that the increase is rapid in the early years and more gradual later. (Data from Kail, 1991)

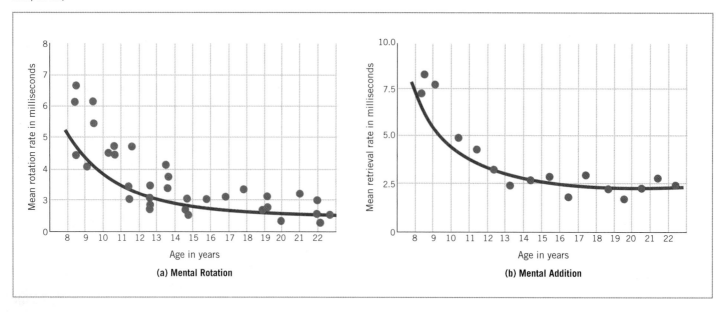

(a) Mental Rotation

(b) Mental Addition

This growth of long-distance connectivity among brain regions is especially prominent in later childhood and adolescence.

STRATEGIES Information-processing theories point to the acquisition and growth of strategies as another major source of the development of memory. Between ages 5 and 8 years, children begin to use a number of broadly useful memory strategies, among them the strategy of **rehearsal,** the repeating of information multiple times in order to remember it. The following newspaper item illustrates the usefulness of rehearsal for remembering information verbatim:

> A 9-year-old boy memorized the licence plate number of a getaway car following an armed robbery, a court was told Monday. … The boy and his friend … looked in the drug store window and saw a man grab a 14-year-old cashier's neck. … After the robbery, the boys mentally repeated the licence number until they gave it to police.
>
> (*Edmonton Journal*, Jan. 13, 1981, cited in Kail, 1984)

Had the boys witnessed the same event when they were 5-year-olds, they probably would not have rehearsed the numbers and would have forgotten the licence number before the police arrived.

Another widely used memory strategy that becomes increasingly prevalent in the early elementary school years is **selective attention**, the process of intentionally focusing on the information that is most relevant to the current goal. If 7- and 8-year-olds are shown objects from two different categories (e.g., several toy animals and several household items) and are told that they later will need to remember the objects in only one category (e.g., "You'll need to remember the animals"), they focus their attention on the objects in the specified category and remember more of them. In contrast, given the same instructions, 4-year-olds pay roughly equal attention to the objects in both categories, which reduces their memory for the objects they need to remember (DeMarie-Dreblow & Miller, 1988).

CONTENT KNOWLEDGE With age and experience, children's knowledge about almost everything increases. This increase in knowledge in long-term memory improves recall of new material by making it easier to integrate new material with existing understanding (Pressley & Hilden, 2006). The importance of content knowledge to memory is illustrated by the fact that when children know more about a topic than adults do, their memory for new information about the topic is often superior to the adults' memory. For example, when children and adults are provided new information about children's television programs and books, the children generally remember more of the information than do the adults (M. A. Lindberg, 1980, 1991). Similarly, children who know a lot about soccer learn more from reading new soccer stories than do other children who are both older and have higher IQs but who know less about soccer (Schneider, Körkel, & Weinert, 1989).

Prior content knowledge improves memory for new information in several different ways. One is by improving encoding. In tests of memory of various arrangements of chess pieces on a board, child chess experts remember far more than do adult novices. The reason is that the child experts' greater knowledge of chess leads to their encoding higher-level chunks of information that include the positions of several pieces relative to one another rather than encoding the location of each

rehearsal ■ The process of repeating information multiple times to aid memory of it.

selective attention ■ The process of intentionally focusing on the information that is most relevant to the current goal.

Through repeated visits to doctors' offices and through other experiences that occur in more or less fixed sequences, children gain content knowledge that improves their memory for subsequent, similar events.

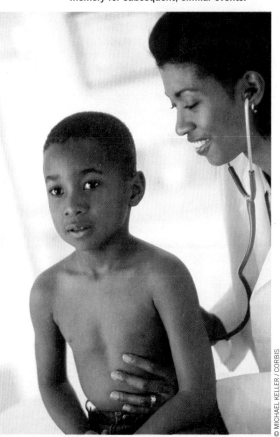

overlapping-waves theory ■ An information-processing approach that emphasizes the variability of children's thinking.

piece separately (Chi & Ceci, 1987). Content knowledge also improves memory by providing useful associations. A child who is knowledgeable about birds knows that type of beak and type of diet are associated, so remembering either one increases memory for the other (Johnson & Mervis, 1994). In addition, content knowledge indicates what is and is not possible and therefore guides memory in useful directions. For instance, when people familiar with baseball are asked to recall a particular inning of a game that they watched and they can remember only two outs in that inning, they recognize that there must have been a third out and search their memories for it; people who lack baseball knowledge do not (Spilich et al., 1979).

The Development of Problem Solving

As noted earlier, information-processing theories depict children as active problem solvers whose use of strategies often allows them to overcome limitations of knowledge and processing capacity. In this section, we present an information-processing perspective on the development of problem solving—the overlapping-waves theory.

Piaget's theory depicted children of a given age as using a particular strategy to solve a particular class of problems. For example, he described 5-year-olds as "solving" conservation-of-number problems (see Figure 4.6) by choosing the longer row of objects, and 7-year-olds as solving the same problems by reasoning that if nothing was added or subtracted, the number of objects must remain the same. According to **overlapping-waves theory,** however, children actually use a variety of approaches to solve this and other problems (Siegler, 1996). For instance, examining 5-year-olds' reasoning on repeated trials of the conservation-of-number problem reveals that most children use at least three different strategies (Siegler, 1995). The same child who on one trial incorrectly reasons that the longer row must have more objects will on other trials correctly reason that just spreading a row does not change the number of objects, and on yet other trials will count the number of objects in the two rows to see which has more.

Figure 4.10 presents the typical pattern of development envisioned by the overlapping-waves approach, with strategy 1 representing the simplest strategy, and strategy 5, the most advanced. At the youngest age depicted, children usually use strategy 1, but they sometimes use strategy 2 or 4. With age and experience, the strategies that produce more successful performances become more prevalent; new strategies are also generated and, if they are more effective than previous approaches, are used increasingly. Thus, by the middle of the age range in Figure 4.10, children have added strategies 3 and 5 to the original group and have almost stopped using strategy 1.

This model has been shown to accurately characterize children's problem solving in a wide range of contexts, including arithmetic, telling time, reading, spelling, scientific

FIGURE 4.10 The overlapping-waves model The overlapping-waves model proposes that, at any one age, children use multiple strategies; that with age and experience, they rely increasingly on more advanced strategies (the ones with the higher numbers); and that development involves changes in use of existing strategies as well as discovery of new approaches.

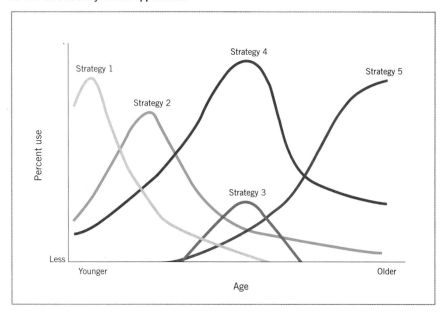

experimentation, biological understanding, tool use, and recall from memory (Chen & Siegler, 2000; Kuhn & Franklin, 2006; Lee & Karmiloff-Smith, 2002; Miller & Coyle, 1999).

The overlapping-waves approach specifies several ways in which problem solving improves over the course of development. Children discover new strategies that are more effective than their previous ones, they learn to execute both new and old strategies more efficiently, and they choose strategies that are more appropriate to the particular situation (Miller & Coyle, 1999; Siegler, 2006).

All these sources of cognitive growth are evident in learning addition. During kindergarten and the first few years of elementary school, children's knowledge of single-digit addition improves greatly. One reason is that children discover new strategies, such as counting-on (e.g., solving 2 + 9 by thinking "9, 10, 11"). Another source of improvement is faster and more accurate execution of all the strategies that children know (e.g., retrieval of answers from memory, counting from one, and counting-on). A third source of improvement is that children choose among strategies increasingly adaptively (e.g., using counting-on most often on problems with a large difference between the addends, such as 2 + 9, and counting from one on problems such as 7 + 8, which are difficult for them to solve correctly by using the other strategies they know) (Geary, 2006; Siegler, 1987; Siegler & Jenkins, 1989). (Box 4.2 illustrates how information-processing analyses can improve education.)

Planning Problem solving is often more successful if people plan before acting. Children benefit from planning how to get to friends' houses, how to get their way with parents, and how to break bad news to others in ways that are least likely to trigger angry reactions (Hudson, Sosa, & Schapiro, 1997). Despite the advantages of planning, however, children, and even adolescents, often fail to plan in situations in which it would help their problem solving (Berg et al., 1997). The question is why.

Information-processing analyses suggest that one reason planning is difficult for children is that it requires inhibiting the desire to solve the problem immediately in favour of first trying to construct the best strategy. Starting to work on an assigned paper without planning what will be written in the paper is one familiar example.

A second reason planning is difficult for young children is that they tend to be overly optimistic about their abilities and think that they can solve problems more effectively than their capabilities actually allow (Bjorklund, 1997; Schneider, 1998). This overconfidence can lead them to not plan, because they think they will succeed without doing so. Such over-optimism can lead young children to act rashly. For instance, 6-year-olds who overestimate their physical abilities have more accidents than do peers who evaluate their abilities more realistically, presumably because their confidence leads them not to plan how to avoid potential dangers (Plumert, 1995). Over time, maturation of the prefrontal cortex, a part of the brain that is especially important for planning, along with experiences that reduce over-optimism or demonstrate the value of planning, lead to increases in the frequency and quality of planning, which improves problem solving (Chalmers & Lawrence, 1993). The improvements in the planning process take a long time, however; even 12-year-olds leave less distance between themselves and oncoming vehicles than adults do (Plumert, Kearney, & Cremer, 2004).

Young children's over-optimism sometimes leads them to engage in dangerous activities. This particular plan worked out fine, but not all do.

BOX 4.2: applications

EDUCATIONAL APPLICATIONS OF INFORMATION-PROCESSING THEORIES

Children's knowledge of numbers when they begin kindergarten predicts their mathematics achievement years later—in elementary school, middle school, and even high school (Duncan et al., 2007; Stevenson & Newman, 1986). It is especially unfortunate, then, that kindergartners from low-income families lag far behind middle-income peers in counting, number recognition, arithmetic, and knowledge of numerical magnitudes (e.g., understanding that 7 is less than 9 and that both are closer to 10 than to 0 on a number line).

What might account for these early differences in numerical knowledge of children from different economic backgrounds? An information-processing analysis suggested that experience playing numerical board games such as Snakes and Ladders might be important. In Snakes and Ladders, players must move a token across 100 consecutively numbered squares, advancing on each of their turns by the number of spaces determined by a spinner. The higher the number of the square on which a child's token rests at any given point in the game, the greater the number of number names the child will have spoken and heard, the greater

the distance the child will have moved the token from the first square, the greater the time the child will have been playing the game, and the greater the number of discrete hand movements with the token the child will have made. These verbal, spatial, temporal, and kinesthetic cues provide a broadly based, multisensory foundation for knowledge of numerical magnitudes, a type of knowledge that is closely related to mathematics achievement test scores (Booth & Siegler, 2006, 2008; Geary, 2011).

Ramani and Siegler (2008) applied this information-processing analysis to improving the numerical understanding of low-income preschoolers. The researchers randomly assigned 4- and 5-year-olds from low-income families to either an experimental number-board condition or a control colour-board condition. The number-board condition was virtually identical to the first row of the Snakes and Ladders board; it included 10 squares numbered consecutively from left to right. On each turn, the child spun a spinner that yielded a "1" or a "2" and moved his or her token the corresponding number of squares on the board, stating the number on each square in the

process. For instance, if a player's token was on the square with the "4," and the player spun a "2," the player would say, "5, 6" while moving the token from the "4" to the "6." Children in the colour-board condition played the same game, except that their board had no numbers and the players would say the name of the colour of each square as they advanced their token. Children in both conditions were given a pretest that examined their knowledge of numbers before playing the game, and then played the game for four 15-minute sessions over a 2-week period. At the end of the fourth session, the children were given a posttest on their knowledge of numbers; 9 weeks later, they were given a follow-up test identical to the pretest and posttest.

On the posttest, children who played the number board game showed improved knowledge of the numbers 1 through 10 on all four tasks that were presented—counting, reading of numbers, magnitude comparisons (e.g., "Which is bigger, 8 or 3?"), and estimates of the locations of numbers on a number line. Significantly, all the gains were maintained on the follow-up test 9 weeks later. In contrast, children who played the colour board game showed no improvement in any aspect of number knowledge. Moreover, children's reports of how often they played Snakes and Ladders and other board games at home was positively correlated with their initial knowledge on all four numerical tasks, and middle-income children reported playing numerical board games (though not video games) much more often than children from low-income backgrounds.

Subsequent studies demonstrated that playing the 1–10 board game also improves preschoolers' ability to learn the answers to arithmetic problems, such as that 2 + 4 = 6 (Siegler & Ramani, 2009). Taken together, the evidence suggests that numerical board games represent a quick, effective, and inexpensive means of improving the numerical knowledge of low-income children before they start school.

ROBERT SIEGLER

Playing this number board game improves preschoolers' numerical knowledge.

review:

Information-processing theories envision children as active learners and problem solvers who continuously devise means for overcoming their processing limits and reaching their goals. The capacity and processing speed of working memory and long-term memory influence all information processing. Executive functioning uses information in working memory and long-term memory to flexibly shift goals and inhibit impulses to behave in ways that are inappropriate in the situation; it also updates the contents of working memory so that new goals can be pursued effectively. Cognitive growth in general, and development of memory and learning in particular, are seen as involving increasingly efficient execution of basic processes, construction of more effective strategies, and acquisition of new content knowledge. Overlapping-waves theory indicates that individual children use multiple strategies to solve the same type of problem, that children choose adaptively among these strategies, and that problem solving improves through the discovery of more effective strategies, more efficient execution of the strategies, better choices of when to use the strategies, and improved planning.

sociocultural theories ■ Approaches that emphasize that other people and the surrounding culture contribute greatly to children's development.

guided participation ■ A process in which more knowledgeable individuals organize activities in ways that allow less knowledgeable people to learn.

Sociocultural Theories

A mother and her 4-year-old daughter, Sadie, assemble a toy, using a diagram to guide them:

> *Mother:* Now you need another one like this on the other side. Mmmmm … there you go, just like that.
>
> *Sadie:* Then I need this one to go like this? Hold on, hold on. Let it go. There. Get that out. Oops.
>
> *M:* I'll hold it while you turn it. *(Watches Sadie work on toy.)* Now you make the end.
>
> *S:* This one?
>
> *M:* No, look at the picture. Right here *(points to diagram)*. That piece.
>
> *S:* Like this?
>
> *M:* Yeah.
>
> (Gauvain, 2001, p. 32)

This interaction probably strikes you as completely unexceptional—and it is. From the perspective of **sociocultural theories,** however, it and thousands of other everyday interactions like it are of the utmost importance, because they are the engines of development.

One noteworthy characteristic of the event, from the sociocultural perspective, is that Sadie is learning to assemble the toy in an interpersonal context. Sociocultural theorists emphasize that much of cognitive development takes place through direct interactions between children and other people—parents, siblings, teachers, playmates, and so on—who want to help children acquire the skills and knowledge valued by their culture. Thus, whereas Piagetian and information-processing theories emphasize children's own efforts to understand the world, sociocultural theories emphasize the developmental importance of children's interactions with other people.

The interaction between Sadie and her mother is also noteworthy because it exemplifies **guided participation,** a process in which more knowledgeable individuals organize activities in ways that allow less knowledgeable people to engage in them at a higher level than they

Through guided participation, parents can help children not only accomplish immediate goals but also learn skills, such as how to use written instructions and diagrams to assemble objects.

cultural tools ■ The innumerable products of human ingenuity that enhance thinking.

could manage on their own (Rogoff, 2003). Sadie's mother, for example, holds one part of the toy so that Sadie can screw in another part. On her own, Sadie would be unable to screw the two parts together and therefore could not improve her skill at the task. Similarly, Sadie's mother points to the relevant part of the diagram, enabling Sadie to decide what to do next and also to learn how diagrams convey information. As this episode illustrates, guided participation often occurs in situations in which the explicit purpose is to achieve a practical goal, such as assembling a toy, but in which learning occurs as a by-product of the goal-directed activity.

A third noteworthy characteristic of the interaction between Sadie and her mother is that it occurs in a broader cultural context. This context includes not only other people but also the innumerable products of human ingenuity that sociocultural theorists refer to as **cultural tools**: symbol systems, artifacts, skills, values, and so on. In the example of Sadie and her mother, the relevant symbol systems include the language they use to convey their thoughts and the diagram they use to guide their assembly efforts; the relevant artifacts include the toy and the printed sheet on which the diagram appears; the relevant skills include the proficiency in language that allows them to communicate with each other and the procedures they use to interpret the diagram; and the values include the culture's approval of parents interacting with their children in the way that Sadie's mother does and of young girls' learning mechanical skills. In the background are an array of broader technological, economic, and historical factors: the technology needed to manufacture toys and print diagrams, for example; an economy that allows parents the leisure time for such interactions; and a history leading up to the symbol systems, artifacts, skills, and values reflected in the interactions between Sadie and her mother. Thus, sociocultural theories can help us appreciate the many aspects of culture embodied in even the smallest everyday interactions.

View of Children's Nature

The giant of the sociocultural approach to cognitive development, and in many ways its originator, was the Russian psychologist Lev Semyonovich Vygotsky. Although Vygotsky and Piaget were contemporaries, much of Vygotsky's most important work was largely unknown outside Russia until the 1970s. Its appearance created a stir, in part because Vygotsky's view of children's nature was so different from Piaget's.

Vygotsky's Theory

As noted earlier, Piaget depicted children as little scientists, trying to understand the world on their own. Vygotsky, in contrast, portrayed them as social learners, intertwined with other people who are eager to help them gain skills and understanding. Whereas Piaget viewed children as intent on mastering physical, mathematical, and logical concepts that are the same in all times and places, Vygotsky viewed them as intent on participating in activities that happen to be prevalent in their local setting. Whereas Piaget emphasized qualitative changes in thinking, Vygotsky emphasized continuous, quantitative changes. These Vygotskian views gave rise to the central metaphor of sociocultural theories: children as social learners, shaped by, and shaping, their cultural contexts.

Vygotsky's emphasis on children as social learners is evident in his perspective on the relation between language and thought. Whereas Piaget viewed the two as

The Russian psychologist Lev Vygotsky, the founder of the sociocultural approach to child development.

largely unrelated, Vygotsky (1934/1962) viewed them as integrally related. In particular, he believed that thought is internalized speech and that thought originates in large part in statements that parents and other adults make to children.

To illustrate the process of internalizing speech, Vygotsky described three phases of its role in the development of children's ability to regulate their own behaviour and problem solving. At first, children's behaviour is controlled by other people's statements (as in the example of Sadie and her mother assembling the toy); then, children's behaviour is controlled by their own **private speech,** in which they tell themselves aloud what to do, much as their parents might have done earlier; and then, their behaviour is controlled by internalized private speech (thought), in which they silently tell themselves what to do. The transition between the second and third phases often involves whispers or silent lip movements; in Vygotsky's terms, the speech "goes underground" and becomes thought. Private speech is most prevalent between ages 4 and 6 years, although older children and adults also use it on challenging tasks, such as assembling model airplanes or following complex directions (Winsler et al., 2003). In addition, the progression from external to internalized speech emerges not only with age but also with experience; children generate a considerable amount of overt private speech when they first encounter a challenging task, but the amount lessens as they master it (Berk, 1994).

Children as Teachers and Learners

Contemporary sociocultural theorists, such as Michael Tomasello (2001, 2009), have extended Vygotsky's insights. Tomasello proposed that the human species has two unique characteristics that are crucial to the ability to create complex, rapidly changing cultures. One of these is the inclination to teach others of the species; the other is the inclination to attend to and learn from such teaching. In every human society, adults communicate facts, skills, values, and traditions to their young. This is what makes culture possible; as Isaac Newton noted, it enables the new generation to stand on the shoulders of the old and thus to see farther. The inclination to teach emerges very early: all typically developing 2-year-olds spontaneously point to and name objects to call other people's attention to what they themselves find interesting. Only humans engage in such rudimentary teaching behaviours that are not directly tied to survival. This inclination to teach and to learn from teaching is what enables children to be socialized into their culture and to pass that culture on to others.

Children as Products of Their Culture

Sociocultural theorists believe that many of the *processes* that produce development, such as guided participation, are the same in all societies. However, the *content* that children learn—the particular symbol systems, artifacts, skills, and values—vary greatly from culture to culture and shape thinking accordingly.

One example of the impact of culturally specific content comes from a study of analogical reasoning, a process in which experience with previously

The inclination to teach and the ability to learn from teaching are among the most distinctly human characteristics.

GALLO IMAGES / DANITA DELIMONT / GETTY IMAGES

As illustrated by this photo of an East Asian father teaching his children to use an abacus, the tools available in a culture shape the learning of children within that culture.

ARIEL SKELLEY / CORBIS

encountered problems is applied to new problems. In the study (Chen, Mo, & Honomichl, 2004), American and Chinese college students were asked to solve two problems. One problem required a solution analogous to the strategy of leaving a trail of white pebbles to follow home from the woods in "Hansel and Gretel," a tale well known to the American students but unknown to the Chinese. The American students were far more successful in solving that problem, and many of them alluded to the fairy tale even though they had not heard it in many years. The other problem required a solution analogous to that in a fairy tale that was well known to the Chinese students but unknown to the Americans. In this case, the Chinese students were vastly superior in solving the problem, and many alluded to the relevant fairy tale.

Children's memories of their own experiences also reflect their culture. When 4- to 8-year-olds from China and the United States were asked to describe their earliest memories, their descriptions differed in ways that reflected their culture's attitudes and values (Wang, 2007). Chinese culture prizes and promotes interdependence among people, especially among close relatives. European-American culture, in contrast, prizes and promotes the independence of individuals. Consistent with these cultural emphases, the Chinese children's reports of their earliest memories included more references to other people than did those of American children, and the American children's reports included more references to the child's own feelings and reactions. Thus, the attitudes and values of a culture, as well as its artifacts and technologies, shape the thoughts and memories of people in that culture.

Central Developmental Issues

Vygotsky and contemporary sociocultural theorists have proposed a number of specific ideas about *how change occurs* through social interaction. One of these ideas—guided participation—has already been discussed. In this section, we examine two related concepts that play prominent roles in sociocultural analyses of change: *intersubjectivity* and *social scaffolding*.

Intersubjectivity

Sociocultural theorists believe that the foundation of human cognitive development is our ability to establish **intersubjectivity,** the mutual understanding that people share during communication (Gauvain, 2001; Rommetveit, 1985). The idea behind this imposing term is both simple and profound: effective communication requires participants to focus on the same topic, and also on one another's reaction to whatever is being communicated. Such a "meeting of the minds" is indispensable for effective teaching and learning.

The roots of intersubjectivity are evident early in infancy. By age 6 months, infants can learn novel behaviours by observing another person's behaviour, which requires attending to the same actions as the person executing the actions (Collie & Hayne, 1999).

This and related developments in early infancy set the stage for the emergence of a process that is at the heart of intersubjectivity—**joint attention.** In this process, infants and their social partners intentionally focus on a common referent in the external environment. The emergence of joint attention is evident in numerous ways. Around their first birthday, infants increasingly look toward objects that are the targets of their social partner's gaze, even if the partner is not acting on the objects, and actively direct a partner's attention toward objects that they themselves find interesting (Adamson, Bakeman, & Deckner, 2004; Akhtar & Gernsbacher, 2008; Moore, 2008).

Joint attention greatly increases children's ability to learn from other people. One important example involves language learning. When an adult tells a toddler the name of an object, the adult usually looks or points directly at it; children who are looking at the same object are in a better position to learn what the word means than ones who are not (Baldwin, 1991). Indeed, the degree of success infants have in following other people's gaze predicts their later vocabulary development (Brooks & Meltzoff, 2008) and their subsequent language development more generally (Carpenter, Nagell, & Tomasello, 1998).

Intersubjectivity continues to develop well beyond infancy, as children become increasingly able to take the perspectives of other people. For example, 4-year-olds are more likely than 3-year-olds to reach agreement with peers on the rules of a game they are about to play and the roles that each child will assume in the game (Göncü, 1993). The continuing development of such perspective-taking abilities also leads to school-age children's increasing ability to teach and learn from one another (Gauvain, 2001).

Social Scaffolding

When putting up tall buildings, construction workers use metal frameworks called scaffolds, which allow them to work high above the ground. Once a building's main structure is in place, it can support further work on its own, thus allowing the scaffolding to be removed. In an analogous fashion, children's learning is aided by **social scaffolding,** in which more competent people provide a temporary framework that supports children's thinking at a higher level than children could manage on their own (Wood, Bruner, & Ross, 1976). Ideally, supplying this framework

Joint attention, the process through which social partners focus on the same external object, underlies the human capacity to teach and to learn from teaching.

intersubjectivity ■ The mutual understanding that people share during communication.

joint attention ■ A process in which social partners intentionally focus on a common referent in the external environment.

social scaffolding ■ A process in which more competent people provide a temporary framework that supports children's thinking at a higher level than children could manage on their own.

© SIMON MARCUS / CORBIS

By providing their children with social scaffolding, parents enable them to play with toys and other objects in more advanced ways than would otherwise be possible, which helps the children learn.

includes explaining the goal of the task, demonstrating how the task can be done, and helping the child with the most difficult parts of the task. This, in fact, is the way parents tend to teach their children (Pratt et al., 1988; Saxe, Guberman, & Gearhart, 1987; Wood, 1986).

Through the process of social scaffolding, children become capable of working at a higher level than if they had not received such help. At first, this higher-level functioning requires extensive support, then it requires less and less support, and eventually it becomes possible without any support. The higher the quality of the scaffolding—that is, the more that instructional efforts are directed at the upper end of the child's capabilities—the greater the learning (Conner, Knight, & Cross, 1997; Gauvain, 2001). The goal of social scaffolding—to allow children to learn by doing—is the same as that of guided participation, but scaffolding tends to involve more explicit instruction and explanation, whereas guided participation tends to involve adults' organizing tasks so that children can take increasingly active and responsible roles in them.

One particularly important way in which parents use scaffolding is in helping children form **autobiographical memories,** that is, explicit memories of events that took place at specific times and places in the individual's past (Nelson & Fivush, 2004). Autobiographical memories include information about one's goals, intentions, emotions, and reactions relative to these events. Over time, these memories become strung together into a more or less coherent narrative about one's life.

When discussing past experiences with their young children, some mothers encourage them to provide many details about past events and often expand on the children's statements. Such a mother might reply to her toddler's statement "Bird fly away" by saying, "Yes, the bird flew away because you got close to it and scared it." Such statements help children remember their experiences by improving their encoding of key information (distance from the bird) and their appreciation of the causal relations among events (Boland, Haden, & Ornstein, 2003; McGuigan & Salmon, 2004). Other mothers ask fewer questions and rarely elaborate on what their children say. Children whose mothers use the more elaborative style remember more about the events than do children whose mothers rarely elaborate (Haden, Haine, & Fivush, 1997; Harley & Reese, 1999; Leichtman et al., 2000). (As discussed in Box 4.3, concepts from sociocultural theories have also proved useful for improving education in classrooms.)

review:

Sociocultural approaches view children as social learners, shaped by, and shaping, their cultural contexts. These approaches emphasize that children develop in a cultural context of other people and human inventions, such as symbol systems, artifacts, skills, and values. Through guided participation, more knowledgeable people help children gain skills in using these cultural tools; children's use of the tools, in turn, further transforms their thinking. Culture is made possible by the human propensity to teach and learn and to establish intersubjectivity with other people. Through processes such as social scaffolding and the creation of communities of learners, older and more skilled individuals help children acquire the skills, knowledge, and values of their culture.

autobiographical memories ■ Memories of one's own experiences, including one's thoughts and emotions.

BOX 4.3: applications

EDUCATIONAL APPLICATIONS OF SOCIOCULTURAL THEORIES

For some time, the educational system in North America has been criticized for promoting rote memorization of facts rather than deep understanding; for promoting competition rather than cooperation among students; and for generally failing to create enthusiasm for learning (National Association for the Education of Young Children, 2011; Pellegrino, Chudowsky, & Glaser, 2001). The emphasis of sociocultural theories on the role of culture in learning implies that one way to improve schooling is to change the culture of schools. The culture should be one in which instruction is aimed at helping children gain deep understanding, in which learning is a cooperative activity, and in which learning a little makes children want to learn more.

One impressive attempt to meet these goals is Ann Brown's (1997) *community-of-learners* program. Its efforts to build communities of learners have focused on 6- to 12-year-olds, most of them African-American children attending inner-city schools in Boston, Massachusetts, and Oakland, California. The main curriculum consists of projects that require research on some large topic, such as interdependence between animals and their habitats. The class divides into small groups, each of which focuses on a particular aspect of the topic. With the topic of the interdependence between animals and habitats, for example, one group might study predator–prey relations; another, reproductive strategies; another, protection from the elements; and so on.

At the end of roughly 10 weeks, new groups are formed, each including one child from every original group. Children in the new groups are asked to solve a problem that encompasses all the aspects studied by the previous groups, such as designing an "animal of the future" that would be particularly well adapted to its habitat. Because each child's participation in the previous group has resulted in the child's gaining expertise on the aspect of the problem studied by that group, and because no other child in the new group has that expertise, all of the children's contributions are essential for the new group to succeed. Aronson (1978) labelled this technique the *jigsaw approach*, because, as in a jigsaw puzzle, each piece is necessary for the solution.

A variety of people help foster such communities of learners. Classroom teachers introduce the big ideas of the unit, encourage children to pool their knowledge to achieve deeper understanding, push them to provide evidence for their opinions, and ask them to summarize what they know and to identify new learning goals. Outside experts are at times brought to classrooms to lecture and answer questions about the topic. Children at other schools, who are working on the same problem, are contacted via email to see how they are approaching issues that arise.

Communities of learners provide both cognitive and motivational benefits for children. Participation in such groups helps children become increasingly adept at constructing high-quality solutions to the problems they try to solve. It also helps them learn such general skills as identifying key questions and comparing alternative solutions to a problem. Finally, because the children all depend on one another's contributions, the community-of-learners approach encourages mutual respect and individual responsibility for the success of the entire group. In short, the approach creates a culture of learning.

Community-of-learners programs are used in Canadian schools. Drawing heavily on both discovery-based learning approaches as well as more didactic teaching, teachers are facilitators or guides for children's learning. This approach puts the onus on the guides or teachers to regularly check students' understanding and readiness to learn, as well as to model, foster, and guide the discovery process (Brown & Campione, 1994).

LWA / DANN TARDIF / BLEND IMAGES / GETTY IMAGES

dynamic-systems theories ■ A class of theories that focus on how change occurs over time in complex systems.

Dynamic-Systems Theories

Like all biological processes, thinking serves an adaptive purpose: it enables people and other animals to devise plans for attaining goals. However, attaining goals also requires the ability to take effective action; without this ability, thinking would be pointless. For instance, what purpose would planning serve for an organism that could not implement the plans through action (see Figure 4.11)? Despite this inherent connection between thinking and acting, however, most theories of cognitive development have ignored the development of the skilled actions that allow children to realize the fruits of their mental labour.

One increasingly influential exception to this generalization is **dynamic-systems theories,** a class of theories that focuses on how change occurs over time in complex systems. Research that reflects the dynamic-systems perspective indicates that detailed analyses of the development of infants' basic actions, such as crawling, walking, reaching, and grasping, yield surprising and impressive insights into how development occurs. For example, dynamic-systems research has shown that improved reaching allows infants to play with objects in more advanced ways, such as organizing them into categories or interesting configurations (Spencer et al., 2006; Thelen & Corbetta, 1994). Dynamic-systems research also has shown that the onset of crawling changes infants' relationships with family members, who may be thrilled to see their baby attain an important motor milestone but also find themselves having to be much more watchful and controlling to avoid harm to the child and to the objects in the child's path (Campos, Kermoian, & Zumbahlen, 1992).

Another contribution of dynamic-systems research has been to demonstrate that the development of seemingly simple actions is far more complex and interesting than previously realized. For instance, such research has overturned the traditional belief that physical maturation leads infants to attain motor milestones in stages, at roughly the same age, in the same way, and in a steady progression. It has shown instead that individual children acquire skills at different ages and in different ways, and that their development entails regressions as well as progress (Adolph & Berger, 2011). One example of this type of research is a longitudinal study of the development of infants' reaching conducted by Esther Thelen,

FIGURE 4.11 Problem solving often requires motor skills A major insight of dynamic-systems theories is that thinking would be pointless without motor capabilities. In these photos, a 9-month-old surveys the barrier in the way of her desired toy (left frame). She then contorts her body, reaching under the barrier to retrieve the toy (right frame). If the infant lacked the motor ability to twist her body and reach her arm under the chair, her problem-solving processes would have been fruitless.

BOTH: MYRLEEN PEARSON / PHOTO EDIT

who, along with her colleague Linda Smith, was the co-founder of the dynamic-systems approach to cognitive development. In this particular study, Thelen and colleagues (1993) repeatedly observed the reaching efforts of four infants during their first year. Using high-speed motion-capture systems and computer analysis of the infants' muscle movements, they found that because of individual differences in such factors as the infants' physiology, activity level, arousal, motivation, and experience, each child faced different challenges in his or her attempts to master reaching. The following observations illustrate some of the complexities these researchers discovered, including variability in the ages at which infants reach developmental milestones, their patterns of change, and the differing challenges they must overcome:

> Infants differed dramatically in the ages of the transition (from no reaching to reaching). Whereas Nathan reached first at 12 weeks, Hannah and Justin did not attain this milestone until 20 weeks of age. [In addition,] the infants showed periods of rapid change, plateaus, and even regressions in performance. ... There was in Nathan, Justin, and Hannah a rather discontinuous shift to better, less variable performance. ... Gabriel's transition to stability was more gradual.
>
> (Thelen & Smith, 1998, pp. 605, 607)

> Infants must individually discover the appropriate [reaching] speeds from the background of their characteristic styles. Gabriel, for example, had to damp down his very vigorous movements in order to successfully reach, and he did. In contrast, Hannah, who moved slowly and spent considerable time with her hands flexed near her face, had to activate her arms more to extend them out in front of her. ... Reaching is thus sculpted from ongoing movements of the arms, through a process of modulating what is in place. ... As infants become older, their attention becomes more focused, and their perceptual discrimination improves, and their memories get better, and their movements become more skilled. A rich, complex, and realistic account of change must include this dynamic interplay.
>
> (Thelen, 2001, pp. 172, 182)

These descriptions help convey what is meant by the label "dynamic systems." As suggested by the term *dynamic*, dynamic-systems theories depict development as a process in which change is the only constant. Whereas some approaches to cognitive development hypothesize that development entails long periods of relatively stable stages or ways of thinking separated by relatively brief transition periods, dynamic-systems theories propose that at all points in development, thought and action change from moment to moment in response to the current situation, the child's immediate past history, and the child's longer-term history of actions in related situations. Thus, Thelen and Smith (1998) noted that the development of reaching included regressions as well as improvements, and Thelen (2001) described how differences in Hannah's and Gabriel's early reaches influenced their later paths to skilled reaching.

As suggested by the second term in the label, dynamic-systems theories depict each child as a well-integrated system, in which many subsystems—perception, action, attention, memory, language, social interaction, and so on—work together to determine behaviour. For instance, success on tasks viewed as measures of conceptual understanding, such as object permanence, is influenced by perception, attention, motor skills, and a host of other factors (Smith et al., 1999). The assumptions that development is dynamic and that it functions as an organized system are central to the theory's perspective on children's nature.

View of Children's Nature

Dynamic-systems theories are the newest of the four types of theories discussed in this chapter, and their view of children's nature incorporates influences from each of the others. Like Piaget's theory, dynamic-systems theories emphasize children's innate motivation to explore the environment; like information-processing theories, they emphasize precise analyses of problem-solving activity; and like sociocultural theories, they emphasize the formative influence of other people. These similarities to other theories, as well as the differences from them, are evident in dynamic-systems theories' emphasis on motivation and the role of action.

Motivators of Development

To a greater extent than any of the other theories except Piaget's, dynamic-systems theories emphasize that from infancy onward, children are strongly motivated to learn about the world around them and to explore and expand their own capabilities (von Hofsten, 2007). This motivation to explore and learn is clearly apparent in the fact that children persist in practising new skills even when they possess well-practised skills that are more efficient. Thus, toddlers persist in their first unsteady efforts to walk, despite the fact that crawling would get them where they want to go more quickly and without the risk of falling (Adolph & Berger, 2011).

© KLAUS LIBERTUS

Reaching with Velcro-covered mittens for Velcro-covered objects improved infants' later ability to grab and explore ordinary objects without the mittens.

Like sociocultural approaches, but unlike Piagetian theory, dynamic-systems theories emphasize infants' interest in the social world as a crucial motivator of development. As noted in our discussion of the *active child* in Chapter 1, even newborns prefer attending to the sounds, movements, and features of the human face over almost any alternative stimuli. By 10 to 12 months of age, infants' interest in the social world is readily apparent in the emergence of intersubjectivity (page 159), as infants look to where the people interacting with them are looking and direct the attention of others to things they themselves find interesting (Deák, Flom, & Pick, 2000; von Hofsten, Dahlström, & Fredricksson, 2005). Dynamic-systems theorists have emphasized that observing other people, imitating their actions, and attracting their attention are all potent motivators of development (Fischer & Bidell, 2006; von Hofsten, 2007).

The Centrality of Action

Dynamic-systems theories are unique in their pervasive emphasis on how children's specific actions shape their development. Piaget's theory asserts the role of actions during infancy, but dynamic-systems theories emphasize that actions contribute to development throughout life. This focus on the developmental role of action has led to a number of interesting discoveries. For example, infants' own reaching for objects helps them infer the goals of other people's reaches; infants who can skilfully reach are more likely to look at the probable target of another person's reaching just after the other person's reach begins (von Hofsten, 2007). Another example of infants' learning from actions comes from research in which infants were outfitted with Velcro mittens that enabled them to "grab" and explore Velcro-covered objects that they otherwise could not have picked up. After 2 weeks of grabbing the Velcro-covered objects with the Velcro-covered mittens, infants showed greater ability to grab and explore ordinary objects without the mittens than did other infants of the same ages (Needham, Barrett, & Peterman, 2002).

The ways in which children's actions shape their development extend well beyond reaching and grasping in infancy. Actions influence categorization: in one study, encouraging children to move an object up and down led to their categorizing it as one of a group of objects that were easiest to move in that way, whereas encouraging children to move the same object from side to side led them to categorize it as one of a group of objects that were easiest to move in that way (Smith, 2005). Actions also affect vocabulary acquisition and generalization (Gershkoff-Stowe, Connell, & Smith, 2006; Samuelson & Horst, 2008): for example, experimental manipulations that lead children to state an incorrect name for an object impair the child's future attempts to learn the object's correct name. In addition, actions shape memory, as demonstrated by research in which children's past attempts to locate and dig up objects they had earlier seen being hidden in a sandbox altered their recall of the objects' new location after they had seen them being re-hidden. That is, the child's new searches tend to be in between the past and present locations, as if the new searches involved a compromise between memories of the new hiding place and of the location where he or she had originally looked (Schutte, Spencer, & Schöner, 2003; Zelazo, Reznick, & Spinazzola, 1998). Thus, just as thinking shapes actions, actions shape thinking.

Central Development Issues

Two developmental issues that are especially prominent in dynamic-systems theories are how the cognitive system organizes itself and how it changes.

Self-Organization

Dynamic-systems theories view development as a process of self-organization that involves bringing together and integrating attention, memory, emotions, and actions as needed to adapt to a continuously changing environment (Spencer et al., 2006). The organizational process is sometimes called *soft assembly*, because the components and their organization change from moment to moment and situation to situation, rather than being governed by rigid stages that are consistently applied across time and situations.

The types of research to which this perspective leads are illustrated particularly well by certain studies of the A-not-B error that 8- to 12-month-olds typically make in Piaget's classic object-permanence task. As noted earlier, this error involves infants' searching for a toy where they had previously found it (location A), rather than where they last saw it being hidden (location B). Piaget (1954) explained the A-not-B error by hypothesizing that before their 1st birthday, infants lack a clear concept of the permanent existence of objects.

In contrast, viewing the A-not-B error from a dynamic-systems perspective suggested that many factors other than conceptual understanding influence performance on the object-permanence task. In particular, Smith and colleagues (1999) argued that infants' previous reaching toward location A produces a habit of reaching there, which influences their behaviour when the object is subsequently hidden at location B. On the basis of this premise, the researchers made several predictions that were later borne out. One was that the more often infants had found an object by reaching to one location, the more likely they would be to reach there again when the object was hidden at a different location. Also supported was the prediction that increasing the memory demands of the task by not allowing infants to search for the object for 3 seconds after it was hidden at the B location would increase the likelihood of infants' reaching to location A (Clearfield et al., 2009). The reasoning here was that the strength of the new memory would fade rapidly relative to the fading of the habit of reaching to the previous hiding place. The dynamic-systems perspective also suggested that infants' attention would influence their object-permanence performance. Consistent with this view, manipulating infants' attention by tapping one of the locations just as the infants were about to reach usually resulted in their reaching to the tapped location, regardless of where the object was actually hidden.

In perhaps the most striking test of such predictions, researchers demonstrated that putting small weights on infants' wrists after the infants had reached to location A but before the object was hidden at location B improved object-permanence performance (Diedrich et al., 2000). The researchers had reasoned that the addition of the wrist weights would require the infants to use different muscle tensions and forces than they had previously used to reach for the object and consequently would disrupt the infants' habit of reaching to location A. Thus, rather than providing a pure measure of conceptual understanding, infants' performance on the object-permanence task appears to reflect the combined influence of the strength of the habit of reaching to location A, the memory demands of the current task, the infant's current focus of attention, and the match between the muscular forces required to reach in the old and new situations.

How Change Occurs

Dynamic-systems theories posit that changes occur through mechanisms of variation and selection that are analogous to those that produce biological evolution (Fischer & Bidell, 2006; Steenbeek & Van Geert, 2008). In this context, *variation* refers to the use of different behaviours to pursue the same goal. For instance, to descend a ramp, a toddler will sometimes walk, sometimes crawl, sometimes do a belly slide, sometimes do a sitting slide feet first, and so on (Adolph, 1997; Adolph & Berger, 2011). *Selection* involves increasingly frequent choice of behaviours that are effective in meeting goals and decreasing reliance on less effective behaviours. For example, when children first learn to walk, they are too optimistic about being able to walk down ramps, and often fall, but when they gain a few more months of walking experience, they more accurately judge the steepness of ramps and whether they can descend them while remaining upright.

Children's selection among alternative approaches reflects several influences. Most important is the *relative success* of each approach in meeting a particular goal: as children gain experience, they increasingly rely on approaches that produce desired outcomes. Another important consideration is *efficiency:* children increasingly choose approaches that meet goals more quickly or with less effort than do other approaches. A third consideration is *novelty,* the lure and challenge of trying something new. Children sometimes choose new approaches that are no more efficient, or even less efficient, than an established alternative but that have the potential to become more efficient. For instance, when they first learn the memory strategy of rehearsal, it does not improve their memory, but they use

BOX 4.4: applications

EDUCATIONAL APPLICATIONS OF DYNAMIC-SYSTEMS THEORIES

As noted in Chapter 2, children born prematurely with low birth weight are more likely than other children to encounter developmental difficulties, among them slower emergence and refinement of reaching (Fallang et al., 2003). These delays in reaching slow the development of brain areas involved in reaching (Martin et al., 2004), limiting infants' ability to explore and learn about objects (Lobo, Galloway, & Savelsbergh, 2004). A variety of seemingly reasonable efforts to improve preterm infants' reaching, such as guiding their arms through reaching movements, have yielded discouraging results (Blauw-Hospers & Hadders-Algra, 2005).

In contrast, a recent intervention based on dynamic-systems research was quite successful. This intervention, designed by Heathcock, Lobo, and Galloway (2008), was inspired by two findings we have discussed: (1) the finding by Thelen and colleagues (1993) that some infants' slowness to initiate arm activity impedes their development

of reaching, and (2) the finding by Needham and colleagues (2002) that providing young infants with experience in reaching for and grabbing Velcro-patched objects while wearing Velcro-covered mittens improves the infants' later ability to reach for and grab ordinary objects bare-handed.

Heathcock, Lobo, and Galloway began their intervention by requesting that caregivers of preterm infants in an experimental group provide the infants with special movement experiences. Specifically, they asked the caregivers to encourage infants' arm movements by (1) tying a bell to the infants' wrists so that arm movements would make it ring, presumably motivating further movements, and (2) placing Velcro mittens on the infants' hands to allow them to reach for and grab Velcro-patched toys held in front of them. The caregivers were asked to do this at home 5 times per week for 8 weeks.

Caregivers of preterm infants in a control group were asked to provide their infants

with special social experiences that included singing to and talking with the infants on the same intervention schedule as that of children in the experimental group. Periodically, the infants in both groups were brought to the lab to allow project personnel to observe their reaching and exploration under controlled circumstances and during free play.

As might be expected, the reaching of preterm infants in both groups improved over the 8 weeks of the study. However, the infants in the experimental group improved to a greater degree. They more often touched toys that were held in front of them, and more often did so with the inside rather than the outside part of their hand, as is needed for grasping objects. Such interventions may also help preterm infants avoid other types of cognitive and motor impairments that are partially caused by delayed development of reaching.

it anyway, and eventually it does improve their recall of rehearsed information (Miller & Seier, 1994). Such a novelty preference tends to be adaptive, because with practice, a strategy that is initially less efficient than existing approaches often becomes more efficient (Wittmann et al., 2008). As discussed in Box 4.4, the insights of dynamic-systems theories have led to useful applications as well as theoretical progress.

review:

Dynamic-systems theories view children as ever-changing, well-integrated organisms that combine perception, action, attention, memory, language, and social influences to produce actions that satisfy goals. From this perspective, children's actions are shaped by both their remote and recent history, their current physical capabilities, and their immediate physical and social environment. The actions, in turn, are viewed as shaping the development of categorization, conceptual understanding, memory, language, and other capabilities. Dynamic-systems theories are unique in their emphasis on how children's actions shape their development, as well as in the range of developmental influences they consider with regard to particular capabilities.

chapter summary:

Theories of development are important because they provide a framework for understanding important phenomena, raise major issues regarding human nature, and motivate new research. Four major theories of cognitive development are Piagetian, information-processing, sociocultural, and dynamic-systems.

Piaget's Theory

■ Among the reasons for the longevity of Piaget's theory are that it vividly conveys the flavour of children's thinking at different ages, extends across a broad range of ages and content areas, and provides many fascinating and surprising observations of children's thinking.

■ Piaget's theory is often labelled "constructivist," because it depicts children as actively constructing knowledge for themselves in response to their experience. The theory posits that children learn through two processes that are present from birth—assimilation and accommodation—and that the contribution of these processes is balanced through a third process, equilibration. These processes produce continuities across development.

■ Piaget's theory divides cognitive development into four broad stages: the sensorimotor stage (birth to age 2), the preoperational stage (ages 2 to 7), the concrete operational stage (ages 7 to 12), and the formal operational stage (age 12 and beyond). These stages reflect discontinuities in development.

■ In the sensorimotor stage, infants' intelligence is expressed primarily through motor interactions with the environment. During this period, infants gain understanding of concepts such as object permanence and become capable of deferred imitation.

■ In the preoperational stage, children become able to represent their experiences in language, mental imagery, and thought, but because of cognitive limitations such as egocentrism and centration, they have difficulty solving many problems, including Piaget's various tests of conservation and tasks related to taking the perspective of others.

■ In the concrete operational stage, children become able to reason logically about concrete objects and events but have difficulty reasoning in purely abstract terms and in succeeding on tasks requiring hypothetical thinking, such as the pendulum problem.

■ In the formal operational stage, children gain the cognitive capabilities of hypothetical thinking.

■ Four weaknesses of Piaget's theory are that it depicts children's thinking as being more consistent than it is, underestimates infants' and young children's cognitive competence, understates the contribution of the social world to cognitive development, and only vaguely describes the mechanisms that give rise to thinking and cognitive growth.

Information-Processing Theories

■ Information-processing theories focus on the specific mental processes that underlie children's thinking. Even in infancy, children are seen as actively pursuing goals, encountering processing limits, and devising strategies that allow them to surmount the processing limits and attain the goals.

■ The memory system includes working memory, long-term memory, and executive functioning.

■ Working memory is a system for actively attending to, gathering, maintaining, storing, and processing information.

■ Long-term memory is the enduring knowledge accumulated over a lifetime.

■ Executive functioning is crucial for controlling thought and action, develops greatly during the preschool and early elementary school years, and is related to later academic achievement and occupational success.

■ The development of memory and learning in large part reflects improvements in basic processes, strategies, and content knowledge.

■ Basic cognitive processes allow infants to learn and remember from birth onward. Among the most important basic processes are association, recognition, generalization, and encoding.

■ The use of strategies enhances learning and memory beyond the level that basic processes alone could provide. Rehearsal and selective attention are two important strategies.

■ Increasing content knowledge enhances memory and learning of all types of information.

■ One important contributor to the growth of problem solving is the development of planning.

Sociocultural Theories

■ Starting with Vygotsky's theory, sociocultural theories have focused on the way that the social world moulds development. These theories emphasize that development is shaped not only by interactions with other people and the skills learned from them, but also by the artifacts with which children interact and the beliefs, values, and traditions of the larger society.

■ Sociocultural theories view humans as differing from other animals in their propensity to teach and their ability to learn from teaching.

■ Establishing intersubjectivity between people through joint attention is essential to learning.

■ Sociocultural theories describe people as learning through guided participation and social scaffolding, in which others who are more knowledgeable support the learner's efforts.

Dynamic-Systems Theories

■ Dynamic-systems theories view change as the one constant in development. Rather than depicting development as being organized into long periods of stability and brief periods of dramatic change, these theories propose that there is no period in which substantial change is not occurring.

■ These theories also view each person as a unified system that, in order to meet goals, integrates perception, action, categorization, motivation, memory, language, conceptual understanding, and knowledge of the physical and social worlds.

■ Dynamic-systems theories view development as a self-organizing process that brings together components as needed to adapt to a continuously changing environment.

■ Attaining goals requires action as well as thought. Thought shapes action, but action also shapes thought.

■ Just as variation and selection produce biological evolution, they also produce cognitive development.

Critical Thinking Questions

1. Piaget's theory has been prominent for more than 80 years. Do you think it will continue to be prominent for the next 20 years as well? Why or why not?

2. Do you think that the term *egocentric* is a good description of preschoolers' overall way of seeing the world? On the basis of what you learned in this chapter and your own experience, explain your answer and indicate in what ways preschoolers are egocentric and in what ways they are not.

3. Information-processing analyses tend to be more specific about cognitive processes than are analyses generated by other theories. Do you see this specificity as an advantage or a disadvantage? Why?

4. Do new behaviours, like new species, grow out of the processes of variation and selection, as depicted within dynamic-systems theories?

5. Imagine that you are trying to help a 6-year-old learn a skill that you possess. Using the ideas of guided participation and social scaffolding, describe how you might go about this task.

6. Dynamic-systems theories reflect influences of each of the other theories reviewed in this chapter. Which theoretical influence do you think is strongest: Piagetian, information-processing, or sociocultural? Explain your reasoning.

Key Terms

accommodation, p. 133

A-not-B error, p. 136

assimilation, p. 133

autobiographical memories, p. 160

basic processes, p. 149

centration, p. 139

concrete operational stage, p. 135

conservation concept, p. 139

cultural tools, p. 156

deferred imitation, p. 137

dynamic-systems theories, p. 162

egocentrism, p. 138

encoding, p. 149

equilibration, p. 133

formal operational stage, p. 135

guided participation, p. 155

information-processing theories, p. 145

intersubjectivity, p. 159

joint attention, p. 159

long-term memory, p. 147

object permanence, p. 136

overlapping-waves theory, p. 152

preoperational stage, p. 135

private speech, p. 157

problem solving, p. 146

rehearsal, p. 151

selective attention, p. 151

sensorimotor stage, p. 135

social scaffolding, p. 159

sociocultural theories, p. 155

symbolic representation, p. 138

task analysis, p. 145

working memory, p. 147

MARY STEVENSON CASSATT, *Mother and Child*, 1900

chapter 5:

Seeing, Thinking, and Doing in Infancy

Four-month-old Benjamin, perched on the kitchen counter in his infant seat, is watching his parents wash the dinner dishes. What he observes includes two people who move on their own, as well as a variety of glass, ceramic, and metal objects of differing sizes and shapes that move only when picked up and manipulated by the people. Other elements of the scene never move. As the people go about their task, distinctive sounds emanate from their moving lips, while different sounds occur as they deposit cutlery, skillets, glasses, and sponges on the kitchen counter. At one point, Benjamin sees a cup completely disappear from view when his father places it on the counter behind a cooking pot; it reappears a moment later when the pot is moved. He also sees objects disappear as they pass through the suds and into the water, but he never sees one object pass through another. The objects that are placed on the counter stay put, until Benjamin's father puts a crystal goblet on the counter with more than half of its base hanging over the counter's edge. The crashing sound that follows startles all three people in the room, and Benjamin is further startled when the two adults begin emitting sharp, loud sounds toward each other, quite unlike the soft, pleasant sounds they had been producing before. When Benjamin begins crying in response, the adults rush to him, patting him and making soft, especially pleasant sounds to him.

This example, to which we will return throughout the chapter, illustrates the enormous amount of information that is available for an infant to observe and learn from in even the most everyday situations. In learning about the world, Benjamin, like most infants, avidly explores everything and everyone around him, using every tool he has: he gathers information by looking and listening, as well as by tasting, smelling, and touching. His explorations will gradually expand as he becomes capable first of reaching for objects and then of manipulating them, making it possible for him to discover more about them. When he starts to move around under his own power, even more of the world will become available to him, including things his parents would prefer that he not investigate, such as electrical outlets and kitty litter. Never will Benjamin explore so voraciously or learn so rapidly as in the first few years of his young life.

In this chapter, we discuss development in four closely related areas: perception, action, learning, and cognition. Our discussion focuses primarily on infancy. One reason for concentrating on this period is that extremely rapid change occurs in all four areas during the first two years of a child's life. A second reason is the fact that infant development in these four domains is particularly intertwined: the mini-revolutions that transform infants' behaviour and experience in one domain lead to mini-revolutions in others. For example, the dramatic improvements in visual abilities that occur in their first few months enable infants to see more of the people and objects around them, thereby greatly increasing the opportunities they have to learn new information.

A third reason for concentrating on infancy in this chapter is the fact that the majority of recent research on perceptual and motor development has been done with infants and young children. There is also a large body of fascinating research on learning and cognition in the first few years. We will review some of this research here and cover subsequent development in these areas in

Like Benjamin, this infant will take in a great deal of perceptual information just observing her mother preparing her food.

YELLOW DOG PRODUCTIONS / GETTY IMAGES

later chapters. A final reason for focusing on infants in this chapter is that the methods used to investigate infants' development in these four domains are, of necessity, quite different from those that researchers are able to use to study older children.

Our examination of key developments in infancy will feature several enduring themes. The *active child* theme is vividly embodied by infants' eager exploration of their environment. *Continuity/discontinuity* arises repeatedly in research that addresses the relation between behaviour in infancy and subsequent development. In some sections, the *mechanisms of change* theme is also prominent, as we explore the role that variability and selection play in infants' development. In our discussion of early motor development, we will examine contributions made by the *sociocultural context*.

Underlying much of this chapter, of course, is the theme of *nature and nurture*. For at least 2000 years, an often-contentious debate has existed between those philosophers and scientists who have emphasized innate knowledge in accounting for human development and those who have emphasized learning (Spelke & Newport, 1998). The desire to shed light on this age-old debate is one reason that an enormous amount of research has been conducted with infants over the past few decades. As you will see, these discoveries have revealed that infant development is even more complicated and remarkable than previously suspected.

Perception

Parents of new babies cannot help wondering what their children experience—how much they can see, how well they can hear, whether they connect sight and sound (as in our opening vignette), and so on. William James, one of the first psychologists, referred to the world of the newborn as a "big blooming, buzzing confusion" (1890, p. 462). Because of remarkable advances in the study of early sensation and perception, modern researchers do not share his view. They have demonstrated that infants come into the world with all their sensory systems functioning to some degree and that subsequent development occurs at a very rapid pace. **Sensation** refers to the processing of basic information from the external world by the sensory receptors in the sense organs (eyes, ears, skin, and so forth) and the brain. **Perception** is the process of organizing and interpreting sensory information about the objects, events, and spatial layout of the world around us. In our opening example, sensation involved light and sound waves activating receptors in Benjamin's eyes, ears, and brain; an instance of perception involved, for example, his experiencing the visual and auditory stimulation provided by the crashing goblet as a single coherent event.

In this section, we devote the most attention to vision, both because of its fundamental importance to humans and because so much more research has been conducted on vision than on the other senses. We will also discuss hearing and, to a lesser degree, taste, smell, and touch, as well as the coordination between these multiple sensory modalities. Although these abilities often seem commonplace to us as adults, they are actually some of the most remarkable achievements attained during the first year of life.

Vision

Humans rely more heavily on vision than most species do: roughly 40% to 50% of our mature cerebral cortex is involved in visual processing (Kellman & Arterberry, 2006). As recently as a few decades ago, it was generally assumed that newborns'

sensation ■ The processing of basic information from the external world by the sensory receptors in the sense organs (eyes, ears, skin, mouth, nose) and brain.

perception ■ The process of organizing and interpreting sensory information.

preferential-looking technique ■ A method for studying visual attention in infants that involves showing infants two patterns or two objects at a time to see if the infants have a preference for one over the other.

visual acuity ■ The sharpness of visual discrimination.

contrast sensitivity ■ The ability to detect differences in light and dark areas in a visual pattern.

cones ■ The light-sensitive neurons that are highly concentrated in the fovea (the central region of the retina).

FIGURE 5.1 Testing infants' visual acuity Paddles like those depicted here can be used to assess young infants' visual acuity. Two paddles are shown to the infant simultaneously, one with stripes and one in plain grey. If the infant can detect the contrast difference between the black and white stripes, the infant's gaze should, because of infants' preference for a patterned visual field over a plain one, become oriented toward the striped paddle. The ophthalmologist or researcher presents the infant a succession of paddles with increasingly narrow stripes, with increasingly narrow gaps between them, until the infant can no longer distinguish between the striped paddle and the plain grey one. The degree of grating on the last paddle discriminated provides an indication of the infant's visual acuity.

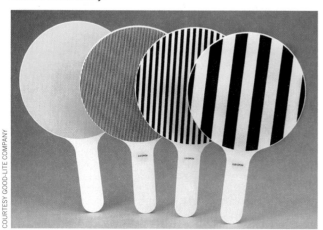

COURTESY GOOD-LITE COMPANY

vision was so poor as to be barely functional. However, once researchers started carefully studying the looking behaviour of newborns and young infants, they discovered that this assumption was incorrect. In fact, newborns begin visually exploring the world minutes after leaving the womb. They scan the environment, and when their gaze encounters a person or object, they pause to look at it. Although newborns do not see as clearly as adults do, their vision improves extremely rapidly in their first months. And as you will learn, recent studies have revealed that despite their immature visual systems, even the youngest infants have some surprisingly sophisticated visual abilities.

The evidence that enables us to say this so confidently was made possible by the invention of a variety of ingenious research methods. Since young infants are unable to understand and respond to instructions, investigations of infant abilities required researchers to devise methods that are quite different from those used with older children and adults. The first breakthrough was achieved with the **preferential-looking technique,** a method for studying visual attention in infants. In this technique, pioneered by Robert Fantz (1961), two different visual stimuli are typically displayed on side-by-side screens. If an infant looks longer at one of the two stimuli, the researcher can infer that the baby is able to discriminate between them and has a preference for one over the other. Fantz established that newborns, just like everyone else, would rather look at something than at nothing. When a pattern of any sort—black and white stripes, newsprint, a bull's-eye, a schematic face—was paired with a plain surface, the infants preferred (i.e., looked longer at) the pattern.

Another method that is used to study sensory and perceptual development in infants is *habituation,* which you encountered in Chapter 2 as a research tool used in studying fetal development. This procedure involves repeatedly presenting an infant with a particular stimulus until the infant's response to it habituates, that is, declines. Then a novel stimulus is presented. If the infant's response increases, the researcher infers that the baby can discriminate between the old and new stimulus. Despite their simplicity, habituation and preferential-looking procedures have turned out to be enormously powerful for studying infants' perception and understanding of the world.

Visual Acuity

The preferential-looking method enables researchers (and eye-care professionals) to assess infants' **visual acuity,** that is, to determine how clearly they can see. This method builds on research showing that infants who can see the difference between a simple pattern and a solid grey field consistently prefer to look at the pattern (Figure 5.1). By varying the patterns and assessing infants' preferences, researchers have learned a great deal about not only infants' early visual abilities but also their looking preferences. For example, young infants generally prefer to look at patterns of high visual contrast—such as a black-and-white checkerboard (Banks & Dannemiller, 1987). This is because young infants have poor **contrast sensitivity:** they can detect a pattern only when it is composed of highly contrasting elements.

One reason for this poor contrast sensitivity is the immaturity of infants' **cones,** the light-sensitive neurons that are highly concentrated in the *fovea* (the central region of the retina) and are involved in seeing fine detail and colour. In infancy, the cones have a different size and shape and are spaced farther apart than in adulthood (Kellman & Arterberry, 2006). As a consequence, newborns' cones catch only 2% of the light striking the fovea, compared with 65% for adults (Banks & Shannon, 1993). This is partly why in their first month, babies have only about 20/120 vision (a level of acuity that would enable an adult to read the large E at the top of a standard eye chart). Subsequently, visual acuity develops so rapidly that by 8 months of age, infants' vision approaches that of adults, with full adult acuity present by around 6 years of age (Kellman & Arterberry, 2006).

Another restriction on young infants' visual experience is that, for the first month or so, they do not share adults' experience of a richly colourful world. At best, they can distinguish some shades from white (Adams, 1995). By 2 or 3 months of age, infants' colour vision is similar to that of adults (Kellman & Arterberry, 2006). Indeed, it is similar to the extent that 4- and 5-month-olds prefer (look longest at) the same basic colours that adults rate as most pleasant—red and blue (Bornstein, 1975). They also perceive the boundaries between colours in more or less the same way as adults do: they respond equivalently to two shades that adults label as the same colour (e.g., "blue"), but they discriminate between two shades that adults refer to with different colour names (e.g., "blue" and "green") (Bornstein, Kessen, & Weiskopf, 1976).

The blurred image on the right is roughly what a 1-month-old infant would perceive. The infant's relatively low level of visual acuity leads some features of the image to pop out—those with higher contrast (e.g., the woman's eyes and hairline).

Visual Scanning

As noted, newborns start visually scanning the environment right away. From the beginning, they are attracted to moving stimuli. However, they have trouble tracking these stimuli because their eye movements are jerky and often do not stay with whatever they are trying to visually follow. Not until 2 or 3 months of age are infants able to track moving objects smoothly, and then they are able to do so only if an object is moving slowly (Aslin, 1981). This developmental achievement appears to be less a function of visual experience than of maturation. Preterm infants, whose neural and perceptual systems are immature, develop smooth visual tracking later than full-term infants do (Strand-Brodd et al., 2011).

Another limitation on young infants' visual experience of the world (and therefore on what they can learn) is that their visual scanning is restricted. With a simple figure like a triangle, infants younger than 2 months old look almost exclusively at one corner. With more complex shapes, they tend to scan only the outer edges (Haith, Bergman, & Moore, 1977; Milewski, 1976). Thus, as Figure 5.2 shows, when 1-month-olds look at a line drawing of a face, they tend to fixate on the perimeter—on the hairline or chin, where there is relatively high contrast with the background. By 2 months of age, infants scan much more broadly, enabling them to pay attention to both overall shape and inner details (see Box 5.1).

FIGURE 5.2 Visual scanning The lines superimposed on these face pictures show age differences in where two babies fixated on the images. (a) A 1-month-old looked primarily at the outer contour of the face and head, with a few fixations of the eyes. (b) A 2-month-old fixated primarily on the internal features of the face, especially the eyes and mouth. (From Maurer & Salapatek, 1976)

Pattern Perception

Accurate visual perception of the world requires more than acuity and systematic scanning; it also requires analyzing and integrating the separate elements of a visual display into a coherent pattern. To perceive the face in Figure 5.2, as 2-month-olds apparently do, they must integrate the separate elements.

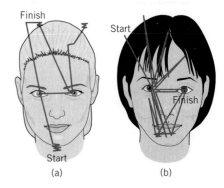

(a)   (b)

BOX 5.1: a closer look

INFANTS' FACE PERCEPTION

A particularly fascinating aspect of infant perception has to do with the reaction of human infants to that most social of all stimuli—the human face. As we have noted, infants are drawn to faces from birth, leading researchers to ask what initially attracts their attention. The answer, it seems, is a very general bias toward configurations with more elements in the upper half than in the lower half—something that characterizes all human faces (Macchi Cassia, Turati, & Simion, 2004; Simion et al., 2002) (see the left image in each pair of stimuli, below). Evidence in support of a general bias to attend to facelike stimuli comes from studies showing that newborn humans are equally interested in human faces and monkey faces—as long as they are presented right-side up (Di Giorgio et al., 2012).

From paying lots of attention to faces, infants very quickly come to recognize and prefer their own mother's face. After exposure to Mom over the first few days after birth, infants look longer at her face than at the face of another woman, even when controlling for olfactory cues (a necessary step because, as discussed in Chapter 2, newborns are highly attuned to their mother's scent) (Bushnell, Sai, & Mullin, 2011).

Over the ensuing months, infants develop a preference for faces depicting the gender of the caregiver they see most often, whether female or male (Quinn et al., 2002).

With exposure to many different faces over their first months, infants gradually develop a well-organized perceptual prototype for human faces. The formation of this detailed face prototype then facilitates discrimination between different faces. Evidence for the formation of a general face prototype in the first year comes from an intriguing study of infants' and adults' ability to discriminate between individual human faces and individual monkey faces. Adults, 9-month-olds, and 6-month-olds can all readily discriminate between two human faces. However, adults and 9-month-olds have a great deal of difficulty telling the difference between one monkey face and another (Pascalis, de Haan, & Nelson, 2002). Surprisingly, 6-month-olds are just as good at discriminating between monkey faces as they are at discriminating between human faces.

The researchers concluded that the 9-month-olds and adults rely on a detailed prototype of the human face to discriminate between people, but this prototype does not help them tell the difference between

monkeys. The fact that the 6-month-olds discriminated among monkey faces just as well as they discriminated among human faces suggests that these younger infants have not yet developed a tightly organized prototype for human faces. Although 6-month-olds are certainly knowledgeable about faces, they do not yet privilege the details of human faces over the details of monkey faces.

Consistent with this account is research showing the effects of experience on face recognition. In one study, from the age of 6 months to 9 months, infants were shown a set of pictures of monkey faces on a regular schedule for 1 to 2 minutes. When they were tested at 9 months of age, they demonstrated that they had retained their ability to distinguish between monkey faces, unlike a control group of 9-month-olds who had not had the exposure to monkey faces (Pascalis et al., 2005).

Another type of experience that shapes infant face perception is exposure to individuals of different races. The *other-race effect (ORE)* is a well-established finding, initially observed in adults, in which individuals find it easier to distinguish between faces of individuals from their own racial

 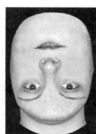 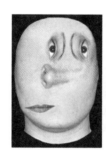 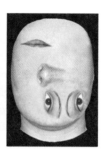  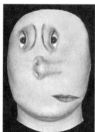

| Upright face (UF) | Inverted face (IF) | Scrambled Top-heavy (ST) | Scrambled Bottom-heavy (SB) | Upright face (UF) | Scrambled Top-heavy (ST) |

When presented with each of these three pairs of stimuli, newborns look longer at the left image, revealing a general preference for top-heavy stimuli that contributes to their preference for human faces (Macchi Cassia et al., 2004; Simion et al., 2002). Notice that this simple preference is all that is needed to result in newborns spending more time looking at their mother's face than at anything else. By 3 months of age, however, infants no longer discriminate between the faces in the middle pair of pictures, suggesting that their visual attention is no longer guided by a general top-heavy bias (Macchi Cassia et al., 2006).

COURTESY OF OLIVIER PASCALIS

Do the photographs of the men show the same person or different people? How about the two monkey photos? As an adult human, you no doubt can tell the two men apart quite easily, but you may still not be sure whether the two monkey photos are of different individuals. (They are.)

group than between faces from other racial groups. An international team of researchers, including Kang Lee at the University of Toronto, later determined that the ORE emerges in infancy. Whereas newborns show no preference for own-race faces over other-race faces, 3-month-old white, African, and Chinese infants prefer own-race faces (Kelly, Liu, et al., 2007; Kelly et al., 2005). Over the second half of the first year, infants' face processing continues to become more specialized, as shown by the emergence of the ORE; by 9 months of age, infants have more difficulty discriminating between other-race faces than between own-race faces (Kelly, Quinn, et al., 2007; Kelly et al., 2009).

What drives these effects is not the infant's own race per se but, rather, the features of individuals in the infant's immediate environment. For instance, 3-month-old African emigrants to Israel who were exposed to both African and white caregivers showed equal interest in African and white faces (Bar-Haim et al., 2006). Further evidence of effects of visual experience on face perception comes from a study suggesting that the facial-scanning abilities of biracial infants—who are exposed to the facial features characteristic of two races in the home—are more mature than those of monoracial infants (Gaither, Pauker, & Johnson, 2012).

One of the most intriguing aspects of infants' facial preferences is the fact that, along with all the rest of us, babies like a pretty face. From birth, infants look longer at faces that are judged by adults to be highly attractive than at faces judged to be less appealing (Langlois et al., 1987; Langlois et al., 1991; Rubenstein, Kalakanis, & Langlois, 1999; Slater et al., 1998, 2000).

Older infants' preference for prettiness, like adults', also affects their behaviour toward real people. This was demonstrated in a study in which 12-month-olds interacted with a woman whose face was either very attractive or very unattractive (Langlois, Roggman, & Rieser-Danner, 1990). The first key feature of this study was that the attractive woman and the unattractive woman were one and the same! This duality of appearance was achieved through the use of extremely natural-looking professional masks that were applied before the woman interacted with the infants. On a given day, the young woman who would test the babies emerged from her makeup session looking either fabulous or not so fabulous, depending on which mask she was wearing. The masks conformed to what adults judge to be a very attractive face and a relatively unattractive one.

When interacting with the woman, infant participants behaved differently as a function of which mask she was wearing. They were more positive, became more involved in play, and were less likely to withdraw when she was wearing the attractive mask than when she had on the unattractive one. This study was particularly well designed because the young woman never knew on any given day which mask she had on. Thus, the children's behaviour could not have been cued by her behaviour; it could only have been due to her pretty or homely appearance.

It is important to note that face perception continues to develop well beyond infancy, as demonstrated by Daphne Maurer of McMaster University and Catherine Mondloch of Brock University. These researchers and their colleagues have shown that sensitivity to differences in the spacing of features, which helps people recognize individual faces, continues to develop well after 8 years of age (Maurer, LeGrand, & Mondloch, 2002; Mondloch et al., 2004).

perceptual constancy ■ The perception of objects as being of constant size, shape, colour, and so on, in spite of physical differences in the retinal image of the object.

FIGURE 5.3 Subjective contour When you look at this figure, you no doubt see a square—what is called a subjective contour, because it does not actually exist on the page. Seven-month-olds also detect the illusory square. (From Bertenthal et al., 1980)

FIGURE 5.4 Size constancy If this infant looks longer at the larger but farther-away cube, researchers will conclude that the child has size constancy.

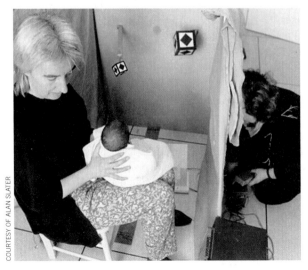

A striking demonstration of integrative pattern perception in infancy comes from research using the stimulus shown in Figure 5.3. When you look at it, you no doubt perceive a square, even though no square actually exists. This perception of subjective contour results from your active integration of the separate elements in the stimulus into a single pattern. If you simply looked at the individual shapes in turn, no square would pop out. Like you, 7-month-olds perceive the subjective square in Figure 5.3 (Bertenthal, Campos, & Haith, 1980), indicating that they integrate the separate elements to perceive the whole. Even newborns can do so if motion cues are added to the display, such as arranging it so that the illusory square appears to move back and forth (Valenza & Bulf, 2007).

Infants are also able to perceive coherence among moving elements. In research by Bertenthal and his colleagues (Bertenthal, 1993; Bertenthal, Proffitt, & Kramer, 1987), infants watched a film of moving points of light. Adults who watch this film immediately and confidently identify what they see as a person walking; the moving lights appear to be (and are) attached to the major joints and head of an adult. Five-month-olds apparently see the same thing; they look longer at the point-light displays that suggest human movement than at ones that do not. As with the research on newborns' response to the illusory square in Figure 5.3, recent studies have confirmed that even newborns show a preference for a moving-lights depiction of biological motion over one of non-biological motion (Bardi, Regolin, & Simion, 2011). Taken together, these results suggest that despite their limited acuity and lack of visual experience, newborns are already attentive to the configurations of elements in their visual world.

Object Perception

One of the most remarkable things about our perception of objects in the world around us is how stable the world appears to be. When a person approaches or moves away from us, or slowly turns in a circle, our retinal image of the person changes in size and shape, but we do not have the impression that the person changes in size and shape. Instead, we perceive a constant shape and size, a phenomenon known as **perceptual constancy.** For a good demonstration of size constancy, look in the mirror and notice that the image of your face seems to be the normal size of a face. Then steam up the mirror and trace the outline of your face on the mirror. You will find that the outline is actually a great deal smaller than your face. But because of perceptual constancy, you perceive the image in the mirror as being the same size as any other adult face.

The origin of perceptual constancy was a traditional component in the debates between *empiricists* and *nativists*. Briefly, empiricists maintain that all knowledge arises from experience, whereas nativists hold that certain aspects of knowledge are, in fact, innate, or hard-wired. Thus, empiricists argue that our perception of the constant size and shape of objects develops as a function of spatially experiencing our environment, whereas nativists argue that this perceptual regularity stems from inherent properties of the nervous system.

The nativist view is supported by evidence of perceptual constancy in newborns and very young infants. In a study of size constancy (Slater, Mattock, & Brown, 1990), newborns were repeatedly shown either a large or a small cube at varying distances. Although the cube's actual size remained the same, the size of the retinal image projected by the cube changed from one trial to the next (see Figure 5.4).

COURTESY OF ALAN SLATER

The question was whether the newborns would perceive these events as multiple presentations of the same object or as presentations of similar objects of different sizes.

To answer this question, the researchers subsequently presented the newborns with the original cube and a second one that was identical except that it was twice as large. The crucial factor was that the second cube was located twice as far away as the original one, so it produced the same-size retinal image as the original. The infants looked longer at the new cube, indicating that they saw it as different in size from the original one. This, in turn, revealed that they had perceived the multiple presentations of the original cube as a single object of a constant size, even though its retinal size varied. Thus, visual experience is not necessary for size constancy (Granrud, 1987; Slater & Morison, 1985).

Another crucial perceptual ability is **object segregation,** the perception of the boundaries between objects. To appreciate the importance of this ability, look around and try to imagine that you are seeing the scene and the objects in it for the first time. How can you tell where one object ends and another begins? If the objects are separated by a gap, the boundaries between the objects are obvious. But what if there are no visible gaps? Suppose, for example, that as baby Benjamin watches his parents washing dishes, he sees a cup sitting on a saucer. An adult would perceive this arrangement as two distinct objects, but will Benjamin? Lacking experience with china, Benjamin may be unsure: the difference in shape suggests two objects, but the common texture suggests only one. Now suppose that Ben's mother picks up the cup to dip it in the suds, leaving the saucer on the table. Will he still be uncertain? No, because even infants treat the independent motion of cup and saucer (or any objects) as a signal that they are separate entities. Is this knowledge innate, or do infants acquire it from observing everyday events in their environment?

The importance of motion as a cue indicating the boundaries between objects was initially demonstrated in a classic experiment by Kellman and Spelke (1983). First, 4-month-olds were presented with the display shown in Figure 5.5a. This display could be perceived either as two pieces of a rod moving on each end of a block of wood or as a single rod moving back and forth behind the block. Importantly, adults perceive displays of this type the latter way. After habituating to the display, the infants were shown the two test displays in Figure 5.5b: a whole rod and a rod broken into two pieces. The investigators reasoned that if the infants, like adults, assumed that there was a single intact rod moving behind the block during habituation, they would look longer at the broken rod because that display would be relatively novel. And that is exactly what the babies did.

What caused the infants to perceive the two rod segments presented during habituation as parts of a unitary object? The answer is *common motion,* that is, the fact that the two segments always moved together in the same direction and at the same speed. Four-month-olds who saw a display that was the same as the one in Figure 5.5a, except that the rod was stationary, looked equally long at the two test displays. In other words, in the absence of common motion, the display was ambiguous.

Common motion is such a powerful cue that it leads infants to perceive disparate elements moving together as parts of a unitary object. It does not matter if the two parts of the object moving behind the block differ in colour, texture, and shape, nor does it make much difference how they move (side to side, up and down, and so forth) (Kellman & Spelke, 1983; Kellman, Spelke, & Short, 1986). For infants, common motion may have this effect, in part, because it draws their attention to the relevant aspects of the scene—the moving pieces rather than the block (S. P. Johnson et al., 2008). Strikingly, however, even this seemingly very basic

object segregation ■ The identification of separate objects in a visual array.

FIGURE 5.5 **Object segregation** Infants who see the combination of elements in (a) perceive two separate objects, a rod moving behind a block. After habituating to the display, they look longer at two rod segments than at a single rod (b), indicating that they find the single rod familiar but the two segments novel. If they first see a display with no movement, they look equally long at the two test displays. This result reveals the importance of movement for object segregation. (From Kellman & Spelke, 1983)

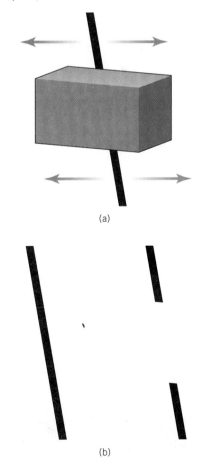

(a)

(b)

FIGURE 5.6 Knowledge and object segregation (a) It is impossible to know for sure whether what you see here is one object or two. (b) Because of your knowledge about gravity and support, you can be sure that this figure is a single (albeit very odd) object. (From Needham, 1997)

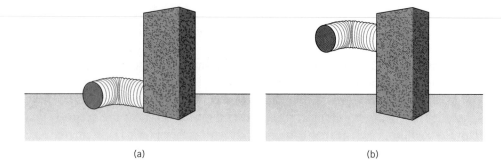

(a)   (b)

feature of visual perception must be learned. Newborn infants, tested using displays similar to those described above and shown in Figure 5.5, do not appear to make use of common motion as a cue to object identity (Slater et al., 1990, 1996). Only at 2 months of age do infants show any evidence that they use common motion to interpret the occluded rod as a single object (S. P. Johnson & Aslin, 1995). Thus, as powerful a cue as common motion may be, infants must develop the ability to exploit it.

As they get older, infants use additional sources of information for object segregation, including their general knowledge about the world (Needham, 1997; Needham & Baillargeon, 1997). Look at the displays shown in Figure 5.6. The differences in colour, shape, and texture between the box and the tube in Figure 5.6a suggest that there are two separate objects, although you cannot really be sure. However, your knowledge that objects cannot float in mid-air tells you that Figure 5.6b has to be a single object; that is, the tube must be attached to the box.

Like you, 8-month-olds interpret these two displays differently. When they see a hand reach in and pull on the tube in Figure 5.6a, they look longer (presumably they are more surprised) if the box and tube move together than if the tube comes apart from the box, indicating that they perceive the display as two separate objects. However, the opposite pattern occurs in Figure 5.6b: now the infants look longer if the tube alone moves, indicating that they perceive a single object. Follow-up studies using the displays in Figure 5.6 with younger infants suggest that younger infants (4½-month-olds) exhibit the adult-like interpretation of these displays, but only when they have been familiarized previously with the box or the tube (Needham & Baillargeon, 1998). Thus, it appears that experience with specific objects helps infants understand their physical properties. We will return to this idea later in this chapter when we discuss the implications of motor development for infants' knowledge about objects (particularly with respect to reaching, on page 192).

Depth Perception

To navigate through our environment, we need to know where we are with respect to the objects and landmarks around us. We use many sorts of depth and distance cues to tell us whether we can reach the coffee cup on our desk or whether the approaching car is far enough away that we can safely cross in front of it. From the beginning, infants are sensitive to some of these cues, and they rapidly become sensitive to the rest.

One cue that infants are sensitive to very early on is **optical expansion,** in which the visual image of an object increases in size as the object comes toward us, occluding more and more of the background. When an image of an approaching object expands symmetrically, we know that the object is headed right for us, and

optical expansion ■ A depth cue in which an object occludes increasingly more of the background, indicating that the object is approaching.

a sensible response is to duck. Babies cannot duck, but they can blink. Timing this blinking response is critical; if infants blink too soon or too late, they risk having the oncoming object hit their open eye. If you think about it, though, it's not at all obvious how infants would know how to correctly time a blink. Doing so requires infants to rapidly exploit information present in the visual image looming before them, including how rapidly the image is expanding and amount of the visual field taken up by the image. Rather remarkably, infants as young as 1 month of age blink defensively at an expanding image that appears to be an object heading toward them (Ball & Tronick, 1971; Náñez & Yonas, 1994; Yonas, 1981). Preterm infants show a delayed developmental pattern of blinks to looming objects, suggesting that maturation, and not solely postnatal visual experience, is crucial for this developmental achievement (Kayed, Farstad, & van der Meer, 2008).

Another depth cue that emerges early is due to the simple fact that we have two eyes. Because of the distance between them, the retinal image of an object at any instant is never quite the same in both eyes. Consequently, the eyes never send quite the same signal to the brain—a phenomenon known as **binocular disparity.** The closer the object we are looking at, the greater the disparity between the two images; the farther away the object, the less the disparity. In a process known as **stereopsis,** the visual cortex computes the degree of disparity between the eyes' differing neural signals and produces the perception of depth. This form of depth perception emerges quite suddenly at around 4 months of age and is generally complete within a few weeks (Held, Birch, & Gwiazda, 1980), presumably due to maturation of the visual cortex.

At around 6 or 7 months of age, infants begin to become sensitive to a variety of **monocular depth cues** (so called because they denote depth even if only one eye is open) (Yonas, Elieff, & Arterberry, 2002). These cues are also known as pictorial cues, because they can be used to portray depth in pictures. Three of

binocular disparity ■ The difference between the retinal image of an object in each eye that results in two slightly different signals being sent to the brain.

stereopsis ■ The process by which the visual cortex combines the differing neural signals caused by binocular disparity, resulting in the perception of depth.

monocular depth (or pictorial) cues ■ The perceptual cues of depth (such as relative size and interposition) that can be perceived by one eye alone.

FIGURE 5.7 Pictorial cues This Renaissance painting contains multiple examples of pictorial cues. One is interposition—nearer objects occlude ones farther away. The convergence of lines in the distance is another. To appreciate the effectiveness of a third cue—relative size—compare the actual size of the man on the steps in the foreground to the actual size of the woman in the blue dress.

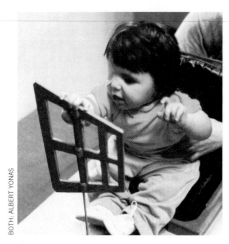

BOTH: ALBERT YONAS

FIGURE 5.8 Monocular depth cues This 7-month-old infant is using the monocular depth cue of relative size. Wearing an eye patch to take away binocular depth information, he is reaching to the longer side of a trapezoidal window. This behaviour indicates that the baby sees it as the nearer, and hence more readily reachable, side of a regular rectangular window. (From Yonas et al., 1978)

them, including relative size, are presented in Figure 5.7.

In one of the earliest studies of infants' sensitivity to monocular depth cues, Yonas, Cleaves, and Pettersen (1978) capitalized on the fact that infants will reach toward whichever of two objects is nearer. The investigators put a patch over one eye of 5- and 7-month-olds (so binocular depth information would not be available) and presented them with a trapezoidal window with one side considerably longer than the other (Figure 5.8). (When viewed by an adult with one eye closed, the window appears to be a standard rectangular window sitting at an angle with one side closer to the viewer.) The 7-month-olds (but not the younger babies) reached toward the longer side, indicating that they, as you would, perceived it as being nearer, providing evidence that they used relative size as a cue to depth. (Box 5.2 reviews research on infants' perception of pictures.)

Auditory Perception

Another rich source of infants' information about the world is sound. As we discussed in Chapter 2, fetuses can hear sufficiently well to learn basic features of their auditory environment (their mother's heartbeat, the rhythmic patterns of her native language, and so forth). At birth, the human auditory system is well developed relative to the visual system. That said, although the inner ear structures appear to be mature and adult-like, the conduction of sound through the outer parts of the ear is inefficient (Keefe et al., 1993). Over the course of infancy, there are vast improvements in sound conduction from the outer and middle ear to the inner ear. Similarly, over the first year, auditory pathways in the brain mature significantly. Taken together, these developments in the ear and in the brain greatly improve the infant's ability to respond to, and learn from, sound.

Other factors add to infants' auditory improvement. One example involves **auditory localization,** the perception of the spatial location of a sound source. When they hear a sound, newborns tend to turn toward it. However, newborns and young infants are far worse at determining the spatial location of a sound than older infants and toddlers are. To localize a sound, listeners rely on differences in the sounds that arrive at both of their ears: a sound played to their right will arrive at their right ear before reaching their left ear, and will be louder at their right ear than at their left ear, thereby signalling the direction the sound is coming from. Young infants may have more difficulty using this information because their heads are small, and thus the differences in timing and loudness in information arriving at each ear are smaller for infants than for toddlers and children with larger heads. Another reason that this information may be difficult for infants to use is that the development of an auditory spatial map (that is, a mental representation of how sounds are organized in physical space—right versus left, up versus down) requires multimodal experiences, through which infants become able to integrate information from what they hear with information from what they see and touch. The development of an auditory spatial map must therefore await the improvements in visual and motor skills that emerge later in infancy (Saffran, Werker, & Werner, 2006).

auditory localization ■ Perception of the location in space of a sound source.

BOX 5.2: a closer look

PICTURE PERCEPTION

A special case of perceptual development concerns pictures. Paintings, drawings, and photographs are ubiquitous in modern societies, and we acquire an enormous amount of information through them. When can infants perceive and understand these important cultural artifacts?

Even young infants perceive pictures in much the same way that you do. In a classic study, Hochberg and Brooks (1962) raised their own infant son with no exposure to pictures at all: no art or family photos; no picture books; no patterns on sheets, clothing, or toys. They even removed the labels from canned foods. Nevertheless, when tested at 18 months, the child readily identified people and objects in photographs and line drawings. Later research established that

infants as young as 5 months old can recognize people and objects in photographs and drawings (e.g., DeLoache, Strauss, & Maynard, 1979; Dirks & Gibson, 1977), and even newborns can recognize two-dimensional versions of three-dimensional objects (Slater, Morison, & Rose, 1984).

Despite their precocious perception of pictures, infants do not understand their nature. The four babies shown here—two from the United States and two from a rural village in West Africa—are all manually exploring depicted objects. Although these 9-month-old babies can perceive the difference between pictures and objects, they do not yet understand what two-dimensionality means; hence, they attempt to treat pictured objects as if they were real objects—with an

inevitable lack of success. By 19 months of age and after substantial experience with pictures, American infants no longer manually investigate pictures, apparently having learned that pictures are to look at and talk about, but not to feel, pick up, or eat (DeLoache et al., 1998; Pierroutsakos & DeLoache, 2003). In short, they have come to understand the symbolic nature of pictures and appreciate that a depicted object stands for a real object (Preissler & Carey, 2003).

Whereas most Western infants live in environments filled with pictured objects, infants in other cultures often lack experience with such images. Fascinating cross-cultural research suggests that, in fact, infants who grow up in homes and communities without pictured objects do not show the same trajectory of understanding that pictures are representations of real objects. In one study, Canadian toddlers and preschoolers outstripped their peers from rural India and Peru in their ability to match line drawings of objects to toy objects (Callaghan et al., 2011). Similarly, toddlers from rural Tanzania, who had no prior exposure to pictures, had greater difficulty than did North American toddlers in generalizing the names of objects in colour photographs to the objects themselves (Walker, Walker, & Ganea, 2013). These studies suggest that understanding the relationship between 2D images and 3D objects requires experience with pictorial media.

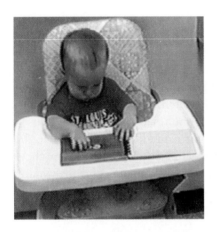
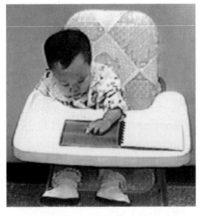

ALL: COURTESY OF DELOACHE ET AL., 1998

These 9-month-old infants—two from the United States and two from West Africa—are responding to pictures of objects as if they were real objects. They do not yet know the true nature of pictures. (From DeLoache et al., 1998)

Infants are adept at perceiving patterns in the streams of sound they hear. They are remarkably proficient, for example, at detecting subtle differences in the sounds of human speech, an ability we will review in detail in our discussion of language development in Chapter 6. Here we will focus on another realm in which infants display an impressive degree of auditory sensitivity—music.

Music Perception

Infants are sensitive to music, as shown by the fact that caregivers around the world sing while caring for their infants (Trehub & Schellenberg, 1995). In Canada, for example, 72% of mothers and 26% of fathers sing to their infants frequently (Trehub et al., 1997). As can be seen in Table 5.1, singing is usually accompanied by other activities.

When adults sing to their infants, they do so in a characteristic fashion which, like the infant-directed speech register we will discuss in Chapter 6 (pages 222–223), tends to be slower and higher-pitched, and to suggest more positive affect, than does singing directed toward adult listeners. Perhaps because of these characteristics, infants prefer infant-directed singing over adult-directed singing, as demonstrated by McMaster University researcher Laurel Trainor (1996). Indeed, infant-directed singing even appears to trump infant-directed speech as a preferred stimulus, as suggested by a study in which 6-month-old infants were more attentive to videos of their own mother singing than to videos of her speaking (Nakata & Trehub, 2004).

Beyond their interest in music, infants are also able to remember what they hear, recognizing musical excerpts several weeks after first being exposed to them (Saffran, Loman, & Robertson, 2000; Trainor, Wu, & Tsang, 2004; Volkova, Trehub, & Schellenberg, 2006). These memories are surprisingly detailed, and include aspects of the pitch, timbre, and tempo of the original performances. For example, when 7-month-old Canadian infants were tested on songs that they had heard in a particular key 2 weeks earlier, they listened longer when the same songs were sung in a new key than when they were sung in the original key (Volkova et al., 2006). This indicates that infants not only discriminated between performances of the same song in two different keys but also continued to remember the original key of the song 2 weeks after they had last heard it sung.

In many ways, infant music perception is adult-like. One well-studied example is the preference for consonant intervals (e.g., octaves, or perfect fifths like the opening notes of the ABCs song) over dissonant intervals (e.g., augmented fourths like the opening of "Maria" from the musical *West Side Story*, or minor seconds like the theme from the film *Jaws*). From Pythagoras to Galileo to the present day, many scientists and scholars, including University of Toronto researchers Sandra Trehub and Glen Schellenberg, have argued that consonant tones are inherently pleasing to human ears, whereas dissonant tones are unpleasant (Schellenberg & Trehub, 1996; Trehub & Schellenberg, 1995). To see if infants agree, researchers employ a simple but reliable procedure. They draw infants' attention toward an audio speaker by using a visually interesting stimulus (e.g., a flashing light) and then play music through the speaker. The length of time infants look at the speaker (actually, at the visual stimulus located in the same position as the speaker) is taken as a measure of their interest in, or preference for, the music emanating from the speaker.

Studies have shown that infants pay more attention to a consonant version of a piece of music, whether a folk song or a minuet, than to a dissonant one (Trainor

TABLE 5.1

Incidence of Song Context and Song Type

Classification	Percentage
Song context	
Play	36
Feeding	19
Sleep preparation	19
Travelling by car	10
Diaper changing	6
Bathing	6
Other	4
Song type	
Play	62
Lullaby	11
Popular	10
Invented	8
Other (religious, folk, unknown)	9

Source: Trehub et al., 1997

& Heinmiller, 1998; Zentner & Kagan, 1996, 1998). A study by Masataka (2006) revealed that even 2-day-old infants show this pattern of preference. This study is particularly notable in that it was conducted with hearing infants whose mothers were deaf, making it unlikely that the infants would have had prenatal exposure to singing. These results suggest that preferences for consonant music as opposed to dissonant music are not due to musical experience. Indeed, other species (including chicks, macaque monkeys, and chimps) also show preferences for consonant music, supporting the view that preferences for consonance over dissonance are unrelated to musical experience (e.g., Chiandetti & Vallortigara, 2011; Sugimoto et al., 2010).

Although this toddler may not become the next Canadian Idol, early exposure to music may help her be a better learner, be less fussy, and know more about music.

In certain other aspects of music perception, infants diverge markedly from adult listeners. One of the most interesting differences is in the area of melodic perception, in which infants can make perceptual discriminations that adults cannot. In one set of studies, 8-month-old infants and adults listened to a brief repeating melody that was consistent with the harmonic conventions of Western music. Then, in a series of test trials, they heard the melody again—but with one note changed. On some trials, the changed note was in the same key as the melody; on others, it fell outside the key. Both infants and adults noticed changes that violated the key of the melody, but only the infants noticed the changes that stayed within the key of the melody (Trainor & Trehub, 1992). Does this mean that infants are more musically attuned than adults? Probably not. What appeared to be a heightened musical sensitivity in the infant participants was more likely a reflection of their relative lack of implicit knowledge about Western music. Because it takes years to acquire culture-specific familiarity with musical key structures, the within-key and out-of-key changes were equally salient to the infant listeners (Trainor & Trehub, 1994). For adults, years of hearing music makes it very difficult to detect note changes that stay within a key.

In a similar way, infants are also more "sensitive" to aspects of musical rhythm than adults are. Musical systems vary in the complexity of their rhythmic patterning; the rhythms of Western music, for example, are relatively simple compared with those of some cultures in Africa, India, and Europe. Hannon and Trehub (2005a, 2005b) tested adults and 6-month-olds on their ability to detect metre-disrupting changes in simple rhythms versus complex rhythms. Notably, some of the adults lived in the Balkans, where the local music contains complex rhythmic patterns, and others lived in North America, where popular music is characterized by simpler rhythmic patterns. The results revealed that all groups detected changes in the simple rhythms, but only the North American infants and the Balkan adults detected changes in the complex rhythms. Thus, North American 6-month-olds outperformed North American adults on this task. A follow-up study asked whether North American 12-month-olds and adults could be trained to detect such changes in the complex rhythms. After 2 weeks of exposure to the Balkan rhythms, the 12-month-olds were able to detect changes in complex rhythms, but the adults still failed to do so.

These examples from the musical domain suggest that, with experience, there is a process of perceptual narrowing. Infants, who are relatively inexperienced with music, can detect differences between musical stimuli that adults cannot.

Developmental changes in which experience fine-tunes the perceptual system are observed across numerous domains. Indeed, you saw this process of perceptual narrowing in our discussion of face perception in Box 5.1, and you will see the same pattern of development when we examine intermodal aspects of speech perception (page 187) and, quite prominently, when we take up language acquisition in Chapter 6. Across all these examples and in other domains, experience leads the young learner to begin to "lose" the ability to make distinctions that he or she could make at earlier points in development. In each case, this perceptual narrowing permits the developing child to become especially attuned to patterns in biological and social stimuli that are important in their environment.

Taste and Smell

As you learned in Chapter 2 (page 53), sensitivity to taste and smell develops before birth, and newborns prefer sweet flavours. Preferences for smells are also present very early in life. Newborns prefer the smell of the natural food source for human infants—breast milk (Marlier & Schaal, 2005). Smell plays a powerful role in how a variety of infant mammals learn to recognize their mothers. It probably does the same for humans, as shown by studies in which infants chose between the scent of their own mother and that of another woman. A pad that an infant's mother had worn next to her breast was placed on one side of the infant's head and a pad worn by a different woman was placed on the other side. Two-week-old infants turned more often and spent more time oriented to the pad infused with their mother's unique scent (Macfarlane, 2008; Porter et al., 1992).

Initially, every object that a baby can pick up gets directed to his or her mouth for oral exploration—whether it will fit or not. Later, infants are more inclined to explore objects visually, thereby showing an interest in the object itself.

Touch

Another important way that infants learn about the environment is through active touch, initially through their mouth and tongue, and later with their hands and fingers. Oral exploration dominates for the first few months, as infants mouth and suck on their own fingers and toes, as well as virtually any object they come into contact with. (This is why it is so important to keep small, swallowable objects away from babies.) Through their ardent oral exploration, babies presumably learn about their own bodies (or at least the parts they can get their mouths on), as well as about the texture, taste, and other properties of the objects they encounter.

From around the age of 4 months, as infants gain greater control over their hand and arm movements, manual exploration increases and gradually takes precedence over oral exploration. Infants actively rub, finger, probe, and bang objects, and their actions become increasingly specific to the properties of the objects. For example, they tend to rub textured objects and bang rigid ones. Increasing manual control facilitates visual exploration in that infants can hold interesting objects in order to examine them more closely, rotating the objects to view them from different angles and transferring them from hand to hand to get a better view (Bushnell & Boudreau, 1991; Lockman & McHale, 1989; Rochat, 1989; Ruff, 1986).

SERGEJS NESCERECKIS / ALAMY

GARETH BROWN / CORBIS

Intermodal Perception

Most events that both adults and infants experience involve simultaneous stimulation through multiple sensory modalities. In the crystal-goblet-falling-on-tile-floor event witnessed by Benjamin, the shattering glass provided both visual and auditory stimulation. Through the phenomenon of **intermodal perception,** the combining of information from two or more sensory systems, Ben's parents perceived the auditory and visual stimulation as a unitary, coherent event. It is likely that 4-month-old Ben did, too.

According to Piaget (1954), information from different sensory modalities is initially separate, and only after some months do infants become capable of forming associations between how things look and how they sound, taste, feel, and so on. However, it has become abundantly clear that from very early on, infants integrate information from different senses. Research has shown, for example, that very young infants link their oral and visual experiences. In studies with newborns (Kaye & Bower, 1994) and 1-month-olds (Meltzoff & Borton, 1979), infants sucked on a pacifier that they were prevented from seeing. They were then shown a picture of the pacifier that had been in their mouth and a picture of a novel pacifier of a different shape or texture. The infants looked longer at the pacifier they had sucked on. Thus, these infants could visually recognize an object they had experienced only through oral exploration.

When infants become capable of exploring objects manually, they readily integrate their visual and tactile experience. In one study, for example, 4-month-olds were allowed to hold and feel, but not see, a pair of rings that were connected by either a rigid bar or a string. When the babies were shown both types of rings, they recognized the ones they had previously explored with their hands (Streri & Spelke, 1988). At this age, infants can also draw more abstract connections between sights and sounds. For instance, 3- to 4-month-olds look longer at visual displays in which dimensions in each modality are congruent, such as a ball rising and falling at the same rate as a whistle rising and falling in pitch (P. Walker et al., 2010).

Researchers have also discovered that infants possess a variety of forms of auditory–visual intermodal perception. In studies of this mode of perception, infants simultaneously view two different videos, side by side, while listening to a soundtrack that is synchronized with one of the videos but not the other. If an infant responds more to the video that goes with the soundtrack, it is taken as evidence that the infant detects the common structure in the auditory and visual information.

In a classic study using this procedure, Spelke (1976) showed 4-month-olds two videos, one of a person playing peekaboo and the other of a hand beating a drumstick against a block. The infants responded more to the film that matched the sounds they were hearing. When they heard a voice saying "Peekaboo," they looked more at the person, but when they heard a beating sound, they looked longer at the hand. In subsequent studies, infants showed finer discriminations. For example, 4-month-olds responded more to a film of a "hopping" toy animal in which the sounds of impact coincided with the animal's landing on a surface than they did to a film in which the impact sounds occurred while the animal was in mid-air (Spelke, 1979).

Similar studies have found that infants are especially sensitive to the relation between human faces and voices. Between 5 and 7 months of age, infants notice the connection between emotional expressions in faces and voices (Soken & Pick, 1992; Walker-Andrews, 1997). When infants hear a happy voice, they look longer at a smiling face, and they look longer at an angry face when they hear an angry

intermodal perception ■ The combining of information from two or more sensory systems.

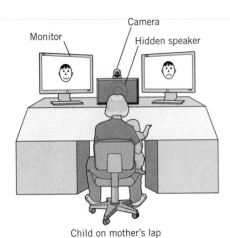

Camera
Monitor
Hidden speaker

Child on mother's lap

A set-up like this one enables researchers to study auditory–visual intermodal perception. The two monitors display different films, one of which is coordinated with a soundtrack. The video camera records the infant's looking toward the two screens.

voice. Infants are also attuned to the match between faces producing speech and the sounds of speech. When 4-month-olds are shown side-by-side films of a person talking while they are listening to a soundtrack that matches one of the films, they look longer at the face whose lip movements are synchronized with the speech they hear (Spelke & Cortelyou, 1981; Walker-Andrews, 1997). Four-month-olds even detect the relation between specific speech sounds, such as /r/ and /l/, and the specific lip movements associated with them (Kuhl & Meltzoff, 1982, 1984).

However, the processes of perceptual narrowing that we have noted elsewhere also occur in intermodal perception. Young infants can detect correspondences between speech sounds and facial movements for non-native speech sounds (those not present in their native language), but older infants cannot (Pons et al., 2009). Similarly, young infants can detect the correspondence between monkey facial movements and monkey vocalizations, but older infants are unable to do so (Lewkowicz & Ghazanfar, 2006). Experience thus fine-tunes the types of intermodal correspondences that infants detect.

Infants can do more than detect relationships between information across modalities: they can use information in one modality to interpret ambiguous information in another modality. In an ingenious series of experiments, 7-month-old Canadian infants listened to a musical rhythm that was ambiguous and could be interpreted in either duple or triple time (Phillips-Silver & Trainor, 2005). While infants were listening, they were bounced up and down at a rate matching either a duple- or triple-time interpretation of the ambiguous rhythm. When tested, infants preferred to listen to the version of the rhythm that fit the pattern in which they were bouncing. These results indicate that infants readily integrate vestibular information with auditory information: how infants were bounced altered how infants interpreted what they were hearing.

review:

Using a variety of special techniques, developmental psychologists have discovered an enormous amount about perceptual development in infancy. They have documented rapid development of basic visual abilities from birth over the next few months, discovering that by approximately 8 months of age infants' visual acuity, scanning patterns, and colour perception are similar to those of adults. Some forms of depth perception are present at birth, whereas others develop in the ensuing months. By 5 to 7 months of age, infants actively integrate separate elements of visual displays to perceive coherent patterns. They use many sources of information, including movement and their knowledge of their surroundings, for object segregation. Faces are of particular interest to infant perceivers.

Research on auditory perception has shown that right from birth, babies turn toward the sounds they hear. They are quite sensitive to music and display some of the same musical preferences adults do, such as a preference for consonance over dissonance. Infants also show perceptual abilities for music that exceed those of adults, whose auditory processing has been shaped by years of musical listening. Smell and touch both play an important role in infants' interaction with the world around them. The crucial ability to link what they perceive in separate modalities in order to experience coherent unitary events is present in a simple form at birth, but more complex associations develop gradually.

There is much in recent research to encourage anyone of a nativist persuasion: neonates show remarkable perceptual abilities that cannot be due to experience, even prenatal experience. At the same time, most perceptual skills also show development over time, much of which clearly involves learning. Infants gradually become more adult-like in their perceptual abilities through perceptual narrowing: as expertise increases (via learning) within and across modalities, infants lose the ability to distinguish between less familiar sights and sounds, becoming increasingly attuned to their native environment.

Motor Development

As you learned in Chapter 2, human movement starts well before birth, as the fetus floats weightlessly in amniotic fluid. After birth, the newborn's movements are jerky and relatively uncoordinated, in part because of physical and neurological immaturity and in part because the baby is experiencing the full effects of gravity for the first time. As you will see in this section, the story of how the uncoordinated newborn, a prisoner of gravity, becomes a competent toddler confidently exploring the environment is remarkably complicated.

reflexes ■ Innate, fixed patterns of action that occur in response to particular stimulation.

Reflexes

Newborns start off with some tightly organized patterns of action known as neonatal **reflexes.** Some reflexes, such as withdrawal from a painful stimulus, have clear adaptive value; others have no known adaptive significance. In the *grasping* reflex, newborns close their fingers around anything that presses against the palm of their hand. When stroked on the cheek near their mouth, infants exhibit the *rooting* reflex, turning their head in the direction of the touch and opening their mouth. Thus, when their cheek comes into contact with their mother's breast, they turn toward the breast, opening their mouth as they do. Oral contact with the nipple then sets off a *sucking* reflex, fol-

lowed by the *swallowing* reflex, both of which increase the baby's chance of getting nourishment and ultimately of surviving. These reflexes are not *fully* automatic; for example, a rooting reflex is more likely to occur when an infant is hungry.

No benefit is known to be associated with other reflexes, such as the *tonic neck* reflex: when an infant's head turns or is turned to one side, the arm on that side of the body extends, while the arm and knee on the other side flex. It is thought that the tonic neck reflex involves an effort by the baby to get and keep its hand in view (von Hofsten, 2004).

The presence of strong reflexes at birth is a sign that the newborn's central nervous system is in good shape. Reflexes that are either unusually weak or unusually vigorous may signal brain damage. Most of the neonatal reflexes disappear on a regular schedule, although some—including coughing, sneezing, blinking, and withdrawing from pain—remain throughout life. Persistence of a neonatal reflex beyond the point at which it is expected to disappear can indicate a neurological problem.

Neonatal reflexes: (a) Grasping   **(b) Rooting**

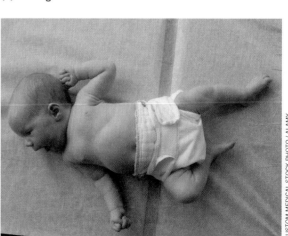

(c) Sucking   **(d) Tonic neck reflex**

Motor Milestones

Infants progress quickly in acquiring the basic movement patterns of our species, shown in Figure 5.9. As you will see, the achievement of each of the major "motor milestones" of infancy, especially walking, constitutes a major advance, and provides new ways for infants to interact with the world.

The average ages that Figure 5.9 gives for the development of each of these important motor skills are based on research with Western, primarily North American, infants. There are, of course, tremendous individual differences in the ages at which these milestones are achieved. Of particular interest is the fact that the degree to which motor skills are encouraged varies from one culture to another, and such variation can affect the course of motor development. Indeed, some cultures actively *discourage* early locomotion. In modern urban China, for example, infants are typically placed on beds and surrounded by thick pillows to keep them from crawling away (Campos et al., 2000). These restrictions make it difficult for infants to develop the muscle strength required to support their upper trunk, which is necessary for crawling. Among the Aché, a nomadic people who live in the rainforest of Paraguay, infants spend almost all of their first 3 years of life being carried by their mothers or kept very close to her because of safety concerns. These infants thus get relatively little opportunity early on to exercise their locomotor skills (Kaplan & Dove, 1987).

In direct contrast, the Kipsigis people in rural Kenya actively encourage the motor development of their infants; for example, they help their babies practise sitting by propping them up in shallow holes dug in the ground to support their backs (Super, 1976). Other groups, in West Africa and the West Indies, institute

FIGURE 5.9 The major milestones of motor development in infancy The average age and range of ages for achievement of each milestone are shown. Note that these age norms are based on research with healthy, well-nourished North American infants.

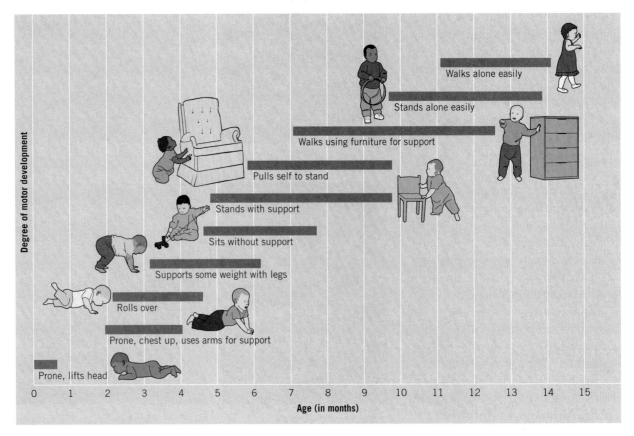

Walks alone easily

Stands alone easily

Walks using furniture for support

Pulls self to stand

Stands with support

Sits without support

Supports some weight with legs

Rolls over

Prone, chest up, uses arms for support

Prone, lifts head

Degree of motor development

Age (in months)

0 1 2 3 4 5 6 7 8 9 10 11 12 13 14 15

an aggressive program of massage, manipulation, and stimulation designed to facilitate their infants' motor development (A. Gottlieb, 2004; Hopkins & Westra, 1988).

These widely varying cultural practices can affect infants' development. Researchers have documented somewhat slower motor development in Aché and Chinese infants compared with the norms shown in Figure 5.9; Kipsigis babies and the infants who undergo exercise regimes, on the other hand, are advanced in their motor-skill development compared with North American infants. Even aspects of infant life that we take for granted in our own culture have an effect on motor development. In a recent study, researchers asked whether diapers—a relatively recent cultural invention—have an impact on walking behaviour (Cole, Lingeman, & Adolph, 2012) (see Figure 5.10). The researchers found that the same infants exhibited more mature walking behaviour when tested naked than when tested diapered, despite the fact that these infants were accustomed to wearing diapers and had rarely walked naked. These data beautifully demonstrate that cultural practices that are undertaken in one domain (toileting) can have unforeseen consequences in another domain (walking behaviour).

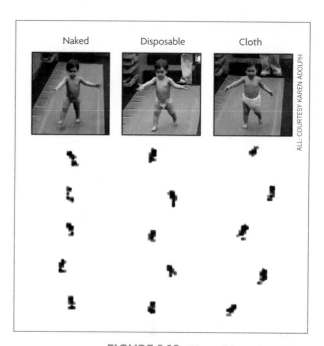

FIGURE 5.10 **Diapers' impact on walking behaviour** These images depict the footprint paths for a single infant participant who was tested walking naked, wearing lightweight disposable diapers, and wearing bulkier cloth diapers. The most mature walking behaviour was seen in the left-most path, in the absence of diapers (Cole et al., 2012).

Current Views of Motor Development

Impressed by the orderly acquisition of skills reflected in Figure 5.9, two early pioneers in the study of motor development, Arnold Gesell and Myrtle McGraw, concluded that infants' motor development is governed by brain maturation (Gesell & Thompson, 1938; McGraw, 1943). In contrast, current theorists, many of whom take a dynamic-systems approach (see Chapter 4, pages 162–167), emphasize that early motor development results from a confluence of numerous factors that include developing neural mechanisms, increases in infants' strength, posture control, balance, and perceptual skills, as well as changes in body proportions and motivation (Bertenthal & Clifton, 1998; Lockman & Thelen, 1993; von Hofsten, 2004). (Box 5.3 offers a detailed account of a program of research exemplifying this approach.)

Think for a moment about how each of these factors plays a part in infants' gradual transition from newborns unable even to lift their head to toddlers who walk independently, holding their upper body erect while coordinating the movement of their legs that have grown strong enough to support their weight. Every milestone in this transition is fuelled by what infants can perceive of the external world and their motivation to experience more of it. The vital role of motivation is especially clear in infants' determined efforts to attempt to walk when they can get around much more efficiently by crawling. Most parents—and many researchers—have the impression that infants derive pleasure from pushing the envelope of their motor skills.

The Expanding World of the Infant

Infants' mastery of each of the milestones shown in Figure 5.9 greatly expands their world: there is more to see when they can sit up, more to explore when they can reach for things themselves, and even more to discover when they can move about on their own. In this section, we consider some of the ways that motor development affects infants' experience of the world.

BOX 5.3: a closer look

"THE CASE OF THE DISAPPEARING REFLEX"

One of the primary proponents of the dynamic-systems point of view we discussed in Chapter 4 was Esther Thelen. Early research by Thelen and her colleagues provides an excellent example of this approach to investigating motor development, as well as a good example of how to formulate hypotheses and test them in general. In one study, they held infants under the arms and submerged them waist-deep in water. As you read the following paragraphs, see how soon you can figure out the rationale for this somewhat strange-sounding, but, in fact, extremely informative, experiment.

This particular study was one in a series of investigations of what Thelen (1995) referred to as "the case of the disappearing reflex." The reflex in question, the **stepping reflex,** can be elicited by holding a newborn under the arms so that his or her feet touch a surface; the baby will reflexively perform stepping motions, lifting first one leg and then the other in a coordinated pattern, as in walking. The reflex typically disappears at around 2 months of age. It was long assumed that the stepping reflex disappears from the infant's motor repertoire as a result of cortical maturation.

However, the results of a classic study by Zelazo, Zelazo, and Kolb (1972) were inconsistent with this view. In that research, 2-month-old infants were given extra practice exercising their stepping reflex; as a result, the infants continued to show the reflex long after it would otherwise have disappeared. Other research also showed persistence of the stepping pattern long beyond 2 months of age. For one thing, the rhythmical kicking that babies engage in when they are lying down on their back involves the same pattern of alternating leg movement as stepping does. However, unlike stepping, kicking continues throughout infancy (Thelen & Fisher, 1982). For another, when 7-month-olds (who neither walk nor typically show the stepping reflex) are supported on a moving treadmill, they step smartly (Thelen, 1986). If the stepping reflex can be prolonged or elicited long after it is supposedly scheduled to disappear, cortical maturation cannot account for its vanishing. Why then does it normally disappear?

A clue was provided by the observation that chubbier babies generally begin walking (and crawling) somewhat later than do slimmer ones. Thelen reasoned that infants' very rapid weight gain in the first few weeks after birth may cause their legs to get heavier faster than they get stronger. More strength is needed to step while upright than to kick while lying down, and more is needed to lift a fat leg than a thin one. Thus, Thelen hypothesized that the solution to the mystery might have more to do with brawn than with brains.

Thelen and her colleagues conducted two elegant experiments to test this hypothesis (Thelen, Fisher, & Ridley-Johnson, 1984). In one, the researchers put weights on the ankles of very young infants who still had a stepping reflex. The amount of weight was roughly equivalent to the amount of fat typically gained in the first few months. When the weight was added, the babies suddenly stopped stepping. In the second study, older infants who no longer showed a stepping reflex were suspended waist-deep in a tank of water. As predicted, the babies resumed stepping when the buoyancy of the water supported their weight. Thus, the scientific detective work of these investigators established that the normal disappearance of the stepping reflex is not caused by cortical maturation, as previously assumed. Rather, the movement pattern (and its neural basis) remains but is masked by the changing ratio of leg weight to strength. Only by considering multiple variables simultaneously was it possible to solve the mystery of the disappearing reflex.

Reaching

The development of reaching sets off a mini-revolution in the infant's life: "once infants can reach for and grasp objects, they no longer have to wait for the world to come to them" (Bertenthal & Clifton, 1998). However, reaching takes time to develop. That is because, as discussed in Chapter 4, this seemingly simple behaviour actually involves a complex interaction of multiple, independent components, including muscle development, postural control, development of various perceptual and motor skills, and so on.

Initially, infants are limited to **pre-reaching movements**—clumsy swiping toward the general vicinity of objects they see (von Hofsten, 1982). At around 3 to 4 months of age, they begin successfully reaching for objects, although their movements are initially somewhat jerky and poorly controlled, and their grabs fail more often than not.

Earlier, we noted that infants' achievements in motor development pave the way for new experiences and opportunities to learn. A particularly compelling example comes from studies (described in Chapter 4) in which pre-reaching infants were

stepping reflex ■ A neonatal reflex in which an infant lifts first one leg and then the other in a coordinated pattern like walking.

pre-reaching movements ■ Clumsy swiping movements by young infants toward the general vicinity of objects they see.

given Velcro-patched mittens and Velcro-patched toys that allowed them to pick up objects (Needham, Barrett, & Peterman, 2002). The manual exploration of objects made possible by these "sticky mittens" led to the infants' increased interest in objects and the earlier emergence of their ability to reach independently for them. Interestingly, a related study found that the effects of the "sticky mittens" intervention extended beyond objects (Libertus & Needham, 2011). Improved ability to interact with objects gives infants additional opportunities to learn about the social world—namely, how people interact with objects. Such improvement also provides infants with new ways to interact with caregivers through shared play with objects. Together, these factors serve to increase infants' interest in social partners.

At around 7 months of age, as infants gain the ability to sit independently, their reaching becomes quite stable, and the trajectory of their reaches is consistently smooth and straight to the target (Spencer et al., 2000; Thelen et al., 1993; von Hofsten, 1979, 1991). The achievement of stable sitting and reaching enables infants to enlarge their sphere of action because they can now lean forward to capture objects previously out of reach (Bertenthal & Clifton, 1998; Rochat & Goubet, 1995). These increased opportunities for object exploration have ramifications for visual perception. For example, consider the difficulty of perceiving 3D objects as whole objects. By their very nature, the front portions of 3D objects block perception of their back portions. Nevertheless, even without X-ray vision, adults readily fill in the non-visible portions of 3D objects and perceive them as solid volumes. It turns out that having more experience manipulating objects helps infants become better at this process of 3D object completion. Infants with better sitting and manual skills are better at perceiving complete 3D objects from a limited view than infants with weaker sitting and manual skills (Soska, Adolph, & Johnson, 2010).

These sources of evidence suggest that there is a great deal of interaction between visual development and motor development. At the same time, infants can perform quite well on some motor tasks in the absence of vision by using auditory or vestibular cues instead. For instance, vision is not necessary for accurate reaching: infants in a completely dark room can successfully nab an invisible object that is making a sound (Clifton et al., 1991). In addition, when reaching for objects they can see, infants rarely reach for ones that are too distant, suggesting that they have some sense of how long their arms are (Bertenthal & Clifton, 1998).

With age and practice, infants' reaching shows increasingly clear signs of anticipation; for example, when reaching toward a large object, infants open their fingers widely and adjust their hand to the orientation of the desired object (Lockman, Ashmead, & Bushnell, 1984; Newell et al., 1989). Furthermore, like an outfielder catching a fly ball, infants can make contact with a moving object by anticipating its trajectory and aiming their reach slightly ahead of it (Robin, Berthier, & Clifton, 1996; von Hofsten et al., 1998). Most impressive, 10-month-olds' approach to an object is affected by what they intend to do after they get their hands on it. Like adults, they reach faster for an object that they plan to throw than for one they plan to use in a more precise fashion (Claxton, Keen, & McCarty, 2003). However, as Figure 5.11 illustrates, infants' anticipation skills remain quite limited for some time.

FIGURE 5.11 Reaching behaviour This right-handed 14-month-old—a participant in research by Rachel Keen and colleagues—is having a hard time getting the applesauce he has been offered into his mouth. On the stand is a spoon with its handle to his left, but the 14-month-old has grabbed it with his dominant right hand, which makes it extremely difficult to keep the spoon upright on its way to his mouth. A spill ensues.

self-locomotion ■ The ability to move oneself around in the environment.

Self-Locomotion

At around 8 months of age, infants become capable for the first time in their lives of **self-locomotion,** that is, of moving around in the environment on their own. No longer limited to being only where someone else carries or puts them, their world must seem vastly larger to them.

Infants' first success at moving forward under their own power typically takes the form of crawling. (Box 5.4 describes a recent increase in variability in the onset of crawling.) Many (perhaps most) infants begin by belly crawling or using other idiosyncratic patterns of self-propulsion, one of which researchers refer to as the "inchworm belly-flop" style (Adolph, Vereijken, & Denny, 1998). Most belly crawlers then shift to hands-and-knees crawling, which is less effortful and faster. Other styles of crawling also have colourful names: bear crawls, crab crawls, spider crawls, commando crawls, and bum shuffles (Adolph & Robinson, 2013). The broader point is that infants are remarkably good at finding ways to get around prior to their being able to walk.

When infants first begin walking independently, at around 11 to 12 months, they keep their feet relatively wide apart, which increases their base of support; they flex slightly at the hip and knee, thereby lowering their centre of gravity; they keep their hands in the air to facilitate balance; and they have both feet on the ground 60% of the time (as opposed to only 20% for adults) (Bertenthal & Clifton, 1998). As they grow stronger and gain experience, their steps become longer, straighter, and more consistent. Practice is vital to infants' gradual mastery over their initially weak muscles and precarious balance (Adolph, Vereikjen, & Shrout, 2003). And practise they do: Adolph and colleagues (2012) found that their sample of 12- to 19-month-olds in New York City averaged 2368 steps (and 17 falls) per hour!

The everyday life of the newly mobile crawler or walker is replete with challenges to locomotion—slippery floors, spongy carpets, paths cluttered with objects and obstacles, stairs, sloping lawns, and so on. Infants must constantly evaluate whether their developing skills are adequate to enable them to travel from one point to another. Eleanor Gibson and her colleagues found that infants adjust their mode of locomotion according to their perception of the properties of the surface they want to traverse (Gibson et al., 1987; Gibson & Schmuckler, 1989). For example, an infant who had promptly walked across a rigid plywood walkway would prudently revert to crawling in order to get across a waterbed. Box 5.5 summarizes a program of research on the early development of locomotion and other forms of motor behaviour in infancy, focusing specifically on the integration of perception and locomotion.

The challenge that young children experience in integrating perceptual

Van Gogh's painting *First Steps* may have been inspired by the joy that most parents feel at seeing their baby walk alone for the first time and the joy the baby feels taking those first steps.

BOX 5.4: applications

A RECENT SECULAR CHANGE IN MOTOR DEVELOPMENT

In the late 1990s, pediatricians noticed a surprising increase in the number of visits they received from parents worried because their infants either began crawling quite late or never crawled at all. Many babies had simply gone from sitting to walking.

The cause for this genuine secular change in motor development seems to be traceable to the campaign, described in Box 2.4 (page 63), to get parents to put their babies to sleep on their backs (Davis et al., 1998). As we discussed in Chapter 2,

this public health effort has been very successful in changing parents' behaviour and has resulted in a remarkable reduction in the incidence of sudden infant death syndrome. However, it appears that regularly lying on their backs makes infants less likely to turn over on schedule. One source of this effect may be motivational: the better view of the environment that they have on their backs may lessen infants' motivation to roll over onto their stomachs, where the view is quite restricted. But, spending

less time on their tummies, the babies have less opportunity to discover that they can propel themselves forward by squirming. With less practice pushing themselves up from lying on their stomachs, the infants' arm strength may develop somewhat more slowly.

In any event, the research is reassuring: when observed at 18 months, there was no developmental difference between infants who had crawled on schedule and those who had not.

---

information in the planning and execution of actions sometimes results in quite surprising behaviours, especially when children fail to meet the challenge. A particularly dramatic example of failure in the integration of perception and action is provided by **scale errors** (Brownell, Zerwas, & Ramani, 2007; DeLoache, Uttal, & Rosengren, 2004; Ware et al., 2006). In this kind of error, very young children try to do something with a miniature replica object that is far too small for the action to be at all possible. Toddlers will attempt, in all seriousness, to sit in a tiny, dollhouse-sized chair or to get into a small toy car (see Figure 5.12). In committing a scale error, the child momentarily fails to take into account the relation between his or her own body and the size of the target object. These errors are hypothesized to result from a failure to integrate visual information represented in two different areas of the brain in the service of action. With development, the incidence of scale errors diminishes, although even adults make a variety of action errors (e.g., putting a cup of water into the cupboard instead of the microwave or trying to squeeze into a too-tight pair of pants).

scale error ▪ The attempt by a young child to perform an action on a miniature object that is impossible due to the large discrepancy in the relative sizes of the child and the object.

FIGURE 5.12 **Scale errors** These three children are making scale errors, treating a miniature object as if it were a much larger one. The girl on the left has just fallen off the toy slide she was trying to go down; the boy in the middle is persistently trying to get into a very small car; and the boy on the right is attempting to sit in a miniature chair. (From DeLoache et al., 2004)

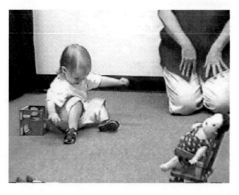

COURTESY OF JUDY DELOACHE

BOX 5.5: a closer look

"GANGWAY—I'M COMING DOWN"

The interdependence of different developmental domains is beautifully illustrated by a rich and fascinating series of experiments conducted over five decades. This work started with a landmark study by Eleanor Gibson and Richard Walk (1960) that addressed the question of whether infants can perceive depth. It has culminated in research linking depth perception, locomotion, cognitive abilities, emotion, and the social context of development.

To answer the depth-perception question, Gibson and Walk used an apparatus known as the "visual cliff." As the photo shows, the visual cliff consists of a thick sheet of Plexiglass that can support the weight of an infant or toddler. A platform across the middle divides the apparatus into two sides. A checked pattern right under the glass on one side makes it look like a solid, safe surface. On the other side, the same pattern is far beneath the glass, and the contrast in the apparent size of the checks makes it look as though there is a dangerous drop-off—a "cliff"—between the two sides.

Gibson and Walk reported that 6- to 14-month-old infants would readily cross the shallow side of the visual cliff. They would not, however, cross the deep side, even when a parent was beckoning to them to come across it. The infants were apparently unwilling to venture over what looked like a precipice—strong evidence that they perceived and understood the significance of the depth cue of relative size.

Karen Adolph, who was a student of Gibson, has conducted extensive research on the relation between perception and action in infancy. Adolph and her colleagues have discovered surprising discontinuities in infants' learning of what they can and cannot accomplish with their developing locomotor and postural skills (Adolph, 1997, 2000; Adolph, Eppler, & Gibson, 1993; Adolph et al., 2003; Eppler, Adolph, & Weiner, 1996). This research exemplifies our theme of *mechanisms of change,* in which variation and selection produce developmental change.

As a way of studying the relation between early motor abilities and judgment, the

investigators asked parents to try to entice their infants to lean over or crawl across gaps of varying widths in an elevated surface or to crawl or walk down sloping walkways that varied in how steep they were. Some of these tasks were possible for a given infant; the baby would have no trouble, for example, negotiating a slope of a particular steepness. Other tasks, however, were impossible for that infant. Would the babies identify which tasks were which? (An experimenter always hovered nearby to catch any infant who misjudged his or her prowess.)

The photos on the next page show how infants behaved on slopes when beckoned by an adult (usually their mother). In their first weeks of crawling, infants (averaging around 8½ months in age) unhesitatingly and competently went down shallow slopes. Confronted with slopes that were too steep to crawl down, the babies typically paused for a moment, but then launched themselves headfirst anyway (requiring the experimenter to catch hold of them). With

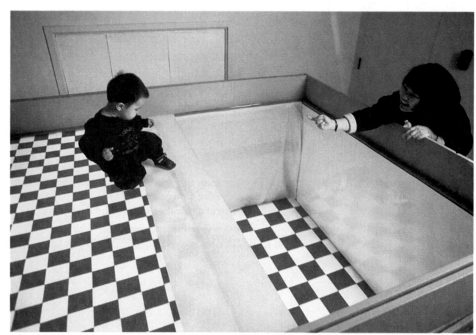

This infant is refusing to cross the deep side of the visual cliff, even though his mother is calling and beckoning to him from the other side.

 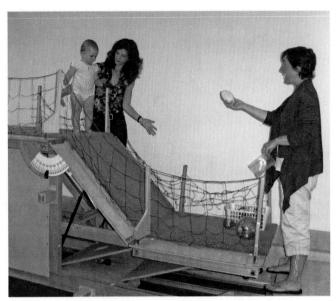

Integrating perceptual information with new motor skills. Researcher Karen Adolph will need to rescue the newly crawling young infant on the left, who does not realize that this slope is too steep for her current level of crawling expertise. In contrast, the experienced walker on the right is judiciously deciding that the slope is too steep for him to walk down.

more weeks of crawling practice, the babies got better at judging when a slope was simply too steep and should be avoided. They also improved at devising strategies to get down somewhat steep slopes, such as turning around and cautiously inching backward down the slope.

However, when the infants started walking, they again misjudged which slopes they could get down using their new mode of locomotion and tried to walk down slopes that were too steep for them. In other words, they failed to transfer what they had learned about crawling down slopes to walking down them. Thus, infants apparently have to learn through experience how to integrate perceptual information with each new motor behaviour they develop. With experience comes increased flexibility, allowing access to multiple strategies for solving previously intractable problems, including laboratory-created challenges such as descending impossibly steep slopes or crossing narrow bridges with wobbly handrails (Adolph & Robinson, 2013).

Infants' decisions in such situations also depend on social information. Infants who are close to being able to make it down a relatively steep walkway can be rather easily discouraged from trying to do so by their mother telling them, "No! Stop!" Conversely, enthusiastic encouragement from a parent can lead an inexperienced crawler or walker to attempt a currently too-steep slope. Thus, the child uses both perceptual and social information in deciding what to do. In this case, the information is obtained through *social referencing,* the child's use of another person's emotional response to an uncertain situation to decide how to behave (see Chapter 10, page 417).

A key finding of Adolph's research is that infants have to learn from experience what they can and cannot do with respect to each new motor skill that they master. Just like the new crawlers and walkers who literally plunge ahead when put atop a sloping walkway, an infant who has just developed the ability to sit will lean too far out over a gap in a platform in an attempt to snag an out-of-reach toy and would fall over the edge if not for the ever-present researcher–catcher. And, like the experienced crawlers and walkers who pause to make a prudent judgment about whether to try a descent, an infant who has been capable of sitting unsupported for some time can judge whether the gap is too wide to lean across and will stay put if it appears to be so. These highly consistent findings across a variety of motor skills have made a very important contribution to our understanding of how infants learn to interact successfully with their environment.

review:

Infants who develop typically display a similar sequence of milestones in the development of motor behaviour, starting with a common set of neonatal reflexes. Although the timing of these milestones may differ across infants, and is affected by cultural differences, their order rarely varies. Researchers emphasize the pervasive interconnectedness between infants' motor behaviour, perception, and motivation, as well as the many ways that infants' experience of the world changes as motor skills improve. In the development of self-locomotion (crawling, walking), infants adopt a variety of different movement patterns and strategies to get around and to cope with different environmental challenges. With experience, infants begin to develop the crucial ability to make accurate judgments about what actions they are and are not capable of performing.

Learning

Who do you think learned more today—you or a 10-month-old infant? We'd bet on the baby, just because there is so much that is new to an infant. Think back to baby Benjamin in the kitchen with his parents. A wealth of learning opportunities was embedded in that everyday scene. Benjamin was, for example, gaining experience with some of the differences between animate and inanimate entities, with the particular sights and sounds that occur together in events, with the consequences of objects' losing support (including the effect of this event on his parents' emotional state), and so on. He also experienced consequences of his own behaviour, such as his parents' response to his crying.

In this section, we review seven different types of learning by which infants profit from their experience and acquire knowledge of the world. Some of the questions that developmental psychologists have addressed with respect to infants' learning include at what age the different forms of learning appear and in what ways learning in infancy is related to later cognitive abilities. Another important question concerns the extent to which infants find some things easier or more difficult to learn. The learning abilities described below are implicated in developmental achievements across every domain of human functioning, from visual perception to social skills. It is thus impossible to think about development without considering the nature of the learning mechanisms that support developmental change.

Habituation

The simplest form of learning is recognizing something that has been experienced before. As we discussed in Chapter 2 and again earlier in this chapter, babies—like everybody else—tend to respond relatively less to stimuli they have previously experienced, and relatively more to novel stimuli (see Figure 5.13). The occurrence of habituation in response to repeated stimulation reveals that learning has taken place; the infant has formed a memory representation of the repeated, and now familiar, stimulus. Habituation is highly adaptive: diminished attention to what is familiar enables infants to pay attention to, and learn about, what is new.

The speed with which an infant habituates is believed to reflect the general efficiency of the infant's processing of information. Related measures of attention, including duration of looking and degree of novelty preference, also indicate speed and efficiency of processing. A substantial and surprising degree of continuity has been found between these measures in infancy and general cognitive ability later in life. Infants who habituate relatively rapidly, who take relatively short looks at

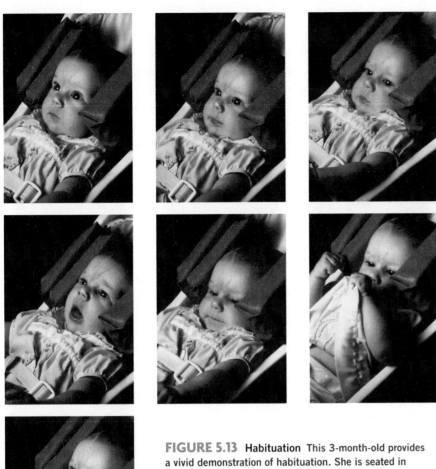

FIGURE 5.13 **Habituation** This 3-month-old provides a vivid demonstration of habituation. She is seated in front of a screen on which photographs are displayed. At the first appearance of a photo of a face, her eyes widen and she stares intently at it. With three more presentations of the same picture, her interest wanes and a yawn appears. By its fifth appearance, other things are attracting the baby's attention, and by the sixth even her dress is more interesting. When a new face finally appears, her interest in something novel is evident. (From Maurer & Maurer, 1988)

ALL: CHARLES E. MAURER

visual stimuli, and/or who show a greater preference for novelty tend to have higher IQs when tested as much as 18 years later (Colombo et al., 2004; Rose & Feldman, 1997). Thus, habituation, one of the earliest and simplest forms of human learning, is fundamental to basic cognitive development.

Perceptual Learning

From their first moments of life, infants actively search for order and regularity in the world around them, and they learn a great deal from simply paying close attention to the objects and events they perceive. According to Eleanor Gibson (1988), the key process in perceptual learning is **differentiation**—extracting from the events in the environment the relation between those elements that are constant. For example, infants learn the association between tone of voice and facial expression because, in their experience, a pleasant, happy, or eagerly excited tone of voice occurs with a smiling face—not a frowning one—and a harsh, angry tone of voice occurs with a frowning face—not a smiling one.

differentiation ■ The extraction from the constantly changing stimulation in the environment of those elements that are invariant, or stable.

GERI ENGBERG / THE IMAGE WORKS

The objects surrounding this baby offer a variety of affordances. Some can be picked up, but others are too big for the infant's small hands or too heavy for her limited strength. The rattle makes noise when shaken, the piano, when banged. Small objects can be inserted into the yellow container, but larger ones won't fit. The stuffed toy can be enjoyably cuddled, but not the telephone. Through interacting with the world around them, infants discover these and many other types of affordances.

A particularly important part of perceptual learning is the infant's discovery of **affordances**—that is, the possibilities for action offered, or afforded, by objects and situations (Gibson, 1988). They discover, for example, that small objects—but not large ones—afford the possibility of being picked up, that liquid affords the possibility of being poured and spilled, that chairs of a certain size afford the possibility of being sat on, and so forth. Infants discover affordances by figuring out the relations between their own bodies and abilities and the things around them. As we discussed earlier, for example, infants learn that solid, flat surfaces afford stable walking, whereas squishy, slick, or steeply sloping ones do not (e.g., Adolph, 2008).

Perceptual learning underlies the development of some, but not all, aspects of intermodal perception. As we noted previously, learning is not required to detect an event involving sight and sound as unitary; thus, baby Benjamin naturally perceives a single, coherent event the first time he sees and hears a crystal goblet crashing on the floor. However, one does have to learn what particular sights and sounds go together, so only through experience does Ben know that a particular tinkling sound means a glass is being broken. As you have seen, young infants are sensitive early on to the synchrony of lip movements and vocal sounds, but they have to learn to relate the unique sight of their mother's face with the unique sound of her voice, which they accomplish by 3½ months of age (Spelke & Owsley, 1979). The necessity for perceptual learning is especially clear with regard to events that involve arbitrary relations, such as an association between the colour of a cup and the taste of the food inside. The fact that 7-month-olds can be taught colour–taste associations in the lab (Reardon & Bushnell, 1988) would come as no surprise to those parents whose infants clamp their mouths shut at the sight of a spoon conveying anything green.

Statistical Learning

A related type of learning also involves simply picking up information from the environment—specifically, detecting statistically predictable patterns (Aslin, Saffran, & Newport, 1998; Kirkham, Slemmer, & Johnson, 2002; Saffran, Aslin, & Newport, 1996). Our natural environment contains a high degree of regularity and redundancy; certain events occur in a predictable order, certain objects appear at the same time and place, and so on. A common example for a baby is the regularity with which the sound of Mom's voice is followed by the appearance of her face.

From quite early on, infants are highly sensitive to the regularity with which one event follows another. In one study, 2- to 8-month-olds were habituated to six simple visual shapes that were presented one after another with specified levels of probability (Kirkham et al., 2002). For instance, three pairs of coloured shapes always occurred together in the same order (e.g., a square was always followed by a cross), but the next stimulus could be any of three different shapes (e.g., a cross was followed by a circle, triangle, or square equally often). Thus, the probability that the cross would follow the square was 100%, but the probability that the circle (or triangle or square) would follow the cross was 33%. In a test, the order of appearance of one or more of the shapes was changed. The infants looked longer when the structure inherent in the initial set was violated (e.g., square followed by circle).

affordances ■ The possibilities for action offered by objects and situations.

Statistical learning abilities have been measured across numerous domains, including music, action, and speech (Roseberry et al., 2011; Saffran & Griepentrog, 2001; Saffran et al., 1996). Even newborn infants track statistical regularities in these domains, suggesting that statistical learning mechanisms are available at birth if not before (Bulf, Johnson, & Valenza, 2011; Kudo et al., 2011; Teinonen et al., 2009). Finally, statistical learning has been proposed to be of vital importance in language learning, as we will discuss in Chapter 6.

Several recent studies suggest that infants prefer to attend to certain types of statistical patterns over others. In particular, they appear to prefer patterns that have some variability over patterns that are very simple (perfectly predictable) or very complex (random) (Gerken, Balcomb, & Minton, 2011; Kidd et al., 2012). This "Goldilocks effect"—avoiding patterns that are either too easy or too hard, while continuing to focus on those that are just right, given the infant's learning abilities—suggests that infants allocate attention differently to different learning problems, preferentially attending to those patterns that are the most informative.

Classical Conditioning

Another type of learning, **classical conditioning,** was first discovered by Ivan Pavlov in his famous research with dogs (who learned an association between the sound of a bell and the arrival of food and gradually came to salivate at the sound of the bell alone). Classical conditioning plays a role in infants' everyday learning about the relations between environmental events that have relevance for them. Consider young babies' mealtimes, which occur frequently and have a predictable structure. A breast or bottle contacts the infant's mouth, eliciting the sucking reflex. The sucking causes milk to flow into the infant's mouth, and the infant experiences the pleasurable sensations of a delicious taste and the satisfaction of hunger. Learning is revealed when an infant's sucking motions begin to occur at the mere sight of the bottle or breast.

In terms of classical conditioning, the nipple in the infant's mouth is an **unconditioned stimulus (UCS)** that reliably elicits a reflexive, unlearned response—in this case, the sucking reflex—the **unconditioned response (UCR).** Learning, or conditioning, occurs when an initially neutral stimulus—the breast or bottle, which is the **conditioned stimulus (CS)**—repeatedly occurs just before the unconditioned stimulus (the baby sees the breast or bottle before receiving the nipple). Gradually, the originally reflexive response becomes a learned behaviour, or **conditioned response (CR),** triggered by exposure to the CS (anticipatory sucking movements now begin as soon as the baby sees the breast or bottle). In other words, the sight of the bottle or breast has become a signal of what will follow. Gradually, the infant may also come to associate caregivers with the entire sequence, including the pleasurable feelings that result from feeding. If so, these feelings could eventually be evoked simply by the presence of a caregiver. It is thought that many emotional responses are initially learned through classical conditioning.

Instrumental Conditioning

A key form of learning for infants (and everyone else) is learning the consequences of one's own behaviour. In everyday life, infants learn that shaking a rattle produces an interesting sound, that cooing at Dad gets him to coo back, and that exploring the dirt in a potted plant leads to a parental reprimand. This kind of learning, referred to as **instrumental conditioning** (or *operant conditioning*), involves learning the relationship between one's own behaviour and the reward or punishment it results in. Most research on instrumental conditioning in infants involves **positive reinforcement,** that

classical conditioning ■ A form of learning that consists of associating an initially neutral stimulus with a stimulus that always evokes a particular reflexive response.

unconditioned stimulus (UCS) ■ In classical conditioning, a stimulus that evokes a reflexive response.

unconditioned response (UCR) ■ In classical conditioning, a reflexive response that is elicited by the unconditioned stimulus.

conditioned stimulus (CS) ■ In classical conditioning, the neutral stimulus that is repeatedly paired with the unconditioned stimulus.

conditioned response (CR) ■ In classical conditioning, the originally reflexive response that comes to be elicited by the conditioned stimulus.

instrumental (or operant) conditioning ■ Learning the relation between one's own behaviour and the consequences that result from it.

positive reinforcement ■ A reward that reliably follows a behaviour and increases the likelihood that the behaviour will be repeated.

TABLE 5.2

Studying Instrumental Conditioning in Infants

Age Group	Learned Response	Reinforcement
Newborns	Head turn to side	Drink of sucrose water
3 weeks	Sucking pattern	Interesting visual display
5–12 weeks	Sucking pattern	Keep a movie in focus
6 months	Push a lever	Cause a toy train to move along a track

Sources: Bruner, 1973; Hartshorn & Rovee-Collier, 1997; Siqueland & DeLucia, 1969; Siqueland & Lipsitt, 1966

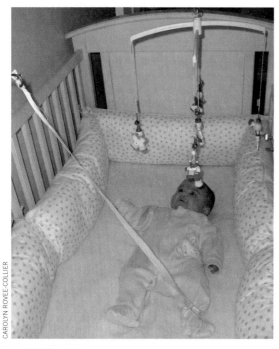

CAROLYN ROVEE-COLLIER

FIGURE 5.14 **Contingency** This young infant learned within minutes that kicking her leg would cause the mobile to move in an interesting way; she learned the contingency between her own behaviour and an external event.

is, a reward that reliably follows a behaviour and increases the likelihood that the behaviour will be repeated. Such research features a *contingency* relation between the infant's behaviour and the reward: if the infant makes the target response, *then* he or she receives the reinforcement. Table 5.2 shows a few examples of the great variety of ingenious situations that researchers have engineered in order to examine instrumental learning in infants.

Carolyn Rovee-Collier (1997) developed an instrumental-conditioning procedure for studying learning and memory in young infants. In this method, experimenters tie a ribbon around a baby's ankle and connect it to a mobile hanging above the infant's crib (Figure 5.14). In the course of naturally kicking their legs, infants as young as 2 months of age quickly learn the relation between their leg movements and the enjoyable sight of the jiggling mobile. They then quite deliberately and often joyfully increase their rate of foot kicking. The interesting mobile movement thus serves as reinforcement for the kicking. An additional feature of this procedure is that the intensity of the reward—the amount of movement of the mobile—depends on the intensity of the baby's behaviour. This task has been used extensively to investigate age-related changes in how long, and under what circumstances, infants continue to remember that kicking will activate the mobile (e.g., Rovee-Collier, 1999). Among the findings: (1) 3-month-olds remember the kicking response for about 1 week, whereas 6-month-olds remember it for 2 weeks; (2) infants younger than about 6 months of age remember the kicking response only when the test mobile is identical to the training mobile, whereas older infants remember it with novel mobiles.

Infants' intense motivation to explore and master their environment, which we have emphasized in our *active child* theme, shows up in instrumental-learning situations: infants work hard at learning to predict and control their experience, and once control has been established, they dislike losing it. Infants as young as 2 months of age display facial expressions of joy and interest while learning a contingency relation, and display expressions of anger when a learned response no longer produces the expected results (Lewis, Alessandri, & Sullivan, 1990; Sullivan, Lewis, & Alessandri, 1992). In one study, for example, seven out of eight newborns cried when they failed to receive the sweet liquid they had learned would follow a head-turn response (Blass, 1990).

Infants may also learn that there are situations over which they have no control. For example, infants of depressed mothers tend to smile less and show lower levels of positive affect than do infants whose mothers are not depressed. In part, this may be because infants of depressed mothers learn that their smiling is rarely rewarded by their preoccupied parent (Campbell, Cohn, & Meyers, 1995). More generally, through contingency situations, whether in a lab or an everyday setting, infants learn more than just the particular contingency relations to which they are exposed. They also learn about the relation between themselves and the world and the extent to which they can have an impact on it.

Observational Learning/Imitation

A particularly potent source of infants' learning is their observation of other people's behaviours. Parents, who are often amused and sometimes embarrassed by their toddler's reproduction of their own behaviour, are well aware that their offspring learn a great deal through simple observation.

The ability to imitate the behaviour of other people appears to be present very early in life, albeit in an extremely limited form. Meltzoff and Moore (1977, 1983) found that after newborns watch an adult model slowly and repeatedly stick out his or her tongue, they often stick out their own tongue. By the age of 6 months, infant imitation is quite robust. Six-month-old infants not only imitate tongue protrusion, but they also attempt to poke their tongue out to the side when that is what they have seen an adult do (Meltzoff & Moore, 1994). From this age on, the scope of infant imitation expands. Infants begin to imitate novel, and sometimes quite strange, actions they have seen performed on objects. In one such study, infants observed an experimenter performing unusual behaviours with objects, such as leaning over from the waist to touch his or her forehead to a box, causing the box to light up. The infants were later presented with the same objects the experimenter had acted on. Infants as young as 6 to 9 months imitated some of the novel actions they witnessed, even after a delay of 24 hours (Barr, Dowden, & Hayne, 1996; Bauer, 2002; Hayne, Barr, & Herbert, 2003; Meltzoff, 1988b). Fourteen-month-olds imitated such actions a full week after first seeing them (Meltzoff, 1988a).

In choosing to imitate a model, infants seem to analyze the reason for the person's behaviour. If infants see a model lean over and touch a box with her forehead, they later do the same. If, however, the model remarks that she's cold and tightly clutches a shawl around her body as she leans over and touches a box with her forehead, infants reach out and touch the box with their hand instead of their head (Gergely, Bekkering, & Kiraly, 2002). They apparently reason that the model wanted to touch the box and would have done so in a standard way if her hands had been free. Their imitation is thus based on their analysis of the person's intentions. In general, infants are flexible in learning through imitation: as in the case of touching the box, they can copy either the specific behaviour through which a model achieves a goal, or they can employ different behaviours to achieve the same goal the model achieved (Buttelmann et al., 2008).

Not only do infants analyze the reason for a person's behaviour but they also pay attention to the credibility of the person. In one study, Concordia University researchers first had an adult behave in either a reliable way (i.e., the adult looked happy when looking inside a container that held a toy) or in an unreliable way (i.e., the adult looked happy when looking inside an empty container). The researchers then tested whether 14-month-olds would imitate the adult's unusual behaviour of switching on a light by touching her forehead to it. As can be seen in Figure 5.15, babies are skeptics; they were more likely to imitate the head touch behaviour of the reliable experimenter but not of the unreliable experimenter. In the latter case, they tended to turn on the lights in the more usual way, using their hands (Poulin-Dubois et al., 2011)!

Further evidence of infants' attention to intention comes from research in which 18-month-olds observed an adult attempting, but failing, to pull apart a small dumbbell toy (Meltzoff, 1995a). The adult pulled on the two ends, but his hand "slipped off," and the dumbbell remained in one piece (Figure 5.16a). When the infants were subsequently given the toy, they pulled the two ends apart, imitating what the adult had *intended* to do, not what he had actually done. This research also established that infants' imitative actions are limited to human acts. A different group of 18-month-olds watched a mechanical device with pincers grasp the two ends of the dumbbell. The pincers either pulled apart the dumbbell or slipped off the ends (Figure 5.16b). Regardless of what the infants had seen the mechanical device do, they rarely attempted to pull apart the dumbbell themselves. Thus, infants attempt to reproduce the behaviour and intentions of other people, but not of inanimate objects.

FIGURE 5.15 Skeptical babies Babies are highly selective in whom they imitate. Babies were more likely to imitate the experimenter, who switched on a light with her head, when her earlier emotional responses made sense. When the experimenter's earlier responses did not make sense, babies were more likely to use their hands to switch on the light. (Adapted from Poulin-Dubois, Brooker, & Polonia, 2011)

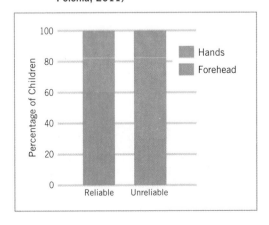

FIGURE 5.16 Imitating intentions
(a) When 18-month-olds see a person apparently try, but fail, to pull the ends off a dumbbell, they imitate pulling the ends off—the action the person intended to do, not what the person actually did. (b) They do not imitate a mechanical device at all. (From Meltzoff, 1995a)

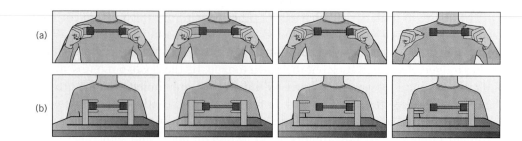

Babies are by no means restricted to learning from the behaviour of live adult models. Infants as young as 15 months of age imitate actions they have seen an adult perform on a video screen (Barr & Hayne, 1999; Meltzoff, 1988a). Peers can also serve as models for young toddlers, as demonstrated by a study in which well-trained 14-month-old "expert peers" performed novel actions (e.g., pushing a button hidden inside a box to sound a buzzer) for their age-mates, either at their preschool or in a laboratory (Hanna & Meltzoff, 1993). When the observer children were tested in their own homes 48 hours later, they imitated what they had seen the child model do earlier.

Current research is focused on the neural underpinnings of imitative learning. One area that has received a good deal of attention as a potential locus for imitation involves the so-called *mirror neuron system,* which was first identified in the ventral premotor cortex in non-human primates (e.g., Gallese et al., 1996; Rizzolati & Craighero, 2004). In research with macaque monkeys, this system becomes activated when the monkey engages in an action; it also is activated when the macaque merely observes another monkey (or a human) engage in an action, as though the macaque itself were engaging in the same action—hence, the name "mirror" neuron system. (Mirror neurons were discovered when neuroscientists who were monitoring the brain activity of a monkey noticed that when the monkey happened to see a lab assistant raising an ice cream cone to his mouth, neurons in the monkey's premotor cortex began firing as though the monkey were about to eat the ice cream cone.)

The degree to which the same system is present in humans, as well as what behavioural domains it might affect, if any at all, is an area of hot debate. Researchers have, however, begun to discover patterns of infant brain activity that are consistent with the hypothesis that mirror neurons are present—namely, patterns of neural firing when infants are observing an action that is similar to those they display when they are performing the same action (Marshall & Meltzoff, 2011). Future studies using neuroscientific techniques should be informative about the roots of imitation, identifying what infants are actually encoding as they observe the actions of others, and how that perceptual information is transformed into self-action.

Rational Learning

As adults, we have many beliefs about the world, and we are usually surprised when the world violates our expectations based on those beliefs. We can then adjust our expectations based on the new information we have just received. For example, you can infer from prior meals at your favourite Chinese restaurant that it will be serving Chinese food the next time you go there, and your expectations would be violated if the restaurant turned out to be serving Mexican food on your next visit. You would then, however, update your expectations about the nature of the cuisine at this establishment. Indeed, scientific reasoning is based on precisely this sort of inference from prior data—for example, using data drawn from a sample of a particular population to make predictions about that population. Infants, too, can use prior experience to generate expectations about what will happen next. This is called **rational learning** because it involves integrating the learner's prior beliefs and biases with what actually occurs in the environment (Xu & Kushnir, 2013).

In an elegant study, Xu & Garcia (2008) demonstrated that 8-month-old Canadian infants could make predictions about simple events. Infants were shown a box containing 75 Ping-Pong balls; 70 were red and 5 were white. The infants then observed an experimenter close her eyes (to suggest a random selection) and draw 5 balls from the box—either 4 red and 1 white or 4 white and 1 red—and put them on display. (The experimenter was actually drawing pre-selected "random samples" from a hidden compartment in the box.) The infants looked longer at the display with the 4 white balls, indicating that they were surprised that the experimenter drew mostly white balls from a box that was mostly filled with red balls. (Later in this chapter, we will further discuss the use of so-called *violation-of-expectation* paradigms, which use infants' "surprise" at unexpected outcomes to draw inferences about their expectations.) It is important to note that the infants showed no such surprise when it was clear that the displayed balls did not come from the box (as when the experimenter took them from her pocket) or when they could see that the red balls were stuck to the box and could not be removed (Denison & Xu, 2010; Teglas et al., 2007; Teglas et al., 2011; Xu & Denison, 2009). Infants as young as 6 months of age appear to be sensitive to the distribution of elements (here, colours) as a source of information upon which to base future expectations (Denison, Reed, & Xu, 2013). Similar findings are emerging across a number of domains, all suggesting that infants generate inferences about the future based on prior data, in tasks ranging from word learning to social interactions, and that infants can use new experiences to adjust these inferences (e.g., Schulz, 2012; Xu & Kushnir, 2013).

rational learning ■ The ability to use prior experiences to predict what will occur in the future.

review:

Infants begin learning about the world immediately. They habituate to repeatedly encountered stimuli, form expectancies for repeated event sequences, and learn associations between particular sights and sounds that regularly occur together. Classical conditioning, which has been demonstrated in newborn and older infants, is believed to be especially important in the learning of emotional reactions. Infants are highly sensitive to a wide range of contingency relations between their own behaviour and what follows it. A particularly powerful form of learning for older infants is observational learning: from 6 months of age on, infants learn many new behaviours simply by watching what other people do. Although an enormous amount of learning goes on during the infancy period, some associations or relations are easier for babies to learn than others are. In observational learning, for example, intentionality is a key factor. Finally, infants are able to use their accumulated experience to make rational predictions about the future.

Cognition

Clearly, infants are capable of learning in a variety of ways. But do they actually think? This is a question that has intrigued parents and developmental psychologists alike. Baby Benjamin's parents have no doubt looked with wonderment at their child, asking themselves, "What is he thinking? *Is* he thinking?" Developmental scientists have been working diligently to find out to what extent infants engage in cognition (knowledge, thought, reasoning). The resulting explosion of fascinating research has established that infants' cognitive abilities are much more impressive than previously believed, although the nature and origin of these impressive skills are a matter of considerable debate. Theorists of cognitive development vary with respect to the relative roles they attribute to nature and nurture, especially in terms of whether development is guided by innate knowledge structures and special-purpose learning mechanisms or by general learning mechanisms relevant to experiences in all domains.

So once again, the primary debate is between nativists and empiricists. Some nativists argue that infants possess innate knowledge in a few domains of particular importance (Carey & Spelke, 1994; Gelman, 2002; Gelman & Williams, 1998; Scholl & Leslie, 1999; Spelke, 2000; Spelke & Kinzler, 2007). As you will see in Chapter 7, for example, these nativists maintain that infants are born with some knowledge about the physical world, such as the fact that two objects cannot occupy the same space, and that physical objects move only if something sets them in motion. They also propose that infants possess rudimentary understandings in the domains of biology and psychology. Other nativists emphasize *specialized* learning mechanisms that enable infants to acquire this kind of knowledge rapidly and efficiently (Baillargeon, 2004; Baillargeon, Kotovsky, & Needham, 1996). According to empiricists, infants' mental representations of the physical world are gradually acquired and strengthened through the *general* learning mechanisms that function across multiple domains (Munakata et al., 1997). The details of this debate are examined in Chapter 7 with respect to conceptual development. In the following sections, we examine findings regarding infants' cognitive abilities and limitations, explanations for which both nativists and empiricists are working to pin down.

Object Knowledge

A large part of what we know about infant cognition has come from research on the development of knowledge about objects, research originally inspired by Piaget's theory of sensorimotor intelligence. As you learned in Chapter 4, Piaget believed that young infants' understanding of the world is severely limited by an inability to mentally represent and think about anything that they cannot currently see, hear, touch, and so on. His tests of *object permanence* led him to infer that when an infant fails to search for an object—even a favourite toy—that has disappeared from sight, it is because the object has also disappeared from the infant's mind.

A substantial body of research has provided strong support for Piaget's original observation that young infants do not manually search for hidden objects. However, as noted in Chapter 4, skepticism gradually arose about his explanation of this fascinating phenomenon, and an overwhelming body of evidence has established that young infants are in fact able to mentally represent and think about the existence of objects and events that are currently out of sight.

The simplest evidence for young infants' ability to represent an object that has vanished from sight is the fact that they will reach for objects in the dark, that is, they reach for objects they cannot see. When young infants are shown an attractive object and the room is then plunged into darkness, causing the object (and everything else) to disappear from view, most babies reach to where they last saw the object, indicating that they expect it to still be there (Perris & Clifton, 1988; Stack et al., 1989).

Young infants even seem to be able to think about some characteristics of invisible objects, such as their size (Clifton et al., 1991). When 6-month-olds sitting in the dark heard the sound of a familiar large object, they reached toward it with both hands (just as they had in the light); but they reached with only one hand when the sound they heard was that of a familiar small object.

The majority of the evidence that young infants can represent and think about invisible objects comes from research using the **violation-of-expectancy procedure.** The logic of this procedure is similar to that of the visual-preference method we discussed earlier (page 174). The basic assumption is that if infants observe an event that violates something they know about the world, they will be surprised or at least interested. Thus, an event that is impossible or inconsistent with respect to the infant's knowledge should evoke a greater response (such as longer looking or a change in heart rate) than does a possible or consistent event.

The violation-of-expectancy technique was first used in a classic series of studies designed by Renée Baillargeon and her colleagues (Baillargeon, Spelke, & Wasserman, 1985) to see if infants too young to search for an invisible object might nevertheless have a mental representation of its existence. In some of these studies, infants were first habituated to the sight of a solid screen rotating back and forth through a 180-degree arc (Figure 5.17). Then a box was placed in the screen's path, and the infants saw two test events. In one, the *possible event*, the screen rotated upward, occluding the box as it did so, and stopped when it contacted the box. In the *impossible event*, the screen continued to rotate a full 180 degrees, appearing to pass through the space occupied by the box (which the experimenter had surreptitiously removed).

Infants as young as 3½ months of age looked longer at the impossible event than at the possible one. The researchers reasoned that the full rotation of the screen (to which the infants had previously been habituated) would be more interesting or surprising than the partial rotation *only* if the infants expected the screen to stop when it reached the box. And the only reason for them to have had that expectation was if they thought the box was still present—that is, if they mentally represented an object they could no longer see. The results also indicate that the infants expected the box to remain in place and did not expect the screen to be able to pass through it.

Other studies have shown that young infants' behaviour in this situation is influenced by some of the characteristics of the occluded objects, including height (Baillargeon, 1987a; Baillargeon, 1987b). They expect the screen to stop sooner for a taller object than for a shorter one. Thus, research using two very different assessments—reaching in the dark and visual attention—provides converging evidence that infants who do not yet search for hidden objects nevertheless can represent their continued existence and some of their properties.

Physical Knowledge

Infants' knowledge about the physical world is not limited to what they know and are learning about objects. Other research has examined what they know about physical phenomena, such as gravity. Even in the first year of life, infants seem to appreciate that objects do not float in mid-air, that an object that is inadequately supported will fall, that a non-round object placed on a stable surface will stay put, and so forth. For instance, in a series of studies in which infants observed a ball being released on a slope, 7-month-olds (but not 5-month-olds) looked longer when the ball moved up the slope than when it moved down, indicating that they had expected the ball to go down (Kim & Spelke, 1992). Similarly, they looked longer at an object that travelled more slowly as it rolled down a slope than at one that picked up speed.

violation-of-expectancy procedure ■ A procedure used to study infant cognition in which infants are shown an event that should evoke surprise or interest if it violates something the infant knows or assumes to be true.

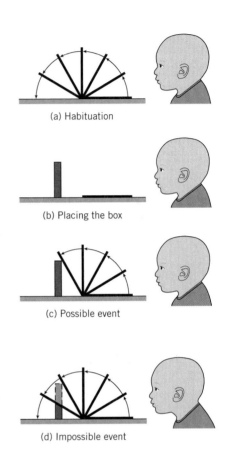

(a) Habituation

(b) Placing the box

(c) Possible event

(d) Impossible event

FIGURE 5.17 Possible versus impossible events In a classic series of tests of object permanence, Renée Baillargeon first habituated young infants to the sight of a screen rotating through 180 degrees. Then a box was placed in the path of the screen. In the possible event, the screen rotated up, occluding the box, and stopped when it reached the top of the box. In the impossible event, the screen rotated up, occluding the box, but then continued on through 180 degrees, appearing to pass through the space where the box was. Infants looked longer at the impossible event, showing that they mentally represented the presence of the invisible box. (From Baillargeon, 1987a)

**Violation detected
at each stage**

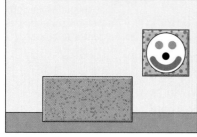

Initial concept:
Contact/No contact

(a)　3 months

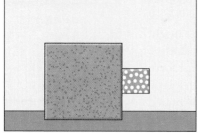

Variable:
Type of contact

(b)　5 months

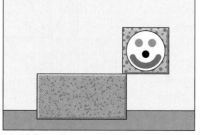

Variable:
Amount of contact

(c)　6.5 months

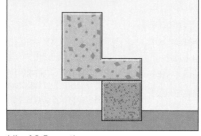

Variable:
Shape of the box

(d)　12.5 months

FIGURE 5.18 **Infants' developing
understanding of support relations** Young
infants appreciate that an object cannot
float in mid-air, but only gradually do they
come to understand under what conditions
one object can be supported by another.
(Adapted from Baillargeon, 1998)

Infants also gradually come to understand under what conditions one object can support another. Figure 5.18 summarizes infants' reactions to simple support problems involving boxes and a platform (Baillargeon, Needham, & DeVos, 1992; Needham & Baillargeon, 1993). At 3 months of age, infants are surprised (they look longer) if a box that is released in mid-air remains suspended (as in Figure 5.18a), rather than falling. However, as long as there is any contact at all between the box and the platform (as in Figure 5.18b and 5.18c), these young infants do not react when the box remains stationary. By approximately 5 months of age, they appreciate the relevance of the type of contact involved in support. They now know that the box will be stable only if it is released on top of the platform, so they would be surprised by the display in Figure 5.18b. Roughly a month later, they recognize the importance of the amount of contact, and hence they look longer when the box in Figure 5.18c stays put with only a small portion of its bottom surface on the platform. Shortly after their 1st birthday, infants also take into account the shape of the object and hence are surprised if an asymmetrical object like that shown in Figure 5.18d remains stable.

Infants presumably develop this progressively refined understanding of support relations between objects as a result of experience. They observe innumerable occasions of adults placing objects on surfaces, and once in a while, as in the crashing crystal observed by baby Benjamin, they see the consequences of inadequate support. And, of course, they collect additional data through their own manipulation of objects, including lots more evidence than their parents would like about what happens when a milk cup is deposited on the very edge of a high-chair tray.

Social Knowledge

In addition to acquiring knowledge about the physical world, infants need to learn about the social world—about people and their behaviour. An important aspect of social knowledge that emerges relatively early is the understanding that the behaviour of others is purposive and goal-directed. In research by Amanda Woodward (1998), 6-month-old infants saw a hand repeatedly reach toward one of two objects sitting side by side in a display (see Figure 5.19). Then the position of the two objects was reversed, and the hand reached again. The question was whether the infants interpreted the reaching behaviour as directed toward a particular object. They did, as shown by their looking longer when the hand went to the new object (in the old place) than when it reached for the old object it had reached to before. Thus, the infants apparently interpreted the reaching behaviour as directed toward a particular object. However, this was true only for a human hand; another group of infants did not react the same way when a mechanical claw did the reaching. (This study may remind you of the one by Meltzoff [1995b] in which older infants imitated the actions of a human but not of a mechanical device.) Shown the same training event (Figure 5.19a), slightly older infants (11-month-olds) were able to correctly

(a)

(b)

(c)

(d)

FIGURE 5.19 **Object-directed reaching** Infants were habituated to the event shown in (a), a hand repeatedly reaching for a ball on one side of a display. When tested later with displays (b), (c), and (d), infants who saw the hand reach for the other object looked longer than did those who saw it reach for the ball (regardless of the ball's position). The pattern of results indicates that the babies interpreted the original reaching as object-directed. (Adapted from Woodward, 1998)

predict what the human hand would do next, moving their eyes to the goal object in the test display *before* the hand actually moved to the goal object (Cannon & Woodward, 2012). Again, though, they did not have the same expectations for the claw as they had for the human hand.

Other research by Sommerville, Woodward, and Needham (2005) established that infants' understanding of the goal-directed nature of another's actions is related to their own experience achieving a goal. Three-month-olds, who were not yet able to pick up objects on their own, were fitted with Velcro "sticky mittens" (like those described earlier in this chapter and in Chapter 4) that enabled them to capture Velcro-patched toys. Their brief experience successfully "picking up" objects enabled them to interpret the goal-directed reaching of others in the procedure in Figure 5.19 a few months earlier than they would otherwise have been able to do.

Further understanding of intentionality is revealed by studies showing that older infants even attribute intentions and goals to inanimate entities if the objects seem to "behave" like humans. In research by Susan Johnson, 12- and 15-month-olds were introduced to a faceless, eyeless blob that "vocalized" and moved in response to what the infant or experimenter did, thus simulating a normal human interaction (S. C. Johnson, 2003; S. C. Johnson et al., 2008; S. C. Johnson, Slaughter, & Carey, 1998) (see Figure 5.20). Subsequently, when the blob turned in one direction, the infants looked in that direction. Thus, they seemed to be following the blob's

FIGURE 5.20 **Intentionality and inanimate objects** When this amorphous blobby object "responds" contingently to infants, they tend to attribute intention to it. (From S. C. Johnson et al., 2008)

"gaze," just as they would do with a human partner, assuming that the person had turned to look at something. They did not behave this way when the blob's initial behaviour was not contingently related to their own.

Older infants even interpret quite abstract displays in terms of intention and goal-directed action (Csibra et al., 1999, 2003; Gergely et al., 2002). For example, 12-month-olds saw a computer animation of a ball repeatedly "jumping" over a barrier toward a ball on the other side. Adults interpret this display as the jumping ball's "wanting" to get to the other ball. So, apparently, did the infants. When the barrier was removed, the infants looked longer when they saw the ball continue to jump, just as it had done before, than when they saw it move straight to the second ball.

Even younger infants seem to attribute intention with respect to simple displays involving small objects. In a study that used a ball, a cube, and a pyramid, all with "googly" eyes attached, 10-month-olds watched as the ball—the "climber"—repeatedly "attempted" to climb up a hill, each time falling back to the bottom (see Figure 5.21) (Hamlin, Wynn, & Bloom, 2007). Then the climber was alternately bumped up the hill by the pyramid or pushed back down by the cube. On the subsequent test event, the infants observed the climber alternately approach the "helper" triangle or the "hinderer" cube. The infants looked longer when the climber approached the "hinderer," indicating by their surprise not only their understanding of the "intentions" of all three objects but also their understanding of what the "climber's" response to the "helper" and "hinderer" might be expected to be.

Infants go beyond attributing intentions to others based on their actions: they exhibit preferences for particular individuals and objects based on the individuals' and objects' actions. Earlier in this chapter, we described research focused on infants' visual preferences (Box 5.1). Infants also exhibit social preferences, as evidenced by their desire to engage with some individuals over others. In one of the first studies to demonstrate early social preferences (Kinzler, Dupoux, & Spelke, 2007), American and French 10-month-olds saw alternating life-sized video projections of two individuals speaking to them, one in English and one in French. They then saw another life-sized video of the same two individuals standing side by side behind a table, both holding an identical plush toy. Silently and simultaneously, they smiled at the infant, then at the toy, then at the infant again, and then leaned forward, holding the toys out as though giving them to the infant. The moment the toys disappeared from view on the screen, they

FIGURE 5.21 The climber, helper, and hinderer Viewers of the "climber" event described above—infants and adults alike—readily interpret it in terms of intentional action. First they see the ball as "trying" to move up a hill, but then rolling back down, thereby "failing" to achieve its goal of reaching the top. On some trials, after the ball starts to roll back down, a triangle appears below the ball and seems to "push" it upward, "helping" it get to the top. On other trials, a cube appears in front of the ball and "hinders" it by seeming to "push" it down the hill.

appeared (through researchers' magic) on a table in front of the infant, creating the impression that they had come directly from the individuals in the video. The infants' responses suggested a social preference for the individual who had spoken their native language: English-learning infants chose the toy offered by the English speaker, whereas French-learning infants chose the toy offered by the French speaker. Crucially, because the toy was offered in silence, these social preferences were attributable to a preference for the individual who shared the infant's language, not for the language itself.

Similar findings emerged in a food-choice paradigm, in which infants were more likely to choose a food offered by a speaker of their language than by a speaker of another language (Shutts et al., 2009). Indeed, even objects similar to those depicted in Figure 5.21 evoke social preferences (Hamlin et al., 2007). In a variation of the "climber" procedure described above, when infants as young as 6 months were presented with the objects they had just observed bumping the "climber" object up the hill or pushing it down the hill, they tended to choose the "helper" object. The social preferences exhibited in studies like these can be quite nuanced. In one recent study that used puppets rather than objects, 5-month-olds uniformly preferred characters who were positive toward "helpers," whereas 8-month-olds preferred characters who were positive toward "helpers" and negative toward "hinderers" (Hamlin et al., 2011).

These and related studies indicate that well before their 1st birthday, infants have already learned a great deal about how humans behave and how their behaviour is related to their intentions and goals. Infants and young children can also draw inferences about other people's knowledge states. For example, 15-month-olds can make inferences about what a person will do based on their knowledge of what the person knows (Onishi & Baillargeon, 2005). In a visual-attention version of the false-belief task (discussed in Chapter 4), infants seem to keep track of what information an adult has about the location of an object. If the object is moved to a new location while an infant—but not the adult—witnesses the move, the infant expects the adult to subsequently search for the object in its *original* location. That is, the infant expects the adult to search where he or she *should believe* the toy to be, rather than in the location where the infant knows it *actually* is. This interpretation is based on the fact that the infants looked longer when the adult searched the object's current location than they did when the adult searched its original location. Thus, this study indicates that 15-month-olds assume that a person's behaviour will be based on what the person *believes* to be true, even if the infant knows that the belief is false. This result suggests that there may be very early precursors of a theory of mind.

Looking Ahead

The intense activity focused on cognition in infancy has produced a wealth of fascinating findings. This new information has not, however, resolved the basic issues about how cognition develops in infancy. The evidence we have reviewed reveals a remarkable constellation of abilities and deficits. Infants can be both surprisingly smart and surprisingly clueless (Keen, 2003; Kloos & Keen, 2005). They can infer the existence of an unseen object but cannot retrieve it. They appreciate that objects cannot float in mid-air but think that any kind and amount of contact at all provides sufficient support. The challenge for theorists is to account for both competence and incompetence in infants' thinking.

review:

Building on the insights and observations of Piaget, and using an array of extremely clever methods, modern researchers have made a host of fascinating discoveries about the cognitive processes of infants. They have demonstrated that infants mentally represent not only the existence of hidden objects but also characteristics such as the object's size, height, and noise-making properties. Infants' understanding of the physical world grows steadily, as shown by their appreciation of support relations and their increasing ability to solve everyday problems. At the same time, their understanding of the social world also increases, as shown, for example, by their interpretation of and preferences concerning the behaviour of actors, both human and animated.

chapter summary:

Perception

- The human visual system is relatively immature at birth; young infants have poor acuity, low contrast sensitivity, and minimal colour vision. Modern research has demonstrated, however, that newborns begin visually scanning the world minutes after birth and that very young infants show preferences for strongly contrasted patterns, for the same colours that adults prefer, and, especially, for human faces.

- Some visual abilities, including perception of constant size and shape, are present at birth; others develop rapidly over the first year. Binocular vision emerges quite suddenly at around 4 months of age, and the ability to identify object boundaries—object segregation—is also present at that age. By 7 months of age, infants are sensitive to a variety of monocular, or pictorial, depth cues; and pattern perception has developed to the point that infants can perceive illusory (subjective) contours, as adults do.

- The auditory system is comparatively well developed at birth, and newborns will turn their heads to localize a sound. Young infants' remarkable proficiency at perceiving pattern in auditory stimulation underlies their sensitivity to musical structure.

- Infants are sensitive to smell from birth. They learn to identify their mother in part by her unique scent.

- Through active touching, using both mouth and hands, infants explore and learn about themselves and their environment.

- Research on the phenomenon of intermodal perception has revealed that from very early on, infants integrate information from different senses, linking their visual with their auditory, olfactory, and tactile experiences.

Motor Development

- Motor development, or the development of action, proceeds rapidly in infancy through a series of "motor milestones," starting with the reflexes displayed by newborn babies. Recent

research has demonstrated that the regular pattern of development results from the confluence of many factors, including the development of strength, posture control, balance, and perceptual skills. Some aspects of motor development vary across cultures as a result of different cultural practices.

- Each new motor achievement, from reaching to self-locomotion, expands the infant's experience of the world but also presents new challenges. Infants adopt a variety of strategies to move around in the world successfully and safely. In the process, they make a variety of surprising mistakes.

Learning

- Various kinds of learning are present in infancy. Infants habituate to repeated stimuli and form expectancies about recurrent regularities in events. Through active exploration, they engage in perceptual learning. They also learn through classical conditioning, which involves forming associations between natural and neutral stimuli, as well as through instrumental conditioning, which involves learning about the contingency between one's own behaviour and some outcome. They can also make use of prior experiences to generate expectations about the future.

- From the second half of the first year on, observational learning—watching and imitating the behaviour of other people—is an increasingly important source of information. Infants' assessment of the intention of a model affects what they imitate.

Cognition

- Powerful new research techniques—most notably the violation-of-expectancy procedure—have established that infants display impressive cognitive abilities. Much of this work on mental representation and thinking was originally inspired by Piaget's concept of object permanence. But it has been revealed that, contrary to Piaget's belief, young infants can mentally represent invisible objects and even reason about observed events.

- Other research, focused on infants' developing knowledge of the physical world, has demonstrated their understanding of some of the effects of gravity. It takes babies several months to work out the conditions under which one object can provide stable support for another.

- What infants know about people is a very active area of research. One clear finding is that infants pay particular attention to the intentions of others.

- Although many fascinating phenomena have been discovered in the area of infant cognition, basic issues about cognitive development remain unresolved. Theorists are sharply divided on how to account for the abilities, on the one hand, and the deficiencies, on the other hand, in infants' thinking.

Critical Thinking Questions

1. The major theme throughout this chapter was nature and nurture. Consider the following research findings discussed in the chapter: infants' preference for consonance (versus dissonance) in music, their preference for faces that adults consider attractive, and their ability to represent the existence and even the height of an occluded object. To what extent do you think these preferences and abilities rest on innate factors, and to what extent might they be the result of experience?

2. As you have seen from this chapter, researchers have learned a substantial amount about infants in the recent past. Were you surprised at some of what has been learned? Describe to a friend something from each of the main sections of the chapter that you would never have suspected an infant could do or would know. Similarly, tell your friend a few things that you were surprised to learn infants do not know or that they fail to do.

3. Studying infants' perceptual and cognitive abilities is especially tricky given their limited abilities to respond in a study—they can't respond verbally or even with a reliable reach or point. Consider some of the methods described in this chapter (preferential looking, conditioning, habituation, violation of expectation, imitation, and so on). Can you match each method up with a study described in the chapter? What kinds of questions are best suited to each method?

4. Explain why researchers did the following things, each of which seems somewhat odd if one does not know the rationale behind it. What hypotheses were they trying to test?

    (a) Suspended infants in water up to their waists

    (b) Put a patch over one eye of infants and showed infants a misshapen window

    (c) Rolled a ball up and down a slope

    (d) Pretended to be unable to pull the end off a dumbbell

Key Terms

affordances, p. 200

auditory localization, p. 182

binocular disparity, p. 181

classical conditioning, p. 201

conditioned response (CR), p. 201

conditioned stimulus (CS), p. 201

cones, p. 174

contrast sensitivity, p. 174

differentiation, p. 199

instrumental (or operant) conditioning, p. 201

intermodal perception, p. 187

monocular depth (or pictorial) cues, p. 181

object segregation, p. 179

optical expansion, p. 180

perception, p. 173

perceptual constancy, p. 178

positive reinforcement, p. 201

preferential-looking technique, p. 174

pre-reaching movements, p. 192

rational learning, p. 205

reflexes, p. 189

scale error, p. 195

self-locomotion, p. 194

sensation, p. 173

stepping reflex, p. 192

stereopsis, p. 181

unconditioned response (UCR), p. 201

unconditioned stimulus (UCS), p. 201

violation-of-expectancy procedure, p. 207

visual acuity, p. 174

Nicola Bealing, *Lucas Talking to a Dog*, 2006 (oil on board)

chapter 6:

Development of Language and Symbol Use

"Woof." (used at age 11 months to refer to a neighbour's dog)

"Hot." (used at age 14 months to refer to a stove, matches, candles, a light reflecting off shiny surfaces, and so forth)

"Read me." (used at age 21 months to ask a mother to read a story)

"Why I don't have a dog?" (27 months old)

"If you give me some candy, I'll be your best friend. I'll be your two best friends." (4 years old)

"Granna, we went to Cagoshin [Chicago]." (5 years, 5 months old)

"It was, like, ya' know, totally awesome, dude." (16 years old)

These utterances were produced by one boy during the process of his becoming a native English speaker (Clore, 1981). Each one reflects the capacity that most sets humans apart from other species: the creative and flexible use of **symbols,** which include language and many kinds of nonlinguistic symbols (print, numbers, pictures, models, maps, and so forth). We use symbols (1) to represent our thoughts, feelings, and knowledge, and (2) to communicate our thoughts, feelings, and knowledge to other people. Our

These children are intent on mastering one of the many important symbol systems in the modern world.

STUART PEARCE / AGE FOTOSTOCK

ability to use symbols vastly expands our cognitive and communicative power. It frees us from the present, enabling us to learn from the generations of people who preceded us and to contemplate the future. Becoming symbol-minded is a crucial developmental task for children around the world (DeLoache, 2005).

In this chapter, we will focus primarily on the acquisition of the pre-eminent symbol system: language. We will then discuss children's understanding and creation of nonlinguistic symbols, such as pictures and models.

The dominant theme in this chapter will once again be the relative contributions of *nature and nurture.* A related issue concerns the extent to which language acquisition is made possible by abilities that are specialized for language learning versus general-purpose mechanisms that support all sorts of learning.

The *sociocultural context* is another prominent theme and features research that examines differences in language acquisition across cultures and communities. This comparative work often provides evidence that is crucial to various theories of language development.

A third recurring theme is *individual differences.* For any given language milestone, some children will achieve it much earlier, and some much later, than others. The *active child* theme also puts in repeated appearances. Infants and young children pay close attention to language and a wide variety of other symbols, and they work hard at figuring out how to use them to communicate.

Language Development

What is the average kindergartener almost as good at as you are? Not much, with one important exception: using language. By 5 years of age, most children have mastered the basic structure of their native language or languages (the possibility of bilingualism is to be assumed whenever we refer to "native language"), whether spoken or manually signed. Although their vocabulary and powers of expression are less

symbols ■ Systems for representing our thoughts, feelings, and knowledge and for communicating them to other people.

sophisticated than yours, their sentences are as grammatically correct as those produced by the average college or university student. This is a remarkable achievement.

Language use requires **comprehension,** which refers to understanding what others say (or sign or write), and **production,** which refers to actually speaking (or signing or writing). As we have observed for other areas of development, infants' and young children's ability to understand precedes their ability to produce. Children understand words and linguistic structures that other people use months or even years before they include them in their own utterances. This is, of course, not unique to young children; you no doubt understand many words that you never actually use. In our discussion, we will be concerned with the developmental processes involved in both comprehension and production, as well as the relation between them.

The Components of Language

How do languages work? Despite the fact that there are thousands of human languages, they share overarching similarities. All human languages are similarly complex, with different pieces combined at different levels to form a hierarchy: sounds are combined to form words, words are combined to form sentences, and sentences are combined to form stories, conversations, and other kinds of narratives. Children must acquire all of these facets of their native language. The enormous benefit that emerges from this combinatorial process is **generativity;** by using the finite set of words in our vocabulary, we can generate an infinite number of sentences, expressing an infinite number of ideas.

However, the generative power of language carries a cost for young language learners: they must deal with its complexity. To appreciate the challenge presented to children learning their first language, imagine yourself as a stranger in a strange land. Someone walks up to you and says, "Jusczyk daxly blickets Mdlangathi." You would have absolutely no idea what this person had just said. Why?

First, you would probably have difficulty perceiving some of the phonemes that make up what the speaker is uttering. **Phonemes** are the units of sound in speech; a change in phoneme changes the meaning of a word. For instance, "rake" and "lake" differ by only one phoneme (/r/ versus /l/), but the two words have quite different meanings to English speakers. Different languages employ different sets of phonemes; English uses just 45 of the roughly 200 sounds found across the world's languages. The phonemes that distinguish meaning in any one language overlap with, but also differ from, those in other languages. For instance, the sounds /r/ and /l/ are a single phoneme in Japanese, and do not carry different meanings. Furthermore, combinations of sounds that are common in one language may never occur in others. When you read the stranger's utterance in the preceding paragraph, you likely were not sure how to pronounce the word "Mdlangathi," because some of its sound combinations do not occur in English (though they do occur in other languages). Thus, the first step in children's language learning is **phonological development:** the mastery of the sound system of their language.

Another reason you would not know what the stranger had said to you, even if you could have perceived the sounds being uttered, is that you would have had no idea what the sounds mean. The smallest units of meaning are called **morphemes.** Morphemes, alone or in combination, constitute words. The word "dog," for example, contains one morpheme. The word "dogs" contains two morphemes, one designating a familiar furry entity ("dog") and the second indicating the plural (–s). Thus, the second component in language acquisition is **semantic development,** that is, learning the system for expressing meaning in a language, including word learning.

comprehension ■ Understanding what others say (or sign or write).

production ■ Speaking (or writing or signing) to others.

generativity ■ The idea that through the use of the finite set of words and morphemes in humans' vocabulary, we can put together an infinite number of sentences and express an infinite number of ideas.

phonemes ■ The elementary units of meaningful sound used to produce languages.

phonological development ■ The acquisition of knowledge about the sound system of a language.

morphemes ■ The smallest units of meaning in a language, composed of one or more phonemes.

semantic development ■ The learning of the system for expressing meaning in a language, including word learning.

syntax ■ Rules in a language that specify how words from different categories (nouns, verbs, adjectives, and so on) can be combined.

syntactic development ■ The learning of the syntax of a language.

pragmatic development ■ The acquisition of knowledge about how language is used.

metalinguistic knowledge ■ An understanding of the properties and function of language—that is, an understanding of language as language.

However, even if you were told the meaning of each individual word the stranger had used, you would still not understand the utterance unless you knew how words are put together in the stranger's language. To express an idea of any complexity, we combine words into sentences, but only certain combinations are allowed in any given language. **Syntax** refers to the permissible combinations of words from different categories (nouns, verbs, adjectives, and so on). In English, for example, the *order* in which words can appear in a sentence is crucial: "Lila ate the lobster" does not mean the same thing as "The lobster ate Lila." Other languages indicate which noun did the eating and which noun was eaten by adding morphemes like suffixes to the nouns. For instance, a Russian noun ending in *a* is likely to refer to the entity doing the eating, while the same noun ending in *u* is likely to refer to the thing that was eaten. The third component in language learning, then, is **syntactic development,** that is, learning how words and morphemes are combined.

Finally, a full understanding of the interaction with the stranger would necessitate having some knowledge of the cultural rules and contextual variations for using language. In some societies, for example, it would be quite bizarre to be addressed by a stranger in the first place, whereas in others it would be commonplace. You would also need to know how to go beyond the speaker's specific words to understand what the speaker was really trying to communicate—to use factors such as the context and the speaker's emotional tone to read between the lines and to learn how to hold a conversation. Acquiring an understanding of how language is typically used is referred to as **pragmatic development.**

Our example of the bewilderment one experiences when listening to an unfamiliar language is useful for delineating the components of language use. However, when we, as adults, hear someone speaking an unfamiliar language, we already know what a language is. We know that the sounds the person is uttering constitute words, that words are combined to form sentences, that only certain combinations are acceptable, and so on. In other words, in contrast with young language learners, adults have considerable **metalinguistic knowledge**—that is, knowledge *about* language and its properties.

Thus, learning language involves phonological, semantic, syntactic, and pragmatic development, as well as metalinguistic knowledge. The same factors are involved in learning a sign language, in which the basic linguistic elements are gestures rather than sounds. In Canada, the two sign languages used most commonly are American Sign Language (ASL) and Langue des Signes Québécoise (LSQ). Around the world, there are over 200 sign languages. These signed languages, which are based on both manual and facial gestures, are true languages in every sense and are as different from one another as spoken languages are. The course of acquisition of a sign language is remarkably similar to that of a spoken language.

By the age of 5, children are capable of generating totally novel sentences that are correct in terms of the phonology, semantics, and syntax of their native language. They are also able to make appropriate pragmatic inferences regarding the content of their partner's utterances.

UDEN / GRAHAM / REDLINK / CORBIS

What Is Required for Language?

What does it take to be able to learn a language in the first place? Full-fledged language is achieved only by humans, so, obviously, one requirement is the human brain. But a single human, isolated from all sources of linguistic experience, could never learn a language; hearing (or seeing) language is a crucial ingredient for successful language development.

A Human Brain

The key to full-fledged language development lies in the human brain. Language is a *species-specific* behaviour: only humans acquire language in the normal course of development. Furthermore, it is *species-universal:* language learning is achieved by typically developing infants across the globe.

In contrast, no other animals naturally develop anything approaching the complexity or generativity of human language, even though they can communicate with one another. For instance, birds claim territorial rights by singing (Marler, 1970), and vervet monkeys can reveal the presence and identity of predators through specific calls (Seyfarth & Cheney, 1993).

Researchers have had limited success in training non-human primates to use complex communicative systems. One early effort was an ambitious project in which a dedicated couple raised a chimpanzee (Vicki) with their own children (Hayes & Hayes, 1951). Although Vicki learned to comprehend some words and phrases, she produced virtually no recognizable words. Subsequent researchers attempted to teach non-human primates sign language. Washoe, a chimpanzee, and Koko, a gorilla, became famous for their ability to communicate with their human trainers and caretakers using manual signs (Gardner & Gardner, 1969; Patterson & Linden, 1981). Washoe could label a variety of objects and could make requests ("more fruit," "please tickle.") The general consensus is that, however impressive Washoe's and Koko's "utterances" were, they do not qualify as language, because they contained little evidence of syntactic structure (Terrace et al., 1979; Wallman, 1992).

The most successful sign-learning non-human is Kanzi, a great ape of the bonobo species. Kanzi's sign learning began when he observed researchers trying to teach his mother to communicate with them by using a lexigram board, a panel composed of a few graphic symbols representing specific objects and actions ("give," "eat," "banana," "hug," and so forth) (Savage-Rumbaugh et al., 1993). Kanzi's mother never caught on, but Kanzi did, and over the years his lexigram vocabulary increased from 6 words to more than 350. He is now very adept at using his lexigram board to answer questions, to make requests, and even to offer comments. He often combines signs, but whether they can be considered syntactically structured sentences is not clear.

There are also several well-documented cases of non-primate animals that have learned to respond to spoken language. Kaminski, Call, and Fischer (2004) found that Rico, a border collie, knew more than 200 words and could learn and remember new words using the same kinds of processes that toddlers use (see pages 236–239). Alex, an African grey parrot, learned to produce and understand basic English utterances, although his skills remained at a toddler level (Pepperberg, 2009).

Whatever the ultimate decision regarding the extent to which trained non-human animals should be credited with language, several things are clear. Even their most basic linguistic achievements come only after a great deal of concentrated human effort, whereas human children master the rudiments of their language with little explicit teaching. Furthermore, while the most advanced non-human communicators do combine symbols, their utterances show limited evidence of syntactic structure, which is a defining feature of language (Tomasello, 1994). In short, only the human brain

Kanzi, who is a male bonobo, and his caretakers communicate with one another by using a specially designed set of symbols that stand for a wide variety of objects, people, and actions.

LAURENTIU GAROFEANU / BARCROFT MEDIA / LANDOV

Rico demonstrates his language comprehension by fetching specific toys on request.

MANUELA HARTLING / REUTERS / CORBIS

acquires a communicative system with the complexity, structure, and generativity of language. Correspondingly, we humans are notoriously poor at learning the communicative systems of other species (Harry Potter's ability to speak Parseltongue with snakes aside). There is an excellent match between the brains of animals of different species and their respective communicative systems.

Brain–language relations A vast amount of research has examined the relationship between language and brain function. It is clear that language processing involves a substantial degree of functional localization. At the broadest level, there are hemispheric differences in language functioning that we discussed to some extent in Chapter 3. For the 90% of people who are right-handed, language is primarily represented and controlled by the left hemisphere.

Left-hemisphere specialization appears to emerge very early in life. Studies using neuroimaging techniques have demonstrated that newborns and 3-month-olds show greater activity in the left hemisphere when exposed to normal speech than when exposed to reversed speech or silence (Bortfeld, Fava, & Boas, 2009; Dehaene-Lambertz, Dehaene, & Hertz-Pannier, 2002; Pena et al., 2003). In addition, EEG studies show that infants exhibit greater left-hemisphere activity when listening to speech but greater right-hemisphere activity when listening to non-speech sounds (Molfese & Betz, 1988). An exception to this pattern of lateralization occurs in the detection of pitch in speech, which in infants, as in adults, tends to involve the right hemisphere (Homae et al., 2006). This specialization for language in the left hemisphere is evident for both spoken and signed languages. Using PET scans, a brain-imaging technique discussed in Chapter 3, researchers at McGill University found similar patterns of brain activation in the left hemisphere for hearing speakers of English and deaf signers of ASL and LSQ, when performing similar language tasks (Petitto et al., 2000).

Although it is evident that the left hemisphere predominantly processes speech from birth, the reasons for this are not yet known. One possibility is that the left hemisphere is innately predisposed to process language but not other auditory stimuli. Another possibility is that speech is localized to the left hemisphere because of its acoustic properties. In this view, the auditory cortex in the left hemisphere is tuned to detect small differences in timing, whereas the auditory cortex in the right hemisphere is tuned to detect small differences in pitch (e.g., Zatorre et al., 1992; Zatorre & Belin, 2001; Zatorre, Belin, & Penhune, 2002). Because speech turns on small differences in timing (as you will see when we discuss voice onset time, page 226), it may be a more natural fit for the left hemisphere.

Critical period for language development If you were to survey your classmates who have studied another language, we predict you would discover that those who learned a foreign language in adolescence found the task to be much more challenging than did those who learned the foreign language in early childhood. A considerable body of evidence suggests that, in fact, the early years constitute a **critical period for language** during which language develops readily. After this period (which ends sometime between age 5 years and puberty), language acquisition is much more difficult and ultimately less successful.

Relevant to this hypothesis, there are several reports of children who barely developed language at all after being deprived of early linguistic experience. The most famous case in modern times is Genie, who was discovered in appalling conditions in Los Angeles in 1970. From the age of approximately 18 months until she was rescued at age 13, Genie's parents kept her tied up and locked alone in a room.

critical period for language ■ The time during which language develops readily and after which (sometime between age 5 and puberty) language acquisition is much more difficult and ultimately less successful.

During her imprisonment, no one spoke to her; when her father brought her food, he growled at her like an animal. At the time of her rescue, Genie's development was stunted—physically, motorically, and emotionally—and she could barely speak. With intensive training, she made some progress, but her language ability never developed much beyond the level of a toddler's: "Father take piece wood. Hit. Cry" (Curtiss, 1977, 1989; Rymer, 1993).

Does this extraordinary case support the critical-period hypothesis? Possibly, but it is difficult to know for sure. Genie's failure to develop full, rich language after her discovery might have resulted as much from the bizarre and inhumane treatment she suffered as from linguistic deprivation.

Other areas of research provide much stronger evidence for the critical-period hypothesis. As noted in Chapter 3, adults, who are well beyond the critical period, are more likely to suffer permanent language impairment from brain damage than are children, presumably because other areas of the young brain (but not the older brain) are able to take over language functions (see M. H. Johnson, 1998). Moreover, adults who learned a second language after puberty use different neural mechanisms to process that language than do adults who learned their second language from infancy (e.g., Kim et al., 1997; Pakulak & Neville, 2011). These results strongly suggest that the neural circuitry supporting language learning operates differently (and better) during the early years.

Further insight into the critical-period hypothesis comes from research with deaf adults who acquired a signed language later in childhood. In one study at McGill University, researchers tested two different groups of adults on an ASL language task: deaf adults who had no exposure to language during early childhood and deaf adults who had learned a spoken language during childhood (both groups were born hearing but later became profoundly deaf) (Mayberry, Lock, & Kazmi, 2002). Both groups began learning ASL at school between the ages of 9 and 15 years. As can be seen in Figure 6.1, those adults who had exposure to a language during infancy, even though it was in a different modality, performed much better on the language task than adults who had received minimal language input during early childhood.

Other studies also highlight the importance of timing of language exposure on later language ability. In an important behavioural study, Johnson and Newport (1989) tested the English proficiency of Chinese and Korean immigrants to the United States who had begun learning English either as children or as adults. The results, shown in Figure 6.2, reveal that knowledge of key aspects of English grammar was related to the age at which these individuals began learning English, but not to the length of their exposure to the language. The most proficient were those who had begun learning English before the age of 7. Johnson and Newport also observed a great deal of variability among "late learners"—those who were acquiring a second language, or a sign language as their first formal language, at puberty or beyond. As in the findings we predicted for your survey of classmates, some individuals achieved native-like skills, whereas the language outcomes for others were quite poor. For reasons that are still unknown, some individuals continue to be talented language learners even after puberty, while most do not.

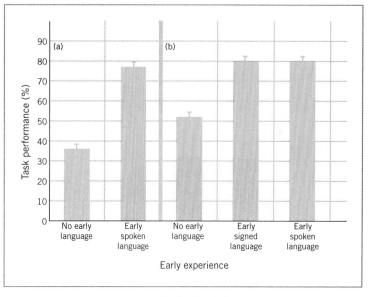

FIGURE 6.1 The importance of early language experience on later language performance (a) The performance of deaf adults who did not experience language in early life is significantly poorer than that of deaf adults who had experienced spoken language in development. (b) Judgments of complex written English sentences are particularly difficult for deaf adults who had no early life language experience. In contrast, the performance of deaf adults who had experience with ASL in infancy and that of hearing adults who had experienced spoken languages other than English in infancy did not differ. (Adapted from Mayberry et al., 2002)

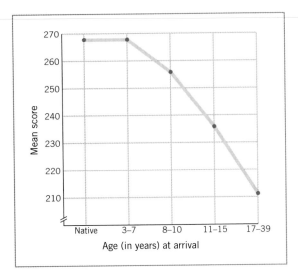

FIGURE 6.2 Test of critical-period hypothesis Performance on a test of English grammar by adults originally from Korea and China was directly related to the age at which they came to the United States and were first exposed to English. The scores of adults who emigrated before the age of 7 were indistinguishable from those of native speakers of English. (Adapted from J. S. Johnson & Newport, 1989)

Newport (1990) proposed an intriguing hypothesis to explain these results and, more generally, to explain why children are usually better language learners than adults. According to her "less-is-more" hypothesis, perceptual and memory limitations cause young children to extract and store smaller chunks of the language than adults do. Because the crucial building blocks of language (the meaning-carrying morphemes) tend to be quite small, young learners' limited cognitive abilities may actually facilitate the task of analyzing and learning language.

The evidence for a critical period in language acquisition has some very clear practical implications. For one thing, deaf children should be exposed to sign language as early as possible. For another, foreign-language exposure at school, discussed in Box 6.1, should begin in the early grades in order to maximize children's opportunity to achieve native-level skills in a second language.

A Human Environment

Possession of a human brain is not enough for language to develop. Children must also be exposed to other people using language—any language, signed or spoken. Adequate experience hearing others talk is readily available in the environment of almost all children around the world. Much of the speech directed to infants occurs in the context of daily routines—during thousands of mealtimes, diaper changes, baths, and bedtimes, as well as in countless games like peekaboo and nursery rhymes like "Itsy Bitsy Spider."

Infants identify speech as something important very early. When given the choice, newborns prefer listening to speech rather than to artificial sounds (Vouloumanos et al., 2010). Intriguingly, newborns also prefer non-human primate (rhesus macaque) vocalizations to non-speech sounds, and show no preference for speech over macaque vocalizations until 3 months of age (Vouloumanos et al., 2010). These results suggest that infants' auditory preferences are fine-tuned through experience with human language during their earliest months.

The infant-directed speech used by this father grabs and holds his baby's attention.

infant-directed speech (IDS) ■ The distinctive mode of speech that adults adopt when talking to babies and very young children.

Infant-directed speech Imagine yourself on a bus listening to a stranger who is seated behind you and speaking to someone. Could you guess whether the stranger was addressing an infant or an adult? We have no doubt that you could, even if the stranger was speaking an unfamiliar language. The reason is that in virtually all cultures, adults adopt a distinctive mode of speech when talking to babies and very young children. This special way of speaking was originally dubbed "motherese" (Newport, Gleitman, & Gleitman, 1977). The current term, **infant-directed speech (IDS)**, recognizes the fact that this style of speech is used by both males and females, including parents and non-parents alike. Indeed, even young children adopt it when talking to babies (Shatz & Gelman, 1973).

CHARACTERISTICS OF INFANT-DIRECTED SPEECH The most obvious quality of IDS is its emotional tone. It is speech suffused with affection—"the sweet music of the species," as Darwin (1877) put it. Another obvious characteristic of IDS is exaggeration. When people speak to babies, their speech is slower and their voice is often higher-pitched than when they speak to adults, and they swoop abruptly from high pitches to low pitches and back again. Even their vowels are clearer (Kuhl et al., 1997). All this exaggerated speech is accompanied by exaggerated facial expressions. Many of these characteristics have been noted in adults speaking such languages as Arabic, French, Italian, Japanese, Mandarin Chinese, and Spanish (see de Boysson-Bardies, 1996/1999), as well as in deaf mothers signing to their infants (Masataka, 1992).

Beyond expressing emotional tone, caregivers can use various pitch patterns of IDS to communicate important information to infants even when infants don't know the meaning of the words uttered. For instance, a word uttered with sharply falling intonation tells the baby that their caregiver disapproves of something, whereas a cooed warm sound indicates approval. These pitch patterns serve the same function in language communities ranging from English and Italian to Japanese (Fernald et al., 1989). Interestingly, infants exhibit appropriate facial emotion when listening to these pitch patterns, even when the language is unfamiliar (Fernald, 1993).

IDS also seems to aid infants' language development. To begin with, it draws infants' attention to speech itself. Indeed, infants prefer IDS to adult-directed speech (Cooper & Aslin, 1994; Pegg, Werker, & McLeod, 1992), even when it is in a language other than their own. In one study, both Cantonese-learning and Canadian English-learning infants listened longer to a Cantonese-speaking Chinese woman talking to a baby than to the same woman talking to an adult friend (Werker, Pegg, & McLeod, 1994). Some studies suggest that infants' preference for IDS may emerge because it is "happy speech"; when speakers' affect is held constant, the preference disappears (Singh, Morgan, & Best, 2002). Perhaps because they pay greater attention to IDS, infants learn and recognize words better when the words are presented in IDS than when they are presented in adult-directed speech (Ma et al., 2011; Singh et al., 2009; Thiessen, Hill, & Saffran, 2005). For instance, Laurel Trainor at McMaster University found that IDS helps young infants discriminate vowel sounds (Trainor & Desjardin, 2002).

Although IDS is very common throughout the world, anthropological data suggest that it may not be universal. In some cultures, such as the Kwara'ae of the Solomon Islands, the Ifaluk of Micronesia, and the Kaluli of Papua New Guinea, it is believed that because infants cannot understand what is said to them, there is no reason for caregivers to speak to them (Le, 2000; Schieffelin & Ochs, 1987; Watson-Gegeo & Gegeo, 1986). For instance, young Kaluli infants are carried facing outward so that they can engage with other members of the group (but not with their caregiver), and if they are spoken to by older siblings, the mother will speak for them (Schieffelin & Ochs, 1987). Thus, even if they are not addressed directly by their caregivers, these infants are still immersed in language.

That infants begin life equipped with the two basic necessities for acquiring language—a human brain and a human environment—is, of course, only the beginning of the story. Of all the things we learn as humans, languages are arguably the most complex—so complex, in fact, that scientists have yet to be able to program computer systems to acquire a human language. The overwhelming complexity of language is further reflected in the difficulty most people have in learning a new language after puberty. How, then, do infants and young children manage to acquire their native language with such astounding success? We turn now to the many steps through which that remarkable accomplishment proceeds.

Around the world, parents in some cultures talk directly to their babies, whereas parents in other cultures do not. Almost everywhere, adults and older children use some form of "baby talk" to address infants.

BOX 6.1: applications

TWO LANGUAGES ARE BETTER THAN ONE

The topic of **bilingualism,** the ability to use two languages, has attracted substantial attention in recent years as increasing numbers of children are developing bilingually. Indeed, almost half of the children in the world are regularly exposed to more than one language, often at home with parents who speak different languages. In Canada, approximately 17% of the population is bilingual, meaning that individuals can carry on conversations in both official languages (French and English). Another 20% of the population reports speaking a first language other than French or English (Statistics Canada, 2011).

Although it was once thought that early exposure to two languages may cause confusion in the young language learner and make the task of language learning more difficult, research on bilingual acquisition gives little cause for concern. In fact, one recent study has demonstrated that bilingual learning can begin in the womb (Byers-Heinlein, Burns, & Werker, 2010). Researchers in Vancouver showed that newborns born to bilingual English/Tagalog mothers prefer listening to these two languages over other languages. Furthermore, a second study demonstrated that newborns were also able to discriminate between the two languages spoken by their mother, setting the stage for their acquisition of both languages. Bilingual infants are also able to discriminate the speech sounds of their two languages at roughly the same pace that monolingual infants distinguish the sounds of their one language (e.g., Albareda-Castellot, Pons, &

Research conducted by Ellen Bialystok at York University on second-language acquisition in Canada reveals a variety of benefits of proficiency in multiple languages. However, the issue of bilingualism in the classroom has been a topic of intense debate in other parts of the world—for example, in the United States which, unlike Canada, has only one official language.

Sebastián-Gallés, 2011; Sundara, Polka, & Molnar, 2008). How might this be, given that bilingual infants have twice as much to learn? One possibility is that bilinguals' attention to speech cues is heightened relative to that of monolinguals. For instance, bilingual infants are better than monolingual infants at using purely visual information (a silent talking face) to discriminate between unfamiliar languages (Sebastián-Gallés et al., 2012).

At a broad level, bilingual children generally seem to follow the same language pathway as monolingual children (see Nicoladis & Genesee, 2007): they produce their first words around the same time as monolingual children, have similar vocabulary sizes (as long as one considers both languages), and use the same types of words. There are some differences in the language development of monolingual and bilingual children, particularly at the early stages of language development. For instance, bilingual infants differentiate between similar-sounding words (e.g., "bin" and "din") in

The Process of Language Acquisition

Acquiring a language involves listening and speaking (or watching and signing) and requires both comprehending what other people communicate and producing intelligible speech (or signs). Infants start out paying attention to what people say or sign, and they know a great deal about language long before their first linguistic productions.

Speech Perception

The first step in language learning is figuring out the sounds of one's native language. As you saw in Chapter 2, the task usually begins in the womb, as fetuses develop a preference for their mother's voice and the language they hear her speak.

bilingualism ■ The ability to use two languages.

word-learning tasks around 3 months later than monolingual infants (Fennell, Byers-Heinlein, & Werker, 2007).

Interestingly, most parents of bilingual children regularly engage in some language mixing during interactions with their young children. Concordia University professor Krista Byers-Heinlein demonstrated that more than 90% of parents did some language mixing, and the degree to which parents mixed language was related to the size of their infants' vocabulary. That is, parents who mixed more frequently had infants with smaller comprehension vocabularies at 18 months (Byers-Heinlein, 2012).

For the most part, children who are acquiring two languages do not seem to confuse them; indeed, they appear to build two separate linguistic systems. Even when bilingual children produce only two words at a time, they show differentiated use of their two languages—for example, they adjust their language to their conversational partner (Genesee, Boivin, & Nicoladis, 1996; Nicoladis & Genesee, 1996). When language mixing does occur, it usually reflects a gap of knowledge in one language that the child is trying to fill in with the other, rather than a confusing of the two language systems (e.g., Deuchar & Quay, 1999; Paradis, Nicoladis, & Genesee, 2000).

There are cognitive benefits to bilingualism, both for the young and the old, as demonstrated by York University professor Ellen Bialystok and Concordia University professor Diane Poulin-Dubois. Children who are competent in two languages perform better on a variety of measures of executive function and cognitive control than do monolingual children (Bialystok, 2009; Bialystok & Craik, 2010; Costa, Hernandez, & Sebastián-Gallés, 2008). Recent results reveal that these effects emerge very early. Bilingual infants and toddlers show greater cognitive flexibility in learning tasks (Kovács & Mehler, 2009a, 2009b; Poulin-Dubois et al., 2011). Finally, being bilingual seems to delay the onset of symptoms in individuals with Alzheimer's disease (Craik, Bialystok, & Freedman, 2010). The link between bilingualism and improved cognitive flexibility likely lies in the fact that bilingual individuals have had to learn to rapidly switch between languages, both in comprehension and production.

Some children learn two languages simultaneously in their homes. In other cases, children learn their second language in a formal school setting. In Canada, French immersion programs, where English-speaking children receive anywhere from 50% to 100% of their instruction in French, were introduced into schools in the 1970s with the goal of encouraging bilingualism across the country. Since that time, other types of second-language immersion programs have been introduced in Canadian public schools, including Mandarin, Spanish, and First Nations languages. According to Statistics Canada (Brockington, 2010), student enrolment in second-language immersion programs increased by 13% between 2003 and 2009, with more than 317 000 students attending a second-language immersion program. These types of programs are voluntary in nature, with parents opting to offer their children the opportunity to learn a second language while already fluent in one of the dominant languages of the country.

Some countries with large but distinct language communities, like Canada, have embraced bilingual education. Others, including the United States, have not. The debate over bilingual education in the United States is tied up with a host of political, ethnic, and racial issues. One side of this debate advocates total immersion, in which children are communicated with and taught exclusively in English, with the goal of helping them become proficient in English as quickly as possible. The other side recommends an approach that initially provides children with instruction in basic subjects in their native language and gradually increases the amount of instruction provided in English (Castro et al., 2011).

In support of the latter view, there is evidence that (1) children often fail to master basic subject matter when it is taught in a language they do not fully understand; and (2) when both languages are integrated in the classroom, children learn the second language more readily, participate more actively, and are less frustrated and bored (Augusta & Hakuta, 1998; Crawford, 1997; Hakuta, 1999). This approach also helps prevent situations where children might become less proficient in their original language as a result of being taught a second one in school.

The basis for this very early learning is **prosody,** the characteristic rhythmic and intonation patterns with which a language is spoken. Differences in prosody are in large part responsible for why languages—from Japanese to French to Swahili—sound so different from one another.

Speech perception also involves distinguishing among the speech sounds that make a difference in a given language. To learn English, for example, one must distinguish between "bat" and "pat," "dill" and "kill," "Ben" and "bed." At the same time, one must learn that the differences in how a speaker in Manitoba versus a speaker in Newfoundland produces the word "boy" do not signal a difference in meaning. As you will see next, young infants do not have to learn to hear these differences: they perceive many speech sounds in very much the same way that adults do.

prosody ■ The characteristic rhythm, tempo, cadence, melody, intonational patterns, and so forth with which a language is spoken.

categorical perception ■ The perception of speech sounds as belonging to discrete categories.

voice onset time (VOT) ■ The length of time between when air passes through the lips and when the vocal cords start vibrating.

Categorical perception of speech sounds Both adults and infants perceive speech sounds as belonging to discrete categories. This phenomenon, referred to as **categorical perception,** has been established by studying people's responses to speech sounds. In this research, a speech synthesizer is used to gradually and continuously change one speech sound, such as /b/, into a related one, such as /p/. These two phonemes are on an acoustic continuum; they are produced in exactly the same way, except for one crucial difference—the length of time between when air passes through the lips and when the vocal cords start vibrating. This lag, referred to as **voice onset time (VOT),** is shorter for /b/ (less than 25 milliseconds [ms]) than for /p/ (greater than 25 ms). (Try saying "ba" and "pa" alternately several times, with your hand on your throat, and you will likely experience this difference in VOT.) To study the perception of VOT, researchers create recordings of speech sounds that vary along this VOT continuum, so that each successive sound is slightly different from the one before, with /b/ gradually changing into /p/. What is surprising is that adult listeners do not perceive this continuously changing series of sounds (Figure 6.3). Instead, they hear /b/ repeated several times and then hear an abrupt switch to /p/. All the sounds in this continuum that have a VOT of less than 25 ms are perceived as /b/, and all those that have a VOT greater than 25 ms are perceived as /p/. Thus, adults automatically divide the continuous signal into two discontinuous categories—/b/ and /p/. This perception of a continuum as two categories is a very useful perceptual ability because it allows one to pay attention to sound differences that are meaningful in one's native language, such as, in English, the difference between /b/ and /p/, while allowing meaningless differences, such as the difference between a /b/ with a 10 ms VOT versus a /b/ with a 20 ms VOT, to be ignored.

Young infants draw the same sharp distinctions between speech sounds. This remarkable fact was established using the habituation technique familiar to you from previous chapters. In the original, classic study (one of the 100 most frequently cited studies in psychology), 1- and 4-month-olds sucked on a pacifier hooked up to a computer (Eimas et al., 1971). The harder they sucked, the more often they'd hear repetitions of a single speech sound. After hearing the same sound repeatedly, the babies gradually sucked less enthusiastically (*habituation*). Then a new sound was played. If the infants' sucking rate increased in response to the new sound, the researchers inferred that the infants discriminated the new sound from the old one (*dishabituation*).

FIGURE 6.3 Categorical perception of speech sounds by adults When adults listen to a tape of artificial speech sounds that gradually change from one sound to another, such as /b/ to /p/ or vice versa, they suddenly switch from perceiving one sound to perceiving the other. (Adapted from C. C. Wood, 1976)

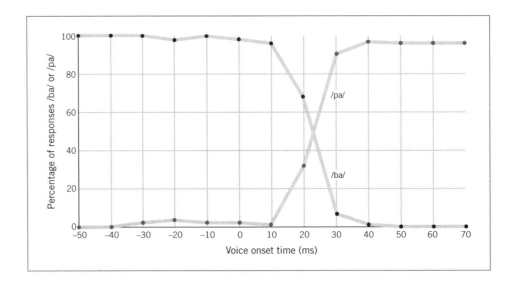

The crucial factor in this study was the relation between the new and old sounds—specifically, whether they were from the same or different phonemic categories. For one group of infants, the new sound was from a different category; thus, after habituation to a series of sounds that adults perceive as /b/, sucking now produced a sound that adults identify as /p/. For the second group, the new sound was within the same category as the old one (i.e., adults perceive them both as /b/). A critical feature of the study is that for both groups, the new and old sounds differed *equally* in terms of VOT.

As Figure 6.4 shows, after habituating to /b/, the infants increased their rate of sucking when the new sound came from a different phonemic category (/p/ instead of /b/). Habituation continued, however, when the new sound was within the same category as the original one. Since this classic study, researchers have established that infants show categorical perception of numerous speech sounds (Aslin, Jusczyk, & Pisoni, 1998).

A fascinating outcome of this research is the discovery that young infants actually make *more* distinctions than adults do. This rather surprising phenomenon occurs because any given language uses only a subset of the large variety of phonemic categories that exist. As noted earlier, the sounds /r/ and /l/ make a difference in English, but not in Japanese. Similarly, speakers of Arabic, but not of English, perceive a difference between the /k/ sounds in "keep" and "cool." Adults simply do not perceive differences in speech sounds that are not important in their native language, which partly accounts for why it is so difficult for adults to become fluent in a second language.

In contrast, infants can distinguish between phonemic contrasts made in all the languages of the world—about 600 consonants and 200 vowels. For instance, Kikuyu infants in Africa are just as good as American babies at discriminating English contrasts not found in Kikuyu (Streeter, 1976). Studies done with infants from English-speaking homes have shown that they can discriminate non-English distinctions made in languages ranging from German and Spanish to Thai, Hindi, and Zulu (Jusczyk, 1997).

This research reveals an ability that is innate, in the sense that it is present at birth, and experience-independent, because infants can discriminate between speech sounds they have never heard before. Being born able to distinguish speech sounds of any language is enormously helpful to infants, priming them to start learning whichever of the world's languages they hear around them. Indeed, the crucial role of early speech perception is reflected in a positive correlation between infants' speech-perception skills and their later language skills. Babies who were better at detecting differences between speech sounds at 6 months scored higher on measures of vocabulary and grammar at 13 to 24 months of age (Tsao, Liu, & Kuhl, 2004).

Developmental changes in speech perception During the last months of their first year, infants increasingly home in on the speech sounds of their native language, and by 12 months of age, they have "lost" the ability to perceive the speech sounds that are not part of it. This shift toward more adult-like speech perception was first demonstrated by Janet Werker and her colleagues at the University of British Columbia (Werker, 1989; Werker & Lalonde, 1988; Werker & Tees, 1984).

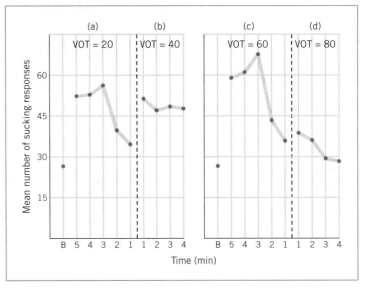

FIGURE 6.4 Categorical perception of speech sounds by infants Infants aged 1 to 4 months were habituated to a tape of artificial speech sounds. (a) One group repeatedly heard a /b/ sound with a VOT of 20, and they gradually habituated to it. (b) When the sound changed to /p/, with a VOT of 40, they dishabituated, indicating that they perceived the difference between the two sounds, just as adults do. (c) A different group was habituated to a /p/ sound with a VOT of 60. (d) When the sound changed to another /p/ with a VOT of 80, the infants remained habituated, suggesting that, like adults, they did not discriminate between these two sounds. (Adapted from Eimas et al., 1971)

FIGURE 6.5 Speech
perception This infant is
participating in a study of speech
perception in the laboratory of
Janet Werker at the University of
British Columbia. The baby has
learned to turn his head to the
sound source whenever he hears a
change from one sound to another.
A correct head turn is rewarded by
an exciting visual display, as well
as by the applause and praise of
the experimenter. To make sure
that neither the mother nor the
experimenter can influence the
child's behaviour, they are both
wearing headphones that prevent
them from hearing what the baby
hears. (From Werker, 1989)

 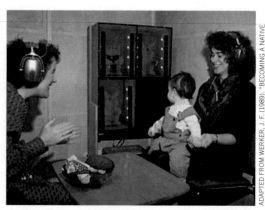

They studied infants ranging in age from 6 to 12 months, all from homes where
Canadian English was spoken. Infants were tested on their ability to discriminate
speech contrasts that are not used in English but that are important in two other
languages—Hindi and Nlaka'pamux (a language spoken by First Nations people
in southcentral British Columbia). The researchers used a simple conditioning
procedure, shown in Figure 6.5. The infants learned that if they turned their head
toward the sound source when they heard a change in the sounds they were listening to, they would be rewarded by an interesting visual display. If the infants
turned their heads in the correct direction immediately following a sound change,
the researchers inferred that they had detected the change.

Figure 6.6 shows that at 6 to 8 months of age, infants learning Canadian English
readily discriminated between the sounds they heard; they could tell one Hindi
syllable from another, and they could also distinguish between two sounds in
Nlaka'pamux. At 10 to 12 months of age, however, the infants no longer perceived
the differences they had detected a few months before. Two Hindi syllables that
had previously sounded different to them now sounded the same. Other research
indicates that a similar change occurs slightly earlier for the discrimination of vowels (Kuhl et al., 1992; Polka & Werker, 1994). Interestingly, this perceptual narrowing does not appear to be an entirely passive process. Kuhl, Tsao, and Liu (2003)
found that infants learned more about the phonetic structure of Mandarin from a
live interaction with a Mandarin speaker than from watching a videotape of one.

Is this process of perceptual narrowing limited to speech? To answer this question, a recent study asked whether this narrowing process also occurs in ASL
(Palmer et al., 2012). The researchers began by determining whether infants who
had never been exposed to ASL were able to discriminate between highly similar ASL signs that are differentiated by the shape of the hand. They found that
4-month-olds could, in fact, discriminate between the signs. However, by 14
months of age, only infants who were learning ASL were able to detect the difference between the hand shapes; those who were not learning ASL had lost their
ability to make this perceptual discrimination. Perceptual narrowing is thus not
limited to speech. Indeed, this narrowing process may be quite broad; recall the
discussion of perceptual narrowing in the domains of face perception (page 186)
and musical rhythm (page 185), discussed in Chapter 5.

Thus, after the age of 8 months or so, infants begin to specialize in their
discrimination of speech sounds, retaining their sensitivity to sounds in the native
language they hear every day, while becoming increasingly less sensitive to non-
native speech sounds. Indeed, becoming a native listener is one of the greatest
accomplishments of the infant's first year of postnatal life.

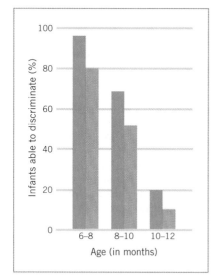

FIGURE 6.6 Percent of infants able
to discriminate foreign-language speech
sounds Infants' ability to discriminate
between speech sounds not in their
native language declines between 6 and
12 months of age. Most 6-month-olds
from English-speaking families readily
discriminate between syllables in Hindi
(blue bars) and Nlaka'pamux (green bars),
but most 10- to 12-month-olds do not.
(Adapted from Werker, 1989)

Word Segmentation

As infants begin to tune into the speech sounds of their language, they also begin to discover another crucial feature of the speech surrounding them: words. This is no easy feat. Unlike the words typed on this page, there are no spaces between words in speech, even in IDS. What this means is that most utterances infants hear are strings of words without pauses between them, like *"Lookattheprettybaby! Haveyoueverseensuchaprettybabybefore?"* They then have to figure out where the words start and end. Remarkably, they begin the process of **word segmentation** during the second half of the first year.

In the first demonstration of infant word segmentation, Jusczyk and Aslin (1995) used a head-turn procedure designed to assess infants' auditory preferences. In this study, 7-month-olds first listened to passages of speech in which a particular word was repeated from sentence to sentence—for example, "The *cup* was bright and shiny. A clown drank from the red *cup*. His *cup* was filled with milk …" After listening to these sentences several times, infants were tested using the head-turn preference procedure to see whether they recognized the words repeated in the sentences. In this method, flashing lights mounted near two loudspeakers located on either side of an infant are used to draw the infant's attention to one side or the other. As soon as the infant turns to look at the light, an auditory stimulus is played through the speaker, and it continues as long as the infant is looking in that direction. The length of time the infant spends looking at the light—and hence listening to the sound—provides a measure of the degree to which the infant is attracted to that sound. Infants in this study were tested on repetitions of words that had been presented in the sentences (such as "cup") or words that had not (such as "bike"). The researchers found that infants listened longer to words that they had heard in the passages of fluent speech, as compared with words that never occurred in the passages. This result indicates that the infants were able to pull the words out of the stream of speech—a task so difficult that even sophisticated speech-recognition software often fails at it.

How do infants find words in pause-free speech? They appear to be remarkably good at picking up regularities in their native language that help them find word boundaries. One example is stress patterning, an element of prosody. In English, the first syllable in two-syllable words is much more likely to be stressed than the second syllable (as in "English," "often," and "second"). By 8 months of age, English-learning infants expect stressed syllables to begin words and can use this information to pull words out of fluent speech (Curtin, Mintz, & Christiansen, 2005; Johnson & Jusczyk, 2001; Jusczyk, Houston, & Newsome, 1999; Thiessen & Saffran, 2003). In contrast, to find words in fluent speech, French-learning infants in Quebec rely on a pattern in which stress falls at the end of a phrase—a pattern that is typical in their native language (Polka & Sundara, 2012).

Another regularity to which infants are surprisingly sensitive concerns the **distributional properties** of the speech they hear. In every language, certain sounds are more likely to appear together than are others. Sensitivity to such regularities in the speech stream was demonstrated in a series of statistical-learning experiments in which babies learned new words based purely on regularities in how often a given sound followed another (Aslin, Saffran, & Newport, 1998; Saffran, Aslin, & Newport, 1996). The infants listened to a 2-minute recording of four different three-syllable "words" (e.g., "tupiro," "golabu," "bidaku," "padoti") repeated in random order with no pauses between the "words." Then, on a series of test trials, the babies were presented with the "words" they had heard (e.g., "bidaku," "padoti") and with sequences that were not words (such as syllable sequences that spanned a word boundary—for example, "kupado," made up from the end of "bidaku" and the

word segmentation ■ The process of discovering where words begin and end in fluent speech.

distributional properties ■ The phenomenon that, in any language, certain sounds are more likely to appear together than are others.

bidakupadotigolabubidakugolabupadotib
idakupadotigolabupadotibidakupadoti...

How quickly could you pick out a word from a stream of speech like the one shown here? It takes 8-month-old infants only 2 minutes of listening.

beginning of "padoti"). Using the same kind of preferential listening test described for the Juscyzk and Aslin (1995) study on the previous page, the researchers found that infants discriminated between the words and the sequences that were not words. To do so, the babies must have registered that certain syllables often occurred together in the sample of speech they heard. For instance, "bi" was always followed by "da" and "da" was always followed by "ku," whereas "ku" could be followed by "tu," "go," or "pa." Thus, the infants used recurrent sound patterns to fish words out of the passing stream of speech. This ability to learn from distributional properties extends to real languages as well; English-learning infants, for example, can track similar statistical patterns when listening to Italian IDS (Pelucchi, Hay, & Saffran, 2009).

Identifying these regularities in speech sounds supports the learning of words. After repeatedly hearing novel "words" such as "timay" and "dobu" embedded in a long stream of speech sounds, 17-month-olds readily learned those sounds as labels for objects (Graf Estes et al., 2007). Similarly, after hearing Italian words like *mela* and *bici* embedded in fluent Italian speech, 17-month-olds who had no prior exposure to Italian readily mapped those labels to objects (Hay et al., 2011). Having already learned the sound sequences that made up the words apparently made it easier for the infants to associate the words with their referents.

Probably the most salient regularity for infants is their own name. Infants as young as 4½ months will listen longer to repetitions of their own name than to repetitions of a different but similar name (Mandel, Jusczyk, & Pisoni, 1995). Just a few weeks later, they can pick their own name out of background conversations (Newman, 2005). This ability helps them find new words in the speech stream. After hearing "It's Jerry's cup!" a number of times, 6-month-old Jerry is more likely to learn the word "cup" than if he had not heard it right after his name (Bortfeld et al., 2005). Over time, infants recognize more and more familiar words, making it easier to pluck new ones out of the speech that they hear.

Infants are exceptional in their ability to identify patterns in the speech surrounding them. They start out with the ability to make crucial distinctions among speech sounds but then narrow their focus to the sounds and sound patterns that make a difference in their native language. This process lays the groundwork for their becoming not just native listeners but also native speakers.

Preparation for Production

In their first months, babies are getting ready to talk. The repertoire of sounds they can produce is initially extremely limited. They cry, sneeze, sigh, burp, and smack their lips, but their vocal tract is not sufficiently developed to allow them to produce anything like real speech sounds. Then, at around 6 to 8 weeks of age, infants begin to coo—producing long, drawn-out vowel sounds, such as "ooohh" or "aaahh." Young infants entertain themselves with vocal gymnastics, switching from low grunts to high-pitched cries, from soft murmurs to loud shouts. They click, smack, blow raspberries, squeal, all with apparent fascination and delight. Through this practice, infants gain motor control over their vocalizations.

As their sound repertoire is expanding, infants become increasingly aware that their vocalizations elicit responses from others, and they begin to engage in dialogues of reciprocal ooohing and aaahing, cooing and gooing, with their parents. With improvement in their motor control of vocalization, they imitate the sounds of their "conversational" partners, even producing higher-pitched sounds when interacting with their mothers and lower-pitched sounds when interacting with their fathers (de Boysson-Bardies, 1996/1999).

Babbling Sometime between 6 and 10 months of age, but on average at around 7 months, a major milestone occurs: babies begin to babble. Standard **babbling** involves producing syllables made up of a consonant followed by a vowel ("pa," "ba," "ma") that are repeated in strings ("papapa"). Contrary to the long-held belief that infants babble a wide range of sounds from their own and other languages (Jakobson, 1941/1968), research has revealed that babies actually babble a fairly limited set of sounds, some of which are not part of their native language (de Boysson-Bardies, 1996/1999). For instance, a longitudinal study of Canadian-English and Parisian-French infants found highly similar patterns in the babble of the two groups of infants (Blake & de Boysson-Bardies, 1992).

Native language exposure is a key component in the development of babbling. Although congenitally deaf infants produce vocalizations similar to those of hearing babies until around 5 or 6 months of age, their vocal babbling occurs very late and is quite limited (Oller & Eilers, 1988). However, some congenitally deaf babies do "babble" right on schedule—those who are regularly exposed to sign language. Infants exposed to ASL babble *manually*. They produce repetitive hand movements that are components of full ASL signs, just as vocally babbled sounds are repeated components of spoken words (Petitto & Marentette, 1991). Thus, like infants learning spoken languages, infants learning signed languages seem to experiment with the elements that are combined to make meaningful words in their native language (Figure 6.7).

As their babbling becomes more varied, it gradually takes on the sounds, rhythm, and intonational patterns of the language infants hear daily. In a simple but clever experiment, French adults listened to the babbling of a French 8-month-old and an 8-month-old from either an Arabic- or Cantonese-speaking family. When asked to identify which baby was the French one in each pair, the adults chose correctly 70% of the time (de Boysson-Bardies, Sagart, & Durand, 1984). Thus, before infants utter their first meaningful words, they are, in a sense, native speakers of a language.

Early interactions Before we turn to the next big step in language production—uttering recognizable words—it is important to consider the social context that promotes language development in most societies. Even before infants start speaking, they display the beginnings of communicative competence: the ability to communicate intentionally with another person.

The first indication of communicative competence is turn-taking. In a conversation, mature participants alternate between speaking and listening. Jerome Bruner and his colleagues (Bruner, 1977; Ratner & Bruner, 1978) have proposed that learning to take turns in social interactions is facilitated by parent–infant games, such as peekaboo and "give-and-take," in which caregiver and baby take turns giving and receiving objects. In these "dialogues," the infant has the opportunity to alternate between an active and a passive role, as in a conversation in which one alternates between speaking and listening. These early interactions give infants practice in bidirectional communication, providing infants with a scaffold to learn how to use language to converse with others. Indeed, recent research suggests that caregivers' responses to infant babbling may serve a similar function. When an adult labels an object for an infant just after the infant babbles, the infant's learning of the label is more greatly enhanced than when the labelling occurs in the absence of babbling (Goldstein et al., 2010). The results of this study suggest that babbling may serve as a signal to the caregiver that the infant is attentive and ready to learn. This early back-and-forth may also provide infants with practice in conversational turn-taking.

babbling ■ Repetitive consonant–vowel sequences ("bababa …") or hand shapes (for learners of signed languages) produced during the early phases of language development.

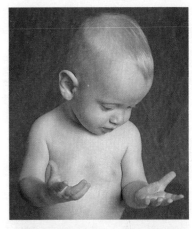

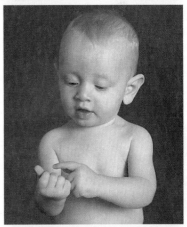

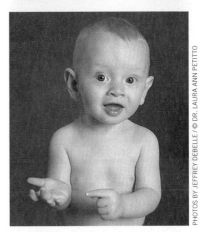

FIGURE 6.7 Manual babbling Babies who are exposed to the sign language of their deaf parents babble with their hands. A subset of their hand movements differs from those of infants exposed to spoken language, and corresponds to the rhythmic patterning of adult signs. (From Petitto et al., 2001)

PHOTOS BY JEFFREY DEBELLE / © DR. LAURA ANN PETITTO

This toddler is pointing to get her father to share her attention—to achieve intersubjectivity. Once the father identifies the focus of his daughter's attention, he may even decide to add it to the shopping basket.

As discussed in Chapter 4, successful communication also requires *intersubjectivity,* in which two interacting partners share a mutual understanding. The foundation of intersubjectivity is *joint attention,* which, early on, is established by the parent's following the baby's lead, looking at and commenting on whatever the infant is looking at. By 12 months of age, infants have begun to understand the communicative nature of pointing, with many also being capable of meaningful pointing themselves (Behne et al., 2012).

We have thus seen that infants spend a good deal of time getting ready to talk. Through babbling, they gain some initial level of control over the production of sounds that are necessary to produce recognizable words. As they do so, they already begin to sound like their parents. Through early interactions with their parents, they develop interactive routines similar to those required in the use of language for communication. We will now turn our attention to the processes that lead to infants' first real linguistic productions: words.

First Words

When babies first begin to segment words from fluent speech, they are simply recognizing familiar patterns of sounds without attaching any meaning to them. But then, in a major revolution, they begin to recognize that words have meaning.

The problem of reference The first step for infants in acquiring the meanings of words is to address the problem of **reference,** that is, to start associating words and meaning. Figuring out which of the multitude of possible referents is the right one for a particular word is, as the philosopher Willard Quine (1960) pointed out, a very complex problem. If a child hears someone say "bunny" in the presence of a rabbit, how does the child know whether this new word refers to the rabbit itself, to its fuzzy tail, to the whiskers on the right side of its nose, or to the twitching of its nose? That the problem of reference is a real problem is illustrated by the case of a toddler who thought "Phew!" was a greeting, because it was the first thing her mother said on entering the child's room every morning (Ferrier, 1978).

Early Word Recognition

A classic problem posed by philosopher Willard Quine was how someone who does not know the word "bunny" could figure out exactly what it refers to. One way this mother could help her son learn a new word is by labelling the referent while it is the focus of her son's attention.

reference ■ In language and speech, the associating of words and meaning.

Infants begin associating highly familiar words with their highly familiar referents surprisingly early on. When 6-month-olds hear either "Mommy" or "Daddy," they look toward the appropriate person (Tincoff & Jusczyk, 1999). Infants gradually come to understand the meaning of less frequently heard words, with the pace of their vocabulary-building varying greatly from one child to another. Remarkably, parents are often unaware of just how many words their infants recognize. Using a computer monitor, Bergelson and Swingley (2012) showed infants pairs of pictures of common foods and body parts and tracked the infants' eye gaze when one of the pictures was named. They found that even 6-month-olds looked to the correct picture significantly more often than would be expected by chance, demonstrating that they recognized the names of these items. Strikingly, most of their parents reported that the infants did not know the meanings of these words. So not only do infants understand far more words than they can produce; they also understand far more words than even their caregivers realize.

One of the remarkable features of infants' early word recognition is how rapidly they understand what they are hearing. To illuminate the age-related dynamics of this understanding, Fernald and her colleagues presented infants with images depicting pairs of familiar objects, such as a dog and a baby, and observed how quickly the infants moved their eyes to the correct object after hearing its label used (e.g., "Where's the *baby*?"). The researchers found that whereas 15-month-olds waited until they had heard the whole word to look at the target object, 24-month-olds looked at the correct object after hearing only the first part of its label, just as adults do (Fernald et al., 1998; Fernald, Perfors, & Marchman, 2006; Fernald, Swingley, & Pinto, 2001). Older infants can also use context to help them recognize words. For instance, those who are learning a language that has a grammatical gender system (like French or Spanish) can use the gender of the article preceding the noun (*la* versus *le* in French; *la* versus *el* in Spanish) to speed their recognition of the noun itself (Lew-Williams & Fernald, 2007; Van Heugten & Shi, 2009). Other visual-fixation research has shown that older infants can even recognize familiar words when they are mispronounced (e.g., "vaby" for "baby," "gall" for "ball," "tog" for "dog," and so on), though their recognition is slower than when they hear the words pronounced correctly (Swingley & Aslin, 2000).

Early word production Gradually, infants begin to say some of the words they understand, with most producing their first words between 10 and 15 months of age. The words a child is able to say are referred to as the child's *productive vocabulary*.

What counts as an infant's "first word"? It can be any specific utterance consistently used to refer to something or to express something. Even with this loose criterion, identification of an infant's earliest few words can be problematic. For one thing, doting parents often misconstrue their child's babbling as words. For another, early words may differ from their corresponding adult forms. For instance, "woof" was one of the first words spoken by the boy whose linguistic progress was illustrated at the beginning of this chapter. It was used to refer to the dog next door—both to excitedly name the animal when it appeared in the neighbours' yard and to wistfully request the dog's presence when it was absent.

Infants' early word productions are limited by their ability to pronounce words clearly enough that an adult can recognize them. To make life easier for themselves, infants adopt a variety of simplification strategies (Gerken, 1994). For instance, they leave out the difficult bits of words, turning "banana" into "nana," or they substitute easier sounds for hard-to-say ones—"bubba" for "brother," "wabbit" for "rabbit." Sometimes they reorder parts of words to put an easier sound at the beginning of the word, as in the common "pasketti" (for "spaghetti") or the more idiosyncratic "Cagoshin" (the way the child quoted at the beginning of the chapter continued for several years to say "Chicago").

When this infant hears the word "mouth," will she look at the picture of the mouth or at the picture of the apple? The speed and accuracy of her looks in response to words provide a useful measure of her vocabulary knowledge.

PHOTO BY ELIKA BERGELSON

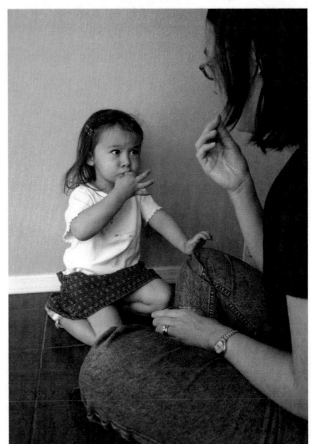

Some parents use baby signs to communicate with their infants before their infants begin to produce spoken words.

CHRISTINA KENNEDY / PHOTOEDIT

Once children start talking, what do they talk about? The early productive vocabularies of English-learning children in the United States and English- and French-learning children in Canada include names for people, objects, and events from the child's everyday life (Clark, 1979; K. Nelson, 1973; Poulin-Dubois, Graham, & Sippola, 1995). Children name their parents, siblings, pets, and themselves, as well as other personally important objects such as cookies, juice, and balls. Frequent events and routines are also labelled—"up," "bye-bye," "night-night." Important modifiers are also used—"mine," "hot," "all gone." Table 6.1 reveals substantial cross-linguistic similarities in the content of the first 10 words of children in the United States, Hong Kong, and Beijing. As the table shows, many of infants' first words in the three societies referred to specific people or were sound effects (Tardif et al., 2008).

In the early productive vocabularies of children learning English, nouns predominate. One reason may be that because nouns label entities—whereas verbs represent *relations* among entities—the meanings of nouns are easier to pick up from observation than are the meanings of verbs (Gentner, 1982). Similarly, words that are easier to picture—that are more imageable—are easier for infants and toddlers to learn (McDonough et al., 2011). Another reason is that middle-class North American mothers (the group most frequently studied) engage in frequent

TABLE 6.1

Rank-Ordered List of Earliest Words in Three Languages*

English	Putonghua (Mandarin)	Cantonese
Daddy	**Daddy**	**Mommy**
Mommy	Aah	**Daddy**
BaaBaa	**Mommy**	*Grandma (paternal)*
Bye	*YumYum*	*Grandpa (paternal)*
Hi	*Sister (older)*	**Hello?/Wei?**
UhOh	**UhOh** (Aiyou)	*Hit*
Grr	*Hit*	Uncle (paternal)
Bottle	**Hello/Wei**	Grab/grasp
YumYum	Milk	*Auntie (maternal)*
Dog	Naughty	**Bye**
No	*Brother (older)*	**UhOh** (Aiyou)
WoofWoof	*Grandma (maternal)*	*Ya/Wow*

*Words in boldface were common across all three languages; those in italics were common for two of the languages.

Source: Tardif et al., 2008

bouts of object-labelling for their infants—"Look, there's a turtle! Do you see the turtle?" (Fernald & Morikawa, 1993)—and the proportion of nouns in very young children's vocabularies is related to the proportion of nouns in their mother's speech to them (Pine, 1994). Significantly, the pattern of object-labelling by mothers differs across cultures and contexts. For instance, Japanese mothers label objects far less often than do American mothers (Fernald & Morikawa, 1993). In the context of toy play, Korean mothers use more verbs than nouns, a pattern very different from that observed in English-speaking mothers (Choi, 2000). And indeed, infants in Korea learn nouns and verbs at the same rate, unlike English-learning infants (Choi & Gopnik, 1995).

Initially, infants say the words in their small productive vocabulary only one word at a time. This phase is referred to as the **holophrastic period,** because the child typically expresses a "whole phrase"—a whole idea—with a single word. For instance, a child might say "Drink!" to express the desire for a glass of juice. Children who produce only one-word utterances are not limited to single ideas; they manage to express themselves by stringing together successive one-word utterances. An example is a little girl with an eye infection who pointed to her eye, saying "Ow," and then after a pause, "Eye" (E. Hoff, 2001).

What young children want to talk about quickly outstrips the number of words in their limited vocabularies, so they make the words they do know perform double duty. One way they do this is through **overextension**—using a word in a broader context than is appropriate, as when children use "dog" for any four-legged animal, "daddy" for any man, "moon" for a dishwasher dial, or "hot" for any reflective metal (Table 6.2). Most overextensions represent an effort to communicate rather than a lack of knowledge, as demonstrated by research in which children who overextended some words were given comprehension tests (Naigles & Gelman, 1995). In one study, children were shown pairs of pictures of entities for which they generally used the same label—for instance, a dog and a sheep, both of which they normally referred to as "dog." However, when asked to point to the sheep, they chose the correct animal. Thus, these children understood the meaning of the word "sheep," but because it was not in their productive vocabulary, they used a related word that they knew how to say in order to talk about the animal.

holophrastic period ■ The period when children begin using the words in their small productive vocabulary one word at a time.

overextension ■ The use of a given word in a broader context than is appropriate.

TABLE 6.2

Examples of Young Children's Overextensions of Word Meaning

Word	Referents
ball	ball, balloon, marble, apple, egg, spherical water tank (Rescorla, 1980)
cat	cat, cat's usual location on top of TV when absent (Rescorla, 1980)
moon	moon, half-moon-shaped lemon slice, circular chrome dial on dishwasher, half a Cheerio, hangnail (Bowerman, 1978)
snow	snow, white flannel bed pad, white puddle of milk on floor (Bowerman, 1978)
baby	own reflection in mirror, framed photograph of self, framed photographs of others (Hoff, 2001)

BOX 6.2: individual differences

THE ROLE OF FAMILY AND SCHOOL CONTEXT IN EARLY LANGUAGE DEVELOPMENT

Within a family, parents often notice significant linguistic differences between their children. Within a given community, such differences can be greatly magnified. In a single kindergarten classroom, for example, there may be a tenfold difference in the number of words used by different children. What accounts for these differences?

The number of words children know is intimately related to the number of words that they hear, which, in turn, is linked to their caregivers' vocabularies. One of the key determinants of the language children hear is the socioeconomic status of their parents. In a seminal study, Hart and Risley (1995) recorded the speech that 42 parents used with their children over the course of 2½ years, from before the infants were talking until they were 3 years of age. Some of the parents were upper-middle class, others were working class, and others were on welfare. The results were astonishing: the received linguistic experience of the average child whose parents were on welfare (616 words per hour) was half that of the average working-class parents' child (1251 words per hour) and less than one-third that of the average child in a professional family (2153 words per hour). The researchers did the math and suggested that after 4 years, an average child with upper-middle-class parents would have accumulated experience

with almost 45 million words, compared with 26 million for an average child in a working-class family and 13 million for an average child with parents on welfare.

How do these differences affect children's language development? Not surprisingly, children from higher-SES groups have larger vocabularies than those of children from lower-SES groups (Fenson et al., 1994; Huttenlocher et al., 1991). Indeed, a study of high-SES and mid-SES mothers and their 2-year-old children found that SES differences in maternal speech (e.g., number and length of utterances, richness of vocabulary, and sentence complexity) predicted some of the differences in children's spoken vocabularies (Hoff, 2003). For instance, higher-SES mothers tended to use longer utterances with their children than did mid-SES parents, giving their children access not only to more words but also to more complex grammatical structures (Hoff, 2003). Such differences in maternal speech even affect how quickly toddlers recognize familiar words: children whose mothers provided more maternal speech at 18 months were faster at recognizing words at 24 months than were children whose mothers provided less input (Hurtado, Marchman, & Fernald, 2008).

Similar findings emerge in the school context. For instance, when preschool children

with low language skills are placed in classrooms with peers who also have low language skills, they show less language growth than do their counterparts who are placed with classmates who have high language skills (Justice et al., 2011). However, there is the possibility that negative peer effects may be offset by positive teacher effects. For instance, one study found that children whose preschool teachers used a rich vocabulary showed better reading comprehension in Grade 4 than did children whose preschool teachers used a more limited vocabulary (Dickinson & Porche, 2011).

These results suggest that for a variety of reasons, parents' SES affects the way they talk to their children; in turn, those individual differences have a substantial influence on the way their children talk. These differences can be intensified by the linguistic abilities of children's peers and teachers. For children in low-SES environments, the potential negative effects of these influences may be offset by interventions ranging from increased access to children's books (which provide enriched linguistic environments) to enhancing teacher training in low-income preschool settings (Dickinson, 2011). Regardless of the source, what goes in is what comes out: we can only learn words and grammatical structures that we hear (or see or read) in the language surrounding us.

Word learning After the appearance of their first words, children typically plod ahead slowly, reaching a productive vocabulary of 50 or so words by around 18 months of age. At this point, the rate of learning appears to accelerate, leading to what appears to be a "vocabulary spurt" (e.g., L. Bloom, 1973; McMurray, 2007). Although scholars disagree about whether learning actually speeds up for all or even most children (Bloom, 2000), it is clear that children's communicative abilities grow rapidly (Figure 6.8).

What accounts for the skill with which young children learn words? When we look closely, we see that there are multiple sources of support for learning new words, some coming from the people around them, and some generated by the children themselves. In Box 6.2 we discuss other influences of family and school context on language development.

ADULT INFLUENCES ON WORD LEARNING In addition to using IDS, which makes word learning easier for infants, adults facilitate word learning by highlighting new words. For instance, they stress new words, or place them at the end of a sentence. They also tend to label objects that are already the focus of the child's attention, thereby reducing uncertainty about the referent (Masur, 1982; Tomasello, 1987; Tomasello & Farrar, 1986). Their repetition of words also helps; young children are more likely to acquire words their parents use frequently (Huttenlocher et al., 1991). Another stimulus to word learning that adults provide involves naming games, in which they ask the child to point to a series of named items—"Where's your nose?" "Where's your ear?" "Where's your tummy?" There is also some evidence that parents may facilitate their children's word learning by maintaining spatial consistency with the objects they are labelling. For instance, in a study in which parents labelled novel objects for their infants, the infants learned the names of the objects more readily when the objects were in the same location each time they were labelled (Samuelson et al., 2011). Presumably, consistency in the visual environment helps children map words onto objects and events in that environment. In Box 6.3, we discuss recent research focused on a currently popular means by which some parents try to "outsource" word learning: technology.

CHILDREN'S CONTRIBUTIONS TO WORD LEARNING When confronted with words they haven't heard before, children actively exploit the context in which the new word was used in order to infer its meaning. A classic study by Carey and Bartlett (1978) demonstrated **fast mapping**—the process of rapidly learning a new word simply from hearing the contrastive use of a familiar word and the unfamiliar word. In the course of everyday activities in a preschool classroom, an experimenter drew a child's attention to two trays—one red, the other an uncommon colour the child would not know by name—and asked the child to get "the *chromium* tray, not the red one." The child was thus provided with a contrast between a familiar term ("red") and an unfamiliar one ("chromium"). From this simple contrast, the participants inferred which tray they were supposed to get and that the name of the colour of that tray was "chromium." After this single exposure to a novel word, about half the children showed some knowledge of it 1 week later by correctly picking out "chromium" from an array of paint chips.

Some theorists have proposed that the many inferences children make in the process of learning words are guided by a number of assumptions (sometimes referred to as principles, constraints, or biases) that limit the possible meanings children entertain for a new word. For instance, children expect that a given entity will have only one name, an expectancy referred to as the *mutual exclusivity* assumption by Woodward and Markman (1998). Early evidence for this assumption came from a study in which 3-year-olds saw pairs of objects—a familiar object for which the children had a name and an unfamiliar one for which they had no name. When the experimenter said, "Show me the blicket," the children mapped the novel label to the novel object, the one for which they had no name (Markman & Wachtel, 1988). Even 16-month-old infants do the same (Graham, Poulin-Dubois, & Baker, 1998). (See Figure 6.9a.) Interestingly, bilingual and trilingual infants, who are accustomed to hearing more than one name for a given object, are less likely to follow the mutual exclusivity principle (Byers-Heinlein & Werker, 2009).

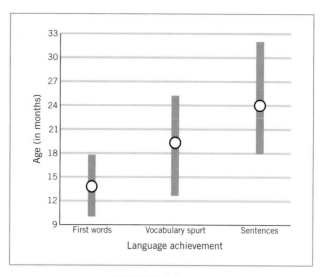

FIGURE 6.8 Language achievement On average, North American children say their first word at around 13 months, experience a vocabulary spurt at around 19 months, and begin to produce simple sentences at around 24 months. However, the bars above and below these means show a substantial amount of variability in when different children achieve each of these milestones. (Adapted from L. Bloom, 1998)

This young Inuit child is playing a naming game; her mother has just asked her to point to her nose.

fast mapping ■ The process of rapidly learning a new word simply from hearing the contrastive use of a familiar and the unfamiliar word.

pragmatic cues ■ Aspects of the social context used for word learning.

Markman and Woodward (Markman, 1989; Woodward & Markman, 1998) also proposed the *whole-object* assumption, according to which children expect a novel word to refer to a whole object rather than to a part, property, action, or other aspect of the object. Thus, in the case of Quine's rabbit problem (see page 232), the whole-object assumption leads children to map the label "bunny" to the whole animal, not just to its tail or the twitching of its nose.

When confronted with novel words, children also exploit a variety of **pragmatic cues** to their meaning by paying attention to the *social contexts* in which the words are used. For instance, children use an adult's focus of attention as a cue to word meaning. In a study by Baldwin (1993), an experimenter showed 18-month-olds

FIGURE 6.9 **Cues for word learning** (a) Mutual exclusivity: Since this child already knows the name of the familiar object on the table, she will pick up the novel object when the adult asks her to "show me the blicket."

(b) Pragmatic cues: This child will assume that the novel word she hears the experimenter saying applies to the novel object the experimenter is looking at, even though the child cannot see the object and is looking at a different novel object when she actually hears the word.

(c) Pragmatic cues: This child will learn "gazzer" as the name of the novel object that the adult smiles at triumphantly after she had previously announced that she wanted to find "the gazzer."

two novel objects and then concealed them in separate containers. Next, the experimenter peeked into one of the containers and commented, "There's a modi in here." The adult then removed and gave both objects to the child. When asked for the "modi," the children picked the object that the experimenter had been looking at when saying the label. Thus, the infants used the relation between eye gaze and labelling to learn a novel name for an object before they had ever seen it (see Figure 6.9b).

Another pragmatic cue that children use to draw inferences about a word's meaning is *intentionality* (Tomasello, 2003). For instance, in one study, 2-year-olds heard an experimenter announce, "Let's dax Mickey Mouse." The experimenter then performed two actions on a Mickey Mouse doll, one carried out in a coordinated and apparently intentional way, followed by a pleased comment ("There!"), and the other carried out in a clumsy and apparently accidental way, followed by an exclamation of surprise ("Oops!"). The children interpreted the novel verb "dax" as referring to the action the adult apparently intended to perform (Tomasello & Barton, 1994). Infants can even use an adult's emotional response to infer the name of a novel object that they cannot see (Tomasello, Strosberg, & Akhtar, 1996). In a study establishing this fact, an adult announced her intention to "find the gazzer." She then picked up one of two objects and showed obvious disappointment with it. When she gleefully seized the second object, the infants inferred that it was "a gazzer." (Figure 6.9c depicts another instance in which a child infers the name of an unseen object from an adult's emotional expression.)

The degree to which preschool children take a speaker's intention into account is shown by the fact that if an adult's labelling of an object conflicts with their knowledge of that object, they will nevertheless accept the label if the adult clearly used it intentionally (Jaswal, 2004). When an experimenter simply used the label "dog" in referring to a picture of a catlike animal, preschool children were reluctant to extend the label to other catlike stimuli. However, they were much more willing to do so when the experimenter made it clear that he really intended his use of the unexpected label by saying, "You're not going to believe this, but this is actually a dog." Similarly, if a child has heard an adult refer to a cat as "dog," the child will be reluctant to subsequently learn a new word used by that "untrustworthy" adult (e.g., Koenig & Harris, 2005; Koenig & Woodward, 2010; Sabbagh & Shafman, 2009).

Another way young children can infer the meaning of novel words is by taking cues from the *linguistic context* in which the words are used. In one of the first experiments on language acquisition, Brown (1957) established that the grammatical form of a novel word influences children's interpretation of it. He showed preschool children a picture of a pair of hands kneading a mass of material in a container (Figure 6.10). The picture was described to one group of children as "sibbing," to another as "a sib," and to a third as "some sib." The children subsequently interpreted "sib" as referring to the action, the container, or the material, depending on which grammatical form (verb, count noun, or mass noun) of the word they had heard.

Two- and 3-year-old children also use the *grammatical category* of novel words to help interpret their meaning (e.g., Hall, 1994; Hall, Waxman, & Hurwitz, 1993; Markman & Hutchinson, 1984; Waxman, 1990). In a number of studies, Geoff Hall and his colleagues at the University of British Columbia have demonstrated that young children are wonderfully sensitive to the way in which a new word is introduced. Hearing "This is a dax," preschoolers assume that "dax" refers to an object, as well as to other objects from the same category. In contrast, "This is a dax one" suggests that "dax" refers to a property of the object (e.g., its colour or

FIGURE 6.10 Linguistic context When Roger Brown, a pioneer in the study of language development, described a drawing like this as "sibbing," "a sib," or "some sib," preschool children made different assumptions about the meaning of "sib."

BOX 6.3: applications

iBABIES: TECHNOLOGY AND LANGUAGE LEARNING

When adults enter a new language culture, they often have access to many technological aids—from pocket dictionaries to smart phone apps for translations—to help them get around and ask for what they need. They can also harness technology to learn a new language, from digital language labs at colleges and universities to commercial training programs like Rosetta Stone.

What about infants? They, too, are often immersed in technology. Indeed, over the past two decades, there was a "brainy-baby" craze in which businesses earned hundreds of millions of dollars marketing all manner of electronic games, toys, and DVDs that claimed to enhance babies' intellectual growth. Some of these claims were laughable. For instance, one of your authors purchased a teething ring for her baby and was astonished to read on the packaging that the ring supposedly improves an infant's language development by enhancing early oral-motor skills. Other claims seemed more plausible but were subsequently called into serious question by developmental research—so much so that the companies producing these products were forced to stop promoting their "educational" value.

However, there is still concern over technology marketed for children younger than 2 years because it reduces the time infants and toddlers spend actively engaged with caregivers and objects, their best source for learning. In a large-scale study that included more than 1000 children younger than 2 years, researchers examined the association between television/DVD viewing and vocabulary development (Zimmerman, Cristakis, & Meltzoff, 2007). Crucially, the authors controlled for family demographics (including parents' education, family income, race/ethnicity, and so forth) that may influence media use. For 8- to 16-month-olds, there was a negative correlation between the amount of time infants watched DVDs and parental reports of the infants' vocabularies: the more the babies watched, the lower their vocabulary scores. Note that this negative relationship was observed only for DVDs marketed as "educational" for babies; other types of programming (including both educational and non-educational children's television programs) showed no association with vocabulary development. For the older infants in the study (between 17 and 24 months of age), the negative relationship disappeared. Contrary to many parents' beliefs, the amount of time parents spent watching television with their children did not affect the children's vocabulary scores. These results are consistent with the Canadian Paediatric Society's recommendation to discourage screen time for children under 2 (Lipnowski & LeBlanc, 2012).

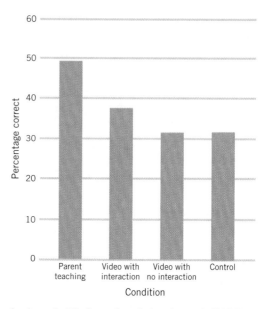

As shown in this figure from DeLoache et al. (2010), the infants who learned from parents (shown in the first column) performed best on the study's measure of word learning. Infants in the two video-learning conditions (middle two columns) did no better than the control group (last column).

---

texture), while "This is dax" suggests that "dax" is a proper noun (a name). Even infants and toddlers can draw on some of these links to interpret the meaning of novel words (e.g., Booth & Waxman, 2009; Waxman & Hall, 1993; Waxman & Markow, 1995, 1998).

Children's interpretation of novel words applied to objects is particularly guided by the objects' shape, possibly because shape is a good cue to category membership. Children readily extend a novel noun to novel objects of the same shape, even when those objects differ dramatically in size, colour, and texture (Graham & Poulin-Dubois, 1999; Landau, Smith, & Jones, 1988; L. B. Smith, Jones, & Landau, 1992). Thus, a child who hears a U-shaped wooden block called "a dax" will assume that "dax" also refers to a U-shaped object covered in blue fur or to a U-shaped piece of red wire—but not to a wooden block of a different shape (Figure 6.11). A shape bias is also evident in young children's spontaneous extension of familiar words to novel objects that are vaguely similar to familiar entities (e.g., a cone

In the most rigorous study to date, DeLoache and colleagues (2010) used random assignment and an objective test of vocabulary to determine whether a bestselling "educational" DVD had an impact on language development. The DVD in question was marketed to infants at least 12 months old. The researchers randomly assigned 12- to 18-month-olds into four groups. Infants in the *video-with-interaction* group watched the video with a parent 5 times a week over 4 weeks; the parent was asked to interact naturally with the infant while watching. Infants in the *video-without-interaction* group received the same amount of exposure, but without a parent watching along with them. This mimics a common situation at home, where parents might be in the same room but are engaged in another activity. Infants in the *parent-teaching group* did not watch the video at all. Instead, their parents were given a list of 25 words featured on the video and asked to teach the infants those words in whatever way felt most natural to them. Finally, infants in the *control* group received no intervention, serving as a baseline for typical vocabulary development.

At the beginning and end of the study, the infants were tested on a subset of the words featured on the DVD. Infants in the DVD-viewing conditions showed no more advancement in vocabulary than the infants in the control group did. The infants who showed the greatest vocabulary development were the infants in the parent-teaching group. Interestingly, the performance of infants in the DVD-viewing conditions was unrelated to how much parents thought their infant had learned from the DVD. However, there was a correlation between how much the parents liked the DVD themselves and how much they thought their infant had learned: the more that parents liked the DVD, the more likely they were to overestimate its positive effects.

Although this area of research is still relatively new, the results thus far suggest that outsourcing infants' vocabulary development to their passive observation of educational media does not match up with how infants actually learn. Even the best technology cannot substitute for a caregiver who is interacting with the child. The importance of such interaction was highlighted by a study in which toddlers learned new words from an adult in one of three conditions: (1) in-person interaction with the adult; (2) interaction with the adult via video link; and (3) observation of a video of the adult interacting with another adult. The word-learning outcomes for the first two conditions were the same—and superior to those in which toddlers were passive observers (O'Doherty et al., 2011). Questions about electronic media for infants are only going to increase, given the delight with which young children, and even infants, have embraced the apps on their parents' smart phones and tablet computers. As with any type of activity, a little here and there probably doesn't hurt. But it is important to approach any claims of "educational value" with a great deal of skepticism.

Whether they are educationally beneficial or not, it is clear that electronic media are of compelling fascination to infants.

might be referred to as a "mountain") (Samuelson & Smith, 2005). This attention to the shared shape of objects is evident in categorization tasks even before infants have acquired many productive words (Graham & Diesendruck, 2010).

Another potentially useful cue to word meaning is the repeated correspondence between words the child hears and objects the child observes in the world. Any single scene is ambiguous. For instance, if the child sees four different novel objects

Exemplar	Shape change	Texture change	Size change
	.50	.76	.82

FIGURE 6.11 Shape bias In one of many studies of the shape bias, children were shown the exemplar at the top of this figure and told that it was a "dax" (or some other nonsense word). Then they were asked which of the objects below the exemplar was also "a dax." The numbers under the objects indicate the proportion of children who thought each object was "a dax." As you can see, they most often thought that the word referred to the object that was of the same shape as the exemplar, even if the surface texture or size was different. (Adapted from Landau, Smith, & Jones, 1988)

syntactic bootstrapping ■ The strategy of using the grammatical structure of whole sentences to figure out meaning.

LETITIA R. NAIGLES, UNIVERSITY OF CONNECTICUT

FIGURE 6.12 **Syntactic bootstrapping** When children in Naigles's (1990) study heard an adult describe this filmed scene as "The duck is kradding the rabbit," they used the syntactic structure of the sentence to infer that "kradding" is what the duck is doing to the rabbit.

together and hears the label "dax," the child has no way of knowing which object is "the dax" (this ambiguity is similar to that in Quine's "bunny" example described earlier). But across experiences, the child might observe that whenever "dax" is said, one of those four objects is always present, and thus that object is probably "the dax." Through this process of *cross-situational word learning,* even infants can narrow down the possible meanings of new words (e.g., L. Smith & Yu, 2008; Vouloumanos & Werker, 2009).

Children also use the grammatical structure of whole sentences to figure out meaning—a strategy referred to as **syntactic bootstrapping** (Fisher, 1999; Fisher, Gleitman, & Gleitman, 1991; Gertner, Fisher, & Eisengart, 2006; Yuan & Fisher, 2009). An early demonstration of this phenomenon involved showing 2-year-olds a videotape of a duck using its left hand to push a rabbit down into a squatting position while both animals waved their right arms in circles (Figure 6.12) (Naigles, 1990). As they watched, some children were told "The duck is kradding the rabbit"; others were told "The rabbit and the duck are kradding." All the children then saw two videos side by side, one showing the duck pushing on the rabbit and the other showing both animals waving their arms in the air. Instructed to "Find kradding," the two groups looked at the event that matched the syntax they had heard while watching the initial video. Those who had heard the first sentence took "kradding" to mean what the duck had been doing to the rabbit, whereas those who had heard the second sentence thought it meant what both animals had been doing. Thus, the children had arrived at different interpretations for a novel verb based on the *structure* of the sentence in which it was embedded.

As you can see, infants and young children have a remarkable ability to learn new words as object names. Under some circumstances, they are also able to learn non-linguistic "labels" for objects. Infants between 13 and 18 months of age map an experimenter's gestures or non-verbal sounds (e.g., squeaks and whistles) onto novel objects just as readily as they map words (Namy, 2001; Namy & Waxman, 1998; Woodward & Hoyne, 1999). By 20 to 26 months of age, however, they accept only words as names. And when novel labels are presented via computer rather than through interaction with an adult, even 12-month-olds accept only words as labels, not other non-verbal sounds (MacKenzie, Graham, & Curtin, 2011). Thus, infants learn quite early on that strings of phonemes are more likely to carry meaning than other types of sounds.

Putting Words Together

A major landmark in early language development is achieved when children start combining words into sentences, an advance that enables them to express increasingly complex ideas. The degree to which children develop syntax, and the speed with which they do it, is what most distinguishes their language abilities from those of non-human primates.

First sentences Most children begin to combine words into simple sentences by the end of their second year. However, in another example of comprehension preceding production, young children know something about word combinations well before they produce any. In one of the first demonstrations of infants' sensitivity to word order, Hirsh-Pasek and Golinkoff (1991) showed infants two videotaped scenes—one of a woman kissing some keys while holding up a ball and the other of the woman holding up the keys while kissing the ball. Thus, the same three elements—kissing, keys, and a ball—were present in both scenes. Yet when the infants heard the sentence "She's kissing the keys" or "She's kissing the ball," they looked preferentially at the appropriate scene.

Children's first sentences are two-word combinations; their separate utterances of "More," "Juice," and "Drink" become "More juice" and "Drink juice." These two-word utterances have been described as **telegraphic speech** because, just as in telegrams, non-essential elements are missing (Brown & Fraser, 1963). Consider the following examples of standard two-word utterances: "Read me," "Mommy tea," "Ride Daddy," "Hurt knee," "All wet," "More boy," "Key door," "Andrew sleep" (Braine, 1976). These primitive sentences lack a number of elements that would appear in adult utterances, including function words (such as "a," "the," "in"), auxiliary verbs ("is," "was," "will," "be"), and word endings (indicating plurals, possessives, or verb tenses). Children's early sentences possess this telegraphic quality in languages as diverse as English, Finnish, Dholuo (Kenya), and Kaluli (Papua New Guinea) (de Boysson-Bardies, 1996/1999). For young children learning languages like English, in which word order is crucial for meaning, their early sentences follow a consistent word order: a child might say "Eat cookie" but would be unlikely ever to say "Cookie eat."

Many children continue to produce one- and two-word utterances for some time, whereas others quickly move on to sentences consisting of three or more words. Figure 6.13 shows the rapid increase in the mean length of utterances of three children in Roger Brown's (1973) classic study of language development. As you can see from the figure, Eve started her explosive increase in sentence length much earlier than the other two children did. The length of children's utterances increases in part because they begin to systematically incorporate some of the elements that were missing from their telegraphic speech.

Once children are capable of producing four-word sentences, typically at around 2½ years of age, they begin to produce complex sentences containing more than one clause (Bowerman, 1979): "Can I do it when we get home?" "I want this doll because she's big" (Limber, 1973).

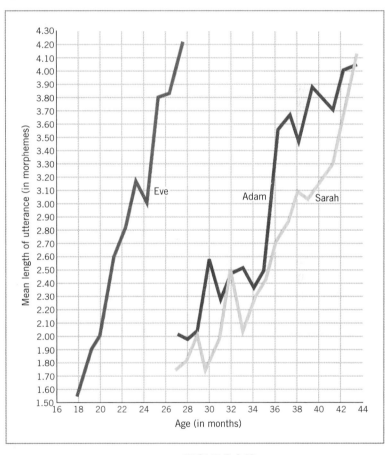

FIGURE 6.13 Length of utterance
This graph shows the relation between age and the mean length of utterance for the three children—Adam, Eve, and Sarah—studied by Roger Brown. (Adapted from Brown, 1973)

Grammar: A tool for building new words and sentences As noted at the beginning of this chapter, human languages are *generative:* through the use of the finite set of words and morphemes in their native vocabulary, individuals can create an infinite number of sentences and express an infinite number of ideas. Each language has a particular set of rules (and exceptions) that governs how linguistic elements can be combined. The power of language derives from the mastery of these regularities, which allows individuals to produce and understand language beyond the specific words and sentences to which they have been exposed. How does this mastery come about, especially in the early years of life?

Much of the research on this topic has focused on morphemes that are added to nouns and verbs. In English, nouns are made plural by adding –*s*, and verbs are put into the past tense by adding –*ed*, with some notable exceptions (e.g., "men,"

overregularization ■ Speech errors in which children treat irregular forms of words as if they were regular.

"went"). Young children recognize these formations and are able to generalize them to novel words. In a classic experiment by Berko (1958), for example, preschoolers were shown a picture of a nonsense animal, which the experimenter referred to as "a wug." Then a picture of two of the creatures was produced, and the experimenter said, "Here are two of them; what are they?" Children as young as 4 readily answered correctly: "Wugs." Since the children had never heard the word "wug" before, their ability to produce the correct plural form for this totally novel word demonstrated that they could generalize beyond the other plurals they had previously heard. The results of this study are taken as evidence that the participants understood how English pluralization works.

Evidence for generalization also comes from the way children treat irregular cases. Consider the plural of "man" and the past tense of "go." Children initially use the correct irregular forms of these words, saying "men" for the plural of "man" and "went" for the past tense of "go." However, they then start making occasional **overregularization** errors, in which they treat irregular forms as if they were regular. For instance, a child who previously said "men" and "went" may begin producing novel forms such as "mans" and "goed," as well as "foots," "feets," "breaked," "broked," and even "branged," and "walkeded" (Berko, 1958; Kuczaj, 1977; Xu & Pinker, 1995). Before eventually mastering irregular forms, children sometimes alternate between these overregularization errors and correct irregular forms (Marcus, 1996; 2004). The following dialogue between a 2½-year-old and his father illustrates this kind of error, as well as the difficulty of correcting it:

> *Child:* I used to wear diapers. When I growed up (pause)
> *Father:* When you grew up?
> *Child:* When I grewed up, I wore underpants.

(Clark, 1993)

Parents play a role in their children's grammatical development, although a more limited one than you might expect. Clearly, they provide a model of grammatically correct speech. In addition, they frequently fill in missing parts of their children's incomplete utterances, as when a parent responds to "No bed" by saying, "You really don't want to go to bed right now, do you?"

One might think that parents also contribute to their children's language development by correcting their grammatical errors. In fact, parents generally ignore even wildly ungrammatical mistakes, accepting sentences such as "I magicked it," "Me no want go," or "I want dessert in front of dinner" (Bryant & Polkosky, 2001; Brown & Hanlon, 1970). It would be hard to do otherwise, since so much of children's speech is like this. And, as the parent who tried to correct his son's use of "growed" discovered, such efforts are largely futile anyway. In general, parents are more likely to correct factual errors than grammatical errors.

Given this lack of correction, how do infants figure out the ways in which the syntax of their native language works? One approach to answering this question in the lab involves creating miniature languages—known as artificial grammars—and determining which types of linguistic patterns infants are able to learn. After just brief exposure, infants as young as 8 months can learn fairly complex patterns, generalizing beyond the specific items they have heard (e.g., Gerken, Wilson, & Lewis, 2005; Gómez, 2002; Lany & Saffran, 2010; Marcus et al., 1999; Saffran et al., 2008). For instance, infants who have heard a list of three-word sequences in which the second word is repeated, such as "le di di, wi je je, de li li …" recognize the pattern when it is presented in new syllables, such as "ko ga ga" (Marcus et al., 1999).

Ongoing research focuses on the degree to which these laboratory studies are tapping into the same processes that infants use to acquire native language syntax.

Learning how to combine words to create interpretable sentences is the crowning achievement in language acquisition. Possibly no linguistic development is more stunning than the progress children make in a few years from simple two-word utterances to grammatically correct complex sentences. Even their errors reveal an increasingly sophisticated understanding of the structure of their native language. This accomplishment is made all the more impressive given the relative lack of parental feedback they receive. The manner in which this learning unfolds is the focus of current research.

Conversational Skills

Although young children are eager to participate in conversations with others, their conversational skills lag well behind their burgeoning language skills. For one thing, much of very young children's speech is directed to themselves, rather than to another person. And this is true not just in solitary play: as much as half of young children's speech in the company of other children or adults is addressed to themselves (Schober-Peterson & Johnson, 1991). Vygotsky (1934/1962) believed that this *private speech* of young children serves an important regulatory function: children talk to themselves as a strategy to organize their actions (Behrend, Rosengren, & Perlmutter, 1992). Gradually, private speech is internalized as thought, and children become capable of mentally organizing their behaviour, so they no longer need to talk out loud to themselves.

As noted in Chapter 4, when young children converse with other children, their conversations tend to be egocentric. Piaget (1923/1926) labelled young children's talk with their peers as **collective monologues.** Even when they take turns speaking, their conversations tend to be a series of non sequiturs, with the content of each child's turn having little or nothing to do with what the other child has just said. The following conversation between two preschoolers is a good example of what Piaget observed:

> *Jenny:* My bunny slippers … are brown and red and sort of yellow and white. And they have eyes and ears and these noses that wiggle sideways when they kiss.
> *Chris:* I have a piece of sugar in a red piece of paper. I'm gonna eat it but maybe it's for a horse.
> *Jenny:* We bought them. My mommy did. We couldn't find the old ones. These are like the old ones. They were not in the trunk.
> *Chris:* Can't eat the piece of sugar, not unless you take the paper off.

(Stone & Church, 1957, pp. 146–147)

Gradually, children's capacity for sustained conversation increases. In a longitudinal study of parent–child conversations of four children from the age of 21 months to 36 months, Bloom, Rocissano, and Hood (1976) found that the proportion of children's utterances that were on the same topic and added new information to what an adult had just said more than doubled (from around 20% to more than 40%). In contrast, the proportion of utterances on unrelated topics fell dramatically (from around 20% to almost 0).

A particular aspect of young children's conversations that changes dramatically in the preschool period is the extent to which they talk about the past. At most, 3-year-olds' conversations include occasional brief references to past events. In

collective monologue ■ Conversation between children that involves a series of non sequiturs, the content of each child's turn having little or nothing to do with what the other child has just said.

narratives ■ Descriptions of past events that have the basic structure of a story.

contrast, 5-year-olds produce **narratives**—descriptions of past events that have the form of a story (Miller & Sperry, 1988; K. Nelson, 1993). One thing that makes longer, more coherent narratives possible is better understanding of the basic structure of stories (Peterson & McCabe, 1988; Shapiro & Hudson, 1991; Stein, 1988).

Parents actively assist their children to develop the ability to produce coherent accounts of past events by providing what has been referred to as *scaffolding* (discussed in Chapter 4) for their children's narratives (Bruner, 1975). An effective way to structure children's conversations about the past is to ask them elaborative questions, that is, questions that enable them to say something—anything—that advances the story:

> *Mother:* And what else happened at the celebrations?
>
> *Child:* I don't know.
>
> *Mother:* We did something special with all the other children.
>
> *Child:* What was it?
>
> *Mother:* There were a whole lot of people over at the beach, and everyone was doing something in the sand.
>
> *Child:* What was it?
>
> *Mother:* Can't you remember what we did in the sand? We were looking for something.
>
> *Child:* Umm, I don't know.
>
> *Mother:* We went digging in the sand.
>
> *Child:* Umm, and that was when um the yellow spade broke.
>
> *Mother:* Good girl, I'd forgotten that. Yes, the yellow spade broke, and what happened?
>
> *Child:* Um, we had to um dig with the other end of the yellow bit one.
>
> *Mother:* That's right. We used the broken bit, didn't we?
>
> *Child:* Yeah.

(Farrant & Reese, 2002)

The child in this conversation does not actually say much, but the parent's questions help the child think about the event, and the parent also provides a conversational model. Those toddlers whose parents scaffold their early conversations by asking useful, elaborative questions produce better narratives on their own a few years later (Fivush, 1991; McCabe & Peterson, 1991; Reese & Fivush, 1993).

A crucial aspect of becoming a good conversational partner is the *pragmatic development* that allows children to understand how language is used to communicate. Such understanding is essential with utterances that require listeners to go beyond the words they are hearing to grasp their actual meaning—as in instances of rhetorical questioning, sarcasm, irony, and the use of hyperbole or understatement to make a point. Children's pragmatic abilities develop over the course of the preschool years, facilitating communication with adults and peers. In particular, they learn to take the perspective of their conversational partner, something that is clearly lacking in the example of the "conversation" between preschoolers Jenny and Chris, quoted earlier. Kindergarten-age listeners are able to make use of a conversational partner's perspective (e.g., by considering what information relevant to the conversation the partner does or doesn't have) to figure out what the partner means, and to provide a pertinent response (Nadig & Sedivy, 2002; Nilsen

DESIGN PICS / DESIGN PICS RF / GETTY IMAGES

Parents typically help young children talk about past events. Such conversations contribute to early language development.

& Graham, 2009). The development of this ability is related to children's level of executive function; as children become more able to control their tendency to assume their own perspective, it becomes easier for them to take the perspective of a conversational partner.

Children also learn to use information other than words to interpret meaning. For instance, older preschoolers can exploit the vocal affect of an ambiguous statement to figure out a speaker's intention (Berman, Chambers, & Graham, 2010). When presented with two birds—one intact, the other broken—and directed to "Look at the bird," 4-year-olds (but not 3-year-olds) looked at the intact bird when the instruction was given with positive affect, and at the broken bird when the instruction was given with negative affect.

We thus see that young children put their burgeoning linguistic skills to good use, becoming more effective communicative partners. Initially, they need substantial support from a more competent partner, but their conversational skills increase quite regularly. Children's growing understanding of narrative structure and their emerging ability to take other people's perspectives are crucial components in the development of their conversational skills.

Later Development

From 5 or 6 years of age on, children continue to develop language skills, although with less dramatic accomplishments. For instance, the ability to sustain a conversation, which grew so dramatically in the preschool years, continues to improve into adulthood. School-age children become increasingly capable of reflecting upon and analyzing language, and they master more complex grammatical structures, such as the use of passive constructions.

One consequence of schoolchildren's more reflective language skills is their increasing appreciation of the multiple meanings of words, which is responsible for the emergence of the endless series of puns, riddles, and jokes with which they delight themselves and torture their parents (Ely & McCabe, 1994). They also are able to learn the meaning of new words simply from hearing them defined (Pressley, Levin, & McDaniel, 1987), a factor that helps their comprehension vocabulary expand—from the 10 000 words that the average 6-year-old knows to the 40 000 words estimated for 5th graders (Anglin, 1993) to the average college- or university-student vocabulary that has been estimated to be as high as 150 000 words (Miller & Gildea, 1987).

Theoretical Issues in Language Development

As you have seen throughout this chapter, there is ample evidence for both nature and nurture in the process of language development. The two key prerequisites for language acquisition are (1) a human brain and (2) experience with a human language. The former clearly falls on the side of nature, and the latter, on the side of nurture. Despite the obvious interaction between the two, the nature–nurture debate continues to rage fiercely in the area of language development. Why?

Chomsky and the Nativist View

The study of language development emerged from a theoretical debate about the processes through which language is acquired. In the 1950s, B. F. Skinner (1957) wrote a book entitled *Verbal Behavior,* in which he presented a behaviourist theory

According to language theorist Noam Chomsky, all these children rely on the same innate linguistic structures in acquiring their various languages.

of language development. As you saw in Chapter 1, behaviourists believed that development is a function of learning through reinforcement and punishment of overt behaviour. Skinner argued that parents teach children to speak by means of the same kinds of reinforcement techniques that are used to train animals to perform novel behaviours.

In what was probably the most influential book review ever published, Noam Chomsky (1959) countered Skinner by pointing out some of the reasons why language cannot be learned through the processes of reinforcement and punishment. One key reason was noted earlier in this chapter: we can understand and produce sentences that we have never heard before (generativity). If language-learning proceeds by means of reinforcement and punishment, how could we know that a sentence like "Colorless green ideas sleep furiously" is a grammatical English sentence, whereas "Green sleep colorless furiously ideas" is not (Chomsky, 1957)? Similarly, how could children produce words they have never heard before, like "wented" or "mouses"? The explanation of such instances must be that we know details about the structure of our native language that we have not been taught—facts that are unobservable and thus impossible to reinforce—contrary to Skinner's proposal.

In his own explanation of language development, Chomsky proposed that humans are born with a **Universal Grammar,** a hard-wired set of principles and rules that govern grammar in all languages. Chomsky's account, which has been central to the development of the modern discipline of linguistics, is consistent with the fact that, despite many surface differences, the underlying structures of the world's languages are fundamentally similar. His strongly nativist account also provides an explanation for why most children learn language with exceptional rapidity, while non-humans (who presumably lack a Universal Grammar) do not. (The Universal Grammar hypothesis has been highly relevant to investigations of emerging languages like the Nicaraguan Sign Language discussed in Box 6.4, a language in which children are creating new grammatical structures.)

Universal Grammar ■ A proposed set of highly abstract, unconscious rules that are common to all languages.

Ongoing Debates in Language Development

Current theories all acknowledge some of Chomsky's crucial observations. For instance, any account of language development must be able to explain why all human languages share so many characteristics. Theories must also explain how it is that language users, from infants to adults, are able to generalize beyond the specific words and sentences they have been exposed to. But the ways in which various accounts handle these facts differ along two key dimensions. The first dimension is the degree to which these explanations lie within the child (*nature*) versus within the environment (*nurture*). The second dimension pertains to the child's contributions: Did the cognitive and neural mechanisms underlying language learning evolve solely to support language learning (*domain-specific*), or are they used for learning many different kinds of things (*domain-general*)?

With respect to the first dimension, theorists have countered Chomsky's argument about the universality of language structure by pointing out that there are also universals in children's environments. Parents all over the world need to communicate about certain things with their children, and these things are likely to be reflected in the language that children learn. For instance, recall Table 6.1, which shows the remarkable overlap in the earliest words acquired across three diverse cultures (Tardif et al., 2008). These similarities reflect what parents want to talk about with their infants, and what infants want to communicate about.

Indeed, accounts focused on social interaction maintain that virtually everything about language development is influenced by its communicative function. Children are motivated to interact with others, to communicate their own thoughts and feelings, and to understand what other people are trying to communicate to them (Bloom, 1991; Bloom & Tinker, 2001; Snow, 1999). According to this position, children gradually discover the underlying regularities in language and its use by paying close attention to the multitude of clues available in the language they hear, the social context in which language is used, and the intentions of the speaker (e.g., Tomasello, 2008). Some of these conventions may be learned by the same kinds of reinforcement methods originally proposed by Skinner. For instance, Goldstein and colleagues have found that both the sounds infants make when babbling and the rate at which they produce them can be influenced by parental reinforcement, such as smiling and touching in response to the babbling (Goldstein, King, & West, 2003; Goldstein & Schwade, 2008). Whether these types of social behaviours can influence less overt aspects of language development, such as the acquisition of syntax, remains unclear.

BOX 6.4: a closer look

"I JUST CAN'T TALK WITHOUT MY HANDS": WHAT GESTURES TELL US ABOUT LANGUAGE

People around the world spontaneously accompany their speech with gestures. The naturalness of gesturing is revealed by the fact that blind people gesture as they speak just as much as sighted individuals do, even when they know their listener is also blind (Iverson & Goldin-Meadow, 1998).

Gesturing starts early: infants often produce recognizable, meaningful gestures before they speak recognizable words. According to Acredolo and Goodwyn (1990), many "baby signs" are invented by children themselves. One child in their research signed "alligator" by putting her hands together and opening and closing them to imitate snapping jaws; another indicated "dog" by sticking her tongue out as if panting; another signalled "flower" by sniffing. Infants gain earlier motor control of their hands than of their vocal apparatus, facilitating the use of signs during the first year.

Interestingly, there is a relationship between early gesturing and later vocabulary (M. L. Rowe, Ozcaliskan, & Goldin-Meadow, 2008). The more children gestured at 14 months, the larger their spoken vocabulary was at 42 months. Moreover, differences in the amount of gesturing by high- and low-SES families are one factor that influences the SES effects discussed in Box 6.2 (M. L. Rowe & Goldin-Meadow, 2009).

Especially dramatic evidence of intimate connections between gesture and language comes from remarkable research on children who have *created* their own gesture-based languages. Goldin-Meadow and colleagues (Feldman, Goldin-Meadow, & Gleitman, 1978; Goldin-Meadow, 2003; Goldin-Meadow & Mylander, 1998) studied congenitally deaf American and Chinese children whose hearing parents had little or no proficiency in any formal sign language. These children and their parents created "home signs" in order to communicate with one another, and the children's gesture vocabulary quickly outstripped that of their parents.

More important, the children (but not the parents) *spontaneously* imposed a structure—a rudimentary grammar—on their gestures. Both groups of children used a grammatical structure that occurs in some languages but not those of their parents. As a result, the sign systems of the children were more similar to one another than to those of their own parents. The children's signs were also more complex than those of their parents. A similar phenomenon occurs when deaf children are learning to sign from parents who themselves learned a conventional sign language, like ASL, but whose signing is ungrammatical (usually because they learned to sign later in life). In such cases, deaf children have been reported to *spontaneously* impose structure that is more consistent than the signs that their parents produce (Singleton & Newport, 2004).

The most extensive and extraordinary example of language creation by children comes from the invention of Nicaraguan Sign Language (NSL), a completely new language that has been evolving over the past 30 years. In 1979, a large-scale education

This young participant in the research of Acredolo and Goodwyn is producing her idiosyncratic "baby sign" for pig.

SUSAN GOODWYN

modularity hypothesis ■ The idea that the human brain contains an innate, self-contained language module that is separate from other aspects of cognitive functioning.

What of the second dimension—the domain-specificity of the processes underlying language acquisition? According to the strongly nativist view espoused by Chomsky, the cognitive abilities that support language development are highly specific to language. As Steven Pinker (1994) describes it, language is "a distinct piece of the biological makeup of our brains … distinct from more general abilities to process information or behave intelligently" (p. 18). This claim is taken one step further by the **modularity hypothesis,** which proposes that the human brain contains an innate, self-contained language module that is separate from other aspects of cognitive functioning (Fodor, 1983). The idea of specialized mental modules is

program for the deaf began in Nicaragua (Senghas & Coppola, 2001). The program brought hundreds of deaf children together in two schools in the city of Managua. For most of the children, it was their first exposure to other deaf people.

The teachers in the schools knew no formal sign language, nor did the children, who had only the simple home signs they had used to communicate with their families. The children quickly began to build on one another's existing informal signs, constructing a "pidgin" sign language—a relatively crude, limited communication system. The language was used by the students, both in and outside school, and was learned by each new group of children who entered the community.

What happened next was astonishing. As younger students entered the schools, they rapidly mastered the rudimentary system used by the older students and then gradually transformed it into a complex, fully consistent language (NSL) with its own grammar. The most fluent signers in the NSL community are currently the youngest children, both because NSL has evolved into a real language and because they acquired it at an earlier age.

Recently, another emerging signed language was discovered in the Negev desert of Israel (Sandler et al., 2005). The Al-Sayyid Bedouin Sign Language (ABSL) is in its third generation and is about 75 years old. Unlike NSL, ABSL is acquired from birth,

COURTESY OF ANN SENGHAS

Nicaraguan deaf children signing together in the language that has emerged in their school community.

because deaf children in this community typically have at least one deaf adult in their extended family. The grammatical structure of ABSL does not resemble those of the local spoken languages (Arabic and Hebrew).

These reports of language invention by deaf children are not just fascinating stories: they provide evidence for the child's contribution to language learning. Over several generations, children have been taking improvised signing that is simple and inconsistent and transforming it into structures much closer to those observed in established languages. Whether this process reflects the operation of a Chomsky-style Universal Grammar or the operation of more general learning mechanisms remains unknown. Regardless, the discovery that children go beyond the linguistic input they receive, spontaneously refining and systematizing these emerging languages, is one of the most fascinating findings in the field of language development.

not limited to language. As you will see in Chapter 7, innate, special-purpose modules have been proposed to underlie a variety of functions, including perception, spatial skills, and social understanding.

An alternative view suggests that the learning mechanisms underlying language development are actually quite general. Although these learning abilities might be innate, their evolutionary development was not restricted to language learning. For instance, researchers have demonstrated that the distributional learning mechanisms discussed earlier in this chapter also help infants track sequences of musical notes, visual shapes, and human actions (e.g., Fiser & Aslin, 2001; Kirkham,

BOX 6.5: individual differences

DEVELOPMENTAL LANGUAGE DISORDERS

Throughout this chapter, we have emphasized both what is similar and what diverges across children and across cultures over the course of language development. The most significant individual differences fall under the category of developmental language disorders. These range from delays that often disappear by school age to lifelong challenges.

Estimates of the number of preschoolers with language disorders range from 2% to 19% (H. D. Nelson et al., 2006). The size of this range reflects the fact that language disorders are often not diagnosed until a child enters school. Of this group, many of the children are considered *late talkers.* This label is applied to toddlers who are developing typically in other domains but whose vocabulary development is lagging at or below the 10th percentile. Some of these children are so-called "late bloomers" who will go on to have normal or near-normal language skills. Recent research shows that late-talking toddlers with better word recognition skills are the most likely to catch up (Fernald & Marchman, 2012). Children who fail to catch up—roughly 7% of school-age children—are diagnosed with *specific language impairment* (SLI). These children exhibit challenges in many language-related tasks, including speech perception, word segmentation, and grammatical comprehension (e.g., Evans, Saffran, & Robe-Torres, 2009; Fonteneau & van der Lely, 2008; Rice, 2004; Ziegler et al., 2005). They may also exhibit more general challenges in working memory, sequence learning, and processing speed (e.g., Leonard et al., 2007; Tomblin, Mainela-Arnold, & Zhang, 2007).

Children diagnosed with Down syndrome, fragile-X syndrome, or autism spectrum disorders (ASD) tend to be significantly delayed across all aspects of language development, including both language production and comprehension. Indeed, challenges in communication are one of the diagnostic criteria for ASD. For children with ASD, early language abilities are predictive of later outcomes, including response to treatment (e.g., Stone & Yoder, 2001; Szatmari et al., 2003). Interestingly, younger siblings of children with ASD, who are themselves at greater risk for ASD, have a higher rate of language delay than do their peers (Gamliel et al., 2009).

Another group of children who may develop language disorders are deaf children. As we noted earlier, if these children have early exposure to a natural sign language like ASL, they will follow a typical language development trajectory. However, 90% of deaf children are born to hearing parents, and many of these children do not have access to sign language. In the absence of hearing, it is very difficult to learn a spoken language. An increasingly popular intervention for profoundly deaf infants, children, and adults is the use of cochlear implants (CIs), surgically implanted devices that translate auditory input into electrical stimulation of the auditory nerve. The signal that CIs provide is quite degraded relative to typical acoustic hearing. Nevertheless, many deaf infants and children are able to learn spoken language with the help of CIs, though the level of success varies widely across individuals. Consistent with other critical-period findings, implantation at a young age (e.g., prior to age 3) is better than at later ages (e.g., Houston & Miyamoto, 2010). Even at the outset of learning, though, deaf infants and toddlers who perceive speech through CIs are less accurate and slower to recognize words than are their hearing peers (Grieco-Calub, Saffran, & Litovsky, 2009). Providing these learners with bilingual input (natural sign language and spoken language through CIs) may offer the most successful route to language acquisition.

Cochlear implants are a surgically implanted device used by some deaf and hearing-impaired individuals.

JAN-MICHAEL CARNEY KRT / NEWSCOM

Slemmer, & Johnson, 2002; Roseberry et al., 2011; Saffran et al., 1999). Similarly, the fast-mapping mechanisms that support rapid word learning are also used by toddlers to learn facts about objects (Markson & Bloom, 1997). Also relevant is the fact that the "less-is-more" hypothesis for the critical period for language development, discussed earlier in this chapter, is not tied specifically to language (Newport, 1990). The ability to extract small chunks of information is likely useful in other domains as well, such as music, which also consists of small pieces (notes, chords) organized into higher-level structures (melody, harmony). Finally, recent theories concerning developmental language disorders (discussed in Box 6.5) invoke aspects of general cognitive function, not just language.

As in other areas of child development, computational modelling has played an important role in the development of modern theoretical perspectives. By using computational models, researchers can specify both the innate structure and the environmental input to a computerized learner and attempt to determine what is crucial when simulating children's language acquisition. One influential perspective oriented around computational modelling is **connectionism,** a type of information-processing theory that emphasizes the simultaneous activity of numerous interconnected processing units. Connectionist researchers have developed computer simulations of various aspects of cognitive development, including language acquisition (e.g., Elman et al., 1996). The software learns from experience, gradually strengthening certain connections among units in ways that mimic children's developmental progress. Connectionist accounts have achieved impressive success with respect to modelling specific aspects of language development, including children's acquisition of the past tense in English and the development of the shape bias for word learning (e.g., Rumelhart & McClelland, 1986; Samuelson, 2002). However, connectionist models are always open to criticism regarding the features that were built into the models in the first place (e.g., do they have the same "innate" constraints as infants?), and how well the input provided to them matches the input received by real children.

connectionism ■ A type of information-processing approach that emphasizes the simultaneous activity of numerous interconnected processing units.

review:

The process of comprehending and producing language, whether spoken or signed, involves the development of many different kinds of knowledge and skills. In the space of a few years, children take giant steps in mastering the phonology, semantics, syntax, and pragmatics of their native language. This remarkable achievement is made possible by the joint prerequisites of a human brain and exposure to human communication.

The current theoretical accounts of language development differ with respect to how much emphasis they put on nature and nurture. Nativists like Chomsky emphasize innate linguistic knowledge and language-specific learning mechanisms, whereas other theorists argue that language learning can emerge from general-purpose learning mechanisms. Children's motivation to understand and interact with other people is also central to many theories. The vast literature on language development provides some support for all of these views, but none of them provide the full story of children's acquisition of this vastly complex and arguably unique of all human abilities.

Nonlinguistic Symbols and Development

Although language is our pre-eminent symbol system, humans have invented a wealth of other kinds of symbols to communicate with one another. Virtually anything can serve as a symbol as long as someone intends it to stand for something other than itself (DeLoache, 2002, 2004). The list of symbols you regularly encounter is long and varied, ranging from the printed words, numbers, graphs, photographs, and drawings in your textbooks to thousands of everyday items such as computer icons, maps, clocks, and so on. Because symbols are so central to our everyday lives, mastering the symbol systems important in their culture is a crucial developmental task for all children.

Symbolic proficiency involves both the mastery of the symbolic creations of others and the creation of new symbolic representations. We will first discuss early symbolic functioning, starting with research on very young children's ability to

dual representation ■ The idea that a symbolic artifact must be represented mentally in two ways at the same time—both as a real object and as a symbol for something other than itself.

exploit the informational content of symbolic artifacts. Then we will focus on children's creation of symbols through drawing. In Chapter 7, we will consider children's creation of symbolic relations in pretend play, and in Chapter 8, we will examine older children's development of two of the most important of all symbolic activities—reading and mathematics.

Using Symbols as Information

One of the vital functions of many symbols is that they provide useful information. For instance, a map—whether a crude pencil sketch on the back of an envelope or a Google map on your smart phone—can be crucial for locating a particular place. To use a symbolic artifact such as a map requires **dual representation;** that is, the artifact must be represented mentally in two ways at the same time, as a real object and as a symbol for something other than itself (DeLoache, 2002, 2004).

Very young children have substantial difficulty with dual representation, limiting their ability to use information from symbolic artifacts (DeLoache, 2004). This has been demonstrated by research in which a young child watches as an experimenter hides a miniature toy in a scale model of the regular-sized room next door (Figure 6.14) (DeLoache, 1987). The child is then asked to find a larger version of the toy that the child is told "is hiding in the same place in the big room." Three-year-olds readily use their knowledge of the location of the miniature toy in the model to figure out where the large toy is in the adjacent room. In contrast, most 2½-year-old children fail to find the large toy; they seem to have no idea that the model tells them anything about the full-size room. Because the model is so salient and interesting as a three-dimensional object, very young children have trouble managing dual representation and fail to notice the symbolic relation between the model and the room it stands for.

This interpretation received strong support in a study with 2½-year-old children in which reasoning between a model and a larger space was not necessary (DeLoache, Miller, & Rosengren, 1997). An experimenter showed each child a "shrinking machine" (really an oscilloscope with lots of dials and lights) and explained that the machine could "make things get little." The child watched as a troll doll was hidden in a movable tentlike room (approximately 2.5 metres by 1.8 metres) and the shrinking machine was "turned on." Then the child and experimenter waited in another room while the shrinking machine did its job. When they returned,

FIGURE 6.14 Scale-model task In a test of young children's ability to use a symbol as a source of information, a 3-year-old child watches as the experimenter (Judy DeLoache) hides a miniature troll doll under a pillow in a scale model of an adjacent room. The child searches successfully for a larger troll doll hidden in the corresponding place in the actual room, indicating that she appreciates the relation between the model and room. The child also successfully retrieves the small toy she originally observed being hidden in the model.

a small-scale model of the tentlike room stood in place of the original. (Assistants had, of course, removed the original tent and replaced it with the scale model.) When asked to find the troll, the children succeeded.

Why should the idea of a shrinking machine enable these 2½-year-olds to perform the task? The answer is that if a child believes the experimenter's claims about the shrinking machine, then in the child's mind the model simply *is* the room. Hence, there is no symbolic relation between the two spaces and no need for dual representation.

The difficulty that young children have with dual representation and symbols is evident in other contexts as well. For instance, investigators often use anatomically detailed dolls to interview young children in cases of suspected sexual abuse, assuming that the relation between the doll and themselves would be obvious. However, children younger than 5 years often fail to make any connection between themselves and the doll, so the use of a doll does not improve their memory reports and may even make them less reliable (Bruck et al., 1995; DeLoache & Marzolf, 1995; Goodman & Aman, 1990).

Increasing ability to achieve dual representation—to immediately interpret a symbol in terms of what it stands for—enables children to discover the abstract nature of various symbolic artifacts. For instance, unlike younger children, school-age children realize that the red line on a road map does not mean that the real road would be red (Liben & Myers, 2007). Older children are also able, when properly instructed, to use objects such as rods and blocks of different sizes that represent different numerical quantities to help them learn to do mathematical operations (Uttal, Liu, & DeLoache, 2006).

Drawing

Creating pictures is a common symbolic activity encouraged by parents in many societies (Goodnow, 1977). When young children first start making marks on paper, their focus is almost exclusively on the activity per se, with no attempt to produce recognizable images. At around 3 or 4 years or age, most children begin trying to draw pictures *of* something; they try to produce representational art (Callaghan, 1999). Exposure to representational symbols affects the age at which children begin to produce them. One cross-cultural study demonstrated that young children growing up in families in Nova Scotia produced representational drawings between 2½ and 3 years of age. In contrast, children growing up in rural Peru and rural India produced these types of drawings somewhat later, as they approached 4 years of age (Callaghan et al., 2011).

Initially, children's artistic impulses outstrip their motor and planning capabilities (Yamagata, 1997). Figure 6.15 shows what at first appears simply to be a classic scribble. However, the 2½-year-old creator of this picture was narrating his efforts as he drew, making it possible to ascertain his artistic intentions. Although he represented the individual elements of his picture reasonably well, he was unable to coordinate them spatially.

The most common subject for young children is the human figure (Goodnow, 1977). Just as infants who are first beginning to speak simplify the words they produce, young children simplify their drawings, as shown in Figure 6.16. Note that to produce these very simple, crude shapes, the child must plan the drawing and must spatially coordinate the individual elements. Even early "tadpole" people have the legs on the bottom and the arms on the side—although often emerging from the head.

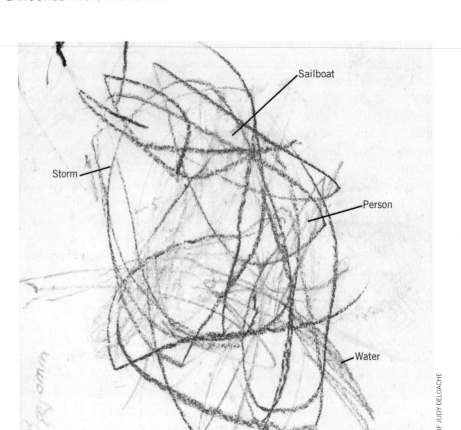

FIGURE 6.15 **Early drawing** Appearances to the contrary, this is not random scribbling, as shown by what the 2½-year-old who produced it said about his work. As he drew a roughly triangular shape, he said it was a "sailboat." A set of wavy lines was labelled "water." Some scribbled lines under the "sailboat" were denoted as the "person driving the boat." Finally, the wild scribbles all over the rest were "a storm." Thus, each element was representational to some degree, even though the picture as a whole was not.

FIGURE 6.16 **Tadpole drawings** Young children's early drawings of people typically take a "tadpole" form.

Figure 6.17 reveals some of the strategies children use to produce more complex pictures. The drawing depicts the route from the artist's home to the local grocery store, with several houses along the way. One strategy the child used was to rely on a well-practised formula for representing houses: a rectangle with a door and a roofline. Another was to coordinate the placement of each house with respect to the

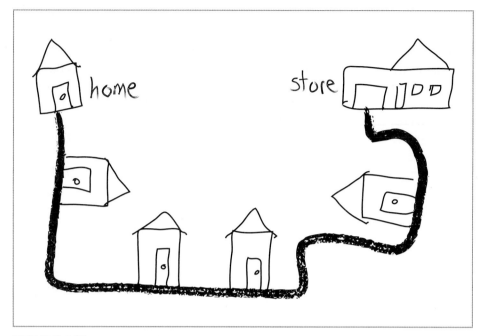

FIGURE 6.17 More complex drawings This child's drawing relies on some well-practised strategies, but the child has not yet worked out how to represent complex spatial relationships.

road, although at the cost of the overall coordination among the houses. Eventually, some children become highly skilled at representing the relations among the multiple elements in their pictures.

review:

Nonlinguistic symbols play an important role in the lives of young children. As they become increasingly sensitive to the informational potential of symbolic objects created by others, children take an important step toward skillful use of the many symbol systems that are key to modern life. A critical factor in understanding and using the symbols created by others is dual representation—the ability to mentally represent both a symbolic object, such as a map or model, and its relation to what it stands for. The ability to *create* symbols is evident in young children's drawings.

chapter summary:

A critical feature of what it means to be human is the creative and flexible use of a variety of languages and other symbols. The enormous power of language comes from generativity—the fact that a finite set of words can be used to generate an infinite number of sentences.

Language Development

- Acquiring a language involves learning the complex system of phonology, semantics, syntax, and pragmatics that govern its sounds, meaning, grammar, and use.

- Language ability is species-specific. The first prerequisite for its full-fledged development is a human brain. Researchers have succeeded in teaching non-human animals remarkable symbolic skills but not full-fledged language.

- The early years constitute a critical period for language acquisition; many aspects of language are more difficult to acquire thereafter.

- A second prerequisite for language development is exposure to language. Much of the language babies hear takes the form of infant-directed speech (IDS), which is characterized by

- a higher-than-normal pitch; extreme shifts in intonation; a warm, affectionate tone; and exaggerated facial expressions.

- Infants have remarkable speech-perception abilities. Like adults, they exhibit categorical perception of speech sounds, perceiving physically similar sounds as belonging to discrete categories.

- Young infants are actually better than adults at discriminating between speech sounds not in their native language. As they learn the sounds that are important in their language(s), infants' ability to distinguish between sounds in other languages declines.

- Infants are remarkably sensitive to the distributional properties of language; they notice a variety of subtle regularities in the speech they hear and use these regularities to segment words from fluent speech.

- Infants begin to babble at around 7 months of age, either repeating syllables ("bababa") or, if exposed to sign language, using repetitive hand movements. Gradually, vocal babbling begins to sound more like the baby's native language.

- During the second half of the first year, infants are learning how to interact and communicate with other people, including developing the ability to establish joint attention.

- Infants begin to recognize highly familiar words at about 6 months of age.

- Infants begin to produce words at around 1 year of age. They initially say just one word at a time, and often make overextension errors, using a particular word in a broader context than is appropriate. Infants make use of a variety of strategies to figure out what new words mean.

- By the end of their second year, most infants produce short sentences. The length and complexity of their utterances gradually increase, and infants spontaneously practise their emerging linguistic skills.

- In the early preschool years, children exhibit generalization, extending such patterns as "add −s to make plural" to novel nouns, and making overregularization errors.

- Children develop their burgeoning language skills as they go from collective monologues to sustained conversation, improving their ability to tell coherent narratives about their experiences.

- All current theories of language development agree that there is an interaction between innate factors and experience.

- Nativists, such as the influential linguist Noam Chomsky, posit innate knowledge of "Universal Grammar," the set of highly abstract rules common to all languages. They believe that language learning is supported by language-specific skills.

- Theorists focused on social interaction emphasize the communicative context of language development and use. They emphasize the impressive degree to which infants and young children exploit a host of pragmatic cues to figure out what others are saying.

- Other perspectives argue that language can develop in the absence of innate knowledge and that language learning requires powerful general-purpose cognitive mechanisms. Connectionist models have been used to support this view.

Nonlinguistic Symbols and Development

- Symbolic artifacts like maps or models require dual representation. To use them, children must represent mentally both the object itself as well as its symbolic relation to what it stands for. Toddlers become increasingly skillful at achieving dual representation and using symbolic artifacts as a source of information.

- Drawing is a popular symbolic activity. Young children's early scribbling quickly gives way to the intention to draw pictures *of* something, with a favourite theme being representations of the human figure.

Critical Thinking Questions

1. Drawing on the many references to parental behaviours relevant to language development that were discussed in this chapter, give some examples of ways parents are known to influence their children's language development.

2. Language development is a particularly complex aspect of child development, and no single theory successfully accounts for all that is known about how children acquire language. Would you weight the child's contributions (nature) or the environment's contributions (nurture) more strongly?

3. What are overregularization errors, and why do they offer strong evidence for the acquisition of grammatical structures by children?

4. Many parallels were drawn between the process of language acquisition in children learning spoken language and in those learning signed language. What do these similarities tell us about the basis for human language?

Key Terms

babbling, p. 231

bilingualism, p. 224

categorical perception, p. 226

collective monologues, p. 245

comprehension, p. 217

connectionism, p. 253

critical period for language p. 220

distributional properties, p. 229

dual representation, p. 254

fast mapping, p. 237

generativity, p. 217

holophrastic period, p. 235

infant-directed speech (IDS), p. 222

metalinguistic knowledge, p. 218

modularity hypothesis, p. 250

morphemes, p. 217

narratives, p. 246

overextension, p. 235

overregularization, p. 244

phonemes, p. 217

phonological development, p. 217

pragmatic cues, p. 238

pragmatic development, p. 218

production, p. 217

prosody, p. 225

reference, p. 232

semantic development, p. 217

symbols, p. 216

syntactic bootstrapping, p. 242

syntactic development, p. 218

syntax, p. 218

telegraphic speech, p. 243

Universal Grammar, p. 249

voice onset time (VOT), p. 226

word segmentation, p. 229

JOHN GEORGE BROWN (1813–1913), *The Little Joker*

chapter 7:

Conceptual Development

THEMES

What does this infant see when looking at this room?

concepts ■ General ideas or understandings that can be used to group together objects, events, qualities, or abstractions that are similar in some way.

Maya, an 8-month-old, crawls into her 7-year-old brother's bedroom. The room contains many objects, among them a bed, a dresser, a dog, a puck, a hockey stick, books, magazines, shoes, and dirty socks. To her older brother, the room includes furniture, clothing, reading material, and sports equipment. But what does the room look like to Maya?

Infants lack concepts of furniture, reading material, and sports equipment, and also lack more specific, relevant concepts such as hockey sticks and books. Thus, Maya would not understand the scene in the same way that her older brother would. However, without knowledge of child development research, it would be difficult to anticipate whether a baby as young as Maya would have formed other concepts relevant to understanding the scene. Would she have formed concepts of living and nonliving things that would help her understand why the dog runs around on its own but the books never do? Would she have formed concepts of heavier and lighter that would allow her to understand why she could pick up a sock but not a dresser? Would she have formed concepts of before and after that would allow her to understand that her brother always puts on his socks before his shoes rather than in the opposite order? Or would it all be a jumble?

As this imaginary scene indicates, concepts are crucial for helping people make sense of the world. But what exactly are concepts, and how do they help us understand?

Concepts are general ideas that organize objects, events, qualities, or relations on the basis of some similarity. There are an infinite number of possible concepts, because there are infinite ways in which objects or events can be similar. For instance, objects can have similar shapes (all football fields are rectangular), materials (all diamonds are made of compressed carbon), sizes (all skyscrapers are large), tastes (all lemons are sour), colours (all colas are brown), functions (all knives are for cutting), and so on.

Concepts help us understand the world and act effectively in it by allowing us to generalize from prior experience. If we like the taste of one carrot, we probably will like the taste of others. Concepts also tell us how to react emotionally to new experiences, as when we fear all dogs after being bitten by one. Life without concepts would be unthinkable: every situation would be new, and we would have no idea what past experience was relevant in the new situation.

Several themes have been especially prominent in research on conceptual development. One is *nature and nurture:* children's concepts reflect the interaction between their specific experiences and their biological predispositions to process information in particular ways. Another recurring theme is the *active child:* from infancy onward, many of children's concepts reflect their active attempts to make sense of the world. A third major theme is *how change occurs:* researchers who study conceptual development attempt to understand not only what concepts children form but also the processes by which they form them. A fourth is the *sociocultural context:* the concepts we form are influenced by the society in which we live.

Although there is widespread agreement that conceptual development reflects the interaction of nature and nurture, the particulars of this interaction are hotly debated. The controversy parallels the nativist/empiricist controversies described previously in the context of perceptual development (page 183) and language development (pages 247–253). Nativists, such as Liz Spelke (2011), Alan Leslie (Scholl & Leslie, 2002), and Karen Wynn (2008), believe that innate understanding of basic concepts plays a central role in development. They argue that infants are born with some sense of fundamental concepts such as time, space, number, causality, and the human mind, or with specialized learning mechanisms that allow them to acquire rudimentary understanding of these concepts unusually quickly and easily. Within the nativist perspective, nurture is important to children's developing the concepts beyond this initial level but not for forming the basic understanding.

In contrast, empiricists, such as Vladimir Sloutsky (2010), Scott Johnson (2010), David Rakison (Rakison & Lupyan, 2008), and Marianella Casasola (2008), argue that nature endows infants with only general learning mechanisms, such as the ability to perceive, associate, generalize, and remember. Within the empiricist perspective, the rapid and universal formation of fundamental concepts such as time, space, causality, number, and mind arises from infants' massive exposure to experiences that are relevant to these concepts. Empiricists also maintain that the data on which many nativist arguments are based—data involving infants' looking times in habituation studies—are not sufficient to support the nativists' conclusions that infants understand the concepts in question (J. J. Campos et al., 2008; Kagan, 2008). The continuing debate between nativists and empiricists reflects a fundamental, unresolved question about human nature: Do children form all concepts through the same learning mechanisms, or do they also possess special mechanisms for forming a few particularly important concepts?

This chapter focuses on the development of fundamental concepts—those that are useful in the greatest number of situations. These concepts fall into two groups. One group of fundamental concepts is used to categorize the kinds of things that exist in the world: human beings, living things in general, and inanimate objects. The other group of fundamental concepts involves dimensions used to represent our experiences: space (where the experience occurred), time (when it occurred), number (how many times it occurred), and causality (why it occurred).

You may have noticed that these fundamental concepts correspond closely to the questions that every news story must answer: Who or what? Where? When? Why? How many? The similarity between the concepts that are most fundamental for children and those that are most important in news stories is no accident. Knowing who or what, where, when, how many, and why is essential for understanding any event.

Because early conceptual development is so crucial, this chapter focuses on development in the first 5 years. This obviously does not mean that conceptual growth ends at age 5. Beyond this age, children form vast numbers of more specialized concepts, and understanding of all types of concepts deepens for many years thereafter. Rather, the focus here on early conceptual development reflects the fact that this is the period in which children acquire a basic understanding of the most crucial concepts—the ones that are universal, that allow children to understand their own and other people's experiences, and that provide the foundations for subsequent conceptual growth.

Understanding Who or What

Dividing Objects into Categories

Beginning early in development, children attempt to understand what kinds of things are in the world. They quickly divide the objects they encounter into three general categories: inanimate objects, people, and other animals (they are unsure for many years whether plants are more like animals or more like inanimate objects)

(S. A. Gelman & Kalish, 2006). Forming these broad divisions is crucial, because different types of concepts apply to different types of objects (Keil, 1979). Some concepts apply to anything—all things, living and nonliving, have height, weight, colour, size, and so on. Other concepts apply only to living things—only living things eat, drink, grow, and breathe, for example. Yet other concepts—reading, shopping, pondering, and talking—apply only to people. Forming these general categories of objects allows children to draw accurate inferences about unfamiliar entities. For instance, when told that a platypus is a kind of animal, children know immediately that a platypus can move, eat, grow, reproduce, and so on.

A number of researchers hypothesize that children organize their observations of these categories of objects into *informal theories* (e.g., Carey, 2009; G. L. Murphy & Medin, 1985; Vosniadou, 2010). Wellman and Gelman (1998) proposed that young children organize their knowledge of the things in the world into three informal theories: a *theory of physics* (inanimate objects), a *theory of psychology* (people), and a *theory of biology* (other living things). These informal theories are viewed as having an innate core but also as incorporating—and in some cases being radically transformed by—learning processes such as association, observation, and the statements of other people (S. A. Gelman & Kalish, 2006). These informal theories are rudimentary, but they share three important characteristics with formal scientific theories:

1. They identify fundamental units for dividing all objects and events into a few basic categories.

2. They explain many phenomena in terms of a few fundamental principles.

3. They explain events in terms of unobservable causes.

Each characteristic is evident in the preschool period (E. M. Evans, 2008; S. A. Gelman, 2003; Inagaki & Hatano, 2008). Consistent with the first characteristic, preschoolers divide all objects into people, other animals, plants, and nonliving things. Consistent with the second characteristic, preschoolers understand broadly applicable principles—that a desire for food and water underlies many behaviours of animals, for example. Consistent with the third characteristic, preschoolers know that many of animals' vital activities, such as reproduction and movement, are caused by something inside the animals as opposed to the external forces that determine the actions of inanimate objects.

When do children first generate such core theories? Spelke (e.g., 2003) speculated that infants begin life with a primitive theory of physics, that is, of inanimate objects. The theory includes the knowledge that the world contains physical objects that occupy space, move only in response to external forces, move in continuous ways through space rather than jumping from one position to another, and cannot simultaneously occupy the same space as another object.

Wellman and Gelman (1998) suggested that children's first theory of psychology emerges at around 18 months of age, and their first theory of biology at around 3 years. The first theory of psychology is organized around the understanding that other people's actions reflect their desires. For example, a 2-year-old boy realizes that his mother will want to eat if she is hungry, regardless of whether the 2-year-old himself is hungry. The first theory of biology is organized around the realization that people and other animals are living things, different from nonliving things and plants. For instance, 3- and 4-year-olds realize that animals, but not inanimate objects, move under their own power (S. A. Gelman, 2003).

Of course, vast development occurs beyond these initial theories. Some of this development builds on the original organization and fills in details. As noted in Chapter 5 (pages 207–208), for example, even 3-month-olds understand that an

TABLE 7.1

Object Hierarchies

Level	Type of Object		
Most General	Inanimate Objects	People	Living Things
General	Furniture, Vehicles …	Europeans, Asians …	Animals, Plants …
Medium	Chairs, Tables …	Spaniards, Finns …	Cats, Dogs …
Specific	La-Z-Boys, Armchairs …	Picasso, Cervantes …	Lions, Lynxes …

category hierarchy ■ Categories that are related by set–subset relations, such as animal/dog/poodle.

object (e.g., a glass) will fall unless at least some of it is supported by another object (e.g., a table), but not until about 5 months of age do infants understand that the object also will fall if only a small portion is supported (Baillargeon, 1994). In other cases, children may replace rudimentary theories with more advanced ones. Their initial biological theory distinguishes animals from inanimate objects and plants; not until the age of 7 years are children convinced that the category *living things* includes plants as well as animals (Inagaki & Hatano, 2008).

Just as these theories help children divide objects into broad categories, forming **category hierarchies**—that is, categories organized according to set–subset relations—helps children make finer distinctions among the objects within each category. The furniture/chair/La-Z-Boy example shown in Table 7.1 is one example. The category "furniture" includes all chairs; the category "chair" includes all La-Z-Boys. Forming such category hierarchies greatly simplifies the world for children by allowing them to draw accurate inferences. Knowing that a La-Z-Boy is a kind of chair allows children to use their general knowledge of chairs to infer that people sit on La-Z-Boys and that La-Z-Boys are neither lazy nor boys.

Of course, infants are not born knowing about La-Z-Boys and chairs, nor are they born knowing the other categories shown in Table 7.1. Thus, one important question is: How do infants and older children form categories that apply to all kinds of objects, living and nonliving?

Categorization of Objects in Infancy

Even in the first months of life, infants form categories of objects. P. C. Quinn and Eimas (1996), for example, found that when shown a series of photographs of very different breeds of cats, 3- and 4-month-olds habituated; that is, they looked at new cat photographs for less and less time. However, when the infants were subsequently shown a picture of a dog, lion, or other animal, they dishabituated; that is, their looking time increased. Their habituation to the cat photographs suggests that the infants saw all the cats, despite their differences, as members of a single category; their subsequent dishabituation to the photo of the dog or other animal suggests that the infants saw those creatures as members of categories other than cats.

Infants also can form categories more general than "cats." Behl-Chadha (1996) found that 6-month-olds habituated after repeatedly being shown pictures of different types of mammals (dogs, zebras, elephants, and so forth.) and then dishabituated when they were shown a picture of a bird or a fish. The infants apparently perceived similarities among the mammals that led to their eventually losing interest in them. The infants also apparently perceived differences between the mammals and the bird or fish that led them to show renewed interest.

perceptual categorization ■ The grouping together of objects that have similar appearances.

superordinate level ■ The most general level within a category hierarchy, such as "animal" in the animal/dog/poodle example.

subordinate level ■ The most specific level within a category hierarchy, such as "poodle" in the animal/dog/poodle example.

basic level ■ The middle level, and often the first level learned, within a category hierarchy, such as "dog" in the animal/dog/poodle example.

As suggested by this example, infants frequently use **perceptual categorization,** the grouping together of objects that have similar appearances (L. B. Cohen & Cashon, 2006; Madole & Oakes, 1999). Prior to participating in the Behl-Chadha (1996) study, few infants would have seen zebras or elephants. Thus, the distinctions the infants made between these mammals and the birds and fish could only have been based on perception of the animals' differing appearances.

Infants categorize objects along many perceptual dimensions, including colour, size, and movement. Often their categorization is largely based on specific parts of an object rather than on the object as a whole; for example, infants younger than 18 months of age rely heavily on the presence of legs to categorize objects as animals, and they rely heavily on the presence of wheels to categorize objects as vehicles (Rakison & Lupyan, 2008; Rakison & Poulin-Dubois, 2001).

One of the key dimensions that infants use to categorize objects is overall shape. This is a useful assumption, because for many objects, shape indeed is similar for different members of a category. If we see a silhouette of a cat, hammer, or chair, we can tell from the shape what the object is. However, we rarely can do the same if we know only the object's colour or size. This reliance on shape emerges early in development. When 15-month-old infants are shown an unfamiliar object with a specific property (e.g., it makes a sound when squeezed), they assume that other objects of the same shape also share that property even when the objects differ from one another in size and colour (Graham & Diesendruck, 2010).

Categorization of Objects Beyond Infancy

As children move beyond infancy, they increasingly grasp not only individual categories but also hierarchical and causal relations among categories.

Category hierarchies The category hierarchies that young children form often include three of the main levels in Table 7.1: the general one, which is called the **superordinate level;** the very specific one, called the **subordinate level;** and the medium or in-between one, called the **basic level** (Rosch et al., 1976). As its name suggests, the basic level is the one that children usually learn first. Thus, they typically form categories of medium generality, such as "tree," before they form more general categories such as "plant" or more specific ones such as "oak."

The reasons why children generally form the basic level first are not hard to understand. A basic-level category such as "tree" has a number of consistent characteristics: bark, branches, large size, and so on. In contrast, the more general category "plant" has fewer consistent characteristics: plants come in a wide range of shapes, sizes, and colours (consider a maple, a rose, and a house plant). Subordinate-level categories have the same consistent characteristics as the basic-level category, and some additional ones—all maples, but not all trees, have rough bark and distinctly shaped leaves, for example. However, it is relatively difficult to discriminate among different subordinate categories within the same basic-level category (maples versus oaks, for example). Thus, it is not surprising that children tend to form basic-level categories first.

Very young children's basic categories do not always match those of adults. For instance, rather than forming separate categories of cars, motorcycles, and buses, young children seem to group these objects together into a category of "objects with wheels" (Mandler & McDonough, 1998). Even in such cases, however, the initial categories are less general than such categories as "moving things" and more general than ones such as "Toyotas."

Having formed basic-level categories, how do children go on to form super-ordinate and subordinate categories? Part of the answer is that parents and others use the child's basic-level categories as a foundation for explaining the more specific and more general categories (S. A. Gelman et al., 1998). When parents teach children superordinate categories such as mammals, they typically illustrate properties of the relevant terms with basic-level examples that the child already knows (Callanan, 1990). They might say, "Mammals are animals, like foxes, bears, and cows, that get milk from their mothers when they are babies."

Parents also refer to basic-level categories to teach children subordinate-level terms (Callanan & Sabbagh, 2004; Waxman & Senghas, 1992). For example, a parent might say, "Belugas are a kind of whale." Preschoolers are sensitive to the nuances of such statements; for example, they generalize more widely from categorical statements such as "Belugas are a kind of whale" than from statements about specific objects, such as "This beluga is a whale" (Cimpian & Scott, 2012). Sensitivity to the differences between these kinds of statements emerges early in development. One study found that 30-month-olds learning Canadian-English were more likely to generalize properties of unfamiliar objects when they heard categorical-type statements (e.g., "Wugs drink milk") versus when they heard more specific sentences (e.g., "These wugs drink milk") (Graham, Nayer, & Gelman, 2011). Thus, statements that specify relations among categories of objects allow children to use what they already know about basic-level categories to form superordinate- and subordinate-level categories and to decide how to generalize properties of objects.

Although parents' explanations clearly enhance children's conceptual understanding, the learning path sometimes involves amusing detours. In one such case, Susan Gelman (2003) gave her 2-year-old son a spoon and a container filled with bite-sized pieces of fruit and said, "This is a fruit cup." The boy responded to her description by picking up the "cup" and attempting to drink from it. Children's active attempts to understand their experiences lead to many short-lived but interesting concepts such as the "fruit cup."

Causal understanding and categorization Toddlers and preschoolers are notorious for their endless questions about causes and reasons. "Why do dogs bark?" "How does the phone know where to call?" "Where does rain come from?" Although parents are often exasperated by such questions, when they respect and answer the inquiries, they help children learn about the world around them (Chouinard, 2007).

Understanding causal relations is crucial in forming many categories. How could children form the category of "light switches," for example, if they did not understand that flipping certain objects causes lights to go on and off? To study how an understanding of causes and effects influences category formation, Krascum and Andrews (1998) told 4- and 5-year-olds about two categories of imaginary animals: wugs and gillies. Some of the preschoolers were provided only physical descriptions of the animals: they were told that wugs usually have claws on their feet, spikes on the ends of their tails, horns on their heads, and armour on their backs; gillies were described as usually having wings, big ears, long tails, and long toes. Other children were provided the same physical descriptions, plus a simple causal story that explained why wugs and gillies are the way they are. These children were told that wugs have claws, spikes, horns, and armour because they like to fight. Gillies, in contrast, do not like to fight; instead, they hide in trees. Their big ears let them hear approaching wugs, their wings let them fly away to treetops, and so on. After the children in both groups were given the information about these animals, they were

FIGURE 7.1 Cause–effect relations
Hearing that wugs are well prepared to fight and gillies to flee helped preschoolers categorize novel pictures such as these as wugs or gillies (Krascum & Andrews, 1998). In general, understanding cause–effect relations helps people of all ages learn and remember.

shown the pictures in Figure 7.1 and asked which animal was a wug and which was a gilly.

The children who were told why wugs and gillies have the physical features they do were better at classifying the pictures into the appropriate categories. When tested the next day, those children also remembered the categories better than did the children who were given the physical descriptions without explanations. Thus, understanding cause–effect relations helps children learn and remember new categories.

Knowledge of Other People and Oneself

Although understanding of oneself and others varies greatly from individual to individual, just about everybody has a commonsensical level of psychological understanding. This **naive psychology** is crucial to normal human functioning and is a major part of what makes us people. Adult chimpanzees are the equal of human 2 ½-year-olds on a wide range of tasks that require physical reasoning, such as how to use tools to obtain food, but fall far short of the toddlers on tasks requiring social reasoning, such as inferring intentions from behaviour (Herrmann et al., 2007; Tomasello, 2008).

At the centre of naive psychology are three concepts that we all use to understand human behaviour: desires, beliefs, and actions (Wellman, 2013). We apply these concepts almost every time we think about why someone did something. For instance, why did Jimmy go to Billy's house? He *wanted* to play with Billy (a desire), he *expected* that Billy would be at home (a belief), so he *went* to Billy's house (an action). Why did Asha turn the television to Channel 5 at 8:00 A.M. on Saturday? She was *interested in* watching *SpongeBob Squarepants* (a desire), she *thought* the program was on Channel 5 at 8 in the morning (a belief), so she *selected* that channel at that time (an action).

Three properties of naive psychological concepts are noteworthy. First, many of them refer to invisible mental states. No one can see a desire, a belief, or other psychological concepts such as a perception or memory. We, of course, can see behaviours related to invisible psychological concepts, such as Jimmy's ringing Billy's doorbell, but we can only infer the underlying mental state, such as Jimmy's desire to see Billy. Second, psychological concepts are linked to one another in cause–effect relations. Jimmy, for example, might get angry if Billy isn't home because he went to a different friend's house, which could later cause Jimmy to be mean to his younger brother. The third noteworthy property of these naive psychological concepts is that they develop surprisingly early in life.

Sharp disagreements have arisen between nativists and empiricists regarding the source of this early psychological understanding. Nativists (e.g., Leslie, 2000) argue that the early understanding is possible only because children are born with an innate basic understanding of human psychology. In contrast, empiricists (e.g., Frye et al., 1996; Ruffman, Slade, & Crowe, 2002) argue that experiences with other people and general information-processing capacities are the key sources of the early understanding of other people. There is evidence to support each view.

Infants' Naive Psychology

As we saw in Chapter 5, infants find people interesting, pay careful attention to them, and learn an impressive amount about them in the first year. Even very young infants prefer to look at people's faces rather than at other objects. Infants also imitate people's facial movements, such as sticking out their tongue, but

naive psychology ■ A commonsensical level of understanding of other people and oneself.

they do not imitate the motions of inanimate objects. And it is not just the face that interests infants; they also prefer to watch human bodies moving instead of other displays with equal amounts of movement (Bertenthal, 1993). Infants also expect humans, but not inanimate objects, to engage in self-propelled movement. For instance, Concordia University researcher Diane Poulin-Dubois and colleagues discovered that 9-month-olds are not surprised when an adult moves in response to another adult's comments, but they are surprised when a robot does (Poulin-Dubois, Lepage, & Ferland, 1996).

This early interest in human faces and bodies helps infants learn about people's behaviour. Imitating other people and forming emotional bonds with them encourages the other people to interact more with the infants, creating additional opportunities for the infants to acquire psychological understanding.

As noted in earlier discussions, many important aspects of psychological understanding emerge late in the first year and early in the second. One is an understanding of intention, the desire to act in a certain way. Other key psychological concepts that emerge at the same time include joint attention, in which two or more people focus intentionally on the same referent; and intersubjectivity, the mutual understanding that people share during communication (Chapter 4, page 159).

One-year-olds' understanding of other people already includes an understanding of their emotions. Consider the following incident:

> Michael, 15 months, is struggling with his friend Paul over a toy. Paul starts to cry. Michael appears concerned and lets go of the toy, so Paul has it. Paul continues crying. Michael pauses, then gives his own teddy bear to Paul; Paul continues crying. Michael pauses again, runs to the next room, gets Paul's security blanket, and gives it to him. Paul stops crying.
>
> (Hoffman, 1976, pp. 129–130)

Although interpreting anecdotes is always tricky, it seems likely that Michael understood that giving Paul something that he liked might make him feel better (or at least stop his crying). Michael's leaving the room, getting Paul's security blanket, and bringing it back to him suggests that Michael had the further insight that Paul's blanket might be especially useful for soothing his hurt feelings. This interpretation is consistent with a variety of evidence suggesting that children as young as 1 year of age offer physical comfort (hugs, kisses, pats) and, by 18–20 months, comforting comments ("You be okay") to unhappy playmates. Presumably, infants' experience of their own emotions and the behaviours that accompany them helps them understand the emotions that accompany others' actions (Harris, 2006).

Development Beyond Infancy

In the toddler and preschool periods, children build on their early-emerging psychological understanding to develop an increasingly sophisticated comprehension of themselves and other people and to interact with others in increasingly complex ways. Two areas of especially impressive development are understanding of other people's minds and play with peers.

The growth of a theory of mind Infants' and preschoolers' naive psychology, together with their strong interest in other people, provides the foundation for a **theory of mind,** an organized understanding of how mental processes such as intentions, desires, beliefs, perceptions, and emotions influence behaviour. Preschoolers'

THE FAMILY CIRCUS   By Bil Keane

"Mommy, how much grape juice would be bad for the rug?"

Indirect ways of breaking bad news are a speciality of young children and reflect their understanding that other people's actions might not be the same as their own.

theory of mind ■ An organized understanding of how mental processes such as intentions, desires, beliefs, perceptions, and emotions influence behaviour.

false-belief problems ■ Tasks that test a child's understanding that other people will act in accord with their own beliefs even when the child knows that those beliefs are incorrect.

FIGURE 7.2 Testing children's theory of mind The Smarties task is frequently used to study preschoolers' understanding of false beliefs. Most 3-year-olds answer the way the child in this cartoon does, which suggests a lack of understanding that people's actions are based on their own beliefs, even when those beliefs deviate from what the child knows to be true.

theory of mind includes, for example, knowledge that beliefs often originate in perceptions, such as seeing an event or hearing someone describe it; that desires can originate either from physiological states, such as hunger or pain, or from psychological states, such as wanting to see a friend; and that desires and beliefs produce actions (S. A. Miller, 2012).

One important component of such a theory of mind—understanding the connection between other people's desires and their actions—emerges by the end of the first year. In a study by Phillips, Wellman, and Spelke (2002), 12-month-olds saw an experimenter look at one of two stuffed kittens and say in a joyful voice, "Ooh, look at the kitty!" Then a screen descended, and when it was raised 2 seconds later, the experimenter was holding either the kitty that she had just gushed over or the other one. The 12-month-olds looked longer when the experimenter was holding the other kitty, suggesting that they expected the experimenter to want to hold the kitty that had just excited her so much and were surprised that she was holding the other one. Eight-month-olds looked for similar amounts of time regardless of which kitty the experimenter held, suggesting that the understanding that people's desires guide their actions develops toward the end of the first year (Phillips et al., 2002). Consistent with this conclusion, 10-month-olds can use information about a person's earlier desires to predict that person's later desires, but only if the earlier and later circumstances are virtually identical (Sommerville & Crane, 2009).

The understanding that desires lead to actions is firmly established by age 2 years. Children of this age, for example, predict that characters in stories will act in accord with their own desires, even when those desires differ from the child's preferences (Gopnik & Slaughter, 1991; Lillard & Flavell, 1992). Thus, if 2-year-olds who would rather play with trucks than with dolls are told that a character in a story would rather play with dolls than with trucks, they predict that, given the choice, the character in the story will choose dolls over trucks.

Although most 2-year-olds understand that *desires* can influence behaviour, they show little understanding that *beliefs* are likewise influential. Thus, when 2-year-olds were told a story in which a character named Sam believed that the only bananas available were in a cupboard, but they themselves knew that there were bananas in a refrigerator as well, they were no more likely than by chance to predict that Sam would act in accord with his own belief and search for bananas only in the cupboard (Wellman & Woolley, 1990).

By age 3 years, children show some understanding of the relation between beliefs and actions. For example, they answer questions such as "Why is Billy looking for his dog?" by referring to beliefs ("He thinks the dog ran away") as well as to desires ("He wants it") (Bartsch & Wellman, 1995). Most 3-year-olds also have some knowledge of how beliefs originate. They know, for example, that seeing an event produces beliefs about it, whereas simply being next to someone who can see the event does not (Pillow, 1988).

At the same time, 3-year-olds' understanding of the relation between people's beliefs and their actions is limited in important ways. These limitations are evident when children are presented with **false-belief problems,** in which another person believes something to be true that the child knows is false. The question is whether the child thinks that the other person will act in accord with his or her own false belief or in accord with the child's correct understanding of the situation. Studying such situations reveals whether children understand that other people's actions are determined by the contents of their own minds rather than by the objective truth of the situation.

In one false-belief problem, preschoolers are shown a box that ordinarily contains Smarties and that has a picture of the candy on it (Figure 7.2). The experimenter then asks what is inside the box. Logically enough, the preschoolers say "Smarties." Next, the experimenter opens the box, revealing that it actually contains pencils. Most 5-year-olds laugh or smile and admit their surprise. When asked what another child would say if shown the closed box and asked to guess its contents, they say the child would answer "Smarties," just as they had. Not 3-year-olds! One study at the University of Toronto demonstrated that a large majority of 3-year-olds claim they always knew what was in the box, and they predict that if another child were shown the box, that child would also believe that the box contained pencils (Gopnik & Astington, 1988). The 3-year-olds' responses show they have difficulty understanding that other people act on their own beliefs, even when those beliefs are false.

This finding is extremely robust. A review of 178 studies of children's understanding of false beliefs showed that similar results emerged with different forms of the problem, different questions, and different societies (Wellman, Cross, & Watson, 2001). In one noteworthy cross-cultural study, false-belief problems were presented to children attending preschools in Canada, India, Peru, Thailand, and Samoa (Callaghan et al., 2005). Performance improved greatly between ages 3 and 5 years in all five societies, from 14% correct for 3-year-olds to 85% correct for 5-year-olds. Especially striking was the consistency of performance across these very different societies: in no country did 3-year-olds answer more than 25% of problems correctly, and in no country did 5-year-olds answer less than 72% correctly.

Although 3-year-olds generally err on false-belief problems when the problems are presented in the standard way, many children of this age succeed if the task is presented in a manner that facilitates understanding. For instance, if an experimenter tells a 3-year-old that the two of them are going to play a trick on another child by hiding pencils in a Smarties box and enlists the child's help in filling the box with pencils, most 3-year-olds correctly predict that the other child will say that the box contains Smarties (K. Sullivan & Winner, 1993). Presumably, assuming the role of deceiver and hiding the pencils in the Smarties box helps 3-year-olds see the situation from the other child's perspective.

Children's theories of mind continue to develop long beyond this early period, with at least some of the development dependent on specific experiences. For instance, 14-year-olds who had experience acting in plays over the course of a school year showed greater understanding of other people's thinking at the end of the year than before their acting experience (T. R. Goldstein & Winner, 2011). In contrast, peers who received other types of arts education (music or visual arts) for the same period did not show comparable gains in understanding other people's thinking.

Explaining the development of theory of mind People's lives clearly would be very different without a reasonably sophisticated theory of mind. However, the findings on the improvement in typical children's theory of mind between ages 3 and 5 do not tell us what causes the improvement. This question has generated enormous controversy, and currently there is great disagreement about how to answer it.

Investigators who take a nativist position have proposed the existence of a **theory of mind module (TOMM),** a hypothesized brain mechanism devoted to understanding other human beings (Baron-Cohen, 1995; Leslie, 2000). Advocates of this

Despite leading very different lives, pygmy children in Africa and same-age peers in industrialized North American and European societies respond to the false-belief task in the same way.

theory of mind module (TOMM) ■ A hypothesized brain mechanism devoted to understanding other human beings.

The child sitting in his mother's lap shows a distinct lack of interest in her affection. Such lack of interest in other people is common among children with autism spectrum disorders and seems related to their very poor performance on tasks that require an understanding of other people's minds.

position argue that among typical children exposed to a typical environment, the TOMM matures over the first 5 years, producing an increasingly sophisticated understanding of people's minds. These investigators cite evidence from brain-imaging studies showing that certain areas of the brain are consistently active in representing beliefs across different tasks, and that the areas are different from those involved in other complex cognitive processes, such as understanding grammar (R. Saxe & Powell, 2006).

Further evidence that is often cited to support the idea of the TOMM comes from children with autism spectrum disorders (ASD). As discussed in Box 7.1, these children have great difficulty with false-belief problems, as well as with understanding people more generally. Consistent with the idea of a TOMM, one reason for these difficulties in understanding the social world appears to be atypical sizes of certain brain areas that are crucial for understanding people (Amaral, Schumann, & Nordahl, 2008)

Theorists who take an empiricist stance suggest a different explanation of the development of theory of mind, maintaining that psychological understanding arises from interactions with other people (Ruffman, Slade, & Crowe, 2002). For instance, Janet Astington and Jennifer Jenkins at the University of Toronto cite evidence that on false-belief tasks, preschoolers who have siblings outperform peers who do not. This finding appears to be strongest when the siblings are older or of the opposite sex, presumably because interacting with people whose interests, desires, and motives are different from their own broadens children's understanding of the mind (Jenkins & Astington, 1996; S. A. Miller, 2012). From this perspective, the tendency of children with ASD not to interact much with other people is a major contributor to their difficulty in understanding others.

A third group of investigators also takes an empiricist stance but emphasizes the growth of general information-processing skills as essential to understanding other people's minds. They cite evidence that children's understanding of false-belief problems is substantially correlated with their ability to reason about complex counterfactual statements (German & Nichols, 2003) and with their ability to inhibit their own behavioural propensities when necessary (S. M. Carlson, Mandell, & Williams, 2004; Frye et al., 1996). The ability to reason about counterfactual statements is important, because false-belief problems require children to predict what a person would do on the basis of a counterfactual belief. The ability to inhibit behavioural propensities is important because false-belief problems also require children to suppress the assumption that the person would act on the truth of the situation. Investigators in this camp argue that typical children younger than 4 years and children with ASD lack the information-processing skills needed to understand others' minds, whereas typical older children can engage in such processing.

All three explanations have merit. Normal development of brain regions relevant to understanding other people, interactions with other people, and improved information-processing capacity all contribute to the growth of psychological understanding during the preschool years. Together, they allow almost all children to achieve a basic, but useful, theory of mind by age 5.

BOX 7.1: individual differences

CHILDREN WITH AUTISM SPECTRUM DISORDERS (ASD)

Although most children readily handle false-belief problems by the age of 5 years, one group continues to find them very difficult even when they are teenagers: children with autism spectrum disorders (ASD). As discussed in Chapter 3 (page 95), this syndrome, which strikes roughly 1 in 100 children in Canada, most of them male (NEDSAC, 2012), involves difficulties in social interaction, communication, and other intellectual and emotional functions.

Children who are on the more severe end of the autism spectrum often engage in solitary, repetitive behaviours, such as continually rocking back and forth or endlessly skipping around a room. They interact minimally with other children and adults, rarely form close relationships, produce little or no language, and tend to be more interested in objects than in people (Willis, 2009). These problems, among others, have led some researchers to speculate that a failure to understand other people underlies these children's limited engagement in the social world.

Recent research supports this hypothesis. Children with ASD tend to have trouble establishing joint attention with other people (Klin et al., 2004). Compared with both typical children and children with developmental delays, children with ASD show less concern when other people appear distressed (Sigman & Ruskin, 1999) or experience circumstances that would lead most people to be distressed (Hobson et al., 2009). These children also tend to have poor language skills (Tager-Flusberg & Joseph, 2005), which both reflects their lack of attention to other people and limits their opportunities to learn about people's thoughts and feelings through conversation. In line with these patterns, children with ASD are strikingly befuddled by false-belief questions (Baron-Cohen, 1991). For example, fewer than half of 6- to 14-year-olds with ASD solve false-belief problems that are easy for typical 4- and 5-year-olds (Peterson, Wellman, & Liu, 2005). Children with ASD have some understanding of how desire affects behaviour, but the ways in which beliefs influence behaviour largely elude them (Harris, 2006; Tager-Flusberg, 2007).

Impaired theory-of-mind mechanisms are not the only source of difficulty that children with ASD encounter in understanding other people. More general deficits in planning, adapting to changing situations, and controlling working memory also contribute (Ozonoff et al., 2004). Nonetheless, impaired theory of mind is a source of particular difficulty, especially in understanding situations in which people's beliefs differ from reality (Baron-Cohen, 1993; Tager-Flusberg, 2007).

Fortunately, many problems caused by ASD can be mitigated by intense and prolonged early treatment. Dawson and colleagues (2010) randomly assigned 1- and 2-year-olds who had been diagnosed with ASD to receive either Early Start Denver Model (ESDM) treatment or community-based treatment (the control condition). The ESDM treatment included roughly 15 hours per week of sessions with trained therapists, during which time the therapists and children practised everyday activities, such as eating and playing, and used operant conditioning techniques to promote desired behaviours. These desired behaviours were chosen by the children's parents, who also were taught how to use the approach and encouraged to use it with their child during common activities such as playing and bathing. The parents reported using the approach for an average of 16 hours/week, beyond the formal ESDM sessions. The effects of ESDM were compared to those of the community-based treatment, which included comprehensive diagnostic evaluations, the provision of resource manuals and reading materials, and referrals for other types of treatment.

After 2 years of treatment, children who received the ESDM treatment showed considerably greater gains in IQ score, language, and daily living skills than did peers who received the community-based treatment. This study and others (e.g., Voos et al., 2012) suggest that early, intensive treatment of ASD can yield large benefits.

The growth of play *Play* refers to activities that are pursued for their own sake, with no motivation other than the enjoyment they bring. The earliest play activities, such as banging a spoon on a high-chair tray, tend to be solitary. Over the next few years, children's increasing understanding of other people contributes to their play becoming more social as well as more complex.

One early milestone in the development of play is the emergence, at around 18 months of age, of **pretend play,** make-believe activities in which children create new symbolic relations. When engaged in pretend play, children act as if they were in a different situation than their actual one. They often engage in **object substitution,** ignoring many of a play object's characteristics so that they can pretend that it is something else. Typical examples of object substitution are a child's treating a cylindrical wooden block as a bottle and pretending to drink from it or treating a plastic soap dish as a boat and floating it on the water while taking a bath.

pretend play ■ Make-believe activities in which children create new symbolic relations, acting as if they were in a situation different from their actual one.

object substitution ■ A form of pretense in which an object is used as something other than itself, for example, using a broom to represent a horse.

sociodramatic play ■ Activities in which children enact miniature dramas with other children or adults, such as "mother comforting baby."

Sociodramatic play, in which children create miniature dramas based on their experiences, both reflects children's understanding of the situation and helps them increase that understanding.

Children often enjoy having a parent join them in sociodramatic play, which tends to be richer and more informative when the parent provides scaffolding for the play episode. Along with helping structure the tea-time conversation, the father in this scenario may also be providing his children with tips on party etiquette.

About a year later, toddlers begin to engage in **sociodramatic play,** a kind of pretend play in which they enact miniature dramas with other children or adults, such as "mother comforting baby" or "doctor helping sick child" (O'Reilly & Bornstein, 1993). Sociodramatic play is more complex and more social than object substitution. Consider, for example, "tea party" rituals, in which a child and parent "pour tea" for each other from an imaginary teapot, daintily "sip" it, "eat" imaginary cookies, and comment on how delicious they are.

Young children's sociodramatic play is typically more sophisticated when they are playing with a parent or older sibling who can scaffold the play sequence than when they are pretending with a peer (Bornstein, 2006; Lillard, 2006). Such scaffolding during play provides children with opportunities for learning, in particular for improving their storytelling skills (Nicolopoulou, 2007). Consider one mother's comments as her 2-year-old played with two action figures:

> Oh look, Lantern Man is chasing Spider Man. Oh no, he is pushing him down. Spider Man says, "Help, Lantern Man is grabbing me." Look, Spider Man is getting away.
>
> (Kavanaugh & Engel, 1998, p. 88)

Such adult elaboration of implicit storylines in children's play provides a useful model for children to follow in later pretend play with peers or by themselves.

By the elementary school years, play becomes even more complex and social. It begins to include activities such as sports and board games that have conventional rules that participants must follow. The frequent quarrels that arise among young elementary school students regarding who is obeying the rules and playing fair attest to the cognitive and emotional challenges posed by these games (Rubin, Fein, & Vandenberg, 1983).

Pretend play is often thought of as limited to early childhood, but it actually continues far beyond that time. In a survey of college students, the majority reported that they had engaged in pretend play at least weekly when they were 10 or 11 years old, and most reported doing so at least monthly when they were 12 or 13 years old (E. D. Smith & Lillard, 2011). Boys and only children tended to report engaging in pretend play at older ages than girls and children with siblings.

In addition to being fun, pretend play may expand children's understanding of the social world. Children who engage in greater amounts of pretend play tend to show greater understanding of other people's thinking (Lillard, 2006) and emotions (Youngblade & Dunn, 1995). The type of pretend play in which children engage also matters: social pretend play is more strongly related to understanding other people's thinking than is non-social pretend play (Harris, 2000). Preschoolers also learn from watching others' pretend play (S. L. Sutherland & Friedman, 2012). Such evidence has led some experts in the area (e.g., Hirsh-Pasek et al., 2009; Tomlinson, 2009) to conclude that high levels of pretend play are causally related to increased social understanding. However, a recent comprehensive review of studies of pretend play (Lillard et al., 2013) found limited evidence for such a causal relation. Instead, frequent

BOX 7.2: individual differences

IMAGINARY COMPANIONS

Many children have an imaginary companion whom they appear to regard as an actual being. Marjorie Taylor (1999) found that 63% of children whom she interviewed at age 3 or 4 years and again at age 7 or 8 years reported having imaginary companions at one or both times. In another study, Taylor and colleagues (2004) found that as many 6- and 7-year-olds as 3- and 4-year-olds said that they had imaginary companions—31% of older children and 28% of younger ones. Hearing a child talk about an invisible friend sometimes leads parents to worry about their child's sanity, but as these statistics suggest, children's creation of such characters is entirely normal.

Most of the imaginary playmates described by children in Taylor's studies were ordinary boys and girls who happened to be invisible. Others were more colourful. They included Derek, a 91-year-old man who was said to be only 60 centimetres tall but able to hit bears; "The Girl," a 4-year-old who always wore pink and was "a beautiful person"; Joshua, a possum who lived in San Francisco; and Nobby, a 160-year-old businessman. Other imaginary companions were modelled after specific people: two examples were MacKenzie, an imaginary playmate who resembled the child's cousin MacKenzie, and "Fake Rachel," who resembled the child's friend Rachel.

As with real friends, children have a variety of complaints about their imaginary companions. In a study of 36 preschoolers with imaginary companions, only one child had no complaints; the other 35 children griped that their imaginary companions argued with them, refused to share, failed to come when invited, and failed to leave when no longer welcome (M. Taylor & Mannering, 2007). In this independence from their creator, the imaginary companions resemble characters invented by novelists, many of whom report that their characters at times seem to act independently, including arguing with and criticizing their creator (M. Taylor & Mannering, 2007).

Contrary to popular speculation, Taylor (1999) found that, in terms of broad characteristics such as personality, intelligence, and creativity, children who invent imaginary playmates are no different from children who do not. However, she and other investigators have identified a few relatively specific differences between these two groups. Children who had created imaginary playmates were more likely (1) to be first-born or only children; (2) to watch relatively little television; (3) to be verbally skillful; and (4) to have advanced theories of mind (Carlson et al., 2003; Taylor & Carlson, 1997; Taylor et al., 2004). These relations make sense. Being without siblings may motivate some first-born and only children to invent friends to keep them company; not watching much television frees time for imaginative play; and being verbally skilled and having an advanced theory of mind may enable children to imagine especially interesting companions and especially interesting adventures with them.

Companionship, entertainment, and enjoyment of fantasy are not the only reasons why children invent imaginary companions. Children also use them to deflect blame ("I didn't do it; Blebbi Ussi did"); to vent anger ("I hate you, Blebbi Ussi"); and to convey information that the child is reluctant to state directly ("Blebbi Ussi is scared of falling into the potty"). As Taylor (1999) noted, "Imaginary companions love you when you feel rejected by others, listen when you need to talk to someone, and can be trusted not to repeat what you say" (p. 63). It is no wonder, then, that so many children invent them.

Although the sight of their child feeding someone who isn't there might worry some parents, the creation of imaginary friends is entirely normal and the majority of children enjoy the company of such characters at some time in early childhood.

pretend play and high levels of social understanding seem to be caused by parents who promote both. Some children with high social skills simply enjoy pretend play and often engage in it. The jury remains out on whether pretend play is a cause of improved social understanding, but it is clear that such play is not harmful and that it enriches many children's lives.

Children's interest in social play is so strong that they do not let the absence of playmates prevent them from engaging in it. For such occasions, and even sometimes when playmates are available, they turn to imaginary companions (Box 7.2).

Knowledge of Living Things

Children are fascinated by living things, especially animals. One sign of their fascination is how often they talk about them. In a study of the first 50 words used by children, the two terms other than "mama" and "dada" that were used by the greatest number of children were "dog" and "cat" (and variants such as "doggie" and "kitty") (K. Nelson, 1973). "Duck," "horse," "bear," "bird," and "cow" also were common early terms. By the time children are 4 or 5 years old, their fascination with living things translates into an impressive amount of knowledge about them, including knowledge of unobservable biological processes such as inheritance, illness, and healing (S. A. Gelman, 2003).

Coexisting with this relatively advanced knowledge, however, are a variety of immature beliefs and types of reasoning. For instance, children often fail to understand the difference between artifacts, such as chairs and cars, which are built by people for specific purposes, and living things, such as monkeys, which are not created by people for any purpose. Thus, when Kelemen and DiYanni (2005) asked 6- to 10-year-olds why the first monkey came to exist, the children often referred to how monkeys serve human purposes, such as "The manager of the zoo-place wanted some" and "So then we had somebody to climb trees."

Another weakness in young children's biological knowledge is their incorrect beliefs about which things are living and which are not. For example, most 5-year-olds believe that plants are not alive, and some believe that the moon and mountains are alive (Hatano et al., 1993; Inagaki & Hatano, 2002). Such erroneous notions have led some investigators to conclude that children have only a shallow and fragmented understanding of living things until they are 7 to 10 years old (Carey, 1999; Slaughter, Jaakkola, & Carey, 1999). In contrast, other investigators believe that by age 5 years, children understand the essential characteristics of living things and what separates them from nonliving things but are confused on just a few points (S. A. Gelman, 2003). A third view is that young children simultaneously possess both mature and immature biological understanding (Inagaki & Hatano, 2008). With this dispute in mind, we will now consider what young children do and do not know about living things and how they acquire knowledge about them.

Distinguishing Living from Nonliving Things

As noted previously, infants in their first year already are interested in people and distinguish them from nonliving things (Figure 7.3). Other animals also attract infants' interest, though infants act differently toward them than they do toward

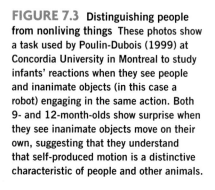

FIGURE 7.3 **Distinguishing people from nonliving things** These photos show a task used by Poulin-Dubois (1999) at Concordia University in Montreal to study infants' reactions when they see people and inanimate objects (in this case a robot) engaging in the same action. Both 9- and 12-month-olds show surprise when they see inanimate objects move on their own, suggesting that they understand that self-produced motion is a distinctive characteristic of people and other animals.

people. Researchers in Montreal have found that 9-month-olds, for example, pay more attention to rabbits than they do to inanimate objects, but they smile less at rabbits than they do at people (Poulin-Dubois, 1999; Ricard & Allard, 1993).

These behavioural reactions indicate that infants in their first year distinguish people from other animals and that they distinguish both from inanimate objects. However, the reactions do not indicate when children construct a general category of living things that includes plants as well as animals or when they recognize humans as a type of animal. It is difficult to assess children's knowledge of these and many other properties of living and nonliving things until the age of 3 or 4 years, when they can comprehend and answer questions about these categories. By this age, they clearly know quite a bit about the similarities among all living creatures and about the differences between living creatures and inanimate objects. This knowledge of living things is not limited to visible properties such as having legs, moving, and making distinctive noises. It also extends to biological processes such as digestion and heredity (S. A. Gelman, 2003). At least through age 5 or 6, however, many children deny that people are animals (Carey, 1985).

Children are interested in living things—plants as well as animals, especially when part of the plant tastes good.

COURTESY OF SUWANNA AND DAVID SIEGLER

Understanding the life status of plants also presents a challenge to young children. On the one hand, most preschoolers know that plants, like animals but unlike inanimate objects, grow (Hickling & Gelman, 1995; Inagaki & Hatano, 1996), heal themselves (Backscheider, Shatz, & Gelman, 1993), and die (Springer, Nguyen, & Samaniego, 1996). On the other hand, most preschoolers believe that plants are not alive; in fact, it is not until age 7 or older that a clear majority of children realize that plants are living things (Hatano et al., 1993). Part of the reason is that children often equate being alive with being able to move in adaptive ways that promote survival; plants do move in this way, but their adaptive movements, such as bending toward sunlight, occur too slowly to observe under ordinary circumstances (Opfer & Gelman, 2001). Consistent with this interpretation, letting 5-year-olds know that plants bend toward sunlight and that their roots grow toward water leads the children to conclude that plants, like animals, are living things (Opfer & Siegler, 2004).

More generally, culture and direct experience influence the age at which children understand that plants are, in fact, alive. For instance, children growing up in rural areas realize that plants are living things at younger ages than do children growing up in cities or suburbs (J. D. Coley, 2000; N. Ross et al., 2003).

Understanding Biological Processes

Preschoolers understand that biological processes, such as growth, digestion, and healing, differ from psychological ones (Wellman & Gelman, 1998). For example, although 3- and 4-year-olds recognize that desires influence what people do, they also recognize that some biological processes are independent of one's desires. Distinguishing between biological and psychological processes, for example, leads preschoolers to predict that people who overeat but wish to lose weight will not get their wish (Inagaki & Hatano, 1993; Schult & Wellman, 1997).

essentialism ■ The view that living things have an essence inside them that makes them what they are.

Preschoolers also recognize that properties of living things often serve important functions for the organism, whereas properties of inanimate objects do not. Thus, 5-year-olds recognize that the green colour of plants is crucial for them to make food, whereas the green colour of emeralds has no function for the emerald (Keil, 1992). The extent of preschoolers' understanding of biological processes can be understood more fully by examining their specific ideas about inheritance, growth, and illness.

Inheritance Although 3- and 4-year-olds obviously know nothing about DNA or the mechanisms of heredity, they do know that physical characteristics tend to be passed on from parent to offspring. If told, for example, that Mr. and Mrs. Bull have hearts of an unusual colour, they predict that Baby Bull also will have a heart of that colour (Springer & Keil, 1991). Similarly, they predict that a baby mouse will eventually have hair of the same colour as its parents, even if it is presently hairless.

Older preschoolers also know that certain aspects of development are determined by heredity rather than by environment. For instance, 5-year-olds realize that an animal of one species raised by parents of another species will become an adult of its own species (S. C. Johnson & Solomon, 1997).

Coexisting with this understanding are numerous misguided beliefs about inheritance. Many preschoolers believe that mothers' desires can play a role in their children's inheritance of physical qualities, such as having blue eyes (Weissman & Kalish, 1999). Many preschoolers also believe that adopted children are at least as likely to look like their adoptive parents as like their birth parents (Solomon et al., 1996). In other situations, preschoolers' belief in heredity is too strong, leading them to deny that the environment has any influence. For example, preschoolers tend to believe that differences between boys and girls in play preferences are due totally to heredity (M. G. Taylor, 1993).

Related to this general belief in the importance of heredity is one of the most basic aspects of children's biological beliefs— **essentialism,** the view that living things have an essence inside them that makes them what they are (S. A. Gelman, 2003). Thus, most preschoolers (as well as most older children and adults) believe that puppies have a certain "dogness" inside them, kittens have a certain "catness," roses have a certain "roseness," and so on. This essence is what makes all members of the category similar to one another and different from members of other categories; for example, their inner "dogness" leads to dogs' barking, chasing cats, and liking to be petted. This essence is viewed as being inherited from one's parents and being maintained throughout the organism's life. Thinking in terms of such essences seems to make it difficult, both for children and for many adults, to understand and accept biological evolution (E. M. Evans, 2008). If animals inherit an unchanging essence from their parents, how, they may wonder, would it be possible, say, for mice and whales to have common ancestors?

Growth, illness, and healing Preschoolers realize that growth, like inheritance, is a product of internal processes. They recognize, for example, that plants and animals become bigger and more complex over time because of something going on inside them (again, preschoolers are not sure what) (Rosengren et al., 1991). Three- and four-year-olds also recognize that the growth of living things generally proceeds in only one direction (smaller to larger) at least until old age, whereas inanimate objects such as balloons can become either smaller or larger at any point in time.

"I've been getting in touch with the puppy in me."

A fanciful representation of the inner essence that children believe makes a dog a dog, a cat a cat, and so on.

Preschoolers also show a basic understanding of illness. Three-year-olds have heard of germs and have a general sense of how they operate. They know that eating food that is contaminated with germs can make a person sick, even if the person is unaware of the germs' presence (Kalish, 1997). Conversely, they realize that psychological processes, such as being aware of germs in one's food, do not cause illness.

Finally, preschoolers know that plants and animals, unlike inanimate objects, have internal processes that often allow them to regain prior states or attributes. For instance, 4-year-olds realize that a tomato plant that is scratched can heal itself and that an animal's hair can grow back after being cut but that a scratched chair cannot heal itself and that a doll's hair cannot grow back (Backscheider et al., 1993). Preschoolers also recognize the limits of living things' recuperative processes: they understand that both illness and old age can cause death, from which no recuperation is possible (Nguyen & Gelman, 2002).

How Do Children Acquire Biological Knowledge?

As with other aspects of conceptual development, nativists and empiricists have very different ideas regarding the development of children's biological understanding. Nativists propose that humans are born with a "biology module" much like the theory of mind module described earlier in the chapter. This brain structure or mechanism helps children learn quickly about living things (Atran, 1990, 2002). Nativists use three main arguments to support the idea that people have a biology module:

- During earlier periods of our evolution, it was crucial for human survival that children learn quickly about animals and plants.

- Children throughout the world are fascinated by plants and animals and learn about them quickly and easily.

- Children throughout the world organize information about plants and animals in very similar ways (in terms of growth, reproduction, inheritance, sickness, and healing).

The feelings of awe experienced by many children (and adults) upon seeing remains of great animals of the past and present, such as dinosaurs, elephants, and whales, were a major reason for the founding of natural history museums. Despite all the depictions of monsters and superheroes on television, in movies, and in video games, these fossils and models inspire the same sense of wonder in children growing up today.

Empiricists, in contrast, maintain that children's biological understanding comes from their personal observations and information they receive from parents, teachers, and the general culture (Callanan, 1990). When mothers read books about animals to their 1- and 2-year-olds, for example, many of the mothers' comments and questions suggest that animals have intentions and goals, that different members of the same species have a lot in common, and that animals differ greatly from inanimate objects (S. A. Gelman et al., 1998). Such teaching is often elicited by children's questions: when 3- to 5-year-olds encounter unfamiliar things, they ask a higher percentage of questions about the functions of things that appear to be man-made but ask a higher percentage of questions about the biological properties of things that look like animals or plants (Margett & Witherington, 2011). Such questions both reflect children's biological knowledge and increase it.

Empiricists also note that children's biological understanding reflects the views of their culture. For instance, 5-year-olds in Japan are more likely than their peers in the United States and Israel to believe that nonliving things and plants are able to feel physical sensations, such as pain and cold (Hatano et al., 1993). This tendency of Japanese children echoes the Buddhist tradition, still influential in Japanese society, which views all objects as having certain psychological properties.

As with the parallel arguments regarding the sources of psychological understanding, both nature and nurture seem certain to play important roles in the acquisition of biological understanding. Young children are innately fascinated by animals and learn about them much more quickly than about aspects of their environment that they find less interesting. At the same time, the particulars of what children learn obviously are influenced by the information, beliefs, and values conveyed to them by their parents and their society. And as always, nurture responds to nature, as parents provide informative answers to their children's many questions about living things, which in turn reflect the children's interest in those things.

review:

From early in infancy, children form categories of similar objects. Such categorization helps them infer the properties of unfamiliar objects within a category. For example, if children learn that a new object is an animal, they know that it will grow, move, and eat. Children form new categories, and include new objects within an existing category, on the basis of similarities between the appearance and function of the new object and objects already known to be category members.

One particularly important category is people. From the first days of life, infants are interested in other people and spend a great deal of time looking at them. By age 3 years, they form a simple theory of mind that includes some understanding of the causal relations among desires, beliefs, and actions. Not until age 4 or 5 years, however, do most children become able to solve false-belief problems that require them to understand that other people will act in accord with their own beliefs, even if the child knows that those beliefs are wrong. The development of understanding of other people's minds during the preschool period has been attributed to biological maturation of a theory of mind module, to interactions with other people, and to the growth of information-processing capabilities that allow children to understand increasingly complex social situations.

Another vital category is living things. During the preschool years, children gain a basic understanding of the properties of biological entities: growth, heredity, illness, and death. Not until children go to school, however, do most of them group plants with animals into a single category of living things. Explanations for children's relatively rapid acquisition of biological knowledge include the extensive exposure to biological information provided by families and the broader culture, children's own questions that elicit from other people useful information about plants and animals, and the existence of brain mechanisms that lead children to be interested in living things and to learn about them quickly and easily.

Understanding Why, Where, When, and How Many

Making sense of our experiences requires accurately representing not only who or what was involved in an event but also why, where, when, and how often the event occurred. To grasp the importance of these latter concepts, imagine what life would be like if you lost your understanding of any one of them—your sense of time, for example. Without a sense of time, you would not even know the order in which events occurred. Did you get dressed and then eat breakfast, or did you eat breakfast and then get dressed? Your whole impression of your life as a continuous stream of events would be shattered. Similar problems would arise if you lost your sense of causality or space or number. Reality would resemble a nightmare in which order and predictability were suspended and chaos reigned.

As described in the previous section, the categories that children need to answer the questions "Who?" and "What?" begin forming in infancy, though the understanding deepens for many years thereafter. Development of understanding of causality, space, time, and number follows a similar path. In each case, development begins in the first year of life, but major improvements continue throughout childhood and adolescence.

Causality

The famed 18th-century Scottish philosopher David Hume described causality as "the cement of the universe." His point was that causal connections unite discrete events into coherent wholes. Consistent with Hume's view, from early in development, children rely heavily on their understanding of causal mechanisms to infer why physical and psychological events occur. When children take apart toys to find out how they work, ask how flipping a switch makes a light go on, or wonder why Mummy is upset, they are trying to understand causal connections. Because we discussed the development of understanding of psychological causes earlier in this chapter, we now focus on the development of understanding of physical causes.

Nativists and empiricists fundamentally disagree about the origins of understanding of physical causes. The difficulty of making sense of the world without some basic causal understanding and the fact that children show some such understanding early in infancy have led nativists to propose that infants possess an innate causal module or core theory that allows them to extract causal relations from the events they observe (e.g., Leslie, 1986; Spelke, 2003). Empiricists, on the other hand, have proposed that infants' causal understanding arises from their observations of innumerable events in the environment (e.g., L. B. Cohen & Cashon, 2006; T. T. Rogers & McClelland, 2004). One fact that both sides agree on is that children show impressive causal reasoning from infancy onward.

Very Early Causal Reasoning

By 6 months of age, infants perceive causal connections among some physical events (L. B. Cohen & Cashon, 2006; Leslie, 1986). In a typical experiment demonstrating infants' ability to perceive such relations, Oakes and Cohen (1995) presented 6- to 10-month-olds a series of video clips in which a moving object collided with a stationary object and the stationary object immediately moved in the way one would expect. Different moving and stationary objects were used in each clip, but the basic "plot" remained the same. After seeing a few of these video clips, infants habituated to the collisions. Then the infants were shown a slightly different clip in which the stationary object started moving shortly before it was struck. Infants looked at this event for a longer time than they had looked during the preceding trials, presumably because the new video clip violated their sense that inanimate objects do not move on their own.

Infants' and toddlers' understandings of physical causality influence not only their expectations about inanimate objects but also their ability to remember and imitate sequences of actions. When 9- to 11-month-olds are shown actions that are causally related (e.g., making a rattle by putting a small object inside two cups that can be pushed together to form a single container), they usually can reproduce the actions (Figure 7.4 shows a toddler performing this procedure) (Carver & Bauer, 1999). In contrast, when similar but causally unrelated actions are shown, babies do not reliably reproduce them until age 20 to 22 months (Bauer, 2007).

By the end of their second year, and by some measures even earlier, children can infer the causal impact of one variable based on indirectly relevant information about another. Sobel and Kirkham (2006), for example, presented 19- and 24-month-olds a box called a "blicket detector" that, the experimenter explained, played music when a type of object called a blicket was placed on it. Then the experimenter placed two objects, A and B, on the blicket detector, and the music played. When the experimenter then placed object A alone on the blicket detector, the music did not play. Then the children were asked to turn on the blicket detector. The 24-month-olds consistently chose object B, indicating that seeing the ineffectiveness of object A led them to infer that object B activated the blicket detector. In contrast, the 19-month-olds chose object A as often as they did object B, suggesting that they did not draw this inference.

FIGURE 7.4 Imitating sequences of events Understanding the actions they are imitating helps toddlers perform the actions in the correct order. In this illustration of the procedure used by Bauer (1995) to demonstrate this point, a toddler imitates a previously observed three-step sequence to build a rattle. The child (a) picks up a small block; (b) puts it into the bottom half of the container; (c) pushes the top half of the container onto the bottom, thus completing the rattle; and (d) shakes it.

(a)

(b)

(c)

(d)

ALL: COURTESY OF PATRICIA BAUER

Another illustration of this growing understanding of causality comes from Z. Chen and Siegler's (2000) study of 1- and 2-year-olds' tool use. The toddlers were presented an attractive toy that was sitting on a table roughly 30 centimetres beyond their reach. Between the child and the toy were six potential tools that varied in length and in the type of head at the end of the shaft (Figure 7.5). To succeed on the task, the toddlers needed to understand the causal relations that would make one tool more effective than the others for pulling in the toy. In particular, they needed to understand that a sufficiently long shaft and a head at right angles to the shaft were essential.

The 2-year-olds succeeded considerably more often than the 1-year-olds did in obtaining the toy, both in their initial efforts to get it on their own and after being shown by the experimenter how they could use the optimal tool to obtain it. One reason for the older toddlers' greater success was that they more often used a tool to try to get the toy, as opposed to reaching for it with their hands or seeking their mother's help. Another reason was that the older toddlers chose the optimal tool in a greater percentage of trials in which they used some tool. A third reason was that the older toddlers more often generalized what they had learned on the first problem to new, superficially different problems involving tools and toys with different shapes, colours, and decorations. All these findings indicate that the older toddlers had a deeper understanding of the causal relations between a tool's features and its usefulness for pulling in the toy.

FIGURE 7.5 Toddlers' problem solving In the task used by Chen and Siegler (2000) to examine toddlers' causal reasoning and problem solving, choosing the right tool for getting the toy required children to understand the importance of both the length of the shaft and the angle of the head relative to the shaft. Compared with younger toddlers, older toddlers had greater understanding of these causal relations, which led them to more often use tools, rather than just reaching for the toy, and to more often choose the right tool for the task.

Causal Reasoning During the Preschool Period

Causal reasoning continues to grow in the preschool period. Preschoolers seem to expect that if a variable causes an effect, it should do so consistently (Schulz & Sommerville, 2006). When 4-year-olds see a potential cause produce an effect inconsistently, they infer that some variable that they cannot see must cause the effect; when the same effect occurs consistently, they do not infer that a hidden variable was important. For instance, if 4-year-olds saw some dogs respond to petting by eagerly wagging their tails and other dogs respond to petting by growling, they might infer that some variable other than the petting, such as the dogs' breed, caused the effect. But if all the dogs they had ever seen looked happy when petted, they would not infer that the dogs' breed was relevant.

Preschoolers' emerging understanding that events must have causes also seems to influence their reactions to magic tricks. Most 3- and 4-year-olds fail to see the point of such tricks; they grasp that something strange has happened but do not find the "magic" humorous or actively try to figure out what caused the strange outcome (Rosengren & Hickling, 2000). By age 5, however, children become fascinated with magic tricks precisely because no obvious causal mechanism could produce the effect (Box 7.3). Many want to search the magician's hat or other apparatus to see how such a stunt was possible. This increasing appreciation that even astonishing events must have causes, along with an increasing understanding of the mechanisms that connect causes and their effects, reflects the growth of causal reasoning.

Most 5-year-olds find magic tricks thrilling, even though they would have been uninterested in them a year or two earlier.

BOX 7.3: a closer look

MAGICAL THINKING AND FANTASY

Lest you conclude that by age 5, children's causal reasoning is as advanced as that of adults, consider the following conversation between two kindergartners and their teacher:

> *Lisa:* Do plants wish for baby plants?
>
> *Deana:* I think only people can make wishes. But God could put a wish inside a plant. …
>
> *Teacher:* I always think of people as having ideas.
>
> *Deana:* It's just the same. God puts a little idea in the plant to tell it what to be.
>
> *Lisa:* My mother wished for me and I came when it was my birthday.
>
> (Paley, 1981, pp. 79–80)

This is not a conversation that would have occurred between 10-year-olds and their teacher. Rather, as noted by Jacqui Woolley, a psychologist who studies preschoolers' fantasies, it reflects one of the most charming aspects of early childhood: preschoolers and young elementary school children "live in a world in which fantasy and reality are more intertwined than they are for adults" (Woolley, 1997).

Young children's belief in fantasy and magic, as well as in normal causes, is evident in many ways. Most 4- to 6-year-olds believe that they can influence other people by wishing them into doing something, such as buying a particular present for their birthday (Vikan & Clausen, 1993). They believe that effective wishing takes a great deal of skill, and perhaps magic, but that it can be done. In related fashion, many believe that getting in good with Santa Claus can make their hopes come true. The fantasies can have a dark side as well, such as when children fear that monsters might hurt them (Woolley, 1997).

Research has shown that young children not only believe in magic but sometimes also act on their belief. In one experiment, preschoolers were told that a certain box was magical and that if they placed a drawing into it and said magical words, the object depicted in the drawing would appear. Then the experimenter left the children alone with the box and a number of drawings. The children put drawings of the most attractive

items into the box, said the "magical words," and were visibly disappointed when they opened the box and found only the drawings (Subbotsky, 1993, 1994).

How can we reconcile preschoolers' understanding of physical causes and effects with their belief in magic, wishing, and Santa Claus? The key is to recognize that here, as in many situations, children simultaneously believe a variety of somewhat contradictory ideas. They may think that magic or the power of their imagination can cause things to happen, but they may not depend on it when doing so could be embarrassing. In one demonstration of this limited belief in magic and the power of the imagination (Woolley & Phelps, 1994), an experimenter showed preschoolers an empty box, closed it, and then asked them to imagine a pencil inside it. The experimenter next asked the children whether there was now a pencil in the box. Many said "yes." Then an adult came into the room and said that she needed a pencil to do her work. Very few of the preschoolers opened the box or handed it to her. Thus, it appeared that many children said the box contained a pencil when no consequences would follow if they were wrong, but they did not believe in magic strongly enough to act in a way that might look foolish to an adult.

How do children move beyond their belief in magic? One means is learning more about real causes: the more children know about the true causes of events, the less likely they are to explain them in magical terms (Woolley, 1997). Another influence is personal experiences that undermine the child's magical beliefs, such as hearing peers dismiss the idea of Santa Claus or seeing two Santa Clauses on the same street. Sometimes, however, children salvage their hopes by distinguishing between flawed manifestations of the magical being and the magical being itself. They may, for

THE FAMILY CIRCUS   **By Bil Keane**

"A real one, or just somebody wearing a funny suit and a painted face?"

example, fervently distinguish between the real Santa Claus and imposters who dress up to look like him.

Although this world of the imagination is most striking between ages 3 and 6, aspects of it remain evident for years thereafter. In one study that demonstrated the persistence of magical thinking, many 9-year-olds and some adults reverted to magical explanations when confronted with a trick that was difficult to explain in physical terms (Subbotsky, 2005). Moreover, in a survey of 1000 Canadian adults, 48% of them said that they believe in ghosts and spirits (Ipsos-Reid, 2007). These beliefs in the supernatural cannot be written off as simply reflecting a lack of education. Subbotsky (2005) found that 0 of 17 American college-student participants were willing to allow someone who was said to be a witch to cast an evil spell on their lives. Innumerable other adults indulge superstitions such as not walking under ladders, avoiding cracks in sidewalks, and knocking on wood. Apparently, we never entirely outgrow magical thinking.

Space

The nativist/empiricist debate has been vigorous with regard to spatial thinking. Nativists argue that children possess an innate module that is specialized for representing and learning about space and that processes spatial information separately from other types of information (Hermer & Spelke, 1996; Hespos & Spelke, 2004). Empiricists argue that children acquire spatial representations through the same types of learning mechanisms and experiences that produce cognitive growth in general, that children adaptively combine spatial and non-spatial information to reach their goals, and that language and other cultural tools, such as puzzles, shape spatial development (Gentner & Boroditsky, 2001; S. C. Levine et al., 2012; Newcombe & Huttenlocher, 2006).

Nativists and empiricists do agree on some issues. One point of agreement is that from early in infancy, children show impressive understanding of some spatial concepts, such as *above, below, left of,* and *right of* (Casasola, 2008; P. C. Quinn, 2005). Another common conclusion is that self-produced movement around the environment stimulates processing of spatial information. A third shared belief is that certain parts of the brain are specialized for coding particular types of spatial information; for example, development of the hippocampus appears to produce improvements in place learning (Sluzenski, Newcombe, & Satlow, 2004; Sutton, Joanisse, & Newcombe, 2010). A fourth common conclusion is that geometric information—information about lengths, angles, and directions—is extremely important in spatial processing. When toddlers and preschoolers are given clues to an object's location, they often weigh such geometric information more strongly than seemingly simpler non-geometric cues, such as the object's being in front of the one blue wall in the room (Hermer & Spelke, 1996; Newcombe & Ratliff, 2007).

Effective spatial thinking requires coding space relative to oneself and relative to the external environment. Next we consider each of these types of spatial coding.

Representing Space Relative to Oneself

From early in infancy, children code the locations of objects in relation to their own bodies. As noted in Chapter 5, when young infants are presented with two objects, they tend to reach for the closer one (van Wermeskerken et al., 2013). This shows that they recognize which object is closer and that they know the direction of that object relative to themselves.

Over the ensuing months, infants' representations of spatial locations become increasingly durable, enabling them to find objects they observed being hidden some seconds earlier. As discussed in Chapter 4, most 7-month-olds reach to the correct location for objects that were hidden 2 seconds earlier under one of two identical opaque covers, but not for objects hidden 4 seconds earlier, whereas most 12-month-olds accurately reach for objects hidden 10 seconds earlier (A. Diamond, 1985). In part, these increasingly enduring object representations reflect brain maturation, particularly of the dorsolateral prefrontal cortex, an area in the frontal lobe that is involved in the formation and maintenance of plans and in the integration of new and previously learned information (A. Diamond & Goldman-Rakic, 1989; J. K. Nelson, 2005). However, the improved object representations reflect learning as well: infants who are provided a learning experience with a hidden object in one situation show improved location of hidden objects in other situations (S. P. Johnson, Amso, & Slemmer, 2003).

egocentric spatial representations ■ Coding of spatial locations relative to one's own body, without regard to the surroundings.

Note that the preceding examples of infants' ability to code space involve infants remaining in a single location and coding locations relative to their bodies. Piaget (1954/1971) proposed that this is the one kind of spatial coding that infants can do. The reason, according to his theory, is that during the sensorimotor period, infants can form only **egocentric spatial representations,** in which the locations of objects are coded relative to the infants' position at the time of the coding. As evidence, Piaget reported experiments showing that if infants repeatedly found a toy located to their right, they would continue to turn right to find it, even if they were repositioned so that the object was now on their left. Subsequent investigators replicated this finding (e.g., L. P. Acredolo, 1978; Bremner, 1978).

Egocentric spatial representation during infancy is not absolute, however. If toys are hidden adjacent to a distinctive landmark, such as a tower, infants usually find the toy despite changes in their own position (Lew, 2011). Still, the question remains: How do young children develop the ability to find objects when their own position has changed and when no landmarks are available to guide their search?

A major factor in helping infants acquire a sense of space independent of their own location appears to be self-locomotion. Infants who crawl or have had experience propelling themselves in walkers more often remember the locations of objects on the object-permanence task (page 165) than do infants of the same age without such locomotor experience (Bertenthal, Campos, & Kermoian, 1994; Campos et al., 2000). Similarly, compared with infants who have not yet moved across rooms on their own, those infants who have done so show an earlier understanding of depth and drop-offs on the surfaces they travel; this is evidenced by acceleration in their heart rate as they approach the visual cliff in the procedure described on page 196.

The reasons why self-locomotion enhances infants' representation of space should be familiar to anyone who has both driven a car and been a passenger in one. Just as driving requires continuous updating of information about the surroundings, so does crawling or walking. In contrast, just as being a passenger in a car does not require such continuous updating of one's location, neither does being carried.

As would be expected from this analysis, self-locomotion also enhances older children's spatial coding. Striking evidence for this conclusion emerged from a study in which kindergarteners were tested in the kitchens of their own homes (Rieser, Garing, & Young, 1994). Some kindergartners were asked to stand in place, imagine themselves walking from their seat in the classroom to the teacher's chair, and turning around to face the class. Then they were asked to point from this imagined position in the classroom to the locations of various objects within it— the fishbowl, the alphabet chart, the coatroom door, and so on. Under these conditions, the 5-year-olds' pointing was inaccurate. Other kindergartners went through the same procedure, except that they were instructed to actually walk through their kitchen and turn around as they imagined themselves walking to the teacher's chair and then turning to face the class. Under these conditions, the children's pointing to the imagined objects in their imagined classroom was far more accurate. This result, like those described above with infants, highlights the interconnectedness of the system that produces self-generated motion and the system that produces mental representations of space (Adolph & Berger, 2006).

Another type of experience that contributes to spatial development beyond infancy is assembling puzzles. Children who played with puzzles more often between their 1st and 4th birthdays than their peers did were found to be more successful as 4 ½-year-olds on the spatial-transformation task shown in Figure 7.6 (Levine et al., 2012). The relation between puzzle play and subsequent spatial reasoning occurred irrespective of parents' education, income, and use of spatial terms

FIGURE 7.6 Measuring early spatial reasoning Levine and colleagues (2012) used these shapes to examine the effects of playing with puzzles on preschoolers' spatial skills. The task was to identify which of the shapes in the top panel could be constructed from the pair of shapes in the bottom panel.

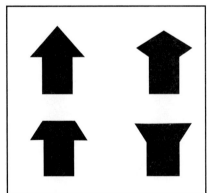

while interacting with their children. This relation between puzzle play and spatial reasoning makes sense. Assembling puzzles requires identifying appropriate pieces for specific locations and physically rotating them into the proper orientation; mentally rotating pieces to identify plausible candidates for filling empty locations allows more efficient puzzle solving than would otherwise be possible. Such practice in mental rotation seems likely to build spatial reasoning skills that can be used in future situations.

Development of Spatial Concepts in People Who Are Blind and Partially Sighted

People often equate spatial thinking with vision, assuming that we can think spatially only about layouts that we have seen. Even in infancy, however, spatial thought can be based on senses other than vision. Thus, when 3-month-olds are brought into a totally dark room in which nothing can be seen, they use sounds emitted by nearby objects to identify the objects' spatial locations and reach for them (Keen & Berthier, 2004).

Although infants can use their auditory sense, among others, to form spatial representations, visual experience during infancy does play an important role in spatial development. Evidence for this conclusion comes from cases in which surgery restored sight to people who were born either blind (S. Carlson, Hyvärinen, & Raninen, 1986) or with severely impaired vision due to cataracts that prevented patterned stimulation from reaching the retina (Le Grand et al., 2001). The surgery was performed early—on average at 4 months of age—and those who underwent it subsequently underwent between 9 and 21 years of postsurgical visual experience before being tested. Despite their extensive visual experience after the corrective surgery, most of these people could not use visual information to represent space as well as other people can; problems remained, even 20 years after the surgery (and thus after 20 years of visual experience). In another study carried out at McMaster University in Hamilton, Ontario, researchers found that adolescents who had undergone surgery for congenital cataracts at least 8 years before testing had impairments in processing faces (Le Grand et al., 2003). The lack of visual experience in the few months of infancy before the surgery limited subsequent visual development.

These findings do not mean that children who are born blind cannot represent space. They actually tend to have a surprisingly good spatial sense. On tasks involving the representation of very small spaces, such as being guided in drawing two sides of a triangle on a piece of paper and then being asked to complete the triangle by drawing the third side themselves, children who are born blind perform as well as sighted children who are blindfolded (Thinus-Blanc & Gaunet, 1997). On tasks involving representation of large spaces, such as those formed by exploring unfamiliar rooms, the spatial representations of people born blind also are surprisingly good, about as good as those formed by sighted people who were blindfolded during the exploration period. Thus, although some spatial skills seem to require early visual experience, many people who are blind develop impressive senses of space without ever seeing the world.

Representing Space Relative to the External Environment

As we have noted, infants as young as 6 months can use landmarks to code the location of objects they observe being hidden (Lew, 2011). However, for such young infants to use a landmark successfully, it must be the only obvious landmark in the environment and must be located right next to the hidden object.

With development, infants become increasingly able to choose among alternative potential landmarks. When 12-month-olds are presented a single yellow cushion, a single green cushion, and a large number of blue cushions, they have little trouble finding an object hidden under either the yellow or the green cushion (Bushnell et al., 1995). At 22 months, but not at 16 months, the presence of a landmark improves children's ability to locate an object that is not hidden adjacent to the landmark (Newcombe et al., 1998). By age 5 years, children can also represent an object's position in relation to multiple landmarks, such as when it is midway between a tree and a street lamp (Newcombe & Huttenlocher, 2006).

Children, like adults, have more difficulty forming a spatial representation when they are moving around in an environment without distinctive landmarks or when the only landmarks are far from the target location. To understand the challenge of such tasks, imagine walking in a forest without cleared paths and not being able to remember exactly how you arrived at your current location. How easily could you find your way back to your starting point?

Even toddlers show the required navigational ability to some degree—good enough to lead them in the right general direction (Loomis et al., 1993). In one experiment, 1- and 2-year-olds first saw a small toy hidden in a long, rectangular sandbox and then saw a curtain descend around the sandbox, thus hiding the toy. The toddlers then walked to a different location, after which they were asked to find the toy. Despite no landmarks being present, the toddlers kept track of the hidden toy's location well enough to show better than chance accuracy in their searches (Newcombe et al., 1998).

However, forming relatively precise coding of locations in the absence of straightforward landmarks continues to be difficult for people well beyond 2 years of age (Bremner, Knowles, & Andreasen, 1994). Six- and seven-year-olds are not very good at it (Overman et al., 1996), and adults vary tremendously in their abilities to perform this type of navigation. For instance, when adults are asked to walk around the perimeter of an unfamiliar college campus and then to walk straight back to the starting point, some are quite accurate, but many choose routes that take them nowhere near the original location (Cornell et al., 1996).

The degree to which people develop spatial skills is strongly influenced by the importance of such skills in their culture. To demonstrate this point, Kearins (1981) compared the spatial abilities of semi-nomadic Aboriginal children growing up in the Australian desert with those of white peers growing up in Australian cities. Spatial ability is essential within Aboriginal culture, because much of life within this culture consists of long treks between distant water holes. Needless to say, the Aboriginal people cannot rely on road signs; they must rely on their sense of space to get to the water. Consistent with the importance of spatial skills within their everyday lives, Aboriginal children are superior to their city-dwelling peers in memory for spatial location, even in board games, a context that is more familiar to the urban children (Kearins, 1981). Thus, consistent with the general importance of the sociocultural context, how people make use of spatial thinking in their everyday activities greatly influences their quality of spatial thinking.

PENNY TWEEDIE / PANOS PICTURES

Spatial skills tend to be especially well developed in cultures in which they are crucial for survival.

Time

What then is time? I know well enough what it is provided nobody asks me; but if I am asked and try to explain, I am baffled.

—*Saint Augustine*

As this quotation suggests, even the deepest thinkers, from Saint Augustine who wrote in the fourth century to Albert Einstein who wrote in the twentieth, have been mystified by the nature of time. Yet even infants in their first half-year have a rudimentary sense of time, including perception of both the order and the duration of events (W. J. Friedman, 2008).

Experiencing Time

Probably the most basic sense of time involves knowledge of temporal order, that is, knowing what happened first, what happened next, and so on. Not surprisingly, given how mystifying life would be without such a basic sense of time, infants represent an understanding of the order in which events occur from as early as the capability can be effectively measured. In one study, 3-month-olds were presented a series of interesting photos, first on their left, then on their right, then on their left, and so on. Within 20 seconds, they began to look to the side where each new photo was to appear even before the photo was presented (Adler et al., 2008; Haith, Wentworth, & Canfield, 1993). This looking pattern indicated that 3-month-olds detected the repetitive sequence of events over time and used the information to form expectations of where the next photo would appear. The same conclusion has arisen using other experimental methods; for example, 4-month-olds who were habituated to three objects falling in a constant order dishabituated when the order changed (Lewkowicz, 2004).

Infants also have an approximate sense of the durations of events. In one study, 4-month-olds saw periods of light and darkness alternate every 5 seconds for eight cycles, at which point the pattern was broken by the light's failing to appear. Within half a second of the break, infants' heart rates decelerated, a change that is characteristic of increased attention. In this case, the heart-rate deceleration suggested that the infants had a rough sense of the 5-second interval, expected the light to go on at the end of the interval, and increased their attention when it did not appear (Colombo & Richman, 2002).

Infants also can discriminate between longer and shorter durations. The ratio of the durations, rather than differences in their absolute length, is critical for these discriminations (Brannon, Suanda, & Libertus, 2007). For instance, 6-month-olds discriminate between two durations when their ratio is 2:1 (1 second versus 0.5 seconds or 3 seconds versus 1.5 seconds) but not when the ratio is 1.5:1 (1.5 seconds versus 1 second or 4.5 seconds versus 3 seconds). Over the course of the first year, the precision of these discriminations increases. Thus, 10-month-olds, unlike 6-month-olds, discriminate when the ratio of the durations is 1.5:1 (though not when it is 1.33:1).

What about longer time periods—periods of weeks, months, or years? It is unknown whether infants have a sense of such long time periods, but preschoolers do possess some knowledge regarding them. For example, when asked which of two past events occurred more recently, most 4-year-olds knew that a specific event that happened a week before the experiment (Valentine's Day) happened more recently than an event that happened 7 weeks earlier (Christmas) (W. J. Friedman, 1991). However, preschoolers correctly answer such questions only when the more recent event is quite close in time and much closer than the less recent one. The ability to distinguish more precisely among the timing of past events develops slowly during middle childhood (W. J. Friedman, 2003). For instance, when children who had been presented a distinctive classroom experience were asked 3 months later to recall the month in which the experience occurred, the percentage of correct recall increased from 20% among 5-year-olds to 46% among 7-year-olds to 64% among 9-year-olds (W. J. Friedman & Lyon, 2005).

Understanding of the timing of future events also increases during this age range (W. J. Friedman, 2000, 2003). Preschoolers often confuse past and future. For example, 5-year-olds predict a week after Valentine's Day that the next Valentine's Day will come sooner than the next Halloween or Christmas; they also predict that their next lunch is the same amount of time in the future regardless of whether they are tested just before lunch or just after it. Six-year-olds, in contrast, generally predict correctly in both cases. The improvement in children's sense of future time between the ages of 5 and 6 years is probably influenced by 5- and 6-year-olds' experience in kindergarten classrooms, where the cycle of seasons, holidays, and daily routines is emphasized.

Children, like adults, are subject to certain illusions about time, in part because of the role attention plays in time perception. When 8-year-olds' attention is focused on the passage of time (for example, when they expect a prize at the end of a 2-minute interval), they perceive the duration as longer than the same interval when they are not anticipating a prize. Conversely, when they have little to do, they perceive the duration as longer than when they are very busy (Zakay, 1992, 1993). Thus, the saying "A watched pot never boils" has psychological merit.

Reasoning About Time

During middle childhood, children become increasingly proficient at reasoning about time. In particular, they become able to infer that if two events started at the same time, but one event ended later than the other, then the event that ended later must have lasted for a longer time.

Children as young as 5 years can sometimes make such logical inferences about time, but only in simple, straightforward situations. For instance, when told that two dolls fell asleep at the same time and that one doll awoke before the other, 5-year-olds reason correctly that the doll that awoke later also slept longer (Levin, 1982). However, when 5-year-olds see two toy trains travel in the same direction on parallel tracks, and one train stops farther down the track, they usually say that the train that stopped farther down the track travelled for a longer time, regardless of when the trains started and stopped moving (C. Acredolo & Schmid, 1981). The problem is that the 5-year-olds' attention is captured by the one train being farther down the track, which leads them to focus on the spatial positions of the trains rather than on their relative starting and stopping times. If this observation reminds you of Piaget's idea of centration (pages 139–140), there is good reason: Piaget's (1969) observations of performance on this task were part of what led him to conclude that children in the preoperational stage often centre on a single dimension and ignore other, more relevant ones.

Number

Like causality, space, and time, number is a central dimension of human experience. It is hard to imagine how the world would appear if we did not have at least a crude sense of number—we would not know how many fingers or family members we have, for example. Unsurprisingly, the nativist/empiricist debate has extended to the concept of number. Nativists argue that children are born with a core concept of number that includes special mechanisms for representing and learning about the relative numbers of objects in sets, counting, and simple addition and subtraction (Wynn, 2000). As evidence, they note that specific brain areas, particularly the intraparietal sulcus, are heavily involved in representing numerical magnitudes (Ansari, 2008; Dehaene & Nieder, 2009) and that specific neurons respond most strongly when particular numbers of objects (e.g., five objects) are displayed (Nieder, 2012). In contrast, empiricists argue that children learn about numbers through the same types of experiences and learning mechanisms that help them acquire other concepts and that infants' numerical competence is not as great as nativists claim (Clearfield, 2006; Mix, Huttenlocher, & Levine, 2002). They also note the existence of large differences in numerical understanding among children of different cultures and document the contributions of instruction, language, and cultural values to these differences (Geary, 2006; K. F. Miller et al., 1995). In this section, we review current evidence regarding numerical development, as well as nativist and empiricist perspectives on the evidence.

Numerical Equality

Perhaps the most basic understanding of numbers involves **numerical equality,** the idea that all sets of *n* objects have something in common. When children recognize, for example, that two dogs, two cups, two balls, and two shoes share the property of "twoness," they have a rudimentary understanding of numerical equality.

Infants as young as 5 months old appear to have some sense of numerical equality, at least as it applies to sets of one, two, or three objects. The evidence for this conclusion comes from studies using the familiar habituation paradigm. In these studies, young infants are shown a sequence of pictures, with each picture having the same number of objects but differing in other ways. For example, infants might be shown three stars arranged vertically, then three circles arranged horizontally, then three diamonds arranged diagonally, and so on. After the infants habituate to the pictures of three objects, they are shown a picture with a different number of objects (such as two squares). These studies indicate that 5-month-olds show renewed interest when the number of objects changes (van Loosbroek & Smitsman, 1990).

This tendency is weak—infants' discriminations are often based on the objects' relative area or perimeter rather than on their number, when both vary (Clearfield & Mix, 1999; Feigenson, Carey, & Spelke, 2002). However, infants also discriminate among small numbers of events, which do not have perimeters or areas, indicating that they have a sense of number independent of spatial concepts. In one demonstration of this numerical understanding, Wynn (1995) showed 6-month-olds a puppet that repeatedly jumped twice. After the infants habituated to this pattern, they were shown the puppet jumping either once or three times. The infants' looking time increased when the number of jumps changed, suggesting that they discriminated between two jumps and one or three.

As with discriminations among temporal durations, infants' discriminations between numerical sets depend in large part on the ratio of the number of entities in them. For instance, as with temporal durations, 6-month-olds discriminate between sets with 2:1 ratios (e.g., 16 versus 8 dots or sounds) but not between sets with ratios of 1.5:1 (e.g., 12 versus 8 dots or sounds) (Brannon, 2002; Lipton & Spelke, 2003). Also as with discriminations between temporal durations, numerical-set discriminations become more precise with age: 6-month-olds do not discriminate between ratios of 1.5:1 objects, but 9-month-olds do (J. N. Wood & Spelke, 2005). However, the absolute number of objects also matters: on some tasks, 9- and 11-month-old infants discriminate between one and two objects but not between two and four or three and six (Feigenson, Carey, & Hauser, 2002).

numerical equality ■ The realization that all sets of *n* objects have something in common.

FIGURE 7.7 Infants' understanding of addition On the task used by Wynn (1992) to examine whether infants have a rudimentary grasp of addition, 5-month-olds saw (1) a single doll placed on a stage, (2) a screen raised to hide the doll, (3) a hand with a doll in it move toward and then behind the screen, and (4) the hand return empty after having been behind the screen. Then the screen dropped, revealing either the possible event of two dolls on the stage (5 and 6) or the seemingly impossible event of one doll on the stage (5* and 6*). Infants younger than 6 months of age looked for a longer time at the seemingly impossible event, suggesting their surprise at seeing one doll rather than two.

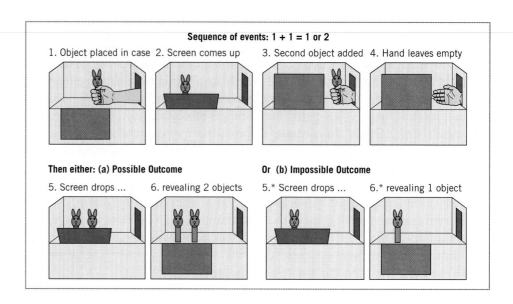

Sequence of events: 1 + 1 = 1 or 2

1. Object placed in case 2. Screen comes up 3. Second object added 4. Hand leaves empty

Then either: (a) Possible Outcome

5. Screen drops ... 6. revealing 2 objects

Or (b) Impossible Outcome

5.* Screen drops ... 6.* revealing 1 object

Infants' Arithmetic

Some experts on early understanding of number have concluded that infants also have a basic understanding of arithmetic (R. Gelman & Williams, 1998; Wynn, 1992). The type of evidence on which they base their conclusion is illustrated in Figure 7.7. A 5-month-old sees a doll on a stage. A screen comes up, hiding the doll from the infant's sight. Next, the infant sees a hand place a second doll behind the screen and then sees the hand emerge from behind the screen without the doll, thus seeming to have left the second doll with the first one. Finally, the screen drops down, revealing either one or two dolls. Most 5-month-olds look longer when there is only one doll, suggesting that they expected that 1 + 1 should equal 2 and that they were surprised when they saw only a single object. Similar results are seen with subtraction: 5-month-olds look longer when the apparent removal of one of two objects results in two objects being present than when the removal results in one object being there (Wynn, 1992).

But do these findings show that infants understand arithmetic? The claim that they do has evoked a great deal of argument. One reason for the controversy is that efforts to replicate the original result have had mixed success. Some studies have replicated it (T. J. Simon, Hespos, & Rochat, 1995), while others have not (Wakeley, Rivera, & Langer, 2000). A more general reason for the controversy is that infants show the precise understanding required by arithmetic only in situations where the total number of objects is three or fewer. Children do not show similar, precise understanding of the effects of adding two objects to two other objects until they are much older—3 to 5 *years* old (J. Huttenlocher, Jordan, & Levine, 1994; Starkey, 1992).

The fact that much of infants' numerical competence is limited to sets of three or fewer objects has led a second group of experts (Clearfield & Mix, 1999; L. B. Cohen & Marks, 2002; T. J. Simon, 1997) to conclude that infants' responses on these tests of arithmetic are based not on an understanding of arithmetic but instead on perception. For instance, Haith and Benson (1998) proposed that infants rely on **subitizing,** a perceptual process by which adults and children can look at one, two, or three objects and almost immediately form a mental image of how many objects there are. According to this interpretation, infants form an image of the object or objects that are initially presented and of the objects that seem to be

subitizing ■ A perceptual process by which adults and children can look at a few objects and almost immediately know how many objects are present.

added to, or subtracted from, them; if the objects that the infants see at the end of the procedure appear different from the image they originally formed, they look for a longer time. Consistent with this interpretation, when 5-month-olds are tested under conditions that increase the difficulty of forming a mental image (e.g., when they see a hand place one object and then another behind the raised screen but, in contrast to the usual procedure, do not see either object's position until the end), the infants do not show surprise when 1 + 1 = 1 (Uller et al., 1999). Thus, under some circumstances, infants show arithmetic competence with small sets of objects, but their competence may stem from an ability to form mental images rather than from an understanding of arithmetic.

Counting

By age 3 years, most children acquire the ability to count, allowing them to precisely establish the number of objects in sets larger than three when the objects are visible. The majority of 3-year-olds can count up to 10 objects correctly. In addition to learning counting procedures, preschoolers also acquire understanding of the principles underlying counting. In particular, they come to understand the following five counting principles (R. Gelman & Gallistel, 1978):

1. *One–one correspondence:* Each object must be labelled by a single number word.

2. *Stable order:* The numbers should always be recited in the same order.

3. *Cardinality:* The number of objects in the set corresponds to the last number stated.

4. *Order irrelevance:* Objects can be counted left to right, right to left, or in any other order.

5. *Abstraction:* Any set of discrete objects or events can be counted.

Much of the evidence that preschoolers understand these principles comes from their judgments when observing two types of counting procedures: incorrect counts and unusual but correct counts. When 4- or 5-year-olds see a puppet counting in a way that violates the one–one correspondence principle—for example, by labelling a single object with two number words (Figure 7.8a)—they consistently say that the counting is incorrect (Frye et al., 1989; R. Gelman, Meck, & Merkin, 1986). In contrast, when they see the puppet count in ways that are unusual but that do not violate any principle—for example, by starting in the middle of a row but counting all the objects (Figure 7.8b)—they judge the counting to be correct, even though they say that they would not count that way themselves. The preschoolers' realization that procedures that they themselves would not use are nonetheless correct shows that they understand the principles that distinguish correct from incorrect counting

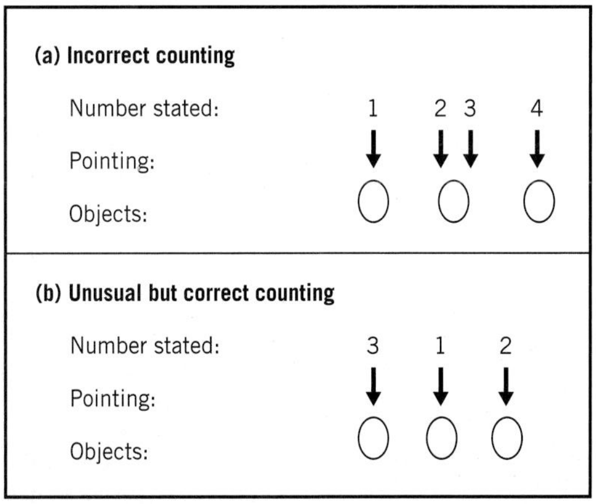

Although children all over the world learn number words, the rate at which they do so is affected by the specifics of the number system used in their culture. As Kevin Miller and his colleagues (1995) note, for example, most 5-year-olds in China can count to 100 or more, whereas most 5-year-olds in North America cannot count nearly as high. Part of the reason for this difference in counting proficiency seems to be the greater regularity of the Chinese number system, particularly with respect to numbers in the teens. In both Chinese and English, the words for numbers greater than 20 follow a regular rule: decade name first, digit name second

FIGURE 7.8 Counting procedures
Counting procedures similar to those used by Frye and colleagues (1989) and Gelman, Meck, and Merkin (1986): (a) an incorrect counting procedure; (b) an unusual but correct procedure.

(a) Incorrect counting

Number stated:	1	2 3	4
Pointing:	↓	↓ ↓	↓
Objects:	○	○	○

(b) Unusual but correct counting

Number stated:	3	1	2
Pointing:	↓	↓	↓
Objects:	○	○	○

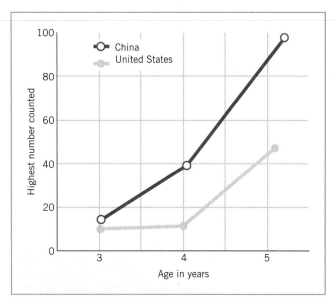

FIGURE 7.9 Counting level Although 3-year-olds in China and the United States can count to about the same point, 4- and 5-year-olds in China can count much higher than their U.S. peers. One reason for the faster development of Chinese children's counting ability appears to be that the Chinese words for numbers in the teens follow a consistent, easily learned pattern, whereas the English words for numbers in the teens must be memorized one by one. (Data from K. F. Miller et al., 1995)

(e.g., twenty-one, twenty-two, and so on). In Chinese, the words for numbers between 11 and 19 follow the same rule (equivalent to ten-one, ten-two, and so on). In English, however, no simple rule indicates the numbers between 11 and 19; each term has to be learned separately.

Figure 7.9 charts the apparent impact of this cultural difference in number systems. Three-year-olds in the United States and China are comparable in their ability to recite the numbers 1 through 10, which do not follow any obvious rule either in the English or the Chinese language. However, Chinese 4-year-olds quickly learn the numbers in the teens and succeeding decades, whereas their U.S. peers experience prolonged difficulty with the teens. The difference in language is not the only reason that the counting skill of U.S. children lags behind that of children in China. Chinese culture places a much greater emphasis on mathematical skill than U.S. culture does, and Chinese pre-schoolers are consequently more advanced than their U.S. peers in numerical skills generally, including arithmetic and number line estimation (Siegler & Mu, 2008). Still, the greater simplicity of the Chinese system for naming numbers in the teens seems to be one contributor to Chinese children's greater counting proficiency.

Relations Among Understanding of Space, Time, and Number

Piaget (1952) hypothesized that infants possess only a general, undifferentiated concept of magnitude and lack specific concepts of space, number, and time. That is, he thought that infants have a concept of "bigness" but do not distinguish among larger size, greater number, or longer time. Subsequent research has shown that infants actually do distinguish among size, number, and time. For example, after habituating to different displays with the same number of objects, infants disha-bituate when the number of objects changes, even though the space occupied by the new objects and the time for which they are displayed is the same as previously (F. Xu & Arriaga, 2007; F. Xu & Spelke, 2000).

However, the fact that infants possess specific concepts of space, time, and number does not mean that they lack the type of undifferentiated magnitude concept that Piaget suggested. Indeed, Lourenco and Longo (2010) found that 9-month-olds have a general sense of magnitude that extends to space, number, and time. The infants in their study were initially habituated to the type of display shown at the top of Figure 7.10, in which a particular decoration (e.g., black with white stripes) consistently accompanied a stimulus that was the larger of two stimuli on one of the three dimensions (e.g., size). Then the infants were presented displays in which the link between decoration and relative magnitude *on a different dimension* either was maintained or changed. For instance, infants who had habituated to a link between black with white stripes and larger size might now see that decoration accompanying either the more numerous set (bottom left in Figure 7.10) or the less numerous one (bottom right in Figure 7.10). Lourenco and Longo found that the infants dishabituated when the decoration that had accompanied the larger stimulus now accompanied the one that was smaller on another dimension, but not when it continued to accompany the larger one.

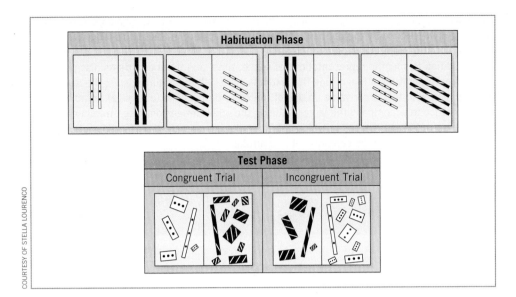

FIGURE 7.10 Infants' general magnitude representations To test whether infants possess a general sense of magnitude, Lourenco and Longo (2010) first presented pairs of figures, such as those in the top panel, in which one decoration (here, black with white stripes) was associated with the larger value of one quantitative dimension (here, larger size). After this habituation phase, the infants were shown either congruent trials (bottom left), in which the same decoration accompanied the choice with the greater quantitative value (here, the greater number of objects), or incongruent trials (bottom right), in which that decoration accompanied the choice with the smaller quantitative value (here, the smaller number of objects). Regardless of the particular pair of quantitative dimensions used during the habituation and test phases, children looked longer on incongruent trials, indicating that they expected that decoration to continue to accompany the choice with the larger value on whichever quantitative dimension varied.

Similar results were obtained regardless of whether the habituated dimension was size, number, or time, and regardless of whether the dimension that subsequently varied was size, number, or time.

Other studies converge on the same conclusion (de Hevia & Spelke, 2010; Srinivasan & Carey, 2010). For instance, the ratios required for infants of a given age to discriminate between two stimuli are similar regardless of whether the discrimination involves time, space, or number (Brannon, Lutz, & Cordes, 2006; Brannon, Suanda, & Libertus, 2007). Moreover, overlapping brain areas in the intraparietal sulcus are involved in representing all three dimensions (Dehaene & Brannon, 2011). Thus, infants appear to have both the general, undifferentiated concept of magnitude that Piaget hypothesized they have and also the more specific concepts of time, space, and number that he hypothesized they lack.

review:

A basic understanding of causality emerges extremely early in development. Infants in their first year distinguish between physical causes, in which actions are produced by direct contact, and psychological causes, in which actions are produced by desires and beliefs. During the preschool and elementary school periods, children become increasingly adept at inferring causal relations, even when the relations are more complex and require deeper understanding of causes, effects, and the mechanisms that link them. However, belief in magic and the supernatural coexist with this growing understanding of causal mechanisms, especially in the preschool years.

People, like other animals, are biologically prepared to code specific types of spatial information in specific parts of the brain. From the first year, children represent spatial locations relative both to their own bodies and to other features of the environment, such as landmarks. Self-produced movement seems crucial in the further development of spatial representations.

A rudimentary sense of time is also present extremely early: by age 3 months, if not earlier, infants possess a sense of the order in which events happened. However, an accurate sense of duration doesn't develop until 3 to 5 years of age, and learning to reason logically about time takes even longer.

A basic recognition of differences between sets of one, two, and three objects or actions is present in the first year, as is the ability to discriminate between larger sets whose numbers differ by substantial ratios. However, not until age 3 or 4 years do children show precise understanding with sets larger than three. During the preschool period, children also learn the principles underlying counting, such as that each object must be counted once and only once. By age 5 years, most also learn the number system of their language. Learning of counting is influenced by the regularity of the number system in the child's language as well as by the culture's emphasis on mathematics.

In addition to specific representations of space, time, and number, infants also possess a general representation of magnitude that extends across all three dimensions. If a decoration is associated with the larger value on one of the three dimensions (e.g., size), infants expect the decoration to accompany the larger value on the other dimensions (e.g., number) as well. The overlap in the brain areas in which the three dimensions are represented probably contributes to this general representation of magnitude.

chapter summary:

- To understand their experiences, children must learn that the world includes several types of objects: people, other living things, and inanimate objects. Children also need a basic understanding of causality, space, time, and number, so that they will be able to code their experiences in terms of why, where, when, and how often events occurred.

Understanding Who or What

- Early categories of objects are based in large part on perceptual similarity, especially similarity in the shapes of the objects.

- By age 2 or 3 years, children form category hierarchies: animal/dog/poodle, furniture/chair/La-Z-Boy, and so on.

- From infancy onward, children differentiate people from other animals and inanimate objects. For example, infants smile more at people than at either rabbits or robots.

- By age 4 or 5 years, preschoolers develop a rudimentary but well-organized theory of mind, within which they organize their understanding of people's behaviour. A key assumption of this theory of mind is that desires and beliefs motivate specific actions.

- Understanding that other people will act on their beliefs, even when the beliefs are false, is very difficult for 3-year-olds; many children do not gain this understanding until age 5.

- Animals and plants, especially animals, are of great interest to young children. When animals are present, infants and toddlers pay careful attention to them.

- By age 4 years, children develop an elaborate understanding of living things, including coherent ideas about invisible processes such as growth, inheritance, illness, and healing. Both their natural fascination with living things and the input they receive from the environment contribute to their knowledge about plants and animals.

Understanding Why, Where, When, and How Many

- The development of causal reasoning about physical events begins in infancy. By 6 to 12 months, infants understand the likely consequences of objects' colliding. Understanding causal relations among actions helps 1-year-olds remember them.

- By 4 or 5 years, children seem to realize that causes are necessary for events to occur. When no cause is obvious, they search for one. However, many preschoolers believe in magic as well as physical cause–effect relations.

- People, like other animals, are biologically prepared to code space. Early in infancy, they code locations of other objects in relation to their own location and to landmarks. As they gain the ability to move around on their own, children gain a sense of locations relative to the overall environment as well as to their own current location.

- Children who are born blind have surprisingly good representations of space, though some aspects of their spatial processing, especially processing of faces, remain poor even if corrective surgery is performed during infancy.

- Just as infants are born with an ability to code some aspects of space, so they are born with an ability to code some aspects of time. Even 3-month-olds code the order in which events occur. Infants of that age also can use consistent sequences of past events to anticipate future events.

- By age 5 years, children also can reason about time, in the sense of inferring that if two events started at the same time, and one stopped later than the other, the event that stopped later took longer. However, they can do this only when interfering perceptual cues are absent.

- Rudimentary understanding of very small numbers is present from early in infancy. Infants notice numerical differences between small sets of objects and between events that are repeated a different number of times. They also notice differences between larger sets when the numbers of objects or events in the sets differ by large ratios.

- By age 3 years, most children learn to count 10 objects. Their counting seems to reflect understanding of certain principles, such as that each object should be labelled by a single number word. Children's subsequent rate of learning about numbers reflects their culture's number system and the degree to which their culture values numerical knowledge.

- From infancy onward, children also possess a general representation of magnitude that extends at least to space, time, and number.

Critical Thinking Questions

1. Why is it useful for people to organize categories into hierarchies, such as animal/dog/poodle or vehicle/car/Prius?

2. Did you have an imaginary companion as a child or know someone who did? What functions did the invisible friend serve, and why do you think that you or the other person stopped imagining the companion?

3. Why do you think 5-year-olds are so much better at false-belief problems than 3-year-olds are?

4. Self-produced movement enhances children's representation of space. What evolutionary purpose might this serve?

5. Describe the thoughts that might go through a 5-year-old's mind when the child sees two Santa Clauses walking past each other.

6. Do you think infants possess a basic understanding of arithmetic? Why or why not?

7. Why might it be useful for children to have a general representation of quantity, as well as specific representations of space, time, and number?

Key Terms

basic level, p. 266

category hierarchy, p. 265

concepts, p. 262

egocentric spatial representations, p. 286

essentialism, p. 278

false-belief problems, p. 270

naive psychology, p. 268

numerical equality, p. 291

object substitution, p. 273

perceptual categorization, p. 266

pretend play, p. 273

sociodramatic play, p. 274

subitizing, p. 292

subordinate level, p. 266

superordinate level, p. 266

theory of mind, p. 269

theory of mind module (TOMM), p. 271

ALICE KENT STODDARD, *On the Chaise*, 1930

chapter 8:

Intelligence and Academic Achievement

In 1904, France's minister of education faced a problem. France, like other western European and North American countries, had recently introduced universal public education, and it was becoming apparent that some children were not learning well. Therefore, the minister wanted a means of identifying children who would have difficulty succeeding in standard classrooms, so that they could be given special education. His problem was how to identify such children.

One obvious way was to ask teachers to indicate which students in their classrooms were encountering difficulty. However, the minister worried that teachers might be biased in their assessments. In particular, he was concerned that some teachers would be prejudiced against poor children and would claim that those children were unable to learn, even if they actually could. He therefore asked Alfred Binet, a French psychologist who had studied intelligence for 15 years, to develop an easy-to-administer, objective test of intelligence.

The prevailing view at the time was that intelligence was based on simple skills, such as associating objects with the sounds they make (e.g., ducks with quacking, bells with ringing), responding quickly to stimuli, and recognizing whether two objects were identical. According to this view, children who were more adept than their peers at such simple skills learned more quickly and thus became more intelligent. The theory was plausible—but wrong. It is now clear that simple skills are only modestly related to broader, everyday indicators of intelligence, such as school performance.

Binet's theory differed from the prevailing wisdom of his time. He believed that the key components of intelligence were high-level abilities, such as problem solving, reasoning, and judgment, and he maintained that intelligence tests should assess such abilities directly. Therefore, on the test that he and his colleague Théophile Simon devised—the *Binet-Simon Intelligence Test*—children were asked (among other things) to interpret proverbs, solve puzzles, define words, and sequence cartoon panels so that the jokes made sense.

Binet's approach was successful in identifying children who would have difficulty learning from classroom instruction. More generally, children's performance on the Binet-Simon test correlated highly not only with their school grades at the time of testing but also with their grades years later. The test was also successful in establishing a goal of intelligence testing that has been pursued ever since—to provide an objective measure of scholastic aptitude that would allow fairer decisions about children's schooling, including which children should be in honours classes, which are in need of special education, which should be admitted to highly selective universities, and so on.

In addition to the practical impact of his test, Binet's theoretical approach to intelligence has continued to influence research on the topic to this day. In most areas of cognitive development—perception, language, conceptual understanding, and so on—the emphasis is on age-related changes: the ways in which younger children differ from older ones. Following Binet's lead, however, research on intelligence has focused on individual differences—on how and why children of the same age differ from one another, and on the continuity of such individual differences over time. The nature of individual differences is an enduring theme throughout the field of child development, but the focus on it is especially intense in the study of intelligence.

Questions regarding the development of intelligence excite strong passions, and no wonder. Research in this area raises many of the most basic issues about human nature: the roles of heredity and environment, the influence of ethnic and racial differences, the effects of wealth and poverty, and the possibility of improvement. Almost everyone has opinions, often heartfelt ones, about why some people are more intelligent than others.

Intelligence research also has added greatly to understanding all the major themes emphasized in this book: the nature and origins of *individual differences,* the contributions of the *active child* and of the *sociocultural context,* the way in which *nature and nurture* together shape development, the degree of *continuity* in a key human trait, the *mechanisms* that produce changes, and the relation between *research and children's welfare.* Before examining research on the development of intelligence, however, we must examine a question that sounds simple but actually lies at the heart of many controversies: What *is* intelligence?

What Is Intelligence?

Intelligence is notoriously difficult to define, but this has not kept people from trying. Part of the difficulty is that intelligence can legitimately be described at three levels of analysis: as one thing, as a few things, or as many things.

Intelligence as a Single Trait

Some researchers view intelligence as a single trait that influences all aspects of cognitive functioning. Supporting this idea is the fact that performance on all intellectual tasks is positively correlated: children who do well on one task tend to do well on others, too (Geary, 2005). These positive correlations occur even among dissimilar intellectual tasks—for example, remembering lists of numbers and folding pieces of paper to reproduce printed designs. Such omnipresent positive correlations have led to the hypothesis that each of us possesses a certain amount of *g,* or **general intelligence,** and that *g* influences our ability to think and learn on all intellectual tasks (A. R. Jensen, 1998; Spearman, 1927).

Numerous sources of evidence attest to the usefulness of viewing intelligence as a single trait. Measures of *g,* such as overall scores on intelligence tests, correlate positively with school grades and achievement test performance (Gottfredson, 2011). At the level of cognitive and brain mechanisms, *g* correlates with information-processing speed (Coyle et al., 2011; Deary, 2000), speed of neural transmission (Vernon et al., 2012), and brain volume (McDaniel, 2005). Measures of *g* also correlate strongly with people's knowledge of subjects that may not be taught in school, such as medicine, law, and art history (Lubinski & Humphreys, 1997). Such evidence supports the view of intelligence as a single trait that involves the ability to think and learn.

Intelligence as a Few Basic Abilities

There are also good arguments for viewing intelligence as more than a single general trait. The simplest such view holds that there are two types of intelligence: *fluid intelligence* and *crystallized intelligence* (Cattell, 1987):

■ **Fluid intelligence** involves the ability to think on the spot—for example, by drawing inferences and understanding relations between concepts that have not been encountered previously. It is closely related to adaptation to novel

g **(general intelligence)** ■ Cognitive processes that influence the ability to think and learn on all intellectual tasks.

fluid intelligence ■ Ability to think on the spot to solve novel problems.

crystallized intelligence ■ Factual knowledge about the world.

primary mental abilities ■ Seven abilities proposed by Thurstone as crucial to intelligence.

three-stratum theory of intelligence ■ Carroll's model that places g at the top of the intelligence hierarchy, eight moderately general abilities in the middle, and many specific processes at the bottom.

tasks, speed of information processing, working-memory functioning, and ability to control attention (C. Blair, 2006; Geary, 2005).

■ **Crystallized intelligence** is factual knowledge about the world: knowledge of word meanings, provincial and territorial capitals, answers to arithmetic problems, and so on. It reflects long-term memory for prior experiences and is closely related to verbal ability.

The distinction between fluid and crystallized intelligence is supported by the fact that tests of each type of intelligence correlate more highly with each other than they do with tests of the other type (J. L. Horn & McArdle, 2007). Thus, children who do well on one test of fluid intelligence tend to do well on other tests of fluid intelligence but not necessarily on tests of crystallized intelligence. In addition, the two types of intelligence have different developmental courses. Crystallized intelligence increases steadily from early in life to old age, whereas fluid intelligence peaks around age 20 and slowly declines thereafter (Salthouse, 2009). The brain areas most active in the two types of intelligence also differ: the prefrontal cortex is usually especially active on measures of fluid intelligence but tends to be much less active in measures of crystallized intelligence (C. Blair, 2006; Jung & Haier, 2007).

A somewhat more differentiated view of intelligence (Thurstone, 1938) proposes that the human intellect is composed of seven **primary mental abilities:** word fluency, verbal meaning, reasoning, spatial visualization, numbering, rote memory, and perceptual speed. The key evidence for the usefulness of dividing intelligence into these seven abilities is similar to that for the distinction between fluid and crystallized intelligence. Scores on various tests of a single ability tend to correlate more strongly with one another than do scores on tests of different abilities. For example, although both spatial visualization and perceptual speed are measures of fluid intelligence, children tend to perform more similarly on two tests of spatial visualization than they do on a test of spatial visualization and a test of perceptual speed. The trade-off between these two views of intelligence is between the simplicity of the crystallized/fluid distinction and the greater precision of the idea of seven primary mental abilities.

Intelligence as Numerous Processes

A third view envisions intelligence as comprising numerous, distinct *processes*. Information-processing analyses of how people solve intelligence test items and how they perform everyday intellectual tasks such as reading, writing, and arithmetic reveal that a great many processes are involved (e.g., Geary, 2005). These include remembering, perceiving, attending, comprehending, encoding, associating, generalizing, planning, reasoning, forming concepts, solving problems, generating and applying strategies, and so on. Viewing intelligence as "many processes" allows more precise specification of the mechanisms involved in intelligent behaviour than do approaches that view it as "a single trait" or "several abilities."

A Proposed Resolution

How can these competing perspectives on intelligence be reconciled? After studying intelligence for more than half a century, John B. Carroll (1993, 2005) proposed a grand integration: the **three-stratum theory of intelligence** (Figure 8.1). At the top of the hierarchy is g; in the middle are several moderately general abilities

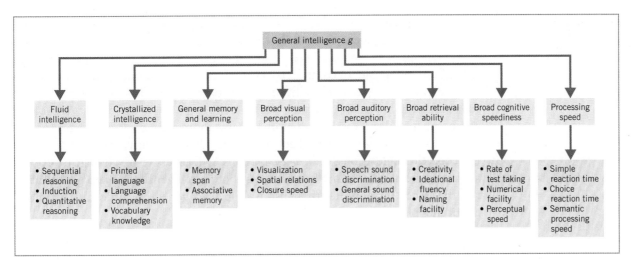

FIGURE 8.1 **Carroll's three-stratum theory of intelligence** In Carroll's hierarchy, general intelligence (*g*) influences several intermediate-level abilities, and each intermediate-level ability influences a variety of specific processes. As this model suggests, intelligence can be usefully viewed as a single entity, as a small set of abilities, or as a very large number of particular processes.

(which include both fluid and crystallized intelligence and other competencies similar to Thurstone's seven primary mental abilities); at the bottom are many specific processes. General intelligence influences all moderately general abilities, and both general intelligence and the moderately general abilities influence the specific processes. For instance, knowing someone's general intelligence allows for a fairly reliable prediction of the person's general memory skills; knowing both of them allows for a quite reliable prediction of the person's memory span; and knowing all three allows for a very accurate prediction of the person's memory span for a particular type of material, such as words, letters, or numbers.

Carroll's comprehensive analysis of the research literature indicated that all three levels of analysis that we have discussed in this section are necessary to account for the totality of facts about intelligence. Thus, for the question "Is intelligence a single trait, a few abilities, or many processes?" the correct answer seems to be "All of the above."

review:

Intelligence can be viewed as a single general ability to think and learn; as several moderately general abilities, such as crystallized and fluid intelligence; or as a collection of numerous specific skills, processes, and content knowledge. All three levels are useful for understanding intelligence.

Measuring Intelligence

Although intelligence is usually viewed as an invisible *capacity* to think and learn, any measure of it must be based on *observable behaviour*. Thus, when we say that a person is intelligent, we mean that the person acts in intelligent ways. One of Binet's profound insights was that the best way to measure intelligence is by observing people's actions on tasks that require a variety of types of intelligence: problem solving, memory, language comprehension, spatial reasoning, and so on. Modern intelligence tests continue to sample these and other aspects of intelligence.

Intelligence testing is highly controversial. Critics such as Ceci (1996) and Sternberg (2008) argue that measuring a quality as complex and multi-faceted as

Wechsler Intelligence Scale for Children (WISC) ■ Widely used test designed to measure the intelligence of children 6 years and older.

intelligence requires assessing a much broader range of abilities than are assessed by current intelligence tests; that current intelligence tests are culturally biased; and that reducing a person's intelligence to a number (the IQ score) is simplistic and ethically questionable. In contrast, advocates (e.g., Gottfredson, 1997; J. L. Horn & McArdle, 2007) argue that intelligence tests are better than any alternative method for predicting important outcomes such as school grades, achievement test scores, and occupational success; that they are valuable for making decisions such as which children should be given special education; and that alternative methods for making educational decisions, such as evaluations by teachers or psychologists, may be subject to greater bias. Knowing the facts about intelligence tests and understanding the issues surrounding their use is crucial to generating informed opinions about these issues.

The Contents of Intelligence Tests

Intelligence is reflected in different abilities at different ages. For example, language ability is not a part of intelligence at 4 months of age, because infants this young neither produce nor understand words, but it is obviously a vital part of intelligence at 4 years of age. The items on tests developed to measure intelligence at different ages reflect these changing aspects. For instance, on the Stanford-Binet intelligence test (a descendant of the original Binet-Simon test), 2-year-olds are asked to identify the objects depicted in line drawings (a test of object recognition), to find an object that they had seen hidden earlier (a test of learning and memory), and to place each of three objects in a hole of the proper shape (a test of perceptual skill and motor coordination). The version of the Stanford-Binet presented to 10-year-olds asks them to define words (a test of verbal ability), to explain why certain social institutions exist (a test of general information and verbal reasoning), and to count the blocks in a picture in which the existence of some blocks must be inferred (a test of problem solving and spatial reasoning).

Intelligence tests have had their greatest success and widest application with children who are at least 5 or 6 years old. The exact abilities examined, and the items used to examine them, vary somewhat from test to test, but there is also considerable similarity among the leading tests.

The most widely used intelligence testing instrument for children 6 years and older is the **Wechsler Intelligence Scale for Children (WISC).** The current edition, the WISC-IV, was revised in 2003 to reflect modern theoretical conceptions of intelligence. In Canada, the WISC-IV-Canadian is used. This version of the test relies on the same test items as the WISC-IV but is normed on a Canadian sample of children. Thus, it captures the abilities of the current population of children in Canada, rather than relying on comparisons to samples of American children.

The conception of intelligence underlying the WISC-IV is consistent with Carroll's three-stratum framework, proposing that intelligence includes general ability (g), several moderately general abilities, and a large number of specific skills. The test yields not only an overall score but also separate scores on four moderately general abilities—verbal comprehension, perceptual reasoning, working memory, and processing speed. The WISC-IV measures these abilities because they reflect skills that are important within information-processing theories, correlate positively with other aspects of intelligence, and are related to important outcomes, notably school grades and later occupational success (Flanagan & Kaufman, 2004). Figure 8.2 provides examples of the four types of items that appear on the WISC-IV (the actual items are protected by copyright and thus cannot be reprinted).

Typical Verbal Comprehension Items

Vocabulary "What is a helicopter?"

Similarities "How are a mountain and a river alike?"

Typical Perceptual Reasoning Items

Block design "Make these nine blocks look exactly like the picture."

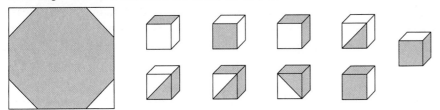

Picture concepts "Pick an object from each pair to make a group of objects that go together."

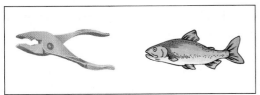

Typical Working Memory Items

Digit span "Repeat the following numbers in order when I'm finished: 5, 3, 7, 4, 9." "Now say these numbers from last to first: 2, 9, 5, 7, 3."

Letter–number sequencing "Repeat the numbers from smallest to biggest, then repeat the letters from earliest to latest in the alphabet: 4, D, 2, G, 7."

Typical Perceptual Speed Items

Coding "Under each square, put a plus; under each circle, put a minus; under each triangle, put an X."

Symbol search "Does the figure to the left of the vertical line also appear to the right of the line?"

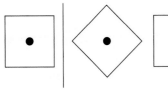

FIGURE 8.2 Four abilities tested by the WISC-IV-Canadian This figure shows examples of the types of items used on the WISC-IV-Canadian to measure four aspects of children's intelligence. On most subtests, the measure of performance is simply whether answers are correct, but on some, such as "perceptual speed," the measure of performance is the number of correct answers that are generated in a limited time. The items shown are not actual items from the test but rather are of the same type; copyright laws prevent the reproduction of the actual items.

IQ (intelligence quotient) ■ Quantitative measure, typically with a mean of 100 and a standard deviation of 15, used to indicate a child's intelligence relative to that of other children of the same age.

normal distribution ■ Pattern of data in which scores fall symmetrically around a mean value, with most scores falling close to the mean and fewer and fewer scores farther from it.

standard deviation (SD) ■ Measure of the variability of scores in a distribution; in a normal distribution, 68% of scores fall within 1 SD of the mean, and 95% of scores fall within 2 SDs of the mean.

The Intelligence Quotient (IQ)

Intelligence tests such as the WISC and the Stanford-Binet provide an overall quantitative measure of a child's intelligence relative to that of other children of the same age. This summary measure is referred to as the child's **IQ (intelligence quotient).**

Understanding how IQ scores are computed, and why, requires a little background. Early developers of intelligence tests observed that many easy-to-measure human characteristics, such as men's heights, women's heights, men's weights, and women's weights, fall into a **normal distribution.** As shown in Figure 8.3, normal distributions are symmetrical around a mean (average) value, with most scores falling relatively near the mean. The farther a score is from the mean, the smaller the percentage of people who obtain it. For example, the mean height of adult males in Canada is around 1.74 metres. Many men are 1.72 metres or 1.76 metres, but few men are 1.6 metres or 1.9 metres. The farther from the mean a height falls, the smaller the number of men of that height.

Similarly, the normal distribution found in intelligence test scores of children of a given age means that most IQ scores are fairly close to the mean, with few children obtaining very high or very low scores. Early designers of IQ tests made an arbitrary decision that has been maintained ever since: a score of 100 is given to children who score exactly at the mean for their age at the time the test is developed. (The mean score can rise or fall in the years after a particular test is developed and, indeed, as discussed later in this chapter, IQ scores on specific tests have risen throughout the industrialized world over the past century.)

IQ scores reflect not only the mean for the test but also its **standard deviation (SD),** a measure of the variability of scores within a distribution. By definition, in a normal distribution, 68% of scores fall between 1 SD below the mean and 1 SD above it, and 95% of scores fall between 2 SDs below the mean and 2 SDs above it.

On most IQ tests, the standard deviation is about 15 points. Thus, as shown in Figure 8.3, a child scoring 1 standard deviation above the mean for his or her age (a score higher than 84% of children) receives a score of 115 (the mean of 100 plus the 15-point SD). Similarly, a child scoring 1 standard deviation below the mean (a score higher than only 16% of children) receives a score of 85 (the mean of 100

FIGURE 8.3 **A normal distribution of IQ scores** Like other measurable human characteristics, IQ scores fall into a normal distribution. Here, the numbers along the base of the graph correspond to IQ scores. The number just below each IQ score indicates how many standard deviation units that score is below or above the mean. Thus, an IQ score of 55 is 3 standard deviations below the mean. The percentages in each interval indicate the percentage of children whose scores fall within that interval; for example, less than 1% of children have IQ scores below 55 and slightly more than 2% score between 55 and 70.

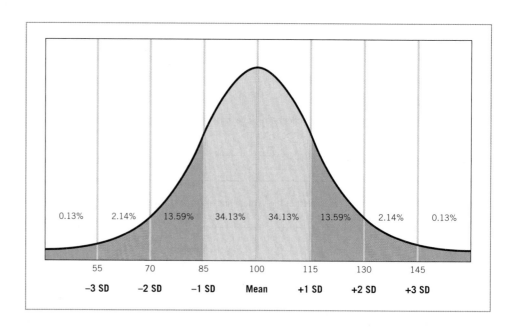

minus the 15-point SD). Figure 8.3 also reflects the fact that about 95% of children obtain IQ scores that fall within 2 standard deviations of the mean (between 70 and 130).

An advantage of this scoring system is that IQ scores at different ages are easy to compare, despite the great increases in knowledge that accompany development in all children. A score of 130 at age 5 means that a child's performance exceeded that of 98% of age peers; a score of 130 at age 10 or 20 means exactly the same thing. This property has facilitated analysis of the stability of individuals' IQ scores over time, a topic we turn to next.

Continuity of IQ Scores

If IQ is a consistent property of a person, then the IQ scores that people obtain at different ages should be highly correlated. Longitudinal studies that have measured the same children's IQ scores at different ages have, in fact, shown impressive continuity from age 5 onward. For example, one large-scale Scottish study indicated that IQ scores at age 5 and 15 correlated 0.67 (Humphreys, 1989). This is a remarkable degree of continuity over a 10-year period. (Recall from Chapter 1 that a correlation of 1.00 indicates that two variables are perfectly correlated.) Indeed, the IQ score has been thought to be the most stable of all psychological traits (N. Brody, 1992).

Several variables influence the degree of stability of IQ scores over time. As might be expected, the closer in time that IQ tests are given, the more stability is found. Thus, the same study that found that IQ scores at ages 5 and 15 correlated 0.67 also found that scores at ages 5 and 9 correlated 0.79 and at ages 5 and 6 correlated 0.87. In addition, for any given length of time between tests, scores are more stable at older ages. For instance, in one study, IQ scores of 4- and 5-year-olds correlated 0.80, those of 6- and 7-year-olds correlated 0.87, and those of 8- and 9-year-olds correlated 0.90 (N. Brody, 1992).

Although a person's IQ scores at different ages tend to be similar, the scores are rarely identical. Children who take an IQ test at age 4 and again at age 17 show an average change, up or down, of 13 points; those who take the test at ages 8 and 17 show an average change of 9 points; and those who take it at ages 12 and 17 show an average change of 7 points (N. Brody, 1992). These changes are due at least in part to random variation in factors such as the child's alertness and mood on the test days. Some of the changes, however, are not random. One recent longitudinal study showed that verbal and nonverbal changes in IQ during the adolescent years were closely related to changes in brain structure (Ramsden et al., 2011). Some of these changes were predicted by reading ability: that is, teenagers with higher reading ability at first assessment showed more improvement in verbal IQ than teenagers with poor reading skills (Ramsden et al., 2013). Changes in the child's environment, for instance, through parental divorce or remarriage or moving to a better or worse neighbourhood, can also produce changes in IQ score (Sameroff et al., 1993).

A question of interest to parents and scientists alike is whether it is possible to identify at young ages children who are superior in intelligence or in specific intellectual or artistic abilities. Research on such children, who are often described as "gifted," is presented in Box 8.1.

The IQ scores of children whose parents take an interest in their academic success tend to increase over time.

BLEND IMAGES / ALAMY

BOX 8.1: **individual differences**

GIFTED CHILDREN

Five-year-old Ryan Wang from West Vancouver has already performed at New York's Carnegie Hall and with the Shanghai Philharmonic, all before beginning Grade 1. Ryan began playing piano around 18 months before his Carnegie Hall debut, quickly mastering complex concertos that are intended for children twice his age. In addition to his musical prowess, Ryan is fluent in Mandarin and English, and excels at his school work.

As noted by Ellen Winner, a psychologist who studies intellectually and artistically gifted children, most gifted children, like Ryan, show astonishing early facility in a single area: numbers, music, drawing, reading, or some other realm. A smaller number of children are exceptional over a wide range of intellectual areas (Winner, 1996). These globally gifted children usually display several signs of giftedness from very early in development (N. M. Robinson & Robinson, 1992):

- Unusual alertness and long attention span in infancy
- Rapid language development
- Curiosity—asking deep questions and being dissatisfied with superficial answers
- High energy levels, often bordering on hyperactivity
- Intense reactions to frustration
- Precocious reading and interest in numbers
- Exceptional logical and abstract reasoning
- Unusually good memory
- Enjoyment of solitary play

Gifted children also show an intense interest or love of learning. Marion Porath of the University of British Columbia interviewed 11- to 12-year-old gifted children, asking them what learning meant to them:

Learning is like a wave of knowledge coming into my head and it just feels good.

[Reading is] an escape. It's something that I love to do, something that I will do at any cost. It's an exploration, and it's a way to learn what I love, expand my vocabulary, expand my concepts, and challenge the way I think. I will read articles by people who have completely different political viewpoints from mine, to see if I can play the devil's advocate. To me, in fact, this is what I like to do.

(Porath, 2004)

Exceptional early ability often foreshadows outstanding later achievement. Consider a long-term study of 320 children who by age 13 took the SAT (Scholastic Assessment Test), a standardized test for college admission in the United States, as part of a national talent search and who scored in the top 1 in 10 000 in verbal or math ability. Among their accomplishments by age 23 were adapting Pink Floyd's *The Wall* into a multimedia rock opera, developing one of the most popular video games in the United States, and inventing a navigation system that was used to land a rocket on Mars (Lubinski et al., 2001). As a group, they had published 11 articles in scientific and medical journals and won numerous major awards in areas ranging from physics to creative writing.

By age 33, more than half of the original sample had received a PhD, MD, or JD (Doctor of Jurisprudence, or doctorate of law) (Lubinski et al., 2006). Their rate of PhDs was more than 50 times higher than that for the general population, and their rate of patents was 11 times that in the general population. Even within this elite sample, higher initial SAT mathematics scores predicted higher achievement.

For example, the higher the score on the SAT math test at age 13, the greater the number of patents and publications in scholarly journals—especially those in science, engineering, and mathematics—at age 33 (Park, Lubinski, & Benbow, 2008).

Exceptional early ability in an area is no guarantee of outstanding adult achievement in it. Factors such as creativity, devotion to the area, ability to work long hours, and perseverance in the face of difficulty are also essential for making exceptional contributions (Lubinski & Benbow, 2006; Wai et al., 2010). Nonetheless, it is remarkable how scores on a single test, given at age 13 years, predict exceptional achievement 20 years later.

Exceptionally early readers, such as this 3½-year-old, often continue to be excellent readers throughout life.

Intelligence tests examine a range of abilities and types of knowledge, including vocabulary, verbal comprehension, arithmetic, memory, and spatial reasoning. The tests are used to obtain a general measure of intelligence: the IQ score. IQ tests are designed to produce average scores of 100, with higher scores indicating above-average intelligence and lower scores below-average intelligence. After age 5 or 6, IQ scores of individual children tend to be quite stable over long periods, but they vary somewhat from one testing to the next.

IQ Scores as Predictors of Important Outcomes

Claims that an IQ score is a strong predictor of academic, economic, and occupational success are based on solid evidence (Sackett, Borneman, & Connelly, 2008; F. L. Schmidt & Hunter, 2004). As noted earlier, IQ scores correlate positively and strongly with school grades and achievement test performance, both at the time of the test and years later (Geary, 2005); for example, IQ and achievement test performance typically correlate between 0.50 and 0.60 (Deary et al., 2007). IQ scores also correlate positively with long-term educational outcomes. A person's IQ score in Grade 6 correlates about 0.60 with the years of education that the person eventually completes (Jencks, 1979). Substantial relations between IQ score and performance in intellectually demanding occupations are present not only when the person is hired but for at least 10 years after entry into the occupation (Sackett et al., 2008).

In part, the positive relation between IQ score and occupational and economic success stems from the fact that standardized test scores serve as gatekeepers, determining which students gain access to the training and credentials required for entry into lucrative professions. Even among people who initially have the same job, however, those with higher IQ scores tend to perform better, earn more money, and receive better promotions (F. L. Schmidt & Hunter, 2004; Wilk, Desmarais, & Sackett, 1995).

A child's IQ score is more closely related to the child's later occupational success than is the socioeconomic status of the child's family, the school the child attends, or any other variable that has been studied (Ceci, 1993). These relations hold even at the top of the test score distribution. Although popular books such as *Outliers* (Gladwell, 2008) claim that people with fairly high test scores achieve grades and occupational success equivalent to those of people with very high scores, empirical research indicates that even at the top of the distribution, the higher the test score, the higher that subsequent achievement is likely to be (Arneson, Sackett, & Beatty, 2011).

As strong a predictor of academic, economic, and occupational success as an IQ score is, intelligence is far from the only influence. A child's other characteristics, such as motivation to succeed, conscientiousness, intellectual curiosity, creativity, physical and mental health, and social skills, also exert important influences (Roberts et al., 2007; Sternberg, 2004; von Stumm, Hell, & Charmorro-Premuzic, 2011). For instance, **self-discipline**—the ability to inhibit actions, follow rules, and avoid impulsive reactions—is more predictive of changes in report card marks between Grades 5 and 9 than is IQ score, though IQ score is more predictive of changes in achievement test scores over the same period (Duckworth, Quinn, & Tsukayama,

self-discipline ■ Ability to inhibit actions, follow rules, and avoid impulsive reactions.

2012). Similarly, "practical intelligence"—skills that are useful in everyday life but that are not measured by traditional intelligence tests, such as accurately reading other people's emotions and intentions and motivating others to work effectively as a team—predicts occupational success beyond the influence of IQ score (Cianciolo et al., 2006; Sternberg, 2003). Characteristics of the environment are similarly influential: parents' encouragement and modelling of productive careers predict their children's occupational success (Kalil, Levine, & Ziol-Guest, 2005).

review:

IQ scores are positively related to grades in school and achievement test performance, both at the time of the test and in the future. They are also positively related to occupational success in adulthood. However, they are not the only influence on these outcomes. Intellectual curiosity, creativity, self-discipline, social skills, practical intelligence, and a variety of other factors also contribute.

Genes, Environment, and the Development of Intelligence

No issue in psychology has produced more acrimonious debate than the issue of how heredity and environment influence intelligence. Even people who recognize that intelligence, like all human qualities, is constructed through the continuous interaction of genes and environment often forget this fact and take extreme positions that are based more on emotions and ideology than on logic and evidence.

A useful starting point for thinking about genetic and environmental influences on intelligence is Bronfenbrenner's (1993) bioecological model of development (detailed in Chapter 9). This model envisions children's lives as embedded within a series of increasingly encompassing environments. The child, with a unique set of qualities including his or her genetic endowment and personal experiences, is at the centre. Surrounding the child is the immediate environment, especially the people

In the movie *My Fair Lady,* Eliza Doolittle found it easier to don the clothing of an upper-class lady than to adopt the haughty reserve viewed as appropriate by that class at that time. This scene, of opening day of Ascot, as well as the movie as a whole, makes the argument that differences that might be attributed to nature are actually the product of nurture.

WARNER BROS / THE KOBAL COLLECTION / ART RESOURCE

and institutions with which the child interacts directly: family, school, classmates, teachers, neighbours, and so on. Surrounding the immediate environment are more distant, and less tangible, forces that also influence development: cultural attitudes, the social and economic system, mass media, the government, and so on. We now examine how qualities of the child, the immediate environment, and the broader society contribute to the development of intelligence.

Qualities of the Child

Children contribute greatly to their own intellectual development, through their genetic endowment, through the reactions they elicit from other people, and through their choice of environments.

Genetic Contributions to Intelligence

As noted in Chapter 3, the genome has a substantial influence on intelligence. This genetic influence varies greatly with age (Figure 8.4): it is moderate in early childhood and becomes large by adolescence and adulthood (Bouchard, 2004; Plomin et al., 2008). Reflecting the same trend, the IQ scores of adopted children and those of their biological parents become increasingly correlated as the children develop, but the scores of adopted children and their adoptive parents become less correlated over the course of development (Plomin et al., 1997).

One reason for this increasing genetic influence is that some genetic processes do not exert their effects until late childhood or adolescence. For example, some connections linking areas in the brain that are distant from one another are not formed until adolescence, and the extent of such connections reflects genetic influences (Thatcher, 1992). Another reason is that children's increasing independence with age allows them greater freedom to choose environments that are compatible with their own genetically based preferences but not necessarily with those of the parents who are raising them (McAdams & Olson, 2010).

Advances in genetics have inspired research aimed at identifying a small set of genes that explain individual differences in intelligence. These efforts have led to identification of almost 300 genes that are associated with mental retardation (Inlow & Restifo, 2004) but none that are consistently related to normal variation in intelligence (Butcher et al., 2008; Chabris et al., 2012). The most likely explanation is that the genetic contribution to intelligence reflects small contributions from each of a very large number of genes, as well as complex interactions among them (Nisbett et al., 2012).

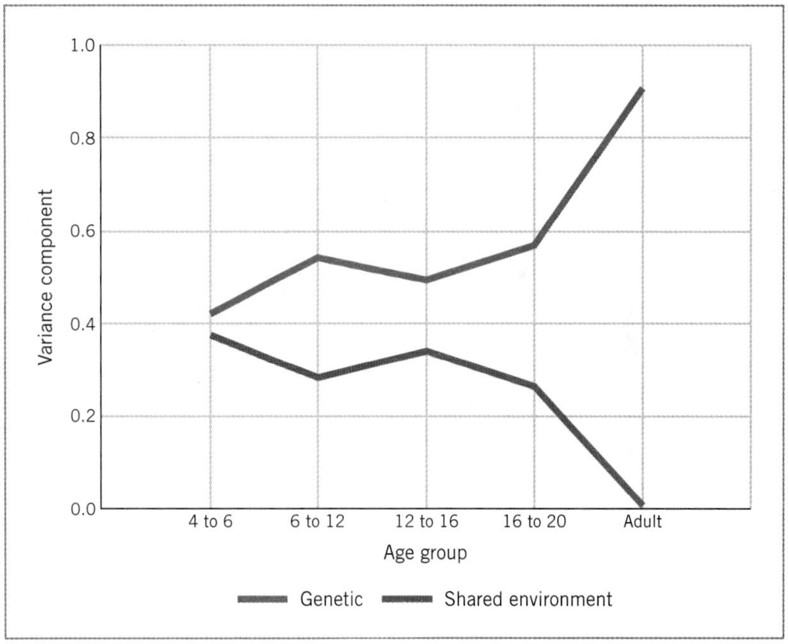

FIGURE 8.4 **Changes with age in factors influencing intelligence** As children grow into adults, the influence of genetics on individual differences in intelligence increases, whereas the influence of shared aspects of family environment decreases. (Data from McGue et al., 1993)

Genotype–Environment Interactions

As noted in Chapter 3, the environments children encounter are influenced by their genotype. Sandra Scarr (1992) proposed that gene–environment relations involve three types of processes: passive, evocative, and active.

PATRICK BENNETT / CORBIS

Children influence their own development: these children's joyous reactions to their father's reading ensure that he will want to read to them in the future.

- *Passive effects* of the genotype arise when children are raised by their biological parents. These effects occur not because of anything the children do but because of the overlap between their parents' genes and their own. Thus, children whose genotypes predispose them to enjoy reading are likely to be raised in homes with plentiful access to reading matter, because their parents also like to read. The passive effects of the genotype help explain why correlations between biological parents' and their children's IQ scores are higher when the children live with their biological parents than when they live with adoptive parents.

- *Evocative effects* of the genotype emerge through children's eliciting or influencing other people's behaviour. For example, even if a child's parents are not avid readers, they will read more bedtime stories to a child who is interested in the stories than to one who is uninterested.

- *Active effects* of the genotype involve children's choosing environments that they enjoy. A high school student who likes reading will borrow books from the library and obtain books in other ways, regardless of whether he or she was read to when young.

The evocative and active effects of the genotype help explain how children's IQ scores become more closely related over time to those of their biological parents, even if the children are adopted and never see their biological parents.

Influence of the Immediate Environment

The influence of nurture on the development of intelligence begins with a child's immediate environment of families and schools.

Family Influences

If asked to identify the most important environmental influence on their intelligence, most people probably would say, "My family." Testing the influence of the family environment on children's intelligence, however, requires some means of assessing that environment. How can something as complex and multi-faceted as a family environment be measured, especially when it can be different for different children in the same family?

Robert Bradley and Bettye Caldwell (1979) tackled this problem by devising a measure known as the HOME (Home Observation for Measurement of the Environment). The HOME samples various aspects of children's home life, including organization and safety of living space; intellectual stimulation offered by parents; whether children have books of their own; amount of parent–child interaction; parents' emotional support of the child; and so on. Table 8.1 shows the items and subscales used in the original HOME, which was designed to assess the family environments of children between birth and 3 years of age. Subsequent versions of the HOME have been developed for application with preschoolers, school-age children, and adolescents (Bradley, 1994).

TABLE 8.1

Sample Items and Subscales on the HOME (Infant Version)

I. Emotional and Verbal Responsivity of Mother

    1. Mother spontaneously vocalizes to child at least twice during visit (excluding scolding).

    2. Mother responds to child's vocalizations with a verbal response.

    3. Mother tells child the name of some object during visit or says name of person or object in a "teaching" style.

II. Avoidance of Restriction and Punishment

    4. Mother does not shout at child during visit.

    5. Mother does not express overt annoyance with or hostility toward child.

    6. Mother does not interfere with child's actions or restrict child's movements more than three times during visit.

III. Organization of Physical and Temporal Environment

    7. When mother is away, care is provided by one of three regular substitutes.

    8. Child is taken regularly to doctor's office or clinic.

    9. Child has a special place in which to keep his or her toys and "treasures."

IV. Provision of Appropriate Play Materials

    10. Child has push or pull toy.

    11. Child has stroller or walker, kiddie car, scooter, or tricycle.

    12. Mother provides learning equipment appropriate to age—cuddly toy or role-playing toys.

V. Maternal Involvement with Child

    13. Mother tends to keep child within visual range and to look at him or her often.

    14. Mother "talks" to child while doing her work.

    15. Mother structures child's play periods.

VI. Opportunities for Variety of Daily Stimulation

    16. Mother reads stories at least three times weekly.

    17. Child eats at least one meal per day with mother and father.

    18. Child has three or more books of his or her own.

Source: Adapted from Bradley & Caldwell, 1984

Stimulating home environments, especially those in which adults and children undertake challenging tasks together, are associated with high IQ scores and high achievement in school.

Throughout childhood, children's IQ scores, as well as their math and reading achievement scores, are positively correlated with the HOME measure of their family environment (Bradley et al., 2001). A large multi-site study, which included a group of children from Hamilton, Ontario, found that HOME scores of 12-month-olds correlated positively with the IQ scores of the same children at 3 years of age (Bradley et al., 1989). Similarly, HOME scores of 2-year-olds correlated positively with IQ scores and school achievement of the same children at age 11 years (Olson, Bates, & Kaskie, 1992). When HOME scores are relatively stable over time, IQ scores also tend to be stable; when HOME scores change, IQ scores also tend to change in the same direction (Bradley, 1989). Thus, assessing varied aspects of a child's family environment allows prediction of the child's IQ score.

Given this evidence, it is tempting to conclude that better-quality home environments cause children to have higher IQ scores. Whether that is actually the case, however, is not yet known. The uncertainty reflects two factors. First, the type of intellectual environment that parents establish in the home is almost certainly influenced by their genetic makeup. Second, almost all studies using the HOME have focused on families in which children live with their biological parents.

These two circumstances may mean that parents' genes influence both the intellectual quality of the home environment and children's IQ scores; thus, the home intellectual environment as such may not cause children to have higher or lower IQ scores. Consistent with this possibility, in the few studies in which the HOME has been used to study adoptive families, the correlations between it and children's IQ scores are lower than in studies of children living with their biological parents (Plomin, Fulker, et al., 1997). Thus, although scores on the HOME clearly correlate with children's IQ scores, whether causal relations exist between the two remains uncertain.

Shared and Non-Shared Family Environments The phrase "family intellectual environment" is often taken to mean characteristics that are the same for all children within the family: the parents' emphasis on education, the number of books in the house, the frequency of intellectual discussions around the dinner table, and so on. As discussed in Chapter 3, however, each child within a given family also encounters unique, non-shared environments. In any family, only one child can be the first-born and receive the intense, undivided parental attention early in life that this status tends to bring. Similarly, a child whose interests or personality characteristics mirror those of one or both parents may receive more positive attention than other children in the family. If homes that are extremely lacking in intellectual stimulation are excluded from consideration, such within-family variations in children's environments may have a greater impact on the development of intelligence than do between-family variations (Petrill et al., 2004). In addition, the influence of the non-shared environment increases with age, and the influence of the shared environment decreases with age, as children become increasingly able to choose their own friends and activities (Bouchard, 2004; Segal et al., 2007).

The relative influence of shared environments and genetics varies with family income. Among children and adolescents from low-income families, the shared environment accounts for more of the variance in IQ scores and academic achievement than genetics does. In contrast, among children and adolescents from middle- and high-income families, the relative influence of shared environment and genetics is reversed (Harden, Turkheimer, & Loehlin, 2007; D. C. Rowe, Jacobson, & Van den Oord, 1999; Turkheimer et al., 2003). These differing patterns are found as early as age 2 years (Tucker-Drob et al., 2011). The reasons for the differences remain to be established.

With age, children increasingly shape their own environments in ways that reflect their personalities and tastes.

Influences of Schooling

Attending school makes children smarter. One type of evidence for this conclusion came from a study that examined IQ scores of older and younger Israeli children in Grades 4 to 6 (Cahan & Cohen, 1989). As indicated by the gradual upward trends in the graphs in Figure 8.5, older children within each grade did somewhat better than younger children within that grade on each part of the test. However, the jumps in the graphs between grades indicate that children who were only slightly older, but who had a year more schooling, did much better than the slightly younger children in the grade below them. For example, on the verbal-oddities sub-test (which involves indicating which word in a series does not belong with the others), the results show a small gap between 123- and 124-month-old 4th graders but a large gap between both of them and 125-month-old 5th graders.

Another type of evidence indicating that going to school makes children smarter is that average IQ and achievement test scores rise during the school year but not during summer vacation (Ceci, 1991; J. Huttenlocher, Levine, & Vevea, 1998). The way in which these changes vary with children's family backgrounds adds further support to the view that schooling makes children smarter. Children from families of low socioeconomic status and those from families of high socioeconomic status make comparable gains in school achievement during the school year. However, over the summer, the achievement test scores of low-SES children tend to stay constant or drop, whereas the scores of high-SES children tend to rise (K. L. Alexander, Entwisle, & Olson, 2007; Burkam et al., 2004). The likely explanation is that during the academic year, schools provide children of all backgrounds with relatively stimulating intellectual environments, but when school is not in session, fewer children from low-SES families have the kinds of experiences that allow them to build on what they learned to increase their academic achievement.

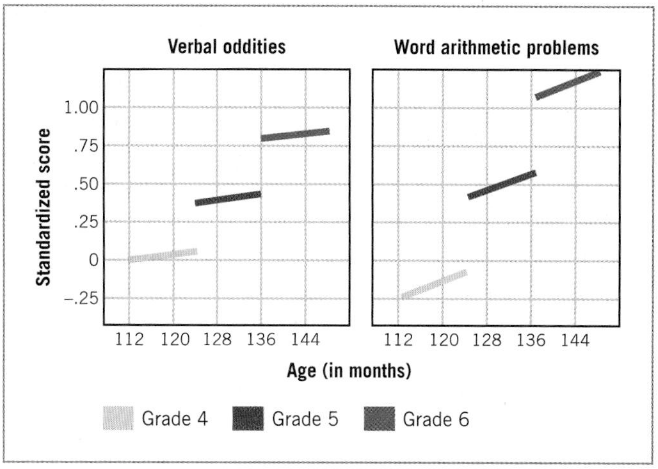

Influence of Society

Intellectual development is influenced not only by characteristics of children, their families, and their schools but also by broader characteristics of the societies within which children develop. One reflection of societal influences is that in many countries throughout the world, average IQ scores have consistently risen over the past 80 years, a phenomenon that has been labelled the **Flynn effect** in honour of James Flynn, the researcher who discovered this widespread trend (Flynn, 1987, 2009). In some countries, including the Netherlands and Israel, average IQ scores have risen as much as 20 points; in the United States, the gains have been roughly 10 points (Dickens & Flynn, 2001; Flynn & Weiss, 2007). Given that the gene pool has not changed appreciably over this period, the increase in IQ scores must be due to changes in society.

The specific source of the Flynn effect remains controversial. Some researchers argue that the key factors are improvements in the lives of low-income families, such as improved nutrition (Lynn, 2009), health (Eppig, Fincher, & Thornhill, 2010), and formal education (C. Blair et al., 2005). These researchers point to evidence that the increase in IQ scores has been greatest among those in the lower part of the IQ score and income distributions. For instance, as shown in Figure 8.6, among Danes born from 1942 to 1980, there was no change in the scores of people in the top 10% of the IQ distribution, but there was a large change among those in the bottom 10% (Geary, 2005). IQ score changes in some other countries, including Spain and Norway, show a similar pattern, but gains in yet other countries, including the United States, France, and Britain, have been comparable throughout the IQ score and income distributions (Nisbett et al., 2012).

FIGURE 8.5 Relations of age and grade to performance on two parts of an IQ test The jumps between grade levels indicate that schooling exerts an effect on intelligence test performance beyond that of the child's age. (Data from Cahan & Cohen, 1989)

Flynn effect ■ Consistent rise in average IQ scores that has occurred over the past 80 years in many countries.

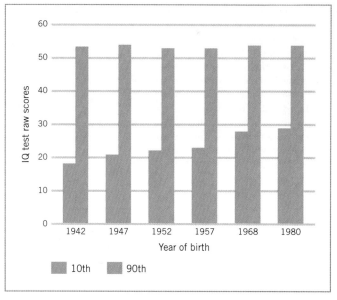

FIGURE 8.6 Changes in IQ score over time among Danish adults with relatively low IQ scores (10th percentile) and relatively high IQ scores (90th percentile) As these data illustrate, IQ scores have improved considerably over the years among Danes near the bottom of the distribution but have remained virtually constant among people near the top. (Adapted from Geary, 2005)

An alternative plausible explanation for the increases in IQ scores is increased societal emphasis on abstract problem solving and reasoning (Flynn, 2009). Supporting this interpretation is the fact that scores on tests of fluid intelligence, which reflects abstract problem solving and reasoning, have increased much more than scores on tests of crystallized intelligence (Nisbett et al., 2012). One source of these recent increases in fluid intelligence might be experience with new technologies, such as video games. Haier and colleagues (2009) found that 3 months of playing a video game (Tetris) led to increased thickness in areas of adolescent girls' brains that are specifically activated by playing the game and that are also active in the types of spatial tasks that are often used to measure fluid intelligence.

One conclusion that sparks no controversy is that poverty hinders intellectual development. In the following sections, we consider how poverty affects children's development in different societies, and how it contributes to differences in IQ scores and school achievement. We will also consider risk factors associated with poverty that adversely affect intelligence, as well as programs that enhance poor children's intellectual development.

Effects of Poverty

The negative effects of poverty or economic disadvantage on children's IQ scores are indisputable. Even after taking into account the mother's education, whether both parents live with the child, and the child's race, the adequacy of family income for meeting family needs is related to children's IQ scores (Bradley & Corwyn, 2002; Duncan et al., 1998). Further, the more years children spend in poverty, the lower their scores tend to be (Korenman, Miller, & Sjaastad, 1995).

Poverty exerts negative effects on intellectual development in numerous ways. Chronic inadequate diet early in life can disrupt brain development; missing meals on a given day (e.g., achievement test day) can impair intellectual functioning on that day; reduced access to health services can result in greater numbers of absences from school; conflicts between adults in the household can produce emotional turmoil that interferes with learning; insufficient intellectual stimulation can lead to a lack of background knowledge needed to understand new material; and so on.

One source of evidence for the relation between poverty and IQ is the fact that in all countries that have been studied, children from wealthier homes score higher on IQ and achievement tests, on average, than do children from poorer homes (Case, Griffin, & Kelley, 1999; Keating & Hertzman, 1999). More telling, in those developed countries where the income gap between rich and poor is widest, such as the United States, the difference between the intellectual achievement of children from rich and poor homes is much larger than in countries in which the gap is smaller, such as the Scandinavian countries and, to a lesser degree, Germany, Canada, and Great Britain. As shown in Figure 8.7, children from affluent families in the United States score, on average, about the same on mathematics achievement tests as children from affluent families in Canada and Japan—two countries with greater income equality. In contrast, children from poor families in the United States have average achievement test scores far below children from poor families in Canada and Japan. The key difference is that poor families in the United States are much poorer, relative to others in their society, than their counterparts in many other developed countries. In Canada, 8.1% of children live in families whose income falls below the low-income cut-off (Statistics

FIGURE 8.7 **Relation in three countries between fathers' occupational status and children's math achievement** As research by Robbie Case at the University of Toronto has demonstrated, Canadian and Japanese children whose fathers hold low-status jobs perform, on average, far better on math achievement tests than do children whose fathers hold comparable jobs in the United States. In contrast, Canadian children whose fathers have high-status jobs perform, on average, as well as children whose fathers hold comparable jobs in the United States and almost as well as children from similar backgrounds in Japan. (Data from Case et al., 1999)

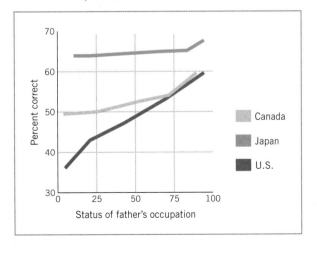

Canada, 2012b). By contrast, in the United States, 23% of children live in families with incomes below half that of the median U.S. family income, and in a set of 35 other developed countries, 11% of children were from families with this low a percentage of the median income in their country (UNICEF, 2012).

Race, Ethnicity, and Intelligence

Few claims stir stronger passions than those surrounding assertions that racial and ethnic groups differ in intelligence. It is therefore especially important to know both the facts about this issue, based on research, and what can and cannot be concluded from these facts.

One fact is that the *average* IQ scores of children from different racial and ethnic groups *do* differ. For example, the average IQ scores of Hispanic-American and Native-American children are a few points higher than those of African-American children, and those of Asian-American children are a few points higher than those of European-Americans (Nisbett et al., 2012). These differences are explained in part by differences in social class backgrounds.

A second fact is that scientific statements about group differences in IQ scores refer to statistical averages rather than to any individual's score. For example, millions of African-American children have IQ scores higher than the average European-American child, and millions of European-American children have IQ scores lower than the average Latino child. Far more variability exists *within* each racial group than *between* groups. Thus, data on the average IQ score of members of an ethnic or racial group tell us nothing about a given individual.

A third crucial fact is that differences in IQ and achievement test scores of children from different racial and ethnic groups describe children's performance only in the environments in which the children live. The findings do not indicate their intellectual potential, nor do they indicate what their scores would be if the children lived in different environments. Indeed, with decreases in discrimination and inequality in the past 40 years, achievement test differences between children of different racial and ethnic backgrounds have decreased considerably. For example, a rigorous analysis of changes over time in intelligence test scores showed that African-American schoolchildren reduced the gap with European-American schoolchildren by 4 to 7 points between 1972 and 2002 (Dickens & Flynn, 2006); achievement test scores have shown the same trend (N. Brody, 1992).

Risk Factors and Intellectual Development

In the popular media, reports on how to help all children reach their intellectual potential often focus on a single factor—the need to eliminate poverty or the need to eliminate racism or the need to preserve two-parent families, or the need for high-quality daycare, or the need for universal preschool education, and so on. However, no single factor, nor even any small group of factors, is *the* key. Instead, a variety of factors in combination contribute to the problem of poor intellectual development.

To capture the impact of these multiple influences, Arnold Sameroff and his colleagues developed an *environmental risk scale* (Sameroff et al., 1993) based on 10 features of the environment that put children at risk for low IQ scores (Table 8.2). Each child's risk score is a simple count of the number of major risks facing the child. Thus, a child growing up with, say, a mother who is unemployed, unmarried, highly anxious, and mentally ill would have an environmental risk score of 4.

TABLE 8.2

Risk Factors Related to IQ Scores

1. Head of household unemployed or working in low-status occupation
2. Mother did not complete high school
3. At least four children in family
4. No father or stepfather in home
5. African-American family
6. Large number of stressful life events in past few years
7. Rigidity of parents' beliefs about child development
8. Maternal anxiety
9. Maternal mental health
10. Negative mother–child interactions

Source: Sameroff et al., 1993

Sameroff and his colleagues measured the IQ scores and environmental risks of more than 100 children when they were 4-year-olds and again when they were 13-year-olds. They found that the more risks in a child's environment, the lower the child's IQ score tended to be. As shown in Figure 8.8, the effect was large. The average IQ score of children whose environments did not include any of the risk factors was around 115; the average score of children whose environments included six or more risks was around 85. The sheer number of risks in the child's environment was a better predictor of the child's IQ score than was the presence of any particular risk. Subsequent studies demonstrated similarly strong relations between the number of risk factors and school grades (Gassman-Pines & Yoshikawa, 2006; Gutman, Sameroff, & Cole, 2003).

The Sameroff (1993) study also provided an interesting perspective on why children's IQ scores are highly stable. It is not just that children's genes remain constant; over time, their environment tends to remain fairly constant as well. The study revealed that there was just as much stability in the number of risk factors in children's environments at ages 4 and 13 years as there was in their IQ scores over that period.

The number of risk factors in a 4-year-old's environment not only correlates highly with the child's IQ score at age 4 but also predicts likely changes in the child's score between ages 4 and 13. That is, if two children have the same IQ score at age 4 but one child lives in an environment with more risk factors, the child facing more risks will, at age 13, probably have an IQ score lower than that of the other child.

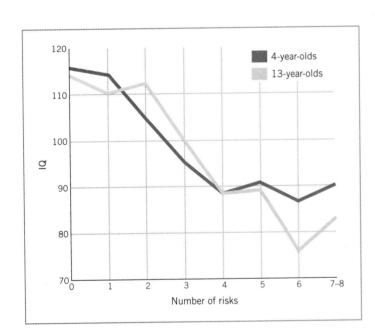

FIGURE 8.8 **Risk factors and IQ score** For both younger and older children, the more risk factors in the environment, the lower the average IQ score. (Data from Sameroff et al., 1993)

Thus, environmental risks seem to have both immediate and long-term effects on children's intellectual development. Genetic contributions cannot be ruled out—anxiety, poor mental health, and other risk factors may be biologically transmitted from parent to child—but a greater number of risk factors is definitely associated with lower IQ scores.

Although Sameroff and his colleagues described their measure as a "risk index," it is as much a measure of the quality of a child's environment as of its potential for harm. High IQ scores are associated with favourable environments as much as low scores are associated with adverse ones. This is true for children from low-income families as well as for children in general. Low-income parents who, relative to others with similar incomes, are responsive to their children and provide them with safe play areas and varied learning materials have children with higher IQ scores (Bradley et al., 1994). Thus, high-quality parenting can help alleviate the risks imposed by poverty.

Programs for Helping Economically Disadvantaged Children

Beginning in the early 1960s, it became clear that children from economically disadvantaged families were at risk for poor outcomes. As a consequence, many intervention programs were initiated to enhance the development of preschoolers from impoverished families.

In a comprehensive analysis of 11 of the most prominent early intervention programs in the United States—all of which focused on 2- to 5-year-old African-American children from low-income families—Irving Lazar and his colleagues found a consistent pattern (Lazar et al., 1982). Participation in the programs, most of which lasted a year or two, initially increased children's IQ scores substantially—by 10 to 15 points. However, over the next 2 or 3 years, the gains decreased, and by the 4th year after the end of the programs, no differences were apparent between the IQ scores of participants and those of non-participants from the same neighbourhoods and backgrounds. Similar patterns emerged in an analysis of programs that emphasized mathematics and reading achievement (McKey et al., 1985).

Fortunately, other effects of these experimental programs were more enduring. Only half as many program participants as non-participants were later assigned to special education classes—14% versus 29%. Similarly, fewer participants were held back in school, more participants subsequently graduated from high school, and fewer had been arrested by age 18 (Reynolds et al., 2001).

This combination of findings may seem puzzling. If the intervention programs did not result in lasting increases in IQ or achievement test scores, why would they have led to fewer children being assigned to special education classes or being held back in school? A likely reason is that the interventions had long-term effects on children's motivation and behaviour. These effects would help children do well enough in the classroom to be promoted with their classmates, which in turn might make them less likely to drop out of high school and less likely to turn to criminal activity, even if their IQ scores were unchanged.

Participation also led to benefits after children finished school. As adults, former participants in some of the programs used the welfare system less and earned larger salaries than did non-participants (Haskins, 1989; McLoyd, 1998). Positive effects such as these suggest that early intervention programs not only can help participants lead more successful lives but might also more than repay their costs by reducing the need for social services. In Box 8.2, we discuss one prevention program in Canada—**Better Beginnings, Better Futures (BBBF)**—and one in the United States—the **Carolina Abecedarian Project**—that have shown the possibility of producing enduring gains in both IQ scores and school achievement.

Children who participate in early intervention programs, like the youngsters pictured here, are in later years less likely to be held back in the same grade and more likely to graduate from high school than are children from similar backgrounds who do not participate in these programs.

MICHAEL STUPARYK / TORONTO STAR VIA GETTY IMAGES

Better Beginnings, Better Futures (BBBF) ■ Successful early intervention program aimed at disadvantaged communities in Ontario.

Carolina Abecedarian Project ■ Comprehensive and successful enrichment program for children from low-income families.

BOX 8.2: applications

SUCCESSFUL PREVENTION AND EARLY INTERVENTION PROJECTS: THE BETTER BEGINNINGS, BETTER FUTURES PROJECT AND THE CAROLINA ABECEDARIAN PROJECT

The difficulty of producing enduring gains in poor children's IQ and achievement test scores led some evaluators to conclude that intelligence is unalterable (A. R. Jensen, 1973; Westinghouse Learning Corporation, 1969). However, the same findings motivated other researchers to find out if interventions that started early, continued for a number of years, and attempted to improve many aspects of children's lives might produce enduring increases in IQ, even though briefer, less intensive, later-starting interventions had not. Two such projects, The *Better Beginnings, Better Futures (BBBF)* project and the *Carolina Abecedarian Project* clearly demonstrate that enduring changes can be achieved.

BBBF began in 1991 as a 25-year longitudinal prevention project, in response to the results of the 1983 Ontario Child Health Study. This study indicated that 1 in 6 children had an emotional or behavioural problem, and that children from socioeconomically disadvantaged homes were at higher risk for these problems (Peters, Bradshaw, et al., 2010a).

BBBF was based on a universal prevention approach. That is, rather than identifying particular children and families who were at risk for adverse outcomes, the project focused on communities in Ontario that were defined as "at risk." These communities were considered economically disadvantaged: they had high numbers of families living below the low-income line, high levels of unemployment, high numbers of children on social assistance, and high numbers of children living in subsidized housing. In addition, factors existed that were considered indicators for poor child development: infant mortality, low birth weight, lone-parent families, adolescent pregnancy, low maternal educational achievement, high

rates of high school dropout, and immigration (see Peters, Bradshaw, et al., 2010 for further details). The three Ontario sites chosen for participation in BBBF were Cornwall, Highfield (in the greater Toronto area), and Sudbury. Following selection of the BBBF sites, two comparison sites with similar characteristics were selected: Ottawa-Vanier and Etobicoke (in Toronto).

All children between the ages of 4 and 8 who were living in one of the selected neighbourhoods could participate in the program, as could the children's families. Drawing on the ecological model of development advanced by Bronfenbrenner (detailed in Chapter 9), the project targeted child development in a variety of areas, including physical, social, and cognitive development, and mental health. Furthermore, in keeping with the ecological model, family, school, and neighbourhoods were targeted for change. The specific programming delivered at each site varied; it was developed within the specific communities, with extensive consultation from community members. The table to the right provides a list of programs that were offered at all three sites. Programming was offered for a total of 4 years.

The impact of programming was measured at Grades 3, 6, and 9. For the purposes of this chapter, we will focus on school functioning and academic achievement, which were assessed at Grades 6 and 9. At Grade 6, children from the BBBF sites had higher math achievement and fewer school suspensions than those from the comparison sites. At Grade 9, children in the BBBF programs required fewer special education services, were less likely to repeat grades, and were rated by teachers as better prepared to learn and have greater potential to go further in school (Peters, Bradshaw, et al., 2010a). A recent follow-up of children at

Better Beginnings, Better Futures Programs Common to the Three Sites

Program type	Program Description
Child-focused	In-class and in-school programs
	Child-care enhancements
	Before and after school activities
	School "breakfast club"
	Recreation programs
Parent-focused	Home visitors
	Parent support groups
	Parenting workshops
	One-on-one support
	Child care for parent relief
Family- and community-focused	Community leadership development
	Special community events and celebrations
	Safety initiatives in neighbourhood
	Community field trips
	Adult education
	Family camps
	Outreach to families

Source: Peters et al., 2010

Grade 12 indicated that the positive effects continued, with children from BBBF sites requiring fewer special education services (Peters, Nelson, et al., 2010b).

One successful early intervention program in the United States was the Carolina Abecedarian Project, which operated at one North Carolina site between 1972 and 1985. In the Abecedarian (pronounced "a-bee-cee-darian") program, children who were at high risk for poor outcomes due to

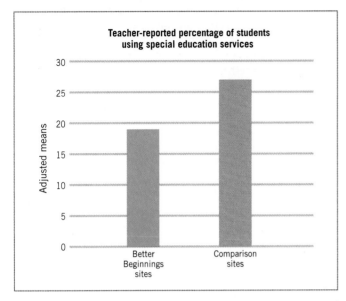

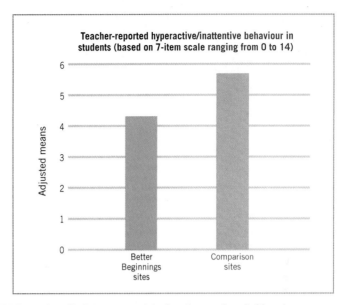

As illustrated in these graphs, at Grade 9, children who had taken part in BBBF were less likely to use special education services (left) and display hyperactive/inattentive behaviours in class (right) than children from comparably disadvantaged backgrounds from the comparison sites. The benefits of participating in BBBF remained evident 6 years after the end of the program. (Data from Roche, Petrunka, & Peters, 2008)

low family income, the absence of a father in the home, low maternal IQ score and education, and other factors began attending a special daycare centre by the time they were 6-month-olds and continued to do so through the age of 5 years. Children aged 3 years and younger received a program that emphasized general social, cognitive, and motor development; for 4- and 5-year-olds, the program also provided systematic instruction in math, science, reading, and music. At all ages, the program emphasized language development and ensured extensive verbal communication between teachers and children. Program personnel also worked with the children's mothers outside the daycare centre to improve their understanding of child development. Families of children in the experimental program were provided with nutritional supplements and access to high-quality health care. Families of children in a comparison group received similar nutritional and health benefits, but the children did not attend the daycare centre.

This well-planned, multi-faceted program proved to have lasting positive effects on the IQ scores and achievement levels of children in the experimental group. At the age of 21 years, 15 years after the program had ended, these children had mean IQ scores 5 points higher than the children in the control group: 90 versus 85 (F. A. Campbell et al., 2001). Participants' achievement test scores in math and reading were also higher. As with less encompassing intervention programs, fewer participants were ever held back in school or placed in special education classes. At age 30, a higher percentage of children in the experimental group than in the control group had graduated from college: 23% versus 6% (F. A. Campbell et al., 2012). A replication of the program demonstrated that the lower the mother's educational level, the greater the difference the program made (Ramey & Ramey, 2004).

What lessons can be drawn from these early intervention projects? One important lesson is the benefit of starting

interventions early and continuing them for substantial periods. A version of the Abecedarian program that ended at age 3 did not produce long-term effects on intelligence, nor did a program that provided educational support from kindergarten through Grade 2 (Burchinal et al., 1997; Ramey et al., 2000). A more recent study demonstrated that two years, versus one year, of enhanced preschool programming led to greater improvements in the early literacy and numeracy skills of economically disadvantaged children (Domitrovich et al., 2013). A second crucial lesson is that the gains produced by successful early-intervention programs are likely due at least as much to improvements in children's self-control and perseverance as to changes in children's IQ scores (Heckman, 2011; Knudsen et al., 2006). Probably the most important lesson is the most basic: it is possible to design interventions that have substantial, lasting, positive effects on economically disadvantaged children's intellectual development.

review:

review:

The development of intelligence is influenced by qualities of the child, the immediate environment, and the broader society. The child's genetic inheritance exerts a large influence, especially for children from middle- and upper-income families; this influence steadily increases over the course of development. The intellectual environment provided by the child's family and the schooling the child encounters are also influential, as are the family's economic status and educational level and whether one or two parents are present. For children from low-income backgrounds, these shared aspects of the environment exert a stronger influence than do children's genes on differences in their intellectual development. The impact of society is evident in the Flynn effect, which reflects the consistent rise in IQ scores in all economically advanced countries.

Some projects have failed to produce enduring gains in poor children's IQ and achievement test scores, which has led some evaluators to conclude that intelligence is unalterable. However, two programs, the Better Beginnings, Better Futures project and the Carolina Abecedarian Project, report enduring positive effects on school achievement and other areas of functioning.

Mozart's musical genius was evident from early in childhood, leading some of the greatest musicians of his day to play music with him when he was still a child.

multiple intelligences theory ■ Gardner's theory of intellect, based on the view that people possess at least eight types of intelligence.

Alternative Perspectives on Intelligence

The discussions of intellectual development in this chapter have relied on IQ tests as their main measure. Research using these tests has revealed a great deal about the development of intelligence. However, a number of contemporary theorists have noted that many important aspects of intelligence are not measured by IQ tests. The tests assess verbal, mathematical, and spatial capabilities, but they do not directly examine other abilities that seem to be inherent parts of intelligence: creativity, social understanding, knowledge of one's own strengths and weaknesses, and so on. This perspective has led Howard Gardner and Robert Sternberg to formulate theories of intelligence that encompass a wider range of human abilities than do traditional theories.

Howard Gardner (1993) labelled his approach **multiple intelligences theory.** Its basic claim is that people possess eight kinds of intelligence: the linguistic, logical–mathematical, and spatial abilities emphasized in previous theories and measured on IQ tests, as well as musical, naturalistic, bodily–kinesthetic, intrapersonal, and interpersonal abilities (see Table 8.3).

Gardner used several types of evidence to arrive at this set of intelligences. One involved deficits shown by people with brain damage. For example, some patients with brain damage function well in most respects but have no understanding of other people (Damasio, 1999). This phenomenon suggested to Gardner that interpersonal intelligence was distinct from other types of intelligence. A second type of evidence that Gardner used to identify this set of intelligences was the existence of prodigies—people who, from early in life, show exceptional ability in one area but not necessarily in others. One such example is Wolfgang Amadeus Mozart, who displayed musical genius while still a child but was unexceptional in many other ways. The existence of highly specialized musical talents such as Mozart's provides evidence for viewing musical ability as a separate intelligence. Although Gardner's theory of multiple intelligences is backed by less supporting evidence than traditional theories of intelligence, its optimistic message—that children have a variety of strengths on which parents and teachers can build—has led to its having a large influence on education.

TABLE 8.3

Gardner's Theory of Multiple Intelligences

Type of Intelligence	Description	Examples
Linguistic intelligence	Sensitivity to the meanings and sounds of words; mastery of syntax; appreciation of the ways language can be used	Poet, political speaker, teacher
Logical–mathematical intelligence	Understanding of objects and symbols, of the actions that can be performed on them, and of the relations between these actions; ability for abstraction; ability to identify problems and seek explanations	Mathematician, scientist
Spatial intelligence	Capacity to perceive the visual world accurately, to perform transformations upon perceptions, and to re-create aspects of visual experience in the absence of physical stimuli; sensitivity to tension, balance, and composition; ability to detect similar patterns	Artist, engineer, chess master
Musical intelligence	Sensitivity to individual tones and phrases of music; an understanding of ways to combine tones and phrases into larger musical rhythms and structures; awareness of emotional aspects of music	Musician, composer
Naturalistic intelligence	Sensitivity to, and understanding of, plants, animals, and other aspects of nature	Biologist, farmer, conservationist
Bodily–kinesthetic intelligence	Use of one's body in highly skilled ways for expressive or goal-directed purposes; capacity to handle objects skilfully	Dancer, athlete, actor
Intrapersonal intelligence	Access to one's own feelings; ability to draw on one's emotions to guide and understand one's behaviour	Novelist, therapist, parent
Interpersonal intelligence	Ability to notice and make distinctions among the moods, temperaments, motivations, and intentions of other people and potentially to act on this knowledge	Political leader, religious leader, parent, teacher, therapist

Source: H. Gardner, 1993

Robert Sternberg (1999) also argued that the emphasis of IQ tests on the type of intelligence needed to succeed in school is too narrow. However, the alternative view of intelligence that he proposed differs from that proposed by Gardner. Sternberg's **theory of successful intelligence** envisions intelligence as "the ability to achieve success in life, given one's personal standards, within one's sociocultural context" (p. 4). In his view, success in life reflects people's ability to build on their strengths, to compensate for their weaknesses, and to select environments in which they can succeed. When people choose a job, for instance, their understanding of the conditions that will motivate them may be crucial to their success.

Sternberg proposed that success in life depends on three types of abilities: analytic, practical, and creative. *Analytic abilities* involve the linguistic, mathematical, and spatial skills that are measured by traditional intelligence tests. *Practical abilities* involve reasoning about everyday problems, such as how to resolve conflicts with other people. *Creative abilities* involve intellectual flexibility and innovation that allow adaptation to novel circumstances.

The theories proposed by Gardner and Sternberg have inspired a rethinking of long-held assumptions about intelligence. Intelligence and success in life clearly involve a broader range of capabilities than traditional intelligence tests measure, and measuring these broader capabilities may allow a more encompassing assessment of intelligence. There is not now, nor will there ever be, a single correct theory of intelligence, nor a single best measure of it. What is possible is a variety of theories, and tests based on them, that together reveal the varied ways in which people can be intelligent.

review:

Howard Gardner and Robert Sternberg have formulated novel theories of intelligence. Gardner's multiple intelligences theory proposes that there are eight intelligences: linguistic, logical–mathematical, spatial, musical, naturalistic, bodily–kinesthetic, intrapersonal, and interpersonal. Sternberg's theory of successful intelligence proposes that success in life depends on three types of abilities: analytic, practical, and creative. Both theories conceive of intelligence as a broader set of abilities than those included in traditional theories.

theory of successful intelligence ■ Sternberg's theory of intellect, based on the view that intelligence is the ability to achieve success in life.

phonemic awareness ■ Ability to identify component sounds within words.

phonological recoding skills ■ Ability to translate letters into sounds and to blend sounds into words; informally called *sounding out*.

Acquisition of Academic Skills: Reading, Writing, and Mathematics

One important goal to which children apply their intelligence is learning the skills and concepts taught at school. Because these skills and concepts are necessary for normal intellectual development in modern societies, because they are central to success in adulthood, and because they can be difficult to master, children spend more than 2000 days in school from Grades 1 through 12. Much of this time is devoted to acquiring proficiency in reading, writing, and mathematics. In this section, we focus on how children learn these skills, why some children have such difficulty mastering them, and how children's learning can be improved.

Reading

Many children learn to read effortlessly, but others do not. You can no doubt remember the painful times classmates—and perhaps you, yourself—seemed to take forever to read aloud simple sentences, even in Grades 2 and 3. Why is it that some children learn to read so easily, whereas others experience great difficulty and frustration? To answer this question, we must examine the typical path of reading development as well as how and why children deviate from it.

Chall (1979) described five stages of reading development. These stages provide a good overview of the typical path to mastery:

1. *Stage 0* (birth until the beginning of Grade 1): During this time, many children acquire key prerequisites for reading. These include knowing the letters of the alphabet and gaining **phonemic awareness,** that is, knowledge of the individual sounds within words.

2. *Stage 1* (Grades 1 and 2): Children acquire **phonological recoding skills,** the ability to translate letters into sounds and to blend the sounds into words (informally referred to as "sounding out").

3. *Stage 2* (Grades 2 and 3): Children gain fluency in reading simple material.

4. *Stage 3* (Grades 4 through 8): Children become able to acquire reasonably complex, new information from written text. To quote Chall, "In the primary grades, children learn to read; in the higher grades, they read to learn" (1979, p. 24).

5. *Stage 4* (Grades 8 through 12): Adolescents acquire skill not only in understanding information presented from a single perspective but also in coordinating multiple perspectives. This ability enables them to appreciate the subtleties in sophisticated novels and plays, which almost always include multiple viewpoints.

This description of developmental stages provides a general sense of the reading acquisition process and a framework for understanding how particular developments fit into the broader picture.

Prereading Skills

Before formal schooling begins, preschoolers begin to develop important skills that set the stage for the development of reading. Many of these important skills are acquired through the home or preschool literacy environment. Through looking at books and having books read to them, preschoolers acquire basic information about reading. They learn that (in English and other European languages) text is read from left to right; that after they reach the right end of a line, the text continues at the extreme left of the line below; and that words are separated by small spaces.

Having books in the home and being read to, however, are not enough. As Carleton University researchers Monique Sénéchal and Jo-Anne LeFevre, and University of Alberta and University of British Columbia researchers Linda Phillips, Stephen Norris, and Jim Anderson, have demonstrated, these activities alone are not directly related to eventual reading outcomes (Phillips, Norris, & Anderson, 2008; Sénéchal & LeFevre, 2002). For example, in one comprehensive Ontario study, general reading activities at home did not predict kindergarten children's early literacy skills (Evans, Shaw, & Bell, 2007). Instead, the frequency with which parents taught their young children letters and sounds of letters, and engaged in printing activities, predicted how much children knew about letter names and sounds—key ingredients for later literacy. Although kindergartners' mastery of letter names is positively correlated with their later reading achievement through at least Grade 7 (Sénéchal & LeFevre, 2002; Vellutino & Scanlon, 1987), there does not appear to be a causal relation between the two: teaching the *names* of the letters to randomly chosen preschoolers does not increase their subsequent reading achievement (Piasta & Wagner, 2010). Instead, it appears that other variables, such as children's interest in books and parents' interest in and expectations about their children's reading, stimulate both early knowledge of the alphabet and later high reading achievement (Martini & Sénéchal, 2012).

Phonemic awareness, on the other hand, is both correlated with later reading achievement and a cause of it. To measure awareness of the component sounds within words, researchers ask children to decide whether two words start with the same sound, to identify component sounds within a word, and to indicate what would remain if a given sound were removed from a word. Kindergartners' performance on these measures of phonemic awareness is the strongest predictor of their ability to sound out and spell words in the early grades—stronger even than IQ score or social class background (Nation, 2008; Rayner et al., 2001)—and it continues to be related to reading achievement as much as 11 years later, above and beyond the influence of the child's social class background (MacDonald & Cornwall, 1995).

Even more impressive, a review of 52 well-controlled experimental studies indicated that teaching phonemic-awareness skills to 4- and 5-year-olds causes them to become better readers and spellers, with the effects enduring for years after the training (National Reading Panel, 2000). Instructing young children to break words into their component sounds and then writing the letter that best matches each successive sound causes especially large gains in spelling (Levin & Aram, 2013).

Although explicit training can help foster phonemic awareness, most children do not receive such training. Where, then, does phonemic awareness come from in the natural environment? One relevant experience is hearing nursery rhymes. Many nursery rhymes highlight the contribution of individual sounds to differences among words (e.g., "I do not like green eggs and *ham;* I do not like them, *Sam* I *am.*") Consistent with this hypothesis, 3-year-olds' knowledge of nursery rhymes correlates positively with their later phonemic awareness, above and beyond their IQ scores and their mother's educational level (Maclean, Bryant, & Bradley, 1987). Other factors that contribute to the development of phonemic awareness include growth of working memory, increasingly efficient processing of language, and, especially, reading itself (Anthony & Francis, 2005; McBride-Chang, 2004). Children with greater phonemic awareness read more and read better, which, in turn, leads to further increases in their phonemic awareness and in the quantity and quality of their reading.

The appeal of nursery rhymes to young children has always been obvious, but only recently have the benefits of such rhymes for phonemic awareness and reading acquisition become known.

visually based retrieval ■ Proceeding directly from the visual form of a word to its meaning.

strategy–choice process ■ Procedure for selecting among alternative ways of solving problems.

Word Identification

Rapid, effortless word identification is crucial not only to reading comprehension but also to its enjoyment. One remarkable finding makes the point: 40% of Grade 4 students who were poor at identifying words said they would rather clean their rooms than read (Juel, 1988). One child went as far as to volunteer, "I'd rather clean the mould around the bathtub than read." Thus, not only does poor word identification make the reading process slow and laborious, it also leads children to read no more than is absolutely necessary, which, in turn, hinders improvement in their reading skills.

Words can be identified in two main ways: *phonological recoding* and *visually based retrieval*. As previously indicated, phonological recoding involves converting the visual form of a word into a verbal, speech-like form and using the speech-like form to determine the word's meaning. **Visually based retrieval** involves processing a word's meaning directly from its visual form.

Most young children use both approaches (Share, 2004), choosing adaptively between them from Grade 1 onward. They do so through a **strategy–choice process,** in which they choose the fastest approach that is likely to allow correct word identification. In the context of reading, this means that on easy words, children rely heavily on the fast but not always accurate approach of visually based retrieval; on hard words, they resort to the slower but surer strategy of phonological recoding. As shown in Figure 8.9, 1st graders are very skillful in adjusting their strategies to the difficulty of a particular word.

FIGURE 8.9 Young children's strategy choices in reading A strong positive correlation exists between the difficulty of a word, as defined by the percentage of errors children make on it, and the frequency of young children's use of an overt strategy, such as audible phonological recoding, to read it. Thus, on words that 1st graders find easy, such as "in," they generally retrieve the word's pronunciation, but on words they find difficult, such as "parade," they often use overt strategies such as sounding out. (Siegler, 1986)

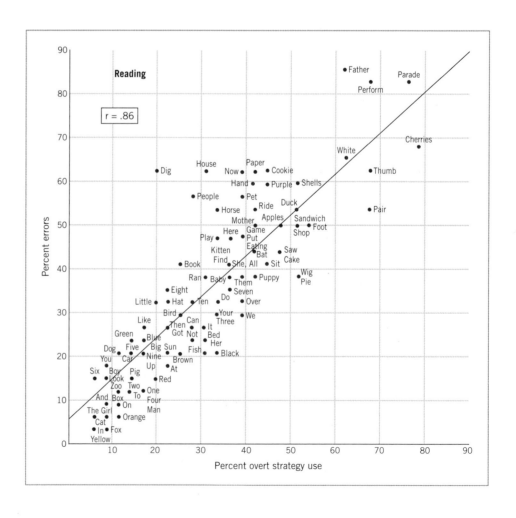

The mechanisms underlying this adaptive strategy choice involve a form of associative learning in which children's past behaviour shapes their future behaviour (Siegler, 1996). Beginning readers rely heavily on phonological recoding, because the associations between words' visual forms and their sounds are too weak to allow much use of retrieval. Correct use of phonological recoding increases the associations between words' visual forms and their sounds, which in turn allows greater use of visually based retrieval. Consistent with this view, the shift to retrieval occurs most rapidly for words on which children most often execute phonological recoding correctly—words that are short, that have regular letter–sound relations, and that children encounter frequently. Also consistent with this view, children who are better at phonological recoding stop using that approach earlier, because their past success with it enables them to shift more rapidly to visually based retrieval. A third correct implication is that reading instruction that emphasizes phonics, and the strategy of phonological recoding, should help produce fast and accurate word identification (M. J. Adams, Treiman, & Pressley, 1998; Xue & Meisels, 2004).

With age and experience, vocabulary knowledge becomes an increasingly important influence on word identification, particularly on words with irregular sound–symbol correspondences (Nation, 2008). However, phonological recoding skill also continues to be important, even for adults when they encounter unfamiliar words. Box 8.3 discusses the relation between poor phonological recoding skills and the reading disability known as *dyslexia*.

Comprehension

The point of learning to read individual words is to comprehend the text in which the words appear. Reading comprehension involves forming a **mental model** to represent the situation or idea being depicted in the text and continuously updating it as new information appears (Oakhill & Cain, 2000). All the types of mental operations that influence cognitive development in general—basic processes, strategies, metacognition (knowledge about people's thinking), and content knowledge—also influence the development of reading comprehension.

Basic processes such as encoding (identification of key features of an object or event) and automatization (executing a process with minimal demands on cognitive resources) are crucial to reading comprehension. The reason is simple: children who are able to identify the key features of stories will understand the story better, and children who are able to automatically identify the key features of words will have more cognitive resources left to devote to comprehension. Fast, accurate word identification correlates positively with reading comprehension at all points from Grade 1 through adulthood (Cunningham & Stanovich, 1997).

Development of reading comprehension is also aided by acquisition of reading strategies. For example, good readers proceed slowly when they need to master written material in depth and speed up when they need only a rough sense of it (Pressley & Hilden, 2006). Proficiency in making such adjustments develops surprisingly late. Even when 10-year-olds are told that some material is crucial and other material is not, they tend to read all the material at the same speed. In contrast, 14-year-olds skim the non-essential parts and spend more time on the important ones (Kobasigawa, Ransom, & Holland, 1980).

Increasing metacognitive knowledge also contributes to improved reading comprehension. With age and experience, readers increasingly monitor their ongoing understanding and reread passages they do not understand (Nicholson, 1999). Such **comprehension monitoring** differentiates good readers from poor ones at all ages

mental model ■ Cognitive processes used to represent a situation or sequence of events.

comprehension monitoring ■ Process of keeping track of one's understanding of a verbal description or text.

BOX 8.3: **Individual differences**

DYSLEXIA

Some children of normal intelligence whose parents encourage reading nonetheless read very poorly. Such poor reading despite normal intelligence is referred to as **dyslexia** and affects 5% to 10% of children (Anthony & Francis, 2005). The causes of dyslexia are not well understood, but genetics are clearly part of the story. If one of a pair of monozygotic twins is diagnosed as dyslexic, the probability of the other twin receiving a similar diagnosis is 84%, whereas if the twins are dizygotic, the corresponding probability is 48% (Kovas & Plomin, 2007; Oliver et al., 2004). The extent of genetic influences varies with parental educational level: as with IQ score, genetic influences on dyslexia are larger with children of highly educated parents than with children of less educated parents (Friend, DeFries, & Olson, 2008).

At a cognitive level of analysis, dyslexia stems primarily from weak ability to discriminate between phonemes, from poor short-term memory for verbal material (as indicated, for example, by poor ability to recall an arbitrary list of words), and from slow recall of the names of objects (Vellutino, Scanlon, & Spearing, 1995; Wimmer, Mayringer, & Raberger, 1999). Determining the sounds that go with vowels is especially difficult for children with dyslexia, at least in English, where a single vowel can be pronounced in many ways (consider the sounds that accompany the letter "a" in "ha," "hat," "hall," and "hate.") Because of these weaknesses, dyslexic children have great difficulty mastering the letter–sound correspondences used in phonological recoding, especially in languages, such as English, with irregular sound–symbol correspondences (Sprenger-Charolles, 2004).

For instance, as shown in the figure, when asked to read pseudowords such as "parding," dyslexic 13- and 14-year-olds perform at the same level as typical 7- and 8-year-olds (Siegel, 1993). As would be expected from the strategy–choice model described on page 326, this difficulty with phonological processing causes most dyslexic children to be poor at visually based retrieval, as well as at sounding out words (Manis et al., 1996).

The problem can be a lasting one: most individuals who have poor phonological processing skills in early elementary school remain poor readers as adults (Wagner et al., 1997). This is especially the case for children who are from disadvantaged backgrounds and who attend inferior schools: children with dyslexia who come from more advantaged family backgrounds and who attend better schools are more likely to show substantial improvements (S. E. Shaywitz, Mody, & Shaywitz, 2006).

Studies of brain functioning support the view that poor phonological processing is at the heart of dyslexia. When dyslexic children read, two areas of their brains are less active than the corresponding areas in typical children reading the same words (Schlaggar & Church, 2009; Tanaka et al., 2011). One such area is directly involved in discriminating phonemes; the other area is involved in integrating visual and auditory data (in this case, integrating letters on the page with accompanying sounds).

How can dyslexic children be helped? One tempting idea is that because these children have difficulty learning phonics, they would learn better through an approach that de-emphasizes letter–sound relations and instead emphasizes either visually based retrieval or reliance on context. These alternative methods work poorly, however (Lyon, 1995); there is simply no substitute for

dyslexia ■ Inability to read and spell well despite having normal intelligence.

from Grade 1 through adulthood. Instructional approaches that focus on comprehension monitoring and other metacognitive skills, such as anticipating questions that a teacher might ask about the material, improve reading comprehension (Magnusson & Palincsar, 2001; Rosenshine & Meister, 1994).

Another powerful influence on the development of reading comprehension is increasing content knowledge. Relevant content knowledge frees cognitive resources for focusing on what is new or complex in the text and allows readers to draw reasonable inferences about information left unstated. Thus, when reading the headline "Leafs thump Habs," readers knowledgeable about hockey realize that the headline concerns a hockey game; it is unclear how readers who lack hockey knowledge would interpret such a headline.

The path to strong or weak reading comprehension begins even before children start school. Hearing stories told or read by their parents helps preschoolers learn how such stories tend to go, facilitating their understanding of new stories once they read themselves. It also enhances their general level of language development (Raikes et al., 2006; Whitehurst & Lonigan, 1998). The amount that parents read to their children during the preschool years also partially accounts for the differences between the reading comprehension skills of children from middle- and

being able to sound out unfamiliar words. Indeed, what seems to work best is to teach children with dyslexia to use strategies that enhance their phonological recoding (Lovett et al., 1994). Effective strategies include drawing analogies to known words with similar spellings; generating alternative pronunciations of vowels when the first attempt at sounding out does not yield a plausible word; and, with long words, "peeling off" prefixes and suffixes and then trying to identify the rest of the word. Another promising strategy involves drawing upon children's *invented spelling:* their early, often unconventional, attempts to spell words (e.g., "prpul" for "purple"). A recent study found that kindergarteners in Ottawa who were at risk for poor reading achievement benefitted significantly from an 8-week program that capitalized on this invented spelling, offering individualized feedback to make the spelling more phonologically sensitive (Sénéchal et al., 2012). For example, a child who spelled the word "lady" as "ledi" would be shown a spelling with one change at a time (e.g., replacing the "e" in "ledi" with an "a" and then, on another occasion, replacing the "i" with a "y").

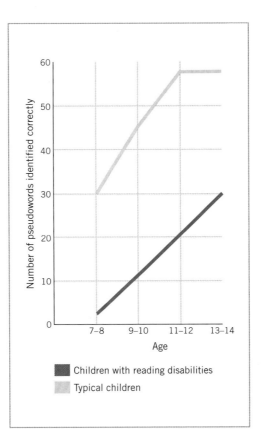

Children with reading disabilities

Typical children

This chart shows the number of pseudowords identified correctly by 7- to 14-year-olds with and without reading disabilities. Note that 13- and 14-year-olds with reading disabilities correctly identified no more items than did typical 7- and 8-year-olds. The poor phonological recoding skills of children with reading disabilities lead them to have special difficulty with pseudowords that, because they are totally unfamiliar, can be pronounced only by using phonological recoding. (Data from Siegel, 1993)

low-income families. For example, a study conducted in Israel showed that in an affluent school district with high reading achievement scores, 96% of parents of preschoolers read to them daily. The same was true of only 15% of parents of preschoolers in a poor district with low scores (Feitelson & Goldstein, 1986).

Although the straightforward implication of these findings is that if preschoolers from lower-income families were read to daily, they too would become better readers, this is only part of the equation. As noted above, how parents engage their children while reading to them also matters (Phillips et al., 2008). Thus, encouraging lower-income parents to actively engage their children in the reading process, such as by asking them to relate what is being read to their own experiences or to explain the characters' goals and motivations, helps even more (Zevenbergen & Whitehurst, 2003). Persuading parents to enrol in programs that teach them about the importance of reading to their children on a daily basis is not easy because of time demands and, in many cases, the pressures of being a single parent (Whitehurst et al., 1999); but when parents do so, their children's reading comprehension benefits.

Once children enter school, the amount of material they read varies greatly and has a large effect on their reading comprehension. For instance, 5th graders whose reading achievement test scores are in the 90th percentile for their grade report roughly 200 times as much discretionary reading as peers who score in the 10th percentile (Anderson, Wilson, & Fielding, 1988). High reading ability leads children to read more; children who read more, in turn, show greater gains over time in reading comprehension than do children of equal ability who read less (Guthrie et al., 1999).

Individual Differences

Individual differences in reading ability tend to be stable over time. Children who have relatively advanced reading skills when they enter kindergarten tend to be better readers through elementary, middle, and high school (Duncan et al., 2007; Harlaar, Dale, & Plomin, 2007). Studies of adoptive and non-adoptive siblings and of monozygotic and dizygotic twins indicate that these continuities of individual differences reflect both shared genes and shared environments (Petrill et al., 2007; Wadsworth et al., 2006). As we have noted, genetic and environmental influences are mutually reinforcing: parents who are good and frequent readers are likely to provide both genes and environments that make it likely that their children will be relatively good readers when they are young, which makes it more likely that the children will seek out reading opportunities, which will further improve their reading, and so on (Petrill et al., 2005).

Writing

Much less is known about the development of children's writing than about the development of their reading, but what is known shows interesting parallels between the two.

Prewriting Skills

The development of writing, like the development of reading, begins before children receive formal schooling. Figure 8.10 displays writing efforts typical of a 3½-year-old. The marks are not conventional letters of the alphabet, but they look vaguely like them and are arranged along a roughly horizontal line. By age 4, children's "writing" is sufficiently advanced that adults have no trouble distinguishing it from the figures 4-year-olds produce when asked to draw a flower or a house (Tolchinsky, 2003).

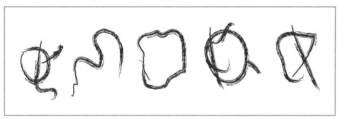

FIGURE 8.10 A 3½-year-old's effort at writing The child's symbols, although unconventional, indicate an understanding that words require separate symbols.

Preschoolers' "writing" indicates that they expect meaning to be reflected in print. They use more marks to represent words that signify many objects, such as "forest," than to represent words that signify a single object, such as "tree" (Levin & Korat, 1993). Similarly, when asked to guess which of several words is the name for a particular object, they generally choose longer words for larger objects (Bialystok, 2000). Although written language does not work this way, the children's guess seems reasonable.

Generating Written Text

Learning to write, in the sense of writing an essay or story, is a good deal more difficult than learning to read. This is not surprising, because writing requires focusing simultaneously on numerous goals, both low level and high level. The low-level goals include forming letters, spelling words, and using correct capitalization and punctuation. The high-level goals include making arguments comprehensible without the intonations and gestures that help us communicate when we speak, organizing individual points in a coherent framework, and providing the background information that readers need to understand the writing (Berninger & Richards, 2002). The difficulties children have in meeting both the low-level and high-level goals result in their often writing the type of flat story illustrated in Figure 8.11.

As with development of reading comprehension, growth of writing proficiency reflects improvements in basic processes, strategies, metacognition, and content knowledge. Automatizing low-level skills, such as spelling and punctuation, aids writing not only because correct spelling and punctuation make writing easier to understand but also because automatizing the low-level skills frees cognitive resources for pursuing the higher-level communicative goals of writing. Consistent with this conclusion, children's proficiency at low-level skills such as spelling correlates positively with the quality of the children's essays (Juel, 1994).

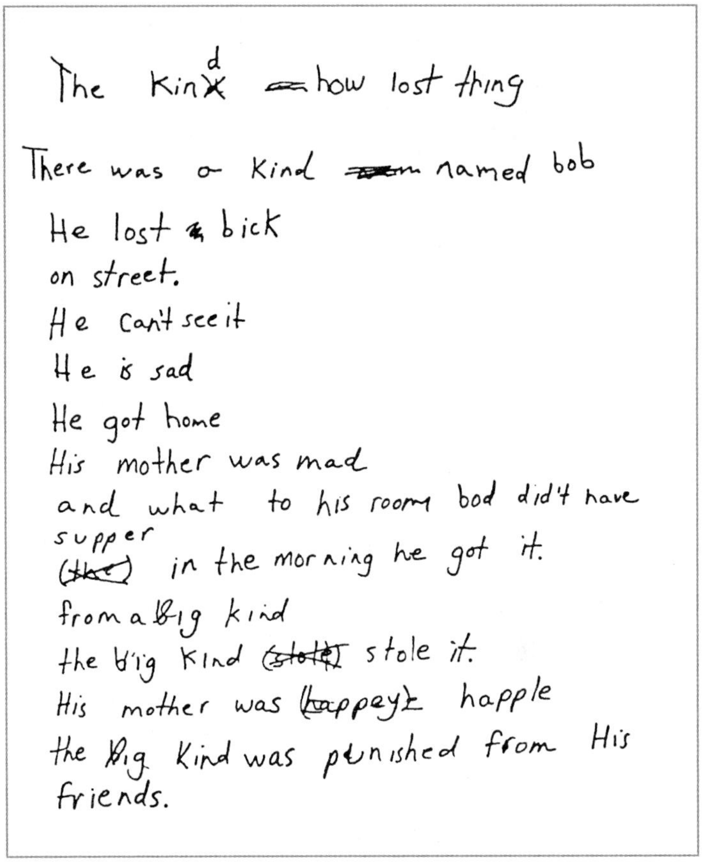

Acquisition of strategies also contributes to improvements in writing. One common strategy is to sequence high-level goals in a standard organization, or **script,** a set of actions or events that occurs repeatedly. Harriet Waters, a psychologist whose proud mother saved all her daughter's "class news" assignments from Grade 2, was one child who employed such an approach (Waters, 1980). As shown in Table 8.4, in each class news essay, Waters first noted the date, then described the weather, and then discussed events of the school day—a strategy that greatly simplified her writing task. For older children, formulating outlines serves a similar purpose of dividing the task of writing into manageable parts: first figure out what you want to say, then figure out the best order for making your main points, then figure out how to make each point.

Metacognitive understanding plays several crucial roles in writing. Perhaps the most basic type of metacognitive understanding is recognizing that readers may not have the same knowledge as the writer and that one therefore should include all the information that readers will need to allow them to grasp what is being said. Good writers consistently exhibit such understanding by high school; poor writers often do not (Berninger & Richards, 2002). A second crucial type of metacognitive knowledge involves understanding the need to plan one's writing rather than just jumping in and starting to write. Good writers spend much more time than do poor writers planning what they will say before they begin writing—making notes, constructing outlines, and so on (Kellogg, 1994). Understanding the need for revision is a third key type of metacognitive knowledge. Good writers spend more time revising their already relatively good first drafts than poor writers spend revising their poorer ones (Fitzgerald, 1992).

Fortunately, as with reading, instruction aimed at inculcating metacognitive understanding can enhance writing skills (S. Graham & Harris, 1996). In particular, the writing of both typical children and children with learning disabilities

The Kin^d ⟶ how lost thing

There was a Kind ~~~~ named bob
He lost a bick
on street.
He can't see it
He is sad
He got home
His mother was mad
and what to his room bod did't have
supper
(the) in the morning he got it.
from a big kind
the big kind (stole) stole it.
His mother was (happey) happle
the big kind was punished from His
friends.

FIGURE 8.11 A 4th grader's story The intended title of this story was *The Kid Who Lost Things.* See if you can figure out the rest. (From Berninger & Richards, 2002)

script ■ Typical sequence of actions used to organize and interpret repeated events, such as eating at restaurants, going to doctors' appointments, and writing reports.

TABLE 8.4

Stories Written at Beginning, Middle, and End of Year for Class News Assignment

SEPTEMBER 24, 1956

Today is Monday, September, 24, 1956. It is a rainy day. We hope the sun will shine. We got new spelling books. We had our pictures taken. We sang Happy Birthday to Barbara.

JANUARY 22, 1957

Today is Tuesday, January 22, 1957. It is a foggy day. We must be careful crossing the road. This morning, we had music. We learned a new song. Linda is absent. We hope she comes back soon. We had arithmetic. We made believe that we were buying candy. We had fun. We work in our English books. We learned when to use is and are.

MAY 27, 1957

Today is Monday, May 27, 1957. It is a warm, cloudy day. We hope the sun comes out. This afternoon, we had music. We enjoyed it. We went out to play. Carole is absent. We hope she comes back soon. We had a spelling lesson, we learned about a dozen. Tomorrow we shall have show and tell. Some of us have spelling sentences to do for homework. Danny brought in a cocoon. It will turn into a butterfly.

Source: H. S. Waters, 1980

improves when they are taught to revise other children's work and to ask themselves several basic questions: Who is the main character in this story? What does the main character do? How do the other characters respond? How does the main character respond to the other characters' responses? What happens in the end? Asking children to reflect on the relative quality of essays written by other children and on why some essays are better than others also can improve writing (Braaksma et al., 2004).

Finally, as in reading, content knowledge plays a crucial role in writing. Children generally write better when they are familiar with the topic than when they are not (Bereiter & Scardamalia, 1982). Thus, the standard advice "Write what you know" applies to children as well as to aspiring authors.

Mathematics

In Chapter 7, we examined infants' early-developing nonverbal number sense and the emergence of counting between age 2 and 4 years. Here we examine the development of arithmetic, which builds on both types of knowledge.

Arithmetic

People often think of arithmetic learning as a process of rote memorization, but it actually is far more complex and interesting. How well children learn arithmetic depends on the strategies that they use, the precision of their representations of numerical magnitudes, and their understanding of basic mathematical concepts and principles.

Strategies From age 4 or 5 years, when most children begin to learn arithmetic, they use a variety of problem-solving strategies. The most common initial strategies are counting from one (e.g., solving 2 + 2 by putting up two fingers on each hand and counting "1, 2, 3, 4") and retrieval (recalling answers from memory). At first, children can use these strategies only to answer a few simple problems, such as 1 + 2 and 2 + 2, but they gradually expand their use to a wider range of single-digit problems (Geary, 2006).

FIGURE 8.12 **Young children's strategy choices in (a) addition, (b) subtraction, and (c) multiplication** As illustrated previously with reading (Figure 8.9), a strong positive correlation exists between the difficulty of a problem, as defined by the percentage of errors it elicits, and the frequency of using an overt strategy, such as counting on one's fingers. Thus, for problems that 4- and 5-year-olds found easy, such as 2 + 2, they usually used retrieval. For problems they found difficult, such as 4 + 3, they usually used overt strategies, such as counting from 1 (Siegler, 1986).

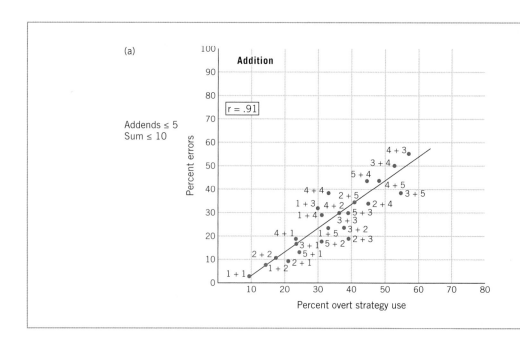

When children begin to do arithmetic on a daily basis, in kindergarten or Grade 1, they add several new strategies. One is *counting on from the larger addend* (e.g., solving 3 + 9 by counting "9, 10, 11, 12"). Another fairly common strategy is *decomposition*, which involves dividing a problem into two easier ones (e.g., solving 3 + 9 by thinking "3 + 10 = 13; 13 − 1 = 12"). Children continue to use the earlier developing strategies as well; most 1st graders use three or more strategies to add single-digit numbers (Siegler, 1987).

Similarly varied strategy use is present on all four arithmetic operations. For example, one study of Canadian schoolchildren demonstrated that they used a wide variety of strategies to solve a multiplication problem such as 3 × 4: they sometimes wrote three 4s and added them, sometimes made three bundles of four hatch marks and counted them, and sometimes retrieved 12 from memory (Mabbott & Bisanz, 2003). Use of these arithmetic strategies is surprisingly enduring: even Canadian university students use strategies other than retrieval on 15% to 30% of single-digit problems (LeFevre et al., 1996).

Just as children's choices among word-identification strategies are highly adaptive, so are their choices among arithmetic strategies (Siegler, 1996). Even 4-year-olds choose in sensible ways, usually solving easy problems such as 2 + 2 quickly and accurately by using retrieval and usually solving harder problems such as 5 + 2 less quickly but still accurately by counting from 1 (Figure 8.12). As children gain experience with the answers to single-digit arithmetic problems, their strategy choices shift increasingly toward using retrieval of those answers. The learning process seems to be the same as with the corresponding shift toward visually based retrieval in reading. The more often children generate the correct answer to a problem, regardless of the strategy they use to generate it, the more often they will be able to retrieve that answer, thereby avoiding the need to use slower counting strategies.

THE FAMILY CIRCUS   **By Bil Keane**

Daddy, how many fingers do I hold up for five and a half?

Learning arithmetic is harder than it looks.

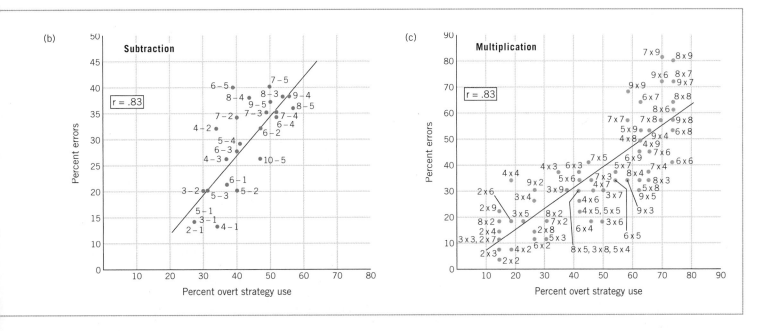

numerical magnitude representations ■ Mental models of the sizes of numbers, ordered along a less-to-more dimension.

symbolic numerical magnitudes ■ Numbers expressed orally or in writing, such as "7" or "seven."

Understanding numerical magnitudes **Numerical magnitude representations** are mental models of the way quantities are ordered along a less-to-more dimension. Regardless of whether "7" refers to a distance (7 kilometres), a weight (7 kilograms), a duration (7 hours), or a set size (7 people), the magnitude represented by "7" is larger than that indicated by "6"—and smaller than that indicated by "8"—of the same unit.

The idea that symbolically expressed numbers represent magnitudes might seem obvious, but accurately linking such numbers and the magnitudes they represent actually constitutes a major challenge over a prolonged period of development. Here are some examples: many preschoolers who can count flawlessly from 1 to 10 do not know whether 4 or 8 indicates the greater number of objects (Le Corre & Carey, 2007); many elementary school children estimate the location of 150 as being near the midpoint of a number line with 0 and 1000 at the two ends (Siegler & Opfer, 2003); many adolescents and adults have no idea whether 3/5 is larger or smaller than 5/11 (Meert, Grégoire, & Noël, 2010). What is lacking in all these cases is accurate representations of numerical magnitudes.

Understanding **symbolic numerical magnitudes** is closely related to understanding arithmetic and indeed to mathematics achievement in general. This relation is evident in arithmetic errors, whose magnitudes usually are close to the correct answer (8 × 7 = 54) rather than far from it (8 × 7 = 24). Similarly, when asked whether answers to arithmetic problems are correct, both children and adults identify incorrect answers more quickly when the magnitude of error is considerable (8 + 4 = 18) than when it is small (8 + 4 = 14) (Ashcraft, 1982; Siegler, 1988).

The range of numbers whose magnitudes children represent reasonably precisely, as indicated by the accuracy of their magnitude comparisons and number-line estimates, changes greatly with age and experience (Figure 8.13). Accuracy of magnitude representations of the numbers 1–10 increases greatly between ages 3 and 6 (Berteletti et al., 2010); that of numbers 1–100, between ages 6 and 8 (Geary et al., 2007); that of numbers 1–1000, between ages 8 and 12 (Siegler & Opfer, 2003); and so on.

Children of any given age differ considerably in their knowledge of numerical magnitudes. These differences are related to the children's overall mathematical knowledge. During elementary school, children who more accurately

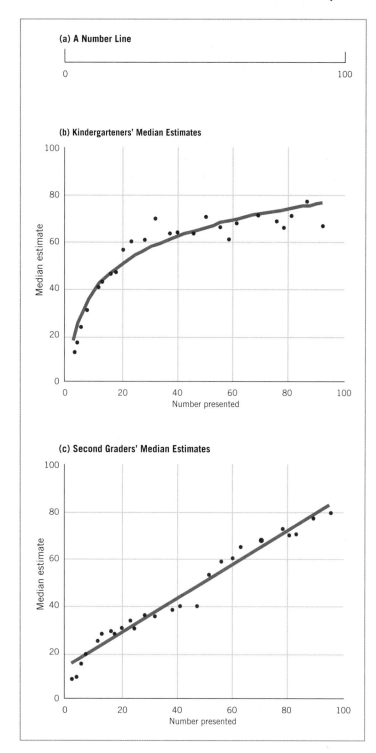

FIGURE 8.13 **The number-line task and typical developmental changes on it** (a) On each trial with a 0–100 number line, children need to estimate a different number's location on the line. (b) Kindergartners' median estimates for each number on the 0–100 number-line task increased with the number being estimated, but in a way that involved overestimates of relatively small numbers and underestimates of large ones, as with a logarithmic function. (c) Second graders' median estimates for each number on the same task increased linearly with the size of the number being estimated, and were quite accurate. (Data from Siegler & Booth, 2004)

estimate whole-number magnitudes on number lines have higher math achievement. During middle school, the same is true for children who accurately estimate fraction magnitudes (Figure 8.14) (D. H. Bailey et al., 2012; Jordan et al., 2013; Siegler & Pyke, 2013).

Part of the reason for this relation is that more accurate magnitude representations help children learn arithmetic. The more precisely a child understands numerical magnitudes, as measured by his or her accuracy in estimating the position of numbers on a number line, the greater the child's arithmetic proficiency (J. L. Booth & Siegler, 2006, 2008; Geary et al., 2007). Moreover, instruction that improves the accuracy of children's symbolic numerical magnitude representations also improves their subsequent learning of arithmetic (J. L. Booth & Siegler, 2008; L. S. Fuchs et al., 2013; Siegler & Ramani, 2009). Accurate magnitude representations may enhance arithmetic learning by suggesting plausible answers and eliminating implausible ones from consideration.

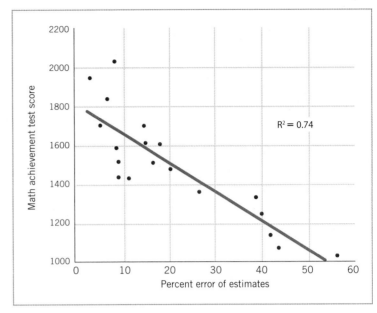

FIGURE 8.14 **Relation between 8th graders' number-line estimation accuracy and their math achievement test scores** Accuracy of number-line estimation is closely related to overall mathematics achievement. These data show the relation between middle school children's math achievement test scores and the accuracy of their estimates of fraction magnitudes. Similar relations have been found between elementary school children's math achievement test scores and their estimates of whole-number magnitudes. The correlation is negative, because estimates that are less distant from numbers' correct locations indicate greater knowledge of the numerical magnitudes. (Data from Siegler, Thompson, & Schneider, 2011)

Conceptual understanding of arithmetic Understanding why some arithmetic procedures are appropriate and others inappropriate poses a major challenge for many children, even those who have memorized the correct procedure. Such conceptual understanding of arithmetic begins developing during the preschool period; for example, many 4-year-olds understand the *commutative law of addition*, the principle that adding a + b is the same as adding b + a (Canobi, Reeve, & Pattison, 2002). Not until years later, however, do they master more advanced arithmetic concepts, such as **mathematical equality**—the idea that the values on the two sides of the equal sign must balance. On almost all problems in which young children encounter the equal sign, numbers appear only to the left of it (e.g., 3 + 4 = __; 3 + 4 + 5 = __). For purposes of solving such problems, children can interpret the equal sign merely as a signal to start adding.

Eventually, however, children encounter arithmetic problems with numbers on both sides of the equal sign, such as 3 + 4 + 5 = __ + 5. As late as Grade 4, most children answer such problems incorrectly (Goldin-Meadow, Cook, & Mitchell, 2009). The most common incorrect approach is to add all the numbers to the left of the equal sign, which in the above problem sum to 12, and to assume that this sum is the answer to the problem. Such errors reflect not only a lack of understanding that the equal sign means that the values on both sides of it must be equivalent but also interference from the vast amount of practice children have had solving typical addition problems, which have no number following the equal sign (McNeil et al., 2011).

In many cases, children's hand gestures reveal that they have somewhat better understanding of mathematical equality than is revealed by their answers or explanations. For example, on the problem 3 + 4 + 5 = __ + 5, children often answer "12" and explain that they solved the problem by adding 3 + 4 + 5, but during their explanation, they point to all four numbers rather than just to the three preceding the equal sign. This pointing suggests an implicit recognition that the fourth number might be important, even though they did not include it in their calculation (Goldin-Meadow & Alibali, 2002). Children who initially show such **gesture–speech mismatches,** in which their gesturing conveys more information than their

mathematical equality ■ Concept that the values on each side of the equal sign must be equivalent.

gesture–speech mismatches ■ Phenomenon in which hand movements and verbal statements convey different ideas.

verbal statements, learn more from instruction on mathematical equality problems than do peers whose gesturing and speech before the instruction were consistent (that is, those who said "12" and pointed only to the three numbers preceding the equal sign).

The gestures play a causal role in learning as well: children who are encouraged to gesture appropriately while explaining answers to mathematical equality problems learn more than children encouraged not to gesture (Goldin-Meadow, Cook, & Mitchell, 2009). The positive relation between gesture–speech mismatches and subsequent learning has emerged on number conservation and physics problems as well as on mathematical equality problems. These findings illustrate a common conclusion: variability of thought and action (for example, generating diverging gestures and speech or advancing multiple explanations of a phenomenon rather than just one) often indicates heightened readiness to learn (Church, 1999; Siegler, 2006; Thelen & Smith, 2006).

Mathematics Anxiety

Many children experience *mathematics anxiety,* a negative emotional state that leads to fear and avoidance of math (Ashcraft & Ridley, 2005). Such anxiety can be evident as early as Grade 1 (Ramirez et al., 2012) and for many people presents a lifelong problem. Mathematics evokes more anxiety than other school subjects, probably because of the unambiguous right/wrong status of answers to many mathematics problems, the widespread belief that mathematics is closely linked to intelligence, and the frustrating periods with no apparent progress that mathematics learning often entails.

Mathematics anxiety is considerably more prevalent in girls than in boys (Devine et al., 2012). It is correlated with poor mathematics achievement, but some people experience it despite having high mathematics achievement and not suffering from high anxiety in general (Ashcraft & Krause, 2007; Maloney & Beilock, 2012). The feelings of dread that math can inspire contribute to the negative outcomes that are feared; a likely reason is that the anxiety reduces the working memory resources needed to solve mathematics problems (Beilock & DeCaro, 2007). Consistent with this interpretation, when presented with mathematics tasks, people with math anxiety show both unusually great activity on the right side of the amygdala, a part of the brain involved in processing negative emotions, and depressed activity in brain areas crucial to working memory (C. B. Young, Wu, & Menon, 2012).

How do some children become anxious about math? The mechanisms are not well understood, but one contributor appears to be the views of adults who are important in the children's lives. Parents and teachers who are themselves anxious about mathematics tend to convey their beliefs and feelings to their children. The problem seems to be especially great for girls whose parents and teachers are pessimistic about girls' mathematical abilities (Beilock et al., 2010; Meece, Wigfield, & Eccles, 1990).

The negative impact of anxiety on mathematics learning has prompted efforts to find ways of reducing it. One promising intervention is surprisingly simple: have students write a brief description of their emotions just before taking a test. Such expressive writing reduces anxiety and boosts performance in a variety of areas in which negative emotions interfere with learning and performance, including mathematics (Ramirez & Beilock, 2011). Putting the negative thoughts on paper might help students think about the situation more objectively and thus allow them to concentrate on the math problems.

BOX 8.4: applications

MATHEMATICS DISABILITIES

Between 5% and 8% of children perform so poorly in math that they are classified as having a mathematics disability (Shalev, 2007). These children have IQ scores in the normal range (85 or higher) but perform extremely poorly in mathematics. In the first few grades, they tend to be slow to learn to count, to learn the relative magnitudes of numbers, and to accurately solve single-digit arithmetic problems (Geary et al., 2008; Jordan, 2007). Their performance improves with experience, but even in later grades and adulthood, most continue to be slow at single-digit arithmetic and to have difficulty with the many mathematical skills that build on it, such as multi-digit arithmetic, fractions, and algebra (Geary et al., 2012; Hecht & Vagi, 2010).

Although people often think of mathematics as a type of knowledge necessary for school but not afterward, the experience of adults with mathematics disabilities illustrates the lifelong debilitating effects of this problem:

> I worked for Nabisco. As a mixer, you had to know the correct scale and formulas. I kept messing up. I lost my job.

(Curry, Schmitt, & Waldron, 1996, p. 63)

> Dairy Queen wouldn't hire me because I couldn't make change in my head.

(Curry, Schmitt, & Waldron, 1996, p. 63)

> For as long as I can remember, numbers have not been my friend.

(Blackburn, cited in M. McCloskey, 2007, p. 415)

Several specific problems contribute to mathematics disabilities (Geary et al., 2012). In severe cases, damage to one or more brain areas that are central to numerical processing, such as the intraparietal sulcus, is often the cause (Butterworth, 2010; T. J. Simon & Rivera, 2007). In less severe cases, minimal exposure to numbers prior to beginning school often contributes. Children who start school lacking knowledge of the key mathematical concepts and skills that their peers possess tend to lag far behind throughout school (Duncan et al., 2007). Other variables that are associated with, and might cause, mathematics disabilities are poor working memory for numbers, poor executive functioning, slow processing of numerical information, and mathematics anxiety (C. Blair & Razza, 2007; Lyons & Beilock, 2012; Mazzocco & Kover, 2007; Raghubar, Barnes, & Hecht, 2010).

A variety of programs have been designed to improve the mathematics knowledge of children with mathematics disabilities. One particularly successful program (L. S. Fuchs et al., 2013) emphasized learning of fraction magnitudes through instruction in magnitude comparison (e.g., "Which is larger: ½ or ⅕?") and number-line estimation (e.g., "Where would ⅕ go on this number line?"). The instruction, which was implemented with 9- and 10-year-olds, not only improved their learning of these capabilities but also improved that of learning of fraction arithmetic, relative to that of children who received a greater amount of fraction arithmetic instruction in the classroom but less instruction in understanding fraction magnitudes. Such findings indicate that effective instruction can reduce the problems associated with mathematics disabilities.

Even among children with mathematics anxiety, most learn the basics reasonably well. However, as noted in Box 8.4, the learning process goes seriously awry with certain children who suffer from the general difficulty in thinking about numbers that is known as *mathematics disability*.

review:

Learning to read begins in preschool, when many children come to recognize the letters of the alphabet and gain phonemic awareness. Early in elementary school, children learn to identify words through two main processes—phonological recoding and visually based retrieval—and they choose adaptively between these strategies. Reading comprehension improves through automatization of word identification, development of strategies, and acquisition of metacognition and content knowledge. How much parents read to their children and, later, how much children themselves read also influence reading development.

Learning to write well is difficult. It requires focusing simultaneously on low-level goals (proper spelling, punctuation, and capitalization) and high-level goals (making arguments clear and persuasive). Many Western children enter school knowing that writing proceeds in a horizontal sequence from left to right, that the text on one line continues on the next, and that words are separated by small spaces. Improvements in writing with age and experience reflect automatization of low-level goals, new organizational strategies, growing metacognitive understanding of what readers need to be told, and increasing content knowledge.

Mathematical development follows a similar general pattern. Most children enter school with some useful knowledge, such as knowing how to count from 1 to solve addition problems. Once in school, children learn a wide range of strategies for solving arithmetic and other mathematical problems, and they generally choose among these strategies in sensible ways. They also learn about an increasing range of numerical magnitudes, which improves their arithmetic learning. Understanding underlying concepts and principles also is an essential part of learning mathematics. On the other hand, mathematics anxiety can interfere with performance and learning, because the heightened emotions reduce working-memory resources.

chapter summary:

- Alfred Binet and his colleague Théophile Simon developed the first widely used intelligence test. Its purpose was to identify children who were unlikely to benefit from standard instruction in the classroom. Modern intelligence tests are descendants of the Binet-Simon test.

- One of Binet's key insights was that intelligence includes diverse high-level capabilities that need to be assessed in order to measure intelligence accurately.

What Is Intelligence?

- Intelligence can be viewed as a single trait, such as *g;* as a few separate abilities, such as Thurstone's primary mental abilities; or as a very large number of specific processes, such as those described in information-processing analyses.

- Intelligence is often measured through use of IQ tests, such as the Stanford-Binet and the WISC. These tests examine general information, vocabulary, arithmetic, language comprehension, spatial reasoning, and a variety of other intellectual abilities.

Measuring Intelligence

- A person's overall score on an intelligence test, the IQ score, is a measure of general intelligence. It reflects the individual's intellectual ability relative to age peers.

- Most children's IQ scores are quite stable over periods of years, though scores do vary somewhat over time.

IQ Scores as Predictors of Important Outcomes

- IQ scores correlate positively with long-term educational and occupational success.

- Other factors, such as social understanding, creativity, and motivation, also influence success in life.

Genes, Environment, and the Development of Intelligence

- Development of intelligence is influenced by the child's own qualities, by the immediate environment, and by the broader societal context.

- Genetic inheritance is one important influence on IQ score. This influence tends to increase with age, in part due to some genes not expressing themselves until late childhood or adolescence, and in part due to genes influencing children's choices of environments.

- A child's family environment, as measured by the HOME, is related to the child's IQ score. The relation reflects within-family influences, such as parents' intellectual and emotional support for the particular child, as well as between-family influences, such as differences in parental wealth and education.

- Schooling positively influences IQ score and school achievement.

- Broader societal factors, such as poverty and discrimination against racial and ethnic minorities, also influence children's IQ scores.

- To alleviate the harmful effects of poverty, Canada and the United States have undertaken both small-scale and larger-scale intervention programs. Both have initial positive effects on intelligence and school achievement, though the effects fade over time. On the other hand, the programs have enduring positive effects on the likelihood of not being held back in a grade and the likelihood of completing high school.

- Intensive early prevention and intervention programs, such as Better Beginnings, Better Futures and the Carolina Abecedarian Project, that begin early in children's lives and provide structured academic curricula; programming for children, parents, families, and communities; and/or optimal child-care circumstances have produced increases in intelligence that continue into adolescence and adulthood.

Alternative Perspectives on Intelligence

■ Novel approaches to intelligence, such as Gardner's multiple intelligences theory and Sternberg's theory of successful intelligence, attempt to broaden traditional conceptions of intelligence.

Acquisition of Academic Skills: Reading, Writing, and Mathematics

■ Many children learn letter names and gain phonemic awareness before they start school. Both skills correlate with later reading achievement, and phonemic awareness also is causally related to it.

■ Word identification is achieved by two main strategies: phonological recoding and visually based retrieval.

■ Reading comprehension benefits from automatization of word identification, because it frees cognitive resources for understanding the text. Use of strategies, metacognitive understanding, and content knowledge also influence reading comprehension, as does the amount that parents read to their children and the amount that children themselves read.

■ Although many children begin to write during the preschool period, writing well remains difficult for many years. Much of the difficulty comes from the fact that writing well requires children to attend simultaneously to low-level processes, such as punctuation and spelling, and to high-level processes, such as anticipating what readers will and will not know.

■ As with reading, automatization of basic processes, use of strategies, metacognitive understanding, and content knowledge influence development of writing.

■ Most children use several strategies to learn arithmetic, such as adding by counting from 1, counting from the larger addend, and retrieving answers from memory. Children typically choose in adaptive ways, using more time-consuming and effortful strategies only on the more difficult problems where such approaches are needed to generate correct answers.

■ Precise representations of numerical magnitudes are crucial for learning arithmetic and other mathematical skills.

■ As children encounter more advanced math, conceptual understanding becomes increasingly important. Understanding mathematical equality, for example, is essential for grasping advanced arithmetic and algebra problems.

Critical Thinking Questions

1. Intelligence can be viewed as a single ability, several abilities, or many processes. List the characteristics that you think are the most important components of intelligence and explain their relevance.

2. Individual differences in intelligence are more stable than individual differences in other areas of psychological functioning such as emotional regulation or aggression. Why do you think this is so?

3. Among children from middle- and upper-income families, genetics are more influential than the shared environment on individual differences in intelligence, but among children from low-income families, the opposite is the case. Why do you think that is?

4. Explain Chall's (1979) statement: "In the primary grades, children learn to read; in the higher grades, they read to learn."

5. The development of reading, writing, and mathematics shows a number of similarities. What are these similarities, and why do you think development occurs in similar ways in the three areas?

Key Terms

DOROTHEA SHARP, *Building a Sandcastle*

chapter 9:

Theories of
Social Development

magine yourself interacting face to face with an infant. What would it be like? You naturally smile and speak in an affectionate tone of voice, and the infant probably smiles and makes happy sounds back at you. If for some reason you speak in a loud, harsh voice, the baby becomes quiet and wary. If you look off to the left, the infant follows your gaze, as though assuming there is something interesting to see in that direction. Of course, the baby does not just respond to what you do; the baby also engages in independent behaviours, examining various objects or events in the room or maybe fussing for no obvious reason. Your interaction with the baby evokes emotions in you—joy, affection, frustration, and so on. Over time, through repeated interactions, you and the infant learn about each other and smile and vocalize more readily to each other than to someone else.

Now, imagine that you are asked to interact with Kismet, the robot pictured below, just as you would with a human infant. Although the request might seem strange, Kismet's facelike features make you willing to give it a try. So you smile and speak in an affectionate tone—"Hi, Kismet, how are you?" Kismet smiles back at you and gurgles happily. You speak harshly, "Kismet, stop that right now." The robot looks surprised—even a bit frightened—and makes a whimpering sound. You find yourself spontaneously attempting to console Kismet: "I'm sorry; I didn't mean it." After just a few moments, you have lost your feeling of self-consciousness and find the interaction with your new metallic friend remarkably natural. You may even start to feel fond of Kismet.

Kismet exists, and the robot's behaviour is pretty much as we have just described it. One of the world's first "social robots," Kismet was designed by a team of scientists headed by Cynthia Breazeal. Their primary goal was to develop robots that, instead of being programmed to behave in specific ways, are programmed to learn from their social interactions with humans, just as infants do. Accordingly, they designed Kismet as a sociable, "cute" infant-like robot that could elicit the attention of, and "nurturing" from, humans. Kismet's behaviour is readily interpretable

Like a face-to-face interaction between a mother and her infant, a face-to-face interaction between Kismet and its designer involves talking, cooing back and forth, and responding to each other's facial expressions.

PETER MENZEL / SCIENCE SOURCE

in human terms, and the robot even seems to have internal mental and emotional states and a personality. Kismet learns from its interactions with people—from the instructions it receives from them and from their reactions to its behaviour. Through these interactions with others, Kismet figures out how to interpret facial expressions, how to communicate, what behaviours are acceptable and unacceptable, and so on. Thus, Kismet develops over time as a function of the interaction between the "innate" structure built into it and its subsequent socially mediated experience. Just like a baby!

The challenge for Kismet's designers was, in many ways, like the task of developmental scientists who attempt to account for how children's development is shaped through their interactions with other people. Any successful account of social development must include the many ways we influence one another, starting with the simple fact that no human infant can survive without intensive, long-term care by other people. We learn how to behave on the basis of how others respond to our behaviour; we learn how to interpret ourselves according to how others treat us; and we interpret other people by analogy to ourselves—all in the context of social interaction and human society. Over the past few years, Kismet's designers, as well as other pioneers in the field, have made important strides in their efforts to allow their increasingly sophisticated robot infants to develop and learn from others. Indeed, some researchers predict that, within a few years, they will have developed cyberbabies that can acquire the cognitive and social abilities of a typical 3-year-old human child.

In this chapter, we review some of the most important and influential general theories of social development, theories that attempt to account for how children's development is affected by the people and social institutions around them. In our survey of cognitive theories in Chapter 4, we discussed some of the reasons why theories are important (pages 130–131); those reasons apply equally well to theories of social development.

Theories of social development attempt to account for many important aspects of development, including emotion, personality, attachment, self, peer relationships, morality, and gender. In this chapter, we will describe four types of theories that address these topics, reflecting, in turn, the psychoanalytic, learning, social cognitive, and ecological perspectives. We will discuss the basic tenets of each theory and examine some of the relevant evidence.

Every one of our seven themes appears in this chapter, with three of them being particularly prominent. The theme that pervades this chapter most extensively is *individual differences*, as we examine how the social world differentially affects children's development. The theme of *nature and nurture* helps us distinguish between the theories, because they vary in the degree to which they emphasize biological and environmental factors. The *active child* theme is also a major focus: some of the theories emphasize children's active participation in, and effect on, their own socialization, whereas others view children's development as shaped primarily by external forces.

Psychoanalytic Theories

No psychological theory has had a greater impact on Western culture and on thinking about personality and social development than the psychoanalytic theory of Sigmund Freud (1856–1939). A successor to Freud's theory, the lifespan developmental theory of Erik Erikson (1902–1994), has also been quite influential.

View of Children's Nature

In both Freud's and Erikson's theories, development is largely driven by biological maturation. For Freud, behaviour is motivated by the need to satisfy basic drives. These drives, and the motives that arise from them, are mostly unconscious, and individuals often have only the dimmest understanding of why they do what they do. In Erikson's theory, development is driven by a series of developmental crises related to age and biological maturation. To achieve healthy development, the individual must successfully resolve these crises.

Central Developmental Issues

Three of our seven themes—*continuity/discontinuity*, *individual differences*, and *nature and nurture*—play prominent roles in psychoanalytic theory. Like Piaget's theory of cognitive development that you encountered in Chapter 4, the developmental accounts of Freud and Erikson are stage theories. However, within the framework of discontinuous development, psychoanalytic theories stress the continuity of individual differences, emphasizing that children's early experiences have a major impact on their subsequent development. The interaction of nature and nurture arises in terms of Freud and Erikson's emphasis on the biological underpinnings of developmental stages and how they interact with the child's experience.

Freud's Theory of Psychosexual Development

Freud began his career as a neurologist and soon became interested in the origins and treatment of mental illness. He was particularly intrigued by the fact that sometimes his patients' symptoms—such as loss of feeling in a hand or blindness—had no apparent physical cause. After listening to his patients talk about their problems, he came to the conclusion that these unexplained symptoms could be attributed to completely unconscious but powerful feelings of guilt, anxiety, or fear—such as the fear of touching or seeing something forbidden. Freud's interest in psychological development grew as he became increasingly convinced that the majority of his patients' emotional problems originated in their early childhood relationships, particularly those with their parents. Freud made fundamental, lasting contributions to developmental psychology, although, as we will discuss later, they had to do with certain broad psychological concepts, not with the specifics of his theory.

In our discussion of Freud's theoretical views, we will focus primarily on their developmental aspects, especially the broad themes that remain influential today.

Basic Features of Freud's Theory

Freud's theory of development is referred to as a theory of *psychosexual* development because he thought that even very young children have a sexual nature that motivates their behaviour and influences their relationships with other people. He proposed that children pass through a series of universal developmental stages. According to Freud, in each successive stage, **psychic energy**—the biologically based, instinctual drives that fuel behaviour, thoughts, and feelings—becomes focused in different **erogenous zones**, that is, areas of the body that are erotically sensitive (e.g., the mouth, the anus, and the genitals). Freud believed that in each stage, children encounter conflicts related to a particular erogenous zone, and he maintained that their success or failure in resolving these conflicts affects their development throughout life.

Sigmund Freud, the father of psychoanalysis, has had a lasting influence on developmental psychology through his emphasis on the lifelong impact of early relationships.

DIZ MUENCHEN GMBH, SUEDDEUTSCHE ZEITUNG PHOTO / ALAMY

psychic energy ■ Freud's term for the collection of biologically based instinctual drives that he believed fuel behaviour, thoughts, and feelings.

erogenous zones ■ In Freud's theory, areas of the body that become erotically sensitive in successive stages of development.

The Developmental Process

In Freud's view, development starts with a helpless infant beset by instinctual drives, foremost among them hunger, which creates tension. The young infant has no knowledge of how to reduce it, so the distress associated with hunger is expressed through crying, prompting the mother to breastfeed the baby. (In Freud's day, virtually all babies were breastfed.) The resulting satisfaction of the infant's hunger, as well as the experience of nursing, is a source of intense pleasure for the infant.

The instinctual drives with which the infant is born constitute the **id**—the earliest and most primitive of three personality structures posited by Freud. The id, which is totally unconscious, is the source of psychic energy. It is the "dark, inaccessible part of our personality … a cauldron full of seething excitations" in need of satisfaction (Freud, 1933/1964). The id is ruled by the *pleasure principle*—the goal of achieving maximal gratification as quickly as possible. Whether the gratification involves eating, drinking, eliminating, or physical comfort, the id wants it *now*. The id remains the source of psychic energy throughout life, with its operation most apparent in selfish or impulsive behaviour in which immediate gratification is sought with little regard for consequences.

During the first year of life, the infant is in Freud's first stage of psychosexual development, the **oral stage**, so called because the primary source of gratification and pleasure is oral activity, such as sucking and eating. "If the infant could express itself, it would undoubtedly acknowledge that the act of sucking at its mother's breast is far and away the most important thing in life" (Freud, 1920/1965). The pleasure associated with breastfeeding is so intense that other oral activities—sucking on a thumb or pacifier, for instance—also provide pleasure.

For Freud, the baby's feelings for his or her mother are "unique, without parallel," and, through them, the mother is "established unalterably for a whole lifetime as the first and strongest love-object and as the prototype for all later love-relations" (1940/1964).

The infant's mother is also a source of security. However, this security does not come without costs. As always with Freud, there is a dark side: infants "pay for this security by a fear of loss of love" (Freud, 1940/1964). For Freud, common fearful reactions to being alone or in the dark are based on "missing someone who is loved and longed for" (1926/1959).

Later in the first year, the second personality structure, the **ego**, begins to emerge. It arises out of the need to resolve conflicts between the id's unbridled demands for immediate gratification and the restraints imposed by the external world. Whereas "the id stands for the untamed passions," the ego "stands for reason and good sense" (1933/1964). The ego operates under the *reality principle*, trying to find ways to satisfy the id that accord with the demands of the real world. Over time, as it continually seeks resolution between the demands of the id and those of the real world, the ego begins to develop into the individual's sense of self. Nevertheless, the ego is never fully in control:

> The ego's relation to the id might be compared with that of a rider to his horse. The horse supplies the locomotive energy, while the rider has the privilege of deciding on the goal and of guiding the powerful animal's movement. But only too often … the rider [is] obliged to guide the horse along the path by which it itself wants to go.
> (Freud, 1933/1964, p. 77)

During the infant's second year, maturation facilitates the development of control over some bodily processes, including urination and defecation. At this point, the infant enters Freud's second stage, the **anal stage**, which lasts until roughly

id ■ In psychoanalytic theory, the earliest and most primitive personality structure. It is unconscious and operates with the goal of seeking pleasure.

oral stage ■ The first stage in Freud's theory, occurring in the first year, in which the primary source of satisfaction and pleasure is oral activity.

ego ■ In psychoanalytic theory, the second personality structure to develop. It is the rational, logical, problem-solving component of personality.

anal stage ■ The second stage in Freud's theory, lasting roughly from 1 to 3 years of age, in which the primary source of pleasure comes from defecation.

phallic stage ■ The third stage in Freud's theory, lasting from age 3 to age 6, in which sexual pleasure is focused on the genitalia.

superego ■ In psychoanalytic theory, the third personality structure, consisting of internalized moral standards.

internalization ■ The process of adopting as one's own the attributes, beliefs, and standards of another person.

Oedipus complex ■ Freud's term for the conflict experienced by boys in the phallic period because of their sexual desire for their mother and their fear of retaliation by their father. (The complex is named for the king in Greek mythology who unknowingly murdered his father and married his mother.)

Electra complex ■ Freud's term for the conflict experienced by girls in the phallic stage when they develop unacceptable romantic feelings for their father and see their mother as a rival. (The complex is named after a figure in Greek mythology who arranged for the murder of her mother.)

Through identifying with his father, this young boy should, according to Freud's theory, develop a strong superego.

age 3. In this stage, the child's erotic interests focus on the pleasurable relief of tension derived from defecation. Conflict ensues when, for the first time, the parents begin to make specific demands on the infant, most notably their insistence on toilet training. In the years to come, parents and others will increase their demands on the child to control his or her impulses and to delay gratification.

Freud's third stage of development, the **phallic stage**, spans the ages of 3 to 6. In this stage, the focus of sexual pleasure again migrates, as children become interested in their own genitalia and curious about those of parents and playmates. Both boys and girls derive pleasure from masturbation, an activity that the parents of Freud's time and place often punished severely.

Freud believed that during the phallic stage, children identify with their same-sex parent, giving rise to gender differences in attitudes and behaviour. This identification begins with children's discovery of the vital difference between having and lacking a penis. At this time, a boy takes a strong interest in his penis, "so easily excitable and changeable, and so rich in sensations" (Freud, 1923/1960, p. 246). Freud supposed that girls notice and resent the fact that they do not have one, experiencing what he called *penis envy*.

Freud also believed that young children experience intense sexual desires during the phallic stage, and he proposed that their efforts to cope with them leads to the emergence of the third personality structure, the **superego**. The superego is essentially what we think of as conscience. It enables a child to control his or her own behaviour on the basis of beliefs about right and wrong. The superego is based on the child's **internalization**, or adoption, of the parents' rules and standards for acceptable and unacceptable behaviour. The superego guides the child to avoid actions that would result in guilt, which the child experiences when violating these internalized rules and standards.

For boys, the path to superego development is through the resolution of the **Oedipus complex**, a psychosexual conflict in which a boy experiences a form of sexual desire for his mother and wants an exclusive relationship with her. Although this idea may seem outlandish, many family stories are consistent with it. For example, when one of the authors' sons was a 5-year-old, he told his mother that he wanted to marry her someday. She said that she was sorry, but she was already married to Daddy, so he would have to marry someone else. The boy replied, "I have a good idea. I'll put Daddy in a big box and mail him away somewhere. Then we can get married!"

In Freud's account of the Oedipal conflict, the son's desire for his mother and his hostility toward his father are highly threatening. In response, the boy's ego protects him through *repression*, banishing his dangerous feelings to the *unconscious*, the mental storehouse where anxiety-producing thoughts and impulses are held hidden from conscious awareness. A consequence of this widespread repression, according to Freud, is *infantile amnesia*—the lack of memories from our first few years that we all suffer. In addition, the boy increases his *identification* with his father: through striving to be like him, the boy *internalizes* his father's values, beliefs, and attitudes, leading to the development of a strong conscience. Freud thought that girls experience a similar but less intense conflict—the **Electra complex**, involving erotic feelings toward the father—which results in their developing a weaker conscience than boys do.

The fourth developmental stage, the **latency period**, lasts from about age 6 to age 12. It is, as its name implies, a time of relative calm. Sexual desires are safely hidden away in the unconscious, and psychic energy gets channelled into constructive, socially acceptable activities, including both intellectual and social pursuits.

The fifth and final stage, the **genital stage**, begins with the advent of sexual maturation. The sexual energy that had been kept in check for several years reasserts itself with full force, although it is now, for the majority of individuals, directed toward other-sex peers. Ideally, the individual has developed a strong ego that facilitates coping with reality and a superego that is neither too weak nor too strong.

Freud thought that healthy development culminates in the ability to invest oneself in, and derive pleasure from, both love and work. This outcome can be compromised in many ways, however. If fundamental needs are not met during any of the stages of psychosexual development, children may become *fixated* on those needs, continually attempting to satisfy them and to resolve associated conflicts. In Freud's view, these unsatisfied needs, and the person's ongoing attempts to fulfill them, are unconscious and are expressed in indirect or symbolic ways. For example, if an infant's needs for oral gratification are not adequately satisfied during the oral stage, later in life the individual may repeatedly engage in substitute oral activities, such as excessive eating, nail-biting, smoking, and so on. Similarly, if toddlers are subjected to very harsh toilet training during the anal stage, they may remain preoccupied with issues related to cleanliness, becoming compulsively tidy and psychologically rigid or extremely sloppy and lax. Thus, in Freud's view, the nature of the child's passage through the stages of psychosexual development shapes the individual's personality for life. (With regard to oral and anal fixations, it is interesting that Freud smoked 20 cigars a day for more than 50 years—in fact, he found it impossible to work without them—and over the same period followed the same ritualized schedule nearly every day.)

Erikson's Theory of Psychosocial Development

Of the many followers of Freud, none has had greater influence in developmental psychology than Erikson. Erikson accepted the basic elements of Freud's theory but incorporated social factors into it, including cultural influences and contemporary issues, such as juvenile delinquency, changing sexual roles, and the generation gap. Consequently, his theory is regarded as a theory of *psychosocial* development.

The Developmental Process

Erikson proposed eight age-related stages of development that span infancy to old age. Each of Erikson's stages is characterized by a specific *crisis*, or set of developmental issues, that the individual must resolve. If the dominant issue of a given stage is not successfully resolved before the onset of the next stage, the person will continue to struggle with it. In the following summary of Erikson's stages, we discuss only the first five stages, which focus on development in infancy, childhood, and adolescence.

1. *Basic Trust Versus Mistrust (the first year).* In Erikson's first stage (which corresponds to Freud's oral stage), the crucial issue for the infant is developing a sense of trust—"an essential trustfulness of others as well as a fundamental sense of one's own trustworthiness" (Erikson, 1969, p. 96). If the mother is warm, consistent, and reliable in her caregiving, the infant learns that she can be trusted. More generally, the baby comes to feel good and reassured by

latency period ■ The fourth stage in Freud's theory, lasting from age 6 to age 12, in which sexual energy gets channelled into socially acceptable activities.

genital stage ■ The fifth and final stage in Freud's theory, beginning in adolescence, in which sexual maturation is complete and sexual intercourse becomes a major goal.

TED STRESHINSKY / CORBIS

Erik Erikson, who was born in Germany, took a long time to settle into a career. Instead of attending college or university, he wandered around Europe for several years, pursuing his interest in art. Eventually, he was hired as an art instructor in a school run by Anna Freud, Sigmund Freud's daughter, and became an analyst. He moved to the United States in the early 1930s, when fascism was on the rise in Germany.

being close to other people. If the ability to trust others when it is appropriate to do so does not develop, the person will have difficulty forming intimate relationships later in life.

2. *Autonomy Versus Shame and Doubt (ages 1 to 3½).* The challenge for the child between ages 1 year and 3½ years (Freud's anal stage) is to achieve a strong sense of autonomy while adjusting to increasing social demands. Going well beyond Freud's focus on toilet training, Erikson pointed out that during this period, the dramatic increases that occur in every realm of children's real-world competence—including motor skills, cognitive abilities, and language—foster children's desires to make choices and decisions for themselves. Infants' newfound ability to explore the environment on their own (as we discussed in Chapter 5) changes the family dynamics, initiating a long-running battle of wills in which parents try to restrict the child's freedom and teach the child which behaviours are acceptable and unacceptable. If parents provide a supportive atmosphere that allows children to achieve self-control without the loss of self-esteem, children gain a sense of autonomy. In contrast, if children are subjected to severe punishment or ridicule, they may come to doubt their abilities or to feel a general sense of shame.

3. *Initiative Versus Guilt (ages 4 to 6).* Like Freud, Erikson saw the time between ages 4 and 6 years as a period during which children come to identify with, and learn from, their parents: "[The child] hitches his wagon to nothing less than a star: he wants to be like his parents, who to him appear very powerful and very beautiful" (Erikson, 1959/1994). The child in this third stage of development is constantly setting goals (building a high tower of blocks, learning the alphabet) and working to achieve them. Like Freud, Erikson believed that a crucial attainment is the development of conscience—the internalization of the parents' rules and standards, and the experiencing of guilt when failing to uphold them. The challenge for the child is to achieve a balance between initiative and guilt. If parents are not highly controlling or punitive, children can develop high standards and the initiative to meet them without being crushed by worry about not being able to measure up.

4. *Industry Versus Inferiority (age 6 to puberty).* Erikson's fourth stage, which lasts from age 6 to puberty (Freud's latency period), is crucial for ego development. During this stage, children master cognitive and social skills that are important in their culture, and they learn to work industriously and to cooperate with peers. Successful experiences give the child a sense of competence, but failure can lead to excessive feelings of inadequacy or inferiority.

5. *Identity Versus Role Confusion (adolescence to early adulthood).* Erikson accorded great importance to adolescence, seeing it as a critical stage for the achievement of a core sense of *identity*. Adolescents change so rapidly in so many ways that they can hardly recognize themselves, either in the mirror or in their minds. The dramatic physical changes of puberty and the emergence of strong sexual urges are accompanied by new social pressures, including a need to make educational and occupational decisions. Caught between their past identity as a child and the many options and uncertainties of their future, adolescents must resolve the question of who they really are or live in confusion about what roles they should play as adults. As you will see in Chapter 11, developmental scientists have devoted a good deal of attention to the stage of identity versus role confusion in modern multicultural societies.

FINE ART / ALAMY

Many parents witness scenes like the one depicted here. Should this toddler be made to feel shame for his natural exploratory behaviour?

Current Perspectives

The most significant of Freud's contributions to developmental psychology were his emphasis on the importance of early experience and emotional relationships and his recognition of the role of subjective experience and unconscious mental activity. Erikson's emphasis on the quest for identity in adolescence has had a lasting impact, providing the foundation for a wealth of research on this aspect of adolescence. The critical weakness of both theories is that their major theoretical claims are stated too vaguely to be testable, and many of their specific elements, particularly in Freud's theory, are generally regarded as highly questionable. Nevertheless, there is no doubt that Freud's theory has been enormously influential. Furthermore, in recent years, some of Freud's and Erikson's original ideas have re-emerged in modified form in psychological research and thinking.

Freud's identification of infantile amnesia, for example, has been supported by a vast literature on the earliest memories that people can recall (Bauer, Wenner, & Kroupina, 2002; Hayne, 2004; Neisser, 2004). Freud was correct in noting that few of us have conscious memories of our experiences from our first few years. However, although the precise reasons for the absence of autobiographical memory in the first three years are unknown, virtually no one thinks it is due to repression, as Freud claimed.

Erikson's psychosocial stages of development have also received some support from research on autobiographical memory. In one study, adults between the ages of 62 and 89 were asked to recall up to three memories from each decade of their lives, and the researchers classified their reports with respect to Erikson's stages (Conway & Holmes, 2004). The reported memories of these older adults corresponded quite well with Erikson's stages. For example, memories from the second decade of their lives were predominantly of experiences having to do with identity confusion and establishing a sense of identity.

Freud's emphasis on the importance of early experience and close relationships was especially influential in setting the foundation for modern-day attachment theory and research (which you will read about in Chapter 11). The research in this area strongly suggests that the nature of infants' relationships with their parents not only affects behaviour in infancy but also has important long-term effects on close relationships throughout life (Allen et al., 2004; Kobak, Cassidy, & Ziv, 2004; Main, 2000).

In addition, Freud's remarkable insight that much of our mental life occurs outside the realm of consciousness is fundamental to modern cognitive psychology and brain science. Indeed, current research in cognitive and affective neuroscience suggests that a remarkably large proportion of human behaviour stems from unconscious processes. According to this research, we are, to a surprising degree, "strangers to ourselves," often acting on the basis of unconscious processes and only later constructing rational accounts of our behaviour (T. D. Wilson, 2002). In this sense, we experience the "illusion of conscious will," believing that our thoughts are the basis for our behaviour, even though those thoughts often come after the brain has already initiated the behaviour (Wegner, 2002). Many of us cry out and jump back even before we are aware that there is a snake across our path (Öhman & Mineka, 2001).

The vast abundance of cartoons about **Freud** and psychoanalysis testifies to his **enormous** impact on society.

"To this day, I can hear my mother's voice—harsh, accusing, 'Lost your mittens? You naughty kittens! Then you shall have no pie!'"

Our behaviour is also influenced by implicit attitudes of which we are unaware, attitudes that are often antithetical to what we consciously believe. For instance, many individuals who believe that they lack racial prejudice nevertheless unconsciously associate members of some racial groups with a variety of negative characteristics (Greenwald & Banaji, 1995; Nosek & Banaji, 2009). Even children as young as 6 years of age exhibit implicit racial biases (Baron & Banaji, 2006). To experience this phenomenon first hand, visit http://implicit.harvard.edu/implicit and take the Implicit Attitudes Test: the result may surprise you (although it would probably not have surprised Freud).

How might psychoanalytic theories be useful to Kismet's designers? They have already adopted the goal of making Kismet as sociable as possible. Probably the most important further step they can take, based on Freud's and Erikson's theories, is to program Kismet to form a few very close relationships with others. Certain people should become much more important to Kismet than other people with whom it interacts. Ideally, Kismet should derive some sense of security and well-being from those relationships. Furthermore, those relationships should have a lasting effect on Kismet's internal organization so that they continue to influence the robot throughout its "life."

review:

The psychoanalytic theories of Sigmund Freud and Erik Erikson propose that social and emotional development proceed in a series of stages, with each stage characterized by a particular task or crisis that must be resolved for subsequent healthy development. A healthy personality involves an appropriate balance between the three structures of personality—id, ego, and superego. Maturational factors play a key role in both theories. Psychic energy and sexual impulses are emphasized by Freud as major forces in development, whereas Erikson places greater emphasis on social factors. Both theories maintain that early experiences in the context of the family have a lasting effect on the individual's relationships with other people. These theories have had enormous, continuing impact on Western thought and culture.

Learning Theories

I imagine the mind of children as easily turn'd this or that way, as water itself.

—John Locke

As you may recall from Chapter 1, the empiricist philosopher John Locke believed that experience shapes the nature of the human mind. The intellectual descendants of Locke are psychologists who consider learning from experience to be the primary factor in social and personality development.

View of Children's Nature

In contrast to Freud's emphasis on the role of internal forces and subjective experience, most learning theorists have emphasized the role of external factors in shaping personality and social behaviour. They have often made very bold claims about the extent to which development can be guided by how people reward, or reinforce, certain of children's behaviours and punish or ignore others. More contemporary learning theorists have emphasized the importance of cognitive factors and the active role children play in their own development.

Central Developmental Issues

The primary developmental question on which learning theories take a unanimous stand is that of *continuity/discontinuity:* they all emphasize continuity, proposing that the same principles control learning and behaviour throughout life and that therefore there are no qualitatively different stages in development. Like information-processing theorists, learning theorists focus on the role of specific *mechanisms of change*—which, in their view, involve learning principles, such as reinforcement and observational learning. They believe that children become different from one another primarily because they have different histories of reinforcement and learning opportunities. The theme of *research and children's welfare* is also relevant here in that therapeutic approaches based on learning principles have been widely used to treat children with a variety of problems.

Watson's Behaviourism

John B. Watson (1878–1958), the founder of behaviourism, believed that children's development is determined by their social environment and that learning through conditioning is the primary mechanism of development (see Chapter 5, pages 201–202). He also believed that psychologists should study only objectively verifiable behaviour, not the "mind."

The extent of Watson's (1924) faith in the power of conditioning is clear in his famous boast:

> Give me a dozen healthy infants, well-formed, and my own specified world to bring them up in, and I'll guarantee to take any one at random and train him to become any type of specialist I might select—doctor, lawyer, artist, merchant-chief, and yes, even beggar man and thief, regardless of his talents, penchants, tendencies, abilities, vocations, and race of his ancestors.
>
> (p. 104)

On a much less ambitious scale, Watson demonstrated the power of classical conditioning in a famous—and by present standards, unethical—experiment with a 9-month-old infant referred to as "Little Albert" (Watson & Rayner, 1920). Watson first exposed Little Albert to a perfectly nice white rat in the laboratory. Initially, Albert reacted positively to the rat. On subsequent exposures, however, the researchers repeatedly paired the presentation of the rat with a loud noise that clearly frightened Albert. After a number of such pairings, Albert became afraid of the rat itself.

Our everyday lives are filled with examples of conditioned responses. Infants and young children, for example, often show fear at the sight of a doctor or nurse in a white coat, based on their previous association between people wearing white coats and painful injections. (To counteract this problem, many physicians wear street clothes or brightly coloured scrubs, hoping to avoid this association.)

Watson's work on classical conditioning laid the foundation for treatment procedures that are based on the opposite process— the *deconditioning*, or elimination, of fear. A student of Watson's (M. C. Jones, 1924) treated 2-year-old Peter, who was deathly afraid of white rabbits (as well as white rats, white fur coats, white feathers, and a variety of other white things). To decondition Peter's fear, the experimenter first gave him a favourite snack. Then, as Peter ate, a white rabbit in a cage was very slowly brought closer and closer to him—but

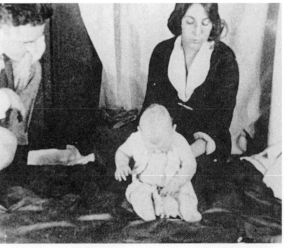

To demonstrate the power of conditioning, John B. Watson and his assistant Rosemary Raynor conditioned "Little Albert" to fear a white rat. Albert had not been afraid of the rat until its presentation was paired several times with a loud, frightening sound.

systematic desensitization ■ A form of therapy based on classical conditioning, in which positive responses are gradually conditioned to stimuli that initially elicited a highly negative response. This approach is especially useful in the treatment of fears and phobias.

never close enough to make him afraid. After repeatedly being exposed to the feared object in a context that was free of distress and provided the positive experience of a snack, Peter got over his fear. Eventually, he was even able to pet the rabbit. This approach, now known as **systematic desensitization**, is still widely used to rid people of fears and phobias of everything from dogs to dentists.

Believing that he had established the power of learning in development, Watson placed the responsibility for guiding children's development squarely on the shoulders of their parents. In his child-rearing manual, *Psychological Care of Infant and Child* (1928), he offered parents stern advice for fulfilling this responsibility. One particular piece of Watson's advice that was widely adopted in North America was to put infants on a strict feeding schedule. The idea was that the baby would become conditioned to expect a feeding at regular intervals and therefore would not cry for attention in between. To help implement this and other of his strict regimens, Watson advised parents to achieve distance and objectivity in their relations with their children (just as he exhorted psychologists to be objective in their research):

> Treat them as though they were young adults. Dress them, bathe them with care and circumspection. Let your behavior always be objective and kindly firm. Never hug and kiss them, never let them sit on your lap. If you must, kiss them once on the forehead when they say good night. Shake hands with them in the morning. Give them a pat on the head if they have made an extraordinarily good job on a difficult task. Try it out. In a week's time you will find how easy it is to be perfectly objective with your child and at the same time kindly. You will be utterly ashamed of the mawkish, sentimental way you have been handling it.
>
> (pp. 81–82)

Watson's overly strict child-rearing advice gradually fell from favour with the publication and widespread success of Dr. Benjamin Spock's *The Common Sense Guide to Baby and Child Care*, first published in 1946 (Spock's thinking about early development and child-rearing was very strongly influenced by Freud). However, Watson's behaviourist emphasis on the environment as the key factor in determining behaviour persisted in the work of B. F. Skinner.

B. F. Skinner, who once appeared in 40th place in a popular magazine's list of the 100 most important people who ever lived (P. H. Miller, 2002), believed that children's development is primarily a matter of their reinforcement history.

NINA LEEN, *LIFE* MAGAZINE © TIME WARNER, INC.

Skinner's Operant Conditioning

B. F. Skinner (1904–1990) was just as forceful as Watson in proposing that behaviour is under environmental control, once claiming that "a person does not act upon the world, the world acts upon him" (Skinner, 1971, p. 211). As described in Chapter 5, a major tenet of Skinner's theory of operant conditioning is that we tend to repeat behaviours that lead to favourable outcomes—that is, reinforcement—and suppress those that result in unfavourable outcomes—that is, punishment. Skinner believed that everything we do in life—every act—is an operant response influenced by the outcomes of past behaviour.

Skinner's research on the nature and function of reinforcement led to many discoveries, including two that are of particular interest to parents and teachers. One is the fact that *attention* can by itself serve as a powerful reinforcer: children often do things "just to get attention" (Skinner, 1953, p. 78). Thus, the best strategy for discouraging a child who throws temper tantrums from continuing to do so is to ignore that behaviour whenever it occurs. The popular behaviour-management strategy of *time out*, or temporary isolation, involves systematically withdrawing attention and thereby removing the reinforcement for inappropriate behaviour, with the goal of extinguishing it.

When the toddler son of one of the authors first graduated to a "big-boy bed," he repeatedly got up after having been put to bed, using one pretext after another to join his parents. This undesirable behaviour was extinguished in just a few nights by his father, who sat in a chair outside the bedroom door. Every time the child appeared, his father gently, but firmly and silently, put him back in his bed. The key to this successful intervention was the fact that there was no reinforcement for getting out of bed—no talking, no yelling, no drink of water, no interaction of any sort—in short, none of the potent reinforcers that parental attention provides.

A second important discovery that Skinner made is the great difficulty of extinguishing behaviour that has been *intermittently reinforced*, that is, that has sometimes been followed by reward and sometimes not. As Skinner discovered in his research with animals, **intermittent reinforcement** makes behaviours resistant to extinction: if the reward for a behaviour is totally withdrawn following intermittent reinforcement, the behaviour persists longer than it would if it had previously been consistently reinforced. In effect, if a given behaviour is not rewarded every time it is performed, an animal is likely to maintain the expectation that the next performance of the behaviour may produce the reward.

Parents often encourage unwanted behaviour in their children by inadvertently applying intermittent reinforcement. They valiantly try not to reward their children's whiny or aggressive demands, but—being human—they sometimes give in. Such intermittent reinforcement is very powerful: if a parent who had occasionally given in to whining never did so again, the child would nevertheless continue to resort to whining for a long time, assuming that because it worked in the past, it might work again. The intermittent-reinforcement effect is one reason most children have at least a few persistent bad habits. Part of the effectiveness of the bedtime example described above was due to the total consistency of the father's behaviour.

Skinner's work on reinforcement has led to a form of therapy known as **behaviour modification**, which has proven quite useful for changing undesirable behaviours. A simple example of this approach involved a preschool child who spent too much of his time in solitary activities. Observers noticed that the boy's teachers were unintentionally reinforcing his withdrawn behaviour: they talked to him and comforted him when he was alone but tended to ignore him when he played with other children. The boy's withdrawal was modified by reversing the reinforcement contingencies: the teachers began paying attention to the boy whenever he joined a group but ignored him whenever he withdrew. Soon the child was spending most of his time playing with his classmates (F. R. Harris, Wolf, & Baer, 1967).

Although scolding has the goal of causing the child to stop doing something that the parent disapproves of, the fact that it is also a form of paying attention to a child may actually reinforce undesirable behaviours and cause them to persist.

intermittent reinforcement ■ Inconsistent response to the behaviour of another person, for example, sometimes punishing an unacceptable behaviour and sometimes ignoring it.

behaviour modification ■ A form of therapy based on principles of operant conditioning in which reinforcement contingencies are changed to encourage more adaptive behaviour.

Social Learning Theory

Social learning theory, like other learning theories, attempts to account for personality and other aspects of social development in terms of learning mechanisms. However, in assessing the influence of the environment on children's development, social learning theory emphasizes observation and imitation, rather than reinforcement, as the primary mechanisms of development. Albert Bandura (1977, 1986), for example, has argued that most human learning is inherently *social* in nature and is based on observation of the behaviour of other

Albert Bandura was born in Mudare, a small town in central Alberta. He completed his undergraduate degree at the University of British Columbia and then moved to the University of Iowa for his graduate training. Bandura has been described as the "greatest living psychologist" in recognition of the impact his social cognitive theory has had on psychology.

vicarious reinforcement ■
Observing someone else receive a reward or punishment.

people. Children learn rapidly and efficiently simply from watching what other people do and then imitating them. Although direct reinforcement can increase the likelihood of imitation, it is not necessary for learning. Children can learn from symbolic models, that is, from reading books and from watching television or movies, in the absence of any reinforcement for their behaviour (see Box 9.1).

Over time, Bandura increasingly emphasized the cognitive aspects of observational learning, eventually renaming his view "social cognitive theory." Observational learning clearly depends on basic cognitive processes of *attention* to others' behaviour, *encoding* what is observed, *storing* the information in memory, and *retrieving* it at some later time in order to reproduce the behaviour observed

BOX 9.1: a closer look

BANDURA AND BOBO

A series of classic studies by Albert Bandura and his colleagues (Bandura, 1965; Bandura, Ross, & Ross, 1963) will give you a good sense of the kind of questions and methods that typify social learning theory research. The investigators began by having preschool children individually watch a short film in which an adult model performed highly unusual aggressive actions on a Bobo doll (an inflatable toy, with a weight in the bottom so it pops back up as soon as it is knocked down). The model punched the doll, hit it with a mallet while shouting "Sockeroo," threw balls at it while shouting "Bang bang," and so on.

In one study, three groups of children observed the adult model receive different consequences for these aggressive behaviours. One group saw the model receive rewards (an adult gave the model candy and pop and praised the "championship performance"). Another group saw the model punished (scolded). The third group saw the model experience no consequences. The question was whether **vicarious reinforcement**—observing someone else

receive a reward or a punishment—would affect the children's subsequent reproduction of the behaviour. After viewing the film, each child was left alone in a playroom with a Bobo doll, and hidden observers recorded whether the child imitated what he or she had seen the model do. Later, whether they had imitated the model or not, the children were offered juice and prizes to reproduce all the model's actions that they could remember.

The results are shown in the figure. The children who had seen the model punished

imitated the behaviour less than did those in the other two groups. However, the children in all conditions had *learned* from observing the model's behaviour and remembered what they had seen; when offered rewards to reproduce the aggressive actions, they did so, even if they had not spontaneously performed them in the initial test.

One particularly interesting feature of this research is the gender differences that emerged: boys were more physically aggressive toward the Bobo doll than girls

This chart shows the average number of aggressive behaviours children imitated after seeing a model rewarded, punished, or receiving no consequences for aggressive behaviour. In the no-incentive test, the children were simply left alone in the room with the Bobo doll and were given no instructions. In the positive-incentive test, they were offered a reward to do what they had seen the model do. The results clearly show that the children had learned from what they observed and that they had learned more than they initially showed. (Adapted from Bandura, 1965)

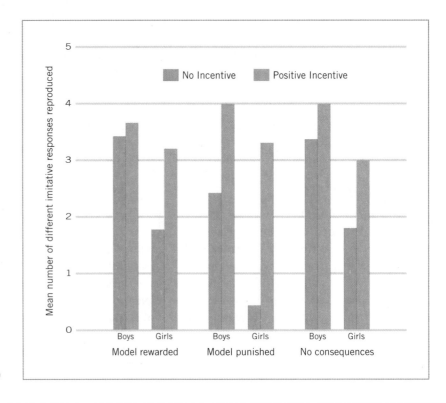

earlier. Thanks to observational learning, many young children know quite a bit about adult activities—such as driving a car (you insert and turn the ignition key or press a button, press on the accelerator, turn the steering wheel)—long before being allowed to engage in them themselves.

Unlike most learning theorists, Bandura emphasized the active role of children in their own development, describing development as a **reciprocal determinism** between children and their social environment. The basic idea of this concept is that every child has characteristics that lead him or her to seek particular kinds of interactions with the external world. The child is affected by these interactions in ways that influence the kinds of interactions he or she seeks in the future. The

reciprocal determinism ■ Bandura's concept that child–environment influences operate in both directions; children are affected by aspects of their environment, but they also influence the environment.

were. However, the girls had learned as much about the modelled behaviours as the boys had, as shown by their increased level of imitation when offered a reward. Presumably, boys and girls generally learn a great deal about the behaviours considered appropriate to both genders but inhibit those they believe to be inappropriate for their own gender.

This classic research thus demonstrates that children can quickly acquire new behaviours simply as a result of observing others, that their tendency to reproduce what they have learned depends on whether the person whose actions they observed was rewarded or punished, and that what children learn from watching others is not necessarily evident in their behaviour.

These photographs show an adult performing a series of aggressive actions on a Bobo doll. The boy, who had observed the adult's behaviour, subsequently imitated it when left alone in the room with the Bobo doll. The girl, who did not initially reproduce the model's aggressive actions, did imitate the model's behaviour when offered a reward to do so.

A good example of observational learning.

perceived self-efficacy ■ An individual's beliefs about how effectively he or she can control his or her own behaviour, thoughts, and emotions in order to achieve a desired goal.

FIGURE 9.1 **Reciprocal determinism** This chart depicts a hypothetical example showing how a child both influences and is influenced by the social environment. (Based on data from C. A. Anderson & Bushman, 2001)

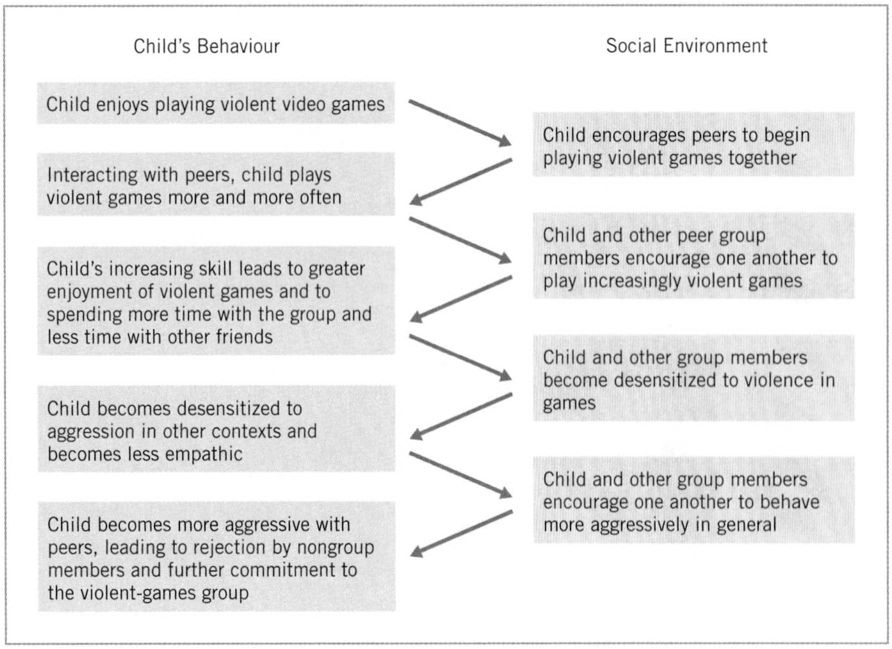

concept is illustrated in Figure 9.1, which depicts how a child's aggressive tendencies can have an impact on the child's playmates and, in turn, be shaped by how those playmates respond.

Bandura has also emphasized the importance of a cognitive factor he calls **perceived self-efficacy**—a person's beliefs about how effectively he or she can control his or her own behaviour, thoughts, and emotions in order to achieve a desired goal (Bandura, 1997; Bandura et al., 2003). For example, your *perceived self-efficacy for affect regulation* has to do with your beliefs about how well you can manage your emotional life. In terms of positive affect, your perceived self-efficacy includes your sense of your ability to express affection for another person and to feel satisfaction with your accomplishments. In terms of negative affect, it includes how well you think you can manage fear or anger in the face of threats and provocations and calm yourself after being upset. Perceived academic self-efficacy concerns students' beliefs about how well they can regulate their learning activities, master their coursework, and fulfill their own and others' expectations. A person with high academic self-efficacy tends, for example, to arrange the environment to be conducive to effective studying and, when necessary, to seek information and help from teachers, parents, and peers.

An individual's perceptions of self-efficacy in various domains often operate in concert (Bandura et al., 2003). For example, adolescents with low self-efficacy for affect regulation tend to also have low self-efficacy with respect to managing their academic performance. In other words, students who lack confidence in their ability to regulate their emotional life see themselves as incapable of taking charge of their academic work. They are also more likely to engage in delinquent behaviour (lying, cheating, theft, aggression, and so forth), presumably because feeling incapable of regulating their own behaviour undermines their ability to resist negative peer pressures.

Current Perspectives

In contrast to psychoanalytic theories, learning theories are based on principles derived from experiments. As a result, they allow explicit predictions that can be empirically tested. Partly for this reason, they have inspired an enormous amount of research yielding a great deal of understanding about parental socialization practices and how children learn social behaviours in many domains. They have also led to important practical applications, including clinical procedures of systematic desensitization and behaviour modification. The primary weakness of the learning approach is its lack of attention to biological influences and, except for Bandura's theory, to the role of cognition in influencing behaviour.

Kismet's designers took learning theories of development to heart from the very beginning by giving the robot the crucial capacity for learning that is mediated by humans. The emotional and verbal reactions of people to its behaviours instruct Kismet regarding the appropriateness of what it has done. Kismet also has the capacity to acquire new behaviours by modelling what it "sees" and "hears" humans do. Kismet's ability to learn from people is a crucial aspect of what makes it seem truly sociable. What would it take for Kismet to acquire a sense of what Bandura refers to as perceived self-efficacy? Could Kismet ever form "beliefs" about what it can and cannot do and base its behaviour on those beliefs?

review:

Learning theorists assume that social development is primarily attributable to what children learn through their interactions with other people. Early behaviourists such as Watson and Skinner emphasized the reinforcement history of the individual, believing that children's social behaviour is shaped by the pattern of rewards and punishments they receive from others. Social learning theorists, most prominently Albert Bandura, emphasize the role of cognition in social learning, noting that children learn a great deal simply from observing the behaviour of other people, including the ramifications of observed behaviour (such as the rewards and punishments observed in the Bobo doll experiments described in Box 9.1). Perceived self-efficacy affects the behaviour of children in many ways, including how well they think they can manage their emotions and schoolwork. Learning approaches have inspired a variety of treatment methods useful for a wide range of behavioural problems in children.

Theories of Social Cognition

Developmental theories of social cognition have to do with children's ability to think and reason about their own and other people's thoughts, feelings, motives, and behaviours. Like adults, children are active processors of social information. They pay attention to what other people do and say, and they are constantly drawing inferences, forming interpretations, constructing explanations, or making attributions regarding what they observe. They process information about their own behaviour and experiences in the same way.

The complexity of children's thinking and reasoning about the social world is related to, and limited by, the complexity of their thought processes in general. After all, the same mind that solves arithmetic and conservation problems also solves problems having to do with making friends and resolving moral dilemmas. With advances in cognitive development in general, the way that children think about themselves and other people deepens and becomes more abstract.

self-socialization ■ The idea that children play a very active role in their own socialization through their activity preferences, friendship choices, and so on.

role taking ■ Being aware of the perspective of another person, thereby better understanding that person's behaviour, thoughts, and feelings.

View of Children's Nature

Social cognitive theories provide a sharp contrast to the emphasis that psychoanalytic and learning theories place on external forces as the primary source of development. Instead, social cognitive theories emphasize the process of **self-socialization**—children's active shaping of their own development. According to this view, children's knowledge and beliefs about themselves and other people lead them to adopt particular goals and standards to guide their own behaviour.

Central Developmental Issues

The central theme of most relevance to social cognitive theories is the *active child*. Another prominent theme is *individual differences*, particularly in the comparisons that are often drawn between the thinking and behaviour of males and females, aggressive and non-aggressive children, and so on. The issue of *continuity/discontinuity* is important in some prominent stage theories that emphasize age-related qualitative changes in how children think about the social world. Information-processing theories, on the other hand, stress continuity in the processes involved in social reasoning. In the following discussions, we will consider these two types of social cognitive theories. The first type is represented by Selman's stage theory of role taking; the second type is represented by Dodge's information-processing theory of social problem solving and by Dweck's attributional account of academic achievement.

Selman's Stage Theory of Role Taking

In formulating his theory of social cognition, Robert Selman (1980; Yeates & Selman, 1989) focused on the development of **role taking**—the ability to adopt the perspective of another person, to think about something from another's point of view. He proposed that such role taking is essential to understanding another person's thoughts, feelings, or motives.

According to Selman, young children's social cognition is quite limited because they lack the ability to engage in role-taking behaviour. Indeed, Selman, like Piaget, suggested that before the age of 6 years, children are virtually unaware that there is any perspective other than their own; they assume that whatever they think, others will think as well. Perhaps failure to recognize the discrepant view of someone else underlies those endless sibling arguments of the familiar form "'Did so,' 'Did not,' 'Did so,' 'Did not.'"

Selman proposed that children go through four increasingly complex and abstract stages in their thinking about other people. In stage 1 (roughly ages 6 to 8), children come to appreciate that someone else can have a perspective different from their own, but they assume that the different perspective is merely due to that person's not possessing the same information they do. In stage 2 (ages 8 to 10), children not only realize that someone else can have a different view, but they also are able to think about the other person's point of view. However, it is not until stage 3 (ages 10 to 12) that children can systematically compare their own and another person's point of view. In this stage, they can also take the perspective of a third party and assess the points of view of two other people. In stage 4 (age 12 and older), adolescents attempt to understand another's perspective by comparing it with that of a "generalized other," assessing whether the person's view is the same as that of most people in their social group.

Notice that in Selman's stages of role taking, as children become less egocentric in their reasoning, they become increasingly capable of considering multiple perspectives simultaneously (e.g., their own, another person's, and "most people's"). This growth in social cognition mirrors the cognitive changes identified by Piaget (and discussed in Chapter 4). Not surprisingly, children's progress through Selman's stages of role taking is strongly related to their progress through Piaget's stages (Keating & Clark, 1980).

Dodge's Information-Processing Theory of Social Problem Solving

The information-processing approach to social cognition emphasizes the crucial role of cognitive processes in social behaviour. This approach is exemplified by Dodge's analysis of children's use of aggression as a problem-solving strategy (Dodge, 1986; Dodge, Dishion, & Lansford, 2008). In the research that originally motivated Dodge's theory, children were presented stories that involved a child who suffers because of another child's actions, the intentions of which are ambiguous. For instance, in one story, as a child is working hard to assemble a puzzle, a peer bumps into the table, scattering the puzzle pieces, and merely says "Oops." The children were then asked to imagine themselves as the victim in this scenario and to describe what they would do and why. Some children interpreted the other child's knocking into the table as an accident and said that they would simply ignore the event. Others concluded that the peer bumped the table on purpose, and they reported that they would find a way to get even (many thought that punching the offender would be a good way to achieve that goal).

Dodge and his colleagues have found that some children have a **hostile attributional bias**, that is, a general expectation that others are antagonistic to them (Crick & Dodge, 1994; S. Graham & Hudley, 1994). This bias leads such children to search for evidence of hostile intent on the part of the peer in the above scenario and to attribute to the peer a desire to harm them. They are likely to conclude that retaliation is the appropriate response to the peer's behaviour. Hostile attributional biases become self-fulfilling prophecies: a child's aggressive retaliation to the presumed hostile act of a peer elicits counterattacks and rejection by his or her peers, further fuelling the child's belief in the hostility of others.

School systems have particular problems in dealing with children who have a hostile attributional bias. One strategy is to remove them from regular classrooms because of their disruptive behaviour and put them into special classrooms in which they can be more closely supervised (Dodge, Lansford, & Dishion, 2007). However, this approach brings together children with hostile attributional biases, causing other negative consequences. First, it provides these youngsters with evidence supporting their existing expectation of hostility from others, raising the possibility that they will reinforce one another's aggressive tendencies. At the same time, it segregates them from more well-adjusted peers from whom they might learn more moderate attitudes and social strategies.

There are many reasons why a child might develop a hostile attributional bias. However, it is noteworthy that children who have been physically abused are

JOHN BIRDSALL PHOTOGRAPHY / AGE FOTOSTOCK

Many of young children's arguments with others stem from their difficulty appreciating that another person can have a different point of view from their own.

hostile attributional bias ■ In Dodge's theory, the tendency to assume that other people's ambiguous actions stem from a hostile intent.

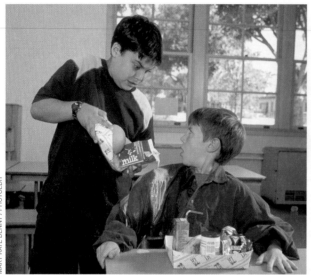

The boy who was spilled on by the other boy seems to have a hostile attributional bias. Since he readily assumes that other people have the intent to harm him, he attributes a hostile intention to the other boy.

particularly likely to attribute anger to others, even in neutral situations (Pollak et al., 2000). It may be that the experience of physical abuse leads children to be especially sensitive to cues to anger. For example, physically abused children are better at recognizing angry facial expressions than are children who have not experienced abuse, and the speed with which they do so is related to the degree of anger and hostility to which they have been subjected (as reported by their parents) (Pollak et al., 2009). Physically abused children also have difficulty reasoning about negative emotions. In one study, abused children had difficulty determining which situations might trigger anger in parents, endorsing both positive and negative events as potential causes of parental anger (Perlman et al., 2008). For example, when presented hypothetical stories about child–parent situations, the abused children saw anger as a plausible response to positive events, such as a child's winning a prize at school or helping around the house. A tendency to assume anger in others (even when it is not present), paired with difficulty understanding what might provoke anger in others, is likely to result in a hostile attributional bias. (We will examine child abuse in more detail later in the chapter.)

Dweck's Theory of Self-Attributions and Achievement Motivation

Imagine two elementary school children, Diane and Megan, both hard at work trying to solve math problems, and both initially failing. Coming to the realization that the problems are quite difficult, Diane feels excited about meeting the challenge and works persistently to get the answers. Megan, in contrast, feels anxious and makes only a half-hearted effort to solve the problems. What explains this difference in the children's reactions to failure?

According to Carol Dweck's social cognition perspective (2006), the difference in their reactions is attributable to a difference in their **achievement motivation**—that is, in whether they are motivated by *learning goals*, seeking to improve their competence and master new material, or by *performance goals*, seeking to receive positive assessments of their competence or to avoid negative assessments. From this perspective, Diane has an *incremental* view of intelligence, the belief that intelligence can be developed through effort. She focuses on mastery—on meeting challenges and overcoming failures—and she generally expects her efforts to be successful. Indeed, her increased effort and persistence following failure will, in all likelihood, improve her subsequent performance.

Megan, on the other hand, has an *entity* view of intelligence, the belief that her intelligence is fixed. Her goal is to be successful, and as long as she is succeeding, all is well. However, when she fails at something, she feels "helpless." Not succeeding causes her to feel bad and to doubt her abilities and self-worth.

Underlying these two patterns of achievement motivation are differences in what attributions children make about themselves, particularly with regard to their sense of self-worth. Children with an **entity/helpless orientation** tend to base their sense of self-worth on the approval they receive (or do not receive) from other people about their intelligence, talents, and personal qualities. To feel good about themselves, they seek out situations in which they can be assured of success and receive praise, and they avoid situations in which they might be criticized. In contrast, the self-esteem of children with an **incremental/mastery orientation**

achievement motivation ■ Whether children are motivated by *learning goals*, seeking to improve their competence and master new material, or by *performance goals*, seeking to receive positive assessments of their competence or to avoid negative assessments.

entity/helpless orientation ■ A general tendency to attribute success and failure to enduring aspects of the self and to give up in the face of failure.

incremental/mastery orientation ■ A general tendency to attribute success and failure to the amount of effort expended and to persist in the face of failure.

is based more on their own effort and learning and not on how others evaluate them. Because they do not equate failure on a task with a personal flaw, they can enjoy the challenge of a hard problem and persist in the attempt to solve it.

These different motivation patterns are evident as early as preschool (Smiley & Dweck, 1994). Given a choice of working on a puzzle they have already solved or on one they had previously failed to solve, some 4- and 5-year-old children strongly prefer the one they already know how to do, whereas others want to continue working on the one they had failed to solve.

Older children's cognitions about themselves and their abilities follow a similar pattern but involve more complex concepts and reasoning than those of younger children. Some have what Dweck and her colleagues (Cain & Dweck, 1995; Dweck, 1999; Dweck & Leggett, 1988) refer to as an **entity theory** of intelligence. This theory, like Megan's entity view of intelligence, is rooted in the idea that a person's level of intelligence is fixed and unchangeable. Over time, it comes to include the belief that success or failure in academic situations depends on how smart one is. When evaluating their own performance, children with an entity theory of intelligence focus on outcomes—success or failure—not on effort or learning from mistakes. Thus, when they experience failure (as everyone does some of the time), they think they are not very smart and that there is nothing they can do about it. They feel helpless.

Other children subscribe to an **incremental theory** of intelligence. This theory, like Diane's view of intelligence, is rooted in the idea that intelligence can grow as a function of experience. Children who hold an incremental theory of intelligence believe that academic success is achievable through effort and persistence. When evaluating their performance, they focus on what they have learned, even when they have failed, and they believe that they can do better in the future by trying harder. They feel hopeful.

Given what you have just read, what kind of praise and criticism do you think would reinforce these two patterns? The answer depends on the focus of the feedback. An incremental/mastery pattern is reinforced by focusing on children's effort, praising them for a good effort ("You really worked hard on that," "I like the way you kept at it") and criticizing them for an inadequate one ("Next time you need to put in some more work," "I think you can do better if you try harder"). In contrast, an entity/helpless pattern is reinforced by both praise and criticism focused on children's enduring traits or on the child as a whole ("You're very smart at these problems. I'm proud of you," "You just can't do math. I'm disappointed in you").

Do these two different types of internal theories have real-world ramifications? Much of the research on this question has been carried out in the domain of math education. In an important study conducted in the New York City public school system, Dweck and her colleagues found that 7th graders with an incremental theory of intelligence showed an upward trajectory in math scores over the next 2 years, while the scores of 7th graders with a fixed theory of intelligence remained flat (Blackwell, Trzesniewski, & Dweck, 2007). The investigators then provided an 8-session intervention to a new group of 7th graders who had a fixed theory of intelligence. Students in

entity theory ■ A theory that a person's level of intelligence is fixed and unchangeable.

incremental theory ■ A theory that a person's intelligence can grow as a function of experience.

The comments this teacher is offering his student on her work could be either beneficial or detrimental, depending on whether he focuses on how smart she is or on the effort she has made.

BLUE JEAN IMAGES / ALAMY

this group were taught an incremental theory of intelligence based on some of the same concepts from basic neuroscience that you read about in Chapter 3: the brain is plastic and always changing; learning forges new connections among synapses; and so on. A control group received training in basic study skills. Remarkably, the children who received the intervention showed a positive change in motivation as well as improvements in grades, while the children in the control group showed a decline in grades.

Another important issue is whether these two types of internal views—entity theories and incremental theories—have implications for children's development in domains beyond intelligence and academic achievement. Recent research by Yeager and colleagues (2013) suggests that they do. For instance, recall the hostile attributional bias discussed in the previous section. Adolescents who maintain an entity theory about personality traits are more likely to demonstrate a hostile attributional bias than are adolescents who endorse an incremental theory. In other words, if they hold the view that people's behaviours are due to fixed personality traits (some people are good, others are bad), rather than due to situations or circumstances, they are more likely to interpret other people's harmful behaviour as hostile rather than as accidental or situational. Assuming that this is the case, learning to take a more incremental view should diminish their tendency to make hostile attributions. And indeed, this is the case: when the experimenters used an intervention (which included a brief introduction to neuroscience concepts, as described in the previous paragraph, but nothing about hostile intent) to shift adolescents' perspectives away from the fixed-entity view and closer to the incremental view, there was a reduction in the participants' hostile attributions. Thus, internal theories about traits of self and others have important implications for diverse aspects of development.

Where might these individual differences in internal theories come from? One obvious source is parents, who often try very hard to enhance their child's self-esteem. Unfortunately, doing something that might seem purely positive—praising a child for being good at something—can actually undermine the child's motivation for improvement. Another obvious source is teachers. One recent study showed that the way teachers comfort poor-performing students when the teacher has an entity perspective (as seen in teacher comments like "It's okay; not everyone can be good at math") can seriously undermine their students' motivation and self-expectations (Rattan, Good, & Dweck, 2012). Parents and teachers alike should be aware that some kinds of praise and comfort are beneficial, whereas others are not.

Current Perspectives

Social cognitive theorists have made several important contributions to the study of social development. One is their strong emphasis on children as active seekers of information about the social world. Another contribution is the insight that the effect of children's social experience depends on their interpretations of those experiences. Thus, children who make different attributions about a given social event (such as someone's causing them harm) or an academic event (such as doing poorly on a test) will respond differently to that event. In addition, a large amount of research has supported the social cognitive position. Although these theories have provided a very healthy antidote to social theories that left children's cognition out of the picture, they too provide an incomplete account. Most notably, they have very little to say about biological factors in social development.

Kismet is designed to shape its own development through its understanding of the behaviour of humans toward it—a form of self-socialization emphasized by social cognition theorists. What would it take, however, for Kismet to go further and draw inferences about others' cognitions, feelings, and motivations? For example, will it ever be possible for Kismet to make different attributions about a given behaviour, based on subtle aspects of the social context of its history with a person? Even more challenging, will Kismet come to know that people can hold points of view different from one another and from its own? Finally, can Kismet develop some sense of self-worth that will affect its attributions about itself? These questions about Kismet's potential to mimic social cognition highlight the vast complexity of human social development and the challenge faced by theorists of social development.

review:

Theories of social cognition stress the role of cognitive processes—attention, knowledge, interpretation, reasoning, attribution, and explanation—in children's social development. A key aspect of these theories is an emphasis on the process of self-socialization, through which children actively shape their own development. Selman's theory of role taking proposes that children go through stages in terms of their ability to appreciate that different people can have different points of view. The information-processing approach taken by Dodge to the study of aggression emphasizes the role of children's interpretation of other people's behaviour. Aggressive children often have a hostile attributional bias, a general expectation that other people will be hostile to them. According to Dweck's theory of achievement motivation, children's response to their success or failure in an academic situation depends on whether they attribute the outcome to their effort or their intelligence.

Ecological Theories of Development

We now turn to a set of theories united by the fact that they take a very broad view of the context of social development. Virtually all psychological theories, and certainly those that we have reviewed in the chapter thus far, emphasize the role of the environment in the development of individual children. However, the "environment" in many of these theories is narrowly construed as immediate contexts—family, peers, schools. The first two approaches discussed here—ethological and evolutionary psychology views—relate children's development to the grand context of the evolutionary history of our species. The third approach—the bioecological model—considers multiple levels of environmental influence that simultaneously affect development.

View of Children's Nature

Ethological and evolutionary theories view children as inheritors of genetically based abilities and predispositions. The focus of these theories is largely on aspects of behaviour that serve, or once served, an adaptive function.

The bioecological model stresses the effects of context on development, but it also emphasizes the child's active role in selecting and influencing those contexts. Children's personal characteristics—temperament, intellectual ability, athletic skill, and so on—lead them to choose certain environments over others, and also influence the people around them.

ethology ■ The study of the evolutionary bases of behaviour.

imprinting ■ A form of learning in which the young of some species of newborn birds and mammals become attached to and follow adult members of the species (usually their mother).

Central Developmental Issues

The developmental issue that is front and centre in ecological theories is the interaction of *nature and nurture*. The importance of the *sociocultural context* and the *continuity/discontinuity* of development are implicitly emphasized in all these theories. The *active role* of children in their own development is another central focus, primarily of the bioecological approach.

Ethological and Evolutionary Theories

Ethological and evolutionary theories are concerned with understanding various aspects of development and behaviour in terms of a given animal's evolutionary heritage. Of particular interest are species-specific behaviours—behaviours that are common to members of a particular species (such as humans) but not typically observed in other species.

Ethology

Ethology, the study of behaviour within an evolutionary context, attempts to understand behaviour in terms of its adaptive or survival value. According to ethologists, a variety of innate behaviour patterns in animals were shaped by evolution just as surely as their physical characteristics were (Crain, 1985).

Ethological approaches have frequently been applied to developmental issues. The prototypical, and best-known, example is the study of imprinting made famous by Konrad Lorenz (1903–1989), who is often referred to as the father of modern ethology (Lorenz, 1935, 1952). **Imprinting** is a process by which newborn birds and mammals of some species become attached to their mother at first sight and follow her everywhere, a behaviour that ensures that the baby will stay near a source of protection and food. For imprinting to occur, the infant has to encounter its mother during a specific *critical period* very early in life.

The basis for imprinting is not actually the baby's mother per se; rather, the infants of some species are genetically predisposed to follow around the first moving object with particular characteristics that they see after emerging into the world. In chickens, for example, imprinting is elicited specifically by the sight of a bird's head and neck regions (M. H. Johnson, 1992). Which particular object the individual will dutifully trail after is thus a matter of experience-expectant processes (discussed in Chapter 3, pages 115–116). Usually, the first moving object any chick sees *is* its mother, so everything works out just fine.

Although human newborns do not "imprint," they do have strong tendencies that draw them to members of their own species. Examples noted in Chapter 5 include an innate visual preference for faces, which seems to result from an attraction to a face shape with more "stuff" in the top half. Even though this attraction is not based on a specific human face template, it gets the infant to pay attention to the most significant entities in the environment. Also, like other mammals, human newborns orient to sounds, tastes, and smells familiar from their experience in the womb—a predisposition that inclines them toward their own mother (see Chapter 5). One of the most influential applications of ethology to human development, which we discuss in Chapter 11, is Bowlby's (1969) extension of the concept of imprinting to the process by which infants form emotional attachments to their mother (pages 428–429).

This famous photograph shows Konrad Lorenz (1952) and a gaggle of greylag goslings that were imprinted on him and followed him all over his farm. Lorenz discovered that mallard ducklings are more discriminating: they would imprint on him only if he squatted low and dragged himself around, quacking all the while, for hours on end. He was a very dedicated scientist.

TIME & LIFE PICTURES / GETTY IMAGES

According to evolutionary psychology, gender differences in play probably have their origin in the evolutionary history of the human species, with males being predisposed to dominance, and females, to nurturing.

Another example of human behaviour to which an ethological perspective has been applied is the existence of differences in the play preferences of males and females (which you will read more about in Chapter 15). For example, many (but not all) boys prefer to play with vehicle toys (trucks and cars, for example), which afford action play, whereas girls prefer dolls, which are conducive to nurturant play. The standard accounts for these differences, which come from social learning and social cognitive theories, maintain that children (especially boys) are encouraged by their parents to play with "gender-appropriate" toys, and they do so because they want to be like others of their own sex.

However, some researchers argue that these accounts are not the whole story and that evolved predispositions fuel these preferences. In one study, for example, newborn girls looked longer at social stimuli—human faces—than at non-social stimuli such as mobiles, whereas the reverse was true for boys (Connellan et al., 2001). Similarly, 1-year-old boys watched a video of moving cars for longer than they watched a video of an active human face, whereas girls did the opposite (Lutchmaya & Baron-Cohen, 2002).

Evolutionary Psychology

A relatively new branch of psychology that is closely related to ethology is evolutionary psychology, which applies the Darwinian concepts of natural selection and adaptation to human behaviour (Bjorklund, 2007; Geary, 2009). The basic idea of this approach is that in the evolutionary history of our species, certain genes predisposed individuals to behave in ways that solved the adaptive challenges they faced (obtaining food, avoiding predators, establishing social bonds), thereby increasing the likelihood that they would survive, mate, and reproduce, passing along their genes to their offspring. These adaptive genes became increasingly common and were passed down to modern humans; thus, many of the ways we behave today are a legacy from our prehistoric ancestors (Geary, 2009).

One of the most important adaptive features of the human species—one that clearly distinguishes us from other species—is the large size of our brains (relative to body size). The trade-off for this is the prolonged period of immaturity and dependence human children go through. We are "a slow-developing, big-brained species" (Bjorklund & Pellegrini, 2002), as illustrated in Figure 9.2. In Chapter 2, we discussed how the size of the human brain at birth is limited by the size of the female pelvis. As modern humans evolved, enlargement of our brains was made possible by birth occurring at a more "premature" stage of development than is

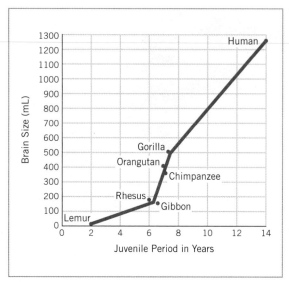

FIGURE 9.2 **Brain sizes of various primates and humans** Humans are "a slow-developing, big-brained species" compared with other primates. The larger the brain size of various primates, the longer their developmental period. (Adapted from Bonner, 1988)

parental-investment theory ■ A theory that stresses the evolutionary basis of many aspects of parental behaviour, including the extensive investment parents make in their offspring.

characteristic of other mammals. These evolutionary changes were made possible by increased social complexity, which is necessary for successful caregiving of extremely helpless offspring. A related consequence of our large brains and slow development is our species-typical high level of neural plasticity that supports our unrivalled capacity for learning from experience. Highlighting the adaptive benefits of our extended immaturity, Bjorklund (1997) has pointed out that

> a prolonged period of youth is necessary for humans [who,] more than any other species, must survive by their wits; human communities are more complex and diverse than those of any other species, and this requires that they have not only a flexible intelligence to learn the conventions of their societies but also *a long time to learn them.*
>
> (p. 153, emphasis added)

Many evolutionary theorists have suggested that *play*, which is one of the most salient forms of behaviour during the period of immaturity of most mammals, is an evolved platform for learning (Bjorklund & Pellegrini, 2002). Children develop motor skills by racing and wrestling with one another, throwing toy spears, or kicking a ball into a goal. They try out and practise a variety of social roles (as mentioned in Chapter 7), enacting what they know about being, say, a parent or a police officer. One of the main virtues of play is that children can experiment in a situation with minimal consequences; no one gets hurt if a baby doll is accidentally dropped on its head or a Nerf gun is fired at a "bad guy."

To benefit from their protracted immature status, children must, of course, survive it, and their survival and development require that parents spend an enormous amount of time, energy, and resources in raising them (Bjorklund, 2007). Why are parents willing to sacrifice so much for the benefit of their offspring? According to **parental-investment theory** (Trivers, 1972), a primary source of motivation for parents to make such sacrifice is the drive to perpetuate their genes in the human gene pool, which can happen only if their offspring survive long enough to pass those genes on to the next generation.

Parental-investment theory also points to a potential dark side of the evolutionary picture—the so-called Cinderella effect—which refers to the fact that rates of child maltreatment are considerably higher for step-parents than for biological parents. McMaster University psychologists Martin Daly and Margo Wilson have provided some of the most detailed examinations of the Cinderella effect. As Figure 9.3 shows, estimates of the rate of murder committed by stepfathers

FIGURE 9.3 **Estimated rates of child homicide committed by genetic fathers versus stepfathers in Canada from 1974 to 1990** As is shockingly clear, stepchildren, especially very young ones, are much more likely to be murdered by a stepfather than other children are likely to be murdered by their biological fathers. (Adapted from Daly & Wilson, 1996)

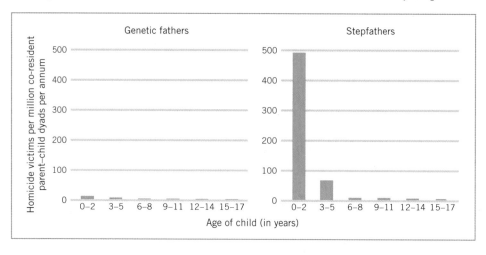

against children residing with them is hundreds of times higher than the rate for fathers and their biological children. Furthermore, in families in which both natural and stepchildren reside, abusive parents typically target their abuse toward their stepchildren (Daly & Wilson, 1996). Similar findings suggest that unintended child fatalities (e.g., drowning) are also more likely to occur in homes with a resident step-parent than in homes with no step-parent, suggesting that there is less commitment to protecting children in step-parent homes (Tooley et al., 2006). Although there are clearly many factors that contribute to these patterns, they are consistent with parent-investment theory; that is, because parenting is so costly, it is not, from an evolutionary point of view, worth investing in children who cannot contribute to the perpetuation of one's own genes.

A clear implication of the evolutionary view of development is that radical departures from the species-typical environment could have negative consequences. It is well established that exposing young and prenatal animals of various species to stimulation that is outside the normal range for their species and age has adverse effects on their development (e.g., G. Gottlieb, 1992; Kenny & Turkewitz, 1986). For example, while developing inside the egg, bobwhite quails experience no light or visual stimulation. If a piece of the shell is removed, letting in light while the embryo develops, the species-typical behaviour of the hatchlings is altered, disrupting normal development (Lickliter, 1995).

Could the same be true for humans? Neonatologist Heideliese Als and colleagues (2003) believe that we should be concerned about this question with regard to babies born prematurely. As discussed in Chapter 2, modern medicine has enabled increasing numbers of premature infants of ever-smaller sizes to survive. However, their first weeks or even months are spent in an environment that is radically different from the species-typical fetal environment. Instead of continued residence in the dark, relatively quiet womb, these babies find themselves in brightly lit, very noisy intensive care units. Believing that many of the brain and behavioural problems common in premature infants may have to do with this atypical early environment, Als has advocated radical changes in newborn nurseries to simulate the womb environment, including reducing illumination and noise levels.

A related area of concern about potential negative effects of species-atypical stimulation is the current craze for providing extra prenatal stimulation that we discussed in Chapter 2. Our species evolved with a certain amount of stimulation available to the fetus in utero, and a substantial increase in prenatal stimulation might very well have negative consequences.

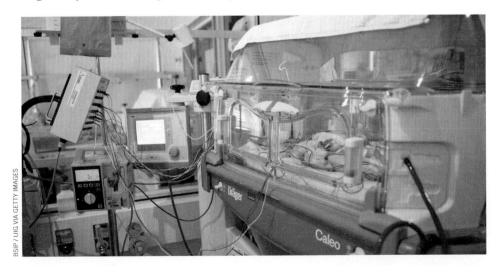

The environment that premature infants encounter in a newborn intensive care unit is radically different from the uterine environment, raising concern that stimulation so different from anything humans encountered in the evolutionary past may be detrimental to development.

Bronfenbrenner's Bioecological Model

The most encompassing model of the general context of development is Urie Bronfenbrenner's bioecological model (Bronfenbrenner, 1979; Bronfenbrenner & Morris, 1998). Bronfenbrenner conceptualizes the environment as "a set of nested structures, each inside the next, like a set of Russian dolls" (1979, p. 22). Each structure represents a different level of influence on development (Figure 9.4). Embedded in the centre of the multiple levels of influences is the individual child, with his or her particular constellation of characteristics (genes, gender, age, temperament, health, intelligence, physical attractiveness, and so on).

Over the course of development, these individual characteristics interact with the environmental forces present at each level. The different levels vary in how immediate their effects are, but Bronfenbrenner emphasizes that *every* level, from the intimate context of a child's nuclear family to the general culture in which the family lives, has an impact on that child's development. Note that each of the levels depicted in Figure 9.4 is labelled as a "system," emphasizing the complexity and interconnectedness of what goes on in each one. This theory is ecological in the sense that, just as in the study of the ecology of other living things, it considers how multiple levels of context influence outcomes. It just happens that instead of the soil microbes or natural predators that might be the relevant ecological contexts for plants or non-human animals, the ecological systems influencing children range from families to neighbourhoods to governments.

The first level in which the child is embedded is the **microsystem**—the activities, roles, and relationships in which the child *directly* participates over time. The child's family is a crucial component of the microsystem, and its influence is predominant in infancy and early childhood. The microsystem becomes richer and more complex as the child grows older and interacts increasingly often with peers, teachers, and others in settings such as school, neighbourhood, organized sports and arts clubs, place of worship, and so on.

Bronfenbrenner stresses the *bidirectional* nature of all relationships within the microsystem. For instance, the parents' marital relationship can affect how they treat their children, and their children's behaviour can, in turn, have an impact on the marital relationship. A good, supportive marital relationship helps parents interact more sensitively and effectively with their children (P. A. Cowan, Powell, & Cowan, 1998; Cox et al., 1989), but a chronically fussy baby can create friction and even damage the relationship between parents (Belsky, Rosenberger, & Crnic, 1995).

The second level in Bronfenbrenner's model is the **mesosystem**, which encompasses the *connections* among various microsystems, such as family, peers, and schools. Supportive relations among these contexts can benefit the child. For example, children's academic success is facilitated when their parents value scholastic endeavours and have positive contact with their teachers (Luster & McAdoo, 1996; Stevenson, Chen, & Lee, 1993) and when their peers encourage academic achievement (Steinberg, Darling, & Fletcher, 1995). When connections in the mesosystem are non-supportive, negative outcomes are more likely.

The third level of social context, the **exosystem**, comprises settings that children may not directly be a part of but that can still influence their development. Their parents' workplaces, for example, can affect children in many ways, from the employer's policies about flexible work hours, parental leave, and on-site child care to the general atmosphere in which parents work. Parents' enjoyment or dislike of their work can affect the emotional relationships within the family

microsystem ■ In the bioecological model, the immediate environment that an individual personally experiences.

mesosystem ■ In the bioecological model, the interconnections among immediate, or microsystem, settings.

exosystem ■ In the bioecological model, environmental settings that a person does not directly experience but that can affect the person indirectly.

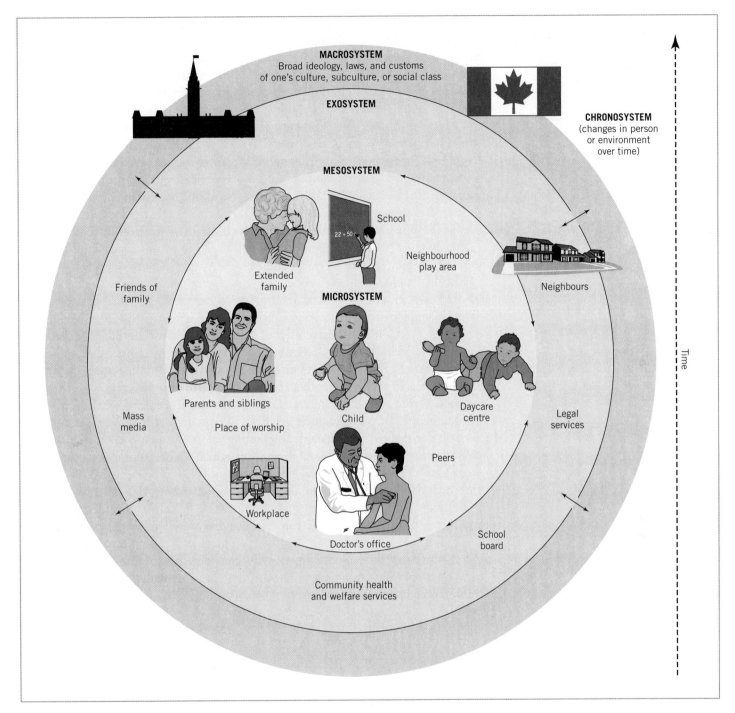

FIGURE 9.4 The bioecological model Urie Bronfenbrenner considers the child's environment as composed of a series of nested structures, including the microsystem (the immediate environment with which the child directly interacts), the mesosystem (the connections that exist among microsystems), the exosystem (social settings the child is not a part of but that still affect him or her), and the macrosystem (the general cultural context in which all the other systems are embedded). This figure illustrates the environment of a child living in North America. (Adapted from Bronfenbrenner, 1979)

(Greenberger, O'Neil, & Nagel, 1994). Even something as seemingly remote from the child as the financial success or failure of a parent's employer can be crucial: job loss, for example, is related to abusive or neglectful parenting (R. E. Emery & Laumann-Billings, 1998).

macrosystem ■ In the bioecological model, the larger cultural and social context within which the other systems are embedded.

chronosystem ■ In the bioecological model, historical changes that influence the other systems.

The outer level of Bronfenbrenner's model is the **macrosystem**, which consists of the general beliefs, values, customs, and laws of the larger society in which all the other levels are embedded. It includes the general cultural, subcultural, or social class groups to which the child belongs. Cultural and class differences permeate almost every aspect of children's lives, including differences in beliefs about what qualities should be fostered in children and how best to foster them.

Cultural influences are apparent even in the earliest memories reported by adults in different parts of the world. In a cross-cultural study (Q. Wang, 2006), European-Americans reported memories from an earlier age than did Taiwanese participants, and their memories focused on specific events and their own role in those events (Q. Wang, 2006). In contrast, the Taiwanese participants more often described everyday events and emphasized the role of other people in the recalled events. Presumably, these differences reflect cultural values that influence what parents encourage their children to talk about, especially with respect to the relative value of focusing on oneself or on others.

Finally, Bronfenbrenner's model also has a temporal dimension, which he has referred to as the **chronosystem**. In any given society, beliefs, values, customs, technologies, and social circumstances change over time, with consequences for children's development. For instance, as a result of technological advances that gave rise to the "digital age," children today have access to a vast realm of information and entertainment unimaginable to previous generations. In addition, the impact of environmental events depends on another chronological variable—the age of the child. For example, divorce has different effects on toddlers and teens; it may make both of them unhappy, but young children are more likely to have the extra burden of thinking that the divorce is their fault (Hetherington & Clingempeel, 1992). Another important aspect of the temporal dimension, which we have noted on several occasions, is the fact that as children get older, they take an increasingly active role in their own development, making their own decisions about their friends, activities, and environments. As Box 9.2 on attention deficit hyperactivity disorder (pages 372–373) suggests, the chronosystem can even be a factor in developmental disorders.

To illustrate the richness of the bioecological model for thinking about and investigating child development, we will consider three examples in which the interactions among multiple levels of the model are particularly clear and relevant: child maltreatment, children and the media, and SES and development.

What different experiences were available to these girls born in different historical times? How did their educational and employment opportunities differ?

Child Maltreatment

One of the most serious threats to children's development is **child maltreatment**, defined as intentional abuse or neglect that endangers the well-being of anyone younger than 18. In 2008, roughly 85 440 children were confirmed to be victims of child maltreatment (Public Health Agency of Canada, 2010). As Figure 9.5 shows, the most common forms of maltreatment were exposure to intimate partner violence, neglect, and physical abuse. The victims included nearly equal numbers of girls (14.5 per 1000) and boys (13.89 per 1000), and the perpetrators were most often a member of the child's own family (Statistics Canada, 2011c). The highest rate of victimization was for infants younger than 1 year: 17.5 per 1000 infant girls and 16.64 per 1000 infant boys were maltreated in 2008 (Statistics Canada, 2011c). More tragic still, in Canada, an average of 35 children per year are killed by a parent, with infants at highest risk (Statistics Canada, 2011c; Trocmé et al., 2007). Consistent with the bioecological model, a variety of factors, including characteristics of the child, the parents, and the community, have been shown to be involved in the causes and consequences of child abuse.

child maltreatment ■ Intentional abuse or neglect that endangers the well-being of anyone under the age of 18.

Causes of maltreatment At the level of the microsystem, certain characteristics of parents increase the risk for maltreatment (R. E. Emery & Laumann-Billings, 1998; Statistics Canada, 2011). Among these are low self-esteem, strong negative reactions to stress, and poor impulse control. Parental alcohol and drug dependence also increase the probability of maltreatment. So does an abusive spousal relationship: mothers who are abused by their partner are more likely to abuse their children. In addition, certain characteristics of children—including low birth weight, physical or cognitive challenges, and difficult temperament—are associated with increased risk for parental abuse (e.g., Bugental & Happaney, 2004).

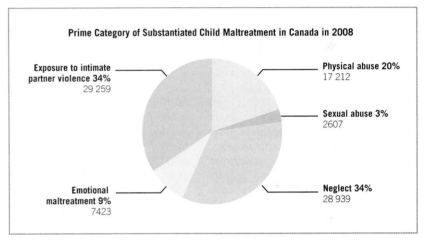

Prime Category of Substantiated Child Maltreatment in Canada in 2008

Exposure to intimate partner violence 34%
29 259

Physical abuse 20%
17 212

Sexual abuse 3%
2607

Emotional maltreatment 9%
7423

Neglect 34%
28 939

FIGURE 9.5 **Primary categories of child maltreatment in Canada in 2008** Neglect and exposure to intimate partner violence are the most common forms of substantiated child maltreatment in Canada, followed by physical abuse. (Adapted from Public Health Agency of Canada, 2010)

Child maltreatment tends to be associated with additional factors in the mesosystem and exosystem that increase stress on parents. Many of these factors are related to low family income. They include high levels of unemployment, inadequate housing, and community violence (R. E. Emery & Laumann-Billings, 1998; Lynch & Cicchetti, 1998).

Often a particularly important exosystem contributor to child maltreatment is a family's social isolation and lack of social support (more common in lower-income families). For example, the Canadian Incidence Study of Reported Child Abuse and Neglect found that 39% of the families where maltreatment had been documented reported having few social supports (Public Health Agency of Canada, 2010). Such isolation may have multiple causes—mistrust of other people, a lack of the social skills needed to maintain positive relationships, frequent moves from place to place because of economic factors, or living in a community characterized by violence and transience. The importance of social support is highlighted by the fact that impoverished parents are less likely to maltreat their children if they live in a neighbourhood in which there is a prevailing sense of community, with neighbours who care about and help one another (Belsky, 1993; Coulton et al., 1995; Garbarino & Kostelny, 1992).

BOX 9.2: individual differences

ATTENTION DEFICIT HYPERACTIVITY DISORDER

Many developmental disorders can be profitably examined with the different levels of the bioecological model in mind. Influences and interventions from different levels can make it easier or harder for children to manage the challenges they face. A good case in point is **attention deficit hyperactivity disorder (ADHD)**.

Although the term "ADHD" is relatively new, the syndrome—variously labelled as "hyperactivity," "minimal brain dysfunction," and "attention deficit disorder" (ADD)—has long been recognized. Children with ADHD tend to be of normal intelligence and do not typically show serious emotional disturbances. However, they have difficulty sticking to plans, following rules and regulations, and persevering in tasks that require sustained attention (especially ones they find uninteresting). Many are hyperactive, constantly fidgeting, drumming on their desks, and moving around. Children with ADHD typically have difficulty acquiring academic skills, such as reading and writing, since these skills require focusing attention for prolonged periods. Many also have problems suppressing aggressive reactions when they are frustrated. All these symptoms seem to reflect an underlying difficulty in inhibiting impulses to act (Barkley, 1997). The difficulty is greatest when interesting distractors are present.

In a large study in British Columbia, 6.9% of boys and 2.2% of girls had received a diagnosis of ADHD (Morrow et al., 2012).

This diagnostic differential may be attributable to the fact that boys with ADHD are more likely than girls to engage in disruptive behaviours that lead to their problem being diagnosed (Gaub & Carlson, 1997). As with autism spectrum disorder (discussed in Chapter 3, page 95), there has been an increase in the diagnosis of ADHD in many countries in the past decade. However, it is currently unclear whether the steep increase in rates of diagnosis of ADHD reflects an actual increase in prevalence, increased awareness of the disorder, changing standards for ADHD diagnoses, or all of the above.

The causes of ADHD are quite varied. Genetic factors clearly play a role. If one identical twin has ADHD, the odds are about 50% that the other twin does too, a rate roughly 10 times that among children in general (Silver, 1999). In addition, ADHD in adopted children is associated with ADHD in the biological parent but not in the adoptive parent (Rhee et al., 1999). Indeed, heritability for ADHD is greater than any other developmental disorder, with the possible exception of autism spectrum disorder.

Environmental factors in the microsystem also influence the development of ADHD. For instance, prenatal exposure to alcohol, which can affect brain development (Chapter 2, pages 61–62), is associated with the development of ADHD (Milberger et al., 1997). Parents' behaviour toward their children may contribute to the early development of ADHD, as shown by a large study with 5-year-olds, half of whom had been of low birth weight (Tully et al., 2004). Those low-birth-weight children whose mothers expressed a high degree of warmth for them ("He's my ray of sunshine," "She's a delight") were less likely than children of less warm mothers to show symptoms of ADHD. However, causal links can be difficult to determine because, as we have noted on numerous occasions, developmental risks tend to cluster together.

Current treatment for ADHD involves agents in the microsystem (the family doctor), the exosystem (the drug industry), and the macrosystem (the government). The most common approach taken by physicians is to prescribe stimulant medications, such as Ritalin. Although it seems paradoxical that stimulants could help children who are already overly active, they improve symptoms in 70% to 90% of children for whom they are prescribed. The reason is that the brain systems in these children are actually underaroused; the children's restless and sometimes disruptive behaviour is actually an attempt to wake up the brain. Appropriate medication, which stimulates neurotransmitter systems, allows children with ADHD to focus their attention better and to be less distractible. This leads to improved academic achievement, better relationships with classmates, and reduced

attention deficit hyperactivity disorder (ADHD) ■ A syndrome that involves difficulty in sustaining attention.

Consequences of maltreatment The consequences of child maltreatment are manifested primarily in the microsystem (although they can extend to, and be moderated by, factors in the mesosystem and exosystem, such as child-protection policies and agencies). In comparison with other children, maltreated children have less secure relationships with their parents, show less empathy for other people, and have lower self-esteem (Cicchetti & Toth, 1998; Main & George, 1985; M. Smith & Walden, 1999). In elementary school, maltreated children are more aggressive and have more conflict with their peers (Bolger & Patterson, 2001; L. A. McCloskey & Stuewig, 2001). Later on, they have difficulty maintaining friendships (Parker & Herrera, 1996; Rogosch, Cicchetti, & Aber, 1995; Salzinger et al., 2001). At school, maltreated children are often anxious and inattentive and overly dependent on their teachers for approval and support. They are more than twice as likely as other children to fail a grade (Eckenrode, Laird, & Doris, 1993; Erickson et al., 1989).

MARY KATE DENNY / PHOTOEDIT

The short attention span of children with ADHD often leads them to distract not only themselves but also other children in their classroom.

activity levels (Barbaresi et al., 2007a, 2007b).

It is important to realize that the benefits of Ritalin continue only as long as children take the medication. Longer-lasting gains require not only medication but also behavioural treatments. A large-scale clinical trial found that high-quality medication management (with careful dosing and extensive follow-up) paired with intensive behavioural treatments (in this case, focused on behavioural management in the context of sports and social skills) led to more positive outcomes than did either medication or behavioural intervention alone (P. S. Jensen et al., 2001). Parents' disciplinary practices also had an impact on the efficacy of these treatments in this study. In particular, ADHD treatment had the greatest impact on children's behaviour in school when parents were

able to improve their previously negative or ineffective parenting behaviour. These findings highlight the importance of considering the impact of multiple systems on developmental outcomes.

The availability of medications helpful to those with ADHD is, of course, the result of a perception on the part of drug companies that they can produce, sell, and make a profit from a drug targeted for this problem. It also depends on the medication's receiving a favourable evaluation from Health Canada, based on research to determine the drug's efficacy and potential side effects. Thus, the fate of a child in need of medication could be quite different, depending on factors far outside the influence of his or her family.

But would any intervention be necessary in the first place if it were not the case that every school-age child is expected to spend a substantial amount of time on most days sitting quietly at a desk concentrating on tasks that he or she may have little interest in? Pointing to the highest level of the bioecological model—the chronosystem—many experts have suggested that ADHD may have emerged as a serious problem only in recent times—specifically, only since the advent of compulsory schooling. Before then, an individual who had attentional difficulties that would have posed problems in a classroom might very well have been able to function successfully in an environment where such difficulties were inconsequential, even unnoticed.

We can further examine the effects of maltreatment at an even more micro level. In our earlier discussion of the hostile attributional bias, we noted that children who are the victims of physical abuse show a heightened response to anger cues. This heightening is observed in behavioural responses, in brain responses such as event-related potentials, or ERPs (e.g., Pollak et al., 1997), and in physiological responses, including heart rate and skin conductance (Pollak et al., 2005). Although such responses might be maladaptive in many social situations, leading children to misinterpret or overreact to emotional cues, an ecological perspective suggests that overattention to negative emotions might be highly adaptive for children growing up in a home marked by threat and danger. By considering children's responses to their environments as adaptive in some contexts, but maladaptive in others, an ecological perspective may help explain why maltreatment has the particular constellation of effects that it does, as well as which interventions might be most effective

With the advent of handheld digital devices and social networking, electronic media have become central to the social lives of many children and teens.

(e.g., Frankenhuis & de Weerth, 2013). Of course, the ideal situation would be to prevent child maltreatment altogether. (For a promising approach to preventing child abuse, see Box 9.3).

Children and the Media: The Good, the Bad, and the Awful

Another good illustration of the multiple levels in which children's development is embedded is the impact of various media—television programs, movies, video games, and popular music. In terms of the bioecological model, media are situated in the exosystem, but they are subject to influences from the chronosystem, as indicated earlier; from the macrosystem (including cultural values and government policies); from other elements in the exosystem (such as economic pressures); and from the microsystem (such as parental monitoring). All these factors are at play every time children tune in or boot up.

Early on, when children's in-home screen viewing was mostly limited to television, some educationally oriented television programming for young children was shown to have beneficial effects (Huston & Wright, 1998). Most notably, watching *Sesame Street* was associated with increases in young children's vocabulary and helped prepare them for school entry, with some positive effects persisting even through high school (D. R. Anderson et al., 2001; Rice et al., 1990). However, as you read in Chapter 6 (Box 6.3: iBabies: Technology and Language Learning), some "educational" DVDs actually have negative effects on language development.

As screens become ever more pervasive, moving from living rooms to bedrooms to children's pockets, concerns about screen time continue to mount. About 50% of Canadian children between ages 12 and 18 spend more than the recommended two hours per day involved in using screen media (Leatherdale & Ahmed, 2011). Use of every type of electronic media has increased during that time, fuelled by social networking (see Box 13.2, pages 530–531), the availability of television programming streamed on demand (rather than presented at a fixed time, as in the past), and an explosion in the use of portable electronics. Even very young children are active participants in this media immersion: children 6 years and younger devote more time to entertainment media than to reading, being read to, and playing outside *combined* (Rideout, Vandewater, & Wartella, 2003).

Concerns about children's exposure to media The nature and amount of children's media exposure have aroused a variety of concerns, ranging from the possible effects of media violence and pornography to those of isolation and inactivity.

MEDIA VIOLENCE Foremost among the concerns that have been raised is fear that a steady diet of watching violent television shows, playing violent video games, and listening to music with violent lyrics will cause children to behave violently. The concern arises from the fact that television is awash in violence. One study of fictional programs on Canadian television in 2001 found that around 40 acts of physical violence occurred per hour of prime-time television (Paquette, 2004). Moreover, aggression in television programs and movies tends to be glamorized and trivialized—particularly the violence perpetrated by heroes, who are rarely punished or condemned for their actions.

Extensive reviews of the vast amount of research on this issue have led researchers to conclude that the scientific debate about whether media violence increases

Researchers have concluded that viewing media violence increases the incidence of aggression and violent behaviour.

BOX 9.3: applications

PREVENTING CHILD ABUSE

Given the multiple factors that contribute to child maltreatment, preventing or ameliorating the problem of abuse is extremely difficult. However, one very promising U.S. intervention program was developed from research financed by federal funding agencies at the macrosystem level and is carried out at the microsystem level.

The program, reflecting a social cognition perspective, was designed and implemented by Daphne Bugental and her colleagues, who found that many abusive parents have inappropriate models of their relationship with their children. They tend to see themselves and their children as locked in a power struggle—a conflict in which they view *themselves* as the victims (Bugental, Blue, & Cruzcosa, 1989; Bugental & Happaney, 2004). Thus, they might interpret their baby's prolonged crying as evidence that the baby is mad at them, and they might think that a child who continues to beg for a withheld toy or treat is intentionally trying to subvert their authority.

The goal of this program was to help parents at risk for abusing their children achieve more realistic interpretations of their difficulties in caring for their children (Bugental et al., 2002). As we discussed in Chapter 2, some children are particularly at risk for abuse, including those born preterm or with other medical complications that make parenting especially challenging. The intervention for families with such children involved frequent home visits in which parents were asked to give examples of recent problems they had had with their children and to indicate what they thought had been the cause of the problem. They were then led to identify a cause that did not focus blame on the children (i.e., something other than deliberate misbehaviour by their children), as well as to come up with potential strategies for solving the problem.

A particularly important factor in assessing this program is that at-risk families were *randomly assigned* to the intervention condition or to two comparison conditions. Thus,

any difference in outcomes could not be due to initial differences among the groups.

The program was remarkably successful: the prevalence of physical abuse in the intervention group was only 4%, compared with around 25% in the two comparison groups. This intervention program, targeted at the microsystem level, suggests that home-visiting programs that focus on altering parents' cognitive interpretations have a high potential for preventing physical abuse. And, consistent with the parent-investment theory discussed earlier in this chapter in the context of evolutionary psychology, the program led parents to begin to invest more caregiving in their at-risk (preterm) infants (Bugental, Beaulieu, & Silbert-Geiger, 2010). As parents developed a greater understanding of the needs—and the potential—of their infants, they subsequently increased their investment in their offspring, who later showed substantial health benefits.

---

aggression and violence is over. The evidence is clear that media violence has negative effects on children. This has led to the imposition of policies developed and implemented by the Canadian Radio-television and Telecommunications Commission (2008) that are designed to limit children's exposure to violence on television. For example, Canadian broadcasters cannot air programs that show violent scenes intended for adult audiences before 9 P.M. In addition, broadcasters are required to provide announcements at the beginning of, and during, programs signalling that the program may contain violent scenes (CRTC, 2012).

Exposure to media violence has an impact in four ways (C. A. Anderson et al., 2003). First, seeing actors engage in aggression teaches aggressive behaviours and inspires imitation of them, as you saw earlier in this chapter in the discussion of Bandura's studies with Bobo. Second, viewing aggression activates the viewer's own aggressive thoughts, feelings, and tendencies. This heightened aggressive mindset makes it more likely that the individual will interpret new interactions and events as involving aggression and will respond aggressively. Furthermore, when aggression-related thoughts are frequently activated, they may become part of the individual's normal internal state. Third, media violence is exciting and arousing for most youth, and their heightened physiological arousal makes them more likely to react violently to provocations right after watching violent films. Finally, frequent long-term exposure to media violence gradually leads to emotional desensitization—a reduction in the level of unpleasant physiological arousal most people experience when observing violence. Because this arousal normally helps inhibit violent behaviour, emotional desensitization can render violent thoughts and behaviours more likely.

PHYSICAL INACTIVITY Another concern has to do with the fact that a child who is glued to a screen is not outside playing or otherwise engaging in robust physical activity. In addition, the thousands of television commercials with which children are bombarded every year (at an advertiser cost of billions of dollars per year) consist largely of advertisements for sugary cereals, candy, and fast-food restaurants. The sedentary nature of screen time, combined with the onslaught of commercials encouraging the consumption of sweet, fatty foods, have been linked to the recent increase in childhood obesity discussed in Chapter 3. Indeed, when a child has a television in the bedroom—as do more than 70% of 8- to 18-year-olds (Rideout et al., 2010)—the child's risk of obesity increases by 31% (Dennison, Erb, & Jenkins, 2002).

EFFECTS ON ACADEMIC ACHIEVEMENT Studies have found a strong relationship between media use and school grades (Rideout, Foehr, & Roberts, 2010). For example, children who are heavy users of screen media (more than 16 hours per day) are far more likely to report fair/poor grades (Cs or below) than are those who are moderate users (3 to 16 hours per day) or light users (less than 3 hours per day). Of course, there are many other confounding factors that might underlie a link between media usage and grades, such as generally poor parental supervision, or a family culture (parents included) that de-emphasizes reading and other academic pursuits in favour of screen time.

However, one cleverly designed study was able to draw causal conclusions about the relation between video games and school achievement (Weis & Cerankosky, 2010). Boys in Grades 1 through 3 who did not already own a video game console were randomly assigned to an experimental group, whose members were given a console at the beginning of the study, or to a comparison group, whose members were, in the name of fairness, given a console after the study was completed. The boys who received the game console at the beginning of the study subsequently spent less time on after-school academic pursuits than the boys in the comparison group, and 4 months into the study, performed more poorly on measures of literacy and had a higher rate of teacher-reported academic problems than did the comparison group. Boys who spent the most time with the games showed the poorest academic outcomes.

SOCIAL INEQUITIES Another area of concern centres on the possibility that socioeconomic inequalities will be exacerbated by the "digital divide"—that is, unequal access to and use of computers as a function of SES. Most children have some degree of access to computers at school, but there are great differences between low-SES and high-SES families in terms of the likelihood that computers are available in their homes. Furthermore, higher-SES families are more likely to have newer, more powerful computers and to have more than one of them. Thus, children from higher-SES families are far more likely to be able to use computers to do homework and to use the Internet than are children from economically disadvantaged families. The disparity in access to computers is less extreme at school, where computers are used extensively in classrooms even in low-SES neighbourhoods.

PORNOGRAPHY A serious concern for many parents is children's exposure to pornography on television and the Internet, whether inadvertent or intentional. Online pornography is particularly problematic because of its ready availability. One study of more than 5000 Canadian children aged 9 to 17 years showed that 16% reported that they had accessed a pornographic website and 9% had accessed an adult chat room during the current school year (Media Awareness Network, 2005). Research suggests that exposure to pornography can make children and teens more tolerant of aggression toward women, as well as more accepting of premarital and extra-marital sex (Greenfield, 2004).

Of special concern is pornography featuring children. Child pornography is a multi-billion-dollar industry and among the fastest-growing criminal segments on the Web (Federal Bureau of Investigation, n. d.). Today, pedophiles commonly use the Web, including chat rooms, to share illegal photographs of children and to lure children into sexual relationships. Furthermore, activities such as divulging personal information, chatting online with strangers, emailing or posting photos, and visiting adult-content websites and chat rooms may actually increase children's risk. According to one study, about 30% of Canadian children aged 9 to 17 years would provide their real names and addresses to sign up for free email or to create a profile on a social networking site (Media Awareness Network, 2005).

The most effective weapons against the various negative effects of media on children operate at the microsystem level, with parents exercising control over their children's access to undesirable media, and at the macrosystem level, with legal controls and government programs designed to minimize the negative features of the media with which children interact. Effective control is complicated, however, by free speech concerns and, in the case of Internet pornography, the global nature of the problem.

SES and Development

As we have frequently noted, the SES of their families has profound effects on children's development. These effects originate at every level of the bioecologi-cal model. In the microsystem, children are affected by the nature of their family's housing and their neighborhood, and in the mesosystem, by the condition of their school and the quality of their teachers. Exosystem influences include the nature of the parents' employment or lack of employment. Macrosystem factors include the government policies that affect employment opportunities and establish programs, such as Better Beginnings, Better Futures, that are geared to families in economi-cally disadvantaged communities.

Chronosystem factors also come into play with respect to changes over time in the kind and number of jobs that are available. For example, in Canada, the num-ber of well-paying manufacturing jobs has been shrinking for many years, ravaging whole communities with skyrocketing unemployment. The shrinking tax base in those communities, and in others affected by the economic downturn of the past several years, has resulted in fewer resources to support schools, health care, and other community resources important for developing children.

The pervasive effects of poverty In many of our discussions throughout this book, we focus on a number of factors that affect the development of children liv-ing in poverty. However, the factors we discuss are only the tip of the iceberg. Table 9.1 lists a wide variety of ways that the environment of economically disadvantaged children in North America differs from that of more affluent children (summarized from G. W. Evans, 2004). Many of the items in the table will be familiar to you, but you may never have considered some of the others. As you look over the table, think about how these various aspects of impoverished environments interact and

J. A. GIORDANO / CORBIS SABA

Would you say that the children who attend this school are from economically disadvantaged or well-to-do families?

what their cumulative impact might be. Also, consider how the many detrimental factors listed in the table relate to the different levels of the bioecological model, from government priorities and policies to the physical health of the individual child growing up in poverty.

As you look over the table, you should also keep in mind two points from our discussion of the multiple-risk model in Chapter 2. First, it is the *accumulated* exposure to multiple environmental risk factors that is crucial (G. W. Evans, 2004). A child whose parents are neglectful might cope reasonably well, but doing so would be more difficult if the child also goes to a poor-quality school in a dangerous neighbourhood. Second, as discussed in Chapters 10 and 11, individual children differ with respect to how susceptible they are to environmental influences, both positive and negative (Belsky, Bakermans-Kranenburg, & van IJzendoorn, 2007).

Because many specific effects of poverty on development are discussed throughout the book, we will not feature them here but, instead, will examine a developmental effect of SES that often goes unnoticed: the costs of affluence.

The costs of affluence Contrary to popular assumption, growing up in highly affluent families can have negative effects on development. The stereotype of the "poor little rich kid" seems to have some basis in fact. For example, compared with inner-city adolescents, affluent youth report higher levels of anxiety, greater depression, and more use of illicit substances (cigarettes, alcohol, marijuana, and other drugs) (Luthar, 2003). Although adolescents' use of illicit substances is linked with depression and anxiety, it is also associated with popularity, suggesting that peer influences may actively promote this behaviour.

TABLE 9.1

The Environment of Childhood Poverty

Some ways that the physical and social environments of children growing up in poverty differ from the environments of more well-off children:

PHYSICAL ENVIRONMENT

Home

Inadequate housing

Structural deficiencies

Inadequate heat

Unsafe drinking water

Poor air quality in house (including parental smoking)

Rodent infestation

Few safety features (e.g., smoke alarms)

Crowding (number of people in home)

Small yards (if any)

Neighbourhood

Exposure to toxins
- Air pollution (e.g., near highways, factories)
- Water, soil pollution (factories, toxic waste dumps)
- Exposure to contaminants (lead, pesticides)

Few parks or open spaces

Few places for informal gatherings

Inadequate municipal services (garbage, police, fire)

Few stores, services, including supermarkets

Less bus, taxi service

More bars, taverns

More physical hazards (traffic volume, street crossings, playground safety)

SOCIAL ENVIRONMENT

Home

Low parental education

Low parental income

Employment instability

Frequent change of residence

Social isolation (small social networks)

Less social support

Lower marital quality (conflict)

More domestic violence (spousal, child abuse)

Higher divorce rate

More single-parent households

Harsher, punitive parenting

Low monitoring of children

Less emotional support

More corporal punishment

Less speech from parents

Less frequent literacy activities

Fewer computers/older computers

Less access to Internet

More television watching

School

Poor-quality daycare

Aggressive, violent peers

Unstable peer relations

Poorer-quality teachers

High teacher turnover

High student absenteeism

Less parent involvement in school

Less sense of belonging to school

Inadequate buildings (plumbing, heating, lighting, etc.)

Overcrowding

Neighbourhood

High crime rates

High level of violence

Widespread unemployment

Fewer positive adult role models

Few social resources

Source: G. W. Evans, 2004

In attempting to account for these findings, Luthar and Becker (2002) note that affluent parents tend to pressure their children to excel both academically and in extracurricular activities. At the same time, these parents often provide their children with little support. For example, because of the career demands of the parents and their children's many after-school activities, family time is diminished in many high-income families (Luthar & Latendresse, 2005; Rosenfeld & Wise, 2000). In addition, when both parents have careers, many preteens from upper-income families are home alone after school, unsupervised, for several hours a week (Capizzano, Tout, & Adams, 2002).

A rather remarkable fact is that, in a national survey, U.S. teens whose family income was fairly low reported higher feelings of closeness with their mothers and fathers than did those whose family income was much higher (Federal Interagency Forum on Child and Family Statistics, 1999). In addition, the level of happiness reported by youth is not directly related to their family's level of affluence (Csikszentmihalyi & Schneider, 2000).

Current Perspectives

The three theoretical positions discussed in this section have all made valuable contributions to developmental science by placing individual development in a much broader context than is typically done in mainstream psychology. All of them challenge researchers to look beyond the lab—far beyond it.

The primary contribution of ethology and evolutionary psychology comes from the emphasis on children's biological nature, including genetic tendencies grounded in evolution. Evolutionary psychology has provided fascinating insights into human development, but it has also come in for serious criticism. One frequent complaint is that, like psychoanalytic theories, many of the claims of evolutionary psychologists are impossible to test. Often, a behavioural pattern that is consistent with an evolutionary account is at least equally consistent with social learning or some other perspective. Finally, evolutionary-psychology theories tend to overlook one of the most remarkable features of human beings, a feature strongly emphasized by Bronfenbrenner—our capacity to transform our environments and ourselves.

Bronfenbrenner's bioecological model has made an important contribution to our thinking about development. His emphasis on the broad context of development and the many different interactions among factors at various levels has highlighted how complex the development of every child is. The main criticism of this model is its lack of emphasis on biological factors.

What is the relevance of ecological theories to Kismet's design? Evolution is basically irrelevant to it. Evolutionary change does not apply to individual development, and, without the possibility for reproduction, it simply cannot occur.

With respect to the bioecological model, Kismet is developing in an extremely limited microsystem—Cynthia Breazeal's lab at the Massachusetts Institute of Technology—populated with a relatively small number of people. It has no mesosystem at present, although that could change in the future. This fact makes Kismet's experience quite different from that of most human children. Kismet could be affected by the macrosystem at any time, if changes in research priorities of the federal government cut off funding for the project. In terms of the chronosystem, such a remarkable robot was unimaginable until recently, and even more remarkable ones are currently being developed to follow in Kismet's footsteps.

It is interesting that the most difficult parallels to draw between Kismet's development and that of children and theories of social development concern the larger context of human development. Part of what is unique about the human species is the fact that every individual is embedded in multiple layers of human interactions, institutions, traditions, and history.

review:

The theories we have grouped under the label "ecological theories" examine development in a much broader context than those found in other theoretical approaches. Theories of development based on ethology and evolutionary psychology emphasize the influence of the evolutionary history of the human species on the development of individual children. Parental-investment theory proposes that the perpetuation of one's genes underlies the enormous effort that parents invest in raising their children.

Other evolutionary theories emphasize the adaptive function of prolonged immaturity in the development of human children. Urie Bronfenbrenner's highly influential bioecological model conceptualizes the environment in which children develop as a set of nested systems, or contexts. The systems range from aspects of the environment that the individual child directly experiences on a daily basis to the broader society and historical time in which the child lives.

chapter summary:

Four major types of social development theories present contrasting views of the social world of children.

Psychoanalytic Theories

- The psychoanalytic theory of Sigmund Freud has had an enormous impact on developmental psychology and psychology as a whole, primarily through Freud's emphasis on the importance of early experience for personality and social development, his depiction of unconscious motivation and processes, and his emphasis on the importance of close relationships.

- Freud posited five biologically determined stages of psychosexual development (oral, anal, phallic, latency, genital) in which psychic energy becomes focused in different areas of the body. Children face specific conflicts at each stage, and these conflicts must be resolved for healthy development to proceed. Freud also posited three structures of personality—id (unconscious urges), ego (rational thought), and superego (conscience).

- Freud believed that the Oedipus complex and the Electra complex form the basis for superego (conscience) development, as children identify with and adopt the values of their same-sex parent. He thought that girls develop a weaker conscience than boys do.

- Erik Erikson extended Freud's theory by identifying eight stages of psychosocial development extending across the entire lifespan. Each stage is characterized by a developmental crisis that, if not successfully resolved, will continue to trouble the individual.

Learning Theories

- John Watson believed strongly in the power of environmental factors, especially reinforcement, to influence children's development.

- B. F. Skinner held that all behaviour can be explained in terms of operant conditioning. He discovered the importance of intermittent reinforcement and the powerful reinforcing value of attention.

- Albert Bandura's social learning theory and his empirical research established that children can learn simply by observing other people. Bandura has increasingly stressed the importance of cognition in social learning.

Theories of Social Cognition

- Social cognitive theories assume that children's knowledge and beliefs are vitally important in social development.

- Robert Selman's theory proposes that children go through four stages in the development of the ability to take the role or perspective of another person. They progress from the simple appreciation that someone can have a view different from their own to being able to think about the view of a "generalized other."

- The social information-processing approach to social cognition emphasizes the importance of children's attributions regarding their own and others' behaviour. The role of such attribution is clearly reflected in the hostile attributional bias, described by Dodge, which leads children to assume hostile intent on the part of others and to respond aggressively in situations in which the intention of others is ambiguous.

■ Dweck's theory of self-attribution focuses on how children's achievement motivation is influenced by their attributions about the reasons for their successes and failures. Children with an incremental/mastery orientation enjoy working on challenging problems and tend to be persistent in trying to solve them, whereas children with an entity/helpless orientation prefer situations in which they expect to succeed and tend to withdraw when they experience failure.

Ecological Theories of Development

■ Ethological theories examine behaviour within the evolutionary context, trying to understand its adaptive or survival value. The research of Konrad Lorenz on imprinting has been particularly relevant to certain theories of social development in children. Sex differences have been documented in children's toy and play preferences.

■ Evolutionary psychologists apply Darwinian concepts of natural selection to human behaviour. Characteristic of their approach are parental-investment theory and the idea that the long period of immaturity and dependence in human infancy enables young children to learn and practise many of the skills needed later in life.

■ Bronfenbrenner's bioecological model conceptualizes the environment as a set of nested contexts, with the child at the centre. These contexts range from the microsystem, which includes the activities, roles, and relationships in which a child directly participates on a regular basis, to the chronosystem, the historical context that affects all the other systems.

Critical Thinking Questions

1. What influences of Freud's theory of development can you identify in modern society?

2. The concept of self-socialization plays a prominent role in social cognitive theories. Explain what is meant by this term. To what extent and in what ways do the other major theories reviewed in the chapter allow for the possibility of self-socialization?

3. Consider your behaviour when preparing for and taking tests and when receiving feedback on your academic performance.

Do you see yourself as having primarily an incremental/mastery orientation or an entity/helpless orientation to academic achievement?

4. Imagine yourself raising a child. Identify one or two things from each of the four types of theories discussed in this chapter that you think might be helpful to you as a parent.

5. Consider Box 9.2 on attention deficit hyperactivity disorder (pages 372–373) and analyze what is discussed there in terms of Bronfenbrenner's bioecological model.

Key Terms

achievement motivation, p. 360

anal stage, p. 345

attention deficit hyperactivity disorder (ADHD), p. 372

behaviour modification, p. 353

child maltreatment, p. 371

chronosystem, p. 370

ego, p. 345

Electra complex, p. 346

entity theory, p. 361

entity/helpless orientation, p. 360

erogenous zones, p. 344

ethology, p. 364

exosystem, p. 368

genital stage, p. 347

hostile attributional bias, p. 359

id, p. 345

imprinting, p. 364

incremental theory, p. 361

incremental/mastery orientation, p. 360

intermittent reinforcement, p. 353

internalization, p. 346

latency period, p. 347

macrosystem, p. 370

mesosystem, p. 368

microsystem, p. 368

Oedipus complex, p. 346

oral stage, p. 345

parental-investment theory, p. 366

perceived self-efficacy, p. 356

phallic stage, p. 346

psychic energy, p. 344

reciprocal determinism, p. 355

role taking, p. 358

self-socialization, p. 358

superego, p. 346

systematic desensitization, p. 352

vicarious reinforcement, p. 354

WILLIAM IRELAND, *The Chase*

chapter 10:

Emotional Development

magine the following situation: a young girl is taken to a room in her preschool where an experimenter shows her some tasty treats, such as Smarties, marshmallows, or pretzels. Then the experimenter tells the girl that he is going to leave the room "for a while" and that she has two choices. If she waits until he returns to the room, she can have two of the treats. Or if she wishes, she can ring a bell and the experimenter will return immediately—but she will get only one treat. The child is then left alone for a considerable period, say 15 to 20 minutes, or until she rings the bell.

Walter Mischel and his colleagues used this procedure in numerous studies with preschoolers and young school-age children to study their ability to delay immediate gratification in order to obtain larger rewards. Videotapes of what the children did during the time they were alone with the treats showed that the children varied in their responses. Some distracted themselves by talking, singing, trying to sleep, or making up games to play. Others kept looking at the rewards or the bell.

Which children do you think were most successful at curbing their desire for the treats and holding out for the larger reward? Of course, it was the children who distracted themselves (Mischel, 1981; Rodriguez, Mischel, & Shoda, 1989). More important, the amount of time children were able to delay requesting the treat proved to be a remarkably good predictor of their social and cognitive competence and their coping skills at an older age. For example, 10 years after the experiment, the children were rated by their parents with regard to their academic and social competence, as well as their verbal fluency, rational thinking, attentiveness, planfulness, and ability to deal with frustration. Those who had waited the longest in Mischel's experiment were rated higher on these dimensions than were those who had summoned the experimenter back after shorter periods (Mischel, Shoda, & Peake, 1988; Peake, Hebl, & Mischel, 2002). In high school, they also obtained higher university admission test scores and scored higher on a behavioural measure requiring control of one's attention and behavioural responses on a computer task (Eigsti et al., 2006; Shoda, Mischel, & Peake, 1990); and at about age 27, they had achieved a higher educational level, had higher self-esteem, and were reported to be better able to cope with stress. Men in this group also were less likely to have used cocaine or crack in the past year (Ayduk et al., 2000; Mischel & Ayduk, 2004; Peake & Mischel, 2000). Furthermore, in computer-task assessments 40 years after the original experiment, those who had been low in delay of gratification in Mischel's study continued to exhibit greater difficulty in delaying responses to rewarding stimuli than did those who had been high in delay (Casey et al., 2011).

That the ability to delay gratification in one situation in preschool predicted social, emotional, and academic competence so many years later illustrates the importance of what has been labelled "emotional intelligence," or "affective social competence." **Emotional intelligence** refers to a set of abilities that are key to competent social functioning. These abilities include being able to motivate oneself and persist in the face of frustration, control impulses and delay gratification, identify and understand one's own and others' feelings, regulate one's moods, regulate the expression of emotion in social interactions, and empathize with others' emotions (Goleman, 1995; Halberstadt, Denham, & Dunsmore, 2001; Matthews, Zeidner, & Roberts, 2002).

BILL ARON / PHOTOEDIT

Many replications of Mischel's delay-of-gratification study have confirmed that children can hold out longer against temptation if they avert their attention from the desired object. This young girl is struggling to resist taking the marshmallow now in front of her in order to get two later, but she seems likely to lose the battle.

emotional intelligence ■ A set of abilities that contribute to competence in the social and emotional domains.

The importance of emotional intelligence is reflected in the fact that, more than almost any other measure, it predicts how well people do in life, especially in their social lives. For example, researchers checked in with 450 boys from economically disadvantaged neighbourhoods when those boys reached middle age and discovered that how well they had done at work and in other areas of their lives had relatively little relation to their IQs. Rather, their success corresponded with their ability to manage their frustration, control their emotions, and get along with others (Felsman & Vaillant, 1987). The similarity between the results of this study and the findings of Mischel and his colleagues underscores the point that our emotions, and how we deal with them, play a huge role in the quality of our lives and in our relationships with others.

In this chapter, we examine the development of children's emotions as well as the development of their ability to regulate their emotions and the behaviour associated with them. In addition, we discuss the development of children's understanding of emotion, which affects how well they can control their emotions and behaviour. In the course of our discussion, we will give particular emphasis to several of our themes. Key among them will be the theme of *individual differences*, as we examine differences among children in various aspects of their emotional functioning. We will also discuss the origins of these differences, including heredity, parental socialization practices, cultural beliefs related to emotion, and how the child's behaviour in a given context affects his or her physiological reactions. Thus, the themes of *nature and nurture* and the *sociocultural context* will also be prominent. The theme of the *active child* is also touched upon with respect to children's attempts to regulate their own emotions and behaviour. Finally, the theme of *continuity versus discontinuity* is discussed briefly in regard to the emergence of self-conscious emotions.

The Development of Emotions in Childhood

Most people take the idea of **emotion** for granted and just equate the term with "feelings." However, developmentalists have a much more complex view of emotions. They see emotions in terms of several components: (1) neural responses involved in emotion; (2) physiological factors, including heart and breath rate and hormone levels; (3) subjective feelings; (4) the cognitions or perceptions that cause or are associated with the aforementioned neural and physiological responses and subjective feelings; and (5) the desire to take action, including the desire to escape, approach, or change people or things in the environment. In addition, emotions can involve expressive behaviour and cognitive interpretations of, or reactions to, the feeling state (Izard, 2010; Saarni et al., 2006).

A simple example illustrates these components in combination: when people experience fear in response to a growling dog, they typically react with heightened physiological arousal, subjective feelings of fearfulness, thoughts about the ways in which the dog might hurt them, and the motivation to get away from the dog. They may also begin calculating their chances of eluding the dog and, finding them slim, imagine the dog to be bigger and more vicious, and themselves more helpless, than previously, thereby increasing their fear.

Although most psychologists share this general view of emotions, they often do not agree on the relative importance of its key components (Lindquist et al., 2013; Mulligan & Scherer, 2012; Tracy & Randles, 2011). For example, some theorists believe that cognition plays a much more important role in the experience of

emotion ■ Emotion is characterized by neural and physiological responses, subjective feelings, cognitions related to those feelings, and the desire to take action.

differential (or discrete) emotions theory ■ A theory about emotions, held by Tomkins, Izard, and others, in which emotions are viewed as innate and discrete from one another from very early in life, and each emotion is believed to be packaged with a specific and distinctive set of bodily and facial reactions.

functionalist approach ■ A theory of emotion, proposed by Campos and others, that argues that the basic function of emotions is to promote action toward achieving a goal. In this view, emotions are not discrete from one another and vary somewhat based on the social environment.

emotion than do other theorists. Moreover, there is considerable debate concerning the degree to which emotions are innate or learned and about when and in what form different emotions emerge during infancy. Before considering the development of specific emotions in childhood, we first need to examine some of the major views that have been proposed regarding the nature and emergence of emotions.

Theories on the Nature and Emergence of Emotion

The debate about the nature and emergence of emotions in children has deep roots. In *The Expression of the Emotions in Man and Animals,* published in 1872, Charles Darwin argued that the facial expressions for certain basic emotional states are innate to the species—and therefore similar across all peoples—and are found even in very young babies. A corresponding view that has been held by some contemporary investigators is **differential** (or **discrete**) **emotions theory,** which has argued that each emotion is innately packaged with a specific set of physiological, bodily, and facial reactions and that distinct emotions can be differentiated very early in life (Ekman & Cordaro, 2011; Izard, 2007, 2011; Tomkins, 1962).

Other researchers maintain that emotions are not distinct from one another at the beginning of life and that environmental factors play an important role in the emergence and expression of emotions. Some argue, for example, that infants experience only excitement and distress in the first weeks of life, and that other emotions emerge at later ages as a function of experience. According to Sroufe (1979, 1995), there are three basic affect systems—joy/pleasure, anger/frustration, and wariness/fear—and these systems undergo developmental change from primitive to more advanced forms during the early years of life. For instance, wariness/fear is first expressed as a startle or pain reaction. At a few months of age, infants start to show wariness of novel situations, and a few months later show clear signs of fear in novel situations. In Sroufe's view, such changes are largely due to infants' expanding social experiences and their increasing ability to understand them.

The role of the environment is also emphasized by theorists who take a **functionalist approach** to understanding emotional development. They propose that the basic function of emotions is to promote action toward achieving a goal in a given context (J. J. Campos et al., 1994; Saarni et al., 2006). The emotion of fear, for example, often causes one to flee or otherwise avoid a stimulus that represents a threat. This action helps achieve the goal of self-preservation (see Table 10.1 for other examples). Functionalists have also argued that emotional reactions are affected by social goals, the immediate context and the individuals involved in it, as well as others' interpretations of events and their reactions to them, both in a given context and in the past (Boiger & Mesquita, 2012; Saarni et al., 2006). For instance, young children's experience of emotions such as shame and guilt is related to the values and standards communicated to them by their parents, the manner in which the values and standards are communicated, and the quality of the children's relationships with their parents.

Although these perspectives differ regarding whether distinct emotions emerge early in life, each with its own set of physiological components, they all agree that cognition and experience shape emotional development. However, few theories within these perspectives offer a detailed description of the emotional processing that accounts for the great variation in emotional experience and developmental trajectories across individuals, even among those who share somewhat similar situations or characteristics.

TABLE 10.1

Characteristics of Some Families of Emotion

Emotion type	Goal connected with the emotion	Meaning regarding the self	Meaning regarding others	Action tendency
Disgust	Avoiding contamination or illness	"This stimulus may contaminate me or make me ill."	—	Active rejection of the thing causing disgust
Fear	Maintaining one's own physical and psychological integrity	"This stimulus is threatening to me."	—	Flight or withdrawal
Anger	Attaining the end state that the individual currently is invested in	"There is an obstacle to my obtaining my goal."	—	Forward movement, especially to eliminate obstacles to one's goal
Sadness	Attaining the end state that the individual currently is invested in	"My goal is unattainable."	—	Disengagement and withdrawal
Shame	Maintaining others' respect and affection; preserving self-esteem	"I am bad (my self-esteem is damaged)."	"Others notice how bad I am."	Withdrawal; avoiding others, hiding oneself
Guilt	Meeting one's own internalized values	"I have done something contrary to my values."	"Someone has been injured by my actions."	Movement to make reparation, to inform others, or to punish self

Source: Adapted from Saarni et al., 1998, p. 239

An emerging perspective that explicitly deals with how the child's characteristics and experiences coalesce in emotional processing is *dynamic-systems theory* (see Chapter 4). From this perspective, novel forms of functioning (emotional or otherwise) arise through the spontaneous coordination of components interacting repeatedly. In these interactions, specific cognitions (including appraisals of events and objects), emotional feelings, and physiological and neural events tend to link together more closely with each repeated occasion, forming coherent "emotional interpretations" that become increasingly coordinated each time they are co-activated (M. D. Lewis, 2005; see also Fogel et al., 1992; Witherington & Crichton, 2007). A dynamic-systems approach postulates that emotional reactions develop differently for each person, based on an individual's emotion-related biology and cognitive capacities, his or her experiences, and how these factors tend to coalesce across time in an increasingly coherent and predictable manner. As you will see in the next section, it is not yet clear to what degree infants' emotions are distinct, emerge early, and can be reliably differentiated. It also is not clear to what degree young children's basic emotions are innate or develop as a consequence of experience.

The Emergence of Emotion in the Early Years and Childhood

Parents are likely to think that they see many emotions in their infants, including interest and joy, as well as anger, fear, and sadness—even in their 1-month-olds. In fact, however, parents often read into their infant's emotional reaction whatever emotion would seem appropriate in the immediate situation. For example, if a parent gives an infant a novel toy and the infant reacts negatively, the parent may assume that the infant's reaction is an expression of fear, when it could just as well be an expression of anger or upset at being overstimulated or at having a current activity disrupted.

To make their own interpretations of infants' emotions more objective, researchers have devised highly elaborate systems for identifying the emotional meaning of infants' facial expressions. These systems involve coding dozens of facial cues—whether an infant's eyebrows are raised or knitted together;

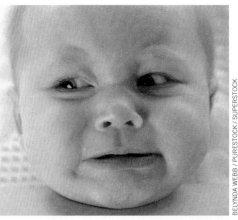

As is evident from this infant's expression, it often is difficult to identify what negative emotion a young infant is feeling.

BELYNDA WEBB / PURESTOCK / SUPERSTOCK

social smiles ■ Smiles that are directed at people. They first emerge as early as 6 to 7 weeks of age.

whether the eyes are wide open, tightly closed, or narrowed; whether the lips are pursed, softly rounded, or retracted straight back; and so on—and then analyzing the combination in which these cues are present. Even with such detailed analysis, however, it is often hard to determine—beyond positive or negative—exactly what emotions infants are experiencing, and it is particularly difficult to differentiate among the various negative emotions that young infants express.

We will begin our examination of the emergence of emotions with the easier task—tracing the early development of positive emotions.

Positive Emotions

The first clear sign of happiness that infants express is a smile. During the 1st month, they exhibit fleeting smiles, primarily during the REM phase of sleep; after the 1st month, they sometimes smile when they are stroked gently. These early smiles may be reflexive and seem to be evoked by some biological state rather than by social interaction (Sroufe & Waters, 1976; Wolff, 1987).

Between the 3rd and 8th week of life, infants begin to smile in reaction to external stimuli, including touching, high-pitched voices, or other stimuli that engage their attention (Sroufe, 1995). More important, by the 3rd month of life, and sometimes as early as 6 or 7 weeks of age, babies begin to exhibit **social smiles,** that is, smiles directed toward people (B. L. White, 1985). Social smiles frequently occur during interactions with a parent or other familiar people and tend to elicit the adult's delight, interest, and affection (Camras, Malatesta, & Izard, 1991; Huebner & Izard, 1988). In turn, this response usually inspires more social smiling from the infant. Thus, the infant's early social smiles likely promote care from parents and other adults and strengthen the infant's relationships with other people.

The social basis of social smiles is highlighted by the fact that although young infants sometimes smile at interesting objects, humans are much more likely to make them smile. This difference was demonstrated in a study by Queen's University researchers in which 3-month-olds smiled and vocalized much more at people, even strangers, than at puppet-like foam balls that resembled people, were animated, and "talked" to the infant (Ellsworth, Muir, & Hains, 1993).

When infants are at least 2 months of age, they also show happiness in both social and non-social contexts in which they can control a particular event. In one study that demonstrated this, researchers divided infants into two groups and attached a string to an arm of each infant. Observing the infants individually, they arranged for infants in one group to hear music whenever they pulled the string and for infants in the other group to hear music at random intervals. The infants who "caused" the music to play by pulling on the string showed more interest and smiling when the music came on than did the infants whose string-pulling had no connection to the music's being played (M. Lewis, Alessandri, & Sullivan, 1990). This pleasure in controlling events is evident in infants' delight when they can consistently make a noise by shaking their rattle or banging a toy on the floor.

At about 7 months of age, infants start to smile primarily at *familiar* people, rather than at people in general. (In fact, as you will see, unfamiliar people often elicit distress at this age.) These selective smiles tend to delight parents and motivate them to continue interacting with the infant. In turn, infants of this age often respond to parents' playfulness and smiles with excitement and joy, which also prolongs their positive social interactions (Weinberg & Tronick, 1994). Such exchanges of positive affect, especially when they occur with parents but not with strangers, make parents feel special to the infant and strengthen the bond between them.

In the first weeks of life, infants' smiles tend to be caused by internal factors and are not social.

Smiles that arise as a function of social interactions, as contrasted with those associated with strictly biological stimuli, typically first appear during the infant's 3rd month.

Children's expression of positive emotion increases across the first year of life (Rothbart & Bates, 2006), perhaps because they are able to understand and respond to more interesting and positive events and stimuli. After about 3 or 4 months of age, infants laugh as well as smile during a variety of activities. For instance, they are likely to laugh when a parent tickles them or blows on their tummy, bounces them on a knee or swings them around in the air, or shares a favourite activity such as bathing with them. By late in the first year of life, children's cognitive development allows them to take pleasure from unexpected or discrepant events such as Mom's making a funny noise or wearing a goofy hat (Kagan, Kearsley, & Zelazo, 1978).

During the second year of life, children start to clown around themselves and are delighted when they can make other people laugh—as in the case of this 18-month-old who looks at his mother and, fully clothed, sits on his potty:

> *Child:* Poo (grunts heavily). Poo! (grunts). Poo! (gets up, looks at Mother,
>   picks up empty potty, and waves it at Mother, laughing)
>
> (Dunn, 1988, p. 154)

Incidents like this are common in the second year of life and demonstrate infants' desire to share positive emotion and activities with parents.

Across the preschool years and elementary school years, children's expression of positive emotion in social interactions, especially intense positive emotion, has been found to decline (Sallquist et al., 2009, 2010). This pattern might be due to children's learning to modulate their expression of positive emotion, especially in contexts in which it might be inappropriate or disruptive to working on tasks (Kochanska et al., 2007).

Negative Emotions

The first negative emotion that is discernible in newborn infants is generalized distress, which can be evoked by a variety of experiences ranging from hunger and pain to overstimulation. Often expressed with piercing cries and a face screwed up in a tight grimace, this type of distress is unmistakable.

The emergence and development of other negative emotions in infancy are, as noted earlier, more difficult to pin down. A number of studies suggest that negative emotion in young infants continues to be expressed as undifferentiated distress (Oster, Hegley, & Nagel, 1992) and that anger and distress/pain are especially likely to be undifferentiated in most contexts (Camras, 1992; Camras & Shutter, 2010). Dynamic-systems theorists have argued that differentiating among infants' expression of emotions is difficult partly because their expressions of emotion are affected by non-emotional factors such as the position of their head, their respiration, and where they are looking (which affects the eyebrow and areas around the eye), as well as by their immediate experience of emotion and interpretation of the context (Camras, 2011). It is also likely that infants' expressions of emotion often reflect a mix of emotions, which makes it additionally difficult to know what infants are feeling (M. Lewis, 2011).

The interpretation of negative emotions is complicated by the fact that infants sometimes display negative emotions that seem incongruent with the situation they are experiencing (Bennett, Bendersky, & Lewis, 2002; Camras, 1992; Hiatt, Campos, & Emde, 1979). In the string-pulling study cited earlier, for example, the infants who could "control" the music by pulling the string attached to their arms fussed and sometimes expressed anger when their pulling of the string no longer produced music. Other times, however, these infants showed fear when pulling

Some theorists believe that young infants can experience sadness and anger, whereas others believe that they only experience an undifferentiated state of distress.

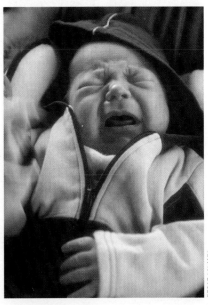

the string no longer produced music (M. Lewis et al., 1990). Incongruities such as these highlight the difficulty of knowing for certain what emotion an infant may be experiencing in certain situations.

In *some* contexts involving relatively intense emotion, however, investigators have been able to differentiate among certain negative emotions in fairly young infants. By 2 months of age, for example, facial expressions that appear to represent anger and sadness have been reliably differentiated from each other and from distress/pain in situations such as getting an injection during a medical procedure (Izard, Hembree, & Huebner, 1987). The correspondence between the context and infants' emotional expressions seems to become more consistent from 5 to 12 months of age. For instance, in research in which experimenters prevented infants from moving their arms, the infants' expressions indicative of anger increased with age, whereas their expressions of interest and surprise decreased (Bennett, Bendersky, & Lewis, 2005).

Fear and distress Although there is little firm evidence of distinct fear reactions in infants during the first months of life (Witherington, Campos, & Hertenstein, 2007), by 4 months of age, infants do seem wary of unfamiliar objects and events (Sroufe, 1995). Then, at around the age of 6 or 7 months, initial signs of fear begin to appear (Camras et al., 1991), most notably the fear of strangers in many circumstances. In part, this shift likely reflects infants' recognition that unfamiliar people do not provide the comfort and pleasure that familiar people do.

Consider the following contrast: at the age of 10 weeks, as Janine was whimpering in her crib, a stranger came over and smiled and talked to her. Janine stopped fussing and smiled at the stranger. At the age of 8 months, Janine is playing on her mother's knee when her mother has to put her down and leave the room to answer the door. A moment later the visitor, a stranger, enters the room without Janine's mother.

> When the visitor enters, Janine cries. The visitor tries to comfort Janine by picking her up and talking softly to her, but she cries still more frantically until her mother returns and holds her. Then Janine calms down and smiles when her mother lifts her high in the air in play.
>
> (Bronson, 1972)

In general, the fear of strangers intensifies and lasts until about age 2 years. However, it should be noted that the fear of strangers is quite variable (Sroufe, 1995), depending on both the infant's temperament (i.e., how fearful the infant is in general) and the specific context, such as whether a parent is present and the manner in which the stranger approaches (e.g., abruptly and excitedly or slowly and calmly).

Other fears are also evident at around the age of 7 months, including fear of novel toys, loud noises, and sudden movements by people or objects, all of which tend to increase until about 12 to 16 months of age (see Figure 10.1) (Braungart-Rieker, Hill-Soderlund, & Karrass, 2010; Kagan et al., 1978; Scarr & Salapatek, 1970). The emergence of such fears is clearly adaptive. Since babies often do not have the ability to escape from potentially dangerous situations on their own, they must rely on their parents to protect them, and expressions of fear and distress are powerful tools for bringing help and support when they are needed. Individual differences in the decline in

Young children who were not afraid of strangers at 6 months of age often suddenly show fear of them at 7 or 8 months of age.

CHRISTINA KENNEDY / PHOTOEDIT

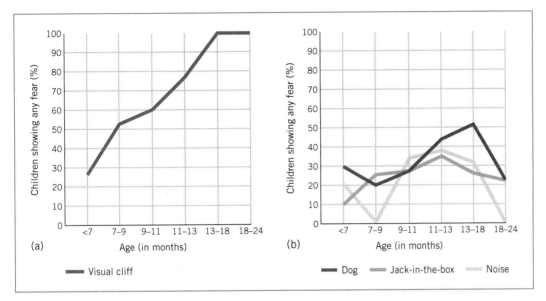

FIGURE 10.1 Percentages of young children showing fear of (a) the visual cliff and (b) dogs, noises, and a jack-in-the-box. Children 1½ to 2 years of age show the most fear of the visual cliff (see Box 5.5, page 196). Children show the most fear of the jack-in-the-box and loud noises at about 1 year of age and the most fear of dogs at 1 to 1½ years of age. (Adapted from Scarr & Salapatek, 1970)

these kinds of fears seem to be related to the quality of children's relationships with their mothers and how effectively their mothers deal with their children's expressions of fear (K. A. Buss & Kiel, 2011; Kochanska, 2001).

An especially salient and important type of fear or distress that emerges at about 8 months of age is **separation anxiety**—distress due to separation from the parent who is the child's primary caregiver. When infants experience separation anxiety, they typically whine, cry, or otherwise express fear and upset. However, the degree to which children exhibit such distress varies with the context. For instance, infants show much less distress when they crawl or walk away from a parent than when the parent does the departing (Rheingold & Eckerman, 1970). Separation anxiety tends to increase from 8 to 13 or 15 months of age, and then begins to decline (Kagan, 1976). This pattern of separation anxiety occurs across many cultures, displayed by infants reared in environments as disparate as Israeli kibbutzim (communal farming communities), !Kung San hunting-and-gathering groups in the Kalahari Desert in Africa, and the U.S. middle class (Kagan, 1976). (Figure 10.2 shows this pattern in Chinese and European-American children.)

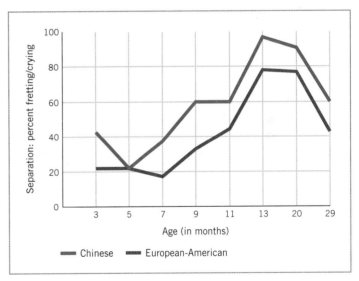

FIGURE 10.2 Percentages of Chinese and European-American children at different ages displaying fretting or crying at the departure of mother Children exhibit the most evidence of separation anxiety at about 13 months of age, and Chinese children have been found to display somewhat more anxiety and distress than do European-American children. (Adapted from Kagan, Kearsley, & Zelazo, 1978)

Anger and sadness It is likely that anger is distinct from other negative emotions by 4 to 8 months of age (Camras et al., 1991; M. W. Sullivan & Lewis, 2003). By their 1st birthday, infants clearly and frequently express anger, often toward other people (Radke-Yarrow & Kochanska, 1990), and their expression of anger typically increases until 16 months of age, although there is considerable variation in this

separation anxiety ■ Feelings of distress that children, especially infants and toddlers, experience when they are separated, or expect to be separated, from individuals to whom they are emotionally attached.

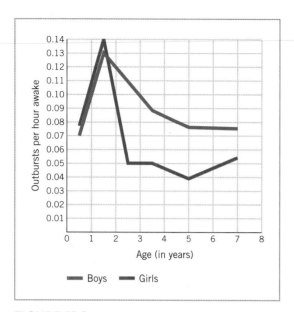

FIGURE 10.3 **Frequency of angry outbursts in the home** Children display the most anger at home during the second year of life. Displays of anger drop sharply thereafter, especially for girls. (Adapted from Goodenough, 1931)

pattern across infants (Braungart-Rieker et al., 2010). Over the course of their second year, as children become better able to control their environments, they are increasingly likely to be upset when control is taken away from them or when they are otherwise frustrated (see Figure 10.3) (Goodenough, 1931).

Infants often exhibit sadness in the same types of situations in which they show anger, such as after a painful event and when they cannot control outcomes in their environment, although displays of sadness appear to be somewhat less frequent than displays of anger or distress (Izard et al., 1987, 1995; M. Lewis et al., 1990; Shiller, Izard, & Hembree, 1986). In addition, when older infants or young children are separated from their parents for extended periods and are not given sensitive care during this period, they often show intense and prolonged displays of sadness (Bowlby, 1973; J. Robertson & Robertson, 1971).

Except in the case of children who have problematic relationships, the expression of negative emotion, and perhaps the experiencing of it, generally decline after the second year of life (Kochanska, 2001). Toddlers are quicker to respond with physical expressions of anger at 18 to 24 months of age than they are at 36 months or older (P. M. Cole et al., 2011); and from age 3 to 6 years, children show less negative emotion on structured laboratory tasks designed to elicit it (Durbin, 2010). The general decline in negative emotionality is likely due to children's increasing ability to express themselves with language (Kopp, 1992), as well as to the increasing ability for the average child to regulate the expression of their negative feelings.

The Self-Conscious Emotions: Embarrassment, Pride, Guilt, and Shame

During the second year of life, children begin to show a range of new emotions: embarrassment, pride, guilt, and shame (Stipek, Gralinski, & Kopp, 1990; R. A. Thompson, 2006; Zahn-Waxler & Robinson, 1995). These emotions often are called **self-conscious emotions** because they relate to our sense of self and our consciousness of others' reactions to us. Some investigators such as Michael Lewis believe that these emotions emerge in the second year because that is when children gain the understanding that they themselves are entities distinct from other people and begin to develop a sense of self (M. Lewis, 1998). Such a view implies an abrupt, qualitative change in children's abilities to experience these emotions and suggests discontinuity in emotional development due to the emergence of an underlying cognitive awareness (M. Lewis, 1998; Mascolo, Fischer, & Li, 2003). The emergence of self-conscious emotions is also fostered by children's growing sense of what adults and society expect of them and their acceptance of these external standards (Lagattuta & Thompson, 2007; M. Lewis, Alessandri, & Sullivan, 1992; Mascolo et al., 2003).

At about 15 to 24 months of age, some children start to show embarrassment when they are made the centre of attention. Asked to show off an ability or a new piece of clothing, for example, they lower their eyes, hang their head, blush, or hide their face in their hands (M. Lewis, 1995).

The first signs of pride are evident in children's smiling glances at others when they have successfully met a challenge or achieved something new, like taking their first step. By 3 years of age, children's pride is increasingly tied to the level of their performance. Children express more pride, for example, when they succeed on difficult tasks than they do when they succeed on easy ones (M. Lewis et al., 1992).

self-conscious emotions ■ Emotions such as guilt, shame, embarrassment, and pride that relate to our sense of self and our consciousness of others' reactions to us.

The two other self-conscious emotions, guilt and shame, are sometimes mistakenly thought of as roughly equivalent, but they are actually quite distinct. Guilt is associated with empathy for others and involves feelings of remorse and regret about one's behaviour, as well as the desire to undo the consequences of that behaviour (M. L. Hoffman, 2000). In contrast, shame does not seem to be related to concern about others. When children feel shame, their focus is on themselves: they feel that they are exposed, and they often feel like hiding (N. Eisenberg, 2000; Tangney, Stuewig, & Mashek, 2007).

Shame and guilt can be distinguished fairly early, as documented by a study in which researchers arranged for 2-year-olds to play with a doll belonging to an adult (the experimenter). The doll had been rigged so that one leg would fall off during play, while the adult was out of the room. When the "accident" occurred, some toddlers displayed a pattern of behaviour that seemed to reflect shame—that is, they avoided the adult when she returned to the room and delayed telling her about the mishap. Other children showed a pattern of behaviour that seemed to reflect guilt—that is, they repaired the doll quickly, told the adult about the mishap shortly after she returned to the room, and showed relatively little avoidance of her (Barrett, Zahn-Waxler, & Cole, 1993). In general, the degree of association of guilt feelings with bad or hurtful behaviour increases in the second to third year (Aksan & Kochanska, 2005), and the individual differences in children's guilt observed at 22 months of age remain relatively stable across the early preschool years (Kochanska, Gross, et al., 2002).

Children in the preschool years often exhibit shame or guilt when they do something wrong.

In everyday life as well, the same situation often elicits shame in some individuals and guilt in others. Which emotion children experience partly depends on parental practices. Studies of North American children have found that they are more likely to experience guilt than shame if, when they have done something wrong, their parents emphasize the "badness" of the behaviour ("You did a bad thing") rather than of the child ("You're a bad boy"). In addition, children are more likely to feel guilt rather than shame if their parents help them understand the consequences their actions have for others, teach them the need to repair the harm they have done, avoid publicly humiliating them, and communicate respect and love for their children even when disciplining them (M. L. Hoffman, 2000; Tangney & Dearing, 2002).

The situations likely to induce self-conscious emotions in children vary across cultures, as does the frequency with which specific self-conscious emotions are likely to be experienced (P. M. Cole, Tamang, & Shrestha, 2006). For instance, among many First Nations peoples, humility is encouraged to emphasize respect for others, rather than a lack of pride in oneself, one's family, and one's community (Blackstock, 2003). Similarly, the Japanese tend to avoid bestowing praise on the individual because they believe that it encourages a focus on the self rather than on the needs of the larger social group (M. Lewis, 1992). Correspondingly, Japanese children, in comparison with U.S. children, are less likely to report experiencing pride as a consequence of personal success (Furukawa et al., 2012). This cultural influence is also powerful in Chinese children: reluctant to demonstrate self-pride, they rate lying about doing good deeds more positively than do Canadian children (K. Lee et al., 1997).

Moreover, in many Asian or Southeast Asian cultures that emphasize the welfare of the group rather than the individual, not living up to social or familial obligations is likely to evoke shame or guilt (Mascolo et al., 2003), and children in these cultures report experiencing guilt and shame more than do children in the United States (Furukawa et al., 2012). In such cultures, parents' efforts to elicit shame from their young children are often direct and disparaging (e.g., "You made your mother lose face," "I've never seen any 3-year-old who behaves like you") (Fung & Chen, 2001). This kind of explicit belittling appears to have a more positive effect on children in these Asian cultures than it does on children in Western cultures.

Typical Emotional Development in Childhood

The causes of emotions continue to change in childhood. For example, the basis of children's self-esteem or self-evaluation changes with cognitive development and experience (see Chapter 11), and the events that make children feel happiness and pride tend to change accordingly. From early to middle childhood, for instance, acceptance by peers and achieving goals become increasingly important, and successes in these areas become key sources of happiness and pride. What makes children smile and laugh also changes with age. As their language skills develop along with their understanding of people and events, children in the preschool years begin to find verbal jokes funny (Dunn, 1988).

Similar examples can be seen in regard to children's negative emotions. For instance, as their cognitive ability to represent imaginary phenomena develops in the preschool years, children often start to fear imaginary creatures such as ghosts or monsters. Such fears are uncommon in elementary school children (Silverman, La Greca, & Wasserstein, 1995), probably because children of this age have a better understanding of reality than do younger children. Instead, school-age children's anxieties and fears are generally related to important, real-life issues (albeit sometimes exaggerated), such as challenges at school (tests and grades, being called on in class, and pleasing teachers), health (their parents' and their own), and personal harm (being bullied or robbed). The causes of anger also change as children develop a better understanding of others' intentions and motives. For instance, in the early preschool years, a child is likely to feel anger when harmed by a peer, whether or not the harm was intentional. In contrast, young school-age children are less likely to be angered if they believe that harm done to them was unintentional or that the motive for some harmful action was benign rather than malicious (Coie & Dodge, 1998; Dodge, Murphy, & Buchsbaum, 1984).

The frequency with which specific emotions are experienced also may change in childhood and adolescence. There is some evidence, for example, that over the course of the preschool and early school years, children generally become less emotionally intense and negative (Guerin & Gottfried, 1994; B. C. Murphy et al., 1999; Sallquist et al., 2009). There is also some support for the common assumption that negative emotion increases after middle childhood. Typically, early to middle adolescence is marked by an increase in the frequency or intensity of negative emotions and a decrease in positive emotions. For most youths, the increase is mild (Larson & Lampman-Petraitis, 1989; Larson et al., 2002; Weinstein et al., 2007), but for a minority, it is quite sharp, often in their relations with their parents (Collins & Steinberg, 2006; Laursen, Coy, & Collins, 1998; see also Chapter 12). This negative shift in average emotions generally appears to end by Grade 10, and older adolescents also experience less emotional lability (i.e., day-to-day change) than do younger adolescents (Larson et al., 2002; Weinstein et al., 2007).

Of course, children's emotional states are highly influenced by the world around them, with negative emotions being intensified by stressful conditions. As might be expected, children and adolescents directly exposed to war or terrorism tend to experience unusually high levels of fear, anxiety, and depression (N. Eisenberg &

SW PRODUCTIONS / GETTY IMAGES

It is common for children to experience a modest increase in the intensity of negative emotions as they move into adolescence.

Silver, 2011; P. T. Joshi & O'Donnell, 2003; Weems et al., 2010). Exposure to lesser stressors, such as conflict between parents in the home, or a single mother's entrance into a new romantic relationship or cohabitation arrangement, also appears to increase children's experience of negative emotions such as fear (Bachman, Coley, & Carrano, 2011; Davies, Cicchetti, & Martin, 2012; Rhoades, 2008).

Depression

Major bouts of depression are much more common in adolescence than in childhood, although a small percentage of preschoolers exhibit depressive symptoms that predict problems with depression in the school years (Luby, 2010). Between 12 and 19 years of age, rates of depression begin to increase.

Major, or clinical, depression is characterized by some combination of at least five of the following symptoms, occurring nearly every day for at least 2 weeks: depressed mood most of the time; marked diminished interest or pleasure in almost all activities; significant weight loss; insomnia or excessive sleeping; motor agitation; fatigue or loss of energy; feelings of worthlessness or excessive or inappropriate guilt; diminished ability to think or concentrate; and recurrent thoughts of death (Hammen & Rudolph, 2003). Besides these specific diagnostic criteria, social withdrawal and bodily complaints are common in depressed youth, as is anxiety (C. M. Turner & Barrett, 2003).

In 2009, 2% of male youth and 3.4% of female youth reported having been diagnosed with a mood disorder, which includes depression, bipolar disorder, and other mental illnesses (Public Health Agency of Canada, 2011). In addition to the adolescents who experience major depression, more than 20% of Canadian children in Grades 6 to 10 report having felt low or depressed at least once per week during the past 6 months (Boyce, 2004). (Box 10.1 discusses the gender differences in depression.)

Some investigators have found that adolescents from a lower socioeconomic level are especially prone to major depression (Hammen & Rudolph, 2003). A review of studies from Canada and the United States found that children between 10 and 15 years who are low in socioeconomic status are 2.5 times more likely to be depressed or anxious than youth who are higher in socioeconomic status (Lemstra et al., 2008). In terms of nonclinical symptoms of depression, however, adolescents' self-reports do not reflect such socioeconomic differences.

There are many possible causes of depression. One is heredity: major depression often runs in families. Children whose mothers are depressed tend to exhibit a pattern of activation in the prefrontal cortex and amygdala that is associated with greater reactivity to the environment, negative emotionality, and withdrawal; they also may have elevated hormone-based stress reactivity (Cicchetti & Toth, 2006; Joormann et al., 2012). These biological correlates likely are partly due to a genetic vulnerability, but they also could be exacerbated by problems in parenting that often accompany maternal depression (Cicchetti & Toth, 2006), including insensitivity and disengagement (Belsky, Schlomer, & Ellis, 2012; S. B. Campbell et al., 2007; Garber & Cole, 2010; Lovejoy et al., 2000).

Other family factors likely also contribute to depression in youth. In particular, whether or not the mother is depressed, children's symptoms of depression are frequently associated with low levels of family engagement, support, and acceptance, and with high levels of negativity (Auerbach et al., 2011; Kiff et al., 2011; O. S. Schwartz et al., 2012). Chronic stress and conflict in the family also predict depression in youths (Brennan et al., 2002; Karevold et al., 2009; H. K. Kim, Capaldi, & Stoolmiller, 2003).

BOX 10.1: individual differences

GENDER DIFFERENCES IN ADOLESCENT DEPRESSION

One of the most striking features of adolescent depression is the gender-related differences in its occurrence (Costello et al., 2008; Twenge & Nolen-Hoeksema, 2002). By age 12, the rate of depression among Canadian girls begins to be higher than that for boys, and by age 19, it is roughly two times as high (Galambos, Leadbeater, & Barker, 2004; Public Health Agency of Canada, 2011). Similar gender differences in the patterns of adolescent depression have been found in numerous countries (Hankin et al., 1998; Wichstrom, 1999).

Why are adolescent girls more likely than boys to experience depression? The biological changes of puberty tend to be more difficult for girls and may contribute to girls' vulnerability (Hilt & Nolen-Hoeksema, 2009). It also seems likely that a key factor is the greater socioemotional stress that adolescence represents for girls (Petersen, Sarigiani, & Kennedy, 1991), at least in certain cultures. Important stressors may include concerns about one's body and appearance (Hankin, Mermelstein, & Roesch, 2007). As discussed in Chapter 15, adolescent girls report greater dissatisfaction with their bodies than boys report with theirs. This dissatisfaction, fuelled by a cultural obsession with an "ideal" body type

attainable only by a few, seems to contribute substantially to low self-esteem and depression in adolescent girls (Compian, Gowen, & Hayward, 2004; Hankin & Abramson, 1999; Harter, 2006; Wichstrom, 1999).

Another stressor for girls can be the social consequences of early puberty, which represent a clear risk for depression (Negriff & Susman, 2011). Early maturity, for example, may lead young adolescent girls to become involved with older adolescent boys, who may pressure them to engage in sexual activity, drinking, or delinquency. Many younger girls often are not cognitively and socially mature enough to cope with these pressures (Ge, Conger, & Elder, 1996; Ge et al., 2003). In contrast, for boys, early puberty has been less consistently related to internalizing problems such as depression. However, recent evidence suggests that boys who enter puberty early and move through it quickly are, in fact, at risk for depression (Ge et al., 2003; Mendle et al., 2010), in part because of a decline in the quality of their relationships with peers (Mendle et al., 2012). For both sexes, early puberty is especially likely to be associated with depressive symptoms if it is accompanied by low popularity (Teunissen et al., 2011). For boys, starting puberty later than one's peers

is a predictor of depression as well (Negriff & Susman, 2011).

Also appearing to contribute to the higher rates of depression for adolescent girls is the fact that they, more than their male peers, are prone to repeatedly focus on causes, consequences, and symptoms of their negative emotions ("I'm so fat" or "I'm so tired") and on the meaning of their distress ("What's wrong with my life?") without engaging in efforts to remedy their situation (Hankin, Stone, & Wright, 2010; Nolen-Hoeksema, Larson, & Grayson, 1999). Such thinking, called **rumination**, seems to increase the chances of becoming depressed, and some researchers have found this relation to be stronger for girls than for boys (Abela et al., 2012; Nolen-Hoeksema, 2012; Nolen-Hoeksema et al., 2007). Moreover, **co-rumination**— that is, extensively discussing and self-disclosing emotional problems with another person (usually a peer)—is more common for girls and seems to further account for the gender difference in depression (A. J. Rose, 2002). However, co-rumination predicts greater severity of depression and anxiety in boys as well as girls (Hankin, et al., 2010; Schwartz-Mette & Rose, 2012; L. B. Stone et al., 2011).

rumination ■ A perseverative focus on one's own negative emotions and on their causes and consequences, without engaging in efforts to improve one's situation.

co-rumination ■ Extensively discussing and self-disclosing emotional problems with another person.

In addition, some investigators emphasize the role that maladaptive belief systems play in the onset and maintenance of depression (Beck, 1983; Hammen & Rudolph, 2003). They argue, for example, that depressed individuals tend to see themselves and others in an excessively negative way and, thus, feel incompetent, flawed, and worthless, and view the world as cruel and unfair (Bohon et al., 2008; K. B. Hoffman et al., 2000; Rudolph & Clark, 2001). They may also feel that they cannot change things for the better because they believe that negative events are beyond their control, and they often do not take credit for their accomplishments (Garber et al., 2002; Gregory et al., 2007; Seligman, 1975). Finally, as noted in Box 10.1, depressed youths also tend to ruminate about the potential causes and negative consequences of their symptoms (Schniering & Rapee, 2004); this rumination can intensify their negative feelings without leading to productive problem solving and solutions (Nolen-Hoeksema, Wisco, & Lyubomirsky, 2008; Silk et al., 2003). All these ideas about the causes of depression have received some support from research (Abela et al., 2011; Hammen & Rudolph, 2003).

Other investigators argue that youths get depressed because they lack the skills needed for appropriate emotional regulation and positive social interactions (e.g., P. M. Cole, Luby, & Sullivan, 2008; Kovacs et al., 2008). Consistent with this view, children and adolescents who experience depression frequently are low in regulation and exhibit behavioural problems such as aggression, stealing, delinquency, and substance abuse (see Chapter 14) (Diamantopoulou et al., 2011; Wiesner & Kim, 2006; Yap et al., 2011). This pattern may contribute to the difficulties depressed youths often tend to have in their relationships with peers (Rudolph, Ladd, & Dinella, 2007; Teunissen et al., 2011).

It has also been proposed that peer victimization and rejection contribute to depression (Hawker & Boulton, 2000; Witvliet et al., 2010), an idea that seems supported by the finding that a sense of connection with peers and school is associated with less depression (Auerbach et al., 2011; D. M. Costello et al., 2008). However, evidence from a recent study that followed children from Grades 4 to 6 suggests that children's depression contributes to peer victimization, which in turn predicts low acceptance by peers, and that problems with peers did not cause depression (Kochel et al., 2012).

In many cases, depression is likely due to a combination of personal vulnerability and external stressful factors (Lewinsohn, Joiner, & Rohde, 2001). In a study of youths making the transition to middle school, for instance, those who felt that they had little control over their success in school and who demonstrated little investment in school were especially likely to show an increase in depressive symptoms if they also experienced the transition as stressful (Rudolph et al., 2001). Other research found that girls who were low in the regulation of sadness were prone to depressive symptoms in preadolescence if their parents were not especially caring and supportive (Feng et al., 2009). In addition, the combination of family difficulties (e.g., separation from parents) in early childhood and high levels of interpersonal stress later on may increase youths' vulnerability to depression (Rudolph & Flynn, 2007), perhaps because early stress can affect the child's ability to adapt physiologically years later (Gunnar & Vazquez, 2006).

A common treatment for depression in youth is drug therapy, but recent concerns have been raised about the possibility that antidepressants may increase the risk of suicidal thinking and behaviour for some adolescents (Calati et al., 2011). Other effective treatments include cognitive-behavioural therapy (Weisz, McCarty, & Valeri, 2006) and programs designed to promote optimistic thinking and teach positive approaches to solving personal problems (Gillham et al., 1995; Jaycox et al., 1994; S. H. Spence, Sheffield, & Donovan, 2003).

In adolescence, depression is much more common among girls than among boys and, in girls, is frequently accompanied by unhappiness with one's appearance and weight.

KALLE SINGER / GETTY IMAGES

review:

Emotions are fundamental for much of human functioning and undergo change in the early months and years of life. Smiles emerge early but do not become social until the 2nd to 3rd month of life, and what makes children smile and laugh changes with age and cognitive development. Distress in newborns involves hunger and various other discomforts; by 6 to 7 months of age, it is often caused by a stranger's approach; by approximately 8 months of age, it is likely to be triggered by a separation from parents. Separation distress develops in similar ways in various cultures.

It is hard to know exactly when anger emerges because distress/pain and anger are difficult to differentiate early in life. Children may experience anger by the 2nd month of life in response to loss of control. In the first months, it is similarly difficult to differentiate fear from distress, but fear likely has emerged by 6 or 7 months of age, when some children appear to display fear of strangers. Young children also exhibit sadness, especially when they are separated from loved ones for extended periods.

emotional self-regulation ■ The process of initiating, inhibiting, or modulating internal feeling states and related physiological processes, cognitions, and behaviours.

The self-conscious emotions—embarrassment, pride, shame, and guilt—emerge somewhat later than do most emotions, probably in the second year of life. Their emergence is tied in part to the development of a rudimentary sense of self and to an appreciation of others' reactions to the self. Situations that evoke these emotions vary across cultures.

Emotions continue to change in their occurrence and causes in childhood and adolescence. Depression increases markedly in adolescence, especially for girls. Age-related cognitive, biological, and experiential factors likely account for these changes.

Regulation of Emotion

Throughout life, being able to regulate one's emotions is crucial to achieving one's goals. **Emotional self-regulation** is a complex process that involves initiating, inhibiting, or modulating the following aspects of emotional functioning:

1. *Internal feeling states* (the subjective experience of emotion)

2. *Emotion-related cognitions* (e.g., thoughts about one's desires or goals; one's interpretation of an evocative situation; self-monitoring of one's emotional states)

3. *Emotion-related physiological processes* (e.g., heart rate and hormonal or other physiological reactions, including neural activation, that can change as a function of regulating one's feeling states and thoughts)

4. *Emotion-related behaviour* (e.g., actions or facial expressions related to one's feelings)

Parents often help young children regulate themselves by physically calming them or distracting them with an object.

© IMAGE SOURCE / SUPERSTOCK

To complicate matters, children's emotionality is difficult to differentiate from their self-regulation (J. J. Gross & Barrett, 2011) and appears to affect the ways in which they regulate both their emotions and behaviour (Ekas et al., 2011; Raikes et al., 2007). For example, when children are fearful, they may have more difficulty managing their thoughts, feelings, and behaviour than when they are calm. Moreover, emotions often may have a regulatory function in that they affect the nature of children's thoughts and behaviours in specific situations, for instance, whether children approach or avoid novel objects or people.

The emergence of emotional regulation in childhood is a long, slow process. Obviously, young infants are not very good at controlling their emotional reactions. They are easily overwhelmed by loud noises, abrupt movements, hunger, and pain and must rely on their caregivers to settle them down. Older infants also have difficulty dealing with intense emotions such as fear of strangers or of being left alone, and they often run to parents for comfort. Indeed, it takes years for children to develop the abilities to reliably regulate their emotions and control the behaviours associated with them.

The Development of Emotional Regulation

The development of emotional regulation is characterized by three general age-related patterns of change. The first pattern involves the transition from infants' relying almost totally on other people to help them regulate their emotions to their being increasingly able to self-regulate during early childhood. The second pattern involves the increasing use of cognitive strategies and planful problem solving to control negative emotions. The third pattern involves the increasing selection and use of appropriate, effective regulating strategies (Zimmer-Gembeck & Skinner, 2011).

The Shift from Caregiver Regulation to Self-Regulation

When young infants are distressed, frustrated, or frightened, their parents typically try to help them regulate their emotional arousal by attempting to soothe or distract them (Gianino & Tronick, 1988). For example, mothers tend to use caressing and other affectionate behaviour to calm a crying 2-month-old. Over the next few months, they increasingly include vocalizations (e.g., talking, singing, "shushing") in their calming efforts, as well as in their attempts to divert the infant's attention. Holding or rocking upset young infants while talking soothingly to them seems to be the most reliable approach, and feeding them if they are not highly upset is also effective (Jahromi, Putnam, & Stifter, 2004).

By 6 months of age, infants show signs of rudimentary emotional self-regulation. In aversively arousing or uncertain situations, they may reduce their distress by unselectively averting their gaze from the source of distress. Occasionally, 6-month-olds can also *self-soothe*—that is, engage in repetitive rubbing or stroking of their body or clothing. Sometimes they can also distract themselves by looking specifically at neutral or positive persons or objects rather than at what has upset them, a strategy that they increasingly use between ages 1 and 2 years (Grolnick, Bridges, & Connell, 1996; Mangelsdorf, Shapiro, & Marzolf, 1995; Parritz, 1996). Such changes in young children's behaviour are probably made possible by their growing ability to control both their own attention and their movements (Ruff & Capozzoli, 2003).

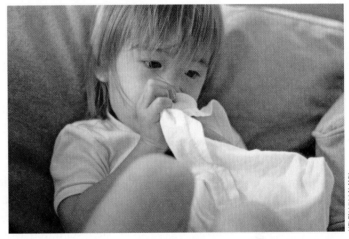

Young children tend to soothe themselves by rubbing their body, sucking a thumb, or clinging to well-loved objects, such as their blanket, that provide a sense of security.

Over the course of the early years, children develop and improve their ability to distract themselves by playing on their own when distressed. They also become less likely to seek comfort from their parents when they are upset (Bridges & Grolnick, 1995). And because of their growing ability to use language, when they are upset by parental demands, they are more likely to discuss and negotiate the situation with the parent than to engage in an emotional outburst (Campos, Frankel, & Camras, 2004; Klimes-Dougan & Kopp, 1999; Kopp, 1992). For instance, if a preschooler is unhappy when told by a parent to stop playing and instead clean up his or her room, the child may verbally protest and lobby for extra playtime or work out a timetable for cleaning up rather than throwing a fit.

These changes in children's self-regulation are at least partly due to the increasing maturation of the neurological systems—including the portion of the frontal lobes that are central to effortfully managing attention and inhibiting thoughts and behaviours (A. Berger, 2011). They are also partly due to changes in what adults expect of children. As children age, adults increasingly expect them to manage their own emotional arousal and behaviour. Once children are capable of crawling, for example, they are viewed as more responsible for their behaviour and for complying with parental expectations (A. Campos, Kermoian, & Zumbahlen, 1992). At about 9 to 12 months of age, children start to show awareness of adults' demands and begin to regulate themselves accordingly (Kopp, 1989). Their compliance

This little girl is using signs to communicate that she wants to take a nap. Children who can indicate their wants and needs with language or signs are less likely to get frustrated and to exhibit unregulated behaviour.

grows rapidly in the second year of life (Kaler & Kopp, 1990), making them increasingly likely to heed simple instructions, such as to not touch dangerous objects.

In the second year of life, children also show increases in the ability to inhibit their motor behaviour when asked to do so—such as slowing down their walking or not touching certain attractive objects (N. P. Friedman et al., 2011; Kochanska, Murray, & Harlan, 2000). Although these abilities are quite limited in the toddler years, they improve considerably by age 3 to 5 (Moilanen et al., 2009; Putnam, Gartstein, & Rothbart, 2006) and further improve in the school years and beyond (Bedard et al., 2002; B. C. Murphy et al., 1999; Sinopoli et al., 2011).

Across the early years, children's ability to regulate their attention improves (Rueda, Posner, & Rothbart, 2011). As a result, children are increasingly able to conform to adults' expectations, such as not hurting others when angry and staying seated at school when they would much prefer to get up and talk or play with classmates. In adolescence, the neurological changes that occur in the cortex (see pages 113–114) further contribute to self-regulation and other cognitive functioning. They also likely contribute to the decline in risk taking and the improvement in judgment that often occur in the transition from adolescence to young adulthood (Steinberg, 2010).

The Use of Cognitive Strategies to Control Negative Emotion

Whereas younger children regulate their negative emotions primarily by using behavioural strategies (e.g., distracting themselves with play), older children are also able to use cognitive strategies and problem solving to adjust to emotionally difficult situations (Zimmer-Gembeck & Skinner, 2011). Finding themselves caught in unpleasant or threatening circumstances, they may rethink their goals or the meaning of events so that they can adapt gracefully to the situation. This ability helps children avoid acting in ways that might be counterproductive. When older children are teased by peers, for instance, they may be able to defuse the situation by downplaying the importance of the teasing rather than reacting to it in a way that would provoke more teasing.

The Selection of Appropriate Regulatory Strategies

In dealing with emotion, children, over time, improve in their ability to select cognitive or behavioural strategies that are appropriate for the particular situation and stressor (Brenner & Salovey, 1997). One reason is that, with age, children are more aware that the appropriateness of a particular coping behaviour depends on their specific needs and goals, as well as on the nature of the problem. For instance, children are increasingly likely to realize that it is better to try to find alternative ways to obtain a goal rather than simply give up in frustration when their initial efforts fail (C. A. Berg, 1989). Another reason is that planning and problem-solving skills, which likely contribute to the selection and use of appropriate strategies, improve across childhood and across adolescence (Albert & Steinberg, 2011; Zimmer-Gembeck & Skinner, 2011).

Children's improving ability to use appropriate strategies for dealing with negative situations is also aided by their growing ability to distinguish between stressors that can be controlled (such as homework) and those that cannot be controlled (such as painful but necessary medical procedures). Older children, for example, are more aware than younger children that in situations they cannot control, it is easier to manage their emotions by simply adapting to the situation rather than trying to change it (e.g., Altshuler et al., 1995; Hoffner, 1993; Rudolph, Dennig, & Weisz, 1995). Faced with having to undergo major surgery, for instance, older children may adapt by trying to think about the benefits of having the surgery, such as being in better health afterward, or by distracting themselves with enjoyable activities. Younger children, in contrast, are more likely to insist that they do not need the operation.

The Relation of Emotional Self-Regulation to Social Competence and Adjustment

As we noted earlier, the development of emotional self-regulation has important consequences for children, especially with regard to their social competence. **Social competence** refers to a set of skills that help individuals achieve their personal goals in social interactions while maintaining positive relationships with others (Rubin, Bukowski, & Parker, 1998). A variety of studies indicate that children who have the ability to inhibit inappropriate behaviours, delay gratification, and use cognitive methods of controlling their emotion and behaviour tend to be well-adjusted and liked by their peers and by adults (Diener & Kim, 2004; Doan, Fuller-Rowell, & Evans, 2012; N. Eisenberg, Spinrad, & Eggum, 2010; Olson et al., 2011).

Moreover, children and adolescents who are able to deal constructively with stressful situations—negotiating with others to settle conflicts, planning strategies to resolve upsetting situations, seeking social support, and so on—generally are better adjusted than are children who lack these skills, including those who avoid dealing with stressful situations altogether (K. A. Blair et al., 2004; Compas et al., 2001; Jaser et al., 2007). Well-regulated children also do better in school than their less regulated peers do, likely because they are better able to pay attention, are better behaved and better liked by teachers and peers, and, consequently, like school better (Denham et al., 2012; Duckworth, Quinn, & Sukayama, 2012; Ponitz et al., 2009; Rimm-Kaufman et al., 2009).

social competence ■ The ability to achieve personal goals in social interactions while simultaneously maintaining positive relationships with others.

FRANCISCO VILLAFLOR / ALAMY

Children who exhibit positive affect and laughter tend to be well liked by peers.

review:

Children's efforts to regulate their emotions and emotionally driven behaviour change with age. Whereas young infants must rely on adults to manage their emotions, older infants and young children increasingly regulate their own emotions and behaviour through such methods as averting their attention, self-soothing, and distracting themselves with activities. Their ability to inhibit their actions also improves with age. Improvements in children's regulatory capacities likely are based on increases in brain maturation that allow them to better control their attention and their own bodies, as well as on changes in adults' expectations of them.

In contrast to young children, who often try to cope with their emotions by taking direct action, older children also are able to use cognitive modes of coping, such as focusing on positive aspects of a negative situation or trying to think about something else altogether. In addition, they are increasingly able to select and use ways of regulating themselves and coping with stress that are appropriate to the requirements of specific situations.

The abilities to regulate one's emotions and related behaviour, and to deal constructively with stressful situations, are associated with high social competence and low levels of problem behaviour.

Individual Differences in Emotion and Its Regulation

Although the overall development of emotions and self-regulatory capabilities is roughly similar for most children, there also are very large individual differences in children's emotional functioning. Some infants and children are relatively mellow: they do not become upset easily and they usually do not have difficulty calming down when they are upset. Other children are quite emotional; they get upset quickly and intensely, and their negative emotion persists for a long time. Moreover, children differ in their timidity, in their expression of positive emotion, and in the ways they deal with their emotions. Compare these two 3-year-old children, Maria and Bruce, as they react to Teri, an adult female stranger:

> When Teri walks over to Maria and starts to talk with her, Maria smiles and is eager to show Teri what she is doing. When Teri asks Maria if she would like to go down the hall to the play room (where experiments are conducted), Maria jumps up and takes Teri's hand.
>
> In contrast, when Teri walks over to Bruce, Bruce turns away. He doesn't talk to her and averts his eyes. When Teri asks him if he wants to play a game, Bruce moves away, looks timid, and softly says "no."
>
> (N. Eisenberg, laboratory observations)

Children also vary in the speed with which they express their emotions, as illustrated by the differences in these two preschool boys:

> When someone crosses Taylor, his wrath is immediate. There is no question how he is feeling, no time to correct the situation before he erupts. Douglas, though, seems almost to consider the ongoing emotional situation. One can almost see annoyance building until he finally sputters, "Stop that!"
>
> (Denham, 1998, p. 21)

The differences among children in their emotionality and regulation of emotion almost certainly have a basis in heredity. For instance, identical twins are more similar to each other in these aspects of their emotion and regulation than are fraternal twins (Rasbash et al., 2011; Saudino & Wang, 2012). However, environmental stressors, including factors as diverse as negative parenting and instability in an adopted child's placement (E. E. Lewis et al., 2007), are related to problems children may have with self-regulation and the expression of emotion. Undoubtedly, a combination of genetic and environmental factors jointly contributes to individual differences in children's emotions and related behaviours (C. S. Barr, 2012; Rasbash et al., 2011; Saudino & Wang, 2012).

Temperament

Because infants differ so much in their emotional reactivity, even from birth, it is commonly assumed that children are born with different emotional characteristics. Differences in various aspects of children's emotional reactivity that tend to emerge early in life are labelled as dimensions of **temperament.** Mary Rothbart and John Bates, two leaders in the study of temperament, define temperament as

> constitutionally based individual differences in emotional, motor, and attentional reactivity and self-regulation. Temperamental characteristics are seen to demonstrate consistency across situations, as well as relative stability over time.
>
> (Rothbart & Bates, 1998, p. 109)

Although characteristics of temperament have generally been thought to be evident fairly early in life, there is now evidence that some may not emerge until childhood or adolescence and may change considerably at different ages (Saudino & Wang, 2012; Shiner et al., 2012). For example, *incentive motivation*—the vigour and rate of responding to anticipated rewards—seems to become stronger in early adolescence, which may account for reduced self-regulation in regard to rewarding but risky activities (e.g., the use of drugs and alcohol), and then drops after adolescence (Luciana & Collins, 2012; Luciana et al., 2012). Changes in when and how much temperament is expressed at different ages likely occur because genes switch on and off throughout development, so there are changes in the degree to which behaviours are affected by genes (Saudino & Wang, 2012).

The phrase "constitutionally based" in Rothbart and Bates's definition of temperament refers, of course, to genetically inherited characteristics. But it also refers to aspects of biological functioning, such as neural development and hormonal responding, that can be affected by the environment during the prenatal period and after birth. For example, nutritional deficiencies or exposure to cocaine during the prenatal period (T. Dennis et al., 2006), maternal stress and anxiety during pregnancy (Huizink, 2008, 2012), and a premature birth (C. A. C. Clark et al., 2008) all appear to have the potential to affect infants' and young children's ability to regulate their attention and behaviour. Similar negative effects can result from sustained elevations of *cortisol* (a stress-related hormone that activates energy reserves) because of maternal insensitivity or child abuse during the early years of life (Bugental, Martorell, & Barraza, 2003; Gunnar & Cheatham, 2003). Thus, the construct of temperament is highly relevant to our themes of *individual differences* and the role of *nature and nurture* in development.

The pioneering work in the field of temperament research was the New York Longitudinal Study, conducted by Alexander Thomas and Stella Chess (Thomas & Chess, 1977; Thomas,

temperament ■ Constitutionally based individual differences in emotional, motor, and attentional reactivity and self-regulation that demonstrate consistency across situations, as well as relative stability over time.

Who could resist this toddler? Children who smile easily in new situations—who have an easy temperament—are likely to elicit more positive reactions from adults than are children who express a high level of negative emotion.

SUSAN GRAHAM

Chess, & Birch, 1968). These researchers began by interviewing a sample of parents, repeatedly and in depth, about their infants' specific behaviours. To reduce the possibility of bias in the parents' reports, the researchers asked that instead of interpretive characterizations such as "he's often cranky" or "she's interested in everything," the parents provide detailed descriptions of their infant's specific behaviours. On the basis of those interviews, nine characteristics of children were identified, including such traits as quality of mood, adaptability, activity level, and attention span and persistence. Further analyzing the interview results in terms of these characteristics, the researchers classified the infants into three groups: easy, difficult, and slow to warm up.

1. *Easy babies* adjusted readily to new situations, quickly established daily routines such as sleeping and eating, and generally were cheerful in mood and easy to calm.

2. *Difficult babies* were slow to adjust to new experiences, tended to react negatively and intensely to novel stimuli and events, and were irregular in their daily routines and bodily functions.

3. *Slow-to-warm-up babies* were somewhat difficult at first but became easier over time as they had repeated contact with new objects, people, and situations.

In the initial study, 40% of the infants were classified as easy, 10% as difficult, and 15% as slow to warm up. The rest did not fit into one of these categories. Of particular importance, some dimensions of children's temperament showed relative stability over time, with temperament in infancy predicting how children were doing years later. For instance, "difficult" infants tended to have problems with adjustment at home and at school, whereas few of the "easy" children had such problems. (We will return to the issue of stability of temperament and its social and emotional correlates shortly.)

Since the groundbreaking efforts of Thomas and Chess, researchers have devoted a great deal of effort to refining both the definition of temperament and its measurement (see Box 10.2). Unlike Thomas and Chess, many contemporary researchers differentiate among types of negative emotionality and assess different types of regulatory capacities. More recent research suggests that infant temperament is captured by six dimensions (Rothbart & Bates, 1998, 2006):

1. *Fearful distress/inhibition*—distress and withdrawal, and their duration, in new situations.

2. *Irritable distress*—fussiness, anger, and frustration, especially if the child is not allowed to do what he or she wants to do.

3. *Attention span and persistence*—duration of orienting toward objects or events of interest.

4. *Activity level*—how much an infant moves (e.g., waves arms, kicks, crawls).

5. *Positive affect/approach*—smiling and laughing, approach to people, degree of cooperativeness and manageability.

6. *Rhythmicity*—the regularity and predictability of the child's bodily functions such as eating and sleeping.

The terms used by investigators to refer to these dimensions vary somewhat—for example, "irritable distress" may be called "frustration" or "anger"—but these dimensions generally include most of the aspects of temperament that have been studied extensively.

TABLE 10.2

Examples of Items in Mary Rothbart's Temperament Scales

Response scale for items:

1	2	3	4	5	6	7	X
Never	Very rarely	Less than half the time	About half the time	More than half the time	Almost always	Always	Does not apply

Temperament dimension	Sample items in infant scale	Sample items in child scale
Fearful distress	How often during the last week did the baby: —cry or show distress at a loud sound (blender, vacuum cleaner, etc.)? —cry or show distress at a change in parents' appearance (glasses off, shower cap on, etc.)?	—Is not afraid of large dogs and/or other animals (reversed for scoring) —Is afraid of loud noises
Irritability (or distress at limitations in infancy and anger/frustration in childhood)	When having to wait for food or liquids during the last week, how often did the baby: —seem not bothered? —show mild fussing? —cry loudly?	—Has temper tantrums when s/he doesn't get what s/he wants —Gets mad when even mildly criticized
Attention span	How often during the last week did the baby: —look at pictures in books and/or magazines for 5 minutes or longer at a time? —play with one toy or object for 10 minutes or longer?	—When drawing or colouring in a book, shows strong concentration —When building or putting something together, becomes very involved in what s/he is doing, and works for long periods
Activity level	During feeding (during the last week), how often did the baby: —lie or sit quietly? —squirm or kick? —wave arms?	—Tends to run, rather than walk, from room to room —When outside, often sits quietly (reversed for scoring)
Positive affectivity (smiling and laughter)	When tossed around playfully (during the last week), how often did the baby: —smile? —laugh?	—Smiles and laughs during play with parents —Usually has a serious expression, even during play (reversed for scoring)

Source: Adapted from Rothbart Infant Behavior Questionnaire and Child Behavior Questionnaire (Rothbart & Gartstein, 1998)

In childhood, the first five of these dimensions (see Table 10.2) are particularly important in classifying children's temperament and predicting their behaviour (Rothbart & Bates, 1998). In addition, there is some evidence that a dimension referred to as agreeableness/adaptability may be another important aspect of temperament (Knafo & Israel, 2012; Rothbart & Bates, 2006). Agreeableness involves exhibiting positive emotions and behaviours toward others (e.g., getting along with others and caring about them versus being aggressive and manipulative), as well as the tendency to affiliate with others. Adaptability involves being able to adjust to specific conditions, including the needs and desires of others.

Due partly to variations in temperament, children often show very different reactions to the same situation.

ANDREW AITCHISON / IN PICTURES / CORBIS

BOX 10.2: a closer look

MEASUREMENT OF TEMPERAMENT

Currently, a number of different methods are used to assess temperament. In one method, similar to that used by Thomas and Chess, parents or other adults (usually teachers or observers) report on aspects of a child's temperament, such as fearfulness, anger/frustration, and positive affect. These reports, based on adults' observations of the children in various contexts (see Table 10.2), tend to be fairly stable over time and predict general later development in such areas as behavioural problems, anxiety disorders, and social competence (A. Berger, 2011; Rothbart, 2012; Rothbart & Bates, 2006).

Laboratory observations have also been used to assess aspects of temperament such as behavioural inhibition, emotionality, and regulatory capacities. In a longitudinal study conducted by Jerome Kagan and his colleagues, for example, the investigators observed children's reactions to a variety of novel experiences in early infancy, at age 2, and at age 4½. Across all three ages, about 20% of the children were consistently quite inhibited and reactive when exposed to the unfamiliar stimuli. As infants, they cried and thrashed about when brightly coloured toys were moved back and forth in front of their faces or when a cotton swab dipped in dilute alcohol was applied to their nose. At age 2, one-third of these inhibited children were highly fearful in unfamiliar laboratory situations—such as being exposed to a loud noise, the smell of alcohol, and an unfamiliar woman dressed in a clown outfit—and nearly all showed at least some fear in these situations. Other children were less reactive: as infants, they rarely fussed when they encountered the novel experiences, and at age 2, two-thirds showed little or no fear in the unfamiliar situations.

At the age of 4½, the children who had been reactive to unfamiliar situations were more subdued, less social, and less positive in their behaviour than were the uninhibited children, who were relatively spontaneous, asked questions of the researchers when being evaluated, commented on events happening around them, and smiled and laughed more (Kagan, 1997; Kagan & Fox, 2006; Kagan, Snidman, & Arcus, 1998). Even in adolescence, individuals who were

inhibited as children exhibited some evidence of heightened worrying and unease with strangers (Kagan, 2012). Thus, laboratory observations appear to be good measures of behavioural inhibition.

Physiological measures also have proved useful for assessing some aspects of children's temperament. For instance, researchers have found that high-reactive and low-reactive children exhibit differences in the variability of their heart rate (Kagan, 1998; Kagan & Fox, 2006). Heart-rate variability—how much an individual's heart rate normally fluctuates—is believed to reflect, in part, the way the central nervous system responds to novel situations and the individual's ability to regulate emotion (Porges, 2007; Porges, Doussard-Roosevelt, & Maiti, 1994). Investigators often measure this fluctuation of heart rate in terms of *vagal tone,* an index of how effectively the vagus nerve—which regulates autonomic nervous system functioning—modulates heart rate in respiratory inhalation and exhalation (inhalation suppresses vagal tone, increasing heart rate; exhalation restores vagal tone, decreasing heart rate). Children who have heart rates that are constantly high and that vary little as a function of breathing are said to have low vagal tone. These children tend to be negatively reactive and inhibited in response to novel situations.

In contrast, children who have variable and often lower heart rates are said to have high vagal tone. After the first year of life, these children tend to exhibit positive emotions and few negative reactions in novel or even stressful situations, such as when dealing with a new preschool. Vagal tone after infancy has been linked with levels of interest and attention, as well as with levels of positive expressiveness (Beauchaine, 2001; Calkins & Swingler, 2012; R. Feldman, 2009; Fox & Field, 1989; Oveis et al., 2009).

A vital component of emotional regulation is the modulation of vagal tone in challenging situations that require an organized response (Porges, 2007). This modulation involves autonomic physiological processes, referred to as *vagal suppression,* that allow the child to shift away from the physiological responses triggered by the situation and to focus on processing information relevant

to the situation and generating coping strategies. Vagal suppression also allows for higher physiological arousal that can be used to deal with the situation at hand.

Vagal suppression during challenging situations has been related to a variety of positive outcomes over the course of childhood, including better regulation of state and more attentional control in infancy (Huffman et al., 1998); fewer behaviour problems, higher status with peers, and more appropriate emotional regulation in the preschool years (Calkins & Dedmon, 2000; Calkins & Keane, 2004); and sustained attention in the school years (Suess, Porges, & Plude, 1994; see also R. A. Thompson, Lewis, & Calkins, 2008). In addition, children with higher vagal tone in general or greater vagal suppression during challenges appear less likely to have problem behaviours and anxiety if exposed to stressors such as conflict between their parents (El-Sheikh, Harger, & Whitson, 2001; El-Sheikh & Whitson, 2006), especially if they live in environments that otherwise are not especially high in stress and risk (Obradović et al., 2010). Findings such as these support the idea that vagal tone and its suppression assess some capacity related to adaptation and emotional regulation.

Another commonly used physiological measure of temperament is electroencephalographic recordings (see Chapter 3, page 110) of frontal lobe activity. Activation of the left frontal lobe of the cortex as measured with an electroencephalograph (EEG) has been associated with approach behaviour, positive affect, exploration, and sociability. In contrast, activation of the right frontal lobe has been linked to withdrawal, a state of uncertainty, fear, and anxiety (Kagan & Fox, 2006). Thus, when confronted with novel stimuli, situations, or challenges, infants and children who show greater right frontal activation on the EEG are more likely to react with anxiety and avoidance (Calkins, Fox, & Marshall, 1996; Kagan & Fox, 2006), whereas individuals who show left frontal activation are more likely to exhibit a relaxed, often happy mood and an eagerness to engage new experiences or challenges (Kagan & Fox, 2006; L. K. White et al., 2012). EEG activation patterns are associated with children's ongoing temperament, not just with their reactions in these specific situations. For example, compared with uninhibited peers, inhibited preschoolers showed greater activation in the right frontal area even under resting conditions, and children who were inhibited as 2-year-olds exhibited greater right than left hemisphere activation at age 11 (Kagan et al., 2007).

A third physiological measure of temperament is cortisol level. In reaction to stress, the adrenal cortex secretes steroid hormones, including cortisol, which, as noted previously, helps activate energy reserves (C. S. Carter, 1986). Sometimes individual differences in children's cortisol baseline—that is, their typical cortisol level—have been related to levels of internalizing problems such as inhibition, anxiety, and social withdrawal (Granger et al., 1994; Smider et al., 2002), and to regulation (Gunnar et al., 2003) and the acting out of behavioural problems (Gunnar & Vazquez, 2006; Shirtcliff et al., 2005; Shoal, Giancola, & Kirillova, 2003). For instance, 2-year-olds who, in a mildly threatening situation, exhibit extremely fearful reactions—such as freezing up in their behaviour—tend to have higher levels of cortisol in general, not just in such situations (K. A. Buss et al., 2004).

In addition, *cortisol reactivity*—the amount of cortisol produced *in a given situation*—has been linked to temperament differences in emotionality, inhibition, regulation, and maladjustment (Ashman et al., 2002; C. Blair et al., 2008; Granger et al., 1998). For example, in child-care settings, children high in temperamental negative emotionality and low in regulation show larger increases in cortisol levels than do other children (Dettling et al., 2000). Cortisol reactivity is related to internalizing problems such as anxiety primarily if a child displays a heightened response to a familiar stressor (Gunnar & Vazquez, 2006).

When attempting to find links between children's cortisol levels and aspects of their temperament, it is important to consider the children's experience in a particular context. This was highlighted in a study by Gunnar (1994), which compared the cortisol levels of two groups of children—outgoing and active versus anxious and withdrawn—in their 1st year of group care. At the start of the school year, the active and outgoing children showed higher cortisol levels; later in the school year, however, the reverse was true. According to teachers' reports at the time of the second cortisol testing, the former group was higher in popularity and had fewer problems interacting socially. Presumably, the less inhibited children had actively dealt with the new situation, initially exposing themselves to stress and raising their cortisol levels but subsequently adapting successfully. The inhibited children, in contrast, had avoided the challenges (and stress) of the new situation and were still not well adjusted to it (Gunnar, 1994).

One exception was uninhibited children who were also unregulated; they exhibited relatively high cortisol levels at preschool even later in the year, perhaps because their impulsive behaviour led to peer rejection (Gunnar et al., 2003). Another exception tends to be for exuberant children who are less socially integrated (Tarullo et al., 2011); they tend to maintain higher levels of cortisol over the school year, perhaps because they are often dealing with stressful social interactions.

Each type of measure of temperament has advantages and disadvantages, and there is considerable debate regarding the merits of the various methods (Kagan, 1998; Kagan & Fox, 2006; Rothbart & Bates, 1998, 2006). The key advantage of parents' reports of temperament is that parents have extensive knowledge of their children's behaviour in many different situations. One important disadvantage of this method is that parents may not always be objective in their observations, as suggested by the fact that their reports sometimes do not correspond with what is found with laboratory measures (Seifer et al., 1994). Another disadvantage is that many parents do not have wide knowledge of other children's behaviour to use as a basis for comparison when reporting on their own children (what is irritability to some parents, for example, may be near-placidness to others).

The key advantage of laboratory observational data is that such data are less

COURTESY OF NATHAN A. FOX, DEPT. OF HUMAN DEVELOPMENT AND QUANTITATIVE METHODOLOGY, UNIVERSITY OF MARYLAND

Nathan Fox and his colleagues have found that children's brain activity, measured by EEG, varies as a function of whether they are experiencing positive or negative emotions. Children who are experiencing positive emotions, or who have an exuberant temperament, display more left-sided EEG activation, whereas children who are experiencing negative emotions, or who have a fearful temperament, display more right-sided activation. These different patterns, found in infants as young as 9 months, appear to reflect an underlying approach-avoidance motivation system in the brain.

likely to be biased than is an adult's personal view of the child. A key disadvantage is that children's behaviour usually is observed in only a limited set of circumstances. Consequently, laboratory observational measures may reflect a child's mood or behaviour at a given moment, in a particular context, rather than reflecting the child's general temperament.

Physiological measures such as an EEG and vagal tone are also relatively objective and unlikely to be biased, but there is no way to tell whether the processes reflected by physiological measures are a cause or consequence of the child's emotion and behaviour in the specific situation. It is unclear, for example, whether left and right frontal lobe activity triggers, or is triggered by, a particular emotional response. Thus, no measure of temperament is foolproof, and it is prudent to assess temperament with a variety of methods.

Stability of Temperament Over Time

As you have seen, temperament, by definition, involves traits that remain fairly stable over time, and in some cases, seem to increase in stability with age (Roberts & DelVecchio, 2000). One example of trait stability comes from research indicating that children who exhibited inhibition or fearful distress when presented with novel stimuli as infants also were prone to exhibit elevated levels of fear in novel situations at age 2 and elevated levels of social inhibition at age 4½. Similarly, children who at age 3 are more prone to negative emotion than their peers tend at ages 6 and 8 to be more emotionally negative than their peers (Guerin & Gottfried, 1994; Rothbart, Derryberry, & Hershey, 2000), and, across the same age range, those prone to positive affect remain relatively positive (Durbin et al., 2007; Sallquist et al., 2009).

Research further indicates that children who are high in the ability to focus attention in the preschool years are high in this ability in early adolescence (B. C. Murphy et al., 1999); and that there also is stability in attentional and behavioural regulation from childhood into adolescence (N. Eisenberg, Hofer, et al., 2008) and across adolescence (Ganiban et al., 2008). As noted, some aspects of temperament tend to be more stable than others. For example, over the course of infancy, positive emotionality, fear, and distress/anger activity level may be more stable than activity level (Lemery et al., 1999).

A fetus's activity level in the womb appears to be related to some aspects of postnatal temperament. Infants who were more active as fetuses tend to be active, difficult, and non-adaptive in the first half-year of life.

The Role of Temperament in Children's Social Skills and Maladjustment

One of the reasons for researchers' deep interest in temperament is that it plays an important role in determining children's social adjustment. Consider a boy who is prone to anger and has difficulty controlling this emotion. Compared with other boys, he is likely to sulk, to yell at others, and to be defiant with adults and aggressive with peers. Such behaviours often lead to long-term adjustment problems. Consequently, it is not surprising that differences in aspects of temperament such as anger/irritability, positive emotion, and the ability to inhibit behaviour—aspects reflected in the difference between difficult and easy temperament—have been associated with differences in children's social competence and maladjustment (Coplan & Bullock, 2012; Eiden et al., 2009; N. Eisenberg et al., 2010; Kagan, 2012; Kochanska et al., 2008). One study at Carleton University demonstrated that shy children were more likely to display socioemotional adjustment issues in Grade 1 than children who were more outgoing, but that close teacher–child relationships could act as a buffer against negative outcomes (Arbeau, Coplan, & Weeks, 2010).

Such differences in temperaments and outcomes are further highlighted by a large longitudinal study in New Zealand conducted by Caspi, Moffitt, Henry, and colleagues. These researchers found that participants who were negative and unregulated as young children tended as adolescents or young adults to have more problems with adjustment, such as not getting along with others, than did peers with different temperaments. They also were more likely to engage in illegal behaviours and to get in trouble with the law (Caspi et al., 1995; Caspi & Silva, 1995; B. Henry et al., 1996). At age 21, they reported getting along less well with whomever they were living with (e.g., roommates) and being unemployed more often. They also tended to have few people from whom they could get social support (Caspi, 2000) and were prone to negative emotions like anxiety (Caspi et al., 2003). At age 32, they had poorer physical health and personal resources, greater substance dependence, more criminal offences, and more problems with gambling (Moffitt et al., 2011; Slutske et al., 2012).

It is important to note, however, that aspects of temperament like negative emotionality may not always be associated with children's negative outcomes such as having problem behaviours and poor social relationships. It seems that some children with certain temperamental characteristics are especially sensitive to their social environments, whether positive or negative. There is some evidence, for example, that, in highly stressful social environments (i.e., poverty, exposure to harsh parenting), children who are prone to negative emotions tend to do worse than children who are not, but that, in supportive social environments, they often tend to do better than their more emotionally positive peers (Belsky & Pluess, 2009). Evolutionarily oriented theorists argue that this "for better or for worse" pattern of findings, labelled *differential susceptibility,* occurs because aspects of temperament and behaviour that are adaptive for survival vary across positive and negative social contexts (B. J. Ellis et al., 2011). For instance, in harsh environments, expressing negative emotion may help children obtain attention and vital resources needed for survival (even though the negative emotion often results in negative social consequences over time), whereas in supportive environments, proneness to negative emotions might make children more sensitive to parents' attempts to socialize positive behaviours, which may lead to higher social and moral competence (Kochanska, 1997a).

Researchers also have found stability with regard to **behavioural inhibition,** the tendency to be high in fearful distress and restrained when dealing with novel or stressful situations. Children who are behaviourally inhibited are more likely than other children to have problems such as anxiety, depression, phobias, and social withdrawal at older ages (Biederman et al., 1990; Fox & Pine, 2012; Hirshfeld-Becker et al., 2007; Moffitt et al., 2007). Thus, different problems with adjustment seem to be associated with different temperaments.

However, how children ultimately adjust depends not only on their temperament but also on how well their temperament fits with the particular environment they are in—what is often called **goodness of fit.** On the basis of their data, Chess and Thomas (1990) argued, for example, that children with difficult temperaments have better adjustment if they receive parenting that is supportive and consistent rather than punitive, rejecting, or inconsistent. In support of their argument, research indicates that children who are impulsive or low in self-regulation seem to have more problems and are less sympathetic to others if exposed to hostile, intrusive, and/or negative parenting rather than to supportive parenting (Hastings & De, 2008; Kiff et al., 2011; Lengua et al., 2008; Valiente et al., 2004; see also Rothbart & Bates, 2006). Similarly, children prone to negative emotions such as anger are more likely to have behavioural problems such as aggression if exposed to hostile parenting or low levels of positive parenting (Calkins, 2002; Lengua, 2008; Mesman et al., 2009; Morris et al., 2002; see also Bates

behavioural inhibition ■ A temperamentally based style of responding characterized by the tendency to be particularly fearful and restrained when dealing with novel or stressful situations.

goodness of fit ■ The degree to which an individual's temperament is compatible with the demands and expectations of his or her social environment.

Not only does temperament play a role in social adjustment, but it also predicts kindergartners' literacy and numeracy skills. A study by Canadian researchers Robert Coplan, Ann Barber, and Daniel Lagacé-Séguin (1999) demonstrated that children who have longer attention spans, lower activity levels, and less negative emotionality performed better in assessments of early vocabulary, print, counting, and numeracy skills.

AMI PARIKH / SHUTTERSTOCK

FIGURE 10.4 **Interaction between a child's shyness/reticence and maternal warmth/supportive parenting** Parenting can interact with the child's characteristics to influence **(a)** internalizing problems (such as depression and anxiety); **(b)** problems with peers; and **(c)** adjustment to school. (Adapted from Coplan, Arbeau, & Armer, 2008)

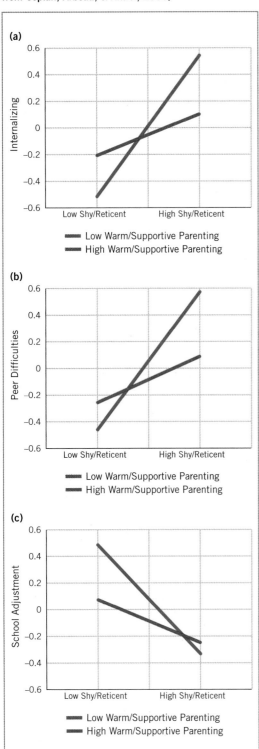

et al., 2012, for a review). Thus, children exposed to suboptimal parenting do worse if they have unregulated or reactive temperaments.

Other research indicates that supportive parenting can moderate some of the negative effects of behavioural inhibition. For instance, research conducted by Coplan and his colleagues at Carleton University found that shy children with warm and supportive mothers showed better psychosocial adjustment in kindergarten than shy children with fretful mothers (see Figure 10.4) (Coplan, Arbeau, & Armer, 2008).

Not only are children's maladjustment and social competence predicted by the combination of their temperament and their parents' child-rearing practices, but the child's temperament and parents' socialization efforts also seem to affect each other over time (Belsky et al., 2007; N. Eisenberg et al., 1999; K. J. Kim et al., 2001; E. H. Lee et al., 2013). For instance, parents of negative, unregulated children may eventually become less patient and more punitive with their children; in turn, this intensification of disciplining may cause their children to become even more negative and unregulated. Thus, temperament plays a role in the development of children's social and psychological adjustment, but that role is complex and varies as a function of the child's social environment and the degree to which a child represents a challenge to the parent (Ganiban et al., 2011).

review:

Temperament refers to individual differences in various aspects of children's emotional reactivity, regulation, and other characteristics such as behavioural inhibition and activity level. Temperament is believed to have a constitutional (biological) basis, but it is also affected by experiences in the environment, including social interactions. Temperament tends to be somewhat stable over time, although the degree of its stability varies across the dimensions of temperament and individuals.

Temperament plays an important role in adjustment and maladjustment. A difficult and unmanageable temperament in childhood tends to predict problem behaviours and low social competence in childhood and adulthood, and children who as infants are fearful and negatively reactive to novel objects, places, and people sometimes have later difficulties in interactions with others, including peers. However, children whose temperaments put them at risk for poor adjustment often do well if they receive sensitive and appropriate parenting and if there is a good fit between their temperament and their social environment.

Children's Emotional Development in the Family

It is clear that the dimensions of temperament related to emotional development are linked to heredity. Twin and adoption studies show that, compared with fraternal twins, identical twins are more similar in the intensity of their emotional reactions, shyness, and sociability, as well as in other aspects of temperament and personality. Furthermore, biological siblings tend to be more similar to one another in some aspects of temperament than do siblings who are not biologically related. On the basis of such studies, it is estimated that genes account for a substantial portion of the variation in some aspects of temperament (Saudino & Wang, 2012).

In addition, recent studies of specific genes have shown connections between an individual's genes and aspects of temperament such as self-regulatory capacities and emotionality (Depue & Fu, 2012; Goldsmith, Pollak, & Davidson, 2008; Saudino & Wang, 2012). For instance, genes related to the functioning of dopamine and other neurotransmitters that affect voluntary attentional processes (executive attention) appear to be especially relevant for self-regulation (Posner, Rothbart, & Sheese, 2007). The expression of these genes appears to be affected by environmental factors such as quality of parenting or stress. Sometimes genetic tendencies toward certain temperamental traits (and related behaviours) are most likely expressed when the environment is suboptimal—for example, when parenting is unsupportive or harsh (Bakermans-Kranenburg & van IJzendoorn, 2006; Kochanska, Philibert, & Barry, 2009; Sheese et al., 2007; H. J. Smith et al., 2012), and sometimes when the environment is optimal (Krueger et al., 2008; Pluess & Belsky, 2013).

Findings in behavioural genetics research also suggest that various environmental factors play an important role in shaping individual differences in temperament generally (Deater-Deckard, Petrill, & Thompson, 2007; Saudino & Wang, 2012). Chief among these factors are children's relationships with their parents and their parents' socialization practices.

Quality of the Child's Relationships with Parents

The quality of a child's relationship with his or her parents can affect the child's emotional development in several ways. As is discussed fully in Chapter 11, the parent–child relationship seems to influence children's sense of security and how they feel about themselves and other people (R. A. Thompson, 2006). In turn, these feelings affect children's emotionality. For instance, children who are *securely attached*—that is, who have high-quality, trusting relationships with their parents— tend to show more positive emotion and less social anxiety and anger than do children who are *insecurely attached*—that is, whose relationships with their parents are low in trust and support (e.g., Bohlin, Hagekull, & Rydell, 2000; Borelli et al., 2010; Kochanska, 2001). Securely attached children also tend to be more open and honest in their expression of emotion (Becker-Stoll, Delius, & Scheitenberger, 2001; Zimmerman et al., 2001) as well as more advanced in their understanding of emotion (Steele, Steele, & Croft, 2008), perhaps because their parents are more likely to discuss feelings and other mental states with them (McElwain, Booth-LaForce, & Wu, 2011; McQuaid et al., 2007; Raikes & Thompson, 2006). This enhanced understanding of emotion is likely to help these children recognize when and how to regulate their emotion.

Parental Socialization of Children's Emotional Responding

In addition to being affected by the overall parent–child relationship, children's emotional development is influenced by parents' **socialization** of their children—that is, their direct and indirect influence on their children's standards, values, and ways of thinking and feeling. Parents socialize their children's emotional development through (1) their expression of emotion with their children and other people, (2) their reactions to their children's expression of emotion, and (3) the discussions they have with their children about emotion and emotional regulation. These avenues of socialization, which are often interrelated, can affect not only children's emotional development but also their social competence (J. K. Baker, Fenning, & Crnic, 2011).

socialization ■ The process through which children acquire the values, standards, skills, knowledge, and behaviours that are regarded as appropriate for their present and future role in their particular culture.

Parents' Expression of Emotion

How parents express their own emotions can have a powerful socializing effect on their children in several ways. To begin with, the emotions expressed in the home may influence children's views about themselves and others in their social world (Dunsmore & Halberstadt, 1997). For example, children exposed to a lot of anger and hostility may come to view themselves as individuals who anger people and may eventually believe that most people are hostile. In addition, parents' expression of emotion provides children with a model of when and how to express emotion (Denham, Zoller, & Couchoud, 1994; Dunn & Brown, 1994). This modelling also may affect children's understanding of what types of emotional expressions are appropriate and effective in interpersonal relations (Halberstadt et al., 1995; Morris et al., 2007). In families in which parents tend not to express emotions, children may get the message that emotions are basically bad and should be avoided or inhibited (Gottman et al., 1997). Finally, the parental emotions to which children are exposed may affect their general level of distress and arousal in social interactions, in turn affecting their ability to process important information about the interactions (e.g., others' verbal and non-verbal cues) that would help them moderate their behaviour (N. Eisenberg, Cumberland, & Spinrad, 1998; M. L. Hoffman, 2000).

Whatever the underlying reason, it is clear that the consistent and open expression of positive or negative emotion in the home is associated with specific outcomes for children. In a review of a considerable number of studies, Halberstadt and colleagues found that when positive emotion is prevalent in the home, children tend to express positive emotion themselves. They are socially skilled, well adjusted, low in aggression, and able to understand others' emotions (at least in childhood), and they tend to have high self-esteem (Halberstadt, Crisp, & Eaton, 1999; see also Barry & Kochanska, 2010; Brophy-Herb et al., 2011; McCoy & Raver, 2011).

In contrast, when negative emotion is prevalent in the home, especially intense and hostile emotion, children tend to exhibit low levels of social competence and to experience and express negative emotion themselves, including depression and anxiety (Crockenberg & Langrock, 2001; N. Eisenberg et al., 2001; Raval & Martini, 2011; Stocker et al., 2007). Even when the conflict and anger in the home involve the adults rather than the children directly, there is an increased likelihood that the children will develop anger, behaviour problems, and deficits in social competence and self-regulation (Grych & Fincham, 1997; Kouros, Cummings, & Davies, 2010; Rhoades, 2008; Rhoades et al., 2011). These outcomes are also more likely when

Children who are exposed to relatively high levels of positive emotion in the family tend to express more positive emotion and are more socially skilled and better adjusted than children who are exposed to high levels of negative emotion.

children are exposed to high levels of parental depression (Blandon et al., 2008; Cicchetti & Toth, 2006; Downey & Coyne, 1990).

Of course, parental expression of emotion is not always causally related to positive or negative outcomes in children: children themselves undoubtedly influence the expression of emotion in the home. For example, children who have difficult temperaments or are unmanageable are likely to evoke negative emotion from their parents (N. Eisenberg et al., 2008; K. J. Kim et al., 2001). Moreover, genetic factors may contribute to some of the associations between parental emotion and children's emotions or behaviour (Burt et al., 2005; Reiss, 2010; Rhoades et al., 2011). That is, because of heredity, both parent and child may be prone to anger and impulsive behaviour, which affects the quality of both parenting and children's socioemotional competence. Thus, both heredity and the kinds of emotions children see and experience in the home undoubtedly play roles in children's emotional and social development.

Parents' Reactions to Children's Emotions

Parents' reactions to their children's negative emotions also seem to affect children's emotional expressivity, as well as their social competence and adjustment. Consider, for example, the different parental messages conveyed in the following two instances:

> Jeremy … watched the movie *Jaws*, against his mother's better judgment. He fearfully, animatedly asked many questions about the movie afterwards, and anxiously discussed it in great detail (e.g., "What was that red stuff?"). His mother and father answered all the questions and supported him as he resolved these things in his mind. Jeremy's emotions were accepted, and he was able to regulate them, as well as to learn about what makes things "scary."
>
> (Denham, 1998, p. 106)

> Scott's parents, who are punitive socializers, show disregard and even contempt when his best friend moves away. These parents tease Scott for his tender feelings, so that in the end he is let down not only by the disappearance of his friend, but by their reactions as well. … [H]e is very lonely and still feels very bad.
>
> (Denham, 1998, p. 120)

Parents who, like Scott's, dismiss or criticize their children's expressions of sadness and anxiety communicate to their children that their feelings are not valid. Parents send similar messages when they react to their children's anger with threats, belligerence, or dismissive comments. In turn, their children are likely to be less emotionally and socially competent than are children whose parents are emotionally supportive. They tend, for example, to be lower in sympathy for others, less skilled at coping with stress, and more prone to negative emotions and problem behaviours such as aggression (N. Eisenberg, Fabes, & Murphy, 1996; Engle & McElwain, 2010; Luebbe, Kiel, & Buss, 2011; Lunkenheimer, Shields, & Cortina, 2007; J. Snyder, Stoolmiller, et al., 2003).

In contrast, parents who are supportive when their children are upset help their children to regulate their emotional arousal and to find ways to express their emotions constructively. In turn, their children tend to be better adjusted and more competent both with peers and academically (Gottman, Katz, & Hooven, 1997; Klimes-Dougan et al., 2007; Raval & Martini, 2011). Parents' supportive reactions to their young children's emotional upsets may be especially helpful in reducing problem behaviours for those children who have difficulty regulating their physiological responses to challenges (see Box 10.2) (Hastings & De, 2008).

Parents' Discussion of Emotion

As you will shortly see, children's emotional understanding is a key part of their emotional development and self-regulation. Family conversations about emotion are therefore an important aspect of children's emotional socialization. Parents who discuss emotions with their children teach them about the meanings of emotions, the circumstances in which they should and should not be expressed, and the consequences of expressing or not expressing them (N. Eisenberg et al., 1998; LaBounty et al., 2008; R. A. Thompson, 2006). An additional help in emotional socialization is *emotion coaching*, in which parents not only discuss emotions with their children but also help them learn ways of coping with their emotions and expressing them appropriately (Gottman et al., 1997; Power, 2004). Children who receive these types of guidance tend to display better emotional understanding than children who do not.

A longitudinal study by Judy Dunn and her colleagues found, for example, that the degree to which children are exposed to, and participate in, discussions of emotions with family members at ages 2 and 3 predicts their understanding of others' emotions until at least age 6 (J. R. Brown & Dunn, 1996; Dunn, Brown, & Beardsall, 1991; Dunn, Brown, et al., 1991). In two similar studies, mothers' references to their children's desires at 15 months of age predicted their children's understanding of emotions and use of emotion language at 24 months. In fact, mothers' verbal references to others' thoughts and knowledge when describing a series of pictures to their children at 24 months of age predicted children's use of emotion language and understanding of emotion at 33 months of age (Taumoepeau & Ruffman, 2006, 2008). Indeed, in these same two studies, as well as in another (Ensor & Hughes, 2008), mothers' references to others' mental states predicted children's emotion understanding better than did mothers' references to emotions themselves, perhaps because references to mental states help children understand the thoughts that accompany and motivate emotional states.

Researchers have also found that children whose parents use emotion coaching are more socially competent with peers, more empathic, and less likely to exhibit problem behaviours or depression than are children who do not receive such guidance (Brophy-Herb et al., 2011; Katz, Maliken, & Stettler, 2012; Stocker et al., 2007). Of course, children's own characteristics—such as their ability to sustain attention and their initial understanding of emotions—may affect the degree to which adults talk about emotion with them. For instance, in one study, parents engaged in more conversations about emotional past events with their 5- and 6-year-olds if the children were relatively well regulated and if their expression of negative emotion was consistent with what their parents expected from a child of their age (Bird, Reese, & Tripp, 2006). In another study, researchers at Mount Saint Vincent University, in Halifax, found that parents' emotional style (i.e., whether they took more of a coaching versus a dismissing approach) and children's temperament together predicted children's coping styles (Lagace-Seguin & Gionet, 2009).

review:

Children's emotional development is influenced by their relationship with their parents: children who have secure relations with their parents tend to show more positive emotion and greater emotional understanding than do children who have insecure relations with their parents. Another influence on children's emotional development is their parents' socialization of emotional responding—including what emotions parents express with their children and others, and how they express them; how parents respond to their children's negative emotions; and whether and how parents discuss emotions with their children.

Culture and Children's Emotional Development

Although people in all cultures appear to experience most of the same basic emotions, there is considerable cultural variation in the degree to which certain emotions are expressed. One reason for this may be genetic, in that people in different racial or ethnic groups may tend, on average, to have somewhat different temperaments. This possibility has been tentatively suggested by cross-cultural studies that were conducted with young infants to minimize the potential for the results to be affected by socialization. One such study found that, in general, 11-month-old European-American infants react more strongly to unfamiliar stimuli than do Chinese or Chinese-American babies, and they cry or smile more in response to evocative events (e.g., scary toys or a vanishing object) (Freedman & Freedman, 1969). Another study found that, compared with Chinese infants, American infants respond more quickly to negative emotion-inducing events such as having their arm held down so they cannot move it (Camras et al., 1998).

A more obvious contributor to cross-cultural differences in infants' emotional expression is the diversity of parenting practices. In Central Africa, for instance, infants in an Ngandu community fuss and cry more than do infants in an Aka community. This may be attributable to differences in caregiving practices related to the contrasting lifestyles of these two groups. Aka infants are almost always within arm's reach of someone who can feed or hold them when the need arises. The Ngandu leave their infants alone more often. Thus, Aka infants may cry and fuss less because they have more physical contact with caregivers and their needs are met more quickly (Hewlett et al., 1998).

The influence of cultural factors on emotional expression is strikingly revealed by a comparison of East Asian and American children. In one study, Japanese and American preschoolers were asked to say what they would do in hypothetical situations of conflict and distress, such as being hit or seeing a peer knock down a tower of blocks they had just built. American preschoolers expressed more anger and aggression in response to these vignettes than did Japanese children. This difference may have to do with the fact that American mothers appear to be more likely than Japanese mothers to encourage their children to express their emotions in situations such as these (Zahn-Waxler et al., 1996). These tendencies are in keeping with the high value European-American culture places on independence, self-assertion, and expressing one's emotions, even negative ones (Zahn-Waxler et al., 1996). In contrast, Japanese culture emphasizes interdependence, the subordination of oneself to one's group, and, correspondingly, the importance of maintaining harmonious interpersonal relationships. A similar contrast is found in other East Asian cultures, such as in China, where mothers often discourage their children from expressing negative emotion, especially anger (Markus & Kitayama, 1991; Matsumoto, 1996; Mesquita & Frijda, 1992). As a consequence, children in such societies learn not to communicate certain negative feelings (Raval & Martini, 2009).

Cultures also differ in the degree to which they promote or discourage specific emotions, and these differences are often reflected in parents' socialization of emotion. For instance, Chinese culture strongly emphasizes the need to be aware of oneself as embedded in a larger group and to maintain a positive image within that group. Thus, shame would be expected to be a powerful emotion—important for self-reflection and self-perfection (Fung, 1999; Fung & Chen, 2001) and particularly useful for inducing compliance in children. In fact, Chinese (Taiwanese) parents frequently try to induce shame in their preschool children when they transgress, typically pointing out that the child's behaviour is judged negatively by people

Interviews with children in remote villages in Nepal allowed Pamela Cole and her colleagues to examine how Buddhist and Hindu values contribute to children's understanding of emotion.

COURTESY OF PAMELA COLE

outside the family and that the child's shame is shared by other family members (Fung & Chen, 2001). Because of this cultural emphasis, it is likely that children in this society experience shame more frequently than do children in many Western cultures. Moreover, when children in Western cultures do experience shame or sadness, their mothers seem to be most concerned with helping them feel better about themselves. In contrast, Chinese mothers more often than Western mothers use the situation as an opportunity to teach proper conduct and help their child understand how to conform to social expectations and norms—for example, asking "Isn't it wrong for you to get mad at Papa?" (Cheah & Rubin, 2004; Friedlmeier, Corapci, & Cole, 2011; Q. Wang & Fivush, 2005).

Another striking example of cultural influences on emotional socialization is provided by the Tamang in rural Nepal. The Tamang are Buddhists who place great value on keeping one's *sem* (mind-heart) calm and clear of emotion, and they believe that people should not express much negative emotion because of its disruptive effects on interpersonal relationships. Consequently, although Tamang parents are responsive to the distress of infants, they often ignore or scold children older than age 2 when those children express anger, and they seldom offer explanations or support to reduce children's anger. Such parental reactions are not typical of all Nepali groups, however; for example, parents of Brahman Nepali children respond to children's anger with reasoning and yielding.

Of particular interest is the fact that although non-supportive parental behaviour comparable to that of the Tamang has been associated with low social competence in North American children, it does not seem to have a negative effect on the social competence of Tamang children. Because of the value placed on controlling the expression of emotion in Tamang culture, parental behaviours that would seem dismissive and punitive to North American parents likely take on a different meaning for Tamang parents and children and probably have different consequences (P. M. Cole & Dennis, 1998; P. M. Cole et al., 2006).

Parents' ideas about the usefulness of various emotions also vary in different cultural and regional groups. In a study of African-American mothers living in dangerous neighbourhoods, mothers valued and promoted their daughters' readiness to express anger and aggressiveness in situations related to self-protection because they wanted their daughters to act quickly and decisively to defend themselves when necessary. One way they did this was to play-act the role of an adversary, teasing, insulting, or challenging their daughters in the midst of everyday interactions. An example of this is provided by Beth's mother, who initiated a teasing event by challenging Beth (27 months old) to fight:

> "Hahahaha, Hahaha. Hahahahah. [Provocative tone:] You wanna fight about it?" Beth laughed. Mother laughed. Mother twice reiterated her challenge and then called Beth an insulting name, "Come on, then, chicken." Beth retorted by calling her mother a chicken. The two proceeded to trade insults through the next 13 turns, in the course of which Beth marked three of her utterances with teasing singsong intonation and aimed a shaming gesture (rubbing one index finger across the other) at her mother. The climax occurred after further mock provocation from the mother, when Beth finally raised her fists (to which both responded with laughter) and rushed toward her mother for an exchange of ritual blows.
>
> (P. Miller & Sperry, 1987, pp. 20–21)

It is unlikely that mothers in a less difficult and dangerous neighbourhood would try to promote the readiness to express aggression in their children, especially in their daughters. Thus, the norms, values, and circumstances of a culture or subcultural group likely contribute substantially to differences among groups in their expression of emotion.

review:

Children's tendencies in regard to experiencing and regulating emotions may be affected by differences in temperament among different groups of people. These tendencies may also be influenced by differences in parenting practices, which in turn are often affected by cultural differences in beliefs about what emotions are valued, and when and where emotions should be expressed.

Children's Understanding of Emotion

Another key influence on children's emotional reactions and regulation of emotion is their *understanding* of emotion—that is, their understanding of how to identify emotions, as well as their understanding of what emotions mean, their social functions, and what factors affect emotional experience. Since an understanding of emotion affects social behaviour, it is critical to the development of social competence. Children's understanding of emotions is primitive in infancy but develops rapidly over the course of childhood.

Identifying the Emotions of Others

The first step in the development of emotional knowledge is the recognition of different emotions in others. By 3 months of age, infants can distinguish facial expressions of happiness, surprise, and anger (Grossmann, 2010; Serrano, Iglesias, & Loeches, 1992; Walker-Andrews & Dickson, 1997). If, for example, 3- or 4-month-olds are habituated to pictures of happy faces and then are presented with a picture of a face depicting surprise, they dishabituate, showing renewed interest by looking longer at the new picture. By 7 months of age, infants appear to discriminate a number of additional expressions such as fear, sadness, and interest (Grossmann, 2010). For example, 7-month-olds exhibit different patterns of brain waves when they observe fearful and angry facial expressions, a finding that suggests some ability to discriminate these emotions (Kobiella et al., 2008).

By this age or a bit earlier, infants also start to perceive others' emotional expressions as meaningful. For instance, if infants at this age are shown a video in which a person's facial expression and voice are consistent in their emotional expression (e.g., a smiling face and a bubbly voice) and a video in which a person's facial expression and voice are emotionally discrepant (e.g., a sad face and a bubbly voice), they will attend more to the presentation that is emotionally consistent (Walker-Andrews & Dickson, 1997). Infants much younger than 7 months generally do not seem to notice the difference between the two presentations.

As discussed in Chapter 5, at about 5½ months of age, some children begin to demonstrate that they can relate facial expressions of emotion and emotional tones of voice to events in the environment, although this ability is often not seen until 7 to 12 months of age (Saarni et al., 2006; Vaillant-Molina & Bahrick, 2012). Such skills are evident in children's **social referencing**—that is, their use of a parent's or other adult's facial expression or vocal cues to decide how to deal with novel, ambiguous, or possibly threatening situations. In laboratory studies of this phenomenon, infants are typically exposed to novel people or toys while their mother, at the experimenter's direction, shows a happy, fearful, or neutral facial expression. In studies of this type, 12-month-olds tend to stay near their mother when she shows fear; to move toward the novel person or object if she expresses positive

social referencing ■ The use of a parent's or other adult's facial expression or vocal cues to decide how to deal with novel, ambiguous, or possibly threatening situations.

The ability to read peers' facial expressions provides children with information about a peer's motives, which helps children respond appropriately in potentially conflictual situations.

emotion; and to move partway toward the person or object if she shows no emotion (L. J. Carver & Vaccaro, 2007; Moses et al., 2001; Saarni et al., 2006). Similar results have been found in research on 12-month-olds' ability to read their mother's tone of voice. When prevented from seeing their mother's face as they were being presented with novel toys, infants were more cautious and exhibited more fear when the mother's voice was fearful than when it was neutral (Mumme, Fernald, & Herrera, 1996).

By 14 months of age, the emotion-related information obtained through social referencing has an effect on children's touching of the object even an hour later (Hertenstein & Campos, 2004). Children seem to be better at social referencing if they receive both vocal and facial cues of emotion from the adult, and vocal cues seem to be more effective than just visual cues (Vaish & Striano, 2004; Valliant-Molina & Bahrick, 2012).

By the age of 3, children in laboratory studies demonstrate a rudimentary ability to label a fairly narrow range of emotional expressions displayed in pictures or on puppets' faces (Bullock & Russell, 1985; Denham, 1986; J. A. Russell & Bullock, 1986). Young children—even 2-year-olds—are skilled at labelling happiness (usually by pointing to pictures of faces that reflect happiness) (Michalson & Lewis, 1985). The ability to label anger, fear, and sadness emerges and increases in the next year or two, with the ability to label surprise and disgust gradually appearing in the late preschool and early school years (N. Eisenberg, Murphy, & Shepard, 1997; J. A. Russell & Widen, 2002; Widen & Russell, 2003, 2010a). Most children cannot label more complex emotions such as pride, shame, and guilt until early to mid-elementary school (Saarni et al., 2006), but the scope and accuracy of emotion labelling improve thereafter into adolescence (Montirosso et al., 2010).

The ability to discriminate and label different emotions helps children respond appropriately to their own and others' emotions. If a child understands that he or she is experiencing guilt, for example, the child may understand the need to make amends to diminish the guilt. Similarly, a child who can see that a peer is angry can devise ways to avoid or appease that peer. In fact, children who are more skilled than their peers at labelling and interpreting others' emotions are also higher in social competence (Denham et al., 2003; R. S. Feldman, Philippot, & Custrini, 1991; Izard et al., 2008) and lower in behaviour problems or social withdrawal (Alonso-Alberca et al., 2012; Fine et al., 2003; Schultz et al., 2001).

Understanding the Causes and Dynamics of Emotion

Knowing the causes of emotions is also important for understanding one's own and others' behaviour and motives (Saarni et al., 2006). It likewise is key for regulating one's own behaviour and, hence, for social competence (Denham et al., 2003; Izard et al., 2008; Schultz et al., 2001). Consider, for instance, a child who is being rebuffed or insulted by a friend whom the child has just bested in a game or on an exam. If the child understands that, in this situation, the friend may be lashing out not because the friend is nasty but because the friend feels threatened and inadequate, the child may be much better able to control his or her own response.

A variety of studies have shown rapid development over the preschool and school years in children's understanding of the kinds of emotions that certain situations tend to evoke in others. In a typical study of this understanding, children are told short stories about characters in situations such as having a birthday party or losing a pet. Children are then asked how the character in the story feels. By age 3, children are quite good at identifying situations that make people feel happy. At age 4, they are fairly accurate at identifying situations that make people sad (Borke, 1971; Denham & Couchoud, 1990), and at age 4 to 5, they can identify situations likely to elicit anger, fear, or surprise (N. Eisenberg et al., 1997; Widen & Russell, 2010b).

Children's ability to understand the circumstances that evoke complex social emotions such as pride, guilt, shame, embarrassment, and jealousy often emerges after age 7, and, according to cross-cultural research that involved children from both Western nations and a remote Himalayan village, this ability is considerable by late elementary school and early adolescence (P. L. Harris et al., 1987; Widen & Russell, 2010b; Wiggers & van Lieshout, 1985). From age 4 until at least age 10, children are generally better at identifying emotions from stories depicting the cause of an emotion than from pictures of facial expressions such as fear, disgust, embarrassment, and shame (an exception is for surprise) (Widen & Russell, 2010a). This is probably because facial expressions of emotions such as anger, fear, sadness, and disgust are often interpreted as indicating more than one emotion (Widen & Naab, 2012).

Another way to assess children's understanding of the causes of emotions is to record what they say about emotions in their everyday conversations and to ask them to discuss and explain others' emotions. In this kind of research, even 28-month-olds mention emotions such as happiness, sadness, anger, fear, crying, and hurting in appropriate ways in their conversations (e.g., "You sad, Daddy?" or "Don't be mad.") and sometimes even mention their causes (e.g., "Santa will be happy if I pee in the potty." or "Grandma mad. I wrote on wall.") (Bretherton & Beeghly, 1982).

By age 4 to 6, children can give accurate explanations for why their peers expressed negative emotions in their preschool (e.g., because they were teased or lost the use of a toy) (Fabes et al., 1988). Children get more skilled at explaining the causes of emotion across the preschool and school years (Fabes et al., 1991; Sayfan & Lagattuta, 2009; Strayer, 1986). For example, 3rd and 6th graders are more likely than kindergartners to believe that someone caught being dishonest will be scared (Barden et al., 1980).

With age, children also come to understand that people can feel particular emotions brought on by reminders of past events. For instance, in one study, 3- to 5-year-olds were told stories about children who experienced a negative event and later saw reminders of that event. One story was about a girl named Mary who has a pet rabbit that lives in a typical rabbit cage. One day Mary's rabbit is chased away by a dog and is never seen again. In different versions of the story, Mary later sees one of three reminders of her loss—the culprit dog, her rabbit's cage, or a photograph of her rabbit. At this point, the children were told that Mary started to feel sad and were asked "Why did Mary start to feel sad right now?" On stories such as these, 39% of 3-year-olds, 83% of 4-year-olds, and 100% of 5-year-olds understood that the story characters were sad because a memory cue had made them think about a previous unhappy event (Lagattuta, Wellman, & Flavell, 1997). Similarly, from ages 3 to 5, children increasingly can explain that when people are in a situation that reminds them of a past negative event, they may worry and change their behaviour to avoid future negative events (Lagattuta, 2007). Understanding that memory cues can trigger emotions associated with past events helps children explain their own and others' emotional reactions in situations that in themselves seem emotionally neutral.

In the elementary school years, children become increasingly sophisticated in their understanding about how, when, and why emotions occur. For instance, they become more aware of cognitive processes related to regulating emotion and of the fact that emotional intensity wanes over time. They also come to recognize that people can experience more than one emotion at the same time, including both positive and negative emotions arising from the same source (P. L. Harris, 2006; Harter & Buddin, 1987; F. Pons & Harris, 2005). In addition, they increasingly understand how the mind can be used to both increase and reduce fears and that thinking positively can improve one's emotion while thinking negatively can worsen it (Bamford & Lagattuta, 2012; Sayfan & Lagattuta, 2009). At around age 10, children begin to understand emotional ambivalence and realize that people can have mixed feelings about events, others, and themselves (Donaldson & Westerman, 1986; Reissland, 1985). Taken together, these developments allow children to better understand the complexities of emotional experience in context.

Children's Understanding of Real and False Emotions

An important component in the development of emotional understanding is the realization that the emotions people express do not necessarily reflect their true feelings (Figure 10.5). The beginnings of this realization are seen in 3-year-olds' occasional (and usually transparent) attempts to mask their negative emotions when they receive a disappointing gift or prize (P. M. Cole, 1986). By age 5, children's

FIGURE 10.5 Facial display figures used in the assessment of expression regulation The figures on the girl's chest indicate how she feels inside. Children select from the different pictures of facial expressions to indicate what expression the girl would show on her face, as well as how she would feel inside. (Adapted from D. C. Jones, Abbey, & Cumberland, 1998)

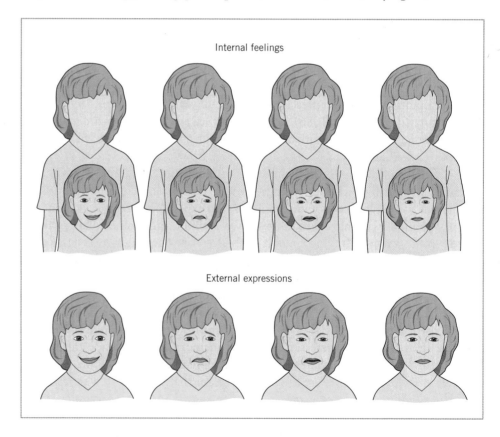

Internal feelings

External expressions

understanding of false emotion has improved considerably, as demonstrated in a study that used six stories such as the following:

> Michelle is sleeping over at her cousin Johnny's house today. Michelle forgot her favorite teddy bear at home. Michelle is really sad that she forgot her teddy bear. But, she doesn't want Johnny to see how sad she is because Johnny will call her a baby. So, Michelle tries to hide how she feels.

(M. Banerjee, 1997)

After children were questioned to ensure that they understood the story, they were presented with illustrations of various emotional expressions and given instructions such as "Show me the picture for how Michelle really feels" and "Show me the picture for how Michelle will try to look on her face." Whereas about half of 3- and 4-year-olds chose the appropriate pictures on four or more of the stories, more than 80% of 5-year-olds chose correctly. Studies with both Japanese and Western children also confirm that between 4 and 6 years of age, children increasingly understand that people can be misled by others' facial expressions (D. Gardner et al., 1988; D. Gross & Harris, 1988).

Part of the improvement in understanding false emotion involves a growing understanding of **display rules**—a social group's informal norms about when, where, and how much one should show emotions and when and where displays of emotion should be suppressed or masked. Over the preschool and elementary school years, children develop a more refined understanding of when and why display rules are used (M. Banerjee, 1997; Rotenberg & Eisenberg, 1997; Saarni, 1979). They increasingly understand, for example, that people use verbal and facial display rules to protect others' feelings or their own, as when they pretend to like someone's cooking so as not to hurt the cook's feelings (labelled a *prosocial motive*) or hide their emotions when they themselves are being teased or lose a contest (labelled a *self-protective motive*) (Gnepp & Hess, 1986). (Figure 10.6 shows age-related changes in these types of motives.) With age, children also better understand that people tend to break eye contact and avert their gaze when lying, and they are increasingly able to use this knowledge to conceal their own deception (McCarthy & Lee, 2009).

These age-related advances in children's understanding of real versus false emotion and display rules are apparently linked to increases in children's cognitive capacities (Flavell, 1986; P. L. Harris, 2000). However, social factors also seem to affect children's understanding of display rules. For example, in most cultures, display rules are somewhat different for males and females and reflect societal beliefs about how males and females should feel and behave (Ruble, Martin, & Berenbaum, 2006; van Beek, van Dolderen, & Demon Dubas, 2006). Elementary school girls in the United States, for instance, are more likely than boys to feel that openly expressing emotions such as pain is acceptable (Zeman & Garber, 1996). In most cultures, girls are also somewhat more attuned than boys to the need to inhibit emotional displays that might hurt others' feelings (P. M. Cole, 1986; Saarni, 1984). This is especially true for girls from cultures such as India, in which females are expected to be deferential and to express only socially appropriate emotions (M. S. Joshi & MacLean, 1994). These findings obviously are consistent with the gender stereotypes that girls are more likely both to try to protect others' feelings and to be more emotional than boys.

display rules ■ A social group's informal norms about when, where, and how much one should show emotions and when and where displays of emotion should be suppressed or masked by displays of other emotions.

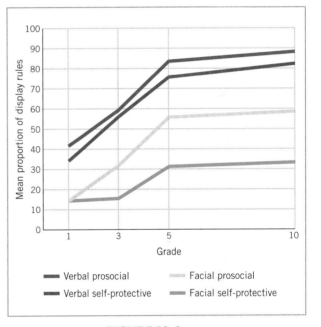

FIGURE 10.6 Mean proportion of display rules as a function of mode of expression (verbal or facial), story type (prosocial or protective), and grade Children in Grades 1, 3, 5, and 10 listened to stories designed to elicit display rules. Then they were asked to predict and explain what the story protagonists would say and what facial expressions the protagonists would show in the emotion-laden situations. Children's knowledge of how and when to control emotional displays increased between Grades 1 and 5 and then levelled off. Their understanding was greater for verbal display rules, whereby children monitor, falsify, and inhibit their speech, than for facial display rules. Children also understood prosocial display rules (used to protect another's feelings) better than self-protective display rules (used for personal gain). (Adapted from Gnepp & Hess, 1986)

Parents' beliefs and behaviours—which often reflect cultural beliefs—likely contribute to children's understanding and use of display rules (Friedlmeier et al., 2011). As discussed earlier, the emphasis placed on controlling emotional displays in Nepal varies by subculture. Correspondingly, the degree to which Nepali children report masking negative emotions varies with the degree to which mothers in different Nepali subcultures report teaching their children how to manage emotions (P. M. Cole & Tamang, 1998). Thus, children seem to be attuned to display rules that are valued in their culture or that serve an important function in the family.

review:

Children's understanding of emotions plays an important role in their emotional functioning. Although infants can detect differences in various emotional expressions such as happiness and surprise by 3 to 7 months of age, it is not until they are about 6 months of age that they start to treat others' emotional expressions as meaningful. At about 5½ to 12 months of age, children begin to connect facial expressions of emotion or an emotional tone of voice with other events in the situation, as evidenced by their use of social referencing. By age 3, children demonstrate a rudimentary ability to label facial expressions and understand simple situations that are likely to cause happiness.

As children move through the preschool and elementary school years, their understanding of emotions and situations that cause emotions grows in range and complexity. In addition, they increasingly appreciate that the emotions people show may not reflect their true feelings.

chapter summary:

The Development of Emotions in Childhood

- Discrete-emotions theorists believe that each emotion is packaged with a specific set of bodily and facial reactions and that distinct emotions are evident from early in life. In contrast, functionalists believe that emotions reflect what individuals are trying to do in specific situations—that is, their concerns and goals at the moment—and that there is not a set of innate, discrete emotions but many emotions based on people's many different interactions with the social world.

- From early in life, emotions play an important role in both survival and social communication. Although infants show negative and positive affect from birth, it is not clear whether young infants experience different types of negative emotions such as anger, fear, and sadness.

- Emotions undergo change in the early months and years of life. Smiles become social around the 2nd to 3rd month of life, and what makes children smile and laugh changes with cognitive development.

- Newborns exhibit distress due to discomfort and hunger. By 6 to 7 months of age, they often are distressed when strangers approach them, and by approximately 8 months of age, they tend to get distressed when separated from their parents.

- The social emotions—embarrassment, pride, shame, and guilt—emerge in the second year of life. Their emergence is tied in part to the development of a rudimentary sense of self and to an appreciation of others' reactions to the self.

- In childhood, emotional reactions are increasingly influenced by a growing cognitive understanding of events and emotions. For some children, there is an increase in the experience of negative emotion from childhood to adolescence. Rates of clinical and subclinical depression are much higher in adolescence than at younger ages, especially for girls.

Regulation of Emotion

- Emotional self-regulation involves the process of initiating, inhibiting, or modulating internal feeling states and emotion-related neural and physiological processes, cognitions, and behaviour in the service of accomplishing one's goals.

- Young infants are not very skilled at regulating themselves and must rely on adults to manage their emotions. However, children's self-regulation improves with age as they increasingly use cognitive strategies and more appropriate and effective means of managing their emotions and behaviour. Improvements in children's regulatory capacities are based on increases in both their cognitive development and their ability to control their own bodies, as well as on changes in others' expectations of them.

■ Emotional self-regulation is generally associated with high social competence and low problem behaviour.

Individual Differences in Emotion and Its Regulation

■ Both biological and environmental factors contribute to the differences we see in children's emotions and related behaviours. Temperament, which is believed to have a constitutional basis but can also be affected by social experiences, predicts adjustment in childhood and adulthood. However, children with difficult temperaments often do well if they receive sensitive and appropriate parenting.

Children's Emotional Development in the Family

■ Children's emotional development is affected by the quality of their early social relationships and their parents' discussion of emotion. High levels of positive emotion in the home are associated with favourable outcomes for children, whereas high levels of negative emotion and punitive reactions to children's displays of negative emotion are often linked to negative developmental outcomes (the latter pattern may be especially likely in Western cultures). Parental discussion of emotion or other internal states (e.g., desires, cognitions) may promote children's understanding of emotion and increase their social competence, although the discussion of emotions per se may be less associated with social competence in some cultures.

Culture and Children's Emotional Development

■ There may be differences in temperament across some cultures, which affect children's tendencies to experience and regulate emotions.

■ There are cultural differences in beliefs about what emotions are valued and when emotions should be expressed, and these shape children's expression of emotion.

Children's Understanding of Emotion

■ To interact with others effectively, a person must be able to identify others' emotions and have some knowledge of their causes and significance. By 5½ to 7 months of age, infants start to treat others' emotional expressions as meaningful. Between 5½ and 12 months of age, children start to exhibit social referencing.

■ By age 2 to 3 years, children demonstrate a rudimentary ability to label facial expressions and simple situations associated with happiness. Children's understanding of facial expressions, the situations that cause emotions, display rules, and the complexities of emotional experience increases in the preschool and elementary school years.

Critical Thinking Questions

1. How might differences in children's intelligence contribute to (a) the emotions they display and (b) their understanding of emotions? What other factors might contribute to children's understanding of their own and others' emotions?

2. List at least five aspects of children's temperament. What aspects of adults' personality might each predict?

3. Suppose that you wanted to assess changes with age in children's regulation of emotion. Think of five different tasks you could use to assess age-related changes. Which would be best to use in early childhood and which would better reflect changes at older ages?

4. Recall from Chapter 7 the development of children's theory of mind. How might advances in children's understanding of theory of mind relate to their understanding of emotion? What aspects of understanding emotion might be mostly associated with an understanding of theory of mind?

Key Terms

behavioural inhibition, p. 409

co-rumination, p. 396

differential (or discrete) emotions theory, p. 386

display rules, p. 421

emotion, p. 385

emotional intelligence, p. 384

emotional self-regulation, p. 398

functionalist approach, p. 386

goodness of fit, p. 409

rumination, p. 396

self-conscious emotions, p. 392

separation anxiety, p. 391

social competence, p. 401

social referencing, p. 417

social smiles, p. 388

socialization, p. 411

temperament, p. 403

HECTOR MCDONNELL (b. 1947), *Refugee Mother and Baby, Goma,* 1997 (oil on canvas)

chapter 11:

Attachment to Others and Development of Self

Between 1937 and 1943, numerous child-care professionals reported instances of a disturbing phenomenon: children who seemed to have no concern or feeling for anyone but themselves. Some of the children were withdrawn and isolated; others were overactive and abusive toward their peers. By the time they were adolescents, these children often had histories of persistent stealing, violence, and sexual misdemeanours. Many of these children had been reared in institutions in which they received adequate physical care but experienced little social interaction; others had been shifted from foster home to foster home in infancy and early childhood (Bowlby, 1953).

At about the same time, similar disturbances were being observed among children who had been orphaned or separated from their parents during World War II and were in refugee camps or other institutional settings. John Bowlby, an English psychoanalyst who worked with many of these children, reported that they were very listless, depressed or otherwise emotionally disturbed, and mentally stunted. Older refugee children often seemed to have lost all interest in life and were possessed by feelings of emptiness (Bowlby, 1953). These children, like the Romanian orphans discussed in Chapter 1 (pages 6–7), tended not to develop typical emotional attachments with other people.

On the basis of such observations, René Spitz, a French psychoanalyst who had worked with Freud, conducted a series of classic studies of how the lack of adequate caregiving affects development (Spitz, 1945, 1946, 1949). Spitz filmed infants (a methodological innovation) residing in orphanages, most of whom had been born to unmarried mothers and had been given up for adoption. The films were extremely poignant and painful to watch. They documented the fact that, despite receiving good institutional care, the infants were generally sickly and developmentally impaired. In many cases, the infants seemed unmotivated to live: their death rate was about 37% over 2 years' time, compared with no deaths in an institution where children had daily contact with their mothers. The most important contribution of the films, however, was their evidence of intense and prolonged grief and depression in infants who had been separated from their mothers after developing a loving relationship with them. Psychologists of the time did not believe that infants could experience such emotions (Emde, 1994).

Taken together, these early observations also challenged the more central belief, then held by many child-care professionals, that if children in institutions such as orphanages received good physical care, including proper nourishment and health care, they would develop as expected. These professionals placed little emphasis on the emotional dimensions of caregiving. As a result of the studies of children who lost their parents in the 1940s, it became generally recognized that, no matter how hygienic and competently managed, institutions like orphanages put babies at high risk because they did not provide the kind of caregiving that enables infants to form close socioemotional bonds. Adoption—the earlier the better—came to be viewed as a far better option.

Another important outcome of the work of Bowlby and others who studied institutionalized children was the beginning of systematic research on how the quality of parent–child interactions affects children's development in families, especially their development of emotional attachments to other people. This research, which continues today, has led to a much deeper understanding of the ways in which the early parent–child emotional bond likely influences children's interactions with others from infancy into adulthood. It has also provided new insight into the development of children's sense of self, as well as of their emotions, including their feelings of self-worth.

In this chapter, we will first explore how children develop **attachments,** close and enduring emotional bonds to parents or other primary caregivers. Then we will examine the ways in which the nature of these attachments to others seems to set the stage for the child's immediate and long-term development. As you will see, the attachment process appears to be biologically based yet unfolds in different ways, depending on the familial and cultural context. Thus, the themes of *nature and nurture* and the *sociocultural context* will be important in our discussion of this topic. You will also see that although most children in typical social circumstances develop attachments to their parents, the quality of these attachments differs in important ways and has implications for each child's social and emotional development. The theme of *individual differences* will therefore figure prominently in our discussion as well. The theme of *research and children's welfare* is also relevant to our examination of experimental interventions designed to enhance the quality of mother–child attachment.

Next we will examine a related issue—the development of children's sense of self, that is, their self-understanding, self-identity, and self-esteem. Although many factors influence these areas of development, the quality of children's early attachments lays the foundation for how children feel about themselves, including their sense of security and well-being. Over time, children's self-understanding, self-esteem, and self-identity are also shaped by how others perceive and treat them, by biologically based characteristics of the child, and by children's developing abilities to think about and interpret their social worlds. Thus, the themes of *nature and nurture, individual differences,* the *sociocultural context,* and the *active child* will be evident in our discussion of the development of self.

attachment ■ An emotional bond with a specific person that is enduring across space and time. Usually, attachments are discussed in regard to the relation between infants and specific caregivers, although they can also occur in adulthood.

The Caregiver–Child Attachment Relationship

Following the very disturbing observations made in the 1930s and 1940s regarding children separated from their parents early in life, researchers began to conduct systematic studies of this phenomenon. Much of the early research, such as that conducted by Spitz, focused on how the development of young children who had been orphaned or otherwise separated from their parents was affected by the quality of the caregiving they subsequently received. The research on children adopted from Romania (discussed in Chapter 1) is probably the best known of recent studies on this topic, all of which support the idea that institutional care in the first years of life typically hinders optimal social, emotional, and cognitive development (McCall et al., 2011; Rutter et al., 2010).

Another line of research in this area involved experimental work with monkeys. In some of the most famous research in psychology, Harry Harlow and his colleagues (Harlow & Harlow, 1965; Harlow & Zimmerman, 1959; E. E. Nelson, Herman, et al., 2009; L. D. Young et al., 1973) reared infant rhesus monkeys in isolation from birth, comparing their development with that of monkeys reared normally with their mothers. The isolated babies were well fed and kept healthy, but they had no exposure to their mother or other monkeys.

Harlow's female monkeys who were raised in isolation were poor mothers as adults, turning their backs on their infants, literally and figuratively, and often attacking them. This outcome suggested that "mother love" is essential to normal social and emotional development.

HARLOW PRIMATE LABORATORY, UNIVERSITY OF WISCONSIN

attachment theory ■ A theory based on John Bowlby's work that posits that children are biologically predisposed to develop attachments to caregivers as a means of increasing the chances of their own survival.

secure base ■ Refers to the idea that the presence of a trusted caregiver provides an infant or toddler with a sense of security that makes it possible for the child to explore the environment.

When they finally were placed with other monkeys 6 months later, they compulsively bit and rocked themselves and avoided other monkeys completely, apparently incapable of communicating with, or learning from, others. They also showed high levels of fear when exposed to threatening stimuli such as loud sounds. As adults, formerly isolated females had no interest in sex. If they were artificially impregnated, they did not know what to do with their babies. At best, they tended to ignore or reject them; at worst, they attacked them. This research, although examining the effects of the lack of all early social interaction (and not just that with parents), strongly supported the view that children's healthy social and emotional development is rooted in their early social interactions with adults.

Attachment Theory

The findings from observations of children and monkeys separated from their parents were so dramatic that psychiatrists and psychologists were compelled to rethink their ideas about early development. Foremost in this effort were John Bowlby, who proposed **attachment theory,** and his colleague, Mary Ainsworth, who extended and tested Bowlby's ideas.

COURTESY OF SIR JOHN BOWLBY

John Bowlby, who laid the foundations of attachment theory, was influenced by psychoanalytic work and research on animals' social behaviour.

Bowlby's Attachment Theory

Bowlby's theory of attachment was strongly influenced by several key tenets of Freud's theories, especially the idea that infants' earliest relationships with their mothers shape their later development. However, Bowlby replaced the psychoanalytic notion of a "needy, dependent infant" with the idea of a "competence-motivated infant" who uses his or her primary caregiver as a **secure base** (E. Waters & Cummings, 2000). The general idea of the secure base is that the presence of a trusted caregiver provides the infant or toddler with a sense of security that allows the child to explore the environment and hence to become generally knowledgeable and competent. In addition, the primary caregiver serves as a haven of safety when the infant feels threatened or insecure, and the child derives comfort and pleasure from being near the caregiver.

Bowlby's idea of the primary caregiver as a secure base was directly influenced by ethological theories, particularly the ideas of Konrad Lorenz (see Chapter 9, page 364). Bowlby proposed that the attachment process between infant and caregiver is rooted in evolution and increases the infant's chance of survival. Just like imprinting, this attachment process develops from the interaction between species-specific learning biases (such as infants' strong tendency to look at faces) and the infant's experience with his or her caregiver. Thus, the attachment process is viewed as having an innate basis, but the development and quality of infants' attachments are highly dependent on the nature of their experiences with caregivers.

According to Bowlby, the initial development of attachment takes place in four phases.

- *Pre-attachment* (birth to age 6 weeks). In this phase, the infant produces innate signals, most notably crying, that summon caregivers, and the infant is comforted by the ensuing interaction.

- *Attachment-in-the-making* (age 6 weeks to 6 to 8 months). During this phase, infants begin to respond preferentially to familiar people. Typically they smile, laugh, or babble more frequently in the presence of their primary caregiver and are more easily soothed by that person. Like Freud and Erik Erikson, Bowlby saw this phase as a time when infants form expectations about how their caregivers will respond to their needs and, accordingly, do or do not develop a sense of trust in them.

- *Clear-cut attachment* (between 6 to 8 months and 1½ years). In this phase, infants actively seek contact with their regular caregivers. They happily greet their mother when she appears and, correspondingly, may exhibit *separation anxiety or distress* when she departs (see Chapter 10, page 391). For the majority of children, the mother now serves as a secure base, facilitating the infant's exploration and mastery of the environment.

- *Reciprocal relationships* (from 1½ or 2 years on). During this final phase, toddlers' rapidly increasing cognitive and language abilities enable them to understand their parents' feelings, goals, and motives and to use this understanding to organize their efforts to be near their parents. As a result, a more mutually regulated relationship gradually emerges as the child takes an increasingly active role in developing a working partnership with his or her parents (Bowlby, 1969). Correspondingly, separation distress declines.

The usual outcome of these phases is an enduring emotional tie uniting the infant and caregiver. In addition, the child develops an **internal working model of attachment,** a mental representation of the self, of attachment figures, and of relationships in general. This internal working model is based on the young child's discovering the extent to which his or her caregiver could be depended on to satisfy the child's needs and provide a sense of security. Bowlby believed that this internal working model guides the individual's expectations about relationships throughout life. If caregivers are accessible and responsive, young children come to expect interpersonal relationships to be gratifying and they feel worthy of receiving care and love. As adults, they look for, and expect to find, satisfying and security-enhancing relationships similar to the ones they had with their attachment figures in childhood. If children's attachment figures are unavailable or unresponsive, children develop negative perceptions of relationships with other people and of themselves (Bowlby, 1973, 1980; Bretherton & Munholland, 1999). Thus, children's internal working models of attachment are believed to influence their overall adjustment, social behaviour, perceptions of others, and the development of their self-esteem and sense of self (R. A. Thompson, 2006).

internal working model of attachment ■ The child's mental representation of the self, of attachment figure(s), and of relationships in general that is constructed as a result of experiences with caregivers. The working model guides children's interactions with caregivers and other people in infancy and at older ages.

Ainsworth's Research

Mary Ainsworth, who began working with John Bowlby in 1950, provided empirical support for Bowlby's theory, extending it in important ways and bringing the concept of the primary caregiver as a secure base to the fore. In research conducted in both Uganda (Ainsworth, 1967) and the United States, Ainsworth studied mother–infant interactions during infants' explorations and separations from their mother. On the basis of her observations, she came to the conclusion that two key measures provide insight into the quality of the infant's attachment to the caregiver: (1) the extent to which an infant is able to use his or her primary caregiver as a secure base, and (2) how the infant reacts to brief separations from, and reunions with, the caregiver (Ainsworth, 1973; Ainsworth et al., 1978).

Strange Situation ■ A procedure developed by Mary Ainsworth to assess infants' attachment to their primary caregiver.

Measurement of Attachment Security in Infancy

With these measures in mind, Ainsworth designed a laboratory test for assessing the security of an infant's attachment to his or her parent. This test is called the **Strange Situation** because it is conducted in a context that is unfamiliar to the child and likely to heighten the child's need for his or her parent. In this test, the infant, accompanied by the parent, is placed in a laboratory playroom equipped with interesting toys. After the experimenter introduces the parent and child to the room, the child is exposed to seven episodes, including two separations from, and reunions with, the parent, as well as two interactions with a stranger—one when the parent is out of the room and one when the parent is present (see Table 11.1). Each episode lasts approximately 3 minutes unless the child becomes overly upset. Throughout these episodes, observers rate infants' behaviours, including their attempts to seek closeness and contact with the parent, their resistance to or avoidance of the parent, their interactions with the stranger, and their interactions with the parent from a distance using language or gestures.

Through her use of the Strange Situation, Ainsworth (1973) discerned three distinct patterns in infants' behaviour that seemed to indicate the quality or security of their attachment bond. These patterns—which are reflected in the infant's behaviour throughout the Strange Situation, but especially during the *reunions* with the parent—have been replicated many times in research with mothers, and sometimes with fathers. On the basis of these patterns, Ainsworth identified three attachment categories.

TABLE 11.1

Episodes in Ainsworth's Strange Situation Procedure

Episode	Events	Aspect of Attachment Behaviour Assessed
1	Experimenter introduces caregiver and infant to the unfamiliar room; shows toys to baby; then leaves.	None
2	Caregiver and child are alone; caregiver is told not to initiate interaction but to respond to baby as appropriate.	Exploration and use of parent as a secure base
3	Stranger enters and is seated quietly for 1 minute; then talks to caregiver for 1 minute; then tries to interact with the baby for 1 minute.	Reaction to the stranger
4	Mother leaves child alone with the stranger, who lets baby play but offers comfort if needed. Segment is shortened if the baby becomes too distressed.	Separation distress and reaction to stranger's comforting
5	Caregiver calls to baby from outside door, enters the room, and pauses by the door. Stranger leaves. Caregiver lets infant play or may comfort infant if distressed.	Reaction to reunion with parent
6	Parent leaves infant alone in the room. Segment is ended if infant is too distressed.	Separation distress
7	Stranger enters room, greets infant, and pauses. She sits or comforts infant if the infant is upset. Segment is ended if the infant is very upset.	Ability to be soothed by stranger
8	Caregiver calls from outside the door, enters and greets infant, and pauses. Caregiver sits if infant is not upset but may provide comfort if infant is distressed. Caregiver allows infant to return to play if interested.	Reaction to reunion

Source: Adapted from Ainsworth et al., 1978

The first attachment category—the one into which the majority of infants fall—is **secure attachment**. Babies in this category use their mother as a secure base during the initial part of the session, leaving her side to explore the many toys available in the room. As they play with the toys, these infants occasionally look back to check on their mother or bring a toy over to show her. They are usually, but by no means always, distressed to some degree when their mother leaves the room, especially when they are left totally alone. However, when their mother returns, they make it clear that they are glad to see her, either by simply greeting her with a happy smile or, if they have been upset during her absence, by going to her to be picked up and comforted. If they have been upset, their mother's presence comforts and calms them, often enabling them to explore the room again. About 60% of typical middle-class children in North America whose mother is not clinically disturbed fall into this category; for infants from lower socioeconomic groups, the rate is significantly lower—slightly less than 50% for children under 24 months of age (K. Chisholm, 1998; R. A. Thompson, 1998; van IJzendoorn, Schuengel, & Bakermans-Kranenburg, 1999).

The other two attachment categories that Ainsworth originally identified involve children who are considered to have an **insecure attachment,** that is, who have less positive attachment to their caregivers than do securely attached children. One type of insecurely attached infant is classified as having an **insecure/resistant (or ambivalent) attachment.** Infants in this category are often clingy from the beginning of the Strange Situation, staying close to the mother instead of exploring the toys. When their mother leaves the room, they tend to get very upset, often crying intensely. In the reunion, the insecure/resistant infant typically re-establishes contact with the mother, only to then rebuff her efforts at offering comfort. For example, the infant may rush to the mother bawling, with outstretched arms, signalling the wish to be picked up—but then, as soon as the child is picked up, he or she arches away from the mother or begins squirming to get free from her embrace. About 9% of typical middle-class children in North America fall into the insecure/resistant category, but the percentage appears to be somewhat higher in many non-Western cultures (van IJzendoorn et al., 1999).

The other type of insecurely attached infant is classified as having an **insecure/avoidant attachment.** Children in this category tend to avoid their mother in the Strange Situation. For example, they often fail to greet her during the reunions and ignore her or turn away while she is in the room. Approximately 15% of typical middle-class children fall into the insecure/avoidant category (van IJzendoorn et al., 1999).

Subsequent to Ainsworth's original research, attachment investigators found that the reactions of a small percentage of children in the Strange Situation did not fit well into any of Ainsworth's three categories. These children seem to have no consistent way of coping with the stress of the Strange Situation. Their behaviour is often confused or even contradictory. For example, they may exhibit fearful smiles and look away while approaching their mother, or they may seem quite calm and contented and then suddenly display angry distress. They also frequently appear dazed or disoriented and may freeze in their behaviour and remain still for a substantial period of time. These infants, labelled as having a **disorganized/disoriented attachment,** seem to have an unsolvable problem: they want to approach their mother, but they also seem to regard her as a source of fear from which they want to withdraw (Main & Solomon, 1990). About 15% of middle-class infants fall into this category. However, this percentage may be considerably

secure attachment ■ A pattern of attachment in which infants or young children have a high-quality, relatively unambivalent relationship with their attachment figure. In the Strange Situation, a securely attached infant, for example, may be upset when the caregiver leaves but may be happy to see the caregiver return, recovering quickly from any distress. When children are securely attached, they can use caregivers as a secure base for exploration.

insecure attachment ■ A pattern of attachment in which infants or young children have a less positive attachment to their caregiver than do securely attached children. Insecurely attached children can be classified as insecure/resistant (ambivalent), insecure/avoidant, or disorganized/disoriented.

insecure/resistant (or ambivalent) attachment ■ A type of insecure attachment in which infants or young children are clingy and stay close to their caregiver rather than exploring their environment. In the Strange Situation, insecure/resistant infants tend to get very upset when the caregiver leaves them alone in the room. When their caregiver returns, they are not easily comforted and both seek comfort and resist efforts by the caregiver to comfort them.

insecure/avoidant attachment ■ A type of insecure attachment in which infants or young children seem somewhat indifferent toward their caregiver and may even avoid the caregiver. In the Strange Situation, they seem indifferent toward their caregiver before the caregiver leaves the room and indifferent or avoidant when the caregiver returns. If the infant gets upset when left alone, he or she is as easily comforted by a stranger as by a parent.

disorganized/disoriented attachment ■ A type of insecure attachment in which infants or young children have no consistent way of coping with the stress of the Strange Situation. Their behaviour is often confused or even contradictory, and they often appear dazed or disoriented.

adult attachment models ■ Working models of attachment in adulthood that are believed to be based on adults' perceptions of their own childhood experiences—especially their relationships with their parents—and of the influence of these experiences on them as adults.

higher among maltreated infants (van IJzendoorn et al., 1999) and among infants whose parents are having serious difficulties with their own working models of attachment (van IJzendoorn, 1995) (see Box 11.1), and among preschoolers from lower socioeconomic backgrounds (van IJzendoorn et al., 1999).

A key question, of course, is whether there is some similarity between infants' behaviour in the Strange Situation and their behaviour at home. The answer is yes (J. Solomon & George, 1999). For example, Western University researchers David Pederson and Greg Moran (1996) found that 12-month-olds who are

BOX 11.1: individual differences

PARENTAL ATTACHMENT STATUS

According to attachment theorists, parents have "working models" of attachment relationships that guide their interactions with their children and thereby influence the security of their children's attachment. These **adult attachment models** are based on adults' perceptions of their own childhood relationships with their parents and on the continuing influence of those relationships (Main, Kaplan, & Cassidy, 1985).

Parental models of attachment often are measured with the Adult Attachment Interview (AAI), developed by Mary Main, Carol George, and their colleagues. In this interview, adults are asked to discuss their early childhood attachments and to evaluate them from their current perspectives (Hesse, 1999). For example, they are asked to describe their childhood relationship with each parent, including what their parent did for them when they were hurt or upset; what they remember about separations from the parent; if they ever felt rejected by the parent; and how their adult personalities were shaped by these experiences. These descriptions are used to classify the adults into four major attachment groups—autonomous (or secure), dismissing, preoccupied, and unresolved/disorganized.

Adults who are rated *autonomous* or secure are those whose descriptions are coherent, consistent, and relevant to the questions. Generally, autonomous adults describe their past in a balanced manner, recalling both positive and negative features of their parents and of their relationships with them. They also report that their early attachments were influential in their development.

Autonomous adults discuss their past in a consistent and coherent manner even if they did not have supportive parents.

Adults in the other three categories are considered to be insecure in their attachment status. *Dismissing* adults often insist that they cannot remember attachment-related interactions with their parents, or they minimize the impact that these experiences had on them. They may also contradict themselves when describing their attachment-related experiences and seem unaware of their inconsistencies. For example, they may describe their mother in glowing terms and later talk about how she got angry at them whenever they hurt themselves (Hesse, 1999).

Preoccupied adults are intensely focused on their parents and tend to give confused and angry accounts of attachment-related experiences. A prototypical response is "I got so angry [at my mother] that I picked up the soup bowl and threw it at her" (Hesse, 1999, p. 403). Preoccupied adults often seem to be so caught up in their attachment memories that they cannot provide a coherent description of them. *Unresolved/disorganized* adults appear to be suffering the aftermath of past traumatic experiences of loss or abuse. Their descriptions of their childhood show striking lapses in reasoning and may not make sense. For example, an unresolved/disorganized adult may indicate that he or she believes that a dead parent is still alive or that the parent died because of negative thoughts that the adult had about the parent (Hesse, 1999). In North American samples of Caucasian mothers

who have no diagnosed psychological disturbance, approximately 58% are classified as secure, 23% as dismissing, and 19% as preoccupied. This distribution is generally similar in samples in other countries such as India and China, and in countries in Africa and South America (van IJzendoorn & Bakermans-Kranenburg, 2010).

Parents' attachment classification predicts both their sensitivity toward their own children and their children's attachment to them. Autonomous parents tend to be sensitive, warm parents, and their infants usually are securely attached to them (Magai et al., 2000; Steele, Steele, & Fonagy, 1996; van IJzendoorn, 1995). Correspondingly, parents in the other three categories tend to have insecurely attached infants, although the relation is not very strong for preoccupied parents (see figure). Unresolved parents are particularly likely to have disorganized infants (Hesse & Main, 2006; Madigan et al., 2007), probably due, in part, to their low sensitivity, including either a negative and controlling, or a disengaged and inattentive, style of parenting (H. N. Bailey et al., 2007; Busch, Cowan, & Cowan, 2008; Whipple, Bernier, & Mageau, 2011). This general pattern of findings has emerged in studies in a number of different Western cultures, including a number of studies with Canadian mother–infant dyads (Madigan et al., 2007; Raval et al., 2001).

The reason for the association between parents' attachment models and the security of their children's attachments is not clear. Autonomous parents appear to be more sensitively attuned to their children,

securely attached exhibit more enjoyment of physical contact, are less fussy or difficult, and are better able to use their mothers as a secure base for exploration at home compared with infants who are insecurely attached. Thus, they are more likely to learn about their environments and to enjoy doing so. In addition, children's behaviour in the Strange Situation correlates with attachment scores derived from observing children's interactions with their mother over several hours (van IJzendoorn et al., 2004). As you will shortly see, attachment measurements derived from the Strange Situation also correlate with later behaviour patterns.

which likely contributes to their children's being securely attached (Mills-Koonce et al., 2011; Pederson et al., 1998; Verschueren et al., 2006). For example, securely attached parents are less angry and intrusive in their interactions with their children than are preoccupied parents (Adam, Gunnar, & Tanaka, 2004). And it may very well be that autonomous adults, who tend to have been securely attached as infants or children (E. Waters et al., 2000), are more sensitive and skilled parents because of their own early experience with sensitive parenting (Benoit & Parker, 1994), although the evidence for this is somewhat inconsistent (H. N. Bailey et al., 2007).

However, it is not clear what adults' responses on the AAI actually represent. Although attachment theorists claim that the content and coherence of adults' discussions of their own early childhood experiences reflect the effects of these early experiences, there is little evidence to prove (or disprove) this theory (Fox, 1995; R. A. Thompson, 1998). Rather than reflecting their own childhood experiences, adults' discussions of them may instead reflect their personal theories about development and child-rearing, their current level of psychological functioning, or their personality—all of which also may affect their parenting. Regardless of the reason, the relation between parents' attachment models and their infants' attachment suggests that parents' beliefs about parenting and about relationships have a powerful influence on the bond between them and their children (R. A. Thompson, 1998).

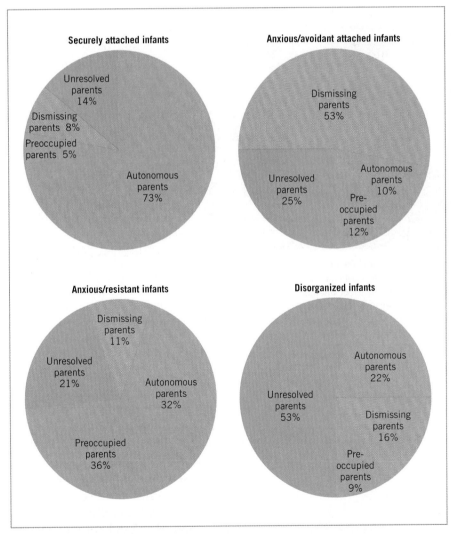

Parents with secure adult attachments tend to have securely attached children. (Adapted from van IJzendoorn, 1995)

Cultural Variations in Attachment

Because human infants are believed to be biologically predisposed to form attachments with their caregivers, one might expect attachment behaviours to be similar in different cultures. In fact, in large measure, infants' behaviours in the Strange Situation are similar across numerous cultures, including those of China, Western Europe, and various parts of Africa. In all these cultures, there are securely attached, insecure/resistant, and insecure/avoidant infants, with the average percentages for these groupings being approximately 53%, 18%, and 21%, respectively (van IJzendoorn & Sagi, 1999; van IJzendoorn et al., 1999). Although relatively few studies in non-Western cultures have included the category "disorganized/disoriented," the findings of those that have suggest that the percentage of babies who fall into this category is roughly 21%, which is not statistically different from the rates in Western countries (Behrens, Hesse, & Main, 2007; van IJzendoorn et al., 1999).

The degree to which children are encouraged to be independent varies across cultures and can affect whether children are categorized as insecure/resistant.

Despite these general consistencies in attachment ratings, some interesting and important differences in children's behaviour in the Strange Situation have been noted in certain other cultures (van IJzendoorn & Sagi-Schwartz, 2008; Zevalkink, Riksen-Walraven, & Van Lieshout, 1999). For example, while Japanese infants in one study showed roughly the same percentage of secure attachment in the Strange Situation as middle-class U.S. infants do (about 62% to 68%), in some research there was a notable difference in the types of insecure attachment they displayed. All the insecurely attached Japanese infants were classified as insecure/resistant, which is to say that none exhibited insecure/avoidant behaviour (Takahashi, 1986). Similarly, in a sample of Korean families, insecure/avoidant children were very rare (Jin et al., 2012).

One possible explanation for this is that Japanese culture exalts the idea of oneness between mother and child; correspondingly, its child-rearing practices, compared with those in North America, foster greater mother–infant closeness and physical intimacy, as well as infants' greater dependency on their mother (Rothbaum et al., 2000). Thus, in the Strange Situation, Japanese children may desire more bodily contact and reassurance than do U.S. children and therefore may be more likely to exhibit anger and resistance to their mother after being deprived of contact with her (Mizuta et al., 1996).

Another explanation is that the Strange Situation might not always have been a valid measure because it is possible that some Japanese parents were self-conscious and inhibited in the Strange Situation setting, which, in turn, could have affected their children's behaviour. It is also possible that how young children react in the Strange Situation is affected by their prior experience with unfamiliar situations and people. Thus, part of the difference in the rates of insecure/resistant attachment shown by Japanese and U.S. infants may be due to the fact that, at the time that many of the studies in question were conducted (the 1980s), very few infants in Japan were enrolled in daycare and thus did not experience frequent separations from their mother. Consistent with this argument, a more recent study, which looked at the reunion behaviours of 6-year-old Japanese children who had all attended preschool, did not find a high number of insecure/resistant attachments (Behrens, Hesse, & Main, 2007). It is therefore possible that differences in children's experiences with separation within or across cultures contribute substantially to the variability in children's behaviour in the Strange Situation.

Factors Associated with the Security of Children's Attachment

One obvious question that arises in trying to explain differences in attachment patterns is whether the parents of securely attached and insecurely attached children differ in the way they interact with their children. Evidence suggests that they do.

Parental Sensitivity

Attachment theorists have argued that the most crucial parental factor contributing to the development of a secure attachment is **parental sensitivity** (Ainsworth et al., 1978). One key aspect of parental sensitivity is *consistently responsive* caregiving. The mothers of securely attached 1-year-olds tend to read their babies' signals accurately, responding quickly to the needs of a crying baby and smiling back at a beaming one. Positive exchanges between mother and child, such as mutual smiling and laughing, making sounds at each other, or engaging in coordinated play, are a characteristic of sensitive parenting that may be particularly important in promoting secure attachment (De Wolff & van IJzendoorn, 1997; Nievar & Becker, 2008).

In contrast, the mothers of insecure/resistant infants tend to be inconsistent in their early caregiving: they sometimes respond promptly to their infants' distress, but sometimes they do not. These mothers often seem highly anxious and overwhelmed by the demands of caregiving. Mothers of insecure/avoidant infants tend to be indifferent and emotionally unavailable, sometimes rejecting their baby's attempts at physical closeness (Isabella, 1993; Leerkes, Parade, & Gudmundson, 2008).

Mothers of disorganized/distressed infants sometimes exhibit abusive, frightening, or disoriented behaviour and may be dealing with unresolved loss or trauma (L. M. Forbes et al., 2007; Madigan, Moran, & Pederson, 2006; van IJzendoorn et al., 1999). For example, Madigan and colleagues found that Canadian adolescent mothers with unresolved attachment were more likely to exhibit disrupted behaviour with their infants (e.g., not soothing their infant when distressed, using a loud voice, removing an interesting toy from the infant) than mothers with organized attachment patterns. In response to their mothers' behaviour, infants often appear to be confused or frightened (E. A. Carlson, 1998; Hesse & Main, 2006). By age 3 to 6 years, perhaps in an attempt to manage their emotions, these children often try to control their mother's activities and conversation, either in an excessively helpful and emotionally positive way, basically trying to cheer her up, or in a hostile or aggressive way (Moss et al., 2004; J. Solomon, George, & De Jong, 1995).

The association between maternal sensitivity and the quality of infants' and children's attachment has been demonstrated in numerous studies involving a variety of cultural groups (Beijersbergen et al., 2012; Mesman et al., 2012; Posada et al., 2004; Valenzuela, 1997; van IJzendoorn et al., 2004). Particularly striking is the finding that infants whose mothers are insensitive show only a 38% rate of secure attachment, which is much lower than the typical rate (van IJzendoorn & Sagi, 1999). An association between fathers' sensitivity and the security of their children's attachment has also been found, though it is somewhat weaker than that for mothers (G. L. Brown, Mangelsdorf, & Neff, 2012; Lucassen et al., 2011; van IJzendoorn & De Wolff, 1997).

parental sensitivity ■ An important factor contributing to the security of an infant's attachment. Parental sensitivity can be exhibited in a variety of ways, including responsive caregiving when an infant is distressed or upset and engaging in coordinated play with the infant.

The mothers of securely attached infants generally respond warmly to their offspring and are sensitive to their needs.

Given that all the research discussed above involves correlations between parental sensitivity and children's attachment status, it is impossible to determine whether parents' sensitivity was actually responsible for their children's security of attachment or was merely associated with it. It could be that some other factor, such as the presence or absence of marital conflict, affected both the parents' sensitivity and the child's security of attachment. However, evidence that parental sensitivity does in fact have a causal effect on infants' attachment has been provided by short-term experimental interventions designed to enhance the sensitivity of mothers' caregiving. These interventions, discussed in Box 11.2, have been found to increase not only mothers' sensitivity with their infants but also the security of their infants' attachment (Bakermans-Kranenburg, van IJzendoorn, & Juffer, 2003; van IJzendoorn, Juffer, & Duyvesteyn, 1995). Moreover, in twin studies of infants' attachment, nearly all the variation in attachments was due to environmental factors (Bokhorst et al., 2003; Roisman & Fraley, 2008).

BOX 11.2: applications

INTERVENTIONS AND ATTACHMENT

To determine whether parental sensitivity is *causally* related to differences in security of attachment, researchers have designed special intervention studies. In these studies, parents in an experimental group are first trained to be more sensitive in their caregiving. Later, the attachment statuses of their infants are compared with those of children whose parents, as members of a control group, experienced no intervention (van IJzendoorn et al., 1995).

An intervention study of this sort was conducted in the Netherlands by Daphna van den Boom (1994, 1995). Infants who were rated as irritable shortly after their birth were selected for the study because some investigators (but not all) have found that irritable infants may be at risk for insecure attachment. When the infants were about 6 months of age, half of their mothers were randomly chosen to be in the experimental group for 3 months. These mothers were taught to be attuned to their infants' cues regarding their wants and needs and to respond to them in a manner that fostered positive exchanges between mother and child. The remaining mothers in the control group received no special training.

At the end of the intervention, mothers in the experimental group were more attentive, responsive, and stimulating to their infants than those in the control group. In turn, their infants were more sociable, explored the environment more, were better able to soothe themselves, and cried less than infants whose mothers did not receive the intervention. Especially significant, the rates of secure attachment were notably higher for infants whose mothers were in the experimental group—62% compared with 22%.

In a longitudinal follow-up at 18 months of age, 72% of the children in the intervention group were securely attached, compared with 26% of the children in the control group. When their infants were 24 months old, mothers in the intervention group were, as earlier, more accepting, accessible, cooperative, and sensitive with their infants than were the control-group mothers, and their children were more cooperative. Similar findings were obtained when the children were 3½ years old.

Experimental interventions have also been used to improve depressed mothers' attachments to their children. The assumption underlying these interventions is that depressed mothers, whose relationship with their children is often impaired, can be taught skills and information that improve the quality of the mother–infant relationship. In one study, for example, investigators taught depressed mothers parenting skills and provided them with information about child development to enhance their coping and social-support skills (Toth et al., 2006). In another study (van Doesum et al., 2008), depressed mothers were videotaped bathing or feeding their infant and then, after viewing the film, were trained to respond to the infant with more sensitive and appropriate communicative behaviours. In addition, this intervention included such techniques as having a home visitor model positive caregiving, encouraging the mother to change her negative patterns of thinking about her infant and about her own parenting skills, and providing practical information on child development. Both studies were successful in improving the quality of the mother–infant attachment relationship.

Other interventions that used similar techniques have also succeeded in reducing the rate of disorganized attachment, and increasing the rate of secure attachment, for children who were at risk for maternal maltreatment (Bernard et al., 2012). For example, in one study, parents in Montreal who had been reported for maltreatment were provided with a short-term home visiting intervention focused on improving parental sensitivity (Moss et al., 2011). The 8-week intervention was successful in improving both parental sensitivity and child attachment security. From the evidence of experimental studies such as those conducted by Bernard and colleagues and Moss and colleagues, it seems clear that sensitive parenting contributes to infants' and young children's security of attachment.

Nonetheless, recent research findings indicate that some individual differences in attachment behaviours may be linked in complex ways to specific genes (S. C. Johnson & Chen, 2011). One study, for instance, focused on the possible influence that allelic variants of the serotonin transporter gene, SLC6A4 (formerly named 5HTT), might have on behaviour in the Strange Situation. The participants were Ukrainian preschoolers, some of whom had been raised in institutions and some of whom had been raised in their biological family. The researchers found that children with an SLC6A4 variant frequently associated with reactivity and vulnerability in the face of stress exhibited less attachment security and more attachment disorganization if they grew up in an institution than did preschoolers with the same variant who lived with their family. In contrast, preschoolers who were raised in an institution but had a different SLC6A4 genotype, one that is frequently associated with less reactivity and less vulnerability, did not exhibit adverse attachment behaviour (Bakermans-Kranenburg, Dobrova-Krol, & van IJzendoorn, 2012).

There is also some research indicating that a gene involved in the dopamine system, called DRD4, is associated with disorganized attachment when an infant is in a stressful environment (as when the mother is suffering from trauma or loss) but is associated with greater attachment security in a less stressful context (Bakermans-Kranenburg & van IJzendoorn, 2007). This research, along with the study discussed above and other recent work, highlights the concept of *differential susceptibility* discussed in Chapter 10 (page 409). That is, it suggests that certain genes result in children's being differentially susceptible to the quality of their rearing environment, such that those with the "reactive" genes benefit more from having a secure attachment (e.g., are better adjusted and more prosocial than their peers) but do more poorly if they have an insecure attachment (Bakermans-Kranenburg & van IJzendoorn, 2007, 2011; Kochanska, Philibert, & Barry, 2009). Although this theory needs more validation, it appears that infants' genetic makeup affects the degree to which their rearing environment alters their adjustment and social functioning.

Does Security of Attachment Have Long-Term Effects?

The reason that developmentalists are so interested in children's attachment status is that securely attached infants appear to grow up to be better adjusted and more socially skilled than do insecurely attached children. One explanation for this may be that children with a secure attachment are more likely to develop positive and constructive internal working models of attachment. (Recall that children's working models of attachment are believed to shape their adjustment and social behaviour, their self-perceptions and sense of self, and their expectations about other people, and there is some direct evidence for this belief [e.g., S. C. Johnson & Chen, 2011; S. C. Johnson, Dweck, & Chen, 2007].) In addition, children who experience the sensitive, supportive parenting that is associated with secure attachment are likely to learn that it is acceptable to express emotions in an appropriate way and that emotional communication with others is important (Cassidy, 1994; Riva Crugnola et al., 2011; Kerns et al., 2007). In contrast, insecure/avoidant children, whose parents tend to be nonresponsive to their signals of need and distress, are likely to learn to inhibit emotional expressiveness and to not seek comfort from other people (Bridges & Grolnick, 1995).

Consistent with these patterns, children who were securely attached in infancy or early childhood later seem to have closer, more harmonious relationships with peers than do children who were insecurely attached (McElwain, Booth-LaForce,

Toddlers who were securely attached as infants are more likely to engage in prosocial behaviour, such as trying to comfort someone who is sad, than are those who were insecurely attached as infants.

& Wu, 2011). For example, they are somewhat more regulated, sociable, and socially competent with peers (Lucas-Thompson & Clarke-Stewart, 2007; Panfile & Laible, 2012; Vondra et al., 2001). Correspondingly, they are less anxious, depressed, or socially withdrawn (Brumariu & Kerns, 2010)—especially compared with children who had insecure/resistant attachments (Groh et al., 2012)—as well as less aggressive and delinquent (Fearon et al., 2010; Groh et al., 2012; Hoeve et al., 2012; NICHD Early Child Care Research Network, 2006). They are also better able to understand others' emotions (Steele, Steele, & Croft, 2008; R. A. Thompson, 2008) and display more helping, sharing, and concern for peers (N. Eisenberg, Fabes, & Spinrad, 2006; Kestenbaum, Farber, & Sroufe, 1989; Panfile & Laible, 2012). Securely attached children are also more likely to report positive emotion and to exhibit typical rather than atypical patterns of reactivity to stress (Bernard & Dozier, 2010; Borelli et al., 2010; Luijk et al., 2010). Secure attachment in infancy even predicts positive peer and romantic relationships and emotional health in adolescence (E. A. Carlson, Sroufe, & Egeland, 2004; Collins et al., 1997) and early adulthood (Englund et al., 2011). Finally, attachment also predicts academic performance. A study of French-Canadian children demonstrated that securely attached children scored higher on measures of communication, mastery motivation, and engagement in problem solving than did their insecure peers (Moss & St-Laurent, 2001).

Although there are only a few studies in which infants' attachments to both parents were assessed, it appears that children may be most at risk if they have insecure attachments to both their mother and their father. In a study in which attachment was assessed at 15 months of age, children with insecure attachments to both parents were especially prone to problem behaviours such as aggression and defiance in elementary school. Having either one secure attachment or secure attachments with both parents was associated with low levels of problem behaviours (Kochanska & Kim, 2013). However, it is not clear yet if having one secure attachment buffers against other types of negative outcomes, such as internalizing problems (e.g., anxiety, depression) or problems in interpersonal relations.

Clearly, then, children's security of attachment is related to their later psychological, social, and cognitive functioning. However, experts disagree on the meaning of this relationship. As noted, some theorists believe that early security of attachment has important effects on later development because it provides enduring working models of positive relationships (Bowlby, 1973; Fraley, 2002; Sroufe, Egeland, & Kreutzer, 1990). This view implies that the effects of early attachment remain stable over time. Other theorists believe that early security of attachment predicts later development primarily to the degree that the child's environment—including the quality of parent–child interactions—does not change (M. E. Lamb et al., 1985). In other words, early security of attachment predicts children's functioning at an older age because "good" parents tend to remain good parents and "bad" parents tend to remain bad parents.

Empirical findings support both perspectives to some degree. One study reported that even if children functioned poorly during the preschool years, those who had a secure attachment and adapted well during infancy and toddlerhood were more socially and emotionally competent in middle childhood than were their peers who had been insecurely attached (Sroufe et al., 1990). This suggests that a child's early attachment has some effects over time. However, although there is often considerable stability in attachment security (Fraley, 2002; C. E. Hamilton, 2000), there is also evidence that children's security of attachment can change somewhat as their environment changes—for example, with the onset or termination of stress and conflict in the home (Frosch, Mangelsdorf, & McHale, 2000; M. Lewis, Feiring, & Rosenthal, 2000; Moss et al., 2005) or a pronounced shift in the mother's typical behaviour with the child (L. M. Forbes et al., 2007) or in her sensitivity (Beijersbergen et al., 2012). In such cases, current parent–child interactions or parenting behaviours predict the child's social and emotional competence at that age better than measures of attachment taken at younger ages (R. A. Thompson, 1998; Youngblade & Belsky, 1992). Indeed, children's development can be predicted better from the combination of both their early attachment status and the quality of subsequent parenting (e.g., maternal sensitivity at an older age) than from either factor alone (Belsky & Fearon, 2002). Finally, it must be emphasized again that most of the research on attachment is correlational, so it is difficult to pin down causal relations.

review:

Evidence revealing the poor development of infants who are deprived of consistent, caring relationships with an adult led to the systematic study of infants' early attachments. John Bowlby proposed that a secure attachment provides children with a secure base for exploration and contributes to a positive internal working model of relationships in general. According to attachment research, pioneered by Mary Ainsworth, children's attachment relationships with caregivers can be classified as secure, insecure/avoidant, insecure/resistant, and disorganized/disoriented. Children in these categories display similarities across cultures, although the percentage of children in different attachment groups sometimes varies across cultures or subcultures.

Factors that appear to influence the security of attachment include parents' sensitivity and responsiveness to their children's needs and the parents' own attachment status. Children's security of attachment to their caregivers predicts the quality of their relationships with family members, which is likely to affect how children feel about and evaluate themselves. These relations may hold not only because the sensitivity of parenting in the early years of life has long-term effects but also because sensitive parents usually continue to provide effective parenting, whereas less sensitive parents continue to interact with the children in ways that undermine children's optimal development.

Conceptions of the Self

As we have noted, children's security of attachment to caregivers affects their feelings about themselves, especially in regard to their relationships with other people. Thus, it is not surprising that children's attachment experiences early in life likely colour their early sense of self, which emerges in infancy and carries over into childhood (R. A. Thompson, 2008). However, the development of a sense of self is an ongoing, very complex process that involves much more than early-childhood attachments and notions of the self.

When we speak of the **self,** we are referring to a conceptual system made up of one's thoughts and attitudes about oneself. This conceptual system can include thoughts about one's own physical being (e.g., body, possessions), social characteristics (e.g., relationships, personality, social roles), and "spiritual" or internal characteristics (e.g., thoughts and psychological functioning). It also may include notions

self ■ A conceptual system made up of one's thoughts and attitudes about oneself.

about how the self changes or remains the same over time, beliefs about one's own role in shaping these processes, and even reflections on one's own consciousness of selfhood (Damon & Hart, 1988). The development of the self is important because individuals' self-conceptions, including the ways they view and feel about themselves, appear to influence their overall feelings of well-being and competence.

The Development of Conceptions of Self

Children's sense of self changes in fairly dramatic ways across infancy, childhood, and adolescence. It continues to develop into adulthood, becoming more complex as the individual's emotional and cognitive development deepens.

The Self in Infancy

There is compelling evidence that infants have a rudimentary sense of self in the first months of life. As noted in Chapters 5 and 10, by 2 to 4 months of age, infants have a sense of their ability to control objects outside themselves, as is clear both from their enthusiasm when they can make a mobile move by pulling a string attached to their arm and from their anger when their efforts no longer have an effect. They also seem to have some understanding of their own bodily movements. For instance, when viewing live video images of their own leg movements, 3- to 5-month-old infants looked longer and moved their legs more when the video showed their leg movements from a perspective other than their own (e.g., when the right and left legs in the video image appeared to move in opposition to the leg movements the infants were performing) than when the video image showed leg movements as the infants themselves saw them (Rochat & Morgan, 1995). Perhaps their longer looking reflected their surprise at, or interest in, seeing the reversal of their leg movements (Rochat & Striano, 2002).

A sense of self becomes much more distinct at about 8 months of age, when infants react with separation distress if parted from their mother, suggesting that they recognize that they and their mother are separate entities. Further indications that children view others as beings different from themselves are apparent by age 1. As discussed in Chapter 4 (page 159), around their 1st birthday, infants begin to show joint attention with respect to objects in the environment. For example, they will visually follow a caregiver's pointing finger to find the object that the caregiver is calling attention to, and then turn back to the caregiver to confirm that they are indeed looking at the intended object (Stern, 1985). They sometimes will also give objects to an adult in an apparent effort to engage the adult in their activities (M. J. West & Rheingold, 1978).

Infants' emerging recognition of the self becomes more directly apparent by 18 to 20 months of age, when many children can look into a mirror and realize that they are looking at themselves (Asendorpf, Warkentin, & Baudonnière, 1996; M. Lewis & Brooks-Gunn, 1979; Nielsen, Suddendorf, & Slaughter, 2006). In studies that test this ability, an experimenter surreptitiously puts a dot of rouge on a child's face, places the child in front of a mirror, and then asks the child who the person with the red spot is, or tells the child to clean

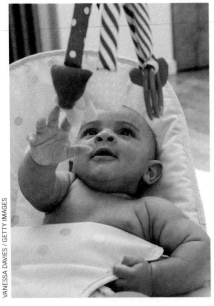

Even young infants seem to experience a sense of mastery and control when they can make a mobile do their bidding by moving their arm.

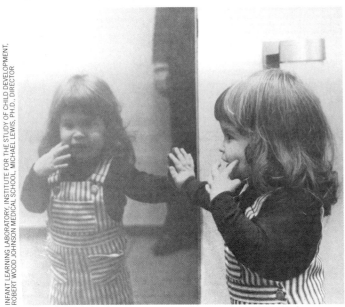

In this photo from the original research of Lewis and Brooks-Gunn, the girl recognizes that the child in the mirror with a spot on her cheek is herself.

the spot off the person in the mirror. Children younger than 18 months often respond by trying to touch the image in the mirror, or they do nothing. By about the age of 18 months, however, many children touch the rouge on their own face, so it is assumed that they realize that the mirror image is a self-reflection.

By age 2, many children can recognize themselves in photographs. In one study, 63% of a group of 20- to 25-month-olds picked themselves out when presented with pictures of themselves and two same-sex, same-age children. By approximately age 30 months, 97% of the children immediately picked their own photograph (Bullock & Lütkenhaus, 1990).

During their third year, children's self-awareness becomes quite clear in other ways as well. As you saw in Chapter 10 (pages 392–394), 2-year-olds exhibit embarrassment and shame—emotions that obviously require a sense of self (M. Lewis, 1995, 1998). The strength of 2-year-olds' awareness of self is even more evident in their notorious self-assertion, which has led to the period between ages 2 and 3 being called the "terrible twos." During this time, children often try to determine their activities and goals independent of, and often in direct opposition to, what their parents (and other adults) want them to do (Bullock & Lütkenhaus, 1990).

Two-year-olds' self-awareness is also evident in, and is enhanced by, their use of language. They can, for example, use pronouns to refer to themselves ("me," "mine") and can label themselves by name (e.g., "Daddy take Julia's book") (E. Bates, 1990). Young children can also use language to store in memory their own experiences and behaviour, giving them access to information about themselves and their past. Thus, language makes it possible for children to construct a narrative of their own "life story" and develop a more enduring picture of the self (Harter, 2012; R. A. Thompson, 2006).

Parents contribute to the child's expanding self-image by providing descriptive information about the child ("You're such a big boy"), evaluative descriptions of the child ("You're so smart"), and information about the degree to which the child has met rules and standards ("Good girls don't hit their baby sisters"). As noted in Chapter 4 (page 160), parents also collaborate in children's construction of autobiographical memory by reminding them of their past experiences (Snow, 1990).

The Self in Childhood

As children progress through childhood, their conception of themselves becomes increasingly complex and encompassing. This developmental pattern in self-understanding has been vividly illustrated by Susan Harter, a leading researcher on children's emerging sense of self. Combining statements made by a wide array of children in a number of empirical studies, Harter has constructed composite examples of children's typical self-descriptive statements at different ages. The following is a composite example of how 3- to 4-year-olds describe themselves:

> I'm three years old and I live in a big house with my mother and father and my brother, Jason, and my sister, Lisa. I have blue eyes and a kitty that is orange and a television in my room. I know all of my ABC's, listen: A, B, C, D, E, F, G, H, J, L, K, O, M, P, Q, X, Z. I can run real fast. I like pizza, and I have a nice teacher at preschool. I can count up to 10, want to hear me? I love my dog, Skipper. I can climb to the top of the jungle gym—I'm not scared! I'm never scared! I'm always happy. … I'm really strong. I can lift this chair, watch me!
>
> (Quoted in Harter, 1999, p. 37)

In describing themselves, young children often make reference to their preferences and possessions such as a family pet.

PURESTOCK / THINKSTOCK / GETTY IMAGES

social comparison ■ The process of comparing aspects of one's own psychological, behavioural, or physical functioning to that of others in order to evaluate oneself.

As this composite self-description demonstrates, at age 3 to 4, children understand themselves in terms of concrete, observable characteristics related to physical attributes ("I have blue eyes"), physical activities and abilities ("I can run real fast"), social relationships ("my brother, Jason, and my sister, Lisa"), and psychological traits ("I'm always happy") (Damon & Hart, 1988; Harter, 1999). Their focus on observable features is further reflected by the fact that the prototypical 3-year-old in the example bragged about particular skills such as running fast and did not make generalizations about his or her overall ability as an athlete. Even when the child made a general statement about himself or herself ("I'm really strong"), this statement was closely tied to actual behaviour (lifting a chair). Young children also describe themselves in terms of their preferences ("I love my dog, Skipper") and possessions ("I have … a kitty … and a television").

The composite example reflects another characteristic typical of children's self-concept during the preschool years: their self-evaluations are unrealistically positive (Trzesniewski, Kinal, & Donnellan, 2010). Young children seem to think that they are really like what they want to be (Harter & Pike, 1984; Stipek, Roberts, & Sanborn, 1984). For example, the child in the composite self-description claimed mastery of the ABCs but clearly lacked it. Maintaining positive illusions about themselves is relatively easy for young children because they usually do not consider their own prior successes and failures when assessing their abilities. Even if they have failed badly at a task several times, they are likely to believe that they will succeed on the next try (Ruble et al., 1992).

Children begin to refine their conceptions of self in elementary school, in part because they increasingly engage in **social comparison,** comparing themselves with others in terms of their characteristics, behaviours, and possessions ("He is bigger than me"). At the same time, they increasingly pay attention to discrepancies between their own and others' performance on tasks ("She got an A on the test and I only got a C") (Chayer & Bouffard, 2010; Frey & Ruble, 1985). By middle to late elementary school, children's conceptions of self have begun to become integrated and more broadly encompassing, as is illustrated by the following composite self-description that would be typical of a child between the ages of 8 and 11:

RADIUS IMAGES / ALAMY

In middle childhood, children start to refine their sense of self by comparing their own attributes and behaviour with those of peers. This process of social comparison involves a variety of areas, ranging from physical abilities and academic achievement to material well-being.

I'm pretty popular, at least with the girls. That's because I'm nice to people and helpful and can keep secrets. Mostly I am nice to my friends, although if I get in a bad mood I sometimes say something that can be a little mean. … At school, I'm feeling pretty smart in certain subjects like Language Arts and Social Studies. … But I'm feeling pretty dumb in Math and Science, especially when I see how well a lot of the other kids are doing. Even though I'm not doing well in those subjects, I still like myself as a person, because Math and Science just aren't that important to me. How I look and how popular I am are more important. I also like myself because I know my parents like me and so do other kids. That helps you like yourself.

(Quoted in Harter, 1999, p. 48)

The developmental changes in older children's conceptions of self reflect cognitive advances in their ability to use higher-order concepts that integrate more specific behavioural features of the self. For example, the child in the preceding self-description was able to relate being "popular" to several behaviours, such as being "nice to others" and being able to "keep secrets." In addition, older children can coordinate opposing self-representations ("smart" and "dumb") that, at a younger age, they would have considered mutually exclusive (Harter, 1999, 2012; Marsh, Craven, & Debus, 1998). The newfound cognitive capacity to form higher-order conceptions of the self allows older children to construct more global views of themselves and to evaluate themselves as a person overall. These abilities result in a more balanced and realistic assessment of the self, although they also can result in feelings of inferiority and helplessness (see the discussion of achievement motivation in Chapter 9, pages 360–362).

The preceding self-description also reflects the fact that schoolchildren's self-concepts are increasingly based on others' evaluations of them, especially those of their peers. Consequently, their self-descriptions often contain a pronounced social element and focus on characteristics that may influence their place in their social networks, as reflected in the following interview:

> WHAT ARE YOU LIKE? I am friendly.
> WHY IS THAT IMPORTANT? Other kids won't like you if you aren't.
>
> (Damon & Hart, 1988, p. 60)

Because older school-age children's conceptions of self are strongly influenced by the opinions of others, children at this age are vulnerable to low self-esteem if others view them negatively or as less competent than their peers (Harter, 2006).

The Self in Adolescence

Children's conceptions of self change in fundamental ways across adolescence, due in part to the emergence of abstract thinking during this stage of life (see Chapter 4, pages 141–142). The ability to use this kind of thinking allows adolescents to conceive of themselves in terms of abstract characteristics that encompass a variety of concrete traits and behaviours. Consider the following composite self-description of a young adolescent, 11 to 13 years old:

> I'm an extrovert with my friends: I'm talkative, pretty rowdy, and funny. … All in all, around people I know pretty well I'm awesome, at least I think my friends think I am. I'm usually cheerful when I'm with my friends, happy and excited to be doing things with them. … With my parents … I feel sad as well as mad and also hopeless about ever pleasing them. … At school, I'm pretty intelligent. I know that because I'm smart when it comes to how I do in classes, I'm curious about learning new things, and I'm also creative when it comes to solving problems. My teacher says so. … I can be a real introvert around people I don't know well—I'm shy, uncomfortable, and nervous. Sometimes I'm simply an airhead, I act really dumb, and say things that are just plain stupid.
>
> (Quoted in Harter, 1999, p. 60)

As is evident in this composite example, young people's concern over their social competence and their social acceptance, especially by peers, intensifies in early adolescence (Damon & Hart, 1988). The example also illustrates young adolescents' ability to arrive at higher-level, abstract self-descriptions such as "extrovert" based on personal traits such as "talkative," "rowdy," and "funny."

personal fable ■ A form of adolescent egocentrism that involves beliefs in the uniqueness of one's own feelings and thoughts.

imaginary audience ■ The belief, stemming from adolescent egocentrism, that everyone else is focused on the adolescent's appearance and behaviour.

Particularly notable is the fact that adolescents can conceive of themselves in terms of a variety of selves, depending on the context. The adolescent in the composite, for instance, describes himself or herself as a somewhat different person with friends and with parents, as well as with familiar and unfamiliar people. In part, this may be because young adolescents tend to think about each of their abstract representations of the self separately from other abstractions and cannot integrate them (Higgins, 1991). Consequently, in terms of their overall sense of themselves, it does not overly concern young adolescents that the person they appear to be can vary according to the context (see Figure 11.1).

According to David Elkind (1967), thinking about the self in early adolescence is characterized by a form of egocentrism called the **personal fable,** in which adolescents overly differentiate their feelings from those of others and come to regard themselves, and especially their feelings, as unique and special. They may believe that only they can experience whatever misery or rapture or confusion they are currently feeling. This belief is typified in the adolescent assertions "But you don't know how it feels" and "My parents don't understand me, what do *they* know about what it's like to be a teenager?" (Elkind, 1967; Harter, 1999, p. 76). The tendency to exhibit this type of egocentrism is often still evident in late adolescence and may even increase in boys (P. D. Schwartz, Maynard, & Uzelac, 2008).

The kind of egocentrism that underlies adolescents' personal fables also causes many adolescents to be preoccupied with what others think of them (Elkind, 1967; Harter, 1999; Rosenberg, 1979). This preoccupation is exhibited in what Elkind (1967) has labelled as the adolescent's belief in an **imaginary audience.** According to Elkind, because adolescents are so concerned with their own appearance and behaviour, they assume that everyone else is, too. Wherever they are, whatever they are doing, they think that all eyes are on them, scrutinizing their every blemish

FIGURE 11.1 Developmental differences in adolescents' perceptions of opposing and conflicting self-attributes When asked about their characteristics, 7th graders were much less likely than older adolescents to report contradictions in their characteristics. Older adolescents, especially 9th graders, reported that such contradictions caused them to feel internal conflict such as confusion or negative emotion. (Adapted from Harter & Monsour, 1992)

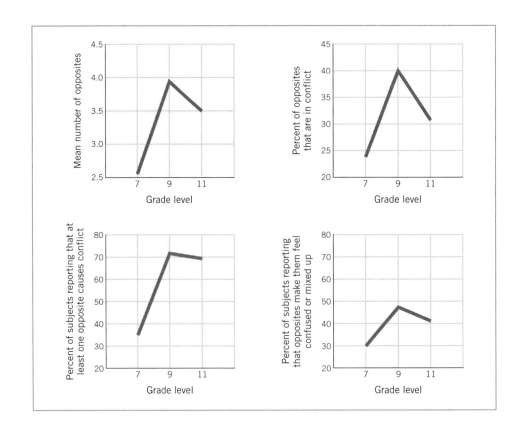

or social misstep. This dimension of adolescent egocentrism, like the personal fable, has been found to become stronger across adolescence for boys but not girls (P. D. Schwartz et al., 2008).

In their middle teens, adolescents often begin to agonize over the contradictions in their behaviour and characteristics. They tend to become introspective and concerned with the question "Who am I?" (Broughton, 1978). Their concern with this question is reflected in the following composite self-description of a 15-year-old:

> What am I like as a person? You're probably not going to understand. I'm complicated! With my really *close* friends, I am very tolerant, I mean I'm understanding and caring. With a *group* of friends I'm rowdier. I'm also usually friendly and cheerful, but I can be pretty obnoxious and intolerant if I don't like how they're acting. … I really don't understand how I can switch so fast from being cheerful with my friends, then coming home and feeling anxious, and then getting frustrated and sarcastic with my parents. Which one is the *real* me?
>
> (Quoted in Harter, 1999, p. 67)

Although adolescents in their middle teens are better than younger adolescents at identifying contradictions in themselves (see Figure 11.2) and often feel conflicted about these inconsistencies, most still do not have the cognitive skills needed to integrate their recognition of these contradictions into a coherent conception of self. As a consequence, adolescents of this age often feel confused and concerned about who they really are. As one teen put it, "It's not right, it should all fit together in one piece!" (Harter, 1999, p. 71; Harter et al., 1998).

In late adolescence and early adulthood, the individual's conception of self becomes both more integrated and less determined by what others think. Both of these shifts are captured by Harter's composite representation of a Grade 12 student:

> I'd like to be an ethical person who treats other people fairly. That's the kind of lawyer I'd like to be, too. I don't always live up to that standard; that is, sometimes I do something that doesn't feel that ethical. When that happens I get a little depressed because I don't like myself as a person. But I tell myself that it's natural to make mistakes, so I don't really question the fact that deep down inside, the real me is a moral person. Basically, I like who I am. … Being athletic isn't that high on my own list of what is important, even though it is for a lot of the kids in our school. But I don't really care what they think anymore. I *used* to, but now what *I* think is what counts. After all, I have to live with myself as a person and to respect that person, which I do now, more than a few years ago.
>
> (Quoted in Harter, 1999, p. 78)

As in the case of this prototypical Grade 12 student, older adolescents' conceptions of self frequently reflect internalized personal values, beliefs, and standards. Many of these were instilled by others in the child's life but are now accepted and generated by adolescents as their own. Thus, older adolescents place less emphasis

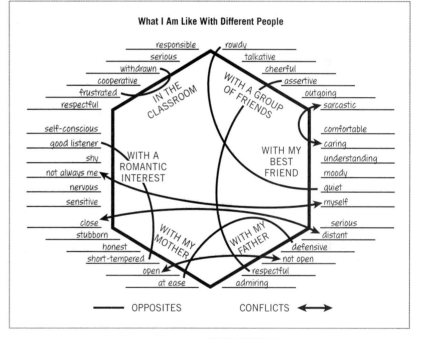

FIGURE 11.2 The multiple selves of a prototypical 15-year-old girl The girl represented by this diagram viewed herself as being different in different contexts or with different people. For example, she described herself as open with her mother but not her father, and as quiet with her best friend but rowdy with a group of friends. (Adapted from Harter, 1999)

Feelings of self-worth develop partly from the child's feelings of acceptance in the family.

on what other people think than they did at younger ages and are more concerned with meeting their own standards and with their future self—what they are becoming or are going to be (Harter, 1999, 2012; Higgins, 1991).

Older adolescents are also more likely to have the cognitive capacity to integrate opposites or contradictions in the self that occur in different contexts or at different times (Higgins, 1991). They may explain contradictory characteristics in terms of the need to be flexible, and may view variations in their behaviour with different people as "adaptive" because one cannot act the same with everyone. Similarly, they may integrate changes in emotion under the characteristic "moody." Moreover, they are likely to view their contradictions and inconsistencies as a normal part of being human, which likely reduces feelings of conflict and upset.

Whether older adolescents are able to successfully integrate contradictions in themselves likely depends not only on their own cognitive capacities but also on the help they receive from parents, teachers, and others in understanding the complexity of personalities. The support and tutelage of others in this regard allow adolescents to internalize values, beliefs, and standards that they feel committed to and to feel comfortable with who they are (D. Hart & Fegley, 1995; Harter, 1999, 2012).

Identity in Adolescence

Clearly, the question "Who am I?" is a central and often disturbing one for many adolescents. It is also a question that, for many older adolescents, expands well beyond the issue of multiple selves and inconsistent behaviour. As they begin to approach adulthood, adolescents must begin to develop a sense of personal identity that incorporates numerous aspects of self, including their values, their belief systems, their goals for the future, and, for some, their sexual identity.

As noted in Chapter 9, Erik Erikson argued that the resolution of these many identity issues is the chief developmental task in adolescence. He referred to the resolution of these issues as the crisis of **identity versus identity confusion.** In his view, the challenge is as follows: "From among all possible and imaginable relations, [the person] must make a series of ever-narrowing selections of personal, occupational, sexual, and ideological commitments" (1968, p. 245). Successful resolution of this crisis results in **identity achievement**—that is, an integration of various aspects of the self into a coherent whole that is stable over time and across events.

Erikson's Theory of Identity Formation

According to Erikson, adolescents who fail to attain identity achievement can experience one of several negative outcomes. One such outcome is **identity confusion,** an incomplete and sometimes incoherent sense of self that may cause the adolescent to feel lost, isolated, and depressed. Erikson suggested that some form of identity confusion is very common in adolescence and that it generally lasts for a relatively short time, although, according to Erikson, it sometimes persists and turns into a more severe psychological disturbance.

Another negative outcome related to the struggle for identity can arise if adolescents commit themselves to an identity prematurely, that is, without adequately considering alternative possibilities. This identity choice is called **identity foreclosure.** An example of this category might be a 17-year-old who quits school and goes to

identity versus identity confusion ■ The psychosocial stage of development, described by Erikson, that occurs during adolescence. During this stage, the adolescent or young adult either develops an identity or experiences an incomplete and sometimes incoherent sense of self.

identity achievement ■ An integration of various aspects of the self into a coherent whole that is stable over time and across events.

identity confusion ■ An incomplete and sometimes incoherent sense of self that often occurs in Erikson's stage of identity versus identity confusion.

identity foreclosure ■ Premature commitment to an identity without adequate consideration of other options.

work in a dead-end job because he or she does not envision any other options, or a young adolescent who, never considering other available career tracks, decides to become a physician simply because his or her parent is one.

A different self-defeating outcome of the search for an identity is a **negative identity,** one that is chosen because it represents the opposite of what is valued by people around the adolescent. A typical example would be a minister's child's willfully engaging in blatant immoral behaviour, or a professor's child's rebelliously dropping out of high school with no occupational goal in mind. For some adolescents, Erikson suggested, taking on a negative identity is a way of getting noticed by significant others when more conventional attempts have failed.

Erikson (1968) argued that because of all the "possible and imaginable" role options that are available in modern society, attaining identity achievement is highly complex and difficult. In light of the negative consequences of failing to achieve a coherent identity, he proposed the importance of a **psychosocial moratorium**—a time-out period during which the adolescent is not expected to take on adult roles and is free to pursue activities that lead to self-discovery. During this period, adolescents can try out new looks, new ways of acting, new ideas about what they want to do for a living, and so forth.

Although Erikson argued that this period of experimentation is important to adolescents' finding the best identity for themselves, a moratorium of this sort is possible or acceptable only in some cultures. Even then, it is often a luxury reserved for the middle and upper classes (i.e., those can who afford the moratorium provided by the college and university years). If adolescents must work full time to help support their families and themselves, many identity options will be closed to them because of limits on their time and schooling. In addition, in traditional societies where there are few role choices available, a moratorium is unheard of and unnecessary: children know from a very young age what their adult identity will be, and people generally live their lives in the same manner as their parents have.

Research on Identity Formation

Following up on Erikson's depiction of identity formation, a number of researchers looked for ways to measure the identity status of adolescents and to trace the outcome of the various statuses proposed by Erikson. The method most often used for this purpose was devised by James Marcia (1980). In this method, study participants are interviewed to determine the extent of their exploration of, and commitment to, issues related to occupation, ideology (e.g., religion, politics), and sexual behaviour. On the basis of their responses, they are classified into one of the following four categories of identity status:

- **Identity-diffusion status.** The individual does not have firm commitments regarding the issues in question and is not making progress toward developing them.
- **Foreclosure status.** The individual has not engaged in any identity experimentation and has established a vocational or ideological identity based on the choices or values of others.
- **Moratorium status.** The individual is exploring various occupational and ideological choices and has not yet made a clear commitment to them.
- **Identity-achievement status.** The individual has achieved a coherent and consolidated identity based on personal decisions regarding occupation, ideology, and the like. The individual believes that these decisions were made autonomously and is committed to them.

Trying out various "looks" can be an aspect of the self-discovery that occurs among many adolescents in some cultures.

negative identity ■ Identity that stands in opposition to what is valued by people around the adolescent.

psychosocial moratorium ■ A time out during which the adolescent is not expected to take on adult roles and can instead pursue activities that may lead to self-discovery.

identity-diffusion status ■ A category of identity status in which the individual does not have firm commitments and is not making progress toward them.

foreclosure status ■ A category of identity status in which the individual is not engaged in any identity experimentation and has established a vocational or ideological identity based on the choices or values of others.

moratorium status ■ A category of identity status in which the individual is in the phase of experimentation with regard to occupational and ideological choices and has not yet made a clear commitment to them.

identity-achievement status ■ A category of identity status in which, after a period of exploration, the individual has achieved a coherent and consolidated identity based on personal decisions regarding occupation, ideology, and the like. The individual believes that these decisions were made autonomously and is committed to them.

More recently, researchers have delineated some additional distinctions in identity status. They propose, for example, that, during the moratorium, certain individuals explore possible commitments in two different ways. Some may explore them in *breadth*, trying out a variety of candidate identities before choosing one (Luyckx, Goossens, & Soenens, 2006; Luyckx, Goossens, et al., 2006). For example, a person might consider being a musician, artist, or historian. (This type of exploration is similar to Marcia's notion of moratorium.) Others may make an initial commitment and explore it in *depth*, through continuous monitoring of current commitments in order to make them more conscious (Meeus et al., 2010). Thus, they may try out various types of art (painting, sculpture) before committing to being an artist.

Researchers using methods similar to Marcia's have found that most young adolescents seem to be in identity diffusion or identity foreclosure and that the percentage of youth in moratorium status is highest at ages 17 to 19 (Nurmi, 2004; Waterman, 1999). In the course of adolescence and early adulthood, individuals generally progress slowly toward identity achievement (Kroger et al., 2010; Meeus, 2011). The most typical sequences of change appear to be from diffusion → early foreclosure → achievement, or from diffusion → moratorium → closure → achievement; few move in the opposite direction (Meeus, 2011). There is little evidence that many adolescents have the kind of sustained identity confusion that Erikson maintained could lead to severe psychological disturbance (Meeus, 2011).

Researchers generally have found that, at least in modern Western societies, the identity status of adolescents and young adults is related to their adjustment, social behaviour, and personality. Those who have made a commitment, whether through foreclosure or identity achievement, tend to be emotionally stable and high in self-esteem (Crocetti et al., 2008), low in depression and anxiety, and extroverted and agreeable (Luyckx et al., 2005; Luyckx et al., 2006; Meeus, 1996). Young adults who explore possible commitments more in depth than in breadth tend to be extroverted, agreeable, and conscientious (reliable, regulated), whereas those who explore more in breadth tend to be prone to negative emotionality but open to experience (Dunkel & Anthis, 2001; Luyckx et al., 2006). Individuals who have made commitments through foreclosure tend to be low on substance use (Luyckx et al., 2005) and aggression (Crocetti et al., 2008; Luyckx et al., 2008). In contrast, adolescents who are in moratorium, especially when they are experimenting in breadth, seem to be relatively likely to take drugs or to have unprotected sex (J. T. Hernandez & DiClemente, 1992; R. M. Jones, 1992; Luyckx, Goossens, et al., 2006).

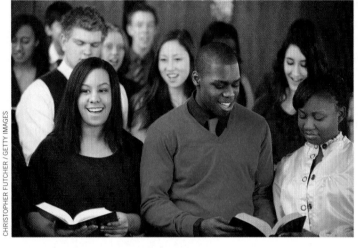

During late adolescence, re-examination of one's value system is common. Often the outcome is either renewed commitment to previously held beliefs or total rejection of them.

Influences on Identity Formation

A number of factors influence adolescents' identity formation. One key factor is the approach parents take with their offspring. Adolescents who experience warmth and support from parents tend to have a more mature identity and less identity confusion (Meeus, 2011; S. J. Schwartz et al., 2009). In addition, parents tend to react with support when young college and university students explore in depth and make identity commitments (Beyers & Goossens, 2008), and this support may reinforce their children's choices. Youths who are subject to parental psychological control tend to explore in breadth and are lower in making commitment to an identity (Luyckx et al., 2007). Adolescents are also more likely to explore identity options rather than go into foreclosure if they have at least one parent who encourages in them both a sense of connection with the parent and a striving for autonomy and individuality (Grotevant, 1998).

Identity formation is also influenced by both the larger social context and the historical context (Bosma & Kunnen, 2001). As already noted, adolescents from economically challenged communities may have fewer career options because of low-quality schooling, financial limitations, and a lack of career information and role models. Such limitations likely affect some aspects of these adolescents' identity formation.

The historical context plays a role in identity formation as well, because of the changes it brings about in identity options over time. Until a few decades ago, for instance, most adolescent girls focused their search for identity on the goal of marriage and family. Even in developed societies, few career opportunities were available to women. Today, women in many cultures are more likely to base their identity on both family and career. Thus, familial, individual, socioeconomic, historical, and cultural factors all contribute to identity development.

In some traditional cultures, adolescents have few role options and, consequently, know from a young age what their adult identity will be.

review:

Children's self-conceptions change greatly with age, shifting from being very concrete—based on physical characteristics and overt behaviour—to being based on internal qualities and the nature of one's relationships with others. Young children tend to view themselves in uniformly positive ways and to overestimate their abilities. Older children are more likely to evaluate themselves on their general level of competence and to assess their own strengths and weaknesses realistically. In late childhood, children increasingly incorporate others' perceptions of themselves into their self-image, and, with age, their conceptions of self also become much more complex and integrated.

Adolescents' self-conceptions are more abstract than younger children's and include the existence of different selves in different contexts. Young adolescents usually are not upset when they perceive discrepancies in their behaviour and characteristics across contexts. However, according to Elkind, many young adolescents do develop a form of egocentrism that expresses itself as the "personal fable" and the critical "imaginary audience." In mid-adolescence, teenagers often agonize over the discrepancies they see in themselves and tend to become concerned with the question "Who am I?" and with what others think of them. In late adolescence and early adulthood, concepts of the self become much more integrated and are more likely to include personal attributes that reflect internalized personal values, beliefs, and standards.

According to Erikson, adolescence is the time of the crisis of identity versus identity confusion, in which the young person must form an identity by making a series of ever-narrowing selections of personal, occupational, sexual, and ideological commitments. Exploration of choices relevant to one's identity, especially exploration in depth, appears to be a healthy option in Western cultures but may not be a viable one in some cultures and subcultures. Most youths eventually move toward identity achievement, some with more exploration than others; this process is usually slow, and youths are fairly stable in their identity status over time. How and when young people construct their identity are affected by a variety of influences, ranging from personal and familial factors to cultural and historical ones.

ethnic identity ■ Individuals' sense of belonging to an ethnic or racial group, including the degree to which they associate their thinking, perceptions, feelings, and behaviour with membership in that group.

Ethnic Identity

The development of identity can present special challenges for minority-group adolescents because it often involves complications related to ethnicity and/or race. In certain contexts, a legitimate distinction can be drawn between the concept of ethnicity (which refers to shared cultural traditions) (M. B. Spencer & Markstrom-Adams, 1990) and the concept of race (which refers to a shared biological ancestry). In the context of identity formation, however, the two concepts are, for practical purposes, quite similar. Thus, for the present discussion, we will use the term **ethnic identity** to refer to the degree to which an individual has a sense of belonging to an ethnic or racial group and associates his or her thinking, feelings, and behaviour with membership in that ethnic or racial group (Rotheram & Phinney, 1987).

SERGEI BACHLALOV / SHUTTERSTOCK

Much of young children's learning about their ethnic group takes place in the family. Parents teach their children the specific practices associated with their group and can instill in them pride in their ethnic heritage.

Ethnic Identity in Childhood

Children's ethnic identity can be viewed as having five components (Bernal et al., 1993):

- *Ethnic knowledge.* Children's knowledge that their ethnic group has certain distinguishing characteristics—behaviours, traits, values, customs, styles, and language—that set it apart from other groups.
- *Ethnic self-identification.* Children's categorization of themselves as members of their ethnic group.
- *Ethnic constancy.* Children's understanding that the distinguishing characteristics of their ethnic group do not change across time and place and that they themselves will always be a member of their ethnic group.
- *Ethnic-role behaviours.* Children's engagement in the behaviours that reflect the distinguishing characteristics of their ethnic group.
- *Ethnic feelings and preferences.* Children's feelings about belonging to their ethnic group and their preferences for the group's members and the characteristics that distinguish the group.

Ethnic identity develops gradually during childhood, although it does not develop for all ethnic-minority children. Preschool children do not really understand the significance of being a member of an ethnic group, although they may be able to label themselves as "Cree," "African-Canadian," "Indo-Canadian," or the like. Even if they engage in behaviours that characterize their ethnic group and have some simple knowledge about the group, they do not understand that ethnicity is a lasting feature of the self (Bernal et al., 1993) (see Table 11.2).

By the early school years, ethnic-minority children know the common characteristics of their ethnic group, start to have feelings about being members of the group, and may have begun to form ethnically based preferences regarding foods, traditional holiday activities, language use, and so forth (Ocampo, Bernal, & Knight, 1993). Children tend to identify themselves according to their ethnic group between the ages of 5 and 8 and shortly thereafter begin to understand that their race or ethnicity is an unchanging feature of themselves (Bernal et al., 1990; Ocampo, Knight, & Bernal, 1997).

TABLE 11.2

Examples of Components of Ethnic Identity in Preschool and the Early School Years

Ethnic-Identity Components	Preschool Level	Early School Level
Ethnic knowledge	Simple, global knowledge	More complex and specific knowledge, including cultural traits
Ethnic self-identification	Empty labels: "I'm Mexican because my mother said so."	Meaningful labels: "I'm Mexican because my parents come from Mexico."
Ethnic constancy	Don't understand	Understand permanence of their ethnicity
Ethnic-role behaviours	Engage in and describe behaviours; may not know why behaviours are ethnic	Engage in more role behaviours; know more about their ethnic relevance
Ethnic feelings and preferences	Undeveloped; do as their families do	Have feelings and preferences

Source: Adapted from Bernal et al., 1993

The family and the larger social environment play a major role in the development of children's ethnic identity. Parents and other family members and adults can be instrumental in teaching their children about the strengths and unique features of their ethnic culture and instilling them with ethnic pride (A. B. Evans et al., 2012; Hughes et al., 2006; Vera & Quintana, 2004). Such instruction can be especially important for the development of a positive ethnic identity when the child's racial or ethnic group is the object of prejudice and discrimination in the larger society (Gaylord-Harden, Burrows, & Cunningham, 2012; M. B. Spencer & Markstrom-Adams, 1990).

Ethnic Identity in Adolescence

The issue of ethnic or racial identity often becomes more central in adolescence, as young people try to forge their overall identity (French et al., 2006). Minority-group members in particular may be faced with difficult and painful decisions as they try to decide the degree to which they will adopt the values of their ethnic group or those of the dominant culture (Phinney, 1993; Spencer & Markstrom-Adams, 1990).

One difficulty for ethnic-minority adolescents is that they are more likely than they were at younger ages to be aware of discrimination against their group and consequently may feel ambivalent about the group and their own ethnic status (M. L. Greene, Way, & Pahl, 2006; Seaton et al., 2008; Szalacha et al., 2003). Ethnic-minority children may also be faced with basic conflicts between the values of their ethnic group and those of the dominant culture (Parke & Buriel, 2006; Qin, 2009). For example, many ethnic groups place a premium on family obligation, including values and behaviours related to children's assisting, supporting, and respecting members of the nuclear and extended family. Thus, adolescents in Canadian-Chinese families, for instance, may be expected to spend after-school time helping take care of elderly or young family members or earning money for the family. At the same time, the majority culture may be urging them to participate in school-related activities—such as sports, clubs, or study groups—that can lead to expanded opportunities.

Extending the work of Erikson, Jean Phinney (Phinney & Kohatsu, 1997) has identified three phases of ethnic-identity development that minority youth often experience:

■ *Ethnic-identity diffusion/foreclosure.* In this phase, many ethnic-minority adolescents have not examined their ethnicity and are not particularly interested in it. Some others have internalized the majority society's negative views of their ethnic group.

■ *Ethnic-identity search/moratorium.* Minority youth in this phase develop an interest in learning about their ethnic or racial culture and begin to consider the effects that their ethnicity may have on their life in the present and future. In some cases, this exploration eventually leads to the third phase, ethnic-identity achievement (K. A. Whitehead et al., 2009).

■ *Ethnic-identity achievement.* This phase is characterized by a more conscious awareness of, and commitment to, one's ethnic group and ethnic identity (M. B. Spencer & Markstrom-Adams, 1990).

Research suggests that higher levels of ethnic identity are generally associated with high self-esteem, well-being, and low levels of emotional and behaviour problems (Berkel et al., 2009; M. D. Jones & Galliher, 2007; Kiang et al., 2006; Neblett, Rivas-Drake, & Umaña-Taylor, 2012). For example, youth from immigrant Chinese families in British Columbia who had higher levels of ethnic identity were less likely to show symptoms of depression, performed better in school, and had higher self-esteem (Costigan et al., 2010). Adolescents with a positive ethnic identity appear to be buffered from the negative effects of discrimination (Gaylord-Harden et al., 2012; Tynes et al., 2012).

Most ethnic-minority adolescents either have stable ethnic identities or progress through the sequence of ethnic-identity development outlined above (Meeus, 2011; Umaña-Taylor, Gonzales-Backen, & Guimond, 2009). The exploration of ethnic identity does not always follow this pattern, however. For some ethnic-minority adolescents, an identity search leads to an exploration of majority identities and a lessening of commitment to the ethnic group. Establishing a clear ethnic identification may be more difficult and less consistent for some adolescents, such as multi-ethnic youth, who could develop identifications with more than one ethnic or racial group (Marks et al., 2011; Nishina et al., 2010). However, when ethnic-minority parents actively socialize their children into their ethnic culture through teaching about the culture and instilling pride, children tend to have a more positive ethnic identity (Neblett et al. 2012; Umaña-Taylor, Bhanot, & Shin, 2006; Umaña-Taylor & Guimond, 2010) and are less susceptible to the negative effects of discrimination (Harris-Britt et al., 2007; Neblett et al., 2008; M. T. Wang & Huguley, 2012).

Ethnic Identity in a Bicultural Environment

In light of Canada's official federal policy on multiculturalism and a high rate of immigration, understanding the development of ethnic identity is highly relevant for the Canadian context. With a focus on bicultural integration, rather than assimilation, our national context is one that encourages and values the retention of a strong sense of ethnic identity for immigrant and ethnic minority children (Berry & Kalin, 1995; Costigan, Su, & Hua, 2009).

A *bicultural identity* includes a comfortable identification with both the majority culture and one's own ethnic culture. The ease with which individuals develop and maintain a bicultural identity depends, to some extent, on the two cultures involved and the individual's level of identification with each culture. For example, bicultural

Engaging in activities that promote the welfare of others in their ethnic or racial group may contribute to adolescents' having a positive sense of ethnic identity. The adolescents shown here are members of a youth-development group that carries out community projects ranging from cleaning parks and painting neighbourhood murals to tending community gardens and working in a food pantry for the needy.

Canadian youth who view their two cultures as very similar are more likely to simultaneously identify with both cultures (Stroink & Lalonde, 2009). The development of a bicultural identity is also easier for second-generation youth versus new immigrants. Costigan and Su (2004) found that second-generation Chinese-Canadian youth from immigrant families were more successful at developing bicultural identities than first-generation youth.

Although trying to straddle two cultures can be stressful, it is not always so, and for some minority youths it can provide certain benefits, such as positive perceptions of opportunities in the majority society (Fuligni, Yip, & Tseng, 2002; Kiang & Harter, 2008; Kiang, Yip, & Fuligni, 2008; LaFromboise, Coleman, & Gerton, 1993). However, for adolescents in some traditional cultures, a bicultural identity can be associated with lower levels of some strengths that are part of successful identity development—for example, bicultural First Nations adolescents had lower levels of certain traditional values, such as fidelity (loyalty and commitment) and wisdom, than adolescents who strongly identified with their indigenous culture (Gfellner & Armstrong, 2012).

review:

The development of identity may be especially complicated for many ethnic-minority youth because it involves incorporating ideas and feelings about their ethnicity and/or race. The development of an ethnic identity begins in childhood and involves acquiring knowledge about one's ethnic group, identifying oneself as a member of that group, developing an understanding of ethnic constancy, engaging in ethnic-role behaviours, and developing feelings and preferences with regard to belonging to one's ethnic group. Family and community influence these aspects of development.

The achievement of an identity during adolescence can be difficult and painful for minority youth due to their awareness of prejudice against their group. Possible clashes between the values and goals of the group and those of the majority culture can further complicate the process. In adolescence, some minority youth start to actively explore the meaning of their ethnicity and its role in their identity. As a result of this exploration, some adolescents embrace their ethnicity; others gravitate toward the majority culture; and still others identify with both cultures.

sexual orientation ■ A person's preference in regard to males or females as objects of erotic feelings.

sexual-minority youth ■ Young people who experience same-sex attractions.

Sexual Identity or Orientation

In childhood and especially adolescence, an individual's identity includes his or her **sexual orientation**—that is, a person's preference in regard to erotic feelings toward males or females. The majority of youth are attracted to individuals of the other sex; a sizable minority are not. Dealing with new feelings of sexuality can be a difficult experience for any adolescent, but the issue of establishing a sexual identity is much harder for some adolescents than for others.

The Origins of Youths' Sexual Identity

Puberty, during which there are large rises in gonadal hormones (Buchanan, Eccles, & Becker, 1992; C. T. Halpern, Udry, & Suchindran, 1997), is the most likely time for youth to begin experiencing feelings of sexual attraction to others. Most current theorists believe that whether those feelings are inspired by members of the other sex or one's own is based primarily on biological factors, although the environment may also be a contributing factor (Savin-Williams & Cohen, 2004). Twin and adoption studies, as well as DNA studies, indicate that a person's sexual orientation is at least partly hereditary: identical twins, for example, are more likely to exhibit similar sexual orientations than are fraternal twins (J. Bailey & Pillard, 1991; J. Bailey et al., 1993; Hamer et al., 1993).

Sexual Identity in Sexual-Minority Youth

For the majority of youth everywhere, the question of personal sexual orientation never arises, at least at a conscious level. They feel themselves to be unquestioningly heterosexual. For a minority of youth, however, the question of personal sexual identity is a vital one that, initially at least, can be confusing and painful. These are the **sexual-minority youth,** who experience same-sex attractions.

It is difficult to know precisely how many youths are in this category. Although current estimates indicate that only 2% to 4% of high school students identify themselves as gay, lesbian, or bisexual (Busseri et al., 2008; Rotheram-Borus & Langabeer, 2001; Savin-Williams & Ream, 2007; T. S. Williams et al., 2003), the number of youths with same-sex attractions is considerably larger because many sexual-minority youth do not identify themselves as such until early adulthood or later (Savin-Williams & Ream, 2007). It is true that, growing up, sexual-minority youth often feel "different" (a difference possibly reflected in their frequently being labelled "sissies" or "tomboys") (Savin-Williams & Cohen, 2007), and some even display cross-gender behaviour—for example, in regard to preferences for toys, clothes, or leisure activities—from a relatively early age (Drummond et al., 2008). However, it sometimes takes them a long time to recognize that they are lesbian, gay, or bisexual.

Another complicating fact is that, especially for females, there is considerable instability in adolescents' and young adults' reports of same-sex attraction or sexual behaviour (Savin-Williams & Ream, 2007). By college or university age, for example, a notable number of young women identify themselves as "mostly straight"—that is, mostly heterosexual but somewhat attracted to females (E. M. Thompson & Morgan, 2008). One longitudinal study that followed 79 lesbian, bisexual, and unlabelled (those with

Sexual-minority youth deal with many of the same family and identity issues as do other adolescents, and they are generally equally as adjusted as other teens. However, they face special challenges if their peers and family do not accept their sexual identity. In what may be a sign of changing attitudes, these two Grade 12 students were allowed to walk together as a couple in the opening procession of their school's royal court. Their appearance together in the procession brought cheers from many of their schoolmates.

some same-sex involvement who were unwilling to attach a label to their sexuality) women aged 18 to 25 found that, over a 10-year period, two-thirds changed the identity labels they had claimed at the beginning of the study and one-third changed labels two or more times (L. M. Diamond, 2008). University of British Columbia professor Elizabeth Saewyc noted that, overall, females are more likely to describe themselves as bisexual or "mostly heterosexual" than are males (Saewyc, 2011). Male youth who have engaged in same-sex sexual experiences show an increasing preference for males from adolescence to early adulthood (Smiler, Frankel, & Savin-Williams, 2011).

In most ways, sexual-minority children and adolescents are developmentally indistinguishable from their heterosexual peers: they deal with many of the same family and identity issues in adolescence and generally function just as well. However, they do face some special challenges. Since being gay, lesbian, or bisexual is viewed negatively by many members of society, it is often difficult for sexual-minority youth to recognize or accept their own sexual preferences. It is usually even more difficult for them to reveal their sexual identity to others—that is, to "come out." However, with the media's increasing attention to, and positive portrayals of, sexual-minority people, as well as increasing legal and cultural acceptance of sexual minorities, more sexual-minority youths are coming out today than did any previous cohort (Savin-Williams, 2005).

The Process of Coming Out

In many cases, the coming-out process for sexual-minority youth involves several developmental phases, some of which occur in varying sequences. It begins with the *first recognition*—an initial realization that one is somewhat different from others, accompanied by feelings of alienation from oneself and others. At this point, there generally is some awareness that same-sex attractions may be the relevant issue, but the individual does not reveal this to others. A number of sexual-minority youth have some awareness of their sexual attractions by middle childhood (Savin-Williams & Diamond, 2000) (see Table 11.3).

TABLE 11.3

Ages of Identity Milestones for Gay/Bisexual Male Youth in Savin-Williams's Study (all are gay youth who have acknowledged their sexual-minority identity)

Event	Mean Age in Years	Age Range	Percent Who Had Not Experienced the Event
Awareness of same-sex attractions	8	3–17	0%
Knew meaning of *homosexuality*	10	4–19	0%
Applied the term *homosexual* to own attractions	13	5–20	0%
First gay sex	14	5–24	7%
First heterosexual sex	15	5–22	48%
Recognized self as gay/bisexual	17	8–24	0%
First disclosed to another	18	13–25	0%
First same-sex romance	18	11–25	29%
First disclosed to:			
Sibling	19	13–25	38%
Father	19	13–25	44%
Mother	19	13–25	31%
Developed positive sexual identity	19	10–25	23%

These numbers do not apply to samples of young men who have not acknowledged their same-sex attractions.

Source: Savin-Williams, 1998a

One gay male reported the following:

> Maybe it was the third grade and there was an ad in the paper about an all-male cast for a movie. This confused me but fascinated—intrigued—me, so I asked the librarian and she looked all flustered, even mortified, and mumbled that I ought to ask my parents.
>
> (Quoted in Savin-Williams, 1998a, p. 24)

However, there is great variability in the age at which same-sex attractions are first noticed. In one recent study of a large sample of gay, lesbian, and bisexual adults, researchers differentiated three age groups for initial recognition of same-sex attraction (Calzo et al., 2011). The largest group, labelled the early-onset group (75% of the sample), reported, on average, that their first same-sex attraction was at about 12 to 14 years of age, with roughly 30% of this group reporting initial same-sex attractions at 7 or 8 years of age. The second largest group, labelled the middle group (19% of the sample), reported that their first same-sex attraction occurred in late adolescence. The third group, labelled the late-onset group (6% of the sample), reported same-sex attractions beginning at an average age of 29 years for men and 34 years for women. Women were much more likely than men to be in the middle and late-onset groups, and within each of these onset groups, women reported somewhat later onset of same-sex attractions. In all three groups, the initial same-sex attractions reported by bisexuals occurred about 1 or 2 years later than those reported by gay and lesbian individuals.

The length of time between recognition of same-sex attractions and self-identification as gay, lesbian, or bisexual varies. For the early-onset group in the study just mentioned, the identification typically occurred about 4 years after the initial recognition of same-sex attractions; for the other two groups, it occurred between 5 and 8 years after initial recognition (see Table 11.3).

Sometimes self-identification as gay, lesbian, or bisexual does not occur until after the individual has engaged in same-sex sexual activities. During this period, referred to as *test and exploration*, the individual may feel ambivalent about his or her same-sex attractions but eventually has limited sexual contact with gays or lesbians and starts to feel alienated from heterosexuality (Savin-Williams, 1998a). This contact may eventually lead to *identity acceptance*, which is marked by a preference for social and sexual interaction with other sexual-minority individuals and the person's coming to feel more positive about his or her sexual identity and disclosing it for the first time to heterosexuals (e.g., family or friends). (As noted, this latter stage, which involves self-identification, sometimes precedes sexual exploration.)

Evidence regarding the sequencing of self-identification as a sexual-minority member and the commencement of same-sex sexual activity is mixed. The majority of individuals in all three groups in the above study self-identified prior to engaging in same-sex sexual activities. However, in a large study of gay men, same-sex sexual encounters were more likely to precede self-identification as gay (M. S. Friedman et al., 2008). Moreover, for many gay, lesbian, and bisexual youth and young adults, especially females, heterosexual activities occur prior to, or overlapping with, same-sex activities (L. M. Diamond, Savin-Williams, & Dube, 1999), which might affect the age of self-identification.

The final step for some youth and adults is *identity integration*, in which gay, lesbian, and bisexual individuals firmly view themselves as such, feel pride in themselves and their particular sexual community, and publicly come out to many people. Often, arrival at this milestone is accompanied by anger over society's prejudice against members of sexual minorities (Savin-Williams, 1996; Sophie, 1986).

Of course, not all individuals go through all these steps or go through them in the same order; some never fully accept their own sexuality or discuss it with others. Others—about one-third in one study—are "discovered" by their parents and do not disclose their sexual identity by choice (Rotheram-Borus & Langabeer, 2001).

Consequences of Coming Out

For the most part, sexual-minority youth typically do not disclose their same-sex preferences until late adolescence or a few years later (see Table 11.3) (Calzo et al., 2011; M. S. Friedman et al., 2008), with only a minority revealing their sexual orientation before the age of 19 (D'Augelli & Hershberger, 1993; Herdt & Boxer, 1993; Savin-Williams & Diamond, 2000). When they do come out, sexual-minority youths usually disclose their same-sex preferences to a best friend (typically a sexual-minority friend), to a peer to whom they are attracted, or to a sibling, and they do not tell their parents until a year or more later, if at all (Savin-Williams, 1998b). If they do reveal their sexual identity to their parents, they usually tell their mothers before telling their fathers, often because the mother asked or because they wanted to share that aspect of their life with their mother (Savin-Williams & Ream, 2003a).

If sexual-minority youths are from communities or religious or ethnic backgrounds that are relatively low in acceptance of same-sex attractions, they are less likely than other sexual-minority youth to disclose their sexual preference to family members. For example, there is some evidence that non-white families in the United States, including Latino and Asian-American families, are less accepting of same-sex attractions than are European-American families (Dube et al., 2001). The effects of such low cultural acceptance are reflected in this statement from a young Asian-American man:

> I am first generation from Southeast Asia. I am still very culturally bound and my … mother can't fathom homosexuality, and many of our friends are the same. So I can't express myself to my culture or to my family. It probably delayed my coming out. I wish I could have done it in high school like other kids.
>
> (Quoted in Savin-Williams, 1998a, pp. 216–217)

Although many parents react in a supportive or only slightly negative manner to their children's coming out, there is good reason for many sexual-minority youth to fear disclosing their sexual identity to their family. It is not unusual for parents to initially respond to such a disclosure with anger, disappointment, and especially denial (Heatherington & Lavner, 2008; Savin-Williams & Ream, 2003a). Surveys indicate that a substantial portion of sexual-minority youth experience threats or insults from relatives when they reveal their sexual orientation, and a small percent experience physical violence (Berrill, 1990; D'Augelli, 1998). Sexual-minority youth who disclose their sexual identity at a relatively early age, and those who are publicly open about their sexual identity, are often subjected to abuse in the home or community (Pilkington & D'Augelli, 1995). As might be expected, sexual-minority youth whose parents are accepting of their child's sexual orientation report higher self-esteem and lower levels of depression and anxiety (Floyd et al., 1999; Savin-Williams, 1989a, 1989b).

Fear of being harassed or rejected outside the home is one reason many sexual-minority youth hide their sexual identity from heterosexual peers. In fact, many heterosexual adolescents are unaccepting of same-sex preferences in their peers (Bos et al., 2008; L. M. Diamond & Lucas, 2004; Pilkington & D'Augelli, 1995) and many sexual-minority youth report that having sexual-minority friends is important in providing social support and acceptance (Savin-Williams, 1994, 1998a).

For a variety of reasons, sexual-minority youth are vulnerable to a number of social and psychological problems. In one Canadian study, sexual-minority adolescents reported experiencing more symptoms of depression, more acting-out behaviours, more bullying, more sexual harassment, and less connection with their best friends than heterosexual adolescents (T. Williams et al., 2005). Other studies have shown that sexual-minority adolescents are prone to experience negative affect, depression, low self-esteem, and low feelings of control in their romantic relationships (Bos et al., 2008; Coker, Austin, & Schuster, 2010; L. M. Diamond & Lucas, 2004). They also report higher levels of school-related problems and substance abuse than do other youth (Bos et al., 2008; Marshal et al., 2008; Saewyc et al., 2007). They are also more likely to be homeless or involved in street life, frequently because they have run away from, or been kicked out of, their home (Coker et al., 2010). Finally, sexual-minority youth have higher reported rates of attempted suicide than do their heterosexual peers (D'Augelli, Hershberger, & Pilkington, 2001; M. S. Friedman et al., 2011; Savin-Williams & Ream, 2003b).

Some of these problems appear to be at least partly due to factors we have already noted, including poor relationships with, and sometimes physical abuse from, family members (Bos et al., 2008; M. S. Friedman et al., 2011; Ryan, 2009), along with victimization and harassment by peers and others in the community (Coker et al., 2010; M. S. Friedman et al., 2011; Martin-Storey & Crosnoe, 2012; Toomey et al., 2010; T. Williams et al., 2005). Additional contributing factors range from sexual abuse in childhood (M. S. Friedman et al., 2011) and discrimination (e.g., bullying from peers) (Saewyc, 2011) to a heightened tendency to engage in behaviours that pose a health threat (e.g., substance use, eating disorders, and, among those who are sexually active, unprotected sex) (Busseri et al., 2008; Coker et al., 2010; Savin-Williams, 2006). Thus, it is likely that what contributes to these social and psychological problems can be attributed to the consequences of being in the sexual minority rather than to same-sex attraction in itself.

It must be noted, however, that the seemingly high rates of problems experienced by sexual-minority youth may be misrepresentative because they are often derived from studies of youth who openly identify themselves as gay and who therefore, as mentioned earlier, are at increased risk of abuse or rejection by their family or community. In fact, estimates of suicide and other problems of adjustment are considerably lower in samples representative of sexual-minority youth overall (Savin-Williams, 2008) and in samples of youth who are attracted to same-sex individuals but have not yet identified themselves as gay (Savin-Williams, 2001a). Moreover, it is important to realize that, despite increased exposure to discrimination, abuses, and victimization, most sexual-minority youth achieve levels of adjustment similar to those of their heterosexual peers (Saewyc, 2011).

review:

Although in most respects, sexual-minority youths differ little from their peers, they may face special challenges in regard to their identity and disclosing their same-sex preferences to others. Typically, but not always, they move through the milestones of *first recognition, test and exploration, identity acceptance* (the order of the second and third milestones varies), and *identity integration*. Most sexual-minority youth have a sense of their sexual attractions by late adolescence, although some individuals report that they first experienced same-sex attractions in middle childhood or as late as their 30s. Because many sexual-minority youth initially have difficulty accepting their sexuality and fear revealing their sexual identity to others, they often do not tell others about their sexual preferences until mid- to late adolescence or older.

Parents sometimes have difficulty accepting their children's same-sex orientation, and a minority of parents abuse or reject their children for this reason. Although sexual-minority youth usually come out first to a friend, they often fear harassment from peers. Perhaps because of the pressures associated with adjusting to their sexual identity, sexual-minority youth who have openly identified themselves as such to others appear to be more likely than other youth to attempt suicide, be depressed, and engage in risky behaviour.

Self-Esteem

A key element of self-concept is **self-esteem,** or one's overall evaluation of the self and the feelings engendered by that evaluation (Crocker, 2001). Self-esteem is important because it is related to how satisfied people are with their lives and their overall outlook. Individuals with high self-esteem tend to feel good about themselves and hopeful in general, whereas individuals with low self-esteem tend to feel worthless and hopeless (Harter, 1999). In particular, low self-esteem in childhood and adolescence is associated with problems such as aggression, depression, substance abuse, social withdrawal, suicidal ideation (Boden, Fergusson, & Horwood, 2008; Donnellan et al., 2005; Rubin, Coplan, & Bowker, 2009; Sowislo & Orth, 2013), and cyberbullying (Modecki, Barber, & Vernon, 2013; S. J. Yang et al., 2013).

Low self-esteem also predicts certain problems in adulthood, including mental health problems, substance abuse and dependence, criminal behaviour, weak economic prospects, and low levels of satisfaction with life and with relationships (Boden et al., 2008; Orth, Robins, & Roberts 2008; Trzesniewski et al., 2006). However, it is not entirely clear if low self-esteem actually causes such problems or if both are due to a third factor. For instance, low self-esteem in children is often associated with their parents' having such characteristics as low education, low income, and teenage maternity, as well as a history of alcohol or illicit drug use and criminal behaviour. It may be that these parental characteristics, perhaps partly based on heredity, underlie both the children's low self-esteem and their high rates of behavioural and psychological problems (Boden et al., 2008).

It should also be noted that high self-esteem, especially if not based on positive self-attributes, may have costs for children and youths (K. Lee & Lee, 2012). For example, high self-esteem in aggressive children is associated with their increasingly valuing the rewards that they derive from their aggression and their belittlement of victims (Menon et al., 2007). The combination of high self-esteem and narcissism—grandiose views of the self, inflated feelings of superiority and entitlement, and exploitative interpersonal attitudes—has been associated with especially high levels of aggression in young adolescents (Thomaes et al., 2008).

Sources of Self-Esteem

A number of factors are related to the development of children's self-esteem. These include their genetic inheritance, the quality of their relationships with others, their appearance and competence, their school and neighbourhood, and various cultural factors that impinge on their lives. In addition, how children think about themselves in a wide variety of contexts contributes to their feelings of overall self-worth. Thus, the development of self-esteem offers a highly transparent example of the interaction of *nature and nurture,* including the *sociocultural context.* Moreover, it is a domain of functioning marked by large *individual differences.*

self-esteem ■ One's overall evaluation of the worth of the self and the feelings that this evaluation engenders.

TABLE 11.4

Sample Items from Susan Harter's Self-Perception Profile for Children, a Commonly Used Measure of Self-Esteem and Self-Perceptions

Really True for Me	Sort of True for Me				Sort of True for Me	Really True for Me
		Scholastic Competence				
☐	☐	Some kids feel that they are very *good* at their school work.	BUT	Other kids *worry* about whether they can do the school work assigned to them.	☐	☐
		Social Acceptance				
☐	☐	Some kids find it *hard* to make friends.	BUT	Other kids find it's pretty *easy* to make friends.	☐	☐
		Athletic Competence				
☐	☐	Some kids do very *well* at all kinds of sports.	BUT	Other kids *don't* feel that they are very good when it comes to sports.	☐	☐
		Physical Appearance				
☐	☐	Some kids are *happy* with the way they look.	BUT	Others kids are *not* happy with the way they look.	☐	☐
		Behavioural Conduct				
☐	☐	Some kids often do *not like* the way they *behave.*	BUT	Other kids usually *like* the way they behave.	☐	☐
		Global Self-Esteem				
☐	☐	Some kids are often *unhappy* with themselves.	BUT	Other kids are pretty *pleased* with themselves.	☐	☐

Source: Adapted from Harter, 1985

To measure children's self-esteem, researchers ask children, verbally or by questionnaire, about their perceptions of themselves. As reflected in Table 11.4, the questions assess children's sense of their own physical attractiveness, athletic competence, social acceptance, scholastic ability, and the appropriateness of their behaviour. In addition, the researchers ask children about their global self-esteem—how they feel about themselves in general.

Heredity

Heredity contributes to children's sense of self-worth in several ways. The most obvious of these involve physical appearance and athletic ability, both of which are strongly related to self-esteem. In childhood and adolescence, attractive individuals are much more likely to report high self-esteem than are those who are less attractive (Erkut et al., 1999; Harter, 2012), possibly because attractive people are viewed more positively by others and are treated better than unattractive people. Perhaps as a consequence, attractive people behave in more socially competent ways and are well-adjusted, which likely enhances their appeal to others (Langlois et al., 2000). The association between self-esteem and attractiveness may be stronger for girls than for boys, particularly in late childhood and adolescence, because girls are much more likely to report concerns about their appearance (see Figure 11.3). This gender difference may partly explain why boys report slightly higher self-esteem than do girls, especially in late adolescence (Kling et al., 1999).

In addition, genetically based intellectual abilities and aspects of personality, such as sociability, no doubt play a part in academic and social self-esteem (Harter, 1983;

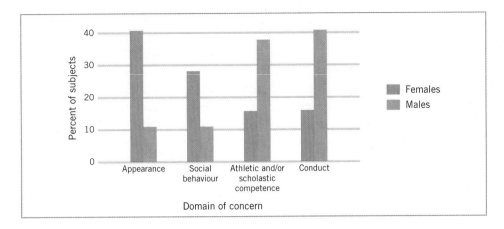

FIGURE 11.3 **Gender differences in adolescents' concerns about their appearance, social behaviour (how they treat significant others with whom they have a relationship), competence (athletic and/or scholastic), and conduct (not behaving in ways that are not morally sanctioned)** Girls report more concerns about their appearance and social behaviour, and boys report more concerns about athletic and/or scholastic competence and conduct. (Adapted from Harter, 1999)

E. A. Skinner, Zimmer-Gembeck, & Connell, 1998), although self-esteem may also affect academic competence (X. Chen, He, & Li, 2004). The hereditary contribution to self-esteem is underscored by the fact that on a variety of dimensions, self-esteem is more similar in identical twins than in fraternal twins and in non-twin siblings than in stepsiblings (McGuire et al., 1994).

Interestingly, the genetic contribution to self-esteem appears to be stronger for boys than for girls (Raevuori et al., 2007), perhaps, in part, because of the power and pervasiveness of certain environmental influences on girls' self-esteem. Chief among these are the social norms and media messages regarding the importance of female beauty (Harter, 2012). A telling example of this is the emphasis that the media and peers put on the desirability of thinness, an emphasis that appears to contribute to some girls' dissatisfaction with their bodies and themselves by the age of 8 (Dohnt & Tiggemann, 2006).

Others' Contributions to Self-Esteem

One of the most important influences on children's self-esteem is the approval and support they receive from others. This idea goes back more than a century to Charles Cooley's (1902) proposal of the "looking glass self," the concept that people's self-esteem is a reflection of what others think of them (see Figure 11.4). More specifically, Cooley maintained that we develop our sense of self-esteem by internalizing the views that important others have of us.

Similar ideas were proposed by Erikson (1950) and Bowlby (1969), who argued that children's sense of self is grounded in the quality of their relationships with others. If children feel loved when young, they come to believe that they are lovable and worthy of others' love; if they feel unloved when young, they come to believe the opposite. This view is supported by links between attachment status and children's self-esteem or positive self-perceptions (Boden et al., 2008; Cassidy et al., 2003; Verschueren, Marcoen, & Schoefs, 1996). Moreover, parents who tend to be accepting and involved with their children and who use supportive yet firm child-rearing practices tend to have children and adolescents with high self-esteem (Awong, Grusec, & Sorenson, 2008; Behnke et al., 2011; S. M. Cooper & McLoyd, 2011; Lamborn et al., 1991). Support from non-parental adults such as teachers has likewise been associated with higher self-esteem in adolescents (Sterrett et al., 2011). In contrast, parents who regularly react to their children's unacceptable behaviour with belittlement or rejection—in effect, condemning the child rather than the behaviour—are likely to instill in their children a sense of worthlessness and of being loved only to the extent that they meet parental standards (Harter, 1999, 2006; Heaven & Ciarrochi, 2008).

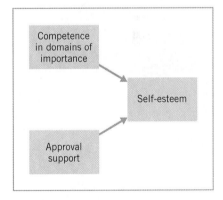

FIGURE 11.4 **Factors contributing to children's self-esteem** Children's self-esteem is affected by the approval and support they receive from parents, friends, and other people in their communities, as well as by their physical, social, behavioural, and academic competence, which are affected by both environmental and genetic factors. (Adapted from Harter, 1999)

Although far from being the only factors in shaping a child's self-esteem, the quality and nature of interactions with parents and other caregivers are among the more important influences.

Over the course of childhood, children's self-esteem is increasingly affected by peer acceptance (Harter, 1999). Indeed, in late childhood, children's feelings of competence about their appearance, athletic ability, and likeability may be affected more by their peers' evaluations than by their parents'. This tendency to evaluate the self on the basis of peers' perceptions has been associated with a preoccupation with approval, fluctuations in self-esteem, lower levels of peer approval, and lower self-esteem (Harter, 2012). At the same time, children's self-esteem likely affects how peers respond to them. Youth who see themselves as competent in their peer relationships tend to be well liked (M. S. Caldwell et al., 2004), perhaps because their behaviour is confident and socially engaging.

In contrast to children, adolescents increasingly evaluate themselves on the basis of their own internalized standards rather than on the approval of others (Connell & Wellborn, 1991; Higgins, 1991). Adolescent girls' self-esteem, for example, is increasingly linked to their feeling that they can have *relationship authenticity*—that is, that they can be themselves in terms of their thoughts and feelings in their social interactions (Impett et al., 2008). Experts agree that adolescents who continue to base their self-evaluations on others' standards and approval are at risk for psychological problems, at least in Western industrialized cultures where an autonomous, relatively stable sense of self is valued (Damon & Hart, 1988; Harter, 2012; Higgins, 1991).

School and Neighbourhood

Children's and adolescents' self-esteem can also be affected by their school and neighbourhood environments. The effect of the school environment is most apparent in the decline in self-esteem that is associated with the transition from elementary school to junior high (Eccles et al., 1989). The junior high environment often is not a good developmental match for 11- and 12-year-olds because many children of that age are distressed by the switch from having one teacher whom they know well and who is well acquainted with their skills and weaknesses to having many teachers who know little about them. In addition, the transition to junior high forces students to enter a new group of peers and to go from the top of one school's pecking order to the bottom of another's. Especially in poor, overcrowded, urban schools, young adolescents often do not receive the attention, support, and friendship they need to do well and to feel good about themselves (Seidman et al., 1994; Wigfield et al., 2006).

That children's self-esteem can be affected by their neighbourhood is suggested by the evidence that living in poverty in an urban environment, especially in violent neighbourhoods, is associated with lower self-esteem among adolescents in the United States (Behnke et al., 2011; Ewart & Suchday, 2002; Paschall & Hubbard, 1998; Turley, 2003). This may be due to high levels of stress that undermine the quality of parenting, prejudice from more affluent peers and adults, and inadequate material and psychological resources (Behnke et al., 2011; K. Walker et al., 1995). Interestingly, this relation between poverty and self-esteem does not hold in Canada and Britain, perhaps due to universal health care and social services (Fagg et al., 2013).

Children who do poorly in school tend to have lower self-esteem than do their more successful peers. However, children's perceptions of their academic competence tend to be less important to their overall self-esteem than are their perceptions of their appearance.

Self-Esteem in Minority Children

Minority children generally are more likely than majority children to be exposed to poverty and subjected to prejudice from both adults and peers, which can undermine children's self-esteem (e.g., M. L. Greene et al., 2006; Seaton & Yip,

2009). Because children's self-esteem is strongly influenced by the evaluations of others, it often is assumed that minority children have lower self-esteem than do majority children.

Although discrimination can have a negative effect on adolescents' self-esteem, how minority children and adolescents think about themselves is influenced much more strongly by acceptance from their family, neighbours, and friends than by reactions from strangers and the society at large (Galliher, Jones, & Dahl, 2011; Seaton, Yip, & Sellers, 2009). Thus, minority-group parents can help their children develop high self-esteem and a sense of well-being by instilling them with pride in their culture and by being generally supportive (Bámaca et al., 2005; Berkel et al., 2009; S. M. Cooper & McLoyd, 2011). For instance, in children from immigrant Chinese families in Canada, those with stronger ethnic identities had higher self-esteem (Costigan et al., 2010). Having positive peer and adult role models from their own ethnic group also contributes to children's positive feelings about themselves and their ethnicity (A. R. Fischer & Shaw, 1999; K. Walker et al., 1995).

Culture and Self-Esteem

In various cultures, the sources of self-esteem, as well as its form and function, may be different, and the criteria that children use to evaluate themselves may vary accordingly. Between Asian and Western cultures, for example, there are fundamental differences that appear to affect the very meaning of self-esteem. In Western cultures, it is argued, self-esteem is related to individual accomplishments and self-promotion. In contrast, in Asian societies such as Japan and China, which traditionally have had a collectivist (or group) orientation, self-esteem is believed to be more related to contributing to the welfare of the larger group and affirming the norms of social interdependence. In this cultural context, self-criticism and efforts at self-improvement may be viewed as evidence of commitment to the group (Heine et al., 1999). But in terms of standard measures of self-esteem (i.e., those used by North American researchers), this motivation toward self-criticism is reflected as lower self-evaluation (Harter, 2012).

Cultures differ in the skills they value. Children learn what abilities are valued in their group through participation in the family and larger community and evaluate their own competence accordingly.

It is not surprising, then, that scores on standard measures of self-esteem vary considerably across these cultures. Except perhaps in the area of social competence, for instance, self-esteem scores tend to be lower in China, Japan, and Korea than in Canada, the United States, Australia, and some parts of Europe (Harter, 1999). These differences seem to be partly due to the greater emphasis that the Asian cultures place on modesty and self-effacement—which results in less positive self-descriptions (Cai et al., 2007; Suzuki, Davis, & Greenfield, 2008; Q. Wang, 2004). Indeed, the fact that North American adolescents tend to be more comfortable with being praised and with events that make them look good and cause them to stand out than are Asian-American and Latino adolescents (K. Lee et al., 1997; Suzuki et al., 2008) could affect the degree to which they report high self-esteem, and hence account for the pattern of ethnic differences in self-esteem (Harter, 2012).

In addition, in some Asian societies, people tend to be more comfortable acknowledging discrepancies in themselves—for example, the existence of both good and bad personal characteristics—than are people in Western cultures, and this tendency results in reports of lower self-esteem in late adolescence and early adulthood (Hamamura, Heine, & Paulhus, 2008; Spencer-Rodgers et al., 2004). The same types of cultural influences may affect measures of self-esteem in North American subcultures that have maintained traditional non-Western ideas about the self and its relation to other people.

review:

Many factors affect children's and adolescents' self-esteem. Genetic predispositions, the support and approval of parents and peers, physical attractiveness, academic competence, and social factors such as the neighbourhood and school environments all affect how children and youth feel about themselves. Although minority children may be exposed to prejudice and poverty, supportive families and communities can buffer and even enhance their self-esteem. The sources of self-esteem, as well as its form and function, may differ across cultures, and self-evaluations may differ accordingly.

chapter summary:

The Caregiver–Child Attachment Relationship

■ According to Bowlby's theory, attachment is a biologically based process that is rooted in evolution and increases the helpless infant's chance of survival. A secure attachment also provides children with a secure base for exploration. An outcome of early parent–caregiver interactions is an internal working model of relationships.

■ The quality of children's attachment to their primary caregiver has been assessed using Ainsworth's Strange Situation. Children typically are categorized as securely attached, insecurely attached (insecure/resistant, insecure/avoidant), or disorganized/disoriented. Children are more likely to be securely attached if their caregivers are sensitive and responsive to their needs.

■ There are similarities in children's attachments across many cultures, although the percentages of children in different attachment categories sometimes vary across cultures or subcultures.

■ Parents' attachment status and their working models of relationships are related to the quality of their attachment to their infants. There appears to be some continuity in attachment from childhood to adulthood, unless hardships such as divorce, illness, child maltreatment, or maternal depression occur between childhood and adulthood.

■ Intervention programs demonstrate that parents can be trained to be more sensitive, attentive, and stimulating in their parenting and that these changes are associated with increases in infants' sociability, exploration, ability to soothe themselves, and security of attachment.

■ Children's security of attachment to their caregivers predicts quality of their future interpersonal relationships.

Conceptions of the Self

■ Young children's conceptions of themselves are very concrete—based on physical characteristics and overt behaviour—and usually positive. With age, conceptions of self increasingly become based on internal qualities and the quality of relationships with others; they also become more realistic, integrated, abstract, and complex.

■ According to Elkind, because of their focus on what others think of them, young adolescents think about an "imaginary audience" and develop "personal fables."

■ According to Erikson, adolescence is marked by the crisis of identity versus identity confusion. The individual's attempt to construct an identity, as well as whether and when the individual experiences a particular identity status (psychosocial moratorium, identity foreclosure, identity diffusion, or identity achievement), is influenced by personal characteristics and familial and cultural factors.

Ethnic Identity

■ In childhood, the development of an ethnic identity involves identifying oneself as a member of an ethnic group, developing an understanding of ethnic constancy, engaging in ethnic-role behaviours, acquiring knowledge about one's ethnic group, and developing a sense of belonging to the ethnic group. Family and community influence these aspects of development.

■ In adolescence, minority youth often start to explore the meaning of their ethnicity and its role in their identity.

Many ethnic-minority youth initially tend to be diffused or foreclosed in regard to their identities; then they become increasingly interested in exploring their ethnicity (search/moratorium). Some come to embrace their ethnicity (ethnic-identity achievement); others gravitate toward the majority culture; still others become bicultural.

Sexual Identity or Orientation

- Sexual-minority (gay, lesbian, or bisexual) youth are similar to other youth in their development of identity and self, although they face special difficulties. Many have some awareness of their same-sex attractions by middle childhood. The process of self-labelling and disclosure among sexual-minority youth may involve several phases: first recognition, test and exploration, identity acceptance, and identity integration. However, not all sexual-minority individuals go through all these stages,

or go through them in the same order, and some individuals have difficulty accepting their sexuality-minority identity and revealing it to others.

Self-Esteem

- Children's self-esteem is affected by many factors, including genetic predispositions, the quality of parent–child and peer relationships, physical attractiveness, academic competence, and various social factors.
- Although minority children may be exposed to prejudice and poverty, supportive families and communities can buffer and even enhance their self-esteem.
- Concepts of how a person should think and behave differ across cultures, with the consequence that self-evaluations and self-esteem scores differ in different cultures.

Critical Thinking Questions

1. Some theorists believe that early attachment relationships have enduring long-term effects. Others think that such effects depend on the quality of the ongoing parent–child relationship, which tends to be correlated with the security of children's early attachment to parents. How do you think researchers might go about examining this issue?

2. Based on what you have read about attachment and the development of the self, what negative effects might children experience as a result of being placed in a series of different foster-care homes? How might these effects vary with the age of the child?

3. What are the similarities and differences in the stages or phases of identity development as discussed by Erikson or

Marcia (general identity development), Phinney (ethnic identity), and Savin-Williams (sexual-minority identity)? What factors might contribute to similarities and differences? What variables might be especially relevant for ethnic identity and for identity in regard to sexual orientation?

4. What are some of the practical and conceptual difficulties of determining when children first recognize that they are physically attracted to same-sex or other-sex individuals?

5. Recall Erikson's psychosocial stages of development (Chapter 9, pages 347–348). How might a person's self-esteem be affected by the events and outcomes associated with each of the stages?

Key Terms

adult attachment models, p. 432

attachment, p. 427

attachment theory, p. 428

disorganized/disoriented attachment, p. 431

ethnic identity, p. 450

foreclosure status, p. 447

identity achievement, p. 446

identity confusion, p. 446

identity foreclosure, p. 446

identity versus identity confusion, p. 446

identity-achievement status, p. 447

identity-diffusion status, p. 447

imaginary audience, p. 444

insecure attachment, p. 431

insecure/avoidant attachment, p. 431

insecure/resistant (or ambivalent) attachment, p. 431

internal working model of attachment, p. 429

moratorium status, p. 447

negative identity, p. 447

parental sensitivity, p. 435

personal fable, p. 444

psychosocial moratorium, p. 447

secure attachment, p. 431

secure base, p. 428

self, p. 439

self-esteem, p. 459

sexual orientation, p. 454

sexual-minority youth, p. 454

social comparison, p. 442

Strange Situation, p. 430

BERNARD FLEETWOOD-WALKER, *The Family*, c. 1932

chapter 12:

The Family

The one-child policy in China provided an opportunity to assess the effects of being an only child. In general, only children in China are as well-adjusted as children from larger families and tend to do better in school. However, the one-child policy has resulted in the birth and survival of far more male children than female children, apparently due to selective abortion or female infanticide in order to have the opportunity to have a son. During the period of 2000 to 2004, approximately 124 boys were born for every 100 girls. It is estimated that in 2005 there were 32 million more males than females in China younger than age 20. This trend is changing, however, with increased government attention to illegal prenatal gender tests and selective abortions, as well as attempts to improve opportunities for, and the social status of, females. By 2012, the rate had decreased to 117.7 boys born for every 100 girls.

ADRIAN BRADSHAW / EPA / NEWSCOM

控制人口数量 提高人口素质
Control the growth of the Population   Improve the qualities of the Population

As noted in Chapter 2, in 1979, the People's Republic of China announced a sweeping new policy that would affect Chinese families dramatically. Because of the many problems associated with the country's overpopulation, the government ordered a limit of one child per family. Backed up by a system of economic rewards for those who complied and financial and social sanctions against those who did not, this policy was quite effective, especially in urban areas. For example, in Shanghai in 1985, 98% of births were first births; across the country, the figure was 68% (Poston & Falbo, 1990). The Chinese government estimates that, as of 2009, the policy had prevented 250 to 300 million births (Y. Wang & Fong, 2009).

The one-child policy is controversial at a number of levels and has had a consequence that was unintended and grim: an epidemic of female abortion and infanticide arising from the cultural preference for male offspring. The controversies aside, however, the one-child policy provided developmental psychologists with an opportunity to study how a particular family structure might affect children's development. Think about the differences in upbringing that might occur when parents have one child as opposed to two or more. To begin with, an only child is likely to receive more individual attention from parents and more of the family's resources. In addition, an only child does not have to cooperate and share with siblings. Because of differences such as these, many people predicted that the new generation of single children raised in the People's Republic of China would be overindulged and have little experience in compromising and cooperating with others. Thus, there was concern that these single children (called "onlies") would become spoiled "little emperors" (Falbo & Poston, 1993).

There is, however, no consistent support for this concern. There is some evidence that onlies in China, especially in urban areas, perform better on tests of academic performance and intelligence than do children from families with more than one child (Falbo & Poston, 1993; Falbo et al., 1989; Jiao, Ji, & Jing, 1996). Furthermore, although some initial studies found that only children in China were viewed by peers as more self-interested and less cooperative than children with siblings (e.g., Jiao, Ji, & Jing, 1986), later studies found little evidence that only children have more behavioural problems (Hesketh et al., 2011; D. Wang et al., 2000; S. Zhang, 1997).

Moreover, large survey studies do not indicate that onlies are more prone to depression and anxiety (G. D. Edwards et al., 2005; Hesketh & Ding, 2005), despite the potential for heightened family pressures on them to fulfill parental goals and needs. In fact, there appears to be virtually no difference between onlies and other children in regard to personality or social behaviour, including positive behaviours needed for getting along with others, negative behaviours such as aggression and lying, and respect and support for other family members (Deutsch, 2006; Falbo & Poston, 1993; Fuligni & Zhang, 2004; Poston & Falbo, 1990). The difference between the early and later findings may be due to a change in parents' behaviours toward only children as one-child families have become more common and expected, with the consequence that onlies are less likely to be spoiled.

The one-child policy in China is a good example of how the structure of families can change and of how, consistent with Bronfenbrenner's model discussed in Chapter 9 (pages 368–370), the larger world affects what goes on within families. Culture, as well as social and economic events, can have a tremendous effect on the structure of families and interactions among family members. In industrialized Western societies as well, a variety of social changes in the past 50 years have had marked effects on the structure of the family. For instance, families are smaller than in the past, and many more people are choosing to have children outside of marriage. In addition, it is not uncommon today for children to be reared by one biological parent or to live in a family that has experienced one or more divorces (Human Resources and Skills Development Canada, 2013). Such changes in the family can affect the resources available to the child, as well as the parents' child-rearing practices and behaviour.

In this chapter, we examine many developmental aspects of family interaction, including the ways in which parents' approach to parenting can influence their children's development, the ways in which children can influence their parents' parenting, and the ways in which siblings may influence one another. In addition, we consider how family functioning and children's development may have been affected by certain social changes that have occurred in North America over the past seven decades— from the increased age of first-time parenthood to increased rates of divorce, maternal employment, and use of out-of-home child care. We will also consider the impact that factors such as poverty and culture may have on developmental outcomes.

As you will see, the theme of *nature and nurture* is central to the study of the role of the family because a child's heredity and rearing influence each other and jointly affect the child's development. In addition, the theme of the *active child* is evident in our discussion of how children influence the way their parents socialize them. The theme of the *sociocultural context* is also key, in that parenting practices are strongly influenced by cultural beliefs, biases, and goals and are related to different outcomes for children in different cultures. Furthermore, the issue of *individual differences* is a major theme in this chapter because different styles of parenting, child-rearing practices, and family structures are associated with differences in children's social and emotional functioning. Finally, because parenting influences the

Among the many changes that have occurred in the Canadian family over the past seven decades is a rise in the age of first marriage.

family dynamics ■ The way in which the family operates as a whole.

quality of children's day-to-day experience, as well as children's beliefs and behaviours, understanding patterns of family functioning has relevance for our theme of *research and children's welfare*.

Family Dynamics

Families fulfill several vital functions, including ensuring the survival of children to maturity, providing the means for children to acquire skills needed to be economically productive, and teaching children the basic values of the culture (R. A. LeVine, 1988). How well a family fulfills these basic child-rearing functions obviously depends on a great many factors. Not the least of these is **family dynamics**, that is, how the family operates as a whole. In subsequent sections, we discuss the ways in which individual family members contribute to a child's development. However, it is important to frame these discussions with a clear appreciation of the overall impact of family dynamics. Families are complex social units whose members are all interdependent and who reciprocally influence one another.

Consider the diverse ways in which family members affect one another in the following scenario. A man loses his job because of company cutbacks, and the ensuing stress causes him to become very irritable with his wife and children. His wife, in turn, has to work extra hours to make ends meet, and her increasing fatigue makes her less patient with the children. The mother's increased workload also means that the couple's 8-year-old daughter is expected to do more of the household chores. This makes the daughter angry because her 6-year-old brother is not required to help her out. Soon the daughter becomes hostile to both her parents and her brother. Not surprisingly, the brother starts to fight with his sister, further upsetting the parents. Over time, tension and conflict among all family members increase, adding to the stress created by the family's economic situation.

As researchers have increasingly focused on the complexity of family dynamics, a number of factors have become clear (Parke & Buriel, 1998). First, as illustrated by the foregoing example, all family members influence one another, both directly and indirectly, through their behaviours. Second, family functioning is influenced by the social support that parents receive from kin, friends, neighbours, and social institutions such as schools and places of worship (C.-Y. Lee, Lee, & August, 2011; Leidy, Guerra, & Toro, 2010; McConnell, Breitkreuz, & Savage, 2011) and is undermined by economic stresses (Riina & McHale, 2012). Thus, the sociocultural context is important for understanding family dynamics and their possible effects on children. Finally, family dynamics must be looked at developmentally. As children grow older, the nature of parent–child interactions changes. For example, as you saw in Chapter 5, when infants become independently mobile, parents start to discipline them more to keep them out of harm's way, and this can lead to tension and anger between parent and child (J. J. Campos, Kermoian, & Zumbahlen, 1992). Similarly, as children experience increasing independence in adolescence, there sometimes is an increase in conflict between them and their parents over what is acceptable behaviour (Laursen, Coy, & Collins, 1998). (See Box 12.1.)

Family dynamics may also be altered by changes in parents (for example, in their beliefs about child-rearing), in the marital relationship (for example, how well the parents are getting along), or in the relationships of other family members (for example, in the level of conflict between siblings). Alterations in the family structure due to births, deaths, divorce, remarriage, or other factors can also influence interactions among family members and may affect family routines and norms, as well as children's emotional well-being (Bachman, Coley, & Carrano, 2012; Dush,

BOX 12.1: **a closer look**

PARENT–CHILD RELATIONSHIPS IN ADOLESCENCE

A common stereotype about adolescence is that, inevitably, conflict between parents and their children escalates dramatically and that parents and their adolescent children typically become alienated from one another. However, a good deal of research has shown that this simply is not true in most families (Fuligni, 1998; Laursen & Collins, 1994).

As children advance through adolescence, they do, obviously, become more willing to disagree openly with their parents and feel that their parents should have less authority over them in personal matters (Fuligni, 1998; Youniss & Smollar, 1985). However, for the most part, disagreements between parents and adolescents, though fairly frequent and often intense in early and middle adolescence (Laursen et al., 1998), are usually over mundane topics such as chores and attire. Moreover, the increase in mild conflict and bickering between adolescents and their parents in early adolescence is typically followed by the establishment of a relationship that is less contentious and volatile, and more egalitarian (Steinberg, 1990; Steinberg & Morris, 2001; van Doorn et al., 2011).

In a minority of families, however, parent–child conflict in adolescence runs hotter and deeper, often involving issues such as sex, drugs, and choice of friends (Arnett, 1999; Papini & Sebby, 1988). Higher levels of conflict seem especially likely when a child attains puberty earlier than his or her peers do (Collins & Steinberg, 2006; J. P. Hill, 1988; Steinberg, 1987, 1988). This may be because early maturation widens the gap between how much autonomy adolescents themselves think they deserve and how much autonomy their parents are willing to

Most adolescents and their parents do not experience high levels of conflict.

MONIKA GRAFF / THE IMAGE WORKS

grant them. In addition, unlike their better-regulated peers, children who are unregulated and prone to negative emotions are likely to have particularly heated conflicts with their parents in adolescence about issues such as doing chores and respecting and getting along with other family members (N. Eisenberg et al., 2008). Such conflicts between adolescents and their parents are associated with delinquency and externalizing problems in youths (N. Eisenberg et al., 2008; A. M. Klahr et al., 2011; Sentse & Laird, 2010; van Doorn et al., 2008).

Although most parents and their adolescents are not alienated, feelings of closeness and support between them often decline, especially from the beginning of

puberty through mid-adolescence (Fuligni, 1998; Shanahan et al., 2007; Steinberg, 1988). This decline is especially likely if the mother–child relationship is fairly negative just prior to adolescence (Laursen, DeLay, & Adams, 2010). In addition, adolescents spend less time with their parents and more time with peers than do younger children (Dubas & Gerris, 2002; Larson & Richards, 1991). Thus, the decline in feelings of closeness seems due in part to the desire by adolescents to be more autonomous and to an increase in their activities outside the home. Nonetheless, although peers are important confidants for adolescents (see Chapter 13), parents remain a primary source of support.

Kotila, & Schoppe-Sullivan, 2011; Lam, McHale, & Crouter, 2012). In many cases, the effects of such shifts in family dynamics tend to be gradual and continuous. However, a single event such as a traumatic divorce or the death of a parent may cause a fairly dramatic change in a child's behaviour and emotional adjustment.

In thinking about family dynamics, it is also important to keep in mind that the biological characteristics (e.g., temperament) of both children and parents, as well as parental behaviours, contribute to the nature of family interactions (Denissen, van Aken, & Dubas, 2009; Ganiban et al., 2011; Rasbash et al., 2011).

For example, mothers' negativity toward their children and the degree of parenting control they use appear to be affected partly by children's heredity (including, perhaps, their tendency to experience and express negative emotion), whereas the degree to which mothers are close and affectionate with their children appears to be partly due to the mothers' own genetic inheritance (Narusyte et al., 2008; Neiderhiser et al., 2004).

With this larger framework of family dynamics in mind, we now turn to the role that parents play in the socialization of their children.

review:

Families are complex social units that serve diverse functions, including helping offspring to survive, to acquire the skills needed to be economically productive adults, and to learn the values of the culture. Family members' behaviours influence one another and can alter the functioning of the entire family. Moreover, family dynamics are affected by a number of factors, including changes in the parents, changes in the child over the course of development, and changes in family circumstances.

The Role of Parental Socialization

Socialization is the process through which children acquire the values, standards, skills, knowledge, and behaviours that are regarded as appropriate for their present and future roles in their particular culture. Parents typically contribute to their children's socialization in at least three different ways (Parke & Buriel, 1998, 2006):

- *Parents as direct instructors.* Parents may directly teach their children skills, rules, and strategies and explicitly inform or advise them on various issues.

- *Parents as indirect socializers.* Parents provide indirect socialization through their own behaviours with and around their children. For instance, in everyday actions, parents unintentionally demonstrate skills, communicate information and rules, and model attitudes and behaviours toward others.

- *Parents as social managers.* Parents manage their children's experiences and social lives, including their exposure to various people, activities, and information, especially when children are young. If parents decide to place their child in a daycare centre, for example, the child's daily experience with peers and adult caregivers will likely differ dramatically from that of children whose daily care is provided at home.

Parents use all these ways of socializing their children's behaviour and development. However, as you will see, parents differ considerably in how they do so.

Parenting Styles and Practices

As you undoubtedly recognize from your own experience, parents in different families exhibit quite different **parenting styles**, that is, parenting behaviours and attitudes that set the emotional climate of parent–child interactions. Some parents, for example, are strict rule setters who expect complete and immediate compliance from their children. Others are more likely to allow their children some leeway in following the standards they have set for them. Still others seem oblivious to

parenting styles ■ Parenting behaviours and attitudes that set the emotional climate in regard to parent–child interactions, such as parental responsiveness and demandingness.

what their children do. Parents also differ in the overall emotional tone they bring to their parenting, especially with regard to the warmth and support they convey to their children. In trying to understand the impact that parents can have on children's development, researchers have identified two dimensions of parenting style that are particularly important: (1) the degree of parental warmth, support, and acceptance, and (2) the degree of parenting control and demandingness (Maccoby & Martin, 1983).

The pioneering research on parenting style was conducted by Diana Baumrind (1973), who differentiated among four styles of parenting related to the dimensions of support and control. These styles are referred to as *authoritative, authoritarian, permissive*, and *rejecting-neglecting* (Baumrind, 1973, 1991b) (Figure 12.1). The differences in these parenting styles are reflected in the following examples, which depict the way four different parents respond when they observe their child taking away another child's toy.

1. *Authoritative.* When Vikram takes away Troy's toy, Vikram's father takes him aside and points out that the toy belongs to Troy and that Vikram has made Troy upset. He also says, "Remember our rule about taking other people's belongings. Now think about how to make things right with Troy." His tone is firm but not hostile, and he waits to see if Vikram returns the toy.

2. *Authoritarian.* When Elene takes Marc's toy, Elene's mother comes over, grabs her arm, and says in an angry voice, "Haven't I warned you about taking other people's belongings? Return that toy now or you will not be able to watch TV tonight. I'm tired of you disobeying me!"

3. *Permissive.* When Ethan takes away Angelina's toy, Ethan's mother does not intervene. She doesn't like to discipline her son and usually does not try to control his actions. However, she is not detached as a parent and is affectionate with him in other situations.

4. *Rejecting-neglecting.* When Heather takes away Mika's toy, Heather's father, as he does in most situations, pays no attention. He generally is not very involved with his child. Even when Heather behaves well, her father rarely hugs her or expresses approval of Heather or her behaviour.

According to Baumrind, parents, like Vikram's father, who have an **authoritative parenting** style, tend to be demanding but also warm and responsive. They set clear standards and limits for their children, monitor their children's behaviour, and are firm about enforcing important limits. However, they allow their children considerable autonomy within those limits, are not restrictive or intrusive, and are able to engage in calm conversation and reasoning with their children. They are attentive to their children's concerns and needs and communicate openly with their children about them. They are also measured and consistent, rather than harsh or arbitrary, in disciplining them. Authoritative parents usually want their

authoritative parenting ■ A parenting style that is high in demandingness and supportiveness. Authoritative parents set clear standards and limits for their children and are firm about enforcing them; at the same time, they allow their children considerable autonomy within those limits, are attentive and responsive to their children's concerns and needs, and respect and consider their children's perspective.

FIGURE 12.1 Parental demandingness and responsiveness The relations of parental demandingness and responsiveness in Baumrind's typology of parenting styles.

	Responsiveness	
	high	low
Demandingness high	Authoritative parenting	Authoritarian parenting
low	Permissive parenting	Rejecting-neglecting parenting

Positive social and academic outcomes seem more likely when levels of parental warmth and control are both high.

SUSAN GRAHAM

authoritarian parenting ■ A parenting style that is high in demandingness and low in responsiveness. Authoritarian parents are unresponsive to their children's needs and tend to enforce their demands through the exercise of parental power and the use of threats and punishment. They are oriented toward obedience and authority and expect their children to comply with their demands without question or explanation.

permissive parenting ■ A parenting style that is high in responsiveness but low in demandingness. Permissive parents are responsive to their children's needs and do not require their children to regulate themselves or act in appropriate or mature ways.

children to be socially responsible, assertive, and self-controlled. Baumrind found that children of authoritative parents tend to be competent, self-assured, and popular with peers. According to a recent Canadian study, mothers and fathers who had authoritative parenting styles were more likely to have toddlers with higher levels of adaptive skills, including social skills and functional communication (Rinaldi & Howe, 2012). Children of authoritative parents are also able to behave in accordance with adults' expectations and are low in antisocial behaviour. As adolescents, they tend to be relatively high in social and academic competence, self-reliance, and coping skills, and relatively low in drug use and problem behaviour (Baumrind, 1991a; Driscoll, Russell, & Crockett, 2008; Hoeve et al., 2011; Lamborn et al., 1991).

Parents who have an **authoritarian parenting** style, much like Elene's mother, tend to be cold and unresponsive to their children's needs. They are also high in control and demandingness and expect their children to comply with their demands without question. Authoritarian parents tend to enforce their demands through the exercise of parental power, especially the use of threats and punishment. A study of Ontario mothers demonstrated that authoritarian mothers tend to respond with more negative emotion than authoritative mothers to a wide variety of child-rearing contexts. Furthermore, authoritarian mothers tend to view negative child behaviour as caused by the child but positive behaviour as caused by external events (Coplan et al., 2002). Children of authoritarian parents tend to be relatively low in social and academic competence, unhappy and unfriendly, and low in self-confidence, with boys being more negatively affected than girls in early childhood (Baumrind, 1991b). High levels of authoritarian parenting are associated with youths' experiencing negative events at school (e.g., being teased by peers, doing poorly on tests) and ineffective coping with everyday stressors (Zhou et al., 2008), along with depression, aggression, delinquency, and alcohol problems (Bolkan et al., 2010; Driscoll et al., 2008; Kerr, Stattin, & Özdemir, 2012; Rinaldi & Howe, 2012).

In studies by Baumrind and many others, parents' control of children's behaviour has been measured mostly in terms of the setting and enforcing of limits. Another type of control is psychological control—control that constrains, invalidates, and manipulates children's psychological and emotional experience and expression. Examples include parents' cutting off children when they want to express themselves, threatening to withdraw love and attention if they do not behave as expected, exploiting children's sense of guilt, belittling their worth, and discounting or misinterpreting their feelings. These kinds of psychological control are more likely to be reported by children in relatively poor families. Their use by parents predicts children's depression in late middle childhood and adolescence, as well as externalizing problems (e.g., aggression and delinquency) (Barber, 1996; Kuppens et al., 2012; Li, Putallaz, & Su, 2011; Soenens et al., 2008). However, parental use of psychological control may not always be a causal factor in children's problem behaviours. For example, some adolescents who exhibit high levels of problem behaviours also engage in high levels of conflict with their mothers, which in turn, appears to elicit their mothers' use of psychological control (Steeger & Gondoli, 2013).

Parents with a **permissive parenting** style are responsive to their children's needs and wishes and are lenient with them. Like Ethan's mother, they do not require their children to regulate themselves or act in appropriate ways. Their children tend to be impulsive, lacking in self-control, prone to externalizing problems, and low in school achievement (Baumrind, 1973, 1991a, 1991b; Rinaldi & Howe, 2012). As adolescents, they engage in more school misconduct and drug or alcohol use than do peers with authoritative parents (Driscoll et al., 2008; Lamborn et al., 1991).

When parents have a **rejecting-neglecting parenting** style, such as Heather's father has, they are disengaged parents, low in both demandingness and responsiveness to their children. They do not set limits for them or monitor their behaviour and are not supportive of them. Sometimes they are rejecting or neglectful of their children altogether. These parents are focused on their own needs rather than their children's. Children who experience rejecting-neglecting parenting tend to have disturbed attachment relationships when they are infants or toddlers and problems with peer relationships as children (Parke & Buriel, 1998; R. A. Thompson, 1998). In adolescence, they tend to exhibit a wide range of problems, from antisocial behaviour and low academic competence to internalizing problems (e.g., depression, social withdrawal), substance abuse, and risky or promiscuous sexual behaviour (Baumrind, 1991a, 1991b; Driscoll et al., 2008; Hoeve et al., 2011; Lamborn et al., 1991). The negative effects of this type of parenting appear to continue to accumulate and worsen over the course of adolescence (Steinberg et al., 1994).

In addition to the broad effects that different parenting styles seem to have for children, they also establish an emotional climate that affects the impact of whatever specific parenting practices may be employed (Darling & Steinberg, 1993). For example, children are more likely to view punishment as being justified and indicating serious misbehaviour when it comes from an authoritative parent than when it comes from a parent who generally is punitive and hostile. Moreover, parenting style affects children's receptiveness to parents' practices. Children are more likely to listen to, and care about, their parents' preferences and demands if their parents are generally supportive and reasonable than if they are distant, neglectful, or expect obedience in all situations (Grusec, Goodnow, & Kuczynski, 2000; M. L. Hoffman, 1983).

Although parenting style appears to have an effect on children's adjustment, it is important to keep in mind that children's behaviour sometimes shapes parents' typical parenting style. In a recent study, adolescents' reports of relatively high levels of externalizing problems (e.g., delinquency, loitering, and intoxication) and internalizing problems (e.g., low self-esteem, depressive symptoms) predicted a decline in parents' authoritative parenting styles (as reported by the youths) 2 years later, whereas an increase or decline in authoritative parenting over the same 2 years did not predict a change in the adolescents' adjustment (Kerr et al., 2012). As noted previously, the family is a dynamic system, with each member having an effect on other members.

Ethnic and Cultural Influences on Parenting

In keeping with our theme of the *sociocultural context*, it is important to note that parenting styles and practices may vary somewhat across ethnic groups (C. Ho, Bluestein, & Jenkins, 2008). For instance, European-Canadian mothers tend to be more authoritative and sensitive and more responsive to their children during play than East Asian immigrant mothers in Canada (K. Chan et al., 2010). Furthermore, particular parenting styles and practices may have different meanings, and different effects, in different ethnic groups and cultures. In European-Canadian families, authoritative parenting, as noted, seems to be associated with a close relationship between parent and child and with children's positive psychological adjustment and academic success. Although a somewhat similar relation between authoritative

rejecting-neglecting parenting ■ A disengaged parenting style that is low in both responsiveness and demandingness. Rejecting-neglecting parents do not set limits for or monitor their children's behaviour, are not supportive of them, and sometimes are rejecting or neglectful. They tend to be focused on their own needs rather than their children's needs.

parenting and adjustment has been found in China, it tends to be weaker (Chang et al., 2004; Cheah et al., 2009; C. A. Nelson, Thomas, & de Haan, 2006; Zhou et al., 2004, 2008). In fact, some features of parenting that are considered appropriate in traditional Chinese culture are more characteristic of authoritarian parenting than of authoritative parenting. Compared with European-American mothers, for example, Chinese-American mothers are more likely to believe that children owe unquestioning obedience to their parents and thus use scolding, shame, and guilt to control them (Chao, 1994). Although such a pattern of parental control generally fits the category of authoritarian parenting, it appears to have few negative effects for Chinese-American and Chinese children, at least prior to adolescence. Rather, for younger Chinese children, it is primarily physical punishment that is related to negative outcomes (N. Eisenberg, Chang, et al., 2009; Zhou et al., 2004, 2008).

A likely explanation is that in Chinese culture, children (but perhaps not adolescents) view parental strictness and emphasis on obedience as signs of parental involvement and caring, and as important for family harmony (Chao, 1994; Yau & Smetana, 1996). Consistent with this idea, parents' directiveness with their preschoolers—for example, telling the child what to do—is positively related to parental warmth/acceptance in China, whereas it is negatively related to this dimension in the United States (Wu et al., 2002). However, it is interesting to note that in some urban areas of China today, parental use of control appears to be relatively low compared with that in a number of other cultures (Deater-Deckard et al., 2011), probably as a result of exposure to Western child-rearing values.

Cultural variation in the relation of parental warmth to parental control was highlighted by a study of families in the United States and 12 other countries. In this study, high levels of both warmth and control were found in African-American and Latino-American families, as well as in a number of other cultures in countries such as Italy, Kenya, Sweden, Colombia, Jordan, the Philippines, and Thailand. In contrast, European-American families were characterized by moderately high warmth and low control, and these two dimensions of parenting were not correlated with each other. Although it is not clear why high warmth and high control go together in all the different groups mentioned above *except* European-Americans, it is likely related to differences in the degree to which various cultures value high levels of parental control (Deater-Deckard et al., 2011).

Because of variations such as these, findings regarding parenting styles in North America—especially findings that involve primarily European-Canadian or European-American middle-class families—cannot automatically be generalized to other cultures or subcultures. Rather, the relation of parenting to children's development must be considered in terms of the cultural context in which it occurs. Nonetheless, it should be noted that there are probably more similarities than differences in the parenting values and behaviours of various ethnic groups, as is strongly suggested by research that controls for socioeconomic status (e.g., N. E. Hill, Bush, & Roosa, 2003; Julian, McKenry, & McKelvey, 1994; Whiteside-Mansell et al., 2003).

The Child as an Influence on Parenting

Among the strongest influences on a mother and father's parenting style and practices are the characteristics of their children, such as their appearance, behaviour, and attitudes. Thus, *individual differences* in children contribute to the parenting they receive, which, in turn, contributes to differences among children in their behaviour and personalities.

Attractive children tend to elicit positive interactions from adults, which likely helps foster their social and emotional development.

Attractiveness

Although you might not want to think it is true, children's physical appearance can influence the way their parents respond to them. For example, mothers of very attractive infants are more affectionate and playful with their infants than are mothers of infants with unappealing faces. Moreover, mothers of unappealing infants, compared with mothers of appealing ones, are more likely to report that their infants interfere with their lives (Langlois et al., 1995). Thus, from the first months of life, unattractive infants may experience somewhat different parenting than attractive infants. And this pattern continues throughout childhood, with attractive children tending to elicit more positive responses from adults than unattractive children do (Langlois et al., 2000).

Children's Behaviours and Temperaments

Children's influence on parenting through their appearance is, of course, a passive contribution. Consistent with the theme of the *active child*, children also actively shape the parenting process through their behaviour and expressions of temperament. Children who are disobedient, angry, or challenging, for example, make it more difficult for parents to use authoritative parenting than do children who are compliant and positive in their behaviour (Cook, Kenny, & Goldstein, 1991; Crouter & Booth, 2003; Kerr et al., 2012).

Differences in children's behaviour with their parents—including the degree to which they are emotionally negative, unregulated, and disobedient—can be due to a number of factors. The most prominent of these are genetic factors related to temperament (Saudino & Wang, 2012). At the same time, studies with twins indicate that environmental factors, likely including social interactions with family members, also affect infants' and children's temperament (Rasbash et al., 2011; Roisman & Fraley, 2006; Saudino & Wang, 2012). In addition, there appear to be genetically based differences in how children respond to their environment, including their parents' caregiving. In line with our discussion of *differential susceptibility* in Chapter 10 (page 409), some children may be more reactive to the quality of parenting they receive than are others. For instance, children with a difficult temperament often react worse (e.g., have more problems with adjustment or are less

bidirectionality of parent–child interactions ■ The idea that parents and their children are mutually affected by one another's characteristics and behaviours.

socially competent) when they receive non-supportive or non-optimal parenting; however, these same children sometimes respond better when they receive supportive parenting (Beach et al., 2012; Kiff, Lengua, & Zalewski, 2011; Pluess & Belsky, 2010).

Children's non-compliance and externalizing problems offer further insight into the complex ways in which children can affect their parents' behaviour toward them. In resisting their parents' demands, for example, children may become so whiny, aggressive, or hysterical that their parents back down, leading the children to resort to the same behaviour when resisting future demands (G. R. Patterson, 1982). By adolescence, those youths who are non-compliant and acting out, in part due to their heredity, appear to evoke negativity from their parents to a greater degree than their parents' negativity affects the youths' externalizing problems (Marceau et al., 2013).

Over time, the mutual influence, or **bidirectionality of parent–child interactions,** reinforces and perpetuates each party's behaviour (Combs-Ronto et al., 2009; Morelen & Suveg, 2012). One study, for example, found that children's low self-regulation at age 6 to 8 (which may have been influenced by maternal behaviours at an earlier age) predicted mothers' punitive reactions (e.g., scolding and rejection) to their children's expressions of negative emotion at age 8 to 10. In turn, mothers' punitive reactions when their children were age 8 to 10 predicted low levels of self-regulation in the children at age 10 to 12 (N. Eisenberg, Fabes, et al., 1999) (Figure 12.2).

A similar self-reinforcing and escalating negative pattern is common when parents are hostile and inconsistent in enforcing standards of conduct with their adolescent children; their children, in turn, are hostile, insensitive, disruptive, and inflexible with them (Conger & Ge, 1999; Rueter & Conger, 1998) and exhibit increased levels of problem behaviours (Roche et al., 2011; Scaramella et al., 2008). Bidirectional interaction is also a likely key factor in parent–child relationships that exhibit a pattern of cooperation, positive affect, harmonious communication, and coordinated behaviour, with the positive behaviour of each partner eliciting analogous positive behaviour from the other (Aksan, Kochanska, & Ortmann, 2006; Denissen et al., 2009).

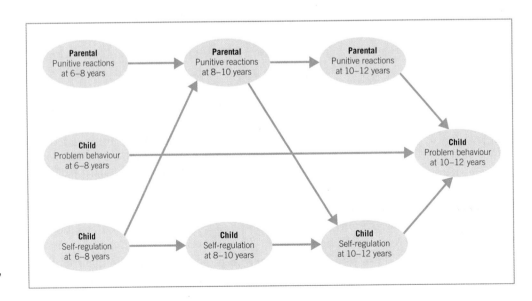

FIGURE 12.2 Bidirectional parent–child interactions In a study of elementary school children, children's low self-regulation at ages 6 to 8 predicted parents' punitive reactions when the children were 8 to 10 years of age, which, in turn, predicted the children's relatively low self-regulation at ages 10 to 12. Both parental punitive reactions and children's relatively low self-regulation at ages 10 to 12, as well as children's problem behaviour at a younger age, predicted externalizing problem behaviour at ages 10 to 12. In addition, parental punitive reactions, children's self-regulation, and children's problem behaviour were all correlated across time. (Adapted from N. Eisenberg, Fabes, et al., 1999)

Socioeconomic Influences on Parenting

Another factor that is associated with parenting styles and practices is socio-economic status. Parents with low SES are more likely than higher-SES parents to use an authoritarian and punitive child-rearing style; higher-SES parents tend to use a style that is more authoritative, accepting, and democratic (McConnell et al., 2011; Pinderhughes et al., 2000; D. S. Shaw et al., 2004). Higher-SES mothers, for example, are less likely than low-SES mothers to be controlling, restrictive, and dis-approving in their interactions with their young children (Jansen et al., 2012), even in non-Western cultures (X. Chen, Dong, & Zhou, 1997; von der Lippe, 1999). In addition, as discussed in Chapter 6 (page 236), higher-SES mothers talk more to their children, and they more readily discuss emotion (Garrett-Peters et al., 2008, 2011). They also elicit more talk from their children, and follow up more directly on what their children say. This greater use of language by higher-SES mothers may foster better communication between parent and child, as well as promote the child's verbal skills (B. Hart & Risley, 1995; E. Hoff, Laursen, & Tardif, 2002).

Some of the SES differences in parenting style and practices are related to dif-ferences in parental beliefs and values (Bornstein & Bradley, 2003; E. A. Skinner, 1985). Higher-SES parents are more likely than lower-SES parents to view them-selves as teachers rather than as providers or disciplinarians (S. A. Hill & Sprague, 1999) and to feel more capable as young parents (Jahromi et al., 2012). In Western countries, parents from lower-SES families often promote conformity in chil-dren's behaviour, whereas higher-SES parents are more likely to want their chil-dren to become self-directed and autonomous (Alwin, 1984; Luster, Rhoades, & Haas, 1989).

It is likely that level of education is an important aspect of SES associated with differences in parental values and knowledge. Highly educated parents have more knowledge about parenting (Bornstein et al., 2010) and tend to hold a more com-plex view of development than do parents with less education. They are more likely, for example, to view children as active participants in their own learning and development (J. Johnson & Martin, 1985; E. A. Skinner, 1985). Such a view may make high-SES parents more inclined to allow children to have a say in matters that involve them, such as family rules and the consequences for breaking them.

It is important to recognize that SES differences in parenting styles and prac-tices may partly reflect differences in the environments in which families live. Many low-SES parents may adopt a controlling, authoritarian parenting style to protect their children from harm in poor, unsafe neighbourhoods, especially those with high rates of violence and substance abuse. Correspondingly, it may be that higher-SES parents—being less economically stressed and freer of the need to protect their children from violence—have more time and energy to focus on complex issues in child-rearing and may be in a better position to adopt an authoritative style, interacting with their children in a controlled yet flexible and stimulating manner (Hoff-Ginsberg & Tardif, 1995).

Economic Stress and Parenting

Protracted economic stress is a strong predictor of quality of parenting, famil-ial interactions, and children's adjustment, and the outcome for each is generally negative (McLoyd, 1998; Valenzuela, 1997). Moreover, economic pressures tend to increase the likelihood of marital conflict and parental depression, which, in turn, make parents more likely to be uninvolved with, or hostile to, their children

(Benner & Kim, 2010; Conger et al., 2002; Parke et al., 2004) and less likely to cooperate and support each other's parenting (L. F. Katz & Low, 2004; Margolin, Gordis, & John, 2001; J. P. McHale et al., 2004). For both children and adolescents, the non-supportive, inconsistent parenting associated with economic hardship and living in a poor neighbourhood correlates with increased risk for depression, loneliness, unregulated behaviour, delinquency, academic problems, and substance use (Benner & Kim, 2010; Doan, Fuller-Rowell, & Evans, 2012; Kohen et al., 2008; Scaramella et al., 2008).

The quality of parenting and family interactions is especially likely to be compromised for families at the poverty level. In Canada, 8.1% of children live in families whose income falls below the low-income cut-off. When children live in lone-parent families headed by a woman, the rate jumps to almost 22% (Statistics Canada, 2012b). At one time or another, a substantial number of families in poverty experience homelessness, which obviously makes effective parenting extremely difficult (see Box 12.2).

One factor that can help moderate the potential impact of economic stress on parenting is having supportive relationships with relatives, friends, neighbours, or others who can provide material assistance, child care, advice, approval, or a sympathetic ear. Such positive connections can help parents feel more successful and

BOX 12.2: a closer look

HOMELESSNESS

It is impossible to know the precise number of homeless children and families in Canada, much less in the world. In some countries, such as India, Brazil, and the United States, the figure is in the millions (Diversi, Filho, & Morelli, 1999; Verma, 1999). In Canada, one way to estimate the number of homeless people is to examine the use of homeless shelters. In 2009, it was estimated that 1 in 230 Canadians (approximately 147 000 people) made use of an emergency homeless shelter. Although the majority of shelter clients are male and over 16, a growing number of children in Canada are using shelters. Between 2005 and 2009, the number of children in shelters increased from 6205 to 9459. Children are also spending more time in shelters. In 2005, the median length of stay was 16 days; in 2009, it was 24 days (Human Resources and Skills Development Canada, 2012).

Homeless children are at risk in a variety of ways. At the most basic level, they are often malnourished and lack adequate medical care. Frequently, they are also exposed to the chaotic and unsafe conditions found in many shelters. They are also

Children in homeless families are at risk for depression, behavioural problems, and academic failure.

Homeless youth are at high risk for becoming involved in drugs and prostitution.

satisfied as parents and actually be better parents (C.-Y. Lee et al., 2011; MacPhee et al., 1996; McConnell et al., 2011). Although social support for parents is generally associated with better parental functioning and child outcomes (Cardoso, Padilla, & Sampson, 2010; R. Feldman & Masalha, 2007; R. D. Taylor, Seaton, & Dominguez, 2008), it may be less beneficial for low-income parents in the poorest, most dangerous neighbourhoods (Ceballo & McLoyd, 2002) and for depressed parents (R. Taylor, 2011).

In considering the effects of economic stress on parenting, it is important to bear in mind that individuals contribute to their own socioeconomic situation through their traits, dispositions, and goals, and these same traits, dispositions, and goals are likely to influence their relations with their children and their children's behaviour. For instance, when investigators took into account adolescents' initial level of socioeconomic status, they found that youths with personality characteristics that reflected positive social skills, regulation, goal-setting, and hard work were more likely to attain a higher income and educational level at an older age than were youths who lacked those traits; and their children, in turn, exhibited high levels of positive development (Schofield et al., 2011). Similarly, adolescents with lower levels of problem behaviour tended, over time, to attain higher socioeconomic status and to be more emotionally invested in their children, and their children, in

at increased risk both of being sexually abused (Buckner et al., 1999) and of ending up in foster care (Zlotnick et al., 1998). As might be expected, homeless children's school performance tends to be poor and is commonly accompanied by absenteeism and serious behavioural problems (Masten et al., 1997; Obradović et al., 2009; Tyler et al., 2003). Exceptions to this pattern tend to include children who have a close relationship with their parents, especially if their parents are involved in their education (Masten & Sesma, 1999; Miliotis et al., 1999), and children who are temperamentally well regulated (Obradović, 2010). Compared with economically disadvantaged children who are not homeless, homeless children also experience more internalizing problems, such as depression, social withdrawal, and low self-esteem (Buckner et al., 1999; DiBiase & Waddell, 1995; Rafferty & Shinn, 1991). However, those who are well regulated tend to be better adjusted and to get along better with peers (Obradović, 2010).

In adolescence, numerous youths either choose to leave their homes or are kicked out, and many of them live on the streets.

Some estimates place the number of homeless, runaway, or "thrown away" adolescents in Canada at around 150 000 (Public Health Agency of Canada, 2006). Predictors of youths' running away include their living in lower-income families and neighbourhoods, living in a home without two biological parents, and experiencing peer victimization and school suspension (Tyler & Bersani, 2008; Tyler, Hagewen, & Melander, 2011). In comparison with other adolescents from the same neighbourhoods, these homeless youths generally report having experienced more conflict with, and rejection by, their parents and more parental maltreatment, including physical abuse, not infrequently due to their sexual orientation. They also often exhibited problem behaviours when they were at home (Tyler et al., 2011). However, these differences seem to be based in part on differences in the parents' behaviour toward the children or in levels of stress in the home; they do not seem to be due merely to more adjustment problems in the homeless children (American Psychological Association, 2013; Tyler et al., 2011; Wolfe, Toro, & McCaskill, 1999).

In many developing countries, homeless children often live with other children on the streets and report doing so because of the loss of their parents or because of sexual, mental, or physical abuse at home (Aptekar & Ciano-Federoff, 1999). In many cases, children living on the streets reside at least part of the time with a parent or other relative (Diversi et al., 1999; Verma, 1999). Some youths report that they stay on the streets in order to enjoy freedom with their friends (J. J. Campos et al., 1994; Sampa, 1997).

Life on the streets in most developing countries is even riskier than it is in Canada. In one study of Brazilian street youth, 75% were engaged in illegal activities such as stealing and prostitution (J. J. Campos et al., 1994). The longer these children were on the streets, the more likely they were to be involved in illegal activities. Compared with peers who hung out on the street but usually slept in homes, street children also were at greater risk for drug abuse and began sexual activities at a younger age. Thus, it is clear that homelessness, wherever it occurs, takes a tremendous toll on the welfare of children and on the larger society.

turn, exhibited fewer problem behaviours (M. J. Martin et al., 2010). Such findings support an *interactionist* model of socioeconomic influence on human development, in which the association between SES and developmental outcomes reflects both social causation (SES influences developmental outcomes) and social selection (individual characteristics influence SES) (Conger, Conger, & Martin, 2010).

review:

Styles of parenting are associated with important developmental outcomes. Researchers have delineated four basic parenting styles varying in parental warmth and control: authoritative (relatively high in control and high in warmth); authoritarian (high in control but low in warmth); permissive (high in warmth and low in control); and rejecting-neglecting (low in both warmth and control). Particular styles of parenting can affect the meaning and impact of specific parenting practices, as well as children's receptiveness to these practices. In addition, the significance and effects of different parenting styles or practices may vary somewhat across cultures.

Education and income are associated with variations in parenting. Economic stressors can undermine the quality of marital interactions and parent–child interactions. Children in economically disadvantaged and homeless families are at a greater risk for serious adjustment problems, such as depression, academic failure, disruptive behaviour at school, and drug use.

Mothers, Fathers, and Siblings

As part of their focus on family dynamics, developmentalists have examined differences in children's interactions with mothers, fathers, and siblings. They have been particularly interested in these two questions: How do mothers and fathers differ in their parenting? How do siblings affect one another?

Differences in Mothers' and Fathers' Interactions with Their Children

In the last 25 years, there has been growing attention to the importance of fathers and their interactions with their children. To support these interactions, programs have been designed to increase father involvement (e.g., J. Ball & Daly, 2012; Devault et al., 2005; Magill-Evans et al., 2007) and changes to social policies have promoted fathers' engagement in child care. For example, in 1990, Canadian maternity leave policies were changed to a parental benefits program, allowing either parent to claim parental leave after childbirth or adoption (K. Marshall, 2008).

Despite the increased involvement of fathers and their changing role in the family, there are differences between mothers' and fathers' interactions with their children, although these differences do appear to be decreasing over time (M. E. Lamb & Lewis, 2013). In most Western cultures today, spouses share child-care responsibilities to some degree; however, in the majority of families, mothers—including those who work outside the home—still spend considerably more time with their children than fathers do (Biehle & Mickelson, 2012; Dubas & Gerris, 2002; Gaertner et al., 2007).

Fathers' participation in child care differs from that of mothers not only in amount but also in kind. Mothers are more likely to provide physical care and emotional support than are fathers (M. Moon & Hoffman, 2008; G. Russell & Russell, 1987). In contrast, fathers in modern industrialized cultures spend a greater proportion of their available time playing with their children than do mothers, both in infancy and childhood, and the type of play they engage in differs from mothers' play as well (M. E. Lamb & Lewis, 2013; Parke & Buriel, 1998). In an Australian study, for example, fathers were more likely to engage their children in physical and outdoor play activities (e.g., rough-and-tumble play and playing ball) than were mothers (G. Russell & Russell, 1987). Mothers, on the other hand, were more likely to play more reserved games with their children (e.g., peekaboo), to read to them, and to join them in play with toys indoors (Parke, 1996; G. Russell & Russell, 1987).

Although these general patterns prevail in many cultures, there are also cultural variations. Fathers in Sweden, Malaysia, and India, for example, do not report playing much at all with their children (C. P. Hwang, 1987; Roopnarine, Lu, & Ahmeduzzaman, 1989). Indeed, both mothers and fathers in some cultures simply play less with their children than North American parents do (Göncü, Mistry, & Mosier, 2000; Roopnarine & Hossain, 1992). In a study of Gusii infants and parents in Kenya, fathers were seldom seen within 1.5 metres of their infants, and mothers spent 60% less time playing with infants than American mothers typically do (R. A. LeVine et al., 1996). The degree of maternal and paternal involvement in parenting and the nature of parents' interactions with children doubtlessly vary as a function of cultural practices and such factors as the amount of time parents work away from home and children spend at home.

Economic and educational factors also seem to be related to the degree to which mothers engage in various caregiving activities. In a study of mothers in 28 developing countries who had children younger than 5 years, those in countries that had higher levels of education and higher gross national product were more likely to engage in caregiving activities that were cognitively stimulating (e.g., reading books, counting, naming objects) and were less likely to leave their children alone or in the care of another child younger than 10. It is likely that cultural differences in the importance placed on literacy and cognitive growth account for these differences in mothers' caregiving activities (Bornstein & Putnick, 2012).

Fathers tend to engage in more physical play with their children than do mothers.

Sibling Relationships

Siblings influence one another's development and the functioning of the larger family system in many ways, both positive and negative. They serve not only as playmates for one another but also as sources of support, instruction, security, assistance, and caregiving (G. H. Brody et al., 1985; Gamble et al., 2011; Gass, Jenkins, & Dunn, 2007; N. Howe & Recchia, 2005). The quality of the sibling relationship plays a key role in the influence that siblings have on one another. For example, researchers at Concordia University in Montreal have demonstrated that siblings with a positive relationship are more likely to compromise with on another when resolving a conflict than siblings who have a less positive relationship (N. Howe et al., 2002; Karavasilis Karos, Howe, & Aquan-Assee, 2007; Recchia & Howe, 2009). Siblings, of course, also can be rivals and sources of mutual conflict and irritation (Vandell, 2008). And, in some cases, they can contribute to the development of one another's undesirable behaviours, such as disobedience, delinquency, and drinking (Bank, Patterson, & Reid, 1996; Low, Shortt, & Snyder, 2012; Slomkowski et al.,

2001), especially if they live in disadvantaged neighbourhoods (G. H. Brody et al., 2003). Low-quality sibling relationships also are associated with higher levels of siblings' depression, anxiety, and social withdrawal (Compton et al., 2003; S. M. McHale et al., 2007; Morgan et al., 2012). In addition, sibling aggression and conflict are related to children's lack of self-regulation (Padilla-Walker, Harper, & Jensen, 2010) and risky sexual behaviour (S. M. McHale, Bissell, & Kim, 2009), as well as externalizing problems (Bascoe, Davies, & Cummings, 2012; Natsuaki et al., 2009; Padilla-Walker et al., 2010).

Numerous factors affect whether siblings get along with one another. Siblings' relationships tend to be less hostile and more supportive, for example, when their parents are warm and accepting of them (Grych, Raynor, & Fosca, 2004; Ingoldsby, Shaw, & Garcia, 2001; J.-Y. Kim et al., 2006). Siblings also have closer, more positive relationships with one another if their parents treat them similarly (G. H. Brody et al., 1992; S. M. McHale et al., 1995). If parents favour one child over another, the sibling relationship may suffer, and the less favoured child may experience distress, depression, and other problems with adjustment, especially if the child does not have a positive relationship with his or her parents (Feinberg & Hetherington, 2001; Meunier et al., 2013; Shanahan et al., 2008; Solmeyer et al., 2011).

Differential treatment by parents is particularly influential in early and middle childhood, with less favoured siblings being likelier to experience worry, anxiety, or depression than are their more favoured siblings (Coldwell, Pike, & Dunn, 2008; Dunn, 1992). By early adolescence, however, children often view parents' differential treatment of them as justified because of differences they perceive between themselves and their siblings in age, needs, and personal characteristics. When children view differential treatment by parents as justified, they report more positive relationships with their sibling and their parents than when they feel that differential parental treatment is unfair (Kowal & Kramer, 1997; Kowal, Krull, & Kramer, 2004; S. M. McHale et al., 2000).

Cultural values may play a role in children's evaluations of, and reactions to, differential parental treatment. For example, in a study of Mexican-American families, older siblings who embraced the cultural value of *familism*, which emphasizes

The quality of parents' relationships with their children is related to how well siblings interact.

interdependence, mutual support, and loyalty among family members, were not put at risk of higher levels of depressive symptoms or risky behaviours by their parents' preferential treatment of younger siblings (S. M. McHale et al., 2005).

Another factor that can affect the quality of siblings' interactions is the nature of the parents' relationship with each other. Siblings get along better if their parents are getting along with each other (Erel, Margolin, & John, 1998; McGuire, S. M. McHale, & Updegraff, 1996). In contrast, siblings whose parents fight with each other are likely to have more hostile interactions because their parents not only model negative behaviour for their children but also may be less sensitive and appropriate in their efforts to manage their children's interactions with one another (N. Howe, Aquan-Assee, & Bukowski, 2001).

Rivalry and conflict between siblings tend to be higher in divorced families and in remarried families than in non-divorced families, even between biological siblings. Although some siblings turn to one another for support when their parents divorce or remarry (Jenkins, 1992), they may also compete for parental affection and attention, which often are scarce in these situations. Relationships between half-siblings can be especially emotionally charged, perhaps because the older sibling may resent the younger sibling who is born to both parents in the new marital relationship (Hetherington, 1999). In general, the more a child in a blended family perceives a parent's preferential treatment of a sibling—whether a full sibling or a half-sibling—the worse the child's relationship is with that sibling (Baham et al., 2008).

Thus, the quality of sibling relationships differs across families depending on the ways that parents interact with each child and with each other and children's perceptions of their treatment by other family members. Such differences highlight the fact that families are complex, dynamic social systems and that all members contribute to one another's functioning.

review:

Mothers typically interact with their children more than fathers do. The nature of mother–child and father–child interactions also tends to differ, although these differences are decreasing. Parent–child interactions differ across cultures; for example, in some cultures, parents play little or not at all with their children.

Siblings are important contributors to one another's socialization and development. They can be sources of learning and support, as well as rivalry and conflict. Siblings get along better if they have good relationships with their parents and if they do not feel that their parents treat them differently. Sibling relationships are, on average, more hostile and conflicted in divorced and remarried families than in non-divorced families. Thus, sibling relationships, like all family relationships, must be viewed in the context of the larger family system.

Changes in Families in Canada

The family in Canada has changed dramatically since the middle of the twentieth century. For instance, from the 1960s to 2008, the average age at which people first married rose from age 22 to nearly 29 for women and from age 25 to over 31 for men (Human Resources and Skills Development Canada, 2013). Over this same period, the economic arrangement of the Canadian family also changed quite strikingly. In the 1970s, 39% of women with children younger than 16 worked outside the home compared to about 73% in 2009 (Ferrao, 2010).

A third change that occurred in the family, partly as a result of the previous two, was that the average age at which women bore children increased, especially within marriages. In 2009, the average age of mothers was 29.4 years, compared to 26.9 years in 1974 (Human Resources and Skills Development Canada, 2013). At the same time, the number of births to mothers between 14 and 19 years declined from 29.9 per 1000 female adolescents in 1974 to 12.0 in 2009 (Human Resources and Skills Development Canada, 2013) (see Box 12.3).

Two of the most far-reaching changes in the Canadian family in the past half-century have been the upsurge in divorce and decrease in the number of marriages. In 1986, a change to Canada's Divorce Act allowed for divorce after only one year of separation (previously, 3 years of separation had been necessary). In 1987, the divorce rate reached a high of 50.6%. Since that time, the divorce

BOX 12.3: individual differences

ADOLESCENTS AS PARENTS

The incidence of teenage pregnancy in Canada has declined substantially in recent years, from 29.9 per 1000 female teens in 1974 to 12.0 per 1000 female teens in 2009 (Human Resources and Skills Development Canada, 2013). This rate is significantly lower than the rates in England (54.6 per 1000) and the United States (58 per 1000) (McKay, 2012).

Results from longitudinal studies with participants from different countries and cultures, including Canada, Great Britain, the United States, and Scandinavia, have offered insight into the factors that affect girls' risk of child-bearing during adolescence (Serbin & Karp, 2003). Factors that reduce the risk are living with both biological parents and being involved in school activities and religious organizations (B. J. Ellis et al., 2003; K. A. Moore et al., 1998), as well as being successful in school and having parents with supportive parenting styles (Serbin & Karp, 2004). Factors that substantially increase the risk of child-bearing during adolescence include being raised in poverty by a single or adolescent mother, being of low socioeconomic status, not having a partner, having a history of aggressive and withdrawn behaviour in childhood, having previously experienced physical or sexual abuse, having low school achievement, and dropping out of school (Al-Sahad et al., 2012; R. L. Coley & Chase-Lansdale, 1998; Hardy et al., 1998; Serbin et al., 1991; Serbin & Karp, 2004).

For young adolescent girls, having a mother who is cold and uninvolved may increase the risk of their becoming pregnant in later adolescence. In part, this may be because girls whose mothers fit this pattern tend to do poorly in school and hang out with peers who get into trouble, which often leads to risk taking and pregnancy (Scaramella et al., 1998). In fact, girls who are at risk for becoming mothers as teenagers tend to have many friends who are sexually active (East, Felice, & Morgan, 1993; Scaramella et al., 1998). It is likely that girls' willingness to engage in sex is influenced by its acceptability in their group of friends.

Having a child in adolescence is associated with many negative consequences for both the adolescent mother and the child (Jaffee, 2002). Motherhood curtails the mother's opportunities for education, career development, and normal relationships with peers. Even if teenage mothers marry, they are very likely to get divorced and to spend many years as single mothers (R. L. Coley & Chase-Lansdale, 1998; M. E. Lamb & Teti, 1991; M. R. Moore & Brooks-Gunn, 2002). In addition, adolescent mothers often have poor parenting skills and are more likely than older mothers to provide low levels of verbal stimulation to their infants, to expect their children to behave in ways that are beyond their years, and to neglect and abuse them (Culp et al., 1988; Ekéus, Christensson, & Hjern, 2004; M. E. Lamb & Ketterlinus, 1991).

Given these challenges in parenting, it is not surprising that children of teenage mothers are more likely than children of older mothers to exhibit disorganized attachment status, low impulse control, problem behaviours, and delays in cognitive development in the preschool years and thereafter. As adolescents themselves, children born to teenagers have higher rates of academic failure, delinquency, incarceration, and early sexual activity than do adolescents born to older mothers (R. L. Coley & Chase-Lansdale, 1998; M. R. Moore & Brooks-Gunn, 2002; Wakschlag et al., 2000). Not surprisingly, they also tend to have less education, income, and life satisfaction as young adults (Lipman et al., 2011).

This does not mean that all children born to adolescent mothers are destined to poor developmental outcomes. Those whose mothers have more knowledge about child development and parenting and who exhibit more authoritative parenting than most teen mothers do tend to display fewer problem behaviours and better intellectual development (L. Bates, Luster, & Vandenbelt, 2003; C. L. Miller et al., 1996). In addition, those who experience a positive mother–child relationship, including consistent and sensitive parenting, appear more likely to stay in school and obtain employment in early adulthood (Jaffee et al., 2001). Supportive parents and other relatives are also likely to provide child care so that young mothers have the opportunity to continue their schooling.

rate has remained relatively stable, fluctuating between 35% and 42% (Human Resources and Skills Development Canada, 2013). Along with an upsurge in divorce, there has been a decline in marriage. In 2008, the marriage rate was at its lowest level in the past century, at 4.4 marriages per 1000 people (Human Resources and Skills Development Canada, 2013). This decline in marriage is likely related to an increase in common-law relationships. For example, the number of common-law couples in Canada rose 13.9% between 2006 and 2011 (Statistics Canada, 2012b).

As a reflection of changes in families, the percentage of children living with two married parents is declining and the percentage of children living in lone-parent families is increasing. In 2011, lone-parent families with children accounted for 16.3% of all families in Canada, compared to 8.4% in 1961 (Statistics Canada,

A number of factors likewise affect adolescent males' risk of becoming fathers. Chief among these are being economically disadvantaged, being prone to substance abuse and behavioural problems, being involved with deviant peers, and having a police record (Fagot et al., 1998; Miller-Johnson et al., 2004; D. R. Moore & Florsheim, 2001).

Many young unmarried or absent fathers see their children regularly, at least during the first few years, but rates of contact decrease over time (R. L. Coley & Chase-Lansdale, 1998; Marsiglio et al., 2000). In one study, 40% of adolescent fathers had no contact with their 2-year-old children (Fagot et al., 1998). Contact is less likely to be maintained when the unmarried non-cohabiting father is an adolescent (M. Wilson & Brooks-Gunn, 2001). Young unmarried fathers remain more involved with their children if they have a warm, supportive relationship with the mother in the weeks after delivery and if the mother does not experience many stressful life events (particularly financial problems) during and soon after the pregnancy (Cutrona et al., 1998). They are also more likely to be involved with their infants if they have social support from their own parents for the parenting role, and if their level of stress related to fatherhood or other factors is low (Fagan, Bernd, & Whiteman, 2007).

The presence and support of the father can be beneficial to both the child and the mother. Adolescent mothers feel more competent as parents and less likely to be depressed when they are satisfied with the level of the fathers' involvement (Fagan & Lee, 2010). The children of adolescent mothers fare better in their own adolescence if they have a good relationship with their biological father (or a stepfather), especially if he lives with the child. However, exposure to a fathering figure may have little beneficial effect on children of adolescent mothers if the father–child relationship is not positive or the father figure has a criminal history (Furstenberg & Harris, 1993; Jaffee et al., 2001).

Teenage mothers tend to be daughters of teenage mothers. Teen mothers who have lower levels of stress and better social support are more likely to have secure attachments with their infants (J. Emery, Paquette, & Bigras, 2008).

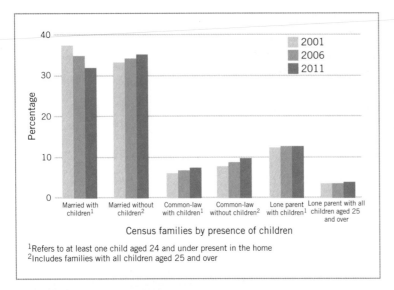

FIGURE 12.3 **Family configuration in Canada** The most common family configurations in Canada continue to be married couples, either with or without children; however, there is a continuing decline in this group, from 37.4% of all census families in 2001 to 31.9% in 2011. (Adapted from Ferrao, 2010)

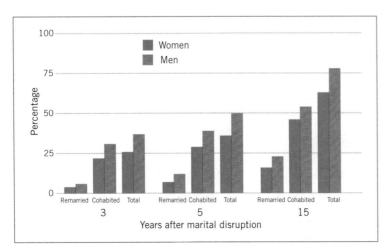

FIGURE 12.4 **Re-partnering after marital disruption** Even though the divorce rate has risen, many people re-partner after marital disruption. Men are more likely to find a new partner sooner than women. (Data from Wu & Shimmele, 2009, p. 173)

2012b). (Figure 12.3 shows other changes in families over time.) Although people are more likely to divorce than in the past, most people also re-partner after divorce, either marrying again or entering into a common-law relationship. Indeed, as Figure 12.4 shows, 36% of divorced Canadian women and more than 50% of divorced Canadian men re-partner after 5 years, and more than 52% of divorced Canadian women and 69% of divorced Canadian men re-partner after 10 years. Thus, the number of families including children from one or both parents' prior marriages has increased substantially.

All these changes in the structure and composition of families have vast implications for the understanding of child development and family life. In the following sections, we will give detailed consideration to the impact of delayed parenthood, the effects of divorce, remarriage, and new common-law relationships on children's development, and the issues surrounding maternal employment and child care. We will also consider an additional change in family structure that has recently received a good deal of public attention: the increase in the number of families with lesbian or gay parents.

Older Parents

In the last two decades, there has been a significant increase in the number of women in Canada having their first child after age 35. In 1987, women over 35 were responsible for only 4% of live births in Canada (Bushnik & Garner, 2008). In contrast, in 2010, almost 19% of live births occurred among women over the age of 35 (Statistics Canada, 2013d). Within limits, having children at a later age has decided parenting advantages. Older first-time parents tend to have more education, higher-status occupations, and higher incomes than younger parents do. Older parents also are more likely to have planned the birth of their children and to have fewer children overall. Thus, they have more financial resources for raising a family. They are also less likely to get divorced within 10 years if they are married (Bramlett & Mosher, 2002).

Older parents also tend to be more positive in their parenting of infants than younger parents are—unless they already have several children. For example, one study found that, compared with people who became parents between the ages of 18 and 25, older mothers and fathers had lower rates of observed harsh parenting with their 2-year-olds, which, in turn, predicted fewer problem behaviours a year later (Scaramella et al., 2008). In another study, this one of mothers aged 16 to 38 who had recently given birth, older mothers expressed greater satisfaction with parenting and commitment to the parenting role, displayed more positive emotion toward the baby, and showed greater sensitivity to the baby's cues. However, these positive outcomes did not extend to mothers who already had two or more children. Perhaps because they had less energy to deal with so many children, these mothers tended to exhibit less positive affect and sensitive behaviour with their infants than did younger mothers with two or more other children (Ragozin et al., 1982).

Men who delay parenting until approximately age 30 or later are likewise more positive about the parenting role than are younger fathers (Cooney et al., 1993; NICHD Early Child Care Research Network, 2000a). On average, they tend to be more responsive, affectionate, and cognitively and verbally stimulating with their infants. They are also more likely to provide a moderate amount of child care (Neville & Parke, 1997; NICHD Early Child Care Research Network, 2000a; Volling & Belsky, 1991). These differences may be partly due to older fathers' more secure establishment in their careers, allowing them to focus on their role as father and to be more flexible in their beliefs about acceptable roles and activities for fathers (Coltrane, 1996; Parke & Buriel, 1998).

On average, older fathers engage in more verbal interactions with their preschool-age children than do younger fathers.

Divorce

Most experts agree that children of divorce are at greater risk for a variety of short-term and long-term problems than are most children who are living with both their biological parents. Compared with the majority of their peers in intact families, for example, they are more likely to experience depression and sadness, to have lower self-esteem, and to be less socially responsible and competent (Amato, 2001; Ge, Natsuaki, & Conger, 2006; Hetherington, Bridges, & Insabella, 1998). In addition, children of divorce, especially boys, may be prone to higher levels of externalizing problem behaviours such as aggression and antisocial behaviour, both soon after the divorce and years later (Burt et al., 2008; Hartman, Magalhães, & Mandich, 2011; Malone et al., 2004). Problems such as these may contribute to the drop in academic achievement that children of divorce often exhibit (Potter, 2010). Adolescents whose parents divorce exhibit a greater tendency toward dropping out of school, engaging in delinquent activities and substance abuse, and having children out of wedlock (Amato & Keith, 1991; Hetherington et al., 1998; Simons & Johnson, 1996; Song, Benin, & Glick, 2012).

The Potential Impact of Divorce

As adults, children from divorced and remarried families are at greater risk for divorce than are their peers from intact families (Bumpass, Martin, & Sweet, 1991; Mustonen et al., 2011; Rodgers, Power, & Hope, 1997). Within this group, women, but not men, appear to also be at risk for poorer-quality intimate relationships, lower self-esteem, and lower satisfaction with social support from friends, family members, and other people (Mustonen et al., 2011). Being less likely to have completed high school or college or university, children of divorce often earn lower incomes in early adulthood than do their peers from intact families (Hetherington, 1999; Song et al., 2012). As adults, they are also at slightly greater risk for serious emotional disorders such as depression, anxiety, and phobias (Chase-Lansdale, Cherlin, & Kiernan, 1995).

Despite all these greater risks, most children whose parents divorce do not suffer significant, enduring problems as a consequence (Amato & Keith, 1991). In fact, although divorce can be a very painful experience for children, the differences between children from divorced families and children from intact families in terms of their psychological and social functioning are small overall (e.g., Burt et al., 2008). In addition, these differences often reflect an extension of the differences in the children's and/or their parents' psychological functioning that existed for years prior to the divorce (Clarke-Stewart et al., 2000; R. E. Emery & Forehand, 1996).

Factors Affecting the Impact of Divorce

A variety of interacting factors seem to predict whether the painful experiences of divorce and remarriage will cause children significant or lasting problems. The question here is one of individual differences: Why do some children of divorce fare better than others?

Parental conflict One influence on children's adjustment to divorce is the level of parental conflict prior to, during, and after the divorce (Amato, 2010; Buchanan, Maccoby, & Dornbusch, 1996). In fact, the level of parental conflict may predict the outcomes for children more than the divorce itself does. Not only is parental conflict distressing for children to observe, but it also may cause them to feel insecure about their own relationships with their parents, even making them fear that their parents will desert them or stop loving them (Davies & Cummings, 1994; Grych & Fincham, 1997). In addition, when there is parental conflict, fathers tend to have lower-quality relationships with their children, which may contribute to children's adjustment problems (Pruett et al., 2003). In contrast, when parents are cooperative and communicate with each other, children exhibit fewer behaviour problems and are closer with their non-residential father (Amato, 2010).

Conflict between parents often increases when the divorce is being negotiated and may continue for years after the divorce. This ongoing conflict is especially likely to have negative effects on children if they feel caught in the middle of it, as when they are forced to act as intermediaries between their parents or to inform one parent about the other's activities. Similar pressures may arise if children feel the need to hide from one parent information about, or their loyalty to, the other parent—or if the parents inappropriately disclose to them sensitive information about the divorce and each other. Adolescents who feel that they are caught up in their divorced parents' conflict are at increased risk for being depressed or anxious and for engaging in problematic behaviour such as drinking, stealing, cheating at school, fighting, or using drugs (Afifi et al., 2007, 2008, 2009; Afifi & McManus 2010; Buchanan, Maccoby, & Dornbusch, 1991; Kenyon & Koerner, 2008).

Stress A second factor that affects children's adjustment to divorce is the stress experienced by the custodial parent and children in the new family arrangement. Not only must custodial parents juggle household, child-care, and financial responsibilities that usually are shared by two parents, but they often must do so isolated from those who might otherwise help. This isolation typically occurs when custodial parents have to change their residence and lose access to established social networks, or when friends and relatives—especially in-laws—take sides in the

Divorced parents who are single often have to deal with increased levels of stress, which can affect the quality of their parenting.

BRUCE AYRES / STONE / GETTY IMAGES

divorce and turn against them. In addition, custodial mothers usually experience a substantial drop in their income, and this financial stress is often associated with problems in their physical health (Wickrama et al., 2006). Given that some of these stressors are similar to those experienced by lone parents more generally, it is no surprise that the quality of parenting, as well as children's adjustment, tends to be highest when the parents are married and are the biological parents of the children (S. L. Brown & Rinelli, 2010; Gibson-Davis & Gassman-Pines, 2010; Magnuson & Berger, 2009).

As a result of all these factors, the parenting of newly divorced mothers and fathers can be less than optimal. For example, studies have shown that the parenting of newly divorced mothers, compared with that of mothers in two-parent families, often tends to be characterized by more irritability and coercion and less warmth, emotional availability (e.g., parental sensitivity, structuring, non-intrusiveness, and non-hostility), consistency, and supervision of children (Hetherington, 1993; Hetherington et al., 1998; Simons & Johnson, 1996; K. E. Sutherland, Altenhofen, & Biringen, 2012). This is unfortunate because children tend to be most adjusted during and after the divorce if their custodial parent is supportive, is emotionally available, and uses authoritative parenting (Altenhofen, Sutherland, & Biringen, 2010; DeGarmo, 2010; Hetherington, 1993; Simons & Associates, 1996; Steinberg et al., 1991).

Making parenting even more difficult for the mother, non-custodial fathers often are permissive and indulgent with their children (Hetherington, 1989; Parke & Buriel, 1998), increasing the likelihood that children will resent and resist their mother's attempts to control their behaviour. (On an optimistic note, intervention efforts among divorced mothers and children that focus on improving mother–child interactions and establishing the mother's use of consistent discipline have been found to enhance the quality of the mother–child relationship and improve the children's adjustment [McClain et al., 2010].)

Thus, stressful life experiences during and after divorce often undermine the quality of parenting and of family interactions, which affects children's adjustment (Ge et al., 2006). These stressful life experiences can also have a direct effect on the child's adjustment (Figure 12.5). Having to change residences because of reduced

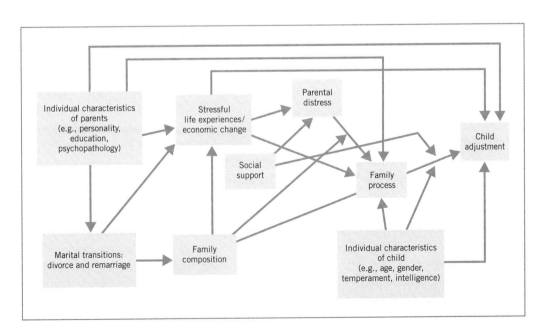

FIGURE 12.5 A model of the predictors of children's adjustment following divorce and remarriage Children's adjustment to parental divorce depends on many interrelated factors. These include characteristics of the parents and children; factors such as remarriage or new common-law relationships and economic changes; family composition (e.g., who is living in the home); the degree of social support; parental response to stressful events; and family processes that reflect these dynamics. (Adapted from Hetherington, Bridges, & Insabella, 1998)

household income, for example, may mean that at a time of high emotional vulnerability, a child also has to go through a wrenching transition to a new home, neighbourhood, school, and peer group (Braver, Ellman, & Fabricius, 2003; Fabricius & Braver, 2006). Disruptions such as these due to reduced family income are likely to contribute to the problems some children of divorce experience, including declines in school performance (Sun & Li, 2011).

Age of the child An additional factor that influences the impact of divorce is the child's age at the time of the divorce. Compared with older children and adolescents, younger children may have more trouble understanding the causes and consequences of divorce. They are especially more likely to be anxious about abandonment by their parents and to blame themselves for the divorce (Hetherington, 1989). As an 8-year-old boy explained, a year after his parents' divorce:

> My parents didn't get along. … They used to argue about me all the time when they were married. I guess I caused them a lot of trouble by not wanting to go to school and all. I didn't mean to make them argue. …
>
> (Wallerstein & Blakeslee, 1989, p. 73)

This boy firmly believed that he caused the divorce.

The following clinical report presents a picture of how divorce often affects young children:

> When we first saw seven-year-old Ned, he brought his family album to the office. He showed us picture after picture of himself with his father, his mother, and his little sister. Smiling brightly, he said, "It's going to be all right. It's really going to be all right." A year later, Ned was a sad child. His beloved father was hardly visiting and his previously attentive mother was angry and depressed. Ned was doing poorly in school, was fighting on the playground, and would not talk much to his mother.
>
> (Wallerstein & Blakeslee, 1989, p. xvi)

Although older children and adolescents are better able to understand a divorce than are younger children, they are nonetheless particularly at risk for problems with adjustment, including poor academic achievement and negative relationships with their parents. Adolescents who live in neighbourhoods characterized by a high crime rate, poor schools, and an abundance of antisocial peers are at especially high risk (Hetherington et al., 1998), most likely because the opportunities to get into trouble are amplified when there is only one parent—who most likely is at work during the day—to monitor the child's activity. College and university students are less reactive to their parents' divorce, probably because of their maturity and relative independence from the family (Amato & Keith, 1991). With regard to their parents' remarriage, young adolescents appear to be more negatively affected than younger children. One possible explanation for this is that young adolescents' struggles with the issues of autonomy and sexuality are heightened by the presence of a new parent who has authority to control them and is a sexual partner of their biological parent (Hetherington, 1993; Hetherington et al., 1992).

Contact with non-custodial parents Most non-custodial parents in Canada are involved in their children's lives, for example, contacting their children by telephone or email or participating in their children's recreational or day-to-day activities (P. Robinson, 2009). Although some studies show that frequency of contact with the non-custodial parent matters for the child's well-being (e.g., Pagani-Kurtz & Derevensky, 1997), other studies show that frequency itself may not be a significant factor (Amato & Gilbreth, 1999; Trinder, Kellet, & Swift, 2008). In studies that examine non-custodial fathers, what does seem to affect children's adjustment after divorce is the quality of the contact with the non-custodial father: children who have contact with competent, supportive, authoritative non-custodial fathers show better adjustment and do better in school than children who have frequent but superficial or disruptive contact with their non-custodial fathers (Amato & Gilbreth, 1999; Hetherington, 1989; Hetherington et al., 1998; Whiteside & Becker, 2000). In contrast, contact with non-residential fathers who have antisocial traits (e.g., who are vengeful, prone to getting into fights, manipulative, discourteous) predicts an increase in children's non-compliance with their fathers (DeGarmo, 2010).

Less is known about non-custodial mothers. However, studies have shown that they provide more emotional support for their children than non-custodial fathers do and are more likely to maintain contact through text messages, phone calls, and overnight visits. The more the non-custodial mothers maintain such involvement with their children and are close to their children, the better adjusted their children are (Gunnoe & Hetherington, 2004; King, 2007).

Children of divorce benefit from interaction with non-custodial fathers only if that interaction is of high quality.

The contribution of long-standing characteristics As noted earlier, it is important to recognize that the greater frequency of problem behaviours in children in divorced and remarried families may not be solely due to the divorce and remarriage. Rather, it sometimes may be related to characteristics of the parents or the children that existed long before the divorce. For instance, the parents may have difficulty coping with stress or forming positive social relationships, as suggested by the fact that parents who divorce are more likely than non-divorced parents to be depressed, alcoholic, or antisocial; to hold dysfunctional beliefs about relationships; or to lack skills for regulating conflict and negative emotion (R. E. Emery et al., 1999; Jocklin, McGue, & Lykken, 1996; Kurdek, 1993). Any one of these characteristics would be likely to undermine the quality of parenting the child receives.

The idea that the greater frequency of problem behaviours in children of divorce may be related to long-standing characteristics of the children themselves is supported by the finding that children of divorce tend to be more poorly adjusted prior to the divorce than are children from non-divorced families (Block, Block, & Gjerde, 1986; Hetherington & Stanley-Hagan, 2002). Interestingly, a longitudinal study conducted in Canada showed that children whose parents divorced over the course of the study showed higher levels of anxiety and depression even before the divorce than children in intact families. The subsequent divorce led to a further increase in these symptoms, likely in response to the divorce itself (Strohschein, 2005). This difference may be due to stress in the home, poor parenting, or parental conflict prior to divorce. Alternatively or additionally, it may be due to the children's own inherited characteristics, such as a lack of self-regulation or a predisposition to negative emotion (T. G. O'Connor, et al., 2000). Such characteristics would not only underlie children's adjustment problems but, when expressed in both children and their parents, would also increase the likelihood of divorce (Hetherington et al., 1998; Jocklin et al., 1996). Children with difficult personalities and limited coping capacities may also react more adversely to the negative events associated with divorce than would other children. However, although heredity seems to contribute to children's adjustment after divorce through its effect on children's characteristics, heredity probably is not the most important factor in how children cope with divorce (Amato, 2010).

Custody of Children After Divorce

It is increasingly common for divorced parents in Canada to have joint custody of their children. This arrangement is generally associated with better adjustment in children than is sole custody (Bauserman, 2002), but its effects depend in part on the degree of cooperation between ex-spouses. When parents cooperate with each other and keep the children's best interests in mind, children are unlikely to feel caught in the middle (Maccoby et al., 1993). Unfortunately, mutually helpful parenting is not the norm (Bretherton & Page, 2004): researchers have found that once parents have been separated for a while, most either engage in conflict or do not deal much with each other (Amato, Kane, & James, 2011; Maccoby et al., 1993).

An Alternative to Divorce: Ongoing Marital Conflict

On the basis of the publicity given to the negative effects that divorce can have on children, some people have argued that it would be better for families if it were more difficult for parents to obtain a divorce. When considering this argument, it is important to realize that sustained marital conflict has negative effects on children at all ages. Infants and children can be harmed by marital conflict because it may cause parents to be less warm and supportive, undermining their emotional involvement with the child and the security of the early parent–child attachment (El-Sheikh & Elmore-Staton, 2004; Frosch, Mangelsdorf, & McHale, 2000; Sturge-Apple, Davies, & Cummings, 2006; Sturge-Apple et al., 2012; Taylor et al., 2008). Preschoolers and older children are especially likely to feel threatened and helpless when there is ongoing parental conflict—more so if the conflict involves

Because ongoing marital conflict poses a variety of risks for children, the idea of staying married "for the sake of the children" may be a questionable one.

high levels of verbal and physical aggression (Davies, Cummings, & Winter, 2004; Grych, Harold, & Miles, 2003). Even adolescents often feel threatened by, and responsible for, parental conflict (Buehler, Lange, & Franck, 2007).

Perhaps as a consequence of these negative effects, interparental conflict and aggression are associated with children's and adolescents' reduced attentional skills, negative emotion, behavioural problems, and abnormal cortisol responses to distress (Grych et al., 2004; Lindahl et al., 2004; Schermerhorn et al., 2010; Sturge-Apple et al., 2012; Towe-Goodman et al., 2011). All these outcomes are likely to be exacerbated if the sustained marital conflict leads—as it frequently does—to parental hostility toward the children themselves (Buehler et al., 1997; Harold & Conger, 1997).

Further complicating matters is the fact that the relation between marital conflict and children's problem behaviour seems to be partly due to genetic factors that affect both parents' and children's behaviour (Harden et al., 2007; Schermerhorn et al., 2011) and partly due to the link between marital conflict and compromised parenting behaviour (Ganiban et al., 2011). Consistent with the aforementioned pattern of relations, Amato and colleagues (1995) found that among children raised in high-conflict families, those whose parents were divorced were better adjusted than those whose parents stayed together, whereas the reverse was true for low-conflict families.

Step-Parenting

In 2011, there were 464 335 stepfamilies in Canada (Vézina, 2012). For many children, the entry of a step-parent into the family is a very threatening event. As described by one long-term study, the child's world is suddenly full of anxious questions:

> What will this new man do for me? Will he threaten my position in the family? Will he interfere with my relationship with Mom and Dad? … Is he good for my mom? Will she be in a better mood? Will she treat me better? … Will my dad be angry? Will having a stepfather around make Dad want to visit me more or less? … Will Mom and Dad ever get remarried now that someone else is in the picture?
> (Wallerstein & Blakeslee, 1989, p. 246)

The answers to specific questions like these obviously vary case by case. Nevertheless, investigators have found some general patterns in the adjustments that are required of both children and adults when a parent remarries or enters a new common-law relationship.

Factors Affecting Children's Adjustment in Stepfamilies

Children's adjustment to living with a step-parent is influenced by a number of factors, including the child's age at the time of the remarriage or new common-law relationship. Very young children tend to accept step-parents more easily than do older children and adolescents (Amato & Keith, 1991; Hetherington et al., 1989). In addition, children generally adjust better and do better academically when all the children are full siblings (Hetherington et al., 1999; Tillman, 2008). One indicator of this is the fact that, in adolescence, children born into blended families have higher rates of delinquency, depression, and detachment from school tasks and relationships than do full siblings living with their biological parents, perhaps because there may be more sibling conflict in blended families (Halpern-Meekin & Tach, 2008).

The challenges in stepfamilies may differ somewhat for families with step-fathers and those with stepmothers. Most research has focused on stepfathers and their stepchildren. Although most stepfathers want their new families to thrive, they generally feel less close to their stepchildren than do fathers in intact families (Hetherington, 1993). At first, stepfathers tend to be polite and ingratiating toward their stepchildren and are less involved in monitoring or controlling their stepchildren than fathers in intact families (Kurdek & Fine, 1993). Nevertheless, on average, conflict between stepfathers and stepchildren tends to be greater than that between fathers and their biological offspring (Bray & Berger, 1993; Hakvoort et al., 2011; Hetherington et al., 1992, 1999), perhaps in part because stepfathers are more likely to see the children as burdens than their biological fathers are (A. O'Connor & Boag, 2010). It is thus not surprising that children with stepfathers tend to have higher rates of depression, withdrawal, and disruptive problem behaviours than do children in intact families (Hetherington & Stanley-Hagan, 1995).

Preadolescent girls in particular are likely to have problems with their step-fathers. Often the difficulty arises from the fact that prior to the remarriage or new common-law relationship, divorced or separated mothers have had a close, confiding relationship with their daughters, and the entry of the stepfather into the family disrupts this relationship. These changes can lead to resentment in the daughter and conflict with both her mother and the stepfather (Hetherington et al., 1992; Hetherington & Stanley-Hagan, 2002).

Despite these potential difficulties, the presence of an involved stepfather can enhance children's well-being, substantially improve family finances, and serve as a welcome source of emotional support and assistance for the custodial parent. A new stepfather may be especially helpful both in parenting his stepson and in providing a male role model (Parke & Buriel, 1998). One sign of this is that the increase of delinquency associated with children of divorce is lessened if the adolescent's parent remarries (Burt et al., 2008). Overall, with time, children often become as close to their stepfathers as they are to their non-residential biological fathers, sometimes even closer (Falci, 2006), usually without affecting their relationship with the biological father (King, 2009). For adolescents, having a close relationship with both their stepfather and their biological father, and believing that they matter to both, is associated with better adolescent outcomes (Schenck et al., 2009).

Because there are decidedly fewer stepmothers than stepfathers, much less research has been devoted to their role as step-parents. However, it appears that stepmothers generally have more difficulty with their stepchildren than do stepfathers (Gosselin & David, 2007) and are at risk for depressive symptoms (D. N. Shapiro & Stewart, 2011). Often fathers expect stepmothers to take an active role in parenting, including monitoring and disciplining the child, although children frequently resent the stepmother's being the disciplinarian and may reject her authority or accept it only grudgingly. This may help explain why stepmothers are more likely than biological mothers to feel resentment toward their stepchildren and view them as a burden (A. O'Connor & Boag, 2010). Despite these problems, when it is possible for stepmothers to use authoritative parenting successfully, step-children may be better adjusted (Hetherington et al., 1998). Indeed, children of both sexes are most adjusted in stepfamilies when their custodial parent is authoritative in his or her parenting style and the step-parent is warm and involved and supports the custodial parent's decisions rather than trying to exert control over the children independently (Bray & Berger, 1993; Hetherington et al., 1998).

An additional factor in children's adjustment in stepfamilies is the attitude of the non-custodial biological parent toward the step-parent and the level of conflict between the two (Wallerstein & Lewis, 2007). If the non-custodial parent has hostile feelings toward the new step-parent and communicates these feelings to the child, the child is likely to feel caught in the middle, increasing his or her adjustment problems (Buchanan et al., 1991). The non-custodial parent's hostile feelings may also encourage the child to behave in a hostile or distant manner with the step-parent. Not surprisingly, children in stepfamilies fare best when the relations between the non-custodial parent and the step-parent are supportive and the relations between the biological parents are cordial (Golish, 2003). Thus, the success or failure of step-families is affected by the behaviour and attitudes of all involved parties.

Lesbian and Gay Parents

Another way that Canadian families have changed in recent decades is that more lesbian and gay adults are parents. The 2011 Census reported that among individuals living in same-sex cohabiting partnerships (married or common-law), 16% of women and 3% of men had children living with them (Statistics Canada, 2011).

Most children of lesbian or gay parents are born when their parents are in a heterosexual marriage or relationship. In many cases, the parents divorce when one parent comes out as lesbian or gay. In addition, an increasing number of single and coupled lesbians and gay men are choosing to become biological parents through the use of artificial insemination or surrogacy. Other lesbians or gay men choose to become foster or adoptive parents, although in some countries there are legal barriers to such adoptions. In some cases, gay men act as stepfathers to the biological children of their partners (C. J. Patterson, 2002; C. J. Patterson & Chan, 1997).

A growing body of research suggests that the development of children of gay and lesbian parents differs little, if at all, from that of children of heterosexual parents.

The question that concerns many people is whether children raised by gay and lesbian parents grow up to be different from other children. According to a growing body of research, they are, in fact, very similar in their development to children of heterosexual parents in terms of adjustment, personality, and relationships with peers (Farr et al., 2010; Gartrell & Bos, 2010; Golombok, Spencer, & Rutter, 1983; Golombok et al., 2013; Wainright & Patterson, 2006, 2008). They are also similar in their sexual orientation and in the degree to which their behaviour is gender-typed (J. M. Bailey et al., 1995; Fulcher, Sutfin, & Patterson, 2008; Golombok et al., 2003), as well as in their romantic involvements and sexual behaviour as adolescents (Wainright, Russell, & Patterson, 2004). Generally, children of lesbian and gay parents report low levels of stigmatization and teasing (Bos & Gartrell, 2010; Tasker & Golombok, 1995), although they sometimes feel excluded, or gossiped about, by peers (Bos & van Balen, 2008).

Just as in families with heterosexual parents, the adjustment of children with lesbian and gay parents seems to depend on family dynamics, including the closeness of the parent–child relationship (Wainright & Patterson, 2008), how well the parents get along, parental supportiveness, regulated discipline, and the degree of stress parents experience in their parenting (Farr, Forssell, & Patterson, 2010; Farr & Patterson, 2013). In addition, children of lesbian parents are better adjusted when their mother and her partner are not highly stressed (R. W. Chan, Raboy, & Patterson, 1998), when they report sharing child-care duties evenly (C. J. Patterson, 1995), and when they are satisfied with the division of labour in the home (R. W. Chan et al., 1998).

When gay adoptive fathers have low levels of social support and a less positive gay identity, they experience more stress regarding parenting and are more likely to have poor relationships with their children (Tornello et al., 2011)—responses that are likely to affect their children's adjustment. In families with a gay father and his partner, a son's happiness with his family life is related to the inclusion of the partner in family activities and the son's having a good relationship with the partner as well as with his biological father (Crosbie-Burnett & Helmbrecht, 1993).

review:

The Canadian family has changed dramatically in recent decades. Adults are marrying later and having children later; more children are born to single mothers; and divorce is a more common occurrence.

Parental divorce and remarriage or new common-law relationships have been associated with enduring negative outcomes, such as behavioural problems, for only a minority of children. The major factor contributing to negative outcomes for children of divorce is dysfunctional family interactions in which parents deal with each other in hostile ways and children feel caught in the middle. Parental depression and upset, as well as economic pressures and other types of stress associated with lone parenting, often compromise the quality of parents' interactions with each other and with their children.

Stepfamilies present special challenges. Conflict is common in stepfamilies, especially when the children are adolescents, and step-parents usually are less involved with their stepchildren than are biological parents. Children do best if all parents are supportive and use an authoritative parenting style.

An increasing number of children live in families in which at least one parent is lesbian or gay. Research indicates that the children of lesbian or gay parents are very similar in their development to children of heterosexual parents in terms of adjustment, personality, relationships with peers, sexual orientation, gender-typed behaviour, romantic involvements, and sexual behaviour as adolescents.

FIGURE 12.6 **Workforce participation rate of mothers by age of youngest child** Over the past 18 years, the percentage of Canadian mothers who are employed has increased. The sharpest increase is among women with children between 0 and 2 years of age. (Adapted from Ferrao, 2010)

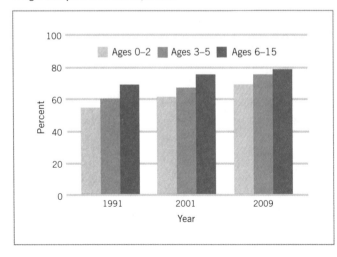

Maternal Employment and Child Care

Paralleling many of the other changes that have occurred in the Canadian family over the past half-century, the employment rate for mothers has increased steadily (see Figure 12.6). In 1976, only 39% of mothers with children younger than 16 were employed outside the home. In 2009, around 65% of mothers of children younger than 3 years, 66% of mothers with children younger than 6, and 73% of mothers with children younger than 16 worked outside the home (Ferrao, 2010). These changes in the rates of maternal employment reflect a variety of factors, including greater acceptance of mothers who work outside the home, more opportunities in the workplace for women, greater focus on career development for women, and increased financial need.

The dramatic rise in the number of mothers working outside the home raised a variety of concerns. Some experts predicted that maternal employment, especially in an infant's first year, would seriously diminish the quality of maternal caregiving and that the mother–child relationship would suffer accordingly. Others worried that "latchkey" children who were left to their own devices after school would get into serious trouble, academically and socially. Over the past two decades, much research has been devoted to addressing such concerns. For the most part, the findings have been reassuring.

The Effects of Maternal Employment

Taken as a whole, research does not support the idea that maternal employment per se has negative effects on children's development. There is little consistent evidence, for example, that the quality of mothers' interactions with their children necessarily diminishes substantially as a result of their employment (Gottfried, Gottfried, & Bathurst, 2002; Huston & Aronson, 2005; Paulson, 1996). Although working mothers typically spend less time with their children than do non-working mothers, the difference is largely offset by the fact that, compared with non-working mothers, working mothers spend a greater portion of their child-care time engaged in social interactions with their infants rather than in straightforward caregiving activities (Huston & Aronson, 2005). Even in the area of greatest debate—the effects of maternal employment on infants in their first year of life—when negative relations between maternal work and children's cognitive or social behaviour have been found, the results have not been consistent across studies, ethnic groups, or the type of analyses applied to the data (L. Berger et al., 2008; Brooks-Gunn, Han, & Wadlfogel, 2010; Burchinal & Clarke-Stewart, 2007).

Over the past 30 years, there has been a dramatic rise in the number of mothers in paid employment, working either from home or outside the home. Although change led to worries about the impact that maternal employment would have on children's development, research suggests there is no cause for concern.

Overall, what the evidence does suggest is that maternal employment may be associated with negative outcomes for some children under certain circumstances and that it may be associated with positive outcomes in other circumstances. As will be discussed shortly, the quality of child care provided while mothers work is undoubtedly a critical factor affecting whether maternal employment is associated with cognitive, language, or social problems in young children. In addition, if children are not adequately supervised and monitored after school, their academic performance may suffer (Muller, 1995). However, if employed mothers are involved with their children and arrange for their after-school supervision, the children tend to do as well in school as children of mothers who are not employed outside the home (Beyer, 1995).

Studies of maternal employment extending beyond infancy also reveal contextual variation in the effects that maternal employment can have on children's development. For instance, a study of 3- to 5-year-olds found that those whose mother worked a night shift (starting at 9:00 P.M. or later) tended to exhibit more aggressive behaviour, anxiety, and depressive symptoms than did the children whose mothers worked a typical daytime schedule (Dunifon et al., 2013). In another study, researchers found that mothers who worked more often at night (starting at 9:00 P.M. or later) spent less time with their adolescents, and that their adolescents had a lower-quality home environment (e.g., in terms of the quality of mother–child interactions, the cleanliness and safety of the home, and so on), which in turn predicted higher levels of adolescents' risky behaviours. These effects were especially strong for boys in low-income families. However, similar negative effects were not found in the case of mothers who worked evening shifts that ended by midnight or who had other non-standard work schedules (e.g., those with varying hours) that allowed them greater knowledge of their children's whereabouts (Han, Miller, & Waldfogel, 2010).

There appear to be costs and benefits of maternal employment for low-income families, depending on the circumstances. Adolescents in lone-parent, mother-led families report feeling more positive emotions and higher self-esteem if their mothers are employed full time (Duckett & Richards, 1995), perhaps because maternal employment is critical for pulling mother-led, poor families out of poverty (Harvey, 1999; Lichter & Lansdale, 1995). Nonetheless, there is also some evidence that unmarried mothers with poor-paying jobs may become less supportive of their children and provide a less stimulating home environment after they start working, compared with when they were at home full time (Menaghan & Parcel, 1995). This drop in supportiveness is no doubt linked to the fact that single mothers with low-paying jobs are particularly likely to be stressed, unhappy with their jobs, and unable to afford services to assist them with child-rearing.

Maternal employment may have specific benefits for girls. Children of employed mothers are also more likely than children of non-employed mothers to reject the confining aspects of traditional gender roles, and they are also more likely to see more benefits of maternal employment (Goldberg et al., 2012; L. W. Hoffman, 1984, 1989). For instance, children of employed mothers are more likely to be exposed to egalitarian parental roles in the family, and this experience seems to affect girls' feelings of effectiveness (L. W. Hoffman & Youngblade, 1999). In addition, compared with peers whose mothers are not employed, daughters of employed mothers tend to have higher aspirations (Gottfried et al., 2002).

The impact that maternal employment—or the lack thereof—can have on children also depends in part on how the mother is affected by her employment status (Kalil & Ziol-Guest, 2005). For example, mothers who want to work but do not are sometimes depressed (Gove & Zeiss, 1987), whereas for those who want to work and do, employment can have a positive effect on their mood and sense of effectiveness (L. W. Hoffman & Youngblade, 1999), which would be expected to affect the quality of their parenting (Bugental & Johnston, 2000).

For many mothers, part-time work may be ideal. Recent research on mothers who were employed full-time, part-time, or not at all indicates that compared with unemployed mothers, mothers who worked part-time had fewer depressive symptoms and better health. And compared with mothers who worked full-time, mothers who worked part-time showed more sensitive parenting during the preschool years, were more involved in their children's schooling and learning in general, and their children exhibited fewer externalizing problems (Brooks-Gunn et al., 2010; Buehler & O'Brien, 2011).

As already noted, a factor that is key to how maternal employment affects children's development is the nature and quality of the care that children receive. But there, too, the effects vary as a function of the context and the individuals involved.

The Effects of Child Care

Because so many mothers work outside the home, a large number of infants and young children receive care on a regular basis from someone besides their parents. In Canada, over half of children between the ages of 6 months and 5 years are in some form of non-parental care (Bushnik, 2006), with the most common arrangements being care outside the home by a non-relative and centre-based care.

In Canada, over half of children between the ages of 6 months and 5 years are in some form of non-parental care.

In regard to the debate over potential risks and benefits of non-parental child care, some experts have argued that, especially for children from deprived backgrounds, group care, with its wide variety of activities, can provide greater cognitive stimulation than care at home (Consortium for Longitudinal Studies, 1983). Some have also suggested that children in group care learn important social skills through their interactions with peers (Clarke-Stewart, 1981; Volling & Feagans, 1995). Critics counter that enriched cognitive stimulation is provided only by high-quality child care and that much of the child care that is currently available does not provide as much stimulation as care by a parent at home does. Critics also point out that although children in child care may learn social skills from interactions with their peers, they also learn negative behaviours, such as aggression, because of the need to assert oneself in the group setting (J. E. Bates et al., 1994; Haskins, 1985).

Probably the greatest concern about child care initially was that it might undermine the early mother–child relationship (e.g., Belsky, 1986). For example, on the basis of attachment theory (see Chapter 11, pages 428–430), it has been argued that young children who are frequently separated from their mothers are more likely to develop insecure attachments to their mothers than are children whose daily care is provided by their mothers. As you will now see, that concern is largely unwarranted.

Attachment and the Parent–Child Relationship

The issue of whether non-parental child care in the early years interferes with children's attachment relationships to their parents has been examined in many studies. A variety of those involving infants and preschoolers show no evidence overall that children in child care are less securely attached than other children or that they display less positive behaviour in interactions with their mothers (Erel, Oberman, & Yirmiya, 2000). Other research indicates that in a small minority of cases, extensive child care is associated with negative effects on attachment, but these cases tend to involve other care-related risk factors, such as frequent turnover in outside caregivers, a high ratio of infants per caregiver, and poor-quality care at home (M. E. Lamb, 1998; Sagi et al, 2002).

Similar findings have been shown in a major in-depth study funded by the National Institute of Child Health and Development (NICHD) that has followed the development of approximately 1300 children in various child-care arrangements and in elementary school. This study, begun in 1991, includes families who are from 10 locations around the United States and who vary considerably in their economic status, ethnicity, and race. The study measures (1) characteristics of the families and the child-care setting, (2) children's attachment to, and interactions with, their mothers, and (3) children's social behaviour, cognitive development, and health status.

A particularly important finding in this study is that how children fare in a non-maternal care situation is much more strongly related to characteristics of the family—such as level of income, maternal education, maternal sensitivity, and the like—than to the nature of the child care itself. Moreover, any effects, positive or negative, that child care might have on development appear to be very limited in magnitude. Indeed, insecure attachments of a notable degree were predicted only when two conditions existed *simultaneously*—that is, (1) when the children experienced poor-quality child care, had 10 or more hours of child care per week, or had more than one child-care arrangement; *and* (2) when their mothers were not very sensitive or responsive to them (NICHD Early Child Care Research Network, 1997a).

When children were 24 and 36 months old, the quality of mother–child interaction was, to a slight degree, predicted by the number of hours in child care. Compared with mothers who did not use child care or who put their child in care for fewer hours, mothers of children who were in daycare for longer hours tended to be less sensitive with their children, and their children tended to be less positive in interactions with them (NICHD Early Child Care Research Network, 1999). Even in these circumstances, the magnitudes of the effects were small.

Adjustment and Social Behaviour

The possible effects of child care on children's self-control, compliance, and social behaviour have also been a focus of much concern and research. Here, the findings are mixed and sometimes depend on the specific mode of analysis (e.g., Crosby et al., 2010) and the country in which the research was conducted. A number of investigators have found that children who are in child care do not differ in problem behaviour from those reared at home (Barnes et al., 2010; Erel et al., 2000; M. E. Lamb, 1998). Indeed, in two recent large studies in Norway, a country in which the quality of child care is uniformly high, researchers found little consistent relation between amount of time in child care and children's externalizing problems, such as aggression and non-compliance, or social competence (Solheim et al., 2013; Zachrisson et al., 2013).

These findings are in notable contrast to those from the NICHD study in the United States, where the quality of child care is more variable. The NICHD study indicates that many hours a day in child care or a number of changes in caregivers in the first 2 years of life predicted lower social competence and more non-compliance with adults at age 2 (NICHD Early Child Care Research Network, 1998a). At 4½ years of age, children in extensive child care were viewed by care providers (but not by mothers) as exhibiting more problem behaviours, such as aggression, non-compliance, and anxiety/depression (NICHD Early Child Care Network, 2006). The relation between more hours in centre care and teacher-reported externalizing problems (e.g., aggression, defiance) was also found in the elementary school years but generally was not significant by Grade 6 (Belsky et al., 2007). However, more hours of non-relative care predicted greater risk taking and impulsivity at age 15 (Vandell et al., 2010).

Significantly, the finding that greater time in child care is related to increased risk for adjustment problems appears not to apply to children from very low-income, high-risk families (Côté et al., 2008). In fact, longer time in child care has been found to be positively related to the better adjustment of such children, unless the quality of care is very poor (Votruba-Drzal, Coley, & Chase-Lansdale, 2004). Similarly, in a large study of children from high-risk families in Canada, physical aggression was less common among children who were in group daycare than among those who were looked after by their own families (Borge et al., 2004). High-quality child care that involves programs designed to promote children's later success at school may be especially beneficial for disadvantaged children (Keys et al., 2013; M. E. Lamb, 1998; Peisner-Feinberg et al., 2001; Webster-Stratton, 1998; Zhai, Brooks-Gunn, & Waldfogel, 2011).

Thus, it appears that most children in child care never develop significant behaviour problems, but for some, the risk that they will develop such problems increases with an increase in hours spent in child care, especially centre care (R. L. Coley et al., 2013). In the NICHD study, this risk was higher when children spent many hours with a large group of peers and in low-quality child care (the overall risk was modest and was not due to the characteristics of children who are put in child care for longer hours) (McCartney et al., 2010). More generally, higher-quality child care in the NICHD study was related to fewer externalizing problems in the early years (McCartney et al., 2010) and at age 15 (Vandell et al., 2010)—a relation primarily seen in children and adolescents who were prone to negative emotion (Belsky & Pluess, 2012; Pluess & Belsky, 2010) or who had a particular variant of gene DRD4, which, as discussed in Chapter 11 (page 437), is associated with being susceptible to the effects of the environment (Belsky & Pluess, 2013).

In addition, it must be remembered that the background characteristics (e.g., family income, parental education, parental personality) of children who are in daycare for long hours likely differ in a variety of ways from those of children in daycare for fewer hours. Therefore, cause-and-effect relations cannot be assumed, even when the effects of some of these factors are taken into account (Bolger & Scarr, 1995; NICHD Early Child Care Research Network, 1997b). Furthermore, the number of hours spent in child care is less relevant than the quality of child care provided: no matter what their SES background, children in high-quality child-care programs tend to be well adjusted and to develop social competencies (Love et al., 2003; NICHD Early Child Care Research Network, 2003; Votruba-Drzal et al., 2004).

As noted earlier, another factor related to the effects of child care on children's adjustment is the number of changes in the child care. In the NICHD study, increases in the number of non-parental child-care arrangements were associated with increases in children's problem behaviours and lower levels of positive behaviour such as compliance and constructive expression of emotion (Morrissey, 2009). Instability of child care was also related to poorer adjustment in an Australian study (Love et al., 2003).

ELKE VAN DE VELDE / GETTY IMAGES

For low-income students, some of the positive academic outcomes associated with high-quality preschool child care have been found to persist into elementary grades.

Cognitive and Language Development

The possible effects of child care on children's cognitive and language performance are of particular concern to educators as well as to parents. Research suggests that high-quality child care can have a modest, positive effect on these aspects of children's functioning (Keys et al., 2013), although the effects sometimes weaken over time (Côté et al., 2013). The NICHD study found that, overall, the number of hours in child care did not correlate with cognitive or language development when demographic variables such as family income were taken into account. However, higher-quality child care that included specific efforts to stimulate children's language development was linked to better cognitive and language development in the first 3 years of life (NICHD Early Child Care Research Network, 2000b). Children in higher-quality child care (especially centre care) scored higher on tests of pre-academic cognitive skills, language abilities, and attention than did those in lower-quality care (NICHD Early Child Care Research Network, 2002, 2006; NICHD Early Child Care Research Network & Duncan, 2003). Higher-quality care also predicted mothers' greater involvement in their children's schooling when the children were in kindergarten. This would be expected to foster children's school performance (Crosnoe et al., 2012); promote higher vocabulary (but not reading and math) scores in elementary school (Belsky et al., 2007); and cultivate higher cognitive and academic achievement at age 15 (Vandell et al., 2010). Moreover, for children in high-quality care, low income was less likely to predict underachievement at 4½ to 11 years of age (Dearing et al., 2009).

Other research also suggests that child care may have positive effects on cognition and that these effects are larger for higher-quality centres (Peisner-Feinberg et al., 2001). For instance, in Sweden and the United States, a number of researchers have found that children enrolled in out-of-home child care perform better on cognitive tasks, even in elementary school (Erel et al., 2000; M. E. Lamb, 1998). In addition, children from low-income families who spend long hours in child care, compared with those who spend fewer hours, tend to show increases in quantitative skills (Votruba-Drzal et al., 2004). Finally, researchers in Quebec have found that socially disadvantaged children who attended formal child care score higher on measures of academic readiness and achievement than socially disadvantaged children who do not attend child care (Geoffroy et al., 2010). It is likely that child care, unless it is of low quality, provides greater cognitive stimulation than is available in some low-income homes.

Quality of Child Care

In Canada, each province regulates child-care centres and sets minimum standards for care. Alberta is the only province to develop an accreditation process for child care programs (see Table 12.1). In addition, organizations like the Canadian Child Care Federation provide resources for parents seeking high-quality child care.

Studies from Canada, the United States, Chile, and Sweden have demonstrated that the quality of child care influences children's development (Broberg et al., 1997; Herrera et al., 2005; NICHD Early Child Care Research Network, 1998b). For example, a recent study in Quebec found that quality child care was related to better cognitive development in preschoolers. Interestingly, the best predictor of overall child-care quality in this study was the type of language stimulation that teachers and caregivers used—that is, whether they responded to children's vocalizations, praised children, asked questions, and were positive in the language they directed to children (Côté et al., 2013).

TABLE 12.1

Alberta Child Care Accreditation Standards

Experts in early childhood education recommend that parents assess child-care programs before selecting one for their children. Following are the Alberta Child Care Accreditation Standards; Alberta is the only province to develop an accreditation process for childcare programs. These standards apply to licensed daycare centres, approved family day homes, and licensed out-of-school care. The standards are divided into four categories: outcomes for children, for families, for staff, and for the community. (Note that these standards are more stringent than the basic provincial/territorial regulatory requirements.)

Outcomes for Children

Standard 1: Positive, supportive relationships and enriched physical and emotional environments foster children's well-being and development.

1.1 Child care programs promote and nurture children's positive sense of self and belonging through supportive relationships.

1.2 Child care programs demonstrate respectful, positive interactions and communications with children.

1.3 Child care programs incorporate well-designed physical indoor learning environments to foster the optimal development in children.

1.4 Children's development is supported through outdoor environments with active play spaces and opportunities to experience and learn about the natural world.

Standard 2: Program planning and practices support every child's optimal development in an inclusive early learning and care environment that incorporates the value and importance of play.

2.1 Child care programs incorporate inclusive approaches that respect children's diversity and value children's individual needs and backgrounds.

2.2 Child care programs promote physical wellness in all children and incorporate physical literacy in everyday programming.

2.3 Child care programs promote competence, active exploration, and learning through play.

2.4 Child care programs use observation, recording, and documentation to plan the program based on the needs, abilities, and interests of children and their experiences with families and communities.

Outcomes for Families

Standard 3: Relationships with families are supportive and respectful.

3.1 Child care programs work in partnership with families and respect their beliefs and expertise in their child-rearing role as primary caregivers.

3.2 Child care programs implement clear, simple practices that promote regular exchange of information with families.

3.3 Child care programs support families through parental involvement, sharing of resources, and providing information regarding additional supports for their children.

Outcomes for Staff

Standard 4: Child care programs create a supportive work environment to maintain a qualified team of child care professionals and assist them in providing high quality child care services through its philosophy, policies, procedures, and practices.

4.1 Child care programs have clear and current statements of program philosophy, policies, goals, and strategies in place to assist child care professionals in providing quality care.

4.2 Child care programs have well-defined human resources and management practices to support a qualified team of child care professionals and maintain a positive work environment.

4.3 Child care programs demonstrate a positive workplace environment and organizational culture that support the well-being and educational development of child care professionals.

Outcomes for Community

Standard 5: Child care programs collaborate with community organizations and services to respond to the needs of children and families they serve.

5.1 Child care programs are responsive to the diverse needs of the children and families they serve.

5.2 Child care programs establish working relationships with organizations and services within the community.

5.3 Child care programs have a clearly defined process for involving community stakeholders.

Standard 6: Continuous quality improvement is demonstrated through ongoing self-monitoring and evaluation processes.

6.1 Child care programs engage in ongoing monitoring and evaluation processes involving administrative staff, families, child care professionals, and other stakeholders to support continuous quality improvement.

6.2 Child care programs use a Quality Enhancement Plan to set program goals annually.

6.3 Child care programs have sound administrative policies and procedures in place to support quality services.

Source: Accreditation of Early Learning and Care Services, 2014.

review:

The bulk of recent research on maternal employment indicates that it often benefits children and mothers and that it has few negative effects on children if they are in child care of acceptable quality and are supervised and monitored. Unfortunately, however, in low-income families, especially those headed by a lone parent, adequate child care and supervision may not always be possible.

Because so many mothers work, a large proportion of children receive some care from adults other than their parents. Recent research on child care indicates that, on the whole, non-maternal care has small, if any, effect on the quality of the mother–child relationship. Children who spend long hours in centres tend to exhibit more aggressive behaviour at schools, but the effects are modest and likely are non-significant for high-quality child care. High-quality care does appear to have some modest benefits for cognitive development and especially language development. Whether child care has positive or negative effects on children's functioning probably depends on the characteristics of the child, the number of hours in care, the quality of parenting at home, and the quality of the care situation.

chapter summary:

Family Dynamics

- How well a family fulfills its functions depends on its family dynamics: all the family members influence one another, and the nature of their interactions shapes children's development.

The Role of Parental Socialization

- Parents socialize their children's development through direct instruction; through their modelling of skills, attitudes, and behaviour; and through their managing of children's experiences and social lives.

- Researchers have identified several types of parenting styles related to the dimensions of warmth and control. Authoritative parents are supportive and relatively high in control; their children tend to be socially and academically competent. Authoritarian parents are low in warmth and high in control; their children tend to be relatively low in social and academic competence, unhappy, and low in self-confidence. Permissive parents are responsive to their children's needs and wishes and low on control; their children tend to be low in self-control and in school achievement. Rejecting-neglecting parents are low in demandingness, support, and control; their children tend to have disturbed attachment relationships during infancy, poor peer relations during childhood, and poor adjustment in adolescence.

- The significance and effects of different parenting styles or practices may vary somewhat across cultures.

- Parenting styles and practices are affected by characteristics of the children, including their attractiveness, behaviour, and temperament.

- Parents' beliefs and values tend to differ across social classes, such that lower socioeconomic status tends to be associated with authoritarian parenting.

- Economic stressors can undermine the quality of marital and parent–child interactions, increasing children's risk for depression, academic failure, disruptive behaviour, and drug use.

- Homeless children are more likely than other children to show delays in cognitive and language development, to have academic difficulties, and to show problems in adjustment.

Mothers, Fathers, and Siblings

- Mothers typically interact with their children more than fathers do, and fathers' play tends to be more physical than mothers' play. However, the nature of parent–child interactions differs across cultures.

- Siblings learn from one another, can be sources of support for one another, and sometimes engage in conflict. Siblings get along better if they have good relationships with their parents and if one of them does not feel that their parents treat him or her less well than they treat his or her siblings.

Changes in Families in Canada

- In Canada today, adults are marrying later, more children are being born to single mothers, divorce is becoming a more common occurrence, and more couples are entering into common-law relationships.

- Adolescent parents come disproportionately from impoverished backgrounds and families with cold, uninvolved parents. Adolescent mothers tend to be less effective parents than older parents, and their children are at risk for behavioural and academic problems, delinquency, and early sexual activity. Children of adolescent mothers fare better if their mothers have more knowledge about parenting and if the children themselves have a warm, involved relationship with their fathers.

- Mothers who delay child-bearing tend to be more responsive with their children and to enjoy motherhood more than do mothers who have their first children in their teens and 20s.

- Parental divorce/separation and remarriage/new common-law relationships have been associated with enduring negative outcomes such as behavioural problems for a minority of children. The major factor contributing to negative outcomes for children of divorce is hostile, dysfunctional family interactions, including continuing conflict between ex-spouses.

- Parental depression and upset, as well as other types of stress associated with lone parenting, often compromise the quality of divorced parents' interactions with their children.

- Conflict is common in stepfamilies. Children often are hostile toward step-parents, and step-parents usually are less involved with their stepchildren than are biological parents. Children do best if all parents are supportive and use an authoritative parenting style.

- Children raised by lesbian or gay parents are very similar in their development to children of heterosexual parents.

Maternal Employment and Child Care

- Children and mothers reap some benefits from maternal employment, and maternal employment has few negative effects on children if they are in child care of acceptable quality and are supervised and monitored by adults.

- Experience with non-maternal care has small negative effects on the quality of the mother–child relationship for some young children, especially if they are in child care for long hours, the quality of care is low, and their mother is insensitive.

- Child care is associated with a small increase in negative problem behaviour for children from working- and middle-class families, especially if they are not in a high-quality program, but it may be associated with improvements in adjustment for low-income children.

- Children in high-quality care do better in their cognitive and language development than children in low-quality care. Whether child care has positive or negative effects on children's functioning probably depends in part on the characteristics of the child, the child's relationship with his or her mother, and the quality of the child-care situation.

Critical Thinking Questions

1. It often is assumed that parental socialization of children's behaviour is a bidirectional process, with the parent affecting the child's behaviour and the child's behaviour also evoking some socialization practices or behaviours. Provide examples of bidirectional causality in regard to (a) the relation between parental punitive practices and children's aggression, and (b) the relation between parental use of punitive control and children's self-regulation.

2. In some cultures, respect for authority, including the authority of parents in general, is valued more than in many Western industrialized countries. How might this cultural variation affect interactions between parents and children and the relation of parenting styles to children's social and emotional development? Similarly, how might living in a culture in which men and women often are separated (e.g., do not eat together) and women are discouraged from going out in public affect parent–child relationships and interactions?

3. Think about the ways your parents interacted with you when you were a child. Based on Baumrind's categories of parenting style, which type of parenting did your mother and/or father display? What specific behaviours did you use to classify their parenting?

4. Make a list of the advantages and disadvantages of joint custody for children of divorce. How would the advantages and disadvantages vary for families in which the parents either (a) argue a lot or get along and (b) live 50 kilometres apart or 5 kilometres apart after the divorce?

Key Terms

authoritarian parenting, p. 474

authoritative parenting, p. 473

bidirectionality of parent–child interactions, p. 478

family dynamics, p. 470

parenting styles, p. 472

permissive parenting, p. 474

rejecting-neglecting parenting, p. 475

KOMI CHEN, *Show Off*, 1994 (gouache on silk)

chapter 13:

Peer Relationships

Themes

In Chapters 1 and 11, we described the plight of institutionalized orphans who, lacking consistent interaction with a caring adult, developed social, emotional, and cognitive deficits. After World War II, an interesting exception to this pattern was noted by Anna Freud—the daughter of Sigmund Freud—and Sophie Dann (1972/1951). They observed six young German-Jewish children who had been victims of the Hitler regime. Soon after these children were born, their parents were deported to Poland and killed. The children were subsequently moved from one refuge to another until, between the ages of approximately 6 and 12 months, they were placed in a ward for motherless children in a concentration camp. The care they received in this ward was undoubtedly compromised by the fact that their caregivers were themselves prisoners who were undernourished and overworked. Moreover, the rates of deportation and death among the prisoners were high, so it is likely that the children's caregivers changed frequently.

In 1945, approximately 2 to 3 years after the children's arrival at the concentration camp, the camp was liberated; within a month, the six children were sent to Britain. After spending 2 months in a reception facility, the children, as a group, were sent to various shelters and then, finally, to a country house that had been converted to accommodate orphans.

Given the conditions of their early lives, it is not surprising that these children initially showed a variety of problem behaviours in their new home:

> During the first days after arrival they destroyed all the toys and damaged much of the furniture. Toward the staff they behaved either with cold indifference or with active hostility, making no exception for the young assistant Maureen who had accompanied them from Windermere and was their only link with the immediate past. At times they ignored the adults so completely that they would not look up when one of them entered the room. … In anger, they would hit the adults, bite or spit … shout, scream, and use bad language.
>
> (Freud & Dann, 1972, p. 452)

These children, however, behaved quite differently among themselves. They obviously were deeply attached to one another, sensitive to one another's feelings, and they exhibited almost a complete lack of envy, jealousy, and rivalry. They shared possessions and food, helped and protected one another, and admired one another's abilities and accomplishments. The children's closeness is reflected in this brief selection from Freud and Dann's daily observations:

> November 1945—John cries when there is no cake left for a second helping for him. Ruth and Miriam offer him what is left of their portions. While John eats their pieces of cake, they pet him and comment contentedly on what they have given him. …
>
> (p. 134)

> December 1945—Paul loses his gloves during a walk. John gives him his own gloves, and never complains that his hands are cold. …
>
> (p. 135)

> April 1946—On the beach in Brighton, Ruth throws pebbles into the water. Peter is afraid of the waves and does not dare to approach them. In spite of his fear, he suddenly rushes to Ruth, calls out: "Water coming, water coming," and drags her back to safety. …
>
> (p. 136)

Freud and Dann concluded that the children, although aggressive and difficult for adults to handle, were "neither deficient, delinquent nor psychotic" (p. 473) and that their relationships with one another helped them master their anxiety and develop the capacity for social relationships.

Freud and Dann's observations provided some of the first evidence that relationships with peers can help very young children develop some of the social and emotional capacities that usually emerge in the context of adult–child attachments. Two decades later, similar findings were obtained in research with monkeys. As discussed in Chapter 11, Harry Harlow and his colleagues raised laboratory monkeys in isolation from other monkeys from birth to 6 months of age. By the end of this period, the isolate monkeys had developed significant abnormalities in behaviour, such as compulsive rocking and a reluctance to explore. Some of the isolate monkeys were subsequently placed with one or two normal, playful monkeys who were 3 months younger. Over the course of the next several months, the isolate monkeys' abnormal behaviours diminished greatly, and they began to explore their environment and engage in social interactions, demonstrating that peers can provide some of the social and emotional experiences required for typical development in monkeys (Suomi & Harlow, 1972).

Findings such as these do not suggest that peers alone can produce optimal development in young children. However, they do suggest that peers can contribute to children's development in meaningful ways. In fact, in Western societies, children's relationships with other children—their friends and acquaintances at school and in the neighbourhood—usually play a very important role in their lives. By Grade 6, for example, 25 to 30% of Canadian children report spending time with friends after school four or five days a week (McCuaig Edge & Craig, 2011). Thus, peer interactions are a context in which children develop social skills and test new behaviours, both positive and negative.

In this chapter, we consider the special nature of peer interactions and their implications for children's social development. First, we discuss theoretical views on what makes peer interactions special. Then we look at friendships, the most intimate form of peer relationships, and consider questions such as: How do children's interactions with friends differ from those with other peers (non-friends)? How do friendships change with age? What do children get out of friendships and how do they think about them?

Next, we consider children's relationships in the larger peer group. These relationships are discussed separately from friendships because they appear to play a somewhat different role in children's development, particularly in regard to the provision of intimacy. We try to answer questions such as: What are the differences among children who are liked, disliked, or not noticed by their peers? Does children's acceptance or rejection by peers have long-term implications for their behaviour and psychological adjustment?

In our discussions of friendships as well as more general peer relationships, we will examine *individual differences* among children in their relationships with peers and the ways in which these differences may cause differences in development. In

Anna Freud's study of children who lived together in a concentration camp provided evidence of the importance of early peer relationships.

peers ■ People of approximately the same age and status.

addition, we will focus on the influence that the *sociocultural context* has on peer relationships, the contributions that both *nature and nurture* make to the quality of children's peer relationships, and the role of the *active child* in choosing friends and activities with peers. We will also consider the question of whether changes in children's thinking about friendships exhibit *continuity or discontinuity*. Finally, as an example of *research and children's welfare*, we will examine interventions to improve children's interactions with other children.

What Is Special About Peer Relationships?

Many theorists have argued that peer relationships provide special opportunities for children's development. To begin with, **peers** are, by definition, individuals who are close in age to one another, closer usually than siblings. Thus, in contrast to their status in most of their other relationships, especially those with adults, children are relatively equal in terms of power when they interact with their peers (Furman & Buhrmester, 1985).

Piaget (1932/1965) suggested that because of this relative equality, children tend to be more open and spontaneous with peers when expressing their ideas and beliefs than they are with adults. As Piaget noted, children often accept adults' beliefs and rules on the basis of mere obedience rather than on the basis of understanding or agreement (Youniss, 1980). With peers, on the other hand, children are more likely to openly criticize another's ideas, clarify and elaborate their own ideas, and ask for feedback (A. C. Kruger & Tomasello, 1986). In this way, peers jointly construct their own explanations and rules for why or how things work or should work.

Similarly, Vygotsky (1978) suggested that children learn new skills and develop their cognitive capacities in peer interactions. However, unlike Piaget, Vygotsky highlighted the role of cooperation among peers. In particular, he emphasized the ways in which children's working together helps to build new skills and abilities, as well as to convey the knowledge and skills valued by the culture.

Other researchers have emphasized the social and emotional gains provided by peer interaction. In the preschool and school years, peers are an important source of companionship and assistance with problems and tasks (Youniss, 1980). As children

Both disagreement and cooperation within the context of peer relationships have been emphasized by theorists as important contributors to children's cognitive development. Even something as seemingly simple as establishing the ground rules for an informal game of softball can hone children's skills in debate and compromise.

ROBIN SACHS / PHOTOEDIT

become older, peers may become more important as a source of emotional support and provide children with their first experience of an intimate interpersonal relationship based on reciprocity and exchange between equals (H. S. Sullivan, 1953).

In summary, theorists such as Piaget, Vygotsky, and others have argued that peer relationships provide a unique context for cognitive, social, and emotional development. In their view, the equality, reciprocity, cooperation, and intimacy that can develop in peer relationships, especially friendships, enhance children's reasoning ability and their concern for others. In the next section, we will focus particularly on what friendships are like, how they change with age, and what possible benefits and costs they carry with them.

friendship ■ An intimate, reciprocated positive relationship between two people.

Friendships

> Kay and Sarah are my *best* friends—we talk and share secret things … and we sometimes do things with Jo and Kerry and Sue. Then there's all the rest of the girls— some are nice. But the boys—yuk!
>
> (Annie, aged 8, cited by Dunn, personal communication, 1999)

Annie, the speaker above, clearly differentiates her close friends from other children she knows and with whom she may also interact. Researchers generally agree that friends are people who like to spend time together and feel affection for one another. In addition, as noted by Bill Bukowski from Concordia University and his colleagues, friends' interactions are characterized by *reciprocities;* that is, friends have mutual regard for one another, exhibit give-and-take in their behaviour (such as cooperation and negotiation), and benefit in comparable ways from their social exchanges (Bukowski, Newcomb, & Hartup, 1996). In brief, a **friendship** is an intimate, reciprocated positive relationship between two people. As we will discuss next, the degree to which the conditions of friendship become evident in peer interactions increases with age during childhood.

Early Peer Interactions and Friendships

Very young children usually cannot verbally indicate who they like, so researchers must make inferences about children's friendships from observing their behaviour with peers. In doing so, researchers have focused particularly on such issues as the age at which friendships first develop, the nature of early friendships, and age-related changes in friendships.

Do Very Young Children Have Friends?

Some investigators have argued that children can have friends by or before the age of 2 (C. Howes, 1996). Consider the following example:

> Anna and Suzanne are not yet 2 years old. Their mothers became acquainted during their pregnancies and from their earliest weeks of life the little girls have visited each other's houses. When the girls were 5 months old they were enrolled in the same child-care center. They now are frequent play partners, and sometimes insist that their naptime cots be placed side by side. Their greetings and play are often marked by shared smiles. Anna and Suzanne's parents and teachers identify them as friends.
>
> (C. Howes, 1996, p. 66)

Even 12- to 18-month-olds seem to select and prefer some children over others, touching them, smiling at them, and engaging in positive interactions with them

ELIZABETH CREWS

Some researchers believe that friendships may begin at 2 years of age or even earlier.

more than they do with other peers (D. F. Hay, Caplan, & Nash, 2009; C. Howes, 1983; Shin, 2010). In addition, when a preferred peer shows distress, toddlers are three times more likely to respond by offering comfort or by alerting an adult than they are when a non-preferred peer is upset (C. Howes & Farver, 1987). University of Waterloo psychologist Hildy Ross and University of Guelph psychologist Susan Lollis (1989) note that starting at around 20 months of age, children increasingly initiate more interactions with some children than with others and contribute more when playing games with those children. By age 3 or 4, children can make and maintain friendships with peers (Dunn, 2004), and most have at least one friendship (Quinn & Hennessy, 2010). By age 3 to 7 years, it is not uncommon for children to have "best friends" who retain that status over at least several months' time (Sebanc et al., 2007). As an example, one recent study showed that 40% of kindergartners in Quebec maintained at least one friendship from the early fall to the springtime (Proulx & Poulin, 2013).

Differences in Young Children's Interactions with Friends and Non-Friends

By the age of 2, children begin to develop several skills that allow greater complexity in their social interactions, such as imitating peers' and other people's social behaviour (Seehagen & Herbert, 2011), engaging in cooperative problem solving, and trading roles during play (C. A. Brownell, Ramani, & Zerwas, 2006; C. Howes, 1996; C. Howes & Matheson, 1992). These more complex skills tend to be in greater evidence in the play of friends than of non-friends (acquaintances) (Werebe & Baudonnière, 1991).

Especially with friends, cooperation and coordination in children's interactions continue to increase substantially from the toddler to the preschool years (C. Howes & Phillipsen, 1998). This is especially evident in shared pretend play (Dunn, 2004), which occurs more often among friends than among non-friends (C. Howes & Unger, 1989). As discussed in Chapter 7, pretend play involves symbolic actions that must be mutually understood by the play partners, as in the following example:

> Johnny, 30 months, joins his friend Kevin who is pretending to go on a picnic. Johnny, on instruction from 3-year-old Kevin, fills the car with gas, "drives" the car, then gets the food out, pretends to eat it, saying he doesn't like it! Both boys pretend to spit out the food, saying "yuk!," laughing. …
>
> (Dunn, personal communication, 1999)

Pretend play may occur more often among friends because friends' experiences with one another allow them to trust that their partner will work to interpret and share the meaning of symbolic actions (C. Howes, 1996). The degree to which preschoolers engage in, and are competent at, such pretend play is related to their prosocial behaviours such as kindness, cooperation, sharing, and empathy (Spivak & Howes, 2011).

Although the rate of cooperation and positive interactions among young friends is higher than among non-friends, so is the rate of conflict. Preschool friends quarrel as much or more with one another as do non-friends and also more often express hostility by means of assaults, threats, and refusing requests (Fabes et al., 1996; D. C. French et al., 2005; Hartup et al., 1988). The higher rate of conflict for friends is likely due, in part, to the greater amount of time friends spend with one another.

Although preschool friends are more likely than non-friends to fight, they also are more likely to resolve conflicts in controlled ways, such as by negotiating, asserting themselves non-aggressively, acquiescing, or simply ceasing the activity that is causing the conflict (Fabes et al., 1996; Hartup et al., 1988) (see Table 13.1). Moreover, friends are more likely than non-friends to resolve conflicts in ways that result in equal outcomes rather than in one child's winning and another's losing. Thus, after a conflict, friends are more likely than non-friends to resume their interactions and to have positive feelings for one another.

Developmental Changes in Friendship

In the school years, many of the patterns apparent in the interactions among preschool-age friends and non-friends persist and become more sharply defined. As earlier, friends, in comparison with non-friends, communicate more and better with one another and cooperate and work together more effectively (Hartup, 1996). They also fight more often—but again, they are also more likely to negotiate their way out of the conflict (Laursen, Finkelstein, & Betts, 2001). In addition, they now have the maturity to take responsibility for the conflict and to give reasons for their disagreement, increasing the likelihood of their maintaining the friendship (Fonzi et al., 1997; Hartup et al., 1993; Whitesell & Harter, 1996).

Although children's friendships remain similar in many aspects as the children grow older, they do change in one important dimension: the level and importance of intimacy. The change is reflected both in the nature of friends' interactions with one another and in the way children conceive of friendship. Between ages 6 and 8, for example, children define friendship primarily on the basis of actual activities with their peers and tend to define "best" friends as peers with whom they play all the time and share everything (Gummerum & Keller, 2008; Youniss, 1980). At this age, children also tend to view friends in terms of rewards and costs (Bigelow, 1977). In this respect, friends tend to be close by, have interesting toys, and have similar expectations about play activities. Non-friends tend to be uninteresting or difficult to get along with. Thus, in the early school years, children's views of friendship are instrumental and concrete (Rubin, Bukowski, & Parker, 2006) (see Table 13.2).

In contrast, between the early school years and adolescence, children in both Asian and Western countries increasingly define their friendships in terms of deeper characteristics (Furman & Buhrmester, 1992; Gummerum & Keller, 2008). At about 9 years of age, children seem to become more sensitive to the needs of others and to the inequalities among people. Children define friends in terms of taking care of one another's physical and material needs, providing general assistance and help with school work, reducing loneliness and the sense of being excluded, and sharing feelings. The following descriptions of friends are typical:

female, 10: If you're hurt, they come over and visit.

male, 9: Help someone out. If the person is stuck, show them the answer but tell them why it's the answer.

male, 9: You're lonely and your friend on a bike joins you. You feel a lot better because he joined you.

(Youniss, 1980, pp. 177–178)

TABLE 13.1

Strategies Chosen by Schoolchildren When a Peer Says Something Mean to, or About, Them

	Percent of Children Selecting Each Strategy When the Peer Is:	
	Their Best Friend	Classmate (Neither a Friend nor Enemy)
Talk to friend/classmate	43%	19%
Think about what to do	24%	14%
Hit, kick, yell	9%	10%
Hold anger in	8%	5%
Quit thinking about it	6%	20%
Get away from what happened	4%	17%
Talk to someone else about it	4%	11%
Do nothing	1%	4%

Source: Adapted from Whitesell & Harter, 1996

TABLE 13.2

Dimensions on Which Elementary School Children Often Evaluate Their Friendships

Validation and Caring

Makes me feel good about my ideas.

Tells me I am good at things.

Conflict Resolution

Make up easily when we have a fight.

Talk about how to get over being mad at each other.

Conflict and Betrayal

Argue a lot.

Doesn't listen to me.

Help and Guidance

Help each other with school work a lot.

Loan each other things all the time.

Companionship and Recreation

Always sit together at lunch.

Do fun things together a lot.

Intimate Exchange

Always tell each other our problems.

Tell each other secrets.

Source: Adapted from Parker & Asher, 1993

When children are about 10 years old, loyalty, mutual understanding, and self-disclosure become important components of children's conceptions of friendship (Bigelow, 1977). In addition, both preadolescents and adolescents emphasize cooperative reciprocity (doing the same things for one another), equality, and trust between friends (Youniss, 1980). The following descriptions are indicative of how children in this age range view their friends:

> *female, 10:* Somebody you can keep your secrets with together. Two people who are really good to each other.
>
> *male, 12:* A person you can trust and confide in. Tell them what you feel and you can be yourself with them.
>
> *female, 13:* They'll understand your problems. They won't always be the boss. Sometimes they'll let you decide; they'll take turns. If you did something wrong, they'll share the responsibility.
>
> *male, 14:* They have something in common. You hang around with him. … We're more or less the same; the same personalities.

(Youniss, 1980, pp. 180–182)

One study of Canadian children aged 8 to 18 found that children of all ages characterized friends as people "to have fun with" and people who make the necessary efforts to keep the friendship going. But older children, compared to younger children, were more likely to focus on the characteristics of their friend, such as similarity in attitudes/interests, and more abstract dimensions of friendship such as acceptance, intimacy, trust, genuineness, and loyalty (McDoughall & Hymel, 2007).

More than younger children, adolescents use friendship as a context for self-exploration and working out personal problems (Gottman & Mettetal, 1986). Thus, friendships become an increasing source of intimacy and disclosure with age, as well as a source of honest feedback. These changes may explain why adolescents perceive the quality of their friendships as improving from middle to late adolescence and why they value them so highly (Way & Greene, 2006).

What accounts for the various age-related changes that occur in children's friendships, particularly with regard to their concept of friendship? Some researchers have argued that the changes in children's thinking about friendship are qualitative, or *discontinuous*. For example, Selman (1980) suggested that changes in children's reasoning about friendships are a consequence of age-related qualitative changes in their ability to take others' perspectives (see Chapter 9, pages 358–359). In the view of Selman, as well as of Piaget and others, young children have limited awareness that others may feel or think about things differently than they themselves do. Consequently, their thinking about friendships is limited in the degree to which they consider issues beyond their own needs. As children begin to understand others' thoughts and feelings, they realize that friendships involve consideration of both parties' needs so that the relationship is mutually satisfying.

Other researchers argue that the age-related changes in children's conceptions of friendships reflect differences in how children think and express their ideas rather than age-related differences in the basic way they view friendships. Hartup and Stevens (1997) maintain that children of all ages consider their friendships "to be marked by reciprocity and mutuality—the giving and taking, and returning in kind or degree" (p. 356). What differs with age is merely the complexity with which children view friendship and describe its dimensions. Nonetheless, these differences likely have important effects on children's behaviour with friends and on their reactions to friends' behaviour. For example, because 6th graders are more

During the elementary school years, the willingness to lend support and help, including with homework, becomes an important dimension of friendship.

Adolescent friends are more likely to share confidences with one another than are younger friends.

likely than 2nd graders to report that intimacy and support are important features of friendships (Furman & Bierman, 1984), they are more likely to evaluate their own and their friends' behaviours in terms of these dimensions.

The Functions of Friendships

As is clear from their statements about the meaning of friendships, having friends provides numerous potential benefits for children. The most important of these, noted by Piaget, Vygotsky, and others, are emotional support and the validation of one's own thoughts, feelings, and worth, as well as opportunities for the development of important social and cognitive skills.

Support and Validation

Friends can provide a source of emotional support and security, even at an early age. Consider the following fantasy play interaction between Eric and Naomi, two 4-year-olds who have been best friends for some time. In the course of their play, Eric expresses his ongoing fear that other children do not like him and think he is stupid:

> *Eric:* I'm the skeleton! Whoa! [screams] A skeleton, everyone! A skeleton!
> *Naomi:* I'm our friend, the dinosaur.
> *Eric:* Oh, hi Dinosaur. [subdued] You know, no one likes me.
> *Naomi:* [reassuringly] But I like you. I'm your friend.
> *Eric:* But none of my other friends like me. They don't like my new suit. They don't
> like my skeleton suit. It's really just me. They think I'm a dumb-dumb.
> *Naomi:* I know what. He's a good skeleton.
> *Eric:* [yelling] I am not a dumb-dumb!
> *Naomi:* I'm not calling you a dumb-dumb. I'm calling you a friendly skeleton.

(Parker & Gottman, 1989, p. 95)

In this fantasy play situation, Naomi clearly served as a source of support and validation for Eric. When he expressed concern that others do not like him, she reassured him that she does. And when he confessed that the other children think he, not the skeleton, is dumb, she shifted the focus from him to the fantasy skeleton character, praising the skeleton character to make Eric feel competent ("He's a good skeleton") (Gottman, 1986).

Friends also can provide support when a child feels lonely. School-age children with best friends and with intimate, supportive friendships experience less loneliness compared with children who do not have a best friend or whose friends are less caring and intimate (Asher & Paquette, 2003; Erdley et al., 2001; Kingery, Erdley, & Marshall, 2011). Correspondingly, chronic friendlessness predicts internalizing problems such as depression and social withdrawal, which often cause or accompany loneliness (Engle, McElwain, & Lasky, 2011; Ladd & Troop-Gordon, 2003; Palmen et al., 2011). One study of more than 500 children from Quebec found that loneliness was strongly related to depressive symptoms and peer rejection (S. Pedersen et al., 2007).

The support of friends can be particularly important during difficult periods of transition that involve peers. For example, young children have more positive initial attitudes toward school if they begin school with a large number of established friends as classmates (Ladd & Coleman, 1997; Ladd & Kochenderfer, 1996). In part, this may be because the presence of established friends in the early weeks of school reduces the strangeness of the new environment. Similarly, as 6th graders move into junior high, they are more likely to increase their levels of sociability and leadership if they have stable, high-quality, intimate friendships during this period (Berndt, Hawkins, & Jiao, 1999).

Friendships may also serve as a buffer against unpleasant experiences, such as being yelled at by the teacher, being excluded or victimized by peers (Bukowski, Laursen, & Hoza, 2010; Ladd, Kochenderfer, & Coleman, 1996; Waldrip, Malcolm, & Jensen-Campbell, 2008), or being socially isolated (i.e., having low levels of involvement with peers more generally) (Laursen et al., 2007). In one study that demonstrated this effect, 5th and 6th graders from the greater Montreal area reported on their negative experiences over a 4-day period, indicating shortly after each such experience how they felt about themselves and whether a best friend had been present during each experience. The researchers also recorded the children's cortisol levels multiple times each day, as a measure of the children's stress reactions. The study showed that when a best friend was not present, the more negative that children's everyday experiences were, the greater the increase in their cortisol levels and the greater the decline in their sense of self-worth following each experience. In contrast, when a best friend was present, there was less change in cortisol responding and in the child's self-worth due to negative experiences (R. E. Adams, Santo, & Bukowski, 2011).

This buffering effect of friends is especially clear for victimized children. Victimized children fare better if they have a number of reciprocated friendships (Hodges et al., 1999; D. Schwartz et al., 1999), if their friends are capable of defending them and are liked by peers (Hodges et al., 1997), and if their friendships are of high quality—that is, friends are perceived as providing intimacy, security, and help when needed (Kawabata, Crick, & Hamaguchi, 2010; M. E. Schmidt & Bagwell, 2007).

As noted previously, the degree to which friends provide caring and support generally increases from childhood into adolescence (De Goede, Branje, & Meeus, 2009). Indeed, around age 16, adolescents, especially girls, report that friends are more important confidantes and providers of support than their parents are (Bokhorst, Sumter, & Westenberg, 2010; Furman & Buhrmester, 1992; Helsen, Vollebergh, & Meeus, 2000; Hunter & Youniss, 1982) (Figure 13.1).

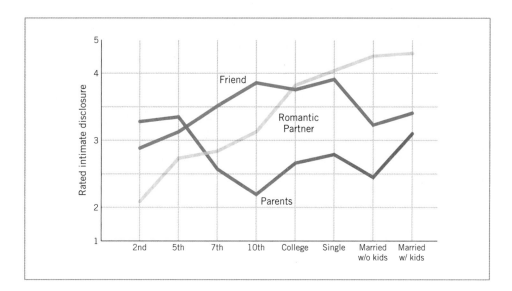

FIGURE 13.1 **Age trends in reports of self-disclosure to parents and peers** By early adolescence, children disclose more to friends than to their parents. Young adults continue to disclose much more to friends than to their parents, but by college age they disclose most to romantic partners. (Adapted from Burmeister, 1996)

The Development of Social and Cognitive Skills

Friendships provide a context for the development of social skills and knowledge that children need in order to form positive relationships with other people. As discussed earlier, young children seem to first develop more complex play in interactions with friends; and throughout childhood, cooperation, negotiation, and the like are all more common among friends than among non-friends. In addition, young children who discuss emotions with their friends and interact with them in positive ways develop a better understanding of others' mental and emotional states than do children whose peer relationships are less close (C. Hughes & Dunn, 1998; Maguire & Dunn, 1997). These skills can be brought to bear when helping their friends. In a study of 3rd to 9th graders over the course of the school year, those with high-quality friendships improved in the quality of their reported strategies for helping friends deal with social stressors. For instance, they reported becoming more likely to be emotionally engaged in talking with their friend about a problem and less likely to act as though the problem did not exist (Glick & Rose, 2011).

Friendship provides other avenues to social and cognitive development. Through interaction with friends, for example, children learn about peer norms, including how, why, and when to display or control the expression of emotions and other behaviours (Gottman, 1986; McDonald et al., 2007). As Piaget pointed out, friends are more likely than non-friends to criticize and elaborate on one another's ideas and to expand and clarify their own ideas (Azmitia & Montgomery, 1993; J. Nelson & Aboud, 1985).

This kind of openness promotes cognitive skills and enhances performance on creative tasks (Miell & MacDonald, 2000; Rubin et al., 2006). One demonstration of this was provided by a study in which teams of 10-year-olds, half of them made up of friends and the other half made up of non-friends, were assigned to write a story about rainforests. The teams consisting of friends engaged in more constructive conversations (e.g., they posed alternative approaches and provided elaborations more frequently) and were more focused on the task than were teams of non-friends. In addition, the stories written by friends were of higher quality than those written by non-friends (Hartup, 1996).

Interactions with friends provide children with opportunities to get constructive feedback regarding their behaviour and ideas.

Gender Differences in the Functions of Friendships

As children grow older, gender differences emerge in what girls and boys feel they want and get from their friendships. Girls are more likely than boys to desire closeness and dependency in friendships, and to worry about abandonment, loneliness, hurting others, peers' evaluations, and loss of relationships if they express anger (A. J. Rose & Rudolph, 2006). By late elementary school, girls, compared with boys, feel that their friendships are more intimate and provide more validation, caring, help, and guidance (Bauminger et al., 2008; A. J. Rose & Rudolph, 2006; Zarbatany, McDougall, & Hymel, 2000). For instance, girls are more likely than boys to report that they rely on their friends for advice or help with homework, that they and their friends share confidences and stick up for one another, and that their friends tell them that they are good at things and make them feel special.

Probably as a consequence of this intimacy, girls also report getting more upset than do boys when friends betray them, are unreliable, or do not provide support and help (MacEvoy & Asher, 2012). Girls also report more friendship-related stress, such as when a friend breaks off a friendship or reveals their secrets or problems to other friends, and greater stress from dealing emotionally with stressors that their friends experience (A. J. Rose & Rudolph, 2006). Ironically, the very intimacy of girls' close friendships may make them more fragile, and therefore of shorter duration, than those of boys (Benenson & Christakos, 2003; A. Chan & Poulin, 2007; C. L. Hardy, Bukowski, & Sippola, 2002).

As discussed in Chapter 10 (page 396), girls are also more likely than boys to *co-ruminate* with their close friends, that is, to extensively discuss problems and negative thoughts and feelings (R. L. Smith & Rose, 2011). And compared with their male counterparts, girls who are socially anxious or depressed seem more susceptible to the anxiety or depression of their friends (Giletta et al., 2011; M. H. van Zalk et al., 2010; N. van Zalk et al., 2011). Unfortunately, while providing support, a co-ruminating anxious or depressed friend may also reinforce the other friend's anxiety or depression, especially in young adolescent girls (A. J. Rose, Carlson, & Waller, 2007; Schwartz-Mette & Rose, 2012).

Girls and boys are less likely to differ in the amount of conflict they experience in their best friendships (A. J. Rose & Rudolph, 2006). Boys' and girls' friendships also do not differ much in terms of the recreational opportunities they provide (e.g., doing things together, going to one another's house) (Parker & Asher, 1993), although they often differ in the time spent together in various activities (e.g., sports versus shopping) (A. J. Rose & Rudolph, 2006). For example, Canadian preadolescent girls tend to focus more heavily on socializing with their best friends than do preadolescent boys (Zarbatany et al., 2000).

Effects of Friendships on Psychological Functioning and Behaviour over Time

Since friendships fill important needs for children, it might be expected that having friends enhances children's social and emotional health. In fact, having close, reciprocated friendships in elementary school has been linked to a variety of positive psychological and behavioural outcomes for children, not only during the school years but also years later in early adulthood. However, there also may be costs to having friends, if the friends engage in or encourage negative behaviours rather than positive ones (Simpkins, Eccles, & Becnel, 2008).

The Possible Long-Term Benefits of Having Friends

Longitudinal research provides the best data concerning the possible long-term benefits of having friends in elementary school. Since this research is generally correlational, however, it is difficult to determine if having friends influences long-term outcomes such as psychological adjustment, or if characteristics of the child (such as psychological adjustment) affect whether the child has friends (Klima & Repetti, 2008).

Typical of this research is a study that examined the relation between the quality of friendship and the development of aggression. In this study, researchers followed a large group of Quebec children from kindergarten to Grade 2 and found that children with high-quality friendships became less physically aggressive over time (Salvas et al., 2011). In another, broader, longitudinal study, researchers looked at children when they were 5th graders and when they were young adults. They found that, compared with their peers who did not have **reciprocated best friendships**, or friendships in which two children view each other as best or close friends, 5th graders who did have reciprocated best friendships were viewed by classmates as more mature and competent, less aggressive, and more socially prominent (e.g., they were liked by everyone or were picked for such positions as class president or team captain). At approximately age 23, those individuals who had reciprocated best friendships in Grade 5 reported higher levels of doing well in college and in their family and social life than did individuals who did not have reciprocated best friendships. They also reported higher levels of self-esteem, fewer problems with the law, and less psychopathology (e.g., depression) (Bagwell, Newcomb, & Bukowski, 1998). Thus, having a reciprocated best friendship in preadolescence relates not only to positive social outcomes in middle childhood but also to self-perceived competence and adjustment in adulthood.

The Possible Costs of Friendships

Although friendships are usually associated with positive outcomes, sometimes they are not. Friends who have behavioural problems may exert a detrimental influence, contributing to the likelihood of a child's or adolescent's engaging in violence, drug use, or other negative behaviours. And, as previously noted, friends who are depressed may foster depression in their close friends, in part through a contagion effect (Dishion & Tipsord, 2011).

Aggression and disruptiveness In the elementary school years and early adolescence, children who have antisocial and aggressive friends tend to exhibit antisocial, delinquent, and aggressive tendencies themselves, even across time (Brendgen, Vitaro, & Bukowski, 2000; J. Snyder et al., 2008). However, the research in this area is correlational, so it is difficult to know to what degree this pattern reflects *socialization* or *individual selection*. With regard to individual selection, aggressive and disruptive children may gravitate toward peers who are similar to themselves in temperament, preferred activities, or attitudes, thereby taking an active role in creating their own peer group (Knecht et al., 2010; Mrug, Hoza, & Bukowski, 2004). A longitudinal study of children in northwestern Quebec demonstrated that friends affect one another's disruptive and deviant behaviour (Vitaro, Pedersen, & Brendgen, 2007). Through their talk and behaviour, youths who are antisocial may socialize and reinforce aggression and deviance in one another by making these behaviours seem acceptable (Dishion & Tipsord, 2011; Piehler & Dishion, 2007). This pattern is more likely to occur with those adolescents who are easily

reciprocated best friendship ■
A friendship in which two children view each other as best or close friends.

influenced by peers holding high status in the peer group (Prinstein, Bechwald, & Cohen, 2011) or by friends whose peer-group status is higher than their own (Laursen et al., 2012).

The factors accounting for the association between friends' antisocial behaviour may change with age. One longitudinal study found that both selection and socialization processes were in play in mid-adolescence, but that from ages 16 to 20, antisocial behaviour was reinforced only through socialization by friends. After age 20, an age past which youths become more resistant to peer influence, there was little evidence of either process occurring (Monahan, Steinberg, & Cauffman, 2009).

Alcohol and substance abuse As in the case of aggression, adolescents who abuse alcohol or drugs tend to have friends who do so also (Jaccard, Blanton, & Dodge, 2005; Scholte et al., 2008; Urberg, Değirmencioğlu, & Pilgrim, 1997). And again, as in the case of aggression, it is not clear if friends' substance abuse is a cause or merely a correlate of adolescents' substance abuse, or if the relation between the two is bidirectional.

On the one hand, there is some evidence that adolescents tend to select friends who are similar to themselves in terms of drinking and the use of drugs (Knecht et al., 2011). For example, one recent study conducted in Quebec showed that adolescents who used cigarettes, alcohol, and marijuana were more likely to select new friends who also used these substances (Poulin et al., 2011). The tendency to select substance-using friends may be especially true for those youths who are highly susceptible to peer pressure (Schulenberg et al., 1999). However, there is also evidence that peer socialization influences drug and alcohol use (Branstetter, Low, & Fuman, 2011). For example, adolescents who start drinking or smoking tend to have a close friend who has been using alcohol or tobacco (Selfhout, Branje, & Meeus, 2008; Urberg et al., 1997). Youths who are highly susceptible to the influence of their close friends seem particularly vulnerable to any pressure from them to use drugs and alcohol (Allen, Porter, & McFarland, 2006), and, as in the case of aggression, this is especially the case if those friends have high status in the peer group (Allen et al., 2012). There is also evidence that adolescents' use of alcohol and drugs and their friend's alcohol and substance use mutually reinforce each other, often resulting in an escalation of use (Bray et al., 2003; Popp et al., 2008; Poulin et al., 2011).

Yet another factor in the association between adolescents' abuse of drugs and alcohol and that of their friends is their genetic makeup. Youths with similar genetically based temperamental characteristics such as risk taking may be drawn both to one another and to alcohol or drugs (Dick et al., 2007; J. Hill et al., 2008). Thus, friends' alcohol and drug abuse may be correlated because of their similarity in genetically based characteristics as well as in their socialization experiences, although the effect of a group of friends on youths' drinking is not due solely to genetics (Cruz, Emery, & Turkheimer, 2012).

Peers can encourage youths to use alcohol, but it is also the case that youths who are prone to drinking may seek out peers who are similarly inclined.

OCEAN / CORBIS

The extent to which friends' use of drugs and alcohol may put adolescents at risk for use themselves seems to depend, in part, on the nature of the child–parent relationship. An adolescent with a substance-using close friend is at risk primarily if the adolescent's parents are cold, detached, and uninclined to monitor and supervise the adolescent's activities (Kiesner, Poulin, & Dishion, 2010; Mounts & Steinberg, 1995; Pilgrim et al., 1999). If the adolescent's parents are authoritative in their parenting—monitoring their child's behaviour and setting firm limits, but also being warm and receptive to the adolescent's viewpoint (see Chapter 12, pages 473–475)—the adolescent is more likely to be protected against peer pressure to use drugs (Mounts, 2002).

Children's Choice of Friends

What factors influence children's choices of friends? As noted earlier, for young children, proximity is an obvious key factor. Preschoolers tend to become friends with peers who are nearby physically, as neighbours or playgroup members. (As Box 13.1 points out, young children's access to peers can vary widely by culture.) Although proximity becomes less important with age, it continues to play a role in individuals' choices of friends in adolescence (Clarke-McLean, 1996; Dishion, Andrews, & Crosby, 1995). This is partly because one form of proximity is involvement in similar activities at school (e.g., sports, academic activities, arts), which appears to promote the development of new friendships. In one study, when two adolescents participated in the same activity, they were on average 2.3 times more likely to be friends than were adolescents who did not participate in the same activity (Schaefer et al., 2011).

In most industrialized countries, similarity in age is also a major factor in friendship, with most children tending to make friends with age-mates (Aboud & Mendelson, 1996; Dishion et al., 1995). In part, this may be due to the fact that in most industrialized societies, children are segregated by age in school: in societies where children do not attend school or otherwise are not segregated by age, they are more likely to develop friendships with children of different ages.

Another powerful factor in friend selection is a child's gender: girls tend to be friends with girls, and boys, with boys (Knecht et al., 2011; C. L. Martin et al., 2013; A. J. Rose & Rudolph, 2006). Cross-gender friendships, though not uncommon, tend to be more fragile (L. Lee, Howes, & Chamberlain, 2007; Maccoby, 2000) (see Chapter 15). The preference for same-gender friends emerges in preschool and continues through childhood (Hartup, 1983). The liking of other-gender peers also increases over the course of childhood and into early adolescence (Poulin & Pedersen, 2007), with other-gender close friendships increasing in frequency from Grade 8 to Grade 11 (Arndorfer & Stormshak, 2008).

To a lesser degree, children tend to be friends with peers of their own racial/ethnic group, although this tendency varies across groups and contexts (Knecht et al., 2011). For instance, a study that examined friendships in French-English integrated primary schools in Montreal demonstrated that most students had similar numbers of friends from each ethnolinguistic group (Aboud & Sankar, 2007). Similarly, in a study of inter-ethnic friendship in Toronto, students in Grades 7 and 8 listed similar numbers of in-group and out-group friends, although there was a tendency for best friends to be from the same ethnic group (A. Smith & Schneider, 2000).

In general, efforts to establish friendships outside one's own racial/ethnic group are less likely to be reciprocated than are efforts within the group (Vaquera & Kao, 2008); and when they are reciprocated, they often are not as long-lasting

BOX 13.1: **individual differences**

CULTURE AND CHILDREN'S PEER EXPERIENCE

Young children's contact with unrelated peers varies considerably around the world. In some communities, such as one in Okinawa, Japan, Beatrice Whiting and Carolyn Edwards (1988) found that children were free to wander in the streets and public areas of town and had extensive contact with peers. In contrast, in some sub-Saharan African societies, children were confined primarily to the family yard and therefore had relatively little contact with peers other than their siblings.

As might be expected, Whiting and Edwards found that children's access to the wider community, including peers, increased with age. However, even when children were aged 6 to 10, there were marked differences in the extent to which their social interactions extended beyond the family. In large measure, these differences were based on parents' attitudes toward childhood peer relationships. For example, in kin-based societies such as Kenya, peer interactions were discouraged:

> Parents feared the inherent potential for competition and conflict; they did not want their children to fight with outsiders and engender spiteful relations or become vulnerable to aggression and sorcery. Moreover, as their children did not attend school,

they had no need for them to easily acquire skills of affiliating, negotiating, and competing with nonfamily agemates.

> (C. P. Edwards, 1992, p. 305)

However, Edwards noted that the situation in Kenya is changing as the economy modernizes and literacy becomes an increasingly valued skill. Parents usually want their children to be educated, and education involves contact with peers. Indeed, in numerous kin-based societies, levels of interaction with peers who are not from the child's family or clan increased dramatically when Westernized schooling was established (Rogoff, 2003; Tietjen, 2006), although in some cases, this contact has been restricted primarily to the school setting.

Cultures differ in terms of the total number of hours that children typically spend with peers. In many cultures, especially in unschooled, nonindustrial populations, boys tend to spend more time with peers than girls do, likely because they are less closely monitored and are allowed greater freedom to be away from home (Larson & Verma, 1999). For example, 6- to 12-year-old Indian boys were found to spend three times as much time with their peers outside their families than girls did (Saraswati & Dutta, 1988).

Among postindustrial schooled populations, European-American, African-American, and European adolescents have been found to spend much more time with peers, especially other-gender peers, than Asian adolescents do (Larson & Verma, 1999). In one study, for example, U.S. adolescents spent 18.4 hours per week with friends outside the classroom, whereas the time their Japanese and Taiwanese counterparts spent in out-of-school peer contact was, respectively, 12.4 and 8.8 hours per week (Fuligni & Stevenson, 1995). Moreover, East Asians tended to spend more of their time with peers studying than did U.S. youths, who were more inclined to engage in leisure activities with peers. Similar differences were evident in time spent dating, with Japanese and Taiwanese 11th graders devoting roughly an hour a week to dating, compared with 4.7 hours per week for U.S. youths.

The cross-cultural differences in the amount of peer interaction adolescents engage in is likely due, at least in part, to cultural differences in values about what is important. A recent study of adolescents in 11 countries found that the greater the importance of traditional family values—defined as high feelings of family obligations, acceptance of children's duty to be obedient, and an orientation toward the

(L. Lee et al., 2007). A study of junior high students in Montreal and Toronto demonstrated that 70% of co-ethnic friendships lasted for a 6-month testing interval versus 57% of inter-ethnic friendships (Schneider, Dixon, & Udvari, 2007). Those youths with cross-racial/ethnic friendships tend to be leaders and relatively inclusive in their social relationships (Kawabata & Crick, 2008), as well as socially competent and high in self-esteem (N. Eisenberg, Valiente, et al., 2009; Fletcher, Rollins, & Nickerson, 2004; Kawabata & Crick, 2011). For majority-group children, having cross-ethnic friendships has been associated with positive attitudes toward people in other groups in the future (Feddes, Noack, & Rutland, 2009).

Beyond these basic factors, a key determinant of liking and friendship is similarity of interests and behaviour. By age 7, children tend to like peers who are similar to themselves in the cognitive maturity of their play (Rubin et al., 1994) and in the level of their aggressive behaviour (Poulin et al., 1997). Between Grade 4

In some groups in Kenya, children are discouraged from forming relationships with peers who are not related. Thus, children interact primarily with siblings and adult relatives.

the degree to which parents expect their children to develop such social skills as negotiating, taking the initiative, and standing up for their rights with peers. European-American and European-Australian mothers expect their children to develop such skills earlier than do Japanese mothers (Hess et al., 1980) and Lebanese-Australian mothers (Goodnow et al., 1984). This is probably because the European-American and European-Australian mothers are influenced by their respective culture's emphasis on personal autonomy and independence and believe that the aforementioned skills are important for success.

Correspondingly, Japanese mothers and Australian mothers of Lebanese heritage are likely to be similarly influenced by their respective cultures' emphasis on the interdependence of family members; therefore, they may be more likely to accept or even encourage dependency in young children (F. A. Johnson, 1993; M. I. White & LeVine, 1986). Thus, differences in parents' expectations regarding what social skills their children will develop and by what age likely influence what parents teach their children about social interactions with peers.

family instead of a focus on autonomy and individualism—the less that peer acceptance was related to adolescents' life satisfaction (Schwarz et al., 2012). Thus, in cultures with traditional family values, the peer group appears less important, and adolescents' well-being is less related to how well liked they are by peers.

Adults' expectations in regard to the nature of children's interactions with peers also tend to differ across cultures. For instance, there are cultural differences in

and Grade 8, friends are more similar than non-friends in their cooperativeness, antisocial behaviour, acceptance by peers, and shyness (X. Chen, Cen, et al., 2005; Haselager et al., 1998; A. J. Rose, Swenson, & Carlson, 2004). They are also more similar in their level of academic motivation and self-perceptions of competence (Altermatt & Pomerantz, 2003). Much the same pattern holds for adolescents (Dijkstra, Cillessen, & Borch, 2012; Gavin & Furman, 1996; Rubin et al., 2006), with the added dimensions that friends also tend to share similar levels of negative emotions such as distress and depression (Haselager et al., 1998; Hogue & Steinberg, 1995) and are similar in their tendency to attribute hostile intentions to others (Halligan & Philips, 2010).

Thus, birds of a feather do tend to flock together. The fact that friends tend to be similar on a number of dimensions underscores the difficulty of knowing whether friends actually affect one another's behaviour or whether children simply seek out peers who think, act, and feel as they do.

review:

Peers, especially friends, provide intimacy, support, and rich opportunities for the development of play and for the exchange of ideas. Children engage in more complex and cooperative play, and in more conflict, with friends than with non-friends, and they tend to resolve conflicts with friends in more appropriate ways. With age, the dimensions of children's friendships change somewhat. Whereas young children define friendship primarily on the basis of actual activities with their peers and on the rewards and costs involved, older children increasingly rely on their friends to provide a context for self-disclosure, intimacy, self-exploration, and problem solving. As was suggested by Piaget and Vygotsky, friends also provide opportunities for the development of important social and cognitive skills. However, friends can have negative effects on children if they engage in problematic behaviours such as aggression or substance abuse.

Children tend to become friends with peers who are similar in age, sex, race, and social behaviour. This makes it especially difficult to distinguish between characteristics that children bring to friendships and the effects of friends on one another.

Peers in Groups

Most children usually have one or a few very close friends and some less close additional friends with whom they spend time and share activities. These groups tend to exist within a larger social network of peers that hangs together loosely. Developmentalists have been especially interested in how these peer groups emerge and change with age and how they affect the development of their members.

The Nature of Young Children's Groups

When in a setting with a number of their peers, very young children, including toddlers, sometimes interact in small groups. One striking feature of these first peer groups is the early emergence of status patterns within them, with some children being more dominant and central to group activities than are others (Rubin et al., 2006). By the time children are preschool age, there is a clear dominance hierarchy among the members of a peer group. Certain children are likely to prevail over other group members when there is conflict, and there is a consistent pattern of winners and losers in physical confrontations.

As we will discuss shortly, by middle childhood, status in the peer groups involves much more than dominance, and children become very concerned about their peer-group standing. Before examining peer status, however, we need to consider the nature of social groups in middle childhood and early adolescence.

Cliques and Social Networks in Middle Childhood and Early Adolescence

Starting in middle childhood, most children are part of a clique. **Cliques** are friendship groups that children voluntarily form or join themselves. In middle childhood, clique members are usually of the same sex and race and typically number between 3 and 10 (X. Chen, Chang, & He, 2003; Kwon, Lease, & Hoffman, 2012; Neal, 2010; Rubin et al., 2006). Boys' groups tend to be larger than those of girls (Benenson, Morganstein, & Roy, 1998), although this difference decreases with age (Neal, 2010). By age 11, many of children's social interactions—from

cliques ■ Friendship groups that children voluntarily form or join themselves.

gatherings in the school lunchroom to outings at the mall—occur within the clique (Crockett, Losoff, & Peterson, 1984). Although friends tend to be members of the same clique, many members of a clique do not view one another as close friends (Cairns et al., 1995).

A key feature that underlies cliques and binds their members together is the similarities the members share. Like friends, members of cliques tend to be similar in their degree of academic motivation (Kindermann, 2007; Kiuru et al., 2009); in their aggressiveness and bullying; and in their shyness, attractiveness, popularity, and adherence to conventional values such as politeness and cooperativeness (Espelage, Holt, & Henkel, 2003; Kiesner, Poulin, & Nicotra, 2003; Leung, 1996; Salmivalli & Voeten, 2004; Witvliet et al., 2010). Not only do like individuals tend to group together in cliques, but membership in a clique also seems to increase the likelihood that children will exhibit behaviours similar to those of other group members (Espelage et al., 2003).

Despite the social glue of similarity, the membership of cliques tends to be relatively unstable (Cairns et al., 1995). A study of 4th and 5th graders, for example, found the turnover rate of cliques to be about 50% over 8 months (Kindermann, 1993); and in a study of 6th graders, only about 60% of the members of cliques maintained their group ties over the school year (Kindermann, 2007). The degree to which cliques remain stable appears to depend in large part on whether children are assigned to the same classroom from one year to the next (Neckerman, 1996).

In contrast to the tendency of dominant children to be the central figures in young children's groups, during the school years, girls and boys who are central to the peer group are likely to be popular, athletic, cooperative, seen as leaders, and studious relative to other peers (Farmer & Rodkin, 1996). However, especially in the case of boys, and more especially in the case of aggressive groups of youths, the central figures are sometimes domineering, aggressive, and viewed by peers as "tough" or "cool" (Estell et al., 2002; Rodkin et al., 2006).

Cliques in middle childhood serve a variety of functions: they provide a ready-made pool of peers for socializing; they offer validation of the characteristics that the group members have in common; and, perhaps most important, they provide a sense of belonging. By middle childhood, children are quite concerned about being accepted by peers, and issues of peer status become a common topic of children's conversation and gossip (Gottman, 1986; Kanner et al., 1987; Rubin et al., 1998). Being accepted by others who are similar to oneself in various ways may provide a sense of personal affirmation, as well as of being a welcomed member of the larger peer group.

Cliques and Social Networks in Adolescence

From ages 11 to 18, there is a marked drop in the number of students who belong to a single clique and an increase in the number of adolescents who have ties to many cliques or to students at the margins of cliques (Shrum & Cheek, 1987). In addition, membership in a clique is fairly stable across the school year by Grade 10 (Değirmencioğlu et al., 1998).

Although cliques at younger ages contain mostly same-sex members, by Grade 7, about 10% of cliques contain both boys and girls (Cairns et al., 1995). Thereafter, dyadic dating relationships become increasingly common (Dunphy, 1963; Richards et al., 1998); thus, by high school, cliques of friends often include adolescents of both genders (J. L. Fischer, Sollie, & Morrow, 1986; La Greca, Prinstein, & Fetter, 2001).

MARTIN THOMAS PHOTOGRAPHY / ALAMY

Children and adolescents in cliques tend to spend a lot of time together and often dress similarly.

crowds ■ Groups of adolescents who have similar stereotyped reputations; among North American high school students, typical crowds may include the "brains," "jocks," "loners," "burnouts," "punks," "populars," "elites," "freaks," or "nonconformists."

The dynamics of cliques also vary at different ages in adolescence. During early and middle adolescence, children report placing a high value on being in a popular group and in conforming to the group's norms regarding dress and behaviour. Failure to conform—even something as seemingly trivial as wearing the wrong brand or style of jeans or belonging to an after-school club that is viewed as uncool—can result in being ridiculed or shunned by the group. In comparison with older adolescents, younger adolescents also report more interpersonal conflict with members of their group as well as with members of other groups. In later adolescence, the importance of belonging to a clique and of conforming to its norms appears to decline, which may account for the decline in friction and antagonism within and between groups. With increasing age, adolescents not only are more autonomous but they also tend to look more to individual relationships than to group relationships to fulfill their social needs (Gavin & Furman, 1989; Rubin et al., 1998).

Although older adolescents seem less tied to cliques, they still often belong to crowds. **Crowds** are groups of people who have similar stereotyped reputations. Among high school students, typical crowds may include the "brains," "jocks," "loners," "burnouts," "punks," "populars," "elites," "freaks," "hip-hoppers," "geeks," "normals," and "metalheads" (B. B. Brown & Klute, 2003; Delsing et al., 2007; Doornwaard et al., 2012; La Greca et al., 2001). Which crowd adolescents belong to is often not their choice; crowd "membership" is frequently assigned to the individual by the consensus of the peer group, even though the individual may actually spend little time with other members of that designated crowd (B. B. Brown, 1990).

Being associated with a crowd may enhance or hurt adolescents' reputations and influence how they are treated by peers. Someone labelled a freak, for example, may be ignored or ridiculed by people in groups such as the jocks or the populars (S. S. Horn, 2003). Thus, it is not surprising that youths in high-status groups tend to have higher self-esteem than do youths in less desirable crowds (B. B. Brown, Von Bank, & Steinberg, 2008). Being labelled as part of a particular crowd also may limit adolescents' options with regard to exploring their identities (see Chapter 11). This is because crowd membership may "channel" adolescents into relationships with other members of the same crowd rather than with a diverse group of peers (B. B. Brown, 2004; Eckert, 1989). Adolescents in one crowd, for instance, might be exposed to their peers' acceptance of violence or drug use, whereas members of another crowd may find that their peers value success in academics or sports (La Greca et al., 2001).

An example of the potential consequences of such channelling comes from a large study in Holland that found that adolescents' persistent identification with non-conventional crowds (e.g., hip-hoppers, nonconformists, and metalheads) was associated with more consistent problem behaviours throughout adolescence, whereas adolescents' consistent identification with conventional groups was generally associated with less problematic behaviour (Doornwaard et al., 2012). Thus, experiences in a crowd, like interactions with friends, may help shape youths' behaviour.

A relatively new dimension in which peers interact, one that they have used with increasing frequency in recent years, is cyberspace. As Box 13.2 explains, youths' most frequent form of contact with friends and peers is now digital communication, and the role and effects, both positive and negative, of this venue have become subjects of considerable debate.

Negative Influences of Cliques and Social Networks

Like close friends, members of the clique or the larger peer network can sometimes lead the child or adolescent astray. Preadolescents and adolescents are more likely to goof off in school, smoke, drink, use drugs, or engage in violence, for example, if members of their peer group do so and if they hang out with peers who have been in trouble (Lacourse et al., 2003; Loukas et al., 2008). (Figure 13.2 shows the connection between risky peer group activities and students' mental health.) Adolescents who have an extreme orientation to peers—that is, who are willing to do anything to be liked by peers—are particularly at risk for such behaviours if engaging in them secures peer acceptance (Fuligni et al., 2001). Adolescents who are low in self-regulation are also at increased risk if their peers are antisocial (T. W. Gardner, Dishion, & Connell, 2008).

Perhaps the greatest potential for negative peer-group influence comes with membership in a **gang**, which is a loosely organized group of adolescents or young adults who identify as a group and often engage in illegal activities. Gang members often say that they join or stay in a gang for protection from other gangs. One male gang member explained that "being cool with a gang" meant that "you don't have to worry about nobody jumping you. You don't got to worry about getting beat up" (quoted in Decker, 1996, p. 253).

Gangs also provide members with a sense of belonging and a way to spend their time. Gang members frequently report that the most common gang activities are "hanging out" together and engaging in fairly innocuous behaviours (e.g., drinking beer, playing sports, cruising, looking for girls, and having parties) (Decker & van Winkle, 1996). Nonetheless, adolescents tend to engage in more illegal activities such as delinquency and drug abuse when they are in a gang than when they are not (Alleyne & Wood, 2010; Bjerregaard & Smith, 1993; Craig et al., 2002; Esbensen & Huizinga, 1993) (see Chapter 14, pages 587–588), and the heightened risk for such activities seems to be due to both pre-existing characteristics of the adolescents who join gangs and their experience of being in a gang (Barnes, Beaver, & Miller, 2010; DeLisi et al., 2009).

The potential for peer-group influence to promote problem behaviour is affected by family and cultural influences. As noted in our discussion of friendship, having authoritative, involved parents helps protect adolescents from peer pressure to use drugs, whereas having authoritarian, detached parents increases adolescents' susceptibility to such pressure. Correspondingly, youths who have poor relationships with their mothers may be especially vulnerable to pressure from the peer group (Farrell & White, 1998).

At the same time, the strength of peer influence on problem behaviour can vary by culture and subculture. For example, compared with its strength among European-American adolescents, peer influence on the use of drugs, drinking, aggression, or school misconduct appears to be weaker for Native American youths who live on a reservation and for adolescents in mainland China or Taiwan (C. Chen et al., 1998; Swaim et al., 1993), perhaps because family sanctions against such behaviours play a more important role in these groups. Although the precise reasons for all these differences in peer-group influence are not yet known, it is clear from findings such as these that family and cultural factors can affect the degree to which peers' behaviours are associated with adolescents' problem behaviour.

gang ■ A loosely organized group of adolescents or young adults who identify as a group and often engage in illegal activities.

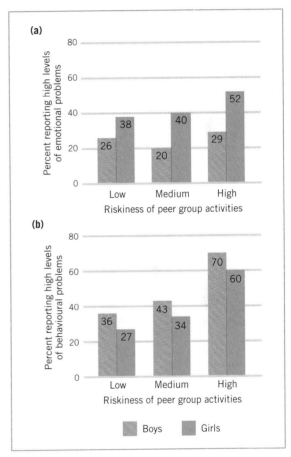

FIGURE 13.2 The relation of risky peer group activities and youths' mental health Girls whose peer groups engaged in higher levels of risky activities, such as smoking, drinking, sexual relationships, and using drugs, experienced more emotional problems (a) and behavioural problems (b). For boys, this relation held true for behavioural problems only. (Adapted from McCuaig Edge & Craig, 2011)

BOX 13.2: a closer look

CYBERSPACE AND CHILDREN'S PEER EXPERIENCE

Social media, instant messaging, texting, and other means of communication that rely on technology are playing an increasing role in peer interactions of children and adolescents. The figure below shows the percentage of Canadian students in Grades 6 to 10 who talk to friends on the phone or send them text or email messages five or more times a week (McCuaig Edge & Craig, 2011). In addition, according to a 2012 Ipsos Reid report, 67% of Canadian teens own their own cellphone, 69% of online teens have joined a social networking site such as Facebook, and, daily, teens' most frequent means of communication are texting (54%) and social networking (48%).

Given youths' tremendous use of digital technologies for their social interactions,

social and behavioural scientists, as well as parents, have expressed considerable concern about the effects that these modes of communication may have on children's and adolescents' social development—and especially on their social relationships. Two major perspectives have guided research on this issue. One view is the rich-get-richer hypothesis, which proposes that those youths who already have good social skills benefit from the Internet and related forms of technology when it comes to developing friendships (Peter, Valkenburg, & Schouten, 2005). In contrast, according to the social-compensation hypothesis, social media may be especially beneficial for lonely, depressed, and socially anxious adolescents. Specifically, because they can take their time thinking about, and revising, what they say and reveal in their messages, these youths may be more likely to make personal disclosures online than offline, which eventually fosters the formation of new friendships.

In support of the rich-get-richer hypothesis, researchers have found that adolescents who are not socially anxious or lonely use the Internet for communication more often

than do adolescents who are (Valkenburg & Peter, 2007b; Van den Eijnden et al., 2008). Moreover, youths who were better adjusted at age 13 to 14 were found to use social networking more at ages 20 to 22 and to exhibit a similarity in their online and offline social competence (e.g., in peer relationships, friendship quality, adjustment) (Mikami et al., 2010). Thus, socially competent people may benefit most from the Internet because they are more likely to interact in appropriate and positive ways when engaged in social networking.

However, consistent with the social-compensation hypothesis, lonely and socially anxious youths seem to prefer online communication over face-to-face communication (Peter et al., 2005; Pierce, 2009). There is also evidence that online communication is used by youths with high levels of depressive symptoms to make friends and express their feelings (J. M. Hwang, Cheong, & Feeley, 2009), and that such use is associated with less depression for youths with low-quality best-friend relationships (Selfhout et al., 2009). Thus, the use of online technology often may provide depressed youths or those with low-quality offline friendships a means of obtaining communication and emotional intimacy with peers.

Another issue is how online communication may affect youths' existing friendships. Some investigators have hypothesized that online communication impairs the quality of existing friendships because it displaces the time that could be spent strengthening the affection and commitment these friendships can provide (Kraut et al., 1998; see

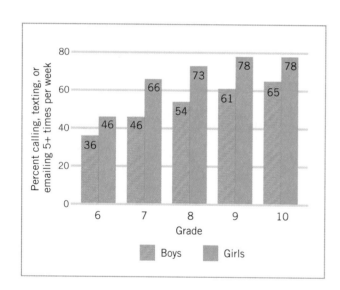

Percent calling, texting, or emailing 5+ times per week, by Grade. Boys: Grade 6 = 36, Grade 7 = 46, Grade 8 = 54, Grade 9 = 61, Grade 10 = 65. Girls: Grade 6 = 46, Grade 7 = 66, Grade 8 = 73, Grade 9 = 78, Grade 10 = 78.

Romantic Relationships with Peers

In Canada, 26% of 12-year-olds and 75% of 16-year-olds report having a current or recent romantic relationship (Connolly & McIsaac, 2009; Connolly et al., 2004). Similar rates have been reported for youth in the United States and Europe (K. Carver, Joyner, & Udry, 2003; Zani, 1991). For adolescents 15 years or younger, two-thirds of these romantic relationships, on average, do not last more than 11 months. For more than half of the older adolescents, they do (Collins, 2003).

Valkenburg & Peter, 2011). Alternatively, other investigators have hypothesized that recent Internet-based communication technologies are designed to facilitate communication among existing friends, allowing them to maintain and enhance the closeness of their relationships (J. A. Bryant, Sanders-Jackson, & Smallwood, 2006; Peter et al., 2005; Valkenburg & Peter, 2007a, 2011; Wang, Jackson, & Zhang, 2011).

Overall, the latter view has received more support. Brock University researchers found that teenage girls who interacted with their friends on the computer more often had better friendships than girls who did not often use the computer with their friends (Desjarlais & Willoughby, 2010). In existing friendships, online communication seems to foster self-disclosure, which enhances friendship quality (Valkenburg & Peter, 2009a). In fact, many adolescents tend to use social networking sites to connect with people they know offline and to strengthen these pre-existing relationships (Reich, Subrahmanyam, & Espinoza, 2012). Similarly, the use of instant messaging has been associated with an increase in the quality of adolescents' existing friendships over time (Valkenburg & Peter, 2009b). In contrast, high levels of using the Internet primarily for entertainment (e.g., playing games, surfing) or for communication with strangers can harm the quality of friendships (Blais et al., 2008; Punamäki et al., 2009; Valkenburg & Peter, 2007b) and predicts increases in anxiety and depression (Selfhout et al., 2009).

Another potential risk of online use—one that is quite serious—is cyberbullying among adolescents (Kiriakidis & Kavoura, 2010; Kowalski, Limber, & Agatston, 2008; Tokunaga, 2010). Internet applications can be used by youths to intimidate, insult, and humiliate peers, and they ensure a much larger group of peer witnesses than is possible in everyday face-to-face interactions. A recent Canadian study of 529 students from Grades 6 to 11 demonstrated that around 20% had been the victims of at least one type of cyberbullying behaviour in the past 3 months. In addition, close to 30% of the students reported having engaged in some type of cyberbullying, including calling people names or spreading rumours (Wade & Beran, 2011).

Cyberbullies and cybervictims tend to be the same youths who are bullies or victims offline (Twyman et al., 2010). Cybervictims, like victims offline, tend to be high in social anxiety, psychological distress, and symptoms of depression, as well as to have aggressive tendencies, poor anger management, and problems at school (Valkenburg & Peter, 2011). However, nearly all the relevant research is correlational, so it is not clear if youths with these characteristics elicit cyberbullying, if cyberbullying causes emotional and behavioural problems, or if both factors come into play. Interestingly, one recent Canadian study found that involvement in cyberbullying, either as a bully or a victim, was related to students' reports of depression symptoms and suicidal thoughts (Bonanno & Hymel, 2013).

Although social media are often used to bully peers, they also may be helpful in countering the effects of peer rejection. In an experimental study, adolescents and young adults played what they were led to believe was an online interactive game with unfamiliar peers (Reijntjes et al., 2011). Actually, the game is a standardized laboratory computer program designed to elicit feelings of social inclusion or exclusion in the only real player—the research participant. In the exclusion version, the "other players" eventually begin to play among themselves, completely ignoring the participant. In this study, after the game ended, the excluded participants showed lower levels of self-esteem and higher levels of anger and shame than did the included participants. Next, the excluded participants spent 12 minutes either playing a computer puzzle game by themselves or engaging in instant messaging with an unfamiliar other-sex person, with whom they were free to discuss anything *except* the just-completed game.

The researchers found that excluded participants who engaged in the text messaging showed greater recovery from exclusion in terms of self-esteem and negative affect than did the excluded participants who played the puzzle game. These findings are consistent with the previously mentioned benefits of cybercommunication for shy, anxious, or depressed individuals and suggest that Internet relationships can have benefits for children and youths who have difficulties with peer relationships.

The path to heterosexual romantic relationships in adolescence typically begins in mixed-gender peer groups, with dating emerging out of mixed-gender affiliations in these groups (Collins & Steinberg, 2006; Connolly et al., 2004). From ages 14 to 18, youth tend to balance the time they spend with romantic partners and with same-gender cliques, gradually decreasing the percent of time they spend in mixed-gender groups (Richards et al., 1998). However, by early adulthood, the time spent with romantic partners increases to the level that it is at the expense of involvement with friends and crowds (Reis et al., 1993). Less is known about the emergence of romantic relationships among sexual-minority youths: although most

The importance of compatibility and caring in romantic relationships increases with age in adolescence.

report some sexual activity in adolescence (Savin-Williams & Diamond, 2000), whether they date depends on the level of acceptance in their social environment (L. M. Diamond, Savin-Williams, & Dube, 1999).

Young adolescents tend to be drawn to, and choose, partners on the basis of characteristics that bring status—such as being stylish and having the approval of peers (Pellegrini & Long, 2007). By middle to late adolescence, traits such as kindness, honesty, intelligence, and interpersonal skills are also important factors in selecting a romantic partner (Ha et al., 2010; Regan & Joshi, 2003). Older adolescents are more likely than younger ones to select partners based on compatibility and characteristics that enhance intimacy, such as caring and compromise (Collins, 2003).

For many adolescents, being in a romantic relationship is important for a sense of belonging and status in the peer group (W. Carlson & Rose, 2007; Connolly et al., 1999). By late adolescence, having a high-quality romantic relationship is also associated with feelings of self-worth and a general sense of competence (Collins, Welsh, & Furman, 2009; Connolly & Konarski, 1994), and it can improve functioning in adolescents who are prone to depression, sadness, or aggression (V. A. Simon, Aikins, & Prinstein, 2008).

However, romantic relationships can also have negative effects on development, particularly in early adolescence. Early dating and sexual activity, for example, are associated with increased rates of current and later problem behaviours, such as drinking and using drugs, as well as with social and emotional difficulties (e.g., Davies & Windle, 2000; Zimmer-Gembeck, Siebenbruner, & Collins, 2001). One study of Canadian 12- to 14-year-olds found that teenagers who were currently or recently in a romantic relationship were more likely to use illegal substances, be sexually active, and commit delinquent acts (Doyle et al., 2003). This relation is especially true if the romantic partner is prone to delinquent behaviour (Lonardo et al., 2009; S. Miller et al., 2009). When a romantic relationship does not work out, hurt feelings for one or both partners are par for the course, but girls who are treated badly or are rejected in a relationship seem particularly prone to depression and anxiety (W. E. Ellis, Crooks, & Wolfe, 2009).

The quality of adolescents' romantic relationships appears to mirror the quality of their other relationships. Adolescents who have had poor-quality relationships with parents and peers are likely to have romantic relationships characterized by low levels of intimacy and commitment (Ha et al., 2010; Oriña et al., 2011; Seiffge-Krenke, Overbeek, & Vermulst, 2010) and by aggression (Stocker & Richmond, 2007; Zimmer-Gembeck, Siebenbruner, & Collins, 2004).

It is also believed that adolescents' working models of relationships with their parents tend to be reflected in their romantic relationships. This belief is supported by the finding that children who were securely attached at age 12 months were more socially competent in elementary school, which predicted more secure relationships with friends at age 16. The security of these friendships, in turn, predicted more positive daily emotional experiences in romantic relationships at ages 20 to 23 and less negative affect in conflict resolution and collaborative tasks with romantic partners (J. A. Simpson et al., 2007). Related research suggests that individuals who were securely attached in infancy, in contrast to those with insecure attachments, rebound better from conflicts with their romantic partners in early adulthood (Salvatore et al., 2011). Thus, romantic relationships appear to be affected in multiple ways by youths' history of relationships with parents and peers (Rauer et al., 2013).

review:

Very young children often interact with peers in groups, and dominance hierarchies emerge in these groups by preschool age. By middle childhood, most children belong to cliques of same-gender peers who often are similar in their aggressiveness and orientation toward school.

In adolescence, the importance of cliques tends to diminish, and adolescents typically belong to more than one group. The degree of conformity to the norms of the peer group regarding dress, talk, and behaviour decreases over the high school years. Nonetheless, adolescents often are members of crowds, such as the jocks or brains—that is, groups of people with similar reputations. Even though adolescents often do not choose what crowd they belong to, belonging to a particular crowd may affect their reputations, their treatment by peers, and their exploration of identities.

Peer groups sometimes contribute to the development of antisocial behaviour and the use of alcohol and drugs, although children and adolescents may also select peers with problem behaviours that are similar to their own. Membership in a gang is particularly likely to encourage problem behaviour. The degree to which the peer group influences adolescents' antisocial behaviour or drug abuse appears to vary according to family and cultural factors.

Involvement in romantic relationships increases with age in adolescence, and youths increasingly select partners based on intimacy, compatibility, and caring rather than on criteria such as social status and stylishness. Involvement in romantic relationships often is related to a sense of belonging, high self-esteem, and reduced depressive feelings, but can also lead to involvement in risky behaviours, such as drinking and using drugs, and to feelings of rejection if one partner treats the other poorly. The quality of youths' romantic relationships tends to mirror the quality of their relationships with parents and friends.

Status in the Peer Group

As noted in the preceding section, older children and adolescents often are extremely concerned with their peer status: being popular is of great importance, and peer rejection can be a devastating experience. Rejection by peers is associated with a range of developmental outcomes for children, such as dropping out of school and problem behaviours, and these relations can hold independent of any effects of having, or not having, close friends (Gest et al., 2001). Because of the central role that peer relations play in children's lives, developmental researchers have devoted a good deal of effort to studying the concurrent and long-term effects associated with peer status.

In this section, we will examine children's status in the peer group, including how it is measured, its stability, the characteristics that determine it, and the long-term implications of being popular with, or being rejected by, peers.

Measurement of Peer Status

The most common method developmentalists use to assess peer status is to ask children to rate how much they like or dislike each of their classmates. Alternatively, they may ask children to nominate some of those whom they like the most and the least, or whom they do or do not like to play with. The information from these procedures is used to calculate the children's **sociometric status,** or peer acceptance—that is, the degree to which the children are liked or disliked by their peers as a group. The most commonly used sociometric system classifies children into one of five groups: popular, rejected, neglected, average, or controversial (see Table 13.3) (Coie & Dodge, 1988).

sociometric status ■ A measurement that reflects the degree to which children are liked or disliked by their peers as a group.

TABLE 13.3

Common Sociometric Categories

Popular—Children are designated as popular if they receive many positive nominations (e.g., for being liked) and few negative nominations (e.g., for being disliked).

Rejected—Children are designated as rejected if they receive many negative nominations and few positive nominations.

Neglected—Children are designated as neglected if they are low in social impact—that is, if they receive few positive or negative nominations. These children are not especially liked or disliked by peers; they simply go unnoticed.

Average—Children are designated as average if they receive an average number of both positive and negative nominations.

Controversial—Children are designated as controversial if they receive many positive and many negative nominations. They are noticed by peers and are liked by a quite a few children and disliked by quite a few others.

Characteristics Associated with Sociometric Status

Why are some children liked better than others? One obvious factor is physical attractiveness. From early childhood through adolescence, attractive children are much more likely to be popular, and are less likely to be victimized by peers, than are children who are unattractive (Langlois et al., 2000; Rosen, Underwood, & Beron, 2011; Vannatta et al., 2009). Athleticism is also related to high peer status, albeit more strongly for boys than for girls (Vannatta et al., 2009). Further affecting peer status is the status of one's friends: having popular friends appears to boost one's own popularity (Eder, 1985; Sabongui, Bukowski, & Newcomb, 1998). Beyond these simple determiners, sociometric status also seems to be affected by a variety of other factors, including children's social behaviour, personality, cognitions about others, and goals when interacting with peers.

Popular Children

Popular children—those who, in sociometric procedures, are predominantly nominated as liked by peers—tend to have a number of social skills in common. To begin with, they tend to be skilled at initiating interaction with peers and at maintaining positive relationships with others (Rubin et al., 2006). For example, when popular children enter a group of children who are already talking or playing, they first try to see what is going on in the group and then join in by talking about the same topic or engaging in the same activity as the group, rather than drawing unwarranted attention to themselves (Dodge et al., 1983; Putallaz, 1983).

At a broader level, popular children tend to be cooperative, friendly, sociable, helpful, and sensitive to others, and they are perceived that way by their peers, teachers, and adult observers (Dodge et al., 1997; Lansford et al., 2006; Newcomb, Bukowski, & Pattee, 1993; Rubin et al., 2006). They also regulate themselves well (N. Eisenberg et al., 1993; Kam et al., 2011), are not prone to intense negative emotions, and tend to have a relatively high number of low-conflict reciprocated friendships (Litwack, Wargo Aikins, & Cillessen, 2012).

Although popular children often are less aggressive overall than are rejected children (Newcomb et al., 1993), in comparison with children designated as *average* (i.e., those who receive an average number of both positive and negative nominations), they are less aggressive only with respect to aggression related to generalized anger, vengefulness, or satisfaction in hurting others (Dodge et al., 1990). With respect to assertive aggressiveness, including pushing and fighting, popular children

popular (peer status) ▪ A category of sociometric status that refers to children or adolescents who are viewed positively (liked) by many peers and are viewed negatively (disliked) by few peers.

often do not differ from average children (Newcomb et al., 1993). Highly aggressive children may even have high peer acceptance in some special cases, such as among adolescent males (but not females) who perform poorly in school (Kreager, 2007), in peer groups in which the popular members tend to be relatively aggressive (Dijkstra, Lindenberg, & Veenstra, 2008), or in classrooms that have a strong hierarchy in terms of peer status (Garandeau, Ahn, & Rodkin, 2011).

On the question of aggression and popularity, it is important to differentiate between children who are popular in terms of sociometric, or social-preference, measures—that is, who are *well liked* by peers—and those who are perceived by peers as being popular or high status in the group. Although children who are well liked by peers tend not to be particularly aggressive, children who are perceived as having high status in the group—those who are often labelled "popular" by other children and often seen as "cool"—tend to be viewed as above average in aggression and use it to obtain their goals (P. H. Hawley, 2003; Kuryluk, Cohen, & Audley-Piotrowski, 2011; Prinstein & Cillessen, 2003). To illustrate, a study by Tracy Vaillancourt of McMaster University and Shelley Hymel of University of British Columbia (2006) demonstrated that children tended to dislike physically and relationally aggressive adolescents but tended to perceive those adolescents as both popular and powerful. This association between aggression and perceived popularity, although seen to some degree even in preschool (Vaughn et al., 2003), is quite strong in early adolescence; indeed, high-status individuals, particularly girls, are likely to engage in **relational aggression**, such as excluding others from the group, withholding friendship to inflict harm, and spreading rumours to ruin a peer's reputation (Cillessen & Mayeux, 2004; K. E. Hoff et al., 2009; Prinstein & Cillessen, 2003).

Especially if they are aware that they are perceived as popular, youth who are perceived as having high status tend to increasingly use relational and physical aggression across adolescence, perhaps because they tend to be arrogant and can get away with it (Cillessen & Mayeux, 2004; Mayeux & Cillessen, 2008; A. J. Rose, Swenson, & Waller, 2004). By the middle-school years, children with the reputation of being popular sometimes start to shun less popular peers. As a result, they are considered "stuck-up," "mean," and "snobby" and begin to be viewed with ambivalence by their peers and sometimes even become resented or disliked (Closson, 2009; Mayeux, 2011; Merten, 1997; D. L. Robertson et al., 2010).

Rejected Children

A majority of **rejected** children tend to fall into one of two categories: those who are overly aggressive and those who are withdrawn.

Aggressive-rejected children According to reports from peers, teachers, and adult observers, 40% to 50% of rejected children tend to be aggressive. These **aggressive-rejected** children are especially prone to hostile and threatening behaviour, physical aggression, disruptive behaviour, and delinquency (Lansford et al., 2010; Newcomb et al., 1993; S. Pedersen et al., 2007; Rubin et al., 2006). When they are angry or want

BLEND IMAGES / AGE FOTOSTOCK

Physically attractive children and teens tend to be more popular than their less attractive peers.

relational aggression ■ A kind of aggression that involves excluding others from the social group and attempting to do harm to other people's relationships; it includes spreading rumours about peers, withholding friendship to inflict harm, ignoring peers when angry or frustrated, and trying to get one's own way.

rejected (peer status) ■ A category of sociometric status that refers to children or adolescents who are liked by few peers and disliked by many peers.

aggressive-rejected (peer status) ■ A category of sociometric status that refers to children who are especially prone to physical aggression, disruptive behaviour, delinquency, and negative behaviour such as hostility and threatening others.

their own way, many rejected children also engage in relational aggression (Cillessen & Mayeux, 2004; Crick, Casas, & Mosher, 1997; Tomada & Schneider, 1997).

Most of the research on the role of aggression in peer status is correlational, so it is impossible to know for certain whether aggression causes peer rejection or results from it. However, some research supports the view that frequent aggressive behaviour often underlies rejection by peers. For example, observation of unfamiliar peers getting to know one another has shown that those who are aggressive become rejected over time (Coie & Kupersmidt, 1983). In addition, longitudinal research has shown that children who are aggressive, negative, and disruptive tend to become increasingly disliked by peers across the school year (S. A. Little & Garber, 1995; Maszk, Eisenberg, & Guthrie, 1999).

Nonetheless, other research suggests that the experience of rejection may trigger or increase children's aggression. In an experimental study, 5th and 6th graders were led to believe that they had been entered in an online popularity contest and had been evaluated by peer judges on the basis of a personal photograph and information about their preferences and personality traits. They were then presented with their "peers'" evaluations—which were actually standardized assessments devised by the researchers to be either neutral or mostly negative and rejecting. After receiving their evaluations, the participants were given the opportunity to reduce the payments that would be made to the judges and to post negative comments about the judges on the contest's website. Those youths who were rejected by the judges, compared with those who were not, imposed deeper cuts on judges' payments and posted more negative comments about them on the website (Reijntjes et al., 2011). Taken together, these and other studies suggest that the relation between peer rejection and youths' aggression is bidirectional—that aggression predicts more peer rejection over time *and* that more peer rejection predicts more aggression (Lansford et al., 2010).

As you have seen, however, not all aggressive children are rejected by their peers and some are even perceived as popular (Farmer et al., 2011; D. L. Robertson et al., 2010). Aggressive children sometimes develop a network of aggressive friends and are accepted in their peer group (Xue & Meisels, 2004), and some elementary school and preadolescent children who start fights and get into trouble are viewed as "cool" and are central in their peer group (K. E. Hoff et al., 2009; Rodkin et al., 2000, 2006). Many of these children are among those designated as *controversial*—liked by numerous peers and disliked by numerous others.

Withdrawn-rejected children The second group of rejected children includes **withdrawn-rejected** children. These children, who make up 10% to 25% of the rejected category, are socially withdrawn and wary and, according to some research, are often timid and socially anxious (Booth-LaForce et al., 2012; Cillessen et al., 1992; Rubin et al., 2006). They frequently are victimized by peers, and many feel isolated and lonely (Booth-LaForce & Oxford, 2008; Rubin, Coplan, & Bowker, 2009; Woodhouse, Dykas, & Cassidy, 2012). Friendlessness, friendship instability, and exclusion in Grade 5 predict increases in socially withdrawn behaviour through Grade 8, whereas low peer exclusion in Grade 5 predicts a decline in social withdrawal across time (Oh et al., 2008). Thus, as with aggression, social withdrawal may be both a cause and consequence of peer exclusion and rejection.

However, not all socially withdrawn children are rejected or socially excluded (Gazelle, 2008; Gazelle & Ladd, 2003). Rather, it is *active isolates*—withdrawn children who display immature, unregulated, or angry, defiant behaviour such as bullying, boasting, and meanness—who are the most likely to be rejected by their peers. Research suggests that children who are withdrawn with peers but are

withdrawn-rejected (peer status) ■ A category of sociometric status that refers to rejected children who are socially withdrawn, wary, and often timid.

relatively socially competent tend to be merely neglected—that is, they are not nominated as either liked or disliked by peers (Harrist et al., 1997). Similarly, children and adolescents who are simply not social and prefer solitary activities may not be especially prone to peer rejection (J. C. Bowker & Raja, 2011; Coplan & Armer, 2007).

Over the course of childhood, withdrawn behaviour, regardless of the underlying motivation, seems to become a more reliable predictor of peer rejection. By the middle to late elementary school years, children who are quite withdrawn stand out, tend to be disliked, and appear to become increasingly alienated from the group as time goes on (Rubin et al., 1998). One recent study with Ontario children aged 9 to 12 years demonstrated that all forms of social withdrawal (i.e., shyness, unsociability, social avoidance) were all associated with negative peer relations (Coplan et al., 2013). In some cases, however, children who are not initially socially withdrawn have social isolation forced upon them as they progress through school (A. Bowker et al., 1998). That is, children who are disliked and rebuffed by peers, often because of their disruptive or aggressive behaviour, may increasingly isolate themselves from the group even if they initially were not withdrawn (Coie, Dodge, & Kupersmidt, 1990; Rubin et al., 1998).

Children who are socially withdrawn because they enjoy being by themselves do not necessarily experience rejection from peers.

Social cognition and social rejection Rejected children, particularly those who are aggressive, tend to differ from more popular children in their social motives and in the way they process information related to social situations (Lansford et al., 2010). For instance, rejected children are more likely than better-liked peers to be motivated by goals such as "getting even" with others or "showing them up" (Crick & Dodge, 1994; Rubin et al., 2006). As discussed in Chapter 9 (pages 358–360), they also are relatively likely to attribute malicious intent to others in negative social situations, even when the intent of others is uncertain or benign (Crick & Dodge, 1994).

Rejected children also have more trouble than other children do in finding constructive solutions to difficult social situations, such as wanting to take a turn on a swing when someone else is using it. When asked how they would deal with such situations, rejected children suggest fewer strategies than do their more popular peers, and the ones they suggest are more hostile, demanding, and threatening (Dodge et al., 2003; Harrist et al., 1997; Rubin et al., 1998). (Box 13.3 discusses programs designed to help rejected children gain peer acceptance.) Perhaps one reason rejected children are more likely to select inappropriate strategies is that their theory of mind is less developed than that of their better-liked peers, and they may therefore have greater difficulty understanding others' feelings and thoughts (Caputi et al., 2012) (see Chapter 7, pages 269–270).

Neglected Children

As noted earlier, some withdrawn children are categorized as **neglected** because they are not nominated by peers as either liked or disliked (Booth-LaForce & Oxford, 2008). These children tend to be both less sociable and less disruptive than average children (Rubin et al., 1998) and are likely to back away from peer interactions that involve aggression (Coie & Dodge, 1988). Neglected children perceive that they receive less support from peers (S. Walker, 2009; Wentzel, 2003),

neglected (peer status) ■ A category of sociometric status that refers to children or adolescents who are infrequently mentioned as either liked or disliked; they simply are not noticed much by peers.

BOX 13.3: applications

FOSTERING CHILDREN'S PEER ACCEPTANCE

Given the difficult and often painful outcomes commonly associated with a child's being rejected or having few friends, a number of researchers have designed programs to help children in these categories gain acceptance from peers. Their approaches have varied according to what they believe to be the causes of social rejection, but a number of approaches have proven to be useful, at least to some degree.

One common approach involves **social skills training**. The assumption behind this approach is that rejected children lack social skills that promote positive peer relations. These deficits are viewed as occurring at three levels (Mize & Ladd, 1990):

1. *Lack of social knowledge*—Rejected children lack social knowledge regarding the goals, strategies, and normative expectations that apply in specific peer contexts. For example, children engaged in a joint activity usually expect a newcomer to the group to blend in slowly and not to begin immediately pushing his or her own ideas or wishes. Lacking an understanding of this,

aggressive-rejected children are likely to barge in on a conversation or to try to control the group's choice of activities. In contrast, a withdrawn-rejected child may not know how to start a conversation or contribute to the group's activities when the opportunity arises.

2. *Performance problems*—Some rejected children possess the social knowledge required for being successful in various peer contexts, but they may still act inappropriately because they are unable or unmotivated to use their knowledge to guide their performance.

3. *Lack of appropriate monitoring and self-evaluation*—To behave in a way that is consistent with the interests and actions of their peers, children need to monitor their own and others' social behaviour. Such monitoring requires them to accurately interpret social cues regarding what is occurring, what others are feeling and thinking, and how their own behaviour is being perceived. Rejected children often cannot engage in such

monitoring and thus cannot modify their behaviour in appropriate ways.

To help children overcome such deficits, some social skills training programs teach children to pay attention to what is going on in a group of peers and help them develop skills related to participating with peers. Interventions may include coaching and rehearsing children on how to start a conversation with an unfamiliar peer, how to compliment a peer, how to smile and offer help, and how to take turns and share materials (Oden & Asher, 1977). In other interventions, the emphasis is primarily on teaching children to think about alternative ways to achieve a goal, evaluate the consequences of each alternative, and then select an appropriate strategy. Children may be asked to think about or act out a situation in which they are excluded or teased by peers and to come up with various strategies for handling the situation. The children are then helped to evaluate the strategies and to understand the specific costs and benefits of each (e.g., Coleman, Wheeler, & Webber, 1993).

---

social skills training ■ Training programs designed to help rejected children gain peer acceptance; they are based on the assumption that rejected children lack important knowledge and skills that promote positive interaction with peers.

controversial (peer status) ■ A category of sociometric status that refers to children or adolescents who are liked by quite a few peers and are disliked by quite a few others.

yet they are not particularly anxious about their social interactions (Hatzichristou & Hopf, 1996; Rubin et al., 1998). In fact, other than being less socially interactive, neglected children display few behaviours that differ greatly from those of many other children (Bukowski et al., 1993; S. Walker, 2009). They appear to be neglected primarily because they are simply not noticed by their peers.

Controversial Children

In some ways, the most intriguing group of children are **controversial** children, who, as indicated, are liked by numerous peers and disliked by numerous others. Controversial children tend to have characteristics of both popular and rejected children (Rubin et al., 1998). For example, they tend to be aggressive, disruptive, and prone to anger, but they also tend to be cooperative, sociable, good at sports, and humorous (Bukowski et al., 1993; Coie & Dodge, 1988). In addition, they are very socially active and tend to be group leaders (Coie et al., 1990). At the same time, controversial children also tend to be viewed by peers as arrogant and snobbish (Hatzichristou & Hopf, 1996), which could explain why they are disliked by some peers even if they are perceived as having high status in the peer group (D. L. Robertson et al., 2010).

Recent forms of this sort of program are often multi-faceted, including such components as communication skills, anger management, and training in perspective taking (Reid, Webster-Stratton, & Hammond, 2007; Webster-Stratton, Reid, & Stoolmiller, 2008). Their primary focus is on helping children to better understand and communicate about their own and others' emotions and to regulate their behaviour (Domitrovich, Cortes, & Greenberg, 2007; Izard et al., 2008; P. C. McCabe & Altamura, 2011), although training in social skills strategies also usually occurs to some degree. The general assumption underlying these programs is that children act in more appropriate ways and, consequently, are better liked if their behaviour takes into account the feelings of others and is modulated in a manner that is both sensitive and socially appropriate to those feelings.

A notable example of this approach is the PATHS (Promoting Alternative Thinking Strategies) curriculum, in which children learn to identify emotional expressions (using pictures, for example) and to think about the causes and consequences of different ways of expressing emotions (Domitrovich et al., 2007, 2010). In addition, the program provides children with opportunities to develop conscious strategies for self-control through verbal mediation (self-talk) and to practise ways to self-regulate. The PATHS approach is illustrated by the Control Signals Poster (CSP), which, like the turtle technique discussed in Chapter 1, is designed to remind children how to deal with troubling social situations:

> The CSP is modeled after a traffic signal, with red, yellow, and green lights. The red light signals children to "Stop—Calm Down." Here, youth are instructed that as challenging social situations occur, they should first "take a long deep breath," calm down, and "say the problem and how they feel." The yellow light signals children to "Slow Down—Think." Here, youth make a plan by considering possible solutions and then selecting the best option. Finally, the green light signals children to "Go—Try My Plan." Below the illustration of the stoplight are the words "Evaluate—How Did My Plan Work?" Students may then formulate and try new plans if necessary.
>
> (Riggs et al., 2006, p. 94)

Programs like this one tend to be successful in fostering knowledge about emotions, self-regulation, prosocial behaviour, and social competence—and sometimes in reducing social withdrawal and aggression as well (e.g., Bierman et al., 2010; Domitrovich et al., 2007; Izard et al., 2008; Riggs et al., 2006). Such improvements have been found especially for children with numerous problem behaviours and for children in disadvantaged schools (Bierman et al., 2010; Greenberg et al., 1995). The increases in social competence that often result as a consequence of participation in such an intervention would be expected to promote children's social status, although this issue usually has not been specifically tested.

Stability of Sociometric Status

Do popular children always remain at the top of the social heap? Do rejected children sometimes become better liked? In other words, how stable is a child's sociometric status in the peer group? The answer to this question depends in part on the particular time span and sociometric status that are in question.

Over relatively short periods such as weeks or a few months, children who are popular or rejected tend to remain so, whereas children who are neglected or controversial are likely to acquire a different status (Asher & Dodge, 1986; X. Chen, Rubin, & B. Li, 1995b; Newcomb & Bukowski, 1984; S. Walker, 2009). Over longer periods, children's sociometric status is more likely to change. In one study in which children were rated by their peers in Grade 5 and again 2 years later, only those children who had initially been rated average maintained their status overall, whereas nearly two-thirds of those who had been rated popular, rejected, or controversial received a different rating later on (Newcomb & Bukowski, 1984). Over time, sociometric stability for rejected children is generally higher than for popular, neglected, or controversial children (Harrist et al., 1997; Parke et al., 1997; S. Walker, 2009) and may increase with the age of the child (Coie & Dodge, 1983; Rubin et al., 1998).

Cross-Cultural Similarities and Differences in Factors Related to Peer Status

Most of the research on behaviours associated with sociometric status has been conducted in Canada and the United States, but findings similar to those discussed here have been obtained in a wide array of cross-cultural research. In countries ranging from Italy, Australia, the Netherlands, and Greece to Indonesia, Hong Kong, Japan, and China, for example, socially rejected children tend to be aggressive and disruptive, and, in most countries, popular (i.e., well-liked) children tend to be described as prosocial and as having leadership skills (Attili, Vermigli, & Schneider, 1997; Chung-Hall & Chen, 2010; D. C. French, Setiono, & Eddy, 1999; Gooren et al., 2011; Hatzichristou & Hopf, 1996; Kawabata, Crick, & Hamaguchi, 2010; D. Schwartz et al., 2010; Tomada & Schneider, 1997; Walker, 2009; Y. Xu et al., 2004).

Similar cross-cultural parallels have been found with regard to withdrawal and rejection. Various studies done in Germany, Italy, and Hong Kong, for example, have shown that, as in North America, withdrawal becomes linked with peer rejection in preschool or elementary school (Asendorpf, 1990; Attili et al., 1997; Casiglia, Lo Coco, & Zappulla, 1998; D. A. Nelson et al., 2010; D. Schwartz et al., 2010).

Research has also demonstrated that there are certain cultural and historical differences in the characteristics associated with children's sociometric status. One notable example involving both types of differences is the status associated with shyness among Chinese children. In studies conducted in the 1990s, Chinese children who were shy, sensitive, and cautious or inhibited in their behaviour were—unlike their inhibited or shy Western counterparts—viewed by teachers as socially competent and as leaders, and they were liked by their peers (X. Chen, Rubin, & B. Li, 1995; X. Chen, Rubin, & Z.-y. Li, 1995; X. Chen et al., 1999; X. Chen, Rubin, & Sun, 1992). A probable explanation for this difference is that Chinese culture traditionally values self-effacing, withdrawn behaviour, and Chinese children are encouraged to behave accordingly (Ho, 1986).

In contrast, because Western cultures place great value on independence and self-assertion, withdrawn children in these cultures are likely to be viewed as weak, needy, and socially incompetent. However, Chen found that since the early 1990s, shy, reserved behaviour in Chinese elementary school children has become

Children who are well liked tend to have similar characteristics in many cultures, as do children who are rejected by their peers.

JANET WISHNETSKY / CORBIS

increasingly associated with lower levels of peer acceptance, at least for urban children (X. Chen, Chang, et al., 2005). Chen argues that the economic and political changes in China in the past decade have been accompanied by an increased valuing of assertive, less inhibited behaviour. For children from rural areas who have had only limited exposure to the dramatic cultural changes in China in recent years, shyness is associated with high levels of both peer liking and disliking, albeit more to liking; thus, for groups somewhat less exposed to cultural changes, shyness is viewed with some ambivalence by peers (X. Chen, Wang, & Cao, 2011; X. Chen, Wang, & Wang, 2009). In addition, for the rural children, being unsociable—that is, uninterested in social interaction—is associated with peer rejection (X. Chen et al., 2009), whereas among North American children it often is not, at least for younger children. Thus, culture and changes in culture appear to affect children's evaluations of what is desirable behaviour.

Peer Status as a Predictor of Risk

Having an undesirable peer status has been associated with a variety of short-term and long-term risks and negative outcomes for children, including inferior academic performance, loneliness, delinquency, and poor adjustment.

Academic Performance

Research in a variety of regions, including North America, China, and Indonesia, indicates that rejected children, especially those who are aggressive, are more likely than their peers to have academic difficulties (X. Chen et al., 2011; Chung-Hall & Chen, 2010; D. C. French et al., 1999; Véronneau et al., 2010; Wentzel, 2009). In particular, they have higher rates of school absenteeism (DeRosier, Kupersmidt, & Patterson, 1994) and lower grade-point averages (Wentzel & Caldwell, 1997). Those who are aggressive are especially likely to be uninterested in school and to be viewed by peers and teachers as poor students (Hymel, Bowker, & Woody, 1993; Wentzel & Asher, 1995).

Longitudinal research, conducted mostly in the United States, indicates that students' classroom participation is lower during periods in which they are rejected by peers than during periods when they are not, and that the tendency of rejected children to do relatively poorly in school worsens across time (Coie et al., 1992; Ladd, Herald-Brown, & Reiser, 2008; Ollendick et al., 1992). In one study that followed children from Grade 5 through the high school years, rejected children were much more likely than other children, especially popular children, to be required to repeat a grade or to be suspended from school, to be truants, or to drop out (Kupersmidt & Coie, 1990) (Figure 13.3). They were also more likely to have difficulties with the law—in many cases, no doubt, deepening their academic difficulties. All told, approximately 25% to 30% of rejected children drop out of school, compared with approximately 8% or less of other children (Parker & Asher, 1987; Rubin et al., 1998).

FIGURE 13.3 The relation of children's sociometric status to academic and behavioural problems Children's sociometric status is related to their future problem behaviours. Rejected children are far more likely to be suspended from school; to be held back a grade; to be truants; to drop out; and to have problems with the police. (Adapted from Kupersmidt & Coie, 1990)

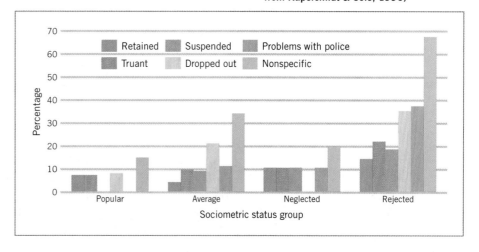

Problems with Adjustment

Children who are rejected in the elementary school years—especially aggressive-rejected boys—are at risk for increases in externalizing symptoms such as aggression, delinquency, hyperactivity and attention deficit disorders, conduct disorder, and substance abuse (Criss et al., 2009; Lansford et al., 2010; Ollendick et al., 1992; Sturaro et al., 2011; Vitaro et al., 2007). In one longitudinal study that followed more than 1000 U. S. children from Grade 3 to Grade 10 (Coie et al., 1995), boys and girls who were assessed as rejected in Grade 3 were, according to parent reports, higher than their peers in externalizing symptoms 3 years and 7 years later. In addition, aggressive boys (both rejected and non-rejected) increased in parent-reported externalizing symptoms between Grades 6 and 10, whereas other boys did not; and by Grade 10, aggressive-rejected boys themselves reported an average of more than twice the number of symptoms reported by all other boys (Figure 13.4).

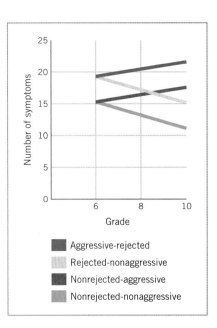

FIGURE 13.4 Rates of parent-reported externalizing symptoms in adolescent males as a function of rejection and aggression in Grade 3 According to parent reports, boys who were assessed as rejected in Grade 3 showed more externalizing symptoms than did their peers years later. Aggressive boys (both rejected and non-rejected) showed an increase in parent-reported externalizing symptoms between Grades 6 and 10, whereas other boys did not. By Grade 10, aggressive-rejected boys had an especially high number of externalizing symptoms. (Adapted from Coie et al., 1995)

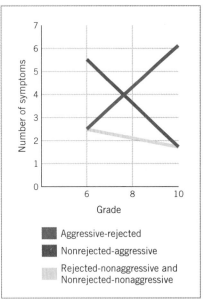

FIGURE 13.5 Rates of boys' self-reported internalizing symptoms as a function of rejection and aggression in Grade 3 Aggressive-rejected boys' reports of internalizing problems increased from Grade 6 to Grade 10, whereas such reports decreased over the same period for all other boys. (Adapted from Coie et al., 1995)

Other research provides evidence that peer rejection may also be associated with internalizing problems such as loneliness, depression, withdrawn behaviour, and obsessive-compulsive behaviour (Gooren et al., 2011; Prinstein et al., 2009), even 10 to 40 years later (Modin, Östberg, & Almquist, 2011). In the longitudinal study of more than 1000 children mentioned above, girls and boys who were rejected in Grade 3 were, as reported by parents, higher than their peers in internalizing symptoms by Grade 6 and Grade 10. Moreover, aggressive-rejected boys themselves reported a marked increase in internalizing symptoms from Grade 6 to Grade 10, whereas all other boys reported a drop in these symptoms (Figure 13.5). Aggressive-rejected girls were viewed by parents as most prone to internalizing problems by Grade 10. Thus, both boys and girls who were assessed as rejected in Grade 3—especially if they also were aggressive—were at risk for developing internalizing problems years later (Coie et al., 1995).

Also at risk for internalizing problems in Western cultures are children who are very withdrawn but non-aggressive with their peers. As you have seen, although these children tend to become rejected by the middle to late elementary school years, they are generally not at risk for the behavioural problems that aggressive-rejected children often experience. However, a consistent pattern of social withdrawal, social anxiety, and wariness with familiar people, including peers, is associated with symptoms such as depression, low self-worth, and loneliness in childhood and into early adulthood (Hoza et al., 1995; S. J. Katz et al., 2011; Rubin et al., 2009).

Children who are socially withdrawn amid familiar peers may differ in important ways from their peers even in adulthood. In a longitudinal study of American children born in the late 1920s, boys who were rated by their teachers as reserved and unsociable were less likely to marry and to have children than were less reserved boys. They also tended to begin their careers at later ages, had less success in their careers, and were less stable in their jobs. Reserved men who were late in establishing stable careers had twice the rate of divorce and marital separation by mid-life as did their less reserved peers.

In contrast, reserved girls were more likely than their less reserved peers to have a conventional lifestyle of marriage, parenthood, and homemaking rather than working outside the home. Thus, a reserved style of interaction at school during childhood was associated with more negative outcomes for men than for women, perhaps because a reserved style was more compatible with the feminine homemaker role of the times than with the demands of achieving outside the home (Caspi, Elder, & Bem, 1988).

A final group of rejected children who may be especially at risk for loneliness and other internalizing problems is **victimized** children, who are targets of their peers' aggression and demeaning behaviour. Although the sequence of events is not entirely clear, it appears that children in this group are more likely to be rejected first and then victimized rather than the reverse (Hanish & Guerra, 2000a; D. Schwartz et al., 1999).

Victimized children tend to be aggressive, as well as withdrawn and anxious (Barker et al., 2008; D. Schwartz et al., 1998; J. Snyder, Brooker, et al., 2003; Tom et al., 2010), and the relation between victimization and aggression appears to be bidirectional (Reijntjes et al., 2011; van Lier et al., 2012). Aggression sometimes appears to elicit victimization by peers (Barker et al., 2008; Kawabata et al., 2010).

Other factors might also contribute to victimization. For instance, immigrant children are more likely to be victimized than are peers who are part of the majority group, likely because they are seen as different (Strohmeier, Kärnä, & Salmivalli, 2011; von Grünigen et al., 2010). In addition, hereditary factors associated with aggression appear to predict peer victimization, suggesting that temperamental or other personal characteristics may increase the likelihood of children becoming both aggressive and victimized (Brendgen et al., 2011). For example, low self-regulation is related to both aggression and peer victimization (N. Eisenberg, Sallquist, et al., 2009; Iyer et al., 2010) and may contribute to both.

Unfortunately, peer victimization is not an uncommon event and can begin quite early. In one study of peer victimization across 40 countries, including Canada, 12% of adolescents reported being bullied and a further 3.6% reported being both a victim and a perpetrator of bullying (Craig et al., 2009). Over time, victimization by peers likely increases children's aggression, withdrawal, depression, and loneliness (Nylund et al., 2007; D. Schwartz et al., 1998), leading to hanging out with peers who are engaged in deviant behaviours (Rudolph et al., 2013), as well as problems at school and absenteeism (Juvonen, Nishina, & Graham, 2000; Kochenderfer & Ladd, 1996; Nakamoto & Schwartz, 2010). Peer victimization is a serious problem that warrants concern, especially since the same children tend to be victimized again and again (Hanish & Guerra, 2000b). According to a study of more than 1200 Ontario children, among the factors that put children at risk for further victimization are anxiety and low-quality friendships (Goldbaum et al., 2003).

victimized (peer status) ■ With respect to peer relationships, this term refers to children who are targets of their peers' aggression and demeaning behaviour.

Paths to Risk

Clearly, children who are rejected by peers are at risk for academic and adjustment problems. The key question is whether peer rejection actually *causes* problems at school and in adjustment, or whether children's maladaptive behaviour (e.g., aggression) leads to both peer rejection and problems in adjustment (Parker et al., 1995; L. J. Woodward & Fergusson, 1999). Although conclusive evidence is not yet available, findings suggest that peer status and the quality of children's social behaviour have partially independent effects on subsequent adjustment (Coie et al., 1992; DeRosier et al., 1994). Moreover, as demonstrated by Bonnie Leadbeater at the University of Victoria and Wendy Hoglund at the University of Alberta (2009), early maladjustment, such as internalizing problems, may contribute to both future maladaptive behaviour (e.g., aggression) and peer victimization, which in turn may lead to more internalizing problems over time. Thus, it is likely that there are complex bidirectional relations among children's adjustment, social competencies, and peer acceptance (Boivin et al., 2010; Fergusson, Woodward, & Horwood, 1999; Lansford et al., 2010; Obradović & Hipwell, 2010).

Once children are rejected by peers, they may be denied opportunities for positive peer interactions and thus for learning social skills. Moreover, cut off from desirable peers, they may be forced to associate with other rejected children, and rejected children may teach one another, and mutually reinforce, deviant norms and behaviours. The lack of social support from peers also may increase rejected children's vulnerability to the effects of stressful life experiences (e.g., poverty, parental conflict, divorce), negatively influencing their social behaviour even further, which in turn affects both their peer status and adjustment.

review:

Children's sociometric status is assessed by peers' reports of their liking and disliking of one another. On the basis of such reports, children typically have been classified as popular, rejected, average, neglected, or controversial.

Well-liked, popular children tend to be attractive, socially skilled, prosocial, well regulated, and low in aggression that is driven by anger, vengefulness, or satisfaction in hurting others. However, some children who are viewed as popular by their peers are aggressive and not especially well-liked. Some rejected children tend to be relatively aggressive, disruptive, and low in social skills; they also tend to make hostile attributions about others' intentions and have trouble dealing with difficult social situations in a constructive manner. Withdrawn children who are aggressive and hostile as well are also rejected by peers by kindergarten age. In contrast, most children who are withdrawn from their peers but are not hostile and aggressive are at somewhat less risk, although they sometimes become rejected later in elementary school.

Neglected children interact less frequently with peers than do children who are average in sociometric status, and they display relatively few behaviours that differ greatly from those of many other children. Controversial children display characteristics of both popular and rejected children and tend to be very socially active. Children who are neglected or controversial, unlike rejected children, are particularly likely to change their status, even over short periods.

Rejection by peers in childhood—especially rejection due to aggression—predicts relatively high levels of subsequent academic problems and externalizing behaviours. Rejected children also tend to become more withdrawn and are prone to loneliness and depression. It is likely that children's maladaptive behaviour as well as their low status with peers contribute to these negative developmental outcomes.

The Role of Parents in Children's Peer Relationships

Cliff is having a hard time … he just doesn't have any good friends, says he has no one to do things with … he's just not part of the gang. … I hate to see him having troubles with the other kids—I keep wondering if I should do something about it, or if he just has to sort it out hisself. … And it reminds me of *my* troubles at school.
(cited by Dunn, personal communication, 1999)

The speaker, the mother of 8-year-old Cliff, not only worries about Cliff's problems with his peers but also feels that she may have contributed to them—a common reaction of parents of lonely and rejected children. The idea that parents influence children's ability to relate to peers has a long history, beginning with Freud's emphasis on the importance of the mother–child relationship as a foundation for later personality development and interpersonal relationships. Moreover, attachment theorists (see Chapter 11) as well as social learning theorists (see Chapter 9) have asserted that early parent–child interactions are linked to children's peer interactions at an older age. It also seems likely that children's ongoing relationships with their parents can affect their relationships with their peers.

Relations Between Attachment and Competence with Peers

Attachment theory maintains that whether a child's attachment to the parent is secure or insecure affects the child's future social competence and the quality of the child's relationships with others, including peers. Attachment theorists have suggested that a secure attachment between parent and child promotes competence with peers in at least three ways (Elicker, Englund, & Sroufe, 1992). First, children with a secure attachment develop positive social expectations. They are thus inclined to interact readily with other children and expect these interactions to be positive and rewarding. Second, because of their experience with a sensitive and responsive caregiver, they develop the foundation for understanding reciprocity in relationships. Consequently, they learn to give and take in relationships and to be empathic to others. Finally, children who are securely attached are likely to be confident, enthusiastic, and emotionally positive—characteristics that are attractive to other children and that facilitate social interaction.

Conversely, attachment theorists argue, an insecure attachment is likely to impair a child's competence with peers. If parents are rejecting and hostile or neglectful, young children are likely to become hostile themselves and to expect negative behaviour from other people. They may be predisposed to perceive peers as hostile and, consequently, are likely to be aggressive toward them. These children may also expect rejection from other people and may try to avoid experiencing it by withdrawing from peer interaction (Furman et al., 2002; Renken et al., 1989).

There is a good deal of evidence to support these theoretical views. Children who are not securely attached do, in fact, tend to have difficulties with peer relationships. Toddlers and preschoolers who were insecurely attached as infants tend to be aggressive, whiny, socially withdrawn, and low in popularity in elementary school (Bohlin, Hagekull, & Rydell, 2000;

Children who have secure attachment relationships with their parents tend to develop better social skills than do their peers who are not securely attached.

Burgess et al., 2003; Erickson, Sroufe, & Egeland, 1985). Throughout childhood, these children, in comparison with securely attached children, express less positive emotion with peers, as well as less sympathy and prosocial behaviour, and they demonstrate poorer skills in resolving conflicts (Elicker et al., 1992; Fox & Calkins, 1993; Kestenbaum, Farber, & Sroufe, 1989; Panfile & Laible, 2012; Raikes & Thompson, 2008).

Securely attached children, on the other hand, tend to exhibit positive emotions and good social skills and, not surprisingly, tend to have high-quality friendships and to be relatively popular with peers—both as preschoolers (LaFreniere & Sroufe, 1985; McElwain, Booth-LaForce, & Wu, 2011) and in elementary school and adolescence (Granot & Mayseless, 2001; Kerns, Klepac, & Cole, 1996; B. H. Schneider, Atkinson, & Tardif, 2001) (see Chapter 11). Even in late childhood and early adolescence, children with more and higher-quality (e.g., more intimate and supportive) friendships tend to be those with a history of a secure attachment (Dwyer et al., 2010; Freitag et al., 1996; B. H. Schneider et al., 2001; J. A. Simpson et al., 2007). Some studies, including one by Concordia University researchers Anna-Beth Doyle, Heather Lawford, and Dorothy Markiewicz (2009), suggest that the security of attachment with fathers may be especially important for the quality of children's and adolescents' friendships.

Thus, security of the parent–child relationship is linked with quality of peer relationships. This link probably arises from both the early and the continuing effect that parent–child attachment has on the quality of social behaviour, as well as their working models of relationships (Shomaker & Furman, 2009). However, it is also possible that the individual characteristics of each child, such as sociability, influence both the quality of attachments and the quality of his or her relationships with peers.

Quality of Ongoing Parent–Child Interactions and Peer Relationships

Ongoing parent–child interactions are associated with peer relations in much the same way that attachment patterns are. For example, socially competent, popular children tend to have mothers who are warm in general, discuss feelings with them, and who use warm control, positive verbalizations, reasoning, and explanations in their approach to parenting (C. H. Hart et al., 1992; Kam et al., 2011; McDowell & Parke, 2009; Updegraff et al., 2010). Fathers' warmth and expression of positive rather than negative emotion with their children has been linked to the positivity of children's interactions with close friends in the preschool years (Kahen, Katz, & Gottman, 1994; Youngblade & Belsky, 1992) and to children's peer acceptance in elementary school (McDowell & Parke, 2009).

Overall, research in this area suggests that when the family is generally characterized by a warm, involved, and harmonious family style, young children tend to be sociable, socially skilled, liked by peers, and cooperative in child care (R. Feldman & Masalha, 2010). These associations may occur because such parenting fosters children's self-regulation (Eiden et al., 2009; N. Eisenberg, Zhou, et al., 2005; Kam et al., 2011). In contrast, parenting that is characterized by harsh, authoritarian discipline and low levels of child monitoring is often associated with children's being unpopular and victimized (Dishion, 1990; Duong et al., 2009; C.H. Hart, Ladd, & Burleson, 1990; Ladd, 1992).

In considering findings such as these, it is generally assumed that quality of parenting influences the degree to which children behave in socially competent ways, which in turn affects whether children are accepted by peers. But as in the case of attachment, it is difficult to prove that quality of parenting actually has a causal influence on children's social behaviour with peers. As we noted in Chapter 12, it may be that children who are aggressive and disruptive because of constitutional factors (e.g., heredity, prenatal influences) elicit both negative parenting and negative peer responses (Rubin et al., 1998) or it may be that both harsh parenting and the children's negative behaviour with peers are due to heredity. The most likely possibility is that the causal links are bidirectional—that parents' behaviour affects their children's social competence and vice versa—and that both environmental and biological factors play a role in the development of children's social competence with peers.

Parental Beliefs

Parents of socially competent children think about parenting and their children somewhat differently than do parents of children who have low social competence. For one thing, they are more likely to believe that they should play an active role in teaching their children social skills and in providing them with opportunities for peer interaction. They also tend to believe that when their children display inappropriate or maladaptive behaviour with a peer (e.g., aggression, hostility, social withdrawal), it is because of the circumstances of the *specific situation,* such as a provocation by the peer or a mutual misunderstanding. In contrast, parents of less socially competent children tend to believe that when their children behave in socially inappropriate ways, it is because of something in their children's nature and that it would thus be very hard to alter such behaviour (Rubin et al., 2006). In other words, they tend to believe that their children "were born that way." Of course, it is difficult to know the degree to which parents' beliefs about their children's social competencies are based on realistic perceptions of their offspring or on their own belief systems and personal history (such as the troubles Cliff's mother experienced when she was a schoolchild).

ANNA MOLLER / GETTY IMAGES

Parents may contribute to their children's development of social competence by arranging opportunities for their children to interact with peers.

Gatekeeping and Coaching

Other dimensions of parent–child interactions may influence children's competencies in peer relationships. Two of the more salient ones are parents' gatekeeping role in their children's social life and their coaching of their children in social skills.

Gatekeeping

As noted in Chapter 12, parents, especially those of young children, act as gatekeepers, controlling where their children go, with whom they interact, and how much time they spend with peers doing various activities. However, some parents are more thoughtful and active in this role than are others (Mounts, 2002). Preschoolers whose parents arrange and oversee opportunities for them to interact with peers tend to be more positive and social with peers, have a larger and more stable set of play partners, and more easily initiate social interactions with peers than do other children—as long as their parents are not overly controlling in this gatekeeping role (Ladd & Golter, 1988; Ladd & Hart, 1992). Similarly, elementary school children whose parents allow them to engage in numerous social activities in the neighbourhood and extracurricular activities at school are more socially competent and liked by peers (McDowell & Parke, 2009).

In adolescence, gatekeeping may be affected by parents' cultural orientation. For example, in Mexican-American families, parents who had a stronger orientation toward Mexican culture and the traditional Mexican value of familism—which emphasizes closeness in the family, family obligations, and consideration of the family in making decisions—placed more restrictions on adolescents' peer relationships than did parents whose orientation was less traditional. They were also more likely to restrict their adolescents'—especially a daughter's—contact with peers if the adolescent reported associating with deviant peers (Updegraff et al., 2010).

Coaching

Preschool children tend to be more socially skilled and more likely to be accepted by peers if their parents effectively coach them on how to interact with unfamiliar peers (Laird et al., 1994; McDowell & Parke, 2009). Mothers of accepted children tend to teach their children group-oriented strategies for gaining entry into a group of peers: they may make suggestions about what to say when entering the group, for example, or they may discourage the child from disrupting the group's current activities. In contrast, mothers of children who are low in sociometric status often try to direct the group's activity themselves or urge their child to initiate activities that are inconsistent with what the group is currently doing (Finnie & Russell, 1988; A. Russell & Finnie, 1990).

Children may also benefit in their peer relations when their parents provide emotion coaching—that is, explanations about the acceptability of emotions and how to appropriately deal with them (L. F. Katz, Maliken, & Stettler, 2012). Children whose parents use high levels of emotion coaching are, for example, more likely to use appropriate conflict-avoidance strategies, such as laughter, to deflect teasing, and they are less likely to display socially inappropriate behaviours when dealing with peers' provocations (L. F. Katz, Hunter, & Klowden, 2008). Some evidence suggests that a fairly high level of parental advice giving is sometimes associated with low levels of children's social competence and peer acceptance; but, in part, this may be because parents are more likely to try to help when their children are experiencing a high level of problems (McDowell & Parke, 2009). It is likely that coaching needs to be provided in a sensitive, skilled manner to be effective; that is, it should convey clear, useful information about others' feelings and behaviour, along with strategies for dealing with them, and it should be presented in a way that does not overwhelm children or derogate them. For reasons that are not yet clear, mothers' coaching may be especially important for enhancing girls' social skills (Pettit et al., 1998).

Family Stress and Children's Social Competence

As discussed in Chapter 12 (pages 479–480), parents who are preoccupied and distressed by problems related to poverty are more likely to be negative and less likely to be warm and supportive and to monitor their children's behaviour (Lengua, Honorado, & Bush, 2007; McLoyd, 1998). Thus, it is not surprising that children from families with fewer economic resources and higher levels of stress (e.g., unemployment, health problems) exhibit less social competence, have fewer friends, and are more likely than other children to be rejected by their peers (Brophy-Herb et al., 2007; Criss et al., 2002; Dishion, 1990; C. J. Patterson et al., 1992). For instance, in a longitudinal study, elementary school children from low-income families were considerably more likely to be rejected than were children from middle-class families (boys also were rejected more than girls; see Figure 13.6). It is likely that the effects of poverty and stress on parenting are reflected in children's compromised social competence.

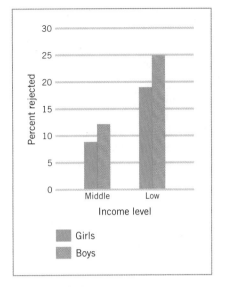

FIGURE 13.6 **Percentages of children rejected by peers as a function of gender and family income** As can be seen in these data from a longitudinal study, elementary school children from families with low incomes are considerably more likely to be rejected than are children from middle-class families. (Adapted from C. J. Patterson et al., 1992)

review:

Although differences in children's social behaviour likely are based in part on constitutional factors that influence temperament and personality, parents appear to influence children's competence with peers. Attachment theorists have suggested that a secure attachment between parent and child promotes peer competence because securely attached children develop positive social expectations, the foundation for understanding reciprocity in relationships, and a sense of self-worth and self-efficacy. In fact, securely attached children tend to be more positive in their behaviour and affect, more socially skilled, and better liked than insecurely attached children. Ongoing parent–child interactions show similar associations with peer relations.

Parents can also influence their children's competence with peers through their beliefs, their role as gatekeepers, and the social behaviours they teach their children. It is probable that the causal links between quality of parenting and children's social competence are bidirectional and that both environmental (e.g., parenting, poverty) and biological factors play a role in the development of children's social competence with peers.

chapter summary:

What Is Special About Peer Relationships?

- Theorists such as Piaget, Vygotsky, and Sullivan have argued that the equality, reciprocity, cooperation, and intimacy that characterize many peer relationships enhance children's ability to reason and their concern for others.

Friendships

- Consistent with theorists' arguments, peers (especially friends) provide intimacy, support, and rich opportunities for the development of play and for exchange of ideas.

- Even very young children prefer some children over others. Toddlers engage in more complex and cooperative play with friends than with non-friends, and those who engage in such play exhibit more positive and social behaviour with peers when they are older.

- As children grow, friends rely on one another and increasingly provide a context for self-disclosure and intimacy. Adolescent friends, more than younger friends, use friendship as a context for self-exploration, for personal problem solving, and as a source of honest feedback.

- Children's conceptions of friends change with age. Young children define friendship primarily on the basis of actual activities with their peers. With age, issues such as loyalty, mutual understanding, trust, cooperative reciprocity, and self-disclosure become important components of friendship.

- As was suggested by Piaget, Vygotsky, and Sullivan, friends provide emotional support; validation or confirmation of the legitimacy of one's own thoughts, feelings, and worth; and opportunities for the development of important social and cognitive skills.

- Having friends is associated with positive developmental outcomes, such as social competence and adjustment. However, friends also may have negative effects on children if they engage in problematic behaviours such as violence or substance abuse.

- Intervention programs can be helpful in teaching children social skills. One common approach, social skills training, involves teaching children skills related to three types of deficits: lack of social knowledge, problems in performing appropriate behaviours, and a lack of appropriate monitoring and self-evaluation. Many recent programs include procedures to foster children's understanding and communication of emotion and their self-regulation.

- Children tend to become friends with peers who are similar in age, sex, and race, and who are similar in behaviours such as aggression, sociability, and cooperativeness.

- The degree to which adults encourage children to play with unrelated peers varies greatly in different cultures, as does the degree to which parents expect their children to develop social skills (e.g., negotiating, taking initiative, standing up for their rights) with peers. In addition, the hours children spend with unrelated peers varies considerably across cultures.

Peers in Groups

- The size of very young children's playgroups increases with age, and dominance hierarchies emerge by preschool age.

- By middle childhood, most children belong to cliques of same-sex peers, and members of cliques often are similar in their aggressiveness and orientation toward school. Membership in these cliques is not very stable over time.

- In adolescence, the importance of cliques tends to diminish, and adolescents tend to belong to more than one group. With increasing age, adolescents are not only more autonomous but also tend to look more to individual relationships rather than to a social group to fulfill their social needs. Nonetheless, adolescents often are members of crowds. In adolescence, girls and boys associate with one another more with increasing age, both as members of social groups and in dyadic relationships.

- In some circumstances, the peer group may contribute to the development of antisocial behaviour, alcohol consumption, and substance use, although youths may also actively seek out peers who engage in similar levels of these behaviours.

Status in the Peer Group

- On the basis of their sociometric ratings, children typically have been classified as popular, rejected, neglected, average, or controversial.

- Children's status in the larger peer group varies as a function of their social behaviour and thinking about their social interactions, as well as their physical attractiveness.

- Popular children—those who rank high on sociometric measures—tend to be socially skilled, prosocial, and well regulated in their expression of emotion and behaviour. In contrast, children who are perceived as popular in terms of high status often are aggressive and not always well liked.

- Children who are rejected by their peers often (but not always) are aggressive and/or socially withdrawn. Rejected-aggressive children are low in social skills, tend to make hostile attributions about others' intentions, and have trouble coming up with constructive strategies for dealing with difficult social situations. Withdrawn children who are rejected during preschool tend to be aggressive and hostile.

- Children who are withdrawn from their peers but are not hostile or aggressive are at less risk for rejection during the early school years, although they tend to become rejected later in elementary school.

- Neglected children—those who are not nominated by peers as either liked or disliked—tend to be less sociable, aggressive, and disruptive than average children. They display relatively few behaviours that differ greatly from those of many other children.

- Controversial children tend to have characteristics of both popular and rejected children: they tend to be aggressive, disruptive, and prone to anger, as well as helpful, cooperative, sociable, good at sports, and humorous.

- Although children's status with their peers frequently changes over time, those children who are rejected frequently remain rejected. Children who are neglected or controversial are particularly likely to change their status, even over short periods.

- In general, in numerous cultures, children who are popular or rejected share similar characteristics. However, reticent behaviour may be more valued in some East Asian cultures and has, at least until recently, been related in China to others' perceptions of a child's social competence.

- Rejection by peers in childhood—especially rejection because of aggression—predicts subsequent academic problems, delinquency, substance abuse, social withdrawal, and loneliness and depression. Children who are consistently withdrawn, reticent, and wary with familiar people, including peers, are more likely than less withdrawn children to experience internalizing problems such as depression, low self-worth, and loneliness concurrently and at older ages. It is likely that children's maladaptive behaviour and their peer status both play a causal role in their future adjustment—separately and in combination.

The Role of Parents in Children's Peer Relationships

- Consistent with the predictions of attachment theorists, securely attached children tend to be more positive in their behaviour and affect, more socially skilled, and better liked than insecurely attached children.

- Parents of socially competent and popular children are more likely than parents of less competent children to use warm control, positive verbalizations, reasoning, and explanations in interactions with their children. They also hold more positive beliefs about their children's abilities. It is likely that the causal links between quality of parenting and children's social competence are bidirectional and that both environmental and biological factors play a role in the development of children's social competence with peers.

- Parents are the gatekeepers of young children's peer interactions in the sense that they organize and control their children's social experiences.

- Some parents provide emotional coaching for their children to help them in their social interactions with peers. Such coaching, if appropriate and sensitive, often is associated with children's social competence.

- Stressors such as poverty and marital conflict appear to have a negative effect on the quality of parenting, which in turn is linked to low peer competence in children.

Critical Thinking Questions

1. What are some of the ways in which same-age peer relationships and relationships with older or younger siblings might differ? On what dimensions are they typically the same? What might Piaget and Vygotsky say about the different costs and benefits of interactions with same-age friends and differently aged siblings?

2. What procedures and methods might someone use to assess which 2-year-old playmates in a group are close friends? How would these methods be the same or different if one were assessing close friendships at ages 6, 11, and 17?

3. List at least five ways in which interactions among friends and among non-friends in elementary school likely differ (e.g., type of activities, style of interaction). In what ways might such differences, if they exist, influence children's socioemotional development?

4. Consider a child who is growing up in an isolated area with few peers nearby and is being schooled at home. In what ways might his or her daily experience differ from that of children attending school? How might this affect his or her development, positively or negatively? What factors might mitigate or increase these effects?

Key Terms

aggressive-rejected (peer status), p. 535

cliques, p. 526

controversial (peer status), p. 538

crowds, p. 528

friendship, p. 513

gang, p. 529

neglected (peer status), p. 537

peers, p. 512

popular (peer status), p. 534

reciprocated best friendship, p. 521

rejected (peer status), p. 535

relational aggression, p. 535

social skills training, p. 538

sociometric status, p. 533

victimized (peer status), p. 543

withdrawn-rejected (peer status), p. 536

VICTOR GILBERT, *Make Believe*

chapter 14:

Moral Development

THEMES

- Nature and Nurture
- The Active Child
- Continuity/Discontinuity
- Mechanisms of Change
- The Sociocultural Context
- Individual Differences
- Research and Children's Welfare

I n April 1999, Eric Harris and Dylan Klebold, two students at Columbine High School in Littleton, Colorado, killed a dozen students and a teacher and injured 23 other persons. As terrible as this incident was, it could have been much worse. The two adolescents, who had planned the massacre carefully for months, had actually prepared 95 explosive devices, which did not go off due to an electronic failure. One set of explosives was supposed to go off in the cafeteria, killing many students and forcing others to flee into the schoolyard, where Harris and Klebold had planned to hide in wait and gun them down. Another set of explosives in the killers' cars in the school parking lot was timed to explode after the police and paramedics arrived on the scene, causing more death and chaos.

In videotapes made weeks before the attacks, the boys gleefully predicted that they would kill 250 people and bragged about the publicity they would get for their actions. They also made it clear that their attack was payback for having been humiliated and rejected by their peers: on one videotape, Harris, holding a sawed-off shotgun, declared, "Isn't it fun finally to get the respect that we are going to deserve?" (quoted in Aronson, 2000, p. 86).

In striking contrast to the lethally self-centred actions of Harris and Klebold, in the midst of the carnage, some students stayed with and tried to assist a teacher and other students who were shot. One boy running for his life helped a badly wounded girl get to an exit. Another boy draped himself over his sister and her friend to protect them from being shot (Gibbs, 1999). These students were concerned with others' lives even when their own were at risk.

One week after that shooting in Colorado, a 14-year-old boy entered W. R. Myers High School in Taber, Alberta, and began shooting with a 22-calibre rifle. He killed one student and injured a second one. Fortunately, the second student subsequently recovered.

The Columbine and Taber tragedies, and more recent incidents, like the 2012 Sandy Hook school slayings in Connecticut, are additions to a long list of incidents that raise questions about why some adolescents become involved in antisocial and illegal behaviour, ranging from vandalism and other forms of delinquency to horrific violent crime. The starting point for finding answers to these questions is understanding the aspects of children's thinking and behaviour that contribute to morality.

To act in moral ways on a regular basis, children must have an understanding of right and wrong and the reasons why certain actions are moral or immoral. In addition, they must have a conscience, that is, they must be concerned about acting in a moral manner and feel guilty when they do not. When studying moral development, researchers have focused on a number of different questions related to these requirements. How do children think about moral issues and how does that thinking change with age? Does children's reasoning about moral issues relate to their behaviour? How early do caring and sharing, or aggression and cruelty, first appear in children? What factors contribute to differences among children in the degree to which they display helpful and caring or antisocial behaviours? Can steps be taken to help children develop caring and helpful behaviours and reduce the likelihood of their developing immoral or antisocial behaviours?

GARY CASKEY / REUTERS NEW MEDIA INC. / CORBIS

Although many contributing factors to the Columbine tragedy have been identified, the precise reasons for the actions of Harris and Klebold may never be known. As you will discover in this chapter, moral development—and whether an individual is inclined to prosocial or aggressive, antisocial behaviour—depends on the interaction of a great many variables.

We start our discussion of moral development by examining children's moral judgment—that is, how children think about situations involving moral decisions. Then we examine findings on the early emergence of conscience and the development of *prosocial* behaviours—behaviours that benefit others, such as helping and sharing. Next, we turn to aggression and other antisocial behaviours such as stealing. As you will see, children's moral development is influenced by advances in their social and cognitive capacities, as well as by genetic factors and environmental factors, including family and cultural influences. Therefore, the themes of *individual differences, nature and nurture,* and the *sociocultural context* will be prominent in our discussions.

Theory and research on moral judgment grew out of Piaget's work in this area, which, like his theory on cognitive development (see Chapter 4), involves stages of development and assumes that children actively try to understand the world around them. Consequently, the themes of *continuity/discontinuity, mechanisms of change,* and the *active child* are evident in our consideration of the development of moral judgment. Also in play is the theme of *research and children's welfare,* as we survey intervention programs that are designed to promote prosocial thinking and behaviour and prevent antisocial behaviour.

Moral Judgment

The morality of a given action cannot be determined at face value. Consider a girl who steals food to feed her starving sister. Stealing is usually regarded as an immoral behaviour, but obviously the morality of this girl's behaviour is not so clear. Or consider an adolescent male who offers to help fix a peer's bike but does so because he wants to borrow it later, or perhaps he wants to find out if the bike is worth stealing. Although this adolescent's behaviour may appear altruistic on the surface, it is morally ambiguous, at best, in the first instance and clearly immoral in the second. These examples illustrate that the morality of a behaviour is based partly on the cognitions—including conscious intentions and goals—that underlie the behaviour.

Indeed, some psychologists (as well as philosophers and educators) believe that the reasoning behind a given behaviour is critical for determining whether that behaviour is moral or immoral, and they maintain that changes in moral reasoning form the basis of moral development. As a consequence, much of the research on children's moral development has focused on how children think when they try to resolve moral conflicts and how their reasoning about moral issues changes with age. The most important contributors to the current understanding of the development of children's moral reasoning are Piaget and Lawrence Kohlberg, both of whom took a cognitive developmental approach to studying the development of morality.

Piaget's Theory of Moral Judgment

The foundation of cognitive theories about the origin of morality is Piaget's book *The Moral Judgment of the Child* (1932/1965). In it, Piaget describes how children's moral reasoning changes from a rigid acceptance of the dictates and rules of authorities to an appreciation that moral rules are a product of social interaction and are therefore modifiable. Piaget believed that interactions with peers, more than adult influence, account for advances in children's moral reasoning.

Piaget initially studied children's moral reasoning by observing children playing games, such as marbles, in which they often deal with issues related to rules and fairness. In addition, Piaget interviewed children to examine their thinking about issues such as transgressions of rules, the role of intentionality in morality, fairness of punishment, and justness when distributing goods among people. In these open-ended interviews, he typically presented children with pairs of short vignettes such as the following:

> A little boy who is called John is in his room. He is called to dinner. He goes into the dining room. But behind the door there was a chair, and on the chair there was a tray with fifteen cups on it. John couldn't have known that there was all this behind the door. He goes in, the door knocks against the tray, bang go the fifteen cups, and they all get broken!

> Once there was a little boy whose name was Henry. One day when his mother was out he tried to get some jam out of the cupboard. He climbed up on to a chair and stretched out his arm. But the jam was too high up and he couldn't reach it and have any. But while he was trying to get it he knocked over a cup. The cup fell down and broke.

> (Piaget, 1932/1965, p. 122)

Piaget (1932/1965) argued that through games children learn that rules are a creation of human beings—that they are not absolute but are interpreted, and they can be changed, by the consensus of the peer group.

After children heard these stories, they were asked which boy was naughtier, and why. Children younger than 6 years typically said that the child who broke 15 cups was naughtier. In contrast, older children said that the child who was trying to sneak jam was naughtier, even though he broke only one cup. Partly on the basis of children's responses to such vignettes, Piaget concluded that there are two stages of development in children's moral reasoning, as well as a transitional period between the stages.

The Stage of the Morality of Constraint

The first stage of moral reasoning, referred to as the *morality of constraint*, is most characteristic of children who have not achieved Piaget's stage of concrete operations—that is, children younger than 7 years (see Chapter 4). Children in this stage regard rules and duties to others as unchangeable "givens." In their view, justice is whatever authorities (adults, rules, or laws) say is right, and authorities' punishments for noncompliance are always justified. Acts that are not consistent with rules and authorities' dictates are "bad"; acts that are consistent with them are "good." It is in this stage that children believe that what determines whether an action is good or bad are the consequences of the action, not the motives or intentions behind it.

Piaget suggested that young children's belief that rules are unchangeable is due to two factors, one social and one cognitive. First, Piaget argued that parental control of children is coercive and unilateral, leading to children's unquestioning respect for rules set by adults. Second, children's cognitive immaturity causes them to believe that rules are "real" things, like chairs or gravity, that exist outside people and are not the product of the human mind.

The Transitional Period

According to Piaget, the period from about age 7 or 8 to age 10 represents a transition from the morality of constraint to the next stage. During this transitional period, children typically have more interactions with peers than previously, and these interactions are more egalitarian, with more give-and-take, than are their interactions with adults. In games with peers, children learn that rules can be constructed and changed by the group. They also increasingly learn to take one another's perspective and to cooperate. As a consequence, children start to value fairness and equality and begin to become more autonomous in their thinking about moral issues. Piaget viewed children as taking an active role in this transition, using information from their social interactions to figure out how moral decisions are made and how rules are constructed.

The Stage of Autonomous Morality

By about age 11 or 12, Piaget's second stage of moral reasoning emerges. In this stage, referred to as the stage of *autonomous morality* (also called *moral relativism*), children no longer accept blind obedience to authority as the basis of moral decisions. They fully understand that rules are the product of social agreement and can be changed if the majority of a group agrees to do so. In addition, they consider fairness and equality among people as important factors to consider when constructing rules. Children at this stage believe that punishments should "fit the crime" and that punishment delivered by adults is not necessarily fair. They also consider individuals' motives and intentions when evaluating their behaviour; thus, they view breaking one cup while trying to sneak jam as worse than accidentally breaking 15 cups.

According to Piaget, all normal children progress from the morality of constraint to autonomous moral reasoning. Individual differences in the rate of their progress are due to numerous factors, including differences in children's cognitive maturity, in their opportunities for interactions with peers and for reciprocal role taking, and in how authoritarian and punitive their parents are.

Evaluation of Piaget's Theory

Piaget's general vision of moral development has received some support from empirical research. Studies of children from many countries and various racial or ethnic groups have shown that with age, boys and girls increasingly take motives and intentions into account when judging the morality of actions (N. E. Berg & Mussen, 1975; Lickona, 1976). In addition, parental punitiveness, which would be expected to reinforce a morality of constraints, has been associated with less mature moral reasoning and moral behaviour (M. L. Hoffman, 1983). Finally, consistent with Piaget's belief that cognitive development plays a role in the development of moral judgment, children's performance on tests of perspective-taking skills, Piagetian logical tasks, and IQ tests have all been associated with their level of moral judgment (N. E. Berg & Mussen, 1975; Lickona, 1976).

Some aspects of Piaget's theory, however, have been soundly faulted. For example, there is little evidence that peer interaction per se stimulates moral development (Lickona, 1976). Rather, it seems likely that the quality of peer interactions—for example, whether or not they involve cooperative interactions—is more important than mere quantity of interaction with peers. Piaget also underestimated young children's ability to appreciate the role of intentionality in morality (Nobes, Panagiotaki, & Pawson 2009). When Piagetian moral vignettes are presented in ways that make the individuals' intentions more obvious—such as by using videotaped dramas—preschoolers and early elementary school children are more likely to recognize individuals with bad intentions (Chandler et al., 1973; Grueneich, 1982; Yuill & Perner, 1988). It is probable that in Piaget's research, young children focused primarily on the *consequences* of the individuals' actions because consequences (e.g., John's breaking the 15 cups) were very salient in his stories.

In addition, many 4- and 5-year-olds do *not* think that a person caused a negative outcome "on purpose" if they have been explicitly told that the person had no foreknowledge of the consequences of his or her action or believed that the outcome of the action would be positive rather than negative (Pellizzoni, Siegal, & Surian, 2009). Moreover, even younger children seem to use knowledge of intentionality to evaluate others' behaviour. In one study, 3-year-olds who saw an adult intend (but fail) to hurt another adult were less likely to help that person than they were if the person's behaviour toward the other adult was neutral (intended to neither help nor hurt the other). In contrast, they helped an adult who accidently caused harm as much as they helped an adult whose behaviour was neutral (Vaish, Carpenter, & Tomasello, 2010). Equally impressive, a study conducted at Queen's University demonstrated that 21-month-olds were more likely to help an adult who had tried (but failed) to assist them in retrieving a toy than an adult who had been unwilling to assist them. They were also more likely to help an adult who had tried (but failed) to assist them than an adult whose intentions had not been clear (Dunfield & Kuhlmeier, 2010). Finally, as you will see later in the chapter, it is clear that young children do not believe that some actions, such as hurting others, are right even when adults say they are.

Whatever its shortcomings, Piaget's theory provided the basis for subsequent research on the development of moral judgment. The most notable example is the more complexly differentiated theory of moral development formulated by Kohlberg.

Kohlberg's Theory of Moral Judgment

Heavily influenced by the ideas of Piaget, Kohlberg was primarily interested in the sequences through which children's moral reasoning develops (Colby & Kohlberg, 1987a; Kohlberg, 1976). On the basis of a 20-year longitudinal study in which he first assessed boys' moral reasoning at ages 10, 13, and 16, Kohlberg proposed that moral development proceeds through a specific series of stages that are discontinuous and hierarchical. That is, each new stage reflects a qualitatively different, more adequate way of thinking than the one before it.

Kohlberg assessed moral judgment by presenting children with hypothetical moral dilemmas and then questioning them about the issues these dilemmas involved. The most famous of these dilemmas concerns a man named Heinz, whose wife was dying from a rare form of cancer:

Kohlberg (pictured here), like Piaget, argued that stages of moral reasoning involve a qualitative change in reasoning and that each stage represents a new way of thinking that replaces the child's thinking at prior, lower levels.

LEE LOCKWOOD / TIMEPIX

> There was one drug that the doctors thought might save her. It was a form of radium that a druggist in the same town had recently discovered. The drug was expensive to make, but the druggist was charging 10 times what it cost him to make. The sick woman's husband, Heinz, went to everyone he knew to borrow the money and tried every legal means, but he could only get together about $2,000, which is half of what it cost. He told the druggist his wife was dying, and asked him to sell it cheaper or let him pay later. But the druggist said, "No, I discovered the drug and I'm going to make money from it." So having tried every legal means, Heinz gets desperate and considers breaking into the man's store to steal the drug for his wife.
>
> (Colby & Kohlberg 1987b, p. 1)

After relating this dilemma to children, Kohlberg asked them questions such as: Should Heinz steal the drug? Would it be wrong or right if he did? Why? Is it a husband's duty to steal the drug for his wife if he can get it no other way? For Kohlberg, the reasoning behind choices of what to do in the dilemma, rather than the choices themselves, is what reflects the quality of children's moral reasoning. For example, the response that "Heinz should steal the drug because he probably won't get caught and put in jail" was considered less advanced than "Heinz should steal the drug because he wants his wife to feel better and to live."

Kohlberg's Stages

On the basis of the reasoning underlying children's responses, Kohlberg proposed three levels of moral judgment—preconventional, conventional, and postconventional (or principled). *Preconventional moral reasoning* is self-centred: it focuses on getting rewards and avoiding punishment. *Conventional moral reasoning* is centred on social relationships: it focuses on compliance with social duties and laws. *Postconventional moral reasoning* is centred on ideals: it focuses on moral principles. Each of these three levels involves two stages of moral judgment (see Table 14.1). However, so few people ever attained the highest stage (Stage 6— Universal Ethical Principles) of the postconventional level that Kohlberg (1978) eventually stopped scoring it as a separate stage, and many theorists consider it an elaboration of Stage 5 (Lapsley, 2006).

TABLE 14.1

Kohlberg's Levels and Stages of Moral Reasoning

Preconventional Level

Stage 1: Punishment and Obedience Orientation. At Stage 1, what is seen as right is obedience to authorities. Children's "conscience" (what makes them decide what is right or wrong) is fear of punishment, and their moral action is motivated by avoidance of punishment. The child does not consider the interests of others or recognize that they differ from his or her own interests. Examples of reasoning for (pro) and against (con) Heinz's stealing the drug for his wife are as follows:

> *Pro:* If you let your wife die, you will get in trouble. You'll be blamed for not spending the money to save her and there'll be an investigation of you and the druggist for your wife's death.

> *Con:* You shouldn't steal the drug because you'll be caught and sent to jail if you do. If you do get away, your conscience would bother you thinking how the police would catch up with you at any minute (Kohlberg, 1969, p. 381).

Stage 2: Instrumental and Exchange Orientation. At Stage 2, what is right is what is in one's own best interest or involves equal exchange between people (tit-for-tat exchange of benefits).

> *Pro:* If you do happen to get caught, you could give the drug back and you wouldn't get much of a sentence. It wouldn't bother you much to serve a little jail term, if you have your wife when you get out.

> *Con:* He may not get much of a jail term if he steals the drug, but his wife will probably die before he gets out so it won't do him much good. If his wife dies, he shouldn't blame himself, it wasn't his fault she has cancer (Kohlberg, 1969, p. 381).

Conventional Level

Stage 3: Mutual Interpersonal Expectations, Relationships, and Interpersonal Conformity ("Good Girl, Nice Boy") Orientation. In Stage 3, good behaviour is doing what is expected by people who are close to the person or what people generally expect of someone in a given role (e.g., "a son"). Being "good" is important in itself and means having good motives, showing concern about others, and maintaining good relationships with others.

> *Pro:* No one will think you're bad if you steal the drug, but your family will think you're an inhuman husband if you don't. If you let your wife die, you'll never be able to look anybody in the face again.

> *Con:* It isn't just the druggist who will think you're a criminal, everyone else will, too. After you steal it, you'll feel bad thinking how you've brought dishonor on your family and yourself; you won't be able to face anyone again (Kohlberg, 1969, p. 381).

Stage 4: Social System and Conscience ("Law and Order") Orientation. Right behaviour in Stage 4 involves fulfilling one's duties, upholding laws, and contributing to society or one's group. The individual is motivated to keep the social system going and to avoid a breakdown in its functioning.

> *Pro:* In most marriages, you accept the responsibility to look after one another's health and after their life and you have the responsibility when you live with someone to try and make it a happy life (Colby & Kohlberg, 1987b, p. 43).

In the revised coding manual, Colby and Kohlberg (1987b) provide virtually no examples of Stage 4 reasoning supporting the decision that Heinz should not steal the drug for his wife. However, they provide reasons for not stealing the drug for a pet: Heinz should not steal for a pet because animals cannot contribute to society (p. 37).

Postconventional or Principled Level

Stage 5: Social Contract or Individual Rights Orientation. At Stage 5, right behaviour involves upholding rules that are in the best interest of the group ("the greatest good for the greatest number"), are impartial, or were agreed upon by the group. However, some values and rights, such as life and liberty, are universally right and must be upheld in any society, regardless of majority opinion. It is difficult to construct a Stage 5 reason that justifies not stealing the drug.

> *Pro:* Heinz should steal the drug because the right to life supersedes or transcends the right to property (Colby & Kohlberg, 1987b, p. 11).

> *Pro:* Heinz is working from a hierarchy of values, in which life (at least the life of his wife) is higher than honesty. ... Human life and its preservation—at least as presented here—must take precedence over other values, like Heinz's desire to be honest and law abiding, or the druggist's love of money and his rights. All values stem from the ultimate value of life (Colby & Kohlberg, 1987b, p. 54).

Stage 6: Universal Ethical Principles. Right behaviour in Stage 6 is commitment to self-chosen ethical principles that reflect universal principles of justice (e.g., equality of human rights, respect for the dignity of each human being). When laws violate these principles, the individual should act in accordance with these universal principles rather than with the law.

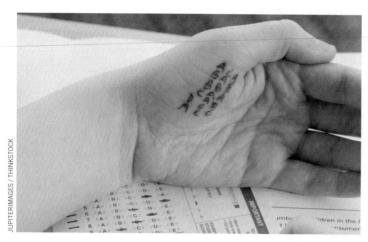

Children's and adolescents' moral reasoning can be quite low-level. Moreover, even if their reasoning is at the conventional level, they sometimes act in ways that do not reflect their highest level of moral reasoning.

Kohlberg argued that people in all parts of the world move through his stages in the same order, although they differ in how many stages they attain. As in Piaget's theory, age-related advances in cognitive skills, especially perspective taking, are believed to underlie the development of higher-level moral judgment. Consistent with Kohlberg's theory, people who have higher-level cognitive and perspective-taking skills and who are better educated exhibit higher-level moral judgment (Colby et al., 1983; Mason & Gibbs, 1993; Rest, 1983).

In their initial longitudinal study, Kohlberg and his colleagues (Colby et al., 1983) followed 58 boys into adulthood and found that moral judgment changed systematically with age (see Figure 14.1). When the boys were 10 years old, they used primarily Stage 1 reasoning (blind obedience to authority) and Stage 2 reasoning (self-interest). Thereafter, reasoning in these stages dropped off markedly. For most adolescents aged 14 and older, Stage 3 reasoning (being "good" to earn approval or maintain relationships) was the primary mode of reasoning, although some adolescents occasionally used Stage 4 reasoning (fulfilling duties and upholding laws to maintain social order). Only a small number of participants, even by age 36, ever achieved Stage 5 (upholding the best interests of the group while recognizing life and liberty as universal values).

Critique of Kohlberg's Theory

Kohlberg's work is important because it demonstrated that children's moral judgment changes in relatively systematic ways with age. In addition, because individuals' levels of moral judgment have been related to their moral behaviour, especially for people reasoning at higher levels (e.g., Kutnick, 1986; B. Underwood & Moore, 1982), Kohlberg's work has been useful in understanding how cognitive processes contribute to moral behaviour.

Kohlberg's theory and findings have also produced controversy and criticism. One criticism is that Kohlberg did not sufficiently differentiate between truly moral issues and issues of social convention (Nucci & Gingo, 2011) (we examine this differentiation on pages 563–565). Another criticism pertains to cultural differences.

FIGURE 14.1 **Mean percentage of moral reasoning at each stage for each age group** This graph shows age trends in moral reasoning in Kohlberg's longitudinal sample. (Adapted from Colby et al., 1983)

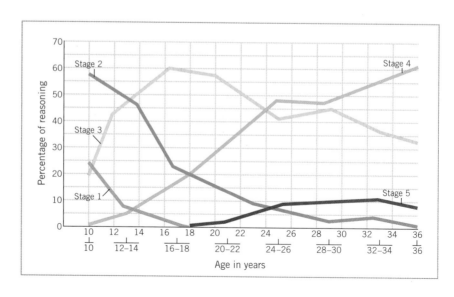

Although children in many non-Western, nonindustrialized cultures start out reasoning much the way Western children do in Kohlberg's scoring system, their moral judgment within this system generally does not advance as far as that of their Western peers (e.g., Nisan & Kohlberg, 1982; Snarey, 1985). This finding has led to the objection that Kohlberg's stories and scoring system reflect an intellectualized conception of morality that is biased by Western values (E. L. Simpson, 1974). In many non-Western societies, in which the goal of preserving group harmony is of critical importance and most conflicts of interest are worked out through face-to-face contact, issues of individual rights and civil liberties may not be viewed as especially relevant. Moreover, in some societies, obedience to authorities, elders, and religious dictates are valued more than principles of freedom and individual rights.

Another criticism has to do with Kohlberg's argument that change in moral development is discontinuous. Kohlberg asserted that because each stage is more advanced than the previous one, once an individual attains a new stage, he or she seldom reasons at a lower stage. However, research has shown that children and adults alike often reason at different levels on different occasions—or even on the same occasion (Rest, 1979). As a consequence, it is not clear that the development of moral reasoning is qualitatively discontinuous. Rather, children and adolescents may gradually acquire the cognitive skills to use increasingly higher stages of moral reasoning, but they also may use lower stages when it is consistent with their goals, motives, or beliefs in a particular situation. For example, even an adolescent who is capable of using Stage 4 reasoning may well use Stage 2 reasoning to justify a decision to break the law for personal gain.

A hotly debated issue regarding Kohlberg's theory is whether there are gender differences in moral judgment. As noted previously, Kohlberg developed his conception of moral-reasoning stages on the basis of interviews with a sample of boys. Carol Gilligan (1982) argued that Kohlberg's classification of moral judgment is biased against females because it does not adequately recognize differences in the way males and females reason morally. Gilligan suggested that because of the way they are socialized, males tend to value principles of justice and rights, whereas females value caring, responsibility for others, and avoidance of exploiting or hurting others (Gilligan & Attanucci, 1988). This difference in moral orientation, according to Gilligan, causes males to score higher on Kohlberg's dilemmas than females do.

Contrary to Gilligan's theory, there is little evidence that boys and girls, or men and women, score differently on Kohlberg's stages of moral judgment (Turiel, 1998; L. J. Walker, 1984, 1991). However, consistent with Gilligan's arguments, during adolescence and adulthood, females focus somewhat more on issues of caring about other people in their moral judgment (Garmon et al., 1996; Jaffee & Hyde, 2000). Differences in males' and females' moral reasoning seem to be most evident when individuals report on moral dilemmas in their own lives (Jaffee & Hyde, 2000). Thus, Gilligan's work has been very important in broadening the focus of research on moral reasoning and in demonstrating that males and females differ somewhat in the issues they focus on when confronting moral dilemmas.

Although Kohlberg's stages probably are not as invariant in sequence nor as universal as he claimed, they do describe changes in children's moral reasoning that are observed in many Western societies. These changes are important because people with higher-level moral reasoning are more likely to behave in a moral manner (Kohlberg & Candee, 1984; Matsuba & Walker, 2004) and to assist others (Blasi, 1980), and they are less likely to engage in delinquent activities (Stams et al., 2006). Thus, understanding developmental changes in moral judgment provides insight into why, as children grow older, they tend to engage in more prosocial behaviour.

prosocial behaviour ■ Voluntary behaviour intended to benefit another, such as helping, sharing with, and comforting others.

Prosocial Moral Judgment

When children respond to Kohlberg's dilemmas, they are choosing between two acts that are wrong—for example, stealing or allowing someone to die. However, there are other types of moral dilemmas that children encounter in which the choice is between personal advantage and fairness to, or the welfare of, others (Damon, 1977; N. Eisenberg, 1986; Skoe, 1998).

To determine how children resolve these dilemmas, researchers present children with stories in which the characters must choose between helping someone or meeting their own needs. These dilemmas are called *prosocial* moral dilemmas and concern **prosocial behaviour**—that is, voluntary behaviour intended to benefit others, such as helping, sharing with, and comforting others. The following story illustrates the type of dilemma used with children 4 years or older (with slight modifications for the latter group):

NANCY EISENBERG

> One day a boy named Eric was going to a friend's birthday party. On his way he saw a boy who had fallen down and hurt his leg [see Figure 14.2]. The boy asked Eric to go to his house and get his parents so the parents could come and take him to a doctor. But if Eric did run and get the child's parents, he would be late to the birthday party and miss the ice cream, cake, and all the games.
>   What should Eric do? Why?
>
> (Eisenberg-Berg & Hand, 1979, p. 358)

FIGURE 14.2 Moral reasoning: Eric's dilemma This is one of the pictures that accompany the prosocial moral-reasoning vignette of Eric's birthday-party dilemma.

On these tests, children and adolescents use five levels of prosocial moral reasoning, delineated by Eisenberg (1986), that resemble Kohlberg's stages (see Table 14.2). Preschool children express primarily hedonistic reasoning (Level 1) in which their own needs are central. They typically indicate that Eric should go to the party because he wants to. However, preschoolers also often mention other people's physical needs, which suggests that some preschoolers are concerned about other people's welfare (Level 2). (For example, they may indicate that Eric should help because the other boy is bleeding or hurt.) Such recognition of others' needs increases in the elementary school years. In addition, in elementary school, children increasingly express concern about social approval and acting in a manner that is considered "good" by other people and society (e.g., they indicate that Eric should help "to be good"; Level 3).

In late childhood and adolescence, children's judgments begin to be based, in varying degrees, on explicit perspective taking (Level 4a—e.g., "Eric should think about how he would feel in that situation") and morally relevant affect such as sympathy, guilt, and positive feelings due to the real or imagined consequences of performing beneficial actions (e.g., "Eric would feel bad if he didn't help and the boy was in pain"). The judgments of a minority of older adolescents reflect internalized values and affect (Levels 4b and 5) related to not living up to those values (e.g., self-censure).

In general, this pattern of changes in prosocial moral reasoning has been found for children in Brazil, Germany, Israel, and Japan (Carlo et al., 1996; N. Eisenberg et al., 1985; I. Fuchs et al., 1986; Munekata & Ninomiya, 1985). Nevertheless, children from different cultures do vary somewhat in their prosocial moral reasoning. For example, stereotypic and internalized reasoning were not clearly different factors for Brazilian older adolescents and adults, whereas the two types of reasoning were somewhat more different for similar groups in the United States (Carlo et al., 2008). Moreover, older children (and adults) in some traditional societies in Papua New Guinea exhibit higher-level reasoning less often than do people of the same age in Western cultures. However, the types of reasoning they frequently use— reasoning that pertains to others' needs and the relationship between people—are

TABLE 14.2

Levels of Prosocial Behaviour

Level 1: Hedonistic, self-focused orientation.

The individual is concerned with his or her own interests rather than with moral considerations. Reasons for assisting or not assisting another include the prospects of direct personal gain or future reciprocation and whether one needs or likes the other person. (Predominant mode primarily for preschoolers and younger elementary school children.)

Level 2: Needs-based orientation.

The individual expresses concern for the physical, material, and psychological needs of others even when those needs conflict with his or her own. This concern is expressed in the simplest terms, without clear evidence of self-reflective role taking, verbal expressions of sympathy, or reference to such emotions as pride or guilt. (Predominant mode for many preschoolers and many elementary school children.)

Level 3: Approval and/or stereotyped orientation.

The individual justifies engaging or not engaging in prosocial behaviour on the basis of others' approval or acceptance and/or on stereotyped images of good and bad persons and behaviour. (Predominant mode for some elementary school and high school students.)

Level 4a: Self-reflective empathic orientation.

The individual's judgments include evidence of self-reflective sympathetic responding or role taking, concern with the other's humanness, and/or guilt or positive emotion related to the consequences of one's actions. (Predominant mode for a few older elementary school children and many high school students.)

Level 4b: Transitional level.

The individual's justifications for helping or not helping involve internalized values, norms, duties, or responsibilities. They may also reflect concerns for the condition of the larger society or refer to the necessity of protecting the rights and dignities of other persons. These ideals, however, are not clearly or strongly stated. (Predominant mode for a minority of people of high school age or older.)

Level 5: Strongly internalized stage.

The individual's justifications for helping or not helping are based on internalized values, norms, or responsibilities; the desire to maintain individual and societal contractual obligations or improve the condition of society; and the belief in the rights, dignity, and equality of all individuals. This level is also characterized by positive or negative emotions related to whether one succeeds in living up to one's own values and accepted norms. (Predominant mode for only a small minority of high school students.)

Source: Adapted from N. Eisenberg, 1986

consistent with the values of a culture in which people must cooperate with one another in face-to-face interactions in order to survive (Tietjen, 1986). In nearly all cultures, reasoning that reflects the needs of others and global concepts of good and bad behaviour (Kohlberg's Stage 3 and Eisenberg's Level 3) emerges at somewhat younger ages on prosocial dilemmas than on Kohlberg's moral dilemmas.

With age, children's prosocial moral judgment, like their reasoning on Kohlberg's moral dilemmas, becomes more abstract and is based more on internalized principles and values (N. Eisenberg, 1986; N. Eisenberg et al., 1995). Paralleling the case with moral reasoning on Kohlberg's measure, in numerous cultures those children, adolescents, and young adults who use higher-level prosocial moral reasoning tend to be more sympathetic and prosocial in their behaviour than do peers who use lower-level prosocial moral judgment (Carlo, Knight, et al., 2010; N. Eisenberg, 1986; Janssens & Dekovic, 1997; Kumru et al., 2012).

Domains of Social Judgment

In everyday life, children make decisions about many kinds of actions, including whether to follow rules and laws or break them, whether to fight or walk away from conflict, whether to dress formally or informally, whether to study or goof off after

moral judgments ■ Decisions that pertain to issues of right and wrong, fairness, and justice.

social conventional judgments ■ Decisions that pertain to customs or regulations intended to secure social coordination and social organization.

personal judgments ■ Decisions that refer to actions in which individual preferences are the main consideration.

school, and so on. Some of these decisions involve *moral judgments;* others involve *social conventional judgments;* and still others involve *personal judgments* (Nucci, 1981; Turiel, 2006).

Moral judgments pertain to issues of right and wrong, fairness, and justice. **Social conventional judgments** pertain to customs or regulations intended to ensure social coordination and social organization, such as choices about modes of dress, table manners, and forms of greeting (e.g., using "Sir" when addressing a male teacher). **Personal judgments** pertain to actions in which individual preferences are the main consideration. For example, within Western culture, the choice of friends or recreational activities usually is considered a personal choice (Nucci & Weber, 1995). These distinctions are important because whether children perceive particular judgments as moral, social conventional, or personal affects the importance they accord them.

Children's Use of Social Conventional Judgment

In many cultures, children begin to differentiate between moral and social conventional issues at an early age (J. G. Miller & Bersoff, 1992; Nucci, Camino, & Sapiro, 1996; Smetana et al., 2012; Tisak, 1995). By age 3, they generally believe that moral violations (e.g., stealing another child's possession or hitting another child) are more wrong than social conventional violations (e.g., not saying "please" when asking for something or wearing your clothes inside out). By age 4, they believe that moral transgressions, but not social conventional transgressions, are wrong even if an adult does not know about them and even if adult authorities have not said they are wrong (Smetana & Braeges, 1990). This distinction is reflected in the following excerpt from an interview with a 5-year-old boy:

> *Interviewer:* This is a story about Park School. In Park School the children are allowed to hit and push others if they want. It's okay to hit and push others. Do you think it is all right for Park School to say children can hit and push others if they want to?
>
> *Boy:* No. It is not okay.
>
> *Interviewer:* Why not?
>
> *Boy:* Because that is like making other people unhappy. You can hurt them that way. It hurts other people, hurting is not good.

This boy is firm in his belief that hurting others is wrong, even if adults say it is acceptable. Children tend to justify their condemnation of moral violations by referring to violations of fairness and harm to others' welfare (Turiel, 2008). Compare that reasoning with the boy's response to a question about the acceptability of a school policy that allows children to take off their clothes in hot weather.

> *Interviewer:* I know another school in a different city. … Grove School … At Grove School the children are allowed to take their clothes off if they want to. Is it okay or not okay for Grove School to say children can take their clothes off if they want to?
>
> *Boy:* Yes. Because this is the rule.
>
> *Interviewer:* Why can they have that rule?
>
> *Boy:* If that's what the boss wants to do, he can do that. … He is in charge of the school.

(Turiel, 1987, p. 101)

With regard to both moral and social conventional issues in the family, children and, to a lesser degree, adolescents believe that parents have authority (Smetana,

1988; Yau, Smetana, & Metzger, 2009), unless the parent gives commands that violate moral and conventional principles (Yamada, 2009). With respect to matters of personal judgment, however, even preschoolers tend to believe that they themselves should have control, and older children and adolescents are quite firm in their belief that they should control choices in the personal domain (e.g., their appearance, how they spend their money, their choice of friends) at home and at school (Lagattuta et al., 2010; Nucci & Gingo, 2011). At the same time, parents usually feel that they should have some authority over their children's personal choices, even into adolescence, so parents and teenagers frequently do battle in this domain—battles that parents often lose (Lins-Dyer & Nucci, 2007; Smetana, 1988; Smetana & Asquith 1994).

Cultural and Socioeconomic Differences

People in different cultures sometimes vary in whether they view decisions as moral, social conventional, or personal (Shweder et al., 1987). Take the question of whether one engages in self-promotion. Children from mainland China consider telling modest lies about having done a good deed more acceptable than European-Canadian children (i.e., children from mainland China deny having done a good deed that they did). Furthermore, both children from mainland China and Chinese-Canadian children considered telling truthful but self-promoting statements (e.g., telling someone that you cleaned up the classroom) less acceptable than did European-Canadian children (Cameron et al., 2012). Cultural differences exist even within Western societies. For example, Canadian girls score higher than Canadian boys on a care-based morality measure, but there are no such gender differences among Norwegian boys and girls (Skoe et al., 1999).

Cultural differences with regard to which events are considered moral, social conventional, or personal sometimes arise from religious beliefs (Turiel, 2006; Wainryb & Turiel, 1995). For example, devout Hindus believe that if a widow eats fish, she has committed an immoral act. In Hindu society, fish is viewed as a "hot" food, and eating "hot" food is believed to stimulate the sexual appetite. Consequently, traditional Hindu adults and children assume that a widow who eats fish will behave immorally and offend her husband's spirit. Underlying this belief is the obligation that Hinduism places on a widow to seek salvation and be reunited with the soul of her husband rather than initiating another relationship (Shweder et al., 1987). Of course, for most other people in the world, a widow's eating fish would be considered a matter of personal choice. Thus, beliefs regarding the significance and consequences of various actions in different cultures can influence the designation of behaviours as moral, social conventional, or personal.

Even within a given culture, different religious beliefs may affect what is considered a moral or a social conventional issue. In Finland, for example, conservative religious adolescents are less likely to make a distinction between the moral and social conventional domain than are non-religious youths. For the religious youths, the most crucial deciding factor for non-moral (conventional) issues is God's word as written in the Bible (i.e., whether or not the Bible says a particular social convention is wrong) (Vainio, 2011).

Socioeconomic class can also influence the way children make such designations. Research in the United States and Brazil indicates that children of lower-income families are somewhat less likely than middle-class children to differentiate sharply between moral and social conventional actions and, prior to adolescence, are also less likely to view personal issues as a matter of choice. These differences may be

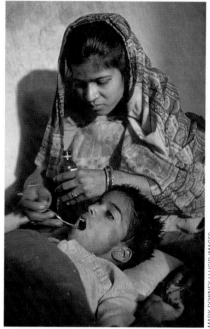

Children in India are much more likely than children in Canada to say that helping other people is a moral obligation, not a matter of personal choice.

due to the tendency of individuals of low socioeconomic status both to place a greater emphasis on submission to authority and to allow children less autonomy (Nucci, 1997). This social-class difference in children's views may evaporate as youths approach adolescence, although Brazilian mothers of lower-income youths still claim more control over personal issues than do mothers of middle-income youths (Lins-Dyer & Nucci, 2007).

review

How children think about moral issues provides one basis for their moral or immoral behaviour. Piaget delineated two moral stages—morality of constraint and autonomous morality—separated by a transitional stage. In the first stage, children regard rules as fixed and tend to weigh consequences more than intentions in evaluating actions. According to Piaget, a combination of cognitive growth and egalitarian, cooperative interactions with peers brings children to the autonomous stage, in which they recognize that rules can be changed by group consent and judge the morality of actions on the basis of intentions more than consequences. Aspects of Piaget's theory have not held up well to criticism—for example, children use intentions to evaluate behaviour at a younger age than Piaget believed they could—but his theory provided the foundation for Kohlberg's work on stages of moral reasoning.

Kohlberg outlined three levels of moral judgment—preconventional, conventional, and postconventional—each initially containing two stages (Stage 6 was subsequently dropped). He hypothesized that his sequence of stages reflected age-related discontinuous changes in moral reasoning and that children everywhere go through the same stage progression (although they may stop development at different points). Several aspects of Kohlberg's theory are controversial, including whether children's moral reasoning moves through discontinuous stages of development, whether the theory is valid for all cultures, and whether there are gender differences in moral judgment. Research on other types of moral judgment, such as prosocial moral judgment, suggests that children's concerns about the needs of others emerge at a younger age than Kohlberg's work indicates. However, with age, prosocial moral reasoning, like Kohlberg's justice-oriented moral reasoning, becomes more abstract and based on internalized principles.

There are important differences among the moral, social conventional, and personal domains of behaviour and judgment—differences that even children recognize. For example, young children believe that moral transgressions, but not social conventional or personal violations, are wrong regardless of whether adults say they are unacceptable. There are some cultural differences in whether a given behaviour is viewed as having moral implications, but it is likely that people in all cultures differentiate among moral, social conventional, and personal domains of functioning.

The Early Development of Conscience

We all are familiar with the notion of a conscience—that voice inside us that pushes us to behave in moral ways and makes us feel guilty if we do not. Stated more formally, **conscience** is an internal regulatory mechanism that increases the individual's ability to conform to standards of conduct accepted in his or her culture. Consistent with Freud's theory (see Chapter 9), it is likely that the conscience of a young child reflects primarily internalized parental standards (although probably the standards of both parents, not just of the same-gender parent, as Freud suggested). The conscience restrains antisocial behaviour or destructive impulses and promotes a child's compliance with adults' rules and standards, even when no one is monitoring the child's behaviour (Kochanska, 2002). The conscience can also promote prosocial behaviour by causing the child to feel guilty when

conscience ■ An internal regulatory mechanism that increases the individual's ability to conform to standards of conduct accepted in his or her culture.

engaging in uncaring behaviour or failing to live up to internalized values about helping others (N. Eisenberg, 2000; M. L. Hoffman, 1982).

Factors Affecting the Development of Conscience

Contrary to Freud's idea that the conscience emerges as an outcome of identification with the same-gender parent at about age 4 to 6, children actually develop a conscience slowly over time. By age 2, toddlers start to show an appreciation for moral standards and rules and begin to exhibit signs of guilt when they do something wrong (Kopp, 2001; R. A. Thompson & Newton, 2010; Zahn-Waxler & Robinson, 1995). These two components of conscience—the desire to comply with rules and feelings of guilt when failing to do so—are quite stable in their early development from 22 to 45 months of age (Aksan & Kochanska, 2005; Kochanska et al., 2002). Children's growing understanding of others' emotions and goals, and their increasing capacity for empathic concern, are likely contributors to the development of conscience (R. A. Thompson, 2012).

Young children often have not yet internalized some of their parents' prohibitions and values. The degree to which they do so appears to depend in part on the quality of the parenting they receive and, in part, on their temperament.

As they mature, children are more likely to take on their parents' moral values, and to exhibit guilt for violating those values, if their parents use disciplinary practices that de-emphasize parental power and include rational explanations that help children understand and learn the parents' values (Kochanska & Aksan, 2006; Laible et al., 2008; Volling et al., 2009). Children's adoption of their parents' values is also facilitated by a secure, positive parent–child relationship, which inclines children to be open to, and eager to internalize, their parents' communication of their values (Bretherton et al., 1997; Kochanska et al., 2005, 2008).

Children may develop a conscience in different ways according to their temperament. Toddlers who are prone to fear (e.g., who are fearful of unfamiliar people or situations) tend to exhibit more guilt at a young age than do less fearful children (Kochanska et al., 2002). Moreover, for those infants who are prone to fear, the development of conscience seems to be promoted by the mother's use of gentle discipline that includes reasoning with the child and providing non-material incentives for compliance (Kochanska & Aksan, 2006). When mothers use gentle discipline, fearful children do not become so apprehensive and anxious that they tune out their mother's messages about desired behaviour. Gentle discipline arouses fearful children just enough that they attend to and remember what their mothers tell them (Kochanska, 1993).

In contrast, gentle discipline seems to be unrelated to the development of conscience in fearless young children, perhaps because it is insufficient to arouse their attention (Kochanska, 1997a). What does seem to foster the development of conscience in fearless children is a parent–child relationship characterized by secure attachment and mutual cooperation (Kochanska, 1995; Kochanska & Aksan, 2006). Fearless children appear motivated more by the desire to please their mother than by a fear of her (Kochanska, 1997b). Unfortunately, research on this topic seldom has been conducted with fathers, so it is not known whether the findings for the effects of mothers' discipline also generalize to fathers' discipline.

The effects of parenting on children's conscience also vary with their genes, which, as discussed in Chapter 10, affect temperament. This can be seen in the dynamic between maternal responsiveness—the mother's acceptance of, and sensitivity to, the child—and the child's genotype for the serotonin transporter gene, SLC6A4. As discussed in Chapter 11 (page 437), a particular allele variant of SLC6A4 is believed to make children especially reactive to their rearing environment. For children with this allele variant, high maternal responsiveness is associated with high levels of conscience at 15 to 52 months of age. Conversely, for children with this same variant, low maternal responsiveness is associated with low conscience. For children with a different genotype for SLC6A4, their level of conscience is unrelated to their mother's responsiveness (Kochanska et al., 2011). This pattern is an example of differential susceptibility, whereby some children are more reactive than others are to the quality of parenting they receive, be it of high or low quality.

The early development of conscience undoubtedly contributes to whether children come to accept the moral values of their parents and society. Indeed, in a longitudinal assessment of children's behavioural and affective expression of guilt (in which they were led to believe that they had broken a valuable object), the children's levels of guilt at 22 and 45 months of age predicted their morality at 54 months of age (e.g., their violating rules about touching prohibited toys, cheating on tasks, and expressing selfish and antisocial themes when discussing vignettes with morally relevant topics) (Kochanska et al., 2002). This, in turn, predicted whether they engaged in hurtful or problematic social behaviour at 67 months (Kochanska et al., 2008). In a related study, children's internalization of parental rules at 2 to 4 years of age predicted their self-perceptions as being moral at 67 months (Kochanska et al., 2010). Therefore, the nature of early parent–child disciplinary interactions sets the stage for children's subsequent moral development.

review

The conscience is believed to reflect internalized moral standards; it restrains the child from engaging in immoral behaviour and involves feelings of guilt for misbehaviour. Contrary to Freud's beliefs, the conscience emerges slowly over time, beginning before age 2. Children are more likely to internalize parental standards if they have secure attachments with their parents and if their parents use rational explanations in their discipline rather than excessive parental power. Factors that promote the development of conscience differ somewhat for children depending on their temperament and genetic inheritance.

Prosocial Behaviour

As noted earlier, moral behaviour is as important for moral development as are moral thinking and moral emotions. The same is true for prosocial behaviour; all children are capable of prosocial behaviours, but children differ in how often they engage in these behaviours and in their reasons for doing so. Consider the behaviour of the following three preschool children:

Sara is drawing a picture and has a box of crayons. Erin is sitting across from her, and wants to draw. But Erin has only a single crayon and all the rest are in use by other children. She looks around for crayons of other colors. After a short time, Erin looks somewhat distressed. Sara notices that Erin is looking for crayons and is distressed, so she smiles and hands Erin a few of her own crayons, saying, "Here, do you want to use these?"

Marc is sitting at a table drawing with crayons when Manuel comes over and wants to draw. Manuel can't find any crayons and shows signs of upset. Marc looks at Manuel and then returns to his own drawing. Finally, Manuel asks Marc, "Can I have some crayons?" At first Marc ignores Manuel. After Manuel asks for crayons again, Marc hands Manuel three crayons without any comment or display of emotion.

Sakina is drawing when Darren comes to the table, picks up a piece of paper, and looks around for crayons. When Darren can't find any, he exhibits mild distress and then asks Sakina for some crayons. Sakina just ignores him. When Darren tries to take a crayon that Sakina is not using, Sakina angrily pushes him away.

(Eisenberg, unpublished laboratory observations)

Seeing that someone else is sad or in distress, Sara gladly shares without even being asked. Marc shares only if asked repeatedly. Sakina doesn't share at all and does not seem to care if other children are upset. Do these differences in behaviour forecast consistent differences in Sara's, Marc's, and Sakina's positive moral behaviour as they are growing up?

The answer is yes: there is some developmental consistency in children's readiness to engage in prosocial behaviours, such as sharing, helping, and comforting (N. Eisenberg & Fabes, 1998; Knafo et al., 2008). In fact, children who, like Sara, share spontaneously with peers tend to be more concerned with others' needs throughout childhood and adolescence and even in early adulthood. One longitudinal study found that, in comparison with their peers, for example, children who spontaneously engage in prosocial behaviours were more likely to assist other people even when doing so involved a cost to themselves. As young adults, they reported that they felt responsible for the welfare of others and that they usually tried to suppress aggression toward others when angered. This view of themselves was supported by friends, who rated them as more sympathetic than study participants who engaged in less spontaneous prosocial behaviours in preschool (N. Eisenberg et al., 2002; N. Eisenberg, Guthrie, et al., 1999). In contrast, children like Sakina are unlikely to be concerned with others' needs and feelings when they are older.

Of course, not all prosocial behaviours are of equal worth. Sometimes children help or share to get something in return, to gain social acceptance from peers, or to avoid their anger ("I'll share my doll if you'll be my friend"). However, most parents and teachers want children to perform prosocial behaviours not for rewards or social approval but for altruistic motives. **Altruistic motives** initially include empathy or sympathy for others and, at later ages, the desire to act in ways consistent with one's own conscience and moral principles (N. Eisenberg, 1986).

altruistic motives ■ Helping others for reasons that initially include empathy or sympathy for others and, at later ages, the desire to act in ways consistent with one's own conscience and moral principles.

In their second year, most children are willing to share objects and treats with their parents and with other children.

HOWARD SAYER / ALAMY

The Development of Prosocial Behaviour

The origins of altruistic prosocial behaviour are rooted in the capacity to feel empathy and sympathy. As discussed in Chapter 10, *empathy* is an emotional reaction to another's emotional state or condition (e.g., sadness, poverty) that is highly similar to (or consistent with) the other person's state or condition (N. Eisenberg, 1986; M. L. Hoffman, 2000). For example, if a child becomes sad upon observing another person's sadness or pain, the child is experiencing empathy. To experience empathy, children must be able to identify the emotions of others (at least to some degree) and understand that another person is feeling an emotion or is in some kind of need.

Charitable activities in schools have become part of the regular curriculum, with an eye to increasing prosocial behaviour and citizenship. This group of students participated in the Terry Fox Run to raise money for cancer research.

DIANA MARTIN / CHATHAM DAILY NEWS / QMI AGENCY

Young children who view another child's distress sometimes respond with looks of concern or attempts to console or help the distressed peer—about 20% of the time in a study of 16- to 33-month-olds (C. Howes & Farver, 1987). Even young infants sometimes show interest in a peer's distress.

Sympathy is a feeling of concern for another in reaction to the other's emotional state or condition. Although sympathy often is an outcome of empathizing with another's negative emotion or negative situation, what distinguishes sympathy from empathy is the element of concern: people who experience sympathy for another person are not merely feeling the same emotion as the other person.

An important factor contributing to empathy or sympathy is, obviously, the ability to take the perspective of others. Although early theorists such as Piaget believed that children are unable to do this until age 6 to 7 (Piaget & Inhelder, 1956/1977), it is now clear that children have some ability to understand others' perspectives much earlier (Vaish, Carpenter, & Tomasello, 2009). By 10 to 14 months of age, and occasionally between age 8 and 12 months, children sometimes become disturbed and upset when they view other people who are upset (Knafo et al., 2008; Roth-Hanania et al., 2011).

Of course, it may be that infants are not really sympathizing with others' distress; they may become upset merely because they do not differentiate clearly between another person's emotional distress and their own (M. L. Hoffman, 2000). Indeed, young children sometimes seek comfort from a parent when they see someone else upset or when they are upset both for another person and for themselves (Zahn-Waxler, Radke-Yarrow, & King, 1979).

By 18 to 25 months of age, toddlers in laboratory studies sometimes share a personal object with an adult whom they have viewed being harmed by another (for example, by having a piece of personal property taken away or destroyed). They also will sometimes comfort an adult who appears to be injured or distressed, or help an adult retrieve a dropped object or obtain food (Dunfield et al., 2011; Vaish et al., 2009). Such behaviours are especially likely to occur if the adult explicitly and emotionally communicates his or her need (C. A. Brownell, Svetlova, & Nichols, 2009), but they sometimes occur even when the adult does not express an emotional reaction (Vaish et al., 2009). (It should be noted that in studies like these, toddlers seem particularly likely to help adults achieve a task or goal, like retrieving a dropped object [Warneken & Tomasello, 2006], but are much less likely to share one of their own objects [Svetlova, Nichols, & Brownell, 2010].) In displaying empathy, children in the second year of life also are more likely to try to comfort someone who is upset than to become upset themselves, indicating that they know who is suffering. Consider the following example:

> A neighbor's baby boy cries. Jenny (18 months old) looked startled, her body stiffened. She approached and tried to give the baby cookies. She followed him around and began to whimper herself. She then tried to stroke his hair, but he pulled away. Later, Jenny approached her mother, led her to the baby, and tried to put her mother's hand on the baby's head. He calmed down a little, but Jenny still looked worried. She continued to bring him toys and to pat his head and shoulders.
>
> (Radke-Yarrow & Zahn-Waxler, 1984, p. 89)

In the second and third years of life, the frequency and variety of young children's prosocial behaviours increase. In a study conducted at Queen's University, researchers examined three types of prosocial behaviours in children 2, 3, and 4 years of age. All three age groups were consistent in helping an experimenter complete a puzzle by handing her pieces (instrumental need). Between 2 and 3 years of age, there was an increase in children's tendency to help someone experiencing emotional distress. Finally, across all three ages, children were least likely to share their food or stickers with the experimenter (material desire) (see Figure 14.3) (Dunfield & Kuhlmeier, 2013).

During their second year of life, children not only increasingly comfort others (see Table 14.3) and share objects but also assist adults with various tasks such as sweeping, carrying objects, or setting the table (Rheingold, 1982; Warneken, Chen, & Tomasello, 2006). Moreover, their prosocial behaviours at home often seem to be motivated by concern for others because they frequently show expressions of sympathy when they help or comfort others (Knafo et al., 2008; Radke-Yarrow & Zahn-Waxler, 1984). As shown in Table 14.3, 25% of 23- to 25-month-olds showed concern when they observed someone in distress that they had not caused themselves.

As should be clear from Table 14.3, however, young children do not regularly act in prosocial ways (S. Lamb & Zakhireh, 1997). Between the ages of 2 and 3, children most often ignore their siblings' distress or need, or they simply watch without intervening. Occasionally, they even make the situation worse with teasing or aggression (see "Aggressive behaviour" in Table 14.3) (Dunn, 1988). In one study of children in a playgroup setting, for instance, 16- to 33-month-olds responded to peers' distress only 22% of the time, usually by attempting to intervene on the peer's behalf, comforting the peer, or bringing the peer's distress to the attention of the caregiver (C. Howes & Farver, 1987). Consistent with our discussion in Chapter 13, these children were much more likely to help a friend than to help a child who was not a friend (N. Eisenberg, Fabes, & Spinrad, 2006; Fujisawa, Kutsukake, & Hasegawa, 2008).

Children's prosocial behaviours, such as helping, sharing, and donating, increase in frequency in the toddler years and from the preschool years through childhood (N. Eisenberg & Fabes, 1998; Knafo et al., 2008). However, prosocial behaviour seems to stabilize or even decline in early to mid-adolescence and rebounds somewhat in late adolescence and early adulthood (Carlo et al., 2007; N. Eisenberg et al., 2005; Luengo Kanacri et al., 2013; Nantel-Vivier et al., 2009).

The Origins of Individual Differences in Prosocial Behaviour

Although children's prosocial behaviours change with age, consistent with the theme of *individual differences,* there is great variation among children of the same age in their propensity to help, share with, and comfort others. Recall the behaviours of Sara, Marc, and Sakina, the three children described earlier in this section. Why do children of the same ages differ so much in their prosocial behaviour? To identify the origins of these individual differences, we must consider the themes of *nature and nurture* and the *sociocultural context.*

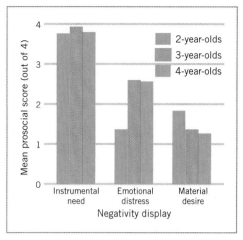

FIGURE 14.3 **Performance of three types of prosocial behaviours by age** Researchers at Queen's University have demonstrated that different types of prosocial behaviour—responding to instrumental need, emotional distress, and material desire—emerge at different ages and develop differently over time. (Adapted from Dunfield & Kuhlmeier, 1998)

Children display helping behaviours at home, often with chores, from an early age.

TABLE 14.3

Mothers' Reports of the Proportion of Times Children Responded to Others' Distress During the Second Year of Life

	When the child witnessed another's distress			When the child caused another's distress		
	13–15 months	18–20 months	23–25 months	13–15 months	18–20 months	23–25 months
Prosocial behaviour	.09	.21	.49	.07	.10	.52
Empathy or sympathy	.09	.10	.25	.03	.03	.14
Aggressive behaviour	.01	.01	.03	.01	.04	.19
Self-distress (personal distress)	.15	.12	.07	.34	.41	.33

Source: Adapted from Zahn-Waxler et al., 1992

Biological Factors

Many biologists and psychologists have proposed that humans are biologically predisposed to be prosocial (Hastings, Zahn-Waxler, & McShane, 2005). They believe that humans have evolved the capacity for empathy and altruism because these traits increase the likelihood of an individual's genes being passed on to the next generation (M. L. Hoffman, 1981). According to this view, people who help others are more likely than less helpful people to be assisted when they themselves are in need and, thus, are more likely to survive and reproduce (Trivers, 1983). In addition, assisting those with whom they share genes increases the likelihood that those genes will be passed on to the next generation (E. O. Wilson, 1975). Evolutionary explanations for prosocial behaviour, however, pertain to the human species as a whole and do not explain individual differences in empathy, sympathy, and prosocial behaviour.

Nonetheless, genetic factors do contribute to individual differences in these characteristics (e.g., Waldman et al., 2011). In twin studies with adults, twins' reports of their own empathy and prosocial behaviour are considerably more similar for identical twins than for fraternal twins (Gregory et al., 2009; Knafo & Israel, 2010). In one of the few twin studies of children's prosocial behaviour, researchers observed young twins' reactions to adults' simulations of distress in the home and in the laboratory. They also had the twins' mothers report on their everyday prosocial behaviour. On the basis of heritability estimates derived from this study, it appears that the role that genetic factors play in children's prosocial concern for others and in their prosocial behaviour increases with age (Knafo et al., 2008).

Recently, researchers have identified specific genes that might contribute to individual differences in prosocial tendencies (Knafo & Israel, 2010). For example, certain genes are associated with individual differences in oxytocin, a hormone that plays a role in a variety of social behaviours and emotions, including pair bonding and parenting, and that has been associated with parental attachment, empathy, and prosocial behaviour (N. Eisenberg, Spinrad, & Knafo, under revision; R. Feldman, 2012; K. MacDonald & MacDonald, 2010; Striepens et al., 2011).

How else might genetic factors affect empathy, sympathy, and prosocial behaviour? Most likely, their effects are related to differences in temperament. For instance, differences in children's ability to regulate emotion are related to children's empathy and sympathy. Children who tend to experience emotion without getting overwhelmed by it are especially likely to experience sympathy and to enact prosocial behaviour (N. Eisenberg, Fabes, & Murphy, 1996; N. Eisenberg et al., 2007; Trommsdorff, Friedlmeier, & Mayer, 2007). Moreover, children who are not responsive to others' emotions or are too inhibited to help others may be relatively unlikely to enact prosocial behaviours (Liew et al., 2011; S. K. Young, Fox, & Zahn-Wexler, 1999). Regulation is also related to children's theory of mind (see page 269), and theory of mind predicts children's prosocial behaviour (Caputi et al., 2012). Thus, the effect of heredity on sympathy and prosocial behaviour might be through individual differences in children's social cognition. It seems, then, that genetic factors likely affect when and how children assist others through their effect on a number of different aspects of children's functioning.

The Socialization of Prosocial Behaviour

A number of environmental factors also contribute to sympathy and prosocial behaviour (Knafo & Plomin, 2006a, 2006b; Volbrecht et al., 2007). The primary environmental influence on children's development of prosocial behaviour probably

Children are more likely to donate to charity if they see others donate and if adults explain to them how donating helps others.

is their socialization in the family. Researchers have identified three ways in which parents socialize prosocial behaviour in their children: (1) through their modelling and teaching of prosocial behaviour; (2) through their arranging opportunities for their children to engage in prosocial behaviour; and (3) through their methods of disciplining their children and eliciting prosocial behaviour from them. Parents also communicate and reinforce cultural beliefs about the value of prosocial behaviour (see Box 14.1).

BOX 14.1: a closer look

CULTURAL CONTRIBUTIONS TO CHILDREN'S PROSOCIAL AND ANTISOCIAL TENDENCIES

The amount of prosocial and antisocial behaviour that children display can be influenced by the particular culture they are part of (Graves & Graves, 1983; Turnbull, 1972). For example, one study found that Canadian children were more competitive than Italian children during a car race game and were more likely to break rules (B. H. Schneider et al., 2000). Other studies have found that children from traditional communities and subcultures (e.g., Mexicans and Mexican-Americans) are more likely to cooperate on laboratory tasks than are children from urban, Westernized groups (N. Eisenberg & Mussen, 1989; Knight, Cota, & Bernal, 1993). Similar patterns have been found in observations of children interacting at home and in their neighbourhoods (Whiting & Edwards, 1988; Whiting & Whiting, 1975): children in traditional societies in Kenya, Mexico, and the Philippines helped, shared with, and offered support to others in their families and communities more than did children in the United States, India, and Japan. In the more prosocial cultures, children often lived in extended families with many relatives. At a young age, they were assigned chores that were very important for the welfare of other family members, such as caring for younger children and tending herds. As a result of taking on these duties, children may have learned that they were responsible for others and that their helping behaviour was expected and valued by adults.

However, there may be cultural differences in the people toward whom children's caring behaviour is directed. For example, in the research just discussed, Philippine children were more prosocial toward relatives that toward non-relatives, that is, they were more likely to share with, comfort, or help relatives than non-relatives, whereas U.S. children were more prosocial toward non-relatives than toward relatives (de Guzman, Carlo, & Edwards, 2008). Children in traditional cultures may be socialized to help people with whom they have close ties but may be relatively disinclined to help people with whom they don't have a close connection.

The multicultural study cited above also revealed cultural differences in children's aggression (Whiting & Whiting, 1975). Children's tendencies to assault, berate, and scold others were related primarily to family structure and interactions among parents. Children with lower rates of assaulting and reprimanding tended to live in cultures in which fathers were closely involved with their wives and children, helped their wives with the care of infants, and were relatively unlikely to assault their wives. In such family circumstances, children may have learned non-aggressive modes of social interaction from their fathers and were relatively unlikely to have been exposed to aggressive adult models.

Even in various industrial societies today, there are differences in cultural values regarding prosocial and antisocial behaviour. For instance, Mexican-American youths are more prosocial if they espouse the traditional Mexican value of familism—a set of norms that promotes emotional and economic interdependence within an extended network of kin—rather than mainstream U.S. norms of individualism (Armenta et al., 2011). Along similar lines, the incidence of children's sharing, helping, and comforting is higher in Taiwan and Japan than it is in the United States (Rao & Stewart, 1999; Stevenson, 1991). Again, in contrast to the North American valuing of self and competition,

Chinese and Japanese cultures traditionally place great emphasis on teaching children to share and to be responsible for the needs of others in the group (the family, class, or community). In Japan, there also is an emphasis on creating a "community of learners" in the elementary school classroom—that is, teaching children to respond supportively to one another's thoughts and feelings (M. Lewis, 1995). However, the traditional emphasis on prosocial behaviour in many Asian cultures seems to be eroding (L. C. Lee & Zhan, 1991), perhaps due to increasing economic modernization and exposure to Western culture and values. This may explain why Asian children have not been found to be more prosocial than Western children in several relatively recent studies outside the classroom (Kärtner, Keller, & Chaudhary, 2010; Trommsdorff et al., 2007).

Cross-cultural research has shown that girls who live in societies in which they are expected to take care of younger children are more prosocial than are girls who live in societies that do not have this expectation.

Modelling and the communication of values Just as they imitate many other behaviours, children tend to imitate other people's helping and sharing behaviour, including even that of unknown peers or adults (N. Eisenberg & Fabes, 1998). Children are especially likely to imitate the prosocial behaviour of adults with whom they have a positive relationship (D. Hart & Fegley, 1995; Yarrow, Scott, & Zahn-Waxler, 1973). This may help explain the fact that parents and children tend to be similar in their levels of prosocial behaviour and sympathy (Clary & Miller, 1986; N. Eisenberg et al., 1991; Stukas et al., 1999), although heredity may also contribute to the similarity between parent and child in sympathy and helpfulness.

In a particularly interesting study, individuals who had risked their lives to rescue Jews from the Nazis in Europe during World War II were interviewed many years later, along with "bystanders" from the same communities who had not been involved in rescue activities (Oliner & Oliner, 1988). As shown in Table 14.4, when recalling the values that they had learned from their parents and other influential adults, 44% of the rescuers mentioned generosity and caring for others, whereas only 21% of bystanders mentioned the same values. In addition, bystanders were almost twice as likely as rescuers to cite economic competence as a value learned from their parents.

Bystanders also reported that their parents emphasized ethical obligations to family, community, church, and country, but not to other groups of people. In contrast, rescuers were seven times more likely than bystanders to report that their parents taught them that values related to caring should be applied to everyone (28% of rescuers; 4% of bystanders):

> "They taught me to respect all human beings."

> "He taught me to love my neighbor—to consider him my equal whatever his nationality or religion."

> (Oliner & Oliner, 1988, p. 165)

Thus, the values parents convey to their children may influence not only *whether* children are prosocial but also *toward whom* they are prosocial.

One effective way for parents to teach their children prosocial values and behaviours is to have discussions with them that appeal to their ability to sympathize. In laboratory studies, when elementary school children heard adults explicitly point out the positive consequences of prosocial actions for others (e.g., "Poor children … would be so happy and excited if they could buy food and toys"), they were relatively

TABLE 14.4

Values Learned from Parents by Rescuers and Bystanders (Percent of Rescuers and Bystanders Who Reported Learning a Given Type of Value from Parents)

Type of value	Rescuers (%)	Bystanders (%)
Economic competence	19	34
Independence	6	8
Fairness/equity (including reciprocity)	44	48
Fairness/equity applied universally	14	10
Caring	44	21
Caring applied universally	28	4

Source: Adapted from Oliner & Oliner, 1988

likely to donate money anonymously to help other people (Eisenberg-Berg & Geisheker, 1979; Perry, Bussey, & Freiberg, 1981). Children were less likely to donate anonymously if adults simply said that helping is "good" or "nice" and did not provide sympathy-arousing rationales for helping or sharing (Bryan & Walbek, 1970; N. Eisenberg & Fabes, 1998).

Opportunities for prosocial activities Providing children with opportunities to engage in helpful activities can increase their willingness to take on prosocial tasks at a later time (N. Eisenberg et al., 1987; Staub, 1979). In the home, opportunities to help others include routinely performing household tasks that benefit others (Richman et al., 1988; Whiting & Whiting, 1975). A study of Australian and Canadian families found that performance of household tasks may foster prosocial actions primarily toward family members (Grusec, Goodnow, & Cohen, 1996). For adolescents, voluntary community service such as working in homeless shelters or other community agencies also can be a way of gaining experience in helping others and deepening feelings of prosocial commitment (M. K. Johnson et al., 1998; Lawford et al., 2005; Pratt et al., 2003; Yates & Youniss, 1996).

Participation in prosocial activities may also provide opportunities for children and adolescents to take others' perspectives, to increase their confidence that they are competent to assist others, and to experience emotional rewards for helping. A two-year longitudinal study of Ontario high school students showed that those students who were involved in community helping activities at age 17 subsequently placed more importance on holding prosocial values (Pratt et al., 2003). Even mandatory school-based community service has been associated with future prosocial values (D. Hart et al., 2007), as well as with increased voluntary service at a later date for those high school youths who were not initially inclined to engage in such activities (Metz & Youniss, 2003). It should be noted, however, that forcing older adolescents or young adults into community service can sometimes backfire and undermine their motivation to help (Stukas, Snyder, & Clary, 1999).

Volunteering helps children learn the value of giving back to their community, increases their self-esteem and sense of pride as they discover that they can make a difference, and gives them a broader perspective of the diverse ways in which people live.

JIM WILKES / TORONTO STAR VIA GETTY IMAGES

Discipline and parenting style High levels of prosocial behaviour and sympathy in children tend to be associated with constructive and supportive parenting, including authoritative parenting (Day & Padilla-Walker, 2009; Knafo & Plomin, 2006a; Michalik et al., 2007). When parents are involved with and are close to their children, children are higher in sympathy and regulation, which in turn predicts higher levels of prosocial behaviour (Padilla-Walker & Christensen, 2011). For example, Maayan Davidov and Joan Grusec of the University of Toronto (2006) found that the degree to which mothers were responsive to their children's distress predicted children's empathy and their prosocial behaviour toward distressed others. As was noted on page 567, parental support of, and attachment to, the child have been found to be especially predictive of prosocial behaviour for youths who are low in fearfulness (Padilla-Walker & Nelson, 2010). It is important to note, however, that not only might supportive, authoritative parenting promote sympathy and prosocial behaviour, but prosocial, sympathetic children might also elicit more support from their parents (Miklikowska, Duriez, & Soenens 2011; Padilla-Walker et al., 2012). In contrast, a parenting style that involves physical punishment, threats, and an authoritarian approach (see Chapter 12) tends to be associated with a lack of sympathy and prosocial behaviour in children (Asbury et al., 2003; Hastings et al., 2000; Krevans & Gibbs, 1996; Laible et al., 2008).

The way in which parents attempt to directly elicit prosocial behaviour from their children is also important. If children are regularly punished for failing to engage in prosocial behaviour, they may start to believe that the reason for helping others is primarily to avoid punishment (Dix & Grusec, 1983; M. L. Hoffman, 1983). Similarly, if children are given material rewards for prosocial behaviours, they may come to believe that they helped solely for the rewards and, thus, may be less motivated to help when no rewards are offered (Fabes et al., 1989; Warneken & Tomasello, 2008).

What does seem particularly likely to foster children's voluntary prosocial behaviour is discipline that involves reasoning (Carlo, Mestre, et al., 2010). This is especially true when the reasoning points out the consequences of the child's behaviour for others (Krevans & Gibbs, 1996), encourages perspective taking (B. M. Farrant et al., 2012), and is used by parents who generally are warm and supportive (M. L. Hoffman, 1963). Such reasoning also encourages sympathy with others and provides guidelines children can refer to in future situations (C. S. Henry, Sager, & Plunkett, 1996; M. L. Hoffman, 1983). Maternal use of reasoning (e.g., "Can't you see that Tim is hurt? Don't pull hair") seems to increase prosocial behaviour even for 1- to 2-year-olds, as long as mothers state their reasoning in an emotional tone of voice (Zahn-Waxler et al., 1979). Emotion in the mother's voice likely catches her toddler's attention and communicates that she is very serious about what she is saying.

The combination of parental warmth and certain parenting practices—not parental warmth by itself— seems to be especially effective for fostering prosocial tendencies in children. Thus, children tend to be more prosocial when their parents are not only warm and supportive but also model prosocial behaviour, include reasoning and references to moral values and responsibilities in their discipline, and expose their children to

When adults point out the consequences of a child's transgressions for others, children are more likely to respond with sympathy and prosocial behaviour in other situations (N. Eisenberg & Fabes, 1998; Krevans & Gibbs, 1996).

SUSIE FITZHUGH

prosocial models and activities (i.e., use authoritative parenting) (Hastings et al., 2007; Janssens & Dekovic, 1997; Yarrow et al., 1973).

Since most of the research on the socialization of prosocial responding is correlational in design, it does not allow firm conclusions about cause-and-effect relations. However, some school interventions have been effective at promoting prosocial behaviour in children, so environmental factors must contribute to its development (see Box 14.2). The research underlying such interventions indicates that experience in helping and cooperating with others, and exposure to prosocial values and behaviours jointly contribute to the development of prosocial behaviour.

BOX 14.2: applications

SCHOOL-BASED INTERVENTIONS FOR PROMOTING PROSOCIAL BEHAVIOUR: ROOTS OF EMPATHY

Knowledge about the socialization of helping and sharing behaviour has been used to design school interventions aimed at fostering such behaviour. One notable program is the Roots of Empathy program, a program for children in kindergarten through Grade 8 (M. Gordon, 2005). The program began as a small project in Toronto in 1996 but is now delivered in every province in Canada, in rural, urban, and remote communities, including Aboriginal communities. It is also available in three U.S. states, the United Kingdom, Germany, the Isle of Man, the Republic of Ireland, and New Zealand.

The core aims of Roots of Empathy are to

1. develop children's social and emotional understanding

2. promote children's prosocial behaviours and decrease their aggressive behaviours

3. increase children's knowledge about infant development and effective parenting practices (Schonert-Reichl et al., 2012, p. 2).

The program, which lasts for the school year, is built around a monthly class visit by an infant and parent. The infant and parent are "adopted" by the class at the beginning of the school year. During the monthly visit, children learn about the baby's development by interacting with and observing the infant. A Roots of Empathy program instructor, who visits the classroom three times each month—before the visit, during the visit, and after the visit—provides lessons that focus on developing emotional

understanding, empathy, problem solving, perspective taking, effective parenting, infant development, and caring for others. The lessons and activities vary with the age of the baby and the developmental level of the students in the classroom. Apart from the instructor visits, classroom teachers incorporate information and ideas from the Roots of Empathy lessons into their regular lessons (Schonert-Reichl et al., 2012).

A recent evaluation of the program, which studied 585 children from Grades 4 to 7 and included reports from peers and teachers, yielded promising results. Children

who participated in Roots of Empathy demonstrated a greater understanding of why infants cry. Peer reports indicated increases in prosocial behaviour, and teacher reports pointed to more proactive behaviour and less relational aggression. Children's own reports of empathy and perspective taking did not show significant changes (Schonert-Reichl et al., 2012). Results from a Manitoba-based study of Roots of Empathy suggest that a decrease in teacher-reported aggression is maintained for up to three years after students' participation in the program (Santos et al., 2011).

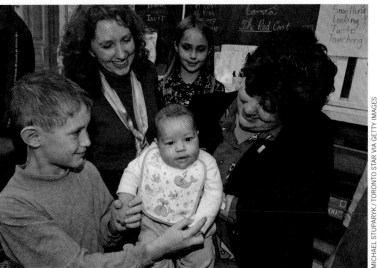

Roots of Empathy is a program designed to reduce aggression and promote empathy in elementary school children. It was developed by Mary Gordon (left), who is seen here in a Roots of Empathy classroom.

MICHAEL STUPARYK / TORONTO STAR VIA GETTY IMAGES

review

Prosocial behaviours emerge by the second year of life and increase in frequency during the toddler years. At least some types of prosocial behaviour continue to increase in frequency and sensitivity in the preschool years and elementary school years. Early individual differences in prosocial behaviour predict differences among children in these types of behaviours years later.

Prosocial behaviour may increase with age in childhood partly because of children's developing abilities to sympathize and take others' perspectives. Differences among children in their empathy, sympathy, distress reactions to others' distress, and perspective taking also contribute to individual differences in children's prosocial behaviour. Furthermore, biological factors, which may contribute to differences among children in temperament, likely affect how empathic and prosocial children become.

The development of prosocial behaviour also is related to children's upbringing. In general, a positive relationship between parents and children is linked to prosocial moral development, especially when supportive parents use effective parenting practices. Authoritative, positive discipline—including the use of reasoning by parents and teachers and exposure to prosocial models, values, and activities—is associated with the development of sympathy and prosocial behaviour. Cultures differ in the degree to which they value and teach prosocial behaviour, and these differences are reflected in how much children help, share with, and are concerned about other people and perhaps whom they assist.

Intervention programs in schools designed to foster prosocial behaviour sometimes have been found to increase children's prosocial behaviour and prosocial moral reasoning; whether a given intervention is effective probably depends on its content, length, and the degree to which it is effectively administered. Such findings convincingly demonstrate that social factors (as well as heredity) contribute to the development of prosocial tendencies.

Antisocial Behaviour

Youth crime in Canada has been declining over the past 10 years. Most of the crimes for which youths were sentenced during 2010/2011 were nonviolent (61%), while 39% were violent offences (Munch, 2012). In spite of these declining rates, violence in youth does occur, especially in urban, industrialized countries—particularly in Western societies. When events such as the Columbine and Taber tragedies, described at the beginning of the chapter, do occur, questions are raised, such as, Are youths who commit violent acts already aggressive in childhood? How do levels of aggression change with development? What factors contribute to individual differences in children's antisocial behaviour? As we address these issues, the themes of *individual differences, nature and nurture,* the *sociocultural context,* and *research and children's welfare* will be particularly salient.

The Development of Aggression and Other Antisocial Behaviours

Aggression is behaviour aimed at harming others (Parke & Slaby, 1983), and it is behaviour that emerges quite early. How early? Instances of aggression over the possession of objects occur between infants before 12 months of age—especially behaviours such as trying to tug objects away from each other (D. F. Hay, Mundy, et al., 2011)—but most do not involve bodily contact such as hitting (Coie & Dodge, 1998; D. F. Hay & Ross, 1982). Beginning at around 18 months of age, physical aggression such as hitting and pushing—particularly over the possession of objects—increases in frequency until about age 2 or 3 (Alink et al., 2006; D. F. Hay, Hurst, et al., 2011; D. S. Shaw et al., 2003). Then, with the growth of language

aggression ■ Behaviour aimed at harming or injuring others.

skills, physical aggression decreases in frequency. Results from the Quebec Newborn Twin Study, discussed in Chapter 3, suggest that physical aggression and vocabulary are negatively correlated in 19-month-olds: that is, those 19-month-olds with larger vocabularies were less likely to be physically aggressive (Dionne et al., 2003). As physical aggression decreases, verbal aggression, such as insults and taunting, increases (Bonica et al., 2003; Mesman et al., 2009; Miner & Clarke-Stewart, 2008).

Among the most frequent causes of aggression in the preschool years are conflicts between peers over possessions (Fabes & Eisenberg, 1992; Shantz, 1987) and conflict between siblings over most anything (Abramovitch, Corter, & Lando, 1979). Conflict over possessions often is an example of **instrumental aggression,** that is, aggression motivated by the desire to obtain a concrete goal, such as gaining possession of a toy or getting a better place in line. Preschool children sometimes also use *relational aggression* (Crick, Casas, & Mosher, 1997), which, as explained in Chapter 13, is intended to harm others by damaging their peer relationships. Among preschoolers, this typically involves excluding peers from a play activity or a social group (M. K. Underwood, 2003). This relational or indirect aggression has been linked to theory-of-mind skills, particularly for those children with low levels of prosocial skills. For instance, a longitudinal study of young children in Quebec demonstrated that theory-of-mind skills at age 5 predicted levels of indirect aggression one year later, but only for those children who were rated as low to average on prosocial behaviour (Renouf et al., 2010).

The drop in physical aggression in the preschool years is likely due to a variety of factors, including not only children's increasing ability to use verbal and relational aggression but also their developing ability to use language to resolve conflicts and to control their own emotions and actions (Coie & Dodge, 1998). Thus, overt physical aggression continues to remain low or to decline in frequency for most children during elementary school, although a relatively small group of children—primarily boys (Moffitt & Caspi, 2001; NICHD Early Child Care Research Network, 2004)—develop frequent and serious problems with aggression and antisocial behaviour at this age (Cairns et al., 1989; S. B. Campbell et al., 2010; D. S. Shaw et al., 2003) or in early adolescence (Xie, Drabick, & Chen, 2011).

Whereas aggression in young children is usually instrumental, aggression in elementary school children often is hostile, arising from the desire to hurt another person or the need to protect oneself against a perceived threat to self-esteem (Dodge, 1980; Hartup, 1974). Children who engage in physical aggression tend to also engage in relational aggression (Card et al., 2008), with the degree to which they use one or the other tending to be consistent across childhood (Ostrov et al., 2008). A study of more than 3000 Canadian children found that children between the ages of 4 and 11 years were consistent in the type of aggression that they exhibited, be it physical or relational (Vaillancourt et al., 2003). Overall, the frequency of overt aggression decreases for most teenagers (Di Giunta et al., 2010; Loeber, 1982), at least after mid-adolescence (Karriker-Jaffe et al., 2008).

In childhood, covert types of antisocial behaviours, such as stealing, lying, and cheating, also occur with considerable frequency and begin to be characteristic of some children with behavioural problems (Loeber & Schmaling, 1985). Compared with overt antisocial behaviour, a high level of such covert behaviour in the early school years has been found to be an even better predictor of a range of antisocial behaviour 3 to 4 years later (J. J. Snyder et al., 2012).

instrumental aggression ■ Aggression motivated by the desire to obtain a concrete goal.

Aggressive conflicts over objects are very common among young children.

MYRLEEN PEARSON / PHOTOEDIT

In mid-adolescence, serious acts of violence increase markedly, as do property offences and status offences such as drinking and truancy (Lahey et al., 2000). Adolescent crime peaks at age 17, with more males than females reporting committing at least one serious violent offence. In addition, male adolescents and adults engage in much more violent behaviour and crime than do females (Coie & Dodge, 1998; Elliott, 1994).

Consistency of Aggressive and Antisocial Behaviour

There is considerable consistency in both girls' and boys' aggression across childhood and adolescence. Children who are the most aggressive and prone to conduct problems such as stealing in middle childhood tend to be more aggressive and delinquent in adolescence than children who develop conduct problems at a later age (Broidy et al., 2003; Burt et al., 2011; Lahey, Goodman, et al., 1999; Schaeffer et al., 2003). This holds especially true for boys (Fontaine et al., 2009). In one 19-year longitudinal study of Quebec children, physical aggression during the early school years was the strongest predictor of criminal charges at 25 years of age (Pingault et al., 2013). In another study of girls only, relational aggression in childhood was related to subsequent *conduct disorders* (Keenan et al., 2010). (Conduct disorders are discussed in Box 14.3.)

Many children who are aggressive from early in life have underlying neurological deficits (i.e., brain dysfunctions) such as difficulty in paying attention and hyperactivity (Gatzke-Kopp et al., 2009; Moffitt, 1993a; Speltz et al., 1999; Viding & McCrory, 2012). These deficits, which may become more marked with age (Aguilar et al., 2000), can result in troubled relations with parents, peers, and teachers that further fuel the child's aggressive, antisocial pattern of behaviour. Problems with attention are particularly likely to have this effect because they make it difficult for aggressive children to carefully consider all the relevant information in a social situation before deciding how to act; thus, their behaviour often is inappropriate for the situation. In addition, callous, unemotional traits, which often accompany aggression and conduct disorder (e.g., Keenan et al., 2010), appear to be associated with a delay in cortical maturation in brain areas involved in decision making, morality, and empathy (De Brito et al., 2009).

Early-onset conduct problems are also associated with a range of family risk factors. These include the mother's being single at the time of her child's birth, the mother's being stressed prenatally and during the child's preschool years; the mother's being psychologically unavailable in the preschool years; parental antisocial tendencies; low maternal education and poverty; and child neglect and physical abuse (S. B. Campbell et al., 2010; D. F. Hay et al., 2011; K. M. McCabe et al., 2001; NICHD Early Child Care Research Network, 2004; M. Robinson et al., 2011).

Adolescents with a long childhood history of troubled behaviour represent only a minority of adolescents who engage in the much broader problem of "juvenile delinquency" (Hämäläinen & Pulkkinen, 1996). Indeed, most adolescents who perform delinquent acts have no history of aggression or antisocial behaviour before age 11 (Elliott, 1994). For some, delinquency may occur in response to the normal pressures of adolescence, as when they attempt to assert their independence from adults or win acceptance from their peers. However, the onset of antisocial behaviour in adolescence is also predicted by economic disadvantage, being a member of an ethnic minority, interacting with deviant peers (see Chapter 13), and having a difficult, irritable temperament from infancy onward (K. M. McCabe et al., 2001, 2004; Roisman et al., 2010).

Youths who develop problem behaviours in adolescence typically stop engaging in antisocial behaviour later in adolescence or early adulthood (Moffitt, 1993a). However, some—especially those who have low impulse control, poor regulation of aggression, and a weak orientation toward the future (Monahan et al., 2009)—continue to engage in problem behaviours and to have some problems with their mental health and substance dependence until at least their mid-20s (Moffitt et al., 2002).

oppositional defiant disorder (ODD) ■ A disorder characterized by age-inappropriate and persistent displays of angry, defiant, and irritable behaviours.

conduct disorder (CD) ■ A disorder that involves severe antisocial and aggression behaviours that inflict pain on others or involve destruction of property or denial of the rights of others.

BOX 14.3: a closer look

OPPOSITIONAL DEFIANT DISORDER AND CONDUCT DISORDER

If a child's problem behaviours become serious, the child is likely to be diagnosed by psychologists and physicians as having a clinical disorder. Two such disorders that involve antisocial behaviour are oppositional defiant disorder and conduct disorder. **Oppositional defiant disorder (ODD)** is characterized by angry, defiant behaviour that is age-inappropriate and persistent (lasting at least 6 months). Children with ODD typically lose their temper easily, arguing with adults and actively defying their requests or rules. They are also prone to blame others for their own mistakes or misbehaviour and are often spiteful or vindictive. **Conduct disorder (CD)** includes more severe antisocial and aggression behaviours that inflict pain on others (e.g., initiating fights, cruelty to animals) or involve the destruction of property or the violation of the rights of others (e.g., stealing, robberies). Other diagnostic signs include frequently running away from home, frequently staying out all night before age 13 despite parental prohibitions, or persistent school truancy beginning prior to age 13. To warrant a diagnosis of ODD or CD, children must exhibit multiple, persistent symptoms that are clearly impairing, distinguishing them from those youngsters who display the designated behaviours on an infrequent or inconsistent basis (American Psychiatric Association, 2000; Hinshaw & Lee, 2003).

There is debate in the field regarding how antisocial behaviour, including ODD and CD, should be conceptualized. Some experts argue that antisocial behaviour should be viewed in terms of a continuum from infrequent to frequent displays of externalizing symptoms. Others argue that extreme forms of antisocial behaviour are qualitatively different from garden-variety types of externalizing behaviours. In other words, there is a question regarding whether children with ODD or CD simply have more, or more severe, externalizing problems than do better-adjusted youth, or whether their problems are of an altogether different type. The answer to this question is not clear. However, the fact that more externalizing symptoms at a younger age predict serious diagnosed problems in adolescence or adulthood (Biederman et al., 2008; Côté et al., 2001; Hinshaw & Lee, 2003) is viewed by some as evidence that serious externalizing problems differ in their origins from less severe types of such behaviour.

Estimates of the prevalence of ODD and CD range widely (Hinshaw & Lee, 2003). A systematic review completed by McMaster University researchers found that ODD prevalence estimates ranged from 2% to 14% in community samples and from 28% to 50% in clinical samples (Boylan et al., 2007). In one large study in Canada, the rates of ODD and CD were approximately 8% for boys and 5% for girls (Romano et al., 2001). The average age of onset for ODD is approximately 6 years of age; for CD it is 9 years of age (Hinshaw & Lee, 2003).

Although there is debate in regard to the relation between ODD and CD, some children develop both CD and ODD, whereas others do not. A minority of youth with ODD later develop CD; however, those children or adolescents with CD often, but not always, had ODD first (Loeber & Burke, 2011; van Lier et al., 2007). In many instances, youth with ODD or CD also have been diagnosed with other disorders such as anxiety disorder or attention deficit hyperactivity disorder (about half of youth with ODD or CD also have attention deficit hyperactivity disorder) (Hinshaw & Lee, 2003). The two disorders also seem to differ somewhat in their prediction of later problem behaviours: CD has been found to predict primarily behavioural problems in early adulthood, including antisocial behaviour, whereas ODD shows stronger prediction of emotional disorders in early adulthood (Loeber & Burke, 2011; R. Rowe et al., 2010).

The factors related to the development of CD or ODD are similar to those related to the development of aggression. Genetics play a role, although heritability seems to be stronger for early-onset and overt types of antisocial behaviour (such as aggression) than for later-onset or covert forms of antisocial behaviour (such as stealing) (Hinshaw & Lee, 2003; Lahey, Goodman, et al., 2009; Maes et al., 2007; Meier et al., 2011). Environmental risks for these disorders include such factors as living in a disadvantaged, risky neighbourhood or in a stressed, lower-SES family; parental abuse; poor parental supervision; and harsh and inconsistent discipline (Goodnight et al., 2012; Hinshaw & Lee, 2003; R. Rowe et al., 2010). Peer rejection and associating with deviant peers are also linked with ODD and CD (Hinshaw & Lee, 2003; Loeber & Stouthamer-Loeber, 1986). It is likely that a variety of these factors jointly contribute to children's developing ODD or CD and that the most important factors vary according to the age of onset, the specific problem behaviours, and individual characteristics of the children, including their temperament and intelligence.

Characteristics of Aggressive-Antisocial Children and Adolescents

Aggressive-antisocial children and adolescents differ, on average, from their non-aggressive peers in a variety of characteristics. These include having a difficult temperament and the tendency to process social information in negative ways.

Temperament and Personality

Children who develop problems with aggression and antisocial behaviour tend to exhibit a difficult temperament and a lack of self-regulatory skills from a very early age (Espy et al., 2011; Rothbart, 2012; Yaman et al., 2010). Longitudinal studies have shown, for example, that infants and toddlers who frequently express intense negative emotion and demand much attention tend to have higher levels of problem behaviours such as aggression from the preschool years through high school (J. E. Bates et al., 1991; Joussemet et al., 2008; Olson et al., 2000). Similarly, preschoolers who exhibit lack of control, impulsivity, high activity level, irritability, and distractibility are prone to fighting, delinquency, and other antisocial behaviour at ages 9 through 15; to aggression and criminal behaviour in late adolescence; and, in the case of men, to violent crime in adulthood (Caspi et al., 1995; Caspi & Silva, 1995; Tremblay et al., 1994). In a large-scale study in Quebec, Nathalie Fontaine and colleagues (2008) found that girls who exhibited high levels of physical aggression and hyperactivity between the ages of 6 and 12 years are more likely to be physically aggressive with their partners, be in mutually psychologically aggressive relationships, become pregnant early, and receive welfare assistance than are females who did not exhibit both high levels of physical aggression and hyperactivity. However, children who use aggression to achieve instrumental goals are less prone to unregulated negative emotion and physiological responding than those who exhibit angry responses to provocation (Scarpa et al., 2010; Vitaro et al., 2006).

Some aggressive children and adolescents tend to feel neither guilt nor empathy or sympathy for others (de Wied et al., 2012; Lotze et al., 2010; R. J. McMahon, Witkiewitz, & Kotler, 2010; Pardini & Byrd, 2012; Stuewig et al., 2010). They are often charming, but insincere and callous. The combination of impulsivity, problems with attention, and callousness in childhood is especially likely to predict aggression, antisocial behaviour, and run-ins with the police in adolescence (Christian et al., 1997; Frick & Morris, 2004; Hastings et al., 2000) and perhaps in adulthood as well (Lynam, 1996). A large-scale Canadian study found that teacher ratings of hurtful and uncaring behaviours in children ages 6 and 10 predicted criminal convictions at age 24, for both boys and girls (Hodgins et al., 2013).

Social Cognition

In addition to their differences in temperament, aggressive children differ from non-aggressive children in their social cognition. As discussed in Chapter 9, aggressive children tend to interpret the world through an "aggressive" lens. They are more likely than non-aggressive children to attribute hostile motives to others in contexts in which the other person's motives and intentions are unclear (the "hostile attributional bias") (Dodge et al., 2006; Lansford et al., 2010; MacBrayer et al., 2003; D. A. Nelson, Mitchell, & Yang, 2008). Compared with the goals of non-aggressive peers, their goals in such social encounters are also more likely to be hostile and inappropriate to the situation, typically involving attempts to intimidate or get back at a peer (Crick & Dodge, 1994; Slaby & Guerra, 1988). Correspondingly, when asked to come up with possible solutions to a negative social situation, aggressive children generate fewer options than do non-aggressive children, and those options are more likely to involve aggressive or disruptive behaviour (Deluty, 1985; Slaby & Guerra, 1988).

In line with these tendencies, aggressive children are also inclined to evaluate aggressive responses more favourably, and competent, prosocial responses less favourably, than do their non-aggressive peers (Crick & Dodge, 1994; Dodge et al., 1986), especially as they get older (Fontaine et al., 2010). In part, this is because they feel more confident of their ability to perform acts of physical and verbal aggression (Barchia & Bussey, 2011; Quiggle et al., 1992), and they expect their aggressive behaviour to result in positive outcomes (e.g., getting their way) as well as to reduce negative treatment by others (Dodge et al., 1986; Perry, Perry, & Rasmussen, 1986). Given all this, it is not surprising that aggressive children are predisposed to aggressive behavioural choices (Calvete & Orue, 2012; Dodge et al., 2006). This aggressive behaviour, in turn, appears to increase children's subsequent tendency to positively evaluate aggressive interpersonal behaviours, further increasing the level of future antisocial conduct (Fontaine et al., 2008).

It is important to note, however, that although all these aspects of functioning contribute to the prediction of children's aggression, not all aggressive children exhibit the same biases in social cognition. Children who are prone to emotionally driven, hostile aggression—labelled **reactive aggression**—are particularly likely to perceive others' motives as hostile (Crick & Dodge, 1996), to initially generate aggressive responses to provocation, and to evaluate their responses as morally acceptable (Arsenio, Adams, & Gold, 2009; Dodge et al., 1997). In contrast, children who are prone to **proactive aggression**—which, like instrumental aggression, is aimed at fulfilling a need or desire—tend to anticipate more positive social consequences for aggression (Arsenio et al., 2009; Crick & Dodge, 1996; Dodge et al., 1997; Sijtsema et al., 2009).

The Origins of Aggression

What are the causes of aggression in children? Key contributors include genetic makeup, socialization by family members, the influence of peers, and cultural factors.

Biological Factors

Biological factors undoubtedly contribute to individual differences in aggression, but their precise role is not very clear. Twin studies suggest that antisocial behaviour runs in families and is partially due to genetic factors (Arseneault et al., 2003; Rhee & Waldman, 2002; Waldman et al., 2011). In addition, heredity appears to play a stronger role in aggression in early childhood and adulthood than it does in adolescence, when environmental factors are a major contributor to aggression (Rende & Plomin, 1995; J. Taylor, Iacono, & McGue, 2000). Heredity also contributes to both proactive and reactive aggression, but in terms of stability of individual differences in aggression and the association of aggression with psychopathic traits (e.g., callousness, lack of affect, including lack of remorse and manipulativeness), the influence of heredity is greater for proactive aggression (Bezdjian et al., 2011; Tuvblad et al., 2009).

We have already noted one genetically influenced contributor to aggression—difficult temperament. Hormonal factors are also assumed to play a role in aggression, although the evidence for this assumption is mixed. For example, testosterone levels seem to be related to activity level and responses to provocation, and high testosterone

reactive aggression ■ Emotionally driven, antagonistic aggression sparked by one's perception that other people's motives are hostile.

proactive aggression ■ Unemotional aggression aimed at fulfilling a need or desire.

Proactive aggression (purposeful aggression not evoked by emotion) is used by children to bully others and to get what they want from them.

levels sometimes have been linked to aggressive behaviour (Archer, 1991; Hermans, Ramsey, & van Honk, 2008). However, the relation of testosterone to aggression, although statistically significant, is quite small (Book, Starzyk, & Quinsey, 2001).

Another biological contributor to aggression discussed earlier is neurological deficits that affect attention and regulatory capabilities (Moffitt, 1993b): children who are not well regulated are likely to have difficulty controlling their tempers and inhibiting aggressive impulses (N. Eisenberg, Spinrad, & Eggum, 2010; N. Eisenberg, Valiente, et al., 2009; Y. Xu, Farver, & Zhang, 2009).

Whatever their specific role, the biological correlates of aggression probably are neither necessary nor sufficient to cause aggressive behaviour in most children. Genetic, neurological, or hormonal characteristics may put a child at risk for developing aggressive and antisocial behaviour, but whether the child becomes aggressive will depend on numerous factors, including experiences in the social world. We return to the joint role of genetics and the environment in aggression shortly.

Socialization of Aggression and Antisocial Behaviour

Many people, including some legislators and judges, feel that the development of aggression can be traced back to socialization in the home. And, in fact, the quality of parenting experienced by antisocial children is poorer than that experienced by other children (Dodge et al., 2006; Scaramella et al., 2002). For example, children in chaotic homes—characterized by a lack of order and structure, few predictable routines, and noise—tend to be relatively high in disruptive behaviour, and this relation appears not to be due to genetics (Jaffee et al., 2012). Although it is unclear to what degree poor parenting and chaotic homes, in and of themselves, may account for children's antisocial behaviour, it is clear that they comprise several factors that can promote such behaviour.

Parental punitiveness Many children whose parents often use harsh but nonabusive physical punishment are prone to problem behaviours in the early years, aggression in childhood, and criminality in adolescence and adulthood (Burnette et al., 2012; Gershoff, 2002; Gershoff et al., 2010, 2012; Olson et al., 2011). This is especially true when the parents are cold and punitive in general (Deater-Deckard & Dodge, 1997), when the child does not have an early secure attachment (Kochanska et al., 2009; Kochanska & Kim, 2012), and when the child has a difficult temperament and is chronically angry and unregulated (Kochanska & Kim, 2012; Mulvaney & Mebert, 2007; Y. Xu et al., 2009; Yaman et al., 2010).

It is important to note, however, that the relation between physical punishment and children's antisocial behaviour varies across racial, ethnic, and cultural groups. As discussed in Chapter 12, in some cultures and subcultures, physical punishment and controlling parental behaviours are viewed as part of responsible parenting when coupled with parental support and normal demands for compliance. When this is the case, parental punishment tends not to be associated with antisocial behaviour because children might see authoritarian parenting as protective and caring (Lansford et al., 2006). Although corporal punishment, as well as yelling and screaming, tends to be associated with higher levels of aggression in children in a number of diverse cultures, including China, India, Kenya, Italy, the Philippines, and Thailand, this relation is weaker if children view such parenting as normative (Gershoff et al., 2010).

In contrast, abusive punishment is likely to be associated with the development of antisocial tendencies regardless of the group in question (Deater-Deckard et al., 1995; Luntz & Widom, 1994; Weiss et al., 1992). Very harsh physical discipline appears to lead to the kinds of social cognition that are associated with aggression, such as assuming that others have hostile intentions, generating aggressive solutions to interpersonal problems, and expecting aggressive behaviour to result in positive outcomes (Alink et al., 2012; Dodge et al., 1995).

In addition, parents who use abusive punishment provide salient models of aggressive behaviour for their children to imitate (Dogan et al., 2007). Ironically, children who are subjected to such punishment are likely to be anxious or angry and therefore are unlikely to attend to their parents' instructions or demands or to be motivated to behave as their parents wish them to (M. L. Hoffman, 1983).

There probably is a reciprocal relation between children's behaviour and their parents' punitive discipline (Arim et al., 2011; N. Eisenberg, Fabes, et al., 1999). That is, children who are high in antisocial behaviour exhibit psychopathic traits (e.g., are callous, unemotional, manipulative, remorseless), or are low in self-regulation tend to elicit harsh parenting (Lansford et al., 2009; Salihovic et al., 2012); in turn, harsh parenting increases the children's problem behaviour (Sheehan & Watson, 2008). However, some recent research suggests that harsh physical punishment has a stronger effect on children's externalizing problems than vice versa (Lansford et al., 2011).

There is probably a reciprocal relation between children's behaviour and their parents' punitive discipline. That is, children who are high in antisocial behaviour or low in self-regulation tend to elicit harsher parenting. The harsher parenting in turn elicits more problematic behaviour from the child.

The relation between punitive parenting and children's aggression can, of course, have a genetic component. Parents whose children are antisocial and aggressive often are that way themselves and are predisposed to punitive parenting (Davies et al., 2012; Dogan et al., 2007; Thornberry et al., 2003). At the same time, however, twin studies indicate that the relation between punitive, negative parenting and children's aggression and antisocial behaviour is not entirely due to hereditary factors (Boutwell et al., 2011; Jaffee et al., 2004a, 2004b). In one study, for example, differences in punitive parenting with adolescent identical twins were related to differences in the twins' aggression (Caspi et al., 2004). In another study, parent–adolescent conflict predicted more conduct problems over time (but not vice versa), even in adoptive families (Klahr et al., 2011). In neither of these studies can genetics explain the effects of parents' behaviours on their children's problem behaviours.

Ineffective discipline and family coercion Another factor that can increase children's antisocial behaviour is ineffective parenting. Parents who are inconsistent in administering discipline are more likely than other parents to have aggressive and delinquent children (Côté et al., 2006; Dumka et al., 1997; Frick, Christian, & Wootton, 1999; Sampson & Laub, 1994). So too are parents who fail to monitor their children's behaviour and activities. One reason parental monitoring may be important is that it reduces the likelihood that older children and adolescents will associate with deviant, antisocial peers (Dodge et al., 2008; G. R. Patterson, Capaldi, & Bank, 1991). It also makes it more likely that parents will know if their children are engaging in antisocial behaviour. At the same time, however, parents of difficult, aggressive youth sometimes find that monitoring leads to such conflict with their children that they are forced to back off (Laird et al., 2003).

Ineffective discipline is often evident in the pattern of troubled family interaction described by G. R. Patterson (1982, 1995; J. Snyder et al., 2005) and discussed in Chapter 1. In this pattern, the aggression of children who are out of control may be unintentionally reinforced by parents who, once their efforts to coerce compliance have failed, give in to their children's fits of temper and demands (J. Snyder, Reid, & Patterson, 2003). This is especially probable in the case of out-of-control boys, who are much more likely than other boys to react negatively to their mother's attempts to discipline them (G. R. Patterson, Reid, & Dishion, 1992). Whether maternal coercion elicits the same pattern of response from girls as from boys is not yet known because most of the relevant research has been done with boys, but there is some reason to believe that it does not (McFadyen-Ketchum et al., 1996).

Parental conflict Children who are frequently exposed to verbal and physical violence between their parents tend to be more antisocial and aggressive than other children (Cummings & Davies, 2002; R. Feldman, Masalha, & Derdikman-Eiron, 2010; Keller et al., 2008; Van Ryzin & Dishion, 2012). This relation holds true even when genetic factors that might have caused it are taken into account (Jaffee et al., 2002). One obvious reason for this is that embattled parents model aggressive behaviour for their children. Another is that children whose mothers are physically abused tend to believe that violence is an acceptable, even natural part of family interactions (Graham-Bermann & Brescoll, 2000). Compared with spouses who get along well with each other, embattled spouses also tend to be less skilled and responsive, and more hostile and controlling, in their parenting (Buehler et al., 1997; Davies et al., 2012; R. E. Emery, 1989; Gonzales et al., 2000), which, in turn, can increase their children's aggressive tendencies (Li et al., 2011). This pattern, in which marital hostility predicts hostile parenting, which, in turn, predicts children's aggression, has also been found in families with an adopted child, so these relations cannot be due solely to genes shared by parents and children (Stover et al., 2012).

Children are more likely to develop aggressive and antisocial behaviour if they are exposed to marital conflict, especially violence. Parents who are in unhappy marriages tend to be withdrawn and non-supportive with their children, which appears to contribute to their children's problems with adjustment.

Socioeconomic status and children's antisocial behaviour Children from low-income families tend to be more antisocial and aggressive than children from more prosperous homes (Goodnight et al., 2012; Keiley et al., 2000; NICHD Early Child Care Research Network, 2004; Stouthamer-Loeber et al., 2002). A large-scale Canadian study demonstrated that this pattern was particularly true for boys—that is, being male, being from an economically disadvantaged home, and having a mother with a low level of education predicted high levels of aggression for children between 2 and 11 years of age (Côté et al., 2006). Furthermore, studies have shown that when families escaped from poverty, 4- to 7-year-old children tended to become less aggressive and antisocial, whereas families' remaining in poverty or moving into poverty for the long-term was associated with an increase in children's antisocial behaviour (Macmillan et al., 2004). There are many reasons that might account for such differences in trajectories.

One major reason is the greater amount of stressors experienced by children in poor families, including stress in the family (illness, domestic violence, divorce, legal problems) and neighbourhood violence (Vanfossen et al., 2010). In addition, as discussed in Chapter 12, low SES tends to be associated with living in a single-parent family or being an unplanned child of a teenage parent; stressors of these sorts are linked to increased aggression and antisocial behaviour (Dodge, Pettit, & Bates, 1994; Linares et al., 2001; Tolan, Gorman-Smith, & Henry, 2003; Trentacosta et al., 2008). Also, because of the many stressors that economically disadvantaged parents face, they are more likely than other parents to be rejecting and low in warmth; to use erratic, threatening, and harsh discipline; and to be lax in supervising their children (Conger et al., 1994; Dodge et al., 1994; Odgers et al., 2012).

In addition to all these low-SES risk factors, conditions such as the presence of gangs, the lack of jobs for juveniles, and few opportunities to engage in constructive activities (e.g., clubs and sports) also likely contribute to the antisocial behaviour of many youths in economically disadvantaged neighbourhoods.

Peer Influence

As we discussed in Chapter 13, aggressive children tend to socialize with other aggressive children and often become more delinquent over time if they have close friends who are aggressive. Moreover, the expression of a genetic tendency toward aggression is stronger for individuals who have aggressive friends (Brendgen et al., 2008).

The larger peer group with whom older children and adolescents socialize may influence aggression even more than their close friends do (Coie & Dodge, 1998). In one study, boys exposed to peers involved in overt antisocial behaviours, such as violence and the use of a weapon, were more than three times as likely as other boys to engage in such acts themselves (Keenan et al., 1995). Associating with delinquent peers tends to increase delinquency because these peers model and reinforce antisocial behaviour in the peer group. At the same time, participating in delinquent activities brings adolescents into contact with more delinquent peers (Dishion et al., 2010, 2012; Lacourse et al., 2003; Thornberry et al., 1994).

Although research findings vary somewhat, it appears that children's susceptibility to peer pressure to become involved in antisocial behaviour increases in the elementary school years, peaks at about Grade 8 or 9, and declines thereafter (Berndt, 1979; B. B. Brown, Clasen, & Eichler, 1986; Steinberg & Silverberg, 1986). Although not all adolescents are susceptible to negative peer influence (Allen, Porter, & McFarland, 2006), even popular youth in early adolescence tend to increase participation in minor levels of drug use and delinquency if these behaviours are approved by peers (Allen et al., 2005). Peer approval of relational aggression increases in middle school, and students in peer groups supportive of relational aggression become increasingly aggressive (N. E. Werner & Hill, 2010). However, there are exceptions to this overall pattern that appear to be related to cultural factors. For example, Mexican-American immigrant youth who are less acculturated, and therefore more tied to traditional values, appear to be less susceptible to peer pressure toward antisocial behaviour than are Mexican-American children who are more acculturated. Thus, it may be that peers play less of a role in promoting antisocial behaviour for adolescents who are embedded in a traditional culture oriented toward adults' expectations (e.g., deference and courtesy toward adults and adherence to adult values) (Wall et al., 1993).

Gangs An important peer influence on antisocial behaviour can be membership in a gang. Gangs tend to be composed of young people who are similar in ethnic and racial background. One study of Toronto high school students and street youth showed that the majority of Toronto gang members are Canadian-born whites, although black, Hispanic, and Aboriginal youth are overrepresented relative to their population (Wortley & Tanner, 2006) Across the Prairie provinces, First Nations youth are particularly vulnerable to gang recruitment (Totten, 2009). The average age of gang members is between 17 and 18 years, with about half being 18 or older and a small portion being as young as 12 (Egley & Howell, 2012).

Studies conducted in Canada and the United Kingdom show that adolescents are more likely to join gangs if they come from a neighbourhood with a high rate of resident turnover, if they have an antisocial personality, and if they have psychopathic tendencies such as a combination of high hyperactivity, low anxiety, and low prosociality (Dupéré et al., 2007; Egan & Beadman, 2011). Adolescents who join gangs also tend to have engaged in antisocial activities and to have had delinquent friends before they joined. However, being in a gang appears to increase adolescents' delinquent and antisocial behaviour above their prior levels (Barnes, Beaver, & Miller, 2010; DeLisi et al., 2009; Dishion et al., 2010; Lahey, Gordon, et al., 1999). Not surprisingly, the longer adolescents remain in a gang, the more

Gangs often provide youth with a sense of belonging, emblemized by specific gang signs.

likely they are to engage in delinquent and antisocial behaviour (Craig et al., 2002; R. A. Gordon et al., 2004). A study conducted in the Montreal area found that those boys who belonged to a gang at both 13 and 14 years of age were more likely to report drug and alcohol abuse, stealing, and vandalism (Craig et al., 2002).

Biology and Socialization: Their Joint Influence on Children's Antisocial Behaviour

As should be clear by now, it is very difficult to separate the specific biological, cultural, peer, and familial factors that affect the development of children's antisocial behaviour (Van den Oord et al., 2000). Nonetheless, it is clear that parents' treatment of their children affects children's aggression and antisocial behaviour. Direct evidence of the role of parental effects can be found in intervention studies. When parents are trained to deal with their children in an effective manner, there are improvements in their children's conduct problems (A. Connell et al., 2008; Dishion et al., 2008; Hanish & Tolan, 2001). Similar effects have been obtained in intervention studies in schools (see Box 14.4). Effects such as these indicate that socialization in and of itself plays a role in the development of antisocial behaviour.

BOX 14.4: applications

THE FAST TRACK INTERVENTION

Psychologists interested in the prevention of antisocial behaviour and violence have designed numerous school-based intervention programs. One of the most intensive was Fast Track—a program designed to prevent the development of serious conduct problems in children in Grades 1 and 2. Fast Track is based on a large, federally funded study that was tested in high-risk schools in four U.S. cities (Conduct Problems Prevention Research Group, 1999a, 1999b). This program was initially implemented for 3 successive years with almost 400 Grade 1 classes, half of which received the intervention and half of which served as a control group. The children in both groups tended to come from low-income families, about half of which were minority families (Slough, McMahon, & the Conduct Problems Prevention Research Group, 2008). A replication project is currently running in six Calgary elementary schools.

There were two major parts of the U.S. intervention. In the first part, all children in the intervention classes were trained with a special curriculum designed to promote understanding and communication of emotions, positive social behaviour, self-control, and social problem solving (Greenberg et al., 1995). The children were taught to recognize emotional cues in themselves and to distinguish appropriate and inappropriate behavioural reactions to emotions. They were also taught how to make and keep friends, how to share, how to listen to others, and how to calm themselves down and to inhibit aggressive behaviour when they became upset or frustrated.

In the second part of the program, children with the most serious problem behaviours (about 10% of the group) participated in a more intensive intervention. In addition to the school intervention, they attended special meetings throughout the year, receiving social skills training similar to what they experienced in the classroom. They were also tutored in their school work. Their parents received group training that was designed to build their self-control and promote developmentally appropriate expectations for their child's behaviour. In addition, the program promoted parenting skills that would improve parent–child interaction, decrease children's disruptive behaviour, and establish a positive relationship between parents and the child's school. After Grade 1, the curriculum was continued in the classrooms; other aspects of the intervention outside the classroom were adjusted to the needs of each family and child (Conduct Problems Prevention Research Group, 2004). Meetings with children and parents continued through Grade 9.

The program was quite successful. In the Grade 1 classrooms as a whole, there was less aggression and disruptive behaviour and a more positive atmosphere than in the control classes. More important, the children in the intervention group improved in their social and emotional skills (such as recognizing and coping with emotions), as well as in academic skills. They had more positive interactions with peers, were liked more by their classmates, and exhibited fewer conduct problems than the control children. Their parents improved in their parenting skills and were more involved with their children's schooling.

In a follow-up at the end of Grade 3, 37% of the children in the intervention group were found to be free of serious conduct problems, whereas only 27% of the children who did not receive the intervention were free of problems (Conduct Problems Prevention Research Group, 2002a). Teachers' and parents' reports, as well as school records, likewise indicated that there was a modest positive effect, both at home

Nonetheless, recent genetically informed research illustrates that often it is the combination of genetic and environmental factors that predict children's antisocial, aggressive behaviour and that some children are more sensitive to the quality of parenting than are others. As noted in our previous discussions of differential susceptibility (pages 409, 437, and 568), children with certain gene variants related to serotonin or dopamine, which affect neurotransmission, appear to be more reactive to their environment than are children with different variants. For example, under adverse conditions (e.g., chronic stress, poor parenting, socioeconomic deprivation), children with a particular variant of the serotonin transporter gene (SLC6A4) or the dopamine receptor gene (DRD4) tend to be more aggressive than children with different variants of these genes (C. C. Conway et al., 2012)—but, compared with those children, they tend to be less aggressive when they are in a supportive, resource-rich environment (Conway et al., 2012; Simons et al., 2011, 2012). In other cases, such gene variants are related to higher risk for more aggression in adverse situations like maltreatment and divorce, but are not related to aggression in the absence of the adverse conditions (Cicchetti, Rogosch, & Thibodeau, 2012; Nederhof et al., 2012). Regardless of the exact nature of the gene–environment interaction, it seems clear that the degree of aggression is affected by a combination of heredity and the environment.

and in school, including the intervention group's using special education services less and showing greater improvement in academic engagement. The intervention group also showed a modest increase in prosocial behaviour. These effects generally were stronger in less disadvantaged schools, and effects on aggression were larger in students who showed higher baseline levels of aggression. In Grades 4 and 5, children in the intervention group still exhibited modest improvements in terms of conduct problems, peer acceptance, and lower levels of association with deviant peers. These positive outcomes seemed to be due, in part, to the effects of the intervention on reducing children's hostile attribution biases, fostering their problem-solving skills, and reducing the levels of harsh parental discipline (Bierman et al., 2010; Conduct Problems Prevention Research Group, 2002b, 2004).

Across Grades 3 to 12, the prevalence of externalizing problems such as conduct disorder, oppositional defiant disorder, and attention deficit hyperactivity disorder was reduced, although only for the youths most at risk (Conduct Problems Prevention Research Group, 2007, 2011). In addition, juvenile arrests were reduced, as were

high-severity arrests in early adulthood for youths with the highest initial behavioural risk (Conduct Problems Prevention Research Group, 2010). In terms of cost, it appears that, given the funds available, the program was not cost-efficient relative to the total sample but was likely cost-effective for the subgroup of children at high risk for externalizing problems (Foster & Jones, 2007). Thus, it is important that children be screened for inclusion in high-cost programs such as Fast Track (Conduct Problems Prevention Research Group, 2007).

Many interventions besides Fast Track have been devised to reduce children's aggression and other externalizing problems. For example, numerous programs have been used to combat bullying in schools and the high-quality programs appear to reduce the incidence of bullying considerably (Cross et al., 2011; Salmivalli, Kärnä, & Poskiparta, 2011; Ttofi & Farrington, 2011). More intensive programs tend to be more effective, and the most important elements of successful programs included parent meetings and training; teacher training and an emphasis on classroom management; firm disciplinary practices at school, including the enforcement of classroom rules; and a

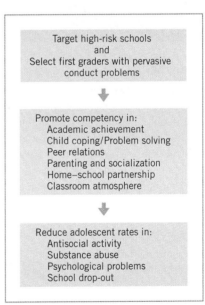

Objectives of the Fast Track project

whole-school policy to eliminate bullying, improve playground supervision, and have children work in cooperative groups (Ttofi & Farrington, 2011). Anti-bullying interventions appear to be more effective for adolescents than for younger children (Ttofi & Farrington, 2011).

review

Aggressive behaviour emerges by the second year of life and increases in frequency during the toddler years. Physical aggression starts to decline in frequency in the preschool years; in elementary school, children tend to exhibit more non-physical aggression (e.g., relational aggression) than at younger ages, and some children increasingly engage in antisocial behaviours such as stealing. Early individual differences in aggression and conduct problems predict antisocial behaviour in later childhood, adolescence, and adulthood. Children who first engage in aggressive, antisocial acts in early to mid-adolescence are less likely to continue their antisocial behaviour after adolescence than are children who are aggressive and antisocial at a younger age.

Biological factors, including those related to temperament and neurological problems, likely affect children's degree of aggression. Social cognition is also associated with aggressiveness in a variety of ways, including the attribution of hostile motives to others, having hostile goals, constructing and enacting aggressive responses in difficult situations, and evaluating aggressive responses favourably.

Children's aggression is affected by a range of environmental factors, as well as by heredity. In general, low parental support, poor monitoring, or the use of disciplinary practices that are abusive or inconsistent are related to high levels of children's antisocial behaviour. Parental conflict in the home and many of the stresses associated with family transitions (e.g., divorce) and poverty can increase the likelihood of children's aggression. In addition, involvement with antisocial peers likely contributes to antisocial behaviour, although aggressive children also seek out antisocial peers. Cultural values and practices, as communicated in the child's social world, also contribute to differences among children in aggressive behaviour. Intervention programs can be used to reduce aggression, which provides evidence of the role of environmental factors in children's aggression.

chapter summary:

Moral Judgment

■ Piaget delineated two age-related moral stages and a transitional period. In the first stage, morality of constraint, young children tend to believe that rules are unchangeable and tend to weigh consequences more than intentions in evaluating the morality of actions. In the autonomous stage, children realize that rules are social products that can be changed, and they consider motives and intentions when evaluating behaviour. Several aspects of Piaget's theory have not held up well to scrutiny, but his theory provided the foundation for subsequent work on moral reasoning.

■ Kohlberg outlined three levels of moral judgment—preconventional, conventional, and postconventional—each originally containing two stages (Stage 6 was eventually dropped from Kohlberg's scoring procedure). Kohlberg hypothesized that his sequence of stages reflects age-related, discontinuous (qualitative) changes in moral reasoning that are universal. According to Kohlberg, these changes stem from cognitive advances, particularly in perspective taking. Although there is support for the idea that higher levels of moral reasoning are related to cognitive growth, it is not clear that children's moral reasoning moves through discontinuous stages of development or develops the same way in all cultures and for all kinds of moral issues (e.g., prosocial moral reasoning).

■ There are important differences among the moral, social conventional, and personal domains of behaviour and judgment. Young children, like older children, differentiate among different domains of social judgment. Which behaviours are considered matters of moral, social conventional, or personal judgment varies somewhat across cultures.

The Early Development of Conscience

■ The conscience involves internalized moral standards and feelings of guilt for misbehaviour: it restrains the individual from engaging in unacceptable behaviour. The conscience develops slowly over time, beginning before age 2. Depending on their temperament, children are more likely to internalize parental standards if they are securely attached and if their parents do not rely on excessive parental power in their discipline.

Prosocial Behaviour

■ Prosocial behaviour is voluntary behaviour intended to benefit another, such as helping, sharing with, and comforting others. Young children who are prosocial, especially those who spontaneously engage in sharing that is personally costly, tend to be prosocial when older.

■ Prosocial behaviours emerge by the second year of life and increase in frequency with age, probably due to age-related increases in children's abilities to sympathize and take others' perspectives. Differences among children in these abilities contribute to individual differences in children's prosocial behaviour.

- Heredity, which contributes to differences among children in temperament, likely affects how empathic and prosocial children are.

- A positive parent–child relationship, authoritative parenting, the use of reasoning by parents and teachers, and exposure to prosocial models, values, and activities are associated with the development of sympathy and prosocial behaviour. Cultural values and expectations also appear to affect the degree to which children exhibit prosocial behaviour and toward whom.

- School-based intervention programs designed to promote cooperation, perspective taking, helping, and prosocial values are associated with increased prosocial tendencies in children.

Antisocial Behaviour

- Aggressive behaviour emerges by the second year of life and increases in frequency during the toddler years; physical aggression starts to decline in frequency in the preschool years. In elementary school, children tend to exhibit more non-physical aggression (e.g., relational aggression) than at younger ages, and some children increasingly engage in antisocial behaviours such as stealing.

- From preschool on, boys are more physically aggressive than girls and more likely to engage in delinquent behaviour.

- Early individual differences in aggression and conduct problems predict antisocial behaviour in later childhood, adolescence, and adulthood.

- Biological factors that contribute to differences among children in temperament and neurological functioning likely affect how aggressive children become. Social cognition also affects aggression: aggressive children tend to attribute hostile motives to others and to have hostile goals themselves.

- Children's aggression is promoted by a range of environmental factors, including low parental support; chaotic families; poor monitoring; abusive, coercive, or inconsistent disciplining; and stress or conflict in the home. In addition, involvement with antisocial peers likely contributes to antisocial behaviour, although it is also likely that aggressive children seek out antisocial peers. Aggression also varies somewhat across cultures, suggesting that cultural values, norms, and socialization practices may also contribute to individual differences in aggression and antisocial behaviour.

- Children who are diagnosed with antisocial behaviour such as conduct disorder and oppositional defiant disorder display relatively severe forms of problematic externalizing behaviours.

- In high-risk schools, interventions designed to promote understanding and communication of emotions, positive social behaviour, self-control, and social problem solving can reduce the likelihood that children will develop behaviour problems, including aggression.

Critical Thinking Questions

1. Recall a recent moral dilemma in your own life. What sorts of reasoning did you use when thinking about the dilemma? On what dimensions did it differ from Kohlberg's Heinz dilemma? How might these differences have affected your reasoning about this dilemma?

2. How would you design a study to determine why aggressive children and adolescents have aggressive friends? How would you determine whether aggressive youth simply choose aggressive friends or whether aggressive friends tend to make youth become more aggressive?

3. Suppose you wanted to assess children's helping behaviour that was altruistic and not due to factors such as the expectation of personal gain or concern about others' approval. How would you design a study to assess altruistic helping in 5-year-olds? Might the procedure differ if you wanted to assess altruistic helping in 16-year-olds?

4. Freud believed that morality does not emerge until the child develops a superego at around 4 to 6 years of age. What evidence contradicts his theory?

5. Using the tenets of social learning theory (see Chapter 9), outline ways that parents might deter the development of aggression in their children.

Key Terms

aggression, p. 578

altruistic motives, p. 569

conduct disorder (CD), p. 581

conscience, p. 566

instrumental aggression, p. 579

moral judgments, p. 564

oppositional defiant disorder (ODD), p. 581

personal judgments, p. 564

proactive aggression, p. 583

prosocial behaviour, p. 562

reactive aggression, p. 583

social conventional judgments, p. 564

P.J. CROOK, *Playground* (acrylic on canvas)

chapter 15:

Gender Development

One late autumn afternoon, two children were playing in the backyard as their mothers, best friends for many years, were having tea on the deck. Colin, who was 5 years old, and Catherine, who was 4½, had played together since infancy. Even though they shared many of the same interests, they were also different in many ways. For example, Catherine hated movies that were the least bit violent or scary: as a toddler, she would not even watch *Sesame Street* because she was frightened of Oscar the Grouch. In contrast, Colin loved action films full of car chases, fires, and explosions.

Colin and Catherine exhibit some of the behavioural differences in *assertion* and *affiliation* that are often seen between boys and girls. **Assertion** refers to one's attempts to exert influence over the environment, whereas **affiliation** refers to making connections with others. The traditional masculine role in most societies stresses self-assertion over interpersonal affiliation, with corresponding emphases on independence, competition, and task orientation. In contrast, the traditional feminine role stresses affiliation over assertion, with corresponding emphases on interpersonal sensitivity, supportiveness, and affection (Bassen & Lamb, 2006; Leaper & Smith, 2004).

However, the goals of assertion and affiliation are not mutually exclusive: they are often blended together in a style known as **collaboration** (Leaper, 1991; Leaper, Tenenbaum, & Shaffer, 1999). Collaboration is associated with gender-role flexibility and, on average, is more common among girls than among boys. As with most gender differences, however, there is also, on average, considerable overlap between girls and boys in collaboration. Indeed, although some children act in gender-stereotypical ways, many girls and boys are, as you will soon see, quite similar to one another in a wide variety of behaviours.

In this chapter, we consider what might account for gender differences or similarities between girls and boys. Why do they have different preferences? How representative is their behaviour compared with other children of their gender? Do they consistently demonstrate gender-stereotypical behaviours across different situations?

Developmental psychologists generally acknowledge the combined influences of biological, psychological, and cultural processes on gender development (Leaper, 2013) but differ in how much they stress particular factors. Some researchers argue that certain differences in boys' and girls' behaviour reflect underlying biological differences that emerged over the course of human evolution (Bjorklund & Pellegrini, 2002; Geary, 1998). In their view, average gender differences in assertion and affiliation are partly attributable to genetic sex differences in brain structures and hormone effects. In contrast, other psychologists place more emphasis on social and cognitive influences (Bussey & Bandura, 1999; C. L. Martin, Ruble, & Szkrybalo, 2002). In general, most developmental psychologists contend that the role of biology in the development of gender-related differences must be considered in the context of the social influences of family, peers, teachers, and the culture at large.

We examine two main questions in this chapter: (1) How similar or different are girls and boys in terms of psychological variables? and (2) What might account for

JOHN GERLACH

Although this boy and girl are siblings, growing up in the same household, some differences in their behaviour, attitudes, and interests are apparent. In this chapter, we compare girls' and boys' development and consider different theoretical perspectives on the development of gender differences.

assertion ■ Tendency to take action on behalf of the self through competitive, independent, or aggressive behaviours.

affiliation ■ Tendency to affirm connection with others through being emotionally open, empathetic, or cooperative.

collaboration ■ Coordination of assertion and affiliation in behaviour, which is associated with gender-role flexibility; more common among girls than boys.

any differences? We first consider the biological, cognitive-motivational, and cultural influences that may contribute to gender development. Next, we outline the major milestones in children's development of gender stereotypes and gender-typed behaviour. Then we compare what actually is known about the similarities and differences between girls and boys in specific areas of development, including physical development, cognitive abilities and achievement, and personality and social behaviour.

Throughout our discussion, we use the terms *sex* and *gender* in distinct ways. *Sex* tends to imply biological origins for any differences between males and females. Therefore, we follow the convention of using *gender* as a more neutral term that refers simply to one's social categorization as either female or male, and we use the term *sex* only when referring explicitly to biological processes, such as those involving sex hormones or genetic sex. In addition, the terms **gender-typed** and **cross-gender-typed** refer, respectively, to behaviours associated with a given person's gender and to behaviours associated with the gender other than that of a given person. For example, playing with dolls is gender-typed for girls and cross-gender-typed for boys. Finally, the term **gender typing** refers broadly to the process of gender socialization and development.

Four of our seven themes are particularly prominent in this chapter. The theme of *nature and nurture* appears repeatedly, as perspectives vary in emphasizing the roles played by biological and environmental factors in gender development. The theme of the *active child* is apparent in cognitive theories of gender development that emphasize children's roles in discovering what it means to be male or female and in socializing their peers into gender-appropriate roles. The *sociocultural context* is reflected in theories that emphasize the central roles that parents, teachers, peers, and the media play in shaping children's gender development. Finally, the theme of *individual differences* also pervades the chapter as we attempt to account for the ways in which males and females are similar and different.

Theoretical Approaches to Gender Development

Researchers variously point to the influences of biological, cognitive-motivational, and cultural factors on gender development. First, biological differences between females and males—including the influence of sex hormones and brain structure differences—may partly account for average gender differences in some behaviours. Second, cognition and motivation—learning gender-typed roles through observation and practice—can shape children's gender development. As highlighted in cognitive-motivational explanations, boys and girls are systematically provided different role models, opportunities, and incentives for gender-typed behaviour by parents, teachers, peers, and the media. Finally, cultural factors, including the relative status of women and men in society, may shape children's gender development.

As you will see in this section, there is empirical evidence for the role of each type of influence in certain behaviours. Indeed, it is likely that most aspects of gender development result from the complex interaction of all three sets of factors.

Biological Influences

Some researchers interested in biological influences on development consider possible ways that gender differences in behaviour may have emerged during the course of human evolution. Other biologically oriented researchers focus more directly on identifying hormonal factors and differences in brain functioning as possible influences on gender differences in behavioural development.

gender-typed ■ Traditionally associated with a given person's gender.

cross-gender-typed ■ Traditionally associated with the gender other than that of a given person.

gender typing ■ The process of gender socialization and development.

Evolutionary Approaches

As discussed in Chapter 9, evolutionary theory proposes that certain characteristics that facilitate survival and the transmission of genes to succeeding generations have been favoured over the course of human evolution. Developmental psychologists generally agree that evolution is important for understanding children's development. However, there are different views regarding the proposal that females and males evolved different behavioural dispositions. Two examples are *evolutionary psychology theory* and *biosocial theory*.

Evolutionary psychology theory According to evolutionary psychology theory, certain behavioural tendencies occur because they helped humans survive during the course of evolution. Some evolutionary psychology theorists propose that particular gender differences in behaviour reflect evolved personality dispositions. These theorists argue that sex-linked dispositions evolved to increase the chances that women and men would successfully mate and protect their offspring (Bjorklund & Pellegrini, 2002; D. M. Buss, 1999; Geary, 1998; Kenrick, Trost, & Sundie, 2004).

As noted in Chapter 9, studies of children's play behaviour show average gender differences that have been interpreted as consistent with the evolutionary perspective. For example, more boys than girls tend to engage in physically active, rough-and-tumble, and competitive types of play. Many boys devote considerable effort to jockeying with their male peers for dominance in groups. Geary (1999) proposed that boys' play-fighting may represent an "evolved tendency to practice the competencies that were associated with male–male competition during human evolution" (p. 31). A propensity to engage in physical aggression is thought to have provided reproductive advantages for males in competition with other males for resources, including access to females (Geary, 1999, 2004).

In contrast, girls devote much effort to establishing and maintaining positive social relations, spend time in smaller groups of close female friends, and tend to avoid open conflict in their interactions. Girls also engage in much more play-parenting, including play with dolls, than boys do. From the evolutionary psychology perspective, these behaviours reflect evolved dispositions because maternal care in the form of breastfeeding was required for infants' survival. In addition, nurturance and other affiliative behaviours may have increased the probability that their offspring would survive long enough to reproduce.

Evolutionary psychology theory is a popular approach, but a number of its proposals regarding gender differences are controversial. Some biologists and psychologists argue that many of evolutionary psychology theory's claims about sex differences in personality traits cannot be tested (S. J. Gould, 1997; Lickliter & Honeycutt, 2003; W. Wood & Eagly, 2002). These critics also argue that some of the theory's explanations are based on circular reasoning: if an average sex difference in behaviour occurs—such as women being more likely than men to express nurturance—it is seen as having helped humans survive during the course of evolution, and it is considered adaptive during evolution because the average gender difference exists today. Such an argument merely asserts its premise as its conclusion and therefore is a

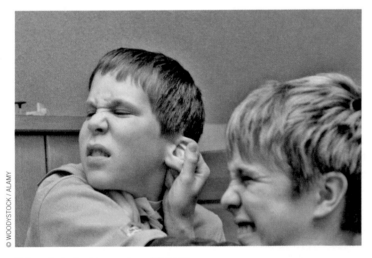

© WOODYSTOCK / ALAMY

Rates of physical aggression with peers tend to be higher for boys than for girls in all cultures that have been studied, although the magnitude of the average gender difference varies across cultures.

difficult argument to test. Perhaps the clearest way to establish evidence of evolutionary influences would be to link sex differences in particular behaviours to genetic variations on sex chromosomes. We review work in this area later in the chapter.

Keep in mind that evolutionary psychology theory is not synonymous with all evolutionary approaches. An alternative evolutionary view emphasizes human evolution as maximizing our capacity for behavioural flexibility as an adaptation to environmental variability (S. J. Gould, 1997; Lickliter & Honeycutt, 2003). This view also points out that, because of their focus on biological constraints in gender development, some versions of evolutionary psychology theory can be construed as a rationalization for the status quo in traditional gender roles (Angier, 1999; S. J. Gould, 1997). As reviewed next, biosocial theory is an evolutionary approach that places more emphasis on the potential for behavioural flexibility while also acknowledging the impact of evolution on sex differences in physical characteristics.

Biosocial theory Wood and Eagly (2002) have offered biosocial theory as an alternative evolutionary approach to understanding gender development. Biosocial theory focuses on the evolution of *physical* differences between the sexes and proposes that these differences have behavioural and social consequences. For much of human history, the most important physical differences have been (1) men's greater average size, strength, and foot speed and (2) women's child-bearing and nursing capacities. Men's physical abilities gave them an advantage in activities such as hunting and combat and, in turn, tended to confer status and social dominance in the society. In contrast, bearing and nursing children limited women's mobility and involvement in many forms of economic subsistence such as hunting.

However, according to biosocial theory, biology does not necessarily determine destiny. Nowadays in technological societies, men's strength and other physical qualities are not relevant for most means of subsistence. For example, strength is irrelevant to succeeding as a manager, a lawyer, a physician, or an engineer. All these high-status occupations are now performed by women as well as by men (although gender equality is not fully realized in any of these occupations). Also, reproductive control and child care provide women greater flexibility to maintain their involvement in the labour force. Thus, according to biosocial theory, both physical sex differences and social ecology shape the different gender roles assigned to men and women—as well as the socialization of boys and girls.

As we have seen, some claims associated with evolutionary psychology theory are criticized for emphasizing biological determinants of gender differences. However, evolutionary psychologists take issue with biosocial theory, asserting that the body and the mind evolved together and that biosocial theory addresses only the body's impact on gender development (Archer & Lloyd, 2002; Luxen, 2007). In sum, evolutionary psychology theory and biosocial theory both acknowledge the importance of the physical differences between women and men. But evolutionary psychology theorists additionally argue for the impact of sex differences in evolved behavioural dispositions.

Neuroscience Approaches

Researchers who take a neuroscience approach focus on testing whether and how hormones and brain functioning relate to variations in gender development (Berenbaum, 1998; Hines, 2004). Some neuroscience researchers also frame their work in terms of an evolutionary psychology perspective (Geary, 1998, 2004).

androgens ■ Class of steroid hormones that normally occur at higher levels in males than in females and that affect physical development and functioning from the prenatal period onward.

organizing influences ■ Potential result of certain sex-linked hormones affecting brain differentiation and organization during prenatal development or at puberty.

activating influences ■ Potential result of certain fluctuations in sex-linked hormone levels affecting the contemporaneous activation of the nervous system and corresponding behavioural responses.

Hormones and brain functioning In the study of gender development, much attention has been paid to the possible effects of **androgens,** a class of steroid hormones that includes testosterone (Box 15.1). As discussed in Chapter 2, during normal prenatal development, the presence of androgens leads to the formation of male genitalia in genetic males; in their absence, female genitalia are formed in genetic females.

Androgens can also have *organizing* or *activating* influences on the nervous system. **Organizing influences** occur when certain sex-linked hormones affect brain differentiation and organization during prenatal development or at puberty. For example, sex-related differences in prenatal androgens may influence the organization and functioning of the nervous system; in turn, this may be related to later average gender differences in certain play preferences (see Berenbaum, 1998). **Activating influences** occur when fluctuations in sex-linked hormone levels influence the contemporaneous activation of certain brain and behavioural responses

BOX 15.1: a closer look

GENDER IDENTITY: MORE THAN SOCIALIZATION?

Most children's gender identification is consistent with their observable genitalia and gender socialization. That is, children's view of themselves as "a girl" or "a boy" is consistent with their genetic sex and the gender-role expectations others hold for them. However, in some cases, children believe that their gender is not the one that others take it to be. Studies of such cases suggest that, once established, the child's initial gender identification is often impervious to parental attempts to socialize the child as a member of what the child perceives as the "wrong" gender.

The potential power of children's preferences over gender socialization is evident when children identify with the other gender. Some boys indicate a preference to identify as a girl, and some girls express a preference to identify as a boy. These children usually favour cross-gender-typed play activities and clothing and dislike gender-typed activities (Zucker & Bradley, 1995). Such discrepant gender identity usually appears very early in development, mostly occurs in boys, and can be difficult to alter even with parental socialization efforts. These cases suggest that gender identification has a biological component. The biological perspective points to the prenatal impact of sex hormones on the developing fetal brain. Such biological influences seem to contribute to gender identity as well as to behavioural gender differences.

There is currently a debate in psychology over whether children with discrepant gender identities should be classified as having a psychiatric disorder. In the DSM-5, the latest version of the American Psychiatric Association's (2013) compendium, these children receive the diagnosis of **gender dysphoria disorder** (formerly "gender identity disorder"). Some clinicians, such as Kenneth Zucker at the Centre for Addiction and Mental Health in Toronto, contend that children with discrepant gender identity are distressed and require care (Zucker, 2006). Other psychologists, such as Nancy Bartlett, a clinical psychologist in Halifax, Paul Vasey from the University of Lethbridge, and Bill Bukowski from Concordia University, argue that applying a disorder label to children with cross-gender-typed interests merely reflects societal pressures for gender-role conformity (Bartlett, Vasey, & Bukowski, 2000).

Along these lines, some people argue for a broader notion of gender that goes beyond thinking only of the two categories of "female" or "male." This includes acceptance of **transgender** youth and adults, individuals whose gender identity does not match their genetic sex. Some transgendered individuals prefer to identify with the other gender, with both genders, or with neither gender.

Another group of individuals who seek to broaden the gender spectrum include those born with intersex conditions (Preves, 2003). *Intersex* conditions are due to recessive genes that cause, in rare instances, a person of one genetic sex to develop genital characteristics typical of the other genetic sex. (Intersex individuals may also consider themselves transgender.) Two such intersex conditions are *congenital adrenal hyperplasia* and *androgen insensitivity syndrome.*

High levels of androgens produced during the prenatal development of genetic females can lead to **congenital adrenal hyperplasia (CAH),** a condition that involves the formation of male (or partly masculinized) genitalia. Researchers have studied girls with CAH to infer the possible influence of androgens on gender development. They have found that, compared with other girls, those with CAH are more likely to choose physically active forms of play, such as rough-and-tumble play, and to avoid sedentary forms of play, such as playing with dolls (Berenbaum & Hines, 1992; Nordenström et al., 2002). This evidence has been used to support the idea that prenatal androgens may partly contribute to boys' and girls' gender identities and to gender-typed play preferences. In addition, this kind of evidence is sometimes used to support evolutionary accounts of gender development (G. M. Alexander, 2003).

In contrast, **androgen insensitivity syndrome (AIS),** a rare syndrome in genetic males, causes androgen receptors to malfunction. In these cases, genetic males may be born with female external genitalia.

(Collaer & Hines, 1995). For example, as discussed later, the body increases androgen production in response to perceived threats, with possible implications for gender differences in aggression.

Brain structure and functioning Male and female brains show some small differences in physical structure (Hines, 2004). One such difference is in the corpus callosum (the connection between the brain's two hemispheres), which tends to be larger and to include more dense nerve bundles in women than in men (Driesen & Raz, 1995). When engaged in cognitive tasks (e.g., deciding whether words rhyme or navigating a maze), the male brain tends to show activations in one hemisphere or the other, whereas the female brain tends to show activations in both hemispheres (B. A. Shaywitz et al., 1995). However, this particular difference does not appear to result in any advantage to cognitive performance (D. F. Halpern, 2012).

One limitation of research documenting sex differences in brain structure is that it is mostly based on brain-imaging studies performed on adults. Given the continual interaction of genes and experience during brain development, it is unclear to what extent any differences in the brain's structure or functioning seen in adults are due to genetic or environmental influences. It is also unclear to what extent these small differences in brain structure determine any gender differences in ability and behaviour (D. F. Halpern, 2012).

Cognitive and Motivational Influences

Cognitive theories of gender development emphasize the ways that children learn gender-typed attitudes and behaviours through observation, inference, and practice. According to these explanations, children form expectations about gender that guide their behaviour. Cognitive theories stress children's active **self-socialization:** individuals use their beliefs, expectations, and preferences to guide how they perceive the world and the actions that they choose. Self-socialization occurs in gender development when children seek to behave in accord with their gender identity as a girl or a boy. However, cognitive theories also emphasize the role of the environment—the different role models, opportunities, and incentives that girls and boys might experience. We next discuss four pertinent cognitive theories of gender development: cognitive developmental theory, gender schema theory, social identity theory, and social cognitive theory.

Cognitive Developmental Theory

Lawrence Kohlberg's (1966) cognitive developmental theory of gender-role development reflects a Piagetian framework (reviewed in Chapter 4). Kohlberg proposed that children actively construct gender knowledge in the same way, in the Piagetian view, that they construct knowledge about the physical world.

Kohlberg maintained that children's understanding of gender involves a three-stage process that occurs between approximately 2 to 6 years of age. First, by around 30 months of age, young children acquire a **gender identity:** they categorize themselves either as a girl or a boy (Fagot & Leinbach, 1989). However, they do not yet realize that gender is permanent. For example, young children may believe that a girl could grow up to be a father (Slaby & Frey, 1975). The second stage, which begins at around 3 or 4 years of age, is **gender stability:** children come to realize that gender remains the same over time ("I'm a girl, and I'll always be a girl"). However, they are still not clear that gender is independent of superficial

gender dysphoria disorder ■ Psychiatric diagnosis included in the DSM-5 to refer to children who identify with the other gender and indicate cross-gender-typed interests.

transgender ■ A person whose gender identity does not match the person's genetic sex; includes individuals who identify either with the other sex, with both sexes, or with neither sex.

congenital adrenal hyperplasia (CAH) ■ Condition during prenatal development in which the adrenal glands produce high levels of androgens; sometimes associated with masculinization of external genitalia in genetic females, and sometimes associated with higher rates of masculine-stereotyped play in genetic females.

androgen insensitivity syndrome (AIS) ■ Condition during prenatal development in which androgen receptors malfunction in genetic males, impeding the formation of male external genitalia; in these cases, the child may be born with female external genitalia.

self-socialization (gender development) ■ Individuals' use of their beliefs, expectations, and preferences to guide how they perceive the world and what actions they choose.

gender identity ■ Awareness of oneself as a boy or a girl.

gender stability ■ Awareness that gender remains the same over time.

JULIA CUMES / THE IMAGE WORKS

As predicted by cognitive theories, children learn a great deal about gender roles by observing other people. Television, movies, and video games provide many examples of gender stereotypes for both sexes.

appearance and think that a boy who has put on a dress and now looks like a girl has become a girl.

The basic understanding of gender is completed in the third stage, around 6 years of age, when children achieve **gender constancy,** the understanding that gender is invariant across situations ("I'm a girl, and nothing I do will change that"). Kohlberg noted that this is the same age at which children begin to succeed on Piagetian conservation problems and argued that both achievements reflect the same stage of thinking. Kohlberg maintained that children's understanding that gender remains constant even when superficial changes occur is similar to their understanding that the amount of a substance is conserved even when its appearance is altered (a ball of clay that has been mashed flat is still the same amount of clay; a girl who gets her hair cut short and starts wearing baseball shirts instead of dresses is still a girl). According to Kohlberg, once gender constancy is attained, children begin to seek out and attend to same-gender models to learn how to behave ("Since I'm a girl, I should like to do girl things, so I need to find out what those are").

Subsequent research has supported the idea that children's understanding of gender develops in the sequence Kohlberg hypothesized and that the attainment of gender constancy occurs at more or less the same age as success on conservation problems (e.g., D. E. Marcus & Overton, 1978; Munroe, Shimmin, & Munroe, 1984). Studies also indicate that acquiring gender constancy increases the likelihood of many gender-typed behaviours (C. L. Martin et al., 2002). Gender schema theory, reviewed next, also addresses ways that attaining a concept of gender can affect children's gender development.

Gender Schema Theory

Martin and Halverson (1981) proposed gender schema theory as an alternative to Kohlberg's explanation of children's gender development (also see Bem, 1981). In contrast to Kohlberg's view that gender-typed interests emerge after gender constancy is achieved, gender schema theory holds that the motivation to enact gender-typed behaviour begins as soon as children can label other people's and their own gender—in other words, when they are toddlers.

Accordingly, children's understanding of gender develops through their construction of **gender schemas,** mental representations incorporating everything the child knows about gender. Gender schemas include memories of one's own experiences with males and females, gender stereotypes transmitted directly by adults and peers ("boys don't cry," "girls play with dolls"), and messages conveyed indirectly through the media. Children use an *in-group/out-group* gender schema to classify other people as being either "the same as me" or not. The motivation for cognitive consistency leads them to prefer, pay attention to, and remember more about others of their own gender. As a consequence, an *own-gender schema* is formed, consisting of detailed knowledge about how to do things that are consistent with one's own gender. Simply learning that an unfamiliar object is "for my gender" makes children like it more. Figure 15.1 illustrates how this process leads children to acquire greater knowledge and expertise with gender-consistent entities.

gender constancy ■ Realization that gender is invariant despite superficial changes in a person's appearance or behaviour.

gender schemas ■ Organized mental representations (concepts, beliefs, memories) about gender, including gender stereotypes.

To test the impact of gender schemas on children's information processing, 4- to 9-year-olds were given three boxes. Each contained unfamiliar, gender-neutral objects, and each was separately labelled as "boys," "girls," or "boys and girls/girls and boys." The children spent more time exploring objects in boxes labelled for their own gender (or for both genders) than objects in the box labelled only for the other gender. One week later, not surprisingly, they remembered more details about the objects they had explored than about the ones they had spent less time with (Bradbard et al., 1986).

Children regularly look to their peers to infer gender-appropriate behaviour. In an observational study conducted in a preschool classroom, boys were influenced by the number and the proportion of same-gender children who were playing with a set of toys: they approached toys that were being played with primarily by boys and shunned those that seemed popular mainly with girls (Shell & Eisenberg, 1990).

Gender schemas are also responsible for *biased* processing and remembering of information about gender. Consistent with the research described above, children tend to remember more about what they observe from same-gender than from cross-gender role models (Signorella, Bigler, & Liben, 1997; Stangor & McMillan, 1992). They are also more likely to accurately encode and remember information about story characters that behave in gender-consistent ways and to forget or distort information that is gender-inconsistent (Liben & Signorella, 1993; C. L. Martin & Halverson, 1983). For example, children who heard a story that featured a girl sawing wood often remembered it later as a story about a boy sawing wood. Similarly, children who saw pictures that showed a boy playing with a doll and a girl playing with a truck tended to misremember the gender of the children performing these respective actions (C. L. Martin & Halverson, 1983). This tendency to retain information that is schema-consistent and to ignore or distort schema-inconsistent information helps perpetuate gender stereotypes that have little or no basis in reality.

Liben and Bigler (2002) have added another component to gender schema theory. They proposed that children use two kinds of filters when processing information about the world. One is a **gender schema filter** ("Is this information relevant for my gender?") and the other is an **interest filter** ("Is this information interesting?"). When encountering a new toy, for example, children may decide that it is something for girls or for boys and explore or ignore the toy on the basis of their gender schema filter. This is the same process emphasized in Martin and Halverson's gender schema theory. However, Liben and Bigler noted that children sometimes find a new toy attractive without initially evaluating its appropriateness for their gender. In these instances, they use their interest filter to evaluate information. Furthermore, children sometimes use their interest filter to modify their gender schemas ("If I like this toy, it must be something that is okay for my gender"). Liben and Bigler's modification to gender schema theory helps account for findings indicating that children are often inconsistent in their gender-typed interests (for example, they are often more traditional in some areas than others). It also allows for the fact that some children actively pursue certain cross-gender-typed activities simply because they enjoy them.

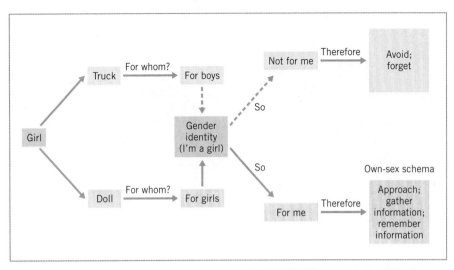

FIGURE 15.1 **Gender schema theory** According to gender schema theory, children classify new objects and activities as "for boys" or "for girls." They tend to investigate objects and activities that are relevant to their gender and to ignore those that are associated with the other gender.

gender schema filter ■ Initial evaluation of information as relevant for one's own gender.

interest filter ■ Initial evaluation of information as being personally interesting.

Children's stereotyped beliefs about gender can be changed through cognitive intervention programs. Children who learned that a person's interests and abilities were important for the kind of job the person could have showed significant reductions in gender stereotyping.

Although gender schemas are resistant to change, the contents of children's gender schemas can be modified through explicit instruction. Such an approach was demonstrated by Bigler and Liben, who created a cognitive intervention program in which elementary school children learned that a person's interests and abilities (but not gender) are important for the kind of job that the person could have (Bigler & Liben, 1990; Liben & Bigler, 1987). (The children were encouraged to see, for example, that if Mary was strong and liked to build things, a good job for her would be to work as a carpenter.) Children who participated in this week-long program showed decreased gender stereotyping and also had better memory for gender-inconsistent stimuli (such as a picture of a girl holding a hammer). However, a limitation of interventions aimed at reducing gender stereotyping is the fact that their impact typically fades once the intervention ends (Bigler, 1999). That is, children gradually revert back to their old gender stereotypes. Given the pervasiveness of gender stereotyping in children's everyday lives, cognitive interventions need to be sustained to have a longer-lasting effect.

Social Identity Theory

Developmental psychologists have highlighted the importance of gender as a social identity in children's development (e.g., Bigler & Liben, 2007; J. R. Harris, 1995; Leaper, 2000; Nesdale, 2007; Powlishta, 1995). Indeed, gender may be the *most* central social identity in children's lives (Bem, 1993). Children's commitment to gender as a social identity is most readily apparent through their primary affiliation with same-gender peers (Leaper, 1994; Maccoby, 1998).

Henri Tajfel and John Turner's (1979) social identity theory addresses the influence of group membership on people's self-concepts and behaviour with others. Two influential processes that occur when a person commits to an in-group are *in-group bias* and *in-group assimilation*. **In-group bias** refers to the tendency to evaluate individuals and characteristics associated with the in-group as superior to those associated with the out-group. For example, Kimberly Powlishta (1995) observed that children showed same-gender favouritism when rating peers on likeability and favourable traits. In-group bias is related to the process of **in-group assimilation**, whereby individuals are socialized to conform to the group's norms. That is, peers expect in-group members to demonstrate the characteristics that define the in-group. Thus, they anticipate in-group approval for preferring same-gender peers and same-gender-typed activities, as well as for avoiding other-gender peers and cross-gender-typed activities (R. Banerjee & Lintern, 2000; C. L. Martin et al., 1999). As a result, children tend to become more gender-typed in their preferences as they assimilate into their same-gender peer groups (C. L. Martin & Fabes, 2001).

A corollary of social identity theory is that the characteristics associated with a high-status group are typically valued more than those of a low-status group. In male-dominated societies, masculine-stereotyped attributes such as assertiveness and competition tend to be valued more highly than feminine-stereotyped attributes such as affiliation and nurturance (Hofstede, 2000). Related to this pattern is the tendency of cross-gender-typed behaviour to be more common among girls than among boys. Indeed, masculine-stereotyped behaviour in a girl can sometimes enhance her status, whereas feminine-stereotyped behaviour in a boy typically tarnishes his status (see Leaper, 1994).

in-group bias ■ Tendency to evaluate individuals and characteristics of the in-group as superior to those of the out-group.

in-group assimilation ■ Process whereby individuals are socialized to conform to the group's norms, demonstrating the characteristics that define the in-group.

Social identity theory helps explain why gender-typing pressures tend to be more rigid for boys than for girls (Leaper, 2000). Members of high-status groups, for example, are usually more invested in maintaining group boundaries than are members of low-status groups. In most societies, males are accorded greater status and power than are females. Consistent with social identity theory, boys are more likely than girls to initiate and maintain role and group boundaries (Fagot, 1977; Sroufe et al., 1993). Boys are also more likely to endorse gender stereotypes (Rowley et al., 2007) and to hold sexist attitudes (C. S. Brown & Bigler, 2004).

Social Cognitive Theory

Kay Bussey and Albert Bandura (1999) proposed a theory of gender development based on Bandura's (1986, 1997) social cognitive theory (see pages 353–356). The theory depicts a *triadic model of reciprocal causation* among personal factors, environmental factors, and behaviour patterns. Personal factors include cognitive, motivational, and biological processes. Although the theory acknowledges the potential influence of biological factors, it primarily addresses cognition and motivation. Among its key features are sociocognitive modes of influence, observational learning processes, and self-regulatory processes.

According to social cognitive theory, learning occurs through *tuition, enactive experience,* and *observation.* **Tuition,** which refers to direct teaching, occurs during gender socialization—for example, when a father shows his son how to throw a baseball, or a mother teaches her daughter how to change a baby's diaper. **Enactive experience** occurs when children learn to guide their behaviour by taking into account the reactions their past behaviour has evoked in others. For instance, girls and boys usually get positive reactions for behaviours that are gender-stereotypical and negative reactions for behaviours that are counter-stereotypical (Fagot, 1977), and they tend to use this feedback to regulate their behaviour in relevant situations. Finally, **observational learning**—the most common form of learning—occurs through seeing and encoding the consequences other people experience as a result of their actions. Thus, children learn a great deal about gender simply through observing the behaviour of their parents, siblings, teachers, and peers. (Some examples of gender socialization in the family are described in Box 15.2.) Children also learn about gender roles through media such as television, films, and computer and video games (see Box 15.3).

Observational learning of gender-role information involves four key processes: attention, memory, production, and motivation. To learn new information, it must, of course, be attended to (noticed) and then stored in memory. As we have noted, children often notice information that is consistent with their existing gender stereotypes. (This is the main premise of gender schema theory.) Next, children need to practise the behaviour (production) that they have observed (assuming that the behaviour is within their capabilities). Finally, children's motivation to repeat a gender-typed behaviour will depend on the incentives or disincentives they experience relative to the behaviour. These sanctions can be experienced either directly (as when a parent praises a daughter for helping prepare dinner) or indirectly (as when a boy observes another boy getting teased for playing with a doll). Over time, external sanctions are usually internalized as personal standards and become self-sanctions that motivate behaviour.

According to the social cognitive theory, children monitor their behaviour and evaluate how well it matches personal standards. After making this evaluation, children may feel pride or shame, depending on whether they meet their standards.

tuition ■ Learning through direct teaching.

enactive experience ■ Learning to take into account the reactions one's past behaviour has evoked in others.

observational learning ■ Learning through watching other people and the consequences others experience as a result of their actions.

gender-essentialist statements ■
Remarks about males' and females' activities and characteristics phrased in language that implies they are inherent to the group as a whole.

When individuals experience positive self-reactions for their behaviour, they gain the sense of personal agency referred to as *self-efficacy* (see page 356). Self-efficacy can develop gradually through practice (as when a son regularly plays catch with his father), through social modelling (as when a girl observes a female friend do well in math and thinks that maybe she could do well herself), and by social persuasion (as when a coach gives a pep talk to push the boys' performances on the baseball field). Researchers consistently find a strong relation between feelings of self-efficacy and motivation. For example, self-efficacy in math predicts girls' as well as boys' likelihood of taking advanced math courses (Stevens et al., 2007).

BOX 15.2: a closer look

GENDER TYPING AT HOME

Parents convey messages about gender in many ways. One is in the division of household labour. Most Canadian parents share responsibilities, particularly if both parents work outside the home; however, the division of labour is not even. According to one recent survey of Canadian dual-earner couples with children, men spend about 1.2 hours a day on household work while women spend 2.1 hours (K. Marshall, 2011). Furthermore, the household work of mothers and fathers in two-parent families tends to mirror traditional roles. Mothers are more likely to be primarily responsible for basic child care and cleaning; fathers are more likely to be responsible for household maintenance. Analogous patterns tend to hold in parents' assignment of household chores to daughters and sons. In general, boys are more likely than girls to take out the trash, help wash the car, mow the lawn, and perform other tasks outside the home. Girls are more likely than boys to help care for younger siblings and to perform other tasks inside the home (Grusec, Goodnow, & Cohen, 1996). This gender-based role modelling and assignment of chores implies a natural division of labour and may influence boys' and girls' emerging interests and preferences (Leaper, 2002).

In conversations between parents and children, parents often convey relatively subtle messages about gender through the use of **gender-essentialist statements** phrased in the timeless present tense, such as "Boys play football" and "Girls take ballet." This linguistic form implies that the activities and implied characteristics in question are and always will be generally true of the group as a whole. In contrast, non-essentialist statements such as "Those girls are taking ballet lessons" carry no such implications. In a study of the comments that mothers made as they read stories to their toddlers or preschool children, nearly all (96%) used gender-essentialist language when referring to the gender of the story characters and activities (S. A. Gelman, Taylor, & Nguyen, 2004). They also used gender to distinguish the characters' activities ("Does that look more like a boy job or a girl job?"). Such language use may convey the idea that gender is an important distinction and that gender-related characteristics are universal and stable (Leaper & Bigler, 2004).

Another difference in how parents talk to boys and to girls was found in a study that used naturalistic observation to document parent–child conversations in a science museum. While using interactive exhibits, parents were three times more likely to offer explanations to boys about what they were observing than they were to girls (Crowley et al., 2001). In a different study, researchers observed that when demonstrating a physics task to their school-age children, fathers used more instructional talk (explanations, technical vocabulary) with sons than with daughters (Tenenbaum & Leaper, 2003). Presumably, both sets of findings occurred because adults assumed that boys are more scientifically inclined than are girls.

Finally, research by Carole Peterson at Memorial University in Newfoundland has documented differences in how parents talk about their children (Peterson, 2004). In this study, parents were interviewed a few days after they and their children had visited a hospital emergency room for treatment of an injury that the child had incurred. Although the mother's and father's narratives were similar in many ways, parents provided more information and description when talking about their daughters' injuries than their sons' injuries. Furthermore, fathers tended to emphasize a lack of emotional reaction in their sons (e.g., "He didn't cry too much"), but not in their daughters. These differences in narratives are consistent with stereotypes of males as unemotional.

In many Canadian households, children's chores are assigned in ways that differ by gender: girls are responsible for tasks performed inside the home, whereas boys are more often assigned chores that involve machinery and that are performed outside the home.

BOX 15.3: applications

WHERE ARE SPONGESALLY SQUAREPANTS AND CURIOUS JANE?

Before reading further, take a moment to list your five favourite television programs. Now count the number of major characters in them who are female and male. Which characters are highly active and/or have positions of power on the show? How would you characterize the general nature of your programs—action-packed adventures, romantic comedies, sports shows, reality series? What would be different if you made a list of the programs you liked best as a child?

We would be willing to bet that your list of major characters includes more males than females, probably by a substantial degree. We also suspect that more male than female readers would list action and sports as favourite programs, whereas more female than male readers would have romantic shows on their lists. The imbalance in female and male characters in your current favourite shows is probably not much different from what you would find in the shows you watched in your youth.

The reason we feel such confidence in our predictions is that differences in the gender representation of characters on television have been well documented, are very large, and have changed relatively little over the past three decades (Huston & Wright, 1998; Leaper et al., 2002; Signorielli, 2001; T. L. Thompson & Zerbinos, 1995). A recent study of 1613 main characters on children's programs in Canada found that 61% were male, 36% were female, and 3% were gender non-specified (The Centre for Youth and Media Studies, 2010). One study of children's television cartoons, however, did indicate that female and male characters were more equal in number and less gender-stereotyped in their portrayals on public television than on commercial television (Leaper et al., 2002).

The differential treatment of the sexes in the media is not limited to numbers. Portrayals of males and females tend to be highly stereotypical in terms of appearance, personal characteristics, occupations, and the nature of the characters' roles. On average, male characters tend to be

Computer and online games are displacing television as the primary source of children's media entertainment. Unfortunately, like television programming, many computer games portray the sexes in highly stereotyped ways.

older and in more powerful roles; females tend to be young, attractive, and provocatively dressed (Diekman & Murnen, 2004; Gooden & Gooden, 2001; Leaper et al., 2002; Signorielli, 2012; T. L. Thompson & Zerbinos, 1995).

Do the large differences in both the number and nature of the portrayals of the sexes on television matter? Keep in mind that the average Canadian child between 2 and 6 years of age spends about 19 hours a week watching television (BBM Canada, 2009). In addition, for most young children, television is a major source of information about the world at large (Gerbner et al., 2002). From a gender-typing perspective, the fact that children have so much exposure to highly stereotyped gender models matters a great deal. For example, children who watch a lot of television have more highly stereotypic beliefs about males and females and prefer gender-typed activities to a greater extent than do children who are less avid viewers (Oppliger, 2007). Furthermore, several experimental studies have established a causal relationship between television

viewing and gender stereotyping (Oppliger, 2007). For example, when children are randomly assigned to watch television shows with either gender-stereotyped or neutral content, they are more likely to endorse gender stereotypes themselves after watching gender-stereotyped programs.

Children are, of course, exposed to media other than television, but similar gender disparities have been documented in them as well. For example, children's books still contain far more male than female characters, and characters of both sexes are often portrayed in gender-stereotypic ways. Males tend to be depicted as active and effective in the world at large, whereas females are frequently passive and prone to problems that require the help of males to solve (DeWitt, Cready, & Seward, 2013; Diekman & Murnen, 2004; Gooden & Gooden, 2001; Hamilton et al., 2006). Thus, although it is now possible to find more counter-stereotypical role models in children's media (e.g., Hermione in the *Harry Potter* series), most female and male characters continue to be gender-stereotyped.

opportunity structure ■ The economic and social resources offered by the macrosystem in the bioecological model, and people's understanding of those resources.

Cultural Influences

The theoretical approaches that we have discussed so far emphasize biological and cognitive-motivational processes involved in gender development. Complementing these approaches are theories that address the larger cultural and social-structural factors that can shape gender development. Two relevant theories that reflect this approach are the bioecological model and social role theory. Both emphasize how cultural practices mirror and perpetuate the gender divisions that are prevalent in a society.

Bioecological Model

As described in Chapter 9, Urie Bronfenbrenner's bioecological model of human development differentiates among interconnected systems, from the micro-system (the immediate environment) to the macrosystem (the culture), that influence children's development over time (see Figure 9.4) (Bronfenbrenner, 1979; Bronfenbrenner & Morris, 1998). A fundamental feature of the macrosystem is its **opportunity structure,** that is, the economic resources it offers and people's understanding of those resources (Ogbu, 1981). Opportunities for members of a cultural community can vary depending on gender, income, and other factors and are reflected by the dominant adult roles within that cultural community.

According to the bioecological approach, child socialization practices in particular microsystems serve to prepare children for these adult roles. Thus, traditional gender-typing practices perpetuate as well as reflect the existing opportunity structures for women and men in a particular community at a particular time in history (Whiting & Edwards, 1988). To the extent that children's development is largely an adaptation to their existing opportunities, changes in children's macrosystems and microsystems can lead to greater gender equality (see Leaper, 2000). For example, increased academic and professional opportunities for girls have led to a dramatic narrowing of the gender gap in math and science within the past 30 years (D. F. Halpern et al., 2007).

Social Role Theory

A fundamental premise of Alice Eagly's social role theory is that different expectations for each gender stem from the division of labour between men and women in a given society (Eagly, 1987; Eagly, Wood, & Diekman, 2000). To the extent that family and occupational roles are allocated on the basis of gender, different behaviours (roles) are expected of women and men (as well as of girls and boys). An obvious example, alluded to above, was the traditional exclusion of women from many occupations in North America and similar societies. Women were under-represented in politics, business, science, technology, and various other fields. In turn, girls were not expected to develop interests and skills that lead toward professions in those fields. Thus, somewhat similar to the bioecological model, social role theory highlights ways that institutionalized roles impose both opportunities and constraints on people's behaviour and beliefs in the home, schools, the labour force, and political institutions.

review

To varying degrees, biological, cognitive-motivational, and cultural factors relate to different aspects of gender development. In their theories and work, researchers tend to focus on one set of factors—although they usually acknowledge that other influences are also important.

In trying to explain gender differences in behaviour, some researchers focus on biological factors. Those who adopt an evolutionary perspective argue that gender differences in behaviour emerged over the course of human evolution because they offered reproductive advantages to males and females. Disagreement exists, however, regarding the degree that evolution led to different behavioural predispositions for females and males. Other biological approaches focus on measureable physiological processes that may be related to variations in development, such as sex-related hormonal influences and sex differences in brain functioning.

Researchers who focus on cognitive-motivational processes emphasize how children's gender-related beliefs, expectations, and preferences guide their behaviour. Once children begin to identify with members of their own gender, they are typically motivated to acquire interests, values, and behaviour in accord with their social identity as girls or boys. Self-socialization plays a prominent role in cognitive theories because it is primarily children themselves who initiate and enforce many forms of gender-typed behaviour.

Cross-cultural comparisons and historical change within Canada, the United States, and other countries underscore ways that gender roles are tied to culture. Societal values and cultural practices can limit or enhance the role models and opportunities that girls and boys experience during development.

Milestones in Gender Development

Developmental psychologists have identified general patterns that tend to occur over the course of children's gender development. As reviewed next, gender-related changes are evident in children's physical, cognitive, and social development. Recall that these changes begin during prenatal development, when sexual differentiation occurs.

Infancy and Toddlerhood

During their first year, infants' perceptual abilities allow them to figure out that there are two groups of people in the world: females and males. As we saw in Chapter 5, much research indicates that infants can detect complex regularities in perceptual information. Clothing, hairstyle, height, body shape, motion patterns, vocal pitch, and activities all tend to vary with gender, and these differences provide infants with gender cues. For example, habituation studies of infant perception and categorization indicate that by about 6 to 9 months of age, infants can distinguish males and females, usually on the basis of hairstyle (Intons-Peterson, 1988). Infants can also distinguish male and female voices and make intermodal matches on the basis of gender (C. L. Martin et al., 2002). For instance, they expect a female voice to go with a female face rather than with a male face. Although we cannot conclude that infants understand anything about what it *means* to be female or male, it does appear that older infants recognize the physical difference between females and males by using multiple perceptual cues.

Shortly after entering toddlerhood, children begin exhibiting distinct patterns of gender development. By the latter half of their second year, children have begun to form gender-related expectations about the kinds of objects and activities typically associated with males and females. For example, research by Diane Poulin-Dubois, Lisa Serbin, and their colleagues at Concordia University in Montreal showed that 18-month-olds looked longer at a doll than at a toy car after viewing a series of female faces, and they looked longer at a toy car than at a doll after habituating to male faces (Serbin et al., 2001). Another study with 24-month-olds found that counter-stereotypical matches of gender and action (e.g., a man putting on lipstick, a woman hammering a nail) led to longer looking times; it appeared that the children were surprised by people demonstrating gender-inconsistent behaviours (Serbin et al., 2002).

The clearest evidence that children have acquired the concept of gender occurs around 2½ years of age, when they begin to label other people's genders. For example, researchers might assess this ability by asking children to put pictures of children into "boys" and "girls" piles. Toddlers can also make simple gender matches, such as choosing a toy train over a doll when asked to point to the "boy's toy" (A. Campbell, Shirley, & Caygill, 2002). Children typically begin to show understanding of their own *gender identity* within a few months after labelling other people's gender. By age 3, most children use gender terms such as "boy" and "girl" in their speech and correctly refer to themselves as a boy or girl (Fenson et al., 1994).

MICHELLE D. BRIDWELL / PHOTOEDIT

In North America, children's play becomes differentiated by gender during the preschool period, with most girls preferring to play with soft toys and to spend time in the "housekeeping" area, and most boys preferring to play with blocks and transportation toys.

Preschool Years

During the preschool years, children quickly learn gender stereotypes—the activities, traits, and roles associated with each gender. By around 3 years of age, most children begin to attribute certain toys and play activities to each gender. By around 5 years of age, they usually stereotype affiliative characteristics to females and assertive characteristics to males (Best & Thomas, 2004; Biernat, 1981; Liben & Bigler, 2002; Serbin, Powlishta, & Gulko, 1993). During this period, children usually lack gender constancy.

Gender-Typed Behaviour

Many children begin to demonstrate preferences for some gender-typed toys by around 2 years of age. These preferences become stronger for most children during the preschool years (Cherney & London, 2006; Pomerleau et al., 1990; Rheingold & Cook, 1975). Indeed, during childhood, one of the largest average gender differences is in toy and play preferences. Girls are more likely than boys to favour dolls, toy cooking sets, and dress-up materials. Girls are also more likely to invoke domestic themes (such as playing house) in their fantasy play. In contrast, boys are more likely than girls to prefer cars, trucks, building toys, and sports equipment. Boys also are more likely than girls to engage in rough-and-tumble play and to enact action-and-adventure themes (such as playing superheroes) in their fantasy play.

The preschool period is also when **gender segregation** emerges, as children start to prefer playing with same-gender peers and to avoid other-gender peers (Leaper, 1994; Maccoby, 1998). Gender segregation increases steadily between around 3 and 6 years of age, and then remains stable throughout childhood (Figure 15.2). Children's preference for same-gender peers is seen across different cultures; however, there are some cultural variations in the degree that children play exclusively with their own gender (Whiting & Edwards, 1988).

Gender-segregated peer groups are a laboratory for children to learn what it means to be a girl or a boy. Peers are both role models and enforcers of gender-typed behaviour. Martin and Fabes (2001) identified what they termed a "social dosage effect" of belonging to same-gender peer groups during early childhood. The amount of time that preschool or kindergarten children spent with same-gender peers predicted subsequent changes in gender-typed behaviour over 6 months. For example, boys

gender segregation ■ Children's tendency to associate with same-gender peers and to avoid other-gender peers.

FIGURE 15.2 **Gender segregation in play** This graph reflects the increase in social playtime between preschool and Grade 1 that children spent with playmates of their own gender and the decrease in playtime with playmates of the other gender. (Adapted from Maccoby, 1998)

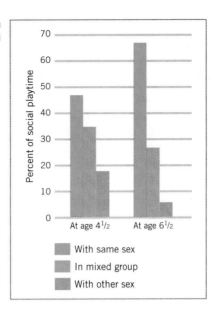

who spent more time playing with same-gender peers showed increases over time in aggression, rough-and-tumble play, activity level, and gender-typed play. Girls who spent more time playing with same-gender peers showed increases in gender-typed play and decreases in aggression and activity level.

The reasons for children's same-gender peer preferences seem to involve a combination of temperamental, cognitive, and social forces (Maccoby, 1998). Their relative influences change over time. At first, children appear to prefer same-gender peers because they have more compatible behavioural styles and interests. For instance, girls may avoid boys because boys tend to be rough and unresponsive to girls' attempts to influence them, and boys may prefer the company of other boys because they share similar activity levels. Around the time that children begin to exhibit a same-gender peer preference, they also are establishing a gender identity and therefore are further drawn to peers who belong to the same in-group.

As they get older, peer pressures may additionally motivate children to favour same-gender peers. Thus, behavioural compatibility may become a less important factor with age. For example, physically active girls may frequently play with boys during early childhood; however, as these girls get older, they tend to affiliate more with girls—even though their activity preferences may be more compatible with those of boys than with those of girls (Pellegrini et al., 2007). Therefore, in-group identity and conformity pressures may supersede behavioural compatibility as reasons for gender segregation as children get older.

Middle Childhood

By around 7 years of age, children have attained gender constancy, and their ideas about gender are more consolidated. At this point, children often show a bit more flexibility in their gender stereotypes and attitudes than they did in their younger years (P. A. Katz & Ksansnak, 1994; Liben & Bigler, 2002; Serbin, Powlishta, & Gulko, 1993). For example, they may recognize that some boys don't like playing baseball and that some girls don't wear dresses. However, most children continue to be highly gender-stereotyped in their views.

Around 9 or 10 years of age, children start to show an even clearer understanding that gender is a social category. They typically recognize that gender roles are social conventions as opposed to biological outcomes (D. B. Carter & Patterson, 1982; Stoddart & Turiel, 1985). As children come to appreciate the social basis of gender roles, they may recognize that some girls and boys may not want to do things that are typical for their gender. Some children may even argue that, in such cases, other girls and boys should be allowed to follow their personal preferences. For instance, Damon (1977) found that children would say that a boy who liked to play with dolls should be allowed to do so. However, children also recognized that the boy would probably be teased and that they themselves would not want to play with him. That

During preschool, children begin to avoid peers who violate gender-role norms, and by age 5 to 7 years, they will actively tease peers who cross gender-role boundaries. This is especially true for boys: the boy in this photo is likely to experience peer rejection if he continues to play with dolls and other toys strongly stereotyped as appropriate for girls.

is, children understood the notion of individual variations in gender typing, but they were also aware that violating gender role norms would have social costs.

Another development in children's thinking is realizing that gender discrimination is unfair and noticing when it occurs (C. S. Brown & Bigler, 2005; Killen, 2007). Killen and Stangor (2001) demonstrated this when they told children stories about a child who was excluded from a group because of the child's gender. Examples included a boy who was kept out of a ballet club and a girl who was kept out of a baseball-cards club. Eight- and 10-year-olds consistently judged it unfair for a child to be excluded from a group solely because of gender. Despite their capacity to see this as wrong, children commonly exclude other children from activities based on their gender (Killen, 2007; Maccoby, 1998).

Brown and Bigler (2005) identified various factors that affect whether children recognize gender discrimination. First among them are cognitive prerequisites, such as having an understanding of cultural stereotypes, being able to make social comparisons, and having a moral understanding of fairness and equity. These abilities are typically reached by middle childhood. People's awareness of sexism can also be influenced by individual factors such as their self-concepts or beliefs. For example, girls with gender-egalitarian beliefs were more likely to recognize sexism (C. S. Brown & Bigler, 2004; Leaper & Brown, 2008). Finally, the specific situation can affect children's likelihood of noticing discrimination. For instance, children are more likely to notice discrimination directed toward someone else than toward themselves. Also, they are more apt to recognize gender discrimination in someone known to be prejudiced (C. S. Brown & Bigler, 2005).

During the elementary school years, girls' and boys' groups rarely mix. Children themselves enforce gender segregation; this tendency does not seem to be due to adult influences.

Gender-Typed Behaviour

In middle childhood, many boys' and girls' peer groups establish somewhat different gender-role norms for behaviour (A. J. Rose & Rudolph, 2006). For this reason, some researchers have suggested that each gender usually constructs its own "culture" during childhood (Maccoby, 1998; Maltz & Borker, 1982; Thorne & Luria, 1986). In line with their tendency to value self-assertion over affiliation, boys' peer groups are more likely to reflect norms of dominance, self-reliance, and hiding vulnerability. Conversely, in line with their greater tendency to value affiliative goals (or a balance of affiliative and assertive goals), girls' peer groups are more likely to reflect norms of intimacy, collaboration, and emotional sharing (A. J. Rose & Rudolph, 2006).

As we have noted, when children violate gender-role norms, their peers often react negatively (Fagot, 1977), including mercilessly teasing someone who has crossed gender "borders." The following description of an event in an elementary school clearly illustrates the degree to which children enforce gender segregation on their own:

In the lunchroom, when the two second-grade tables were filling, a high-status [popular] boy walked by the inside table, which had a scattering of both boys and girls, and said loudly, "Oooo, too many girls," as he headed for a seat at the far table. The boys at the inside table picked up their trays and moved, and no other boys sat at the inside table, which the pronouncement had effectively made taboo.

(Thorne, 1986, p. 171)

Although most children typically favour same-gender peers, in certain contexts friendly cross-gender contacts regularly occur in North American and other Western cultures (Sroufe et al., 1993; Strough & Covatto, 2002; Thorne, 1993; Thorne & Luria, 1986). At home and in the neighbourhood, the choice of play companions is frequently limited. As a result, girls and boys often play cooperatively with one another. In more public settings, the implicit convention is that girls and boys can be friendly if they can attribute the reason for their cross-gender contact to an external cause. For example, this might occur when a teacher assigns them to work together on a class project or when they are waiting in line together at the cafeteria. However, beyond such exceptions, the risk of peer rejection is high when children violate the convention to avoid cross-gender contact (Sroufe et al., 1993).

Overall, gender typing during childhood tends to be more rigid among boys than among girls (Leaper, 1994; Levant, 2005). As noted earlier, boys are more likely to endorse gender stereotypes than are girls, who tend to endorse gender-egalitarian attitudes (C. S. Brown & Bigler, 2004). In addition, girls are less gender-typed in their behaviour. Girls are more likely than boys to play with cross-gender-typed toys, for example. Also, girls tend to be more flexible in coordinating interpersonal goals. For instance, girls commonly coordinate both affiliative and assertive goals in their social interactions (Leaper, 1991; Leaper & Smith, 2004). That is, girls are more likely than boys to use collaborative communication that affirms both the self and the other (e.g., proposals for joint activity), whereas boys are more likely than girls to use power-assertive communication that primarily affirms the self (e.g., giving commands). Girls, however, also frequently pursue play activities traditionally associated with boys, as in sports such as soccer and basketball. In contrast, it is relatively rare to see boys engage in activities traditionally associated with girls, such as playing house.

Gender segregation persists through childhood. Cross-gender teasing is used to maintain gender boundaries.

Adolescence

For some girls and boys, adolescence can be a period of either increased *gender-role intensification* (Galambos, Almeida, & Petersen, 1990; J. P. Hill & Lynch, 1983) or increased *gender-role flexibility* (D. B. Carter & Patterson, 1982; P. A. Katz & Ksansnak, 1994). **Gender-role intensification** refers to heightened concerns with adhering to traditional gender roles. Factors associated with adolescence, such as concerns with romantic attractiveness or conventional beliefs regarding adult gender roles, may intensify some youths' adherence to traditional gender roles. Alternatively, advances in cognitive development can lead to greater **gender-role flexibility,** whereby adolescents may reject traditional gender roles as social conventions and pursue a flexible range of attitudes and interests (see Box 15.4). As in childhood, greater gender-role flexibility during adolescence is more likely among girls than among boys. For example, many girls and young women in North America and elsewhere participate in sports and pursue careers in business (traditionally male-dominated domains), whereas relatively few boys and young men show similar levels of interest in child care or homemaking.

gender-role intensification ■ Heightened concerns with adhering to traditional gender roles that may occur during adolescence.

gender-role flexibility ■ Recognition of gender roles as social conventions and adoption of more flexible attitudes and interests.

BOX 15.4: a closer look

GENDER FLEXIBILITY AND ASYMMETRY

Gender typing is more rigid for boys than for girls at all ages. Most boys engage almost exclusively in activities considered to be either masculine or gender-neutral, while many girls engage in activities stereotyped for boys (Bussey & Bandura, 1992; Fagot & Leinbach, 1993). This difference in gender flexibility seems to stem in large part from males' *avoidance* of feminine-stereotyped activities in addition to their preference for masculine-stereotyped ones (Bussey & Bandura, 1992; C. L. Martin, Eisenbud, & Rose, 1995; Powlishta, Serbin, & Moller, 1993). By age 5, boys are more likely than girls to say that they *dislike* cross-gender-typed toys (Bussey & Bandura, 1992; Eisenberg-Berg, Murray, & Hite, 1982). The rigid preference for gender-typed objects and activities—along with the bias against cross-gender-typed objects and activities—declines during the school years; however, boys remain relatively stricter about gender typing than do girls (Serbin et al., 1993).

One reason for boys' greater avoidance of feminine-stereotyped activities is an asymmetry in the extent to which most people find it acceptable for boys and girls to engage in activities deemed more appropriate for the other gender. Generally, parents, peers, and teachers respond more negatively to boys who do "girl things" than vice versa. A child of one of this book's authors, for instance, attended preschool with a girl who spent most of her time in the block-building area

and a boy who, almost every day, selected a pink tutu from the dress-up corner to wear over his clothes. The teachers, parents, and other adults who observed these two children were concerned about the boy's behaviour but not the girl's behaviour.

Suppose you had a daughter who liked to play with toy soldiers and a son who liked to play with a baby doll. Would you find one of these more acceptable than the other? Also, imagine you heard another child call your daughter a "tomboy" or you heard someone refer to your son as a "sissy." Would your reactions be different? According to one study, adults tended to find a "tomboy" girl considerably more acceptable than a "sissy" boy (C. L. Martin, 1990).

Many fathers play an active role in instilling male behaviours in their sons and in enforcing the avoidance of feminine behaviours (Jacklin, DiPietro, & Maccoby, 1984; Leve & Fagot, 1997; Turner & Gervai, 1995). They generally react negatively to their sons for doing anything "feminine," such as crying or playing with dolls. Consider the difference in what this mother and father say to their son when he hurts himself:

Mother: "Come here, honey. I'll kiss it better."

Father: "Oh, toughen up. Quit your bellyaching."

(Gable, Belsky, & Crnic, 1993, p. 32)

Why are many parents and other adults more upset when boys engage in cross-gender-typed behaviours than they are when girls do? According to social identity theory (pages 602–603) and social role theory (page 606), the asymmetry is tied to men's higher status in society and the emphasis on dominance in the traditional male gender role. When boys show interest in feminine-stereotyped characteristics, people with traditional attitudes view the boys' behaviour as a loss in status. Conversely, when girls exhibit certain masculine-stereotyped qualities, those qualities are more likely to be seen as conferring status (Leaper, 1994). For example, a boy who wants to babysit may be ridiculed for being "soft," but a girl who wants to play ice hockey may be praised for being "strong."

In many cultures, caring for children is viewed as a *strength.* Among the Aka hunter-gatherers in Africa, for example, child care is not viewed as a solely feminine activity and is in fact shared by men and women (Hewlett, 1991). A similar pattern is emerging among dual-career heterosexual parents in North America and other Western cultures. Many fathers are more involved in child care these days than was true in previous generations (S. N. Davis & Greenstein, 2004). However, in most heterosexual families, mothers are usually responsible for most child care and housework (Sayer, 2005).

Parents, peers, and teachers are much more tolerant of girls who engage in masculine-stereotyped activities than they are of boys who engage in feminine-stereotyped activities.

Fathers play an important role in encouraging boys to learn masculine-stereotyped behaviours.

During late childhood and adolescence, as children increasingly develop an understanding that norms about gender roles are social conventions, they may nevertheless endorse the conventions. Thus, adolescents may believe it is legitimate to exclude cross-gender peers from their peer group, because they feel that to include them would be violating the group's gender norms and social conventions (Killen, 2007). Researchers also find that girls tend to perceive more gender discrimination during the course of adolescence (Leaper & Brown, 2008). This trend is likely due to a combination of experiencing increased sexism (American Association of University Women, 2011; S. E. Goldstein et al., 2007; McMaster et al., 2002) and having an increased awareness of sexism (C. S. Brown & Bigler, 2005; Leaper & Brown, 2008).

Gender-Typed Behaviour

During early adolescence, peer contacts are primarily members of the same gender. However, cross-gender interactions and friendships usually become more common during adolescence (see Figure 15.3) (Poulin & Pedersen, 2007). As described in Chapter 13, these interactions can open the way to romantic relationships. Adolescence is also a period of increased intimacy in same-gender friendships. For many girls and boys, increased emotional closeness is often attained through sharing personal feelings and thoughts, although there appears to be more variability among boys in the ways they experience and express closeness in friendships (Camarena, Sarigiani, & Petersen, 1990). Although some boys attain intimacy through shared disclosures with same-gender friends, other boys tend to avoid self-disclosure with same-gender friends because they wish to appear strong. Instead, they usually attain a feeling of emotional closeness with friends through shared activities, such as playing sports. At the same time, many boys who avoid expressing feelings with male friends will do so with their female friends or girlfriends (Youniss & Smollar, 1985).

Self-disclosure and supportive listening are generally associated with relationship satisfaction and emotional adjustment (Leaper & Anderson, 1997; Rubin, Bukowski, & Parker, 2006). However, it is possible to have too much of a good thing. This occurs when friends dwell too long on upsetting events by talking to one another about them over and over. As discussed in Chapter 10, this process of *co-rumination* is more common among girls than among boys (A. J. Rose, Carlson, & Waller, 2007). Although it may foster feelings of closeness between friends, co-rumination appears to increase depression and anxiety in girls (but not in boys).

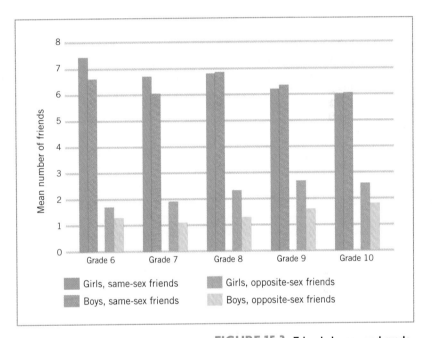

FIGURE 15.3 **Friends by sex and grade** The data shown in this figure demonstrate that younger children tend to be friends with children who are the same sex as they are. As children move into adolescence, the number of friends of the opposite sex tends to increase, for both boys and girls. (Adapted from Poulin & Pedersen, 2007)

review

By about 6 to 9 months of age, infants can distinguish between females and males on the basis of perceptual cues. Between ages 2 and 3 years, children identify their own gender, after which they begin acquiring stereotypes regarding culturally prescribed activities and traits associated with each gender. They also start to demonstrate gender-typed play preferences. During the preschool period, children begin a process of self-initiated gender segregation that lasts through childhood and is strongly enforced by peers.

Around 7 years of age, children have acquired gender constancy and consolidated their understanding of gender. During middle childhood, children are capable of recognizing gender discrimination. Adolescence is a period that can involve increased gender-role rigidity or flexibility. It is also a time when girls are more likely to experience gender discrimination (sexism). Throughout childhood and adolescence, gender-role rigidity tends to be more common among boys, and gender-role flexibility tends to be more common among girls. Friendship intimacy also increases during adolescence, although intimacy is more common among girls than among boys.

Comparing Girls and Boys

effect size ■ Magnitude of difference between two groups' averages and the amount of overlap in their distributions.

Given existing gender stereotypes as well as children's early adoption of gender-typed behaviour, you might assume that the actual differences between girls and boys are many and deep. Contrary to this assumption, as we will see in this section, only a few cognitive abilities, personality traits, and social behaviours actually show consistent gender differences, and most of those gender differences tend to be fairly small.

When evaluating gender comparisons for different behaviours, it is often the case that one gender differs only *slightly* from the other: the overlap between genders is considerable. Substantial variation also appears within each gender: not all members of the same gender are alike. Both these patterns appear in many observed gender differences studied by researchers. Therefore, besides knowing whether a group difference on some attribute is statistically significant—that is, unlikely to be caused by chance—it is important to consider both the *magnitude* of difference between two groups' averages and the *amount* of overlap in their distributions. This statistical index, known as **effect size,** is illustrated in Figure 15.4.

Researchers generally recognize four categories of effect sizes: *trivial* if the two distributions overlap more than 85%; *small* but meaningful if the distributions overlap between 67% and 85% (Figure 15.4a); *medium* if the distributions overlap between 53% and 66% (Figure 15.4b); and *large* if the overlap is less than 53% (Figure 15.4c) (J. Cohen, 1988). Thus, sometimes even a small group difference can be statistically significant.

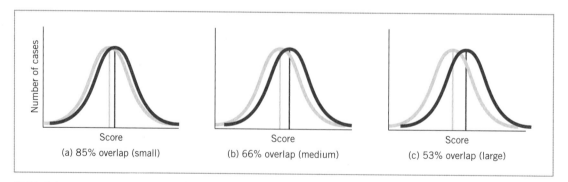

FIGURE 15.4 **Effect sizes in three typical distributions of scores** The effect sizes shown in graphs (a), (b), and (c) depict the overlap between males and females on three hypothetical dimensions and are typical of most gender differences. The distribution shown in yellow on each graph represents one gender, and the distribution shown in red represents the other gender. On many attributes, differences in average performance are statistically significant but very small, and the overlap between the scores for girls and boys is considerable. Note also the considerable variation on each graph *within* each gender, as revealed by the bell-shaped curves.

Across different research studies, contradictory findings are common regarding gender differences or similarities in particular outcomes. Contradictory findings can occur because studies vary in the characteristics of their samples (such as participants' ages and backgrounds) and the methods used (such as surveys, naturalistic observation, or experiments). To infer overall patterns, scientists use a statistical technique known as **meta-analysis** to summarize the average effect size and statistical significance across studies. When available, in this section we have used meta-analyses to summarize research on gender differences and similarities. Table 15.1 on page 616 compiles average gender differences and effect sizes for specific behaviours that we consider in this section.

Because statistically significant gender differences in cognitive abilities and social behaviours are often in the small range of effect sizes, Janet Hyde (2005) has advocated "the gender similarities hypothesis." She argued that, when comparing girls and boys, it is important to appreciate that similarities far outweigh differences on most attributes. When reviewing research findings, we acknowledge this importance by noting in Table 15.1 whether the effect size of any average gender difference in behaviour or cognition is non-existent, trivial, small, medium, large, or very large. Keep in mind, however, that even when there is a large average difference on any particular measure, many girls and boys are similar to one another. Also, some members of the group with the lower average exceed some members of the group with the higher average (see Figure 15.4). For example, there is a very large average gender difference in adult height. At the same time, many women and men are the same height, and some women are taller than the average man.

meta-analysis ■ Statistical technique used to summarize average effect size and statistical significance across several research studies.

Physical Growth: Prenatal Development Through Adolescence

Sex differences in physical development appear early in prenatal development. The most dramatic of these, of course, is the emergence of male or female genitalia. Thereafter, the differences that occur between males and females are relatively subtle—until the onset of puberty. In the following sections, we review the role of androgens in initiating prenatal sex differences; the average differences in male and female size, strength, and physical abilities in childhood; and the development of secondary sex characteristics in adolescence.

Prenatal Development

As should be clear from our earlier discussions, a key prenatal factor in sexual development is the presence or absence of androgens. Their presence, normally triggered by the Y chromosome in genetic males 6 to 8 weeks after conception, stimulates the formation of male external organs and internal reproductive structures; their absence results in the formation of female genital structures. In unusual circumstances known as intersex conditions (see Box 15.1), an overproduction of androgens may occur during prenatal development (congenital adrenal hyperplasia). In genetic females, this can lead to the formation of masculinized genitals. Conversely, a rare syndrome in genetic males (androgen insensitivity syndrome) causes the androgen receptors to malfunction. In these cases, female external genitalia may form.

Research suggests that prenatal exposure to androgens may influence the organization of the nervous system, and these effects may be partly related to some average gender differences in behaviour seen at later ages.

TABLE 15.1

Summary of Average Gender Differences and Effect Sizes for Gender-Typed Cognitions and Behaviours

Statistically significant differences between two groups on any measure can range from trivial to very large. Guidelines for interpreting the effect size (magnitude of average difference) between two groups are based on the amount of overlap between the two groups' distributions of scores (see Figure 15.4). When the overlap is greater than 85%, the difference is considered *trivial*. More meaningful differences are considered *small* if the overlap is between 67% and 85%, *medium* between 53% and 66%, and *large* if less than 53% (J. Cohen, 1988). In this table, an overlap less than 30% indicates a *very large* difference.

Measure	Age Range	Average Finding*	Effect Size[†]	Source
Motor Abilities				
Physical strength	Childhood	B > G	Medium	J. R. Thomas & French, 1985
	Adolescence	B > G	Very large	J. R. Thomas & French, 1985
Running speed	Childhood	B > G	Medium	J. R. Thomas & French, 1985
	Adolescence	B > G	Very large	J. R. Thomas & French, 1985
Achievement and Test Performance				
Overall verbal ability	Childhood	G ≥ B	Trivial	Hyde & Linn, 1988
Reading achievement	Childhood	G > B	Small	Nowell & Hedges, 1998
Writing achievement	Childhood	G > B	Medium	Nowell & Hedges, 1998
Spatial ability (mental rotation and spatial perception)	Childhood and adolescence	B > G	Small	Voyer, Voyer, & Bryden, 1995
Math achievement	Childhood	B = G	None	Else-Quest et al., 2010; S. M. Lindberg et al., 2010
	Adolescence	B ≥ G	Trivial or none	Else-Quest et al., 2010; S. M. Lindberg et al., 2010
Life sciences achievement	Adolescence	B = G	None	D. F. Halpern et al., 2007; S. M. Lindberg et al., 2010
Physical sciences achievement	Adolescence	B > G	Small	D. F. Halpern et al., 2007; S. M. Lindberg et al., 2010
Gender Stereotyping	Childhood	B > G	Small	Signorella et al., 1997
Gender-Typed Play				
Preference for feminine-stereotyped toys	Childhood	G > B	Very large*	Cherney & London, 2006
Preference for masculine-stereotyped toys	Childhood	B > G	Very large*	Cherney & London, 2006
Rough-and-tumble play	Childhood	B > G	Large*	DiPietro, 1981
Ability Beliefs				
Athletic self-concept	Childhood and adolescence	B > G	Small	Wilgenbusch & Merrell, 1999
Verbal self-concept	Childhood and adolescence	G > B	Small	Wilgenbusch & Merrell, 1999
Math self-concept	Childhood and adolescence	B > G	Small	Wilgenbusch & Merrell, 1999
Science self-concept	Childhood and adolescence	B > G	Trivial	Weinburgh, 1997
Computing self-concept	Childhood	B = G	None	Whitley, 1997
	Adolescence	B > G	Medium	Whitley, 1997
Personality Traits				
Activity level	Infancy	B > G	Small	Eaton & Enns, 1986
	Childhood	B > G	Medium	Eaton & Enns, 1986
Self-control	Childhood	G > B	Small to large	Else-Quest et al., 2006
Risk taking	Childhood	B > G	Small	Byrnes et al., 1999
Interpersonal Goals				
Dominance and control goals	Childhood and adolescence	B > G	Small*	A. J. Rose & Rudolph, 2006
Intimacy and support goals	Childhood and adolescence	G > B	Medium*	A. J. Rose & Rudolph, 2006
Communication with Peers				
Talkativeness	Childhood and adolescence	G = B	None	Leaper & Smith, 2004
Directive speech	Childhood and adolescence	B > G	Small	Leaper & Smith, 2004
Collaborative speech	Childhood and adolescence	G > B	Small	Leaper & Smith, 2004
Self-disclosure	Childhood	G > B	Small*	A. J. Rose & Rudolph, 2006
	Adolescence	G > B	Medium*	A. J. Rose & Rudolph, 2006
Aggression				
Direct physical aggression	Childhood and adolescence	B > G	Medium to large	Archer, 2004; Card et al., 2008
Direct verbal aggression	Childhood and adolescence	B > G	Small	Archer, 2004; Card et al., 2008
Indirect aggression	Childhood and adolescence	G ≥ B	Trivial	Card et al., 2008

*B indicates boys; G indicates girls.

[†]Effect size *not* based on a meta-analysis but refers either to magnitude of difference seen in a single study or trend from a few studies summarized in the source.

Infancy

Early in life, males and females are quite similar in size, appearance, and abilities. At birth, males, on average, weigh only about 225 grams more than females do; through infancy, male and female babies look so similar that, if they are dressed in gender-neutral clothing, people cannot guess their gender. Not surprisingly, it is quite easy to mislead people by, for example, dressing an infant boy in a girl's outfit and calling him by a girl's name. In fact, this "Baby X" technique has frequently been used to demonstrate the power of gender stereotypes. Adults who believe that they are playing with a boy are likely to encourage the infant to play with blocks and to offer the infant a toy football, even though the infant is really a girl (Bell & Carver, 1980). The technique is successful at revealing the influence of stereotyped expectations, because there are no consistent or obvious differences in how female and male infants actually look when they are clothed in a neutral manner or in how they behave.

Childhood

As discussed in Chapter 3, during childhood, girls and boys grow at roughly the same rate and are essentially equal in height and weight; however, on average, boys become notably stronger. With the changes in body composition that occur in early adolescence, particularly the substantial increase in muscle mass in boys, the gender gap in physical and motor skills greatly increases. After puberty, average gender differences are very large in strength, speed, and size: few adolescent girls can run as fast or throw a ball as far as most boys can (Malina & Bouchard, 1991; J. R. Thomas & French, 1985). These differences in motor abilities are among the largest seen between females and males (see Table 15.1).

Another average gender difference that increases in magnitude during childhood is activity level, as demonstrated in a meta-analysis conducted by University of Manitoba researchers Warren Eaton and Nancy Enns (1986). As described in Chapter 10, activity level is a temperamental quality that refers to how much children tend to move and expend energy. On average, boys' activity level tends to be higher than that of girls. In infancy, the difference is small, meaning that there is a lot of overlap between the distributions of the two genders (see Figure 15.4a). During childhood, the average gender difference in activity level increases to medium (Figure 15.4b). This increase may result from a combination of practice effects and the greater encouragement commonly given to boys to participate in sports and other physical activities (Leaper, 2013). At the same time, average gender differences in activity level also may contribute to children's preferences for gender-typed play activities.

Adolescence

A series of dramatic bodily transformations during adolescence is associated with **puberty,** the developmental period marked by the ability to reproduce: for boys, to inseminate, and for girls, to menstruate, gestate, and lactate. In girls, puberty typically begins with enlargement of the breasts and the general growth spurt in height and weight, followed by the appearance of pubic hair and then **menarche,** the onset of menstruation. Menarche is triggered in part by the increase in body fat that typically occurs in adolescence. In boys, puberty generally starts with the growth of the testes, followed by the appearance of pubic hair, the general growth spurt, growth of the penis, and the capacity for ejaculation, known as **spermarche** (Gaddis & Brooks-Gunn, 1985; Jorgensen, Keiding, & Skakkebaek, 1991).

puberty ■ Developmental period marked by the ability to reproduce and other dramatic bodily changes.

menarche ■ Onset of menstruation.

spermarche ■ Onset of capacity for ejaculation.

JUSTIN PUMFREY / GETTY IMAGES

In early puberty, girls are typically taller than boys because of girls' earlier physical maturation. By the end of adolescence, boys catch up and surpass girls in average height and weight.

body image ■ An individual's perception of, and feelings about, his or her own body.

adrenarche ■ Period prior to the emergence of visible signs of puberty during which the adrenal glands mature, providing a major source of sex steroid hormones; correlates with the onset of sexual attraction.

For both sexes, there is considerable variability in physical maturation. The variability in physical development is due to both genetic and environmental factors. Genes affect growth and sexual maturation in large part by influencing the production of hormones, especially growth hormone (secreted by the pituitary gland) and thyroxin (released by the thyroid gland). The influence of environmental factors is particularly evident in the changes in physical development that have occurred over generations (see Chapter 3). In many Westernized countries today, girls begin menstruating several years earlier than their ancestors did 200 years ago. This change is thought to reflect improvement in nutrition over the generations.

The physical changes that boys and girls experience as they go through puberty are accompanied by psychological and behavioural changes. For example, in some cultures, the increase in body fat that girls experience in adolescence may be related to gender differences in **body image**—how an individual perceives and feels about his or her physical appearance. On average, girls tend to have more negative attitudes toward their bodies than boys do, and teenage girls typically want to lose several kilograms regardless of how much they actually weigh (Tyrka, Graber, & Brooks-Gunn, 2000). A survey of more than 10 000 U.S. adolescents found that roughly half of boys and two-thirds of girls were dissatisfied with their bodies. Girls were mostly concerned about losing weight; boys, with being more muscular (A. E. Field et al., 2005). Dissatisfaction with body image has long been associated with a host of difficulties, ranging from low self-esteem and depression to eating disorders. This survey added another to the list: the use of unproven and potentially harmful substances to control weight or build muscle—reported by 12% of the boys and 8% of the girls surveyed.

Another change that accompanies physical maturation is the onset of sexual attraction, which usually begins before the physical process of puberty is complete. According to the recollections of a sample of adults, sexual attraction is first experienced at around 10 years of age—regardless of whether the attraction was for individuals of the other sex or the same sex (McClintock & Herdt, 1996). The onset of sexual attraction correlates with the maturation of the adrenal glands, which are the major source of sex steroids other than the testes and ovaries. This stage has been termed **adrenarche,** although the child's body does not yet show any outside signs of maturation. (Sexual identity and romantic relationships are reviewed in Chapters 11 and 13.)

Cognitive Abilities and Academic Achievement

Although average gender differences have been reported for certain aspects of mental functioning, the amount of difference between girls' and boys' averages on achievement and test performance measures is usually small (see Table 15.1) (D. F. Halpern, 2012). Thus, the overlap between the two distributions is large, with girls as well as boys scoring at the top and the bottom of the range. Nevertheless, despite the fact that the effect size of gender differences in abilities tends to be small, larger differences appear when it comes to interest and achievement in particular subjects. The following sections summarize the evidence comparing boys' and girls' cognitive abilities and achievement; then we examine biological, cognitive-motivational, and cultural influences that might account for these findings. Understanding gender differences in this area is especially important because, to the extent that girls and boys develop different cognitive abilities, academic interests, and achievement, gender differences in their future occupations and pay may follow.

General Intelligence

Despite widespread belief to the contrary, boys and girls are equivalent in most aspects of intelligence and cognitive functioning. The average IQ scores of girls and boys are virtually identical (D. F. Halpern, 2004; Hyde & McKinley, 1997). However, proportionally more boys' than girls' scores fall at both the lower and the upper range of scores. That is, somewhat more boys than girls are diagnosed with intellectual disabilities or classified as intellectually gifted (D. F. Halpern, 2012).

Overall Academic Achievement

Although girls and boys are similar in general intelligence, they tend to differ in academic achievement from elementary school through college and university. Recent statistics in Canada indicate that girls tend to show higher levels of school achievement than do boys. For example, in 2009, the high school dropout rate was higher for boys (10%) than for girls (7%) (Turcotte, 2011). In addition, in 2008, 62% of university undergraduates were women (Turcotte, 2011).

In addition to the overall differences in academic achievement, for some specific cognitive abilities and academic subjects, one gender tends to excel slightly more than the other.

Adrenarche, the onset of sexual interest, has been linked to the maturation of the adrenal glands, which produce sex steroid hormones in both boys and girls.

Verbal Skills

Compared with boys, girls tend to be slightly advanced in early language development, including fluency and clarity of articulation and vocabulary development (Gleason & Ely, 2002). On standardized tests of children's overall verbal ability, a negligible average gender difference favours girls (Hyde & Linn, 1988). Larger average differences are seen when specific verbal skills are examined. Girls tend to achieve higher average performance in reading and writing from elementary school into high school; the effect size of the average differences was small for reading and medium for writing (see Table 15.1) (Hedges & Nowell, 1995; Nowell & Hedges, 1998). Boys are more likely to suffer speech-related problems, such as poor articulation and stuttering, as well as more reading-related problems such as dyslexia (D. F. Halpern, 2012).

Spatial Skills

On average, boys tend to perform better than girls do in some aspects of visual-spatial processing (see Table 15.1). This difference emerges between 3 and 4 years of age and becomes more substantial during adolescence and adulthood (D. F. Halpern, 2012). Gender differences are most pronounced on tasks that involve mental rotation of a complex geometric figure in order to decide whether it matches another figure presented in a different orientation (Figure 15.5a). However, other spatial tasks, such as finding a hidden figure embedded within a larger image, show much smaller gender differences (Figure 15.5b). Thus, the conclusion that more males than females have superior spatial ability depends on the particular type of spatial ability.

FIGURE 15.5 Tests of spatial skills
Gender differences vary according to the type of task. Boys tend to perform better than girls do on tasks that involve mental rotation, such as the one in (a), in which children have to determine which response matches the standard. In contrast, gender differences are small or non-existent on tasks like that in (b), which requires children to find the simple geometric figure on the left embedded in the adjoining complex figure. (Adapted from Linn & Peterson, 1985)

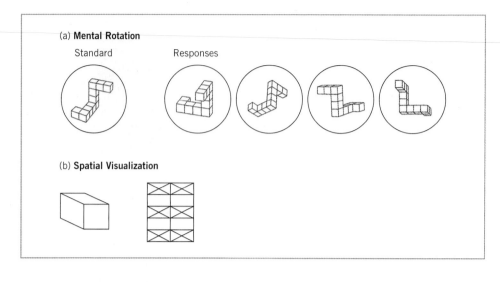

Mathematical and Related Skills

Until recent decades in Canada, boys tended to perform somewhat better on standardized tests of mathematical ability than did girls. Although the gender gap in mathematics achievement is closing as a result of efforts made by schools to improve girls' performance, 15-year-old boys continue to outperform 15-year-old girls on standardized tests of math completed as part of an international study of student achievement (Knighton, Brochu, & Gluszynski, 2010).

Mathematics is considered a key gateway for careers in science, technology, and engineering (D. F. Halpern et al., 2007; Watt, 2006). Patterns of gender differences in these subject areas are mixed in Canada. One study showed that, in 2008, women earned 57% of bachelor's degrees in life and physical sciences (Turcotte, 2011). In contrast, 30% of graduates in mathematics, computer, and information services were women, while women made up 22% of graduates in architecture and engineering (Turcotte, 2011). According to another study, in 2011, women aged 25 to 34 held 39.1% of university degrees in science, engineering, math, and computer sciences compared to 22.6% for women aged 55 to 64 (Statistics Canada, 2013a). Following the attention paid to the gender gap in math achievement a few decades ago, educators and researchers are increasingly addressing the gender gap in the physical sciences and technology.

The number of women in science and engineering has increased significantly in the last 20 years.

Explanations for Gender Differences in Cognitive Abilities and Achievement

Researchers have variously pointed to biological, cognitive-motivational, and cultural factors in relation to gender-related variations in cognitive abilities and achievement. We now examine each possible area of influence.

Biological influences Some researchers have proposed that sex differences in brain structure and function may underlie some differences in how male and female brains process different types of information. However, because the research supporting this interpretation has often been based on adults, it is impossible to determine whether any differences in brain structure and function are due to genetic or environmental influences. Also, a slight biological difference can get exaggerated through differential experience (D. F. Halpern, 2012). For example, boys may initially have a slight average advantage over girls in some types of spatial processing. However, when boys spend more time playing video games and sports than girls do, they practise their spatial skills more (Moreau et al., 2012; I. Spence & Feng, 2010). As a consequence, the magnitude of the gender difference in spatial ability may widen.

Stronger evidence for possible biological influences is suggested by research showing that some sex differences in brain structure may be partly due to the influence of sex-related hormones on the developing fetal brain (Hines, 2004). Androgens may affect parts of the brain associated with spatial skills (Grön et al., 2000), for example. Because males are exposed to higher levels of androgens than are females during normal prenatal development, this difference may lead to greater hemispheric specialization in the male brain and more proficiency in spatial ability later in life. Support for this hypothesis comes from studies that have linked very high levels of prenatal androgens in girls with above-average spatial ability (Grimshaw, Sitarenios, & Finegan, 1995; Hines et al., 2003; Mueller et al., 2008). Conversely, it has been found that males with androgen insensitivity syndrome (see Box 15.1) tend to score lower than average in spatial ability (Imperato-McGinley et al., 1991/2007).

As discussed in Chapters 6 through 9, boys are more vulnerable than girls to developmental disorders of mental functioning such as autism, attention deficit hyperactivity disorder, and language-related and intellectual disabilities (T. Thompson, Caruso, & Ellerbeck, 2003). Some researchers have argued that these differences may be linked to differences in brain organization and sex hormones. For example, higher rates of attention problems and language-related disorders in boys might be linked to unusually high levels of androgen exposure during prenatal development (Tallal & Fitch, 1993).

Attention problems in girls may often go unrecognized because girls' symptoms do not match the standard descriptions, which are based on male symptoms. A girl with attention difficulties may be overlooked or described as a daydreamer by her teacher because her behaviour is not disruptive to the class.

Cognitive and motivational influences The process of self-socialization emphasized in cognitive-motivational theories plays a role in children's academic achievement. According to Eccles's expectancy-value model of achievement (Eccles & Wigfield, 2002), children are most motivated to achieve in areas in which they view themselves as competent (expectations for success) and that they find interesting and important (value). Gender stereotypes can shape the kinds of subjects that girls and boys tend to value. For instance, many children internalize gender stereotypes that science, technology, and math are for boys and that reading, writing, and the arts are for girls (Archer & Macrae, 1991; J. M. Whitehead, 1996). Perhaps it is not surprising then, that average gender differences in interest and ability beliefs exist in these academic areas (see Table 15.1) (Eccles & Wigfield, 2002; Wigfield et al., 1997; Wilgenbusch & Merrell, 1999) and that these self-concepts predict academic achievement and occupational aspirations (Bussey & Bandura, 1999; Eccles & Wigfield, 2002; D. F. Halpern et al., 2007). As discussed next, parents, teachers, peers, and the surrounding culture can influence the development of girls' and boys' academic self-concepts and achievement through the role models, opportunities, and motivations that they provide for practising, or not practising, particular behaviours.

PARENTAL INFLUENCES As noted in Chapter 6, parents' talking to their children is a strong predictor of children's language learning. A meta-analysis found that mothers tended to have higher rates of verbal interaction with daughters than with sons (Leaper, Anderson, & Sanders, 1998). Thus, one possibility is that young girls learn language a bit faster than boys do simply because mothers spend more time talking with daughters than sons. Conversely, girls' faster language acquisition may lead mothers to talk more to them than to their sons (Leaper & Smith, 2004). Finally, both patterns may tend to occur—a possible bidirectional influence whereby both mothers and daughters tend to be talkative and reinforce this behaviour in one another.

Parents' gender stereotyping (see Box 15.2) is also related to children's academic achievement. Many parents accept the prevailing stereotypes about boys' and girls' relative interest in and aptitude for various academic subjects (Eccles et al., 2000; Leaper, 2013), and these gender-typed expectations can affect children's achievement motivation (Eccles et al., 2000). Observational research suggests that parents may communicate their own gender-stereotyped expectations to their children through differential encouragement (Bhanot & Jovanovic, 2005; Crowley et al., 2001; Tenenbaum & Leaper, 2003). You might think that parents' beliefs about their children's academic potential would be based primarily on their children's own self-concepts and achievement, but researchers find that parents often hold these beliefs before any average gender differences in academic interest or performance occur. In fact, longitudinal research indicates that parents' expectations can be a stronger predictor of children's later achievement than the children's earlier performance in particular subject areas (Bleeker & Jacobs, 2004).

Some studies find that mothers are more talkative with daughters than with sons. Studies also find that, on average, girls acquire language at a faster rate than do boys. Does mothers' greater talkativeness with girls contribute to girls' faster language acquisition? Or does girls' faster language acquisition influence mothers' talkativeness with them?

INNOCENTI / CULTURA RM / ALAMY

Teachers are more likely to call on boys than on girls to answer questions in class. One reason may be that, on average, girls earn higher grades than boys; thus, some teachers may tend to focus their attention on lower-achieving students. Another reason may be that boys are more assertive in raising their hands and shouting out answers.

TEACHER INFLUENCES Teachers can influence gender differences in children's academic motivation and achievement in two important ways. First, teachers themselves are sometimes influential gender-role models. Having women as science teachers, for example, may increase girls' interest in science careers (M. A. Evans, Whigham, & Wang, 1995). Second, many teachers hold gender-stereotyped beliefs about girls' and boys' abilities. For example, some teachers may expect higher school achievement in girls than in boys (S. Jones & Myhill, 2004), or they may stereotype boys as being better at math and science (Shepardson & Pizzini, 1992; Tiedemann, 2000). When teachers hold gender-typed expectations, they may differentially assess, encourage, and pay attention to students according to their gender. In this manner, teachers can lay the groundwork for self-fulfilling prophecies that affect children's later academic achievement (see D. F. Halpern et al., 2007; Jussim, Eccles, & Madon, 1996).

PEER INFLUENCES Children's interests often are shaped by the activities and values they associate with their classmates and friends. Consequently, peers can shape children's academic achievement. This influence begins with the kinds of play activities that children practise with their peers. As we have noted, many activities favoured by boys—including construction play, sports, and video games—provide them with opportunities to develop their spatial abilities as well as math- and science-related skills (Serbin et al., 1990; Subrahmanyam et al., 2001). The types of play more common among girls—such as domestic role-play—are talk-oriented and build verbal skills (Taharally, 1991).

Girls and boys may be more likely to achieve in particular school subjects when they are viewed as compatible with peer norms. For example, one study found that high school students who viewed their friends as supportive of science and math were more likely to express interest in a

Peer norms can have a strong impact on girls' and boys' achievement motivation. For example, research indicates that girls are more likely to maintain their interest in science and computers when their friends support achievement in these subjects.

future science-related career (Robnett & Leaper, 2013). The association between friends' science support and science career interest held for both girls and boys—but boys were more likely than girls to report having a friendship group supportive of science. It is also notable that friends' support of English (reading and writing) was not related to science career interest; thus, peer norms regarding particular academic subjects may be related to how likely girls or boys are to value those subjects.

Traditional masculinity norms emphasizing dominance and self-reliance may undermine some boys' academic achievement in Western countries (Levant, 2005; Renold, 2001; Steinmayr & Spinath, 2008; Van Houtte, 2004). That is, some boys may not consider it masculine to do well in certain subjects or possibly in school overall. For example, doing well in school or expressing interest in certain subjects, such as reading, may be devalued as being feminine (Andre et al., 1999; Martinot, Bagès, & Désert, 2012; J. M. Whitehead, 1996). Indeed, some research suggests that boys' endorsement of traditional masculinity is related to lower average performances in reading and writing and lower rates of high school graduation in North America and Europe (Levant, 2005; Renold, 2001; Steinmayr & Spinath, 2008; Van de Gaer et al., 2006; Van Houtte, 2004). At the same time, some research suggests that gender-role flexibility is related to holding more positive scholastic self-concepts in adolescent boys (A. J. Rose & Montemayor, 1994), as well as to stronger interest in non-traditional majors among male undergraduates (Jome & Tokar, 1998; Leaper & Van, 2008).

CULTURAL INFLUENCES Social role theory maintains that socialization practices prepare children for their adult roles in society. If women and men tend to hold different occupations, then different abilities and preferences are apt to be encouraged in girls and boys. Therefore, where there are cultural variations in girls' and boys' academic achievement, there should be corresponding differences in socialization.

A meta-analysis conducted by Else-Quest, Hyde, and Linn (2010) pointed to cultural influences on gender-related variations in mathematics achievement. Gender differences on standardized math tests varied widely across nations: in some, boys scored higher; in others, girls scored higher; and in still others, no gender difference appeared. To assess possible cultural influences, the researchers considered the representation of women in higher education in the country. They found that average gender differences in several math-related outcomes were less likely in nations with higher percentages of women in higher levels of education. This was seen for adolescents' test performance, self-confidence, and intrinsic motivation regarding math.

Other cultural factors have also been found to predict gender-related variations in academic achievement within Western society. Average gender differences in overall academic success and verbal achievement tend to be less common among children from higher-income neighbourhoods and among children of highly educated parents (Burkam, Lee, & Smerdon, 1997; DeBaryshe, Patterson, & Capaldi, 1993; Ferry, Fouad, & Smith, 2000). Gender differences in achievement may also be less common among children of gender-egalitarian parents. One study found that adolescent girls raised by egalitarian parents maintained higher levels of academic achievement in middle school—especially in math and science—compared with girls raised by more traditional parents (Updegraff, McHale, & Crouter, 1996).

Personality Traits

During childhood, average gender differences appear in some personality traits, including activity level, self-regulation, and risk taking (see Table 15.1). Keep in mind, however, that there is much overlap between girls and boys. In other words, many girls and boys express similar personality traits. Also, there is variation *within* each gender in personality. Not all girls are alike, and not all boys are alike.

Activity Level

Higher average activity levels are seen among boys than among girls during childhood. The effect size is medium, which means that there is a meaningful average difference (although there is also much overlap between the two genders). Children's activity levels may partly underlie some average differences between girls and boys in how much they prefer active versus sedentary forms of play—such as sports and doll play, respectively.

Self-Regulation

As discussed in Chapter 10, self-regulation refers to children's ability to control their own emotions and behaviour, to comply with adults' directions, and to make good decisions when adults are not around. Research indicates that girls tend to show higher levels of self-regulation and lower impulsivity than do boys of the same age—with the average gender difference being in the small-to-large range, depending on the type of measure used (Else-Quest et al., 2006). Given the average gender difference in self-regulation, perhaps it is not surprising that, on average, girls are more compliant with adult directives and expectations than boys are (C. L. Smith et al., 2004). As discussed later, average gender differences in self-regulation and impulsivity may partly contribute to higher incidences of direct physical aggression among boys than girls.

Risk Taking

A third personality trait associated with average gender differences during childhood is risk taking. There is a small average difference across studies indicating that boys are more likely than girls to engage in many types of risky behaviour (Byrnes, Miller, & Schafer, 1999). When boys and girls encounter the same hazardous situation, for example, girls are more cautious, on average, and often point out the hazard to a parent. In contrast, boys are more likely to approach and explore the hazard (Fabes, Martin, & Hanish, 2003).

Explanations for Gender Differences in Personality

As with other aspects of gender development, there is evidence for both biological and cognitive-motivational influences on average gender differences in personality. Activity level and impulse control are temperamental qualities that are partly based on genetic predispositions (see Chapter 10). In addition, environmental factors—such as parents' and peers' reactions—can exaggerate or attenuate temperamental dispositions (Goldsmith, Buss, & Lemery, 1997). For instance, some parents encourage athletic participation more in sons than in daughters. Also, peer pressures on boys to participate in sports are often stronger than on girls (see Leaper, 2013). As a consequence of these socialization practices, preferences for physical activity may strengthen in boys and weaken in girls.

Boys tend to be less compliant with adult instructions and expectations than girls are. Boys are also more likely than girls to engage in risky behaviours, leading to higher rates of injury and death for boys.

DENNIS MACDONALD / PHOTOEDIT

Interpersonal Goals and Communication

One of the most popular self-help books about relationships has been John Gray's *Men Are from Mars, Women Are from Venus* (1992). The author (who is not a scientist) purported that gender differences in interpersonal goals and communication style are so great that it is almost as if the sexes came from different planets. The scientific evidence, however, indicates that average gender differences in adults' communication are not nearly as dramatic as Gray portrayed them. Although average gender differences in women's and men's speech have been documented, the magnitude of the differences have usually been in the small-to-medium range (Leaper & Ayres, 2007). The average gender differences in communication and interpersonal goals during childhood and adolescence have likewise been found to be modest (see Table 15.1).

In terms of interpersonal goals, researchers have found average gender differences that are consistent with traditional gender roles (A. J. Rose & Rudolph, 2006). More boys than girls tend to emphasize dominance and power as goals in their social relationships. In contrast, more girls than boys tend to favour intimacy and support as goals in their relationships. The effect sizes for these differences tend to be small to moderate.

BOX 15.5: a closer look

GENDER AND CHILDREN'S COMMUNICATION STYLES

Several studies conducted by Leaper and colleagues have examined gender-related variations in children's and adults' communication patterns (e.g., Leaper, 1991; Leaper et al., 1995, 1999; Leaper & Gleason, 1996; Leaper & Holliday, 1995). In one study of 5- and 7-year-olds, Leaper (1991) placed children in same- or mixed-gender pairs to play with a set of hand puppets. He recorded the children's conversation and classified each statement the children made in terms of affiliation and assertion. As diagrammed in the figure, a statement can be high or low on each dimension, which allows for four speech act (statement) categories:

1. *Collaborative statements* are high in both affiliation (engaging the other person) and assertion (guiding the action). Examples include suggestions for joint activity ("Let's play superheroes") or elaborations on what the other speaker said.

2. *Controlling statements* are high in assertion but low in affiliation. Examples include directives ("Do this") or negative comments.

3. *Obliging statements* are high in affiliation and low in assertion. Examples include expressions of agreement or going along with the other's proposal ("Sure, that's fine").

4. *Withdrawing acts* reflect low assertion and low affiliation. This includes being nonresponsive to another person's statements.

For girls and boys in both age groups, collaborative conversations were the most common. There were no average gender differences in any of the types of statements among the younger children and there were no average differences in obliging statements or withdrawing acts among the older children. However, significant gender differences were seen among the older children in the percentages of collaborative and controlling statements. Among the 7-year-olds, the average percentage of collaborative statements was significantly higher among girl–girl pairs (mean = 56%) than either boy–boy pairs (mean = 39%) or mixed-gender pairs (mean = 43%).

Following is an example of reciprocal collaboration between one pair of girls. The type of speech act is indicated in brackets next to each statement.

> *Jennifer:* Let's go play on the slide. *(Makes sliding noises)* [Collaborate]
>
> *Sally:* Okay. [Oblige] *(Makes sliding noises)* I'll do a choo-choo train with you. [Collaborate]
>
> *Jennifer:* Okay. [Oblige]
>
> *Sally:* You can go first. [Collaborate]
>
> *Jennifer:* Ch ... *(Gasp)* [Collaborate]
>
> *Sally:* Ch ... *(Gasp)* [Collaborate]
>
> (Leaper, 1991, p. 800)

Another average gender difference was the percentage of controlling speech. Rates were significantly lower in girl–girl pairs (mean = 13%) than either boy–boy pairs (mean = 26%) or mixed-gender pairs (mean = 24%).

Within the mixed-gender pairs, no gender differences appeared in collaborative or controlling speech. Thus, it appears that girls tended to decrease their amount of collaborative speech and increase their use of controlling speech when interacting with boys

Researchers have also observed some average gender differences among children in communication style with their peers. Contrary to the stereotypes of talkative girls and taciturn boys, studies generally do not find average differences in talkativeness after early childhood (Leaper & Smith, 2004). However, with regard to self-disclosure about personal thoughts and feelings, there tends to be a small-to-medium gender difference, with higher average rates among girls than boys (A. J. Rose & Rudolph, 2006). Girls also tend to be somewhat more likely than boys to use collaborative statements, which reflect high affiliation and high assertion. In contrast, boys tend to be more likely than girls to use directive statements, which reflect high assertion and low affiliation (see Box 15.5).

Cognitive and motivational influences The average gender differences in interpersonal goals and communication style are related. To the extent that some girls and boys differ in their primary goals for social relationships, they are apt to use different language styles to attain those goals (P. M. Miller, Danaher, & Forbes, 1986; Strough & Berg, 2000). For example, if a boy is especially interested in establishing dominance, using directive statements may help him attain that goal; and if a girl wants to establish intimacy, then talking about personal feelings or elaborating on the other person's thoughts would help realize that goal.

(compared with when they are interacting with girls). Conversely, boys tended to use similar amounts of collaborative and controlling speech in same-gender and mixed-gender interactions.

According to Leaper (1991), it is important to acknowledge, first, that collaboration was the most common type of speech for both girls and boys. Despite this similarity, collaboration was even more frequent in the average speech of girls than of boys. Conversely, controlling speech was more common among boys than among girls. Contrary to old stereotypes of girls being unassertive, girls were not more likely than boys to make statements low in assertion (obliging speech or withdrawing). Instead, girls were more likely to coordinate affiliative and assertive goals in their communication. Finally, in mixed-gender interactions, there was more evidence of girls' accommodating to the speech style of boys than the reverse; that is, girls tended to show more of the pattern associated with boys' same-gender interactions (more controlling and less collaborative speech) during mixed-gender interactions, whereas boys tended to show similar average patterns in same- and mixed-gender interactions.

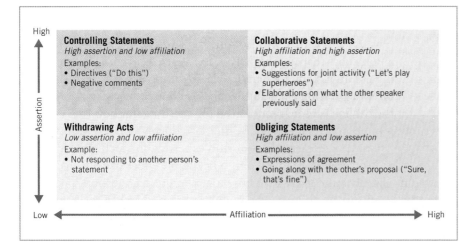

Communication styles The figure illustrates the two-dimensional model of social interaction and communication. Assertion ranges from low to high along the vertical axis, and affiliation ranges from low to high along the horizontal axis. Withdrawing acts are low in both affiliation and assertion. Obliging statements are high in affiliation and low in assertion. Controlling statments are high in assertion and low in affiliation. Collaborative statements are high in both affiliation and assertion.

Parental influences Many children may observe their parents modelling gender-typed communication patterns. A meta-analysis comparing mothers' and fathers' speech to their children indicated small average effect sizes, with mothers more likely than fathers to use affiliative speech; in contrast, fathers were more likely than mothers to use controlling (high in assertion and low in affiliation) speech (Leaper, Anderson, & Sanders, 1998).

Peer influences The social norms and activities traditionally practised within children's gender-segregated peer groups foster different interpersonal goals in girls and boys. For example, many girls commonly engage in domestic scenarios ("playing house") that are structured around collaborative and affectionate interchanges. Boys' play is more likely to involve competitive contexts ("playing war" or sports) that are structured around dominance and power. The impact of same-gender peer norms was implicated in Leaper and Smith's (2004) meta-analysis in which it was found that gender differences in communication were more likely to be detected in studies of same-gender interactions than in mixed-gender interactions.

Rates of indirect aggression are higher for girls than for boys. Indirect aggression includes behaviours such as criticizing and spreading rumours about a peer or excluding a peer from the friendship group.

Aggressive Behaviour

The conventional wisdom is that boys are more aggressive than girls are. In support of this expectation, research studies indicate a reliable gender difference in aggression. However, the magnitude of the gender difference is not as great as many people expect. Also, it depends partly on the type of aggression being considered.

As noted in Chapter 13, researchers distinguish between direct and indirect forms of aggression (Archer & Coyne, 2005; Björkqvist, Österman, & Kaukiainen, 1992). *Direct aggression* involves overt physical or verbal acts openly intended to cause harm, whereas *indirect aggression* (also known as relational or social aggression) involves attempts to damage a person's social standing or group acceptance through covert means such as negative gossip and social exclusion.

Average gender differences in the incidence of physical aggression emerge gradually during the preschool years (D. F. Hay, 2007). In a comprehensive meta-analysis of studies comparing boys' and girls' aggressive behaviour, John Archer (2004) found that both physical and verbal forms of direct aggression occurred more often among boys than among girls. The average difference was small during childhood and moderate to large during adolescence. Although direct aggression generally declines for both boys and girls with age, the decline is more pronounced for girls than for boys.

There appears to be no average gender difference during childhood in the use of indirect aggression. In a meta-analysis of studies testing for such gender differences, Card and colleagues (2008) found only a negligible effect size during adolescence, with girls slightly more likely than boys to use indirect aggression. The trivial effect size may seem surprising given the popular notion of "mean girls" who use indirect strategies such as negative gossip and social exclusion. However, because direct aggression is less likely among girls than boys, girls tend to use proportionally more indirect than direct aggression than boys, on average. Thus, when most girls do express aggression, it may be indirect rather than direct physical or verbal aggression (Leaper, 2013).

Although there may not be much difference between girls and boys in the average use of indirect aggression, being the target of indirect aggression may more often cause problems for girls than boys (Crick & Grotpeter, 1996). This may occur because girls' friendships tend to be exclusive and intimate, whereas boys' friendships tend to be embedded within a larger peer group (Benenson et al., 2002; A. J. Rose & Rudolph, 2006). Nonetheless, all forms of aggression can have negative effects on both girls and boys.

Average gender differences in aggression have been found primarily in research on same-gender interactions. Research conducted with mostly European-American children suggests that different rules may apply when some girls and boys have conflicts with one another. Beginning in early childhood, boys are more likely than girls to ignore the other gender's attempts to exert influence (Jacklin & Maccoby, 1978; Serbin et al., 1982). Thus, when they are more assertive and less affiliative, boys may be more apt to get their way in unsupervised mixed-gender groups (Charlesworth & LaFreniere, 1983).

Studies comparing children's behaviour in same-gender versus cross-gender conflicts revealed an interesting pattern. In same-gender conflicts, boys were more likely to use power-assertive strategies (e.g., threats, demands) and girls were more likely to use conflict-mitigation strategies (e.g., compromise, change the topic). However, in cross-gender conflicts, girls' use of power-assertive strategies increased, but boys' use of conflict-mitigation strategies did not change (P. M. Miller et al., 1986; Sims, Hutchins, & Taylor, 1998). These studies suggest that girls often may find it necessary to play by the boys' rules to gain influence in mixed-gender settings.

Explanations for Gender Differences in Aggression

Possible explanations for gender differences in aggression range from the effects of biological factors to the socializing influences of family, peers, the media, and the culture at large. Each factor likely has a contributing role.

Biological influences It is well known that, on average, males have higher baseline levels of testosterone than do females, and many people assume that this accounts for gender differences in aggression. Contrary to this popular belief, there is *no* direct association between aggression and baseline testosterone levels (Archer, Graham-Kevan, & Davies, 2005). However, there is an indirect one: the body increases its production of testosterone in response to perceived threats and challenges, and this increase can lead to more aggressive behaviour (Archer, 2006). Furthermore, people who are impulsive and less inhibited are more likely to perceive the behaviour of others as threatening. Thus, because boys, on average, have more difficulty regulating emotion (Else-Quest et al., 2006), they may be more prone to direct aggression (D. F. Hay, 2007). Conversely, greater emotional regulation among girls may contribute to higher rates of prosocial behaviour.

Cognitive and motivational influences Average gender differences in empathy and prosocial behaviour may be related to differences in boys' and girls' rates of aggression (Knight, Fabes, & Higgins, 1996; Lemerise & Arsenio, 2000; Levant, 2005; Mayberry & Espelage, 2007). On average, girls are somewhat more likely than boys to report feelings of empathy and sympathy in response to people's distress (N. Eisenberg & Fabes, 1998), and they also tend to display more concern in their behavioural reactions (e.g., looks of concern and attempts to help). Direct aggression may be more likely among children who are less empathetic and have fewer prosocial skills. In support of this explanation, one study found average gender differences, with boys scoring higher on direct aggression and lower on empathy than girls, but both aggressive girls and aggressive boys scored lower on empathy than did non-aggressive girls and boys (Mayberry & Espelage, 2007).

The gender-typed social norms and goals regarding assertion and affiliation may further contribute to the average gender difference in conflict and aggression (see Table 15.1) (P. M. Miller et al., 1986; A. J. Rose & Rudolph, 2006). More boys than girls tend to favour assertive over affiliative goals (e.g., being dominant), whereas more girls than boys tend to endorse affiliative goals or a combination of affiliative and assertive goals (e.g., maintaining intimacy). When some boys focus on dominance goals, they may be more likely to appraise conflicts as competitions that require the use of direct aggression. In addition, some boys may initiate direct aggression as a way to enhance their status.

In contrast, by emphasizing intimacy and nurturance goals, many girls may be more likely to view relationship conflicts as threats that need to be resolved through compromise that preserves harmony (P. M. Miller et al., 1986). The normative social pressures among many girls to act "nice" may also lead them to avoid direct confrontation. However, when girls who adhere to these norms are unable to resolve a conflict, they may try to hurt one another through indirect strategies such as criticizing or excluding the offender or sharing secret information about the offender with other girls (Crick, Bigbee, & Howes, 1996; Galen & Underwood, 1997). This may be one reason for a paradox noted in Chapter 13: even though girls, on average, have more intimate friendships than do boys, girls' same-gender friendships tend to be less stable over time (Benenson & Christakos, 2003). That is, when conflict occurs in same-gender friendships and indirect aggression occurs, girls may be more likely than boys to take it personally and see it as a reason to end the relationship.

Parental and other adult influences In general, most parents and other adults disapprove of physical aggression in both boys and girls. After the preschool years, however, they tend to be more tolerant of aggression in boys and often adopt a "boys will be boys" attitude toward it (J. Martin & Ross, 2005). In an experimental demonstration of this effect, researchers asked people to watch a short film of two children engaged in rough-and-tumble play in the snow and to rate the level of the play's aggressiveness (Condry & Ross, 1985). The children were dressed in gender-neutral snowsuits and filmed at a distance that made their gender undeterminable. Some viewers were told that both children were male; others, that they were both female; and still others, that they were a boy and girl. Viewers who thought that both children were boys rated their play as much less aggressive than did viewers who thought that both children were girls.

Children also appear aware of this "boys will be boys" bias and believe that physical aggression is more acceptable, and less likely to be punished, when enacted by boys than when enacted by girls (Giles & Heyman, 2005; Perry, Perry, & Weiss, 1989). Thus, girls' reliance on strategies of aggression that are covert—and easily denied if detected—may reflect their recognition that displays of physical aggression on their part will attract adult attention and punishment.

Parenting style may also factor into children's manifestations of aggression. Harsh, inconsistent parenting and poor monitoring increase the likelihood of physical aggression in childhood (Leve, Pears, & Fisher, 2002; Vitaro et al., 2006). Children who experience such parenting may learn to mistrust others and make hostile attributions about other people's intentions (Crick & Dodge, 1996).

BOX 15.6: applications

SEXUAL HARASSMENT AND DATING VIOLENCE

Sexual harassment commonly affects both boys and girls and can involve direct (physical or verbal) or indirect (relational) aggression. Physical sexual harassment involves inappropriate touching or forced sexual activity. Verbal sexual harassment involves unwanted, demeaning, or homophobic sexual comments, whether spoken directly to the target or indirectly, behind her or his back. Also, verbal harassment commonly spreads via electronic media (Ybarra & Mitchell, 2007).

Surveys in Canada and the United States indicate that the vast majority of both girls and boys have experienced sexual harassment during adolescence (American Association of University Women, 2011; Leaper & Brown, 2008; McMaster et al., 2002). Most teen sexual harassment occurs in school hallways and classrooms, and the perpetrators are more likely to be peers rather than teachers or other adults. In a large-scale study of Canadian students enrolled in Grades 6 to 8, 38% of girls and 42% of boys reported having experienced sexual harassment at least once during the prior six weeks (McMaster et al., 2002). Other surveys suggest that rates of sexual harassment may be higher for sexual-minority (lesbian, gay, bisexual, transgender, and intersex) youths (Williams et al., 2005). Studies indicate that sexual harassment is also a problem for teens in many parts of the world (see Leaper & Robnett, 2011).

Two of the most frequent forms of reported sexual harassment in the survey conducted by McMaster and colleagues were unwanted sexual comments or gestures (22% of girls, 18% of boys) and being called gay or lesbian in a negative way (11% of girls, 26% of boys).

Girls tend to have more negative reactions to sexual harassment than do boys partly because girls are somewhat more likely than boys to experience repeated sexual harassment. Also, because of traditional masculine socialization, boys may be more reluctant to admit vulnerability. Regardless of the individual's gender, repeated experiences with sexual harassment can have long-term negative consequences on girls' and boys' self-esteem and adjustment (S. E. Goldstein et al., 2007; Gruber & Fineran, 2008).

Sexual harassment and violence also occur in dating relationships. Physical aggression occurs in an estimated one-fourth of adolescent heterosexual dating relationships (Hickman, Jaycox, & Aronoff, 2004; O'Leary et al., 2008), with boys being more likely to be the perpetrators (Swahn et al., 2008; Wolitzky-Taylor et al., 2008). As a consequence, many girls come to regard demeaning behaviours as normal in heterosexual relationships (Witkowska & Gådin, 2005), and they therefore may be at risk for dysfunctional and abusive relationships in adulthood (Larkin & Popaleni, 1994). Although there have been fewer studies of dating violence in lesbian and gay teens' relationships, one survey indicated that the prevalence of dating violence among sexual-minority youths was similar to that among heterosexual youths (Freedner et al., 2002).

The association between harsh parenting and later physical aggression is stronger for boys than for girls. Also, as noted in Chapter 14, poor parental monitoring increases children's susceptibility to negative peer influences and is correlated with higher rates of aggression and delinquency (K. C. Jacobson & Crockett, 2000). Thus, the fact that parents monitor daughters more closely than sons may contribute to gender differences in aggression.

Peer influences Gender differences in aggression are consistent with the gender-typed social norms of girls' and boys' same-gender peer groups. However, it is worth noting that children who are high in aggression *and* low in prosocial behaviour are typically rejected in both male and female peer groups (P. H. Hawley, Little, & Card, 2008). These children tend to seek out marginal peer groups of other similarly rejected peers, and these contacts strengthen the likelihood of physical aggression over time (N. E. Werner & Crick, 2004).

Another peer influence on aggression may be boys' regular participation in aggressive contact sports, which sanction the use of physical force and may contribute to higher rates of direct aggression among boys (Messner, 1998). Support for this proposal is the finding that participation in aggressive sports, such as football, in high school is correlated with a higher likelihood of sexual aggression in college (G. B. Forbes et al., 2006). As explained in Box 15.6, aggressive behaviours may also involve sexual harassment.

Media influences A common question for parents and researchers is whether frequently watching violent television shows and movies or playing violent video games has a negative impact on children. As you might expect, boys are more likely than girls to devote time to these activities (Cherney & London, 2006). One possible inference is that consuming more violent media may contribute to average gender differences in physical aggression.

Our discussion of media violence in Chapter 9 makes clear that viewing aggression in movies, television programs, and video games is associated with children's aggressive behaviour and that this holds true for girls as well as for boys. Several experimental studies point to a causal influence. That is, the likelihood of aggression increases in *some* children after watching violent programs (Paik & Comstock, 1994) or playing violent video games (Ferguson, 2007). Exposure to violent media may lead to increased arousal and decreased inhibition, which may stimulate aggression in some children (Coyne & Archer, 2005). However, rather than causing aggression, the effect might more likely be correlated with children who are also prone toward aggressive behaviour for additional reasons.

Whereas boys are more likely than girls to favour television shows and movies with violent content, one study found that adolescent girls were more likely than boys to prefer shows depicting indirect aggression (Coyne & Archer, 2005). Furthermore, an experimental study demonstrated that observing indirect aggression on television increased the subsequent likelihood of indirect aggressive behaviour but had no impact on direct aggression (Coyne, Archer, & Eslea, 2004).

Other cultural influences Although gender differences in aggression have been observed in all cultures, cultural norms also play an important role in determining the levels of aggression that are observed in boys and girls. Douglas Fry (1988) studied rural communities in the mountains of Mexico and found that the levels of childhood aggression that were considered normal varied widely from one area to another. Boys in each community showed more aggression than girls did. However, girls in the high-aggression communities were more aggressive than boys in the low-aggression communities.

When children are exposed to violence in their homes and communities, boys and girls both experience an increased risk of emotional and behavioural problems and show an increase in aggressive behaviours. However, boys are more likely than girls to be exposed to the highest levels of violence, and the average impact of exposure is also greater for boys than for girls (Guerra, Huesmann, & Spindler, 2003).

review

Gender development begins before birth when the genes program the developing embryo to form female or male genitalia. In the absence of androgen hormones triggered by the Y chromosome, female genitalia form. The higher production of androgens in genetic males (and, in rare cases, in genetic females) may influence brain organization and functioning. Physical changes during puberty typically lead to increased muscle mass in boys as well as large average advantages in strength, speed, and size. Also, puberty leads to bodily transformations that allow for each sex's reproductive ability.

Although the common impression is that girls and boys are inherently and deeply different in their cognitive and social behaviours, in most respects the similarities between them outweigh the differences. As summarized in Table 15.1, even when differences are consistently reported, they tend to be fairly small. Also, many average differences do not emerge until later in childhood or adolescence. The most substantial differences are found in physical strength and speed, specific spatial abilities (e.g., mental rotation), academic achievement, self-regulation, activity level, and physical aggression. Small average gender differences are seen in verbal ability, risk taking, interpersonal goals, and communication style. A combination of biological, cognitive-motivational, and cultural influences are implicated to varying degrees in most of these differences.

Chapter Summary

Theoretical Approaches to Gender Development

■ One major approach to gender development is biological, including evolutionary psychology, biosocial theory, and neuroscience approaches.

■ According to evolutionary psychology theory, *behavioural* differences between males and females served adaptive functions in our evolutionary past and have been passed down as inherited behavioural dispositions. For example, direct aggression in males is interpreted as an advantage in mating competition, whereas nurturance in females is viewed as facilitating the survival of offspring.

■ Biosocial theory focuses on the impact of evolved *physical* differences between females (child-bearing and nursing capacities) and males (greater strength, speed, and size) in relation to the social ecology. For example, men's strength and women's child-bearing may have made certain roles more appropriate for women and men in hunter-gatherer societies, but physical differences impose fewer constraints on roles in technological societies.

■ Other biological researchers take a neuroscience approach to gender development by focusing on sex differences in brain organization and the influences of sex hormones (such as androgens) both before birth and after. A striking example of hormonal influence involves cases of girls with congenital adrenal hyperplasia (CAH), who tend to show a stronger inclination toward play emphasizing physical activity and tend to perform somewhat better on spatial abilities than do girls without CAH.

■ A second approach, which addresses cognitive and motivational influences on gender development, includes cognitive developmental theory, gender schema theory, social identity theory, and social cognitive theory. All emphasize children's active participation in learning gender roles and adopting the preferences and behaviours considered appropriate for their gender, thereby highlighting how gender development is largely a process of self-socialization.

■ According to cognitive developmental theory, once children realize that their gender is consistent across situations (gender constancy), they pay close attention to same-gender models to learn how to behave.

■ Gender schema theory maintains that children construct mental representations of gender based on their own experience and the gender-related ideas they are exposed to and proposes that children begin to acquire same-gender interests and values as soon as they can identify their own gender. Subsequently, children pay greater attention to, and learn more about, those things that they regard as relevant for their own gender.

■ Social identity theory, which also stresses the importance of adopting a gender identity, proposes that children tend to form an in-group bias favouring attributes associated with their own gender and also to enforce conformity to gender-role norms.

■ Social cognitive theory addresses many processes involved in learning gender-typed values and behaviours, including observing others' behaviour and determining the consequences of particular behaviours in relation to one's own or other people's gender. Children internalize gender-typed norms, standards that they use to monitor their own behaviour.

■ The third theoretical approach focuses on cultural influences and includes the bioecological model and social role theory. The bioecological model characterizes children's development as embedded in nested systems ranging from the microsystem (immediate environment) to the macrosystem (society). A key feature of the macrosystem is its opportunity structure and the corresponding roles available to women and men that shape the ways in which girls and boys are socialized. Social role theory similarly addresses the division of labour by gender in society and how it affects girls' and boys' gender-role development.

Milestones in Gender Development

■ Between 6 and 8 weeks of prenatal development, sexual differentiation begins. External and internal genitalia are normally completed by the end of the first trimester.

■ During their first year, infants learn to distinguish male and female faces. Between ages 2 and 3, children learn to identify their own gender, start to acquire stereotypes about males and females, and begin to prefer gender-typed toys and play activities.

■ During preschool, children begin to gravitate toward same-gender peers, and a strong tendency for children to self-segregate by gender persists until adolescence. Preschool children also stereotype certain traits and activities for each gender. Preferences for gender-typed play become stronger from early to middle childhood.

■ Around 6 years of age, children develop gender constancy. In addition, during middle childhood, they come to understand that gender roles are social conventions. They also may understand that gender discrimination is unfair and notice when it occurs. Average gender differences in social behaviour begin to emerge, with boys more likely than girls to stress assertion over affiliation, and girls more apt to emphasize affiliation or a combination of affiliation and assertion.

■ During adolescence, gender roles sometimes become more flexible (due to increased cognitive flexibility) or more rigid (due to concerns with heterosexual roles and adoption of conventional gender attitudes). Intimacy in friendships and romantic relationships also increases for both girls and boys, although friendship intimacy is more common among girls.

■ Throughout childhood and adolescence, gender-role flexibility is more likely among girls than among boys. Peers and parents tend to react more negatively to cross-gender-typed behaviour in boys than in girls. This asymmetry may be related to the higher status and power traditionally accorded males.

Comparing Girls and Boys

■ Actual differences in girls' and boys' psychological functioning are decidedly fewer than commonly portrayed by gender stereotypes. Even on measures in which, on average, one gender scores higher than the other, the effect size often is trivial for many attributes. Moreover, considerable overlap usually occurs in the distribution of scores for males and females even when gender differences in effect size are greater.

■ Boys and girls are quite similar in physical development until puberty, which begins earlier for girls than for boys. Among the largest average gender differences are physical strength, speed, and size after puberty, and a moderate difference exists in physical activity level.

■ Girls and boys score similarly on tests of general intelligence. Slight-to-small average gender differences have been reported in specific cognitive abilities: boys show higher proficiency with certain types of spatial reasoning and mathematic ability, and girls show a small advantage in verbal ability. In academic achievement, girls have tended to do better than boys in reading and writing, whereas boys have tended to do better than girls in the physical sciences. Girls also tend to do better in overall school performance.

■ Biological, cognitive-motivational, and cultural factors may contribute to gender-related variations in academic achievement. Biological processes, such as prenatal hormones, may influence girls' and boys' brain development; however, the degree to which these factors lead to gender differences in cognitive functioning is unclear. The evidence for cognitive-motivational and cultural influences on average gender differences in academic achievement is more clearly established. Researchers find academic achievement in particular domains is related to the expectations of parents, peers, and teachers. The gender gap in math achievement has dramatically closed in recent decades, and such differences are less likely in societies characterized by greater overall gender equality.

■ Average gender differences in personality are seen in self-regulation (girls higher), physical activity (boys higher), and risk taking (boys higher). Biological factors, such as prenatal androgen levels, may be related in part to later gender differences in some or all these personality traits. However, traditional socialization may exaggerate gender differences.

■ Direct (physical and verbal) aggression is associated with an average gender difference of moderate effect size, with higher rates among boys than among girls. No meaningful average gender difference appears in indirect aggression (such as social exclusion or negative gossip). However, indirect aggression constitutes a larger proportion of all aggressive behaviours among girls than among boys. Lower average levels of self-regulation may be partly related to the higher incidence of direct aggression among boys. Cognitive and motivational factors are important as well. For example, boys often practise aggressive themes and behaviours in their play, and aggression is tolerated more in boys than in girls. Some cultural variations in the magnitude of gender difference in direct aggression are related to the degree that behaviours such as sexual harassment are tolerated in a particular culture.

Critical Thinking Questions

1. The two children pictured at the start of the chapter display gender-typed differences in their costumes and interests. How would the different theories outlined in this chapter attempt to explain these differences and similarities? How would different theories account for other children who have more flexible gender-typed behaviours and interests?

2. Think about how females and males were portrayed in television shows, movies, and video games as you were growing up. How might these depictions have affected your gender development?

3. Imagine that you wanted to raise your own children to be as minimally gender-typed as possible. Which of the theoretical perspectives outlined in the chapter would you rely on most? Do you think you would be more likely to achieve your goal with a daughter or a son?

4. Suppose you are speaking with an evolutionary psychology theorist who tells you that biology makes gender differences in behaviour inevitable. What evidence could you use to challenge this view? What evidence could you use to support it?

5. Historically, men have held dominant status in society, but in the last century, women have significantly increased their status and power in Canada and in many other countries. Women now occupy top ranks in many occupations, and men are more involved in child care and housework. Do you think that this trend toward gender equality among adults will affect the kinds of play activities and behaviours in which girls and boys engage in the future?

Key Terms

activating influences, p. 598

adrenarche, p. 618

affiliation, p. 594

androgen insensitivity syndrome (AIS), p. 599

androgens, p. 598

assertion, p. 594

body image, p. 618

collaboration, p. 594

congenital adrenal hyperplasia (CAH), p. 599

cross-gender-typed, p. 595

effect size, p. 614

enactive experience, p. 603

gender constancy, p. 600

gender dysphoria disorder, p. 599

gender identity, p. 599

gender schema filter, p. 601

gender schemas, p. 600

gender segregation, p. 608

gender stability, p. 599

gender typing, p. 595

gender-essentialist statements, p. 604

gender-role flexibility, p. 611

gender-role intensification, p. 611

gender-typed, p. 595

in-group assimilation, p. 602

in-group bias, p. 602

interest filter, p. 601

menarche, p. 617

meta-analysis, p. 615

observational learning, p. 603

opportunity structure, p. 606

organizing influences, p. 598

puberty, p. 617

self-socialization (gender development), p. 599

spermarche, p. 617

transgender, p. 599

tuition, p. 603

LINCOLN SELIGMAN, *Kite Flying*, 2000

chapter 16:

Conclusions

In the preceding 15 chapters, you were presented with a great deal of information about how children develop. You learned about the development of perception, attachment, conceptual understanding, language, intelligence, emotional regulation, peer relations, aggression, morality, gender, and a host of other vital human characteristics. Although these are all important parts of child development, the sheer amount of information may seem daunting: getting lost in the trees and losing a sense of the forest is a real danger. We therefore devote this final chapter to providing an overview of the forest by organizing many of the specifics that you have learned into an integrative framework. A likely side benefit of reading this chapter is that you will probably discover that you understand much more about child development than you realized.

The integrative framework that organizes this chapter consists of the seven themes that were introduced in Chapter 1 and highlighted throughout the book. As we have noted, most child-development research is ultimately aimed at understanding fundamental issues related to these themes. This is true regardless of the type of development that the research addresses and regardless of whether the research focuses on fetuses, infants, toddlers, preschoolers, school-age children, or adolescents. Beneath the myriad details, the seven themes emerge again and again.

Theme 1: Nature and Nurture: All Interactions, All the Time

When people think of a child's nature, they typically focus on the biological characteristics with which the child enters the world. When they think of the child's nurture, they focus on the child-rearing experiences provided by parents, caregivers, and other adults. Within this view, nurture is like a sculptor, shaping the raw material provided by the child's nature into closer and closer approximations of its final form.

Although this metaphor is appealing, the reality is much more complex. Unlike the sculptor's passive media of marble and clay, children are active participants in their own development. They seek out their own experiences, based on their inclinations and interests. They also influence other people's behaviour toward them: from birth onward, their nature influences the nurture they receive. In addition, rather than nature doing its work before birth and nurture doing its work after, nurture influences development even before birth, and nature is just as influential in adolescence and adulthood as earlier. In this section, we review how nature and nurture interact to produce development.

Nature and Nurture Begin Interacting Before Birth

When prenatal development proceeds normally, it is easy to think of it as a simple unfolding of innate potential, one in which the environment matters little. When things go wrong, however, the interaction of nature and nurture is all too evident. Consider the effects of teratogens. Prenatal exposure to these potentially harmful substances—which include toxins in the general environment, such as mercury, radiation, and air pollution, as well as toxins that depend on parental behaviour, such as cigarettes, alcohol, and illegal drugs—can cause a wide variety of physical and cognitive impairments. However, whether a given baby will actually be affected depends on innumerable interactions among the genetics of the parents, the genetics of the fetus, and a host of environmental factors such as the particular teratogen and the timing and amount of exposure.

The interaction of nature and nurture during the prenatal period is also evident in fetal learning. The experience of hearing their mother's voice while in the womb leads newborns to prefer her voice to that of other women once they enter the world. Fetuses can also learn taste preferences from their mother's diet during pregnancy. Thus, even qualities that are present at birth, which are often thought of as being determined purely by nature, reflect the fetus's experience as well.

Infants' Nature Elicits Nurture

Nature equips babies with a host of qualities that elicit appropriate nurture from parents and other caregivers. One big factor in babies' favour is that they are cute; most people enjoy watching and interacting with them. Their looking and smiling at other people motivates others to feel warmly toward them and to care for them. Their emotional expressions—cries, coos, and smiles—guide caregivers' efforts to figure out what to do to make them happy and comfortable. In addition, their attentiveness to sights and sounds that they find interesting encourages others to talk to them and to provide the stimulation necessary for learning. One simple example of this interactive relationship is the fact that parents everywhere sing to their infants; infants throughout the world find singing soothing, bounce in response to rhythm, and respond positively to melodies.

Infants' expressions of contentment and happiness when engaging in certain activities motivate their parents and other adults to engage in the activities with them.

Timing Matters

The effects of an experience on development depend on the state of the organism at the time of the experience. As already noted, timing of exposure to teratogens greatly influences their effects on prenatal development. For example, if a pregnant woman contracts rubella early in pregnancy, when the developing visual and auditory systems are at a particularly sensitive point, her baby may be born deaf or blind; if she contracts rubella later in pregnancy, no damage will occur.

Timing also influences many aspects of development in the months and years following birth. The development of perceptual capabilities presents numerous illustrations of the importance of appropriate experience at the appropriate time. The general rule in such cases is "use it or lose it": for normal development to occur, children must encounter the relevant experiences during a certain window of time.

Auditory development provides a good example. Until 8 months of age, infants can discriminate between phonemes regardless of whether they occur in the language the infants hear daily. By age 12 months, however, infants lose the ability to hear the difference between similar sounds that they do not ordinarily encounter or that are not meaningfully different in their native language.

Similar sensitive periods occur in grammatical development. Children from East Asia who move to North America and begin to learn English as a second language before age 7 acquire grammatical competence in English that eventually matches that of native-born English-speaking children. Those who arrive between ages 7 and 11 learn almost as well. However, individuals who immigrate at later ages rarely gain comparable mastery of English grammar, even after many years of hearing and speaking the language of their adopted land. Deaf children's learning of sign language shows a similar pattern: early exposure results in more complete grammatical mastery.

The importance of normal early experience is also evident in social, emotional, and intellectual development. Infants and toddlers who do not have an emotional connection with any caregiver, such as the children who spent their first years in the infamous orphanages of Romania in the 1980s or in concentration camps during World War II, often continue to interact abnormally with other people after being placed in loving homes. Children who spent their first two years or more in the Romanian orphanages also had unusually high rates of low IQ for many years after they were adopted into loving homes in Canada and Great Britain. Thus, in many aspects of the development of perception, language, intelligence, emotions, and social behaviour, the timing of experience is crucial: normal early experience is vital for successful later development.

Nature Does Not Reveal Itself All at Once

Many genetically influenced properties do not become evident until middle childhood, adolescence, or adulthood. One obvious example is the physical changes that occur at puberty. A less obvious example involves nearsightedness. Many children are born with genes that predispose them to become nearsighted, but most do not become so until late childhood or early adolescence. The more close work, including reading, they do during childhood, the more likely that the genetic predisposition will eventually be realized. A third example involves children who are born with certain types of brain damage. These children's performance on IQ tests is comparable to that of other children through age 6 years, but falls considerably behind thereafter.

Differences in running speeds are partially attributable to genetic differences that are present at birth, but nature takes time to reveal itself. Who could have looked at these children when they were newborns and predicted which would be the best runners?

POLKA DOT IMAGES / THINKSTOCK

The development of schizophrenia follows a similar path. Schizophrenia is highly influenced by genes inherited at conception, but most people who become schizophrenic do not do so until late adolescence or early adulthood. As with other aspects of development, the emergence of schizophrenia reflects a complex interplay between nature and nurture. Children with a schizophrenic biological parent who are raised by non-schizophrenic parents are more likely to become schizophrenic themselves than are the biological children of the non-schizophrenic parents. Children who are raised in troubled homes are also more likely than others to become schizophrenic. However, the only children with a substantial likelihood of becoming schizophrenic are those who have a biological parent who is schizophrenic *and* who grew up in a troubled family. As in other contexts, the interaction between the children's nature and the nurture they receive is crucial.

Perhaps the most surprising and compelling evidence for the interaction of nature and nurture comes from the emerging field of epigenetics. Although people often think of the genotype as being "fixed" at birth, experience can enhance or silence gene expression. Early stressful environments, such as those imposed by poverty, seem to especially influence later gene expression. Thus, adults who grew up in low-income families exhibit different patterns of gene expression decades later than do adults who grew up in high-income homes, regardless of their incomes as adults. Even more remarkably, some of these effects of the early environment on the genome are passed down to the next generation. Thus, not only does nature not reveal itself all at once, but nature itself changes as a result of nurture.

Everything Influences Everything

One common reaction to learning about the complex interactions between nature and nurture is "It sounds like everything influences everything else." This reaction is basically accurate. Consider some of the factors that influence children's and adolescents' self-esteem. Genes matter; the closer the biological relation between two children or adolescents, the more similar their degree of self-esteem is likely to be. A large part of the reason for this genetic influence on self-esteem is that genes influence a wide range of *other* characteristics that themselves influence self-esteem. For example, genes strongly affect attractiveness, athletic talent, and academic success, all of which contribute to self-esteem.

Factors other than genes also play large roles in the development of self-esteem. Support from one's family and peers contribute in a positive way; poverty and unpopularity contribute in a negative way. Unrelated adults also can have positive or negative influences on self-esteem; for example, having a teacher who is supportive can promote a child's self-esteem; conversely, having a teacher who is hostile or demeaning can reduce it. Values of the broader society also are influential. East Asian societies tend to emphasize the importance of self-criticism, and children and adolescents in those societies report lower levels of self-esteem than do peers in Western societies.

Complex interactions are not limited to the development of self-esteem or to social development; they are characteristic of development in all areas. For example, in the development of intelligence, the influence of genetics seems to be greater than that of shared environment for children from middle- and upper-income backgrounds, but the opposite is true for children from impoverished backgrounds. Similarly, parental involvement in school is more closely related to academic achievement in low-income families than in more affluent families. Thus, children's nature—their genes, personal characteristics, and behavioural tendencies—interact with the nurture they receive from parents, teachers, peers, the broader society, and the physical environment in ways that shape their self-esteem, intellect, and other qualities.

Theme 2: Children Play Active Roles in Their Own Development

Children are physically active even before they leave the womb; the fetal kicking that thrills prospective parents is just the most obvious example. Less obvious is that fetuses are also mentally active. While still in the womb, they can learn enough about the sounds in a story their mother repeatedly reads aloud that, as newborns, they are able to discriminate that story from ones their mother did not read aloud. Moreover, from their first minutes outside the womb, infants selectively focus on objects and events that interest them, rather than passively gazing at whatever appears before their eyes.

Infants' and older children's actions also produce reactions in other people, which further shape the children's development. In this section, we examine four ways in which children contribute to their own development—through physically interacting with the environment, interpreting their experience, regulating their behaviour, and eliciting reactions from other people.

Self-Initiated Activity

Even in the womb, normal development depends on the fetus's being active. Fetuses make breathing movements that strengthen their lungs, and they swallow amniotic fluid that prepares their digestive system to function properly after birth. They also "work out" various muscles by tugging on their umbilical cord, sucking their thumb, kicking, and turning somersaults.

As this infant's eager gaze suggests, children's choices of where to look are among the ways in which they shape their own development.

From the day they are born, infants display looking preferences that guide their attention to the most informative aspects of the environment that their processing abilities can handle and thus enhance their learning. They like looking at objects rather than at blank fields. They like looking at moving objects rather than at stationary ones and at the edges of objects rather than at their interiors. And they particularly like looking at faces, especially their mother's.

Infants' ability to interact with the environment expands greatly during the first year. At around 3 months, most infants become able to follow moving objects fairly smoothly with their eyes, which improves their ability to learn about the actions occurring around them. At 6 or 7 months, most become able to crawl on their bellies, and soon after on their hands and knees; as a result, they no longer have to wait for the world to come to them. By 8 or 9 months, most can hold up their heads, which allows them to reach accurately for objects even when they are not being supported. And by 13 or 14 months, most begin to walk independently, opening new frontiers for exploration.

As development proceeds, children's self-initiated activity extends to additional domains such as language. Toddlers delight in telling their parents the names of objects, for no reason beyond the joy of doing so. They practise talking in their cribs, even when nobody else is present to hear them. They and older children, both deaf and hearing, invent gestures and words to represent objects and events. As their language proficiency develops, children become skilled at initiating conversations that bring them information, allow them to express their feelings and desires, and help them regulate their emotions.

Children's choices of activities shape their development. This child's interest in print led him to learn to read and write at age 3; the fact that he is one of the authors' children also probably had something to do with his early interest in these skills. (He also is now the father of the baby in the photo above.)

The effects of self-initiated activities also are seen at older ages in other areas, such as self-socialization and antisocial behaviour. Throughout the world, boys and girls choose to play predominantly with members of their own gender, especially between the ages of 6 and 10 years. The play patterns reflect the children's own choices: gender segregation is rarely imposed by adults but, rather, arises from differences in the kinds of play that boys and girls tend to prefer. Beginning in the school years, these preferences tend to be reinforced by ridicule from peers when a child crosses the "gender border."

In later childhood and adolescence, children's choices of friends and peer groups become important influences on their own behaviour, in that children tend to increasingly act like their friends and others in their social group in both positive and negative ways. Thus, from the prenatal period through adolescence, children's self-initiated activities contribute to their development.

COURTESY OF ROBERT SIEGLER

COURTESY OF ALICE & ROBERT SIEGLER

Active Interpretation of Experience

Children also contribute to their development by trying to understand the world around them. Even in the first year, infants develop a sense of what is possible in the physical world. Thus, they look longer at an "impossible" event—such as when one solid object appears to move through the space occupied by another object, or when an object seems to be suspended in mid-air without support—than they do at an event that is similar but physically possible. Toddlers' and preschoolers' continuous "why" questions, and school-age children's searching for the explanations of magic tricks, provide other compelling examples of children's eagerness to understand the world.

This desire to understand also motivates young children to construct informal theories concerning inanimate objects, living things, and people. These theories allow children to go beyond the data provided by their senses to infer underlying causes. For example, preschoolers reason that there must be something inside animals that causes them to grow, breathe, have babies, get sick, and so on, even though they do not know what that something is. They also reason that inanimate objects must have different material inside them than living things do.

Children's and adolescents' interpretation of their experiences extends to inferences about themselves as well as about the external world. When some children fail on a task, for example, they feel sad and question their ability. Other children who fail on the same task take the failure as a challenge and an opportunity to learn. Similarly, in ambiguous situations, aggressive children tend to attribute hostile intentions to others even when the others' motives are unclear; this interpretation sometimes leads the aggressive children to lash out before the other person can hurt them. Thus, subjective interpretations of experiences, as well as objective reality, shape development.

Self-Regulation

Another way in which children contribute to their development is by regulating their behaviour. Consider how they regulate their emotions. In the first months after they are born, infants rely almost totally on parents and other caregivers to help them cope with fright and frustration. By age 6 months, they learn to cope with some upsetting situations by rubbing their bodies to soothe themselves. During the toddler and preschool periods, children become increasingly adept at using physical strategies, such as looking away, when faced with stressors or temptation. During elementary school, they increasingly use cognitive strategies, such as reminding themselves that an unpleasant experience will soon be over, to cope with negative situations. Across a wide range of ages, children who successfully regulate their emotions tend to be more popular and more socially competent than those who are less skilled at emotional regulation.

These early self-regulation skills are related to long-term developmental outcomes. For example, boys who exhibit strong self-regulation abilities in the preschool and early elementary school periods are less likely as adults to use cocaine and other drugs. Children's early self-control also has been found to be a strong predictor of their later grades in school and of occupational and economic success in adulthood.

Over the course of childhood and adolescence, children increasingly regulate their development through their choice of activities. Whether young children go to sports events, movies, libraries, or religious services depends mainly on whether their parents take them there. Whether adolescents engage in the same activities depends mainly on their own preferences. Selecting moral values, choosing a romantic partner, pursuing an occupation, and deciding whether to have children are just a few of the major decisions that adolescents and young adults face. The wisdom of their choices strongly influences their subsequent lives.

Eliciting Reactions from Other People

Because children of all ages differ from one another in behaviour and appearance, they evoke different reactions from other people. For example, babies with easy temperaments elicit more positive reactions from their parents than do cranky or fussy babies. Similarly, attractive babies elicit more affectionate and playful mothering than do less attractive ones. And in trying times, attractive children are less likely to suffer parental rejection and punishment than are less attractive ones. Other adults also are influenced by children's actions. For example, when children encounter difficulty learning particular material, teachers act in more encouraging ways if the child has generally been well behaved than if the child has been badly behaved in the past.

The effects that children's initial inclinations have on their parents' behaviour toward them multiply over time. Most parents of children who are disobedient, angry, and challenging try to be supportive but firm with them. However, if the bad behaviour and defiance continue, many parents become hostile and punitive. Other parents, faced with belligerence and aggression, back down from confrontations and increasingly give in to their children's demands. Once such negative cycles are established, they are difficult to stop. If teenagers act disruptively, and parents respond with hostility, problems generally worsen over the course of adolescence.

Children's characteristics and behaviour influence not just their parents' and teachers' reactions but also those of their peers. At all ages, children who are cooperative, friendly, sociable, and sensitive to others tend to be popular with their peers, whereas those who are aggressive or disruptive tend to be disliked and rejected. In some cases, peers' reactions to one another's behaviour change with age; for example, kindergartners tend to neither like nor dislike withdrawn peers, but older elementary and middle school students tend to dislike such children. Peer reactions to children's behaviour often have long-term consequences; rejected children are more likely than popular children to have difficulty later in school and to engage in criminal activity. In many ways, then, children influence their development, not only by initiating actions, interpreting their experiences, and regulating their emotions, but also by eliciting reactions from other people that then shape their own subsequent behaviour.

PIXLAND / JUPITERIMAGES / THINKSTOCK

It is all too easy for relations between parents and children to spiral downward, with disobedience and anger from children eliciting anger and hostility from parents, which then elicits more disobedience and anger from children, and so on.

from the prenatal period to early or middle childhood (depending on the particular brain area). By the end of this period of explosive growth, the number of synapses in the area far exceeds the number in the brains of adults. A process of pruning then reduces the number of synapses. The greatest pruning occurs at different times in different brain areas. Those synapses that are frequently used are maintained; those that are not are eliminated ("use it or lose it" at the biological level). The pruning of unused synapses makes information processing more efficient.

The brain includes a number of areas that are specialized for specific functions. This specialization makes possible rapid and universal development of these functions and thus enhances learning of the relevant type of information. Some of the functions are closely linked to sensory and motor systems. The visual cortex is particularly active in processing sights; the auditory cortex is particularly active in processing sounds; the motor cortex is particularly active in making movements; and so on.

Other brain areas are specialized for functions that are not specific to any one sensory or motor system. The limbic system, located in the lower part of the brain, is particularly prominent in producing emotions. The prefrontal cortex is particularly involved in executive functioning. Some areas toward the back of the right hemisphere are particularly active in processing space, time, and number. All of these areas are involved in numerous other types of processing, and all types of processing involve numerous brain areas, but each of the areas is especially active in processing the type of information associated with it. Thus, biological mechanisms underlie both very specific and very general changes.

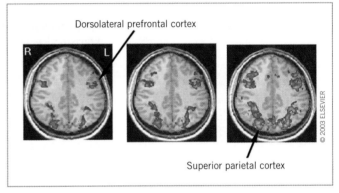

The group average pattern of brain activation for each of three increasingly difficult items (from left to right) on a problem-solving task that requires both executive functioning and spatial processing. As shown, the amount of activation in this slice of the brain increases with difficulty in the prefrontal cortex (toward the front of the brain, often involved in executive functioning) and in the superior parietal cortex (toward the back of the brain, often involved in spatial processing). (Data from S. D. Newman et al., 2003)

Behavioural Change Mechanisms

Behavioural change mechanisms describe responses to environmental contingencies that contribute to development. These learning mechanisms shape behaviour from infants' first days out of the womb onward.

Habituation, Conditioning, Statistical Learning, and Rational Learning

The capacity to habituate to familiar stimuli begins before fetuses leave the womb. By 30 weeks after conception (8 to 10 weeks before the typical time of birth), the central nervous system is sufficiently developed for habituation to occur, as reflected in a fetus's heart rate initially slowing down (a sign of interest) when a bell is rung next to the mother's belly and then its returning toward the typical rate as the bell is rung repeatedly. Habituation continues after birth as well, and it is seen in changes in looking patterns as well as in heart-rate patterns. For example, when a picture of a face is shown repeatedly, infants reduce the time they spend looking at it, but they show renewed interest when a different face appears. Habituation motivates babies to seek new stimulation when they have learned from an experience and thus helps them learn more.

From their first days in the outside world, infants also can learn through classical conditioning. If an initially neutral stimulus is repeatedly presented just before an unconditioned stimulus, it comes to elicit a similar response to that elicited by the unconditioned stimulus. Recall Little Albert, who, after repeatedly seeing a harmless white rat and then hearing a frightening loud noise immediately after, came to fear the white rat (and also came to fear doctors and nurses wearing white lab coats).

The fact that an infant would become afraid not only of the white rat but also of people with white coats illustrates the functioning of another key learning ability that is present from infancy: generalization. Although infants' learning tends to be less general than that of older children, it is never completely literal. Infants generalize the lessons of their past experience to new situations that differ at least in a few details from the original ones.

Like older children, infants also learn through instrumental conditioning; behaviours that are rewarded become more frequent, and behaviours that do not lead to rewards become less frequent. Even young infants appear highly motivated to learn in this way: 2-month-olds express joy and interest while learning a contingency relation, and they often cry and express anger when a learned response no longer produces the expected results.

Yet another mechanism that allows infants to acquire information rapidly is statistical learning. From birth onward, infants quickly learn the likelihood that one sight or sound will follow another. Because many events, including the sounds within words and certain daily activities, occur in predictable orders, statistical learning helps infants anticipate other people's actions and generate similar sequences of behaviour themselves.

Closely related to statistical learning is rational learning, which involves integrating the learner's prior beliefs and biases with what actually occurs in the environment. When, for example, infants observe an adult pulling balls of two different colours out of a box, seemingly at random, and the ratio of the colours of those balls deviates greatly from that of all the balls in the box, the infants' looking times suggest that they are surprised. Together with habituation and classical, instrumental, and statistical learning, such rational learning allows infants to acquire knowledge of the world from the first days following birth.

Social Learning

Children (and adults) learn a great deal from observing and interacting with other people. This social learning pervades our lives to such an extent that it is difficult to think of it as a specific learning capability. However, when we compare humans with other animals, even close relatives such as chimpanzees and other apes, the omnipresence of social learning in people's lives becomes apparent. Humans are far more skillful than any other animal in learning what others are trying to teach them; they also are far more inclined to teach others what they know. Among the crucial contributors to this social learning are imitation, social referencing, language, and guided participation.

The first discernible form of social learning is imitation. At first, the imitation seems limited to behaviours that infants sometimes produce on their own, such as sticking out their tongue. However, by age 6 months, infants begin to imitate novel behaviours that they never make spontaneously. By 15 months, toddlers not only learn novel behaviours but can remember them and continue to produce them for at least a week. This imitation is not just "monkey see, monkey do." When children of this age see a model try to do something but fail, they imitate what the model was trying to do rather than what the model actually did.

Social learning influences socioemotional development as well as acquisition of knowledge. When an unfamiliar person enters the room, 12-month-olds look to

HASSAN KINLEY / DK STOCK / GETTY IMAGES

Imitation starts in infancy.

their mother for guidance. If the mother's face or voice shows fear, the baby tends to stay close to her; if the mother smiles, the baby is more likely to approach the stranger. Similarly, in the laboratory, a baby of this age will cross the visual cliff if the mother smiles but not if she looks worried.

Social learning also shapes children's standards and values. From the second year of life, toddlers internalize their parents' values and standards and use them to guide and evaluate their own conduct. Later in development, peers, teachers, and other adults also influence children's standards and values through the process of social learning. Peers, in particular, play a steadily increasing role over the course of childhood and adolescence.

Imitation is not the only mechanism of social learning. Another is social scaffolding. In this change mechanism, an older and more knowledgeable person provides a learner with an overview of a given task, demonstrates how to do the most difficult parts, provides help with the difficult parts if necessary, and offers suggestions to the learner on how to proceed. Such scaffolding allows a beginner to do more than he or she could without help. Then, as the learner masters the basics of the task, the scaffolder transfers more and more responsibility to the learner until the learner is doing the entire task. Thus, adults and children collaborate to produce social learning.

Activities that involve a series of steps, such as putting up a tent or building something, are common contexts for social scaffolding, in which the older and more experienced person helps the younger and less experienced person to operate at a higher level than would otherwise be possible, as well as to meet goals and acquire skills.

Cognitive Change Mechanisms

Many of the most compelling analyses of developmental change are at the level of cognitive processes. Both general and specific information-processing mechanisms play important roles.

General Information-Processing Mechanisms

Four categories of information-processing mechanisms are especially general and pervasive: basic processes, strategies, metacognition, and content knowledge.

Basic processes are the simplest, most broadly applicable, and earliest-developing general information-processing mechanisms. They overlap considerably with behavioural learning processes and include associating events with each other, recognizing objects as familiar, recalling facts and procedures, encoding key features of events, and generalizing from one instance to another. Changes with age occur in the speed and efficiency of these basic processes, but all of the basic processes are present from infancy onward. These basic processes provide a foundation that allows infants to learn about the world from their very first days.

Strategies also contribute to many types of development. Toddlers, for example, form strategies for achieving such goals as obtaining a toy that is out of reach or descending a steep surface; preschoolers form strategies for counting and solving arithmetic problems; school-age children form strategies for playing games and getting along with others; and so on. Often, children acquire multiple strategies for solving a single kind of problem—for example, strategies for approaching unfamiliar children on a playground or for solving arithmetic problems. Knowing multiple strategies allows children to adapt to the demands of different problems and situations.

Metacognition is a third type of cognitive process that contributes to development in large ways. For instance, increasing use of memory strategies stems in

TOPHAM / THE IMAGE WORKS

Exceptional content knowledge can outweigh all of adults' usual intellectual advantages over children. On the day this photograph was taken, this 8-year-old boy became the youngest person ever to defeat a chess grandmaster (the ranking awarded to the greatest chess players in the world).

large part from children's increasing realization that they are unlikely to remember large amounts of material verbatim without using such strategies. Among the most important applications of metacognition is adaptive choice among alternative strategies, for example, in deciding whether rereading is necessary to understand text, whether to count or state a retrieved answer to solve an arithmetic problem, and whether to write an outline before beginning an essay. The cognitive control involved in executive functioning, such as inhibiting tempting but counterproductive actions, being cognitively flexible, and considering other people's perspectives, is another crucial type of metacognition.

Content knowledge is a fourth pervasive contributor to cognitive change. The more children know about any topic—whether it be chess, soccer, dinosaurs, or language—the better able they are to learn and remember new information about it. Knowledge also facilitates learning of unfamiliar content by allowing children to draw analogies between the new content and content that is familiar to them.

Domain-Specific Learning Mechanisms

Infants acquire some complex competencies surprisingly rapidly, including basic perception and understanding of the physical world, language comprehension and production, interpretation of emotions, and attachment to caregivers. What seems to unite the varied capabilities that children acquire especially rapidly is their apparent evolutionary importance. Virtually everyone quickly and easily acquires abilities that are important to survival.

A number of theorists have posited that the nearly universal, rapid learning in these domains is produced by domain-specific learning mechanisms that operate on everyday experience to produce accurate conclusions about the world in domains of evolutionary importance. For example, even infants in their first year seem to expect bigger moving objects to produce stronger effects than smaller moving objects. Similarly, toddlers' word learning seems to be aided by the whole-object assumption (the idea that words used to label objects refer to the whole object rather than to a part of it) and the mutual exclusivity assumption (the idea that each object has a single name). These assumptions are usually correct for the words that young children hear, thus helping them learn what the words mean.

Children's informal theories about the main types of entities in the world—inanimate objects, people, and other living things—also facilitate their learning about them. The value of learning rapidly about the properties of people, other living things, and inanimate objects is clear; saying "More juice" to another person, for example, is considerably more likely to yield the desired outcome than is saying the same words to the family dog. Crucial in children's informal theories, as in scientists' formal ones, are causal relations that explain a large number of observations in terms of a few basic unobservable processes.

Possessing basic understanding of key concepts—such as inertia and solidity for inanimate objects; goal-directed movement and growth for living things; and intentions, beliefs, and desires for people—helps children act appropriately in new situations. For example, when preschoolers meet an unfamiliar child, they assume that the child will have intentions, beliefs, and desires—an assumption that helps them understand the other child's actions and react appropriately to them. These assumptions about other people's minds aid the social understanding of children in all societies. Thus, both general and domain-specific cognitive learning mechanisms help children understand the world around them.

Change Mechanisms Work Together

Although it is often easiest to discuss different change mechanisms separately, it is crucial to remember that biological, cognitive, and behavioural mechanisms all reflect interactions between the person and the environment and that all types of mechanisms work together to produce change. For instance, consider effortful attention. The development of this capability reflects a combination of biological and environmental factors. On the biological side, genes influence the production of neurotransmitters that affect children's ability to concentrate and ignore distractions. Effortful attention also relies on the development of connections between two parts of the brain—the anterior cingulate, which is active in attention to goals, and the limbic area, which is active in emotional reactions. On the environmental side, the development of effortful attention can be influenced by the quality of parenting a child receives—though this is true primarily for children with a particular genotype. For children with one form of a relevant gene, quality of parenting influences the development of effortful attention, whereas for children with another form of the gene, quality of parenting has little effect on its development. Specific experiences can also be influential; for example, playing specially designed computer games increases the activity of the anterior cingulate and thus the ability to sustain attention on both experimental tasks and intelligence tests. In short, varied types of mechanisms work together to produce development of even a single capability.

Theme 5: The Sociocultural Context Shapes Development

Children develop within a personal context of other people: families, friends, neighbours, teachers, and classmates. They also develop within an impersonal context of historical, economic, technological, and political forces, as well as societal beliefs, attitudes, and values. The impersonal context is as important as the personal one in shaping development. There is little reason to think that parents in developed societies in the twenty-first century love their children more than parents of the past did. Yet their children die less often, get sick less often, eat a more nutritious diet, and receive more formal schooling than did children from even the wealthiest families of 100 or 200 years ago. Thus, when and where children grow up profoundly influences their lives.

Growing Up in Societies with Different Practices and Values

Values and practices that people within a society take for granted as "natural" often vary substantially among societies. These variations considerably influence the rate and form of development. Throughout the book, you encountered examples of this in every aspect of development, including in domains that are commonly thought of as governed entirely by maturation. For example, people often assume that the timing of walking and other motor skills in infancy is determined solely by biology, but babies who grow up in African tribes that strongly encourage infants' motor development tend to walk and reach other motor milestones earlier than do infants in North America. Similarly, infants in societies where babies sleep with their mothers for several years exhibit less fear at bedtime than do children in North America, where babies rarely sleep with their mothers, or even in the same room with them, for more than 6 months.

Emotional reactions provide another example of how cultural practices and values influence behaviour, even when we might not expect them to do so. Infants in all societies that have been studied show the same attachment patterns, but the frequency of occurrence of each pattern varies with the values of the society. Relative to babies in North America, for instance, Japanese babies who are placed in the Strange Situation more often become very upset, showing the insecure-resistant attachment pattern. These differences in attachment patterns appear to be due to differing cultural values and practices. Japanese mothers traditionally encourage dependence in children and rarely leave their babies alone, which may lead the babies to become especially upset when they are left alone in the Strange Situation. In contrast, North American parents emphasize independence to a greater degree and more often leave babies alone in a room or with other people.

Cultural influences such as these continue well beyond infancy. Japanese culture, for example, places a higher value on hiding negative emotions, especially anger, than does North American culture, and Japanese mothers discourage their children from expressing negative emotions. Quite likely because of these cultural influences, Japanese preschoolers and school-age children less often express anger and other negative emotions than do North American peers. Similarly, child-rearing in rural Mexican villages emphasizes cooperation and caring about others, and children raised in these villages are more likely to share their possessions than are children from Mexican cities.

The culture of Mexican villages successfully encourages cooperation and caring among children.

Culture influences not only parents' actions but also children's interpretations of those actions. For example, harsh parenting is associated with more aggressive behaviour at school for children from European-Canadian families, but it is associated with less aggressive behaviour in children from South-Asian Canadian families (C. Ho et al., 2008). The differing effectiveness of the disciplinary approaches may reflect children's interpretations of their parents' behaviour. If children believe that scolding or authoritarian parenting is in their best interest, the behaviours can be effective. However, if children see such disciplinary approaches as reflecting negative parental feelings toward them, the discipline tends to be ineffective or harmful.

Sociocultural differences exert a similar influence on cognitive development. They help determine which skills and knowledge children acquire—for instance, whether children learn to operate abacuses, iPads, or both. They also influence how well children learn skills that everyone acquires to some degree; for example, Australian-Aboriginal children, whose lives will eventually depend on their ability to trek through the desert to distant oases, develop spatial skills superior to those of urban Australian children. Finally, cultural values influence the educational system, which in turn influences what and how deeply children learn. For example, students in community-of-learners classrooms learn about fewer scientific topics than do children in traditional classrooms, but they learn about them in greater depth.

Growing Up in Different Times and Places

When and where children grow up profoundly influences their development. As noted earlier, in modern societies, children's lives are greatly improved over what they were in the past, in terms of health, nutrition, shelter, and so on. Not all of the changes in modern societies have promoted children's well-being, however. For example, in North America and Europe, far more children grow up with divorced parents than in the past, and these children are at risk for many problems. On average, they are more prone to sadness and depression, have lower self-esteem, do less well in school, and are less socially competent than peers who live in intact families. Although most children from divorced families do not have serious problems, a minority do: engaging in delinquent activities, dropping out of school, and having children out of wedlock all are more common among children whose parents are divorced.

Other historical changes may result in children's lives being different, but neither better nor worse. The great expansion of maternal employment outside the home represents one such case. In 1976, only 39% of Canadian mothers with children younger than 16 were employed outside the home. By 2009, that percentage had increased to 73%. As this change was occurring, many people feared that maternal employment and child care outside the home would weaken attachment between babies and mothers. Others expressed hopes that such care would greatly stimulate cognitive development, especially of children from impoverished backgrounds, because of the greater opportunities for interaction with other children and adults. In fact, the data indicate that neither the fears nor the hopes were justified. In almost all respects, children who receive care outside the home tend to develop similarly, both emotionally and cognitively, to those who do not.

More generally, the same cultural or technological change can bring either positive or negative effects, depending on who the child is and how the innovation is used. For instance, the Internet can be used to communicate with friends, which tends to strengthen friendships, but it can also be used for cyberbullying. Playing certain Internet games stimulates development of attention, but very high frequency of playing Internet games can harm the quality of friendships. Thus, in terms of health, comfort, and material well-being, children growing up today in modern societies are, on the whole, better off than those who grew up in the past—but in other ways, the pictures is more mixed.

Growing Up in Different Circumstances Within a Society

Even among children growing up at the same time in the same society, differences in economic circumstances, family relationships, and peer groups lead to large differences in children's lives.

Economic Influences

In every society, the economic circumstances of a child's family considerably influence the child's life. However, the degree of economic inequality within each society influences just how large a difference the economic circumstances make. In societies with large income inequalities, such as the United States, poor children's academic achievement is far lower than that of children from wealthier families. In societies with smaller inequalities, such as Canada, Japan, and Sweden, children from affluent families also do better academically than children from poorer families, but the differences are smaller.

It is not just academic achievement that is influenced by economic circumstances; all aspects of development are. Infants from impoverished families more often are insecurely attached to their mothers. Children and adolescents from impoverished families more often are rejected as friends and more often are lonely. Illegal substance use, crime, and depression also are more common among poor adolescents than among peers from wealthier backgrounds.

These negative outcomes are unsurprising, given the many disadvantages that poor children face. Relative to children who grow up in more affluent environments, poor children more often live in dangerous neighbourhoods; grow up in homes with one or no biological parents; attend inferior daycare centres and schools; and have few books, magazines, and other intellectually stimulating material in their homes. The cumulative burden of these disadvantages, rather than any one of them, poses the greatest obstacle to successful development.

Influences of Family and Peers

Families and peer groups vary considerably in ways other than income, and many of these differences also have a substantial influence on development. In some families, regardless of income, parents are sensitive to babies' needs and form close attachments with them; in others, this practice does not occur. In some families, again regardless of income, parents read to their children each night, thus helping the children learn to read; in others, this does not occur.

The influence of friends, other peers, teachers, and other adults varies in as many ways as that of families. Friends, for example, can provide companionship and feedback, contribute to self-esteem, and serve as a buffer against stress; during adolescence, they can be particularly important sources of sympathy and support. On the other hand, friends can also have a negative influence, drawing children and adolescents into reckless and aggressive behaviour, including crime, drinking, and drug use. Thus, personal relationships, like economic circumstances, culture, and technology, definitely influence development, but the effects of these influences vary with the particulars.

Theme 6: Individual Differences

Children differ on a huge number of dimensions—demographic characteristics (gender, race, ethnicity, SES), psychological characteristics (intellect, personality, artistic ability), experiences (where they grow up; whether their parents are divorced; whether they participate in plays, bands, or organized sports), and so on. How can we tell which individual differences are the crucial ones for understanding children and predicting their futures?

As illustrated in Figure 16.1, three characteristics—breadth of related characteristics, stability over time, and predictive value—are crucial in determining the importance of any dimension of individual differences. First, as shown by the dotted arrows, children's status on the most important dimensions is associated with their status at that time on other important dimensions. Thus, one reason why intelligence is considered a central individual difference is that the higher a child's IQ at a given age, the higher the child's grades, achievement test scores, and general knowledge tend to be at the same time (the dotted arrows in Figure 16.1). A second key characteristic is stability over time (the solid arrows in Figure 16.1). A dimension of individual differences is of greater interest if the higher or lower that children score on it early in development, the higher or lower they are likely to score on it later. Thus, another reason for interest in IQ is that children with high (or low) IQs usually grow into adults with high (or low) IQs. A third characteristic of major dimensions of individual differences is that a child's status on the dimension predicts outcomes on other important characteristics in the future (the dashed arrows in Figure 16.1). Thus, a third reason for interest in IQ scores is that

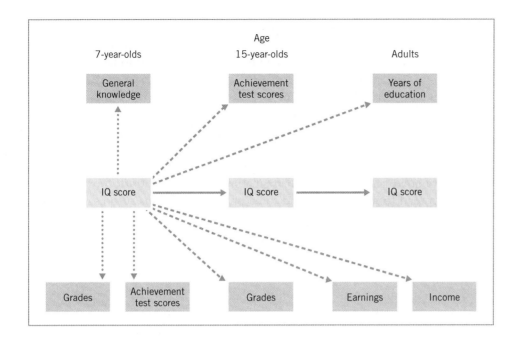

FIGURE 16.1 Intelligence and individual differences Intelligence is considered a crucial dimension of individual differences because IQ scores (1) correlate with other conceptually related dimensions such as general knowledge and grades at any one age (dotted arrows extending from IQ to other outcomes at age 7); (2) show considerable continuity over age (solid arrows); and (3) predict future outcomes, such as years of education and income in adulthood (dashed arrows connecting IQ score at age 7 to other later outcomes).

a person's IQ during middle childhood and adolescence predicts that person's later earnings, occupational status, and years of education.

These three characteristics make clear why demographic variables such as gender, race, ethnicity, and SES are studied so often. Consider gender, for example. Gender differences are related to a wide variety of other differences. Boys tend to be larger, stronger, more physically active, and more aggressive; to play in larger groups; to be better at some forms of spatial thinking; and more often to have ADHD and math or reading disabilities. Girls tend to be more verbal, quicker to perceive emotions, better at writing, and more likely to express sympathy and empathy for people in distress. Being male or female obviously is also stable over time. Finally, being male or female predicts future individual differences. If a newborn is female, it is likely that, compared with males, she will be more self-revealing with friends, more vulnerable to depression, more inclined to prosocial behaviour, and more disposed to using relational aggression.

We next consider the extent to which several other variables show these three key characteristics of major individual differences.

Breadth of Individual Differences at a Given Time

Individual differences are not randomly distributed. Children who are high on one dimension also tend to be high on other, conceptually related dimensions. Thus, children who do well on one measure of intellect—language, memory, conceptual understanding, problem solving, reading, or mathematics—tend to do well on others. Similarly, children who do well on one measure of social or emotional functioning—relations with parents, relations with peers, relations with teachers, self-esteem, prosocial behaviour, and lack of aggression and lying—also tend to do well on others. Sometimes, as with the relation between intelligence and school achievement, the connections are very strong. More often, the relations are moderate. Thus, although children who get along well with their parents also tend to get along well with peers, there are many exceptions.

Beyond intelligence and gender, two other crucial dimensions of individual differences are attachment and self-esteem. Compared with their insecurely attached peers, toddlers who are securely attached to their mother tend to be more enthusiastic and positive about solving problems with her, to comply more often with her directives, and to obey her requests even when she isn't present. Such children also tend to get along better with other toddlers and to be more sociable and more socially competent. Similarly, children and adolescents who are high in self-esteem also tend to be strong on many other dimensions of social and emotional functioning. They tend to be generally hopeful and popular, to have many friends, and to have good academic and self-regulation skills. In contrast, those with low self-esteem tend to feel hopeless and to be prone to problems such as depression, aggression, and social withdrawal.

Stability Over Time

Many individual differences show moderate stability over time. For instance, people who have easy temperaments during infancy tend to continue to have easy temperaments in middle and later childhood. Similarly, elementary school children with ADHD, reading disabilities, or mathematics disabilities usually have lifelong difficulties in those areas.

The reasons for such stability of psychological characteristics are to be found in the stability of both genes and environment. A child's genotype remains identical over the course of development (though particular genes switch on and off at different times). Most children's environments remain fairly stable as well. Families that are middle-class when a child is born tend to remain middle-class; families that value education when the child is born usually continue to value education; families that are sensitive and supportive generally remain that way; and so on. Major changes, such as divorce and unemployment, do occur, and they affect children's happiness, self-esteem, and other characteristics. Nonetheless, the stability of children's environments, like the stability of their genes, contributes to the stability over time of their psychological functioning.

Predicting Future Individual Differences on Other Dimensions

Individual differences on some dimensions are related not only to future status on that dimension but also to future status on other dimensions. For example, children who are securely attached as infants tend as toddlers and preschoolers to have more social ties to their peers than do children who were insecurely attached as infants. When they reach school age, they tend to understand other children's emotions relatively well and to be relatively skilled in resolving conflicts. When they reach adolescence and adulthood, they tend to form close attachments with romantic partners. All of these outcomes are consistent with the view that secure early attachment provides a working model that influences subsequent relationships with other people.

As with stability over time of a single dimension, the relative stability of most children's environments contributes to these long-term continuities of psychological functioning. If children's environments change in important ways, the typical continuities may be disrupted accordingly. Thus, stressful events such as divorce reduce the likelihood that children who were securely attached during infancy will continue to show the positive relations with peers usually associated with secure attachment.

Determinants of Individual Differences

Individual differences, like all aspects of development, are ultimately attributable to the interaction of children's genes and the environments they encounter.

Genetics

For a number of important characteristics—including IQ, prosocial behaviour, and empathy—about 50% of the differences among individuals in a given population are attributable to differences in genetic inheritance. The degree of genetic influence on individual differences tends to increase over the course of development. For example, correlations between the IQs of adopted children and their biological parents steadily increase over the course of childhood and adolescence, even if the children never meet or have any contact with their biological parents. One reason for this is that many genes related to intellectual functioning do not exercise their effects until late childhood or adolescence. Another reason is that over the course of development, children become increasingly free to choose environments that are in accord with their genetic predispositions.

Genetic similarities sometimes produce a striking physical resemblance between parent and child. We can only wonder whether this baby, as she develops, will come to resemble her father in other ways as well.

Experience

Individual differences reflect children's experiences as well as their genes. Consider just one major environmental influence: the parents who raise the children. The more speech that parents address to their toddlers, the more rapidly the toddlers recognize familiar words and learn new ones. The more that parents aim their scaffolding at, but not beyond, the upper end of their children's capabilities, the greater the improvement in their children's problem solving. The more stimulating and responsive the home intellectual environment, the higher children's IQ tends to be.

Parents exert at least as large an influence on their children's social and emotional development as on their intellectual development. For example, the likelihood that children will adopt their parents' standards and values appears to be influenced by the type of discipline their parents use with them. Similarly, parents influence their children's willingness to share, especially if they discuss the reasons for sharing with their children and have good relationships with them.

The effect of different types of parenting, like the effects of children's other experiences, depends on the child. One example of this involves the development of conscience. For fearful children, the key factor determining whether the child internalizes the parents' moral values is gentle discipline. Fearful children may become so anxious in the face of rigorous discipline that they cannot focus on the moral values that the parents are trying to instill. For fearless children, on the other hand, the key factor is a positive relationship with one's parents. Such fearless children often do not respond to gentle discipline; they tend to internalize the parents' values only if they feel close to them. As an old adage states, "It's a wise parent who knows his child."

Theme 7: Child-Development Research Can Improve Children's Lives

One of the few goals shared by virtually everyone is that children be as happy and healthy as possible. Understanding how children develop can contribute to this goal. Theories of development provide general principles for interpreting children's behaviour and for analyzing their problems. Empirical studies yield specific lessons regarding how to promote children's physical well-being, positive relationships with other people, and learning. In this section, we review practical implications of child-development research for raising children, educating them, and helping them overcome problems.

Implications for Parenting

Several principles of good parenting are so obvious that noting them might seem unnecessary. However, the number of children who are harmed each year by poor parenting makes it clear that these principles cannot be stated too often.

Pick a Good Partner

The first principle of good parenting comes into play before parenthood even begins: pick a good partner. Given the importance of genetics, pick a partner whose physical, intellectual, and emotional characteristics suggest that he or she will provide your child with good genes. Given the importance of the environment, pick a partner who will be a good mother or father. In terms of your child's development, no decision is more important than picking a good partner.

Ensure a Healthy Pregnancy

An expectant mother should maintain a healthy diet, have regular checkups, and keep stress levels as low as possible to increase the likelihood of a successful pregnancy. Equally important is avoiding teratogens such as tobacco, alcohol, and illegal drugs.

Know Which Decisions Are Likely to Have a Long-Term Impact

In addition to the joy they feel when their baby is born, new parents face a daunting number of decisions. Fortunately, babies are quite resilient. In the context of a loving and supportive home, a great number of choices work out about equally well. Some decisions that seem minor, however, can have important effects. One such decision involves the baby's sleeping position: having a baby sleep on his or her back, rather than on his or her stomach, reduces the possibility of SIDS.

In other cases, the lesson of child-development research is that early problems are often transitory, so there is no reason to worry about them. Colic, which affects about 10% of babies, is one such problem. A colicky baby's frequent, high-pitched, grating, sick-sounding cries are difficult for parents to bear, but they have no long-term implications for the baby's development. In the short run, the best approach is to soothe the baby to the extent possible and not feel fault if the effort fails. In the longer run, the best path for parents is to relax, seek social support, and obtain babysitting help to allow some time off from caregiving—and to remember that colic usually ends by the time babies are 3 months old.

ASIA IMAGES GROUP PTE LTD / ALAMY

Family activities, such as looking at photo albums and reminiscing about the people and settings they depict, provide both stimulation and warm, positive feelings for many children.

Form a Secure Attachment

Most parents have no difficulty forming a secure attachment with their baby, but some parents and babies do not form such bonds. One reason is genetics: variant forms of certain genes can influence the likelihood of a child's forming a secure parental attachment, in at least some circumstances. Of course, no one can control the genes that babies inherit, but parents and other caretakers can maximize the likelihood of a baby's becoming securely attached by maintaining a positive approach in their caregiving and by being responsive to the baby's needs. This is easier said than done, of course, and other dimensions of a baby's temperament, as well as the parents' attitude and responsiveness, influence the quality of attachment. However, even when babies are initially irritable and difficult, programs that teach parents how to be responsive and positive with them can lead to more secure attachments.

Provide a Stimulating Environment

The home environment has a great deal to do with children's learning. One good example involves reading acquisition. Telling stories to toddlers and preschoolers, being responsive when they tell stories, and reading to them are positively related to later reading achievement. One reason is that such activities promote phonological awareness (the ability to identify the component sounds within words). Rhymes seem to be particularly effective in this regard; children who repeatedly hear *Green Eggs and Ham,* for instance, generally learn to appreciate the similarities and differences in "Sam," "ham," "am," and related words. Phonological awareness helps children learn to sound out words, which, in turn, helps them learn to retrieve the words' identities quickly and effortlessly. Successful early reading leads children to read more, which helps them improve their reading further over the course of schooling. More generally, the more stimulating the intellectual environment, the more eager children will be to learn.

Implications for Education

Theories and research on child development hold a number of further lessons for how to educate children most effectively. Consider the instructional implications of several major theories of cognitive development.

Piaget's theory emphasizes the importance of the child's active involvement, both mental and physical, in the learning process. This active involvement is especially important in helping children master counterintuitive ideas. For example, the physical experience of walking around a pivot while holding a long metal rod at points close to and far from the pivot allowed children to overcome a widely held misconception that previous paper-and-pencil physics lessons had failed to correct—the misconception that all parts of an object must move at the same speed.

Information-processing theories suggest that analyzing the types of information available to children in everyday activities can improve learning. One such analysis indicated that the simple board game Snakes and Ladders provided visual, auditory, kinesthetic, and temporal information that could help children learn the sizes of numbers. Consistent with this analysis, having children from low-income families play a game based on Snakes and Ladders improved the children's understanding of the sizes of numbers, as well as their counting, recognition of numbers, and arithmetic learning.

Sociocultural theories emphasize the need to turn classrooms into communities of learners in which children cooperate with one another in their pursuit of knowledge. Rather than following the traditional model of instruction in which teachers lecture and children take notes, community-of-learners classrooms follow an approach in which teachers provide the minimum guidance needed for children to learn and gradually decrease their directive role as children's competence increases. Such programs also encourage children to make use of the resources of the broader community—children and teachers at other schools, outside experts, reference books, websites, and so on. The approach can be effective not only in building intellectual skills but also in promoting desirable values, such as personal responsibility and mutual respect.

Implications for Helping Children at Risk

Several principles that have emerged from empirical research offer valuable guidance for helping children at risk for serious developmental problems.

The Importance of Timing

Providing interventions at the optimal time is crucial in a variety of developmental contexts. One important example involves efforts to help children at risk for learning difficulties. All theories of cognitive development indicate that such difficulties should be addressed early, before children lose confidence in their ability to learn or become resentful toward schools and teachers. This realization, together with research documenting that many children from impoverished backgrounds have difficulty in school, laid the groundwork for various early intervention and prevention programs. Evaluations of the programs' effects indicate that these programs can increase children's IQs and achievement test scores by the end of the programs and for a few years thereafter. Subsequently, the positive effects on IQ and academic achievement usually fade, but other positive effects continue. At-risk children who participate in such programs are less likely to ever be held back in school

COLIN MCCONNELL / TORONTO STAR VIA GETTY IMAGES

The intellectual stimulation children receive and the academic skills they acquire in classrooms with early intervention programs such as this one boost their **IQ** and achievement test scores at program completion and sometimes for several years thereafter.

or assigned to special education classes than are those who do not participate, and they are more likely to graduate from high school.

Even greater positive effects of early educational programs are possible, as illustrated by the Better Beginnings, Better Futures (BBBF) project and the Carolina Abecedarian Project. BBBF offered a variety of child-, parent-, and family- and community-focused programming to all children between the ages of 4 and 8 years living in four Ontario communities considered "at risk," as well as to these children's families. Similarly, the Carolina Abecedarian Project was designed to show what could be achieved through an optimally staffed, highly funded, and carefully designed program that started during infancy and lasted through age 5. These projects produced gains in school functioning, academic achievement, and social skills that continued throughout childhood and adolescence. Their results demonstrate that it is possible for intensive programs that start early to have substantial, lasting benefits on the academic achievement of children with low family incomes.

Early detection of child maltreatment, and rapid intervention to end it, is also crucial. In Canada, roughly 85 000 of children age 18 and younger are maltreated in a given year, based on 2008 data. Inadequate care, physical abuse, and sexual abuse are the three most common problems. Parents who are stressed economically, have few friends, use alcohol and illegal drugs, or are being abused by their partner are the most likely to mistreat their children.

Knowing the characteristics of abused and neglected children can help teachers and others who come into contact with children recognize potential problems early and alert social service agencies so that they can investigate and remedy the problems. Children who are maltreated tend to have difficult temperaments, to have few friends, to be in poor physical or mental health, to do poorly in school, and to show abnormal aggression or passivity. Adolescents who are maltreated may be depressed or hyperactive, use drugs or alcohol, and have sexual problems such as promiscuity or abnormal fearfulness. Early recognition of such signs of abuse can literally save a child's life.

Biology and Environment Work Together

Another principle with important practical implications is that biology and environment work together to produce all behaviour. This principle has proved important in designing treatments for ADHD. Although stimulant drugs such as Ritalin are the best-known treatment for this problem, research has shown that when medications are used alone, their benefits usually end as soon as children stop taking them. Longer-lasting benefits require behavioural therapy as well as medication. One effective behavioural treatment is to teach the children strategies for screening out distractions. The medications calm children with ADHD sufficiently that they can benefit from the therapy; the therapy helps them learn effective ways for dealing with their problems and for interacting with other people.

Every Problem Has Many Causes

An additional principle that has proven useful for helping children with developmental problems is that trying to identify *the* cause of any particular problem is futile; problems almost always have multiple causes. The greater the number of risks, the more likely children will have low IQs, poor socioemotional skills, and psychiatric disorders. Accordingly, providing effective treatment often requires addressing many particular difficulties. This principle has provided useful guidance for intervening with children who are rejected by other children. Helping these children gain better social skills requires increasing their understanding of other people. It also requires helping them learn new strategies, such as how to enter an ongoing group interaction unobtrusively and how to resolve conflicts without resorting to aggression. It also requires helping them learn from their own experience, for example, by monitoring the success of the different strategies they try. Together, these approaches can help rejected children make friends and become better accepted.

Improving Social Policy

Even if you do not have children of your own and rarely interact with other people's children, your actions as a citizen can influence their lives. Votes in elections and referenda, opinions expressed in informal discussions, and participation in advocacy organizations all can make a difference. Knowledge of child-development research can inform your stances on many issues relevant to children. The conclusions that you reach will, and should, reflect your values as well as the evidence. For example, reductions in class size in kindergarten through Grade 3 classrooms have had variable effects on student achievement. A large-scale, well-implemented study in Tennessee, for instance, indicated positive effects on student achievement (A. B. Krueger, 1999), whereas a large-scale, well-implemented study in California did not show any effect on achievement (Stecher, McCaffrey, & Bugliari, 2003). Teachers and parents appeared to be pleased with the class-size reductions in both cases and believed that the smaller classes helped their children.

Are these outcomes worth the substantial cost of hiring the number of teachers needed to implement such reform? Research cannot answer this question, because the answer depends on values as well as data. How expensive is too expensive? Nonetheless, as the example illustrates, knowing the scientific evidence can help us, as citizens, make better-informed decisions.

Child Care

Should the general society subsidize child-care payments for parents of young children. One argument against such a policy has been the claim that children develop more successfully if they stay at home with one of their parents or other relatives than if they attend daycare. This argument has turned out to be flawed, however. Children who attend good-quality child-care programs develop similarly to children who receive care at home from their parents.

Eyewitness Testimony

Understanding child development is also vital for deciding whether children should be allowed to testify in court cases and for obtaining the most accurate testimony possible from them. Each year, tens of thousands of children in Canada testify in legal cases, either about crimes they experienced or witnessed. Often, the child and the accused are the only ones who witnessed the events. Research indicates that, in general, the accuracy of testimony increases with age; 8-year-olds recall more than do 6-year-olds, and 6-year-olds recall more than do 4-year-olds. However, when children are shielded from misleading and repeated questioning, even 4- and 5-year-olds usually provide accurate testimony about the types of issues that are central in court cases. Given the high stakes in such cases, using the lessons of research to elicit the most accurate possible testimony from children is essential for a just verdict.

Child-development research holds lessons for numerous other social problems as well. Research on the causes of aggression has led to programs such as Fast Track, which are designed to teach aggressive children to manage their anger and avoid violence. Research on the roots of helping and sharing behaviour has led to programs such as Roots of Empathy, designed to promote children's prosocial behaviours and decrease their aggressive behaviours. Research on the effects of poverty has provided the basis for the Better Beginnings, Better Futures project, the Carolina Abecedarian Project, and other early education efforts. There is no end of social problems; understanding child development can help address the ones that affect children's futures.

Children are naturally curious about the world; encouraging this curiosity, and channelling it in fruitful directions, is among the most vital goals facing parents and society alike.

Critical Thinking Questions

1. What qualities of children influence the way that other people act toward them, and how do these actions influence their development?

2. Individual differences show some stability over time. How do genes and environment contribute to this stability?

3. How would growing up in one developed society rather than another—for example, Canada rather than Japan—be expected to influence a child's development?

4. How have the changes that have taken place in Canada over the past century influenced children's development? Has the overall effect of the changes on children been predominantly beneficial or predominantly harmful?

5. What findings that you read about in this book surprised you the most? Were there any findings or conclusions that you just do not believe?

6. What practical lessons have you learned from this course that will influence the way that you raise your children if you have them?

Glossary

accommodation The process by which people adapt current knowledge structures in response to new experiences. (p. 133)

achievement motivation Whether children are motivated by *learning goals,* seeking to improve their competence and master new material, or by *performance goals,* seeking to receive positive assessments of their competence or to avoid negative assessments. (p. 360)

activating influences Potential result of certain fluctuations in sex-linked hormone levels affecting the contemporaneous activation of the nervous system and corresponding behavioural responses. (p. 598)

adrenarche Period prior to the emergence of visible signs of puberty during which the adrenal glands mature, providing a major source of sex steroid hormones; correlates with the onset of sexual attraction. (p. 618)

adult attachment models Working models of attachment in adulthood that are believed to be based on adults' perceptions of their own childhood experiences—especially their relationships with their parents—and of the influence of these experiences on them as adults. (p. 432)

affiliation Tendency to affirm connection with others through being emotionally open, empathetic, or cooperative. (p. 594)

affordances The possibilities for action offered by objects and situations. (p. 200)

aggression Behaviour aimed at harming or injuring others. (p. 578)

aggressive-rejected (peer status) A category of sociometric status that refers to children who are especially prone to physical aggression, disruptive behaviour, delinquency, and negative behaviour such as hostility and threatening others. (p. 535)

alleles Two or more different forms of a gene. (p. 92)

altruistic motives Helping others for reasons that initially include empathy or sympathy for others and, at later ages, the desire to act in ways consistent with one's own conscience and moral principles. (p. 569)

amniotic sac A transparent, fluid-filled membrane that surrounds and protects the fetus. (p. 48)

anal stage The second stage in Freud's theory, lasting roughly from 1 to 3 years of age, in which the primary source of pleasure comes from defecation. (p. 345)

androgen insensitivity syndrome (AIS) Condition during prenatal development in which androgen receptors malfunction in genetic males, impeding the formation of male external genitalia; in these cases, the child may be born with female external genitalia. (p. 599)

androgens Class of steroid hormones that normally occur at higher levels in males than in females and that affect physical development and functioning from the prenatal period onward. (p. 598)

A-not-B error The tendency to reach for a hidden object where it was last found rather than in the new location where it was last hidden. (p. 136)

apoptosis Genetically programmed cell death. (p. 47)

assertion Tendency to take action on behalf of the self through competitive, independent, or aggressive behaviours. (p. 594)

assimilation The process by which people translate incoming information into a form that fits concepts they already understand. (p. 133)

association areas Parts of the brain that lie between the major sensory and motor areas and that process and integrate input from those areas. (p. 109)

attachment An emotional bond with a specific person that is enduring across space and time. Usually, attachments are discussed in regard to the relation between infants and specific caregivers, although they can also occur in adulthood. (p. 427)

attachment theory A theory based on John Bowlby's work that posits that children are biologically predisposed to develop attachments to caregivers as a means of increasing the chances of their own survival. (p. 428)

attention deficit hyperactivity disorder (ADHD) A syndrome that involves difficulty in sustaining attention. (p. 372)

auditory localization Perception of the location in space of a sound source. (p. 182)

authoritarian parenting A parenting style that is high in demandingness and low in responsiveness. Authoritarian parents are unresponsive to their children's needs and tend to enforce their demands through the exercise of parental power and the use of threats and punishment. They are oriented toward obedience and authority and expect their children to comply with their demands without question or explanation. (p. 474)

authoritative parenting A parenting style that is high in demandingness and supportiveness. Authoritative parents set clear standards and limits for their children and are firm about enforcing them; at the same time, they allow their children considerable autonomy within those limits, are attentive and responsive to their children's concerns and needs, and respect and consider their children's perspective. (p. 473)

autobiographical memories Memories of one's own experiences, including one's thoughts and emotions. (p. 160)

axons Neural fibres that conduct electrical signals away from the cell body to connections with other neurons. (p. 108)

babbling Repetitive consonant–vowel sequences ("bababa …") or hand shapes (for learners of signed languages) produced during the early phases of language development. (p. 231)

basic level The middle level, and often the first level learned, within a category hierarchy, such as "dog" in the animal/dog/poodle example. (p. 266)

basic processes The simplest and most frequently used mental activities. (p. 149)

behaviour genetics The science concerned with how variation in behaviour and development results from the combination of genetic and environmental factors. (p. 99)

behaviour modification A form of therapy based on principles of operant conditioning in which reinforcement contingencies are changed to encourage more adaptive behaviour. (p. 353)

behavioural inhibition A temperamentally based style of responding characterized by the tendency to be particularly fearful and restrained when dealing with novel or stressful situations. (p. 409)

Better Beginnings, Better Futures (BBBF) Successful early intervention program aimed at disadvantaged communities in Ontario. (p. 319)

bidirectionality of parent–child interactions The idea that parents and their children are mutually affected by one another's characteristics and behaviours. (p. 478)

bilingualism The ability to use two languages. (p. 224)

binocular disparity The difference between the retinal image of an object in each eye that results in two slightly different signals being sent to the brain. (p. 181)

body image An individual's perception of, and feelings about, his or her own body. (p. 618)

Carolina Abecedarian Project Comprehensive and successful enrichment program for children from low-income families. (p. 319)

categorical perception The perception of speech sounds as belonging to discrete categories. (p. 226)

category hierarchy Categories that are related by set–subset relations, such as animal/dog/poodle. (p. 265)

cell body A component of the neuron that contains the basic biological material that keeps the neuron functioning. (p. 108)

centration The tendency to focus on a single, perceptually striking feature of an object or event. (p. 139)

cephalocaudal development The pattern of growth in which areas near the head develop earlier than areas farther from the head. (p. 48)

cerebral cortex The "grey matter" of the brain that plays a primary role in what is thought to be particularly human-like functioning, from seeing and hearing to writing to feeling emotion. (p. 108)

cerebral hemispheres The two halves of the cortex; for the most part, sensory input from one side of the body goes to the opposite hemisphere of the brain. (p. 109)

cerebral lateralization The specialization of the hemispheres of the brain for different modes of processing. (p. 109)

child maltreatment Intentional abuse or neglect that endangers the well-being of anyone under the age of 18. (p. 371)

chromosomes Molecules of DNA that transmit genetic information; chromosomes are made up of DNA. (p. 89)

chronosystem In the bioecological model, historical changes that influence the other systems. (p. 370)

classical conditioning A form of learning that consists of associating an initially neutral stimulus with a stimulus that always evokes a particular reflexive response. (p. 201)

clinical interview A procedure in which questions are adjusted in accord with the answers the interviewee provides. (p. 25)

cliques Friendship groups that children voluntarily form or join themselves. (p. 526)

cognitive development The development of thinking and reasoning. (p. 15)

colic Excessive, inconsolable crying by a young infant for no apparent reason. (p. 74)

collaboration Coordination of assertion and affiliation in behaviour, which is associated with gender-role flexibility; more common among girls than boys. (p. 594)

collective monologue Conversation between children that involves a series of non sequiturs, the content of each child's turn having little or nothing to do with what the other child has just said. (p. 245)

comprehension Understanding what others say (or sign or write). (p. 217)

comprehension monitoring Process of keeping track of one's understanding of a verbal description or text. (p. 327)

conception The union of an egg from the mother and a sperm from the father. (p. 42)

concepts General ideas or understandings that can be used to group together objects, events, qualities, or abstractions that are similar in some way. (p. 262)

concrete operational stage The period (7 to 12 years) within Piaget's theory in which children become able to reason logically about concrete objects and events. (p. 135)

conditioned response (CR) In classical conditioning, the originally reflexive response that comes to be elicited by the conditioned stimulus. (p. 201)

conditioned stimulus (CS) In classical conditioning, the neutral stimulus that is repeatedly paired with the unconditioned stimulus. (p. 201)

conduct disorder (CD) A disorder that involves severe antisocial and aggression behaviours that inflict pain on others or involve destruction of property or denial of the rights of others. (p. 581)

cones The light-sensitive neurons that are highly concentrated in the fovea (the central region of the retina). (p. 174)

congenital adrenal hyperplasia (CAH) Condition during prenatal development in which the adrenal glands produce high levels of androgens; sometimes associated with masculinization of external genitalia in genetic females, and sometimes associated with higher rates of masculine-stereotyped play in genetic females. (p. 599)

connectionism A type of information-processing approach that emphasizes the simultaneous activity of numerous interconnected processing units. (p. 253)

conscience An internal regulatory mechanism that increases the individual's ability to conform to standards of conduct accepted in his or her culture. (p. 566)

conservation concept The idea that merely changing the appearance of objects does not necessarily change other key properties. (p. 139)

continuous development The idea that changes with age occur gradually, in small increments, like that of a pine tree growing taller and taller. (p. 13)

contrast sensitivity The ability to detect differences in light and dark areas in a visual pattern. (p. 174)

control group The group of children in an experimental design who are not presented the experience of interest but in other ways are treated similarly. (p. 31)

controversial (peer status) A category of sociometric status that refers to children or adolescents who are liked by quite a few peers and are disliked by quite a few others. (p. 538)

corpus callosum A dense tract of nerve fibres that enable the two hemispheres of the brain to communicate. (p. 109)

correlation The association between two variables. (p. 29)

correlational designs Studies intended to indicate how variables are related to one another. (p. 28)

co-rumination Extensively discussing and self-disclosing emotional problems with another person. (p. 396)

counting-on strategy Counting up from the larger addend the number of times indicated by the smaller addend. (p. 33)

critical period for language The time during which language develops readily and after which (sometime between age 5 and puberty) language acquisition is much more difficult and ultimately less successful. (p. 220)

cross-gender-typed Traditionally associated with the gender other than that of a given person. (p. 595)

crossing over The process by which sections of DNA switch from one chromosome to the other;

crossing over promotes variability among individuals. (p. 91)

cross-sectional design A research method in which children of different ages are compared on a given behaviour or characteristic over a short period. (p. 32)

crowds Groups of adolescents who have similar stereotyped reputations; among North American high school students, typical crowds may include the "brains," "jocks," "loners," "burnouts," "punks," "populars," "elites," "freaks," or "nonconformists." (p. 528)

crystallized intelligence Factual knowledge about the world. (p. 302)

cultural tools The innumerable products of human ingenuity that enhance thinking. (p. 156)

deferred imitation The repetition of other people's behaviour a substantial time after it originally occurred. (p. 137)

dendrites Neural fibres that receive input from other cells and conduct it toward the cell body in the form of electrical impulses. (p. 108)

dependent variable A behaviour that is measured to determine whether it is affected by exposure to the independent variable. (p. 31)

developmental resilience Successful development in spite of multiple and seemingly overwhelming developmental hazards. (p. 81)

differential (or discrete) emotions theory A theory about emotions, held by Tomkins, Izard, and others, in which emotions are viewed as innate and discrete from one another from very early in life, and each emotion is believed to be packaged with a specific and distinctive set of bodily and facial reactions. (p. 386)

differentiation The extraction from the constantly changing stimulation in the environment of those elements that are invariant, or stable. (p. 199)

direction-of-causation problem The concept that a correlation between two variables does not indicate which, if either, variable is the cause of the other. (p. 29)

discontinuous development The idea that changes with age include occasional large shifts, like the transition from caterpillar to cocoon to butterfly. (p. 13)

disorganized/disoriented attachment A type of insecure attachment in which infants or young children have no consistent way of coping with the stress of the Strange Situation. Their behaviour is often confused or even contradictory, and they often appear dazed or disoriented. (p. 431)

display rules A social group's informal norms about when, where, and how much one should show emotions and when and where displays of emotion should be suppressed or masked by displays of other emotions. (p. 421)

distributional properties The phenomenon that, in any language, certain sounds are more likely to appear together than are others. (p. 229)

DNA (deoxyribonucleic acid) Molecules that carry all the biochemical instructions involved in the formation and functioning of an organism. (p. 89)

dominant allele The allele that, if present, gets expressed. (p. 92)

dose–response relation A relation in which the effect of exposure to an element increases with the extent of exposure (prenatally, the more exposure a fetus has to a potential teratogen, the more severe its effect is likely to be). (p. 59)

dual representation The idea that a symbolic artifact must be represented mentally in two ways at the same time—both as a real object and as a symbol for something other than itself. (p. 254)

dynamic-systems theories A class of theories that focus on how change occurs over time in complex systems. (p. 162)

dyslexia Inability to read and spell well despite having normal intelligence. (p. 328)

effect size Magnitude of difference between two groups' averages and the amount of overlap in their distributions. (p. 614)

ego In psychoanalytic theory, the second personality structure to develop. It is the rational, logical, problem-solving component of personality. (p. 345)

egocentric spatial representations Coding of spatial locations relative to one's own body, without regard to the surroundings. (p. 286)

egocentrism The tendency to perceive the world solely from one's own point of view. (p. 138)

Electra complex Freud's term for the conflict experienced by girls in the phallic stage when they develop unacceptable romantic feelings for their father and see their mother as a rival. (The complex is named after a figure in Greek mythology who arranged for the murder of her mother.) (p. 346)

embryo The name given to the developing organism from the 3rd to 8th week of prenatal development. (p. 45)

embryonic stem cells Embryonic cells that can develop into any type of body cell. (p. 45)

emotion Emotion is characterized by neural and physiological responses, subjective feelings, cognitions related to those feelings, and the desire to take action. (p. 385)

emotional intelligence A set of abilities that contribute to competence in the social and emotional domains. (p. 384)

emotional self-regulation The process of initiating, inhibiting, or modulating internal feeling states and related physiological processes, cognitions, and behaviours. (p. 398)

enactive experience Learning to take into account the reactions one's past behaviour has evoked in others. (p. 603)

encoding The process of representing in memory information that draws attention or is considered important. (p. 149)

entity theory A theory that a person's level of intelligence is fixed and unchangeable. (p. 361)

entity/helpless orientation A general tendency to attribute success and failure to enduring aspects of the self and to give up in the face of failure. (p. 360)

environment Every aspect of an individual and his or her surroundings other than genes. (p. 89)

epigenesis The emergence of new structures and functions in the course of development. (p. 41)

epigenetics The study of stable changes in gene expression that are mediated by the environment. (p. 12)

equilibration The process by which children (or other people) balance assimilation and accommodation to create stable understanding. (p. 133)

erogenous zones In Freud's theory, areas of the body that become erotically sensitive in successive stages of development. (p. 344)

essentialism The view that living things have an essence inside them that makes them what they are. (p. 278)

ethnic identity Individuals' sense of belonging to an ethnic or racial group, including the degree to which they associate their thinking, perceptions, feelings, and behaviour with membership in that group. (p. 450)

ethology The study of the evolutionary bases of behaviour. (p. 364)

event-related potentials (ERPs) Changes in the brain's electrical activity that occur in response to the presentation of a particular stimulus. (p. 110)

exosystem In the bioecological model, environmental settings that a person does not directly experience but that can affect the person indirectly. (p. 368)

experience-dependent plasticity The process through which neural connections are created and reorganized throughout life as a function of an individual's experiences. (p. 116)

experience-expectant plasticity The process through which the normal wiring of the brain occurs in part as a result of experiences that every human who inhabits any reasonably normal environment will have. (p. 115)

experimental control The ability of researchers to determine the specific experiences that children have during the course of an experiment. (p. 31)

experimental designs A group of approaches that allow inferences about causes and effects to be drawn. (p. 30)

experimental group A group of children in an experimental design who are presented the experience of interest. (p. 31)

external validity The degree to which results can be generalized beyond the particulars of the research. (p. 25)

failure to thrive A condition in which infants become malnourished and fail to grow or gain weight for no obvious medical reason. (p. 121)

false-belief problems Tasks that test a child's understanding that other people will act in accord with their own beliefs even when the child knows that those beliefs are incorrect. (p. 270)

family dynamics The way in which the family operates as a whole. (p. 470)

fast mapping The process of rapidly learning a new word simply from hearing the contrastive use of a familiar and the unfamiliar word. (p. 237)

fetal alcohol spectrum disorder (FASD) The harmful effects of maternal alcohol consumption on a developing fetus. Fetal alcohol syndrome (FAS) involves a range of effects, including facial deformities, mental retardation, attention problems, hyperactivity, and other defects. Fetal alcohol effects (FAE) is a term used for individuals who show some, but not all, of the standard effects of FAS. (p. 61)

fetus The name given to the developing organism from the 9th week to birth. (p. 45)

fluid intelligence Ability to think on the spot to solve novel problems. (p. 301)

Flynn effect Consistent rise in average IQ scores that has occurred over the past 80 years in many countries. (p. 315)

foreclosure status A category of identity status in which the individual is not engaged in any

identity experimentation and has established a vocational or ideological identity based on the choices or values of others. (p. 447)

formal operational stage The period (12 years and beyond) within Piaget's theory in which people become able to think about abstractions and hypothetical situations. (p. 135)

fraternal twins Twins that result when two eggs happen to be released into the fallopian tube at the same time and are fertilized by two different sperm; fraternal twins have only half their genes in common. (p. 47)

friendship An intimate, reciprocated positive relationship between two people. (p. 513)

frontal lobe The lobe of the cortex that is associated with organizing behaviour; the lobe that is thought responsible for the human ability to plan ahead. (p. 109)

functionalist approach A theory of emotion, proposed by Campos and others, that argues that the basic function of emotions is to promote action toward achieving a goal. In this view, emotions are not discrete from one another and vary somewhat based on the social environment. (p. 386)

g (general intelligence) Cognitive processes that influence the ability to think and learn on all intellectual tasks. (p. 301)

gametes (germ cells) Reproductive cells—egg and sperm—that contain only half the genetic material of all the other cells in the body. (p. 42)

gang A loosely organized group of adolescents or young adults who identify as a group and often engage in illegal activities. (p. 529)

gender constancy Realization that gender is invariant despite superficial changes in a person's appearance or behaviour. (p. 600)

gender dysphoria disorder Psychiatric diagnosis included in the DSM-5 to refer to children who identify with the other gender and indicate cross-gender- typed interests. (p. 599)

gender identity Awareness of oneself as a boy or a girl. (p. 599)

gender schema filter Initial evaluation of information as relevant for one's own gender. (p. 601)

gender schemas Organized mental representations (concepts, beliefs, memories) about gender, including gender stereotypes. (p. 600)

gender segregation Children's tendency to associate with same-gender peers and to avoid other-gender peers. (p. 608)

gender stability Awareness that gender remains the same over time. (p. 599)

gender typing The process of gender socialization and development. (p. 595)

gender-essentialist statements Remarks about males' and females' activities and characteristics phrased in language that implies they are inherent to the group as a whole. (p. 604)

gender-role flexibility Recognition of gender roles as social conventions and adoption of more flexible attitudes and interests. (p. 611)

gender-role intensification Heightened concerns with adhering to traditional gender roles that may occur during adolescence. (p. 611)

gender-typed Traditionally associated with a given person's gender. (p. 595)

generativity The idea that through the use of the finite set of words and morphemes in humans' vocabulary, we can put together an infinite number of sentences and express an infinite number of ideas. (p. 217)

genes Sections of chromosomes that are the basic unit of heredity in all living things. (p. 89)

genital stage The fifth and final stage in Freud's theory, beginning in adolescence, in which sexual maturation is complete and sexual intercourse becomes a major goal. (p. 347)

genome Each person's or organism's complete set of hereditary information. (p. 12)

genotype The genetic material an individual inherits. (p. 89)

gesture–speech mismatches Phenomenon in which hand movements and verbal statements convey different ideas. (p. 335)

glial cells Cells in the brain that provide a variety of critical supportive functions. (p. 108)

goodness of fit The degree to which an individual's temperament is compatible with the demands and expectations of his or her social environment. (p. 409)

guided participation A process in which more knowledgeable individuals organize activities in ways that allow less knowledgeable people to learn. (p. 155)

habituation A simple form of learning that involves a decrease in response to repeated or continued stimulation. (p. 54)

heritability A statistical estimate of the proportion of the measured variance on a trait among individuals in a given population that is attributable to genetic differences among those individuals. (p. 103)

heritable Refers to any characteristics or traits that are influenced by heredity. (p. 99)

heterozygous Having two different alleles for a trait. (p. 92)

holophrastic period The period when children begin using the words in their small productive vocabulary one word at a time. (p. 235)

homozygous Having two of the same allele for a trait. (p. 92)

hostile attributional bias In Dodge's theory, the tendency to assume that other people's ambiguous actions stem from a hostile intent. (p. 359)

hypotheses Educated guesses. (p. 23)

id In psychoanalytic theory, the earliest and most primitive personality structure. It is unconscious and operates with the goal of seeking pleasure. (p. 345)

identical twins Twins that result from the splitting in half of the zygote, resulting in each of the two resulting zygotes having exactly the same set of genes. (p. 47)

identity achievement An integration of various aspects of the self into a coherent whole that is stable over time and across events. (p. 446)

identity confusion An incomplete and sometimes incoherent sense of self that often occurs in Erikson's stage of identity versus identity confusion. (p. 446)

identity foreclosure Premature commitment to an identity without adequate consideration of other options. (p. 446)

identity versus identity confusion The psychosocial stage of development, described by Erikson, that occurs during adolescence. During this stage, the adolescent or young adult either develops an identity or experiences an incomplete and sometimes incoherent sense of self. (p. 446)

identity-achievement status A category of identity status in which, after a period of exploration, the individual has achieved a coherent and consolidated identity based on personal decisions regarding occupation, ideology, and the like. The individual believes that these decisions were made autonomously and is committed to them. (p. 447)

identity-diffusion status A category of identity status in which the individual does not have firm commitments and is not making progress toward them. (p. 447)

imaginary audience The belief, stemming from adolescent egocentrism, that everyone else is focused on the adolescent's appearance and behaviour. (p. 444)

imprinting A form of learning in which the young of some species of newborn birds and mammals become attached to and follow adult members of the species (usually their mother). (p. 364)

incremental theory A theory that a person's intelligence can grow as a function of experience. (p. 361)

incremental/mastery orientation A general tendency to attribute success and failure to the amount of effort expended and to persist in the face of failure. (p. 360)

independent variable The experience that children in the experimental group receive and that children in the control group do not receive. (p. 31)

infant mortality Death during the first year after birth. (p. 74)

infant-directed speech (IDS) The distinctive mode of speech that adults adopt when talking to babies and very young children. (p. 222)

information-processing theories A class of theories that focus on the structure of the cognitive system and the mental activities used to deploy attention and memory to solve problems. (p. 145)

in-group assimilation Process whereby individuals are socialized to conform to the group's norms, demonstrating the characteristics that define the in-group. (p. 602)

in-group bias Tendency to evaluate individuals and characteristics of the in-group as superior to those of the out-group. (p. 602)

insecure attachment A pattern of attachment in which infants or young children have a less positive attachment to their caregiver than do securely attached children. Insecurely attached children can be classified as insecure/resistant (ambivalent), insecure/avoidant, or disorganized/disoriented. (p. 431)

insecure/avoidant attachment A type of insecure attachment in which infants or young children seem somewhat indifferent toward their caregiver and may even avoid the caregiver. In the Strange Situation, they seem indifferent toward their caregiver before the caregiver leaves the room and indifferent or avoidant when the caregiver returns. If the infant gets upset when left alone, he or she is as easily comforted by a stranger as by a parent. (p. 431)

insecure/resistant (or ambivalent) attachment A type of insecure attachment in which infants or young children are clingy and stay close to their caregiver rather than exploring their environment. In the Strange Situation, insecure/resistant infants tend to get very upset when the caregiver leaves them alone in the room. When their caregiver returns, they are not easily comforted and both seek comfort and resist efforts by the caregiver to comfort them. (p. 431)

instrumental (or operant) conditioning Learning the relation between one's own behaviour and the consequences that result from it. (p. 201)

instrumental aggression Aggression motivated by the desire to obtain a concrete goal. (p. 579)

interest filter Initial evaluation of information as being personally interesting. (p. 601)

intermittent reinforcement Inconsistent response to the behaviour of another person, for example, sometimes punishing an unacceptable behaviour and sometimes ignoring it. (p. 353)

intermodal perception The combining of information from two or more sensory systems. (p. 187)

internal validity The degree to which effects observed within experiments can be attributed to the factor that the researcher is testing. (p. 24)

internal working model of attachment The child's mental representation of the self, of attachment figure(s), and of relationships in general that is constructed as a result of experiences with caregivers. The working model guides children's interactions with caregivers and other people in infancy and at older ages. (p. 429)

internalization The process of adopting as one's own the attributes, beliefs, and standards of another person. (p. 346)

interrater reliability The amount of agreement in the observations of different raters who witness the same behaviour. (p. 24)

intersubjectivity The mutual understanding that people share during communication. (p. 159)

IQ (intelligence quotient) Quantitative measure, typically with a mean of 100 and a standard deviation of 15, used to indicate a child's intelligence relative to that of other children of the same age. (p. 306)

joint attention A process in which social partners intentionally focus on a common referent in the external environment. (p. 159)

latency period The fourth stage in Freud's theory, lasting from age 6 to age 12, in which sexual energy gets channelled into socially acceptable activities. (p. 347)

lobes Major areas of the cortex associated with general categories of behaviour. (p. 108)

longitudinal design A method of study in which the same children are studied twice or more over a substantial length of time. (p. 32)

long-term memory Information retained on an enduring basis. (p. 147)

low birth weight (LBW) A birth weight of less than 2500 grams. (p. 76)

macrosystem In the bioecological model, the larger cultural and social context within which the other systems are embedded. (p. 370)

mathematical equality Concept that the values on each side of the equal sign must be equivalent. (p. 335)

meiosis Cell division that produces gametes. (p. 42)

menarche Onset of menstruation. (p. 617)

mental model Cognitive processes used to represent a situation or sequence of events. (p. 327)

mesosystem In the bioecological model, the interconnections among immediate, or microsystem, settings. (p. 368)

meta-analysis Statistical technique used to summarize average effect size and statistical significance across several research studies. (p. 615)

metalinguistic knowledge An understanding of the properties and function of language—that is, an understanding of language as language (p. 218)

methylation A biochemical process that influences behaviour by suppressing gene activity and expression. (p. 12)

microgenetic design A method of study in which the same children are studied repeatedly over a short period. (p. 33)

microsystem In the bioecological model, the immediate environment that an individual personally experiences. (p. 368)

mitosis Cell division that results in two identical daughter cells. (p. 45)

modularity hypothesis The idea that the human brain contains an innate, self-contained language module that is separate from other aspects of cognitive functioning. (p. 250)

monocular depth (or pictorial) cues The perceptual cues of depth (such as relative size and interposition) that can be perceived by one eye alone. (p. 181)

moral judgments Decisions that pertain to issues of right and wrong, fairness, and justice. (p. 564)

moratorium status A category of identity status in which the individual is in the phase of experimentation with regard to occupational and ideological choices and has not yet made a clear commitment to them. (p. 447)

morphemes The smallest units of meaning in a language, composed of one or more phonemes. (p. 217)

multifactorial Refers to traits that are affected by a host of environmental factors as well as genetic ones. (p. 99)

multiple intelligences theory Gardner's theory of intellect, based on the view that people possess at least eight types of intelligence. (p. 322)

mutation A change in a section of DNA. (p. 91)

myelin sheath A fatty sheath that forms around certain axons in the body and increases the speed and efficiency of information transmission. (p. 108)

myelination The formation of myelin (a fatty sheath) around the axons of neurons that speeds and increases information- processing abilities. (p. 112)

naive psychology A commonsensical level of understanding of other people and oneself. (p. 268)

narratives Descriptions of past events that have the basic structure of a story. (p. 246)

naturalistic observation Examination of ongoing behaviour in an environment not controlled by the researcher. (p. 26)

nature Our biological endowment; the genes we receive from our parents. (p. 11)

negative identity Identity that stands in opposition to what is valued by people around the adolescent. (p. 447)

neglected (peer status) A category of sociometric status that refers to children or adolescents who are infrequently mentioned as either liked or disliked; they simply are not noticed much by peers. (p. 537)

neural tube A groove formed in the top layer of differentiated cells in the embryo that eventually becomes the brain and spinal cord. (p. 47)

neurogenesis The proliferation of neurons through cell division. (p. 111)

neurons Cells that are specialized for sending and receiving messages between the brain and all parts of the body, as well as within the brain itself. (p. 107)

neurotransmitters Chemicals involved in communication among brain cells. (p. 17)

non-REM sleep A quiet or deep sleep state characterized by the absence of motor activity or eye movements and regular, slow brain waves, breathing, and heart rate. (p. 70)

norm of reaction All the phenotypes that can theoretically result from a given genotype in relation to all the environments in which it can survive and develop. (p. 93)

normal distribution Pattern of data in which scores fall symmetrically around a mean value, with most scores falling close to the mean and fewer and fewer scores farther from it. (p. 306)

numerical equality The realization that all sets of n objects have something in common. (p. 291)

numerical magnitude representations Mental models of the sizes of numbers, ordered along a less-to-more dimension. (p. 334)

nurture The environments, both physical and social, that influence our development. (p. 11)

object permanence The knowledge that objects continue to exist even when they are out of view. (p. 136)

object segregation The identification of separate objects in a visual array. (p. 179)

object substitution A form of pretense in which an object is used as something other than itself, for example, using a broom to represent a horse. (p. 273)

observational learning Learning through watching other people and the consequences others experience as a result of their actions. (p. 603)

occipital lobe The lobe of the cortex that is primarily involved in processing visual information. (p. 108)

Oedipus complex Freud's term for the conflict experienced by boys in the phallic period because of their sexual desire for their mother and their fear of retaliation by their father. (The complex is named for the king in Greek mythology who unknowingly murdered his father and married his mother.) (p. 346)

opportunity structure The economic and social resources offered by the macrosystem in the bioecological model, and people's understanding of those resources. (p. 606)

oppositional defiant disorder (ODD) A disorder characterized by age-inappropriate and persistent displays of angry, defiant, and irritable behaviours. (p. 581)

optical expansion A depth cue in which an object occludes increasingly more of the background, indicating that the object is approaching. (p. 180)

oral stage The first stage in Freud's theory, occurring in the first year, in which the primary source of satisfaction and pleasure is oral activity. (p. 345)

organizing influences Potential result of certain sex-linked hormones affecting brain differentiation and organization during prenatal development or at puberty. (p. 598)

overextension The use of a given word in a broader context than is appropriate. (p. 235)

overlapping-waves theory An information-processing approach that emphasizes the variability of children's thinking. (p. 152)

overregularization Speech errors in which children treat irregular forms of words as if they were regular. (p. 244)

parental sensitivity An important factor contributing to the security of an infant's attachment. Parental sensitivity can be exhibited in a variety of ways, including responsive caregiving when an infant is distressed or upset and engaging in coordinated play with the infant. (p. 435)

parental-investment theory A theory that stresses the evolutionary basis of many aspects of parental behaviour, including the extensive investment parents make in their offspring. (p. 366)

parenting styles Parenting behaviours and attitudes that set the emotional climate in regard to parent–child interactions, such as parental responsiveness and demandingness. (p. 472)

parietal lobe The lobe of the cortex that governs spatial processing and integrates sensory input with information stored in memory. (p. 108)

peers People of approximately the same age and status. (p. 512)

perceived self-efficacy An individual's beliefs about how effectively he or she can control his or her own behaviour, thoughts, and emotions in order to achieve a desired goal. (p. 356)

perception The process of organizing and interpreting sensory information. (p. 173)

perceptual categorization The grouping together of objects that have similar appearances. (p. 266)

perceptual constancy The perception of objects as being of constant size, shape, colour, and so on, in spite of physical differences in the retinal image of the object. (p. 178)

permissive parenting A parenting style that is high in responsiveness but low in demandingness. Permissive parents are responsive to their children's needs and do not require their children to regulate themselves or act in appropriate or mature ways. (p. 474)

personal fable A form of adolescent egocentrism that involves beliefs in the uniqueness of one's own feelings and thoughts. (p. 444)

personal judgments Decisions that refer to actions in which individual preferences are the main consideration. (p. 564)

phallic stage The third stage in Freud's theory, lasting from age 3 to age 6, in which sexual pleasure is focused on the genitalia. (p. 346)

phenotype The observable expression of the genotype, including both body characteristics and behaviour. (p. 89)

phenylketonuria (PKU) A disorder related to a defective recessive gene on chromosome 12 that prevents metabolism of phenylalanine. (p. 96)

phonemes The elementary units of meaningful sound used to produce languages. (p. 217)

phonemic awareness Ability to identify component sounds within words. (p. 324)

phonological development The acquisition of knowledge about the sound system of a language. (p. 217)

phonological recoding skills Ability to translate letters into sounds and to blend sounds into words; informally called *sounding out*. (p. 324)

phylogenetic continuity The idea that because of our common evolutionary history, humans share many characteristics, behaviours, and developmental processes with other animals, especially mammals. (p. 47)

placenta A support organ for the fetus; it keeps the circulatory systems of the fetus and mother separate, but as a semi-permeable membrane permits the exchange of some materials between them (oxygen and nutrients from mother to fetus and carbon dioxide and waste products from fetus to mother. (p. 48)

plasticity The capacity of the brain to be affected by experience. (p. 115)

polygenic inheritance Inheritance in which traits are governed by more than one gene. (p. 93)

popular (peer status) A category of sociometric status that refers to children or adolescents who are viewed positively (liked) by many peers and are viewed negatively (disliked) by few peers. (p. 534)

positive reinforcement A reward that reliably follows a behaviour and increases the likelihood that the behaviour will be repeated. (p. 201)

pragmatic cues Aspects of the social context used for word learning. (p. 238)

pragmatic development The acquisition of knowledge about how language is used. (p. 218)

preferential-looking technique A method for studying visual attention in infants that involves showing infants two patterns or two objects at a time to see if the infants have a preference for one over the other. (p. 174)

premature Any child born at 35 weeks after conception or earlier (as opposed to the normal term of 38 weeks). (p. 76)

preoperational stage The period (2 to 7 years) within Piaget's theory in which children become able to represent their experiences in language, mental imagery, and symbolic thought. (p. 135)

pre-reaching movements Clumsy swiping movements by young infants toward the general vicinity of objects they see. (p. 192)

pretend play Make-believe activities in which children create new symbolic relations, acting as if they were in a situation different from their actual one. (p. 273)

primary mental abilities Seven abilities proposed by Thurstone as crucial to intelligence. (p. 302)

private speech The second phase of Vygotsky's internalization-of-thought process, in which children develop their self-regulation and problem-solving abilities by telling themselves aloud what to do, much as their parents did in the first stage. (p. 157)

proactive aggression Unemotional aggression aimed at fulfilling a need or desire. (p. 583)

problem solving The process of attaining a goal by using a strategy to overcome an obstacle. (p. 146)

production Speaking (or writing or signing) to others. (p. 217)

prosocial behaviour Voluntary behaviour intended to benefit another, such as helping, sharing with, and comforting others. (p. 562)

prosody The characteristic rhythm, tempo, cadence, melody, intonational patterns, and so forth with which a language is spoken. (p. 225)

psychic energy Freud's term for the collection of biologically based instinctual drives that he believed fuel behaviour, thoughts, and feelings. (p. 344)

psychosocial moratorium A time out during which the adolescent is not expected to take on adult roles and can instead pursue activities that may lead to self-discovery. (p. 447)

puberty Developmental period marked by the ability to reproduce and other dramatic bodily changes. (p. 617)

random assignment A procedure in which each child has an equal chance of being assigned to each group within an experiment. (p. 30)

rapid eye movement (REM) sleep An active sleep state characterized by quick, jerky eye movements under closed lids and associated with dreaming in adults. (p. 70)

rational learning The ability to use prior experiences to predict what will occur in the future. (p. 205)

reactive aggression Emotionally driven, antagonistic aggression sparked by one's perception that other people's motives are hostile. (p. 583)

recessive allele The allele that is not expressed if a dominant allele is present. (p. 92)

reciprocal determinism Bandura's concept that child–environment influences operate in both directions; children are affected by aspects of their environment, but they also influence the environment. (p. 355)

reciprocated best friendship A friendship in which two children view each other as best or close friends. (p. 521)

reference In language and speech, the associating of words and meaning. (p. 232)

reflexes Innate, fixed patterns of action that occur in response to particular stimulation. (p. 189)

regulator genes Genes that control the activity of other genes. (p. 91)

rehearsal The process of repeating information multiple times to aid memory of it. (p. 151)

rejected (peer status) A category of sociometric status that refers to children or adolescents who are liked by few peers and disliked by many peers. (p. 535)

rejecting-neglecting parenting A disengaged parenting style that is low in both responsiveness and demandingness. Rejecting-neglecting parents do not set limits for or monitor their children's behaviour, are not supportive of them, and sometimes are rejecting or neglectful. They tend to be focused on their own needs rather than their children's needs. (p. 475)

relational aggression A kind of aggression that involves excluding others from the social group and attempting to do harm to other people's relationships; it includes spreading rumours about peers, withholding friendship to inflict harm, ignoring peers when angry or frustrated, and trying to get one's own way. (p. 535)

reliability The degree to which independent measurements of a given behaviour are consistent. (p. 24)

role taking Being aware of the perspective of another person, thereby better understanding that person's behaviour, thoughts, and feelings. (p. 358)

rumination A perseverative focus on one's own negative emotions and on their causes and consequences, without engaging in efforts to improve one's situation. (p. 396)

scale error The attempt by a young child to perform an action on a miniature object that is impossible due to the large discrepancy in the relative sizes of the child and the object. (p. 195)

scientific method An approach to testing beliefs that involves choosing a question, formulating a hypothesis, testing the hypothesis, and drawing a conclusion. (p. 23)

script Typical sequence of actions used to organize and interpret repeated events, such as eating at restaurants, going to doctors' appointments, and writing reports. (p. 331)

secular trends Marked changes in physical development that have occurred over generations. (p. 120)

secure attachment A pattern of attachment in which infants or young children have a high-quality, relatively unambivalent relationship with their attachment figure. In the Strange Situation, a securely attached infant, for example, may be upset when the caregiver leaves but may be happy to see the caregiver return, recovering quickly from any distress. When children are securely attached, they can use caregivers as a secure base for exploration. (p. 431)

secure base Refers to the idea that the presence of a trusted caregiver provides an infant or toddler with a sense of security that makes it possible for the child to explore the environment. (p. 428)

selective attention The process of intentionally focusing on the information that is most relevant to the current goal. (p. 151)

self A conceptual system made up of one's thoughts and attitudes about oneself. (p. 439)

self-conscious emotions Emotions such as guilt, shame, embarrassment, and pride that relate to our sense of self and our consciousness of others' reactions to us. (p. 392)

self-discipline Ability to inhibit actions, follow rules, and avoid impulsive reactions. (p. 309)

self-esteem One's overall evaluation of the worth of the self and the feelings that this evaluation engenders. (p. 459)

self-locomotion The ability to move oneself around in the environment. (p. 194)

self-socialization The idea that children play a very active role in their own socialization through their activity preferences, friendship choices, and so on. (p. 358)

self-socialization (gender development) Individuals' use of their beliefs, expectations, and preferences to guide how they perceive the world and what they choose. (p. 599)

semantic development The learning of the system for expressing meaning in a language, including word learning. (p. 217)

sensation The processing of basic information from the external world by the sensory receptors in the sense organs (eyes, ears, skin, mouth, nose) and brain. (p. 173)

sensitive period The period of time during which a developing organism is most sensitive to the effects of external factors; prenatally, the sensitive period is when the fetus is maximally sensitive to the harmful effects of teratogens. (p. 57)

sensorimotor stage The period (birth to 2 years) within Piaget's theory in which intelligence is expressed through sensory and motor abilities. (p. 135)

separation anxiety Feelings of distress that children, especially infants and toddlers, experience when they are separated, or expect to be separated, from individuals to whom they are emotionally attached. (p. 391)

sex chromosomes The chromosomes (X and Y) that determine an individual's gender. (p. 90)

sexual orientation A person's preference in regard to males or females as objects of erotic feelings. (p. 454)

sexual-minority youth Young people who experience same-sex attractions. (p. 454)

small for gestational age Babies that weigh substantially less than is normal for whatever their gestational age. (p. 76)

social comparison The process of comparing aspects of one's own psychological, behavioural, or physical functioning to that of others in order to evaluate oneself. (p. 442)

social competence The ability to achieve personal goals in social interactions while simultaneously maintaining positive relationships with others. (p. 401)

social conventional judgments Decisions that pertain to customs or regulations intended to secure social coordination and social organization. (p. 564)

social referencing The use of a parent's or other adult's facial expression or vocal cues to decide how to deal with novel, ambiguous, or possibly threatening situations. (p. 417)

social scaffolding A process in which more competent people provide a temporary framework that supports children's thinking at a higher level than children could manage on their own. (p. 159)

social skills training Training programs designed to help rejected children gain peer acceptance; they are based on the assumption that rejected children lack important knowledge and skills that promote positive interaction with peers. (p. 538)

social smiles Smiles that are directed at people. They first emerge as early as 6 to 7 weeks of age. (p. 388)

socialization The process through which children acquire the values, standards, skills, knowledge, and behaviours that are regarded as appropriate for their present and future role in their particular culture. (p. 411)

sociocultural context The physical, social, cultural, economic, and historical circumstances that make up any child's environment. (p. 18)

sociocultural theories Approaches that emphasize that other people and the surrounding culture contribute greatly to children's development. (p. 155)

sociodramatic play Activities in which children enact miniature dramas with other children or adults, such as "mother comforting baby." (p. 274)

socioeconomic status (SES) A measure of social class based on income and education. (p. 19)

sociometric status A measurement that reflects the degree to which children are liked or disliked by their peers as a group. (p. 533)

spermarche Onset of capacity for ejaculation. (p. 617)

spines Formations on the dendrites of neurons that increase the dendrites' capacity to form connections with other neurons. (p. 112)

stage theories Approaches that propose that development involves a series of discontinuous, age-related phases. (p. 15)

standard deviation (SD) Measure of the variability of scores in a distribution; in a normal distribution, 68% of scores fall within 1 SD of the mean, and 95% of scores fall within 2 SDs of the mean. (p. 306)

state Level of arousal and engagement in the environment, ranging from deep sleep to intense activity. (p.70)

stepping reflex A neonatal reflex in which an infant lifts first one leg and then the other in a coordinated pattern like walking. (p. 192)

stereopsis The process by which the visual cortex combines the differing neural signals caused by binocular disparity, resulting in the perception of depth. (p. 181)

Strange Situation A procedure developed by Mary Ainsworth to assess infants' attachment to their primary caregiver. (p. 430)

strategy–choice process Procedure for selecting among alternative ways of solving problems. (p. 326)

structured interview A research procedure in which all participants are asked to answer the same questions. (p. 25)

structured observation A method that involves presenting an identical situation to each child and recording the child's behaviour. (p. 27)

subitizing A perceptual process by which adults and children can look at a few objects and almost immediately know how many objects are present. (p. 292)

subordinate level The most specific level within a category hierarchy, such as "poodle" in the animal/dog/poodle example. (p. 266)

sudden infant death syndrome (SIDS) The sudden, unexpected death of an infant less than 1 year of age that has no identifiable cause. (p. 63)

superego In psychoanalytic theory, the third personality structure, consisting of internalized moral standards. (p. 346)

superordinate level The most general level within a category hierarchy, such as "animal" in the animal/dog/poodle example. (p. 266)

swaddling A soothing technique, used in many cultures, that involves wrapping a baby tightly in cloths or a blanket. (p. 73)

symbolic numerical magnitudes Numbers expressed orally or in writing, such as "7" or "seven." (p. 334)

symbolic representation The use of one object to stand for another. (p. 138)

symbols Systems for representing our thoughts, feelings, and knowledge and for communicating them to other people. (p. 216)

synapses Microscopic junctions between the axon terminal of one neuron and the dendritic branches or cell body of another. (p. 108)

synaptic pruning The normal developmental process through which synapses that are rarely activated are eliminated. (p. 113)

synaptogenesis The process by which neurons form synapses with other neurons, resulting in trillions of connections. (p. 112)

syntactic bootstrapping The strategy of using the grammatical structure of whole sentences to figure out meaning. (p. 242)

syntactic development The learning of the syntax of a language. (p. 218)

syntax Rules in a language that specify how words from different categories (nouns, verbs, adjectives, and so on) can be combined. (p. 218)

systematic desensitization A form of therapy based on classical conditioning, in which positive responses are gradually conditioned to stimuli that initially elicited a highly negative response. This approach is especially useful in the treatment of fears and phobias. (p. 352)

task analysis The research technique of identifying goals, relevant information in the environment, and potential processing strategies for a problem. (p. 145)

telegraphic speech Children's first sentences that are generally two-word utterances. (p. 243)

temperament Constitutionally based individual differences in emotional, motor, and attentional reactivity and self-regulation that demonstrate

consistency across situations, as well as relative stability over time. (p. 403)

temporal lobe The lobe of the cortex that is associated with memory, visual recognition, and the processing of emotion and auditory information. (p. 108)

teratogen An external agent that can cause damage or death during prenatal development. (p. 57)

test–retest reliability The degree of similarity of a child's performance on two or more occasions. (p. 24)

theory of mind An organized understanding of how mental processes such as intentions, desires, beliefs, perceptions, and emotions influence behaviour. (p. 269)

theory of mind module (TOMM) A hypothesized brain mechanism devoted to understanding other human beings. (p. 271)

theory of successful intelligence Sternberg's theory of intellect, based on the view that intelligence is the ability to achieve success in life. (p. 323)

third-variable problem The concept that a correlation between two variables may stem from both being influenced by some third variable. (p. 29)

three-stratum theory of intelligence Carroll's model that places *g* at the top of the intelligence hierarchy, eight moderately general abilities in the middle, and many specific processes at the bottom. (p. 302)

transgender A person whose gender identity does not match the person's genetic sex; includes individuals who identify either with the other sex, with both sexes, or with neither sex. (p. 599)

tuition Learning through direct teaching. (p. 603)

umbilical cord A tube containing the blood vessels connecting the fetus and placenta. (p. 48)

unconditioned response (UCR) In classical conditioning, a reflexive response that is elicited by the unconditioned stimulus. (p. 201)

unconditioned stimulus (UCS) In classical conditioning, a stimulus that evokes a reflexive response. (p. 201)

Universal Grammar A proposed set of highly abstract, unconscious rules that are common to all languages. (p. 249)

validity The degree to which a test measures what it is intended to measure. (p. 24)

variables Attributes that vary across individuals and situations, such as age, sex, and popularity. (p. 28)

vicarious reinforcement Observing someone else receive a reward or punishment. (p. 354)

victimized (peer status) With respect to peer relationships, this term refers to children who are targets of their peers' aggression and demeaning behaviour. (p. 543)

violation-of-expectancy procedure A procedure used to study infant cognition in which infants are shown an event that should evoke surprise or interest if it violates something the infant knows or assumes to be true. (p. 207)

visual acuity The sharpness of visual discrimination. (p. 174)

visually based retrieval Proceeding directly from the visual form of a word to its meaning. (p. 326)

voice onset time (VOT) The length of time between when air passes through the lips and when the vocal cords start vibrating. (p. 226)

Wechsler Intelligence Scale for Children (WISC) Widely used test designed to measure the intelligence of children 6 years and older. (p. 304)

withdrawn-rejected (peer status) A category of sociometric status that refers to rejected children who are socially withdrawn, wary, and often timid. (p. 536)

word segmentation The process of discovering where words begin and end in fluent speech. (p. 229)

working memory Memory system that involves actively attending to, gathering, maintaining, storing, and processing information. (p. 147)

zygote A fertilized egg cell. (p. 44)

References

Abela, J. R., Hankin, B. L., Sheshko, D. M., Fishman, M. B., & Stolow, D. (2012). Multi-wave prospective examination of the stress-reactivity extension of response styles theory of depression in high-risk children and early adolescents. *Journal of Abnormal Child Psychology, 40,* 277–287. doi:10.1007/s10802-011-9563-x

Abela, J. R., Stolow, D., Mineka, S., Yao, S., Zhu, X. Z., & Hankin, B. L. (2011). Cognitive vulnerability to depressive symptoms in adolescents in urban and rural Hunan, China: A multiwave longitudinal study. *Journal of Abnormal Psychology, 120,* 765–778. doi:10.1037/a0025295

Abelson, P., & Kennedy, D. (2004, June 4). The obesity epidemic. *Science, 304,* 1413.

Aboud, F. E., & Mendelson, M. J. (1996). Determinants of friendship selection and quality: Developmental perspectives. In W. M. Bukowski, A. F. Newcomb, & W. W. Hartup (Eds.), *The company they keep: Friendship in childhood and adolescence* (pp. 87–112). New York, NY: Cambridge University Press.

Aboud, F. E., & Sankar, J. (2007). Friendship and identity in a language-integrated school. *International Journal of Behavioral Development, 31,* 445–453. doi:10.1177/0165025407081469

Abramovitch, R., Corter, C., & Lando, B. (1979). Sibling interaction in the home. *Child Development, 50,* 997–1003. doi:10.2307/1129325

Achenbach, T. M., Phares, V., Howell, C. T., Rauh, V. A., & Nurcombe, B. (1990). Seven-year outcome of the Vermont Intervention Program for Low-Birthweight Infants. *Child Development, 61,* 1672–1681.

Acredolo, C., & Schmid, J. (1981). The understanding of relative speeds, distances, and durations of movement. *Developmental Psychology, 17,* 490–493. doi:10.1037/0012-1649.17.4.490

Acredolo, L. P. (1978). Development of spatial orientation in infancy. *Developmental Psychology, 14,* 224–234.

Acredolo, L. P., & Goodwyn, S. W. (1990). Sign language in babies: The significance of symbolic gesturing for understanding language development. In R. Vasta (Ed.), *Annals of child development* (Vol. 7, pp. 1–42). London, England: Jessica Kingsley.

Adam, E. K., Gunnar, M. R., & Tanaka, A. (2004). Adult attachment, parent emotion, and observed parenting behavior: Mediator and moderator models. *Child Development, 75,* 110–122.

Adams, M. J., Treiman, R., & Pressley, M. (1998). Reading, writing, and literacy. In W. Damon (Series Ed.) & I. E. Sigel & K. A. Renninger (Vol. Eds.), *Handbook of child psychology: Vol. 4. Child psychology in practice* (5th ed., pp. 275–355). Hoboken, NJ: Wiley.

Adams, R. E., Santo, J. B., & Bukowski, W. M. (2011). The presence of a best friend buffers the effects of negative experiences. *Developmental Psychology, 47,* 1786–1791. doi:10.1037/a0025401

Adams, R. J. (1995). Further exploration of human neonatal chromatic-achromatic discrimination. *Journal of Experimental Child Psychology, 60,* 344–360. doi:10.1006/jecp.1995.1045

Adamson, L. B., Bakeman, R., & Deckner, D. F. (2004). The development of symbol-infused joint engagement. *Child Development, 75,* 1171–1187. doi:10.1111/j.1467-8624.2004.00732.x

Adler, S. A., Haith, M. M., Arehart, D. M., & Lanthier, E. C. (2008). Infants' visual expectations and the processing of time. *Journal of Cognition and Development, 9,* 1–25.

Adolph, K. E. (1997). Learning in the development of infant locomotion. *Monographs of the Society for Research in Child Development, 62*(3, Serial No. 251).

Adolph, K. E. (2000). Specificity of learning: Why infants fall over a veritable cliff. *Psychological Science, 11,* 290–295. doi:10.1111/1467-9280.00258

Adolph, K. E. (2008). Learning to move. *Current Directions in Psychological Science, 17,* 213–218. doi:10.1111/j.1467-8721.2008.00577.x

Adolph, K. E., & Berger, S. E. (2006). Motor development. In W. Damon & R. M. Lerner (Series Eds.) & D. Kuhn & R. S. Siegler (Vol. Eds.), *Handbook of child psychology: Vol. 2. Cognition, perception, and language* (6th ed., pp. 161–213). Hoboken, NJ: Wiley.

Adolph, K. E., & Berger, S. E. (2011). Physical and motor development. In M. H. Bornstein & M. E. Lamb (Eds.), *Developmental science: An advanced textbook* (6th ed., pp. 314–302). New York, NY: Psychology Press/Taylor & Francis.

Adolph, K. E., Cole, W. G., Komati, M., Garciaguirre, J. S., Badaly, D., Lingeman, J. M., … Sotsky, R. B. (2012). How do you learn to walk? Thousands of steps and dozens of falls per day. *Psychological Science, 23,* 1387–1394. doi:10.1177/0956797612446346

Adolph, K. E., Eppler, M. A., & Gibson, E. J. (1993). Crawling versus walking infants' perception of affordances for locomotion over sloping surfaces. *Child Development, 64,* 1158–1174. doi:10.1111/j.1467-8624.1993.tb04193.x

Adolph, K. E., & Robinson, S. R. (2013). The road to walking: What learning to walk tells us about development. In P. D. Zelazo (Ed.), *Oxford handbook of developmental psychology: Vol. 1. Body and mind* (pp. 403–446). New York, NY: Oxford University Press.

Adolph, K. E., Vereijken, B., & Denny, M. A. (1998). Learning to crawl. *Child Development, 69,* 1299–1312.

Adolph, K. E., Vereijken, B., & Shrout, P. E. (2003). What changes in infant walking and why. *Child Development, 74,* 475–497.

Afifi, T. D., Afifi, W. A., & Coho, A. (2009). Adolescents' physiological reactions to their parents' negative disclosures about the other parent in divorced and nondivorced families. *Journal of Divorce and Remarriage, 50,* 517–540. doi:10.1080/10502550902970496

Afifi, T. D., Afifi, W. A., Morse, C. R., & Hamrick, K. (2008). Adolescents' avoidance tendencies and physiological reactions to discussions about their parents' relationship: Implications for postdivorce and nondivorced families. *Communication Monographs, 75,* 290–317. doi:10.1080/03637750802342308

Afifi, T. D., & McManus, T. (2010). Divorce disclosures and adolescents' physical and mental health and parental relationship quality. *Journal of Divorce and Remarriage, 51,* 83–107. doi:10.1080/10502550903455141

Afifi, T. D., McManus, T., Hutchinson, S., & Baker, B. (2007). Inappropriate parental divorce disclosures, the factors that prompt them, and their impact on parents' and adolescents' well-being. *Communication Monographs, 74,* 78–102. doi:10.1080/03637750701196870

Aguilar, B., Sroufe, L. A., Egeland, B., & Carlson, E. (2000). Distinguishing the early-onset/persistent and adolescence-onset antisocial behavior types: From birth to 16 years. *Development and Psychopathology, 12,* 109–132.

Ainsworth, M. D. (1967). *Infancy in Uganda: Infant care and the growth of love.* Baltimore, MD: Johns Hopkins Press.

Ainsworth, M. D. S. (1973). The development of infant-mother attachment. In B. M. Caldwell & H. N. Ricciuti (Eds.), *Review of child development research* (Vol. 3, pp. 1–94). Chicago, IL: University of Chicago Press.

Ainsworth, M. D. S., Blehar, M. C., Waters, E., & Wall, S. (1978). *Patterns of attachment: A psychological study of the strange situation.* Hillsdale, NJ: Erlbaum.

Akhtar, N., & Gernsbacher, M. A. (2008). On privileging the role of gaze in infant social cognition. *Child Development Perspectives, 2,* 59–65. doi:10.1111/j.1750-8606.2008.00044.x

Aksan, N., & Kochanska, G. (2005). Conscience in childhood: Old questions, new answers. *Developmental Psychology, 41,* 506–516. doi:10.1037/0012-1649.41.3.506

Aksan, N., Kochanska, G., & Ortmann, M. R. (2006). Mutually responsive orientation between parents and their young children: Toward methodological advances in the science of relationships. *Developmental Psychology, 42,* 833–848. doi:10.1037/0012-1649.42.5.833

Albareda-Castellot, B., Pons, F., & Sebastián-Gallés, N. (2011). The acquisition of phonetic categories in bilingual infants: New data from an anticipatory eye movement paradigm. *Developmental Science, 14,* 395–401.

Albert, D., & Steinberg, L. (2011). Age differences in strategic planning as indexed by the Tower of London. *Child Development, 82,* 1501–1517.

Alexander, G. M. (2003). An evolutionary perspective of sex-typed toy preferences: Pink, blue, and the brain. *Archives of Sexual Behavior, 32,* 7–14. doi:10.1023/A:1021833110722

Alexander, K. L., Entwisle, D. R., & Olson, L. S. (2007). Lasting consequences of the summer learning gap. *American Sociological Review, 72,* 167–180.

Alink, L. R. A., Cicchetti, D., Kim, J., & Rogosch, F. A. (2012). Longitudinal associations among child maltreatment, social functioning, and cortisol regulation. *Developmental Psychology, 48,* 224–236. doi:10.1037/a0024892

Alink, L. R. A., Mesman, J., Van Zeijl, J., Stolk, M. N., Juffer, F., Koot, H. M., ... van IJzendoorn, M. H. (2006). The early childhood aggression curve: Development of physical aggression in 10- to 50-month-old children. *Child Development, 77,* 954–966. doi:10.1111/j.1467-8624.2006.00912.x

Allen, J. P., Chango, J., Szwedo, D., Schad, M., & Marston, E. (2012). Predictors of susceptibility to peer influence regarding substance use in adolescence. *Child Development, 83,* 337–350. doi:10.1111/j.1467-8624.2011.01682.x

Allen, J. P., McElhaney, K. B., Kuperminc, G. P., & Jodl, K. M. (2004). Stability and change in attachment security across adolescence. *Child Development, 75,* 1792–1805. doi:10.1111/j.1467-8624.2004.00817.x

Allen, J. P., Porter, M. R., & McFarland, F. C. (2006). Leaders and followers in adolescent close friendships: Susceptibility to peer influence as a predictor of risky behavior, friendship instability, and depression. *Development and Psychopathology, 18,* 155–172. doi:10.1017/S0954579406060093

Allen, J. P., Porter, M. R., McFarland, F. C., Marsh, P., & McElhaney, K. B. (2005). The two faces of adolescents' success with peers: Adolescent

popularity, social adaptation, and deviant behavior. *Child Development, 76,* 747–760. doi:10.1111/j.1467-8624.2005.00875.x

Alleyne, E., & Wood, J. L. (2010). Gang involvement: Psychological and behavioral characteristics of gang members, peripheral youth, and nongang youth. *Aggressive Behavior, 36,* 423–436. doi:10.1002/ab.20360

Alonso-Alberca, N., Vergara, A. I., Fernández-Berrocal, P., Johnson, S. R., & Izard, C. E. (2012). The adaptation and validation of the Emotion Matching Task for preschool children in Spain. *International Journal of Behavioral Development, 36,* 489–494.

Als, H., Gilkerson, L., Duffy, F. H., McAnulty, G. B., Buehler, D. M., Vandenberg, K., ... Jones, K. J. (2003). A three-center, randomized, controlled trial of individualized developmental care for very low birth weight preterm infants: Medical, neurodevelopmental, parenting, and caregiving effects. *Journal of Developmental and Behavioral Pediatrics, 24,* 399–408.

Al-Sahad, B., Heifetz, M., Tamim, H., Bohr, Y., & Connolly, J. (2012). Prevalence and characteristics of teen motherhood in Canada. *Maternal and Child Health Journal, 16,* 228–234. doi:10.1007/s10995-011-0750-8

Altermatt, E. R., & Pomerantz, E. M. (2003). The development of competence-related and motivational beliefs: An investigation of similarity and influence among friends. *Journal of Educational Psychology, 95,* 111–123. doi:10.1037/0022-0663.95.1.111

Altshuler, J. L., Genevaro, J. L., Ruble, D. N., & Bornstein, M. H. (1995). Children's knowledge and use of coping strategies during hospitalization for elective surgery. *Journal of Applied Developmental Psychology, 16,* 53–76. doi:10.1016/0193-3973(95)90016-0

Alwin, D. F. (1984). Trends in parental socialization values: Detroit, 1958–1983. *American Journal of Sociology, 90,* 359–382.

Amaral, D. G., Schumann, C. M., & Nordahl, C. W. (2008). Neuroanatomy of autism. *Trends in Neurosciences, 31,* 137–145. doi:10.1016/j.tins.2007.12.005

Amato, P. R. (2001). Children of divorce in the 1990s: An update of the Amato and Keith (1991) meta-analysis. *Journal of Family Psychology, 15,* 355–370. doi:10.1037/0893-3200.15.3.355

Amato, P. R. (2010). Research on divorce: Continuing trends and new developments. *Journal of Marriage and Family, 72,* 650–666. doi:10.1111/j.1741-3737.2010.00723.x

Amato, P. R., & Gilbreth, J. G. (1999). Nonresident fathers and children's well-being: A meta-analysis. *Journal of Marriage and the Family, 61,* 557–573.

Amato, P. R., Kane, J. B., & James, S. (2011). Reconsidering the "good divorce." *Family Relations, 60,* 511–524. doi:10.1111/j.1741-3729.2011.00666.x

Amato, P. R., & Keith, B. (1991). Parental divorce and the well-being of children: A meta-analysis. *Psychological Bulletin, 110,* 26–46.

Amato, P. R., Loomis, L. S., & Booth, A. (1995). Parental divorce, marital conflict, and offspring well-being during early adulthood. *Social Forces, 73,* 895–915. doi:10.1093/sf/73.3.895

American Association of University Women. (2011). *Crossing the line: Sexual harassment at school.* Washington, DC: Author.

American Psychiatric Association. (1994). *Diagnostic and statistical manual of mental disorders* (4th ed.). Washington, DC: Author.

American Psychiatric Association. (2013). *Diagnostic and statistical manual of mental disorders* (5th ed.). Arlington, VA: American Psychiatric Publishing.

American Psychological Association. (2013). Effects of poverty, hunger and homelessness on children and youth. Retrieved from http://www.apa.org/pi/families/poverty.aspx

Ames, E. (1997). *The development of Romanian orphanage children adopted to Canada. Final report to Human Resources Development Canada.* Burnaby, BC: Simon Fraser University.

Anderson, C. A., Berkowitz, L., Donnerstein, E., Huesmann, L. R., Johnson, J. D., Linz, D., ... Wartella, E. (2003). The influence of media violence on youth. *Psychological Science in the Public Interest, 4*, 81–110. doi: 10.1111/j.1529-1006.2003.pspi_1433.x

Anderson, C. A., & Bushman, B. J. (2001). Effects of violent video games on aggressive behavior, aggressive cognition, aggressive affect, physiological arousal, and prosocial behavior: A meta-analytic review of the scientific literature. *Psychological Science, 12*, 353–359. doi:10.1111/1467-9280.00366

Anderson, D. R., Huston, A. C., Schmitt, K. L., Linebarger, D. L., & Wright, J. C. (2001). Early childhood television viewing and adolescent behavior: The recontact study. *Monographs of the Society for Research in Child Development, 66* (1, Serial No. 264), vii-147.

Anderson, M. E., Johnson, D. C., & Batal, H. A. (2005). Sudden infant death syndrome and prenatal maternal smoking: Rising attributed risk in the Back to Sleep era. *BMC Medicine, 3*, 4. Retrieved from http://www.biomedcentral.com/1741-7015/3/4

Anderson, R. C., Wilson, P. T., & Fielding, L. G. (1988). Growth in reading and how children spend their time outside of school. *Reading Research Quarterly, 23*, 285–303.

Anderson, V., Godfrey, C., Rosenfeld, J. V., & Catroppa, C. (2012). Predictors of cognitive function and recovery 10 years after traumatic brain injury in young children. *Pediatrics, 129*, e254-e261. Advance online publication. doi:10.1542/peds.2011-0311

Andre, T., Whigham, M., Hendrickson, A., & Chambers, S. (1999). Competency beliefs, positive affect, and gender stereotypes of elementary students and their parents about science versus other school subjects. *Journal of Research in Science Teaching, 36*, 719–747. doi:10.1002/(SICI)1098-2736(199908)36:6<719::AID-TEA8>3.0.CO;2-R

Angier, N. (1999). *Woman: An intimate geography.* Boston, MA: Houghton Mifflin.

Anglin, J. M. (1993). Vocabulary development: A morphological analysis. *Monographs of the Society for Research in Child Development, 58*(10, Serial No. 238).

Ansari, D. (2008). Effects of development and enculturation on number representation in the brain. *Nature Reviews Neuroscience, 9*, 278–291. doi: 10.1038/nrn2334

Anthony, J. L., & Francis, D. J. (2005). Development of phonological awareness. *Current Directions in Psychological Science, 14*, 255–259.

Aptekar, L., & Ciano-Federoff, L. M. (1999). Street children in Nairobi: Gender differences in mental health. In M. Raffaelli & R. W. Larson (Eds.), *New Directions for Child and Adolescent Development: No. 85. Homeless and working youth around the world: Exploring developmental issues* (Vol. 1999, pp. 35–46). San Francisco, CA: Jossey-Bass.

Arbeau, K. A., Coplan, R. J., & Weeks, M. (2010). Shyness, teacher-child relationships, and socio-emotional adjustment in grade 1. *International Journal of Behavioral Development, 34*, 259–269. doi:10.1177/0165025409350959

Archer, J. (1991). The influence of testosterone on human aggression. *British Journal of Psychology, 82*, 1–28. doi:10.1111/j.2044-8295.1991.tb02379.x

Archer, J. (2004). Sex differences in aggression in real-world settings: A meta-analytic review. *Review of General Psychology, 8*, 291–322. doi: 10.1037/1089-2680.8.4.291

Archer, J. (2006). Testosterone and human aggression: An evaluation of the challenge hypothesis. *Neuroscience and Biobehavioral Reviews, 30*, 319–345. doi:10.1016/j.neubiorev.2004.12.007

Archer, J., & Coyne, S. M. (2005). An integrated review of indirect, relational, and social aggression. *Personality and Social Psychology Review, 9*, 212–230. doi:10.1207/s15327957pspr0903_2

Archer, J., Graham-Kevan, N., & Davies, M. (2005). Testosterone and aggression: A reanalysis of Book, Starzyk, and Quinsey's (2001) study. *Aggression and Violent Behavior, 10*, 241–261. doi:10.1016/j.avb.2004.01.001

Archer, J., & Lloyd, B. B. (2002). *Sex and gender* (2nd ed.). New York, NY: Cambridge University Press.

Archer, J., & Macrae, M. (1991). Gender-perceptions of school subjects among 10–11 year-olds. *British Journal of Educational Psychology, 61*, 99–103. doi:10.1111/j.2044-8279.1991.tb00965.x

Arduini, D., Rizzo, G., & Romanini, C. (1995). Fetal behavioral states and behavioral transitions in normal and compromised fetuses. In J.-P. Lecanuet, W. P. Fifer, N. A. Krasnegor, & W. P. Smotherman (Eds.), *Fetal development: A psychobiological perspective* (pp. 83–99). Hillsdale, NJ: Erlbaum.

Arim, R. G., Dahinten, V. S., Marshall, S. K., & Shapka, J. D. (2011). An examination of the reciprocal relations between adolescents' aggressive behaviors and their perceptions of parental nurturance. *Journal of Youth and Adolescence, 40*, 207–220.

Aristotle. (1954). *The Nicomachean ethics* (D. Ross, Trans.). London, England: Oxford University Press.

Arim, R. G., Dahinten, V. S., Marshall, S. K., & Shapka, J. D. (2011). An examination of the reciprocal relationships between adolescents' aggressive behaviors and their perceptions of parental nurturance. *Journal of Youth and Adolescence, 40*, 207–220. doi:10.1007/s10964-009-9493-x

Armenta, B. E., Knight, G. P., Carlo, G., & Jacobson, R. P. (2011). The relation between ethnic group attachment and prosocial tendencies: The mediating role of cultural values. *European Journal of Social Psychology, 41*, 107–115. doi:10.1002/ejsp.742

Arndorfer, C., & Stormshak, E. (2008). Same-sex versus other-sex best friendship in early adolescence: Longitudinal predictors of antisocial behavior throughout adolescence. *Journal of Youth and Adolescence, 37*, 1059–1070. doi:10.1007/s10964-008-9311-x

Arneson, J. J., Sackett, P. R., & Beatty, A. S. (2011). Ability-performance relationships in education and employment settings: Critical tests of the more-is-better and the good-enough hypotheses. *Psychological Science, 22*, 1336–1342. doi:10.1177/0956797611417004

Arnett, J. J. (1999). Adolescent storm and stress, reconsidered. *American Psychologist, 54*, 317–326.

Aronson, E. (2000). *Nobody left to hate: Teaching compassion after Columbine.* New York, NY: Freeman.

Aronson, E., Blaney, N., Stephin, C., Sikes, J., & Snapp, M. (1978). *The jigsaw classroom.* Beverly Hills, CA: Sage.

Arseneault, L., Moffitt, T. E., Caspi, A., Taylor, A., Rijsdijk, F. V., Jaffee, S. R., ... Measelle, J. R. (2003). Strong genetic effects on cross-situational antisocial behaviour among 5-year-old children according to mothers, teachers, examiner-observers, and twins' self-reports. *Journal of Child Psychology and Psychiatry, 44*, 832–848. doi:10.1111/1469-7610.00168

Arsenio, W. F., Adams, E., & Gold, J. (2009). Social information processing, moral reasoning, and emotion attributions: Relations with adolescents' reactive and proactive aggression. *Child Development, 80*, 1739–1755. doi: 10.1111/j.1467-8624.2009.01365.x

Asbury, K., Dunn, J. F., Pike, A., & Plomin, R. (2003). Nonshared environmental influences on individual differences in early behavioral development: A monozygotic twin differences study. *Child Development, 74,* 933–943. doi:10.1111/1467-8624.00577

Asendorpf, J. B. (1990). Development of inhibition during childhood: Evidence for situational specificity and a two-factor model. *Developmental Psychology, 26,* 721–730. doi:10.1037/0012-1649.26.5.721

Asendorpf, J. B., Warkentin, V., & Baudonnière, P.-M. (1996). Self-awareness and other-awareness: II. Mirror self-recognition, social contingency awareness, and synchronic imitation. *Developmental Psychology, 32,* 313–321. doi:10.1037/0012-1649.32.2.313

Ashcraft, M. H. (1982). The development of mental arithmetic: A chronometric approach. *Developmental Review, 2,* 213–236. doi: 10.1016/0273-2297(82)90012-0

Ashcraft, M. H., & Krause, J. A. (2007). Working memory, math performance, and math anxiety. *Psychonomic Bulletin and Review, 14,* 243–248.

Ashcraft, M. H., & Ridley, K. S. (2005). Math anxiety and its cognitive consequences. In J. I. D. Campbell (Ed.), *Handbook of mathematical cognition* (pp. 315–327). New York, NY: Psychology Press.

Asher, S. R., & Dodge, K. A. (1986). Identifying children who are rejected by their peers. *Developmental Psychology, 22,* 444–449. doi: 10.1037/0012-1649.22.4.444

Asher, S. R., & Paquette, J. A. (2003). Loneliness and peer relations in childhood. *Current Directions in Psychological Science, 12,* 75–78. doi: 10.1111/1467-8721.01233

Ashman, S. B., Dawson, G., Panagiotides, H., Yamada, E., & Wilkinson, C. W. (2002). Stress hormone levels of children of depressed mothers. *Development and Psychopathology, 14,* 333–349.

Aslin, R. (1981). Development of smooth pursuit in human infants. In D. F. Fisher, R. A. Monty, & J. W. Senders (Eds.), *Eye movements: Cognition and visual perception* (pp. 31–51). Hillsdale, NJ: Erlbaum.

Aslin, R. N. (2012). Questioning the questions that have been asked about the infant brain using near-infrared spectroscopy. *Cognitive Neuropsychology, 29,* 7–33. doi:10.1080/02643294.2012.654773

Aslin, R. N., Jusczyk, P. W., & Pisoni, D. B. (1998). Speech and auditory processing during infancy: Constraints on and precursors to language. In W. Damon (Series Ed.) & D. Kuhn & R. S. Siegler (Vol. Eds.), *Handbook of child psychology: Vol. 2. Cognition, perception, and language* (5th ed., pp. 147–198). Hoboken, NJ: Wiley.

Aslin, R. N., Saffran, J. R., & Newport, E. L. (1998). Computation of conditional probability statistics by 8-month-old infants. *Psychological Science, 9,* 321–324. doi:10.1111/1467-9280.00063

Ateah, C. A., & Parkin, C. M. (2002). Childhood experiences with, and current attitudes toward, corporal punishment. *Canadian Journal of Community Mental Health, 21*(1), 35–46.

Atran, S. (1990). *Cognitive foundations of natural history: Towards an anthropology of science.* Cambridge, England: Cambridge University Press.

Atran, S. (2002). Modular and cultural factors in biological understanding: An experimental approach to the cognitive basis of science. In P. Carruthers, S. P. Stich, & M. Siegal (Eds.), *The cognitive basis of science* (pp. 41–72). New York, NY: Cambridge University Press.

Attili, G., Vermigli, P., & Schneider, B. H. (1997). Peer acceptance and friendship patterns among Italian schoolchildren within a cross-cultural perspective. *International Journal of Behavioral Development, 21,* 277–288. doi:10.1080/016502597384866

Auerbach, R. P., Bigda-Peyton, J. S., Eberhart, N. K., Webb, C. A., & Ho, M.-H. R. (2011). Conceptualizing the prospective relationship between social support, stress, and depressive symptoms among adolescents. *Journal of Abnormal Child Psychology, 39,* 475–487.

Augusta, D., & Hakuta, K. (1998). *Educating language-minority children.* Washington, DC: National Academy Press.

Awong, T., Grusec, J. E., & Sorenson, A. (2008). Respect-based control and anger as determinants of children's socio-emotional development. *Social Development, 17,* 941–959. doi:10.1111/j.1467-9507.2008.00460.x

Ayduk, O., Mendoza-Denton, R., Mischel, W., Downey, G., Peake, P. K., & Rodriguez, M. (2000). Regulating the interpersonal self: Strategic self-regulation for coping with rejection sensitivity. *Journal of Personality and Social Psychology, 79,* 776–792.

Azmitia, M., & Montgomery, R. (1993). Friendship, transactive dialogues, and the development of scientific reasoning. *Social Development, 2,* 202–221. doi:10.1111/j.1467-9507.1993.tb00014.x

Bachman, H. J., Coley, R. L., & Carrano, J. (2011). Maternal relationship instability influences on children's emotional and behavioral functioning in low-income families. *Journal of Abnormal Child Psychology, 39,* 1149–1161. doi:10.1007/s10802-011-9535-1

Bachman, H. J., Coley, R. L., & Carrano, J. (2012). Low-income mothers' patterns of partnership instability and adolescents' socioemotional well-being. *Journal of Family Psychology, 26,* 263–273. doi:10.1037/a0027427

Backscheider, A. G., Shatz, M., & Gelman, S. A. (1993). Preschoolers' ability to distinguish living kinds as a function of regrowth. *Child Development, 64,* 1242–1257. doi:10.1111/j.1467-8624.1993.tb04198.x

Bagwell, C. L., Newcomb, A. F., & Bukowski, W. M. (1998). Preadolescent friendship and peer rejection as predictors of adult adjustment. *Child Development, 69,* 140–153. doi:10.1111/j.1467-8624.1998.tb06139.x

Baham, M. E., Weimer, A. A., Braver, S. L., & Fabricius, W. V. (2008). Sibling relationships in blended families. In J. Pryor (Ed.), *The international handbook of stepfamilies: Policy and practice in legal, research, and clinical environments* (pp. 175–207). Hoboken, NJ: Wiley.

Bahrick, H. F. (1987). Functional and cognitive memory theory: An overview of some key issues. In D. S. Gorfein & R. R. Hoffman (Eds.), *Memory and learning: The Ebbinghaus Centennial Conference* (pp. 387–395). Hillsdale, NJ: Erlbaum.

Bailey, D. H., Hoard, M. K., Nugent, L., & Geary, D. C. (2012). Competence with fractions predicts gains in mathematics achievement. *Journal of Experimental Child Psychology, 113,* 447–455. doi:10.1016/j.jecp.2012.06.004

Bailey, H. N., Moran, G., Pederson, D. R., & Bento, S. (2007). Understanding the transmission of attachment using variable- and relationship-centered approaches. *Development and Psychopathology, 19,* 313–343.

Bailey, J. M., Bobrow, D., Wolfe, M., & Mikach, S. (1995). Sexual orientation of adult sons of gay fathers. *Developmental Psychology, 31,* 124–129. doi:10.1037/0012-1649.31.1.124

Bailey, J. M., & Pillard, R. C. (1991). A genetic study of male sexual orientation. *Archives of General Psychiatry, 48,* 1089–1096. doi:10.1001/archpsyc.1991.01810360053008

Bailey, J. M., Pillard, R. C., Neale, M. C., & Agyei, Y. (1993). Heritable factors influence sexual orientation in women. *Archives of General Psychiatry, 50,* 217–223. doi:10.1001/archpsyc.1993.01820150067007

Baillargeon, R. (1987a). Object permanence in 3 1/2- and 4 1/2-month-old infants. *Developmental Psychology, 23,* 655–664.

Baillargeon, R. (1987b). Young infants' reasoning about the physical and spatial properties of a hidden object. *Cognitive Development, 2,* 179–200. doi:10.1016/S0885-2014(87)90043-8

Baillargeon, R. (1993). The object concept revisited: New directions in the investigation of infants' physical knowledge. In C. E. Granrud (Ed.), *Visual perception and cognition in infancy* (Vol. 23, pp. 265–315). Hillsdale, NJ: Erlbaum.

Baillargeon, R. (1994). How do infants learn about the physical world? *Current Directions in Psychological Science, 3,* 133–140.

Baillargeon, R. (1998). Infants' understanding of the physical world. In M. Sabourin, F. Craik, & M. Robert (Eds.), *Advances in psychological science: Vol. 2. Biological and cognitive aspects* (pp. 503–529). Hove, England: Psychology Press.

Baillargeon, R. (2004). Infants' reasoning about hidden objects: Evidence for event-general and event-specific expectations. *Developmental Science, 7,* 391–414. doi:10.1111/j.1467-7687.2004.00357.x

Baillargeon, R., Kotovsky, L., & Needham, A. (1995). The acquisition of physical knowledge in infancy. In D. Sperber, D. Premack, & A. J. Premack (Eds.), *Causal cognition: A multidisciplinary debate* (pp. 79–116). Oxford, England: Oxford University Press.

Baillargeon, R., Needham, A., & Devos, J. (1992). The development of young infants' intuitions about support. *Early Development and Parenting, 1,* 69–78. doi:10.1002/edp.2430010203

Baillargeon, R., Spelke, E. S., & Wasserman, S. (1985). Object permanence in five-month-old infants. *Cognition, 20,* 191–208. doi:10.1016/0010-0277(85)90008-3

Baker, J. K., Fenning, R. M., & Crnic, K. A. (2011). Emotion socialization by mothers and fathers: Coherence among behaviors and associations with parent attitudes and children's social competence. *Social Development, 20,* 412–430. doi:10.1111/j.1467-9507.2010.00585.x

Baker, S. T., Friedman, O., & Leslie, A. M. (2010). The opposites task: Using general rules to test cognitive flexibility in preschoolers. *Journal of Cognition and Development, 11,* 240–254. doi:10.1080/15248371003699944

Bakermans-Kranenburg, M. J., Dobrova-Krol, N., & van IJzendoorn, M. (2012). Impact of institutional care on attachment disorganization and insecurity of Ukrainian preschoolers: Protective effect of the long variant of the serotonin transporter gene (5HTT). *International Journal of Behavioral Development, 36,* 11–18. doi:10.1177/0165025411406858

Bakermans-Kranenburg, M. J., & van IJzendoorn, M. H. (2006). Gene-environment interaction of the dopamine D4 receptor (DRD4) and observed maternal insensitivity predicting externalizing behavior in preschoolers. *Developmental Psychobiology, 48,* 406–409. doi:10.1002/dev.20152

Bakermans-Kranenburg, M. J., & van IJzendoorn, M. H. (2007). Research review: Genetic vulnerability or differential susceptibility in child development: The case of attachment. *Journal of Child Psychology and Psychiatry, 48,* 1160–1173. doi:10.1111/j.1469-7610.2007.01801.x

Bakermans-Kranenburg, M. J., & van IJzendoorn, M. H. (2011). Differential susceptibility to rearing environment depending on dopamine-related genes: New evidence and a meta-analysis. *Development and Psychopathology, 23,* 39–52. doi:10.1017/S0954579410000635

Bakermans-Kranenburg, M. J., van IJzendoorn, M. H., & Juffer, F. (2003). Less is more: Meta-analyses of sensitivity and attachment interventions in early childhood. *Psychological Bulletin, 129,* 195–215. doi:10.1037/0033-2909.129.2.195

Baldwin, D. A. (1991). Infants' contribution to the achievement of joint reference. *Child Development, 62,* 874–890. doi:10.1111/j.1467-8624.1991.tb01577.x

Baldwin, D. A. (1993). Early referential understanding: Infants' ability to recognize referential acts for what they are. *Developmental Psychology, 29,* 832–843. doi:10.1037/0012-1649.29.5.832

Ball, J., & Daly, K. (2012). *Father involvement in Canada.* Vancouver, BC: UBC Press.

Ball, W., & Tronick, E. (1971, February 26). Infant responses to impending collision: Optical and real. *Science, 171,* 818–820.

Bámaca, M. Y., Umaña-Taylor, A. J., Shin, N., & Alfaro, E. C. (2005). Latino adolescents' perception of parenting behaviors and self-esteem: Examining the role of neighborhood risk. *Family Relations, 54,* 621–632. doi:10.1111/j.1741-3729.2005.00346.x

Bamford, C., & Lagattuta, K. H. (2012). Looking on the bright side: Children's knowledge about the benefits of positive versus negative thinking. *Child Development, 83,* 667–682. doi:10.1111/j.1467-8624.2011.01706.x

Bandura, A. (1965). Influence of models' reinforcement contingencies on the acquisition of imitative responses. *Journal of Personality and Social Psychology, 1,* 589–595. doi:10.1037/h0022070

Bandura, A. (1977). *Social learning theory.* Englewood Cliffs, NJ: Prentice Hall.

Bandura, A. (1986). *Social foundations of thought and action: A social cognitive theory.* Englewood Cliffs, NJ: Prentice-Hall.

Bandura, A. (1997). *Self-efficacy: The exercise of control.* New York, NY: Freeman.

Bandura, A., Caprara, G. V., Barbaranelli, C., Gerbino, M., & Pastorelli, C. (2003). Role of affective self-regulatory efficacy in diverse spheres of psychosocial functioning. *Child Development, 74,* 769–782. doi:10.1111/1467-8624.00567

Bandura, A., Ross, D., & Ross, S. A. (1963). Imitation of film-mediated aggressive models. *Journal of Abnormal and Social Psychology, 66,* 3–11. doi:10.1037/h0048687

Banerjee, M. (1997). Hidden emotions: Preschoolers' knowledge of appearance-reality and emotion display rules. *Social Cognition, 15,* 107–132. doi:10.1521/soco.1997.15.2.107

Banerjee, R., & Lintern, V. (2000). Boys will be boys: The effect of social evaluation concerns on gender-typing. *Social Development, 9,* 397–408.

Banich, M. T. (1997). *Neuropsychology: The neural bases of mental function.* Boston, MA: Houghton Mifflin.

Banich, M. T., Levine, S. C., Kim, H., & Huttenlocher, P. (1990). The effects of developmental factors on IQ in hemiplegic children. *Neuropsychologia, 28,* 35–47. doi:10.1016/0028-3932(90)90084-2

Bank, L., Patterson, G. R., & Reid, J. B. (1996). Negative sibling interaction patterns as predictors of later adjustment problems in adolescent and young adult males. In G. H. Brody (Ed.), *Advances in applied developmental psychology: Vol. 10. Sibling relationships: Their causes and consequences* (pp. 197–229). Westport, CT: Ablex.

Banks, M. S., & Dannemiller, J. L. (1987). Infant visual psychophysics. In P. Salapatek & L. B. Cohen (Eds.), *Handbook of infant perception* (Vol. 1, pp. 115–184). Orlando, FL: Academic Press.

Banks, M. S., & Shannon, E. (1993). Spatial and chromatic visual efficiency in human neonates. In C. Granrud (Ed.), *Visual perception and cognition in infancy* (pp. 1–46). Hillsdale, NJ: Erlbaum.

Bar-Haim, Y., Ziv, T., Lamy, D., & Hodes, R. M. (2006). Nature and nurture in own-race face processing. *Psychological Science, 17,* 159–163. doi:10.1111/j.1467-9280.2006.01679.x

Barbaresi, W. J., Katusic, S. K., Colligan, R. C., Weaver, A. L., & Jacobsen, S. J. (2007a). Long-term school outcomes for children with attention-deficit/hyperactivity disorder: A population-based perspective. *Journal of Developmental and Behavioral Pediatrics, 28,* 265–273. doi: 10.1097/DBP.0b013e31811ff87d

Barbaresi, W. J., Katusic, S. K., Colligan, R. C., Weaver, A. L., & Jacobsen, S. J. (2007b). Modifiers of long-term school outcomes for children with attention-deficit/hyperactivity disorder: Does treatment with stimulant medication make a difference? Results from a population-based study. *Journal of Developmental and Behavioral Pediatrics, 28,* 274–287. doi: 10.1097/DBP.0b013e3180cabc28

Barber, B. K. (1996). Parental psychological control: Revisiting a neglected construct. *Child Development, 67,* 3296–3319. doi:10.1111/j.1467-8624.1996.tb01915.x

Barchia, K., & Bussey, K. (2011). Individual and collective social cognitive influences on peer aggression: Exploring the contribution of aggression efficacy, moral disengagement, and collective efficacy. *Aggressive Behavior, 37,* 107–120. doi:10.1002/ab.20375

Barden, R. C., Zelko, F. A., Duncan, S. W., & Masters, J. C. (1980). Children's consensual knowledge about the experiential determinants of emotion. *Journal of Personality and Social Psychology, 39,* 968–976.

Bardi, L., Regolin, L., & Simion, F. (2011). Biological motion preference in humans at birth: Role of dynamic and configural properties. *Developmental Science, 14,* 353–359. doi:10.1111/j.1467-7687.2010.00985.x

Barker, E. D., Boivin, M., Brendgen, M., Fontaine, N., Arseneault, L., Vitaro, F., … Tremblay, R. E. (2008). Predictive validity and early predictors of peer-victimization trajectories in preschool. *Archives of General Psychiatry, 65,* 1185–1192. doi:10.1001/archpsyc.65.10.1185

Barkley, R. A. (1997). Behavioral inhibition, sustained attention, and executive functions: Constructing a unifying theory of ADHD. *Psychological Bulletin, 121,* 65–94. doi:10.1037/0033-2909.121.1.65

Barnes, J., Leach, P., Malmberg, L. E., Stein, A., Sylva, K., & The FCCC Team. (2009). Experiences of childcare in England and socioemotional development at 36 months. *Early Child Development and Care, 180,* 1215–1229. doi:10.1080/03004430902943959

Barnes, J. C., Beaver, K. M., & Miller, J. M. (2010). Estimating the effect of gang membership on nonviolent and violent delinquency: A counterfactual analysis. *Aggressive Behavior, 36,* 437–451. doi:10.1002/ab.20359

Baron, A. S., & Banaji, M. R. (2006). The development of implicit attitudes: Evidence of race evaluations from ages 6 and 10 and adulthood. *Psychological Science, 17,* 53–58. doi:10.1111/j.1467-9280.2005.01664.x

Baron-Cohen, S. (1991). The development of a theory of mind in autism: Deviance and delay? *Psychiatric Clinics of North America, 14,* 33–51.

Baron-Cohen, S. (1993). From attention-goal psychology to belief-desire psychology: The development of a theory of mind, and its dysfunction. In S. Baron-Cohen, H. Tager-Flusberg, & D. J. Cohen (Eds.), *Understanding other minds: Perspectives from autism* (pp. 59–82). Oxford, England: Oxford University Press.

Baron-Cohen, S. (1995). *Mindblindness: An essay on autism and theory of mind.* Cambridge, MA: MIT Press.

Barr, C. S. (2012). Temperament in animals. In M. R. Zentner & R. L. Shiner (Eds.), *Handbook of temperament* (pp. 251–272). New York, NY: Guilford Press.

Barr, R., Dowden, A., & Hayne, H. (1996). Developmental changes in deferred imitation by 6- to 24-month-old infants. *Infant Behavior and Development, 19,* 159–170. doi:10.1016/S0163-6383(96)90015-6

Barr, R., & Hayne, H. (1999). Developmental changes in imitation from television during infancy. *Child Development, 70,* 1067–1081. doi: 10.1111/1467-8624.00079

Barr, R. G. (1998). Colic and crying syndromes in infants. In J. G. Warhol (Ed.), *New perspectives in early emotional development* (pp. 147–157). Calverton, NY: Johnson & Johnson Pediatric Institute, Ltd.

Barr, R. G., Quek, V. S. H., Cousineau, D., Oberlander, T. F., Brian, J. A., & Young, S. N. (1994). Effects of intra-oral sucrose on crying, mouthing and hand-mouth contact in newborn and six-week-old infants. *Developmental Medicine and Child Neurology, 36,* 608–618. doi:10.1111/j.1469-8749.1994.tb11898.x

Barrett, K. C., Zahn-Waxler, C., & Cole, P. M. (1993). Avoiders vs. amenders: Implications for the investigation of guilt and shame during toddlerhood? *Cognition and Emotion, 7,* 481–505.

Barry, R. A., & Kochanska, G. (2010). A longitudinal investigation of the affective environment in families with young children: From infancy to early school age. *Emotion, 10,* 237–249.

Bartlett, N. H., Vasey, P. L., & Bukowski, W. M. (2000). Is gender identity disorder in children a mental disorder? *Sex Roles, 43,* 753–785. doi: 10.1023/A:1011004431889

Bartrip, J., Morton, J., & de Schonen, S. (2001). Responses to mother's face in 3-week to 5-month-old infants. *British Journal of Developmental Psychology, 19,* 219–232. doi:10.1348/026151001166047

Bartsch, K., & Wellman, H. M. (1995). *Children talk about the mind.* New York, NY: Oxford University Press.

Bascoe, S. M., Davies, P. T., & Cummings, E. M. (2012). Beyond warmth and conflict: The developmental utility of a boundary conceptualization of sibling relationship processes. *Child Development, 83,* 2121–2138. doi: 10.1111/j.1467-8624.2012.01817.x

Bassen, C. R., & Lamb, M. E. (2006). Gender differences in adolescents' self-concepts of assertion and affiliation. *European Journal of Developmental Psychology, 3,* 71–94.

Bates, E. (1990). Language about me and you: Pronominal reference and the emerging concept of self. In D. Cicchetti & M. Beeghly (Eds.), *The self in transition: Infancy to childhood* (pp. 165–182). Chicago, IL: University of Chicago Press.

Bates, J. E., Bayles, K., Bennett, D. S., Ridge, B., & Brown, M. M. (1991). Origins of externalizing behavior problems at eight years of age. In D. J. Pepler & K. H. Rubin (Eds.), *The development and treatment of childhood aggression* (pp. 93–120). Hillsdale, NJ: Erlbaum.

Bates, J. E., Marvinney, D., Kelly, T., Dodge, K. A., Bennett, D. S., & Pettit, G. S. (1994). Child care history and kindergarten adjustment. *Developmental Psychology, 30,* 690–700. doi:10.1037/0012-1649.30.5.690

Bates, J. E., Schermerhorn, A. C., & Petersen, I. T. (2012). Temperament and parenting in developmental perspective. In M. R. Zentner & R. L. Shiner (Eds.), *Handbook of temperament* (pp. 425–441). New York, NY: Guilford Press.

Bates, L., Luster, T., & Vandenbelt, M. (2003). Factors related to social competence in elementary school among children of adolescent mothers. *Social Development, 12,* 107–124. doi:10.1111/1467-9507.00224

Bauer, P. J. (1995). Recalling past events: From infancy to early childhood. In R. Vasta (Ed.), *Annals of child development* (Vol. 11, pp. 25–71). London, England: Jessica Kingsley.

Bauer, P. J. (2002). Long-term recall memory: Behavioral and neurodevelopmental changes in the first 2 years of life. *Current Directions in Psychological Science, 11,* 137–141. doi:10.1111/1467-8721.00186

Bauer, P. J. (2007). *Remembering the times of our lives: Memory in infancy and beyond.* Mahwah, NJ: Erlbaum.

Bauer, P. J., Wenner, J. A., & Kroupina, M. G. (2002). Making the past present: Later verbal accessibility of early memories. *Journal of Cognition and Development, 3,* 21–47. doi:10.1207/S15327647JCD0301_3

Bauminger, N., Finzi-Dottan, R., Chason, S., & Har-Even, D. (2008). Intimacy in adolescent friendship: The roles of attachment, coherence, and self-disclosure. *Journal of Social and Personal Relationships, 25,* 409–428. doi:10.1177/0265407508090866

Baumrind, D. (1973). The development of instrumental competence through socialization. In A. D. Pick (Ed.), *Minnesota Symposia on Child Psychology* (Vol. 7, pp. 3–46). Minneapolis: University of Minnesota Press.

Baumrind, D. (1991a). The influence of parenting style on adolescent competence and substance use. *Journal of Early Adolescence, 11,* 56–95. doi:10.1177/0272431691111004

Baumrind, D. (1991b). Parenting styles and adolescent development. In R. M. Lerner, A. C. Petersen, & J. Brooks-Gunn (Eds.), *Encyclopedia of adolescence* (pp. 746–758). New York, NY: Garland.

Bauserman, R. (2002). Child adjustment in joint-custody versus sole-custody arrangements: A meta-analytic review. *Journal of Family Psychology, 16,* 91–102. doi:10.1037/0893-3200.16.1.91

Bavelier, D., Dye, M. W., & Hauser, P. C. (2006). Do deaf individuals see better? *Trends in Cognitive Sciences, 10,* 512–518. doi:10.1016/j.tics.2006.09.006

Bavelier, D., & Neville, H. J. (2002). Cross-modal plasticity: Where and how? *Nature Reviews Neuroscience, 3,* 443–452. doi:10.1038/nrn848

BBM Canada. (2009). *TV meter databook 2008–2009.* Toronto, ON: Author.

Beach, S. R. H., Lei, M. K., Brody, G. H., Simons, R. L., Cutrona, C., & Philibert, R. A. (2012). Genetic moderation of contextual effects on negative arousal and parenting in African-American parents. *Journal of Family Psychology, 26,* 46–55. doi:10.1037/a0026236

Beardsall, L., & Dunn, J. (1992). Adversities in childhood: Siblings' experiences, and their relations to self-esteem. *Journal of Child Psychology and Psychiatry, 33,* 349–359.

Beauchaine, T. (2001). Vagal tone, development, and Gray's motivational theory: Toward an integrated model of autonomic nervous system functioning in psychopathology. *Development and Psychopathology, 13,* 183–214.

Beck, A. T. (1979). Cognitive therapy of depression. In P. J. Clayton & J. E. Barrett (Eds.), *Treatment of depression: Old controversies and new approaches* (pp. 265–290). New York, NY: Raven Press.

Beck, A. T. (1983). Cognitive therapy of depression: New perspectives. In P. J. Clayton & J. E. Barrett (Eds.), *Treatment of depression: Old controversies and new approaches* (pp. 265–290). New York: Raven Press.

Becker-Stoll, F., Delius, A., & Scheitenberger, S. (2001). Adolescents' nonverbal emotional expressions during negotiation of a disagreement with their mothers: An attachment approach. *International Journal of Behavioral Development, 25,* 344–353.

Beckett, C., Maughan, B., Rutter, M., Castle, J., Colvert, E., Groothues, C., ... Sonuga-Barke, E. J. (2006). Do the effects of early severe deprivation on cognition persist into early adolescence? Findings from the English and Romanian Adoptees study. *Child Development, 77,* 696–711. doi:10.1111/j.1467-8624.2006.00898.x

Bedard, A.-C., Nichols, S., Barbosa, J. A., Schachar, R., Logan, G. D., & Tannock, R. (2002). The development of selective inhibitory control across the life span. *Developmental Neuropsychology, 21,* 93–111. doi:10.1207/S15326942DN2101_5

Bedny, M., Pascual-Leone, A., Dodell-Feder, D., Fedorenko, E., & Saxe, R. (2011). Language processing in the occipital cortex of congenitally blind adults. *Proceedings of the National Academy of Sciences of the United States of America.* Advance online publication. doi:10.1073/pnas.1014818108

Behl-Chadha, G. (1996). Basic-level and superordinate-like categorical representations in early infancy. *Cognition, 60,* 105–141.

Behne, T., Liszkowski, U., Carpenter, M., & Tomasello, M. (2012). Twelve-month-olds' comprehension and production of pointing. *British Journal of Developmental Psychology, 30,* 359–375. doi:10.1111/j.2044-835X.2011.02043.x

Behnke, A. O., Plunkett, S. W., Sands, T., & Bámaca-Colbert, M. Y. (2011). The relationship between Latino adolescents' perceptions of discrimination, neighborhood risk, and parenting on self-esteem and depressive symptoms. *Journal of Cross-Cultural Psychology, 42,* 1179–1197. doi:10.1177/0022022110383424

Behrend, D. A., Rosengren, K. S., & Perlmutter, M. (1992). The relation between private speech and parental interactive style. In R. M. Diaz & L. E. Berk (Eds.), *Private speech: From social interaction to self-regulation* (pp. 85–100). Hillsdale, NJ: Erlbaum.

Behrens, K. Y., Hesse, E., & Main, M. (2007). Mothers' attachment status as determined by the Adult Attachment Interview predicts their 6-year-olds' reunion responses: A study conducted in Japan. *Developmental Psychology, 43,* 1553–1567.

Beijersbergen, M. D., Juffer, F., Bakermans-Kranenburg, M. J., & van IJzendoorn, M. H. (2012). Remaining or becoming secure: Parental sensitive support predicts attachment continuity from infancy to adolescence in a longitudinal adoption study. *Developmental Psychology, 48,* 1277–1282. doi:10.1037/a0027442

Beilock, S. L., & Decaro, M. S. (2007). From poor performance to success under stress: Working memory, strategy selection, and mathematical problem solving under pressure. *Journal of Experimental Psychology: Learning, Memory, and Cognition, 33,* 983–998. doi:10.1037/0278-7393.33.6.983

Beilock, S. L., Gunderson, E. A., Ramirez, G., & Levine, S. C. (2010). Female teachers' math anxiety affects girls' math achievement. *Proceedings of the National Academy of Sciences of the United States of America, 107,* 1860–1863.

Bell, N. J., & Carver, W. (1980). A reevaluation of gender label effects: Expectant mothers' responses to infants. *Child Development, 51,* 925–927. doi:10.2307/1129489

Belsky, J. (1986). Infant day care: A cause for concern? *Zero to Three, 7*(1), 1–7.

Belsky, J. (1993). Etiology of child maltreatment: A developmental-ecological analysis. *Psychological Bulletin, 114,* 413–434. doi:10.1037/0033-2909.114.3.413

Belsky, J., Bakermans-Kranenburg, M. J., & van IJzendoorn, M. H. (2007). For better and for worse: Differential susceptibility to environmental influences. *Current Directions in Psychological Science, 16,* 300–304. doi:10.1111/j.1467-8721.2007.00525.x

Belsky, J., & Fearon, R. M. P. (2002). Early attachment security, subsequent maternal sensitivity, and later child development: Does continuity in development depend upon continuity of caregiving? *Attachment and Human Development, 4,* 361–387. doi:10.1080/14616730210167267

Belsky, J., & Pluess, M. (2009). Beyond diathesis stress: Differential susceptibility to environmental influences. *Psychological Bulletin, 135,* 885–908. doi:10.1037/a0017376

Belsky, J., & Pluess, M. (2012). Differential susceptibility to long-term effects of quality of child care on externalizing behavior in adolescence? *International Journal of Behavioral Development, 36,* 2–10. doi:10.1177/0165025411406855

Belsky, J., & Pluess, M. (2013). Genetic moderation of early child-care effects on social functioning across childhood: A developmental analysis. *Child Development, 84,* 1209–1225. doi:10.1111/cdev.12058

Belsky, J., Rosenberger, K., & Crnic, K. (1995). Maternal personality, marital quality, social support and infant temperament: Their significance for infant–mother attachment in human families. In C. R. Pryce, R. D. Martin, & D. Skuse (Eds.), *Motherhood in human and nonhuman primates: Biosocial determinants* (pp. 115–124). Basel, Switzerland: Karger.

Belsky, J., Schlomer, G. L., & Ellis, B. J. (2012). Beyond cumulative risk: Distinguishing harshness and unpredictability as determinants of parenting and early life history strategy. *Developmental Psychology, 48,* 662–673. doi:10.1037/a0024454

Belsky, J., Vandell, D. L., Burchinal, M., Clarke-Stewart, K. A., McCartney, K., Owen, M. T., & The NICHD Early Child Care Research Network. (2007). Are there long-term effects of early child care? *Child Development, 78,* 681–701.

Bem, S. L. (1981). Gender schema theory: A cognitive account of sex typing. *Psychological Review, 88,* 354–364. doi:10.1037/0033-295X.88.4.354

Bem, S. L. (1993). *The lenses of gender: Transforming the debate on sexual inequality.* New Haven, CT: Yale University Press.

Benenson, J. F., & Christakos, A. (2003). The greater fragility of females' versus males' closest same-sex friendships. *Child Development, 74,* 1123–1129. doi:10.1111/1467-8624.00596

Benenson, J. F., Maiese, R., Dolenszky, E., Dolensky, N., Sinclair, N., & Simpson, A. (2002). Group size regulates self–assertive versus self–deprecating responses to interpersonal competition. *Child Development, 73,* 1818–1829. doi:10.1111/1467-8624.00508

Benenson, J. F., Morganstein, T., & Roy, R. (1998). Sex differences in children's investment in peers. *Human Nature, 9,* 369–390. doi:10.1007/s12110-998-1015-0

Benner, A. D., & Kim, S. Y. (2010). Understanding Chinese American adolescents' developmental outcomes: Insights from the family stress model. *Journal of Research on Adolescence, 20,* 1–12. doi:10.1111/j.1532-7795.2009.00629.x

Bennett, D. S., Bendersky, M., & Lewis, M. (2002). Facial expressivity at 4 months: A context by expression analysis. *Infancy, 3,* 97–113.

Bennett, D. S., Bendersky, M., & Lewis, M. (2005). Does the organization of emotional expression change over time? Facial expressivity from 4 to 12 months. *Infancy, 8,* 167–187.

Benoit, D., & Parker, K. C. (1994). Stability and transmission of attachment across three generations. *Child Development, 65,* 1444–1456.

Bereiter, C., & Scardamalia, M. (1982). From conversation to composition: The role of instruction in a developmental process. In R. Glaser (Ed.), *Advances in instructional psychology* (Vol. 2, pp. 1–64). Hillsdale, NJ: Erlbaum.

Berenbaum, S. A. (1998). How hormones affect behavioral and neural development: Introduction to the special issue on "Gonadal hormones and sex differences in behavior." *Developmental Neuropsychology, 14,* 175–196. doi:10.1080/87565649809540708

Berenbaum, S. A., & Hines, M. (1992). Early androgens are related to childhood sex-typed toy preferences. *Psychological Science, 3,* 203–206. doi:10.1111/j.1467-9280.1992.tb00028.x

Berg, C. A. (1989). Knowledge of strategies for dealing with everyday problems from childhood through adolescence. *Developmental Psychology, 25,* 607–618.

Berg, C. A., Strough, J., Calderone, K., Meegan, S. P., & Sansone, C. (1997). Planning to prevent everyday problems from occurring. In S. L. Friedman & E. K. Scholnick (Eds.), *The developmental psychology of planning: Why, how, and when do we plan?* (pp. 209–236). Mahwah, NJ: Erlbaum.

Berg, N. E., & Mussen, P. (1975). The origins and development of concepts of justice. *Journal of Social Issues, 31,* 183–201. doi:10.1111/j.1540-4560.1975.tb01003.x

Bergelson, E., & Swingley, D. (2012). At 6–9 months, human infants know the meanings of many common nouns. *Proceedings of the National Academy of Sciences of the United States of America, 109,* 3253–3258. doi:10.1073/pnas.1113380109

Berger, A. (2011). *Self-regulation: Brain, cognition, and development.* Washington, DC: American Psychological Association.

Berger, L., Brooks-Gunn, J., Paxson, C., & Waldfogel, J. (2008). First-year maternal employment and child outcomes: Differences across racial and ethnic groups. *Children and Youth Services Review, 30,* 365–387. doi:10.1016/j.childyouth.2007.10.010

Berk, L. E. (1994, November). Why children talk to themselves. *Scientific American, 271*(5), 78–83.

Berkel, C., Murry, V. M., Hurt, T. R., Chen, Y.-f., Brody, G. H., Simons, R. L., … Gibbons, F. X. (2009). It takes a village: Protecting rural African American youth in the context of racism. *Journal of Youth and Adolescence, 38,* 175–188. doi:10.1007/s10964-008-9346-z

Berko, J. (1958). The child's learning of English morphology. *Word, 14,* 150–177.

Berman, J. M. J., Chambers, C. G., & Graham, S. A. (2010). Preschoolers' appreciation of speaker vocal affect as a cue to referential intent. *Journal of Experimental Child Psychology, 107,* 87–99. doi:10.1016/j.jecp.2010.04.012

Bernal, M. E., Knight, G. P., Garza, C. A., Ocampo, K. A., & Cota, M. K. (1990). The development of ethnic identity in Mexican-American children. *Hispanic Journal of Behavioral Sciences, 12,* 3–24. doi:10.1177/07399863900121001

Bernal, M. E., Knight, G. P., Ocampo, K. A., Garza, C. A., & Cota, M. K. (1993). Development of Mexican American identity. In M. E. Bernal & G. P. Knight (Eds.), *Ethnic identity: Formation and transmission among Hispanics and other minorities* (pp. 31–46). Albany: State University of New York Press.

Bernard, K., & Dozier, M. (2010). Examining infants' cortisol responses to laboratory tasks among children varying in attachment disorganization: Stress reactivity or return to baseline? *Developmental Psychology, 46,* 1771–1778. doi:10.1037/a0020660

Bernard, K., Dozier, M., Bick, J., Lewis-Morrarty, E., Lindhiem, O., & Carlson, E. (2012). Enhancing attachment organization among maltreated children: Results of a randomized clinical trial. *Child Development, 83,* 623–636. doi:10.1111/j.1467-8624.2011.01712.x

Berndt, T. J. (1979). Developmental changes in conformity to peers and parents. *Developmental Psychology, 15,* 608–616. doi:10.1037/0012-1649.15.6.608

Berndt, T. J., Hawkins, J. A., & Jiao, Z. (1999). Influences of friends and friendships on adjustment to junior high school. *Merrill-Palmer Quarterly, 45,* 13–41.

Berninger, V. W., & Richards, T. L. (2002). *Brain literacy for educators and psychologists.* San Diego, CA: Academic Press.

Berninger, V. W., & Richards, T. L. (2002). Building a writing brain neurologically. In V. W. Berninger & T. L. Richards (Eds.), *Brain literacy for educators and psychologists* (pp. 247–271). San Diego, CA: Academic Press.

Berrill, K. T. (1990). Anti-gay violence and victimization in the United States: An overview. *Journal of Interpersonal Violence, 5,* 274–294. doi:10.1177/088626090005003003

Berry, J. W., & Kalin, R. (1995). Multicultural and ethnic attitudes in Canada: An overview of the 1991 national survey. *Canadian Journal of Behavioural Sciences, 27,* 301–320. doi:10.1037/0008-400X.27.3.301

Berteletti, I., Lucangeli, D., Piazza, M., Dehaene, S., & Zorzi, M. (2010). Numerical estimation in preschoolers. *Developmental Psychology, 46,* 545–551. doi:10.1037/a0017887

Bertenthal, B. I. (1993). Infants' perception of biomechanical motions: Intrinsic image and knowledge-based constraints. In C. Granrud (Ed.), *Visual perception and cognition in infancy* (pp. 175–214). Hillsdale, NJ: Erlbaum.

Bertenthal, B. I., Campos, J. J., & Haith, M. M. (1980). Development of visual organization: The perception of subjective contours. *Child Development, 51,* 1072–1080. doi:10.2307/1129546

Bertenthal, B. I., Campos, J. J., & Kermoian, R. (1994). An epigenetic perspective on the development of self-produced locomotion and its consequences. *Current Directions in Psychological Science, 3,* 140–145. doi:10.2307/20182292

Bertenthal, B. I., & Clifton, R. K. (1998). Perception and action. In W. Damon (Series Ed.) & D. Kuhn & R. S. Siegler (Vol. Eds.), *Handbook of child psychology: Vol. 2. Cognition, perception, and language* (5th ed., pp. 51–102). New York, NY: Wiley.

Bertenthal, B. I., Proffitt, D. R., & Kramer, S. J. (1987). Perception of biomechanical motions by infants: Implementation of various processing constraints. *Journal of Experimental Psychology: Human Perception and Performance, 13,* 577–585. doi:10.1037/0096-1523.13.4.577

Best, D. L., & Thomas, J. J. (2004). Cultural diversity and cross-cultural perspectives. In A. H. Eagly, A. E. Beall, & R. J. Sternberg (Eds.), *The psychology of gender* (2nd ed., pp. 296–327). New York, NY: Guilford Press.

Beyer, S. (1995). Maternal employment and children's academic achievement: Parenting styles as mediating variable. *Developmental Review, 15,* 212–253. doi:10.1006/drev.1995.1009

Beyers, W., & Goossens, L. (2008). Dynamics of perceived parenting and identity formation in late adolescence. *Journal of Adolescence, 31,* 165–184. doi:10.1016/j.adolescence.2007.04.003

Bezdjian, S., Raine, A., Baker, L. A., & Lynam, D. R. (2011). Psychopathic personality in children: Genetic and environmental contributions. *Psychological Medicine, 41,* 589–600. doi:10.1017/S0033291710000966

Bhanot, R., & Jovanovic, J. (2005). Do parents' academic gender stereotypes influence whether they intrude on their children's homework? *Sex Roles, 52,* 597–607. doi:10.1007/s11199-005-3728-4

Bialystok, E. (2000). Symbolic representation across domains in preschool children. *Journal of Experimental Child Psychology, 76,* 173–189.

Bialystok, E., & Craik, F. I. M. (2010). Cognitive and linguistic processing in the bilingual mind. *Current Directions in Psychological Science, 19,* 19–23. doi:10.1177/0963721409358571

Biederman, J., Petty, C. R., Dolan, C., Hughes, S., Mick, E., Monuteaux, M. C., & Faraone, S. V. (2008). The long-term longitudinal course of oppositional defiant disorder and conduct disorder in ADHD boys: Findings from a controlled 10-year prospective longitudinal follow-up study. *Psychological Medicine, 38,* 1027–1036. doi:10.1017/S0033291707002668

Biederman, J., Rosenbaum, J. F., Hirshfeld, D. R., Faraone, S. V., Bolduc, E. A., Gersten, M., … Reznick, J. S. (1990). Psychiatric correlates of behavioral inhibition in young children of parents with and without psychiatric disorders. *Archives of General Psychiatry, 47,* 21–26.

Biehle, S. N., & Mickelson, K. D. (2012). First-time parents' expectations about the division of childcare and play. *Journal of Family Psychology, 26,* 36–45. doi:10.1037/a0026608

Bierman, K. L., Coie, J. D., Dodge, K. A., Greenberg, M. T., Lochman, J. E., McMahon, R. J., … Conduct Problems Prevention Research Group. (2010). The effects of a multiyear universal social–emotional learning program: The role of student and school characteristics. *Journal of Consulting and Clinical Psychology, 78,* 156–168. doi:10.1037/a0018607

Biernat, M. (1991). Gender stereotypes and the relationship between masculinity and femininity: A developmental analysis. *Journal of Personality and Social Psychology, 61,* 351–365. doi:10.1037/0022-3514.61.3.351

Bigelow, B. J. (1977). Children's friendship expectations: A cognitive-developmental study. *Child Development, 48,* 246–253.

Bigler, R. S. (1999). Psychological interventions designed to counter sexism in children: Empirical limitations and theoretical foundations. In J. W. B. Swann, J. H. Langlois, & L. A. Gilbert (Eds.), *Sexism and stereotypes in modern society: The gender science of Janet Taylor Spence* (pp. 129–151). Washington, DC: American Psychological Association.

Bigler, R. S., & Liben, L. S. (1990). The role of attitudes and interventions in gender-schematic processing. *Child Development, 61,* 1440–1452.

Bigler, R. S., & Liben, L. S. (2007). Developmental intergroup theory: Explaining and reducing children's social stereotyping and prejudice. *Current Directions in Psychological Science, 16,* 162–166. doi:10.1111/j.1467-8721.2007.00496.x

Birch, L. L., & Fisher, J. A. (1996). The role of experience in the development of children's eating behavior. In E. D. Capaldi (Ed.), *Why we eat what we eat: The psychology of eating* (pp. 113–141). Washington, DC: American Psychological Association.

Bird, A., Reese, E., & Tripp, G. (2006). Parent–child talk about past emotional events: Associations with child temperament and goodness-of-fit. *Journal of Cognition and Development, 7,* 189–210.

Bjerregaard, B., & Smith, C. (1993). Gender differences in gang participation, delinquency, and substance use. *Journal of Quantitative Criminology, 9,* 329–355. doi:10.1007/BF01064108

Bjorklund, D. F. (1997). The role of immaturity in human development. *Psychological Bulletin, 122,* 153–169.

Bjorklund, D. F. (2007). *Why youth is not wasted on the young: Immaturity in human development.* Oxford, England: Blackwell.

Bjorklund, D. F., & Pellegrini, A. D. (2002). *The origins of human nature: Evolutionary developmental psychology.* Washington, DC: American Psychological Association.

Björkqvist, K., Österman, K., & Kaukiainen, A. (1992). The development of direct and indirect aggressive strategies in males and females. In K. Björkqvist & P. Niemelä (Eds.), *Of mice and women: Aspects of female aggression* (pp. 51–64). San Diego, CA: Academic Press.

Blachman, B. A., Schatschneider, C., Fletcher, J. M., Francis, D. J., Clonan, S. M., Shaywitz, B. A., & Shaywitz, S. E. (2004). Effects of intensive reading remediation for second and third graders and a 1-year follow-up. *Journal of Educational Psychology, 96,* 444–461. doi:10.1037/0022-0663.96.3.444

Black, R. E., Allen, L. H., Bhutta, Z. A., Caulfield, L. E., de Onis, M., Ezzati, M., … Rivera, J. (2008, January 19). Maternal and child undernutrition: Global and regional exposures and health consequences. *The Lancet, 371,* 243–260.

Black, S. E., Devereux, P. J., & Salvanes, K. G. (2007). From the cradle to the labor market? The effect of birth weight on adult outcomes. *The Quarterly Journal of Economics, 122,* 409–439. doi:10.1162/qjec.122.1.409

Blackstock, C. (2003). Restoring peace and harmony in First Nations communities. In K. Kuefeldt & B. McKenzie (Eds.), *Child welfare: Connecting research policy and practice* (pp. 331–342). Waterloo, ON: Wilfred Laurier Press.

Blackwell, L. S., Trzesniewski, K. H., & Dweck, C. S. (2007). Implicit theories of intelligence predict achievement across an adolescent transition: A longitudinal study and an intervention. *Child Development, 78,* 246–263. doi:10.1111/j.1467-8624.2007.00995.x

Blair, C. (2006). How similar are fluid cognition and general intelligence? A developmental neuroscience perspective on fluid cognition as an aspect of human cognitive ability. *Behavioral and Brain Sciences, 29,* 109–125. doi:10.1017/S0140525X06009034

Blair, C., Gamson, D., Thorne, S., & Baker, D. (2005). Rising mean IQ: Cognitive demand of mathematics education for young children, population exposure to formal schooling, and the neurobiology of the prefrontal cortex. *Intelligence, 33,* 93–106.

Blair, C., Granger, D. A., Kivlighan, K. T., Mills-Koonce, R., Willoughby, M., Greenberg, M. T., … Family Life Project Investigators. (2008). Maternal and child contributions to cortisol response to emotional arousal in young children from low-income, rural communities. *Developmental Psychology, 44,* 1095–1109. doi:10.1037/0012-1649.44.4.1095

Blair, C., & Razza, R. P. (2007). Relating effortful control, executive function, and false belief understanding to emerging math and literacy ability in kindergarten. *Child Development, 78,* 647–663. doi:10.1111/j.1467-8624.2007.01019.x

Blair, K. A., Denham, S. A., Kochanoff, A., & Whipple, B. (2004). Playing it cool: Temperament, emotion regulation, and social behavior in preschoolers. *Journal of School Psychology, 42,* 419–443.

Blais, J. J., Craig, W. M., Pepler, D., & Connolly, J. (2008). Adolescents online: The importance of internet activity choices to salient relationships. *Journal of Youth and Adolescence, 37,* 522–536. doi:10.1007/s10964-007-9262-7

Blake, J., & De Boysson-Bardies, B. (1992). Patterns in babbling: A cross-linguistic study. *Journal of Child Language, 19,* 51–74. doi:10.1017/S0305000900013623

Blandon, A. Y., Calkins, S. D., Keane, S. P., & O'Brien, M. (2008). Individual differences in trajectories of emotion regulation processes: The effects of maternal depressive symptomatology and children's physiological regulation. *Developmental Psychology, 44,* 1110–1123. doi:10.1037/0012-1649.44.4.1110

Blasi, A. (1980). Bridging moral cognition and moral action: A critical review of the literature. *Psychological Bulletin, 88,* 1–45. doi:10.1037/0033-2909.88.1.1

Blass, E. M. (1990). Suckling: Determinants, changes, mechanisms, and lasting impressions. *Developmental Psychology, 26,* 520–533. doi:10.1037/0012-1649.26.4.520

Blass, E. M., & Camp, C. A. (2003). Biological bases of face preference in 6-week-old infants. *Developmental Science, 6,* 524–536. doi:10.1111/1467-7687.00310

Blass, E. M., & Hoffmeyer, L. B. (1991). Sucrose as an analgesic for newborn infants. *Pediatrics, 87,* 215–218.

Blass, E. M., & Teicher, M. H. (1980, October 3). Suckling. *Science, 210,* 15–22.

Blauw-Hospers, C. H., & Hadders-Algra, M. (2005). A systematic review of the effects of early intervention on motor development. *Developmental Medicine and Child Neurology, 47,* 421–432.

Bleeker, M. M., & Jacobs, J. E. (2004). Achievement in math and science: Do mothers' beliefs matter 12 years later? *Journal of Educational Psychology, 96,* 97–109. doi:10.1037/0022-0663.96.1.97

Block, J. H., Block, J., & Gjerde, P. F. (1986). The personality of children prior to divorce: A prospective study. *Child Development, 57,* 827–840.

Bloom, L. (1973). *One word at a time: The use of single word utterances before syntax.* The Hague, The Netherlands: Mouton.

Bloom, L. (1991). *Language development from two to three.* Cambridge, England: Cambridge University Press.

Bloom, L. (1998). Language acquisition in its developmental context. In W. Damon (Series Ed.) & D. Kuhn & R. S. Siegler (Vol. Eds.), *Handbook of child psychology: Vol. 2. Cognition, perception, and language* (5th ed., pp. 309–370). Hoboken, NJ: Wiley.

Bloom, L., Rocissano, L., & Hood, L. (1976). Adult-child discourse: Developmental interaction between information processing and linguistic knowledge. *Cognitive Psychology, 8,* 521–552. doi:10.1016/0010-0285(76)90017-7

Bloom, L., & Tinker, E. (2001). The intentionality model and language acquisition: Engagement, effort, and the essential tension in development. *Monographs of the Society for Research in Child Development, 66*(4, Serial No. 267).

Bloom, P. (2000). *How children learn the meanings of words.* Cambridge, MA: MIT Press.

Bode, L., Kuhn, L., Kim, H. Y., Hsiao, L., Nissan, C., Sinkala, M., … Aldrovandi, G. M. (2012). Human milk oligosaccharide concentration and risk of postnatal transmission of HIV through breastfeeding. *American Journal of Clinical Nutrition, 96,* 831–839. doi:10.3945/ajcn.112.039503

Boden, J. M., Fergusson, D. M., & Horwood, L. J. (2008). Does adolescent self-esteem predict later life outcomes? A test of the causal role of self-esteem. *Development and Psychopathology, 20,* 319–339. doi:10.1017/S0954579408000151

Bohlin, G., Hagekull, B., & Rydell, A.-M. (2000). Attachment and social functioning: A longitudinal study from infancy to middle childhood. *Social Development, 9,* 24–39. doi:10.1111/1467-9507.00109

Bohon, C., Stice, E., Burton, E., Fudell, M., & Nolen-Hoeksema, S. (2008). A prospective test of cognitive vulnerability models of depression with adolescent girls. *Behavior Therapy, 39,* 79–90.

Boiger, M., & Mesquita, B. (2012). The construction of emotion in interactions, relationships, and cultures. *Emotion Review, 4,* 221–229.

Boismier, J. D. (1977). Visual stimulation and wake-sleep behavior in human neonates. *Developmental Psychobiology, 10,* 219–227. doi:10.1002/dev.420100306

Boivin, M., & Hertzman, C. (Eds.). (2012). *Early childhood development: Adverse experiences and developmental health.* Royal Society of Canada—Canadian Academy of Health Sciences Expert Panel (with Ronald Barr, Thomas Boyce, Alison Fleming, Harriet MacMillan, Candice Odgers, Marla Sokolowski, & Nico Trocmé). Ottawa, ON: Royal Society of Canada.

Boivin, M., Petitclerc, A., Feng, B., & Barker, E. D. (2010). The developmental trajectories of peer victimization in middle to late childhood and the changing nature of their behavioral correlates. *Merrill-Palmer Quarterly, 56,* 231–260.

Bokhorst, C. L., Bakermans-Kranenburg, M. J., Pasco Fearon, R. M., van IJzendoorn, M. H., Fonagy, P., & Schuengel, C. (2003). The importance of shared environment in mother–infant attachment security: A behavioral genetic study. *Child Development, 74,* 1769–1782. doi:10.1046/j.1467-8624.2003.00637.x

Bokhorst, C. L., Sumter, S. R., & Westenberg, P. M. (2010). Social support from parents, friends, classmates, and teachers in children and adolescents aged 9 to 18 years: Who is perceived as most supportive? *Social Development, 19,* 417–426. doi:10.1111/j.1467-9507.2009.00540.x

Boland, A. M., Haden, C. A., & Ornstein, P. A. (2003). Boosting children's memory by training mothers in the use of an elaborative conversational style as an event unfolds. *Journal of Cognition and Development, 4,* 39–65. doi:10.1080/15248372.2003.9669682

Bolger, K. E., & Patterson, C. J. (2001). Developmental pathways from child maltreatment to peer rejection. *Child Development, 72,* 549–568.

Bolger, K. E., & Scarr, S. (1995). Not so far from home: How family characteristics predict child care quality. *Early Development and Parenting, 4,* 103–112. doi:10.1002/edp.2430040303

Bolkan, C., Sano, Y., De Costa, J., Acock, A. C., & Day, R. D. (2010). Early adolescents' perceptions of mothers' and fathers' parenting styles and problem behavior. *Marriage and Family Review, 46,* 563–579. doi:10.1080/01494929.2010.543040

Bonica, C., Arnold, D. H., Fisher, P. H., Zeljo, A., & Yershova, K. (2003). Relational aggression, relational victimization, and language development in preschoolers. *Social Development, 12,* 551–562. doi:10.1111/1467-9507.00248

Bonanno, R. A., & Hymel, S. (2013). Cyber bullying and internalizing difficulties: Above and beyond the impact of traditional forms of bullying. *Journal of Youth and Adolescence, 2,* 685–697. doi:10.1007/s10964-013-9937-1

Bonner, J. T. (1988). *The evolution of culture in animals.* Princeton, NJ: Princeton University Press.

Book, A. S., Starzyk, K. B., & Quinsey, V. L. (2001). The relationship between testosterone and aggression: A meta-analysis. *Aggression and Violent Behavior, 6,* 579–599. doi:10.1016/S1359-1789(00)00032-X

Booth, A. E., & Waxman, S. R. (2009). A horse of a different color: Specifying with precision infants' mappings of novel nouns and adjectives. *Child Development, 80,* 15–22. doi:10.1111/j.1467-8624.2008.01242.x

Booth, J. L., & Siegler, R. S. (2006). Developmental and individual differences in pure numerical estimation. *Developmental Psychology, 42,* 189–201. doi:10.1037/0012-1649.41.6.189

Booth, J. L., & Siegler, R. S. (2008). Numerical magnitude representations influence arithmetic learning. *Child Development, 79,* 1016–1031. doi:10.1111/j.1467-8624.2008.01173.x

Booth-Laforce, C., Oh, W., Kennedy, A. E., Rubin, K. H., Rose-Krasnor, L., & Laursen, B. (2012). Parent and peer links to trajectories of anxious withdrawal from grades 5 to 8. *Journal of Clinical Child and Adolescent Psychology, 41,* 138–149. doi:10.1080/15374416.2012.651995

Booth-LaForce, C., & Oxford, M. L. (2008). Trajectories of social withdrawal from grades 1 to 6: Prediction from early parenting, attachment, and temperament. *Developmental Psychology, 44,* 1298–1313. doi:10.1037/a0012954

Borelli, J. L., Crowley, M. J., David, D. H., Sbarra, D. A., Anderson, G. M., & Mayes, L. C. (2010). Attachment and emotion in school-aged children. *Emotion, 10,* 475–485. doi:10.1037/a0018490

Borge, A. I. H., Rutter, M., Côté, S., & Tremblay, R. E. (2004). Early childcare and physical aggression: Differentiating social selection and social causation. *Journal of Child Psychology and Psychiatry, 45,* 367–376. doi:10.1111/j.1469-7610.2004.00227.x

Borke, H. (1971). Interpersonal perception of young children: Egocentrism or empathy? *Developmental Psychology, 5,* 263–269.

Bornstein, M. H. (1975). Qualities of color vision in infancy. *Journal of Experimental Child Psychology, 19,* 401–419. doi:10.1016/0022-0965(75)90070-3

Bornstein, M. H. (2006). On the significance of social relationships in the development of children's earliest symbolic play: An ecological perspective. In A. Göncü & S. Gaskins (Eds.), *Play and development: Evolutionary, sociocultural, and functional perspectives* (pp. 101–130). Mahwah, NJ: Erlbaum.

Bornstein, M. H. (2007). On the significance of social relationships in the development of children's earliest symbolic play: An ecological perspective. In A. Göncü & S. Gaskins (Eds.), *Play and development: Evolutionary, sociocultural, and functional perspectives* (pp. 101–129). New York, NY: Erlbaum.

Bornstein, M. H., & Bradley, R. H. (Eds.). (2003). *Socioeconomic status, parenting, and child development.* Mahwah, NJ: Erlbaum.

Bornstein, M. H., Cote, L. R., Haynes, O. M., Hahn, C.-S., & Park, Y. (2010). Parenting knowledge: Experiential and sociodemographic factors in European American mothers of young children. *Developmental Psychology, 46,* 1677–1693. doi:10.1037/a0020677

Bornstein, M. H., Kessen, W., & Weiskopf, S. (1976). Color vision and hue categorization in young human infants. *Journal of Experimental Psychology: Human Perception and Performance, 2,* 115–129. doi:10.1037/0096-1523.2.1.115

Bornstein, M. H., & Putnick, D. L. (2012). Cognitive and socioemotional caregiving in developing countries. *Child Development, 83,* 46–61. doi:10.1111/j.1467-8624.2011.01673.x

Borstelmann, L. J. (1983). Children before psychology: Ideas about children from antiquity to the late 1800s. In P. H. Mussen (Series Ed.) & W. Kessen (Vol. Ed.), *Handbook of child psychology: Vol. 1. History, theory, and methods* (4th ed., pp. 1–40). New York, NY: Wiley.

Bortfeld, H., Fava, E., & Boas, D. A. (2009). Identifying cortical lateralization of speech processing in infants using near-infrared spectroscopy. *Developmental Neuropsychology, 34,* 52–65. doi:10.1080/87565640802564481

Bortfeld, H., Morgan, J. L., Golinkoff, R. M., & Rathbun, K. (2005). Mommy and me: Familiar names help launch babies into speech-stream segmentation. *Psychological Science, 16,* 298–304. doi:10.1111/j.0956-7976.2005.01531.x

Bos, H., & Gartrell, N. (2010). Adolescents of the USA national longitudinal lesbian family study: Can family characteristics counteract the negative effects of stigmatization? *Family Process, 49,* 559–572. doi:10.1111/j.1545-5300.2010.01340.x

Bos, H. M. W., Sandfort, T. G. M., de Bruyn, E. H., & Hakvoort, E. M. (2008). Same-sex attraction, social relationships, psychosocial functioning, and school performance in early adolescence. *Developmental Psychology, 44,* 59–68. doi:10.1037/0012-1649.44.1.59

Bos, H. M. W., & van Balen, F. (2008). Children in planned lesbian families: Stigmatisation, psychological adjustment and protective factors. *Culture, Health and Sexuality, 10,* 221–236. doi:10.1080/13691050701601702

Bosma, H. A., & Kunnen, E. S. (2001). Determinants and mechanisms in ego identity development: A review and synthesis. *Developmental Review, 21,* 39–66. doi:10.1006/drev.2000.0514

Bouchard, T. J., Jr. (2004). Genetic influence on human psychological traits: A survey. *Current Directions in Psychological Science, 13*, 148–151. doi:10.1111/j.0963-7214.2004.00295.x

Bouchard, T. J., Jr., Lykken, D. T., McGue, M., Segal, N. L., & Tellegen, A. (1990, October 12). Sources of human psychological differences: The Minnesota Study of Twins Reared Apart. *Science, 250*, 223–228.

Boutwell, B. B., Franklin, C. A., Barnes, J. C., & Beaver, K. M. (2011). Physical punishment and childhood aggression: The role of gender and gene–environment interplay. *Aggressive Behavior, 37*, 559–568. doi: 10.1002/ab.20409

Bowerman, M. (1978). The acquisition of word meaning: An investigation into some current conflicts. In N. Waterson & C. E. Snow (Eds.), *The development of communication* (pp. 263–287). Chichester, England: Wiley.

Bowerman, M. (1979). The acquisition of complex sentences. In P. Fletcher & M. Garman (Eds.), *Language acquisition* (pp. 285–305). Cambridge, England: Cambridge University Press.

Bowker, A., Bukowski, W., Zargarpour, S., & Hoza, B. (1998). A structural and functional analysis of a two-dimensional model of social isolation. *Merrill-Palmer Quarterly, 44*, 447–463. doi:10.2307/23093748

Bowker, J. C., & Raja, R. (2011). Social withdrawal subtypes during early adolescence in India. *Journal of Abnormal Child Psychology, 39*, 201–212. doi:10.1007/s10802-010-9461-7

Bowlby, J. (1953). *Child care and the growth of love* (M. Fry, Ed.). London, England: Penguin Books.

Bowlby, J. (1969). *Attachment and loss: Vol. 1. Attachment.* New York, NY: Basic Books.

Bowlby, J. (1973). *Attachment and loss: Vol. 2. Separation: Anxiety and anger.* New York, NY: Basic Books.

Bowlby, J. (1980). *Attachment and loss: Vol. 3. Loss: Sadness and depression.* New York: Basic Books.

Boyce, W. F. (2004). *Young people in Canada: Their health and well-being.* Retrieved from http://www.phac-aspc.gc.ca/hp-ps/dca-dea/publications/hbsc-2004/pdf/hbsc_report_2004_e.pdf

Boylan, K., Vaillancourt, T., Boyle, M., & Szatmari, P. (2007). Comorbidity of internalizing disorders in children with oppositional defiant disorder. *European Child & Adolescent Psychiatry, 16*, 484–494. doi:10.1007/s00787-007-0624-1

Bos, H., & Gartrell, N. (2010). Adolescents of the USA national longitudinal lesbian family study: Can family characteristics counteract the negative effects of stigmatization? *Family Process, 49*, 559–572. doi:10.1111/j.1545-5300.2010.01340.x

Braaksma, M. A. H., Rijlaarsdam, G., Van den Bergh, H., & van Hout-Wolters, B. H. A. M. (2004). Observational learning and its effects on the orchestration of writing processes. *Cognition and Instruction, 22*, 1–36.

Bradbard, M. R., Martin, C. L., Endsley, R. C., & Halverson, C. F. (1986). Influence of sex stereotypes on children's exploration and memory: A competence versus performance distinction. *Developmental Psychology, 22*, 481–486. doi:10.1037/0012-1649.22.4.481

Bradley, R. H. (1989). The use of the HOME Inventory in longitudinal studies of child development. In M. H. Bornstein & N. A. Krasnegor (Eds.), *Stability and continuity in mental development: Behavioral and biological perspectives* (pp. 191–215). Hillsdale, NJ: Erlbaum.

Bradley, R. H. (1994). The HOME inventory: Review and reflections. In H. W. Reese (Ed.), *Advances in child development and behavior* (Vol. 25, pp. 241–288). San Diego, CA: Academic Press.

Bradley, R. H., & Caldwell, B. M. (1979). Home observation for measurement of the environment: A revision of the preschool scale. *American Journal of Mental Deficiency, 84*, 235–244.

Bradley, R. H., & Caldwell, B. M. (1984). 174 children: A study of the relationship between home environment and cognitive development during the first 5 years. In A. W. Gottfried (Ed.), *Home environment and early cognitive development* (pp. 5–56). New York, NY: Academic Press.

Bradley, R. H., Caldwell, B. M., Rock, S. L., Ramey, C. T., Barnard, K. E., Gray, C., ... & Johnson, D. L. (1989). Home environment and cognitive development in the first 3 years of life: A collaborative study involving six sites and three ethnic groups in North America. *Developmental Psychology, 25*, 217–235. doi:10.1037/0012-1649.25.2.217

Bradley, R. H., & Corwyn, R. F. (2002). Socioeconomic status and child development. *Annual Review of Psychology, 53*, 371–399. doi:10.1146/annurev.psych.53.100901.135233

Bradley, R. H., Convyn, R. F., Burchinal, M., McAdoo, H. P., & García Coll, C. (2001). The home environments of children in the United States: Part II. Relations with behavioral development through age thirteen. *Child Development, 72*, 1868–1886.

Bradley, R. H., Whiteside, L., Mundrom, D. J., Casey, P. H., Kelleher, K. J., & Pope, S. K. (1994). Contribution of early intervention and early caregiving experiences to resilience in low-birthweight, premature children living in poverty. *Journal of Clinical Child Psychology, 23*, 425–434.

Braine, M. D. S. (1976). [Review of the book *The acquisition of phonology*, by N. V. Smith]. *Language, 52*, 489–498.

Bramlett, M. D., & Mosher, W. D. (2002). *Vital and health statistics: Series 22. Cohabitation, marriage, divorce, and remarriage in the United States.* Hyattsville, MD: National Center for Health Statistics.

Brannon, E. M. (2002). The development of ordinal numerical knowledge in infancy. *Cognition, 83*, 223–240. doi:10.1016/S0010-0277(02)00005-7

Brannon, E. M., Lutz, D., & Cordes, S. (2006). The development of area discrimination and its implications for number representation in infancy. *Developmental Science, 9*, F59-F64. doi:10.1111/j.1467-7687.2006.00530.x

Brannon, E. M., Suanda, S., & Libertus, K. (2007). Temporal discrimination increases in precision over development and parallels the development of numerosity discrimination. *Developmental Science, 10*, 770–777. doi:10.1111/j.1467-7687.2007.00635.x

Branstetter, S. A., Low, S., & Furman, W. (2011). The influence of parents and friends on adolescent substance use: A multidimensional approach. *Journal of Substance Use, 16*, 150–160. doi:10.3109/14659891.2010.519421

Braungart-Rieker, J. M., Hill-Soderlund, A. L., & Karrass, J. (2010). Fear and anger reactivity trajectories from 4 to 16 months: The roles of temperament, regulation, and maternal sensitivity. *Developmental Psychology, 46*, 791–804. doi:10.1037/a0019673

Braver, S. L., Ellman, I. M., & Fabricius, W. V. (2003). Relocation of children after divorce and children's best interests: New evidence and legal considerations. *Journal of Family Psychology, 17*, 206–219. doi:10.1037/0893-3200.17.2.206

Bray, J. H., Adams, G. J., Getz, J. G., & McQueen, A. (2003). Individuation, peers, and adolescent alcohol use: A latent growth analysis. *Journal of Consulting and Clinical Psychology, 71*, 553–564. doi:10.1037/0022-006X.71.3.553

Bray, J. H., & Berger, S. H. (1993). Developmental issues in StepFamilies Research Project: Family relationships and parent-child interactions. *Journal of Family Psychology, 7*, 76–90. doi:10.1037/0893-3200.7.1.76

Brazelton, T. B., Nugent, J. K., & Lester, B. M. (1987). Neonatal behavioral assessment scale. In J. D. Osofsky (Ed.), *Handbook of infant development* (2nd ed., pp. 780–817). New York, NY: Wiley.

Bremner, J. G. (1978). Spatial errors made by infants: Inadequate spatial cues or evidence of egocentrism? *British Journal of Psychology, 69,* 77–84. doi:10.1111/j.2044-8295.1978.tb01634.x

Bremner, J. G., Knowles, L., & Andreasen, G. (1994). Processes underlying young children's spatial orientation during movement. *Journal of Experimental Child Psychology, 57,* 355–376. doi:10.1006/jecp.1994.1017

Brendgen, M., Boivin, M., Dionne, G., Barker, E. D., Vitaro, F., Girard, A., … Pérusse, D. (2011). Gene–environment processes linking aggression, peer victimization, and the teacher–child relationship. *Child Development, 82,* 2021–2036. doi:10.1111/j.1467-8624.2011.01644.x

Brendgen, M., Boivin, M., Vitaro, F., Bukowski, W. M., Dionne, G., Tremblay, R. E., & Pérusse, D. (2008). Linkages between children's and their friends' social and physical aggression: Evidence for a gene–environment interaction? *Child Development, 79,* 13–29. doi:10.1111/j.1467-8624.2007.01108.x

Brendgen, M., Vitaro, F., & Bukowski, W. M. (2000). Deviant friends and early adolescents' emotional and behavioral adjustment. *Journal of Research on Adolescence, 10,* 173–189. doi:10.1207/SJRA1002_3

Brendgen, M., Vitaro, F., Bukowski, W. M., Doyle, A. B., & Markiewicz, D. (2001). Developmental profiles of peer social preference over the course of elementary school: Associations with trajectories of externalizing and internalizing behavior. *Developmental Psychology, 37,* 308–320.

Brennan, P. A., Hammen, C., Katz, A. R., & Le Brocque, R. M. (2002). Maternal depression, paternal psychopathology, and adolescent diagnostic outcomes. *Journal of Consulting and Clinical Psychology, 70,* 1075–1085.

Brenner, E. M., & Salovey, P. (1997). Emotion regulation during childhood: Developmental, interpersonal, and individual considerations. In P. Salovey & D. J. Sluyter (Eds.), *Emotional development and emotional intelligence: Educational implications* (pp. 168–195). New York, NY: Basic Books.

Bretherton, I., & Beeghly, M. (1982). Talking about internal states: The acquisition of an explicit theory of mind. *Developmental Psychology, 18,* 906–921.

Bretherton, I., Golby, B., & Cho, E. (1997). Attachment and the transmission of values. In J. E. Grusec & L. Kuczynski (Eds.), *Parenting and children's internalization of values: A handbook of contemporary theory* (pp. 103–134). Hoboken, NJ: Wiley.

Bretherton, I., & Munholland, K. A. (1999). Internal working models in attachment relationships: A construct revisited. In J. Cassidy & P. R. Shaver (Eds.), *Handbook of attachment: Theory, research, and clinical applications* (pp. 89–111). New York, NY: Guilford Press.

Bretherton, I., & Page, T. F. (2004). Shared or conflicting working models? Relationships in postdivorce families seen through the eyes of mothers and their preschool children. *Development and Psychopathology, 16,* 551–575. doi:10.1017/S0954579404004663

Bridges, L. J., & Grolnick, W. S. (1995). The development of emotional self-regulation in infancy and early childhood. In N. Eisenberg (Ed.), *Review of personality and social psychology: Vol. 15. Social development* (pp. 185–211). Thousand Oaks, CA: Sage.

Broberg, A. G., Wessels, H., Lamb, M. E., & Hwang, C. (1997). Effects of day care on the development of cognitive abilities in 8-year-olds: A longitudinal study. *Developmental Psychology, 33,* 62–69. doi:10.1037/0012-1649.33.1.62

Brockington, R. (2010). *Summary public school indicators for Canada, the provinces and territories, 2002/2003 to 2008/2009* (Catalogue No. 81-595-M No. 088). Ottawa, ON: Statistics Canada.

Brody, G. H., Ge, X., Kim, S. Y., Murry, V. M., Simons, R. L., Gibbons, F. X., … Conger, R. D. (2003). Neighborhood disadvantage moderates associations of parenting and older sibling problem attitudes and behavior with conduct disorders in African American children. *Journal of Consulting and Clinical Psychology, 71,* 211–222. doi:10.1037/0022-006X.71.2.211

Brody, G. H., Stoneman, Z., MacKinnon, C. E., & MacKinnon, R. (1985). Role relationships and behavior between preschool-aged and school-aged sibling pairs. *Developmental Psychology, 21,* 124–129. doi:10.1037/0012-1649.21.1.124

Brody, G. H., Stoneman, Z., McCoy, J. K., & Forehand, R. (1992). Contemporaneous and longitudinal associations of sibling conflict with family relationship assessments and family discussions about sibling problems. *Child Development, 63,* 391–400. doi:10.1111/j.1467-8624.1992.tb01635.x

Brody, N. (1992). *Intelligence* (2nd ed.). San Diego, CA: Academic Press.

Broidy, L. M., Nagin, D. S., Tremblay, R. E., Bates, J. E., Brame, B., Dodge, K. A., … Vitaro, F. (2003). Developmental trajectories of childhood disruptive behaviors and adolescent delinquency: A six-site, cross-national study. *Developmental Psychology, 39,* 222–245. doi:10.1037/0012-1649.39.2.222

Bronfenbrenner, U. (1979). *The ecology of human development: Experiments by nature and design.* Cambridge, MA: Harvard University Press.

Bronfenbrenner, U. (1993). The ecology of cognitive development: Research models and fugitive findings. In R. H. Wozniak & K. W. Fischer (Eds.), *Development in context: Acting and thinking in specific environments* (pp. 3–44). Hillsdale, NJ: Erlbaum.

Bronfenbrenner, U., & Morris, P. A. (1998). The ecology of developmental processes. In W. Damon (Series Ed.) & R. M. Lerner (Vol. Ed.), *Handbook of child psychology: Vol. 1. Theoretical models of human development* (5th ed., pp. 993–1028). New York, NY: Wiley.

Bronson, G. W. (1972). Infants' reactions to unfamiliar persons and novel objects. *Monographs of the Society for Research in Child Development, 37*(3, Serial No. 148).

Brooks, R., & Meltzoff, A. N. (2008). Infant gaze following and pointing predict accelerated vocabulary growth through two years of age: A longitudinal, growth curve modeling study. *Journal of Child Language, 35,* 207–220. doi:10.1017/S030500090700829X

Brooks-Gunn, J., Han, W.-J., & Waldfogel, J. (2010). First-year maternal employment and child development in the first 7 years: III. What distinguishes women who work full-time, part-time, or not at all in the 1st year? *Monographs of the Society for Research in Child Development, 75*(2, Serial No. 296), 35–49.

Brophy-Herb, H. E., Lee, R. E., Nievar, M. A., & Stollak, G. (2007). Preschoolers' social competence: Relations to family characteristics, teacher behaviors and classroom climate. *Journal of Applied Developmental Psychology, 28,* 134–148. doi:10.1016/j.appdev.2006.12.004

Brophy-Herb, H. E., Schiffman, R. F., Bocknek, E. L., Dupuis, S. B., Fitzgerald, H. E., Horodynski, M., … Hillaker, B. (2011). Toddlers' social-emotional competence in the contexts of maternal emotion socialization and contingent responsiveness in a low-income sample. *Social Development, 20,* 73–92.

Broughton, J. (1978). Development of concepts of self, mind, reality, and knowledge. In W. Damon (Ed.), *New Directions for Child and Adolescent Development: No. 1. Social cognition* (Vol. 1978, pp. 75–100). San Francisco, CA: Jossey-Bass.

Brown, A. L. (1997). Transforming schools into communities of thinking and learning about serious matters. *American Psychologist, 52,* 399–413. doi: 10.1037/0003-066X.52.4.399

Brown, A. L., & Campione, J. C. (1994). Guided discovery in a community of learners. In K. McGilly (Ed.), *Classroom lessons: Integrating cognitive theory and classroom practice* (pp. 229–270). Cambridge, MA: MIT Press/Bradford Books.

Brown, A. S., Begg, M. D., Gravenstein, S., Schaefer, C. A., Wyatt, R. J., Bresnahan, M., … Susser, E. S. (2004). Serologic evidence of prenatal influenza in the etiology of schizophrenia. *Archives of General Psychiatry, 61,* 774–780. doi:10.1001/archpsyc.61.8.774

Brown, B. B. (1990). Peer groups and peer cultures. In S. S. Feldman & G. R. Elliott (Eds.), *At the threshold: The developing adolescent* (pp. 171–196). Cambridge, MA: Harvard University Press.

Brown, B. B. (2004). Adolescents' relationships with peers. In R. M. Lerner & L. Steinberg (Eds.), *Handbook of adolescent psychology* (2nd ed., pp. 363–394). Hoboken, NJ: Wiley.

Brown, B. B., Von Bank, H., & Steinberg, L. (2008). Smoke in the looking glass: Effects of discordance between self- and peer rated crowd affiliation on adolescent anxiety, depression and self-feelings. *Journal of Youth and Adolescence, 37,* 1163–1177. doi:10.1007/s10964-007-9198-y

Brown, B. B., Clasen, D. R., & Eicher, S. A. (1986). Perceptions of peer pressure, peer conformity dispositions, and self-reported behavior among adolescents. *Developmental Psychology, 22,* 521–530. doi:10.1037/0012-1649.22.4.521

Brown, B. B., & Klute, C. (2003). Friends, cliques, and crowds. In G. R. Adams & M. D. Berzonsky (Eds.), *Blackwell handbook of adolescence* (pp. 330–348). Malden, MA: Blackwell.

Brown, C. S., & Bigler, R. S. (2004). Children's perceptions of gender discrimination. *Developmental Psychology, 40,* 714–726. doi:10.1037/0012-1649.40.5.714

Brown, C. S., & Bigler, R. S. (2005). Children's perceptions of discrimination: A developmental model. *Child Development, 76,* 533–553. doi:10.1111/j.1467-8624.2005.00862.x

Brown, G. L., Mangelsdorf, S. C., & Neff, C. (2012). Father involvement, paternal sensitivity, and father-child attachment security in the first 3 years. *Journal of Family Psychology, 26,* 421–430. doi:10.1037/a0027836

Brown, J. L., & Pollitt, E. (1996, February). Malnutrition, poverty and intellectual development. *Scientific American, 274*(2), 38–43.

Brown, J. R., & Dunn, J. (1996). Continuities in emotion understanding from three to six years. *Child Development, 67,* 789–802.

Brown, R. (1973). *A first language: The early stages.* Cambridge, MA: Harvard University Press.

Brown, R., & Fraser, C. (1963). The acquisition of syntax. In C. N. Cofer & B. S. Musgrave (Eds.), *Verbal behavior and learning: Problems and processes; proceedings* (pp. 158–196). New York, NY: McGraw-Hill.

Brown, R., & Hanlon, C. (1970). Derivational complexity and order of acquisition in child speech. In J. R. Hayes (Ed.), *Cognition and the development of language* (Vol. 8, pp. 11–53). New York, NY: Wiley.

Brown, R. W. (1957). Linguistic determinism and the part of speech. *Journal of Abnormal Psychology and Social Psychology, 55,* 1–5.

Brown, S. L., & Rinelli, L. N. (2010). Family structure, family processes, and adolescent smoking and drinking. *Journal of Research on Adolescence, 20,* 259–273. doi:10.1111/j.1532-7795.2010.00636.x

Brownell, C. A., Ramani, G. B., & Zerwas, S. (2006). Becoming a social partner with peers: Cooperation and social understanding in one- and two-year-olds. *Child Development, 77,* 803–821. doi:10.1111/j.1467-8624.2006.t01-1-.x-i1

Brownell, C. A., Svetlova, M., & Nichols, S. (2009). To share or not to share: When do toddlers respond to another's needs? *Infancy, 14,* 117–130. doi:10.1080/15250000802569868

Brownell, C. A., Zerwas, S., & Ramani, G. B. (2007). "So big": The development of body self-awareness in toddlers. *Child Development, 78,* 1426–1440. doi:10.1111/j.1467-8624.2007.01075.x

Brownell, K. (2004). Overfeeding the future. In A. Heintzman & E. Solomon (Eds.), *Feeding the future: From fat to famine* (pp. 155–190). Toronto, Ontario, Canada: House of Anansi Press.

Brownell, K. D. (2003). Diet, obesity, public policy, and defiance. In R. J. Sternberg (Ed.), *Psychologists defying the crowd: Stories of those who battled the establishment and won* (pp. 47–64). Washington, DC: American Psychological Association.

Bruck, M., Ceci, S. J., Francouer, E., & Renick, A. (1995). Anatomically detailed dolls do not facilitate preschoolers' reports of a pediatric examination involving genital touching. *Journal of Experimental Psychology: Applied, 1,* 95–109. doi:10.1037/1076-898X.1.2.95

Bruck, M., Ceci, S. J., & Principe, G. F. (2006). The child and the law. In W. Damon & R. M. Lerner (Series Eds.) & K. A. Renninger & I. E. Sigel (Vol. Eds.), *Handbook of child psychology: Vol. 4. Child psychology in practice* (6th ed., pp. 776–816). Hoboken, NJ: Wiley.

Brumariu, L. E., & Kerns, K. A. (2010). Parent–child attachment and internalizing symptoms in childhood and adolescence: A review of empirical findings and future directions. *Development and Psychopathology, 22,* 177–203. doi:10.1017/S0954579409990344

Bruner, J. S. (1973). *Beyond the information given: Studies in the psychology of knowing* (J. M. Anglin, Ed.). New York, NY: Norton.

Bruner, J. S. (1975). The ontogenesis of speech acts. *Journal of Child Language, 2,* 1–19. doi:10.1017/S0305000900000866

Bruner, J. S. (1977). Early social interaction and language acquisition. In H. R. Schaffer (Ed.), *Studies in mother-infant interaction* (pp. 271–289). London, England: Academic Press.

Bryan, J. H., & Walbek, N. H. (1970). Preaching and practicing generosity: Children's actions and reactions. *Child Development, 41,* 329–353. doi: 10.2307/1127035

Bryant, J. A., Sanders-Jackson, A., & Smallwood, A. M. K. (2006). IMing, text messaging, and adolescent social networks. *Journal of Computer-Mediated Communication, 11,* 577–592.

Bryant, J. B., & Polkosky, M. (2001, April). *Parents responses to preschoolers' lexical innovations.* Paper presented at the Biennial Meeting of the Society for Research in Child Development, Minneapolis, MN.

Buchanan, C. M., Eccles, J. S., & Becker, J. B. (1992). Are adolescents the victims of raging hormones? Evidence for activational effects of hormones on moods and behavior at adolescence. *Psychological Bulletin, 111,* 62–107. doi:10.1037/0033-2909.111.1.62

Buchanan, C. M., Maccoby, E. E., & Dornbusch, S. M. (1991). Caught between parents: Adolescents' experience in divorced homes. *Child Development, 62,* 1008–1029. doi:10.1111/j.1467-8624.1991.tb01586.x

Buchanan, C. M., Maccoby, E. E., & Dornbusch, S. M. (1996). *Adolescents after divorce.* Cambridge, MA: Harvard University Press.

Buckner, J. C., Bassuk, E. L., Weinreb, L. F., & Brooks, M. G. (1999). Homelessness and its relation to the mental health and behavior of low-income school-age children. *Developmental Psychology, 35,* 246–257. doi:10.1037/0012-1649.35.1.246

Buehler, C., Anthony, C., Krishnakumar, A., Stone, G., Gerard, J., & Pemberton, S. (1997). Interparental conflict and youth problem behaviors: A meta-analysis. *Journal of Child and Family Studies, 6,* 233–247. doi: 10.1023/A:1025006909538

Buehler, C., Lange, G., & Franck, K. L. (2007). Adolescents' cognitive and emotional responses to marital hostility. *Child Development, 78,* 775–789. doi:10.1111/j.1467-8624.2007.01032.x

Buehler, C., & O'Brien, M. (2011). Mothers' part-time employment: Associations with mother and family well-being. *Journal of Family Psychology, 25,* 895–906. doi:10.1037/a0025993

Bugental, D. B., Beaulieu, D. A., & Silbert-Geiger, A. (2010). Increases in parental investment and child health as a result of an early intervention. *Journal of Experimental Child Psychology, 106,* 30–40. doi:10.1016/j.jecp.2009.10.004

Bugental, D. B., Blue, J., & Cruzcosa, M. (1989). Perceived control over caregiving outcomes: Implications for child abuse. *Developmental Psychology, 25,* 532–539. doi:10.1037/0012-1649.25.4.532

Bugental, D. B., Ellerson, P. C., Lin, E. K., Rainey, B., Kokotovic, A., & O'Hara, N. (2002). A cognitive approach to child abuse prevention. *Journal of Family Psychology, 16,* 243–258. doi:10.1037/0893-3200.16.3.243

Bugental, D. B., & Happaney, K. (2004). Predicting infant maltreatment in low-income families: The interactive effects of maternal attributions and child status at birth. *Developmental Psychology, 40,* 234–243.

Bugental, D. B., & Johnston, C. (2000). Parental and child cognitions in the context of the family. *Annual Review of Psychology, 51,* 315–344. doi:10.1146/annurev.psych.51.1.315

Bugental, D. B., Martorell, G. A., & Barraza, V. (2003). The hormonal costs of subtle forms of infant maltreatment. *Hormones and Behavior, 43,* 237–244. doi:10.1016/S0018-506X(02)00008-9

Bukowski, W. M., Gauze, C., Hoza, B., & Newcomb, A. F. (1993). Differences and consistency between same-sex and other-sex peer relationships during early adolescence. *Developmental Psychology, 29,* 255–263. doi:10.1037/0012-1649.29.2.255

Bukowski, W. M., Laursen, B., & Hoza, B. (2010). The snowball effect: Friendship moderates escalations in depressed affect among avoidant and excluded children. *Development and Psychopathology, 22,* 749–757. doi:10.1017/S095457941000043X

Bukowski, W. M., Newcomb, A. F., & Hartup, W. W. (1996). Friendship and its significance in childhood and adolescence: Introduction and comment. In W. M. Bukowski, A. F. Newcomb, & W. W. Hartup (Eds.), *The company they keep: Friendship in childhood and adolescence* (pp. 1–15). Cambridge, England: Cambridge University Press.

Bulf, H., Johnson, S. P., & Valenza, E. (2011). Visual statistical learning in the newborn infant. *Cognition, 121,* 127–132. doi:10.1016/j.cognition.2011.06.010

Bullock, M., & Lütkenhaus, P. (1990). Who am I? Self-understanding in toddlers. *Merrill-Palmer Quarterly, 36,* 217–238.

Bullock, M., & Russell, J. A. (1985). Further evidence on preschoolers' interpretation of facial expressions. *International Journal of Behavioral Development, 8,* 15–38.

Bumpass, L. L., Martin, T. C., & Sweet, J. A. (1991). The impact of family background and early marital factors on marital disruption. *Journal of Family Issues, 12,* 22–42. doi:10.1177/019251391012001003

Bunge, S. A., & Zelazo, P. D. (2006). A brain-based account of the development of rule use in childhood. *Current Directions in Psychological Science, 15,* 118–121.

Burchinal, M. R., Campbell, F. A., Brayant, D. M., Wasik, B. H., & Ramey, C. T. (1997). Early intervention and mediating processes in cognitive performance of children of low-income African American families. *Child Development, 68,* 935–954.

Burchinal, M. R., & Clarke-Stewart, K. A. (2007). Maternal employment and child cognitive outcomes: The importance of analytic approach. *Developmental Psychology, 43,* 1140–1155. doi:10.1037/0012-1649.43.5.1140

Burgess, K. B., Marshall, P. J., Rubin, K. H., & Fox, N. A. (2003). Infant attachment and temperament as predictors of subsequent externalizing problems and cardiac physiology. *Journal of Child Psychology and Psychiatry, 44,* 819–831. doi:10.1111/1469-7610.00167

Burkam, D. T., Lee, V. E., & Smerdon, B. A. (1997). Gender and science learning early in high school: Subject matter and laboratory experiences. *American Educational Research Journal, 34,* 297–331. doi:10.3102/00028312034002297

Burkam, D. T., Ready, D. D., Lee, V. E., & LoGerfo, L. F. (2004). Social-class differences in summer learning between kindergarten and first grade: Model specification and estimation. *Sociology of Education, 77,* 1–31.

Burmeister, D. (1996). Need fulfillment, interpersonal competence, and the developmental contexts of early adolescent friendship. In W. M. Bukowski, A. F. Newcomb, & W. W. Hartup (Eds), *The company they keep. Friendship in childhood and adolescence* (pp. 66–86). Cambridge, England: Cambridge University Press.

Burnette, M. L., Oshri, A., Lax, R., Richards, D., & Ragbeer, S. N. (2012). Pathways from harsh parenting to adolescent antisocial behavior: A multidomain test of gender moderation. *Development and Psychopathology, 24,* 857–870. doi:10.1017/S0954579412000417

Burt, S. A., Barnes, A. R., McGue, M., & Iacono, W. G. (2008). Parental divorce and adolescent delinquency: Ruling out the impact of common genes. *Developmental Psychology, 44,* 1668–1677. doi:10.1037/a0013477

Burt, S. A., Donnellan, M. B., Iacono, W., & McGue, M. (2011). Age-of-onset or behavioral sub-types? A prospective comparison of two approaches to characterizing the heterogeneity within antisocial behavior. *Journal of Abnormal Child Psychology, 39,* 633–644. doi:10.1007/s10802-011-9491-9

Burt, S. A., McGue, M., Krueger, R. F., & Iacono, W. G. (2005). How are parent–child conflict and childhood externalizing symptoms related over time? Results from a genetically informative cross-lagged study. *Development and Psychopathology, 17,* 145–165.

Busch, A. L., Cowan, P. A., & Cowan, C. P. (2008). Unresolved loss in the Adult Attachment Interview: Implications for marital and parenting relationships. *Development and Psychopathology, 20,* 717–735. doi:10.1017/S0954579408000345

Bushnell, E. W., & Boudreau, J. P. (1991). The development of haptic perception during infancy. In M. A. Heller & W. Schiff (Eds.), *The psychology of touch* (pp. 139–161). Hillsdale, NJ: Erlbaum.

Bushnell, E. W., McKenzie, B. E., Lawrence, D. A., & Connell, S. (1995). The spatial coding strategies of one-year-old infants in a locomotor search task. *Child Development, 66,* 937–958.

Bushnell, I. W. R., Sai, F., & Mullin, J. T. (2011). Neonatal recognition of the mother's face. *British Journal of Developmental Psychology, 7,* 3–15. doi:10.1111/j.2044-835X.1989.tb00784.x

Bushnik, T. (2006) *Child care in Canada* (Catalogue No. 89-599-MIE—No. 003). Retrieved from http://publications.gc.ca/Collection/Statcan/89-599-MIE/89-599-MIE2006003.pdf

Bushnik, T., & Garner, R. (2008). *The children of older first-time mothers in Canada: Their health and development*. Retrieved from http://www.statcan.gc.ca/pub/89-599-m/89-599-m2008005-eng.htm

Buss, D. M. (1999). *Evolutionary psychology: The new science of the mind*. Boston, MA: Allyn and Bacon.

Buss, K. A., Davidson, R. J., Kalin, N. H., & Goldsmith, H. H. (2004). Context-specific freezing and associated physiological reactivity as a dysregulated fear response. *Developmental Psychology, 40*, 583–594. doi:10.1037/0012-1649.40.4.583

Buss, K. A., & Kiel, E. J. (2011). Do maternal protective behaviors alleviate toddlers' fearful distress? *International Journal of Behavioral Development, 35*, 136–143. doi:10.1177/0165025410375922

Busseri, M. A., Willoughby, T., Chalmers, H., & Bogaert, A. F. (2008). On the association between sexual attraction and adolescent risk behavior involvement: Examining mediation and moderation. *Developmental Psychology, 44*, 69–80. doi:10.1037/0012-1649.44.1.69

Bussey, K., & Bandura, A. (1992). Self-regulatory mechanisms governing gender development. *Child Development, 63*, 1236–1250. doi:10.1111/j.1467-8624.1992.tb01692.x

Bussey, K., & Bandura, A. (1999). Social cognitive theory of gender development and differentiation. *Psychological Review, 106*, 676–713.

Butcher, L. M., Davis, O. S., Craig, I. W., & Plomin, R. (2008). Genome-wide quantitative trait locus association scan of general cognitive ability using pooled DNA and 500K single nucleotide polymorphism microarrays. *Genes, Brain, and Behavior, 7*, 435–446. doi:10.1111/j.1601-183X.2007.00368.x

Buttelmann, D., Carpenter, M., Call, J., & Tomasello, M. (2008). Rational tool use and tool choice in human infants and great apes. *Child Development, 79*, 609–626. doi:10.1111/j.1467-8624.2008.01146.x

Butterworth, B. (2010). Foundational numerical capacities and the origins of dyscalculia. *Trends in Cognitive Sciences, 14*, 534–541. doi:10.1016/j.tics.2010.09.007

Byers-Heinlein, K. (2012). Parental language mixing: Its measurement and the relation of mixed input to young bilingual children's vocabulary size. *Bilingualism: Language and Cognition, 14*(4), 588–595. doi: 10.1017/S1366728911000010

Byers-Heinlein, K., Burns, T. C., & Werker, J. F. (2010). The roots of bilingualism in newborns. *Psychological Science, 21*, 343–348. doi:10.1177/0956797609360758

Byers-Heinlein, K., & Werker, J. F. (2009). Monolingual, bilingual, trilingual: Infants' language experience influences the development of a word-learning heuristic. *Developmental Science, 12*, 815–823. doi:10.1111/j.1467-7687.2009.00902.x

Byrnes, J. P., Miller, D. C., & Schafer, W. D. (1999). Gender differences in risk taking: A meta-analysis. *Psychological Bulletin, 125*, 367–383. doi:10.1037/0033-2909.125.3.367

Cahan, S., & Cohen, N. (1989). Age versus schooling effects on intelligence development. *Child Development, 60*, 1239–1249.

Cai, H., Brown, J. D., Deng, C., & Oakes, M. A. (2007). Self-esteem and culture: Differences in cognitive self-evaluations or affective self-regard? *Asian Journal of Social Psychology, 10*, 162–170. doi:10.1111/j.1467-839X.2007.00222.x

Cain, K. M., & Dweck, C. S. (1995). The relation between motivational patterns and achievement cognitions through the elementary school years. *Merrill-Palmer Quarterly, 41*, 25–52. doi:10.2307/23087453

Cairns, R. B., Cairns, B. D., Neckerman, H. J., Ferguson, L. L., & Gariépy, J.-L. (1989). Growth and aggression: I. Childhood to early adolescence. *Developmental Psychology, 25*, 320–330. doi:10.1037/0012-1649.25.2.320

Cairns, R. B., Leung, M.-C., Buchanan, L., & Cairns, B. D. (1995). Friendships and social networks in childhood and adolescence: Fluidity, reliability, and interrelations. *Child Development, 66*, 1330–1345. doi:10.2307/1131650

Calati, R., Pedrini, L., Alighieri, S., Alvarez, M. I., Desideri, L., Durante, D., … Pericoli, V. (2011). Is cognitive behavioural therapy an effective complement to antidepressants in adolescents? A meta-analysis. *Acta Neuropsychiatrica, 23*, 263–271.

Caldwell, M. S., Rudolph, K. D., Troop-Gordon, W., & Kim, D.-Y. (2004). Reciprocal influences among relational self-views, social disengagement, and peer stress during early adolescence. *Child Development, 75*, 1140–1154. doi:10.1111/j.1467-8624.2004.00730.x

Calkins, S. D. (2002). Does aversive behavior during toddlerhood matter? The effects of difficult temperament on maternal perceptions and behavior. *Infant Mental Health Journal, 23*, 381–402.

Calkins, S. D., & Dedmon, S. E. (2000). Physiological and behavioral regulation in two-year-old children with aggressive/destructive behavior problems. *Journal of Abnormal Child Psychology, 28*, 103–118.

Calkins, S. D., Fox, N. A., & Marshall, T. R. (1996). Behavioral and physiological antecedents of inhibited and uninhibited behavior. *Child Development, 67*, 523–540.

Calkins, S. D., & Keane, S. P. (2004). Cardiac vagal regulation across the preschool period: Stability, continuity, and implications for childhood adjustment. *Developmental Psychobiology, 45*, 101–112. doi:10.1002/dev.20020

Calkins, S. D., & Swingler, M. M. (2012). Psychobiological measures of temperament in childhood. In M. R. Zentner & R. L. Shiner (Eds.), *Handbook of temperament* (pp. 229–247). New York, NY: Guilford Press.

Callaghan, T., Moll, H., Rakoczy, H., Warneken, F., Liszkowski, U., Behne, T., & Tomasello, M. (2011). Early social cognition in three cultural contexts. *Monographs of the Society for Research in Child Development, 76*(2, Serial No. 299), vii-142. doi:10.1111/j.1540-5834.2011.00603.x

Callaghan, T., Rochat, P., Lillard, A., Claux, M. L., Odden, H., Itakura, S., … Singh, S. (2005). Synchrony in the onset of mental-state reasoning: Evidence from five cultures. *Psychological Science, 16*, 378–384. doi:10.1111/j.0956-7976.2005.01544.x

Callaghan, T. C. (1999). Early understanding and production of graphic symbols. *Child Development, 70*, 1314–1324. doi:10.1111/1467-8624.00096

Callanan, M. A. (1990). Parents' descriptions of objects: Potential data for children's inferences about category principles. *Cognitive Development, 5*, 101–122. doi:10.1016/0885-2014(90)90015-L

Callanan, M. A., & Sabbagh, M. A. (2004). Multiple labels for objects in conversations with young children: Parents' language and children's developing expectations about word meanings. *Developmental Psychology, 40*, 746–762.

Calvete, E., & Orue, I. (2012). Social information processing as a mediator between cognitive schemas and aggressive behavior in adolescents. *Journal of Abnormal Child Psychology, 40*, 105–117. doi:10.1007/s10802-011-9546-y

Calzo, J. P., Antonucci, T. C., Mays, V. M., & Cochran, S. D. (2011). Retrospective recall of sexual orientation identity development among gay, lesbian, and bisexual adults. *Developmental Psychology, 47,* 1658–1673. doi: 10.1037/a0025508

Camarena, P. M., Sarigiani, P. A., & Petersen, A. C. (1990). Gender-specific pathways to intimacy in early adolescence. *Journal of Youth and Adolescence, 19,* 19–32. doi:10.1007/BF01539442

Cameron, C. A., Lau, C., Fu, G., & Lee, K. (2012). Development of children's moral evaluations of modesty and self-promotion in diverse cultural settings. *Journal of Moral Education, 41,* 61–78. doi: 10.1080/03057240.2011.617414

Campbell, A., Shirley, L., & Caygill, L. (2002). Sex-typed preferences in three domains: Do two-year-olds need cognitive variables? *British Journal of Psychology, 93,* 203–217. doi:10.1348/000712602162544

Campbell, F. A., Pungello, E. P., Burchinal, M., Kainz, K., Pan, Y., Wasik, B. H., ... Ramey, C. T. (2012). Adult outcomes as a function of an early childhood educational program: An Abecedarian Project follow-up. *Developmental Psychology, 48,* 1033–1043.

Campbell, F. A., Pungello, E. P., Miller-Johnson, S., Burchinal, M., & Ramey, C. T. (2001). The development of cognitive and academic abilities: Growth curves from an early childhood educational experiment. *Developmental Psychology, 37,* 231–242.

Campbell, S. B., Cohn, J. F., & Meyers, T. (1995). Depression in first-time mothers: Mother-infant interaction and depression chronicity. *Developmental Psychology, 31,* 349–357. doi:10.1037/0012-1649.31.3.349

Campbell, S. B., Matestic, P., von Stauffenberg, C., Mohan, R., & Kirchner, T. (2007). Trajectories of maternal depressive symptoms, maternal sensitivity, and children's functioning at school entry. *Developmental Psychology, 43,* 1202–1215. doi:10.1037/0012-1649.43.5.1202

Campbell, S. B., Spieker, S., Vandergrift, N., Belsky, J., Burchinal, M., & NICHD Early Child Care Research Network. (2010). Predictors and sequelae of trajectories of physical aggression in school-age boys and girls. *Development and Psychopathology, 22,* 133–150.

Campos, J. J., Anderson, D. I., Barbu-Roth, M. A., Hubbard, E. M., Hertenstein, M. J., & Witherington, D. (2000). Travel broadens the mind. *Infancy, 1,* 149–219.

Campos, J. J., Frankel, C. B., & Camras, L. (2004). On the nature of emotion regulation. *Child Development, 75,* 377–394. doi:10.1111/j.1467-8624.2004.00681.x

Campos, J. J., Kermoian, R., & Zumbahlen, M. R. (1992). Socioemotional transformations in the family system following infant crawling onset. In N. Eisenberg & R. A. Fabes (Eds.), *New Directions for Child and Adolescent Development: No. 55. Emotion and its regulation in early development* (pp. 25–40). San Francisco, CA: Jossey-Bass.

Campos, J. J., Mumme, D. L., Kermoian, R., & Campos, R. G. (1994). A functionalist perspective on the nature of emotion. *Monographs of the Society for Research in Child Development, 59*(2-3, Serial No. 240), 284–303.

Campos, J. J., Witherington, D., Anderson, D. I., Frankel, C. I., Uchiyama, I., & Barbu-Roth, M. (2008). Rediscovering development in infancy. *Child Development, 79,* 1625–1632. doi:10.1111/j.1467-8624.2008.01212.x

Campos, R. G. (1989). Soothing pain-elicited distress in infants with swaddling and pacifiers. *Child Development, 60,* 781–792.

Camras, L. A. (1992). Expressive development and basic emotions. *Cognition and Emotion, 6,* 269–283.

Camras, L. A. (2011). Differentiation, dynamical integration and functional emotional development. *Emotion Review, 3,* 138–146.

Camras, L. A., Malatesta, C., & Izard, C. E. (1991). The development of facial expressions in infancy. In R. S. Feldman & B. Rimé (Eds.), *Fundamentals of nonverbal behavior* (pp. 73–105). New York, NY: Cambridge University Press.

Camras, L. A., Oster, H., Campos, J., Campos, R., Ujiie, T., Miyake, K., ... Meng, Z. (1998). Production of emotional facial expressions in European American, Japanese, and Chinese infants. *Developmental Psychology, 34,* 616–628.

Camras, L. A., & Shutter, J. M. (2010). Emotional facial expressions in infancy. *Emotion Review, 2,* 120–129.

Canli, T., Omura, K., Haas, B. W., Fallgatter, A., Constable, R. T., & Lesch, K. P. (2005). Beyond affect: A role for genetic variation of the serotonin transporter in neural activation during a cognitive attention task. *Proceedings of the National Academy of Sciences of the United States of America, 102,* 12224–12229. doi:10.1073/pnas.0503880102

Cannon, E. N., & Woodward, A. L. (2012). Infants generate goal-based action predictions. *Developmental Science, 15,* 292–298. doi:10.1111/j.1467-7687.2011.01127.x

Canobi, K. H., Reeve, R. A., & Pattison, P. E. (2002). Young children's understanding of addition concepts. *Educational Psychology, 22,* 513–532.

Capizzano, J., Tout, K., & Adams, G. (2000). Child care patterns of school-age children with employed mothers. Retrieved from http://www.urban.org/publications/310283.html

Caputi, M., Lecce, S., Pagnin, A., & Banerjee, R. (2012). Longitudinal effects of theory of mind on later peer relations: The role of prosocial behavior. *Developmental Psychology, 48,* 257–270. doi:10.1037/a0025402

Card, N. A., Stucky, B. D., Sawalani, G. M., & Little, T. D. (2008). Direct and indirect aggression during childhood and adolescence: A meta-analytic review of gender differences, intercorrelations, and relations to maladjustment. *Child Development, 79,* 1185–1229. doi:10.1111/j.1467-8624.2008.01184.x

Cardno, A. G., & Gottesman, I. I. (2000). Twin studies of schizophrenia: From bow-and-arrow concordances to Star Wars Mx and functional genomics. *American Journal of Medical Genetics, 97,* 12–17.

Cardoso, J. B., Padilla, Y. C., & Sampson, M. (2010). Racial and ethnic variation in the predictors of maternal parenting stress. *Journal of Social Service Research, 36,* 429–444. doi:10.1080/01488376.2010.510948

Carey, S. (1985). *Conceptual change in childhood.* Cambridge, MA: MIT Press.

Carey, S. (1999). Sources of conceptual change. In E. K. Scholnick, K. Nelson, S. A. Gelman, & P. H. Miller (Eds.), *Conceptual development: Piaget's legacy* (pp. 293–326). Mahwah, NJ: Erlbaum.

Carey, S. (2009). Where our number concepts come from. *Journal of Philosophy, 106,* 220–254.

Carey, S., & Bartlett, E. (1978). Acquiring a single new word. *Papers and Reports on Child Language Development, 15,* 17–29.

Carey, S., & Spelke, E. S. (1994). Domain-specific knowledge and conceptual change. In L. Hirschfeld & S. Gelman (Eds.), *Mapping the mind: Domain specificity in cognition and culture* (pp. 169–200). Cambridge, England: Cambridge University Press.

Carlo, G., Crockett, L. J., Randall, B. A., & Roesch, S. C. (2007). A latent growth curve analysis of prosocial behavior among rural adolescents. *Journal of Research on Adolescence, 17,* 301–324. doi: 10.1111/ j.1532- 7795.2007.00524.x

Carlo, G., Knight, G. P., McGinley, M., Zamboanga, B. L., & Jarvis, L. H. (2010). The multidimensionality of prosocial behaviors and evidence of measurement equivalence in Mexican American and European American early adolescents. *Journal of Research on Adolescence, 20,* 334–358. doi: 10.1111/j.1532-7795.2010.00637.x

Carlo, G., Koller, S. H., Eisenberg, N., Da Silva, M. S., & Frohlich, C. B. (1996). A cross-national study on the relations among prosocial moral reasoning, gender role orientations, and prosocial behaviors. *Developmental Psychology, 32*, 231–240. doi:10.1037/0012-1649.32.2.231

Carlo, G., McGinley, M., Roesch, S. C., & Kaminski, J. W. (2008). Measurement invariance in a measure of prosocial moral reasoning to use with adolescents from the USA and Brazil. *Journal of Moral Education, 37*, 485–502. doi:10.1080/03057240802399368

Carlo, G., Mestre, M. V., Samper, P., Tur, A., & Armenta, B. E. (2010). Feelings or cognitions? Moral cognitions and emotions as longitudinal predictors of prosocial and aggressive behaviors. *Personality and Individual Differences, 48*, 872–877. doi:10.1016/j.paid.2010.02.010

Carlson, E. A. (1998). A prospective longitudinal study of attachment disorganization/disorientation. *Child Development, 69*, 1107–1128. doi: 10.1111/j.1467-8624.1998.tb06163.x

Carlson, E. A., Sroufe, L. A., & Egeland, B. (2004). The construction of experience: A longitudinal study of representation and behavior. *Child Development, 75*, 66–83. doi:10.1111/j.1467-8624.2004.00654.x

Carlson, S., Hyvärinen, L., & Raninen, A. (1986). Persistent behavioural blindness after early visual deprivation and active visual rehabilitation: A case report. *British Journal of Ophthalmology, 70*, 607–611. doi:10.1136/bjo.70.8.607

Carlson, S. M., Gum, J., Davis, A., & Malloy, A. (2003, June). *Predictors of imaginary companion in early childhood.* Poster session presented at the annual meeting of the Jean Piaget Society, Chicago, IL.

Carlson, S. M., Mandell, D. J., & Williams, L. (2004). Executive function and theory of mind: Stability and prediction from ages 2 to 3. *Developmental Psychology, 40*, 1105–1122. doi:10.1037/0012-1649.40.6.1105

Carlson, W., & Rose, A. J. (2007). The role of reciprocity in romantic relationships in middle childhood and early adolescence. *Merrill-Palmer Quarterly, 53*, 262–290.

Carpenter, M., Nagell, K., & Tomasello, M. (1998). Social cognition, joint attention, and communicative competence from 9 to 15 months of age. *Monographs of the Society for Research in Child Development, 63*(4, Serial No. 255).

Carroll, J. B. (1993). *Human cognitive abilities: A survey of factor-analytic studies.* New York, NY: Cambridge University Press.

Carroll, J. B. (2005). The three-stratum theory of cognitive abilities. In D. P. Flanagan & P. L. Harrison (Eds.), *Contemporary intellectual assessment: Theories, tests, and issues* (2nd ed., pp. 69–76). New York, NY: Guilford Press.

Carter, C. S. (1986). The reproductive and adrenal systems. In M. G. H. Coles, E. Donchin, & S. W. Porges (Eds.), *Psychophysiology: Systems, processes, and applications* (pp. 172–182). New York, NY: Guilford Press.

Carter, D. B., & Patterson, C. J. (1982). Sex roles as social conventions: The development of children's conceptions of sex-role stereotypes. *Developmental Psychology, 18*, 812–824. doi:10.1037/0012-1649.18.6.812

Carver, K., Joyner, K., & Udry, J. R. (2003). National estimates of adolescent romantic relationships. In P. Florsheim (Ed.), *Adolescent romantic relations and sexual behavior: Theory, research, and practical implications* (pp. 23–56). Mahwah, NJ: Erlbaum.

Carver, L. J. (1999). When the event is more than the sum of its parts: 9-month-olds' long-term ordered recall. *Memory, 7*, 147–174. doi:10.1080/741944070

Carver, L. J., & Bauer, P. J. (1999). When the event is more than the sum of its parts: 9-month-olds' long-term ordered recall. *Memory, 7*, 147–174.

Carver, L. J., Bauer, P. J., & Nelson, C. A. (2000). Associations between infant brain activity and recall memory. *Developmental Science, 3*, 234–246. doi:10.1111/1467-7687.00116

Carver, L. J., & Vaccaro, B. G. (2007). 12-month-old infants allocate increased neural resources to stimuli associated with negative adult emotion. *Developmental Psychology, 43*, 54–69. doi:10.1037/0012-1649.43.1.54

Casasola, M. (2008). The development of infants' spatial categories. *Current Directions in Psychological Science, 17*, 21–25. doi:10.1111/j.1467-8721.2008.00541.x

Casasola, M. (2010). Infant spatial categorization from an information processing approach. In L. M. Oakes, C. H. Cashon, M. Casasola, & D. H. Rakison (Eds.), *Infant perception and cognition: Recent advances, emerging theories, and future directions* (pp. 179–201). New York, NY: Oxford University Press.

Case, R. (1998). The development of conceptual structures. In W. Damon (Series Ed.) & D. Kuhn & R. S. Siegler (Vol. Eds.), *Handbook of child psychology: Vol. 2. Cognition, perception, and language* (5th ed., pp. 745–800). New York, NY: Wiley.

Case, R., Griffin, S., & Kelly, W. M. (1999). Socioeconomic gradients in mathematical ability and their responsiveness to intervention during early childhood. In D. P. Keating & C. Hertzman (Eds.), *Developmental health and the wealth of nations: Social, biological, and educational dynamics* (pp. 125–149). New York, NY: Guilford Press.

Casey, B. J. (1999). Brain development, XII: Maturation in brain activation. *American Journal of Psychiatry, 156*, 504.

Casey, B. J., Somerville, L. H., Gotlib, I. H., Ayduk, O., Franklin, N. T., Askren, M. K., … Shoda, Y. (2011). Behavioral and neural correlates of delay of gratification 40 years later. *Proceedings of the National Academy of Sciences of the United States of America, 108*, 14998–15003. doi:10.1073/pnas.1108561108

Casiglia, A. C., LoCoco, A., & Zappulla, C. (1998). Aspects of social reputation and peer relationships in Italian children: A cross-cultural perspective. *Developmental Psychology, 34*, 723–730. doi:10.1037/0012-1649.34.4.723

Caspi, A. (2000). The child is father of the man: Personality continuities from childhood to adulthood. *Journal of Personality and Social Psychology, 78*, 158–172.

Caspi, A., Elder, G. H., & Bem, D. J. (1988). Moving away from the world: Life-course patterns of shy children. *Developmental Psychology, 24*, 824–831. doi:10.1037/0012-1649.24.6.824

Caspi, A., Harrington, H., Milne, B., Amell, J. W., Theodore, R. F., & Moffitt, T. E. (2003). Children's behavioral styles at age 3 are linked to their adult personality traits at age 26. *Journal of Personality, 71*, 495–514.

Caspi, A., Henry, B., McGee, R. O., Moffitt, T. E., & Silva, P. A. (1995). Temperamental origins of child and adolescent behavior problems: From age three to age fifteen. *Child Development, 66*, 55–68.

Caspi, A., McClay, J., Moffitt, T. E., Mill, J., Martin, J., Craig, I. W., … Poulton, R. (2002, August 2). Role of genotype in the cycle of violence in maltreated children. *Science, 297*, 851–854.

Caspi, A., Moffitt, T. E., Morgan, J., Rutter, M., Taylor, A., Arseneault, L., … Polo-Tomas, M. (2004). Maternal expressed emotion predicts children's antisocial behavior problems: Using monozygotic-twin differences to identify environmental effects on behavioral development. *Developmental Psychology, 40*, 149–161. doi:10.1037/0012-1649.40.2.149

Caspi, A., & Silva, P. A. (1995). Temperamental qualities at age three predict personality traits in young adulthood: Longitudinal evidence from a birth cohort. *Child Development, 66*, 486–498.

Caspi, A., Williams, B., Kim-Cohen, J., Craig, I. W., Milne, B. J., Poulton, R., ... Moffitt, T. E. (2007). Moderation of breastfeeding effects on the IQ by genetic variation in fatty acid metabolism. *Proceedings of the National Academy of Sciences of the United States of America, 104,* 18860–18865. doi:10.1073/pnas.0704292104

Cassidy, J. (1994). Emotion regulation: Influences of attachment relationships. *Monographs of the Society for Research in Child Development, 59*(2-3, Serial No. 240), 228–249.

Cassidy, J., Ziv, Y., Mehta, T. G., & Feeney, B. C. (2003). Feedback seeking in children and adolescents: Associations with self-perceptions, attachment representations, and depression. *Child Development, 74,* 612–628. doi:10.1111/1467-8624.7402019

Castro, D. C., Páez, M. M., Dickinson, D. K., & Frede, E. (2011). Promoting language and literacy in young dual language learners: Research, practice, and policy. *Child Development Perspectives, 5,* 15–21. doi:10.1111/j.1750-8606.2010.00142.x

Cattell, R. B. (1987). *Intelligence: Its structure, growth, and action.* Amsterdam, The Netherlands: North-Holland.

Ceballo, R., & McLoyd, V. C. (2002). Social support and parenting in poor, dangerous neighborhoods. *Child Development, 73,* 1310–1321. doi:10.1111/1467-8624.00473

Ceci, S. J. (1991). How much does schooling influence general intelligence and its cognitive components? A reassessment of the evidence. *Developmental Psychology, 27,* 703–723.

Ceci, S. J. (1993). Contextual trends in intellectual development. *Developmental Review, 13,* 403–435. doi:10.1006/drev.1993.1019

Ceci, S. J. (1996). *On intelligence: A bioecological treatise on intellectual development.* Cambridge, MA: Harvard University Press.

Ceci, S. J., & Bruck, M. (1998). Children's testimony: Applied and basic issues. In W. Damon (Series Ed.) & I. E. Sigel & K. A. Renninger (Vol. Eds.), *Handbook of child psychology: Vol. 4. Child psychology in practice* (5th ed., pp. 713–774). New York, NY: Wiley.

Central Intelligence Agency. (2012). *The world factbook.* Washington, DC: Author.

Centre for Youth and Media Studies. (2010). *A national study on children's television programming in Canada.* Montreal, QC: Département de communication, Université de Montréal.

Chabris, C. F., Hebert, B. M., Benjamin, D. J., Beauchamp, J., Cesarini, D., van der Loos, M., ... Laibson, D. (2012). Most reported genetic associations with general intelligence are probably false positives. *Psychological Science, 23,* 1314–1323. doi:10.1177/0956797611435528

Chall, J. (1979). The great debate: Ten years later, with a modest proposal for reading stages. In L. B. Resnick & P. A. Weaver (Eds.), *Theory and practice of early reading* (Vol. 1, pp. 29–55). Hillsdale, NJ: Erlbaum.

Chalmers, D., & Lawrence, J. A. (1993). Investigating the effects of planning aids on adults' and adolescents' organisation of a complex task. *International Journal of Behavioral Development, 16,* 191–214.

Champagne, F. A., & Curley, J. P. (2009). Epigenetic mechanisms mediating the long-term effects of maternal care on development. *Neuroscience and Biobehavioral Reviews, 33,* 593–600. doi:10.1016/j.neubiorev.2007.10.009

Chan, A., & Poulin, F. (2007). Monthly changes in the composition of friendship networks in early adolescence. *Merrill-Palmer Quarterly, 53,* 578–602.

Chan, K., Penner, K., Mah, J. W. T., & Johnston, C. (2010). Assessing parenting behaviors in Euro-Canadian and East Asian immigrant mothers: Limitations to observations of responsiveness. *Child & Family Behavior Therapy, 32,* 85–102. doi:10.1080/07317101003776423

Chan, R. W., Brooks, R. C., Raboy, B., & Patterson, C. J. (1998). Division of labor among lesbian and heterosexual parents: Associations with children's adjustment. *Journal of Family Psychology, 12,* 402–419. doi:10.1037/0893-3200.12.3.402

Chan, R. W., Raboy, B., & Patterson, C. J. (1998). Psychosocial adjustment among children conceived via donor insemination by lesbian and heterosexual mothers. *Child Development, 69,* 443–457. doi:10.1111/j.1467-8624.1998.tb06201.x

Chandler, M. J., Greenspan, S., & Barenboim, C. (1973). Judgments of intentionality in response to videotaped and verbally presented moral dilemmas: The medium is the message. *Child Development, 44,* 315–320. doi:10.2307/1128053

Chang, L., Lansford, J. E., Schwartz, D., & Farver, J. M. (2004). Marital quality, maternal depressed affect, harsh parenting, and child externalising in Hong Kong Chinese families. *International Journal of Behavioral Development, 28,* 311–318. doi:10.1080/01650250344000523

Changeux, J.-P., & Danchin, A. (1976, December 23). Selective stabilisation of developing synapses as a mechanism for the specification of neuronal networks. *Nature, 264,* 705–712.

Chao, R. K. (1994). Beyond parental control and authoritarian parenting style: Understanding Chinese parenting through the cultural notion of training. *Child Development, 65,* 1111–1119. doi:10.1111/j.1467-8624.1994.tb00806.x

Chaput, J. P., Lambert, M., Mathieu, M. E., Tremblay, M. S., O'Loughlin, J., & Tremblay, A. (2012). Physical activity vs. sedentary time: Independent associations with adiposity in children. *Pediatric Obesity, 7,* 251–258. doi:10.1111/j.2047-6310.2011.00028.x

Charlesworth, W. R., & LaFreniere, P. (1983). Dominance, friendship, and resource utilization in preschool children's groups. *Ethology and Sociobiology, 4,* 175–186. doi:10.1016/0162-3095(83)90028-6

Chase-Lansdale, P. L., Cherlin, A. J., & Kiernan, K. E. (1995). The long-term effects of parental divorce on the mental health of young adults: A developmental perspective. *Child Development, 66,* 1614–1634. doi:10.1111/j.1467-8624.1995.tb00955.x

Chayer, M.-H., & Bouffard, T. (2010). Relations between impostor feelings and upward and downward identification and contrast among 10- to 12-year-old students. *European Journal of Psychology of Education, 25,* 125–140. doi:10.1007/s10212-009-0004-y

Cheah, C., & Rubin, K. (2004). European American and Mainland Chinese mothers' responses to aggression and social withdrawal in preschoolers. *International Journal of Behavioral Development, 28,* 83–94.

Cheah, C. S. L., Leung, C. Y. Y., Tahseen, M., & Schultz, D. (2009). Authoritative parenting among immigrant Chinese mothers of preschoolers. *Journal of Family Psychology, 23,* 311–320. doi:10.1037/a0015076

Chen, C., Greenberger, E., Lester, J., Dong, Q., & Guo, M.-S. (1998). A cross-cultural study of family and peer correlates of adolescent misconduct. *Developmental Psychology, 34,* 770–781. doi:10.1037/0012-1649.34.4.770

Chen, E., & Miller, G. E. (2012). "Shift-and-persist" strategies: Why being low in socioeconomic status isn't always bad for health. *Perspectives on Psychological Science, 7,* 135–158. doi:10.1177/1745691612436694

Chen, X., Cen, G., Li, D., & He, Y. (2005). Social functioning and adjustment in Chinese children: The imprint of historical time. *Child Development, 76,* 182–195. doi:10.1111/j.1467-8624.2005.00838.x

Chen, X., Chang, L., & He, Y. (2003). The peer group as a context: Mediating and moderating effects on relations between academic achievement and social functioning in Chinese children. *Child Development, 74,* 710–727. doi:10.2307/3696225

Chen, X., Chang, L., He, Y., & Liu, H. (2005). The peer group as a context: Moderating effects on relations between maternal parenting and social and school adjustment in Chinese children. *Child Development, 76*, 417–434. doi:10.1111/j.1467-8624.2005.00854.x

Chen, X., Dong, Q., & Zhou, H. (1997). Authoritative and authoritarian parenting practices and social and school performance in Chinese children. *International Journal of Behavioral Development, 21*, 855–873. doi:10.1080/016502597384703

Chen, X., He, Y., & Li, D. (2004). Self-perceptions of social competence and self-worth in Chinese children: Relations with social and school performance. *Social Development, 13*, 570–589. doi:10.1111/j.1467-9507.2004.00284.x

Chen, X., Rubin, K. H., & Li, B. (1995). Social and school adjustment of shy and aggressive children in China. *Development and Psychopathology, 7*, 337–349. doi:10.1017/S0954579400006544

Chen, X., Rubin, K. H., Li, B.-s., & Li, D. (1999). Adolescent outcomes of social functioning in Chinese children. *International Journal of Behavioral Development, 23*, 199–223. doi:10.1080/016502599384071

Chen, X., Rubin, K. H., & Li, Z.-y. (1995). Social functioning and adjustment in Chinese children: A longitudinal study. *Developmental Psychology, 31*, 531–539. doi:10.1037/0012-1649.31.4.531

Chen, X., Rubin, K. H., & Sun, Y. (1992). Social reputation and peer relationships in Chinese and Canadian children: A cross-cultural study. *Child Development, 63*, 1336–1343. doi:10.1111/j.1467-8624.1992.tb01698.x

Chen, X., Wang, L., & Cao, R. (2011). Shyness-sensitivity and unsociability in rural Chinese children: Relations with social, school, and psychological adjustment. *Child Development, 82*, 1531–1543. doi:10.1111/j.1467-8624.2011.01616.x

Chen, X., Wang, L., & Wang, Z. (2009). Shyness-sensitivity and social, school, and psychological adjustment in rural migrant and urban children in China. *Child Development, 80*, 1499–1513. doi:10.1111/j.1467-8624.2009.01347.x

Chen, Z., Mo, L., & Honomichl, R. (2004). Having the memory of an elephant: Long-term retrieval and the use of analogues in problem solving. *Journal of Experimental Psychology: General, 133*, 415–433.

Chen, Z., & Siegler, R. (2000). Across the great divide: Bridging the gap between understanding of toddlers' and older children's thinking. *Monographs of the Society for Research in Child Development, 65*(2, Serial No. 261).

Cheour, M., Martynova, O., Näätänen, R., Erkkola, R., Sillanpää, M., Kero, P., … Hämäläinen, H. (2002, February 7). Speech sounds learned by sleeping newborns. *Nature, 415*, 599–600.

Cherney, I. D., & London, K. (2006). Gender-linked differences in the toys, television shows, computer games, and outdoor activities of 5- to 13-year-old children. *Sex Roles, 54*, 717–726. doi:10.1007/s11199-006-9037-8

Chess, S., & Thomas, A. (1990). Continuities and discontinuities in temperament. In L. N. Robins & M. Rutter (Eds.), *Straight and devious pathways from childhood to adulthood* (pp. 205–220). Cambridge, England: Cambridge University Press.

Chi, M. T. H., & Ceci, S. J. (1987). Content knowledge: Its role, representation, and restructuring in memory development. In H. W. Reese (Ed.), *Advances in child development and behavior* (Vol. 20, pp. 91–142). San Diego, CA: Academic Press.

Chiandetti, C., & Vallortigara, G. (2011). Chicks like consonant music. *Psychological Science, 22*, 1270–1273. doi:10.1177/0956797611418244

Chiappe, P., & Siegel, L. S. (1999). Phonological awareness and reading acquisition in English- and Punjabi-speaking Canadian children. *Journal of Educational Psychology, 91*, 20–28. doi:10.1037/0022-0663.91.1.20

Chisholm, J. S. (1983). *Navajo infancy: An ethological study of child development.* Hawthorne, NY: Aldine.

Chisholm, K. (1998). A three-year follow-up of attachment and indiscriminate friendliness in children adopted from Romanian orphanages. *Child Development, 69*, 1090–1104. doi:10.1111/j.1467-8624.1998.tb06162.x

Choi, S. (2000). Caregiver input in English and Korean: Use of nouns and verbs in book-reading and toy-play contexts. *Journal of Child Language, 27*, 69–96.

Choi, S., & Gopnik, A. (1995). Early acquisition of verbs in Korean: A cross-linguistic study. *Journal of Child Language, 22*, 497–529.

Chomsky, N. (1957). *Syntactic structures.* The Hague: Mouton.

Chomsky, N. (1959). A review of B. F. Skinner's *Verbal Behavior. Language, 35*, 26–58.

Chouinard, M. M. (2007). Children's questions: A mechanism for cognitive development. *Monographs of the Society for Research in Child Development, 72*(1, Serial No. 286).

Christian, R. E., Frick, P. J., Hill, N. L., Tyler, L., & Frazer, D. R. (1997). Psychopathy and conduct problems in children: II. Implications for subtyping children with conduct problems. *Journal of the American Academy of Child and Adolescent Psychiatry, 36*, 233–241. doi:10.1097/00004583-199702000-00014

Chugani, H. T., Behen, M. E., Muzik, O., Juhasz, C., Nagy, F., & Chugani, D. C. (2001). Local brain functional activity following early deprivation: A study of postinstitutionalized Romanian orphans. *Neuroimage, 14*, 1290–1301. doi:10.1006/nimg.2001.0917

Chung-Hall, J., & Chen, X. (2010). Aggressive and prosocial peer group functioning: Effects on children's social, school, and psychological adjustment. *Social Development, 19*, 659–680. doi:10.1111/j.1467-9507.2009.00556.x

Church, R. B. (1999). Using gesture and speech to capture transitions in learning. *Cognitive Development, 14*, 313–342.

Cianciolo, A. T., Matthew, C., Sternberg, R. J., & Wagner, R. K. (2006). Tacit knowledge, practical intelligence, and expertise. In K. A. Ericsson, N. Charness, P. J. Feltovich, & R. R. Hoffman (Eds.), *The Cambridge handbook of expertise and expert performance* (pp. 613–632). New York, NY: Cambridge University Press.

Cicchetti, D., Rogosch, F. A., & Thibodeau, E. L. (2012). The effects of child maltreatment on early signs of antisocial behavior: Genetic moderation by tryptophan hydroxylase, serotonin transporter, and monoamine oxidase A genes. *Development and Psychopathology, 24*, 907–928.

Cicchetti, D., & Toth, S. L. (1998). Perspectives on research and practice in developmental psychopathology. In W. Damon (Series Ed.) & I. E. Sigel & K. A. Renninger (Vol. Eds.), *Handbook of child psychology: Vol. 4. Child psychology in practice* (5th ed., pp. 479–483). New York, NY: Wiley.

Cicchetti, D., & Toth, S. L. (2006). Developmental psychopathology and preventive intervention. In W. Damon & R. M. Lerner (Series Eds.) & K. A. Renninger & I. E. Sigel (Vol. Eds.), *Handbook of child psychology: Vol. 4. Child psychology in practice* (6th ed., pp. 497–547). Hoboken, NJ: Wiley.

Cillessen, A. H. N., & Mayeux, L. (2004). From censure to reinforcement: Developmental changes in the association between aggression and social status. *Child Development, 75*, 147–163. doi:10.2307/3696572

Cimpian, A., & Scott, R. M. (2012). Children expect generic knowledge to be widely shared. *Cognition, 123,* 419–433. doi:10.1016/j.cognition.2012.02.003

Cismaresco, A. S., & Montagner, H. (1990). Mothers' discrimination of their neonates' cry in relation to cry acoustics: The first week of life. *Early Child Development and Care, 65,* 3–11. doi:10.1080/0300443900650102

Clamp, M., Fry, B., Kamal, M., Xie, X., Cuff, J., Lin, M. F., … Lander, E. S. (2007). Distinguishing protein-coding and noncoding genes in the human genome. *Proceedings of the National Academy of Sciences of the United States of America, 104,* 19428–19433. doi:10.1073/pnas.0709013104

Clark, C. A. C., Woodward, L. J., Horwood, L. J., & Moor, S. (2008). Development of emotional and behavioral regulation in children born extremely preterm and very preterm: Biological and social influences. *Child Development, 79,* 1444–1462.

Clark, E. V. (1979). Building a vocabulary: Words for objects, actions, and relations. In P. Fletcher & M. Garman (Eds.), *Language acquisition* (pp. 149–160). Cambridge, England: Cambridge University Press.

Clark, E. V. (1993). *The lexicon in acquisition.* Cambridge, England: Cambridge University Press.

Clarke-McLean, J. G. (1996). Social networks among incarcerated juvenile offenders. *Social Development, 5,* 203–217. doi:10.1111/j.1467-9507.1996.tb00081.x

Clarke-Stewart, K. A. (1981). Observation and experiment: Complementary strategies for studying day care and social development. In S. Kilmer (Ed.), *Advances in early education and day care* (Vol. 2, pp. 227–250). Greenwich, CT: JAI Press.

Clarke-Stewart, K. A. (1982). Observation and experiment: Complementary strategies for studying day care and social development. In S. Kilmer (Ed.), *Advances in early education and day care* (Vol. 2, pp. 227–250). Greenwich, CT: JAI Press.

Clarke-Stewart, K. A., Vandell, D. L., McCartney, K., Owen, M. T., & Booth, C. (2000). Effects of parental separation and divorce on very young children. *Journal of Family Psychology, 14,* 304–326. doi:10.1037/0893-3200.14.2.304

Clary, E. G., & Miller, J. (1986). Socialization and situational influences on sustained altruism. *Child Development, 57,* 1358–1369. doi:10.2307/1130415

Claxton, L. J., Keen, R., & McCarty, M. E. (2003). Evidence of motor planning in infant reaching behavior. *Psychological Science, 14,* 354–356. doi:10.1111/1467-9280.24421

Clearfield, M. (2006). A dynamic account of infant looking behavior in small and large number tasks. In M. A. Vanchevsky (Ed.), *Focus on cognitive psychology research* (pp. 59–83). New York, NY: Nova Science.

Clearfield, M. W., Dineva, E., Smith, L. B., Diedrich, F. J., & Thelen, E. (2009). Cue salience and infant perseverative reaching: Tests of the dynamic field theory. *Developmental Science, 12,* 26–40. doi:10.1111/j.1467-7687.2008.00769.x

Clearfield, M. W., & Mix, K. S. (1999). Number versus contour length in infants' discrimination of small visual sets. *Psychological Science, 10,* 408–411. doi:10.1111/1467-9280.00177

Clifton, R. K., Rochat, P., Litovsky, R. Y., & Perris, E. E. (1991). Object representation guides infants' reaching in the dark. *Journal of Experimental Psychology: Human Perception and Performance, 17,* 323–329. doi:10.1037/0096-1523.17.2.323

Clore, G. (1981). *The wit and wisdom of Benjamin Clore.* Unpublished manuscript.

Closson, L. M. (2009). Status and gender differences in early adolescents' descriptions of popularity. *Social Development, 18,* 412–426. doi:10.1111/j.1467-9507.2008.00459.x

Coe, C. L., & Lubach, G. R. (2008). Fetal programming: Prenatal origins of health and illness. *Current Directions in Psychological Science, 17,* 36–41. doi:10.1111/j.1467-8721.2008.00544.x

Cohen, J. (1988). *Statistical power analysis for the behavioral sciences* (2nd ed.). Hillsdale, NJ: Erlbaum.

Cohen, L. B., & Cashon, C. H. (2006). Infant cognition. In W. Damon & R. M. Lerner (Series Eds.) & D. Kuhn & R. S. Siegler (Vol. Eds.), *Handbook of child psychology: Vol. 2. Cognition, perception, and language* (6th ed., pp. 214–251). Hoboken, NJ: Wiley.

Cohen, L. B., & Marks, K. S. (2002). How infants process addition and subtraction events. *Developmental Science, 5,* 186–201.

Coie, J., Terry, R., Lenox, K., Lochman, J., & Hyman, C. (1995). Childhood peer rejection and aggression as predictors of stable patterns of adolescent disorder. *Development and Psychopathology, 7,* 697–713. doi:10.1017/S0954579400006799

Coie, J. D., & Dodge, K. A. (1983). Continuities and changes in children's social status: A five-year longitudinal study. *Merrill-Palmer Quarterly, 29,* 261–282.

Coie, J. D., & Dodge, K. A. (1988). Multiple sources of data on social behavior and social status in the school: A cross-age comparison. *Child Development, 59,* 815–829.

Coie, J. D., & Dodge, K. A. (1998). Aggression and antisocial behavior. In W. Damon (Series Ed.) & N. Eisenberg (Vol. Ed.), *Handbook of child psychology: Vol. 3. Social, emotional, and personality development* (5th ed., pp. 779–862). Hoboken, NJ: Wiley.

Coie, J. D., Dodge, K. A., & Kupersmidt, J. B. (1990). Peer group behavior and social status. In S. R. Asher & J. D. Coie (Eds.), *Peer rejection in childhood* (pp. 17–59). New York, NY: Cambridge University Press.

Coie, J. D., & Kupersmidt, J. B. (1983). A behavioral analysis of emerging social status in boys' groups. *Child Development, 54,* 1400–1416. doi:10.2307/1129803

Coie, J. D., Lochman, J. E., Terry, R., & Hyman, C. (1992). Predicting early adolescent disorder from childhood aggression and peer rejection. *Journal of Consulting and Clinical Psychology, 60,* 783–792. doi:10.1037/0022-006X.60.5.783

Coker, T. R., Austin, S. B., & Schuster, M. A. (2010). The health and health care of lesbian, gay, and bisexual adolescents. *Annual Review of Public Health, 31,* 457–477. doi:10.1146/annurev.publhealth.012809.103636

Colby, A., & Kohlberg, L. (1987a). *The measurement of moral judgment* (Vol. 1). New York, NY: Cambridge University Press.

Colby, A., & Kohlberg, L. (1987b). *The measurement of moral judgment* (Vol. 2). New York, NY: Cambridge University Press.

Colby, A., Kohlberg, L., Gibbs, J., Lieberman, M., Fischer, K., & Saltzstein, H. D. (1983). A longitudinal study of moral judgment. *Monographs of the Society for Research in Child Development, 48*(1-2, Serial No. 200), 1–124. doi:10.2307/1165935

Coldwell, J., Pike, A., & Dunn, J. (2008). Maternal differential treatment and child adjustment: A multi-informant approach. *Social Development, 17,* 596–612. doi:10.1111/j.1467-9507.2007.00440.x

Cole, P. M. (1986). Children's spontaneous control of facial expression. *Child Development, 57,* 1309–1321.

Cole, P. M., Bruschi, C. J., & Tamang, B. L. (2002). Cultural differences in children's emotional reactions to difficult situations. *Child Development, 73,* 983–996.

Cole, P. M., & Dennis, T. A. (1998). Variations on a theme: Culture and the meaning of socialization practices and child competence. *Psychological Inquiry, 9*, 276–278.

Cole, P. M., Luby, J., & Sullivan, M. W. (2008). Emotions and the development of childhood depression: Bridging the gap. *Child Development Perspectives, 2*, 141–148.

Cole, P. M., & Tamang, B. L. (1998). Nepali children's ideas about emotional displays in hypothetical challenges. *Developmental Psychology, 34*, 640–646.

Cole, P. M., Tamang, B. L., & Shrestha, S. (2006). Cultural variations in the socialization of young children's anger and shame. *Child Development, 77*, 1237–1251. doi:10.1111/j.1467-8624.2006.00931.x

Cole, P. M., Tan, P. Z., Hall, S. E., Zhang, Y., Crnic, K. A., Blair, C. B., & Li, R. (2011). Developmental changes in anger expression and attention focus: Learning to wait. *Developmental Psychology, 47*, 1078–1089. doi:10.1037/a0023813

Cole, S. W. (2009). Social regulation of human gene expression. *Current Directions in Psychological Science, 18*, 132–137. doi:10.1111/j.1467-8721.2009.01623.x

Cole, W. G., Lingeman, J. M., & Adolph, K. E. (2012). Go naked: Diapers affect infant walking. *Developmental Science, 15*, 783–790. doi:10.1111/j.1467-7687.2012.01169.x

Coleman, M., Wheeler, L., & Webber, J. (1993). Research on interpersonal problem-solving training: A review. *Remedial and Special Education, 14*, 25–37. doi:10.1177/074193259301400205

Coley, J. D. (2000). On the importance of comparative research: The case of folkbiology. *Child Development, 71*, 82–90.

Coley, R. L., & Chase-Lansdale, P. L. (1998). Adolescent pregnancy and parenthood: Recent evidence and future directions. *American Psychologist, 53*, 152–166. doi:10.1037/0003-066X.53.2.152

Coley, R. L., & Lombardi, C. M. (2013). Does maternal employment following childbirth support or inhibit low-income children's long-term development? *Child Development, 84*, 178–197. doi:10.1111/j.1467-8624.2012.01840.x

Coley, R. L., Votruba-Drzal, E., Miller, P. L., & Koury, A. (2013). Timing, extent, and type of child care and children's behavioral functioning in kindergarten. *Developmental Psychology, 49*, 1859–1873. doi:10.1037/a0031251

Collaer, M. L., & Hines, M. (1995). Human behavioral sex differences: A role for gonadal hormones during early development? *Psychological Bulletin, 118*, 55–107. doi:10.1037/0033-2909.118.1.55

Collie, R., & Hayne, H. (1999). Deferred imitation by 6-and 9-month-old infants: More evidence for declarative memory. *Developmental Psychobiology, 35*, 83–90.

Collins, S. A., Surmala, P., Osborne, G., Greenberg, C., Bathory, L. W., Edmunds-Potvin, S., & Arbour, L. (2012). Causes and risk factors for infant mortality in Nunavut, Canada 1999–2011. *BMC Pediatrics, 12*(1), 190. doi:10.1186/1471-2431-12-190

Collins, W. A. (2003). More than myth: The developmental significance of romantic relationships during adolescence. *Journal of Research on Adolescence, 13*, 1–24. doi:10.1111/1532-7795.1301001

Collins, W. A., Hennighausen, K. C., Schmit, D. T., & Sroufe, L. A. (1997). Developmental precursors of romantic relationships: A longitudinal analysis. In S. Shulman & W. A. Collins (Eds.), *New Directions for Child and Adolescent Development: No. 78. Romantic relationships in adolescence: Developmental perspectives* (pp. 69–84). San Francisco, CA: Jossey-Bass.

Collins, W. A., & Steinberg, L. (2006). Adolescent development in interpersonal context. In W. Damon & R. M. Lerner (Series Eds.) & N. Eisenberg (Vol. Ed.), *Handbook of child psychology: Vol. 3. Social, emotional, and personality development* (6th ed., pp. 1003–1067). Hoboken, NJ: Wiley.

Collins, W. A., Welsh, D. P., & Furman, W. (2009). Adolescent romantic relationships. *Annual Review of Psychology, 60*, 631–652. doi:10.1146/annurev.psych.60.110707.163459

Colombo, J., & Richman, W. A. (2002). Infant timekeeping: Attention and temporal estimation in 4-month-olds. *Psychological Science, 13*, 475–479.

Colombo, J., Shaddy, D. J., Richman, W. A., Maikranz, J. M., & Blaga, O. M. (2004). The developmental course of habituation in infancy and preschool outcome. *Infancy, 5*, 1–38. doi:10.1207/s15327078in0501_1

Coltrane, S. (1996). *Family man: Fatherhood, housework, and gender equity.* New York, NY: Oxford University Press.

Combs-Ronto, L., Olson, S., Lunkenheimer, E., & Sameroff, A. (2009). Interactions between maternal parenting and children's early disruptive behavior: Bidirectional associations across the transition from preschool to school entry. *Journal of Abnormal Child Psychology, 37*, 1151–1163. doi:10.1007/s10802-009-9332-2

Compas, B. E., Connor-Smith, J. K., Saltzman, H., Thomsen, A. H., & Wadsworth, M. E. (2001). Coping with stress during childhood and adolescence: Problems, progress, and potential in theory and research. *Psychological Bulletin, 127*, 87–127.

Compian, L., Gowen, L. K., & Hayward, C. (2004). Peripubertal girls' romantic and platonic involvement with boys: Associations with body image and depression symptoms. *Journal of Research on Adolescence, 14*, 23–47.

Compton, K., Snyder, J., Schrepferman, L., Bank, L., & Shortt, J. W. (2003). The contribution of parents and siblings to antisocial and depressive behavior in adolescents: A double jeopardy coercion model. *Development and Psychopathology, 15*, 163–182. doi:10.1017.S0954579403000099

Condry, J. C., & Ross, D. F. (1985). Sex and aggression: The influence of gender label on the perception of aggression in children. *Child Development, 56*, 225–233. doi:10.2307/1130189

Conduct Problems Prevention Research Group. (1999a). Initial impact of the Fast Track prevention trial for conduct problems: I. The high-risk sample. *Journal of Consulting and Clinical Psychology, 67*, 631–647. doi:10.1037/0022-006X.67.5.631

Conduct Problems Prevention Research Group. (1999b). Initial impact of the Fast Track prevention trial for conduct problems: II. Classroom effects. *Journal of Consulting and Clinical Psychology, 67*, 648–657. doi:10.1037/0022-006X.67.5.648

Conduct Problems Prevention Research Group. (2002a). Evaluation of the first 3 years of the Fast Track prevention trial with children at high risk for adolescent conduct problems. *Journal of Abnormal Child Psychology, 30*, 19–35. doi:10.1023/A:1014274914287

Conduct Problems Prevention Research Group. (2002b). Using the Fast Track randomized prevention trial to test the early-starter model of the development of serious conduct problems. *Development and Psychopathology, 14*, 925–943.

Conduct Problems Prevention Research Group. (2004). The effects of the Fast Track program on serious problem outcomes at the end of elementary school. *Journal of Clinical Child and Adolescent Psychology, 33*, 650–661. doi:10.1207/s15374424jccp3304_1

Conduct Problems Prevention Research Group. (2007). Fast Track randomized controlled trial to prevent externalizing psychiatric disorders:

Findings from grades 3 to 9. *Journal of the American Academy of Child and Adolescent Psychiatry, 46*, 1250–1262. doi:10.1097/chi.0b013e31813e5d39

Conduct Problems Prevention Research Group. (2010). Fast Track intervention effects on youth arrests and delinquency. *Journal of Experimental Criminology, 6*, 131–157. doi:10.1007/s11292-010-9091-7

Conduct Problems Prevention Research Group. (2011). The effects of the Fast Track preventive intervention on the development of conduct disorder across childhood. *Child Development, 82*, 331–345. doi:10.1111/j.1467-8624.2010.01558.x

Conger, R. D., Conger, K. J., & Martin, M. J. (2010). Socioeconomic status, family processes, and individual development. *Journal of Marriage and Family, 72*, 685–704. doi:10.1111/j.1741-3737.2010.00725.x

Conger, R. D., & Ge, X. (1999). Conflict and cohesion in parent–adolescent relations: Changes in emotional expression from early to midadolescence. In M. J. Cox & J. Brooks-Gunn (Eds.), *Conflict and cohesion in families: Causes and consequences* (pp. 185–206). Mahwah, NJ: Erlbaum.

Conger, R. D., Ge, X., Elder, G. H., Jr., Lorenz, F. O., & Simons, R. L. (1994). Economic stress, coercive family process, and developmental problems of adolescents. *Child Development, 65*, 541–561. doi:10.2307/1131401

Conger, R. D., Wallace, L. E., Sun, Y., Simons, R. L., McLoyd, V. C., & Brody, G. H. (2002). Economic pressure in African American families: A replication and extension of the family stress model. *Developmental Psychology, 38*, 179–193. doi:10.1037/0012-1649.38.2.179

Conley, D., & Bennett, N. G. (2002). [Peer commentary on "Outcomes in young adulthood for very-low-birth-weight infants" by Hack et al.]. *New England Journal of Medicine, 347*, 141–143. doi:10.1056/NEJM200207113470214

Connell, A., Bullock, B., Dishion, T., Shaw, D., Wilson, M., & Gardner, F. (2008). Family intervention effects on co-occurring early childhood behavioral and emotional problems: A latent transition analysis approach. *Journal of Abnormal Child Psychology, 36*, 1211–1225. doi:10.1007/s10802-008-9244-6

Connell, J. P., & Wellborn, J. G. (1991). Competence, autonomy, and relatedness: A motivational analysis of self-system processes. In M. R. Gunnar & L. A. Sroufe (Eds.), *Minnesota Symposia on Child Psychology: Vol. 23. Self processes and development* (pp. 43–77). Hillsdale, NJ: Erlbaum.

Connellan, J., Baron-Cohen, S., Wheelwright, S., Batki, A., & Ahluwalia, J. (2000). Sex differences in human neonatal social perception. *Infant Behavior and Development, 23*, 113–118. doi:10.1016/S0163-6383(00)00032-1

Conner, D. B., Knight, D. K., & Cross, D. R. (1997). Mothers' and fathers' scaffolding of their 2-year-olds during problem-solving and literacy interactions. *British Journal of Developmental Psychology, 15*, 323–338. doi:10.1111/j.2044-835X.1997.tb00524.x

Connolly, J., Craig, W., Goldberg, A., & Pepler, D. (1999). Conceptions of cross-sex friendships and romantic relationships in early adolescence. *Journal of Youth and Adolescence, 28*, 481–494. doi:10.1023/A:1021669024820

Connolly, J., Craig, W., Goldberg, A., & Pepler, D. (2004). Mixed-gender groups, dating, and romantic relationships in early adolescence. *Journal of Research on Adolescence, 14*, 185–207. doi:10.1111/j.1532-7795.2004.01402003.x

Connolly, J., & McIsaac, C. (2009). Adolescents' explanations for romantic dissolutions: A developmental perspective. *Journal of Adolescence, 32*, 1209–1223. doi: 10.1016/j.adolescence.2009.01.006

Connolly, J. A., & Konarski, R. (1994). Peer self-concept in adolescence: Analysis of factor structure and of associations with peer experience. *Journal of Research on Adolescence, 4*, 385–403. doi:10.1207/s15327795jra0403_3

Consortium for Longitudinal Studies. (1983). *As the twig is bent: Lasting effects of preschool programs.* Hillsdale, NJ: Erlbaum.

Conway, C. C., Keenan-Miller, D., Hammen, C., Lind, P. A., Najman, J. M., & Brennan, P. A. (2012). Coaction of stress and serotonin transporter genotype in predicting aggression at the transition to adulthood. *Journal of Clinical Child and Adolescent Psychology, 41*, 53–63. doi:10.1080/15374416.2012.632351

Conway, M. A., & Holmes, A. (2004). Psychosocial stages and the accessibility of autobiographical memories across the life cycle. *Journal of Personality, 72*, 461–480. doi:10.1111/j.0022-3506.2004.00269.x

Cook, W. L., Kenny, D. A., & Goldstein, M. J. (1991). Parental affective style risk and the family system: A social relations model analysis. *Journal of Abnormal Psychology, 100*, 492–501. doi:10.1037/0021-843X.100.4.492

Cooley, C. H. (1902). *Human nature and the social order.* New York, NY: Charles Scribner's Sons.

Cooney, T. M., Pedersen, F. A., Indelicato, S., & Palkovitz, R. (1993). Timing of fatherhood: Is "on-time" optimal? *Journal of Marriage and the Family, 55*, 205–215.

Cooper, R. P., & Aslin, R. N. (1994). Developmental differences in infant attention to the spectral properties of infant-directed speech. *Child Development, 65*, 1663–1677.

Cooper, S. M., & McLoyd, V. C. (2011). Racial barrier socialization and the well-being of African American adolescents: The moderating role of mother–adolescent relationship quality. *Journal of Research on Adolescence, 21*, 895–903. doi:10.1111/j.1532-7795.2011.00749.x

Coplan, R. J., Arbeau, K. A., & Armer, M. (2008). Don't fret, be supportive! Maternal characteristics linking child shyness to psychosocial and school adjustment in kindergarten. *Journal of Abnormal Child Psychology, 36*, 359–371. doi:10.1007/s10802-007-9183-7

Coplan, R. J., & Armer, M. (2007). A "multitude" of solitude: A closer look at social withdrawal and nonsocial play in early childhood. *Child Development Perspectives, 1*, 26–32. doi:10.1111/j.1750-8606.2007.00006.x

Coplan, R. J., Barber, A. M., & Lagacé-Séguin, D. G. (1999). The role of child temperament as a predictor of early literacy and numeracy skills in preschoolers. *Early Childhood Research Quarterly, 14*, 537–553. doi:10.1016/S0885-2006(99)00025-3

Coplan, R. J., & Bullock, A. (2012). Temperament and peer relationships. In M. R. Zentner & R. L. Shiner (Eds.), *Handbook of temperament* (pp. 442–461). New York, NY: Guilford Press.

Coplan, R. J., Hastings, P. D., Lagacé-Séguin, D. G., & Moulton, C. E. (2002). Authoritative and authoritarian mothers' parenting goals, attributions, and emotions across different childrearing contexts. *Parenting, 2*, 1–26. doi:10.1207/S15327922PAR0201_1

Coplan, R. J., Rose-Krasnor, L., Weeks, M., Kingsbury, A., Kingsbury, M., & Bullock, A. (2013). Alone is a crowd: Social motivations, social withdrawal, and socioemotional functioning in later childhood. *Developmental Psychology, 49*, 861. doi:10.1037/a0028861

Corballis, M. C. (2009). The evolution and genetics of cerebral asymmetry. *Philosophical Transactions of the Royal Society of London, B: Biological Sciences, 364*, 867–879. doi: 10.1098/rstb.2008.0232

Cornell, E. H., Heth, C. D., Kneubuhler, Y., & Sehgal, S. (1996). Serial position effects in children's route reversal errors: Implications for police search operations. *Applied Cognitive Psychology, 10*, 301–326.

Costa, A., Hernández, M., & Sebastián-Gallés, N. (2008). Bilingualism aids conflict resolution: Evidence from the ANT task. *Cognition, 106,* 59–86. doi:10.1016/j.cognition.2006.12.013

Costello, D. M., Swendsen, J., Rose, J. S., & Dierker, L. C. (2008). Risk and protective factors associated with trajectories of depressed mood from adolescence to early adulthood. *Journal of Consulting and Clinical Psychology, 76,* 173–183. doi:10.1037/0022-006X.76.2.173

Costello, E. J., Foley, D. L., & Angold, A. (2006). 10-year research update review: The epidemiology of child and adolescent psychiatric disorders: II. Developmental epidemiology. *Journal of the American Academy of Child and Adolescent Psychiatry, 45,* 8–25.

Costigan, C. L., Koryzma, C. M., Hua, J. M., & Chance, L. J. (2010). Ethnic identity, achievement, and psychological adjustment: Examining risk and resilience among youth from immigrant Chinese families in Canada. *Cultural Diversity and Ethnic Minority Psychology, 16,* 264–278. doi:10.1037/a0017275

Costigan, C. L., & Su, T. (2004). Orthogonal versus linear models of acculturation among immigrant Chinese Canadians: A comparison of mothers, fathers, and children. *International Journal of Behavioral Development, 28,* 518–527. doi:10.1080/01650250444000234

Costigan, C. L., Su, T. F., & Hua, J. M. (2009). Ethnic identity among Chinese Canadian youth: A review of the Canadian literature. *Canadian Psychology, 50,* 261–272. doi:10.1037/a0016880

Côté, S., Vaillancourt, T., LeBlanc, J. C., Nagin, D. S., & Tremblay, R. E. (2006). The development of physical aggression from toddlerhood to pre-adolescence: A nation wide longitudinal study of Canadian children. *Journal of Abnormal Child Psychology, 34,* 68–82. doi:10.1007/s10802-005-9001-z

Côté, S., Zoccolillo, M., Tremblay, R. E., Nagin, D., & Vitaro, F. (2001). Predicting girls' conduct disorder in adolescence from childhood trajectories of disruptive behaviors. *Journal of the American Academy of Child and Adolescent Psychiatry, 40,* 678–684.

Côté, S. M., Borge, A. I., Geoffroy, M.-C., Rutter, M., & Tremblay, R. E. (2008). Nonmaternal care in infancy and emotional/behavioral difficulties at 4 years old: Moderation by family risk characteristics. *Developmental Psychology, 44,* 155–168. doi:10.1037/0012-1649.44.1.155

Côté, S. M., Doyle, O., Petitclerc, A., & Timmins, L. (2013). Child care in infancy and cognitive performance until middle childhood in the Millennium Cohort Study. *Child Development, 84,* 1191–1208. doi:10.1111/cdev.12049

Coulton, C. J., Korbin, J. E., Su, M., & Chow, J. (1995). Community level factors and child maltreatment rates. *Child Development, 66,* 1262–1276. doi:10.2307/1131646

Courage, M. L., & Howe, M. L. (2002). From infant to child: The dynamics of cognitive change in the second year of life. *Psychological Bulletin, 128,* 250–277.

Cowan, N. (2005). *Working memory capacity.* New York, NY: Psychology Press.

Cowan, N., Nugent, L. D., Elliott, E. M., Ponomarev, I., & Saults, J. S. (1999). The role of attention in the development of short-term memory: Age differences in the verbal span of apprehension. *Child Development, 70,* 1082–1097.

Cowan, P. A., Powell, D., & Cowan, C. P. (1998). Parenting interventions: A family systems perspective. In W. Damon (Series Ed.) & I. E. Sigel & K. A. Renninger (Vol. Eds.), *Handbook of child psychology: Vol. 4. Child psychology in practice* (5th ed., pp. 3–72). Hoboken, NJ: Wiley.

Cox, M. J., Owen, M. T., Lewis, J. M., & Henderson, V. K. (1989). Marriage, adult adjustment, and early parenting. *Child Development, 60,* 1015–1024. doi:10.2307/1130775

Coyle, T. R., Pillow, D. R., Snyder, A. C., & Kochunov, P. (2011). Processing speed mediates the development of general intelligence (g) in adolescence. *Psychological Science, 22,* 1265–1269. doi:10.1177/0956797611418243

Coyne, S. M., & Archer, J. (2005). The relationship between indirect and physical aggression on television and in real life. *Social Development, 14,* 324–338. doi:10.1111/j.1467-9507.2005.00304.x

Coyne, S. M., Archer, J., & Eslea, M. (2004). Cruel intentions on television and in real life: Can viewing indirect aggression increase viewers' subsequent indirect aggression? *Journal of Experimental Child Psychology, 88,* 234–253. doi:10.1016/j.jecp.2004.03.001

Craig, W., Harel-Fisch, Y., Fogel-Grinvald, H., Dostaler, S., Hetland, J., Simons-Morton, B., … & Pickett, W. (2009). A cross-national profile of bullying and victimization among adolescents in 40 countries. *International Journal of Public Health, 54,* 216–224. doi:10.1007/s00038-009-5413-9

Craig, W. M., Vitaro, F., Gagnon, L., & Tremblay, R. E. (2002). The road to gang membership: Characteristics of male gang and nongang members from ages 10 to 14. *Social Development, 11,* 53–68. doi:10.1111/1467-9507.00186

Craik, F. I. M., Bialystok, E., & Freedman, M. (2010). Delaying the onset of Alzheimer's disease: Bilingualism as a form of cognitive reserve. *Neurology, 75,* 1726–1729. doi:10.1212/WNL.0b013e3181fc2a1c

Crain, W. C. (1985). *Theories of development: Concepts and applications* (2nd ed.). Englewood Cliffs, NJ: Prentice Hall.

Crawford, J. (1997). *Best evidence: Research foundations of the bilingual education act.* Washington, DC: National Clearinghouse for Bilingual Education.

Crick, N. R., Bigbee, M. A., & Howes, C. (1996). Gender differences in children's normative beliefs about aggression: How do I hurt thee? Let me count the ways. *Child Development, 67,* 1003–1014. doi:10.1111/j.1467-8624.1996.tb01779.x

Crick, N. R., Casas, J. F., & Mosher, M. (1997). Relational and overt aggression in preschool. *Developmental Psychology, 33,* 579–588. doi:10.1037/0012-1649.33.4.579

Crick, N. R., & Dodge, K. A. (1994). A review and reformulation of social information-processing mechanisms in children's social adjustment. *Psychological Bulletin, 115,* 74–101. doi:10.1037/0033-2909.115.1.74

Crick, N. R., & Dodge, K. A. (1996). Social information-processing mechanisms in reactive and proactive aggression. *Child Development, 67,* 993–1002. doi:10.2307/1131875

Crick, N. R., & Grotpeter, J. K. (1996). Children's treatment by peers: Victims of relational and overt aggression. *Development and Psychopathology, 8,* 367–380. doi:10.1017/S0954579400007148

Criminal Intelligence Service Saskatchewan (CISS). (2005). *2005 intelligence trends: Aboriginal-based gangs in Saskatchewan, 1*(1). Retrieved from http://www.cissask.ca/PDF/Public-gang-report.pdf

Criss, M. M., Pettit, G. S., Bates, J. E., Dodge, K. A., & Lapp, A. L. (2002). Family adversity, positive peer relationships, and children's externalizing behavior: A longitudinal perspective on risk and resilience. *Child Development, 73,* 1220–1237.

Criss, M. M., Shaw, D. S., Moilanen, K. L., Hitchings, J. E., & Ingoldsby, E. M. (2009). Family, neighborhood, and peer characteristics as predictors of child adjustment: A longitudinal analysis of additive and mediation models. *Social Development, 18,* 511–535. doi:10.1111/j.1467-9507.2008.00520.x

Crocetti, E., Rubini, M., Luyckx, K., & Meeus, W. (2008). Identity formation in early and middle adolescents from various ethnic groups: From three dimensions to five statuses. *Journal of Youth and Adolescence, 37,* 983–996. doi:10.1007/s10964-007-9222-2

Crockenberg, S., & Langrock, A. (2001). The role of specific emotions in children's responses to interparental conflict: A test of the model. *Journal of Family Psychology, 15,* 163–182.

Crocker, J. (2001). Self-esteem in adulthood. In N. J. Smelser & P. B. Baltes (Eds.), *International encyclopedia of the social and behavioral sciences.* New York, NY: Elsevier.

Crockett, L., Losoff, M., & Petersen, A. C. (1984). Perceptions of the peer group and friendship in early adolescence. *Journal of Early Adolescence, 4,* 155–181. doi:10.1177/0272431684042004

Crosbie-Burnett, M., & Helmbrecht, L. (1993). A descriptive empirical study of gay male stepfamilies. *Family Relations, 42,* 256–262.

Crosby, D. A., Dowsett, C. J., Gennetian, L. A., & Huston, A. C. (2010). A tale of two methods: Comparing regression and instrumental variables estimates of the effects of preschool child care type on the subsequent externalizing behavior of children in low-income families. *Developmental Psychology, 46,* 1030–1048. doi:10.1037/a0020384

Crosnoe, R., Augustine, J. M., & Huston, A. C. (2012). Children's early child care and their mothers' later involvement with schools. *Child Development, 83,* 758–772. doi:10.1111/j.1467-8624.2011.01726.x

Cross, D., Epstein, M., Hearn, L., Slee, P., Shaw, T., & Monks, H. (2011). National Safe Schools Framework: Policy and practice to reduce bullying in Australian schools. *International Journal of Behavioral Development, 35,* 398–404. doi:10.1177/0165025411407456

Crouter, A. C., & Booth, A. (Eds.). (2003). *Children's influence on family dynamics: The neglected side of family relationships.* Mahwah, NJ: Erlbaum.

Crowley, K., Callanan, M. A., Tenenbaum, H. R., & Allen, E. (2001). Parents explain more often to boys than to girls during shared scientific thinking. *Psychological Science, 12,* 258–261. doi:10.1111/1467-9280.00347

Cruz, J. E., Emery, R. E., & Turkheimer, E. (2012). Peer network drinking predicts increased alcohol use from adolescence to early adulthood after controlling for genetic and shared environmental selection. *Developmental Psychology, 48,* 1390–1402. doi:10.1037/a0027515

Csibra, G., Bíró, S., Koós, O., & Gergely, G. (2003). One-year-old infants use teleological representations of actions productively. *Cognitive Science, 27,* 111–133. doi:10.1016/S0364-0213(02)00112-X

Csibra, G., Gergely, G., Bíró, S., Koós, O., & Brockbank, M. (1999). Goal attribution without agency cues: The perception of "pure reason" in infancy. *Cognition, 72,* 237–267.

Csikszentmihalyi, M., & Schneider, B. (2000). *Becoming adult: How teenagers prepare for the world of work.* New York, NY: Basic Books.

Culp, R. E., Appelbaum, M. I., Osofsky, J. D., & Levy, J. A. (1988). Adolescent and older mothers: Comparison between prenatal maternal variables and newborn interaction measures. *Infant Behavior and Development, 11,* 353–362. doi:10.1016/0163-6383(88)90019-7

Cummings, E. M., & Davies, P. T. (2002). Effects of marital conflict on children: Recent advances and emerging themes in process-oriented research. *Journal of Child Psychology and Psychiatry, 43,* 31–63. doi:10.1111/1469-7610.00003

Cunningham, A. E., & Stanovich, K. E. (1997). Early reading acquisition and its relation to reading experience and ability 10 years later. *Developmental Psychology, 33,* 934–945.

Cunningham, A. J., & Stevens, L. (2011). *Helping a child to be a witness in court: 101 things to know, say and do.* Retrieved from http://www.lfcc.on.ca/Helping_a_Child_Witness.pdf

Curry, D., Schmitt, M. J., & Waldron, S. (1996). A framework for adult numeracy standards: The mathematical skills and abilities adults need to be equipped for the future. Retrieved from http://shell04.theworld.com/std/anpn//framewk

Curtin, S., Mintz, T. H., & Christiansen, M. H. (2005). Stress changes the representational landscape: Evidence from word segmentation. *Cognition, 96,* 233–262. doi:10.1016/j.cognition.2004.08.005

Curtiss, S. (1977). *Genie: A psycholinguistic study of a modern-day "wild child."* New York, NY: Academic Press.

Curtiss, S. (1989). The independence and task-specificity of language. In M. H. Bornstein & J. S. Bruner (Eds.), *Interaction in human development* (pp. 105–137). Hillsdale, NJ: Erlbaum.

Cutrona, C. E., Hessling, R. M., Bacon, P. L., & Russell, D. W. (1998). Predictors and correlates of continuing involvement with the baby's father among adolescent mothers. *Journal of Family Psychology, 12,* 369–387. doi:10.1037/0893-3200.12.3.369

D'Augelli, A. R. (1998). Developmental implications of victimization of lesbian, gay, and bisexual youths. In G. M. Herek (Ed.), *Psychological perspectives on lesbian and gay issues: Vol. 4. Stigma and sexual orientation: Understanding prejudice against lesbians, gay men, and bisexuals* (pp. 187–210). Thousand Oaks, CA: Sage.

D'Augelli, A. R., & Hershberger, S. L. (1993). Lesbian, gay, and bisexual youth in community settings: Personal challenges and mental health problems. *American Journal of Community Psychology, 21,* 421–448. doi:10.1007/BF00942151

D'Augelli, A. R., Hershberger, S. L., & Pilkington, N. W. (1998). Lesbian, gay, and bisexual youth and their families: Disclosure of sexual orientation and its consequences. *American Journal of Orthopsychiatry, 68,* 361–371. doi:10.1037/h0080345

D'Augelli, A. R., Hershberger, S. L., & Pilkington, N. W. (2001). Suicidality patterns and sexual orientation-related factors among lesbian, gay and bisexual youths. *Suicide and Life-Threatening Behavior, 31,* 250-265.

Daly, M., & Wilson, M. I. (1996). Violence against stepchildren. *Current Directions in Psychological Science, 5,* 77–80. doi:10.1111/1467-8721.ep10772793

Damasio, A. R. (1999). *The feeling of what happens: Body and emotion in the making of consciousness.* New York, NY: Harcourt Brace.

Damon, W. (1977). *The social world of the child.* San Francisco, CA: Jossey-Bass.

Damon, W., & Hart, D. (1988). *Self-understanding in childhood and adolescence.* Cambridge, England: Cambridge University Press.

Darling, N., & Steinberg, L. (1993). Parenting style as context: An integrative model. *Psychological Bulletin, 113,* 487–496. doi:10.1037/0033-2909.113.3.487

Darwin, C. (1877). A biographical sketch of an infant. *Mind, 2,* 285–294.

Davidov, M., & Grusec, J. E. (2006). Untangling the links of parental responsiveness to distress and warmth to child outcomes. *Child Development, 77,* 44–58. doi:10.1111/j.1467-8624.2006.00855.x

Davidson, R. J. (1994). Asymmetric brain function, affective style, and psychopathology: The role of early experience and plasticity. *Development and Psychopathology, 6*, 741–741.

Davies, P. T., Cicchetti, D., & Martin, M. J. (2012). Toward greater specificity in identifying associations among interparental aggression, child emotional reactivity to conflict, and child problems. *Child Development, 83*, 1789–1804. doi:10.1111/j.1467-8624.2012.01804.x

Davies, P. T., & Cummings, E. M. (1994). Marital conflict and child adjustment: An emotional security hypothesis. *Psychological Bulletin, 116*, 387–411. doi:10.1037/0033-2909.116.3.387

Davies, P. T., Cummings, E. M., & Winter, M. A. (2004). Pathways between profiles of family functioning, child security in the interparental subsystem, and child psychological problems. *Development and Psychopathology, 16*, 525–550. doi:10.1017/S0954579404004651

Davies, P. T., Sturge-Apple, M. L., Cicchetti, D., Manning, L. G., & Vonhold, S. E. (2012). Pathways and processes of risk in associations among maternal antisocial personality symptoms, interparental aggression, and preschooler's psychopathology. *Development and Psychopathology, 24*, 807–832. doi:10.1017/S0954579412000387

Davies, P. T., & Windle, M. (2000). Middle adolescents' dating pathways and psychosocial adjustment. *Merrill-Palmer Quarterly, 46*, 90–118. doi:10.2307/23093344

Davis, B. E., Moon, R. Y., Sachs, H. C., & Ottolini, M. C. (1998). Effects of sleep position on infant motor development. *Pediatrics, 102*, 1135–1140.

Davis, O. S. P., Haworth, C. M. A., & Plomin, R. (2009). Dramatic increase in heritability of cognitive development from early to middle childhood: An 8-year longitudinal study of 8,700 pairs of twins. *Psychological Science, 20*, 1301–1308. doi:10.1111/j.1467-9280.2009.02433.x

Davis, S. N., & Greenstein, T. N. (2004). Cross-national variations in the division of household labor. *Journal of Marriage and Family, 66*, 1260–1271. doi:10.1111/j.0022-2445.2004.00091.x

Dawson, G., Rogers, S., Munson, J., Smith, M., Winter, J., Greenson, J., … Varley, J. (2010). Randomized, controlled trial of an intervention for toddlers with autism: The Early Start Denver Model. *Pediatrics, 125*, e17–e23. doi:10.1542/peds.2009-0958

Day, R. D., & Padilla-Walker, L. M. (2009). Mother and father connectedness and involvement during early adolescence. *Journal of Family Psychology, 23*, 900–904. doi:10.1037/a0016438

de Boysson-Bardies, B. (1999). *How language comes to children: From birth to two years* (M. B. DeBevoise, Trans.). Cambridge, MA: MIT Press. (Original work published 1996)

de Boysson-Bardies, B., Sagart, L., & Durand, C. (1984). Discernible differences in the babbling of infants according to target language. *Journal of Child Language, 11*, 1–15. doi:10.1017/S0305000900005559

De Brito, S. A., Hodgins, S., McCrory, E. J. P., Mechelli, A., Wilke, M., Jones, A. P., & Viding, E. (2009). Structural neuroimaging and the antisocial brain: Main findings and methodological challenges. *Criminal Justice and Behavior, 36*, 1173–1186. doi:10.1177/0093854809342883

De Goede, I. H. A., Branje, S. J. T., & Meeus, W. H. J. (2009). Developmental changes and gender differences in adolescents' perceptions of friendships. *Journal of Adolescence, 32*, 1105–1123. doi:10.1016/j.adolescence.2009.03.002

de Guzman, M. R. T., Carlo, G., & Edwards, C. P. (2008). Prosocial behaviors in context: Examining the role of children's social companions. *International Journal of Behavioral Development, 32*, 522–530. doi:10.1177/0165025408095557

de Heering, A., & Maurer, D. (2012). Face memory deficits in patients deprived of early visual input by bilateral congenital cataracts. *Developmental Psychobiology.* Advance online publication. doi:10.1002/dev.21094

de Hevia, M. D., & Spelke, E. S. (2010). Number-space mapping in human infants. *Psychological Science, 21*, 653–660. doi:10.1177/0956797610366091

De Souza, E., Alberman, E., & Morris, J. K. (2009). Down syndrome and paternal age, a new analysis of case–control data collected in the 1960s. *American Journal of Medical Genetics Part A, 149A*, 1205–1208. doi:10.1002/ajmg.a.32850

de Vries, J. I. P., Visser, G. H. A., & Prechtl, H. F. R. (1982). The emergence of fetal behaviour: I. Qualitative aspects. *Early Human Development, 7*, 301–322. doi:10.1016/0378-3782(82)90033-0

de Wied, M., van Boxtel, A., Matthys, W., & Meeus, W. (2012). Verbal, facial and autonomic responses to empathy-eliciting film clips by disruptive male adolescents with high versus low callous-unemotional traits. *Journal of Abnormal Child Psychology, 40*, 211–223. doi:10.1007/s10802-011-9557-8

De Wolff, M. S., & van IJzendoorn, M. H. (1997). Sensitivity and attachment: A meta-analysis on parental antecedents of infant attachment. *Child Development, 68*, 571–591.

Deák, G. O., Flom, R. A., & Pick, A. D. (2000). Effects of gesture and target on 12- and 18-month-olds' joint visual attention to objects in front of or behind them. *Developmental Psychology, 36*, 511–523.

Dearing, E., McCartney, K., & Taylor, B. A. (2009). Does higher quality early child care promote low-income children's math and reading achievement in middle childhood? *Child Development, 80*, 1329–1349. doi:10.1111/j.1467-8624.2009.01336.x

Deary, I. J. (2000). *Oxford Psychology Series: No. 34. Looking down on human intelligence: From psychometrics to the brain.* Oxford, England: Oxford University Press.

Deary, I. J., Strand, S., Smith, P., & Fernandes, C. (2007). Intelligence and educational achievement. *Intelligence, 35*, 13–21.

Deater-Deckard, K., & Dodge, K. A. (1997). Externalizing behavior problems and discipline revisited: Nonlinear effects and variation by culture, context, and gender. *Psychological Inquiry, 8*, 161–175. doi:10.1207/s15327965pli0803_1

Deater-Deckard, K., Dodge, K. A., Bates, J. E., & Pettit, G. S. (1995, April). *Risk factors for the development of externalizing behavior problems: Are there ethnic group differences in process?* Paper presented at the biennial meeting of the Society for Research in Child Development, Indianapolis, IN.

Deater-Deckard, K., Lansford, J. E., Malone, P. S., Alampay, L. P., Sorbring, E., Bacchini, D., … Al-Hassan, S. M. (2011). The association between parental warmth and control in thirteen cultural groups. *Journal of Family Psychology, 25*, 790–794. doi:10.1037/a0025120

Deater-Deckard, K., & O'Connor, T. G. (2000). Parent–child mutuality in early childhood: Two behavioral genetic studies. *Developmental Psychology, 36*, 561–570. doi:10.1037/0012-1649.36.5.561

Deater-Deckard, K., Petrill, S. A., & Thompson, L. A. (2007). Anger/frustration, task persistence, and conduct problems in childhood: A behavioral genetic analysis. *Journal of Child Psychology and Psychiatry, 48*, 80–87. doi:10.1111/j.1469-7610.2006.01653.x

DeBaryshe, B. D., Patterson, G. R., & Capaldi, D. M. (1993). A performance model for academic achievement in early adolescent boys. *Developmental Psychology, 29*, 795–804. doi:10.1037/0012-1649.29.5.795

DeCasper, A., & Fifer, W. (1980, June 6). Of human bonding: Newborns prefer their mothers' voices. *Science, 208*, 1174–1176.

DeCasper, A. J., & Spence, M. J. (1986). Prenatal maternal speech influences newborns' perception of speech sounds. *Infant Behavior and Development*, 9, 133–150. doi:10.1016/0163-6383(86)90025-1

Decker, S. (1996). Collective and normative features of gang violence. *Justice Quarterly*, 13, 243–264. doi:10.1080/07418829600092931

Decker, S. H., & Van Winkle, B. (1996). *Life in the gang: Family, friends, and violence*. New York, NY: Cambridge University Press.

DeFries, J. C., & Gillis, J. J. (1993). Genetics of reading disability. In R. Plomin & G. E. McClearn (Eds.), *Nature, nurture and psychology* (pp. 121–145). Washington, DC: American Psychological Association.

DeGarmo, D. S. (2010). Coercive and prosocial fathering, antisocial personality, and growth in children's postdivorce noncompliance. *Child Development*, 81, 503–516. doi:10.1111/j.1467-8624.2009.01410.x

Değirmencioğlu, S. M., Urberg, K. A., Tolson, J. M., & Richard, P. (1998). Adolescent friendship networks: Continuity and change over the school year. *Merrill-Palmer Quarterly*, 44, 313–337.

Dehaene, S., & Brannon, E. (Eds.). (2011). *Space, time and number in the brain: Searching for the foundations of mathematical thought*. San Diego, CA: Academic Press.

Dehaene-Lambertz, G., Dehaene, S., & Hertz-Pannier, L. (2002, December 6). Functional neuroimaging of speech perception in infants. *Science*, 298, 2013–2015.

Delaney, C. (2000). Making babies in a Turkish village. In J. S. DeLoache & A. Gottlieb (Eds.), *A world of babies: Imagined childcare guides for seven societies* (pp. 117–144). New York, NY: Cambridge University Press.

DeLisi, M., Barnes, J. C., Beaver, K. M., & Gibson, C. L. (2009). Delinquent gangs and adolescent victimization revisited: A propensity score matching approach. *Criminal Justice and Behavior*, 36, 808–823. doi:10.1177/0093854809337703

DeLoache, J. S. (1987, December 11). Rapid change in the symbolic functioning of very young children. *Science*, 238, 1556–1557.

DeLoache, J. S. (2002). The symbol-mindedness of young children. In W. W. Hartup & R. A. Weinberg (Eds.), *Minnesota Symposia on Child Psychology: Vol. 32. Child psychology in retrospect and prospect: In celebration of the 75th anniversary of the Institute of Child Development* (pp. 73–101). Mahwah, NJ: Erlbaum.

DeLoache, J. S. (2004). Becoming symbol-minded. *Trends in Cognitive Sciences*, 8, 66–70. doi:10.1016/j.tics.2003.12.004

DeLoache, J. S. (2005, August). Mindful of symbols. *Scientific American*, 293(2), 72–77.

DeLoache, J. S., Chiong, C., Sherman, K., Islam, N., Vanderborght, M., Troseth, G. L., ... O'Doherty, K. (2010). Do babies learn from baby media? *Psychological Science*, 21, 1570–1574. doi:10.1177/0956797610384145

DeLoache, J. S., & Marzolf, D. P. (1995). The use of dolls to interview young children: Issues of symbolic representation. *Journal of Experimental Child Psychology*, 60, 155–173.

DeLoache, J. S., Miller, K. F., & Rosengren, K. S. (1997). The credible shrinking room: Very young children's performance with symbolic and nonsymbolic relations. *Psychological Science*, 8, 308–313. doi:10.1111/j.1467-9280.1997.tb00443.x

DeLoache, J. S., Pierroutsakos, S. L., Uttal, D. H., Rosengren, K. S., & Gottlieb, A. (1998). Grasping the nature of pictures. *Psychological Science*, 9, 205–210. doi:10.1111/1467-9280.00039

DeLoache, J. S., Simcock, G., & Macari, S. (2007). Planes, trains, automobiles—and tea sets: Extremely intense interests in very young children. *Developmental Psychology*, 43, 1579–1586. doi:10.1037/0012-1649.43.6.1579

DeLoache, J. S., Strauss, M. S., & Maynard, J. (1979). Picture perception in infancy. *Infant Behavior and Development*, 2, 77–89. doi:10.1016/S0163-6383(79)80010-7

DeLoache, J. S., Uttal, D. H., & Rosengren, K. S. (2004, May 14). Scale errors offer evidence for a perception-action dissociation early in life. *Science*, 304, 1027–1029.

Delsing, M. J. M. H., ter Bogt, T. F. M., Engels, R. C. M. E., & Meeus, W. H. J. (2007). Adolescents' peer crowd identification in the Netherlands: Structure and associations with problem behaviors. *Journal of Research on Adolescence*, 17, 467–480. doi:10.1111/j.1532-7795.2007.00530.x

Deluty, R. H. (1985). Cognitive mediation of aggressive, assertive, and submissive behavior in children. *International Journal of Behavioral Development*, 8, 355–369. doi:10.1177/016502548500800309

DeMarie-Dreblow, D., & Miller, P. H. (1988). The development of children's strategies for selective attention: Evidence for a transitional period. *Child Development*, 59, 1504–1513.

Dempster, F. N. (1995). Interference and inhibition in cognition: An historical perspective. In F. N. Dempster & C. J. Brainerd (Eds.), *Interference and inhibition in cognition* (pp. 3–16). San Diego, CA: Academic Press.

Dempster, F. N., & Corkill, A. J. (1999). Interference and inhibition in cognition and behavior: Unifying themes for educational psychology. *Educational Psychology Review*, 11, 1–88. doi:10.1023/A:1021992632168

Denham, S. A. (1986). Social cognition, prosocial behavior, and emotion in preschoolers: Contextual validation. *Child Development*, 57, 194–201.

Denham, S. A. (1998). *Emotional development in young children*. New York, NY: Guilford Press.

Denham, S. A. (2006). The emotional basis of learning and development in early childhood education. In B. Spodek & O. N. Saracho (Eds.), *Handbook of research on the education of young children* (2nd ed., pp. 85–103). Mahwah, NJ: Erlbaum.

Denham, S. A., Blair, K. A., DeMulder, E., Levitas, J., Sawyer, K., Auerbach-Major, S., & Queenan, P. (2003). Preschool emotional competence: Pathway to social competence? *Child Development*, 74, 238–256.

Denham, S. A., & Burton, R. (1996). A social-emotional intervention for at-risk 4-year-olds. *Journal of School Psychology*, 34, 225–245. doi:10.1016/0022-4405(96)00013-1

Denham, S. A., & Couchoud, E. A. (1990). Young preschoolers' understanding of emotions. *Child Study Journal*, 20, 171–192.

Denham, S. A., Warren-Khot, H. K., Bassett, H. H., Wyatt, T., & Perna, A. (2012). Factor structure of self-regulation in preschoolers: Testing models of a field-based assessment for predicting early school readiness. *Journal of Experimental Child Psychology*, 111, 386–404. doi:10.1016/j.jecp.2011.10.002

Denham, S. A., Zoller, D., & Couchoud, E. A. (1994). Socialization of preschoolers' emotion understanding. *Developmental Psychology*, 30, 928–936.

Denison, S., Reed, C., & Xu, F. (2013). The emergence of probabilistic reasoning in very young infants: Evidence from 4.5- and 6-month-olds. *Developmental Psychology*, 49, 243–249. doi:10.1037/a0028278

Denison, S., & Xu, F. (2010). Integrating physical constraints in statistical inference by 11-month-old infants. *Cognitive Science*, 34, 885–908. doi:10.1111/j.1551-6709.2010.01111.x

Denissen, J. J. A., van Aken, M. A. G., & Dubas, J. S. (2009). It takes two to tango: How parents' and adolescents' personalities link to the quality of their mutual relationship. *Developmental Psychology*, 45, 928–941. doi:10.1037/a0016230

Dennis, T., Bendersky, M., Ramsay, D., & Lewis, M. (2006). Reactivity and regulation in children prenatally exposed to cocaine. *Developmental Psychology, 42,* 688–697. doi:10.1037/0012-1649.42.4.688

Dennison, B. A., Erb, T. A., & Jenkins, P. L. (2002). Television viewing and television in bedroom associated with overweight risk among low-income preschool children. *Pediatrics, 109*(6), 1028–1035.

Després, C., Beuter, A., Richer, F., Poitras, K., Veilleux, A., Ayotte, P., … & Muckle, G. (2005). Neuromotor functions in Inuit preschool children exposed to Pb, PCBS, and Hg. *Neurotoxicology and Teratology, 27,* 245–257. doi:10.1016/j.ntt.2004.12.001

Depue, R. A., & Fu, Y. (2012). Neurobiology and neurochemistry of temperament (adults). In M. R. Zentner & R. L. Shiner (Eds.), *Handbook of temperament* (pp. 368–399). New York, NY: Guilford Press.

DeRosier, M. E., Kupersmidt, J. B., & Patterson, C. J. (1994). Children's academic and behavioral adjustment as a function of the chronicity and proximity of peer rejection. *Child Development, 65,* 1799–1813. doi:10.1111/j.1467-8624.1994.tb00850.x

Desjarlais, M., & Willoughby, T. (2010). A longitudinal study of the relation between adolescent boys and girls' computer use with friends and friendship quality: Support for the social compensation or the rich-get-richer hypothesis? *Computers in Human Behavior, 26,* 896–905. doi:10.1016/j.chb.2010.02.004

Dettling, A. C., Parker, S. W., Lane, S., Sebanc, A., & Gunnar, M. R. (2000). Quality of care and temperament determine changes in cortisol concentrations over the day for young children in childcare. *Psychoneuroendocrinology, 25,* 819–836.

Deuchar, M., & Quay, S. (1999). Language choice in the earliest utterances: A case study with methodological implications. *Journal of Child Language, 26,* 461–475.

Deutsch, F. M. (2006). Filial piety, patrilineality, and China's one-child policy. *Journal of Family Issues, 27,* 366–389. doi:10.1177/0192513x05283097

Devault, A., Gaudet, J., Bolte, C., & St-Denis, M. (2005). A survey and description of projects that support and promote fathering in Canada: Still work to do to reach fathers in their real-life settings. *Canadian Journal of Community Mental Health, 24*(1), 5–17.

Devine, A., Fawcett, K., Szücs, D., & Dowker, A. (2012). Gender differences in mathematics anxiety and the relation to mathematics performance while controlling for test anxiety. *Behavioral and Brain Functions.* doi:10.1186/1744-9081-8-33

DeVries, M. W. (1984). Temperament and infant mortality among the Masai of East Africa. *American Journal of Psychiatry, 141,* 1189–1194.

DeWitt, A. L., Cready, C. M., & Seward, R. R. (2013). Parental role portrayals in twentieth century children's picture books: More egalitarian or ongoing stereotyping? *Sex Roles, 69,* 89–106.

Di Giorgio, E., Leo, I., Pascalis, O., & Simion, F. (2012). Is the face-perception system human-specific at birth? *Developmental Psychology, 48,* 1083–1090. doi:10.1037/a0026521

Di Giunta, L., Pastorelli, C., Eisenberg, N., Gerbino, M., Castellani, V., & Bombi, A. (2010). Developmental trajectories of physical aggression: Prediction of overt and covert antisocial behaviors from self- and mothers' reports. *European Child and Adolescent Psychiatry, 19,* 873–882. doi:10.1007/s00787-010-0134-4

Diamantopoulou, S., Verhulst, F. C., & van der Ende, J. (2011). Gender differences in the development and adult outcome of co-occurring depression and delinquency in adolescence. *Journal of Abnormal Psychology, 120,* 644–655. doi:10.1037/a0023669

Diamond, A. (1985). Development of the ability to use recall to guide action, as indicated by infants' performance on AB⁻. *Child Development, 56,* 868–883. doi:10.2307/1130099

Diamond, A. (2013). Executive functions. *Annual Review of Psychology, 64,* 135–168. doi:10.1146/annurev-psych-113011-143750

Diamond, A., Barnett, W. S., Thomas, J., & Munro, S. (2007). Preschool program improves cognitive control, *Science, 318,* 1387–1388. doi:10.1126/science.1151148

Diamond, A., Briand, L., Fossella, J., & Gehlbach, L. (2004). Genetic and neurochemical modulation of prefrontal cognitive functions in children. *American Journal of Psychiatry, 161,* 125–132.

Diamond, A., & Goldman-Rakic, P. S. (1989). Comparison of human infants and rhesus monkeys on Piaget's AB task: Evidence for dependence on dorsolateral prefrontal cortex. *Experimental Brain Research, 74,* 24–40. doi:10.1007/BF00248277

Diamond, A., Kirkham, N., & Amso, D. (2002). Conditions under which young children can hold two rules in mind and inhibit a prepotent response. *Developmental Psychology, 38,* 352–361.

Diamond, A., & Lee, K. (2011, August 19). Interventions shown to aid executive function development in children 4 to 12 years old. *Science, 333,* 959–964.

Diamond, L. M. (2008). Female bisexuality from adolescence to adulthood: Results from a 10-year longitudinal study. *Developmental Psychology, 44,* 5–14. doi:10.1037/0012-1649.44.1.5

Diamond, L. M., & Lucas, S. (2004). Sexual-minority and heterosexual youths' peer relationships: Experiences, expectations, and implications for well-being. *Journal of Research on Adolescence, 14,* 313–340. doi:10.1111/j.1532-7795.2004.00077.x

Diamond, L. M., Savin-Williams, R. C., & Dube, E. M. (1999). Sex, dating, passionate friendships, and romance: Intimate peer relations among lesbian, gay, and bisexual adolescents. In W. Furman, B. B. Brown, & C. Feiring (Eds.), *The development of romantic relationships in adolescence* (pp. 175–210). Cambridge, England: Cambridge University Press.

DiBiase, R., & Waddell, S. (1995). Some effects of homelessness on the psychological functioning of preschoolers. *Journal of Abnormal Child Psychology, 23,* 783–792. doi:10.1007/BF01447477

Dick, D. M., Pagan, J. L., Holliday, C., Viken, R., Pulkkinen, L., Kaprio, J., & Rose, R. J. (2007). Gender differences in friends' influences on adolescent drinking: A genetic epidemiological study. *Alcoholism: Clinical and Experimental Research, 31,* 2012–2019. doi:10.1111/j.1530-0277.2007.00523.x

Dickens, W. T., & Flynn, J. R. (2001). Heritability estimates versus large environmental effects: The IQ paradox resolved. *Psychological Review, 108,* 346–369.

Dickens, W. T., & Flynn, J. R. (2006). Black Americans reduce the racial IQ gap: Evidence from standardization samples. *Psychological Science, 17,* 913–920. doi:10.1111/j.1467-9280.2006.01802.x

Dickinson, D. K. (2011, August 19). Teachers' language practices and academic outcomes of preschool children. *Science, 333,* 964–967.

Dickinson, D. K., & Porche, M. V. (2011). Relation between language experiences in preschool classrooms and children's kindergarten and fourth-grade language and reading abilities. *Child Development, 82,* 870–886. doi:10.1111/j.1467-8624.2011.01576.x

Diedrich, F. J., Thelen, E., Smith, L. B., & Corbetta, D. (2000). Motor memory is a factor in infant perseverative errors. *Developmental Science, 3,* 479–494. doi:10.1111/1467-7687.00140

Diekman, A. B., & Murnen, S. K. (2004). Learning to be little women and little men: The inequitable gender equality of nonsexist children's literature. *Sex Roles, 50*, 373–385. doi:10.1023/B:SERS.0000018892.26527.ea

Diener, M. (2000). Gift from the gods: A Balinese guide to early child rearing. In J. S. DeLoache & A. Gottlieb (Eds.), *A world of babies: Imagined childcare guides for seven societies* (pp. 96–116). New York, NY: Cambridge University Press.

Diener, M. L., & Kim, D.-Y. (2004). Maternal and child predictors of preschool children's social competence. *Journal of Applied Developmental Psychology, 25*, 3–24.

Dijkstra, J. K., Cillessen, A. H. N., & Borch, C. (2013). Popularity and adolescent friendship networks: Selection and influence dynamics. *Developmental Psychology, 49*, 1242–1252. doi:10.1037/a0030098

Dijkstra, J. K., Lindenberg, S., & Veenstra, R. (2008). Beyond the class norm: Bullying behavior of popular adolescents and its relation to peer acceptance and rejection. *Journal of Abnormal Child Psychology, 36*, 1289–1299. doi:10.1007/s10802-008-9251-7

Dilworth-Bart, J. E., & Moore, C. F. (2006). Mercy mercy me: Social injustice and the prevention of environmental pollutant exposures among ethnic minority and poor children. *Child Development, 77*, 247–265. doi:10.1111/j.1467-8624.2006.00868.x

Dionne, G., Tremblay, R., Boivin, M., Laplante, D., & Pérusse, D. (2003). Physical aggression and expressive vocabulary in 19-month-old twins. *Developmental Psychology, 39*, 261–273. doi:10.1037/0012-1649.39.2.261

DiPietro, J. A. (2012). Maternal stress in pregnancy: Considerations for fetal development. *Journal of Adolescent Health, 51*(2, Suppl.), S3–8. doi:10.1016/j.jadohealth.2012.04.008

DiPietro, J. A., Bornstein, M. H., Costigan, K. A., Pressman, E. K., Hahn, C. S., Painter, K., ... Yi, L. J. (2002). What does fetal movement predict about behavior during the first two years of life? *Developmental Psychobiology, 40*, 358–371.

DiPietro, J. A., Costigan, K. A., Shupe, A. K., Pressman, E. K., & Johnson, T. R. (1998). Fetal neurobehavioral development: Associations with socioeconomic class and fetal sex. *Developmental Psychobiology, 33*, 79–91.

DiPietro, J. A., Hilton, S. C., Hawkins, M., Costigan, K. A., & Pressman, E. K. (2002). Maternal stress and affect influence fetal neurobehavioral development. *Developmental Psychology, 38*, 659–668.

DiPietro, J. A., Suess, P. E., Wheeler, J. S., Smouse, P. H., & Newlin, D. B. (1995). Reactivity and regulation in cocaine-exposed neonates. *Infant Behavior and Development, 18*, 407–414. doi:10.1016/0163-6383(95)90030-6

Dirix, C. E., Nijhuis, J. G., Jongsma, H. W., & Hornstra, G. (2009). Aspects of fetal learning and memory. *Child Development, 80*, 1251–1258. doi:10.1111/j.1467-8624.2009.01329.x

Dirks, J., & Gibson, E. (1977). Infants' perception of similarity between live people and their photographs. *Child Development, 48*, 124–130. doi:10.2307/1128890

Dishion, T. J. (1990). The family ecology of boys' peer relations in middle childhood. *Child Development, 61*, 874–892. doi:10.1111/j.1467-8624.1990.tb02829.x

Dishion, T. J., Andrews, D. W., & Crosby, L. (1995). Antisocial boys and their friends in early adolescence: Relationship characteristics, quality, and interactional process. *Child Development, 66*, 139–151. doi:10.1111/j.1467-8624.1995.tb00861.x

Dishion, T. J., Ha, T., & Véronneau, M.-H. (2012). An ecological analysis of the effects of deviant peer clustering on sexual promiscuity, problem behavior, and childbearing from early adolescence to adulthood: An enhancement of the life history framework. *Developmental Psychology, 48*, 703–717. doi:10.1037/a0027304

Dishion, T. J., Shaw, D., Connell, A., Gardner, F., Weaver, C., & Wilson, M. (2008). The family check-up with high-risk indigent families: Preventing problem behavior by increasing parents' positive behavior support in early childhood. *Child Development, 79*, 1395–1414. doi:10.1111/j.1467-8624.2008.01195.x

Dishion, T. J., & Tipsord, J. M. (2011). Peer contagion in child and adolescent social and emotional development. *Annual Review of Psychology, 62*, 189–214. doi:10.1146/annurev.psych.093008.100412

Dishion, T. J., Véronneau, M.-H., & Myers, M. W. (2010). Cascading peer dynamics underlying the progression from problem behavior to violence in early to late adolescence. *Development and Psychopathology, 22*, 603–619. doi:10.1017/S0954579410000313

Diversi, M., Filho, N. M., & Morelli, M. (1999). Daily reality on the streets of Campinas, Brazil. In M. Raffaelli & R. W. Larson (Eds.), *New Directions for Child and Adolescent Development: No. 85. Homeless and working youth around the world: Exploring developmental issues* (Vol. 1999, pp. 19–34). San Francisco, CA: Jossey-Bass.

DiVitto, B., & Goldberg, S. (1979). The effects of newborn medical status on early parent-infant interaction. In T. Field, A. M. Sostek, S. Goldberg, & H. H. Shuman (Eds.), *Infants born at risk: Behavior and development* (pp. 311–332). New York, NY: Spectrum.

Dix, T., & Grusec, J. E. (1983). Parental influence techniques: An attributional analysis. *Child Development, 54*, 645–652. doi:10.2307/1130051

Doan, S. N., Fuller-Rowell, T. E., & Evans, G. W. (2012). Cumulative risk and adolescent's internalizing and externalizing problems: The mediating roles of maternal responsiveness and self-regulation. *Developmental Psychology, 48*, 1529–1539. doi:10.1037/a0027815

Dobzhansky, T. (1955). *Evolution, genetics, and man.* New York, NY: Wiley.

Dodge, K. A. (1980). Social cognition and children's aggressive behavior. *Child Development, 51*, 162–170. doi:10.2307/1129603

Dodge, K. A. (1986). A social information processing model of social competence in children. In M. Perlmutter (Ed.), *Minnesota Symposia on Child Psychology: Vol. 18. Cognitive perspectives on children's social and behavioral development* (pp. 77–125). Hillsdale, NJ: Erlbaum.

Dodge, K. A., Coie, J. D., Pettit, G. S., & Price, J. M. (1990). Peer status and aggression in boys' groups: Developmental and contextual analyses. *Child Development, 61*, 1289–1309. doi:10.2307/1130743

Dodge, K. A., Dishion, T. J., & Lansford, J. E. (Eds.). (2008). *Deviant peer influences in programs for youth: Problems and solutions.* New York, NY: Guilford Press.

Dodge, K. A., Greenberg, M. T., Malone, P. S., & Conduct Problems Prevention Research Group. (2008). Testing an idealized dynamic cascade model of the development of serious violence in adolescence. *Child Development, 79*, 1907–1927. doi:10.1111/j.1467-8624.2008.01233.x

Dodge, K. A., Lansford, J. E., Burks, V. S., Bates, J. E., Pettit, G. S., Fontaine, R., & Price, J. M. (2003). Peer rejection and social information-processing factors in the development of aggressive behavior problems in children. *Child Development, 74*, 374–393. doi:10.1111/1467-8624.7402004

Dodge, K. A., Lansford, J. E., & Dishion, T. J. (2006). The problem of deviant peer influences in intervention programs. In K. A. Dodge, T. J. Dishion, & J. E. Lansford (Eds.), *Deviant peer influences in programs for youth: Problems and solutions* (pp. 3–13). New York, NY: Guilford Press.

Dodge, K. A., Lochman, J. E., Harnish, J. D., Bates, J. E., & Pettit, G. S. (1997). Reactive and proactive aggression in school children and psychiatrically impaired chronically assaultive youth. *Journal of Abnormal Psychology, 106,* 37–51.

Dodge, K. A., Murphy, R. R., & Buchsbaum, K. (1984). The assessment of intention-cue detection skills in children: Implications for developmental psychopathology. *Child Development, 55,* 163–173.

Dodge, K. A., Pettit, G. S., & Bates, J. E. (1994). Socialization mediators of the relation between socioeconomic status and child conduct problems. *Child Development, 65,* 649–665. doi:10.2307/1131407

Dodge, K. A., Pettit, G. S., Bates, J. E., & Valente, E. (1995). Social information-processing patterns partially mediate the effect of early physical abuse on later conduct problems. *Journal of Abnormal Psychology, 104,* 632–643. doi:10.1037/0021-843X.104.4.632

Dodge, K. A., Pettit, G. S., McClaskey, C. L., Brown, M. M., & Gottman, J. M. (1986). Social competence in children. *Monographs of the Society for Research in Child Development, 51*(2, Serial No. 213), i-85. doi:10.2307/1165906

Dodge, K. A., Schlundt, D. C., Schocken, I., & Delugach, J. D. (1983). Social competence and children's sociometric status: The role of peer group entry strategies. *Merrill-Palmer Quarterly, 29,* 309–336.

Dogan, S. J., Conger, R. D., Kim, K. J., & Masyn, K. E. (2007). Cognitive and parenting pathways in the transmission of antisocial behavior from parents to adolescents. *Child Development, 78,* 335–349. doi:10.1111/j.1467-8624.2007.01001.x

Dohnt, H., & Tiggemann, M. (2006). The contribution of peer and media influences to the development of body satisfaction and self-esteem in young girls: A prospective study. *Developmental Psychology, 42,* 929–936. doi:10.1037/0012-1649.42.5.929

Domitrovich, C. E., Bradshaw, C. P., Greenberg, M. T., Embry, D., Poduska, J. M., & Ialongo, N. S. (2010). Integrated models of school-based prevention: Logic and theory. *Psychology in the Schools, 47,* 71–88. doi:10.1002/pits.20452

Domitrovich, C. E., Cortes, R. C., & Greenberg, M. T. (2007). Improving young children's social and emotional competence: A randomized trial of the preschool "PATHS" curriculum. *Journal of Primary Prevention, 28,* 67–91. doi:10.1007/s10935-007-0081-0

Domitrovich, C. E., Morgan, N. R., Moore, J. E., Rhoades, B. L., Shah, H. K., Jacobson, L., & Greenberg, M. T. One versus two years: Does length of exposure to an enhanced preschool program impact the academic functioning of disadvantaged children in kindergarten? (2013). One versus two years: Does length of exposure *Early Childhood Research Quarterly, 28,* 704–713. doi:10.1016/j.ecresq.2013.04.004

Donaldson, S. K., & Westerman, M. A. (1986). Development of children's understanding of ambivalence and causal theories of emotions. *Developmental Psychology, 22,* 655–662.

Donnellan, M. B., Trzesniewski, K. H., Robins, R. W., Moffitt, T. E., & Caspi, A. (2005). Low self-esteem is related to aggression, antisocial behavior, and delinquency. *Psychological Science, 16,* 328–335. doi:10.1111/j.0956-7976.2005.01535.x

Doornwaard, S. M., Branje, S., Meeus, W. H. J., & ter Bogt, T. F. M. (2012). Development of adolescents' peer crowd identification in relation to changes in problem behaviors. *Developmental Psychology, 48,* 1366–1380. doi:10.1037/a0026994

Downey, G., & Coyne, J. C. (1990). Children of depressed parents: An integrative review. *Psychological Bulletin, 108,* 50–76.

Doyle, A. B., Brendgen, M., Markiewicz, D., & Kamkar, K. (2003). Family relationships as moderators of the association between romantic relationships and adjustment in early adolescence. *The Journal of Early Adolescence, 23,* 316–340. doi:10.1177/0272431603254238

Doyle, A. B., Lawford, H., & Markiewicz, D. (2009). Attachment style with mother, father, best friend, and romantic partner during adolescence. *Journal of Research on Adolescence, 19,* 690–714. doi:10.1111/j.1532-7795.2009.00617.x

Driesen, N. R., & Raz, N. (1995). The influence of sex, age, and handedness on corpus callosum morphology: A meta-analysis. *Psychobiology, 23,* 240–247.

Drillien, C. M. (1964). *The growth and development of the prematurely born infant.* Baltimore, MD: Williams and Wilkins.

Driscoll, A. K., Russell, S. T., & Crockett, L. J. (2008). Parenting styles and youth well-being across immigrant generations. *Journal of Family Issues, 29,* 185–209. doi:10.1177/0192513x07307843

Drummond, K. D., Bradley, S. J., Peterson-Badali, M., & Zucker, K. J. (2008). A follow-up study of girls with gender identity disorder. *Developmental Psychology, 44,* 34–45. doi:10.1037/0012-1649.44.1.34

Dubas, J. S., & Gerris, J. R. M. (2002). Longitudinal changes in the time parents spend in activities with their adolescent children as a function of child age, pubertal status and gender. *Journal of Family Psychology, 16,* 415–426. doi:10.1037/0893-3200.16.4.415

Dubé, E. M., Savin-Williams, R. C., & Diamond, L. M. (2001). Intimacy development, gender, and ethnicity among sexual-minority youths. In A. R. D'Augelli & C. Patterson (Eds.), *Lesbian, gay, and bisexual identities and youth* (pp. 129–152). New York, NY: Oxford University Press.

Duckett, E., & Richards, M. (1995). Maternal employment and the quality of daily experience for young adolescents of single mothers. *Journal of Family Psychology, 9,* 418–432. doi:10.1037/0893-3200.9.4.418

Duckworth, A. L., Quinn, P. D., & Tsukayama, E. (2012). What *No Child Left Behind* leaves behind: The roles of IQ and self-control in predicting standardized achievement test scores and report card grades. *Journal of Educational Psychology, 104,* 439–451. doi:10.1037/a0026280

Dumka, L. E., Roosa, M. W., & Jackson, K. M. (1997). Risk, conflict, mothers' parenting, and children's adjustment in low-income, Mexican immigrant, and Mexican American families. *Journal of Marriage and Family, 59,* 309–323. doi:10.2307/353472

Duncan, G. J., Dowsett, C. J., Claessens, A., Magnuson, K., Huston, A. C., Klebanov, P., … Japel, C. (2007). School readiness and later achievement. *Developmental Psychology, 43,* 1428–1446. doi:10.1037/0012-1649.43.6.1428

Duncan, G. J., Yeung, W. J., Brooks-Gunn, J., & Smith, J. R. (1998). How much does childhood poverty affect the life chances of children? *American Sociological Review, 63,* 406–423.

Dunfield, K., Kuhlmeier, V. A., O'Connell, L., & Kelley, E. (2011). Examining the diversity of prosocial behavior: Helping, sharing, and comforting in infancy. *Infancy, 16,* 227–247. doi:10.1111/j.1532-7078.2010.00041.x

Dunfield, K. A., & Kuhlmeier, V. A. (2010). Intention-mediated selective helping in infancy. *Psychological Science, 21,* 523–527. doi:10.1177/0956797610364119

Dunfield, K. A., & Kuhlmeier, V. A. (2013). Classifying prosocial behavior: Children's responses to instrumental need, emotional distress, and material desire. *Child Development, 84,* 1766–1776. doi:10.1111/cdev.12075

Dunifon, R., Kalil, A., Crosby, D. A., & Su, J. H. (2013). Mothers' night work and children's behavior problems. *Developmental Psychology.* Advance online publication. doi:10.1037/a0031241

Dunkel, C. S., & Anthis, K. S. (2001). The role of possible selves in identity formation: A short-term longitudinal study. *Journal of Adolescence, 24,* 765–776. doi:10.1006/jado.2001.0433

Dunn, J. (1988). *The beginnings of social understanding.* Cambridge, MA: Harvard University Press.

Dunn, J. (1992). Siblings and development. *Current Directions in Psychological Science, 1,* 6–9. doi:10.1111/1467-8721.ep10767741

Dunn, J. (2004). *Children's friendships: The beginnings of intimacy.* Malden, MA: Blackwell.

Dunn, J., & Brown, J. (1994). Affect expression in the family, children's understanding of emotions, and their interactions with others. *Merrill-Palmer Quarterly, 40,* 120–137.

Dunn, J., Brown, J., & Beardsall, L. (1991). Family talk about feeling states and children's later understanding of others' emotions. *Developmental Psychology, 27,* 448–455.

Dunn, J., Brown, J., Slomkowski, C., Tesla, C., & Youngblade, L. (1991). Young children's understanding of other people's feelings and beliefs: Individual differences and their antecedents. *Child Development, 62,* 1352–1366.

Dunphy, D. C. (1963). The social structure of urban adolescent peer groups. *Sociometry, 26,* 230–246. doi:10.2307/2785909

Dunsmore, J. C., & Halberstadt, A. G. (1997). How does family emotional expressiveness affect children's schemas? In K. C. Barrett (Ed.), *New Directions for Child and Adolescent Development: No. 77. The communication of emotion: Current research from diverse perspectives* (pp. 45–68). San Francisco, CA: Jossey-Bass.

Duong, M. T., Schwartz, D., Chang, L., Kelly, B. M., & Tom, S. R. (2009). Associations between maternal physical discipline and peer victimization among Hong Kong Chinese children: The moderating role of child aggression. *Journal of Abnormal Child Psychology, 37,* 957–966. doi:10.1007/s10802-009-9322-4

Dupéré, V., Lacourse, É., Willms, J. D., Vitaro, F., & Tremblay, R. (2007). Affiliation to youth gangs during adolescence: The interaction between childhood psychopathic tendencies and neighborhood disadvantage. *Journal of Abnormal Child Psychology, 35,* 1035–1045. doi:10.1007/s10802-007-9153-0

Durbin, C. E. (2010). Validity of young children's self-reports of their emotion in response to structured laboratory tasks. *Emotion, 10,* 519–535. doi:10.1037/a0019008

Durbin, C. E., Hayden, E. P., Klein, D. N., & Olino, T. M. (2007). Stability of laboratory-assessed temperamental emotionality traits from ages 3 to 7. *Emotion, 7,* 388–399.

Dush, C. M. K., Kotila, L. E., & Schoppe-Sullivan, S. J. (2011). Predictors of supportive coparenting after relationship dissolution among at-risk parents. *Journal of Family Psychology, 25,* 356–365. doi:10.1037/a0023652

Dweck, C. S. (1999). *Self-theories: Their role in motivation, personality, and development.* Philadelphia, PA: Psychology Press.

Dweck, C. S. (2006). *Mindset: The new psychology of success.* New York, NY: Random House.

Dweck, C. S., & Leggett, E. L. (1988). A social-cognitive approach to motivation and personality. *Psychological Review, 95,* 256–273.

Dwyer, K. M., Fredstrom, B. K., Rubin, K. H., Booth-LaForce, C., Rose-Krasnor, L., & Burgess, K. B. (2010). Attachment, social information processing, and friendship quality of early adolescent girls and boys. *Journal of Social and Personal Relationships, 27,* 91–116. doi:10.1177/0265407509346420

Eagly, A. H. (1987). Sex differences in social behavior: A social-role interpretation. Hillsdale, NJ: Erlbaum.

Eagly, A. H., Wood, W., & Diekman, A. B. (2000). Social role theory of sex differences and similarities: A current appraisal. In T. Eckes & H. M. Trautner (Eds.), *The developmental social psychology of gender* (pp. 123–174). Mahwah, NJ: Erlbaum.

East, P. L., Felice, M. E., & Morgan, M. C. (1993). Sisters' and girl-friends' sexual and childbearing behavior: Effects on early adolescent girls' sexual outcomes. *Journal of Marriage and the Family, 55,* 953–963.

Eaton, W. O., & Enns, L. R. (1986). Sex differences in human motor activity level. *Psychological Bulletin, 100,* 19–28. doi:10.1037/0033-2909.100.1.19

Eaton, W. O., & Saudino, K. J. (1992). Prenatal activity level as a temperament dimension? Individual differences and developmental functions in fetal movement. *Infant Behavior and Development, 15,* 57–70. doi:10.1016/0163-6383(92)90006-R

Eccles, J. S., Freedman-Doan, C., Frome, P., Jacobs, J., & Yoon, K. S. (2000). Gender-role socialization in the family: A longitudinal approach. In T. Eckes & H. M. Trautner (Eds.), *The developmental social psychology of gender* (pp. 333–360). Mahwah, NJ: Erlbaum.

Eccles, J. S., & Wigfield, A. (2002). Motivational beliefs, values, and goals. *Annual Review of Psychology, 53,* 109–132. doi:10.1146/annurev.psych.53.100901.135153

Eccles, J. S., Wigfield, A., Flanagan, C. A., Miller, C., Reuman, D. A., & Yee, D. (1989). Self-concepts, domain values, and self-esteem: Relations and changes at early adolescence. *Journal of Personality, 57,* 283–310. doi:10.1111/j.1467-6494.1989.tb00484.x

Eckenrode, J., Laird, M., & Doris, J. (1993). School performance and disciplinary problems among abused and neglected children. *Developmental Psychology, 29,* 53–62. doi:10.1037/0012-1649.29.1.53

Eckert, P. (1989). *Jocks and burnouts: Social categories and identity in the high school.* New York, NY: Teachers College Press.

Edelman, G. M. (1987). *Neural Darwinism: The theory of neuronal group selection.* New York, NY: Basic Books.

Eder, D. (1985). The cycle of popularity: Interpersonal relations among female adolescents. *Sociology of Education, 58,* 154–165. doi:10.2307/2112416

Edwards, C. P. (1992). Cross-cultural perspectives on family-peer relations. In R. D. Parke & G. W. Ladd (Eds.), *Family-peer relationships: Modes of linkage* (pp. 285–316). Hillsdale, NJ: Erlbaum.

Edwards, G. D., Bangert, A. W., Cooch, G., Shinfuku, N., Chen, T., Bi, Y., & Rappe, P. (2005). The impact of sibling status on Chinese college students' quality of life. *Social Behavior and Personality, 33,* 227–242.

Egan, V., & Beadman, M. (2011). Personality and gang embeddedness. *Personality and Individual Differences, 51,* 748–753. doi:10.1016/j.paid.2011.06.021

Egley, A., Jr., & Howell, J. C. (2012, April). Highlights of the 2010 National Youth Gang Survey. Retrieved from http://www.ojjdp.gov/pubs/237542.pdf

Eiden, R. D., Colder, C., Edwards, E. P., & Leonard, K. E. (2009). A longitudinal study of social competence among children of alcoholic and non-alcoholic parents: Role of parental psychopathology, parental warmth, and self-regulation. *Psychology of Addictive Behaviors, 23,* 36–46.

Eigsti, I. M., Zayas, V., Mischel, W., Shoda, Y., Ayduk, O., Dadlani, M. B., … Casey, B. J. (2006). Predicting cognitive control from preschool to late adolescence and young adulthood. *Psychological Science, 17*, 478–484. doi:10.1111/j.1467-9280.2006.01732.x

Eimas, P. D., Siqueland, E. R., Jusczyk, P., & Vigorito, J. (1971, January 22). Speech perception in infants. *Science, 171*, 303–306.

Eisenberg, M. E., Neumark-Sztainer, D., & Story, M. (2003). Associations of weight-based teasing and emotional well-being among adolescents. *Archives of Pediatrics and Adolescent Medicine, 157*, 733–738. doi:10.1001/archpedi.157.8.733

Eisenberg, N. (1986). *Altruistic emotion, cognition, and behavior.* Hillsdale, NJ: Erlbaum.

Eisenberg, N. (2000). Emotion, regulation, and moral development. *Annual Review of Psychology, 51*, 665–697. doi:10.1146/annurev.psych.51.1.665

Eisenberg, N., Boehnke, K., Schuhler, P., & Silbereisen, R. K. (1985). The development of prosocial behavior and cognitions in German children. *Journal of Cross-Cultural Psychology, 16*, 69–82. doi:10.1177/0022002185016001006

Eisenberg, N., Carlo, G., Murphy, B., & van Court, P. (1995). Prosocial development in late adolescence: A longitudinal study. *Child Development, 66*, 1179–1197. doi:10.2307/1131806

Eisenberg, N., Chang, L., Ma, Y., & Huang, X. (2009). Relations of parenting style to Chinese children's effortful control, ego resilience, and maladjustment. *Development and Psychopathology, 21*, 455–477. doi:10.1017/S095457940900025X

Eisenberg, N., Cumberland, A., Guthrie, I. K., Murphy, B. C., & Shepard, S. A. (2005). Age changes in prosocial responding and moral reasoning in adolescence and early adulthood. *Journal of Research on Adolescence, 15*, 235–260. doi:10.1111/j.1532-7795.2005.00095.x

Eisenberg, N., Cumberland, A., & Spinrad, T. L. (1998). Parental socialization of emotion. *Psychological Inquiry, 9*, 241–273.

Eisenberg, N., & Fabes, R. A. (1998). Prosocial development. In W. Damon (Series Ed.) & N. Eisenberg (Vol. Ed.), *Handbook of child psychology: Vol. 3. Social, emotional, and personality development* (5th ed., pp. 701–778). New York, NY: Wiley.

Eisenberg, N., Fabes, R. A., Bernzweig, J., Karbon, M., Poulin, R., & Hanish, L. (1993). The relations of emotionality and regulation to preschoolers' social skills and sociometric status. *Child Development, 64*, 1418–1438. doi:10.1111/j.1467-8624.1993.tb02961.x

Eisenberg, N., Fabes, R. A., & Murphy, B. C. (1996). Parents' reactions to children's negative emotions: Relations to children's social competence and comforting behavior. *Child Development, 67*, 2227–2247. doi:10.1111/j.1467-8624.1996.tb01854.x

Eisenberg, N., Fabes, R. A., Shepard, S. A., Guthrie, I. K., Murphy, B. C., & Reiser, M. (1999). Parental reactions to children's negative emotions: Longitudinal relations to quality of children's social functioning. *Child Development, 70*, 513–534.

Eisenberg, N., Fabes, R. A., & Spinrad, T. L. (2006). Prosocial development. In W. Damon & R. M. Lerner (Series Eds.) & N. Eisenberg (Vol. Ed.), *Handbook of child psychology: Vol. 3. Social, emotional, and personality development* (6th ed., pp. 646–718). Hoboken, NJ: Wiley.

Eisenberg, N., Gershoff, E. T., Fabes, R. A., Shepard, S. A., Cumberland, A. J., Losoya, S. H., … Murphy, B. C. (2001). Mothers' emotional expressivity and children's behavior problems and social competence: Mediation through children's regulation. *Developmental Psychology, 37*, 475–490.

Eisenberg, N., Guthrie, I. K., Cumberland, A., Murphy, B. C., Shepard, S. A., Zhou, Q., & Carlo, G. (2002). Prosocial development in early adulthood: A longitudinal study. *Journal of Personality and Social Psychology, 82*, 993–1006. doi:10.1037/0022-3514.82.6.993

Eisenberg, N., Guthrie, I. K., Murphy, B. C., Shepard, S. A., Cumberland, A., & Carlo, G. (1999). Consistency and development of prosocial dispositions: A longitudinal study. *Child Development, 70*, 1360–1372. doi:10.1111/1467-8624.00100

Eisenberg, N., Hofer, C., Spinrad, T. L., Gershoff, E. T., Valiente, C., Losoya, S. H., … Maxon, E. (2008). Understanding mother-adolescent conflict discussions: Concurrent and across-time prediction from youths' dispositions and parenting. *Monographs of the Society for Research in Child Development, 73*(2, Serial No. 290). doi:10.1111/j.1540-5834.2008.00470.x

Eisenberg, N., Michalik, N., Spinrad, T. L., Hofer, C., Kupfer, A., Valiente, C., … Reiser, M. (2007). The relations of effortful control and impulsivity to children's sympathy: A longitudinal study. *Cognitive Development, 22*, 544–567. doi:10.1016/j.cogdev.2007.08.003

Eisenberg, N., Miller, P. A., Shell, R., McNalley, S., & Shea, C. (1991). Prosocial development in adolescence: A longitudinal study. *Developmental Psychology, 27*, 849–858.

Eisenberg, N., Murphy, B. C., & Shepard, S. (1997). The development of empathic accuracy. In W. J. Ickes (Ed.), *Empathic accuracy* (pp. 73–116). New York, NY: Guilford Press.

Eisenberg, N., & Mussen, P. H. (1989). *The roots of prosocial behavior in children.* Cambridge, England: Cambridge University Press.

Eisenberg, N., Sallquist, J., French, D. C., Purwono, U., Suryanti, T. A., & Pidada, S. (2009). The relations of majority-minority group status and having an other-religion friend to Indonesian youths' socioemotional functioning. *Developmental Psychology, 45*, 248–259. doi:10.1037/a0014028

Eisenberg, N., & Silver, R. C. (2011). Growing up in the shadow of terrorism: Youth in America after 9/11. *American Psychologist, 66*, 468–481. doi:10.1037/a0024619

Eisenberg, N., Spinrad, T. L., & Eggum, N. D. (2010). Emotion-related self-regulation and its relation to children's maladjustment. *Annual Review of Clinical Psychology, 6*, 495–525. doi:10.1146/annurev.clinpsy.121208.131208

Eisenberg, N., Spinrad, T. L., & Knafo, A. (under revision). Prosocial development. In R. M. Lerner (Series Ed.) & M. Lamb & C. Garcia Coll (Vol. Eds.), *Handbook of child psychology and developmental science: Vol. 3. Socioemotional processes* (7th ed.). New York, NY: Wiley.

Eisenberg, N., Valiente, C., Spinrad, T. L., Cumberland, A., Liew, J., Reiser, M., … Losoya, S. H. (2009). Longitudinal relations of children's effortful control, impulsivity, and negative emotionality to their externalizing, internalizing, and co-occurring behavior problems. *Developmental Psychology, 45*, 988–1008. doi:10.1037/a0016213

Eisenberg, N., Zhou, Q., Spinrad, T. L., Valiente, C., Fabes, R. A., & Liew, J. (2005). Relations among positive parenting, children's effortful control, and externalizing problems: A three-wave longitudinal study. *Child Development, 76*, 1055–1071. doi:10.1111/j.1467-8624.2005.00897.x

Eisenberg-Berg, N., & Geisheker, E. (1979). Content of preachings and power of the model/preacher: The effect on children's generosity. *Developmental Psychology, 15*, 168–175.

Eisenberg-Berg, N., & Hand, M. (1979). The relationship of preschoolers' reasoning about prosocial moral conflicts to prosocial behavior. *Child Development, 50*, 356–363. doi:10.2307/1129410

Eisenberg-Berg, N., Murray, E., & Hite, T. (1982). Children's reasoning regarding sex-typed toy choices. *Child Development, 53*, 81–86. doi: 10.2307/1129639

Ekas, N. V., Braungart-Rieker, J. M., Lickenbrock, D. M., Zentall, S. R., & Maxwell, S. M. (2011). Toddler emotion regulation with mothers and fathers: Temporal associations between negative affect and behavioral strategies. *Infancy, 16*, 266-294. doi:10.1111/j.1532-7078.2010.00042.x

Ekéus, C., Christensson, K., & Hjern, A. (2004). Unintentional and violent injuries among pre-school children of teenage mothers in Sweden: A national cohort study. *Journal of Epidemiology and Community Health, 58*, 680–685. doi:10.1136/jech.2003.015255

Ekman, P., & Cordaro, D. (2011). What is meant by calling emotions basic. *Emotion Review, 3*, 364–370.

El-Sheikh, M., & Elmore–Staton, L. (2004). The link between marital conflict and child adjustment: Parent–child conflict and perceived attachments as mediators, potentiators, and mitigators of risk. *Development and Psychopathology, 16*, 631–648. doi:10.1017/S0954579404004705

El-Sheikh, M., & Whitson, S. A. (2006). Longitudinal relations between marital conflict and child adjustment: Vagal regulation as a protective factor. *Journal of Family Psychology, 20*, 30–39.

El-Sheikh, M., Harger, J., & Whitson, S. M. (2001). Exposure to interparental conflict and children's adjustment and physical health: The moderating role of vagal tone. *Child Development, 72*, 1617–1636.

Elbert, T., Pantev, C., Wienbruch, C., Rockstroh, B., & Taub, E. (1995, October 13). Increased cortical representation of the fingers of the left hand in string players. *Science, 270*, 305–307.

Elicker, J., England, M., & Sroufe, L. A. (1992). Predicting peer competence and peer relationships in childhood from early parent-child relationships. In R. D. Parke & G. W. Ladd (Eds.), *Family–peer relationships: Modes of linkage* (pp. 77–106). Hillsdale, NJ: Erlbaum.

Elkind, D. (1967). Egocentrism in adolescence. *Child Development, 38*, 1025–1034.

Elliott, D. S. (1994). Serious violent offenders: Onset, developmental course, and termination: The American Society of Criminology 1993 presidential address. *Criminology, 32*, 1–21. doi:10.1111/j.1745-9125.1994.tb01144.x

Ellis, B. J., Bates, J. E., Dodge, K. A., Fergusson, D. M., Horwood, L. J., Pettit, G. S., & Woodward, L. (2003). Does father absence place daughters at special risk for early sexual activity and teenage pregnancy? *Child Development, 74*, 801–821. doi:10.1111/1467-8624.00569

Ellis, B. J., Boyce, W. T., Belsky, J., Bakermans-Kranenburg, M. J., & van IJzendoorn, M. H. (2011). Differential susceptibility to the environment: An evolutionary-neurodevelopmental theory. *Development and Psychopathology, 23*, 7–28. doi:10.1017/S0954579410000611

Ellis, W. E., Crooks, C. V., & Wolfe, D. A. (2009). Relational aggression in peer and dating relationships: Links to psychological and behavioral adjustment. *Social Development, 18*, 253–269. doi:10.1111/j.1467-9507.2008.00468.x

Ellsworth, C. P., Muir, D. W., & Hains, S. M. (1993). Social competence and person-object differentiation: An analysis of the still-face effect. *Developmental Psychology, 29*, 63–73. doi:10.1037/0012-1649.29.1.63

Elman, J. L., Bates, E., Johnson, M. H., Karmiloff-Smith, A., Parisi, D., & Plunkett, K. (1996). *Rethinking innateness: A connectionist perspective on development.* Cambridge, MA: MIT Press.

Else-Quest, N. M., Hyde, J. S., Goldsmith, H. H., & Van Hulle, C. A. (2006). Gender differences in temperament: A meta-analysis. *Psychological Bulletin, 132*, 33–72. doi:10.1037/0033-2909.132.1.33

Else-Quest, N. M., Hyde, J. S., & Linn, M. C. (2010). Cross-national patterns of gender differences in mathematics: A meta-analysis. *Psychological Bulletin, 136*, 103–127. doi:10.1037/a0018053

Ely, R., & McCabe, A. (1994). The language play of kindergarten children. *First Language, 14*, 19–35. doi:10.1177/014272379401404002

Emde, R. N. (1994). Individual meaning and increasing complexity: Contributions of Sigmund Freud and René Spitz to developmental psychology. In R. D. Parke, P. A. Ornstein, J. J. Rieser, & C. Zahn-Waxler (Eds.), *A century of developmental psychology* (pp. 203–231). Washington, DC: American Psychological Association.

Emery, J., Paquette, D., & Bigras, M. (2008). Factors predicting attachment patterns in infants of adolescent mothers. *Journal of Family Studies, 14*, 65–90. doi: 10.5172/jfs.327.14.1.65

Emery, R. E. (1989). Family violence. *American Psychologist, 44*, 321–328. doi:10.1037/0003-066X.44.2.321

Emery, R. E., & Forehand, R. (1996). Parental divorce and children's well-being: A focus on resilience. In R. J. Haggerty, L. R. Sherrod, N. Garmezy, & M. Rutter (Eds.), *Stress, risk, and resilience in children and adolescents: Processes, mechanisms, and interventions* (pp. 64–99). Cambridge, England: Cambridge University Press.

Emery, R. E., & Laumann-Billings, L. (1998). An overview of the nature, causes, and consequences of abusive family relationships: Toward differentiating maltreatment and violence. *American Psychologist, 53*, 121–135. doi: 10.1037/0003-066X.53.2.121

Emery, R. E., Waldron, M., Kitzmann, K. M., & Aaron, J. (1999). Delinquent behavior, future divorce or nonmarital childbearing, and externalizing behavior among offspring: A 14-year prospective study. *Journal of Family Psychology, 13*, 568–579. doi:10.1037/0893-3200.13.4.568

Employment and Social Development Canada. (2012). *The national shelter study.* Retrieved from http://www.hrsdc.gc.ca/eng/communities/homelessness/reports/shelter_study.pdf

Employment and Social Development Canada. (2013a). *Indicators of well-being in Canada: Family life—Age of mother at childbirth.* Retrieved from http://www4. hrsdc.gc.ca/.3ndic.1t.4r@-eng.jsp?iid=75

Employment and Social Development Canada. (2013b). *Indicators of well-being in Canada: Family life—Divorce.* Retrieved from http://www4.hrsdc.gc. ca/.3ndic.1t.4r@-eng.jsp?iid=76

Employment and Social Development Canada. (2013c). *Indicators of well-being in Canada, Family life—Marriage.* Retrieved from http://www4.hrsdc.gc. ca/.3ndic.1t.4r@-eng.jsp?iid=78

Engle, J. M., & McElwain, N. L. (2011). Parental reactions to toddlers' negative emotions and child negative emotionality as correlates of problem behavior at the age of three. *Social Development, 20*, 251–271.

Engle, J. M., McElwain, N. L., & Lasky, N. (2011). Presence and quality of kindergarten children's friendships: Concurrent and longitudinal associations with child adjustment in the early school years. *Infant and Child Development, 20*, 365–386. doi:10.1002/icd.706

Englund, M. M., Kuo, S. I.-C., Puig, J., & Collins, W. A. (2011). Early roots of adult competence: The significance of close relationships from infancy to early adulthood. *International Journal of Behavioral Development, 35*, 490–496. doi:10.1177/0165025411422994

Ensor, R., & Hughes, C. (2008). Content or connectedness? Mother–child talk and early social understanding. *Child Development, 79*, 201–216.

Eppig, C., Fincher, C. L., & Thornhill, R. (2010). Parasite prevalence and the worldwide distribution of cognitive ability. *Proceedings of the Royal Society B: Biological Sciences, 277*, 3801–3808. doi:10.1098/rspb.2010.0973

Eppler, M. A., Adolph, K. E., & Weiner, T. (1996). The developmental relationship between infants' exploration and action on slanted surfaces. *Infant Behavior and Development, 19*, 259–264. doi:10.1016/S0163-6383(96)90025-9

Erdley, C. A., Nangle, D. W., Newman, J. E., & Carpenter, E. M. (2001). Children's friendship experiences and psychological adjustment: Theory and research. In C. A. Erdley & D. W. Nangle (Eds.), *New Directions for Child and Adolescent Development: No. 91. The role of friendship in psychological adjustment* (Vol. 2001, pp. 5–24). San Francisco, CA: Jossey-Bass.

Erel, O., Margolin, G., & John, R. S. (1998). Observed sibling interaction: Links with the marital and the mother–child relationship. *Developmental Psychology, 34*, 288–298. doi:10.1037/0012-1649.34.2.288

Erel, O., Oberman, Y., & Yirmiya, N. (2000). Maternal versus nonmaternal care and seven domains of children's development. *Psychological Bulletin, 126*, 727–747. doi:10.1037/0033-2909.126.5.727

Erickson, M. F., Egeland, B., & Pianta, R. (1989). The effects of maltreatment on the development of young children. In D. Cicchetti & V. Carlson (Eds.), *Child maltreatment: Theory and research on the causes and consequences of child abuse and neglect* (pp. 647–684). New York, NY: Cambridge University Press.

Erickson, M. F., Sroufe, L. A., & Egeland, B. (1985). The relationship between quality of attachment and behavior problems in preschool in a high-risk sample. *Monographs of the Society for Research in Child Development, 50*(1–2, Serial No. 209), 147–166. doi:10.2307/3333831

Ericsson, K. A., & Kintsch, W. (1995). Long-term working memory. *Psychological Review, 102*, 211–245.

Erikson, E. H. (1950). *Childhood and society.* New York, NY: Norton.

Erikson, E. H. (1968). *Identity: Youth and crisis.* New York, NY: Norton.

Erikson, E. H. (1969). *Gandhi's truth: On the origins of militant nonviolence.* New York, NY: Norton.

Erikson, E. H. (1994). *Identity and the life cycle.* New York, NY: Norton. (Original work published 1959)

Erkut, S., Marx, F., Fields, J. P., & Sing, R. (1999). Raising confident and competent girls: One size does not fit all. In L. A. Peplau, S. DeBro, R. Veniegas, & P. Taylor (Eds.), *Gender, culture, and ethnicity: Current research about women and men* (pp. 83–101). Mountain View, CA: Mayfield.

Esbensen, F.-A., & Huizinga, D. (1993). Gangs, drugs, and delinquency in a survey of urban youth. *Criminology, 31*, 565–589. doi:10.1111/j.1745-9125.1993.tb01142.x

Espelage, D. L., Holt, M. K., & Henkel, R. R. (2003). Examination of peer-group contextual effects on aggression during early adolescence. *Child Development, 74*, 205–220. doi:10.1111/1467-8624.00531

Esposito, G., Yoshida, S., Ohnishi, R., Tsuneoka, Y., Rostagno, M. d. C., Yokota, S., … Kuroda, K. O. (2013). Infant calming responses during maternal carrying in humans and mice. *Current Biology, 23*, 739–745. doi:10.1016/j.cub.2013.03.041

Espy, K. A., Sheffield, T. D., Wiebe, S. A., Clark, C. A. C., & Moehr, M. J. (2011). Executive control and dimensions of problem behaviors in preschool children. *Journal of Child Psychology and Psychiatry, 52*, 33–46. doi:10.1111/j.1469-7610.2010.02265.x

Essex, M. J., Thomas Boyce, W., Hertzman, C., Lam, L. L., Armstrong, J. M., Neumann, S. M. A., & Kobor, M. S. (2013). Epigenetic vestiges of early developmental adversity: Childhood stress exposure and DNA methylation in adolescence. *Child Development, 84*, 58–75. doi:10.1111/j.1467-8624.2011.01641.x

Estell, D. B., Cairns, R. B., Farmer, T. W., & Cairns, B. D. (2002). Aggression in inner-city early elementary classrooms: Individual and peer-group configurations. *Merrill-Palmer Quarterly, 48*, 52–76. doi:10.2307/23093354

Etkin, A., Egner, T., Peraza, D. M., Kandel, E. R., & Hirsch, J. (2006). Resolving emotional conflict: A role for the rostral anterior cingulate cortex in modulating activity in the amygdala. *Neuron, 51*, 871–882. doi:10.1016/j.neuron.2006.07.029

Evans, A. B., Banerjee, M., Meyer, R., Aldana, A., Foust, M., & Rowley, S. (2012). Racial socialization as a mechanism for positive development among African American youth. *Child Development Perspectives, 6*, 251–257. doi:10.1111/j.1750-8606.2011.00226.x

Evans, A. D., Xu, F., & Lee, K. (2011). When all signs point to you: Lies told in the face of evidence. *Developmental Psychology, 47*, 39–49.

Evans, E. M. (2008). Conceptual change and evolutionary biology: A developmental analysis. In S. Vosniadou (Ed.), *International handbook of research on conceptual change* (pp. 263–294). New York, NY: Routledge.

Evans, G. W. (2004). The environment of childhood poverty. *American Psychologist, 59*, 77–92. doi:10.1037/0003-066X.59.2.77

Evans, G. W., Gonnella, C., Marcynyszyn, L. A., Gentile, L., & Salpekar, N. (2005). The role of chaos in poverty and children's socioemotional adjustment. *Psychological Science, 16*, 560–565. doi:10.1111/j.0956-7976.2005.01575.x

Evans, J. L., Saffran, J. R., & Robe-Torres, K. (2009). Statistical learning in children with specific language impairment. *Journal of Speech, Language, and Hearing Research, 52*, 321–335. doi:10.1044/1092-4388(2009/07-0189)

Evans, M. A., Shaw, D., & Bell, M. (2007). Home literacy activities and their influence on early literacy skills. *Canadian Journal of Experimental Psychology, 54*, 65–75. doi:10.1037/h0087330

Evans, M. A., Whigham, M., & Wang, M. C. (1995). The effect of a role model project upon the attitudes of ninth-grade science students. *Journal of Research in Science Teaching, 32*, 195–204. doi:10.1002/tea.3660320208

Ewart, C. K., & Suchday, S. (2002). Discovering how urban poverty and violence affect health: Development and validation of a neighborhood stress index. *Health Psychology, 21*, 254–262. doi:10.1037/0278-6133.21.3.254

Fabes, R. A., & Eisenberg, N. (1992). Young children's coping with interpersonal anger. *Child Development, 63*, 116–128. doi:10.1111/j.1467-8624.1992.tb03600.x

Fabes, R. A., Eisenberg, N., McCormick, S. E., & Wilson, M. S. (1988). Preschoolers' attributions of the situational determinants of others' naturally occurring emotions. *Developmental Psychology, 24*, 376–385.

Fabes, R. A., Eisenberg, N., Nyman, M., & Michealieu, Q. (1991). Young children's appraisals of others' spontaneous emotional reactions. *Developmental Psychology, 27*, 858–866.

Fabes, R. A., Eisenberg, N., Smith, M. C., & Murphy, B. C. (1996). Getting angry at peers: Associations with liking of the provocateur. *Child Development, 67*, 942–956. doi:10.1111/j.1467-8624.1996.tb01775.x

Fabes, R. A., Fultz, J., Eisenberg, N., May-Plumlee, T., & Christopher, F. S. (1989). Effects of rewards on children's prosocial motivation: A socialization study. *Developmental Psychology, 25*, 509–515. doi:10.1037/0012-1649.25.4.509

Fabes, R. A., Martin, C. L., & Hanish, L. D. (2003). Young children's play qualities in same-, other-, and mixed-sex peer groups. *Child Development, 74*, 921–932. doi:10.1111/1467-8624.00576

Fabricius, W. V., & Braver, S. L. (2006). Relocation, parent conflict, and domestic violence: Independent risk factors for children of divorce. *Journal of Child Custody, 3*, 7–27. doi:10.1300/j190v03n03_02

Fagan, J., Bernd, E., & Whiteman, V. (2007). Adolescent fathers' parenting stress, social support, and involvement with infants. *Journal of Research on Adolescence, 17,* 1–22. doi:10.1111/j.1532-7795.2007.00510.x

Fagan, J., & Lee, Y. (2010). Perceptions and satisfaction with father involvement and adolescent mothers' postpartum depressive symptoms. *Journal of Youth and Adolescence, 39,* 1109–1121. doi:10.1007/s10964-009-9444-6

Fagg, J. H., Curtis, S. E., Cummins, A., Stansfield, S. A., & Quesnel-Vallée, A. (2013) Neighbourhood deprivation and adolescent self-esteem: Exploration of the 'socio-economic equalisation in youth' hypothesis in Britain and Canada. *Social Science and Medicine, 91,* 168–177. doi:10.1016/j.socscimed.2013.02.021

Fagot, B. I. (1977). Consequences of moderate cross-gender behavior in preschool children. *Child Development, 48,* 902–907. doi:10.2307/1128339

Fagot, B. I., & Leinbach, M. D. (1989). The young child's gender schema: Environmental input, internal organization. *Child Development, 60,* 663–672. doi:10.2307/1130731

Fagot, B. I., & Leinbach, M. D. (1993). Gender-role development in young children: From discrimination to labeling. *Developmental Review, 13,* 205–224. doi:10.1006/drev.1993.1009

Fagot, B. I., Pears, K. C., Capaldi, D. M., Crosby, L., & Leve, C. S. (1998). Becoming an adolescent father: Precursors and parenting. *Developmental Psychology, 34,* 1209–1219. doi:10.1037/0012-1649.34.6.1209

Falbo, T., & Poston, D. L. (1993). The academic, personality, and physical outcomes of only children in China. *Child Development, 64,* 18–35. doi:10.1111/j.1467-8624.1993.tb02893.x

Falbo, T., Poston, D. L., Ji, G., Jiao, S., Jing, Q., Wang, S., … Liu, Y. (1989). Physical, achievement and personality characteristics of Chinese children. *Journal of Biosocial Science, 21,* 483–496. doi:10.1017/S0021932000018228

Falci, C. (2006). Family structure, closeness to residential and nonresidential parents, and psychological distress in early and middle adolescence. *Sociological Quarterly, 47,* 123–146. doi:10.1111/j.1533-8525.2006.00040.x

Fallang, B., Saugstad, O. D., Grogaard, J., & Hadders-Algra, M. (2003). Kinematic quality of reaching movements in preterm infants. *Pediatric Research, 53,* 836–842. doi:10.1203/01.PDR.0000058925.94994.BC

Fantz, R. L. (1961, May). The origin of form perception. *Scientific American, 204*(5), 66–72.

Farmer, T. W., Hall, C. M., Leung, M.-C., Estell, D. B., & Brooks, D. (2011). Social prominence and the heterogeneity of rejected status in late elementary school. *School Psychology Quarterly, 26,* 260–274. doi:10.1037/a0025624

Farmer, T. W., & Rodkin, P. C. (1996). Antisocial and prosocial correlates of classroom social positions: The social network centrality perspective. *Social Development, 5,* 174–188. doi:10.1111/j.1467-9507.1996.tb00079.x

Farr, R. H., Forssell, S. L., & Patterson, C. J. (2010). Parenting and child development in adoptive families: Does parental sexual orientation matter? *Applied Developmental Science, 14,* 164–178. doi:10.1080/10888691.2010.500958

Farr, R. H., & Patterson, C. J. (2013). Coparenting among lesbian, gay, and heterosexual couples: Associations with adopted children's outcomes. *Child Development, 84,* 1226–1240. doi:10.1111/cdev.12046

Farrant, B. M., Devine, T. A. J., Maybery, M. T., & Fletcher, J. (2012). Empathy, perspective taking and prosocial behaviour: The importance of parenting practices. *Infant and Child Development, 21,* 175–188. doi:10.1002/icd.740

Farrant, K., & Reese, E. (2002). *Attachment security and mother-child reminiscing: Reflections on a shared past.* Manuscript submitted for publication.

Farrell, A. D., & White, K. S. (1998). Peer influences and drug use among urban adolescents: Family structure and parent–adolescent relationship as protective factors. *Journal of Consulting and Clinical Psychology, 66,* 248–258. doi:10.1037/0022-006X.66.2.248

Fearon, R. P., Bakermans-Kranenburg, M. J., van IJzendoorn, M. H., Lapsley, A.-M., & Roisman, G. I. (2010). The significance of insecure attachment and disorganization in the development of children's externalizing behavior: A meta-analytic study. *Child Development, 81,* 435–456. doi:10.1111/j.1467-8624.2009.01405.x

Feddes, A. R., Noack, P., & Rutland, A. (2009). Direct and extended friendship effects on minority and majority children's interethnic attitudes: A longitudinal study. *Child Development, 80,* 377–390. doi:10.1111/j.1467-8624.2009.01266.x

Federal Bureau of Investigation. (n.d.). Innocent images. Retrieved from http://www.fbi.gov/about-us/investigate/vc_majorthefts/innocent

Federal Interagency Forum on Child and Family Statistics. (1999). America's children: Key national indicators of well-being, 1999. Retrieved from http://www.childstats.gov/pdf/ac1999/ac_99.pdf

Feigenson, L., Carey, S., & Spelke, E. (2002). Infants' discrimination of number vs. continuous extent. *Cognitive Psychology, 44,* 33–66.

Feigenson, L., Carey, S., & Hauser, M. (2002). The representations underlying infants' choice of more: Object files versus analog magnitudes. *Psychological Science, 13,* 150–156. doi:10.1111/1467-9280.00427

Feinberg, M., & Hetherington, E. M. (2001). Differential parenting as a within-family variable. *Journal of Family Psychology, 15,* 22–37. doi:10.1037/0893-3200.15.1.22

Feitelson, D., & Goldstein, Z. (1986). Patterns of book ownership and reading to young children in Israeli school-oriented and nonschool-oriented families. *The Reading Teacher, 39,* 924–930.

Feldman, H., Goldin-Meadow, S., & Gleitman, L. R. (1978). Beyond Herodotus: The creation of language by linguistically deprived deaf children. In A. Lock (Ed.), *Action, symbol, and gesture: The emergence of language* (pp. 351–413). New York, NY: Academic Press.

Feldman, R. (2009). The development of regulatory functions from birth to 5 years: Insights from premature infants. *Child Development, 80,* 544–561. doi:10.1111/j.1467-8624.2009.01278.x

Feldman, R. (2012). Oxytocin and social affiliation in humans. *Hormones and Behavior, 61,* 380–391. doi:10.1016/j.yhbeh.2012.01.008

Feldman, R., & Masalha, S. (2007). The role of culture in moderating the links between early ecological risk and young children's adaptation. *Development and Psychopathology, 19,* 1–21. doi:10.1017/S0954579407070010

Feldman, R., & Masalha, S. (2010). Parent–child and triadic antecedents of children's social competence: Cultural specificity, shared process. *Developmental Psychology, 46,* 455–467. doi:10.1037/a0017415

Feldman, R., Masalha, S., & Derdikman-Eiron, R. (2010). Conflict resolution in the parent–child, marital, and peer contexts and children's aggression in the peer group: A process-oriented cultural perspective. *Developmental Psychology, 46,* 310–325. doi:10.1037/a0018286

Feldman, R. S., Philippot, P., & Custrini, R. J. (1991). Social competence and nonverbal behavior. In R. S. Feldman & B. Rimé (Eds.), *Fundamentals of nonverbal behavior* (pp. 329–350). Cambridge, England: Cambridge University Press.

Fell, D. B., & Joseph, K. S. (2012, September). Temporal trends in the frequency of twins and higher-order multiple births in Canada and the United States. *BMC Pregnancy and Childbirth, 12,* 103. doi:10.1186/1471-2393-12-103

Felsman, J. K., & Vaillant, G. E. (1987). Resilient children as adults: A 40-year study. In E. J. Anthony & B. J. Cohler (Eds.), *The invulnerable child* (pp. 289–314). New York, NY: Guilford Press.

Feng, X., Keenan, K., Hipwell, A. E., Henneberger, A. K., Rischall, M. S., Butch, J., ... Babinski, D. E. (2009). Longitudinal associations between emotion regulation and depression in preadolescent girls: Moderation by the caregiving environment. *Developmental Psychology, 45,* 798–808.

Fennell, C. T., Byers-Heinlein, K., & Werker, J. F. (2007). Using speech sounds to guide word learning: The case of bilingual infants. *Child Development, 78,* 1510–1525. doi:10.1111/j.1467-8624.2007.01080.x

Fenson, L., Dale, P. S., Reznick, J. S., Bates, E., Thal, D. J., & Pethick, S. J. (1994). Variability in early communicative development. *Monographs of the Society for Research in Child Development, 59*(5, Serial No. 242), 1–173.

Ferguson, C. J. (2007). The good, the bad and the ugly: A meta-analytic review of positive and negative effects of violent video games. *Psychiatric Quarterly, 78,* 309–316. doi:10.1007/s11126-007-9056-9

Fergusson, D. M., Woodward, L. J., & Horwood, L. J. (1999). Childhood peer relationship problems and young people's involvement with deviant peers in adolescence. *Journal of Abnormal Child Psychology, 27,* 357–369. doi:10.1023/A:1021923917494

Fernald, A. (1993). Approval and disapproval: Infant responsiveness to vocal affect in familiar and unfamiliar languages. *Child Development, 64,* 657–674.

Fernald, A., & Marchman, V. A. (2012). Individual differences in lexical processing at 18 months predict vocabulary growth in typically developing and late-talking toddlers. *Child Development, 83,* 203–222. doi:10.1111/j.1467-8624.2011.01692.x

Fernald, A., & Morikawa, H. (1993). Common themes and cultural variations in Japanese and American mothers' speech to infants. *Child Development, 64,* 637–656.

Fernald, A., Perfors, A., & Marchman, V. A. (2006). Picking up speed in understanding: Speech processing efficiency and vocabulary growth across the 2nd year. *Developmental Psychology, 42,* 98–116. doi:10.1037/0012-1649.42.1.98

Fernald, A., Pinto, J. P., Swingley, D., Weinberg, A., & McRoberts, G. W. (1998). Rapid gains in speed of verbal processing by infants in the 2nd year. *Psychological Science, 9,* 228–231. doi:10.1111/1467-9280.00044

Fernald, A., Swingley, D., & Pinto, J. P. (2001). When half a word is enough: Infants can recognize spoken words using partial phonetic information. *Child Development, 72,* 1003–1015. doi:10.1111/1467-8624.00331

Fernald, A., Taeschner, T., Dunn, J., Papousek, M., de Boysson-Bardies, B., & Fukui, I. (1989). A cross-language study of prosodic modifications in mothers' and fathers' speech to preverbal infants. *Journal of Child Language, 16,* 477–501.

Ferrao, V. (2010, December). *Women in Canada: A gender-based statistical report—paid work.* Retrieved from http://www.statcan.gc.ca/pub/89-503-x/2010001/article/11387-eng.pdf

Ferrier, L. (1978). Some observations of error in context. In N. Waterson & C. E. Snow (Eds.), *The development of communication* (pp. 301–309). Chichester, England: Wiley.

Ferry, T. R., Fouad, N. A., & Smith, P. L. (2000). The role of family context in a social cognitive model for career-related choice behavior: A math and science perspective. *Journal of Vocational Behavior, 57,* 348–364. doi:10.1006/jvbe.1999.1743

Field, A. E., Austin, S. B., Camargo, C. A., Taylor, C. B., Striegel-Moore, R. H., Loud, K. J., & Colditz, G. A. (2005). Exposure to the mass media, body shape concerns, and use of supplements to improve weight and shape among male and female adolescents. *Pediatrics, 116,* e214-e220. doi:10.1542/peds.2004-2022

Field, D. (1987). A review of preschool conservation training: An analysis of analyses. *Developmental Review, 7,* 210–251. doi:10.1016/0273-2297(87)90013-X

Field, T. (2001). Massage therapy facilitates weight gain in preterm infants. *Current Directions in Psychological Science, 10,* 51–54. doi:10.1111/1467-8721.00113

Field, T., Grizzle, N., Scafidi, F., Abrams, S., Richardson, S., Kuhn, C., & Schanberg, S. (1996). Massage therapy for infants of depressed mothers. *Infant Behavior and Development, 19,* 107–112. doi:10.1016/S0163-6383(96)90048-X

Field, T., Hernandez-Reif, M., & Freedman, J. (2004). Stimulation programs for preterm infants. *Social Policy Report, 28*(1), 1, 3–19.

Fields, R. D. (2004, March). The other half of the brain. *Scientific American, 290*(4), 54–61.

Fifer, W. P., Byrd, D. L., Kaku, M., Eigsti, I.-M., Isler, J. R., Grose-Fifer, J., ... Balsam, P. D. (2010). Newborn infants learn during sleep. *Proceedings of the National Academy of Sciences of the United States of America, 107,* 10320–10323. doi:10.1073/pnas.1005061107

Fifer, W. P., & Moon, C. M. (1995). The effects of fetal experience with sound. In J.-P. Lecanuet, W. P. Fifer, N. A. Krasnegor, & W. P. Smotherman (Eds.), *Fetal development: A psychobiological perspective* (pp. 351–366). Hillsdale, NJ: Erlbaum.

Fine, S. E., Izard, C. E., Mostow, A. J., Trentacosta, C. J., & Ackerman, B. P. (2003). First grade emotion knowledge as a predictor of fifth grade self-reported internalizing behaviors in children from economically disadvantaged families. *Development and Psychopathology, 15,* 331–342.

Finnie, V., & Russell, A. (1988). Preschool children's social status and their mothers' behavior and knowledge in the supervisory role. *Developmental Psychology, 24,* 789–801. doi:10.1037/0012-1649.24.6.789

Fischer, A. R., & Shaw, C. M. (1999). African Americans' mental health and perceptions of racist discrimination: The moderating effects of racial socialization experiences and self-esteem. *Journal of Counseling Psychology, 46,* 395–407. doi:10.1037/0022-0167.46.3.395

Fischer, J. L., Sollie, D. L., & Morrow, K. B. (1986). Social networks in male and female adolescents. *Journal of Adolescent Research, 1,* 1–14. doi:10.1177/074355488611002

Fischer, K. W., & Bidell, T. R. (2006). Dynamic development of action and thought. In W. Damon & R. M. Lerner (Series Eds.) & R. M. Lerner (Vol. Ed.), *Handbook of child psychology: Vol. 1. Theoretical models of human development* (6th ed., pp. 313–399). Hoboken, NJ: Wiley.

Fiser, J., & Aslin, R. N. (2001). Unsupervised statistical learning of higher-order spatial structures from visual scenes. *Psychological Science, 12,* 499–504. doi:10.1111/1467-9280.00392

Fisher, C. (1999). From form to meaning: A role for structural alignment in the acquisition of language. *Advances in Child Development and Behavior, 27,* 1–53.

Fisher, C., Gleitman, H., & Gleitman, L. R. (1991). On the semantic content of subcategorization frames. *Cognitive Psychology, 23,* 331–392.

Fisher, S. E., & Scharff, C. (2009). FOXP2 as a molecular window into speech and language. *Trends in Genetics, 25,* 166–177.

Fitzgerald, J. (1992). Variant views about good thinking during composing: Focus on revision. In M. Pressley, K. R. Harris, & J. T. Guthrie (Eds.),

Promoting academic competence and literacy in school (pp. 337–358). Bingley, England: Emerald Group.

Fivush, R. (1991). The social construction of personal narratives. *Merrill-Palmer Quarterly, 37,* 59–81.

Flanagan, D. P., & Kaufman, A. S. (2004). *Essentials of WISC–IV assessment.* Hoboken, NJ: Wiley.

Flavell, J. H. (1971). Stage-related properties of cognitive development. *Cognitive Psychology, 2,* 421–453. doi:10.1016/0010-0285(71)90025-9

Flavell, J. H. (1982). On cognitive development. *Child Development, 53,* 1–10.

Flavell, J. H. (1986). The development of children's knowledge about the appearance-reality distinction. *American Psychologist, 41,* 418–425.

Fletcher, A. C., Rollins, A., & Nickerson, P. (2004). The extension of school-based inter- and intraracial children's friendships: Influences on psychosocial well-being. *American Journal of Orthopsychiatry, 74,* 272–285. doi:10.1037/0002-9432.74.3.272

Fleury, D. (2009). *Low-income children.* Retrieved from http://www.statcan.gc.ca/pub/75-001-x/2008105/article/10578-eng.htm

Floyd, F. J., Stein, T. S., Harter, K. S. M., Allison, A., & Nye, C. L. (1999). Gay, lesbian, and bisexual youths: Separation-individuation, parental attitudes, identity consolidation, and well-being. *Journal of Youth and Adolescence, 28,* 719–739. doi:10.1023/A:1021691601737

Flynn, J. R. (1987). Massive IQ gains in 14 nations: What IQ tests really measure. *Psychological Bulletin, 101,* 171–191.

Flynn, J. R. (2009). *What is intelligence? Beyond the Flynn effect.* Cambridge, England: Cambridge University Press.

Flynn, J. R., & Weiss, L. G. (2007). American IQ gains from 1931 to 2002: The WISC subtests and educational progress. *International Journal of Testing, 7,* 209–224.

Fodor, J. A. (1983). *The modularity of mind: An essay on faculty psychology.* Cambridge, MA: MIT Press.

Fogel, A., Nwokah, E., Dedo, J. Y., Messinger, D., Dickson, K. L., Matusov, E., & Holt, S. A. (1992). Social process theory of emotion: A dynamic systems approach. *Social Development, 1,* 122–142.

Fontaine, N., Carbonneau, R., Barker, E. D., Vitaro, F., Hébert, M., Côté, S. M., ... & Tremblay, R. E. (2008). Girls' hyperactivity and physical aggression during childhood and adjustment problems in early adulthood: A 15-year longitudinal study. *Archives of General Psychiatry, 65,* 320–328. doi:10.1001/archgenpsychiatry.2007.41

Fontaine, R. G., Tanha, M., Yang, C., Dodge, K. A., Bates, J. E., & Pettit, G. S. (2010). Does response evaluation and decision (RED) mediate the relation between hostile attributional style and antisocial behavior in adolescence? *Journal of Abnormal Child Psychology, 38,* 615–626. doi:10.1007/s10802-010-9397-y

Fontaine, R. G., Yang, C., Dodge, K. A., Bates, J. E., & Pettit, G. S. (2008). Testing an individual systems model of response evaluation and decision (RED) and antisocial behavior across adolescence. *Child Development, 79,* 462–475. doi:10.1111/j.1467-8624.2007.01136.x

Fontaine, R. G., Yang, C., Dodge, K. A., Pettit, G. S., & Bates, J. E. (2009). Development of response evaluation and decision (RED) and antisocial behavior in childhood and adolescence. *Developmental Psychology, 45,* 447–459. doi:10.1037/a0014142

Fonteneau, E., & van der Lely, H. K. J. (2008). Electrical brain responses in language-impaired children reveal grammar-specific deficits. *PLoS ONE, 3,* e1832. doi:10.1371/journal.pone.0001832

Fonzi, A., Schneider, B. H., Tani, F., & Tomada, G. (1997). Predicting children's friendship status from their dyadic interaction in structured situations of potential conflict. *Child Development, 68,* 496–506. doi:10.1111/j.1467-8624.1997.tb01954.x

Forbes, G. B., Adams-Curtis, L. E., Pakalka, A. H., & White, K. B. (2006). Dating aggression, sexual coercion, and aggression-supporting attitudes among college men as a function of participation in aggressive high school sports. *Violence Against Women, 12,* 441–455. doi:10.1177/1077801206288126

Forbes, L. M., Evans, E. M., Moran, G., & Pederson, D. R. (2007). Change in atypical maternal behavior predicts change in attachment disorganization from 12 to 24 months in a high-risk sample. *Child Development, 78,* 955–971. doi:10.1111/j.1467-8624.2007.01043.x

Foster, E. M., & Jones, D. E. (2007). The economic analysis of prevention: An illustration involving children's behavior problems. *Journal of Mental Health Policy and Economics, 10,* 165–175.

Fox, N. A. (1995). Of the way we were: Adult memories about attachment experiences and their role in determining infant-parent relationships: A commentary on van IJzendoorn (1995). *Psychological Bulletin, 117,* 404–410. doi:10.1037/0033-2909.117.3.404

Fox, N. A., & Calkins, S. D. (1993). Pathways to aggression and social withdrawal: Interactions among temperament, attachment, and regulation. In K. H. Rubin & J. B. Asendorpf (Eds.), *Social withdrawal, inhibition, and shyness in childhood* (pp. 81–100). Hillsdale, NJ: Erlbaum.

Fox, N. A., & Field, T. M. (1989). Individual differences in preschool entry behavior. *Journal of Applied Developmental Psychology, 10,* 527–540.

Fox, N. A., & Pine, D. S. (2012). Temperament and the emergence of anxiety disorders. *Journal of the American Academy of Child and Adolescent Psychiatry, 51,* 125–128. doi:10.1016/j.jaac.2011.10.006

Fraga, M. F., Ballestar, E., Paz, M. F., Ropero, S., Setien, F., Ballestar, M. L., ... Esteller, M. (2005). Epigenetic differences arise during the lifetime of monozygotic twins. *Proceedings of the National Academy of Sciences of the United States of America, 102,* 10604–10609. doi:10.1073/pnas.0500398102

Fraley, R. C. (2002). Attachment stability from infancy to adulthood: Meta-analysis and dynamic modeling of developmental mechanisms. *Personality and Social Psychology Review, 6,* 123–151. doi:10.1207/s15327957pspr0602_03

Frank, D. A., Augustyn, M., Knight, W. G., Pell, T., & Zuckerman, B. (2001, March 28). Growth, development, and behavior in early childhood following prenatal cocaine exposure: A systematic review. *Journal of the American Medical Association, 285,* 1613–1625.

Frankenhuis, W. E., & de Weerth, C. (2013). Does early-life exposure to stress shape or impair cognition? *Current Directions in Psychological Science, 22,* 407–412. doi:10.1177/0963721413484324

Freedman, D. G., & Freedman, N. C. (1969, December 20). Behavioural differences between Chinese-American and European-American newborns. *Nature, 224,* 1227.

Freedner, N., Freed, L. H., Yang, Y. W., & Austin, S. B. (2002). Dating violence among gay, lesbian, and bisexual adolescents: Results from a community survey. *Journal of Adolescent Health, 31,* 469–474. doi:10.1016/S1054-139X(02)00407-X

Freitag, M. K., Belsky, J., Grossmann, K., Grossmann, K. E., & Scheuerer-Englisch, H. (1996). Continuity in parent-child relationships from infancy to middle childhood and relations with friendship competence. *Child Development, 67,* 1437–1454. doi:10.2307/1131710

French, D. C., Pidada, S., Denoma, J., McDonald, K., & Lawton, A. (2005). Reported peer conflicts of children in the United States and Indonesia. *Social Development, 14,* 458–472. doi:10.1111/j.1467-9507.2005.00311.x

French, D. C., Setiono, K., & Eddy, J. M. (1999). Bootstrapping through the cultural comparison minefield: Childhood social status and friendship in the United States and Indonesia. In W. A. Collins & B. Laursen (Eds.), *Minnesota Symposia on Child Psychology: Vol. 30. Relationships as developmental contexts* (pp. 109–131). Mahwah, NJ: Erlbaum.

French, S. E., Seidman, E., Allen, L., & Aber, J. L. (2006). The development of ethnic identity during adolescence. *Developmental Psychology, 42,* 1–10. doi:10.1037/0012-1649.42.1.1

Freud, A., & Dann, S. (1972). An experiment in group upbringing. In U. Bronfenbrenner (Ed.), *Influences on human development* (pp. 127–168). Hinsdale, IL: Dryden Press. (Reprinted from *The Psychoanalytic Study of the Child* (Vol. 6), pp. 127–168, by R. S. Eissler, A. Freud, H. Hartmann, & E. Kris, Eds., 1951, New York, NY: International Universities Press)

Freud, S. (1959). Inhibitions, symptoms and anxiety. In J. Strachey (Ed.), *Standard edition of the complete psychological works of Sigmund Freud: Vol. XX (1925–1926). An autobiographical study, inhibitions, symptoms and anxiety, the question of lay analysis and other works* (pp. 77–175). London, England: The Hogarth Press and the Institute of Psycho-Analysis. (Original work published 1926)

Freud, S. (1960). *The ego and the id* (J. Riviere, Trans. & J. Strachey, Ed.). New York, NY: Norton. (Original work published 1923)

Freud, S. (1964). *New introductory lectures on psychoanalysis: The standard edition* (J. Strachey, Ed. & Trans.). New York, NY: Norton. (Original work published 1933)

Freud, S. (1964). An outline of psycho-analysis. In J. Strachey (Ed. & Trans.), *The standard edition of the complete psychological works of Sigmund Freud* (Vol. 23, pp. 144–207). London, England: Hogarth Press. (Original work published 1940)

Freud, S. (1965). *A general introduction to psychoanalysis* (J. Riviere, Trans.). New York, NY: Washington Square Press. (Original work published 1920)

Frey, K. S., & Ruble, D. N. (1985). What children say when the teacher is not around: Conflicting goals in social comparison and performance assessment in the classroom. *Journal of Personality and Social Psychology, 48,* 550–562. doi:10.1037/0022-3514.48.3.550

Frick, P. J., Christian, R. E., & Wootton, J. M. (1999). Age trends in the association between parenting practices and conduct problems. *Behavior Modification, 23,* 106–128. doi:10.1177/0145445599231005

Frick, P. J., & Morris, A. S. (2004). Temperament and developmental pathways to conduct problems. *Journal of Clinical Child and Adolescent Psychology, 33,* 54–68. doi:10.1207/S15374424JCCP3301_6

Fried, P. A., & Smith, A. M. (2001). A literature review of the consequences of prenatal marihuana exposure: An emerging theme of a deficiency in aspects of executive function. *Neurotoxicology and Teratology, 23,* 1–11.

Friedlmeier, W., Corapci, F., & Cole, P. M. (2011). Emotion socialization in cross-cultural perspective. *Social and Personality Psychology Compass, 5,* 410–427

Friedman, M. A., & Brownell, K. D. (1995). Psychological correlates of obesity: Moving to the next research generation. *Psychological Bulletin, 117,* 3–20. doi:10.1037/0033-2909.117.1.3

Friedman, M. S., Marshal, M. P., Guadamuz, T. E., Wei, C., Wong, C. F., Saewyc, E. M., & Stall, R. (2011). A meta-analysis of disparities in childhood sexual abuse, parental physical abuse, and peer victimization among sexual minority and sexual nonminority individuals. *American Journal of Public Health, 101,* 1481–1494. doi:10.2105/AJPH.2009.190009

Friedman, M. S., Marshal, M. P., Stall, R., Cheong, J., & Wright, E. R. (2008). Gay-related development, early abuse and adult health outcomes among gay males. *AIDS and Behavior, 12,* 891–902. doi:10.1007/s10461-007-9319-3

Friedman, N. P., Miyake, A., Robinson, J. L., & Hewitt, J. K. (2011). Developmental trajectories in toddlers' self-restraint predict individual differences in executive functions 14 years later: A behavioral genetic analysis. *Developmental Psychology, 47,* 1410–1430.

Friedman, W. J. (1991). The development of children's memory for the time of past events. *Child Development, 62,* 139–155. doi:10.1111/j.1467-8624.1991.tb01520.x

Friedman, W. J. (2000). The development of children's knowledge of the times of future events. *Child Development, 71,* 913–932.

Friedman, W. J. (2003). The development of a differentiated sense of the past and the future. *Advances in Child Development and Behavior, 31,* 229–269.

Friedman, W. J. (2008). Developmental perspectives on the psychology of time. In S. Grondin (Ed.), *Psychology of time* (pp. 345–366). Bingley, England: Emerald.

Friedman, W. J., & Lyon, T. D. (2005). Development of temporal-reconstructive abilities. *Child Development, 76,* 1202–1216. doi:10.1111/j.1467-8624.2005.00845.x

Friend, A., DeFries, J. C., & Olson, R. K. (2008). Parental education moderates genetic influences on reading disability. *Psychological Science, 19,* 1124–1130. doi:10.1111/j.1467-9280.2008.02213.x

Frosch, C. A., Mangelsdorf, S. C., & McHale, J. L. (2000). Marital behavior and the security of preschooler–parent attachment relationships. *Journal of Family Psychology, 14,* 144–161. doi:10.1037/0893-3200.14.1.144

Fry, D. P. (1988). Intercommunity differences in aggression among Zapotec children. *Child Development, 59,* 1008–1019. doi:10.2307/1130267

Frye, D., Braisby, N., Lowe, J., Maroudas, C., & Nicholls, J. (1989). Young children's understanding of counting and cardinality. *Child Development, 60,* 1158–1171.

Frye, D., Zelazo, P. D., Brooks, P. J., & Samuels, M. C. (1996). Inference and action in early causal reasoning. *Developmental Psychology, 32,* 120–131.

Fuchs, I., Eisenberg, N., Hertz-Lazarowitz, R., & Sharabany, R. (1986). Kibbutz, Israeli city, and American children's moral reasoning about prosocial moral conflicts. *Merrill-Palmer Quarterly, 32,* 37–50. doi:10.2307/23086241

Fuchs, L. S., Schumacher, R. F., Long, J., Namkung, J., Hamlett, C. L., Cirino, P. T., … Changas, P. (2013). Improving at-risk learners' understanding of fractions. *Journal of Educational Psychology, 105,* 683–700. doi:10.1037/a0032446

Fujisawa, K. K., Kutsukake, N., & Hasegawa, T. (2008). Reciprocity of prosocial behavior in Japanese preschool children. *International Journal of Behavioral Development, 32,* 89–97. doi:10.1177/0165025407084055

Fulcher, M., Sutfin, E. L., & Patterson, C. J. (2008). Individual differences in gender development: Associations with parental sexual orientation, attitudes, and division of labor. *Sex Roles, 58,* 330–341. doi:10.1007/s11199-007-9348-4

Fuligni, A. J. (1998). Authority, autonomy, and parent–adolescent conflict and cohesion: A study of adolescents from Mexican, Chinese, Filipino, and European backgrounds. *Developmental Psychology, 34,* 782–792. doi:10.1037/0012-1649.34.4.782

Fuligni, A. J., Eccles, J. S., Barber, B. L., & Clements, P. (2001). Early adolescent peer orientation and adjustment during high school. *Developmental Psychology, 37*, 28–36. doi:10.1037/0012-1649.37.1.28

Fuligni, A. J., & Stevenson, H. W. (1995). Time use and mathematics achievement among American, Chinese, and Japanese high school students. *Child Development, 66*, 830–842. doi:10.1111/j.1467-8624.1995.tb00908.x

Fuligni, A. J., Yip, T., & Tseng, V. (2002). The impact of family obligation on the daily activities and psychological well-being of Chinese American adolescents. *Child Development, 73*, 302–314. doi:10.1111/1467-8624.00407

Fuligni, A. J., & Zhang, W. (2004). Attitudes toward family obligation among adolescents in contemporary urban and rural China. *Child Development, 75*, 180–192. doi:10.1111/j.1467-8624.2004.00662.x

Fung, H. (1999). Becoming a moral child: The socialization of shame among young Chinese children. *Ethos, 27*, 180–209.

Fung, H., & Chen, E. C.-H. (2001). Across time and beyond skin: Self and transgression in the everyday socialization of shame among Taiwanese preschool children. *Social Development, 10*, 419–437.

Furman, W., & Bierman, K. L. (1984). Children's conceptions of friendship: A multimethod study of developmental changes. *Developmental Psychology, 20*, 925–931.

Furman, W., & Buhrmester, D. (1985). Children's perceptions of the personal relationships in their social networks. *Developmental Psychology, 21*, 1016–1024. doi:10.1037/0012-1649.21.6.1016

Furman, W., & Buhrmester, D. (1992). Age and sex differences in perceptions of networks of personal relationships. *Child Development, 63*, 103–115. doi:10.1111/j.1467-8624.1992.tb03599.x

Furman, W., Simon, V. A., Shaffer, L., & Bouchey, H. A. (2002). Adolescents' working models and styles for relationships with parents, friends, and romantic partners. *Child Development, 73*, 241–255. doi:10.1111/1467-8624.00403

Furnes, B., & Samuelsson, S. (2011). Phonological awareness and rapid automatized naming predicting early development in reading and spelling: Results from a cross-linguistic longitudinal study. *Learning and Individual Differences, 21*, 85–95. doi:10.1016/j.lindif.2010.10.005

Furstenberg, F. F., & Harris, K. M. (1993). When and why fathers matter: Impacts of father involvement on the children of adolescent mothers. In R. I. Lerman & T. J. Ooms (Eds.), *Young unwed fathers: Changing roles and emerging policies* (pp. 117–138). Philadelphia, PA: Temple University Press.

Furukawa, E., Tangney, J., & Higashibara, F. (2012). Cross-cultural continuities and discontinuities in shame, guilt, and pride: A study of children residing in Japan, Korea and the USA. *Self and Identity, 11*, 90–113.

Gable, S., Belsky, J., & Crnic, K. (1993, March). *Coparenting in the child's second year: Stability and change from 15 to 21 months.* Paper presented at the biennial meeting of the Society for Research in Child Development, New Orleans, LA.

Gaddis, A., & Brooks-Gunn, J. (1985). The male experience of pubertal change. *Journal of Youth and Adolescence, 14*, 61–69. doi:10.1007/BF02088647

Gaertner, B. M., Spinrad, T. L., Eisenberg, N., & Greving, K. A. (2007). Parental childrearing attitudes as correlates of father involvement during infancy. *Journal of Marriage and Family, 69*, 962–976. doi:10.1111/j.1741-3737.2007.00424.x

Gagné, M.-H., Tourigny, M., Joly, J., & Pouliot-Lapointe, J. (2007). Predictors of adult attitudes toward corporal punishment of children. *Journal of Interpersonal Violence, 22*, 1285–1304. doi:10.1177/0886260507304550

Gaither, S. E., Pauker, K., & Johnson, S. P. (2012). Biracial and monoracial infant own-race face perception: An eye tracking study. *Developmental Science, 15*, 775–782. doi:10.1111/j.1467-7687.2012.01170.x

Galambos, N., Leadbeater, B., & Barker, E. (2004). Gender differences in and risk factors for depression in adolescence: A 4-year longitudinal study. *International Journal of Behavioral Development, 28*, 16–25.

Galambos, N. L., Almeida, D. M., & Petersen, A. C. (1990). Masculinity, femininity, and sex role attitudes in early adolescence: Exploring gender intensification. *Child Development, 61*, 1905–1914. doi:10.1111/j.1467-8624.1990.tb03574.x

Galen, B. R., & Underwood, M. K. (1997). A developmental investigation of social aggression among children. *Developmental Psychology, 33*, 589–600. doi:10.1037/0012-1649.33.4.589

Gallese, V., Fadiga, L., Fogassi, L., & Rizzolatti, G. (1996). Action recognition in the premotor cortex. *Brain, 119*, 593–609. doi:10.1093/brain/119.2.593

Galliher, R. V., Jones, M. D., & Dahl, A. (2011). Concurrent and longitudinal effects of ethnic identity and experiences of discrimination on psychosocial adjustment of Navajo adolescents. *Developmental Psychology, 47*, 509–526. doi:10.1037/a0021061

Galton, F. (1962). *Hereditary genius: An inquiry into its laws and consequences.* Cleveland, OH: World. (Original work published 1869)

Gamble, W. C., Yu, J. J., & Kuehn, E. D. (2011). Adolescent sibling relationship quality and adjustment: Sibling trustworthiness and modeling, as factors directly and indirectly influencing these associations. *Social Development, 20*, 605–623. doi:10.1111/j.1467-9507.2010.00591.x

Gamliel, I., Yirmiya, N., Jaffe, D., Manor, O., & Sigman, M. (2009). Developmental trajectories in siblings of children with autism: Cognition and language from 4 months to 7 years. *Journal of Autism and Developmental Disorders, 39*, 1131–1144. doi:10.1007/s10803-009-0727-2

Gandelman, R. (1992). *The psychobiology of behavioral development.* New York, NY: Oxford University Press.

Ganiban, J. M., Saudino, K. J., Ulbricht, J., Neiderhiser, J. M., & Reiss, D. (2008). Stability and change in temperament during adolescence. *Journal of Personality and Social Psychology, 95*, 222–236.

Ganiban, J. M., Ulbricht, J., Saudino, K. J., Reiss, D., & Neiderhiser, J. M. (2011). Understanding child-based effects on parenting: Temperament as a moderator of genetic and environmental contributions to parenting. *Developmental Psychology, 47*, 676–692.

Garandeau, C. F., Ahn, H.-J., & Rodkin, P. C. (2011). The social status of aggressive students across contexts: The role of classroom status hierarchy, academic achievement, and grade. *Developmental Psychology, 47*, 1699–1710. doi:10.1037/a0025271

Garbarino, J., & Kostelny, K. (1992). Child maltreatment as a community problem. *Child Abuse and Neglect, 16*, 455–464. doi:10.1016/0145-2134(92)90062-V

Garber, J., & Cole, D. A. (2010). Intergenerational transmission of depression: A launch and grow model of change across adolescence. *Development and Psychopathology, 22*, 819–830. doi:10.1017/S0954579410000489

Garber, J., Keiley, M. K., & Martin, C. (2002). Developmental trajectories of adolescents' depressive symptoms: Predictors of change. *Journal of Consulting and Clinical Psychology, 70*, 79–95.

Gardner, D., Harris, P. L., Ohmoto, M., & Hamazaki, T. (1988). Japanese children's understanding of the distinction between real and apparent emotion. *International Journal of Behavioral Development, 11,* 203–218.

Gardner, H. (1993). *Multiple intelligences: The theory in practice.* New York, NY: Basic Books.

Gardner, R. A., & Gardner, B. T. (1969, August 15). Teaching sign language to a chimpanzee. *Science, 165,* 664–672.

Gardner, T. W., Dishion, T. J., & Connell, A. M. (2008). Adolescent self-regulation as resilience: Resistance to antisocial behavior within the deviant peer context. *Journal of Abnormal Child Psychology, 36,* 273–284. doi:10.1007/s10802-007-9176-6

Gargus, R. A., Vohr, B. R., Tyson, J. E., High, P., Higgins, R. D., Wrage, L. A., & Poole, K. (2009). Unimpaired outcomes for extremely low birth weight infants at 18 to 22 months. *Pediatrics, 124,* 112–121. doi:10.1542/peds.2008-2742

Garmezy, N. (1983). Stressors of childhood. In N. Garmezy & M. Rutter (Eds.), *Stress, coping, and development in children* (pp. 43–84). New York, NY: McGraw-Hill.

Garmon, L. C., Basinger, K. S., Gregg, V. R., & Gibbs, J. C. (1996). Gender differences in stage and expression of moral judgment. *Merrill-Palmer Quarterly, 42,* 418–437. doi:10.2307/23089870

Garrett-Peters, P., Mills-Koonce, R., Adkins, D., Vernon-Feagans, L., Cox, M., & The Family Life Project Key Investigators. (2008). Early environmental correlates of maternal emotion talk. *Parenting, Science and Practice, 8,* 117–152. doi:10.1080/15295190802058900

Garrett-Peters, P., Mills-Koonce, R., Zerwas, S., Cox, M., Vernon-Feagans, L., & The Family Life Project Key Investigators. (2011). Fathers' early emotion talk: Associations with income, ethnicity, and family factors. *Journal of Marriage and Family, 73,* 335–353. doi:10.1111/j.1741-3737.2010.00810.x

Gartrell, N., & Bos, H. (2010). US National Longitudinal Lesbian Family Study: Psychological adjustment of 17-year-old adolescents. *Pediatrics, 126,* 28–36. doi:10.1542/peds.2009-3153

Gass, K., Jenkins, J., & Dunn, J. (2007). Are sibling relationships protective? A longitudinal study. *Journal of Child Psychology and Psychiatry, 48,* 167–175. doi:10.1111/j.1469-7610.2006.01699.x

Gassman-Pines, A., & Yoshikawa, H. (2006). The effects of antipoverty programs on children's cumulative level of poverty-related risk. *Developmental Psychology, 42,* 981–999. doi:10.1037/0012-1649.42.6.981

Gathercole, S. E., Pickering, S. J., Ambridge, B., & Wearing, H. (2004). The structure of working memory from 4 to 15 years of age. *Developmental Psychology, 40,* 177–190.

Gatzke-Kopp, L. M., Beauchaine, T. P., Shannon, K. E., Chipman, J., Fleming, A. P., Crowell, S. E., … Aylward, E. (2009). Neurological correlates of reward responding in adolescents with and without externalizing behavior disorders. *Journal of Abnormal Psychology, 118,* 203–213. doi:10.1037/a0014378

Gaub, M., & Carlson, C. L. (1997). Gender differences in ADHD: A meta-analysis and critical review. *Journal of the American Academy of Child and Adolescent Psychiatry, 36,* 1036–1045. doi:10.1097/00004583-199708000-00011

Gauvain, M. (2001). *The social context of cognitive development.* New York, NY: Guilford Press.

Gavin, L. A., & Furman, W. (1989). Age differences in adolescents' perceptions of their peer groups. *Developmental Psychology, 25,* 827–834. doi:10.1037/0012-1649.25.5.827

Gaylord-Harden, N. K., Burrow, A. L., & Cunningham, J. A. (2012). A cultural-asset framework for investigating successful adaptation to stress in African American youth. *Child Development Perspectives, 6,* 264–271. doi:10.1111/j.1750-8606.2012.00236.x

Gazelle, H. (2008). Behavioral profiles of anxious solitary children and heterogeneity in peer relations. *Developmental Psychology, 44,* 1604–1624. doi:10.1037/a0013303

Gazelle, H., & Ladd, G. W. (2003). Anxious solitude and peer exclusion: A diathesis–stress model of internalizing trajectories in childhood. *Child Development, 74,* 257–278. doi:10.1111/1467-8624.00534

Ge, X., Conger, R. D., & Elder, G. H., Jr. (1996). Coming of age too early: Pubertal influences on girls' vulnerability to psychological distress. *Child Development, 67,* 3386–3400.

Ge, X., Kim, I. J., Brody, G. H., Conger, R. D., Simons, R. L., Gibbons, F. X., & Cutrona, C. E. (2003). It's about timing and change: Pubertal transition effects on symptoms of major depression among African American youths. *Developmental Psychology, 39,* 430–439.

Ge, X., Natsuaki, M. N., & Conger, R. D. (2006). Trajectories of depressive symptoms and stressful life events among male and female adolescents in divorced and nondivorced families. *Development and Psychopathology, 18,* 253–273. doi:10.1017/S0954579406060147

Geary, D. C. (1998). *Male, female: The evolution of human sex differences.* Washington, DC: American Psychological Association.

Geary, D. C. (1999). Evolution and developmental sex differences. *Current Directions in Psychological Science, 8,* 115–120. doi:10.1111/1467-8721.00027

Geary, D. C. (2004). Mathematics and learning disabilities. *Journal of Learning Disabilities, 37,* 4–15. doi:10.1177/00222194040370010201

Geary, D. C. (2005). *The origin of mind: Evolution of brain, cognition, and general intelligence.* Washington, DC: American Psychological Association.

Geary, D. C. (2006). Development of mathematical understanding. In W. Damon & R. M. Lerner (Series Eds.) & D. Kuhn & R. S. Siegler (Vol. Eds.), *Handbook of child psychology: Vol. 2. Cognition, perception, and language* (6th ed., pp. 777–810). Hoboken, NJ: Wiley.

Geary, D. C. (2009). *Male, female: The evolution of human sex differences* (2nd ed.). Washington, DC: American Psychological Association.

Geary, D. C. (2011). Cognitive predictors of achievement growth in mathematics: A 5-year longitudinal study. *Developmental Psychology, 47,* 1539–1552.

Geary, D. C., Hoard, M. K., Byrd-Craven, J., Nugent, L., & Numtee, C. (2007). Cognitive mechanisms underlying achievement deficits in children with mathematical learning disability. *Child Development, 78,* 1343–1359. doi:10.1111/j.1467-8624.2007.01069.x

Geary, D. C., Hoard, M. K., Nugent, L., & Bailey, D. H. (2012). Mathematical cognition deficits in children with learning disabilities and persistent low achievement: A five-year prospective study. *Journal of Educational Psychology, 104,* 206–223. doi:10.1037/a0025398

Geary, D. C., Hoard, M. K., Nugent, L., & Byrd-Craven, J. (2008). Development of number line representations in children with mathematical learning disability. *Developmental Neuropsychology, 33,* 277–299. doi:10.1080/87565640801982361

Gelman, R. (2002). Animates and other worldly things. In N. L. Stein, P. J. Bauer, & M. Rabinowitz (Eds.), *Representation, memory, and development: Essays in honor of Jean Mandler* (pp. 75–87). Mahwah, NJ: Erlbaum.

Gelman, R., & Gallistel, C. R. (1978). *The child's understanding of number.* Cambridge, MA: Harvard University Press.

Gelman, R., Meck, E., & Merkin, S. (1986). Young children's numerical competence. *Cognitive Development, 1,* 1–29.

Gelman, R., & Williams, E. M. (1998). Enabling constraints for cognitive development and learning: Domain specificity and epigenesis. In W. Damon (Series Ed.) & D. Kuhn & R. S. Siegler (Vol. Eds.), *Handbook of child psychology: Vol. 2: Cognition, perception, and language* (5th ed., pp. 575–630). Hoboken, NJ: Wiley.

Gelman, S. A. (2003). *The essential child: Origins of essentialism in everyday thought.* New York, NY: Oxford University Press.

Gelman, S. A., Coley, J. D., Rosengren, K. S., Hartman, E., & Pappas, A. (1998). Beyond labeling: The role of maternal input in the acquisition of richly structured categories. *Monographs of the Society for Research in Child Development, 63*(1, Serial No. 253).

Gelman, S. A., & Kalish, C. W. (2006). Conceptual development. In W. Damon & R. M. Lerner (Series Eds.) & D. Kuhn & R. S. Siegler (Vol. Eds.), *Handbook of child psychology: Vol. 2. Cognition, perception, and language* (6th ed., pp. 687–733). Hoboken, NJ: Wiley.

Gelman, S. A., Taylor, M. G., & Nguyen, S. P. (2004). Mother-child conversations about gender: Understanding the acquisition of essentialist beliefs. *Monographs of the Society for Research in Child Development, 69*(1, Serial No. 275), i-142. doi:10.2307/3701396

Genesee, F., Boivin, I. & Nicoladis, E. (1996). Bilingual children talking with monolingual adults: A study of bilingual communicative competence. *Applied Psycholinguistics, 17,* 427–442. doi:10.1017/S0142716400008183

Genesee, F., & Nicoladis, E. (2007). Bilingual first language acquisition. In E. Hoff & M. Shatz (Eds.), *Blackwell handbook of language development,* 324–342. Oxford, UK: Blackwell.

Genesee, F., & Nicoladis, E. (2009). Bilingual first language acquisition. In E. Hoff & M. Shatz (Eds.), *Blackwell handbook of language development* (pp. 324–342). Malden, MA: Wiley-Blackwell.

Gentner, D. (1982). Why nouns are learned before verbs: Linguistic relativity versus natural partitioning. In S. A. Kuczaj (Ed.), *Language development: Vol. 2. Language, thought and culture* (pp. 301–334). Hillsdale, NJ: Erlbaum.

Gentner, D., & Boroditsky, L. (2001). Individuation, relativity, and early word learning. In M. Bowerman & S. Levinson (Eds.), *Language acquisition and conceptual development* (pp. 215–256). Cambridge, England: Cambridge University Press.

Geoffroy, M. C., Côté, S., Giguère, C. É., Dionne, G., Zelazo, P. D., Tremblay, R. E., … & Séguin, J. (2010). Closing the gap in academic readiness and achievement: The role of early childcare. *Journal of Child Psychology and Psychiatry, 51,* 1359–1367. doi:10.1111/j.1469-7610.2010.02316.x

Gerbner, G., Gross, L., Morgan, M., Signorielli, N., & Shanahan, J. (2002). Growing up with television: Cultivation processes. In J. Bryant & D. Zillmann (Eds.), *Media effects: Advances in theory and research* (2nd ed., pp. 43–67). Mahwah, NJ: Erlbaum.

Gergely, G., Bekkering, H., & Kiraly, I. (2002, February 14). Developmental psychology: Rational imitation in preverbal infants. *Nature, 415,* 755–755.

Gerken, L. (1994). Child phonology: Past research, present questions, future directions. In M. A. Gernsbacher (Ed.), *Handbook of psycholinguistics* (pp. 781–820). San Diego, CA: Academic Press.

Gerken, L., Balcomb, F. K., & Minton, J. L. (2011). Infants avoid "labouring in vain" by attending more to learnable than unlearnable linguistic patterns. *Developmental Science, 14,* 972–979. doi:10.1111/j.1467-7687.2011.01046.x

Gerken, L., Wilson, R., & Lewis, W. (2005). Infants can use distributional cues to form syntactic categories. *Journal of Child Language, 32,* 249–268. doi:10.1017/S0305000904006786

German, T. P., & Nichols, S. (2003). Children's counterfactual inferences about long and short causal chains. *Developmental Science, 6,* 514–523. doi:10.1111/1467-7687.00309

Gernsbacher, M. A., Dawson, M., & Goldsmith, H. H. (2005). Three reasons not to believe in an autism epidemic. *Current Directions in Psychological Science, 14,* 55–58. doi:10.1111/j.0963-7214.2005.00334.x

Gershkoff-Stowe, L., Connell, B., & Smith, L. (2006). Priming overgeneralizations in two- and four-year-old children. *Journal of Child Language, 33,* 461–486. doi:10.1017/S0305000906007562

Gershoff, E. T. (2002). Corporal punishment by parents and associated child behaviors and experiences: A meta-analytic and theoretical review. *Psychological Bulletin, 128,* 539–579.

Gershoff, E. T., Grogan-Kaylor, A., Lansford, J. E., Chang, L., Zelli, A., Deater-Deckard, K., & Dodge, K. A. (2010). Parent discipline practices in an international sample: Associations with child behaviors and moderation by perceived normativeness. *Child Development, 81,* 487–502. doi:10.1111/j.1467-8624.2009.01409.x

Gershoff, E. T., Lansford, J. E., Sexton, H. R., Davis-Kean, P., & Sameroff, A. J. (2012). Longitudinal links between spanking and children's externalizing behaviors in a national sample of White, Black, Hispanic, and Asian American families. *Child Development, 83,* 838–843. doi:10.1111/j.1467-8624.2011.01732.x

Gertner, Y., Fisher, C., & Eisengart, J. (2006). Learning words and rules: Abstract knowledge of word order in early sentence comprehension. *Psychological Science, 17,* 684–691. doi:10.1111/j.1467-9280.2006.01767.x

Geschwind, D. H. (2011). Genetics of autism spectrum disorders. *Trends in Cognitive Sciences, 15,* 409–416.

Gesell, A., & Thompson, H. (1938). *The psychology of early growth, including norms of infant behavior and a method of genetic analysis.* New York, NY: Macmillan.

Gest, S. D., Graham-Bermann, S. A., & Hartup, W. W. (2001). Peer experience: Common and unique features of number of friendships, social network centrality, and sociometric status. *Social Development, 10,* 23–40. doi:10.1111/1467-9507.00146

Gfellner, B. M., & Armstrong, H. D. (2012). Ego development, ego strengths, and ethnic identity among First Nation adolescents. *Journal of Research on Adolescence, 22,* 225–234. doi:10.1111/j.1532-7795.2011.00769.x

Gianino, A., & Tronick, E. Z. (1988). The mutual regulation model: The infant's self and interactive regulation and coping and defensive capacities. In T. M. Field, P. M. McCabe, & N. Schneiderman (Eds.), *Stress and coping across development* (pp. 47–68). Hillsdale, NJ: Erlbaum.

Gibbs, N. (1999, May 3). The Littleton massacre: … In sorrow and disbelief. *Time, 153*(17), 20–36.

Gibson, E. J. (1988). Exploratory behavior in the development of perceiving, acting, and the acquiring of knowledge. *Annual Review of Psychology, 39,* 1–42. doi:10.1146/annurev.ps.39.020188.000245

Gibson, E. J., Riccio, G., Schmuckler, M. A., Stoffregen, T. A., Rosenberg, D., & Taormina, J. (1987). Detection of the traversability of surfaces by crawling and walking infants. *Journal of Experimental Psychology: Human Perception and Performance, 13,* 533–544. doi:10.1037/0096-1523.13.4.533

Gibson, E. J., & Schmuckler, M. A. (1989). Going somewhere: An ecological and experimental approach to development of mobility. *Ecological Psychology, 1,* 3–25. doi:10.1207/s15326969eco0101_2

Gibson, E. J., & Walk, R. D. (1960, April). The "visual cliff." *Scientific American, 202*(4), 64–71.

Gibson-Davis, C. M., & Gassman-Pines, A. (2010). Early childhood family structure and mother–child interactions: Variation by race and ethnicity. *Developmental Psychology, 46*, 151–164. doi:10.1037/a0017410

Giedd, J. N., Blumenthal, J., Jeffries, N. O., Castellanos, F. X., Liu, H., Zijdenbos, A., … Rapoport, J. L. (1999). Brain development during childhood and adolescence: A longitudinal MRI study. *Nature Neuroscience, 2*, 861–863.

Giles, J. W., & Heyman, G. D. (2005). Young children's beliefs about the relationship between gender and aggressive behavior. *Child Development, 76*, 107–121. doi:10.1111/j.1467-8624.2005.00833.x

Giletta, M., Scholte, R. H., Burk, W. J., Engels, R. C., Larsen, J. K., Prinstein, M. J., & Ciairano, S. (2011). Similarity in depressive symptoms in adolescents' friendship dyads: Selection or socialization? *Developmental Psychology, 47*, 1804–1814. doi:10.1037/a0023872

Gillham, J. E., Reivich, K. J., Jaycox, L. H., & Seligman, M. E. P. (1995). Prevention of depressive symptoms in schoolchildren: Two-year follow-up. *Psychological Science, 6*, 343–351.

Gilligan, C. (1982). *In a different voice: Psychological theory and women's development.* Cambridge, MA: Harvard University Press.

Gilligan, C., & Attanucci, J. (1988). Two moral orientations: Gender differences and similarities. *Merrill-Palmer Quarterly, 34*, 223–237. doi: 10.2307/23086381

Gladwell, M. (2008). *Outliers: The story of success.* New York, NY: Little, Brown.

Glasper, E. R., Schoenfeld, T. J., & Gould, E. (2012). Adult neurogenesis: Optimizing hippocampal function to suit the environment. *Behavioural Brain Research, 227*, 380–383. doi:10.1016/j.bbr.2011.05.013

Gleason, J. B., & Ely, R. (2002). Gender differences in language development. In A. V. McGillicuddy-De Lisi & R. De Lisi (Eds.), *Biology, society, and behavior: The development of sex differences in cognition* (Vol. 21, pp. 127–154). Westport, CT: Ablex.

Glick, G. C., & Rose, A. J. (2011). Prospective associations between friendship adjustment and social strategies: Friendship as a context for building social skills. *Developmental Psychology, 47*, 1117–1132.

Gnepp, J., & Hess, D. L. (1986). Children's understanding of verbal and facial display rules. *Developmental Psychology, 22*, 103–108.

Godlee, F., Smith, J., & Marcovitch, H. (2011). Wakefield's article linking MMR vaccine and autism was fraudulent. *BMJ, 342*. doi:10.1136/bmj.c7452

Gogtay, N., Sporn, A., Clasen, L. S., Nugent, T. F., Greenstein, D., Nicolson, R., … Rapoport, J. L. (2004). Comparison of progressive cortical gray matter loss in childhood-onset schizophrenia with that in childhood-onset atypical psychoses. *Archives of General Psychiatry, 61*, 17–22. doi:10.1001/archpsyc.61.1.17

Goldbaum, S., Craig, W. M., Pepler, D., & Connolly, J. (2003). Developmental trajectories of victimization. *Journal of Applied School Psychology, 19*, 139–156. doi: 10.1300/J008v19n02_09

Goldberg, W. A., Kelly, E., Matthews, N. L., Kang, H., Li, W., & Sumaroka, M. (2012). The more things change, the more they stay the same: Gender, culture, and college students' views about work and family. *Journal of Social Issues, 68*, 814–837. doi:10.1111/j.1540-4560.2012.01777.x

Goldfield, G., Moore, C., Henderson, K., Buchholz, A., Obeid, N., Flament, M. (2010). The relation between weight-based teasing and psychological adjustment in adolescents. *Paediatrics & Child Health, 15*, 283–288. doi:10.1111/josh.12118

Goldin-Meadow, S. (2003). *The resilience of language: What gesture creation in deaf children can tell us about how all children learn language.* New York, NY: Psychology Press.

Goldin-Meadow, S., & Alibali, M. W. (2002). Looking at the hands through time: A microgenetic perspective on learning and instruction. In N. Granott & J. Parziale (Eds.), *Microdevelopment: Transition processes in development and learning* (pp. 80–105). Cambridge, England: Cambridge University Press.

Goldin-Meadow, S., Cook, S. W., & Mitchell, Z. A. (2009). Gesturing gives children new ideas about math. *Psychological Science, 20*, 267–272.

Goldin-Meadow, S., & Mylander, C. (1998, January 15). Spontaneous sign systems created by deaf children in two cultures. *Nature, 391*, 279–281. doi:10.1038/34646

Goldsmith, H. H., Buss, K. A., & Lemery, K. S. (1997). Toddler and childhood temperament: Expanded content, stronger genetic evidence, new evidence for the importance of environment. *Developmental Psychology, 33*, 891–905. doi:10.1037/0012-1649.33.6.891

Goldsmith, H. H., Pollak, S. D., & Davidson, R. J. (2008). Developmental neuroscience perspectives on emotion regulation. *Child Development Perspectives, 2*, 132–140.

Goldstein, M. H., King, A. P., & West, M. J. (2003). Social interaction shapes babbling: Testing parallels between birdsong and speech. *Proceedings of the National Academy of Sciences of the United States of America, 100*, 8030–8035. doi:10.1073/pnas.1332441100

Goldstein, M. H., & Schwade, J. A. (2008). Social feedback to infants' babbling facilitates rapid phonological learning. *Psychological Science, 19*, 515–523. doi:10.1111/j.1467-9280.2008.02117.x

Goldstein, M. H., Schwade, J., Briesch, J., & Syal, S. (2010). Learning while babbling: Prelinguistic object-directed vocalizations indicate a readiness to learn. *Infancy, 15*, 362–391. doi:10.1111/j.1532-7078.2009.00020.x

Goldstein, S. E., Malanchuk, O., Davis-Kean, P. E., & Eccles, J. S. (2007). Risk factors of sexual harassment by peers: A longitudinal investigation of African American and European American adolescents. *Journal of Research on Adolescence, 17*, 285–300. doi:10.1111/j.1532-7795.2007.00523.x

Goldstein, T. R., & Winner, E. (2011). Enhancing empathy and theory of mind. *Journal of Cognition and Development, 13*, 19–37. doi:10.1080/15248372.2011.573514

Goleman, D. (1995). *Emotional intelligence.* New York, NY: Bantam Books.

Golish, T. D. (2003). Stepfamily communication strengths. *Human Communication Research, 29*, 41–80. doi:10.1111/j.1468-2958.2003.tb00831.x

Golombok, S., Perry, B., Burston, A., Murray, C., Mooney-Somers, J., Stevens, M., & Golding, J. (2003). Children with lesbian parents: A community study. *Developmental Psychology, 39*, 20–33. doi:10.1037/0012-1649.39.1.20

Golombok, S., Spencer, A., & Rutter, M. (1983). Children in lesbian and single-parent households: Psychosexual and psychiatric appraisal. *Journal of Child Psychology and Psychiatry, 24*, 551–572. doi:10.1111/j.1469-7610.1983.tb00132.x

Gómez, R. L. (2002). Variability and detection of invariant structure. *Psychological Science, 13*, 431–436.

Göncü, A. (1993). Development of intersubjectivity in the dyadic play of preschoolers. *Early Childhood Research Quarterly, 8*, 99–116.

Göncü, A., Mistry, J., & Mosier, C. (2000). Cultural variations in the play of toddlers. *International Journal of Behavioral Development, 24*, 321–329. doi:10.1080/01650250050118303

Gonzales, N. A., Pitts, S. C., Hill, N. E., & Roosa, M. W. (2000). A mediational model of the impact of interparental conflict on child adjustment in a multiethnic, low-income sample. *Journal of Family Psychology, 14,* 365–379. doi:10.1037/0893-3200.14.3.365

Good, T. L., & Brophy, J. E. (1996). *Looking in classrooms* (7th ed.). New York, NY: Longman.

Gooden, A. M., & Gooden, M. A. (2001). Gender representation in notable children's picture books: 1995–1999. *Sex Roles, 45,* 89–101. doi:10.1023/A:1013064418674

Goodenough, F. L. (1931). *Anger in young children.* Minneapolis: University of Minnesota Press.

Goodman, G. S., & Aman, C. (1990). Children's use of anatomically detailed dolls to recount an event. *Child Development, 61,* 1859–1871. doi:10.1111/j.1467-8624.1990.tb03570.x

Goodnight, J. A., Lahey, B. B., Van Hulle, C. A., Rodgers, J. L., Rathouz, P. J., Waldman, I. D., & D'Onofrio, B. M. (2012). A quasi-experimental analysis of the influence of neighborhood disadvantage on child and adolescent conduct problems. *Journal of Abnormal Psychology, 121,* 95–108. doi:10.1037/a0025078

Goodnow, J. J. (1977). *Children drawing.* Cambridge, MA: Harvard University Press.

Goodnow, J. J., Cashmore, J., Cotton, S., & Knight, R. (1984). Mothers' developmental timetables in two cultural groups. *International Journal of Psychology, 19,* 193–205. doi:10.1080/00207598408247526

Gooren, E. M. J. C., van Lier, P. A. C., Stegge, H., Terwogt, M. M., & Koot, H. M. (2011). The development of conduct problems and depressive symptoms in early elementary school children: The role of peer rejection. *Journal of Clinical Child and Adolescent Psychology, 40,* 245–253. doi:10.1080/15374416.2011.546045

Gopnik, A., & Astington, J. W. (1988). Children's understanding of representational change and its relation to the understanding of false belief and the appearance-reality distinction. *Child Development, 59,* 26–37.

Gopnik, A., & Slaughter, V. (1991). Young children's understanding of changes in their mental states. *Child Development, 62,* 98–110. doi:10.1111/j.1467-8624.1991.tb01517.x

Gordon, M. (2005). *Roots of empathy: Changing the world child by child.* Toronto, ON: Thomas Allen.

Gordon, R. A., Lahey, B. B., Kawai, E., Loeber, R., Stouthamer-Loeber, M., & Farrington, D. P. (2004). Antisocial behavior and youth gang membership: Selection and socialization. *Criminology, 42,* 55–88. doi:10.1111/j.1745-9125.2004.tb00513.x

Gosselin, J., & David, H. (2007). Risk and resilience factors linked with the psychosocial adjustment of adolescents, stepparents and biological parents. *Journal of Divorce and Remarriage, 48,* 29–53. doi:10.1300/j087v48n01_02

Gottesman, I. I. (with Wolfgram, D. L.). (1991). *Schizophrenia genesis: The origins of madness.* New York, NY: Freeman.

Gottesman, I. I., & Goldsmith, H. H. (1994). Developmental psychopathology of antisocial behavior: Inserting genes into its ontogenesis and epigenesis. In C. A. Nelson (Ed.), *Minnesota Symposia on Child Psychology: Vol. 27. Threats to optimal development: Integrating biological, psychological, and social risk factors* (pp. 69–104). Hillsdale, NJ: Erlbaum.

Gottfredson, L. S. (1997). Why g matters: The complexity of everyday life. *Intelligence, 24,* 79–132.

Gottfredson, L. S. (2011). Intelligence and social inequality: Why the biological link. In T. Chamorro-Premuzic, S. von Stumm, & A. Furnham (Eds.), *Handbook of individual differences* (pp. 538–575). Chichester, West Sussex, England: Wiley-Blackwell.

Gottfried, A. E., Gottfried, A. W., & Bathurst, K. (2002). Maternal and dual-earner employment status and parenting. In M. H. Bornstein (Ed.), *Handbook of parenting: Vol. 2. Biology and ecology of parenting* (2nd ed., pp. 207–229). Mahwah, NJ: Erlbaum.

Gottlieb, A. (2004). *The afterlife is where we come from: The culture of infancy in West Africa.* Chicago, IL: University of Chicago Press.

Gottlieb, G. (1992). *Individual development and evolution: The genesis of novel behavior.* New York, NY: Oxford University Press.

Gottlieb, G., Wahlsten, D., & Lickliter, R. (1998). The significance of biology for human development: A developmental psychobiological systems view. In R. M. Lerner (Ed.), *Handbook of child psychology: Vol. 1. Theoretical models of human development* (5th ed., pp. 233–273). Hoboken, NJ: Wiley.

Gottman, J. M. (1986). The world of coordinated play: Same- and cross-sex friendship in young children. In J. M. Gottman & J. G. Parker (Eds.), *Conversations of friends: Speculations on affective development* (pp. 139–191). New York, NY: Cambridge University Press.

Gottman, J. M., Katz, L. F., & Hooven, C. (1997). *Meta-emotion: How families communicate emotionally.* Mahwah, NJ: Erlbaum.

Gottman, J. M., & Mettetal, G. (1986). Speculations about social and affective development: Friendship and acquaintanceship through adolescence. In J. M. Gottman & J. G. Parker (Eds.), *Conversations of friends: Speculations on affective development* (pp. 192–237). New York, NY: Cambridge University Press.

Gougoux, F., Lepore, F., Lassonde, M., Voss, P., Zatorre, R. J., & Belin, P. (2004, July 15). Pitch discrimination in the early blind: People blinded in infancy have sharper listening skills than those who lost their sight later. *Nature, 430,* 309. doi:10.1038/430309a

Gould, E., Beylin, A., Tanapat, P., Reeves, A., & Shors, T. J. (1999). Learning enhances adult neurogenesis in the hippocampal formation. *Nature Neuroscience, 2,* 260–265.

Gould, S. J. (1997, June 12). Darwinian fundamentalism. *New York Review of Books, 44,* 34–37.

Gove, W. R., & Zeiss, C. (1987). Multiple roles and happiness. In F. J. Crosby (Ed.), *Spouse, parent, worker: On gender and multiple roles* (pp. 125–137). New Haven, CT: Yale University Press.

Govindan, R. B., Wilson, J. D., Murphy, P., Russel, W. A., & Lowery, C. L. (2007). Scaling analysis of paces of fetal breathing, gross body and extremity movements. *Physica A: Statistical Mechanics and Its Applications, 386,* 231–239. doi:10.1016/j.physa.2007.08.021

Graf Estes, K., Evans, J. L., & Else-Quest, N. M. (2007). Differences in the nonword repetition performance of children with and without specific language impairment: A meta-analysis. *Journal of Speech, Language, and Hearing Research, 50,* 177–195. doi:10.1044/1092-4388(2007/015)

Graham, S. [Steve], & Harris, K. R. (1996). Self-regulation and strategy instruction for students who find writing and learning challenging. In C. M. Levy & S. Ransdell (Eds.), *The science of writing: Theories, methods, individual differences, and applications* (pp. 347–360). Hillsdale, NJ: Erlbaum.

Graham, S. [Sandra], & Hudley, C. (1994). Attributions of aggressive and nonagressive African-American male early adolescents: A study of construct accessibility. *Developmental Psychology, 30,* 365–373. doi:10.1037/0012-1649.30.3.365

Graham, S. A., & Diesendruck, G. (2010). Fifteen-month-old infants attend to shape over other perceptual properties in an induction task. *Cognitive Development, 25*, 111–123. doi:10.1016/j.cogdev.2009.06.002

Graham, S. A., Nayer, S. L., & Gelman, S. A. (2011). Two-year-olds use the generic/non-generic distinction to guide their inferences about novel kinds. *Child Development, 82*, 493–507. doi:10.1111/j.1467-8624.2010.01572.x

Graham, S. A., & Poulin-Dubois, D. (1999). Infants' reliance on shape to generalize novel labels to animate and inanimate objects. *Journal of Child Language, 26*, 295–320.

Graham, S. A., Poulin-Dubois, D., & Baker, R. K. (1998). Infants' disambiguation of novel object words. *First Language, 18*, 149–164. doi:10.1177/014272379801805302

Graham-Bermann, S. A., & Brescoll, V. (2000). Gender, power, and violence: Assessing the family stereotypes of the children of batterers. *Journal of Family Psychology, 14*, 600–612. doi:10.1037/0893-3200.14.4.600

Granger, D. A., Serbin, L. A., Schwartzman, A., Lehoux, P., Cooperman, J., & Ikeda, S. (1998). Children's salivary cortisol, internalising behaviour problems, and family environment: Results from the Concordia Longitudinal Risk Project. *International Journal of Behavioral Development, 22*, 707–728.

Granger, D. A., Stansbury, K., & Henker, B. (1994). Preschoolers' behavioral and neuroendocrine responses to social challenge. *Merrill-Palmer Quarterly, 40*, 190–211.

Granier-Deferre, C., Ribeiro, A., Jacquet, A. Y., & Bassereau, S. (2011). Near-term fetuses process temporal features of speech. *Developmental Science, 14*, 336–352.

Granot, D., & Mayseless, O. (2001). Attachment security and adjustment to school in middle childhood. *International Journal of Behavioral Development, 25*, 530–541. doi:10.1080/01650250042000366

Granrud, C. E. (1987). Size constancy in newborn human infants. *Investigative Ophthalmology and Visual Science, 28*(Suppl.), 5.

Graves, N. B., & Graves, T. D. (1983). The cultural context of prosocial development: An ecological model. In D. Bridgeman (Ed.), *The nature of prosocial development: Interdisciplinary theories and strategies* (pp. 243–264). New York, NY: Academic Press.

Gray, J. (1992). *Men are from Mars, women are from Venus: A practical guide for improving communication and getting what you want in your relationships.* New York, NY: HarperCollins.

Green, J. A., Jones, L. E., & Gustafson, G. E. (1987). Perception of cries by parents and nonparents: Relation to cry acoustics. *Developmental Psychology, 23*, 370–382.

Green, R. E., Krause, J., Briggs, A. W., Maricic, T., Stenzel, U., Kircher, M., … Pääbo, S. (2010, May 7). A draft sequence of the Neandertal genome. *Science, 328*, 710–722.

Greenberg, M. T., & Kusché, C. A. (2006). Building social and emotional competence: The PATHS curriculum. In S. R. Jimerson & M. J. Furlong (Eds.), *The handbook of school violence and school safety: From research to practice* (pp. 395–412). Mahwah, NJ: Erlbaum.

Greenberg, M. T., Kusché, C. A., Cook, E. T., & Quamma, J. P. (1995). Promoting emotional competence in school-aged children: The effects of the PATHS curriculum. *Development and Psychopathology, 7*, 117–136. doi:10.1017/S0954579400006374

Greenberger, E., O'Neil, R., & Nagel, S. K. (1994). Linking workplace and homeplace: Relations between the nature of adults' work and their parenting behaviors. *Developmental Psychology, 30*, 990–1002. doi:10.1037/0012-1649.30.6.990

Greene, J. G., Fox, N. A., & Lewis, M. (1983). The relationship between neonatal characteristics and three-month mother-infant interaction in high-risk infants. *Child Development, 54*, 1286–1296.

Greene, M. L., Way, N., & Pahl, K. (2006). Trajectories of perceived adult and peer discrimination among Black, Latino, and Asian American adolescents: Patterns and psychological correlates. *Developmental Psychology, 42*, 218–238. doi:10.1037/0012-1649.42.2.218

Greenfield, P. M. (2004). Inadvertent exposure to pornography on the Internet: Implications of peer-to-peer file-sharing networks for child development and families. *Journal of Applied Developmental Psychology, 25*, 741–750. doi:10.1016/j.appdev.2004.09.009

Greenfield, P. M., Suzuki, L. K., & Rothstein-Fisch, C. (2006). Cultural pathways through human development. In W. Damon & R. M. Lerner (Series Eds.) & K. A. Renninger & I. E. Sigel (Vol. Eds.), *Handbook of child psychology: Vol. 4. Child psychology in practice* (6th ed., pp. 655–699). Hoboken, NJ: Wiley.

Greenough, W. T., & Black, J. E. (1992). Induction of brain structure by experience: Substrates for cognitive development. In M. R. Gunnar & C. A. Nelson (Eds.), *Minnesota Symposia on Child Psychology: Vol. 24. Developmental behavioral neuroscience* (pp. 155–200). Hillsdale, NJ: Erlbaum.

Greenough, W. T., Larson, J. R., & Withers, G. S. (1985). Effects of unilateral and bilateral training in a reaching task on dendritic branching of neurons in the rat motor-sensory forelimb cortex. *Behavioral and Neural Biology, 44*, 301–314. doi:10.1016/S0163-1047(85)90310-3

Greenwald, A. G., & Banaji, M. R. (1995). Implicit social cognition: Attitudes, self-esteem, and stereotypes. *Psychological Review, 102*, 4–27.

Gregory, A. M., Light-Häusermann, J. H., Rijsdijk, F., & Eley, T. C. (2009). Behavioral genetic analyses of prosocial behavior in adolescents. *Developmental Science, 12*, 165–174. doi:10.1111/j.1467-7687.2008.00739.x

Gregory, A. M., Rijsdijk, F. V., Lau, J. Y., Napolitano, M., McGuffin, P., & Eley, T. C. (2007). Genetic and environmental influences on interpersonal cognitions and associations with depressive symptoms in 8-year-old twins. *Journal of Abnormal Psychology, 116*, 762–775. doi:10.1037/0021-843X.116.4.762

Grieco-Calub, T. M., Saffran, J. R., & Litovsky, R. Y. (2009). Spoken word recognition in toddlers who use cochlear implants. *Journal of Speech, Language, and Hearing Research, 52*, 1390–1400. doi:10.1044/1092-4388(2009/08-0154)

Grimshaw, G. M., Sitarenios, G., & Finegan, J.-A. K. (1995). Mental rotation at 7 years: Relations with prenatal testosterone levels and spatial play experiences. *Brain and Cognition, 29*, 85–100. doi:10.1006/brcg.1995.1269

Groh, A. M., Roisman, G. I., van IJzendoorn, M. H., Bakermans-Kranenburg, M. J., & Fearon, R. P. (2012). The significance of insecure and disorganized attachment for children's internalizing symptoms: A meta-analytic study. *Child Development, 83*, 591–610. doi:10.1111/j.1467-8624.2011.01711.x

Grolnick, W. S., Bridges, L. J., & Connell, J. P. (1996). Emotion regulation in two-year-olds: Strategies and emotional expression in four contexts. *Child Development, 67*, 928–941.

Grön, G., Wunderlich, A. P., Spitzer, M., Tomczak, R., & Riepe, M. W. (2000). Brain activation during human navigation: Gender-different neural networks as substrate of performance. *Nature Neuroscience, 3*, 404–408.

Gross, D., & Harris, P. L. (1988). False beliefs about emotion: Children's understanding of misleading emotional displays. *International Journal of Behavioral Development, 11*, 475–488.

Gross, J. J., & Barrett, L. F. (2011). Emotion generation and emotion regulation: One or two depends on your point of view. *Emotion Review, 3*, 8–16. doi:10.1177/1754073910380974

Gross, R. T., Spiker, D., & Haynes, C. W. (Eds.). (1997). *Helping low birth weight, premature babies: The infant health and development program.* Stanford, CA: Stanford University Press.

Grossmann, T. (2010). The development of emotion perception in face and voice during infancy. *Restorative Neurology and Neuroscience, 28*, 219–236. doi:10.3233/RNN-2010-0499

Grotevant, H. D. (1998). Adolescent development in family contexts. In W. Damon (Series Ed.) & N. Eisenberg (Vol. Ed.), *Handbook of child psychology: Vol. 3. Social, emotional, and personality development* (5th ed., pp. 1097–1149). New York: Wiley.

Gruber, J. E., & Fineran, S. (2008). Comparing the impact of bullying and sexual harassment victimization on the mental and physical health of adolescents. *Sex Roles, 59*, 1–13. doi:10.1007/s11199-008-9431-5

Grueneich, R. (1982). Issues in the developmental study of how children use intention and consequence information to make moral evaluations. *Child Development, 53*, 29–43. doi:10.2307/1129636

Grusec, J. E., Goodnow, J. J., & Cohen, L. (1996). Household work and the development of concern for others. *Developmental Psychology, 32*, 999–1007.

Grusec, J. E., Goodnow, J. J., & Kuczynski, L. (2000). New directions in analyses of parenting contributions to children's acquisition of values. *Child Development, 71*, 205–211. doi:10.1111/1467-8624.00135

Grych, J. H., & Fincham, F. D. (1997). Children's adaptation to divorce: From description to explanation. In S. A. Wolchik & I. N. Sandler (Eds.), *Handbook of children's coping: Linking theory and intervention* (pp. 159–193). New York, NY: Plenum Press.

Grych, J. H., Harold, G. T., & Miles, C. J. (2003). A prospective investigation of appraisals as mediators of the link between interparental conflict and child adjustment. *Child Development, 74*, 1176–1193. doi:10.1111/1467-8624.00600

Grych, J. H., Raynor, S. R., & Fosco, G. M. (2004). Family processes that shape the impact of interparental conflict on adolescents. *Development and Psychopathology, 16*, 649–665. doi:10.1017/S0954579404004717

Guerin, D. W., & Gottfried, A. W. (1994). Developmental stability and change in parent reports of temperament: A ten-year longitudinal investigation from infancy through preadolescence. *Merrill-Palmer Quarterly, 40*, 334–355.

Guerra, N. G., Huesmann, L. R., & Spindler, A. (2003). Community violence exposure, social cognition, and aggression among urban elementary school children. *Child Development, 74*, 1561–1576. doi:10.1111/1467-8624.00623

Gummerum, M., & Keller, M. (2008). Affection, virtue, pleasure, and profit: Developing an understanding of friendship closeness and intimacy in western and Asian societies. *International Journal of Behavioral Development, 32*, 218–231. doi:10.1177/0165025408089271

Gunnar, M. R. (1994). Psychoendocrine studies of temperament and stress in early childhood: Expanding current models. In J. E. Bates & T. D. Wachs (Eds.), *Temperament: Individual differences at the interface of biology and behavior* (pp. 175–198). Washington, DC: American Psychological Association.

Gunnar, M. R., & Cheatham, C. L. (2003). Brain and behavior interface: Stress and the developing brain. *Infant Mental Health Journal, 24*, 195–211.

Gunnar, M. R., Sebanc, A. M., Tout, K., Donzella, B., & van Dulmen, M. M. (2003). Peer rejection, temperament, and cortisol activity in preschoolers. *Developmental Psychobiology, 43*, 346–358.

Gunnar, M. R., & Vazquez, D. (2006). Stress neurobiology and developmental psychopathology. In D. Cicchetti & D. J. Cohen (Eds.), *Developmental psychopathology: Vol. 2. Developmental neuroscience* (2nd ed., pp. 533–577). Hoboken, NJ: Wiley.

Gunnoe, M. L., & Hetherington, E. M. (2004). Stepchildren's perceptions of noncustodial mothers and noncustodial fathers: Differences in socioemotional involvement and associations with adolescent adjustment problems. *Journal of Family Psychology, 18*, 555–563. doi:10.1037/0893-3200.18.4.555

Gustafson, G. E., & Green, J. A. (1988, April). *A role of crying in the development of prelinguistic communicative competence.* Paper presented at the International Conference on Infant Studies, Washington, DC.

Guthrie, J. T., Wigfield, A., Metsala, J. L., & Cox, K. E. (1999). Motivational and cognitive predictors of text comprehension and reading amount. *Scientific Studies of Reading, 3*, 231–256. doi:10.1207/s1532799xssr0303_3

Gutman, L. M., Sameroff, A. J., & Cole, R. (2003). Academic growth curve trajectories from 1st grade to 12th grade: Effects of multiple social risk factors and preschool child factors. *Developmental Psychology, 39*, 777–790.

Gwiazda, J., Grice, K., Held, R., McLellan, J., & Thorn, F. (2000). Astigmatism and the development of myopia in children. *Vision Research, 40*, 1019–1026.

Ha, T., Overbeek, G., de Greef, M., Scholte, R. H. J., & Engels, R. C. M. E. (2010). The importance of relationships with parents and best friends for adolescents' romantic relationship quality: Differences between indigenous and ethnic Dutch adolescents. *International Journal of Behavioral Development, 34*, 121–127. doi:10.1177/0165025409360293

Haden, C. A., Haine, R. A., & Fivush, R. (1997). Developing narrative structure in parent-child reminiscing across the preschool years. *Developmental Psychology, 33*, 295–307.

Haier, R. J., Karama, S., Leyba, L., & Jung, R. E. (2009). MRI assessment of cortical thickness and functional activity changes in adolescent girls following three months of practice on a visual-spatial task. *BMC Research Notes.* doi:10.1186/1756-0500-2-174

Haines, H. M., Rubertsson, C., Pallant, J. F., & Hildingsson, I. (2012). The influence of women's fear, attitudes and beliefs of childbirth on mode and experience of birth. *BMC Pregnancy Childbirth, 12*, 55. Retrieved from http://www.biomedcentral.com/1471-2393/12/55

Haith, M. M., & Benson, J. B. (1998). Infant cognition. In W. Damon (Series Ed.) & D. Kuhn & R. S. Siegler (Vol. Eds.), *Handbook of child psychology: Vol. 2. Cognition, perception, and language* (5th ed., pp. 199–254). Hoboken, NJ: Wiley.

Haith, M. M., Bergman, T., & Moore, M. J. (1977, November). Eye contact and face scanning in early infancy. *Science, 198*, 853–855.

Haith, M. M., Wentworth, N., & Canfield, R. L. (1993). The formation of expectations in early infancy. In C. Rovee-Collier & L. P. Lipsitt (Eds.), *Advances in infancy research* (Vol. 8, pp. 251–297). Norwood, NJ: Ablex.

Hakak, Y., Walker, J. R., Li, C., Wong, W. H., Davis, K. L., Buxbaum, J. D., … Fienberg, A. A. (2001). Genome-wide expression analysis reveals dysregulation of myelination-related genes in chronic schizophrenia. *Proceedings of the National Academy of Sciences of the United States of America, 98*, 4746–4751. doi:10.1073/pnas.081071198

Hakuta, K. (1999). The debate on bilingual education. *Journal of Developmental and Behavioral Pediatrics, 20,* 36–37.

Hakvoort, E. M., Bos, H. M. W., Van Balen, F., & Hermanns, J. M. A. (2011). Postdivorce relationships in families and children's psychosocial adjustment. *Journal of Divorce and Remarriage, 52,* 125–146. doi:10.1080/10502556.2011.546243

Halberstadt, A. G., Cassidy, J., Stifter, C. A., Parke, R. D., & Fox, N. A. (1995). Self-expressiveness within the family context: Psychometric support for a new measure. *Psychological Assessment, 7,* 93–103.

Halberstadt, A. G., Crisp, V. W., & Eaton, K. L. (1999). Family expressiveness: A retrospective and new directions for research. In P. Philippot, R. S. Feldman, & E. J. Coats (Eds.), *The social context of nonverbal behavior* (pp. 109–155). Cambridge, England: Cambridge University Press.

Halberstadt, A. G., Denham, S. A., & Dunsmore, J. C. (2001). Affective social competence. *Social Development, 10,* 79–119.

Hall, D. G. (1994). Semantic constraints on word learning: Proper names and adjectives. *Child Development, 65,* 1299–1317.

Hall, D. G., Waxman, S. R., & Hurwitz, W. M. (1993). How two- and four-year-old children interpret adjectives and count nouns. *Child Development, 64,* 1651–1664. doi:10.1111/j.1467-8624.1993.tb04205.x

Halligan, S. L., & Philips, K. J. (2010). Are you thinking what I'm thinking? Peer group similarities in adolescent hostile attribution tendencies. *Developmental Psychology, 46,* 1385–1388. doi:10.1037/a0020383

Hallmayer, J., Cleveland, S., Torres, A., Phillips, J., Cohen, B., Torigoe, T., ... Risch, N. (2011). Genetic heritability and shared environmental factors among twin pairs with autism. *Archives of General Psychiatry, 68,* 1095–1102. doi:10.1001/archgenpsychiatry.2011.76

Halpern, C. T., Udry, J. R., & Suchindran, C. (1997). Testosterone predicts initiation of coitus in adolescent females. *Psychosomatic Medicine, 59,* 161–171.

Halpern, D. F. (2004). A cognitive-process taxonomy for sex differences in cognitive abilities. *Current Directions in Psychological Science, 13,* 135–139. doi:10.1111/j.0963-7214.2004.00292.x

Halpern, D. F. (2012). *Sex differences in cognitive abilities* (4th ed.). New York, NY: Psychology Press.

Halpern, D. F., Benbow, C. P., Geary, D. C., Gur, R. C., Hyde, J. S., & Gernsbacher, M. A. (2007). The science of sex differences in science and mathematics. *Psychological Science in the Public Interest, 8,* 1–51. doi:10.1111/j.1529-1006.2007.00032.x

Halpern-Meekin, S., & Tach, L. (2008). Heterogeneity in two-parent families and adolescent well-being. *Journal of Marriage and Family, 70,* 435–451. doi:10.1111/j.1741-3737.2008.00492.x

Hämäläinen, M., & Pulkkinen, L. (1996). Problem behavior as a precursor of male criminality. *Development and Psychopathology, 8,* 443–455. doi:10.1017/S0954579400007185

Hamamura, T., Heine, S. J., & Paulhus, D. L. (2008). Cultural differences in response styles: The role of dialectical thinking. *Personality and Individual Differences, 44,* 932–942. doi:10.1016/j.paid.2007.10.034

Hamer, D. H., Hu, S., Magnuson, V. L., Hu, N., & Pattatucci, A. M. (1993, July 16). A linkage between DNA markers on the X chromosome and male sexual orientation. *Science, 261,* 321–327.

Hamilton, C. E. (2000). Continuity and discontinuity of attachment from infancy through adolescence. *Child Development, 71,* 690–694. doi:10.1111/1467-8624.00177

Hamilton, M. C., Anderson, D., Broaddus, M., & Young, K. (2006). Gender stereotyping and under-representation of female characters in 200 popular children's picture books: A twenty-first century update. *Sex Roles, 55,* 757-765.

Hamlin, J. K., Wynn, K., & Bloom, P. (2007, September 24). Social evaluation by preverbal infants. *Nature, 450,* 557–559. doi:10.1038/nature06288

Hamlin, J. K., Wynn, K., Bloom, P., & Mahajan, N. (2011). How infants and toddlers react to antisocial others. *Proceedings of the National Academy of Sciences of the United States of America, 108,* 19931–19936. doi:10.1073/pnas.1110306108

Hammen, C., & Rudolph, K. D. (2003). Childhood mood disorders. In E. J. Mash & R. A. Barkley (Eds.), *Child psychopathology* (2nd ed., pp. 233–278). New York, NY: Guilford Press.

Han, W.-J., Miller, D. P., & Waldfogel, J. (2010). Parental work schedules and adolescent risky behaviors. *Developmental Psychology, 46,* 1245–1267. doi:10.1037/a0020178

Hanish, L. D., & Guerra, N. G. (2000a). Predictors of peer victimization among urban youth. *Social Development, 9,* 521–543. doi:10.1111/1467-9507.00141

Hanish, L. D., & Guerra, N. G. (2000b). The roles of ethnicity and school context in predicting children's victimization by peers. *American Journal of Community Psychology, 28,* 201–223. doi:10.1023/A:1005187201519

Hanish, L. D., & Tolan, P. H. (2001). Patterns of change in family-based aggression prevention. *Journal of Marital and Family Therapy, 27,* 213–226. doi:10.1111/j.1752-0606.2001.tb01158.x

Hankin, B. L., & Abramson, L. Y. (1999). Development of gender differences in depression: Description and possible explanations. *Annals of Medicine, 31,* 372–379.

Hankin, B. L., Abramson, L. Y., Moffitt, T. E., Silva, P. A., McGee, R., & Angell, K. E. (1998). Development of depression from preadolescence to young adulthood: Emerging gender differences in a 10-year longitudinal study. *Journal of Abnormal Psychology, 107,* 128–140. doi:10.1037/0021-843X.107.1.128

Hankin, B. L., Mermelstein, R., & Roesch, L. (2007). Sex differences in adolescent depression: Stress exposure and reactivity models. *Child Development, 78,* 279–295. doi:10.1111/j.1467-8624.2007.00997.x

Hankin, B. L., Stone, L., & Wright, P. A. (2010). Corumination, interpersonal stress generation, and internalizing symptoms: Accumulating effects and transactional influences in a multiwave study of adolescents. *Development and Psychopathology, 22,* 217–235. doi:10.1017/S0954579409990368

Hanna, E., & Meltzoff, A. N. (1993). Peer imitation by toddlers in laboratory, home, and day-care contexts: Implications for social learning and memory. *Developmental Psychology, 29,* 701–710. doi:10.1037/0012-1649.29.4.701

Hannon, E. E., & Trehub, S. E. (2005a). Metrical categories in infancy and adulthood. *Psychological Science, 16,* 48–55. doi:10.1111/j.0956-7976.2005.00779.x

Hannon, E. E., & Trehub, S. E. (2005b). Tuning in to musical rhythms: Infants learn more readily than adults. *Proceedings of the National Academy of Sciences of the United States of America, 102,* 12639–12643. doi:10.1073/pnas.0504254102

Harada, M. (1995). Minamata disease: Methylmercury poisoning in Japan caused by environmental pollution. *Critical Reviews in Toxicology, 25,* 1–24. doi:10.3109/10408449509089885

Harden, K. P., Turkheimer, E., Emery, R. E., D'Onofrio, B. M., Slutske, W. S., Heath, A. C., & Martin, N. G. (2007). Marital conflict and conduct problems in Children of Twins. *Child Development, 78,* 1–18. doi:10.1111/j.1467-8624.2007.00982.x

Harden, K. P., Turkheimer, E., & Loehlin, J. C. (2007). Genotype by environment interaction in adolescents' cognitive aptitude. *Behavior Genetics, 37,* 273–283. doi:10.1007/s10519-006-9113-4

Hardy, C. L., Bukowski, W. M., & Sippola, L. K. (2002). Stability and change in peer relationships during the transition to middle-level school. *Journal of Early Adolescence, 22,* 117–142. doi:10.1177/0272431602022002001

Hardy, J. B., Astone, N. M., Brooks-Gunn, J., Shapiro, S., & Miller, T. L. (1998). Like mother, like child: Intergenerational patterns of age at first birth and associations with childhood and adolescent characteristics and adult outcomes in the second generation. *Developmental Psychology, 34,* 1220–1232. doi:10.1037/0012-1649.34.6.1220

Harkness, S., Super, C., Keefer, C., Raghavan, C., & Campbell, E. (1996). Ask the doctor: The negotiation of cultural models in American parent-pediatrician discourse. In S. Harkness & C. M. Super (Eds.), *Parents' cultural belief systems: Their origins, expressions and consequences* (pp. 289–310). New York, NY: Guilford Press.

Harkness, S., & Super, C. M. (1995). Culture and parenting. In M. H. Bornstein (Ed.), *Handbook of parenting* (Vol. 2, pp. 211–234). Mahwah, NJ: Erlbaum.

Harlaar, N., Dale, P. S., & Plomin, R. (2007). From learning to read to reading to learn: Substantial and stable genetic influence. *Child Development, 78,* 116–131. doi:10.1111/j.1467-8624.2007.00988.x

Harley, K., & Reese, E. (1999). Origins of autobiographical memory. *Developmental Psychology, 35,* 1338–1348.

Harlow, H. F., & Harlow, M. K. (1965). The affectional systems. In A. M. Schrier, H. F. Harlow, & F. Stollnitz (Eds.), *Behavior of nonhuman primates* (Vol. 2, pp. 287–334). New York, NY: Academic Press.

Harlow, H. F., & Zimmermann, R. R. (1959, August 21). Affectional responses in the infant monkey. *Science, 130,* 421–432.

Harman, C., Rothbart, M. K., & Posner, M. I. (1997). Distress and attention interactions in early infancy. *Motivation and Emotion, 21,* 27–44.

Harold, G. T., & Conger, R. D. (1997). Marital conflict and adolescent distress: The role of adolescent awareness. *Child Development, 68,* 333–350. doi:10.1111/j.1467-8624.1997.tb01943.x

Harris, F. R., Wolf, M. M., & Baer, D. M. (1967). Social reinforcement effects on child behavior. In W. W. Hartup & N. L. Smothergill (Eds.), *The young child: Reviews of research* (pp. 13–26). Washington, DC: National Association for the Education of Young Children.

Harris, J. R. (1995). Where is the child's environment? A group socialization theory of development. *Psychological Review, 102,* 458–489. doi:10.1037/0033-295X.102.3.458

Harris, P. L. (2000). *The work of the imagination.* Oxford, England: Blackwell.

Harris, P. L. (2006). Social cognition. In W. Damon & R. M. Lerner (Series Eds.) & D. Kuhn & R. S. Siegler (Vol. Eds.), *Handbook of child psychology: Vol. 2. Cognition, perception, and language* (6th ed., pp. 811–858). Hoboken, NJ: Wiley.

Harris, P. L., Olthof, T., Terwogt, M. M., & Hardman, C. E. (1987). Children's knowledge of the situations that provoke emotion. *International Journal of Behavioral Development, 10,* 319–343.

Harris-Britt, A., Valrie, C. R., Kurtz-Costes, B., & Rowley, S. J. (2007). Perceived racial discrimination and self-esteem in African American youth: Racial socialization as a protective factor. *Journal of Research on Adolescence, 17,* 669–682. doi:10.1111/j.1532-7795.2007.00540.x

Harrison, Y. (2004). The relationship between daytime exposure to light and night-time sleep in 6–12-week-old infants. *Journal of Sleep Research, 13,* 345–352.

Harrist, A. W., Zaia, A. F., Bates, J. E., Dodge, K. A., & Pettit, G. S. (1997). Subtypes of social withdrawal in early childhood: Sociometric status and social-cognitive differences across four years. *Child Development, 68,* 278–294. doi:10.2307/1131850

Hart, B., & Risley, T. R. (1995). *Meaningful differences in the everyday experience of young American children.* Baltimore, MD: Brookes.

Hart, C. H., DeWolf, D. M., Wozniak, P., & Burts, D. C. (1992). Maternal and paternal disciplinary styles: Relations with preschoolers' playground behavioral orientations and peer status. *Child Development, 63,* 879–892. doi:10.1111/j.1467-8624.1992.tb01668.x

Hart, C. H., Ladd, G. W., & Burleson, B. R. (1990). Children's expectations of the outcomes of social strategies: Relations with sociometric status and maternal disciplinary styles. *Child Development, 61,* 127–137. doi:10.1111/j.1467-8624.1990.tb02766.x

Hart, D., Donnelly, T. M., Youniss, J., & Atkins, R. (2007). High school community service as a predictor of adult voting and volunteering. *American Educational Research Journal, 44,* 197–219. doi:10.3102/0002831206298173

Hart, D., & Fegley, S. (1995). Prosocial behavior and caring in adolescence: Relations to self-understanding and social judgment. *Child Development, 66,* 1346–1359. doi:10.1111/j.1467-8624.1995.tb00939.x

Harter, S. (1983). Developmental perspectives on the self-system. In P. H. Mussen (Series Ed.) & E. M. Hetherington (Vol. Ed.), *Handbook of child psychology: Vol. 4. Socialization, personality and social development* (4th ed., pp. 275–385). New York, NY: Wiley.

Harter, S. (1985). *Manual for the self-perception profile for children.* Unpublished manuscript. University of Denver, CO.

Harter, S. (1999). *The construction of the self: A developmental perspective.* New York, NY: Guilford Press.

Harter, S. (2006). The self. In W. Damon & R. M. Lerner (Series Eds.) & N. Eisenberg (Vol. Ed.), *Handbook of child psychology: Vol. 3. Social, emotional, and personality development* (6th ed., pp. 505–570). Hoboken, NJ: Wiley.

Harter, S. (2012). *The construction of the self: Developmental and sociocultural foundations* (2nd ed.). New York, NY: Guilford Press.

Harter, S., & Buddin, B. J. (1987). Children's understanding of the simultaneity of two emotions: A five-stage developmental acquisition sequence. *Developmental Psychology, 23,* 388–399.

Harter, S., & Monsour, A. (1992). Development analysis of conflict caused by opposing attributes in the adolescent self-portrait. *Developmental Psychology, 28,* 251–260. doi:10.1037/0012-1649.28.2.251

Harter, S., & Pike, R. (1984). The Pictorial Scale of Perceived Competence and Social Acceptance for young children. *Child Development, 55,* 1969–1982.

Hartman, L. R., Magalhães, L., & Mandich, A. (2011). What does parental divorce or marital separation mean for adolescents? A scoping review of North American literature. *Journal of Divorce and Remarriage, 52,* 490–518. doi:10.1080/10502556.2011.609432

Hartshorn, K., & Rovee-Collier, C. (1997). Infant learning and long-term memory at 6 months: A confirming analysis. *Developmental Psychobiology, 30,* 71–85. doi:10.1002/(SICI)1098-2302(199701)30:1<71::AID-DEV7>3.0.CO;2-S

Hartup, W. W. (1974). Aggression in childhood: Developmental perspectives. *American Psychologist, 29,* 336–341. doi:10.1037/h0037622

Hartup, W. W. (1983). Peer relations. In P. H. Mussen (Series Ed.) & E. M. Hetherington (Vol. Ed.), *Handbook of child psychology: Vol. 4. Socialization, personality and social development* (4th ed., pp. 103–196). New York, NY: Wiley.

Hartup, W. W. (1996). The company they keep: Friendships and their developmental significance. *Child Development, 67*, 1–13. doi:10.1111/j.1467-8624.1996.tb01714.x

Hartup, W. W., French, D. C., Laursen, B., Johnston, M. K., & Ogawa, J. R. (1993). Conflict and friendship relations in middle childhood: Behavior in a closed-field situation. *Child Development, 64*, 445–454. doi:10.1111/j.1467-8624.1993.tb02920.x

Hartup, W. W., Laursen, B., Stewart, M. I., & Eastenson, A. (1988). Conflict and the friendship relations of young children. *Child Development, 59*, 1590–1600.

Hartup, W. W., & Stevens, N. (1997). Friendships and adaptation in the life course. *Psychological Bulletin, 121*, 355–370.

Harvey, E. (1999). Short-term and long-term effects of early parental employment on children of the National Longitudinal Survey of Youth. *Developmental Psychology, 35*, 445–459. doi:10.1037/0012-1649.35.2.445

Haselager, G. J. T., Hartup, W. W., van Lieshout, C. F. M., & Riksen-Walraven, J. M. A. (1998). Similarities between friends and nonfriends in middle childhood. *Child Development, 69*, 1198–1208. doi:10.1111/j.1467-8624.1998.tb06167.x

Haskins, R. (1985). Public school aggression among children with varying day-care experience. *Child Development, 56*, 689–703.

Haskins, R. (1989). Beyond metaphor: The efficacy of early childhood education. *American Psychologist, 44*, 274–282.

Hastings, P. D., & De, I. (2008). Parasympathetic regulation and parental socialization of emotion: Biopsychosocial processes of adjustment in preschoolers. *Social Development, 17*, 211–238.

Hastings, P. D., McShane, K. E., Parker, R., & Ladha, F. (2007). Ready to make nice: Parental socialization of young sons' and daughters' prosocial behaviors with peers. *Journal of Genetic Psychology, 168*, 177–200. doi:10.3200/GNTP.168.2.177-200

Hastings, P. D., Zahn-Waxler, C., & McShane, K. E. (2005). We are, by nature, moral creatures: Biological bases of concern for others. In M. Killen & J. Smetana (Eds.), *Handbook of moral development* (pp. 483–516). Hillsdale, NJ: Erlbaum.

Hastings, P. D., Zahn-Waxler, C., Robinson, J., Usher, B., & Bridges, D. (2000). The development of concern for others in children with behavior problems. *Developmental Psychology, 36*, 531–546. doi:10.1037/0012-1649.36.5.531

Hatano, G., Siegler, R. S., Richards, D. D., Inagaki, K., Stavy, R., & Wax, N. (1993). The development of biological knowledge: A multi-national study. *Cognitive Development, 8*, 47–62. doi:10.1016/0885-2014(93)90004-O

Hatzichristou, C., & Hopf, D. (1996). A multiperspective comparison of peer sociometric status groups in childhood and adolescence. *Child Development, 67*, 1085–1102. doi:10.2307/1131881

Hauck, F. R., Thompson, J. M., Tanabe, K. O., Moon, R. Y., & Vennemann, M. M. (2011). Breastfeeding and reduced risk of sudden infant death syndrome: A meta-analysis. *Pediatrics, 128*, 103–110. doi:10.1542/peds.2010-3000

Hawker, D. S. J., & Boulton, M. J. (2000). Twenty years' research on peer victimization and psychosocial maladjustment: A meta-analytic review of cross-sectional studies. *Journal of Child Psychology and Psychiatry, 41*, 441–455.

Hawley, P. H. (2003). Prosocial and coercive configurations of resource control in early adolescence: A case for the well-adapted Machiavellian. *Merrill-Palmer Quarterly, 49*, 279–309.

Hawley, P. H., Little, T. D., & Card, N. A. (2008). The myth of the alpha male: A new look at dominance-related beliefs and behaviors among adolescent males and females. *International Journal of Behavioral Development, 32*, 76–88. doi:10.1177/0165025407084054

Hawley, T. L., & Disney, E. R. (1992, Winter). Crack's children: The consequences of maternal cocaine abuse. *Social Policy Report, 6*(4), 1–23.

Haworth, C. M. A., Wright, M. J., Luciano, M., Martin, N. G., de Geus, E. J. C., van Beijsterveldt, C. E. M., … Plomin, R. (2010). The heritability of general cognitive ability increases linearly from childhood to young adulthood. *Molecular Psychiatry, 15*, 1112–1120. doi:10.1038/mp.2009.55

Hay, D. F. (2007). The gradual emergence of sex differences in aggression: Alternative hypotheses. *Psychological Medicine, 37*, 1527–1537. doi:10.1017/S0033291707000165

Hay, D. F., Caplan, M., & Nash, A. (2009). The beginnings of peer relations. In K. H. Rubin, W. M. Bukowski, & B. Laursen (Eds.), *Handbook of peer interactions, relationships, and groups* (pp. 121–142). New York, NY: Guilford Press.

Hay, D. F., Hurst, S.-L., Waters, C. S., & Chadwick, A. (2011). Infants' use of force to defend toys: The origins of instrumental aggression. *Infancy, 16*, 471–489. doi:10.1111/j.1532-7078.2011.00069.x

Hay, D. F., Mundy, L., Roberts, S., Carta, R., Waters, C. S., Perra, O., … van Goozen, S. (2011). Known risk factors for violence predict 12-month-old infants' aggressiveness with peers. *Psychological Science, 22*, 1205–1211. doi:10.1177/0956797611419303

Hay, D. F., & Ross, H. S. (1982). The social nature of early conflict. *Child Development, 53*, 105–113. doi:10.2307/1129642

Hay, J. F., Pelucchi, B., Graf Estes, K., & Saffran, J. R. (2011). Linking sounds to meanings: Infant statistical learning in a natural language. *Cognitive Psychology, 63*, 93–106. doi:10.1016/j.cogpsych.2011.06.002

Hayes, K. J., & Hayes, C. (1951). The intellectual development of a home-raised chimpanzee. *Proceedings of the American Philosophical Society, 95*, 105–109.

Hayne, H. (2004). Infant memory development: Implications for childhood amnesia. *Developmental Review, 24*, 33–73. doi:10.1016/j.dr.2003.09.007

Hayne, H., Barr, R., & Herbert, J. (2003). The effect of prior practice on memory reactivation and generalization. *Child Development, 74*, 1615–1627. doi:10.2307/3696293

Heathcock, J. C., Lobo, M., & Galloway, J. C. (2008). Movement training advances the emergence of reaching in infants born at less than 33 weeks of gestational age: A randomized clinical trial. *Physical Therapy, 88*, 310–322. doi:10.2522/ptj.20070145

Heatherington, L., & Lavner, J. A. (2008). Coming to terms with coming out: Review and recommendations for family systems-focused research. *Journal of Family Psychology, 22*, 329–343. doi:10.1037/0893-3200.22.3.329

Heaven, P., & Ciarrochi, J. (2008). Parental styles, gender and the development of hope and self-esteem. *European Journal of Personality, 22*, 707–724. doi:10.1002/per.699

Hebb, D. O. (1949). *The organization of behavior: A neuropsychological theory.* New York, NY: Wiley.

Hecht, S. A., & Vagi, K. J. (2010). Sources of group and individual differences in emerging fraction skills. *Journal of Educational Psychology, 102*, 843–859. doi:10.1037/a0019824

Heckman, J. J. (2011, Spring). The economics of inequality. *American Educator, 31*–35, 47.

Hedges, L. V., & Nowell, A. (1995, July 7). Sex differences in mental test scores, variability, and numbers of high-scoring individuals. *Science, 269,* 41–45.

Heine, S. J., Lehman, D. R., Markus, H. R., & Kitayama, S. (1999). Is there a universal need for positive self-regard? *Psychological Review, 106,* 766–794.

Held, R., Birch, E., & Gwiazda, J. (1980). Stereoacuity of human infants. *Proceedings of the National Academy of Sciences of the United States of America, 77,* 5572–5574.

Helsen, M., Vollebergh, W., & Meeus, W. (2000). Social support from parents and friends and emotional problems in adolescence. *Journal of Youth and Adolescence, 29,* 319–335. doi:10.1023/A:1005147708827

Henry, B., Caspi, A., Moffitt, T. E., & Silva, P. A. (1996). Temperamental and familial predictors of violent and nonviolent criminal convictions: Age 3 to age 18. *Developmental Psychology, 32,* 614–623. doi:10.1037/0012-1649.32.4.614

Henry, C. S., Sager, D. W., & Plunkett, S. W. (1996). Adolescents' perceptions of family system characteristics, parent-adolescent dyadic behaviors, adolescent qualities, and adolescent empathy. *Family Relations, 45,* 283–292. doi:10.2307/585500

Hepper, P. G. (1988). Adaptive fetal learning: Prenatal exposure to garlic affects postnatal preferences. *Animal Behaviour, 36,* 935–936. doi:10.1016/S0003-3472(88)80177-5

Herdt, G. H., & Boxer, A. (1993). *Children of Horizons: How gay and lesbian teens are leading a new way out of the closet.* Boston, MA: Beacon Press.

Hermans, E. J., Ramsey, N. F., & van Honk, J. (2008). Exogenous testosterone enhances responsiveness to social threat in the neural circuitry of social aggression in humans. *Biological Psychiatry, 63,* 263–270. doi:10.1016/j.biopsych.2007.05.013

Hermer, L., & Spelke, E. (1996). Modularity and development: The case of spatial reorientation. *Cognition, 61,* 195–232.

Hernandez, D. J., Denton, N. A., & Macartney, S. E. (2008). Children in immigrant families: Looking to America's future. *Social Policy Report, 22*(3), 3–22.

Hernandez, J. T., & Diclemente, R. J. (1992). Self-control and ego identity development as predictors of unprotected sex in late adolescent males. *Journal of Adolescence, 15,* 437–447. doi:10.1016/0140-1971(92)90073-E

Herrera, M. A., Mathiesen, M. E., Merino, J. M., & Recart, I. (2005). Learning contexts for young children in Chile: Process quality assessment in preschool centres. *International Journal of Early Years Education, 13,* 13–27. doi:10.1080/09669760500048253

Herrmann, E., Call, J., Hernàndez-Lloreda, M. V., Hare, B., & Tomasello, M. (2007, September 7). Humans have evolved specialized skills of social cognition: The cultural intelligence hypothesis. *Science, 317,* 1360–1366.

Hertenstein, M. J., & Campos, J. J. (2004). The retention effects of an adult's emotional displays on infant behavior. *Child Development, 75,* 595–613. doi:10.1111/j.1467-8624.2004.00695.x

Hesketh, T., & Ding, Q. J. (2005). Anxiety and depression in adolescents in urban and rural China. *Psychological Reports, 96,* 435–444. doi:10.2466/pr0.96.2.435-444

Hesketh, T., Zheng, Y., Jun, Y. X., Xing, Z. W., Dong, Z. X., & Lu, L. (2011). Behaviour problems in Chinese primary school children. *Social Psychiatry and Psychiatric Epidemiology, 46,* 733–741. doi:10.1007/s00127-010-0240-0

Hespos, S. J., & Spelke, E. S. (2004, July 22). Conceptual precursors to language. *Nature, 430,* 453–456. doi:10.1038/nature02634

Hess, R. D., Kashiwagi, K., Azuma, H., Price, G. G., & Dickson, W. P. (1980). Maternal expectations for mastery of developmental tasks in Japan and the United States. *International Journal of Psychology, 15,* 259–271. doi:10.1080/00207598008246996

Hesse, E. (1999). The Adult Attachment Interview: Historical and current perspectives. In J. Cassidy & P. R. Shaver (Eds.), *Handbook of attachment: Theory, research, and clinical applications* (pp. 395–433). New York, NY: Guilford Press.

Hesse, E., & Main, M. (2006). Frightened, threatening, and dissociative parental behavior in low-risk samples: Description, discussion, and interpretations. *Development and Psychopathology, 18,* 309–343.

Hetherington, E. M. (1989). Coping with family transitions: Winners, losers, and survivors. *Child Development, 60,* 1–14.

Hetherington, E. M. (1993). An overview of the Virginia Longitudinal Study of Divorce and Remarriage with a focus on early adolescence. *Journal of Family Psychology, 7,* 39–56. doi:10.1037/0893-3200.7.1.39

Hetherington, E. M. (1999). Social capital and the development of youth from nondivorced, divorced and remarried families. In W. A. Collins & B. Laursen (Eds.), *Minnesota Symposia on Child Psychology: Vol. 30. Relationships as developmental contexts* (pp. 177–209). Mahwah, NJ: Erlbaum.

Hetherington, E. M., Bridges, M., & Insabella, G. M. (1998). What matters? What does not? Five perspectives on the association between marital transitions and children's adjustment. *American Psychologist, 53,* 167–184. doi:10.1037/0003-066X.53.2.167

Hetherington, E. M., Clingempeel, W. G. (with Anderson, E. R., Deal, J. E., Hagan, M. S., Hollier, E. A., & Lindner, M. S.). (1992). Coping with marital transitions: A family systems perspective. *Monographs of the Society for Research in Child Development, 57*(2–3, Serial No. 227), i-238. doi:10.2307/1166050

Hetherington, E. M., Henderson, S. H., Reiss, D. (with Anderson, E. R., Bridges, M., Chan, R. W., Insabella, G. M., Jodl, K. M., Kim, J. E., Mitchell, A. S., O'Connor, T. G., Skaggs, M. J., & Taylor, L. C.). (1999). Adolescent siblings in stepfamilies: Family functioning and adolescent adjustment, with commentary by James H. Bray. *Monographs of the Society for Research in Child Development, 64*(4, Serial No. 259), i-209.

Hetherington, E. M., & Stanley-Hagan, M. (2002). Parenting in divorced and remarried families. In M. H. Bornstein (Ed.), *Handbook of parenting: Vol. 3. Being and becoming a parent* (2nd ed., pp. 287–315). Mahwah, NJ: Erlbaum.

Hetherington, E. M., Stanley-Hagan, M., & Anderson, E. R. (1989). Marital transitions: A child's perspective. *American Psychologist, 44,* 303–312. doi:10.1037/0003-066X.44.2.303

Hetherington, E. M., & Stanley-Hagan, M. M. (1995). Parenting in divorced and remarried families. In M. H. Bornstein (Ed.), *Handbook of parenting: Vol. 3. Status and social conditions of parenting* (pp. 233–254). Hillsdale, NJ: Erlbaum.

Hewlett, B. S. (1991). *Intimate fathers: The nature and context of Aka pygmy paternal infant care.* Ann Arbor: University of Michigan Press.

Hewlett, B. S., Lamb, M. E., Shannon, D., Leyendecker, B., & Scholmerich, A. (1998). Culture and early infancy among central African foragers and farmers. *Developmental Psychology, 34,* 653–661.

Hiatt, S. W., Campos, J. J., & Emde, R. N. (1979). Facial patterning and infant emotional expression: Happiness, surprise, and fear. *Child Development, 50,* 1020–1035.

Hickling, A. K., & Gelman, S. A. (1995). How does your garden grow? Early conceptualization of seeds and their place in the plant growth cycle. *Child Development, 66,* 856–876. doi:10.1111/j.1467-8624.1995.tb00910.x

Hickman, L. J., Jaycox, L. H., & Aronoff, J. (2004). Dating violence among adolescents: Prevalence, gender distribution, and prevention program effectiveness. *Trauma, Violence, and Abuse, 5,* 123–142. doi:10.1177/1524838003262332

Higgins, E. T. (1991). Development of self-regulatory and self-evaluative processes: Costs, benefits, and tradeoffs. In M. R. Gunnar & L. A. Sroufe (Eds.), *Self processes and development* (pp. 125–165). Hillsdale, NJ: Erlbaum.

Hill, J., Emery, R. E., Harden, K. P., Mendle, J., & Turkheimer, E. (2008). Alcohol use in adolescent twins and affiliation with substance using peers. *Journal of Abnormal Child Psychology, 36,* 81–94. doi:10.1007/s10802-007-9161-0

Hill, J. P. (1988). Adapting to menarche: Familial control and conflict. In M. R. Gunnar & W. A. Collins (Eds.), *Minnesota Symposia on Child Psychology: Vol. 21. Development during the transition to adolescence* (pp. 43–77). Hillsdale, NJ: Erlbaum.

Hill, J. P., & Lynch, M. E. (1983). The intensification of gender-related role expectations during early adolescence. In J. Brooks-Gunn & A. C. Petersen (Eds.), *Girls at puberty: Biological and psychosocial perspectives* (pp. 201–228). New York, NY: Springer.

Hill, N. E., Bush, K. R., & Roosa, M. W. (2003). Parenting and family socialization strategies and children's mental health: Low-income Mexican-American and Euro-American mothers and children. *Child Development, 74,* 189–204. doi:10.1111/1467-8624.t01-1-00530

Hill, S. A., & Sprague, J. (1999). Parenting in black and white families: The interaction of gender with race and class. *Gender and Society, 13,* 480–502. doi:10.1177/089124399013004004

Hilt, L. M., & Nolen-Hoeksema, S. (2009). The emergence of gender differences in depression in adolescence. In S. Nolen-Hoeksema & L. M. Hilt (Eds.), *Handbook of depression in adolescents* (pp. 111–135). New York, NY: Routledge/Taylor & Francis Group.

Hines, M. (2004). *Brain gender.* Oxford, England: Oxford University Press.

Hines, M., Fane, B. A., Pasterski, V. L., Mathews, G. A., Conway, G. S., & Brook, C. (2003). Spatial abilities following prenatal androgen abnormality: Targeting and mental rotations performance in individuals with congenital adrenal hyperplasia. *Psychoneuroendocrinology, 28,* 1010–1026. doi:10.1016/S0306-4530(02)00121-X

Hinshaw, S. P., & Lee, S. S. (2003). Conduct and oppositional defiant disorders. In E. J. Mash & R. A. Barkley (Eds.), *Child psychopathology* (2nd ed., pp. 144–198). New York, NY: Guilford Press.

Hirsh-Pasek, K., & Golinkoff, R. (1991). Language comprehension: A new look at some old themes. In N. A. Krasnegor, D. M. Rumbaugh, R. L. Schiefelbusch, & M. Studdert-Kennedy (Eds.), *Biological and behavioral determinants of language development* (pp. 301–320). Hillsdale, NJ: Erlbaum.

Hirsh-Pasek, K., Golinkoff, R. M., Berk, L. E., & Singer, D. G. (2009). *A mandate for playful learning in preschool: Presenting the evidence.* New York, NY: Oxford University Press.

Hirshfeld-Becker, D. R., Biederman, J., Henin, A., Faraone, S. V., Davis, S., Harrington, K., & Rosenbaum, J. F. (2007). Behavioral inhibition in preschool children at risk is a specific predictor of middle childhood social anxiety: A five-year follow-up. *Journal of Developmental and Behavioral Pediatrics, 28,* 225–233.

Ho, C., Bluestein, D. N., & Jenkins, J. M. (2008). Cultural differences in the relationship between parenting and children's behavior. *Developmental Psychology, 44,* 507–522. doi:10.1037/0012-1649.44.2.507

Ho, D. Y. F. (1986). Chinese patterns of socialization: A critical review. In M. H. Bond (Ed.), *The psychology of the Chinese people* (pp. 1–37). New York, NY: Oxford University Press.

Hobson, J. A., Harris, R., Garcia-Perez, R., & Hobson, R. P. (2009). Anticipatory concern: A study in autism. *Developmental Science, 12,* 249–263. doi:10.1111/j.1467-7687.2008.00762.x

Hochberg, J., & Brooks, V. (1962). Pictorial recognition as an unlearned ability: A study of one child's performance. *American Journal of Psychology, 75,* 624–628. doi:10.2307/1420286

Hodges, E. V., Boivin, M., Vitaro, F., & Bukowski, W. M. (1999). The power of friendship: Protection against an escalating cycle of peer victimization. *Developmental Psychology, 35,* 94–101.

Hodges, E. V., Malone, M. J., & Perry, D. G. (1997). Individual risk and social risk as interacting determinants of victimization in the peer group. *Developmental Psychology, 33,* 1032–1039.

Hodgins, S., Larm, P., Ellenbogen, M., Vitaro, F., & Tremblay, R. E. (2013). Teachers' ratings of childhood behaviours predict adolescent and adult crime among 3016 males and females. *Canadian Journal of Psychiatry, 58,* 143–150.

Hoeve, M., Dubas, J. S., Gerris, J. R. M., van der Laan, P. H., & Smeenk, W. (2011). Maternal and paternal parenting styles: Unique and combined links to adolescent and early adult delinquency. *Journal of Adolescence, 34,* 813–827. doi:10.1016/j.adolescence.2011.02.004

Hoeve, M., Stams, G. J. J. M., Put, C. E., Dubas, J. S., Laan, P. H., & Gerris, J. R. M. (2012). A meta-analysis of attachment to parents and delinquency. *Journal of Abnormal Child Psychology, 40,* 771–785. doi:10.1007/s10802-011-9608-1

Hoff, E. (2001). *Language development* (2nd ed.). Belmont, CA: Wadsworth/Thomson Learning.

Hoff, E. (2003). The specificity of environmental influence: Socioeconomic status affects early vocabulary development via maternal speech. *Child Development, 74,* 1368–1378. doi:10.1111/1467-8624.00612

Hoff, E., Laursen, B., & Tardif, T. (2002). Socioeconomic status and parenting. In M. H. Bornstein (Ed.), *Handbook of parenting: Vol. 2. Biology and ecology of parenting* (2nd ed., pp. 231–252). Mahwah, NJ: Erlbaum.

Hoff, K. E., Reese-Weber, M., Schneider, W. J., & Stagg, J. W. (2009). The association between high status positions and aggressive behavior in early adolescence. *Journal of School Psychology, 47,* 395–426. doi:10.1016/j.jsp.2009.07.003

Hoff-Ginsberg, E., & Tardif, T. (1995). Socioeconomic status and parenting. In M. H. Bornstein (Ed.), *Handbook of parenting, Vol. 2: Biology and ecology of parenting* (pp. 161–188). Hillsdale, NJ: Erlbaum.

Hoffman, K. B., Cole, D. A., Martin, J. M., Tram, J., & Seroczynski, A. (2000). Are the discrepancies between self- and others' appraisals of competence predictive or reflective of depressive symptoms in children and adolescents: A longitudinal study, part II. *Journal of Abnormal Psychology, 109,* 651–662.

Hoffman, L. W. (1984). Work, family, and the socialization of the child. In R. D. Parke (Ed.), *Review of child development research: Vol. 7. The family* (pp. 223–282). Chicago, IL: University of Chicago Press.

Hoffman, L. W. (1989). Effects of maternal employment in the two-parent family. *American Psychologist, 44,* 283–292. doi:10.1037/0003-066X.44.2.283

Hoffman, L. W., Youngblade, L. M. (with Coley, R. L., Fuligni, A. S., & Kovacs, D. D.). (1999). *Mothers at work: Effects on children's well-being.* Cambridge, England: Cambridge University Press.

Hoffman, M. L. (1963). Parent discipline and the child's consideration for others. *Child Development, 34,* 573–588.

Hoffman, M. L. (1976). Empathy, role-taking, guilt and development of altruistic motives. In T. Lickona (Ed.), *Moral development and behavior: Theory, research, and social issues.* New York: Holt, Rinehart, & Winston.

Hoffman, M. L. (1981). Is altruism part of human nature? *Journal of Personality and Social Psychology, 40,* 121–137. doi:10.1037/0022-3514.40.1.121

Hoffman, M. L. (1982). Development of prosocial motivation: Empathy and guilt. In N. Eisenberg (Ed.), *The development of prosocial behavior* (pp. 281–313). New York, NY: Academic Press.

Hoffman, M. L. (1983). Affective and cognitive processes in moral internalization. In E. T. Higgins, D. N. Ruble, & W. W. Hartup (Eds.), *Social cognition and social development: A sociocultural perspective* (pp. 236–274). Cambridge, England: Cambridge University Press.

Hoffman, M. L. (2000). *Empathy and moral development: Implications for caring and justice.* Cambridge, England: Cambridge University Press.

Hoffner, C. (1993). Children's strategies for coping with stress: Blunting and monitoring. *Motivation and Emotion, 17,* 91–106.

Hofstede, G. (2000). Masculine and feminine cultures. In A. E. Kazdin (Ed.), *Encyclopedia of psychology* (Vol. 5, pp. 115–118). Washington, DC: American Psychological Association.

Hogue, A., & Steinberg, L. (1995). Homophily of internalized distress in adolescent peer groups. *Developmental Psychology, 31,* 897–906. doi:10.1037/0012-1649.31.6.897

Holden, C. (1980, March 21). Identical twins reared apart. *Science, 207,* 1323–1325.

Homae, F., Watanabe, H., Nakano, T., Asakawa, K., & Taga, G. (2006). The right hemisphere of sleeping infant perceives sentential prosody. *Neuroscience Research, 54,* 276–280. doi:10.1016/j.neures.2005.12.006

Hopkins, B., & Westra, T. (1988). Maternal handling and motor development: An intracultural study. *Genetic, Social, and General Psychology Monographs, 114,* 377–408.

Horn, J. L., & McArdle, J. J. (2007). Understanding human intelligence since Spearman. In R. Cudeck & R. C. MacCallum (Eds.), *Factor analysis at 100: Historical developments and future directions* (pp. 205–247). Mahwah, NJ: Erlbaum.

Horn, S. S. (2003). Adolescents' reasoning about exclusion from social groups. *Developmental Psychology, 39,* 71–84. doi:10.1037/0012-1649.39.1.71

Horne, R. S., Parslow, P. M., Ferens, D., Watts, A. M., & Adamson, T. M. (2004). Comparison of evoked arousability in breast and formula fed infants. *Archives of Disease in Childhood, 89,* 22–25.

Houston, D. M., & Miyamoto, R. T. (2010). Effects of early auditory experience on word learning and speech perception in deaf children with cochlear implants: Implications for sensitive periods of language development. *Otology and Neurotology, 31,* 1248–1253.

Howe, M. L., & Courage, M. L. (1997). The emergence and early development of autobiographical memory. *Psychological Review, 104,* 499–523.

Howe, N., Aquan-Assee, J., & Bukowski, W. M. (2001). Predicting sibling relations over time: Synchrony between maternal management styles and sibling relationship quality. *Merrill-Palmer Quarterly, 47,* 121–141.

Howe, N., & Recchia, H. (2005). Playmates and teachers: Reciprocal and complementary interactions between siblings. *Journal of Family Psychology, 19,* 497–502. doi:10.1037/0893-3200.19.4.497

Howe, N., Rinaldi, C., Jennings, M., & Petrakos, H. (2002). "No! The lambs can stay out because they got cozies": Constructive and destructive sibling conflict, pretend play, and social understanding. *Child Development, 73,* 1460–1473. doi:10.1111/1467-8624.00483

Howes, C. (1996). The earliest friendships. In W. M. Bukowski, A. F. Newcomb, & W. W. Hartup (Eds.), *The company they keep: Friendship in childhood and adolescence* (pp. 66–86). Cambridge, England: Cambridge University Press.

Howes, C., & Farver, J. (1987). Toddlers' responses to the distress of their peers. *Journal of Applied Developmental Psychology, 8,* 441–452. doi:10.1016/0193-3973(87)90032-3

Howes, C., & Matheson, C. C. (1992). Sequences in the development of competent play with peers: Social and social pretend play. *Developmental Psychology, 28,* 961–974.

Howes, C., & Phillipsen, L. (1998). Continuity in children's relations with peers. *Social Development, 7,* 340–349. doi:10.1111/1467-9507.00071

Howes, C., & Unger, O. (1989). Play with peers in child care settings. In M. N. Bloch & A. D. Pellegrini (Eds.), *The ecological context of children's play* (pp. 104–119). Norwood, NJ: Ablex.

Howes, D. (2012). Hiccups: A new explanation for the mysterious reflex. *Bioessays, 34,* 451–453. doi:10.1002/bies.201100194

Hoza, B., Molina, B. S. G., Bukowski, W. M., & Sippola, L. K. (1995). Peer variables as predictors of later childhood adjustment. *Development and Psychopathology, 7,* 787–802. doi:10.1017/S0954579400006842

Hubbard, F. O. A., & van IJzendoorn, M. H. (1991). Maternal unresponsiveness and infant crying across the first 9 months: A naturalistic longitudinal study. *Infant Behavior and Development, 14,* 299–312. doi:10.1016/0163-6383(91)90024-M

Hudson, J. A., Sosa, B., & Shapiro, L. R. (1997). Scripts and plans: The development of preschool children's event knowledge and event planning. In S. L. Friedman & E. K. Scholnick (Eds.), *The developmental psychology of planning: Why, how, and when do we plan?* (pp. 77–102). Mahwah, NJ: Erlbaum.

Huebner, R. R., & Izard, C. E. (1988). Mothers' responses to infants' facial expressions of sadness, anger, and physical distress. *Motivation and Emotion, 12,* 185–196.

Huffman, L. C., Bryan, Y. E., del Carmen, R., Pedersen, F. A., Doussard-Roosevelt, J. A., & Porges, S. W. (1998). Infant temperament and cardiac vagal tone: Assessments at twelve weeks of age. *Child Development, 69,* 624–635.

Hughes, C., & Dunn, J. (1998). Understanding mind and emotion: Longitudinal associations with mental-state talk between young friends. *Developmental Psychology, 34,* 1026–1037.

Hughes, D., Rodriguez, J., Smith, E. P., Johnson, D. J., Stevenson, H. C., & Spicer, P. (2006). Parents' ethnic-racial socialization practices: A review of research and directions for future study. *Developmental Psychology, 42,* 747–770.

Huizink, A. C. (2008). Prenatal stress exposure and temperament: A review. *International Journal of Developmental Science, 2,* 77–99. doi:10.3233/DEV-2008-21206

Huizink, A. C. (2012). Prenatal factors in temperament: The role of prenatal stress and substance use exposure. In M. R. Zentner & R. L. Shiner (Eds.), *Handbook of temperament* (pp. 297–314). New York, NY: Guilford Press.

Humphreys, L. G. (1989). Intelligence: Three kinds of instability and their consequences for policy. In R. L. Linn (Ed.), *Intelligence* (pp. 193–216). Urbana: University of Illinois Press.

Hunt, E., Streissguth, A. P., Kerr, B., & Olson, H. C. (1995). Mothers' alcohol consumption during pregnancy: Effects on spatial-visual reasoning in 14-year-old children. *Psychological Science, 6,* 339–342. doi:10.1111/j.1467-9280.1995.tb00523.x

Hunter, F. T., & Youniss, J. (1982). Changes in functions of three relations during adolescence. *Developmental Psychology, 18,* 806–811.

Hunziker, U. A., & Barr, R. G. (1986). Increased carrying reduces infant crying: A randomized controlled trial. *Pediatrics, 77,* 641–648.

Hurles, M. (2012). Older males beget more mutations. *Nature Genetics, 44,* 1174–1176.

Hurtado, N., Marchman, V. A., & Fernald, A. (2008). Does input influence uptake? Links between maternal talk, processing speed and vocabulary size in Spanish-learning children. *Developmental Science, 11,* F31-F39. doi:10.1111/j.1467-7687.2008.00768.x

Huston, A. C., & Aronson, S. R. (2005). Mothers' time with infant and time in employment as predictors of mother–child relationships and children's early development. *Child Development, 76,* 467–482. doi:10.1111/j.1467-8624.2005.00857.x

Huston, A. C., & Wright, J. C. (1998). Mass media and children's development. In W. Damon (Series Ed.) & I. E. Sigel & K. A. Renninger (Vol. Eds.), *Handbook of child psychology: Vol. 4. Child psychology in practice* (5th ed., pp. 999–1058). New York, NY: Wiley.

Huttenlocher, J., Haight, W., Bryk, A., Seltzer, M., & Lyons, T. (1991). Early vocabulary growth: Relation to language input and gender. *Developmental Psychology, 27,* 236–248.

Huttenlocher, J., Jordan, N. C., & Levine, S. C. (1994). A mental model for early arithmetic. *Journal of Experimental Psychology: General, 123,* 284–296.

Huttenlocher, J., Levine, S., & Vevea, J. (1998). Environmental input and cognitive growth: A study using time-period comparisons. *Child Development, 69,* 1012–1029.

Huttenlocher, P. R., & Dabholkar, A. S. (1997). Regional differences in synaptogenesis in human cerebral cortex. *Journal of Comparative Neurology, 387,* 167–178.

Hwang, C. P. (1987). The changing role of Swedish fathers. In M. E. Lamb (Ed.), *The father's role: Cross-cultural perspectives* (pp. 115–138). Hillsdale, NJ: Erlbaum.

Hwang, J. M., Cheong, P. H., & Feeley, T. H. (2009). Being young and feeling blue in Taiwan: Examining adolescent depressive mood and online and offline activities. *New Media and Society, 11,* 1101–1121. doi:10.1177/1461444809341699

Hyde, J. S. (2005). The gender similarities hypothesis. *American Psychologist, 60,* 581–592. doi:10.1037/0003-066X.60.6.581

Hyde, J. S., & Linn, M. C. (1988). Gender differences in verbal ability: A meta-analysis. *Psychological Bulletin, 104,* 53–69. doi:10.1037/0033-2909.104.1.53

Hyde, J. S., & McKinley, N. M. (1997). Gender differences in cognition: Results from meta-analyses. In P. J. Caplan, M. Crawford, J. S. Hyde, & J. T. E. Richardson (Eds.), *Gender differences in human cognition* (pp. 30–51). New York, NY: Oxford University Press.

Hymel, S., Bowker, A., & Woody, E. (1993). Aggressive versus withdrawn unpopular children: Variations in peer and self-perceptions in multiple domains. *Child Development, 64,* 879–896. doi:10.1111/j.1467-8624.1993.tb02949.x

Imperato-McGinley, J., Pichardo, M., Gautier, T., Voyer, D., & Bryden, M. P. (2007). Cognitive abilities in androgen-insensitive subjects: Comparison with control males and females from the same kindred. In G. Einstein (Ed.), *Sex and the brain* (pp. 555–560). Cambridge, MA: The MIT Press. (Reprinted from *Clinical Endocrinology, 34,* pp. 341–347, 1991)

Impett, E. A., Sorsoli, L., Schooler, D., Henson, J. M., & Tolman, D. L. (2008). Girls' relationship authenticity and self-esteem across adolescence. *Developmental Psychology, 44,* 722–733. doi:10.1037/0012-1649.44.3.722

Inagaki, K., & Hatano, G. (1993). Young children's understanding of the mind-body distinction. *Child Development, 64,* 1534–1549.

Inagaki, K., & Hatano, G. (1996). Young children's recognition of commonalities between animals and plants. *Child Development, 67,* 2823–2840. doi:10.1111/j.1467-8624.1996.tb01890.x

Inagaki, K., & Hatano, G. (2002). *Young children's naive thinking about the biological world.* New York, NY: Psychology Press.

Inagaki, K., & Hatano, G. (2008). Conceptual change in naïve biology. In S. Vosniadou (Ed.), *International handbook of research on conceptual change* (pp. 240–262). New York, NY: Routledge/Taylor & Francis.

Ingoldsby, E. M., Shaw, D. S., & Garcia, M. M. (2001). Intrafamily conflict in relation to boys' adjustment at school. *Development and Psychopathology, 13,* 35–52.

Inhelder, B., & Piaget, J. (1958). *The growth of logical thinking from childhood to adolescence: An essay on the construction of formal operational structures.* New York, NY: Basic Books.

Inlow, J. K., & Restifo, L. L. (2004). Molecular and comparative genetics of mental retardation. *Genetics, 166,* 835–881.

Intons-Peterson, M. J. (1988). *Children's concepts of gender.* Norwood, NJ: Ablex.

Ipsos-Reid. (2007, December 30). *In the land of the not so living.* Toronto, ON: Author.

Isabella, R. A. (1993). Origins of attachment: Maternal interactive behavior across the first year. *Child Development, 64,* 605–621. doi:10.1111/j.1467-8624.1993.tb02931.x

Ito, T., Ando, H., Suzuki, T., Ogura, T., Hotta, K., Imamura, Y., … Handa, H. (2010, March 12). Identification of a primary target of thalidomide teratogenicity. *Science, 327,* 1345–1350.

Iverson, J. M., & Goldin-Meadow, S. (1998, November 26). Why people gesture when they speak. *Nature, 396,* 228.

Iyer, R. V., Kochenderfer-Ladd, B., Eisenberg, N., & Thompson, M. (2010). Peer victimization and effortful control: Relations to school engagement and academic achievement. *Merrill-Palmer Quarterly, 56,* 361–387.

Izard, C. E. (2007). Basic emotions, natural kinds, emotion schemas, and a new paradigm. *Perspectives on Psychological Science, 2,* 260–280. doi:10.1111/j.1745-6916.2007.00044.x

Izard, C. E. (2010). The many meanings/aspects of emotion: Definitions, functions, activation, and regulation. *Emotion Review, 2,* 363–370.

Izard, C. E. (2011). Forms and functions of emotions: Matters of emotion–cognition interactions. *Emotion Review, 3,* 371–378.

Izard, C. E., Fantauzzo, C. A., Castle, J. M., Haynes, O. M., Rayias, M. F., & Putnam, P. H. (1995). The ontogeny and significance of infants' facial expressions in the first 9 months of life. *Developmental Psychology, 31,* 997–1013. doi:10.1037/0012-1649.31.6.997

Izard, C. E., Hembree, E. A., & Huebner, R. R. (1987). Infants' emotion expressions to acute pain: Developmental change and stability of individual differences. *Developmental Psychology, 23,* 105–113. doi:10.1037/0012-1649.23.1.105

Izard, C. E., King, K. A., Trentacosta, C. J., Morgan, J. K., Laurenceau, J. P., Krauthamer-Ewing, E. S., & Finlon, K. J. (2008). Accelerating the development of emotion competence in Head Start children: Effects on adaptive and maladaptive behavior. *Development and Psychopathology, 20,* 369–397. doi:10.1017/S0954579408000175

Jaccard, J., Blanton, H., & Dodge, T. (2005). Peer influences on risk behavior: An analysis of the effects of a close friend. *Developmental Psychology, 41,* 135–147.

Jacklin, C. N., DiPietro, J. A., & Maccoby, E. E. (1984). Sex-typing behavior and sex-typing pressure in child/parent interaction. *Archives of Sexual Behavior, 13,* 413–425. doi:10.1007/BF01541427

Jacklin, C. N., & Maccoby, E. E. (1978). Social behavior at thirty-three months in same-sex and mixed-sex dyads. *Child Development, 49,* 557–569.

Jacobson, J. L., & Jacobson, S. W. (1996). Intellectual impairment in children exposed to polychlorinated biphenyls in utero. *New England Journal of Medicine, 335,* 783–789. doi:10.1056/NEJM199609123351104

Jacobson, J. L., & Jacobson, S. W. (2002). Effects of prenatal alcohol exposure on child development. *Alcohol Research and Health, 26,* 282–286.

Jacobson, J. L., Jacobson, S. W., Padgett, R. J., Brumitt, G. A., & Billings, R. L. (1992). Effects of prenatal PCB exposure on cognitive processing efficiency and sustained attention. *Developmental Psychology, 28,* 297–306.

Jacobson, K. C., & Crockett, L. J. (2000). Parental monitoring and adolescent adjustment: An ecological perspective. *Journal of Research on Adolescence, 10,* 65–97. doi:10.1207/SJRA1001_4

Jaffe, A. C. (2011). Failure to thrive: Current clinical concepts. *Pediatrics in Review, 32,* 100–108. doi:10.1542/pir.32-3-100

Jaffee, S., Caspi, A., Moffitt, T. E., Belsky, J., & Silva, P. (2001). Why are children born to teen mothers at risk for adverse outcomes in young adulthood? Results from a 20-year longitudinal study. *Development and Psychopathology, 13,* 377–397.

Jaffee, S., & Hyde, J. S. (2000). Gender differences in moral orientation: A meta-analysis. *Psychological Bulletin, 126,* 703–726. doi:10.1037/0033-2909.126.5.703

Jaffee, S. R. (2002). Pathways to adversity in young adulthood among early childbearers. *Journal of Family Psychology, 16,* 38–49. doi:10.1037/0893-3200.16.1.38

Jaffee, S. R., Caspi, A., Moffitt, T. E., Polo-Tomas, M., Price, T. S., & Taylor, A. (2004a). The limits of child effects: Evidence for genetically mediated child effects on corporal punishment but not on physical maltreatment. *Developmental Psychology, 40,* 1047–1058. doi:10.1037/0012-1649.40.6.1047

Jaffee, S. R., Caspi, A., Moffitt, T. E., & Taylor, A. (2004b). Physical maltreatment victim to antisocial child: Evidence of an environmentally mediated process. *Journal of Abnormal Psychology, 113,* 44–55. doi:10.1037/0021-843X.113.1.44

Jaffee, S. R., Hanscombe, K. B., Haworth, C. M. A., Davis, O. S. P., & Plomin, R. (2012). Chaotic homes and children's disruptive behavior: A longitudinal cross-lagged twin study. *Psychological Science, 23,* 643–650. doi:10.1177/0956797611431693

Jaffee, S. R., Moffitt, T. E., Caspi, A., Taylor, A., & Arseneault, L. (2002). Influence of adult domestic violence on children's internalizing and externalizing problems: An environmentally informative twin study.

Journal of the American Academy of Child and Adolescent Psychiatry, 41, 1095–1103. doi:10.1097/00004583-200209000-00010

Jaffee, S. R., & Price, T. S. (2007). Gene-environment correlations: A review of the evidence and implications for prevention of mental illness. *Molecular Psychiatry, 12,* 432–442.

Jahromi, L. B., Putnam, S. P., & Stifter, C. A. (2004). Maternal regulation of infant reactivity from 2 to 6 months. *Developmental Psychology, 40,* 477–487. doi:10.1037/0012-1649.40.4.477

Jahromi, L. B., Umana-Taylor, A. J., Updegraff, K. A., & Lara, E. E. (2012). Birth characteristics and developmental outcomes of infants of Mexican-origin adolescent mothers: Risk and promotive factors. *International Journal of Behavioral Development, 36,* 146–156. doi:10.1177/0165025411430777

Jakobson, R. (1968). *Child language. Aphasia and phonological universals* (A. R. Keiler, Trans.). The Hague, The Netherlands: Mouton. (Original work published 1941)

James, D., Pillai, M., & Smoleniec, J. (1995). Neurobehavioral development in the human fetus. In J.-P. Lecanuet, W. P. Fifer, N. A. Krasnegor, & W. P. Smotherman (Eds.), *Fetal development: A psychobiological perspective* (pp. 101–128). Hillsdale, NJ: Erlbaum.

Jansen, P. W., Raat, H., Mackenbach, J. P., Hofman, A., Jaddoe, V. W. V., Bakermans-Kranenburg, M. J., … Tiemeier, H. (2012). Early determinants of maternal and paternal harsh discipline: The Generation R Study. *Family Relations, 61,* 253–270. doi:10.1111/j.1741-3729.2011.00691.x

Janssens, J. M. A. M., & Deković, M. (1997). Child rearing, prosocial moral reasoning, and prosocial behaviour. *International Journal of Behavioral Development, 20,* 509–527. doi:10.1080/016502597385252

Jaser, S. S., Champion, J. E., Reeslund, K. L., Keller, G., Merchant, M. J., Benson, M., & Compas, B. E. (2007). Cross-situational coping with peer and family stressors in adolescent offspring of depressed parents. *Journal of Adolescence, 30,* 917–932.

Jaswal, V. K. (2004). Don't believe everything you hear: Preschoolers' sensitivity to speaker intent in category induction. *Child Development, 75,* 1871–1885. doi:10.1111/j.1467-8624.2004.00822.x

Jaycox, L. H., Reivich, K. J., Gillham, J., & Seligman, M. E. (1994). Prevention of depressive symptoms in school children. *Behaviour Research and Therapy, 32,* 801–816.

Jegalian, K., & Lahn, B. T. (2001, February). Why the Y is so weird. *Scientific American, 284*(2), 56–61.

Jencks, C. (1979). *Who gets ahead? The determinants of economic success in America.* New York, NY: Basic Books.

Jenkins, J. (1992). Sibling relationships in disharmonious homes: Potential difficulties and protective effects. In F. Boer & J. Dunn (Eds.), *Children's sibling relationships: Developmental and clinical issues* (pp. 125–138). Hillsdale, NJ: Erlbaum.

Jenkins, J. M., & Astington, J. W. (1996). Cognitive factors and family structure associated with theory of mind development in young children. *Developmental Psychology, 32,* 70–78.

Jensen, A. R. (1973). *Educability and group differences.* New York, NY: Harper & Row.

Jensen, A. R. (1998). *The g factor: The science of mental ability.* Westport, CT: Praeger.

Jensen, P. S., Hinshaw, S. P., Swanson, J. M., Greenhill, L. L., Conners, C. K., Arnold, L. E., … Wigal, T. (2001). Findings from the NIMH Multimodal Treatment Study of ADHD (MTA): Implications and applications for primary care providers. *Journal of Developmental and Behavioral Pediatrics, 22,* 60–73.

Jiao, S., Ji, G., & Jing, Q. (1986). Comparative study of behavioral qualities of only children and sibling children. *Child Development, 57,* 357–361.

Jiao, S., Ji, G., & Jing, Q. (1996). Cognitive development of Chinese urban only children and children with siblings. *Child Development, 67,* 387–395. doi:10.1111/j.1467-8624.1996.tb01740.x

Jin, M. K., Jacobvitz, D., Hazen, N., & Jung, S. H. (2012). Maternal sensitivity and infant attachment security in Korea: Cross-cultural validation of the Strange Situation. *Attachment and Human Development, 14,* 33–44. doi:10.1080/14616734.2012.636656

Jocklin, V., McGue, M., & Lykken, D. T. (1996). Personality and divorce: A genetic analysis. *Journal of Personality and Social Psychology, 71,* 288–299. doi:10.1037/0022-3514.71.2.288

Johnson, D. E., & Gunnar, M. R. (2011). IV. Growth failure in institutionalized children. *Monographs of the Society for Research in Child Development, 76*(4, Serial No. 301), 92–126. doi:10.1111/j.1540-5834.2011.00629.x

Johnson, E. K., & Jusczyk, P. W. (2001). Word segmentation by 8-month-olds: When speech cues count more than statistics. *Journal of Memory and Language, 44,* 548–567. doi:10.1006/jmla.2000.2755

Johnson, F. A. (1993). *Dependency and Japanese socialization: Psychoanalytic and anthropological investigations into amae.* New York, NY: New York University Press.

Johnson, J., & Martin, C. (1985). Parents' beliefs and home learning environments: Effects on cognitive development. In I. E. Sigel (Ed.), *Parental belief systems: The psychological consequences for children* (pp. 25–49). Hillsdale, NJ: Erlbaum.

Johnson, J. S., & Newport, E. L. (1989). Critical period effects in second language learning: The influence of maturational state on the acquisition of English as a second language. *Cognitive Psychology, 21,* 60–99.

Johnson, K. E., & Mervis, C. B. (1994). Microgenetic analysis of first steps in children's acquisition of expertise on shorebirds. *Developmental Psychology, 30,* 418–435.

Johnson, M. H. (1992). Imprinting and the development of face recognition: From chick to man. *Current Directions in Psychological Science, 1,* 52–55. doi:10.2307/20182129

Johnson, M. H. (1998). The neural basis of cognitive development. In W. Damon (Series Ed.) & D. Kuhn & R. S. Siegler (Vol. Eds.), *Handbook of child psychology: Vol. 2. Cognition, perception, and language* (5th ed., pp. 1–49). New York, NY: Wiley.

Johnson, M. K., Beebe, T., Mortimer, J. T., & Snyder, M. (1998). Volunteerism in adolescence: A process perspective. *Journal of Research on Adolescence, 8,* 309–332. doi:10.1207/s15327795jra0803_2

Johnson, S., Slaughter, V., & Carey, S. (1998). Whose gaze will infants follow? The elicitation of gaze-following in 12-month-olds. *Developmental Science, 1,* 233–238. doi:10.1111/1467-7687.00036

Johnson, S. C. (2003). Detecting agents. *Philosophical Transactions of the Royal Society of London: Series B: Biological Sciences, 358,* 549–559. doi:10.1098/rstb.2002.1237

Johnson, S. C., Bolz, M., Carter, E., Mandsanger, J., Teichner, A., & Zettler, P. (2008). Calculating the orientation of an unfamiliar agent in infancy. *Cognitive Development, 23,* 24–37. doi:10.1016/j.cogdev.2007.09.002

Johnson, S. C., & Chen, F. S. (2011). Socioemotional information processing in human infants: From genes to subjective construals. *Emotion Review, 3,* 169–178. doi:10.1177/1754073910387945

Johnson, S. C., Dweck, C. S., & Chen, F. S. (2007). Evidence for infants' internal working models of attachment. *Psychological Science, 18,* 501–502. doi:10.1111/j.1467-9280.2007.01929.x

Johnson, S. C., & Solomon, G. E. A. (1997). Why dogs have puppies and cats have kittens: The role of birth in young children's understanding of biological origins. *Child Development, 68,* 404–419. doi:10.1111/j.1467-8624.1997.tb01948.x

Johnson, S. L., & Birch, L. L. (1994). Parents' and children's adiposity and eating style. *Pediatrics, 94,* 653–661.

Johnson, S. P. (Ed.). (2010). *Neoconstructivism: The new science of cognitive development.* New York, NY: Oxford University Press.

Johnson, S. P., Amso, D., & Slemmer, J. A. (2003). Development of object concepts in infancy: Evidence for early learning in an eye-tracking paradigm. *Proceedings of the National Academy of Sciences of the United States of America, 100,* 10568–10573. doi:10.1073/pnas.1630655100

Johnson, S. P., & Aslin, R. N. (1995). Perception of object unity in 2-month-old infants. *Developmental Psychology, 31,* 739–745. doi:10.1037/0012-1649.31.5.739

Johnson, S. P., Davidow, J., Hall-Haro, C., & Frank, M. C. (2008). Development of perceptual completion originates in information acquisition. *Developmental Psychology, 44,* 1214–1224. doi:10.1037/a0013215

Johnson, W., McGue, M., & Iacono, W. G. (2006). Genetic and environmental influences on academic achievement trajectories during adolescence. *Developmental Psychology, 42,* 514–532. doi:10.1037/0012-1649.42.3.514

Jome, L. M., & Tokar, D. M. (1998). Dimensions of masculinity and major choice traditionality. *Journal of Vocational Behavior, 52,* 120–134. doi:10.1006/jvbe.1996.1571

Jones, D. C., Abbey, B. B., & Cumberland, A. (1998). The development of display rule knowledge: Linkages with family expressiveness and social competence. *Child Development, 69,* 1209–1222.

Jones, K. L., & Smith, D. W. (1973, November 3). Recognition of the fetal alcohol syndrome in early infancy. *The Lancet, 302,* 999–1001.

Jones, M. C. (1924). A laboratory study of fear: The case of Peter. *Pedagogical Seminary, 31,* 308–315.

Jones, M. D., & Galliher, R. V. (2007). Ethnic identity and psychosocial functioning in Navajo adolescents. *Journal of Research on Adolescence, 17,* 683–696.

Jones, R. M. (1992). Ego identity and adolescent problem behavior. In G. R. Adams, T. P. Gullotta, & R. Montemayor (Eds.), *Advances in adolescent development: Vol. 4. Adolescent identity formation* (pp. 216–233). Thousand Oaks, CA: Sage.

Jones, S., & Myhill, D. (2004). "Troublesome boys" and "compliant girls": Gender identity and perceptions of achievement and underachievement. *British Journal of Sociology of Education, 25,* 547–561. doi:10.2307/4128701

Joormann, J., Cooney, R. E., Henry, M. L., & Gotlib, I. H. (2012). Neural correlates of automatic mood regulation in girls at high risk for depression. *Journal of Abnormal Psychology, 121,* 61–72. doi:10.1037/a0025294

Jordan, N. C. (2007). Do words count? Connections between mathematics and reading difficulties. In D. B. Berch & M. M. M. Mazzocco (Eds.), *Why is math so hard for some children? The nature and origins of mathematical learning difficulties and disabilities* (pp. 107–120). Baltimore, MD: Paul H. Brookes.

Jordan, N. C., Hansen, N., Fuchs, L. S., Siegler, R. S., Gersten, R., & Micklos, D. (2013). Developmental predictors of fraction concepts and procedures. *Journal of Experimental Child Psychology.* Advance online publication. doi:10.1016/j.jecp.2013.02.001

Jorgensen, M., Keiding, N., & Skakkebaek, N. E. (1991). Estimation of spermarche from longitudinal spermaturia data. *Biometrics, 47,* 177–193. doi:10.2307/2532505

Joseph, K. S., Liu, S., Rouleau, J., Lisonkova, S., Hutcheon, J. A., Sauve, R., ... & Kramer, M. S. (2012, February 12). Influence of definition based versus pragmatic birth registration on international comparisons of perinatal and infant mortality: Population based retrospective study. *BMJ 2012;344*:e746. doi:10.1136bmj.e746

Joseph K. S., Young D. C., Dodds L., O'Connell C. M., Allen V. M., Chandra S., & Allen, A. C. (2003). Changes in maternal characteristics and obstetric practice and recent increases in primary cesarean delivery. *Obstetrics & Gynecology, 102,* 791–800.

Joshi, M. S., & MacLean, M. (1994). Indian and English children's understanding of the distinction between real and apparent emotion. *Child Development, 65,* 1372–1384.

Joshi, P. T., & O'Donnell, D. A. (2003). Consequences of child exposure to war and terrorism. *Clinical Child and Family Psychology Review, 6,* 275–292.

Joussemet, M., Vitaro, F., Barker, E. D., Côté, S., Nagin, D. S., Zoccolillo, M., & Tremblay, R. E. (2008). Controlling parenting and physical aggression during elementary school. *Child Development, 79,* 411–425. doi:10.1111/j.1467-8624.2007.01133.x

Juel, C. (1988). Learning to read and write: A longitudinal study of 54 children from first through fourth grades. *Journal of Educational Psychology, 80,* 437–447. doi:10.1037/0022-0663.80.4.437

Juel, C. (1994). *Learning to read and write in one elementary school.* New York, NY: Springer-Verlag.

Julian, T. W., McKenry, P. C., & McKelvey, M. W. (1994). Cultural variations in parenting: Perceptions of Caucasian, African-American, Hispanic, and Asian-American parents. *Family Relations, 43,* 30–37.

Jung, R. E., & Haier, R. J. (2007). The Parieto-Frontal Integration Theory (P-FIT) of intelligence: Converging neuroimaging evidence. *Behavioral and Brain Sciences, 30,* 135–154. doi:10.1017/S0140525X07001185

Jusczyk, P. W. (1997). *The discovery of spoken language.* Cambridge, MA: MIT Press.

Jusczyk, P. W., & Aslin, R. N. (1995). Infants' detection of the sound patterns of words in fluent speech. *Cognitive Psychology, 29,* 1–23. doi:10.1006/cogp.1995.1010

Jusczyk, P. W., Houston, D. M., & Newsome, M. (1999). The beginnings of word segmentation in English-learning infants. *Cognitive Psychology, 39,* 159–207. doi:10.1006/cogp.1999.0716

Jussim, L., Eccles, J., & Madon, S. (1996). Social perception, social stereotypes, and teacher expectations: Accuracy and the quest for the powerful self-fulfilling prophecy. In M. P. Zanna (Ed.), *Advances in experimental social psychology* (Vol. 28, pp. 281–388). San Diego, CA: Academic Press.

Justice, L. M., Petscher, Y., Schatschneider, C., & Mashburn, A. (2011). Peer effects in preschool classrooms: Is children's language growth associated with their classmates' skills? *Child Development, 82,* 1768–1777. doi:10.1111/j.1467-8624.2011.01665.x

Juvonen, J., Nishina, A., & Graham, S. (2000). Peer harassment, psychological adjustment, and school functioning in early adolescence. *Journal of Educational Psychology, 92,* 349–359. doi:10.1037/0022-0663.92.2.349

Kagan, J. (1976). Emergent themes in human development. *American Scientist, 64,* 186–196.

Kagan, J. (1997). Temperament and the reactions to unfamiliarity. *Child Development, 68,* 139–143.

Kagan, J. (1998). Biology and the child. In W. Damon (Series Ed.) & N. Eisenberg (Vol. Ed.), *Handbook of child psychology: Vol. 3. Social, emotional, and personality development* (5th ed., pp. 177–235). Hoboken, NJ: Wiley.

Kagan, J. (2008). In defense of qualitative changes in development. *Child Development, 79,* 1606–1624. doi:10.1111/j.1467-8624.2008.01211.x

Kagan, J. (2012). The biography of behavioral inhibition. In M. R. Zentner & R. L. Shiner (Eds.), *Handbook of temperament* (pp. 69–82). New York, NY: Guilford Press.

Kagan, J., & Fox, N. A. (2006). Biology, culture, and temperamental biases. In W. Damon & R. M. Lerner (Series Eds.) & N. Eisenberg (Vol. Ed.), *Handbook of child psychology: Vol. 3. Social, emotional, and personality development* (6th ed., pp. 167–225). Hoboken, NJ: Wiley.

Kagan, J., Kearsley, R. B., & Zelazo, P. R. (1978). *Infancy: Its place in human development.* Cambridge, MA: Harvard University Press.

Kagan, J., Snidman, N., & Arcus, D. (1998). Childhood derivatives of high and low reactivity in infancy. *Child Development, 69,* 1483–1493.

Kagan, J., Snidman, N., Kahn, V., & Towsley, S. (2007). The preservation of two infant temperaments into adolescence. *Monographs of the Society for Research in Child Development, 72*(2, Serial No. 287). doi:10.1111/j.1540-5834.2007.00436.x

Kahen, V., Katz, L. F., & Gottman, J. M. (1994). Linkages between parent—child interaction and conversations of friends. *Social Development, 3,* 238–254. doi:10.1111/j.1467-9507.1994.tb00043.x

Kail, R. (1991). Developmental change in speed of processing during childhood and adolescence. *Psychological Bulletin, 109,* 490–501.

Kail, R. (1997). Processing time, imagery, and spatial memory. *Journal of Experimental Child Psychology, 64,* 67–78. doi:10.1006/jecp.1996.2337

Kail, R. V. (1984). *The development of memory in children* (2nd ed.). New York, NY: Freeman.

Kaler, S. R., & Kopp, C. B. (1990). Compliance and comprehension in very young toddlers. *Child Development, 61,* 1997–2003.

Kalil, A., Levine, J. A., & Ziol-Guest, K. M. (2005). Following in their parents' footsteps: How characteristics of parental work predict adolescents' interest in parents' jobs. In B. Schneider & L. J. Waite (Eds.), *Being together, working apart: Dual-career families and the work-life balance* (pp. 422–442). New York, NY: Cambridge University Press.

Kalil, A., & Ziol-Guest, K. M. (2005). Single mothers' employment dynamics and adolescent well-being. *Child Development, 76,* 196–211. doi:10.1111/j.1467-8624.2005.00839.x

Kalish, C. (1997). Preschoolers' understanding of mental and bodily reactions to contamination: What you don't know can hurt you, but cannot sadden you. *Developmental Psychology, 33,* 79–91.

Kalmár, M. (1996). The course of intellectual development in preterm and fullterm children: An 8-year longitudinal study. *International Journal of Behavioral Development, 19,* 491–516. doi:10.1177/016502549601900303

Kam, C.-M., Greenberg, M. T., Bierman, K. L., Coie, J. D., Dodge, K. A., Foster, M. E., ... Pinderhughes, E. E. (2011). Maternal depressive symptoms and child social preference during the early school years: Mediation by maternal warmth and child emotion regulation. *Journal of Abnormal Child Psychology, 39,* 365–377. doi:10.1007/s10802-010-9468-0

Kaminski, J., Call, J., & Fischer, J. (2004, June 11). Word learning in a domestic dog: Evidence for "fast mapping." *Science, 304,* 1682–1683.

Kanner, A. D., Feldman, S. S., Weinberger, D. A., & Ford, M. E. (1987). Uplifts, hassles, and adaptational outcomes in early adolescents. *Journal of Early Adolescence, 7,* 371–394. doi:10.1177/0272431687074002

Kaplan, H., & Dove, H. (1987). Infant development among the Ache of eastern Paraguay. *Developmental Psychology, 23,* 190–198. doi:10.1037/0012-1649.23.2.190

Karavasilis Karos, L., Howe, N., & Aquan-Assee, J. (2007). Reciprocal and complementary sibling interactions, relationship quality and socio-emotional problem solving. *Infant and Child Development, 16,* 577–596. doi:10.1002/icd.492

Karevold, E., Roysamb, E., Ystrom, E., & Mathiesen, K. S. (2009). Predictors and pathways from infancy to symptoms of anxiety and depression in early adolescence. *Developmental Psychology, 45,* 1051–1060. doi:10.1037/a0016123

Karmiloff-Smith, A., Broadbent, H., Farran, E. K., Longhi, E., D'Souza, D., Metcalfe, K., … Sansbury, F. (2012). Social cognition in Williams syndrome: Genotype/phenotype insights from partial deletion patients. *Frontiers in Psychology, 3.* Advance online publication. doi:10.3389/fpsyg.2012.00168

Karriker-Jaffe, K. J., Foshee, V. A., Ennett, S. T., & Suchindran, C. (2008). The development of aggression during adolescence: Sex differences in trajectories of physical and social aggression among youth in rural areas. *Journal of Abnormal Child Psychology, 36,* 1227–1236. doi:10.1007/s10802-008-9245-5

Kärtner, J., Keller, H., & Chaudhary, N. (2010). Cognitive and social influences on early prosocial behavior in two sociocultural contexts. *Developmental Psychology, 46,* 905–914. doi:10.1037/a0019718

Katz, L. F., Hunter, E., & Klowden, A. (2008). Intimate partner violence and children's reaction to peer provocation: The moderating role of emotion coaching. *Journal of Family Psychology, 22,* 614–621. doi:10.1037/a0012793

Katz, L. F., & Low, S. M. (2004). Marital violence, co-parenting, and family-level processes in relation to children's adjustment. *Journal of Family Psychology, 18,* 372–382. doi:10.1037/0893-3200.18.2.372

Katz, L. F., Maliken, A. C., & Stettler, N. M. (2012). Parental meta-emotion philosophy: A review of research and theoretical framework. *Child Development Perspectives, 6,* 417–422. doi:10.1111/j.1750-8606.2012.00244.x

Katz, P. A., & Ksansnak, K. R. (1994). Developmental aspects of gender role flexibility and traditionality in middle childhood and adolescence. *Developmental Psychology, 30,* 272–282. doi:10.1037/0012-1649.30.2.272

Katz, S. J., Conway, C. C., Hammen, C. L., Brennan, P. A., & Najman, J. M. (2011). Childhood social withdrawal, interpersonal impairment, and young adult depression: A mediational model. *Journal of Abnormal Child Psychology, 39,* 1227–1238. doi:10.1007/s10802-011-9537-z

Kavanaugh, R. D., & Engel, S. (1998). The development of pretense and narrative in early childhood. In O. N. Saracho & B. Spodek (Eds.), *Multiple perspectives on play in early childhood education* (pp. 80–99). Albany: State University of New York Press.

Kawabata, Y., & Crick, N. R. (2008). The role of cross-racial/ethnic friendships in social adjustment. *Developmental Psychology, 44,* 1177–1183. doi:10.1037/0012-1649.44.4.1177

Kawabata, Y., & Crick, N. R. (2011). The significance of cross-racial/ethnic friendships: Associations with peer victimization, peer support, sociometric status, and classroom diversity. *Developmental Psychology, 47,* 1763–1775. doi:10.1037/a0025399

Kawabata, Y., Crick, N. R., & Hamaguchi, Y. (2010). Forms of aggression, social-psychological adjustment, and peer victimization in a Japanese sample: The moderating role of positive and negative friendship quality. *Journal of Abnormal Child Psychology, 38,* 471–484. doi:10.1007/s10802-010-9386-1

Kaye, K. L., & Bower, T. G. R. (1994). Learning and intermodal transfer of information in newborns. *Psychological Science, 5,* 286–288. doi:10.1111/j.1467-9280.1994.tb00627.x

Kayed, N. S., Farstad, H., & van der Meer, A. L. H. (2008). Preterm infants' timing strategies to optical collisions. *Early Human Development, 84,* 381–388. doi:10.1016/j.earlhumdev.2007.10.006

Kearins, J. M. (1981). Visual spatial memory in Australian Aboriginal children of desert regions. *Cognitive Psychology, 13,* 434–460.

Keating, D. P., & Clark, L. V. (1980). Development of physical and social reasoning in adolescence. *Developmental Psychology, 16,* 23–30. doi:10.1037/0012-1649.16.1.23

Keating, D. P., & Hertzman, C. (1999). *Developmental health and the wealth of nations: Social, biological, and educational dynamics.* New York, NY: Guilford Press.

Keefe, D. H., Bulen, J. C., Arehart, K. H., & Burns, E. M. (1993). Ear-canal impedance and reflection coefficient in human infants and adults. *Journal of the Acoustical Society of America, 94,* 2617–2638.

Keen, R. (2003). Representation of objects and events: Why do infants look so smart and toddlers look so dumb? *Current Directions in Psychological Science, 12,* 79–83. doi:10.1111/1467-8721.01234

Keen, R. E., & Berthier, N. E. (2004). Continuities and discontinuities in infants' representation of objects and events. In V. K. Robert (Ed.), *Advances in child development and behavior* (Vol. 32, pp. 243–279). San Diego, CA: Elsevier.

Keenan, K., Loeber, R., Zhang, Q., Stouthamer-Loeber, M., & van Kammen, W. B. (1995). The influence of deviant peers on the development of boys' disruptive and delinquent behavior: A temporal analysis. *Development and Psychopathology, 7,* 715–726. doi:10.1017/S0954579400006805

Keenan, K., Wroblewski, K., Hipwell, A., Loeber, R., & Stouthamer-Loeber, M. (2010). Age of onset, symptom threshold, and expansion of the nosology of conduct disorder for girls. *Journal of Abnormal Psychology, 119,* 689–698. doi:10.1037/a0019346

Keil, F. C. (1979). *Semantic and conceptual development: An ontological perspective.* Cambridge, MA: Harvard University Press.

Keil, F. C. (1992). The origins of an autonomous biology. In M. R. Gunnar & M. Maratsos (Eds.), *Minnesota Symposia on Child Psychology: Vol. 25. Modularity and constraints in language and cognition* (pp. 103–137). Hillsdale, NJ: Erlbaum.

Keiley, M. K., Bates, J. E., Dodge, K. A., & Pettit, G. S. (2000). A cross-domain growth analysis: Externalizing and internalizing behaviors during 8 years of childhood. *Journal of Abnormal Child Psychology, 28,* 161–179. doi:10.1023/A:1005122814723

Kelemen, D., & DiYanni, C. (2005). Intuitions about origins: Purpose and intelligent design in children's reasoning about nature. *Journal of Cognition and Development, 6,* 3–31. doi:10.1207/s15327647jcd0601_2

Keller, P. S., Cummings, E. M., Davies, P. T., & Mitchell, P. M. (2008). Longitudinal relations between parental drinking problems, family functioning, and child adjustment. *Development and Psychopathology, 20,* 195–212. doi:10.1017/S0954579408000096

Kelley, M. L., Sanchez-Hucles, J., & Walker, R. R. (1993). Correlates of disciplinary practices in working-to middle-class African-American mothers. *Merrill-Palmer Quarterly, 39,* 252–264.

Kellman, P. J., & Arterberry, M. E. (2006). Infant visual perception. In W. Damon & R. M. Lerner (Series Eds.) & D. Kuhn & R. S. Siegler (Vol. Eds.), *Handbook of child psychology: Vol. 2. Cognition, perception, and language* (6th ed., pp. 109–160). Hoboken, NJ: Wiley.

Kellman, P. J., & Spelke, E. S. (1983). Perception of partly occluded objects in infancy. *Cognitive Psychology, 15,* 483–524. doi:10.1016/0010-0285(83)90017-8

Kellman, P. J., Spelke, E. S., & Short, K. R. (1986). Infant perception of object unity from translatory motion in depth and vertical translation. *Child Development, 57,* 72–86. doi:10.2307/1130639

Kellogg, R. T. (1994). *The psychology of writing.* New York, NY: Oxford University Press.

Kelly, D. J., Liu, S., Ge, L., Quinn, P. C., Slater, A. M., Lee, K., … Pascalis, O. (2007). Cross-race preferences for same-race faces extend beyond the African versus Caucasian contrast in 3-month-old infants. *Infancy, 11,* 87–95.

Kelly, D. J., Liu, S., Lee, K., Quinn, P. C., Pascalis, O., Slater, A. M., & Ge, L. (2009). Development of the other-race effect during infancy: Evidence toward universality? *Journal of Experimental Child Psychology, 104,* 105–114. doi:10.1016/j.jecp.2009.01.006

Kelly, D. J., Quinn, P. C., Slater, A. M., Lee, K., Ge, L., & Pascalis, O. (2007). The other-race effect develops during infancy: Evidence of perceptual narrowing. *Psychological Science, 18,* 1084–1089. doi:10.1111/j.1467-9280.2007.02029.x

Kelly, D. J., Quinn, P. C., Slater, A. M., Lee, K., Gibson, A., Smith, M., … Pascalis, O. (2005). Three-month-olds, but not newborns, prefer own-race faces. *Developmental Science, 8,* F31-F36. doi:10.1111/j.1467-7687.2005.0434a.x

Kenny, P. A., & Turkewitz, G. (1986). Effects of unusually early visual stimulation on the development of homing behavior in the rat pup. *Developmental Psychobiology, 19,* 57–66. doi:10.1002/dev.420190107

Kenrick, D. T., Trost, M. R., & Sundie, J. M. (2004). Sex roles as adaptations: An evolutionary perspective on gender differences and similarities. In A. H. Eagly, A. E. Beall, & R. J. Sternberg (Eds.), *The psychology of gender* (2nd ed., pp. 65–91). New York, NY: Guilford Press.

Kenyon, D. B., & Koerner, S. S. (2008). Post-divorce maternal disclosure and the father–adolescent relationship: Adolescent emotional autonomy and inter-reactivity as moderators. *Journal of Child and Family Studies, 17,* 791–808. doi:10.1007/s10826-008-9190-5

Kerns, K. A., Abraham, M. M., Schlegelmilch, A., & Morgan, T. A. (2007). Mother–child attachment in later middle childhood: Assessment approaches and associations with mood and emotion regulation. *Attachment and Human Development, 9,* 33–53. doi:10.1080/14616730601151441

Kerns, K. A., Klepac, L., & Cole, A. (1996). Peer relationships and preadolescents' perceptions of security in the child-mother relationship. *Developmental Psychology, 32,* 457–466. doi:10.1037/0012-1649.32.3.457

Kerr, M., Stattin, H., & Özdemir, M. (2012). Perceived parenting style and adolescent adjustment: Revisiting directions of effects and the role of parental knowledge. *Developmental Psychology, 48,* 1540–1553. doi:10.1037/a0027720

Kessen, W. (1965). *The child.* New York, NY: Wiley.

Kestenbaum, R., Farber, E. A., & Sroufe, L. A. (1989). Individual differences in empathy among preschoolers: Relation to attachment history. In N. Eisenberg (Ed.), *New Directions for Child and Adolescent Development: No. 44. Empathy and related emotional responses* (pp. 51–64). San Francisco, CA: Jossey-Bass.

Kety, S. S., Wender, P. H., Jacobsen, B., Ingraham, L. J., Jansson, L., Faber, B., & Kinney, D. K. (1994). Mental illness in the biological and adoptive relatives of schizophrenic adoptees: Replication of the Copenhagen Study in the rest of Denmark. *Archives of General Psychiatry, 51,* 442–455.

Keys, T. D., Farkas, G., Burchinal, M. R., Duncan, G. J., Vandell, D. L., Li, W., … Howes, C. (2013). Preschool center quality and school readiness: Quality effects and variation by demographic and child characteristics. *Child Development, 84,* 1171–1190. doi:10.1111/cdev.12048

Kiang, L., & Harter, S. (2008). Do pieces of the self-puzzle fit? Integrated/fragmented selves in biculturally-identified Chinese Americans. *Journal of Research in Personality, 42,* 1657–1662. doi:10.1016/j.jrp.2008.07.010

Kiang, L., Yip, T., & Fuligni, A. J. (2008). Multiple social identities and adjustment in young adults from ethnically diverse backgrounds. *Journal of Research on Adolescence, 18,* 643–670. doi:10.1111/j.1532-7795.2008.00575.x

Kiang, L., Yip, T., Gonzales-Backen, M., Witkow, M., & Fuligni, A. J. (2006). Ethnic identity and the daily psychological well-being of adolescents from Mexican and Chinese backgrounds. *Child Development, 77,* 1338–1350.

Kidd, C., Piantadosi, S. T., & Aslin, R. N. (2012). The Goldilocks effect: Human infants allocate attention to visual sequences that are neither too simple nor too complex. *PLoS ONE, 7*(5), e36399. doi:10.1371/journal.pone.0036399

Kiesner, J., Poulin, F., & Dishion, T. J. (2010). Adolescent substance use with friends: Moderating and mediating effects of parental monitoring and peer activity contexts. *Merrill Palmer Quarterly, 56,* 529–556.

Kiesner, J., Poulin, F., & Nicotra, E. (2003). Peer relations across contexts: Individual-network homophily and network inclusion in and after school. *Child Development, 74,* 1328–1343. doi:10.2307/3696181

Kiff, C. J., Lengua, L. J., & Bush, N. R. (2011). Temperament variation in sensitivity to parenting: Predicting changes in depression and anxiety. *Journal of Abnormal Child Psychology, 39,* 1199–1212.

Kiff, C. J., Lengua, L. J., & Zalewski, M. (2011). Nature and nurturing: Parenting in the context of child temperament. *Clinical Child and Family Psychology Review, 14,* 251–301. doi:10.1007/s10567-011-0093-4

Killen, M. (2007). Children's social and moral reasoning about exclusion. *Current Directions in Psychological Science, 16,* 32–36. doi:10.1111/j.1467-8721.2007.00470.x

Killen, M., & Stangor, C. (2001). Children's social reasoning about inclusion and exclusion in gender and race peer group contexts. *Child Development, 72,* 174–186. doi:10.2307/1132478

Kim, H. K., Capaldi, D. M., & Stoolmiller, M. (2003). Depressive symptoms across adolescence and young adulthood in men: Predictions from parental and contextual risk factors. *Development and Psychopathology, 15,* 469–495.

Kim, I. K., & Spelke, E. S. (1992). Infants' sensitivity to effects of gravity on visible object motion. *Journal of Experimental Psychology: Human Perception and Performance, 18,* 385–393. doi:10.1037/0096-1523.18.2.385

Kim, J.-Y., McHale, S. M., Wayne Osgood, D., & Crouter, A. C. (2006). Longitudinal course and family correlates of sibling relationships from childhood through adolescence. *Child Development, 77,* 1746–1761. doi:10.1111/j.1467-8624.2006.00971.x

Kim, K. H., Relkin, N. R., Lee, K. M., & Hirsch, J. (1997, July 10). Distinct cortical areas associated with native and second languages. *Nature, 388,* 171–174.

Kim, K. J., Conger, R. D., Lorenz, F. O., & Elder, G. H., Jr. (2001). Parent–adolescent reciprocity in negative affect and its relation to early adult social development. *Developmental Psychology, 37,* 775–790. doi:10.1037/0012-1649.37.6.775

Kindermann, T. A. (1993). Natural peer groups as contexts for individual development: The case of children's motivation in school. *Developmental Psychology, 29*, 970–977. doi:10.1037/0012-1649.29.6.970

Kindermann, T. A. (2007). Effects of naturally existing peer groups on changes in academic engagement in a cohort of sixth graders. *Child Development, 78*, 1186–1203. doi:10.1111/j.1467-8624.2007.01060.x

King, V. (2007). When children have two mothers: Relationships with nonresident mothers, stepmothers, and fathers. *Journal of Marriage and Family, 69*, 1178–1193. doi:10.1111/j.1741-3737.2007.00440.x

King, V. (2009). Stepfamily formation: Implications for adolescent ties to mothers, nonresident fathers, and stepfathers. *Journal of Marriage and Family, 71*, 954–968. doi:10.1111/j.1741-3737.2009.00646.x

Kingery, J. N., Erdley, C. A., & Marshall, K. C. (2011). Peer acceptance and friendship as predictors of early adolescents' adjustment across the middle school transition. *Merrill-Palmer Quarterly, 57*, 215–243.

Kinzler, K. D., Dupoux, E., & Spelke, E. S. (2007). The native language of social cognition. *Proceedings of the National Academy of Sciences of the United States of America, 104*, 12577–12580. doi:10.1073/pnas.0705345104

Kiriakidis, S. P., & Kavoura, A. (2010). Cyberbullying: A review of the literature on harassment through the internet and other electronic means. *Family and Community Health, 33*, 82–93. doi:10.1097/FCH. 0b013e3181d593e4

Kirkham, N. Z., Slemmer, J. A., & Johnson, S. P. (2002). Visual statistical learning in infancy: Evidence for a domain general learning mechanism. *Cognition, 83*, B35-B42. doi:10.1016/S0010-0277(02)00004-5

Kisilevsky, B. S., Fearon, I., & Muir, D. W. (1998). Fetuses differentiate vibroacoustic stimuli. *Infant Behavior and Development, 21*, 25–46.

Kisilevsky, B. S., Hains, S. M., Lee, K., Xie, X., Huang, H., Ye, H. H., … Wang, Z. (2003). Effects of experience on fetal voice recognition. *Psychological Science, 14*, 220–224.

Kiuru, N., Nurmi, J.-E., Aunola, K., & Salmela-Aro, K. (2009). Peer group homogeneity in adolescents' school adjustment varies according to peer group type and gender. *International Journal of Behavioral Development, 33*, 65–76. doi:10.1177/0165025408098014

Klahr, A. M., McGue, M., Iacono, W. G., & Burt, S. A. (2011). The association between parent–child conflict and adolescent conduct problems over time: Results from a longitudinal adoption study. *Journal of Abnormal Psychology, 120*, 46–56. doi:10.1037/a0021350

Klahr, A. M., Rueter, M. A., McGue, M., Iacono, W. G., & Burt, S. A. (2011). The relationship between parent-child conflict and adolescent antisocial behavior: Confirming shared environmental mediation. *Journal of Abnormal Child Psychology, 39*, 683–694. doi:10.1007/s10802-011-9505-7

Klahr, D. (1978). Goal formation, planning, and learning by pre-school problem solvers or: "My socks are in the dryer." In R. Siegler (Ed.), *Children's thinking: What develops?* (pp. 181–212). Hillsdale, NJ: Erlbaum.

Klima, T., & Repetti, R. L. (2008). Children's peer relations and their psychological adjustment: Differences between close friendships and the larger peer group. *Merrill-Palmer Quarterly, 54*, 151–178.

Klimes-Dougan, B., Brand, A. E., Zahn-Waxler, C., Usher, B., Hastings, P. D., Kendziora, K., & Garside, R. B. (2007). Parental emotion socialization in adolescence: Differences in sex, age and problem status. *Social Development, 16*, 326–342.

Klimes-Dougan, B., & Kopp, C. B. (1999). Children's conflict tactics with mothers: A longitudinal investigation of the toddler and preschool years. *Merrill-Palmer Quarterly, 45*, 226–241.

Klin, A., Jones, W., Schultz, R., & Volkmar, F. (2004). The enactive mind, or from actions to cognition: Lessons from autism. In U. Frith &

E. L. Hill (Eds.), *Autism, mind, and brain* (pp. 127–160). Oxford, England: Oxford University Press.

Kling, K. C., Hyde, J. S., Showers, C. J., & Buswell, B. N. (1999). Gender differences in self-esteem: A meta-analysis. *Psychological Bulletin, 125*, 470–500.

Kloos, H., & Keen, R. (2005). An exploration of toddlers' problems in a search task. *Infancy, 7*, 7–34. doi:10.1207/s15327078in0701_3

Knafo, A., & Israel, S. (2010). Genetic and environmental influences on prosocial behavior. In M. Mikulincer & P. R. Shaver (Eds.), *Prosocial motives, emotions, and behavior: The better angels of our nature* (pp. 149–167). Washington, DC: American Psychological Association.

Knafo, A., & Israel, S. (2012). Empathy, prosocial behavior, and other aspects of kindness. In M. R. Zentner & R. L. Shiner (Eds.), *Handbook of temperament* (pp. 168–182). New York, NY: Guilford Press.

Knafo, A., & Plomin, R. (2006a). Parental discipline and affection and children's prosocial behavior: Genetic and environmental links. *Journal of Personality and Social Psychology, 90*, 147–164. doi:10.1037/ 0022-3514.90.1.147

Knafo, A., & Plomin, R. (2006b). Prosocial behavior from early to middle childhood: Genetic and environmental influences on stability and change. *Developmental Psychology, 42*, 771–786. doi:10.1037/0012-1649.42.5.771

Knafo, A., Zahn-Waxler, C., Van Hulle, C., Robinson, J. L., & Rhee, S. H. (2008). The developmental origins of a disposition toward empathy: Genetic and environmental contributions. *Emotion, 8*, 737–752. doi: 10.1037/a0014179

Knecht, A., Snijders, T. A. B., Baerveldt, C., Steglich, C. E. G., & Raub, W. (2010). Friendship and delinquency: Selection and influence processes in early adolescence. *Social Development, 19*, 494–514. doi:10.1111/ j.1467-9507.2009.00564.x

Knecht, A. B., Burk, W. J., Weesie, J., & Steglich, C. (2011). Friendship and alcohol use in early adolescence: A multilevel social network approach. *Journal of Research on Adolescence, 21*, 475–487. doi:10.1111/ j.1532-7795.2010.00685.x

Knight, G. P., Cota, M. K., & Bernal, M. E. (1993). The socialization of cooperative, competitive, and individualistic preferences among Mexican American children: The mediating role of ethnic identity. *Hispanic Journal of Behavioral Sciences, 15*, 291–309. doi:10.1177/07399863930153001

Knight, G. P., Fabes, R. A., & Higgins, D. A. (1996). Concerns about drawing causal inferences from meta-analyses: An example in the study of gender differences in aggression. *Psychological Bulletin, 119*, 410–421. doi: 10.1037/0033-2909.119.3.410

Knighton, T., Brochu, P., & Gluszynski, T. (2010). *Measuring up: Canadian results of the OECD PISA study—The performance of Canada's youth in reading, mathematics and science: 2009 first results for Canadians aged 15*. Ottawa, ON: Statistics Canada, Human Resources and Skills Development Canada.

Knudsen, E. I., Heckman, J. J., Cameron, J. L., & Shonkoff, J. P. (2006). Economic, neurobiological, and behavioral perspectives on building America's future workforce. *Proceedings of the National Academy of Sciences of the United States of America, 103*, 10155–10162. doi:10.1073/pnas.0600888103

Kobak, R., Cassidy, J., & Ziv, Y. (2006). Attachment-related trauma and posttraumatic stress disorder: Implications for adult adaptation. In W. S. Rholes & J. A. Simpson (Eds.), *Adult attachment: Theory, research, and clinical implications* (pp. 388–407). New York, NY: Guilford Press.

Kobasigawa, A., Ransom, C. C., & Holland, C. J. (1980). Children's knowledge about skimming. *Alberta Journal of Educational Research, 26*, 169–182.

Kobiella, A., Grossmann, T., Reid, V. M., & Striano, T. (2008). The discrimination of angry and fearful facial expressions in 7-month-old infants: An event-related potential study. *Cognition and Emotion, 22,* 134–146.

Kochanska, G. (1993). Toward a synthesis of parental socialization and child temperament in early development of conscience. *Child Development, 64,* 325–347. doi:10.2307/1131254

Kochanska, G. (1995). Children's temperament, mothers' discipline, and security of attachment: Multiple pathways to emerging internalization. *Child Development, 66,* 597–615. doi:10.1111/j.1467-8624.1995.tb00892.x

Kochanska, G. (1997a). Multiple pathways to conscience for children with different temperaments: From toddlerhood to age 5. *Developmental Psychology, 33,* 228–240.

Kochanska, G. (1997b). Mutually responsive orientation between mothers and their young children: Implications for early socialization. *Child Development, 68,* 94–112. doi:10.2307/1131928

Kochanska, G. (2001). Emotional development in children with different attachment histories: The first three years. *Child Development, 72,* 474–490.

Kochanska, G. (2002). Committed compliance, moral self, and internalization: A mediational model. *Developmental Psychology, 38,* 339–351. doi:10.1037/0012-1649.38.3.339

Kochanska, G., & Aksan, N. (2006). Children's conscience and self-regulation. *Journal of Personality, 74,* 1587–1618. doi:10.1111/j.1467-6494.2006.00421.x

Kochanska, G., Aksan, N., Penney, S. J., & Doobay, A. F. (2007). Early positive emotionality as a heterogeneous trait: Implications for children's self-regulation. *Journal of Personality and Social Psychology, 93,* 1054–1066.

Kochanska, G., Barry, R. A., Aksan, N., & Boldt, L. J. (2008). A developmental model of maternal and child contributions to disruptive conduct: The first six years. *Journal of Child Psychology and Psychiatry, 49,* 1220–1227. doi:10.1111/j.1469-7610.2008.01932.x

Kochanska, G., Barry, R. A., Stellern, S. A., & O'Bleness, J. J. (2009). Early attachment organization moderates the parent-child mutually coercive pathway to children's antisocial conduct. *Child Development, 80,* 1288–1300. doi:10.1111/j.1467-8624.2009.01332.x

Kochanska, G., Coy, K. C., & Murray, K. T. (2001). The development of self-regulation in the first four years of life. *Child Development, 72,* 1091–1111.

Kochanska, G., Forman, D. R., Aksan, N., & Dunbar, S. B. (2005). Pathways to conscience: Early mother–child mutually responsive orientation and children's moral emotion, conduct, and cognition. *Journal of Child Psychology and Psychiatry, 46,* 19–34. doi:10.1111/j.1469-7610.2004.00348.x

Kochanska, G., Gross, J. N., Lin, M. H., & Nichols, K. E. (2002). Guilt in young children: Development, determinants, and relations with a broader system of standards. *Child Development, 73,* 461–482. doi:10.1111/1467-8624.00418

Kochanska, G., & Kim, S. (2012). Toward a new understanding of legacy of early attachments for future antisocial trajectories: Evidence from two longitudinal studies. *Development and Psychopathology, 24,* 783–806. doi:10.1017/S0954579412000375

Kochanska, G., & Kim, S. (2013). Early attachment organization with both parents and future behavior problems: From infancy to middle childhood. *Child Development, 84,* 283–296. doi:10.1111/j.1467-8624.2012.01852.x

Kochanska, G., Kim, S., Barry, R. A., & Philibert, R. A. (2011). Children's genotypes interact with maternal responsive care in predicting children's competence: Diathesis–stress or differential susceptibility? *Development and Psychopathology, 23,* 605–616. doi:10.1017/S0954579411000071

Kochanska, G., Koenig, J. L., Barry, R. A., Kim, S., & Yoon, J. E. (2010). Children's conscience during toddler and preschool years, moral self, and a competent, adaptive developmental trajectory. *Developmental Psychology, 46,* 1320–1332. doi:10.1037/a0020381

Kochanska, G., Murray, K. T., & Harlan, E. T. (2000). Effortful control in early childhood: Continuity and change, antecedents, and implications for social development. *Developmental Psychology, 36,* 220–232.

Kochanska, G., Philibert, R. A., & Barry, R. A. (2009). Interplay of genes and early mother–child relationship in the development of self-regulation from toddler to preschool age. *Journal of Child Psychology and Psychiatry, 50,* 1331–1338. doi:10.1111/j.1469-7610.2008.02050.x

Kochel, K. P., Ladd, G. W., & Rudolph, K. D. (2012). Longitudinal associations among youth depressive symptoms, peer victimization, and low peer acceptance: An interpersonal process perspective. *Child Development, 83,* 637–650.

Kochenderfer, B. J., & Ladd, G. W. (1996). Peer victimization: Cause or consequence of school maladjustment? *Child Development, 67,* 1305–1317. doi:10.2307/1131701

Koenig, M. A., & Harris, P. L. (2005). Preschoolers mistrust ignorant and inaccurate speakers. *Child Development, 76,* 1261–1277. doi:10.1111/j.1467-8624.2005.00849.x

Koenig, M. A., & Woodward, A. L. (2010). Sensitivity of 24-month-olds to the prior inaccuracy of the source: Possible mechanisms. *Developmental Psychology, 46,* 815–826. doi:10.1037/a0019664

Kohen, D. E., Leventhal, T., Dahinten, V. S., & McIntosh, C. N. (2008). Neighborhood disadvantage: Pathways of effects for young children. *Child Development, 79,* 156–169. doi:10.1111/j.1467-8624.2007.01117.x

Kohlberg, L. (1966). A cognitive-developmental analysis of children's sex-role concepts and attitudes. In E. E. Maccoby (Ed.), *The development of sex differences* (Vol. 5, pp. 82–173). Palo Alto, CA: Stanford University Press.

Kohlberg, L. (1969). Stage and sequence: The cognitive-developmental approach to socialization. In D. A. Goslin (Ed.), *Handbook of socialization theory and research* (pp. 347–480). New York, NY: Rand McNally.

Kohlberg, L. (1976). Moral stages and moralization: The cognitive-developmental approach. In T. Lickona (Ed.), *Moral development and behavior: Theory, research, and social issues* (pp. 31–53). New York, NY: Holt, Rinehart and Winston.

Kohlberg, L. (1978). Revisions in the theory and practice of moral development. In W. Damon (Ed.), *New Directions for Child and Adolescent Development: No. 2. Moral development* (Vol. 1978, pp. 83–87). San Francisco, CA: Jossey-Bass.

Kohlberg, L., & Candee, D. (1984). The relationship of moral judgment to moral action. In W. M. Kurtines & J. L. Gewirtz (Eds.), *Morality, moral behavior, and moral development* (pp. 52–73). New York, NY: Wiley.

Kolb, B. (1995). *Brain plasticity and behavior.* Mahwah, NJ: Erlbaum.

Kolb, B., & Whishaw, I.Q. (1996). *Fundamentals of human neuropsychology* (4th ed.). New York: Freeman.

Kopp, C. B. (1989). Regulation of distress and negative emotions: A developmental view. *Developmental Psychology, 25,* 343–354. doi:10.1037/0012-1649.25.3.343

Kopp, C. B. (1990). Risks in infancy: Appraising the research. *Merrill-Palmer Quarterly, 36,* 117–140.

Kopp, C. B. (1992). Emotional distress and control in young children. In R. A. Fabes & N. Eisenberg (Eds.), *New Directions for Child and Adolescent Development: No. 55. Emotion and its regulation in early development* (Vol. 1992, pp. 41–56). San Francisco, CA: Jossey-Bass.

Kopp, C. B. (2001). Self-regulation in childhood. In N. J. Smelser & P. B. Baltes (Eds.), *International encyclopedia of the social and behavioral sciences* (pp. 13862–13866). London, England: Elsevier.

Kopp, C. B., & Kaler, S. R. (1989). Risk in infancy: Origins and implications. *American Psychologist, 44,* 224–230.

Koren, G., Nulman, I., Rovet, J., Greenbaum, R., Loebstein, M., & Einarson, T. (1998). Long-term neurodevelopmental risks in children exposed in utero to cocaine. The Toronto Adoption Study. In J. A. Harvey & B. E. Kosofsky (Eds.), *Annals of the New York Academy of Sciences: Vol. 846. Cocaine: Effects on the developing brain* (pp. 306–313). New York, NY: Blackwell.

Korenman, S., Miller, J. E., & Sjaastad, J. E. (1995). Long-term poverty and child development in the United States: Results from the NLSY [Special Issue on Child Poverty, Public Practices, and Welfare Reform]. *Children and Youth Services Review, 17,* 127–155.

Korner, A. F., & Thoman, E. B. (1970). Visual alertness in neonates as evoked by maternal care. *Journal of Experimental Child Psychology, 10,* 67–78.

Kouros, C. D., Cummings, E. M., & Davies, P. T. (2010). Early trajectories of interparental conflict and externalizing problems as predictors of social competence in preadolescence. *Development and Psychopathology, 22,* 527–537.

Kovács, Á. M., & Mehler, J. (2009a). Cognitive gains in 7-month-old bilingual infants. *Proceedings of the National Academy of Sciences of the United States of America, 106,* 6556–6560. doi:10.1073/pnas.0811323106

Kovács, Á. M., & Mehler, J. (2009b, July 31). Flexible learning of multiple speech structures in bilingual infants. *Science, 325,* 611–612.

Kovacs, M., Joormann, J., & Gotlib, I. H. (2008). Emotion (dys)regulation and links to depressive disorders. *Child Development Perspectives, 2,* 149–155. doi:10.1111/j.1750-8606.2008.00057.x

Kovas, Y., & Plomin, R. (2007). Learning abilities and disabilities: Generalist genes, specialist environments. *Current Directions in Psychological Science, 16,* 284–288. doi:10.1111/j.1467-8721.2007.00521.x

Kowal, A., & Kramer, L. (1997). Children's understanding of parental differential treatment. *Child Development, 68,* 113–126. doi:10.1111/j.1467-8624.1997.tb01929.x

Kowal, A. K., Krull, J. L., & Kramer, L. (2004). How the differential treatment of siblings is linked with parent-child relationship quality. *Journal of Family Psychology, 18,* 658–665. doi:10.1037/0893-3200.18.4.658

Kowalski, R. M., Limber, S., & Agatston, P. W. (2008). *Cyber bullying: Bullying in the digital age.* Malden, MA: Blackwell.

Kramer, M. S., Aboud, F., Mironova, E., Vanilovich, I., Platt, R. W., Matush, L., ... Shapiro, S. (2008). Breastfeeding and child cognitive development: New evidence from a large randomized trial. *Archives of General Psychiatry, 65,* 578–584. doi:10.1001/archpsyc.65.5.578

Krascum, R. M., & Andrews, S. (1998). The effects of theories on children's acquisition of family-resemblance categories. *Child Development, 69,* 333–346. doi:10.1111/j.1467-8624.1998.tb06192.x

Kraut, R., Patterson, M., Lundmark, V., Kiesler, S., Mukophadhyay, T., & Scherlis, W. (1998). Internet paradox: A social technology that reduces social involvement and psychological well-being? *American Psychologist, 53,* 1017–1031. doi:10.1037/0003-066X.53.9.1017

Kreager, D. A. (2007). When it's good to be "bad": Violence and adolescent peer acceptance. *Criminology, 45,* 893–923. doi:10.1111/j.1745-9125.2007.00097.x

Kreppner, J. M., Rutter, M., Beckett, C., Castle, J., Colvert, E., Groothues, C., ... Sonuga-Barke, E. J. (2007). Normality and impairment following profound early institutional deprivation: A longitudinal follow-up into early adolescence. *Developmental Psychology, 43,* 931–946. doi:10.1037/0012-1649.43.4.93

Krevans, J., & Gibbs, J. C. (1996). Parents' use of inductive discipline: Relations to children's empathy and prosocial behavior. *Child Development, 67,* 3263–3277. doi:10.1111/j.1467-8624.1996.tb01913.x

Krishnamoorthy, J. S., Hart, C., & Jelalian, E. (2006). The epidemic of childhood obesity: Review of research and implications for public policy. *Social Policy Report, 20*(2), 1, 3–17.

Kroger, J., Martinussen, M., & Marcia, J. E. (2010). Identity status change during adolescence and young adulthood: A meta-analysis. *Journal of Adolescence, 33,* 683–698. doi:10.1016/j.adolescence.2009.11.002

Krueger, A. B. (1999). Experimental estimates of educational production functions. *Quarterly Journal of Economics, 114,* 497–532.

Krueger, R. F., South, S., Johnson, W., & Iacono, W. (2008). The heritability of personality is not always 50%: Gene-environment interactions and correlations between personality and parenting. *Journal of Personality, 76,* 1485–1522.

Kruger, A. C., & Tomasello, M. (1986). Transactive discussions with peers and adults. *Developmental Psychology, 22,* 681–685. doi:10.1037/0012-1649.22.5.681

Kuczaj, S. A., II. (1977). The acquisition of regular and irregular past tense forms. *Journal of Verbal Learning and Verbal Behavior, 16,* 589–600. doi:10.1016/S0022-5371(77)80021-2

Kudo, N., Nonaka, Y., Mizuno, N., Mizuno, K., & Okanoya, K. (2011). On-line statistical segmentation of a non-speech auditory stream in neonates as demonstrated by event-related brain potentials. *Developmental Science, 14,* 1100–1106. doi:10.1111/j.1467-7687.2011.01056.x

Kuhl, P. K., Andruski, J. E., Chistovich, I. A., Chistovich, L. A., Kozhevnikova, E. V., Ryskina, V. L., ... Lacerda, F. (1997, August 1). Cross-language analysis of phonetic units in language addressed to infants. *Science, 277,* 684–686.

Kuhl, P. K., Conboy, B. T., Coffey-Corina, S., Padden, D., Rivera-Gaxiola, M., & Nelson, T. (2008). Phonetic learning as a pathway to language: New data and native language magnet theory expanded (NLM-e). *Philosophical Transactions of the Royal Society B: Biological Sciences, 363,* 979–1000. doi:10.1098/rstb.2007.2154

Kuhl, P. K., & Meltzoff, A. N. (1982, December 10). The bimodal perception of speech in infancy. *Science, 218,* 1138–1141.

Kuhl, P. K., & Meltzoff, A. N. (1984). The intermodal representation of speech in infants. *Infant Behavior and Development, 7,* 361–381. doi:10.1016/S0163-6383(84)80050-8

Kuhl, P. K., Tsao, F.-M., & Liu, H.-M. (2003). Foreign-language experience in infancy: Effects of short-term exposure and social interaction on phonetic learning. *Proceedings of the National Academy of Sciences of the United States of America, 100,* 9096–9101. doi:10.1073/pnas.1532872100

Kuhl, P. K., Williams, K. A., Lacerda, F., Stevens, K. N., & Lindblom, B. (1992, January 31). Linguistic experience alters phonetic perception in infants by 6 months of age. *Science, 255,* 606–608.

Kuhn, D., & Franklin, S. (2006). The second decade: What develops (and how). In W. Damon & R. M. Lerner (Series Eds.) & D. Kuhn & R. Siegler (Vol. Eds.), *Handbook of child psychology: Vol. 2. Cognition, perception, and language* (6th ed., pp. 953–993). Hoboken, NJ: Wiley.

Kumru, A., Carlo, G., Mestre, M. V., & Samper, P. (2012). Prosocial moral reasoning and prosocial behavior among Turkish and Spanish adolescents. *Social Behavior and Personality, 40,* 205–214. doi:10.2224/sbp.2012.40.2.205

Kupersmidt, J. B., & Coie, J. D. (1990). Preadolescent peer status, aggression, and school adjustment as predictors of externalizing problems in adolescence. *Child Development, 61,* 1350–1362. doi:10.1111/j.1467-8624.1990.tb02866.x

Kuppens, S., Laurent, L., Heyvaert, M., & Onghena, P. (2013). Associations between parental psychological control and relational aggression in children and adolescents: A multilevel and sequential meta-analysis. *Developmental Psychology, 49,* 1697–1712. doi:10.1037/a0030740

Kuppens, P., Sheeber, L. B., Yap, M. B., Whittle, S., Simmons, J. G., & Allen, N. B. (2012). Emotional inertia prospectively predicts the onset of depressive disorder in adolescence. *Emotion, 12,* 283–289. doi:10.1037/a0025046

Kurdek, L. A. (1993). Predicting marital dissolution: A 5-year prospective longitudinal study of newlywed couples. *Journal of Personality and Social Psychology, 64,* 221–242. doi:10.1037/0022-3514.64.2.221

Kurdek, L. A., & Fine, M. A. (1993). Parent and nonparent residential family members as providers of warmth and supervision to young adolescents. *Journal of Family Psychology, 7,* 245–249. doi:10.1037/0893-3200.7.2.245

Kuryluk, A., Cohen, R., & Audley-Piotrowski, S. (2011). The role of respect in the relation of aggression to popularity. *Social Development, 20,* 703–717. doi:10.1111/j.1467-9507.2011.00613.x

Kuschel, C. (2007). Managing drug withdrawal in the newborn infant. *Seminars in Fetal and Neonatal Medicine, 12,* 127–133. doi:10.1016/j.siny.2007.01.004

Kutnick, P. (1986). The relationship of moral judgment and moral action: Kohlberg's theory, criticism and revision. In S. Modgil & C. Modgil (Eds.), *Lawrence Kohlberg: Consensus and controversy* (pp. 125–148). Philadelphia, PA: Falmer Press.

Kwon, K., Lease, A. M., & Hoffman, L. (2012). The impact of clique membership on children's social behavior and status nominations. *Social Development, 21,* 150–169. doi:10.1111/j.1467-9507.2011.00620.x

La Greca, A. M., Prinstein, M. J., & Fetter, M. D. (2001). Adolescent peer crowd affiliation: Linkages with health-risk behaviors and close friendships. *Journal of Pediatric Psychology, 26,* 131–143. doi:10.1093/jpepsy/26.3.131

LaBounty, J., Wellman, H. M., Olson, S., Lagattuta, K., & Liu, D. (2008). Mothers' and fathers' use of internal state talk with their young children. *Social Development, 17,* 757–775.

Lacourse, E., Nagin, D., Tremblay, R. E., Vitaro, F., & Claes, M. (2003). Developmental trajectories of boys' delinquent group membership and facilitation of violent behaviors during adolescence. *Development and Psychopathology, 15,* 183–197. doi:10.1017.S0954579403000105

Ladd, G. W. (1992). Themes and theories: Perspectives on processes in family-peer relationships. In R. D. Parke & G. W. Ladd (Eds.), *Family-peer relationships: Modes of linkage* (pp. 1–34). Hillsdale, NJ: Erlbaum.

Ladd, G. W., & Coleman, C. C. (1997). Children's classroom peer relationships and early school attitudes: Concurrent and longitudinal associations. *Early Education and Development, 8,* 51–66. doi:10.1207/s15566935eed0801_5

Ladd, G. W., & Golter, B. S. (1988). Parents' management of preschooler's peer relations: Is it related to children's social competence? *Developmental Psychology, 24,* 109–117. doi:10.1037/0012-1649.24.1.109

Ladd, G. W., & Hart, C. H. (1992). Creating informal play opportunities: Are parents' and preschoolers' initiations related to children's competence with peers? *Developmental Psychology, 28,* 1179–1187. doi:10.1037/0012-1649.28.6.1179

Ladd, G. W., Herald-Brown, S. L., & Reiser, M. (2008). Does chronic classroom peer rejection predict the development of children's classroom participation during the grade school years? *Child Development, 79,* 1001–1015. doi:10.1111/j.1467-8624.2008.01172.x

Ladd, G. W., & Kochenderfer, B. J. (1996). Linkages between friendship and adjustment during early school transition. In W. M. Bukowski, A. F. Newcomb, & W. W. Hartup (Eds.), *The company they keep: Friendship in childhood and adolescence* (pp. 322–345). Cambridge, UK: Cambridge University Press.

Ladd, G. W., Kochenderfer, B. J., & Coleman, C. C. (1996). Friendship quality as a predictor of young children's early school adjustment. *Child Development, 67,* 1103–1118. doi:10.1111/j.1467-8624.1996.tb01785.x

Ladd, G. W., & Troop-Gordon, W. (2003). The role of chronic peer difficulties in the development of children's psychological adjustment problems. *Child Development, 74,* 1344–1367. doi:10.1111/1467-8624.00611

LaFreniere, P. J., & Sroufe, L. A. (1985). Profiles of peer competence in the preschool: Interrelations between measures, influence of social ecology, and relation to attachment history. *Developmental Psychology, 21,* 56–69. doi:10.1037/0012-1649.21.1.56

LaFromboise, T., Coleman, H. L., & Gerton, J. (1993). Psychological impact of biculturalism: Evidence and theory. *Psychological Bulletin, 114,* 395–412. doi:10.1037/0033-2909.114.3.395

Lagacé-Séguin, D. G., & Gionet, A. (2009). Parental meta-emotion and temperament predict coping skills in early adolescence. *International Journal of Adolescence and Youth, 14,* 367–382. doi:10.1080/02673843.2009.9748015

Lagattuta, K. H. (2007). Thinking about the future because of the past: Young children's knowledge about the causes of worry and preventative decisions. *Child Development, 78,* 1492–1509.

Lagattuta, K. H., Nucci, L., & Bosacki, S. L. (2010). Bridging theory of mind and the personal domain: Children's reasoning about resistance to parental control. *Child Development, 81,* 616–635. doi:10.1111/j.1467-8624.2009.01419.x

Lagattuta, K. H., & Thompson, R. A. (2007). The development of self-conscious emotions: Cognitive processes and social influences. In J. L. Tracy, R. W. Robins, & J. P. Tangney (Eds.), *The self-conscious emotions: Theory and research* (pp. 91–113). New York, NY: Guilford Press.

Lagattuta, K. H., Wellman, H. M., & Flavell, J. H. (1997). Preschoolers' understanding of the link between thinking and feeling: Cognitive cuing and emotional change. *Child Development, 68,* 1081–1104.

Lagercrantz, H., & Slotkin, T. A. (1986, April). The "stress" of being born. *Scientific American, 254*(4), 100–107.

Lahey, B. B., Goodman, S. H., Waldman, I. D., Bird, H., Canino, G., Jensen, P., … Applegate, B. (1999). Relation of age of onset to the type and severity of child and adolescent conduct problems. *Journal of Abnormal Child Psychology, 27,* 247–260.

Lahey, B. B., Gordon, R. A., Loeber, R., Stouthamer-Loeber, M., & Farrington, D. P. (1999). Boys who join gangs: A prospective study of predictors of first gang entry. *Journal of Abnormal Child Psychology, 27,* 261–276.

Lahey, B. B., Hulle, C. A., Rathouz, P. J., Rodgers, J. L., D'Onofrio, B. M., & Waldman, I. D. (2009). Are oppositional-defiant and hyperactive–inattentive symptoms developmental precursors to conduct problems in late childhood? Genetic and environmental links. *Journal of Abnormal Child Psychology, 37,* 45–58. doi:10.1007/s10802-008-9257-1

Lahey, B. B., Schwab-Stone, M., Goodman, S. H., Waldman, I. D., Canino, G., Rathouz, P. J., … Jensen, P. S. (2000). Age and gender differences in oppositional behavior and conduct problems: A cross-sectional household study of middle childhood and adolescence. *Journal of Abnormal Psychology, 109,* 488–503. doi:10.1037/0021-843X.109.3.488

Laible, D., Eye, J., & Carlo, G. (2008). Dimensions of conscience in mid-adolescence: Links with social behavior, parenting, and temperament. *Journal of Youth and Adolescence, 37,* 875–887. doi:10.1007/s10964-008-9277-8

Laird, R. D., Pettit, G. S., Bates, J. E., & Dodge, K. A. (2003). Parents' monitoring-relevant knowledge and adolescents' delinquent behavior: Evidence of correlated developmental changes and reciprocal influences. *Child Development, 74,* 752–768. doi:10.1111/1467-8624.00566

Laird, R. D., Pettit, G. S., Mize, J., Brown, E. G., & Lindsey, E. (1994). Mother-child conversations about peers: Contributions to competence. *Family Relations, 43,* 425–432. doi:10.2307/585374

Lam, C. B., McHale, S. M., & Crouter, A. C. (2012). Parent–child shared time from middle childhood to late adolescence: Developmental course and adjustment correlates. *Child Development, 83,* 2089–2103. doi:10.1111/j.1467-8624.2012.01826.x

Lamb, M. E. (1998). Nonparental child care: Context, quality, correlates, and consequences. In W. Damon (Series Ed.) & I. E. Sigel & K. A. Renninger (Vol. Eds.), *Handbook of child psychology: Vol. 4. Child psychology in practice* (5th ed., pp. 135–210). New York, NY: Wiley.

Lamb, M. E., Hershkowitz, I., Orbach, Y., & Esplin, P. W. (2008). *Tell me what happened: Structured investigative interviews of child victims and witnesses.* Hoboken, NJ: Wiley.

Lamb, M. E., & Ketterlinus, R. D. (1991). Parental behavior, adolescent. In R. M. Lerner, A. C. Petersen, & J. Brooks-Gunn (Eds.), *Encyclopedia of adolescence* (pp. 735–738). New York, NY: Garland.

Lamb, M. E., & Lewis, C. (2013). Father-child relationships. In N. J. Cabrera & C. S. Tamis-LeMonda (Eds.), *Handbook of father involvement* (p. 119). New York, NY: Routledge.

Lamb, M. E., & Teti, D. M. (1991). Parenthood and marriage in adolescence: Associations with educational and occupational attainment. In R. M. Lerner, A. C. Petersen, & J. Brooks-Gunn (Eds.), *Encyclopedia of adolescence* (Vol. 2, pp. 742–745). New York, NY: Garland.

Lamb, M. E., Thompson, R. A., Gardner, W., & Charnov, E. L. (1985). *Infant-mother attachment: The origins and developmental significance of individual differences in Strange Situation behavior.* Hillsdale, NJ: Erlbaum.

Lamb, S., & Zakhireh, B. (1997). Toddlers' attention to the distress of peers in a daycare setting. *Early Education and Development, 8,* 105–118. doi:10.1207/s15566935eed0802_1

Lamborn, S. D., Dornbusch, S. M., & Steinberg, L. (1996). Ethnicity and community context as moderators of the relations between family decision making and adolescent adjustment. *Child Development, 67,* 283–301. doi:10.1111/j.1467-8624.1996.tb01734.x

Lamborn, S. D., Mounts, N. S., Steinberg, L., & Dornbusch, S. M. (1991). Patterns of competence and adjustment among adolescents from authoritative, authoritarian, indulgent, and neglectful families. *Child Development, 62,* 1049–1065. doi:10.1111/j.1467-8624.1991.tb01588.x

Landau, B., Smith, L. B., & Jones, S. S. (1988). The importance of shape in early lexical learning. *Cognitive Development, 3,* 299–321. doi:10.1016/0885-2014(88)90014-7

Lander, E. S. (2011, February 10). Initial impact of the sequencing of the human genome. *Nature, 470,* 187–197. doi:10.1038/nature09792

Landry, S. H., Chapieski, M. L., Richardson, M. A., Palmer, J., & Hall, S. (1990). The social competence of children born prematurely: Effects of medical complications and parent behaviors. *Child Development, 61,* 1605–1616. doi:10.1111/j.1467-8624.1990.tb02887.x

Langlois, J. H., Kalakanis, L., Rubenstein, A. J., Larson, A., Hallam, M., & Smoot, M. (2000). Maxims or myths of beauty? A meta-analytic and theoretical review. *Psychological Bulletin, 126,* 390–423. doi:10.1037/0033-2909.126.3.390

Langlois, J. H., Ritter, J. M., Casey, R. J., & Sawin, D. B. (1995). Infant attractiveness predicts maternal behaviors and attitudes. *Developmental Psychology, 31,* 464–472. doi:10.1037/0012-1649.31.3.464

Langlois, J. H., Ritter, J. M., Roggman, L. A., & Vaughn, L. S. (1991). Facial diversity and infant preferences for attractive faces. *Developmental Psychology, 27,* 79–84. doi:10.1037/0012-1649.27.1.79

Langlois, J. H., Roggman, L. A., Casey, R. J., Ritter, J. M., Rieser-Danner, L. A., & Jenkins, V. Y. (1987). Infant preferences for attractive faces: Rudiments of a stereotype? *Developmental Psychology, 23,* 363–369. doi:10.1037/0012-1649.23.3.363

Langlois, J. H., Roggman, L. A., & Rieser-Danner, L. A. (1990). Infants' differential social responses to attractive and unattractive faces. *Developmental Psychology, 26,* 153–159. doi:10.1037/0012-1649.26.1.153

Lansford, J. E., Criss, M. M., Dodge, K. A., Shaw, D. S., Pettit, G. S., & Bates, J. E. (2009). Trajectories of physical discipline: Early childhood antecedents and developmental outcomes. *Child Development, 80,* 1385–1402. doi:10.1111/j.1467-8624.2009.01340.x

Lansford, J. E., Criss, M. M., Laird, R. D., Shaw, D. S., Pettit, G. S., Bates, J. E., & Dodge, K. A. (2011). Reciprocal relations between parents' physical discipline and children's externalizing behavior during middle childhood and adolescence. *Development and Psychopathology, 23,* 225–238. doi:10.1017/S0954579410000751

Lansford, J. E., Malone, P. S., Dodge, K. A., Pettit, G. S., & Bates, J. E. (2010). Developmental cascades of peer rejection, social information processing biases, and aggression during middle childhood. *Development and Psychopathology, 22,* 593–602. doi:10.1017/S0954579410000301

Lansford, J. E., Putallaz, M., Grimes, C. L., Schiro-Osman, K. A., Kupersmidt, J. B., & Coie, J. D. (2006). Perceptions of friendship quality and observed behaviors with friends: How do sociometrically rejected, average, and popular girls differ? *Merrill-Palmer Quarterly, 52,* 694–720. doi:10.2307/23096030

Lany, J., & Saffran, J. R. (2010). From statistics to meaning: Infants' acquisition of lexical categories. *Psychological Science, 21,* 284–291. doi:10.1177/0956797609358570

Lapsley, D. K. (2006). Moral stage theory. In J. S. Melanie Killen (Ed.), *Handbook of moral development* (pp. 37–66). Mahwah, NJ: Erlbaum.

Largo, R. H., Pfister, D., Molinari, L., Kundu, S., Lipp, A., & Due, G. (1989). Significance of prenatal, perinatal and postnatal factors in the development of AGA preterm infants at five to seven years. *Developmental Medicine and Child Neurology, 31,* 440–456. doi:10.1111/j.1469-8749.1989.tb04022.x

Larkin, J., & Popaleni, K. (1994). Heterosexual courtship violence and sexual harassment: The private and public control of young women. *Feminism and Psychology, 4,* 213–227. doi:10.1177/0959353594042002

Larson, R., & Lampman-Petraitis, C. (1989). Daily emotional states as reported by children and adolescents. *Child Development, 60,* 1250–1260.

Larson, R., & Richards, M. H. (1991). Daily companionship in late childhood and early adolescence: Changing developmental contexts. *Child Development, 62,* 284–300. doi:10.1111/j.1467-8624.1991.tb01531.x

Larson, R. W., Moneta, G., Richards, M. H., & Wilson, S. (2002). Continuity, stability, and change in daily emotional experience across adolescence. *Child Development, 73,* 1151–1165.

Larson, R. W., & Verma, S. (1999). How children and adolescents spend time across the world: Work, play, and developmental opportunities. *Psychological Bulletin, 125,* 701–736. doi:10.1037/0033-2909.125.6.701

Laursen, B., Bukowski, W. M., Aunola, K., & Nurmi, J.-E. (2007). Friendship moderates prospective associations between social isolation and adjustment problems in young children. *Child Development, 78,* 1395–1404. doi:10.1111/j.1467-8624.2007.01072.x

Laursen, B., & Collins, W. A. (1994). Interpersonal conflict during adolescence. *Psychological Bulletin, 115,* 197–209. doi:10.1037/0033-2909.115.2.197

Laursen, B., Coy, K. C., & Collins, W. A. (1998). Reconsidering changes in parent-child conflict across adolescence: A meta-analysis. *Child Development, 69,* 817–832.

Laursen, B., DeLay, D., & Adams, R. E. (2010). Trajectories of perceived support in mother–adolescent relationships: The poor (quality) get poorer. *Developmental Psychology, 46,* 1792–1798. doi:10.1037/a0020679

Laursen, B., Finkelstein, B. D., & Betts, N. T. (2001). A developmental meta-analysis of peer conflict resolution. *Developmental Review, 21,* 423–449. doi:10.1006/drev.2000.0531

Laursen, B., Hafen, C. A., Kerr, M., & Stattin, H. (2012). Friend influence over adolescent problem behaviors as a function of relative peer acceptance: To be liked is to be emulated. *Journal of Abnormal Psychology, 121,* 88–94. doi:10.1037/a0024707

Lavelli, M., & Fogel, A. (2005). Developmental changes in the relationship between the infant's attention and emotion during early face-to-face communication: The 2-month transition. *Developmental Psychology, 41,* 265–280.

Lawford, H., Pratt, M. W., Hunsberger, B., & Pancer, S. M. (2005). Adolescent generativity: A longitudinal study of two possible contexts for learning concern for future generations. *Journal of Research on Adolescence, 15,* 261–273. doi:10.1111/j.1532-7795.2005.00096.x

Lazar, I., Darlington, R., Murray, H., Royce, J., & Snipper, A. (1982). Lasting effects of early education: A report from the Consortium for Longitudinal Studies. *Monographs of the Society for Research in Child Development, 47*(2/3, Serial No. 195).

Le Corre, M., & Carey, S. (2007). One, two, three, four, nothing more: An investigation of the conceptual sources of the verbal counting principles. *Cognition, 105,* 395–438. doi:10.1016/j.cognition.2006.10.005

Le Grand, R., Mondloch, C. J., Maurer, D., & Brent, H. P. (2001, April 19). Early visual experience and face processing. *Nature, 410,* 890. doi:10.1038/35073749

Le Grand, R., Mondloch, C. J., Maurer, D., & Brent, H. P. (2003). Expert face processing requires visual input to the right hemisphere during infancy. *Nature Neuroscience, 6,* 1108–1112. doi:10.1038/nn1121

Le, H.-N. (2000). Never leave your little one alone: Raising an Ifaluk child. In J. S. DeLoache & A. Gottlieb (Eds.), *A world of babies: Imagined childcare guides for seven societies* (pp. 199–220). New York, NY: Cambridge University Press.

Leadbeater, B. J., & Hoglund, W. L. G. (2009). The effects of peer victimization and physical aggression on changes in internalizing from first to third grade. *Child Development, 80,* 843–859. doi:10.1111/j.1467-8624.2009.01301.x

Leaper, C. (1991). Influence and involvement in children's discourse: Age, gender, and partner effects. *Child Development, 62,* 797–811.

Leaper, C. (1994). Exploring the consequences of gender segregation on social relationships: Social relationships in childhood, adolescence and adulthood. In C. Leaper (Ed.), *New Directions for Child and Adolescent Development: No. 65. Childhood gender segregation: Causes and consequences* (pp. 67–86). San Francisco, CA: Jossey-Bass.

Leaper, C. (2000). The social construction and socialization of gender during development. In P. H. Miller & E. K. Scholnick (Eds.), *Toward a feminist developmental psychology* (pp. 127–152). Florence, KY: Taylor & Frances/Routledge.

Leaper, C. (2002). Parenting girls and boys. In M. H. Bornstein (Ed.), *Handbook of parenting: Vol. 1. Children and parenting* (2nd ed., pp. 189–225). Mahwah, NJ: Erlbaum.

Leaper, C. (2013). Gender development during childhood. In P. D. Zelazo (Ed.), *Oxford handbook of developmental psychology: Vol. 2. Self and other* (pp. 326–376). New York, NY: Oxford University Press.

Leaper, C., & Anderson, K. J. (1997). Gender development and heterosexual romantic relationships during adolescence. In S. Shulman & W. A. Collins (Eds.), *New Directions for Child and Adolescent Development: No. 78. Romantic relationships in adolescence: Developmental perspectives* (pp. 85–103). San Francisco, CA: Jossey-Bass.

Leaper, C., Anderson, K. J., & Sanders, P. (1998). Moderators of gender effects on parents' talk to their children: A meta-analysis. *Developmental Psychology, 34,* 3–27. doi:10.1037/0012-1649.34.1.3

Leaper, C., & Ayres, M. M. (2007). A meta-analytic review of gender variations in adults' language use: Talkativeness, affiliative speech, and assertive speech. *Personality and Social Psychology Review, 11,* 328–363. doi:10.1177/1088868307302221

Leaper, C., & Bigler, R. S. (2004). Gendered language and sexist thought. *Monographs of the Society for Research in Child Development, 69,* 128–142. doi:10.1111/j.1540-5834.2004.06901012.x

Leaper, C., Breed, L., Hoffman, L., & Perlman, C. A. (2002). Variations in the gender-stereotyped content of children's television cartoons across genres. *Journal of Applied Social Psychology, 32,* 1653–1662. doi:10.1111/j.1559-1816.2002.tb02767.x

Leaper, C., & Brown, C. S. (2008). Perceived experiences with sexism among adolescent girls. *Child Development, 79,* 685–704. doi:10.1111/j.1467-8624.2008.01151.x

Leaper, C., Carson, M., Baker, C., Holliday, H., & Myers, S. (1995). Self-disclosure and listener verbal support in same-gender and cross-gender friends' conversations. *Sex Roles, 33,* 387–404. doi:10.1007/BF01954575

Leaper, C., & Gleason, J. B. (1996). The relationship of play activity and gender to parent and child sex-typed communication. *International Journal of Behavioral Development, 19,* 689–703. doi:10.1177/016502549601900401

Leaper, C., & Holliday, H. (1995). Gossip in same-gender and cross-gender friends' conversations. *Personal Relationships, 2,* 237–246. doi:10.1111/j.1475-6811.1995.tb00089.x

Leaper, C., & Robnett, R. D. (2012). Sexism. In R. J. R. Levesque (Ed.), *Encyclopedia of adolescence* (pp. 2641–2648). New York, NY: Springer.

Leaper, C., & Smith, T. E. (2004). A meta-analytic review of gender variations in children's language use: Talkativeness, affiliative speech, and assertive speech. *Developmental Psychology, 40,* 993–1027. doi:10.1037/0012-1649.40.6.993

Leaper, C., Tenenbaum, H. R., & Shaffer, T. G. (1999). Communication patterns of African American girls and boys from low-income, urban backgrounds. *Child Development, 70,* 1489–1503. doi:10.1111/1467-8624.00108

Leaper, C., & Van, S. R. (2008). Masculinity ideology, covert sexism, and perceived gender typicality in relation to young men's academic motivation and choices in college. *Psychology of Men and Masculinity, 9,* 139–153. doi: 10.1037/1524-9220.9.3.139

Leatherdale, S. T., & Ahmed, R. (2011). Screen-based sedentary behaviors among a nationally representative sample of youth: Are Canadian kids couch potatoes? *Chronic Diseases and Injuries in Canada, 31,* 141–146.

Lecanuet, J.-P., Granier-Deferre, C., & Busnel, M. C. (1995). Human fetal auditory perception. In J.-P. Lecanuet, W. P. Fifer, N. A. Krasnegor, & W. P. Smotherman (Eds.), *Fetal development: A psychobiological perspective* (pp. 239–262). Hillsdale, NJ: Erlbaum.

Lecanuet, J.-P., & Jacquet, A.-Y. (2002). Fetal responsiveness to maternal passive swinging in low heart rate variability state: Effects of stimulation direction and duration. *Developmental Psychobiology, 40,* 57–67. doi: 10.1002/dev.10013

Lee, C.-Y. S., Lee, J., & August, G. J. (2011). Financial stress, parental depressive symptoms, parenting practices, and children's externalizing problem behaviors: Underlying processes. *Family Relations, 60,* 476–490. doi:10.1111/j.1741-3729.2011.00656.x

Lee, E. H., Zhou, Q., Eisenberg, N., & Wang, Y. (2013). Bidirectional relations between temperament and parenting styles in Chinese children. *International Journal of Behavioral Development, 37,* 57–67. doi:10.1177/0165025412460795

Lee, H., & Barratt, M. S. (1993). Cognitive development of preterm low birth weight children at 5 to 8 years old. *Journal of Developmental and Behavioral Pediatrics, 14,* 242–249.

Lee, K., & Karmiloff-Smith, A. (2002). Macro- and microdevelopmental research: Assumptions, research strategies, constraints, and utilities. In N. Granott & J. Parziale (Eds.), *Microdevelopment: Transition processes in development and learning* (pp. 243–265). Cambridge, UK: Cambridge University Press.

Lee, K., & Lee, J. (2012). Self-esteem and delinquency in South Korean adolescents: Latent growth modeling. *School Psychology International, 33,* 54–68. doi:10.1177/0143034311409856

Lee, L., Howes, C., & Chamberlain, B. (2007). Ethnic heterogeneity of social networks and cross-ethnic friendships of elementary school boys and girls. *Merrill-Palmer Quarterly, 53,* 325–346.

Lee, L. C., & Zhan, G. Q. (1991). Political socialisation and parental values in the People's Republic of China. *International Journal of Behavioral Development, 14,* 337–373. doi:10.1177/016502549101400401

Leerkes, E. M., Parade, S. H., & Gudmundson, J. A. (2011). Mothers' emotional reactions to crying pose risk for subsequent attachment insecurity. *Journal of Family Psychology, 25,* 635–643. doi:10.1037/a0023654

LeFevre, J.-A., Bisanz, J., Daley, K. E., Buffone, L., Greenham, S. L., & Sadesky, G. S. (1996). Multiple routes to solution of single-digit multiplication problems. *Journal of Experimental Psychology: General, 125,* 284–306.

Leichtman, M. D., Pillemer, D. B., Wang, Q., Koreishi, A., & Han, J. J. (2000). When Baby Maisy came to school: Mothers' interview styles and preschoolers' event memories. *Cognitive Development, 15,* 99–114. doi: 10.1016/S0885-2014(00)00019-8

Leidy, M. S., Guerra, N. G., & Toro, R. I. (2010). Positive parenting, family cohesion, and child social competence among immigrant Latino families. *Journal of Family Psychology, 24,* 252–260. doi:10.1037/a0019407

Le Mare, L., & Audet, K. (2006). A longitudinal study of the physical growth and health of postinstitutionalized Romanian adoptees. *Paediatrics & Child Health, 11,* 85–91.

Lemerise, E. A., & Arsenio, W. F. (2000). An integrated model of emotion processes and cognition in social information processing. *Child Development, 71,* 107–118. doi:10.1111/1467-8624.00124

Lemery, K. S., Goldsmith, H. H., Klinnert, M. D., & Mrazek, D. A. (1999). Developmental models of infant and childhood temperament. *Developmental Psychology, 35,* 189–204.

Lemstra, M., Neudorf, C., D'arcy, C., Kunst, A., Warren, L. M., & Bennett, N. R. (2008). A systematic review of depressed mood and anxiety by SES in youth aged 10–15 years. *Canadian Journal of Public Health, 99,* 125–129.

Lengua, L. J. (2008). Anxiousness, frustration, and effortful control as moderators of the relation between parenting and adjustment in middle-childhood. *Social Development, 17,* 554–577.

Lengua, L. J., Bush, N. R., Long, A. C., Kovacs, E. A., & Trancik, A. M. (2008). Effortful control as a moderator of the relation between contextual risk factors and growth in adjustment problems. *Development and Psychopathology, 20,* 509–528.

Lengua, L. J., Honorado, E., & Bush, N. R. (2007). Contextual risk and parenting as predictors of effortful control and social competence in preschool children. *Journal of Applied Developmental Psychology, 28,* 40–55. doi: 10.1016/j.appdev.2006.10.001

Lenhart, A., Ling, R., Campbell, S., & Purcell, K. (2010). Teens and mobile phones. Retrieved from http://www.pewinternet.org/Reports/2010/Teens-and-Mobile-Phones/Summary-of-findings.aspx

Lenroot, R. K., & Giedd, J. N. (2006). Brain development in children and adolescents: Insights from anatomical magnetic resonance imaging. *Neuroscience and Biobehavioral Reviews, 30,* 718–729. doi:10.1016/j.neubiorev.2006.06.001

Leonard, L. B., Ellis Weismer, S., Miller, C. A., Francis, D. J., Tomblin, J. B., & Kail, R. V. (2007). Speed of processing, working memory, and language impairment in children. *Journal of Speech, Language, and Hearing Research, 50,* 408–428. doi:10.1044/1092-4388(2007/029)

Lerner, R. M. (1995). The limits of biological influence: Behavioral genetics as the emperor's new clothes [Review of the book *The limits of family influence: Genes, experience, and behavior,* by David C. Rowe]. *Psychological Inquiry, 6,* 145–156. doi:10.2307/1449785

Leslie, A. M. (1986). Getting development off the ground: Modularity and the infant's perception of causality. In P. van Geert (Ed.), *Theory building in developmental psychology* (pp. 406–437). New York, NY: Elsevier.

Leslie, A. M. (2000). How to acquire a representational theory of mind. In D. Sperber (Ed.), *Metarepresentations: A multidisciplinary perspective* (pp. 197–223). Oxford, UK: Oxford University Press.

Lester, B. M. (1998). The Maternal Lifestyles Study. In J. A. Harvey & B. E. Kosofsky (Eds.), *Annals of the New York Academy of Sciences: Vol. 846. Cocaine: Effects on the developing brain* (pp. 296–305). New York, NY: Blackwell.

Lester, B. M., Anderson, L. T., Boukydis, C. F., García Coll, C. T., Vohr, B., & Peucker, M. (1989). Early detection of infants at risk for later handicap through acoustic cry analysis. *Birth Defects: Original Article Series, 25,* 99–118.

Leung, M.-C. (1996). Social networks and self enhancement in Chinese children: A comparison of self reports and peer reports of group membership. *Social Development, 5,* 146–157. doi:10.1111/j.1467-9507.1996.tb00077.x

Levant, R. F. (2005). The crises of boyhood. In G. E. Good & G. R. Brooks (Eds.), *The new handbook of psychotherapy and counseling with men: A comprehensive guide to settings, problems, and treatment approaches* (Rev. and abridged ed., pp. 161–171). San Francisco, CA: Jossey-Bass.

Leve, L. D., & Fagot, B. I. (1997). Prediction of positive peer relations from observed parent–child interactions. *Social Development, 6*, 254–269. doi:10.1111/j.1467-9507.1997.tb00105.x

Leve, L. D., Pears, K. C., & Fisher, P. A. (2002). Competence in early development. In J. B. Reid, G. R. Patterson, & J. Snyder (Eds.), *Antisocial behavior in children and adolescents: A developmental analysis and model for intervention* (pp. 45–64). Washington, DC: American Psychological Association.

Levin, I. (1982). The nature and development of time concepts in children: The effects of interfering cues. In W. J. Friedman (Ed.), *Developmental psychology of time* (pp. 47–85). New York, NY: Academic Press.

Levin, I., & Aram, D. (2013). Promoting early literacy via practicing invented spelling: A comparison of different mediation routines. *Reading Research Quarterly, 48*, 221–236. doi:10.1002/rrq.48

Levin, I., & Korat, O. (1993). Sensitivity to phonological, morphological, and semantic cues in early reading and writing in Hebrew. *Merrill-Palmer Quarterly, 39*, 213–232.

Levin, I., Siegler, R. S., & Druyan, S. (1990). Misconceptions about motion: Development and training effects. *Child Development, 61*, 1544–1557. doi:10.1111/j.1467-8624.1990.tb02882.x

Levine, J. S., & Suzuki, D. T. (1993). *The secret of life: Redesigning the living world.* Boston, MA: WGBH Educational Foundation.

LeVine, R. A. (1988). Human parental care: Universal goals, cultural strategies, individual behavior. In R. A. LeVine, P. M. Miller, & M. M. West (Eds.), *New Directions for Child and Adolescent Development: No. 40. Parental behavior in diverse societies* (pp. 3–12). San Francisco, CA: Jossey-Bass.

LeVine, R. A., Dixon, S., LeVine, S., Richman, A., Keefer, C. H., Leiderman, P. H., & Brazelton, T. B. (1996). *Child care and culture: Lessons from Africa.* Cambridge, England: Cambridge University Press.

Levine, S. C., Kraus, R., Alexander, E., Suriyakham, L. W., & Huttenlocher, P. R. (2005). IQ decline following early unilateral brain injury: A longitudinal study. *Brain and Cognition, 59*, 114–123. doi:10.1016/j.bandc.2005.05.008

Levine, S. C., Ratliff, K. R., Huttenlocher, J., & Cannon, J. (2012). Early puzzle play: A predictor of preschoolers' spatial transformation skill. *Developmental Psychology, 48*, 530–542. doi:10.1037/a0025913

Lew, A. R. (2011). Looking beyond the boundaries: Time to put landmarks back on the cognitive map? *Psychological Bulletin, 137*, 484–507. doi:10.1037/a0022315

Lew-Williams, C., & Fernald, A. (2007). Young children learning Spanish make rapid use of grammatical gender in spoken word recognition. *Psychological Science, 18*, 193–198. doi:10.1111/j.1467-9280.2007.01871.x

Lewinsohn, P. M., Joiner, T. E., Jr., & Rohde, P. (2001). Evaluation of cognitive diathesis-stress models in predicting major depressive disorder in adolescents. *Journal of Abnormal Psychology, 110*, 203–215.

Lewis, E. E., Dozier, M., Ackerman, J., & Sepulveda-Kozakowski, S. (2007). The effect of placement instability on adopted children's inhibitory control abilities and oppositional behavior. *Developmental Psychology, 43*, 1415–1427. doi:10.1037/0012-1649.43.6.1415

Lewis, M. (1992). *Shame: The exposed self.* New York, NY: Free Press.

Lewis, M. (1995). Embarrassment: The emotion of self-exposure and evaluation. In J. P. Tangney & K. W. Fischer (Eds.), *Self-conscious emotions: The psychology of shame, guilt, embarrassment, and pride* (pp. 198–218). New York, NY: Guilford Press.

Lewis, M. (1998). Emotional competence and development. In D. Pushkar, W. M. Bukowski, A. E. Schwartzman, D. M. Stack, & D. R. White (Eds.), *Improving competence across the lifespan: Building interventions based on theory and research* (pp. 27–36). New York, NY: Plenum Press.

Lewis, M. (2011). Problems in the study of infant emotional development. *Emotion Review, 3*, 131–137.

Lewis, M., Alessandri, S. M., & Sullivan, M. W. (1990). Violation of expectancy, loss of control, and anger expressions in young infants. *Developmental Psychology, 26*, 745–751.

Lewis, M., Alessandri, S. M., & Sullivan, M. W. (1992). Differences in shame and pride as a function of children's gender and task difficulty. *Child Development, 63*, 630–638.

Lewis, M., & Brooks-Gunn, J. (1979). *Social cognition and the acquisition of self.* New York, NY: Plenum Press.

Lewis, M., Feiring, C., & Rosenthal, S. (2000). Attachment over time. *Child Development, 71*, 707–720. doi:10.1111/1467-8624.00180

Lewis, M. D. (2005). Bridging emotion theory and neurobiology through dynamic systems modeling. *Behavioral and Brain Sciences, 28*, 169–193.

Lewkowicz, D. J. (2004). Perception of serial order in infants. *Developmental Science, 7*, 175–184.

Lewkowicz, D. J., & Ghazanfar, A. A. (2006). The decline of cross-species intersensory perception in human infants. *Proceedings of the National Academy of Sciences of the United States of America, 103*, 6771–6774. doi:10.1073/pnas.0602027103

Lewkowicz, D. J., Karmel, B. Z., & Gardner, J. M. (1998). Effects of prenatal cocaine exposure on responsiveness to multimodal information in infants between 4 and 10 months of age. In J. A. Harvey & B. E. Kosofsky (Eds.), *Annals of the New York Academy of Sciences: Vol. 846. Cocaine: Effects on the developing brain* (pp. 408–411). New York, NY: Blackwell.

Lewontin, R. C. (1982). *Human diversity.* New York, NY: Scientific American Library.

Li, Y., Putallaz, M., & Su, Y. (2011). Interparental conflict styles and parenting behaviors: Associations with overt and relational aggression among Chinese children. *Merrill-Palmer Quarterly, 57*, 402–428.

Liaw, F.-R., & Brooks-Gunn, J. (1993). Patterns of low-birth-weight children's cognitive development. *Developmental Psychology, 29*, 1024–1035. doi:10.1037/0012-1649.29.6.1024

Liben, L. S., & Bigler, R. S. (1987). Children's gender schemata. In L. S. Liben & M. L. Signorella (Eds.), *New Directions for Child and Adolescent Development: No. 38. Children's gender schemata* (Vol. 1987, pp. 89–105). San Francisco, CA: Jossey-Bass.

Liben, L. S., & Bigler, R. S. (2002). The developmental course of gender differentiation: Conceptualizing, measuring, and evaluating constructs and pathways. *Monographs of the Society for Research in Child Development, 67*(2, Serial No. 269), i-183. doi:10.2307/3181530

Liben, L. S., & Myers, L. J. (2007). Developmental changes in children's understanding of maps: What, when, and how. In J. M. Plumert & J. P. Spence (Eds.), *The emerging spatial mind* (pp. 193–218). Oxford, England: Oxford University Press.

Liben, L. S., & Signorella, M. L. (1993). Gender-schematic processing in children: The role of initial interpretations of stimuli. *Developmental Psychology, 29*, 141–149. doi:10.1037/0012-1649.29.1.141

Libertus, K., & Needham, A. (2010). Teach to reach: The effects of active vs. passive reaching experiences on action and perception. *Vision Research, 50*, 2750–2757. doi:10.1016/j.visres.2010.09.001

Libertus, K., & Needham, A. (2011). Reaching experience increases face preference in 3-month-old infants. *Developmental Science, 14,* 1355–1364. doi:10.1111/j.1467-7687.2011.01084.x

Lichter, D. T., & Landale, N. S. (1995). Parental work, family structure, and poverty among Latino children. *Journal of Marriage and the Family, 57,* 346–354.

Lickliter, R. (1995). Embryonic sensory experience and intersensory development in precocial birds. In J.-P. Lecanuet, W. P. Fifer, N. A. Krasnegor, & W. P. Smotherman (Eds.), *Fetal development: A psychobiological perspective* (pp. 281–294). Hillsdale, NJ: Erlbaum.

Lickliter, R., & Honeycutt, H. (2003). Developmental dynamics: Toward a biologically plausible evolutionary psychology. *Psychological Bulletin, 129,* 819–835. doi:10.1037/0033-2909.129.6.819

Lickona, T. (1976). Research on Piaget's theory of moral development. In T. Lickona (Ed.), *Moral development and behavior: Theory, research, and social issues* (pp. 219–240). New York, NY: Holt, Rinehart and Winston.

Liew, J., Eisenberg, N., Spinrad, T. L., Eggum, N. D., Haugen, R. G., Kupfer, A., … Baham, M. E. (2011). Physiological regulation and fearfulness as predictors of young children's empathy-related reactions. *Social Development, 20,* 111–134. doi:10.1111/j.1467-9507.2010.00575.x

Lillard, A. (2006). Children's play as cultural interpretation. In A. Göncü & S. Gaskins (Eds.), *Play and development: Evolutionary, sociocultural, and functional perspectives* (pp. 131–154). Mahwah, NJ: Erlbaum.

Lillard, A. (2007). Guided participation: How mothers structure and children understand pretend play. In A. Göncü & S. Gaskins (Eds.), *Play and development: Evolutionary, sociocultural, and functional perspectives* (pp. 131–154). New York, NY: Erlbaum.

Lillard, A. S., & Flavell, J. H. (1992). Children's understanding of different mental states. *Developmental Psychology, 28,* 626–634.

Lillard, A. S., Lerner, M. D., Hopkins, E. J., Dore, R. A., Smith, E. D., & Palmquist, C. M. (2013). The impact of pretend play on children's development: A review of the evidence. *Psychological Bulletin, 139,* 1–34. doi:10.1037/a0029321

Limber, J. (1973). The genesis of complex sentences. In T. Moore (Ed.), *Cognitive development and the acquisition of language* (pp. 169–185). New York, NY: Academic Press.

Linares, L. O., Heeren, T., Bronfman, E., Zuckerman, B., Augustyn, M., & Tronick, E. (2001). A mediational model for the impact of exposure to community violence on early child behavior problems. *Child Development, 72,* 639–652. doi:10.1111/1467-8624.00302

Lindahl, K. M., Malik, N. M., Kaczynski, K., & Simons, J. S. (2004). Couple power dynamics, systemic family functioning, and child adjustment: A test of a mediational model in a multiethnic sample. *Development and Psychopathology, 16,* 609–630.

Lindberg, M. (1991). A taxonomy of suggestibility and eyewitness memory: Age, memory process, and focus of analysis. In J. Doris (Ed.), *The suggestibility of children's recollection: Implications for eyewitness memory* (pp. 47–55). Washington, DC: American Psychological Association.

Lindberg, M. A. (1980). Is knowledge base development a necessary and sufficient condition for memory development? *Journal of Experimental Child Psychology, 30,* 401–410. doi:10.1016/0022-0965(80)90046-6

Lindberg S. M., Hyde J. S., Petersen, J. L., & Linn, M. C. (2010). New trends in gender and mathematics performance: A meta-analysis. *Psychological Bulletin, 10,* 1123–1135.

Lindell, S. G. (1988). Education for childbirth: A time for change. *Journal of Obstetric, Gynecologic, and Neonatal Nursing, 17,* 108–112.

Lindquist, K. A., Siegel, E. H., Quigley, K. S., & Barrett, L. F. (2013). The hundred-year emotion war: Are emotions natural kinds or psychological constructions? Comment on Lench, Flores, and Bench (2011). *Psychological Bulletin, 139,* 255–263. doi:10.1037/a0029038

Linkletter, A. (1957). *Kids say the darndest things!* Englewood Cliffs, NJ: Prentice-Hall.

Linn, M. C., & Petersen, A. C. (1985). Emergence and characterization of sex differences in spatial ability: A meta-analysis. *Child Development, 56,* 1479–1498. doi:10.2307/1130467

Lins-Dyer, M. T., & Nucci, L. (2007). The impact of social class and social cognitive domain on northeastern Brazilian mothers' and daughters' conceptions of parental control. *International Journal of Behavioral Development, 31,* 105–114. doi:10.1177/0165025407073577

Lipman, E. L., Georgiades, K., & Boyle, M. H. (2011). Young adult outcomes of children born to teen mothers: Effects of being born during their teen or later years. *Journal of the American Academy of Child and Adolescent Psychiatry, 50,* 232–241.e4. doi:10.1016/j.jaac.2010.12.007

Lipnowski, S., & LeBlanc, C. M. A. (2012). *Healthy active living: Physical activity guidelines for children and adolescents.* Retrieved from http://www.cps.ca/en/documents/position/physical-activity-guidelines

Lipsitt, L. P. (2003). Crib death: A biobehavioral phenomenon? *Current Directions in Psychological Science, 12,* 164–170. doi:10.1111/1467-8721.01253

Lipton, J. S., & Spelke, E. S. (2003). Origins of number sense large-number discrimination in human infants. *Psychological Science, 14,* 396–401.

Little, J. F., Hepper, P. G., & Dornan, J. C. (2002). Maternal alcohol consumption during pregnancy and fetal startle behaviour. *Physiology and Behavior, 76,* 691–694.

Little, S. A., & Garber, J. (1995). Aggression, depression, and stressful life events predicting peer rejection in children. *Development and Psychopathology, 7,* 845–856. doi:10.1017/S0954579400006878

Litwack, S. D., Wargo Aikins, J., & Cillessen, A. H. N. (2012). The distinct roles of sociometric and perceived popularity in friendship: Implications for adolescent depressive affect and self-esteem. *Journal of Early Adolescence, 32,* 226–251. doi:10.1177/0272431610387142

Llewellyn, C. H., van Jaarsveld, C. H., Boniface, D., Carnell, S., & Wardle, J. (2008). Eating rate is a heritable phenotype related to weight in children. *American Journal of Clinical Nutrition, 88,* 1560–1566. doi:10.3945/ajcn.2008.26175

Lobo, M. A., Galloway, J. C., & Savelsbergh, G. J. (2004). General and task-related experiences affect early object interaction. *Child Development, 75,* 1268–1281. doi:10.1111/j.1467-8624.2004.00738.x

Lockman, J. J., Ashmead, D. H., & Bushnell, E. W. (1984). The development of anticipatory hand orientation during infancy. *Journal of Experimental Child Psychology, 37,* 176–186. doi:10.1016/0022-0965(84)90065-1

Lockman, J. J., & McHale, J. P. (1989). Object manipulation in infancy: Developmental and contextual determinants. In J. J. Lockman & N. L. Hazen (Eds.), *Action in social context: Perspectives on early development* (pp. 129–167). New York, NY: Plenum Press.

Lockman, J. J., & Thelen, E. (1993). Developmental biodynamics: Brain, body, behavior connections. *Child Development, 64,* 953–959. doi:10.1111/j.1467-8624.1993.tb04181.x

Loeber, R. (1982). The stability of antisocial and delinquent child behavior: A review. *Child Development, 53,* 1431–1446. doi:10.2307/1130070

Loeber, R., & Burke, J. D. (2011). Developmental pathways in juvenile externalizing and internalizing problems. *Journal of Research on Adolescence, 21,* 34–46. doi:10.1111/j.1532-7795.2010.00713.x

Loeber, R., & Schmaling, K. B. (1985). Empirical evidence for overt and covert patterns of antisocial conduct problems: A metaanalysis. *Journal of Abnormal Child Psychology, 13,* 337–353. doi:10.1007/BF00910652

Loeber, R., & Stouthamer-Loeber, M. (1986). Family factors as correlates and predictors of juvenile conduct problems and delinquency. In M. Tonry & N. Morris (Eds.), *Crime and justice* (Vol. 7, pp. 29–149). Chicago, IL: University of Chicago Press.

Loewy, J., Stewart, K., Dassler, A.-M., Telsey, A., & Homel, P. (2013). The effects of music therapy on vital signs, feeding, and sleep in premature infants. *Pediatrics, 131,* 902–918. doi:10.1542/peds.2012-1367

Lonardo, R. A., Giordano, P. C., Longmore, M. A., & Manning, W. D. (2009). Parents, friends, and romantic partners: Enmeshment in deviant networks and adolescent delinquency involvement. *Journal of Youth and Adolescence, 38,* 367–383. doi:10.1007/s10964-008-9333-4

Loomis, J. M., Klatzky, R. L., Golledge, R. G., Cicinelli, J. G., Pellegrino, J. W., & Fry, P. A. (1993). Nonvisual navigation by blind and sighted: Assessment of path integration ability. *Journal of Experimental Psychology: General, 122,* 73–91.

Lorenz, K. (1935). Der Kumpan in der Umwelt des Vogels. Der Artgenosse als auslosendes Moment sozialer Verhaltungsweisen. [The companion in the bird's world. The fellow-member of the species as releasing factor of social behavior.]. *Journal fur Ornithologie. Beiblatt. (Leipzig), 83,* 137–213.

Lorenz, K. (1952). *King Solomon's ring: New light on animal ways.* New York, NY: Crowell.

Lotze, G. M., Ravindran, N., & Myers, B. J. (2010). Moral emotions, emotion self-regulation, callous-unemotional traits, and problem behavior in children of incarcerated mothers. *Journal of Child and Family Studies, 19,* 702–713. doi:10.1007/s10826-010-9358-7

Loukas, A., Prelow, H. M., Suizzo, M.-A., & Allua, S. (2008). Mothering and peer associations mediate cumulative risk effects for Latino youth. *Journal of Marriage and Family, 70,* 76–85. doi:10.1111/j.1741-3737.2007.00462.x

Lourenco, S. F., & Longo, M. R. (2010). General magnitude representation in human infants. *Psychological Science, 21,* 873–881. doi:10.1177/0956797610370158

Love, J. M., Harrison, L., Sagi-Schwartz, A., van IJzendoorn, M. H., Ross, C., Ungerer, J. A., ... Chazan-Cohen, R. (2003). Child care quality matters: How conclusions may vary with context. *Child Development, 74,* 1021–1033. doi:10.1111/1467-8624.00584

Lovejoy, M. C., Graczyk, P. A., O'Hare, E., & Neuman, G. (2000). Maternal depression and parenting behavior: A meta-analytic review. *Clinical Psychology Review, 20,* 561–592.

Lovett, M. W., Borden, S. L., DeLuca, T., Lacerenza, L., Benson, N. J., & Brackstone, D. (1994). Treating the core deficits of developmental dyslexia: Evidence of transfer of learning after phonologically- and strategy-based reading training programs. *Developmental Psychology, 30,* 805–822.

Low, S., Shortt, J. W., & Snyder, J. (2012). Sibling influences on adolescent substance use: The role of modeling, collusion, and conflict. *Development and Psychopathology, 24,* 287–300. doi:10.1017/S0954579411000836

Lozoff, B. (1989). Nutrition and behavior. *American Psychologist, 44,* 231–236.

Lubinski, D., & Benbow, C. P. (2006). Study of mathematically precocious youth after 35 years: Uncovering antecedents for the development of math-science expertise. *Perspectives on Psychological Science, 1,* 316–345. doi:10.1111/j.1745-6916.2006.00019.x

Lubinski, D., Benbow, C. P., Webb, R. M., & Bleske-Rechek, A. (2006). Tracking exceptional human capital over two decades. *Psychological Science, 17,* 194–199. doi:10.1111/j.1467-9280.2006.01685.x

Lubinski, D., & Humphreys, L. G. (1997). Incorporating general intelligence into epidemiology and the social sciences. *Intelligence, 24,* 159–201.

Lubinski, D., Webb, R. M., Morelock, M. J., & Benbow, C. P. (2001). Top 1 in 10,000: A 10-year follow-up of the profoundly gifted. *Journal of Applied Psychology, 86,* 718–729.

Luby, J. L. (2010). Preschool depression: The importance of identification of depression early in development. *Current Directions in Psychological Science, 19,* 91–95. doi:10.1177/0963721410364493

Lucas-Thompson, R., & Clarke-Stewart, K. A. (2007). Forecasting friendship: How marital quality, maternal mood, and attachment security are linked to children's peer relationships. *Journal of Applied Developmental Psychology, 28,* 499–514. doi:10.1016/j.appdev.2007.06.004

Lucassen, N., Tharner, A., van IJzendoorn, M. H., Bakermans-Kranenburg, M. J., Volling, B. L., Verhulst, F. C., ... Tiemeier, H. (2011). The association between paternal sensitivity and infant–father attachment security: A meta-analysis of three decades of research. *Journal of Family Psychology, 25,* 986–992. doi:10.1037/a0025855

Luciana, M., & Collins, P. F. (2012). Incentive motivation, cognitive control, and the adolescent brain: Is it time for a paradigm shift? *Child Development Perspectives, 6,* 392–399. doi:10.1111/j.1750-8606.2012.00252.x

Luciana, M., Wahlstrom, D., Porter, J. N., & Collins, P. F. (2012). Dopaminergic modulation of incentive motivation in adolescence: Age-related changes in signaling, individual differences, and implications for the development of self-regulation. *Developmental Psychology, 48,* 844–861. doi:10.1037/a0027432

Luebbe, A. M., Kiel, E. J., & Buss, K. A. (2011). Toddlers' context-varying emotions, maternal responses to emotions, and internalizing behaviors. *Emotion, 11,* 697–703.

Luengo Kanacri, B. P., Pastorelli, C., Eisenberg, N., Zuffianò, A., & Caprara, G. V. (2013). The development of prosociality from adolescence to early adulthood: The role of effortful control. *Journal of Personality, 81,* 302–312. doi:10.1111/jopy.12001

Luijk, M. P. C. M., Saridjan, N., Tharner, A., van IJzendoorn, M. H., Bakermans-Kranenburg, M. J., Jaddoe, V. W. V., ... Tiemeier, H. (2010). Attachment, depression, and cortisol: Deviant patterns in insecure-resistant and disorganized infants. *Developmental Psychobiology, 52,* 441–452. doi:10.1002/dev.20446

Luna, B., Garver, K. E., Urban, T. A., Lazar, N. A., & Sweeney, J. A. (2004). Maturation of cognitive processes from late childhood to adulthood. *Child Development, 75,* 1357–1372. doi:10.1111/j.1467-8624.2004.00745.x

Lunkenheimer, E. S., Shields, A. M., & Cortina, K. S. (2007). Parental emotion coaching and dismissing in family interaction. *Social Development, 16,* 232–248.

Luntz, B. K., & Widom, C. S. (1994). Antisocial personality disorder in abused and neglected children grown up. *American Journal of Psychiatry, 151,* 670–674.

Luo, Z.-C., Wilkins, R., Heaman, M., Smylie, J., Martens, P. J., McHugh, N. G. L., ... Fraser, W. D. (2012). Birth outcomes and infant mortality among First Nations Inuit, and non-Indigenous women by northern versus southern residence, Quebec. *Journal of Epidemiology & Community Health, 66,* 328–333. doi:10.1136/jech.2009.092619

Luo, Z.-C., Wilkins, R., Kramer, M. S. (2006). Effect of neighbourhood income and maternal education on birth outcomes: A population-based study. *Canadian Medical Association Journal, 174*, 1415–1420. doi:10.1503/cmaj.051096

Luster, T., & McAdoo, H. (1996). Family and child influences on educational attainment: A secondary analysis of the High/Scope Perry Preschool data. *Developmental Psychology, 32*, 26–39. doi:10.1037/0012-1649.32.1.26

Luster, T., Rhoades, K., & Haas, B. (1989). The relation between parental values and parenting behavior: A test of the Kohn hypothesis. *Journal of Marriage and the Family, 51*, 139–147.

Lutchmaya, S., & Baron-Cohen, S. (2002). Human sex differences in social and non-social looking preferences, at 12 months of age. *Infant Behavior and Development, 25*, 319–325. doi:10.1016/S0163-6383(02)00095-4

Luthar, S. S. (1999). *Poverty and children's adjustment.* Thousand Oaks, CA: Sage.

Luthar, S. S. (2003). The culture of affluence: Psychological costs of material wealth. *Child Development, 74*, 1581–1593. doi:10.1046/j.1467-8624.2003.00625.x

Luthar, S. S. (2006). Resilience in development: A synthesis of research across five decades. In D. Cicchetti & D. J. Cohen (Eds.), *Developmental psychopathology: Vol. 3. Risk, disorder, and adaptation* (2nd ed., pp. 739–795). Hoboken, NJ: Wiley.

Luthar, S. S., & Becker, B. E. (2002). Privileged but pressured? A study of affluent youth. *Child Development, 73*, 1593–1610. doi:10.1111/1467-8624.00492

Luthar, S. S., & Latendresse, S. J. (2005). Children of the affluent: Challenges to well-being. *Current Directions in Psychological Science, 14*, 49–53. doi:10.1111/j.0963-7214.2005.00333.x

Luxen, M. F. (2007). Sex differences, evolutionary psychology and biosocial theory: Biosocial theory is no alternative. *Theory and Psychology, 17*, 383–394. doi:10.1177/0959354307077289

Luyckx, K., Goossens, L., & Soenens, B. (2006). A developmental contextual perspective on identity construction in emerging adulthood: Change dynamics in commitment formation and commitment evaluation. *Developmental Psychology, 42*, 366–380. doi:10.1037/0012-1649.42.2.366

Luyckx, K., Goossens, L., Soenens, B., & Beyers, W. (2006). Unpacking commitment and exploration: Preliminary validation of an integrative model of late adolescent identity formation. *Journal of Adolescence, 29*, 361–378. doi:10.1016/j.adolescence.2005.03.008

Luyckx, K., Goossens, L., Soenens, B., Beyers, W., & Vansteenkiste, M. (2005). Identity statuses based on 4 rather than 2 identity dimensions: Extending and refining Marcia's paradigm. *Journal of Youth and Adolescence, 34*, 605–618. doi:10.1007/s10964-005-8949-x

Luyckx, K., Schwartz, S. J., Goossens, L., Soenens, B., & Beyers, W. (2008). Developmental typologies of identity formation and adjustment in female emerging adults: A latent class growth analysis approach. *Journal of Research on Adolescence, 18*, 595–619. doi:10.1111/j.1532-7795.2008.00573.x

Luyckx, K., Soenens, B., & Goossens, L. (2006). The personality-identity interplay in emerging adult women: Convergent findings from complementary analyses. *European Journal of Personality, 20*, 195–215.

Luyckx, K., Soenens, B., Vansteenkiste, M., Goossens, L., & Berzonsky, M. D. (2007). Parental psychological control and dimensions of identity formation in emerging adulthood. *Journal of Family Psychology, 21*, 546–550. doi:10.1037/0893-3200.21.3.546

Lynam, D. R. (1996). Early identification of chronic offenders: Who is the fledgling psychopath? *Psychological Bulletin, 120*, 209–234. doi:10.1037/0033-2909.120.2.209

Lynch, M., & Cicchetti, D. (1998). An ecological-transactional analysis of children and contexts: The longitudinal interplay among child maltreatment, community violence, and children's symptomatology. *Development and Psychopathology, 10*, 235–257. doi:10.1017/S095457949800159X

Lynn, R. (2009). What has caused the Flynn effect? Secular increases in the Development Quotients of infants. *Intelligence, 37*, 16–24.

Lyon, G. R. (1995). Toward a definition of dyslexia. *Annals of Dyslexia, 45*, 1–27.

Lyons, I. M., & Beilock, S. L. (2012). When math hurts: Math anxiety predicts pain network activation in anticipation of doing math. *PLoS ONE, 7*, e48076. doi:10.1371/journal.pone.0048076

Ma, W., Golinkoff, R. M., Houston, D. M., & Hirsh-Pasek, K. (2011). Word learning in infant- and adult-directed speech. *Language Learning and Development, 7*, 185–201. doi:10.1080/15475441.2011.579839

Mabbott, D. J., & Bisanz, J. (2003). Developmental change and individual differences in children's multiplication. *Child Development, 74*, 1091–1107.

MacBrayer, E. K., Milich, R., & Hundley, M. (2003). Attributional biases in aggressive children and their mothers. *Journal of Abnormal Psychology, 112*, 698–708. doi:10.1037/0021-843X.112.4.598

Macchi Cassia, V., Kuefner, D., Westerlund, A., & Nelson, C. A. (2006). A behavioural and ERP investigation of 3-month-olds' face preferences. *Neuropsychologia, 44*, 2113–2125. doi:10.1016/j.neuropsychologia.2005.11.014

Macchi Cassia, V., Turati, C., & Simion, F. (2004). Can a nonspecific bias toward top-heavy patterns explain newborns' face preference? *Psychological Science, 15*, 379–383. doi:10.1111/j.0956-7976.2004.00688.x

Maccoby, E. E. (1998). *The two sexes: Growing up apart, coming together.* Cambridge, MA: Harvard University Press.

Maccoby, E. E. (2000). Perspectives on gender development. *International Journal of Behavioral Development, 24*, 398–406. doi:10.1080/016502500750037946

Maccoby, E. E., Buchanan, C. M., Mnookin, R. H., & Dornbusch, S. M. (1993). Postdivorce roles of mothers and fathers in the lives of their children. *Journal of Family Psychology, 7*, 24–38. doi:10.1037/0893-3200.7.1.24

Maccoby, E. E., & Martin, J. A. (1983). Socialization in the context of the family: Parent-child interaction. In P. H. Mussen (Series Ed.) & E. M. Hetherington (Vol. Ed.), *Handbook of child psychology: Vol. 4. Socialization, personality, and social development* (4th ed., pp. 1–101). New York, NY: Wiley.

MacDonald, G. W., & Cornwall, A. (1995). The relationship between phonological awareness and reading and spelling achievement eleven years later. *Journal of Learning Disabilities, 28*, 523–527.

MacDonald, K., & MacDonald, T. M. (2010). The peptide that binds: A systematic review of oxytocin and its prosocial effects in humans. *Harvard Review of Psychiatry, 18*, 1–21. doi:10.3109/10673220903523615

MacEvoy, J. P., & Asher, S. R. (2012). When friends disappoint: Boys' and girls' responses to transgressions of friendship expectations. *Child Development, 83*, 104–119. doi:10.1111/j.1467-8624.2011.01685.x

Macfarlane, A. (2008). Olfaction in the development of social preferences in the human neonate. In R. Porter & M. O'Connor (Eds.), *Ciba Foundation symposium: No. 33. Parent-infant interaction* (pp. 103–117). doi:10.1002/9780470720158.ch7

MacKenzie, H., Graham, S. A., & Curtin, S. (2011). Twelve-month-olds privilege words over other linguistic sounds in an associative learning task. *Developmental Science, 14*, 249–255.

Maclean, M., Bryant, P., & Bradley, L. (1987). Rhymes, nursery rhymes, and reading in early childhood. *Merrill-Palmer Quarterly, 33,* 255–281.

Macmillan, R., McMorris, B. J., & Kruttschnitt, C. (2004). Linked lives: Stability and change in maternal circumstances and trajectories of antisocial behavior in children. *Child Development, 75,* 205–220. doi:10.1111/j.1467-8624.2004.00664.x

MacPhee, D., Fritz, J., & Miller-Heyl, J. (1996). Ethnic variations in personal social networks and parenting. *Child Development, 67,* 3278–3295. doi:10.1111/j.1467-8624.1996.tb01914.x

Madigan, S., Moran, G., & Pederson, D. R. (2006). Unresolved states of mind, disorganized attachment relationships, and disrupted interactions of adolescent mothers and their infants. *Developmental Psychology, 42,* 293–304. doi:10.1037/0012-1649.42.2.293

Madigan, S., Moran, G., Schuengel, C., Pederson, D. R., & Otten, R. (2007). Unresolved maternal attachment representations, disrupted maternal behavior and disorganized attachment in infancy: Links to toddler behavior problems. *Journal of Child Psychology and Psychiatry, 48,* 1042–1050. doi:10.1111/j.1469-7610.2007.01805.x

Madole, K. L., & Oakes, L. M. (1999). Making sense of infant categorization: Stable processes and changing representations. *Developmental Review, 19,* 263–296. doi:10.1006/drev.1998.0481

Maes, H. H., Silberg, J. L., Neale, M. C., & Eaves, L. J. (2007). Genetic and cultural transmission of antisocial behavior: An extended twin parent model. *Twin Research and Human Genetics, 10,* 136–150. doi:10.1375/twin.10.1.136

Magai, C., Hunziker, J., Mesias, W., & Culver, L. C. (2000). Adult attachment styles and emotional biases. *International Journal of Behavioral Development, 24,* 301–309.

Magill-Evans, J., Harrison, M. J., Benzies, K., Gierl, M., & Kimak, C. (2007). Effects of parenting education on first-time fathers' skills in interactions with their infants. *Fathering: A Journal of Theory, Research, and Practice about Men as Fathers, 5,* 42–57. doi:10.3149/fth.0501.42

Magnuson, K., & Berger, L. M. (2009). Family structure states and transitions: Associations with children's well-being during middle childhood. *Journal of Marriage and Family, 71,* 575–591. doi:10.1111/j.1741-3737.2009.00620.x

Magnusson, S. J., & Palincsar, A. S. (2001). The interplay of first-hand and second-hand investigations to model and support the development of scientific knowledge and reasoning. In S. M. Carver & D. Klahr (Eds.), *Cognition and instruction: Twenty-five years of progress* (pp. 151–187). Mahwah, NJ: Erlbaum.

Maguire, M. C., & Dunn, J. (1997). Friendships in early childhood, and social understanding. *International Journal of Behavioral Development, 21,* 669–686. doi:10.1080/016502597384613

Main, M. (2000). The organized categories of infant, child, and adult attachment: Flexible vs. inflexible attention under attachment-related stress. *Journal of the American Psychoanalytic Association, 48,* 1055–1096. doi:10.1177/00030651000480041801

Main, M., & George, C. (1985). Responses of abused and disadvantaged toddlers to distress in agemates: A study in the day care setting. *Developmental Psychology, 21,* 407–412. doi:10.1037/0012-1649.21.3.407

Main, M., Kaplan, N., & Cassidy, J. (1985). Security in infancy, childhood, and adulthood: A move to the level of representation. *Monographs of the Society for Research in Child Development, 50*(1–2, Serial No. 209), 66–104.

Main, M., & Solomon, J. (1990). Procedures for identifying infants as disorganized/disoriented during the Ainsworth Strange Situation. In M. T. Greenberg, D. Cicchetti, & E. M. Cummings (Eds.), *Attachment in the preschool years: Theory, research, and intervention* (pp. 121–160). Chicago, IL: University of Chicago Press.

Malina, R. M., & Bouchard, C. (1991). *Growth, maturation, and physical activity.* Champaign, IL: Human Kinetics.

Malone, P. S., Lansford, J. E., Castellino, D. R., Berlin, L. J., Dodge, K. A., Bates, J. E., & Pettit, G. S. (2004). Divorce and child behavior problems: Applying latent change score models to life event data. *Structural Equation Modeling: A Multidisciplinary Journal, 11,* 401–423. doi:10.1207/s15328007sem1103_6

Maloney, E. A., & Beilock, S. L. (2012). Math anxiety: Who has it, why it develops, and how to guard against it. *Trends in Cognitive Sciences, 16,* 404–406.

Maltz, D. N., & Borker, R. (1982). A cultural approach to male-female miscommunication. In J. J. Gumperz (Ed.), *Language and social identity* (pp. 196–216). Cambridge, England: Cambridge University Press.

Maluccio, J. A., Hoddinott, J., Behrman, J. R., Martorell, R., Quisumbing, A. R., & Stein, A. D. (2009). The impact of improving nutrition during early childhood on education among Guatemalan adults. *The Economic Journal, 119,* 734–763. doi:10.1111/j.1468-0297.2009.02220.x

Mampe, B., Friederici, A. D., Christophe, A., & Wermke, K. (2009). Newborns' cry melody is shaped by their native language. *Current Biology, 19,* 1994–1997.

Mandel, D. R., Jusczyk, P. W., & Pisoni, D. B. (1995). Infants' recognition of the sound patterns of their own names. *Psychological Science, 6,* 314–317. doi:10.1111/j.1467-9280.1995.tb00517.x

Mandler, J. M., & McDonough, L. (1998). Studies in inductive inference in infancy. *Cognitive Psychology, 37,* 60–96. doi:10.1006/cogp.1998.0691

Mangelsdorf, S. C., Shapiro, J. R., & Marzolf, D. (1995). Developmental and temperamental differences in emotion regulation in infancy. *Child Development, 66,* 1817–1828.

Manis, F. R., Seidenberg, M. S., Doi, L. M., McBride-Chang, C., & Petersen, A. (1996). On the bases of two subtypes of development dyslexia. *Cognition, 58,* 157–195.

Marceau, K., Horwitz, B. N., Narusyte, J., Ganiban, J. M., Spotts, E. L., Reiss, D., & Neiderhiser, J. M. (2013). Gene–environment correlation underlying the association between parental negativity and adolescent externalizing problems. *Child Development.* Advance online publication. doi:10.1111/cdev.12094

Marcia, J. E. (1980). Identity in adolescence. In J. Adelson (Ed.), *Handbook of adolescent psychology* (pp. 159–187). New York, NY: Wiley.

Marcus, D. E., & Overton, W. F. (1978). The development of cognitive gender constancy and sex role preferences. *Child Development, 49,* 434–444. doi:10.2307/1128708

Marcus, G. F. (1996). Why do children say "breaked"? *Current Directions in Psychological Science, 5,* 81–85.

Marcus, G. F. (2004). *The birth of the mind: How a tiny number of genes creates the complexities of human thought.* New York, NY: Basic Books.

Marcus, G. F., Vijayan, S., Bandi Rao, S., & Vishton, P. M. (1999, January 1). Rule learning by seven-month-old infants. *Science, 283,* 77–80.

Margett, T. E., & Witherington, D. C. (2011). The nature of preschoolers' concept of living and artificial objects. *Child Development, 82,* 2067–2082. doi:10.1111/j.1467-8624.2011.01661.x

Margolin, G., Gordis, E. B., & John, R. S. (2001). Coparenting: A link between marital conflict and parenting in two-parent families. *Journal of Family Psychology, 15,* 3–21. doi:10.1037/0893-3200.15.1.3

Markman, E. M. (1989). *Categorization and naming in children: Problems of induction.* Cambridge, MA: MIT Press.

Markman, E. M., & Hutchinson, J. E. (1984). Children's sensitivity to constraints on word meaning: Taxonomic versus thematic relations. *Cognitive Psychology, 16,* 1–27. doi:10.1016/0010-0285(84)90002-1

Markman, E. M., & Wachtel, G. F. (1988). Children's use of mutual exclusivity to constrain the meanings of words. *Cognitive Psychology, 20,* 121–157.

Marks, A. K., Patton, F., & García Coll, C. (2011). Being bicultural: A mixed-methods study of adolescents' implicitly and explicitly measured multiethnic identities. *Developmental Psychology, 47,* 270–288. doi:10.1037/a0020730

Markson, L., & Bloom, P. (1997, February 27). Evidence against a dedicated system for word learning in children. *Nature, 385,* 813–815. doi:10.1038/385813a0

Markus, H. R., & Kitayama, S. (1991). Culture and the self: Implications for cognition, emotion, and motivation. *Psychological Review, 98,* 224–253.

Marler, P. (1970, November-December). Birdsong and speech development: Could there be parallels? *American Scientist, 58,* 669–673.

Marlier, L., & Schaal, B. (2005). Human newborns prefer human milk: Conspecific milk odor is attractive without postnatal exposure. *Child Development, 76,* 155–168. doi:10.1111/j.1467-8624.2005.00836.x

Marlier, L., Schaal, B., & Soussignan, R. (1998). Neonatal responsiveness to the odor of amniotic and lacteal fluids: A test of perinatal chemosensory continuity. *Child Development, 69,* 611–623.

Marsh, H. W., Craven, R., & Debus, R. (1998). Structure, stability, and development of young children's self-concepts: A multicohort-multioccasion study. *Child Development, 69,* 1030–1053. doi:10.1111/j.1467-8624.1998.tb06159.x

Marshall, K. (2008). *Fathers' use of paid parental leave* (Catalogue No. 75-001-X). Retrieved from http://www.statcan.gc.ca/pub/75-001-x/2008106/pdf/10639eng.pdf

Marshall, K. (2011). *Generational change in paid and unpaid work* (Catalogue No. 11-008-X). Retrieved from http://www.statcan.gc.ca/pub/11-008-x/2011002/article/11520-eng.pdf

Marshal, M. P., Friedman, M. S., Stall, R., King, K. M., Miles, J., Gold, M. A., … Morse, J. Q. (2008). Sexual orientation and adolescent substance use: A meta-analysis and methodological review. *Addiction, 103,* 546–556. doi:10.1111/j.1360-0443.2008.02149.x

Marshall, P. J., & Meltzoff, A. N. (2011). Neural mirroring systems: Exploring the EEG mu rhythm in human infancy. *Developmental Cognitive Neuroscience, 1,* 110–123.

Marsiglio, W., Amato, P., Day, R. D., & Lamb, M. E. (2000). Scholarship on fatherhood in the 1990s and beyond. *Journal of Marriage and Family, 62,* 1173–1191. doi:10.1111/j.1741-3737.2000.01173.x

Martin, C. L. (1990). Attitudes and expectations about children with nontraditional and traditional gender roles. *Sex Roles, 22,* 151–166. doi:10.1007/BF00288188

Martin, C. L., Eisenbud, L., & Rose, H. (1995). Children's gender-based reasoning about toys. *Child Development, 66,* 1453–1471. doi:10.1111/j.1467-8624.1995.tb00945.x

Martin, C. L., & Fabes, R. A. (2001). The stability and consequences of young children's same-sex peer interactions. *Developmental Psychology, 37,* 431–446. doi:10.1037/0012-1649.37.3.431

Martin, C. L., Fabes, R. A., Evans, S. M., & Wyman, H. (1999). Social cognition on the playground: Children's beliefs about playing with girls versus boys and their relations to sex segregated play. *Journal of Social and Personal Relationships, 16,* 751–771. doi:10.1177/0265407599166005

Martin, C. L., & Halverson, C. F., Jr. (1981). A schematic processing model of sex typing and stereotyping in children. *Child Development, 52,* 1119–1134. doi:10.2307/1129498

Martin, C. L., & Halverson, C. F., Jr. (1983). The effects of sex-typing schemas on young children's memory. *Child Development, 54,* 563–574. doi:10.2307/1130043

Martin, C. L., Kornienko, O., Schaefer, D. R., Hanish, L. D., Fabes, R. A., & Goble, P. (2013). The role of sex of peers and gender-typed activities in young children's peer affiliative networks: A longitudinal analysis of selection and influence. *Child Development, 84,* 921–937. doi:10.1111/cdev.12032

Martin, C. L., Ruble, D. N., & Szkrybalo, J. (2002). Cognitive theories of early gender development. *Psychological Bulletin, 128,* 903–933.

Martin, J., & Ross, H. (2005). Sibling aggression: Sex differences and parents' reactions. *International Journal of Behavioral Development, 29,* 129–138. doi:10.1080/01650250444000469

Martin, J. A., Hamilton, B. E., & Osterman, M. J. K. (2012). *Three decades of twin births in the United States, 1980–2009* (NCHS Data Brief, No. 80). Hyattsville, MD: National Center for Health Statistics.

Martin, J. H., Choy, M., Pullman, S., & Meng, Z. (2004). Corticospinal system development depends on motor experience. *Journal of Neuroscience, 24,* 2122–2132. doi:10.1523/jneurosci.4616-03.2004

Martin, M. J., Conger, R. D., Schofield, T. J., Dogan, S. J., Widaman, K. F., Donnellan, M. B., & Neppl, T. K. (2010). Evaluation of the interactionist model of socioeconomic status and problem behavior: A developmental cascade across generations. *Development and Psychopathology, 22,* 695–713. doi:10.1017/S0954579410000374

Martin-Storey, A., & Crosnoe, R. (2012). Sexual minority status, peer harassment, and adolescent depression. *Journal of Adolescence, 35,* 1001–1011. doi:10.1016/j.adolescence.2012.02.006

Martini, F., & Sénéchal, M. (2012). Learning literacy skills at home: Parent teaching, expectations, and child interest. *Canadian Journal of Behavioural Science, 44,* 210–221. doi: 10.1037/a0026758

Martinot, D., Bagès, C., & Désert, M. (2012). French children's awareness of gender stereotypes about mathematics and reading: When girls improve their reputation in math. *Sex Roles, 66,* 210–219. doi:10.1007/s11199-011-0032-3

Masataka, N. (1992). Motherese in a signed language. *Infant Behavior and Development, 15,* 453–460. doi:10.1016/0163-6383(92)80013-K

Masataka, N. (2006). Preference for consonance over dissonance by hearing newborns of deaf parents and of hearing parents. *Developmental Science, 9,* 46–50. doi:10.1111/j.1467-7687.2005.00462.x

Mascolo, M. F., Fischer, K. W., & Li, J. (2003). Dynamic development of component systems of emotions: Pride, shame, and guilt in China and the United States. In R. J. Davidson, K. R. Scherer, & H. H. Goldsmith (Eds.), *Handbook of affective sciences* (pp. 375–408). Oxford, England: Oxford University Press.

Mason, M. G., & Gibbs, J. C. (1993). Social perspective taking and moral judgment among college students. *Journal of Adolescent Research, 8,* 109–123. doi:10.1177/074355489381008

Masten, A. S. (2007). Resilience in developing systems: Progress and promise as the fourth wave rises. *Development and Psychopathology, 19,* 921–930. doi:10.1017/S0954579407000442

Masten, A. S., Best, K. M., & Garmezy, N. (1990). Resilience and development: Contributions from the study of children who overcome adversity. *Development and Psychopathology, 2,* 425–444. doi:10.1017/S0954579400005812

Masten, A. S., & Sesma, A., Jr. (1999). Risk and resilience among children homeless in Minneapolis. *Center for Urban and Regional Affairs Reporter, 29*(1), 1–6.

Masten, A. S., Sesma, A., Jr., Si-Asar, R., Lawrence, C., Miliotis, D., & Dionne, J. A. (1997). Educational risks for children experiencing homelessness. *Journal of School Psychology, 35,* 27–46. doi:10.1016/S0022-4405(96)00032-5

Masur, E. F. (1982). Mothers' responses to infants' object-related gestures: Influences on lexical development. *Journal of Child Language, 9,* 23–30.

Maszk, P., Eisenberg, N., & Guthrie, I. K. (1999). Relations of children's social status to their emotionality and regulation: A short-term longitudinal study. *Merrill-Palmer Quarterly, 45,* 468–492. doi:10.2307/23092582

Matson, J. L., & Kozlowski, A. M. (2011). The increasing prevalence of autism spectrum disorders. *Research in Autism Spectrum Disorders, 5,* 418–425. doi:10.1016/j.rasd.2010.06.004

Matsuba, M. K., & Walker, L. J. (2004). Extraordinary moral commitment: Young adults involved in social organizations. *Journal of Personality, 72,* 413–436. doi:10.1111/j.0022-3506.2004.00267.x

Matsumoto, D. R. (1996). *Unmasking Japan: Myths and realities about the emotions of the Japanese.* Stanford, CA: Stanford University Press.

Matthews, G., Zeidner, M., & Roberts, R. D. (2002). *Emotional intelligence: Science and myth.* Cambridge, MA: MIT Press.

Mattson, S. N., Riley, E. P., Gramling, L., Delis, D. C., & Jones, K. L. (1998). Neuropsychologicazl comparison of alcohol-exposed children with or without physical features of fetal alcohol syndrome. *Neuropsychology, 12,* 146–153.

Maurer, D., Le Grand, R., & Mondloch, C. J. (2002). The many faces of configural processing. *Trends in Cognitive Sciences, 6,* 255–260. doi:10.1016/S1364-6613(02)01903-4

Maurer, D., & Maurer, C. (1988). *The world of the newborn.* New York, NY: Basic Books.

Maurer, D., & Mondloch, C. (2004). Neonatal synesthesia: A re-evaluation. In L. C. Robertson & N. Sagiv (Eds.), *Attention on synesthesia: Cognition, development and neuroscience* (pp. 193–213). New York, NY: Oxford University Press.

Maurer, D., Mondloch, C. J., & Lewis, T. L. (2007). Sleeper effects. *Developmental Science, 10,* 40–47. doi:10.1111/j.1467-7687.2007.00562.x

Maurer, D., & Salapatek, P. (1976). Developmental changes in the scanning of faces by young infants. *Child Development, 47,* 523–527. doi:10.2307/1128813

Maya-Vetencourt, J. F., & Origlia, N. (2012). Visual cortex plasticity: A complex interplay of genetic and environmental influences. *Neural Plasticity, 2012.* doi:10.1155/2012/631965

Mayberry, M. L., & Espelage, D. L. (2007). Associations among empathy, social competence, & reactive/proactive aggression subtypes. *Journal of Youth and Adolescence, 36,* 787–798. doi:10.1007/s10964-006-9113-y

Mayberry, R. I., Lock, E., & Kazmi, H. (2002). Linguistic ability and early language exposure. *Nature, 417*(6884), 38. doi:10.1038/417038a

Mayeux, L. (2011). Effects of popularity and gender on peers' perceptions of prosocial, antisocial, and jealousy-eliciting behaviors. *Merrill-Palmer Quarterly, 57,* 349–374.

Mayeux, L., & Cillessen, A. H. N. (2008). It's not just being popular, it's knowing it, too: The role of self-perceptions of status in the associations between peer status and aggression. *Social Development, 17,* 871–888. doi:10.1111/j.1467-9507.2008.00474.x

Mazur, E., & Richards, L. (2011). Adolescents' and emerging adults' social networking online: Homophily or diversity? *Journal of Applied Developmental Psychology, 32,* 180–188. doi:10.1016/j.appdev.2011.03.001

Mazzocco, M. M. M., & Kover, S. T. (2007). A longitudinal assessment of executive function skills and their association with math performance. *Child Neuropsychology, 13,* 18–45.

McAdams, D. P., & Olson, B. D. (2010). Personality development: Continuity and change over the life course. *Annual Review of Psychology, 61,* 517–542. doi:10.1146/annurev.psych.093008.100507

McBride-Chang, C. (2004). *Children's literacy development.* New York, NY: Oxford University Press.

McCabe, A., & Peterson, C. (1991). Getting the story: A longitudinal study of parental styles in eliciting narratives and developing narrative skill. In A. McCabe & C. Peterson (Eds.), *Developing narrative structure* (pp. 217–253). Hillsdale, NJ: Erlbaum.

McCabe, K. M., Hough, R., Wood, P. A., & Yeh, M. (2001). Childhood and adolescent onset conduct disorder: A test of the developmental taxonomy. *Journal of Abnormal Child Psychology, 29,* 305–316. doi:10.1023/A:1010357812278

McCabe, K. M., Rodgers, C., Yeh, M., & Hough, R. (2004). Gender differences in childhood onset conduct disorder. *Development and Psychopathology, 16,* 179–192. doi:10.1017/S0954579404044463

McCabe, P. C., & Altamura, M. (2011). Empirically valid strategies to improve social and emotional competence of preschool children. *Psychology in the Schools, 48,* 513–540. doi:10.1002/pits.20570

McCall, R. B., van IJzendoorn, M. H., Juffer, F., Groark, C. J., & Groza, V. K. (2011). Children without permanent parents: Research, practice, and policy. *Monographs of the Society for Research in Child Development, 76*(4, Serial No. 301), 1–318.

McCarthy, A., & Lee, K. (2009). Children's knowledge of deceptive gaze cues and its relation to their actual lying behavior. *Journal of Experimental Child Psychology, 103,* 117–134. doi:10.1016/j.jecp.2008.06.005

McCartney, K., Burchinal, M., Clarke-Stewart, A., Bub, K. L., Owen, M. T., & Belsky, J. (2010). Testing a series of causal propositions relating time in child care to children's externalizing behavior. *Developmental Psychology, 46,* 1–17. doi:10.1037/a0017886

McCarton, C. M., Brooks-Gunn, J., Wallace, I. F., Bauer, C. R., Bennett, F. C., Bernbaum, J. C., … Meinert, C. L. (1997, January 8). Results at age 8 years of early intervention for low-birth-weight premature infants. The Infant Health and Development Program. *Journal of the American Medical Association, 277,* 126–132. doi:10.1001/jama.1997.03540260040033

McClain, D. B., Wolchik, S. A., Winslow, E., Tein, J.-Y., Sandler, I. N., & Millsap, R. E. (2010). Developmental cascade effects of the New Beginnings Program on adolescent adaptation outcomes. *Development and Psychopathology, 22,* 771–784. doi:10.1017/S0954579410000453

McClelland, M. M., & Cameron, C. E. (2012). Self-regulation in early childhood: Improving conceptual clarity and developing ecologically valid measures. *Child Development Perspectives, 6,* 136–142.

McClintock, M. K., & Herdt, G. (1996). Rethinking puberty: The development of sexual attraction. *Current Directions in Psychological Science, 5,* 178–183. doi:10.1111/1467-8721.ep11512422

McCloskey, L. A., & Stuewig, J. (2001). The quality of peer relationships among children exposed to family violence. *Development and Psychopathology, 13,* 83–96.

McCloskey, M. (2007). Quantitative literacy and developmental dyscalculias. In D. B. Berch & M. M. M. Mazzocco (Eds.), *Why is math so hard for some children? The nature and origins of mathematical learning difficulties and disabilities* (pp. 415–429). Baltimore, MD: Paul H. Brookes.

McConnell, D., Breitkreuz, R., & Savage, A. (2011). From financial hardship to child difficulties: Main and moderating effects of perceived social support. *Child: Care, Health and Development, 37,* 679–691. doi: 10.1111/j.1365-2214.2010.01185.x

McCormick, M. C., Brooks-Gunn, J., Buka, S. L., Goldman, J., Yu, J., Salganik, M., … Casey, P. H. (2006). Early intervention in low birth weight premature infants: Results at 18 years of age for the Infant Health and Development Program. *Pediatrics, 117,* 771–780. doi:10.1542/peds.2005-1316

McCoy, D. C., & Raver, C. C. (2011). Caregiver emotional expressiveness, child emotion regulation, and child behavior problems among Head Start families. *Social Development, 20,* 741–761.

McCuaig Edge, H., & Craig, W. (2011). *The health of Canada's young people: A mental health focus.* Retrieved from http://www.phac-aspc.gc.ca/hp-ps/dca-dea/publications/hbsc-mental-mentale/peers-camarades-eng.php

McDaniel, M. A. (2005). Big-brained people are smarter: A meta-analysis of the relationship between in vivo brain volume and intelligence. *Intelligence, 33,* 337–346. doi:10.1016/j.intell.2004.11.005

McDonald, K. L., Putallaz, M., Grimes, C. L., Kupersmidt, J. B., & Coie, J. D. (2007). Girl talk: Gossip, friendship, and sociometric status. *Merrill-Palmer Quarterly, 53,* 381–411.

McDonough, C., Song, L., Hirsh-Pasek, K., Golinkoff, R. M., & Lannon, R. (2011). An image is worth a thousand words: Why nouns tend to dominate verbs in early word learning. *Developmental Science, 14,* 181–189. doi:10.1111/j.1467-7687.2010.00968.x

McDougall, P., & Hymel, S. (2007). Same-gender versus cross-gender friendship conceptions: Similar or different? *Merrill-Palmer Quarterly, 53,* 347–380.

McDowell, D. J., & Parke, R. D. (2009). Parental correlates of children's peer relations: An empirical test of a tripartite model. *Developmental Psychology, 45,* 224–235. doi:10.1037/a0014305

McElwain, N. L., Booth-LaForce, C., & Wu, X. (2011). Infant–mother attachment and children's friendship quality: Maternal mental-state talk as an intervening mechanism. *Developmental Psychology, 47,* 1295–1311. doi:10.1037/a0024094

McEwen, B. S., & Schmeck, H. M. (1994). *The hostage brain.* New York, NY: Rockefeller University Press.

McFadyen-Ketchum, S. A., Bates, J. E., Dodge, K. A., & Pettit, G. S. (1996). Patterns of change in early childhood aggressive-disruptive behavior: Gender differences in predictions from early coercive and affectionate mother-child interactions. *Child Development, 67,* 2417–2433. doi: 10.2307/1131631

McGowan, P. O., Sasaki, A., D'Alessio, A. C., Dymov, S., Labonté, B., Szyf, M., … Meaney, M. J. (2009). Epigenetic regulation of the glucocorticoid receptor in human brain associates with childhood abuse. *Nature Neuroscience, 12,* 342–348. doi:10.1038/nn.2270

McGraw, M. B. (1943). *The neuromuscular maturation of the human infant.* New York, NY: Columbia University Press.

McGue, M., Bouchard, T. J., Jr., Iacono, W. G., & Lykken, D. T. (1993). Behavioral genetics of cognitive ability: A life-span perspective. In R. Plomin & G. E. McClearn (Eds.), *Nature, nurture and psychology* (pp. 59–76). Washington, DC: American Psychological Association.

McGue, M., & Lykken, D. T. (1992). Genetic influence on risk of divorce. *Psychological Science, 3,* 368–373. doi:10.1111/j.1467-9280.1992.tb00049.x

McGuigan, F., & Salmon, K. (2004). The time to talk: The influence of the timing of adult–child talk on children's event memory. *Child Development, 75,* 669–686. doi:10.1111/j.1467-8624.2004.00700.x

McGuire, S., McHale, S. M., & Updegraff, K. (1996). Children's perceptions of the sibling relationship in middle childhood: Connections within and between family relationships. *Personal Relationships, 3,* 229–239. doi: 10.1111/j.1475-6811.1996.tb00114.x

McGuire, S., Neiderhiser, J. M., Reiss, D., Hetherington, E. M., & Plomin, R. (1994). Genetic and environmental influences on perceptions of self-worth and competence in adolescence: A study of twins, full siblings, and step-siblings. *Child Development, 65,* 785–799. doi:10.1111/j.1467-8624.1994.tb00783.x

McHale, J. P., Kazali, C., Rotman, T., Talbot, J., Carleton, M., & Lieberson, R. (2004). The transition to coparenthood: Parents' prebirth expectations and early coparental adjustment at 3 months postpartum. *Development and Psychopathology, 16,* 711–733. doi:10.1017/S0954579404004742

McHale, S. M., Bissell, J., & Kim, J.-Y. (2009). Sibling relationship, family, and genetic factors in sibling similarity in sexual risk. *Journal of Family Psychology, 23,* 562–572. doi:10.1037/a0014982

McHale, S. M., Crouter, A. C., McGuire, S. A., & Updegraff, K. A. (1995). Congruence between mothers' and fathers' differential treatment of siblings: Links with family relations and children's well-being. *Child Development, 66,* 116–128. doi:10.1111/j.1467-8624.1995.tb00859.x

McHale, S. M., Updegraff, K. A., Jackson-Newsom, J., Tucker, C. J., & Crouter, A. C. (2000). When does parents' differential treatment have negative implications for siblings? *Social Development, 9,* 149–172. doi: 10.1111/1467-9507.00117

McHale, S. M., Updegraff, K. A., Shanahan, L., Crouter, A. C., & Killoren, S. E. (2005). Siblings' differential treatment in Mexican American families. *Journal of Marriage and Family, 67,* 1259–1274. doi:10.1111/j.1741-3737.2005.00215.x

McHale, S. M., Whiteman, S. D., Kim, J.-Y., & Crouter, A. C. (2007). Characteristics and correlates of sibling relationships in two-parent African American families. *Journal of Family Psychology, 21,* 227–235. doi:10.1037/0893-3200.21.2.227

McKay, A. (2012). Trends in Canadian national and provincial/territorial teen pregnancy rates: 2001–2010. *The Canadian Journal of Human Sexuality, 21,* 3–4. Retrieved from http://www.sieccan.org/pdf/TeenPregancy.pdf

McKey, R. H., Condelli, L., Ganson, H., Barrett, B. J., McConkey, C., & Plantz, M. C. (1985). *The impact of Head Start on children, families, and communities: Final report of the Head Start Evaluation, Synthesis, and Utilization Project* (DHHS Publication No. (OHDS) 90-31193). Washington, DC: Government Printing Office.

McLoyd, V. C. (1998). Children in poverty: Development, public policy, and practice. In W. Damon (Series Ed.) & I. E. Sigel & K. A. Renninger (Vol. Eds.), *Handbook of child psychology: Vol. 4. Child psychology in practice* (5th ed., pp. 135–210). New York, NY: Wiley.

McMahon, A. W., Iskander, J. K., Haber, P., Braun, M. M., & Ball, R. (2008). Inactivated influenza vaccine (IIV) in children <2 years of age: Examination of selected adverse events reported to the Vaccine Adverse Event Reporting System (VAERS) after thimerosal-free or thimerosal-containing vaccine. *Vaccine, 26,* 427–429. doi:10.1016/j.vaccine.2007.10.071

McMahon, R. J., Witkiewitz, K., & Kotler, J. S. (2010). Predictive validity of callous–unemotional traits measured in early adolescence with respect to multiple antisocial outcomes. *Journal of Abnormal Psychology, 119*, 752–763. doi:10.1037/a0020796

McMaster, L. E., Connolly, J., Pepler, D., & Craig, W. M. (2002). Peer to peer sexual harassment in early adolescence: A developmental perspective. *Development and Psychopathology, 14*, 91–105.

McMurray, B. (2007, August 3). Defusing the childhood vocabulary explosion. *Science, 317*, 631.

McNeil, N. M., Fyfe, E. R., Petersen, L. A., Dunwiddie, A. E., & Brletic-Shipley, H. (2011). Benefits of practicing 4 = 2 + 2: Nontraditional problem formats facilitate children's understanding of mathematical equivalence. *Child Development, 82*, 1620–1633.

McQuaid, N., Bigelow, A. E., McLaughlin, J., & MacLean, K. (2008). Maternal mental state language and preschool children's attachment security: Relation to children's mental state language and expressions of emotional understanding. *Social Development, 17*, 61–83. doi:10.1111/j.1467-9507.2007.00415.x

Meaney, M. J. (2001). Maternal care, gene expression, and the transmission of individual differences in stress reactivity across generations. *Annual Review of Neuroscience, 24*, 1161–1192. doi:10.1146/annurev.neuro.24.1.1161

Meaney, M. J. (2010). Epigenetics and the biological definition of gene × environment interactions. *Child Development, 81*, 41–79.

Media Awareness Network. (2005). *Young Canadians in a wired world phase II: Trends and recommendations.* Ottawa, ON: Author.

Meece, J. L., Wigfield, A., & Eccles, J. S. (1990). Predictors of math anxiety and its influence on young adolescents' course enrollment intentions and performance in mathematics. *Journal of Educational Psychology, 82*, 60–70.

Meert, G., Grégoire, J., & Noël, M.-P. (2010). Comparing the magnitude of two fractions with common components: Which representations are used by 10- and 12-year-olds? *Journal of Experimental Child Psychology, 107*, 244–259. doi:10.1016/j.jecp.2010.04.008

Meeus, W. (1996). Studies on identity development in adolescence: An overview of research and some new data. *Journal of Youth and Adolescence, 25*, 569–598. doi:10.1007/BF01537355

Meeus, W. (2011). The study of adolescent identity formation 2000–2010: A review of longitudinal research. *Journal of Research on Adolescence, 21*, 75–94. doi:10.1111/j.1532-7795.2010.00716.x

Meeus, W., Van De Schoot, R., Keijsers, L., Schwartz, S. J., & Branje, S. (2010). On the progression and stability of adolescent identity formation: A five-wave longitudinal study in early-to-middle and middle-to-late adolescence. *Child Development, 81*, 1565–1581. doi:10.1111/j.1467-8624.2010.01492.x

Mehler, J., Jusczyk, P., Lambertz, G., Halsted, N., Bertoncini, J., & Amiel-Tison, C. (1988). A precursor of language acquisition in young infants. *Cognition, 29*, 143–178.

Meier, M. H., Slutske, W. S., Heath, A. C., & Martin, N. G. (2011). Sex differences in the genetic and environmental influences on childhood conduct disorder and adult antisocial behavior. *Journal of Abnormal Psychology, 120*, 377–388. doi:10.1037/a0022303

Meisels, S. J., & Plunkett, J. W. (1988). Developmental consequences of preterm birth: Are there long-term effects? In P. B. Baltes, D. L. Featherman, & R. M. Lerner (Eds.), *Life-span development and behavior* (Vol. 9, pp. 87–128). Hillsdale, NJ: Erlbaum.

Meltzoff, A. N. (1988a). Imitation of televised models by infants. *Child Development, 59*, 1221–1229.

Meltzoff, A. N. (1988b). Infant imitation and memory: Nine-month-olds in immediate and deferred tests. *Child Development, 59*, 217–225.

Meltzoff, A. N. (1995a). Understanding the intentions of others: Re-enactment of intended acts by 18-month-old children. *Developmental Psychology, 31*, 838–850. doi:10.1037/0012-1649.31.5.838

Meltzoff, A. N. (1995b). What infant memory tells us about infantile amnesia: Long-term recall and deferred imitation. *Journal of Experimental Child Psychology, 59*, 497–515. doi:10.1006/jecp.1995.1023

Meltzoff, A. N., & Borton, R. W. (1979, November 22). Intermodal matching by human neonates. *Nature, 282*, 403–404.

Meltzoff, A. N., & Moore, M. K. (1977, October 7). Imitation of facial and manual gestures by human neonates. *Science, 198*, 75–78.

Meltzoff, A. N., & Moore, M. K. (1983). Newborn infants imitate adult facial gestures. *Child Development, 54*, 702–709.

Meltzoff, A. N., & Moore, M. K. (1994). Imitation, memory, and the representation of persons. *Infant Behavior and Development, 17*, 83–99. doi:10.1016/0163-6383(94)90024-8

Menaghan, E. G., & Parcel, T. L. (1995). Social sources of change in children's home environments: The effects of parental occupational experiences and family conditions. *Journal of Marriage and the Family, 57*, 69–84.

Mendle, J., Harden, K. P., Brooks-Gunn, J., & Graber, J. A. (2010). Development's tortoise and hare: Pubertal timing, pubertal tempo, and depressive symptoms in boys and girls. *Developmental Psychology, 46*, 1341–1353. doi:10.1037/a0020205

Mendle, J., Harden, K. P., Brooks-Gunn, J., & Graber, J. A. (2012). Peer relationships and depressive symptomatology in boys at puberty. *Developmental Psychology, 48*, 429–435. doi:10.1037/a0026425

Mennella, J. A., & Beauchamp, G. K. (1993a). Beer, breast feeding, and folklore. *Developmental Psychobiology, 26*, 459–466.

Mennella, J. A., & Beauchamp, G. K. (1993b). The effects of repeated exposure to garlic-flavored milk on the nursling's behavior. *Pediatric Research, 34*, 805–808.

Mennella, J. A., & Beauchamp, G. K. (1996). The human infants' response to vanilla flavors in mother's milk and formula. *Infant Behavior and Development, 19*, 13–19. doi:10.1016/S0163-6383(96)90040-5

Mennella, J. A., Jagnow, C. P., & Beauchamp, G. K. (2001). Prenatal and postnatal flavor learning by human infants. *Pediatrics, 107*(6), e88. doi:10.1542/peds.107.6.e88

Mennella, J. A., Johnson, A., & Beauchamp, G. K. (1995). Garlic ingestion by pregnant women alters the odor of amniotic fluid. *Chemical Senses, 20*, 207–209.

Menon, M., Tobin, D. D., Corby, B. C., Menon, M., Hodges, E. V., & Perry, D. G. (2007). The developmental costs of high self-esteem for antisocial children. *Child Development, 78*, 1627–1639.

Mereu, G., Fà, M., Ferraro, L., Cagiano, R., Antonelli, T., Tattoli, M., … Cuomo, V. (2003). Prenatal exposure to a cannabinoid agonist produces memory deficits linked to dysfunction in hippocampal long-term potentiation and glutamate release. *Proceedings of the National Academy of Sciences of the United States of America, 100*, 4915–4920. doi:10.1073/pnas.0537849100

Merten, D. E. (1997). The meaning of meanness: Popularity, competition, and conflict among junior high school girls. *Sociology of Education, 70*, 175–191. doi:10.2307/2673207

Mervis, C. B., & Velleman, S. L. (2011). Children with Williams syndrome: Language, cognitive, and behavioral characteristics and their implications for intervention. *Perspectives on Language Learning and Education, 18*, 98–107. doi:10.1044/lle18.3.98

Mesman, J., Stoel, R., Bakermans-Kranenburg, M. J., van IJzendoorn, M. H., Juffer, F., Koot, H. M., & Alink, L. R. (2009). Predicting growth curves of early childhood externalizing problems: Differential susceptibility of children with difficult temperament. *Journal of Abnormal Child Psychology, 37*, 625–636. doi:10.1007/s10802-009-9298-0

Mesman, J., van IJzendoorn, M. H., & Bakermans-Kranenburg, M. J. (2012). Unequal in opportunity, equal in process: Parental sensitivity promotes positive child development in ethnic minority families. *Child Development Perspectives, 6*, 239–250. doi:10.1111/j.1750-8606.2011.00223.x

Mesquita, B., & Frijda, N. H. (1992). Cultural variations in emotions: A review. *Psychological Bulletin, 112*, 179–204.

Messner, M. A. (1998). Boyhood, organized sports, and the construction of masculinities. In M. S. Kimmel & M. A. Messner (Eds.), *Men's lives* (4th ed., pp. 109–121). Boston, MA: Allyn and Bacon.

Metz, E., & Youniss, J. (2003). A demonstration that school-based required service does not deter—but heightens—volunteerism. *Political Science and Politics, 36*, 281–286. doi:10.1017/S1049096503002221

Meunier, J. C., Boyle, M., O'Connor, T. G., & Jenkins, J. M. (2013). Multilevel mediation: Cumulative contextual risk, maternal differential treatment, and children's behavior within families. *Child Development, 84*, 1594–1615. doi:10.1111/cdev.12066

Michalik, N. M., Eisenberg, N., Spinrad, T. L., Ladd, B., Thompson, M., & Valiente, C. (2007). Longitudinal relations among parental emotional expressivity and sympathy and prosocial behavior in adolescence. *Social Development, 16*, 286–309. doi:10.1111/j.1467-9507.2007.00385.x

Michalson, L., & Lewis, M. (1985). What do children know about emotions and when do they know it? In M. Lewis & L. A. Rosenblum (Series Eds.) & M. Lewis & C. Saarni (Vol. Eds.), *Genesis of behavior: Vol. 5. The socialization of emotions* (pp. 117–139). New York, NY: Plenum Press.

Miell, D., & MacDonald, R. (2000). Children's creative collaborations: The importance of friendship when working together on a musical composition. *Social Development, 9*, 348–369. doi:10.1111/1467-9507.00130

Mikami, A. Y., Szwedo, D. E., Allen, J. P., Evans, M. A., & Hare, A. L. (2010). Adolescent peer relationships and behavior problems predict young adults' communication on social networking websites. *Developmental Psychology, 46*, 46–56. doi:10.1037/a0017420

Miklikowska, M., Duriez, B., & Soenens, B. (2011). Family roots of empathy-related characteristics: The role of perceived maternal and paternal need support in adolescence. *Developmental Psychology, 47*, 1342–1352. doi:10.1037/a0024726

Milberger, S., Biederman, J., Faraone, S. V., Guite, J., & Tsuang, M. T. (1997). Pregnancy, delivery and infancy complications and attention deficit hyperactivity disorder: Issues of gene-environment interaction. *Biological Psychiatry, 41*, 65–75. doi:10.1016/0006-3223(95)00653-2

Milewski, A. E. (1976). Infants' discrimination of internal and external pattern elements. *Journal of Experimental Child Psychology, 22*, 229–246. doi:10.1016/0022-0965(76)90004-7

Miliotis, D., Sesma, A., Jr., & Masten, A. S. (1999). Parenting as a protective process for school success in children from homeless families. *Early Education and Development, 10*, 111–133. doi:10.1207/s15566935eed1002_2

Miller, C. L., Miceli, P. J., Whitman, T. L., & Borkowski, J. G. (1996). Cognitive readiness to parent and intellectual-emotional development in children of adolescent mothers. *Developmental Psychology, 32*, 533–541. doi:10.1037/0012-1649.32.3.533

Miller, D. J., Duka, T., Stimpson, C. D., Schapiro, S. J., Baze, W. B., McArthur, M. J., ... Sherwood, C. C. (2012). Prolonged myelination in human neocortical evolution. *Proceedings of the National Academy of Sciences of the United States of America, 109*, 16480–16485. doi:10.1073/pnas.1117943109

Miller, G. A., & Gildea, P. M. (1987, September). How children learn words. *Scientific American, 257*(3), 94–99.

Miller, G. E., Chen, E., Fok, A. K., Walker, H., Lim, A., Nicholls, E. F., ... Kobor, M. S. (2009). Low early-life social class leaves a biological residue manifested by decreased glucocorticoid and increased proinflammatory signaling. *Proceedings of the National Academy of Sciences of the United States of America, 106*, 14716–14721. doi:10.1073/pnas.0902971106

Miller, J. G., & Bersoff, D. M. (1992). Culture and moral judgment: How are conflicts between justice and interpersonal responsibilities resolved? *Journal of Personality and Social Psychology, 62*, 541–554. doi:10.1037/0022-3514.62.4.541

Miller, K. (1984). Child as the measurer of all things: Measurement of procedures and the development of quantitative concepts. In C. Sophian (Ed.), *Origins of cognitive skills: The Eighteenth Annual Carnegie Symposium on Cognition* (pp. 193–228). Hillsdale, NJ: Erlbaum.

Miller, K. F., Smith, C. M., Zhu, J., & Zhang, H. (1995). Preschool origins of cross-national differences in mathematical competence: The role of number-naming systems. *Psychological Science, 6*, 56–60. doi:10.1111/j.1467-9280.1995.tb00305.x

Miller, P., & Sperry, L. L. (1987). The socialization of anger and aggression. *Merrill-Palmer Quarterly, 33*, 1–31.

Miller, P. H. (2002). *Theories of developmental psychology* (4th ed.). New York, NY: Worth.

Miller, P. H. (2011). *Theories of developmental psychology* (5th ed.). New York, NY: Worth.

Miller, P. H., & Coyle, T. R. (1999). Developmental change: Lessons from microgenesis. In E. K. Scholnick, K. Nelson, S. A. Gelman, & P. H. Miller (Eds.), *Conceptual development: Piaget's legacy* (pp. 209–239). Mahwah, NJ: Erlbaum.

Miller, P. H., & Seier, W. L. (1994). Strategy utilization deficiencies in children: When, where, and why. In H. W. Reese (Ed.), *Advances in child development and behavior* (Vol. 25, pp. 108–156). San Diego, CA: Academic Press.

Miller, P. J., & Sperry, L. L. (1988). Early talk about the past: The origins of conversational stories of personal experience. *Journal of Child Language, 15*, 293–315. doi:10.1017/S0305000900012381

Miller, P. M., Danaher, D. L., & Forbes, D. (1986). Sex-related strategies for coping with interpersonal conflict in children aged five and seven. *Developmental Psychology, 22*, 543–548. doi:10.1037/0012-1649.22.4.543

Miller, S., Lansford, J. E., Costanzo, P., Malone, P. S., Golonka, M., & Killeya-Jones, L. A. (2009). Early adolescent romantic partner status, peer standing, and problem behaviors. *Journal of Early Adolescence, 29*, 839–861. doi:10.1177/0272431609332665

Miller, S. A. (2012). *Theory of mind: Beyond the preschool years.* New York, NY: Psychology Press.

Miller-Johnson, S., Winn, D.-M. C., Coie, J. D., Malone, P. S., & Lochman, J. (2004). Risk factors for adolescent pregnancy reports among African American males. *Journal of Research on Adolescence, 14*, 471–495. doi:10.1111/j.1532-7795.2004.00083.x

Mills-Koonce, W. R., Appleyard, K., Barnett, M., Deng, M., Putallaz, M., & Cox, M. (2011). Adult attachment style and stress as risk factors for early maternal sensitivity and negativity. *Infant Mental Health Journal, 32*, 277–285.

Minde, K. (1993). Prematurity and serious medical illness in infancy: Implications for development and intervention. In C. H. Zeanah, Jr. (Ed.), *Handbook of infant mental health* (pp. 87–105). New York, NY: Guilford Press.

Mindell, J. A., Sadeh, A., Wiegand, B., How, T. H., & Goh, D. Y. T. (2010). Cross-cultural differences in infant and toddler sleep. *Sleep Medicine, 11,* 274–280. doi:10.1016/j.sleep.2009.04.012

Miner, J. L., & Clarke-Stewart, K. A. (2008). Trajectories of externalizing behavior from age 2 to age 9: Relations with gender, temperament, ethnicity, parenting, and rater. *Developmental Psychology, 44,* 771–786. doi:10.1037/0012-1649.44.3.771

Mirescu, C., & Gould, E. (2006). Stress and adult neurogenesis. *Hippocampus, 16,* 233–238. doi:10.1002/hipo.20155

Mischel, W. (1981). Metacognition and the rules of delay. In J. H. Flavell & L. Ross (Eds.), *Social cognitive development: Frontiers and possible futures* (pp. 240–271). New York, NY: Cambridge University Press.

Mischel, W., & Ayduk, O. (2004). Willpower in a cognitive-affective processing system: The dynamics of delay of gratification. In R. F. Baumeister & K. D. Vohs (Eds.), *Handbook of self-regulation: Research, theory, and applications* (pp. 99–129). New York, NY: Guilford Press.

Mischel, W., & Ayduk, O. (2011). Willpower in a cognitive affective processing system: The dynamics of delay of gratification. In K. D. Vohs & R. F. Baumeister (Eds.), *Handbook of self-regulation: Research, theory, and applications* (2nd ed., pp. 99–129). New York, NY: Guilford Press.

Mischel, W., Shoda, Y., & Peake, P. K. (1988). The nature of adolescent competencies predicted by preschool delay of gratification. *Journal of Personality and Social Psychology, 54,* 687–696.

Mix, K. S., Levine, S. C., & Huttenlocher, J. (2002). *Quantitative development in infancy and early childhood.* Oxford, England: Oxford University Press.

Miyake, A., & Friedman, N. P. (2012). The nature and organization of individual differences in executive functions: Four general conclusions. *Current Directions in Psychological Science, 21,* 8–14. doi:10.1177/0963721411429458

Mize, J., & Ladd, G. W. (1990). Toward the development of successful social skills training for preschool children. In S. R. Asher & J. D. Coie (Eds.), *Peer rejection in childhood* (pp. 338–361). New York, NY: Cambridge University Press.

Mizuta, I., Zahn-Waxler, C., Cole, P. M., & Hiruma, N. (1996). A cross-cultural study of preschoolers' attachment: Security and sensitivity in Japanese and US dyads. *International Journal of Behavioral Development, 19,* 141–159.

Modecki, K. L., Barber, B. L., & Vernon, L. (2013). Mapping developmental precursors of cyber-aggression: Trajectories of risk predict perpetration and victimization. *Journal of Youth and Adolescence, 42,* 651–661. doi:10.1007/s10964-012-9887-z

Modin, B., Östberg, V., & Almquist, Y. (2011). Childhood peer status and adult susceptibility to anxiety and depression: A 30-year hospital follow-up. *Journal of Abnormal Child Psychology, 39,* 187–199. doi:10.1007/s10802-010-9462-6

Moffitt, T. E. (1993a). Adolescence-limited and life-course-persistent antisocial behavior: A developmental taxonomy. *Psychological Review, 100,* 674–701. doi:10.1037/0033-295X.100.4.674

Moffitt, T. E. (1993b). The neuropsychology of conduct disorder. *Development and Psychopathology, 5,* 135–151. doi:10.1017/S0954579400004302

Moffitt, T. E., Arseneault, L., Belsky, D., Dickson, N., Hancox, R. J., Harrington, H., … Caspi, A. (2011). A gradient of childhood self-control predicts health, wealth, and public safety. *Proceedings of the National Academy of Sciences of the United States of America, 108,* 2693–2698. doi:10.1073/pnas.1010076108

Moffitt, T. E., & Caspi, A. (2001). Childhood predictors differentiate life-course persistent and adolescence-limited antisocial pathways among males and females. *Development and Psychopathology, 13,* 355–375.

Moffitt, T. E., Caspi, A., Harrington, H., & Milne, B. J. (2002). Males on the life-course-persistent and adolescence-limited antisocial pathways: Follow-up at age 26 years. *Development and Psychopathology, 14,* 179–207.

Moffitt, T. E., Harrington, H., Caspi, A., Kim-Cohen, J., Goldberg, D., Gregory, A. M., & Poulton, R. (2007). Depression and generalized anxiety disorder: Cumulative and sequential comorbidity in a birth cohort followed prospectively to age 32 years. *Archives of General Psychiatry, 64,* 651–660. doi:10.1001/archpsyc.64.6.651

Moilanen, K. L., Shaw, D. S., Dishion, T. J., Gardner, F., & Wilson, M. (2009). Predictors of longitudinal growth in inhibitory control in early childhood. *Social Development, 19,* 326–347. doi:10.1111/j.1467-9507.2009.00536.x

Molfese, D. L., & Betz, J. C. (1988). Electrophysiological indices of the early development of lateralization for language and cognition and their implications for predicting later development. In D. L. Molfese & S. J. Segalowitz (Eds.), *Brain lateralization in children: Developmental implications* (pp. 171–190). New York, NY: Guilford Press.

Monahan, K. C., Steinberg, L., & Cauffman, E. (2009). Affiliation with antisocial peers, susceptibility to peer influence, and antisocial behavior during the transition to adulthood. *Developmental Psychology, 45,* 1520–1530.

Monahan, K. C., Steinberg, L., Cauffman, E., & Mulvey, E. P. (2009). Trajectories of antisocial behavior and psychosocial maturity from adolescence to young adulthood. *Developmental Psychology, 45,* 1654–1668. doi:10.1037/a0015862

Mondloch, C. J., Dobson, K. S., Parsons, J., & Maurer, D. (2004). Why 8-year-olds cannot tell the difference between Steve Martin and Paul Newman: Factors contributing to the slow development of sensitivity to the spacing of facial features. *Journal of Experimental Child Psychology, 89,* 159–181. doi:10.1016/j.jecp.2004.07.002

Montirosso, R., Peverelli, M., Frigerio, E., Crespi, M., & Borgatti, R. (2010). The development of dynamic facial expression recognition at different intensities in 4-to 18-year-olds. *Social Development, 19,* 71–92.

Moon, C., Cooper, R. P., & Fifer, W. P. (1993). Two-day-olds prefer their native language. *Infant Behavior and Development, 16,* 495–500.

Moon, C., & Fifer, W. (1990, April). *Newborns prefer a prenatal version of mother's voice.* Poster session presented at the Biannual Meeting of the International Society of Infant Studies, Montreal, Canada.

Moon, M., & Hoffman, C. D. (2008). Mothers' and fathers' differential expectancies and behaviors: Parent × child gender effects. *Journal of Genetic Psychology, 169,* 261–280. doi:10.3200/GNTP.169.3.261-280

Moore, C. (2008). The development of gaze following. *Child Development Perspectives, 2,* 66–70. doi:10.1111/j.1750-8606.2008.00052.x

Moore, C. F. (2003). *Silent scourge: Children, pollution, and why scientists disagree.* New York, NY: Oxford University Press.

Moore, D. R., & Florsheim, P. (2001). Interpersonal processes and psychopathology among expectant and nonexpectant adolescent couples. *Journal of Consulting and Clinical Psychology, 69,* 101–113. doi:10.1037/0022-006X.69.1.101

Moore, K. A., Manlove, J., Glei, D. A., & Morrison, D. R. (1998). Nonmarital school-age motherhood: Family, individual, and school characteristics. *Journal of Adolescent Research, 13,* 433–457. doi:10.1177/0743554898134004

Moore, K. L., & Persaud, T. V. N. (1993). *Before we are born: Essentials of embryology and birth defects* (4th ed.). Philadelphia, PA: Saunders.

Moore, M. R., & Brooks-Gunn, J. (2002). Adolescent parenthood. In M. H. Bornstein (Ed.), *Handbook of parenting: Vol. 3. Being and becoming a parent* (2nd ed., pp. 173–214). Mahwah, NJ: Erlbaum.

Morales, J. R., & Guerra, N. G. (2006). Effects of multiple context and cumulative stress on urban children's adjustment in elementary school. *Child Development, 77,* 907–923. doi:10.1111/j.1467-8624.2006.00910.x

Moreau, D., Clerc, J., Mansy-Dannay, A., & Guerrien, A. (2012). Enhancing spatial ability through sport practice: Evidence for an effect of motor training on mental rotation performance. *Journal of Individual Differences, 33,* 83–88. doi:10.1027/1614-0001/a000075

Morelen, D., & Suveg, C. (2012). A real-time analysis of parent-child emotion discussions: The interaction is reciprocal. *Journal of Family Psychology, 26,* 998–1003. doi:10.1037/a0030148

Morelli, G. A., Rogoff, B., Oppenheim, D., & Goldsmith, D. (1992). Cultural variation in infants' sleeping arrangements: Questions of independence. *Developmental Psychology, 28,* 604–613. doi:10.1037/0012-1649.28.4.604

Morgan, J., Shaw, D., & Olino, T. (2012). Differential susceptibility effects: The interaction of negative emotionality and sibling relationship quality on childhood internalizing problems and social skills. *Journal of Abnormal Child Psychology, 40,* 885–899. doi:10.1007/s10802-012-9618-7

Morris, A. S., Silk, J. S., Steinberg, L., Myers, S. S., & Robinson, L. R. (2007). The role of the family context in the development of emotion regulation. *Social Development, 16,* 361–388. doi:10.1111/j.1467-9507.2007.00389.x

Morris, A. S., Silk, J. S., Steinberg, L., Sessa, F. M., Avenevoli, S., & Essex, M. J. (2002). Temperamental vulnerability and negative parenting as interacting predictors of child adjustment. *Journal of Marriage and Family, 64,* 461–471.

Morrissey, T. W. (2009). Multiple child care arrangements and young children's behavioral outcomes. *Child Development, 80,* 59–76. doi:10.1111/j.1467-8624.2008.01246.x

Morrissey, T. W., Dunifon, R. E., & Kalil, A. (2011). Maternal employment, work schedules, and children's body mass index. *Child Development, 82,* 66–81. doi:10.1111/j.1467-8624.2010.01541.x

Morrow, R. L., Garland, E. J., Wright, J. M., Maclure, M., Taylor, S., & Dormuth, C. R. (2012). Influence of relative age on diagnosis and treatment of attention-deficit/hyperactivity disorder in children. *Canadian Medical Association Journal, 184,* 755–762. doi: 10.1503/cmaj.111619

Moses, L. J., Baldwin, D. A., Rosicky, J. G., & Tidball, G. (2001). Evidence for referential understanding in the emotions domain at twelve and eighteen months. *Child Development, 72,* 718–735.

Moss, E., Cyr, C., Bureau, J. F., Tarabulsy, G., & Dubois-Comtois, K. (2005). Stability of attachment during the preschool period. *Developmental Psychology, 41,* 773–783. doi:10.1037/0012-1649.41.5.773

Moss, E., Cyr, C., & Dubois-Comtois, K. (2004). Attachment at early school age and developmental risk: Examining family contexts and behavior problems of controlling-caregiving, controlling-punitive, and behaviorally disorganized children. *Developmental Psychology, 40,* 519–532. doi: 10.1037/0012-1649.40.4.519

Moss, E., Dubois-Comtois, K., Cyr, C., Tarabulsy, G. M., St-Laurent, D., & Bernier, A. (2011). Efficacy of a home-visiting intervention aimed at improving maternal sensitivity, child attachment, and behavioral

outcomes for maltreated children: A randomized control trial. *Development and Psychopathology, 23,* 195–210. doi:10.1017/S0954579410000738

Moss, E., & St-Laurent, D. (2001). Attachment at school age and academic performance. *Developmental Psychology, 37,* 863–874.

Mounts, N. S. (2002). Parental management of adolescent peer relationships in context: The role of parenting style. *Journal of Family Psychology, 16,* 58–69. doi:10.1037/0893-3200.16.1.58

Mounts, N. S., & Steinberg, L. (1995). An ecological analysis of peer influence on adolescent grade point average and drug use. *Developmental Psychology, 31,* 915–922. doi:10.1037/0012-1649.31.6.915

Mouse Genome Sequencing Consortium. (2002, December 5). Initial sequencing and comparative analysis of the mouse genome. *Nature, 420,* 520–562. doi:10.1038/nature01262

Mrug, S., Hoza, B., & Bukowski, W. (2004). Choosing or being chosen by aggressive–disruptive peers: Do they contribute to children's externalizing and internalizing problems? *Journal of Abnormal Child Psychology, 32,* 53–65. doi:10.1023/B:JACP.0000007580.77154.69

Mueller, S. C., Temple, V., Oh, E., VanRyzin, C., Williams, A., Cornwell, B., ... Merke, D. P. (2008). Early androgen exposure modulates spatial cognition in congenital adrenal hyperplasia (CAH). *Psychoneuroendocrinology, 33,* 973–980. doi:10.1016/j.psyneuen.2008.04.005

Muller, C. (1995). Maternal employment, parent involvement, and mathematics achievement among adolescents. *Journal of Marriage and the Family, 57,* 85–100.

Mulligan, K., & Scherer, K. R. (2012). Toward a working definition of emotion. *Emotion Review, 4,* 345–357.

Mulvaney, M. K., & Mebert, C. J. (2007). Parental corporal punishment predicts behavior problems in early childhood. *Journal of Family Psychology, 21,* 389–397. doi:10.1037/0893-3200.21.3.389

Mumme, D. L., Fernald, A., & Herrera, C. (1996). Infants' responses to facial and vocal emotional signals in a social referencing paradigm. *Child Development, 67,* 3219–3237.

Munakata, Y., McClelland, J. L., Johnson, M. H., & Siegler, R. S. (1997). Rethinking infant knowledge: Toward an adaptive process account of successes and failures in object permanence tasks. *Psychological Review, 104,* 686–713. doi:10.1037/0033-295X.104.4.686

Munakata, Y., Snyder, H. R., & Chatham, C. H. (2012). Developing cognitive control: Three key transitions. *Current Directions in Psychological Science, 21,* 71–77. doi:10.1177/0963721412436807

Munch, C. (2012). *Youth correctional statistics in Canada, 2010/2011.* Retrieved from http://www.statcan.gc.ca/pub/85-002-x/2012001/article/11716-eng.htm

Munekata, H., & Ninomiya, K. (1985). The development of prosocial moral judgments. *Japanese Journal of Educational Psychology, 33,* 157–164.

Munroe, R. H., Shimmin, H. S., & Munroe, R. L. (1984). Gender understanding and sex role preference in four cultures. *Developmental Psychology, 20,* 673–682. doi:10.1037/0012-1649.20.4.673

Muraskas, J., Hasson, A., & Besinger, R. E. (2004). A girl with a birth weight of 280 g, now 14 years old. *New England Journal of Medicine, 351,* 836–837. doi:10.1056/NEJM200408193510826

Murphy, B. C., Eisenberg, N., Fabes, R. A., Shepard, S., & Guthrie, I. K. (1999). Consistency and change in children's emotionality and regulation: A longitudinal study. *Merrill-Palmer Quarterly, 45,* 413–444.

Murphy, G. L., & Medin, D. L. (1985). The role of theories in conceptual coherence. *Psychological Review, 92,* 289–316.

Musolino, J., & Landau, B. (2012). Genes, language, and the nature of scientific explanations: The case of Williams syndrome. *Cognitive Neuropsychology, 29*, 123–148. doi:10.1080/02643294.2012.702103

Mustonen, U., Huurre, T., Kiviruusu, O., Haukkala, A., & Aro, H. (2011). Long-term impact of parental divorce on intimate relationship quality in adulthood and the mediating role of psychosocial resources. *Journal of Family Psychology, 25*, 615–619. doi:10.1037/a0023996

Myowa-Yamakoshi, M., & Takeshita, H. (2006). Do human fetuses anticipate self-oriented actions? A study by four-dimensional (4D) ultrasonography. *Infancy, 10*, 289–301.

Nadig, A. S., & Sedivy, J. C. (2002). Evidence of perspective-taking constraints in children's on-line reference resolution. *Psychological Science, 13*, 329–336. doi:10.1111/j.0956-7976.2002.00460.x

Naigles, L. (1990). Children use syntax to learn verb meanings. *Journal of Child Language, 17*, 357–374. doi:10.1017/S0305000900013817

Naigles, L. G., & Gelman, S. A. (1995). Overextensions in comprehension and production revisited: Preferential-looking in a study of dog, cat, and cow. *Journal of Child Language, 22*, 19–46.

Nakamoto, J., & Schwartz, D. (2010). Is peer victimization associated with academic achievement? A meta-analytic review. *Social Development, 19*, 221–242. doi:10.1111/j.1467-9507.2009.00539.x

Nakata, T., & Trehub, S. E. (2004). Infants' responsiveness to maternal speech and singing. *Infant Behavior and Development, 27*, 455–464. doi:10.1016/j.infbeh.2004.03.002

Namy, L. L. (2001). What's in a name when it isn't a word? 17-month-olds' mapping of nonverbal symbols to object categories. *Infancy, 2*, 73–86. doi:10.1207/S15327078IN0201_5

Namy, L. L., & Waxman, S. R. (1998). Words and gestures: Infants' interpretations of different forms of symbolic reference. *Child Development, 69*, 295–308.

Náñez, J. E., Sr., & Yonas, A. (1994). Effects of luminance and texture motion on infant defensive reactions to optical collision. *Infant Behavior and Development, 17*, 165–174. doi:10.1016/0163-6383(94)90052-3

Nantel-Vivier, A., Kokko, K., Caprara, G. V., Pastorelli, C., Gerbino, M. G., Paciello, M., … Tremblay, R. E. (2009). Prosocial development from childhood to adolescence: A multi-informant perspective with Canadian and Italian longitudinal studies. *Journal of Child Psychology and Psychiatry, 50*, 590–598. doi:10.1111/j.1469-7610.2008.02039.x

Narusyte, J., Neiderhiser, J. M., D'Onofrio, B. M., Reiss, D., Spotts, E. L., Ganiban, J., & Lichtenstein, P. (2008). Testing different types of genotype-environment correlation: An extended children-of-twins model. *Developmental Psychology, 44*, 1591–1603. doi:10.1037/a0013911

Nathanielsz, P. W. (1994). *A time to be born: The life of the unborn child.* Oxford, England: Oxford University Press.

Nation, K. (2008). Learning to read words. *Quarterly Journal of Experimental Psychology, 61*, 1121–1133. doi:10.1080/17470210802034603

National Association for the Education of Young Children. (2011). 2010 NAEYC Standards for Initial & Advanced Early Childhood Professional Preparation Programs. Retrieved from http://www.naeyc.org/ncate/files/ncate/file/faculty/Standards/NAEYC%20Initial%20and%20Advanced%20Standards%203_2012.pdf.

National Council of Welfare. (2012). *Poverty profile: Special edition.* Ottawa, ON: Author.

NEDSAC. (2012). *Findings from the National Epidemiologic Database for the Study of Autism in Canada (NEDSAC): Changes in the prevalence of autism spectrum disorders in Newfoundland and Labrador, Prince Edward Island, and Southeastern Ontario.* Kingston, ON: Queen's University.

National Reading Panel. (2000). *Teaching children to read: An evidence-based assessment of the scientific research literature on reading and its implications for reading instruction: Reports of the subgroups* (NIH Publication No. 00–4754). Washington, DC: National Institute of Child Health and Human Development, National Institutes of Health.

Natsuaki, M. N., Gé, X., Reiss, D., & Neiderhiser, J. M. (2009). Aggressive behavior between siblings and the development of externalizing problems: Evidence from a genetically sensitive study. *Developmental Psychology, 45*, 1009–1018. doi:10.1037/a0015698

Neal, J. W. (2010). Hanging out: Features of urban children's peer social networks. *Journal of Social and Personal Relationships, 27*, 982–1000. doi:10.1177/0265407510378124

Neblett, E. W., Rivas-Drake, D., & Umaña-Taylor, A. J. (2012). The promise of racial and ethnic protective factors in promoting ethnic minority youth development. *Child Development Perspectives, 6*, 295–303. doi:10.1111/j.1750-8606.2012.00239.x

Neblett, E. W., White, R. L., Ford, K. R., Philip, C. L., Nguyên, H. X., & Sellers, R. M. (2008). Patterns of racial socialization and psychological adjustment: Can parental communications about race reduce the impact of racial discrimination? *Journal of Research on Adolescence, 18*, 477–515. doi:10.1111/j.1532-7795.2008.00568.x

Neckerman, H. J. (1996). The stability of social groups in childhood and adolescence: The role of the classroom social environment. *Social Development, 5*, 131–145. doi:10.1111/j.1467-9507.1996.tb00076.x

Nederhof, E., Belsky, J., Ormel, J., & Oldehinkel, A. J. (2012). Effects of divorce on Dutch boys' and girls' externalizing behavior in Gene × Environment perspective: Diathesis stress or differential susceptibility in the Dutch Tracking Adolescents' Individual Lives Survey study? *Development and Psychopathology, 24*, 929–939. doi:10.1017/S0954579412000454

Needham, A. (1997). Factors affecting infants' use of featural information in object segregation. *Current Directions in Psychological Science, 6*, 26–33. doi:10.2307/20182439

Needham, A., & Baillargeon, R. (1993). Intuitions about support in 4.5-month-old infants. *Cognition, 47*, 121–148. doi:10.1016/0010-0277(93)90002-D

Needham, A., & Baillargeon, R. (1997). Object segregation in 8-month-old infants. *Cognition, 62*, 121–149. doi:10.1016/S0010-0277(96)00727-5

Needham, A., & Baillargeon, R. (1998). Effects of prior experience on 4.5-month old infants' object segregation. *Infant Behavior and Development, 21*, 1–24. doi:10.1016/S0163-6383(98)90052-2

Needham, A., Barrett, T., & Peterman, K. (2002). A pick-me-up for infants' exploratory skills: Early simulated experiences reaching for objects using 'sticky mittens' enhances young infants' object exploration skills. *Infant Behavior and Development, 25*, 279–295. doi:10.1016/S0163-6383(02)00097-8

Negriff, S., & Susman, E. J. (2011). Pubertal timing, depression, and externalizing problems: A framework, review, and examination of gender differences. *Journal of Research on Adolescence, 21*, 717–746.

Neiderhiser, J. M., Reiss, D., Pedersen, N. L., Lichtenstein, P., Spotts, E. L., Hansson, K., … Elthammer, O. (2004). Genetic and environmental influences on mothering of adolescents: A comparison of two samples. *Developmental Psychology, 40*, 335–351. doi:10.1037/0012-1649.40.3.335

Neisser, U. (2004). Memory development: New questions and old. *Developmental Review, 24*, 154–158. doi:10.1016/j.dr.2003.09.002

Nelson, C. A., III, Bos, K., Gunnar, M. R., & Sonuga-Barke, E. J. S. (2011). The neurobiological toll of early human deprivation. *Monographs of the Society for Research in Child Development, 76*(4, Serial No. 301), 127–146. doi:10.1111/j.1540-5834.2011.00630.x

Nelson, C. A., III, Thomas, K. M., & de Haan, M. (2006). Neural bases of cognitive development. In W. Damon & R. M. Lerner (Series Eds.) & D. Kuhn & R. S. Siegler (Vol. Eds.), *Handbook of child psychology: Vol. 2. Cognition, perception, and language* (6th ed., pp. 3–57). Hoboken, NJ: Wiley.

Nelson, C. A., III, Zeanah, C. H., Fox, N. A., Marshall, P. J., Smyke, A. T., & Guthrie, D. (2007, December 21). Cognitive recovery in socially deprived young children: The Bucharest Early Intervention Project. *Science, 318,* 1937–1940.

Nelson, D. A., Mitchell, C., & Yang, C. (2008). Intent attributions and aggression: A study of children and their parents. *Journal of Abnormal Child Psychology, 36,* 793–806. doi:10.1007/s10802-007-9211-7

Nelson, D. A., Robinson, C. C., Hart, C. H., Albano, A. D., & Marshall, S. J. (2010). Italian preschoolers' peer-status linkages with sociability and subtypes of aggression and victimization. *Social Development, 19,* 698–720. doi:10.1111/j.1467-9507.2009.00551.x

Nelson, E. A., Schiefenhoevel, W., & Haimerl, F. (2000). Child care practices in nonindustrialized societies. *Pediatrics, 105,* e75. doi:10.1542/peds.105.6.e75

Nelson, E. E., Herman, K. N., Barrett, C. E., Noble, P. L., Wojteczko, K., Chisholm, K., ... Pine, D. S. (2009). Adverse rearing experiences enhance responding to both aversive and rewarding stimuli in juvenile rhesus monkeys. *Biological Psychiatry, 66,* 702–704. doi:10.1016/j.biopsych.2009.04.007

Nelson, H. D., Nygren, P., Walker, M., & Panoscha, R. (2006). Screening for speech and language delay in preschool children: Systematic evidence review for the US Preventive Services Task Force. *Pediatrics, 117,* e298–319. doi:10.1542/peds.2005-1467

Nelson, J., & Aboud, F. E. (1985). The resolution of social conflict between friends. *Child Development, 56,* 1009–1017.

Nelson, J. K. (2005). Interference resolution in the left inferior frontal gyrus. *Dissertation Abstracts International: Section B: The Sciences and Engineering, 66*(10), 5703.

Nelson, K. (1973). Structure and strategy in learning to talk. *Monographs of the Society for Research in Child Development, 38*(1-2, Serial No. 149).

Nelson, K. (1993). The psychological and social origins of autobiographical memory. *Psychological Science, 4,* 7–14. doi:10.1111/j.1467-9280.1993.tb00548.x

Nelson, K., & Fivush, R. (2004). The emergence of autobiographical memory: A social cultural developmental theory. *Psychological Review, 111,* 486–511. doi:10.1037/0033-295X.111.2.486

Nesdale, D. (2007). Children's perceptions of social groups. In J. A. Zebrowski (Ed.), *New research on social perception* (pp. 1–45). Hauppauge, NY: Nova Science.

Neville, B., & Parke, R. D. (1997). Waiting for paternity: Interpersonal and contextual implications of the timing of fatherhood. *Sex Roles, 37,* 45–59. doi:10.1023/A:1025636619455

Newcomb, A. F., & Bukowski, W. M. (1984). A longitudinal study of the utility of social preference and social impact sociometric classification schemes. *Child Development, 55,* 1434–1447. doi:10.2307/1130013

Newcomb, A. F., Bukowski, W. M., & Pattee, L. (1993). Children's peer relations: A meta-analytic review of popular, rejected, neglected, controversial, and average sociometric status. *Psychological Bulletin, 113,* 99–128.

Newcombe, N., & Huttenlocher, J. (2000). *Making space: The development of spatial representation and reasoning.* Cambridge, MA: MIT Press.

Newcombe, N., Huttenlocher, J., Drummey, A. B., & Wiley, J. G. (1998). The development of spatial location coding: Place learning and dead reckoning in the second and third years. *Cognitive Development, 13,* 185–200. doi:10.1016/S0885-2014(98)90038-7

Newcombe, N. S., & Huttenlocher, J. (2006). Development of spatial cognition. In W. Damon & R. M. Lerner (Series Eds.) & D. Kuhn & R. S. Siegler (Vol. Eds.), *Handbook of child psychology: Vol. 2. Cognition, perception, and language* (6th ed., pp. 734–776). Hoboken, NJ: Wiley.

Newcombe, N. S., & Ratliff, K. R. (2007). Explaining the development of spatial reorientation. In J. M. Plumert & J. P. Spencer (Eds.), *The emerging spatial mind* (pp. 53–76). New York, NY: Oxford University Press.

Newell, K. M., Scully, D. M., McDonald, P. V., & Baillargeon, R. (1989). Task constraints and infant grip configurations. *Developmental Psychobiology, 22,* 817–831. doi:10.1002/dev.420220806

Newland, M. C., & Rasmussen, E. B. (2003). Behavior in adulthood and during aging is affected by contaminant exposure in utero. *Current Directions in Psychological Science, 12,* 212–217. doi:10.1046/j.0963-7214.2003.01264.x

Newman, J. (1995, December). How breast milk protects newborns. *Scientific American, 273*(6), 76–79.

Newman, R. S. (2005). The cocktail party effect in infants revisited: Listening to one's name in noise. *Developmental Psychology, 41,* 352–362.

Newman, S. D., Carpenter, P. A., Varma, S., & Just, M. A. (2003). Frontal and parietal participation in problem solving in the Tower of London: fMRI and computational modeling of planning and high-level perception. *Neuropsychologia, 41,* 1668–1682.

Newport, E., Gleitman, H., & Gleitman, L. (1977). Mother, I'd rather do it myself: Some effects and non-effects of maternal speech style. In C. E. Snow & C. A. Ferguson (Eds.), *Talking to children: Language input and acquisition* (pp. 109–150). Cambridge, England: Cambridge University Press.

Newport, E. L. (1990). Maturational constraints on language learning. *Cognitive Science, 14,* 11–28.

Nguyen, S. P., & Gelman, S. A. (2002). Four and 6-year olds' biological concept of death: The case of plants. *British Journal of Developmental Psychology, 20,* 495–513. doi:10.1348/026151002760390918

NICHD Early Child Care Research Network. (1997a). The effects of infant child care on infant-mother attachment security: Results of the NICHD Study of Early Child Care. *Child Development, 68,* 860–879. doi:10.1111/j.1467-8624.1997.tb01967.x

NICHD Early Child Care Research Network. (1997b). Familial factors associated with the characteristics of nonmaternal care for infants. *Journal of Marriage and the Family, 59,* 389–408.

NICHD Early Child Care Research Network. (1998a). Early child care and self-control, compliance, and problem behavior at twenty-four and thirty-six months. *Child Development, 69,* 1145–1170.

NICHD Early Child Care Research Network. (1998b, April-May). *When child care classrooms meet recommended guidelines for quality.* Paper presented at the meeting, "Child Care in the New Policy Context," U.S. Department of Health and Human Services, Bethesda, MD.

NICHD Early Child Care Research Network. (1999). Child care and mother–child interaction in the first three years of life. *Developmental Psychology, 35,* 1399–1413. doi:10.1037/0012-1649.35.6.1399

NICHD Early Child Care Research Network. (2000a). Factors associated with fathers' caregiving activities and sensitivity with young children. *Journal of Family Psychology 14*, 200–219.

NICHD Early Child Care Research Network. (2000b). The relation of child care to cognitive and language development. *Child Development, 71*, 960–980.

NICHD Early Child Care Research Network. (2002). Early child care and children's development prior to school entry: Results from the NICHD Study of Early Child Care. *American Educational Research Journal, 39*, 133–164.

NICHD Early Child Care Research Network. (2003). Social functioning in first grade: Associations with earlier home and child care predictors and with current classroom experiences. *Child Development, 74*, 1639–1662.

NICHD Early Child Care Research Network. (2004). Trajectories of physical aggression from toddlerhood to middle childhood: Predictors, correlates, and outcomes. *Monographs of the Society for Research in Child Development, 69*(4, Serial No. 278), i–143. doi:10.2307/3701390

NICHD Early Child Care Research Network. (2006). Child-care effect sizes for the NICHD Study of Early Child Care and Youth Development. *American Psychologist, 61*, 99–116. doi:10.1037/0003-066X.61.2.99

NICHD Early Child Care Research Network, & Duncan, G. J. (2003). Modeling the impacts of child care quality on children's preschool cognitive development. *Child Development, 74*, 1454–1475. doi:10.1111/1467-8624.00617

Nicholson, T. (1999). Reading comprehension processes. In G. B. Thompson & T. Nicholson (Eds.), *Learning to read: Beyond phonics and whole language* (pp. 127–149). Newark, DE: International Reading Association.

Nicoladis, E., & Genesee, F. (1996). A longitudinal study of pragmatic differentiation in young bilingual children. *Language Learning, 46*, 439–464. doi:10.1111/j.1467-1770.1996.tb01243.x

Nicolopoulou, A. (2007). The interplay of play and narrative in children's development: Theoretical reflections and concrete examples. In A. Göncü & S. Gaskins (Eds.), *Play and development: Evolutionary, sociocultural, and functional perspectives* (pp. 247–273). New York, NY: Erlbaum.

Nieder, A. (2012). Supramodal numerosity selectivity of neurons in primate prefrontal and posterior parietal cortices. *Proceedings of the National Academy of Sciences of the United States of America, 109*, 11860–11865. doi:10.1073/pnas.1204580109

Nieder, A., & Dehaene, S. (2009). Representation of number in the brain. *Annual Review of Neuroscience, 32*, 185–208. doi:10.1146/annurev.neuro.051508.135550

Nielsen, M., Suddendorf, T., & Slaughter, V. (2006). Mirror self-recognition beyond the face. *Child Development, 77*, 176–185. doi:10.1111/j.1467-8624.2006.00863.x

Nievar, M. A., & Becker, B. J. (2008). Sensitivity as a privileged predictor of attachment: A second perspective on De Wolff and van IJzendoorn's meta-analysis. *Social Development, 17*, 102–114.

Nilsen, E. S., & Graham, S. A. (2009). The relations between children's communicative perspective-taking and executive functioning. *Cognitive Psychology, 58*, 220–249. doi:10.1016/j.cogpsych.2008.07.002

Nisan, M., & Kohlberg, L. (1982). Universality and variation in moral judgment: A longitudinal and cross-sectional study in Turkey. *Child Development, 53*, 865–876. doi:10.2307/1129123

Nisbett, R. E., Aronson, J., Blair, C., Dickens, W., Flynn, J., Halpern, D. F., & Turkheimer, E. (2012). Intelligence: New findings and theoretical developments. *American Psychologist, 67*, 130–159. doi:10.1037/a0026699

Nishina, A., Bellmore, A., Witkow, M. R., & Nylund-Gibson, K. (2010). Longitudinal consistency of adolescent ethnic identification across varying school ethnic contexts. *Developmental Psychology, 46*, 1389–1401. doi:10.1037/a0020728

Nobes, G., Panagiotaki, G., & Pawson, C. (2009). The influence of negligence, intention, and outcome on children's moral judgments. *Journal of Experimental Child Psychology, 104*, 382–397. doi:10.1016/j.jecp.2009.08.001

Nolen-Hoeksema, S. (2012). Emotion regulation and psychopathology: The role of gender. *Annual Review of Clinical Psychology, 8*, 161–187. doi:10.1146/annurev-clinpsy-032511-143109

Nolen-Hoeksema, S., Larson, J., & Grayson, C. (1999). Explaining the gender difference in depressive symptoms. *Journal of Personality and Social Psychology, 77*, 1061–1072.

Nolen-Hoeksema, S., Stice, E., Wade, E., & Bohon, C. (2007). Reciprocal relations between rumination and bulimic, substance abuse, and depressive symptoms in female adolescents. *Journal of Abnormal Psychology, 116*, 198–207.

Nolen-Hoeksema, S., Wisco, B. E., & Lyubomirsky, S. (2008). Rethinking rumination. *Perspectives on Psychological Science, 3*, 400–424.

Nordenström, A., Servin, A., Bohlin, G., Larsson, A., & Wedell, A. (2002). Sex-typed toy play behavior correlates with the degree of prenatal androgen exposure assessed by CYP21 genotype in girls with congenital adrenal hyperplasia. *Journal of Clinical Endocrinology and Metabolism, 87*, 5119–5124. doi:10.1210/jc.2001-011531

Nordhov, S. M., Rønning, J. A., Ulvund, S. E., Dahl, L. B., & Kaaresen, P. I. (2011). Early intervention improves behavioral outcomes for preterm infants: Randomized controlled trial. *Pediatrics.* Advance online publication. doi:10.1542/peds.2011-0248

Nosek, B. A., & Banaji, M. R. (2009). Implicit attitude. In T. Bayne, A. Cleeremans, & P. Wilken (Eds.), *The Oxford companion to consciousness* (pp. 84–85). Oxford, England: Oxford University Press.

Nowell, A., & Hedges, L. V. (1998). Trends in gender differences in academic achievement from 1960 to 1994: An analysis of differences in mean, variance, and extreme scores. *Sex Roles, 39*, 21–43. doi:10.1023/A:1018873615316

Nucci, L. (1981). Conceptions of personal issues: A domain distinct from moral or societal concepts. *Child Development, 52*, 114–121. doi:10.2307/1129220

Nucci, L. (1997). Culture, universals, and the personal. In H. D. Saltzstein (Ed.), *New Directions for Child and Adolescent Development: No. 76. Culture as a context for moral development: New perspectives on the particular and the universal* (Vol. 1997, pp. 5–22). San Francisco, CA: Jossey-Bass.

Nucci, L., Camino, C., & Sapiro, C. M. (1996). Social class effects on northeastern Brazilian children's conceptions of areas of personal choice and social regulation. *Child Development, 67*, 1223–1242. doi:10.1111/j.1467-8624.1996.tb01792.x

Nucci, L., & Weber, E. K. (1995). Social interactions in the home and the development of young children's conceptions of the personal. *Child Development, 66*, 1438–1452. doi:10.2307/1131656

Nucci, L. P., & Gingo, M. (2011). The development of moral reasoning. In U. Goswami (Ed.), *The Wiley-Blackwell handbook of childhood cognitive development* (2nd ed., pp. 420–445). Oxford, England: Wiley-Blackwell.

Nurmi, J.-E. (2004). Socialization and self-development: Channeling, selection, adjustment, and reflection. In R. M. Lerner & L. D. Steinberg (Eds.), *Handbook of adolescent psychology* (2nd ed., pp. 85–124). Hoboken, NJ: Wiley.

Nylund, K., Bellmore, A., Nishina, A., & Graham, S. (2007). Subtypes, severity, and structural stability of peer victimization: What does latent class analysis say? *Child Development, 78,* 1706–1722. doi:10.1111/j.1467-8624.2007.01097.x

O'Connor, A., & Boag, S. (2010). Do stepparents experience more parental antagonism than biological parents? A test of evolutionary and socialization perspectives. *Journal of Divorce and Remarriage, 51,* 508–525. doi:10.1080/10502556.2010.504101

O'Connor, T. G., Caspi, A., DeFries, J. C., & Plomin, R. (2000). Are associations between parental divorce and children's adjustment genetically mediated? An adoption study. *Developmental Psychology, 36,* 429–437. doi:10.1037/0012-1649.36.4.429

O'Connor, T. G., Heron, J., Golding, J., Beveridge, M., & Glover, V. (2002). Maternal antenatal anxiety and children's behavioural/emotional problems at 4 years. Report from the Avon Longitudinal Study of Parents and Children. *British Journal of Psychiatry, 180,* 502–508.

O'Connor, T. G., Rutter, M., & English and Romanian Adoptees Study Team. (2000). Attachment disorder behavior following early severe deprivation: Extension and longitudinal follow-up. *Journal of the American Academy of Child and Adolescent Psychiatry, 39,* 703–712.

O'Doherty, K., Troseth, G. L., Shimpi, P. M., Goldenberg, E., Akhtar, N., & Saylor, M. M. (2011). Third-party social interaction and word learning from video. *Child Development, 82,* 902–915. doi:10.1111/j.1467-8624.2011.01579.x

O'Leary, K. D., Slep, A. M. S., Avery-Leaf, S., & Cascardi, M. (2008). Gender differences in dating aggression among multiethnic high school students. *Journal of Adolescent Health, 42,* 473–479. doi:10.1016/j.jadohealth.2007.09.012

O'Reilly, A. W., & Bornstein, M. H. (1993). Caregiver-child interaction in play. In M. H. Bornstein & A. W. O'Reilly (Eds.), *New Directions for Child and Adolescent Development: No. 59. The role of play in the development of thought* (pp. 55–66). San Francisco, CA: Jossey-Bass.

O'Rourke, J. A., Scharf, J. M., Yu, D., & Pauls, D. L. (2009). The genetics of Tourette syndrome: A review. *Journal of Psychosomatic Research, 67,* 533–545.

Oakes, L. M., & Cohen, L. B. (1995). Infant causal perception. In L. P. Lipsitt & C. K. Rovee-Collier (Eds.), *Advances in infancy research* (Vol. 9, pp. 1–54). Norwood, NJ: Ablex.

Oakhill, J., & Cain, K. (2000). Children's difficulties in text comprehension: Assessing causal issues. *Journal of Deaf Studies and Deaf Education, 5,* 51–59. doi:10.1093/deafed/5.1.51

Oberlander, T. F., Weinberg, J., Papsdorf, M., Grunau, R., Misri, S., & Devlin, A. M. (2008). Prenatal exposure to maternal depression, neonatal methylation of human glucocorticoid receptor gene (NR3C1) and infant cortisol stress responses. *Epigenetics, 3,* 97–106.

Obradović, J. (2010). Effortful control and adaptive functioning of homeless children: Variable-focused and person-focused analyses. *Journal of Applied Developmental Psychology, 31,* 109–117. doi:10.1016/j.appdev.2009.09.004

Obradović, J., Bush, N. R., Stamperdahl, J., Adler, N. E., & Boyce, W. T. (2010). Biological sensitivity to context: The interactive effects of stress reactivity and family adversity on socioemotional behavior and school readiness. *Child Development, 81,* 270–289.

Obradović, J., & Hipwell, A. (2010). Psychopathology and social competence during the transition to adolescence: The role of family adversity and pubertal development. *Development and Psychopathology, 22,* 621–634. doi:10.1017/S0954579410000325

Obradović, J., Long, J. D., Cutuli, J. J., Chan, C.-K., Hinz, E., Heistad, D., & Masten, A. S. (2009). Academic achievement of homeless and highly mobile children in an urban school district: Longitudinal evidence on risk, growth, and resilience. *Development and Psychopathology, 21,* 493–518. doi:10.1017/S0954579409000273

Ocampo, K. A., Bernal, M. E., & Knight, G. P. (1993). Gender race and ethnicity: The sequencing of social constancies. In M. E. Bernal & G. P. Knight (Eds.), *Ethnic identity: Formation and transmission among Hispanics and other minorities* (pp. 11–30). Albany: State University of New York Press.

Ocampo, K. A., Knight, G. P., & Bernal, M. E. (1997). The development of cognitive abilities and social identities in children: The case of ethnic identity. *International Journal of Behavioral Development, 21,* 479–500. doi:10.1080/016502597384758

Oden, S., & Asher, S. R. (1977). Coaching children in social skills for friendship making. *Child Development, 48,* 495–506. doi:10.2307/1128645

Odgers, C. L., Caspi, A., Russell, M. A., Sampson, R. J., Arseneault, L., & Moffitt, T. E. (2012). Supportive parenting mediates neighborhood socioeconomic disparities in children's antisocial behavior from ages 5 to 12. *Development and Psychopathology, 24,* 705–721. doi:10.1017/S0954579412000326

Ogbu, J. U. (1981). Origins of human competence: A cultural-ecological perspective. *Child Development, 52,* 413–429. doi:10.2307/1129158

Oh, W., Rubin, K., Bowker, J., Booth-LaForce, C., Rose-Krasnor, L., & Laursen, B. (2008). Trajectories of social withdrawal from middle childhood to early adolescence. *Journal of Abnormal Child Psychology, 36,* 553–566. doi:10.1007/s10802-007-9199-z

Öhman, A., & Mineka, S. (2001). Fears, phobias, and preparedness: Toward an evolved module of fear and fear learning. *Psychological Review, 108,* 483–522. doi:10.1037/0033-295X.108.3.483

Oliner, S. P., & Oliner, P. M. (1988). *The altruistic personality: Rescuers of Jews in Nazi Europe.* New York, NY: Free Press.

Oliver, B., Dale, P. S., & Plomin, R. (2004). Verbal and nonverbal predictors of early language problems: An analysis of twins in early childhood back to infancy. *Journal of Child Language, 31,* 609–631.

Ollendick, T. H., Weist, M. D., Borden, M. C., & Greene, R. W. (1992). Sociometric status and academic, behavioral, and psychological adjustment: A five-year longitudinal study. *Journal of Consulting and Clinical Psychology, 60,* 80–87. doi:10.1037/0022-006X.60.1.80

Oller, D. K., & Eilers, R. E. (1988). The role of audition in infant babbling. *Child Development, 59,* 441–449.

Olson, S. L., Bates, J. E., & Kaskie, B. (1992). Caregiver-infant interaction antecedents of children's school-age cognitive ability. *Merrill-Palmer Quarterly, 38,* 309–330.

Olson, S. L., Bates, J. E., Sandy, J. M., & Lanthier, R. (2000). Early developmental precursors of externalizing behavior in middle childhood and adolescence. *Journal of Abnormal Child Psychology, 28,* 119–133. doi:10.1023/A:1005166629744

Olson, S. L., Lopez-Duran, N., Lunkenheimer, E. S., Chang, H., & Sameroff, A. J. (2011). Individual differences in the development of early peer aggression: Integrating contributions of self-regulation, theory of mind, and parenting. *Development and Psychopathology, 23,* 253–266. doi:10.1017/S0954579410000775

Olson, S. L., Tardif, T. Z., Miller, A., Felt, B., Grabell, A. S., Kessler, D., … Hirabayashi, H. (2011). Inhibitory control and harsh discipline as predictors of externalizing problems in young children: A comparative study of US, Chinese, and Japanese preschoolers. *Journal of Abnormal Child Psychology, 39,* 1163–1175.

Olweus, D. (1994). Bullying at school: Basic facts and effects of a school based intervention program. *Journal of Child Psychology and Psychiatry, 35,* 1171–1190. doi:10.1111/j.1469-7610.1994.tb01229.x

Onishi, K. H., & Baillargeon, R. (2005, April 8). Do 15-month-old infants understand false beliefs? *Science, 308,* 255–258.

Opfer, J. E., & Gelman, S. A. (2001). Children's and adults' models for predicting teleological action: The development of a biology-based model. *Child Development, 72,* 1367–1381.

Opfer, J. E., & Siegler, R. S. (2004). Revisiting preschoolers' *living things* concept: A microgenetic analysis of conceptual change in basic biology. *Cognitive Psychology, 49,* 301–332. doi:10.1016/j.cogpsych.2004.01.002

Oppliger, P. A. (2007). Effects of gender stereotyping on socialization. In R. W. Preiss, B. M. Gayle, N. Burrell, M. Allen, & J. Bryant (Eds.), *Mass media effects research: Advances through meta-analysis* (pp. 199–214). Mahwah, NJ: Erlbaum.

Organisation for Economic Co-operation and Development. (2013). Infant mortality rate, deaths per 1000 live births [Data file]. Available from http://www.oecd.org/els/health-systems/oecdhealthdata2013-frequentlyrequesteddata.htm

Oriña, M. M., Collins, W. A., Simpson, J. A., Salvatore, J. E., Haydon, K. C., & Kim, J. S. (2011). Developmental and dyadic perspectives on commitment in adult romantic relationships. *Psychological Science, 22,* 908–915. doi:10.1177/0956797611410573

Orth, U., Robins, R. W., & Roberts, B. W. (2008). Low self-esteem prospectively predicts depression in adolescence and young adulthood. *Journal of Personality and Social Psychology, 95,* 695–708. doi:10.1037/0022-3514.95.3.695

Osborne, L. R., & Mervis, C. B. (2007). Rearrangements of the Williams-Beuren syndrome locus: Molecular basis and implications for speech and language development. *Expert Reviews in Molecular Medicine, 9,* 1–16. doi:10.1017/S146239940700035X

Oster, H., Hegley, D., & Nagel, L. (1992). Adult judgments and fine-grained analysis of infant facial expressions: Testing the validity of a priori coding formulas. *Developmental Psychology, 28,* 1115–1131.

Ostrov, J. M., Ries, E. E., Stauffacher, K., Godleski, S. A., & Mullins, A. D. (2008). Relational aggression, physical aggression and deception during early childhood: A multimethod, multi-informant short-term longitudinal study. *Journal of Clinical Child and Adolescent Psychology, 37,* 664–675. doi:10.1080/15374410802148137

Otake, M., & Schull, W. J. (1984). In utero exposure to A-bomb radiation and mental retardation: A reassessment. *British Journal of Radiology, 57,* 409–414.

Ouellette-Kuntz, H., Coo, H., Lam, M., Breitenbach, M. M., Hennessey, P. E., Jackman, P. D., ... & Chung, A. M. (2014). The changing prevalence of autism in three regions of Canada. *Journal of Autism and Developmental Disorders, 44,* 120–136. doi:10.1007/s10803-013-1856-1

Oveis, C., Cohen, A. B., Gruber, J., Shiota, M. N., Haidt, J., & Keltner, D. (2009). Resting respiratory sinus arrhythmia is associated with tonic positive emotionality. *Emotion, 9,* 265–270. doi:10.1037/a0015383

Overman, W., Pate, B. J., Moore, K., & Peuster, A. (1996). Ontogeny of place learning in children as measured in the Radial Arm Maze, Morris Search Task, and Open Field Task. *Behavioral Neuroscience, 110,* 1205–1228.

Ozonoff, S., Cook, I., Coon, H., Dawson, G., Joseph, R. M., Klin, A., ... Wrathall, D. (2004). Performance on Cambridge Neuropsychological Test Automated Battery subtests sensitive to frontal lobe function in people with autistic disorder: Evidence from the Collaborative Programs of Excellence in Autism Network. *Journal of Autism and Developmental Disorders, 34,* 139–150. doi:10.1023/B:JADD.0000022605.81989.cc

Padilla-Walker, L. M., Carlo, G., Christensen, K. J., & Yorgason, J. B. (2012). Bidirectional relations between authoritative parenting and adolescents' prosocial behaviors. *Journal of Research on Adolescence, 22,* 400–408. doi:10.1111/j.1532-7795.2012.00807.x

Padilla-Walker, L. M., & Christensen, K. J. (2011). Empathy and self-regulation as mediators between parenting and adolescents' prosocial behavior toward strangers, friends, and family. *Journal of Research on Adolescence, 21,* 545–551. doi:10.1111/j.1532-7795.2010.00695.x

Padilla-Walker, L. M., Harper, J. M., & Jensen, A. C. (2010). Self-regulation as a mediator between sibling relationship quality and early adolescents' positive and negative outcomes. *Journal of Family Psychology, 24,* 419–428. doi:10.1037/a0020387

Padilla-Walker, L. M., & Nelson, L. J. (2010). Parenting and adolescents' values and behaviour: The moderating role of temperament. *Journal of Moral Education, 39,* 491–509. doi:10.1080/03057240.2010.521385

Pagani-Kurtz, L., & Derevensky, J. L. (1997). Access by noncustodial parents: Effects upon children's postdivorce coping resources. *Journal of Divorce & Remarriage, 27,* 43–55. doi:10.1300/J087v27n01_03

Paik, H., & Comstock, G. (1994). The effects of television violence on antisocial behavior: A meta-analysis. *Communication Research, 21,* 516–546. doi:10.1177/009365094021004004

Pakulak, E., & Neville, H. J. (2011). Maturational constraints on the recruitment of early processes for syntactic processing. *Journal of Cognitive Neuroscience, 23,* 2752–2765. doi:10.1162/jocn.2010.21586

Paley, V. G. (1981). *Wally's stories.* Cambridge, MA: Harvard University Press.

Palmen, H., Vermande, M. M., Deković, M., & van Aken, M. A. G. (2011). Competence, problem behavior, and the effects of having no friends, aggressive friends, or nonaggressive friends: A four-year longitudinal study. *Merrill-Palmer Quarterly, 57,* 186–213.

Palmer, S. B., Fais, L., Golinkoff, R. M., & Werker, J. F. (2012). Perceptual narrowing of linguistic sign occurs in the 1st year of life. *Child Development, 83,* 543–553. doi:10.1111/j.1467-8624.2011.01715.x

Panfile, T. M., & Laible, D. J. (2012). Attachment security and child's empathy: The mediating role of emotion regulation. *Merrill-Palmer Quarterly, 58,* 1–21.

Papini, D. R., & Sebby, R. A. (1988). Variations in conflictual family issues by adolescent pubertal status, gender, and family member. *Journal of Early Adolescence, 8,* 1–15. doi:10.1177/0272431688081001

Paquette, G. (2004). Violence on Canadian television networks. *The Canadian Child and Adolescent Psychiatry Review, 13,* 13–15.

Paradis, J., Nicoladis, E., & Genesee, F. (2000). Early emergence of structural constraints on code-mixing: Evidence from French–English bilingual children. *Bilingualism: Language and Cognition, 3,* 245–261.

Pardini, D. A., & Byrd, A. L. (2012). Perceptions of aggressive conflicts and others' distress in children with callous-unemotional traits: 'I'll show you who's boss, even if you suffer and I get in trouble.' *Journal of Child Psychology and Psychiatry, 53,* 283–291. doi:10.1111/j.1469-7610.2011.02487.x

Park, G., Lubinski, D., & Benbow, C. P. (2008). Ability differences among people who have commensurate degrees matter for scientific creativity. *Psychological Science, 19,* 957–961. doi:10.1111/j.1467-9280.2008.02182.x

Parke, R. D. (1996). *Fatherhood.* Cambridge, MA: Harvard University Press.

Parke, R. D., & Buriel, R. (1998). Socialization in the family: Ethnic and ecological perspectives. In W. Damon (Series Ed.) & N. Eisenberg (Vol. Ed.), *Handbook of child psychology: Vol. 3. Social, emotional, and personality development* (5th ed., pp. 463–552). New York, NY: Wiley.

Parke, R. D., & Buriel, R. (2006). Socialization in the family: Ethnic and ecological perspectives. In W. Damon & R. M. Lerner (Series Eds.) & N. Eisenberg (Vol. Ed.), *Handbook of child psychology: Vol. 3. Social, emotional, and personality development* (6th ed., pp. 429–504). Hoboken, NJ: Wiley.

Parke, R. D., Coltrane, S., Duffy, S., Buriel, R., Dennis, J., Powers, J., … Widaman, K. F. (2004). Economic stress, parenting, and child adjustment in Mexican American and European American families. *Child Development, 75,* 1632–1656. doi:10.1111/j.1467-8624.2004.00807.x

Parke, R. D., O'Neil, R., Spitzer, S., Isley, S., Welsh, M., Wang, S., … Cupp, R. (1997). A longitudinal assessment of sociometric stability and the behavioral correlates of children's social acceptance. *Merrill-Palmer Quarterly, 43,* 635–662. doi:10.2307/23093363

Parke, R. D., & Slaby, R. G. (1983). The development of aggression. In P. H. Mussen (Series Ed.) & E. M. Hetherington (Vol. Ed.), *Handbook of child psychology: Vol. 4. Socialization, personality, and social development* (pp. 547–641). New York, NY: Wiley.

Parker, J. G., & Asher, S. R. (1987). Peer relations and later personal adjustment: Are low-accepted children at risk? *Psychological Bulletin, 102,* 357–389. doi:10.1037/0033-2909.102.3.357

Parker, J. G., & Asher, S. R. (1993). Friendship and friendship quality in middle childhood: Links with peer group acceptance and feelings of loneliness and social dissatisfaction. *Developmental Psychology, 29,* 611–621.

Parker, J. G., & Gottman, J. M. (1989). Social and emotional development in a relational context: Friendship interaction from early childhood to adolescence. In T. J. Berndt & G. W. Ladd (Eds.), *Peer relationships in child development* (pp. 95–131). Oxford, England: Wiley.

Parker, J. G., & Herrera, C. (1996). Interpersonal processes in friendship: A comparison of abused and nonabused children's experiences. *Developmental Psychology, 32,* 1025–1038. doi:10.1037/0012-1649.32.6.1025

Parker, J. G., Rubin, K. H., Price, J. M., & DeRosier, M. E. (1995). Peer relationships, child development, and adjustment: A developmental psychopathology perspective. In D. Cicchetti & D. J. Cohen (Eds.), *Developmental psychopathology: Vol. 2. Risk, disorder, and adaptation* (pp. 96–161). New York, NY: Wiley.

Parritz, R. H. (1996). A descriptive analysis of toddler coping in challenging circumstances. *Infant Behavior and Development, 19,* 171–180.

Pascalis, O., de Haan, M., & Nelson, C. A. (2002, May 17). Is face processing species-specific during the first year of life? *Science, 296,* 1321–1323.

Pascalis, O., Scott, L. S., Kelly, D. J., Shannon, R. W., Nicholson, E., Coleman, M., & Nelson, C. A. (2005). Plasticity of face processing in infancy. *Proceedings of the National Academy of Sciences of the United States of America, 102,* 5297–5300. doi:10.1073/pnas.0406627102

Paschall, M. J., & Hubbard, M. L. (1998). Effects of neighborhood and family stressors on African American male adolescents' self-worth and propensity for violent behavior. *Journal of Consulting and Clinical Psychology, 66,* 825–831. doi:10.1037/0022-006X.66.5.825

Pascual-Leone, A., Cammarota, A., Wassermann, E. M., Brasil-Neto, J. P., Cohen, L. G., & Hallett, M. (1993). Modulation of motor cortical outputs to the reading hand of braille readers. *Annals of Neurology, 34,* 33–37. doi:10.1002/ana.410340108

Patterson, C. J. (1995). Families of the baby boom: Parents' division of labor and children's adjustment. *Developmental Psychology, 31,* 115–123. doi:10.1037/0012-1649.31.1.115

Patterson, C. J. (2002). Lesbian and gay parenthood. In M. H. Bornstein (Ed.), *Handbook of parenting: Vol. 3. Being and becoming a parent* (2nd ed., pp. 317–338). Mahwah, NJ: Erlbaum.

Patterson, C. J., & Chan, R. W. (1997). Gay fathers. In M. E. Lamb (Ed.), *The role of the father in child development* (3rd ed., pp. 245–260). New York, NY: Wiley.

Patterson, C. J., Griesler, P. C., Vaden, N. A., & Kupersmidt, J. B. (1992). Family economic circumstances, life transitions, and children's peer relations. In R. D. Parke & G. W. Ladd (Eds.), *Family–peer relationships: Modes of linkage* (pp. 385–424). Hillsdale, NJ: Erlbaum.

Patterson, F., & Linden, E. (1981). *The education of Koko.* New York, NY: Holt, Rinehart, and Winston.

Patterson, G. R. (1982). *Coercive family process.* Eugene, OR: Castalia.

Patterson, G. R. (1995). Coercion as a basis for early age of onset for arrest. In J. McCord (Ed.), *Coercion and punishment in long-term perspectives* (pp. 81–105). New York, NY: Cambridge University Press.

Patterson, G. R., Capaldi, D., & Bank, L. (1991). An early starter model for predicting delinquency. In D. J. Pepler & K. H. Rubin (Eds.), *The development and treatment of childhood aggression* (pp. 139–168). Hillsdale, NJ: Erlbaum.

Patterson, G. R., Reid, J. B., & Dishion, T. J. (1992). *A social interactional approach: Vol. 4. Antisocial boys.* Eugene, OR: Castalia.

Patteson, D. M., & Barnard, K. E. (1990). Parenting of low birth weight infants: A review of issues and interventions. *Infant Mental Health Journal, 11,* 37–56.

Paulson, S. E. (1996). Maternal employment and adolescent achievement revisited: An ecological perspective. *Family Relations, 45,* 201–208.

Paus, T. (2010). Growth of white matter in the adolescent brain: Myelin or axon? *Brain and Cognition, 72,* 26–35. doi:10.1016/j.bandc.2009.06.002

Peake, P. K., Hebl, M., & Mischel, W. (2002). Strategic attention deployment for delay of gratification in working and waiting situations. *Developmental Psychology, 38,* 313–326. doi:10.1037/0012-1649.38.2.313

Peake, P. K., & Mischel, W. (2000). *Adult correlates of preschool delay of gratification.* Unpublished data. Smith College, Northampton, MA.

Pedersen, P. E., & Blass, E. M. (1982). Prenatal and postnatal determinants of the 1st suckling episode in albino rats. *Developmental Psychobiology, 15,* 349–355. doi:10.1002/dev.420150407

Pedersen, S., Vitaro, F., Barker, E. D., & Borge, A. I. H. (2007). The timing of middle-childhood peer rejection and friendship: Linking early behavior to early-adolescent adjustment. *Child Development, 78,* 1037–1051. doi:10.1111/j.1467-8624.2007.01051.x

Pederson, D. R., Gleason, K. E., Moran, G., & Bento, S. (1998). Maternal attachment representations, maternal sensitivity, and the infant-mother attachment relationship. *Developmental Psychology, 34,* 925–933.

Pederson, D. R., & Moran, G. (1996). Expressions of the attachment relationship outside of the Strange Situation. *Child Development, 67,* 915–927.

Pegg, J. E., Werker, J. F., & McLeod, P. J. (1992). Preference for infant-directed over adult-directed speech: Evidence from 7-week-old infants. *Infant Behavior and Development, 15,* 325–345. doi:10.1016/0163-6383(92)80003-D

Peisner-Feinberg, E. S., Burchinal, M. R., Clifford, R. M., Culkin, M. L., Howes, C., Kagan, S. L., & Yazejian, N. (2001). The relation of preschool child-care quality to children's cognitive and social developmental trajectories through second grade. *Child Development, 72,* 1534–1553. doi:10.1111/1467-8624.00364

Peláez-Nogueras, M., Field, T. M., Hossain, Z., & Pickens, J. (1996). Depressed mothers' touching increases infants' positive affect and attention in still-face interactions. *Child Development, 67,* 1780–1792.

Pellegrini, A. D., & Long, J. D. (2007). An observational study of early heterosexual interaction at middle school dances. *Journal of Research on Adolescence, 17,* 613–638. doi:10.1111/j.1532-7795.2007.00538.x

Pellegrino, J. W., Chudowsky, N., & Glaser, R. (Eds.). (2001). *Knowing what students know: The science and design of educational assessment.* Washington, DC: National Academy Press.

Pellizzoni, S., Siegal, M., & Surian, L. (2009). Foreknowledge, caring, and the side-effect effect in young children. *Developmental Psychology, 45,* 289–295. doi:10.1037/a0014165

Pelucchi, B., Hay, J. F., & Saffran, J. R. (2009). Statistical learning in a natural language by 8-month-old infants. *Child Development, 80,* 674–685. doi:10.1111/j.1467-8624.2009.01290.x

Pena, M., Maki, A., Kovacic, D., Dehaene-Lambertz, G., Koizumi, H., Bouquet, F., & Mehler, J. (2003). Sounds and silence: An optical topography study of language recognition at birth. *Proceedings of the National Academy of Sciences of the United States of America, 100,* 11702–11705. doi:10.1073/pnas.1934290100

Pepperberg, I. M. (2009). *The Alex studies: Cognitive and communicative abilities of grey parrots.* Cambridge, MA: Harvard University Press.

Perani, D., Saccuman, M. C., Scifo, P., Anwander, A., Spada, D., Baldoli, C., ... Friederici, A. D. (2011). Neural language networks at birth. *Proceedings of the National Academy of Sciences of the United States of America, 108,* 16056–16061. doi:10.1073/pnas.1102991108

Perlman, S. B., Kalish, C. W., & Pollak, S. D. (2008). The role of maltreatment experience in children's understanding of the antecedents of emotion. *Cognition and Emotion, 22,* 651–670. doi:10.1080/02699930701461154

Perris, E. E., & Clifton, R. K. (1988). Reaching in the dark toward sound as a measure of auditory localization in infants. *Infant Behavior and Development, 11,* 473–491. doi:10.1016/0163-6383(88)90007-0

Perry, D. G., Bussey, K., & Freiberg, K. (1981). Impact of adults' appeals for sharing on the development of altruistic dispositions in children. *Journal of Experimental Child Psychology, 32,* 127–138. doi:10.1016/0022-0965(81)90098-9

Perry, D. G., Perry, L. C., & Rasmussen, P. (1986). Cognitive social learning mediators of aggression. *Child Development, 57,* 700–711. doi:10.2307/1130347

Perry, D. G., Perry, L. C., & Weiss, R. J. (1989). Sex differences in the consequences that children anticipate for aggression. *Developmental Psychology, 25,* 312–319. doi:10.1037/0012-1649.25.2.312

Peter, J., Valkenburg, P. M., & Schouten, A. P. (2005). Developing a model of adolescent friendship formation on the internet. *Cyberpsychology and Behavior, 8,* 423–430. doi:10.1089/cpb.2005.8.423

Peters, R. DeV., Bradshaw, A. J., Petrunka, K., Nelson, G., Herry, Y., Craig, W. M., ... & Rossiter, M. D. (2010). The Better Beginnings, Better Futures Project: Findings from grade 3 to grade 9. *Monographs of the Society for Research in Child Development, 75*(3). doi:10.1111/j.1540-5834.2010.00576.x

Peters, R. DeV., Nelson, G., Petrunka, K., Pancer, S. M., Loomis, C., Hasford, ... & Van Andel, A. (2010). *Investing in our future: Highlights of Better Beginnings, Better Futures research findings at grade 12.* Kingston, ON:

Better Beginnings, Better Futures Research Coordination Unit, Queen's University.

Petersen, A. C., Sarigiani, P. A., & Kennedy, R. E. (1991). Adolescent depression: Why more girls? *Journal of Youth and Adolescence, 20,* 247–271.

Peterson, C. (2004). Mothers, fathers, and gender: Parental narratives about children. *Narrative Inquiry, 14,* 323–346.

Peterson, C., & McCabe, A. (1988). The connective "and" as discourse glue. *First Language, 8,* 19–28. doi:10.1177/014272378800802202

Peterson, C. C., Wellman, H. M., & Liu, D. (2005). Steps in theory-of-mind development for children with deafness or autism. *Child Development, 76,* 502–517. doi:10.1111/j.1467-8624.2005.00859.x

Petitto, L. A., Holowka, S., Sergio, L. E., & Ostry, D. (2001, September 6). Language rhythms in baby hand movements. *Nature, 413,* 35–36. doi:10.1038/35092613

Petitto, L. A., & Marentette, P. F. (1991, March 22). Babbling in the manual mode: Evidence for the ontogeny of language. *Science, 251,* 1493–1496.

Petitto, L. A., Zatorre, R. J., Gauna, K., Nikelski, E. J., Dostie, D., & Evans, A. C. (2000) Speech-like cerebral activity in profoundly deaf people processing signed languages: Implications for the neural basis of human language. *Proceedings of the National Academy of Sciences, 97,* 13961–13966. doi:10.1073/pnas.97.25.13961

Petrill, S. A., Deater-Deckard, K., Schatschneider, C., & Davis, C. (2005). Measured environmental influences on early reading: Evidence from an adoption study. *Scientific Studies of Reading, 9,* 237–259.

Petrill, S. A., Deater-Deckard, K., Thompson, L. A., Schatschneider, C., Dethorne, L. S., & Vandenbergh, D. J. (2007). Longitudinal genetic analysis of early reading: The Western Reserve Reading Project. *Reading and Writing, 20,* 127–146. doi:10.1007/s11145-006-9021-2

Petrill, S. A., Lipton, P. A., Hewitt, J. K., Plomin, R., Cherny, S. S., Corley, R., & DeFries, J. C. (2004). Genetic and environmental contributions to general cognitive ability through the first 16 years of life. *Developmental Psychology, 40,* 805–812. doi:10.1037/0012-1649.40.5.805

Pettit, G. S., Brown, E. G., Mize, J., & Lindsey, E. (1998). Mothers' and fathers' socializing behaviors in three contexts: Links with children's peer competence. *Merrill-Palmer Quarterly, 44,* 173–193. doi:10.2307/23093665

Phillips, A. T., Wellman, H. M., & Spelke, E. S. (2002). Infants' ability to connect gaze and emotional expression to intentional action. *Cognition, 85,* 53–78.

Phillips, L. M., Norris, S. P., & Anderson, J. (2008). Unlocking the door: Is parents' reading to children the key to early literacy development? *Canadian Psychology, 49*(2), 82–88. doi:10.1037/0708-5591.49.2.82

Phillips-Silver, J., & Trainor, L. J. (2005, June 3). Feeling the beat: Movement influences infant rhythm perception. *Science, 308,* 1430.

Phinney, J. S. (1993). Multiple group identities: Differentiation, conflict, and integration. In J. Kroger (Ed.), *Discussions on ego identity* (pp. 47–73). Hillsdale, NJ: Erlbaum.

Phinney, J. S., & Kohatsu, E. L. (1999). Ethnic and racial identity development and mental health. In J. Schulenberg, J. L. Maggs, & K. Hurrelmann (Eds.), *Health risks and developmental transitions during adolescence* (pp. 420–443). Cambridge, England: Cambridge University Press.

Phipps, M. G., Blume, J. D., & DeMonner, S. M. (2002). Young maternal age associated with increased risk of postneonatal death. *Obstetrics and Gynecology, 100,* 481–486.

Piaget, J. (1926). *The language and thought of the child* (M. Warden, Trans.). New York, NY: Harcourt Brace & Company. (Original work published 1923)

Piaget, J. (1951). *Play, dreams, and imitation in childhood* (C. Gattegno & F. M. Hodgson, Trans.). New York, NY: Norton.

Piaget, J. (1952a). *The child's concept of number* (C. Gattegno & F. M. Hodgson, Trans.). London, England: Routledge.

Piaget, J. (1952b). *The origins of intelligence in children* (M. Cook, Trans.). Oxford, England: International Universities Press.

Piaget, J. (1954). *The construction of reality in the child* (M. Cook, Trans.). New York, NY: Basic Books.

Piaget, J. (1964). Development and learning. In R. E. Ripple & V. N. Rockcastle (Eds.), *Piaget rediscovered* (pp. 7–20). Ithaca, NY: Cornell University.

Piaget, J. (1965). *The moral judgment of the child* (M. Gabain, Trans.). New York, NY: Free Press. (Original work published 1932)

Piaget, J. (1969). *The child's conception of time* (A. J. Pomerans, Trans.). London, England: Routledge & K. Paul.

Piaget, J. (1971). *The construction of reality in the child* (M. Cook, Trans.). New York, NY: Ballantine. (Original work published 1954)

Piaget, J. (1972). *Psychology and epistemology: Towards a theory of knowledge* (P. A. Wells, Trans.). Harmondsworth, England: Penguin.

Piaget, J., & Inhelder, B. (1977). The child's conception of space. In H. E. Gruber & J. J. Vonèche (Eds.), *The essential Piaget* (pp. 576–642). New York, NY: Basic Books. (Reprinted from *The child's conception of space* by Piaget, J., & Inhelder, B. (F. J. Langdon & J. L. Lunzer, Trans.), 1956, London, England: Routledge & K. Paul)

Piasta, S. B., & Wagner, R. K. (2010). Developing early literacy skills: A meta-analysis of alphabet learning and instruction. *Reading Research Quarterly, 45,* 8–38. doi:10.1598/RRQ.45.1.2

Piehler, T. F., & Dishion, T. J. (2007). Interpersonal dynamics within adolescent friendships: Dyadic mutuality, deviant talk, and patterns of antisocial behavior. *Child Development, 78,* 1611–1624. doi:10.1111/j.1467-8624.2007.01086.x

Pierce, T. (2009). Social anxiety and technology: Face-to-face communication versus technological communication among teens. *Computers in Human Behavior, 25,* 1367–1372. doi:10.1016/j.chb.2009.06.003

Pierroutsakos, S. L., & DeLoache, J. S. (2003). Infants' manual exploration of pictorial objects varying in realism. *Infancy, 4,* 141–156. doi:10.1207/S15327078IN0401_7

Pilgrim, C., Luo, Q., Urberg, K. A., & Fang, X. (1999). Influence of peers, parents, and individual characteristics on adolescent drug use in two cultures. *Merrill-Palmer Quarterly, 45,* 85–107. doi:10.2307/23093315

Pilkington, N. W., & D'Augelli, A. R. (1995). Victimization of lesbian, gay, and bisexual youth in community settings. *Journal of Community Psychology, 23,* 34–56. doi:10.1002/1520-6629(199501)23:1<34::AID-JCOP2290230105>3.0.CO;2-N

Pillow, B. H. (1988). The development of children's beliefs about the mental world. *Merrill-Palmer Quarterly, 34,* 1–32.

Pinderhughes, E. E., Dodge, K. A., Bates, J. E., Pettit, G. S., & Zelli, A. (2000). Discipline responses: Influences of parents' socioeconomic status, ethnicity, beliefs about parenting, stress, and cognitive-emotional processes. *Journal of Family Psychology, 14,* 380–400. doi:10.1037/0893-3200.14.3.380

Pine, J. M. (1994). Environmental correlates of variation in lexical style: Interactional style and the structure of the input. *Applied Psycholinguistics, 15,* 355–370. doi:10.1017/S0142716400004495

Pingault, J-B., Côté, S. M., Lacourse, E., Galéra, C., Vitaro F., & Tremblay, R. E. (2013). Childhood hyperactivity, physical aggression and criminality: A 19-year prospective population-based study. *PLoS ONE 8*(5): e62594. doi:10.1371/journal.pone.0062594

Pinker, S. (1994). *The language instinct: The new science of language and mind.* Harmondsworth, Middlesex, England: Allen Lane, The Penguin Press.

Plato. (1980). *The laws of Plato* (T. L. Pangle, Trans.). New York, NY: Basic Books.

Plomin, R. (1990). *Nature and nurture: An introduction to human behavioral genetics.* Pacific Grove, CA: Brooks/Cole.

Plomin, R. (2004). Genetics and developmental psychology. *Merrill-Palmer Quarterly, 50,* 341–352.

Plomin, R., & Bergeman, C. S. (1991). The nature of nurture: Genetic influence on "environmental" measures. *Behavioral and Brain Sciences, 14,* 373–386. doi:10.1017/S0140525X00070278

Plomin, R., Corley, R., DeFries, J. C., & Fulker, D. W. (1990). Individual differences in television viewing in early childhood: Nature as well as nurture. *Psychological Science, 1,* 371–377. doi:10.2307/40062829

Plomin, R., & Daniels, D. (1987). Why are children in the same family so different from one another? *Behavioral and Brain Sciences, 10,* 1–16.

Plomin, R., DeFries, J. C., McClearn, G. E., & McGuffin, P. (2008). *Behavioral genetics* (5th ed.). New York, NY: Worth.

Plomin, R., Fulker, D. W., Corley, R., & DeFries, J. C. (1997). Nature, nurture, and cognitive development from 1 to 16 years: A parent-offspring adoption study. *Psychological Science, 8,* 442–447.

Pluess, M., & Belsky, J. (2010). Differential susceptibility to parenting and quality child care. *Developmental Psychology, 46,* 379–390. doi:10.1037/a0015203

Pluess, M., & Belsky, J. (2013). Vantage sensitivity: Individual differences in response to positive experiences. *Psychological Bulletin.* Advance online publication. doi:10.1037/a0030196

Plumert, J. M. (1995). Relations between children's overestimation of their physical abilities and accident proneness. *Developmental Psychology, 31,* 866–876.

Plumert, J. M., Kearney, J. K., & Cremer, J. F. (2004). Children's perception of gap affordances: Bicycling across traffic-filled intersections in an immersive virtual environment. *Child Development, 75,* 1243–1253.

Polka, L., & Sundara, M. (2012). Word segmentation in monolingual infants acquiring Canadian-English and Canadian-French: Native language, cross-dialect, and cross-language comparisons. *Infancy, 17,* 198–232. doi:10.1111/j.1532-7078.2011.00075.x

Polka, L., & Werker, J. F. (1994). Developmental changes in perception of nonnative vowel contrasts. *Journal of Experimental Psychology: Human Perception and Performance, 20,* 421–435.

Pollak, S. D., Cicchetti, D., Hornung, K., & Reed, A. (2000). Recognizing emotion in faces: Developmental effects of child abuse and neglect. *Developmental Psychology, 36,* 679–688.

Pollak, S. D., Cicchetti, D., Klorman, R., & Brumaghim, J. T. (1997). Cognitive brain event-related potentials and emotion processing in maltreated children. *Child Development, 68,* 773–787. doi:10.1111/j.1467-8624.1997.tb01961.x

Pollak, S. D., Messner, M., Kistler, D. J., & Cohn, J. F. (2009). Development of perceptual expertise in emotion recognition. *Cognition, 110,* 242–247. doi:10.1016/j.cognition.2008.10.010

Pollak, S. D., Vardi, S., Putzer Bechner, A. M., & Curtin, J. J. (2005). Physically abused children's regulation of attention in response to hostility. *Child Development, 76,* 968–977. doi:10.1111/j.1467-8624.2005.00890.x

Pollitt, E., Golub, M., Gorman, K., Grantham-McGregor, S., Levitsky, D., Schürch, B., ... Wachs, T. (1996). A reconceptualization of the effects of undernutrition on children's biological, psychosocial, and behavioral development. *Social Policy Report, 10*(5), 1–21.

Pollitt, E., Gorman, K. S., Engle, P. L., Martorell, R., Rivera, J., Wachs, T. D., & Scrimshaw, N. S. (1993). Early supplementary feeding and cognition: Effects over two decades. *Monographs of the Society for Research in Child Development, 58*(7, Serial No. 235), i–118. doi:10.2307/1166162

Pomerleau, A., Bolduc, D., Malcuit, G., & Cossette, L. (1990). Pink or blue: Environmental gender stereotypes in the first two years of life. *Sex Roles, 22*, 359–367. doi:10.1007/BF00288339

Ponitz, C. C., McClelland, M. M., Matthews, J. S., & Morrison, F. J. (2009). A structured observation of behavioral self-regulation and its contribution to kindergarten outcomes. *Developmental Psychology, 45*, 605–619.

Pons, F., & Harris, P. (2005). Longitudinal change and longitudinal stability of individual differences in children's emotion understanding. *Cognition and Emotion, 19*, 1158–1174.

Pons, F., Lewkowicz, D. J., Soto-Faraco, S., & Sebastián-Gallés, N. (2009). Narrowing of intersensory speech perception in infancy. *Proceedings of the National Academy of Sciences of the United States of America, 106*, 10598–10602. doi:10.1073/pnas.0904134106

Poole, D. A., Bruck, M., & Pipe, M. E. (2011). Forensic interviewing aids: Do props help children answer questions about touching? *Current Directions in Psychological Science, 20*, 11–15. doi:10.1177/0963721410388804

Popkin, B. M., & Doan, R. M. (1990). Women's roles, time allocation, and health. In J. C. Caldwell, S. Findley, P. Caldwell, G. Santow, W. Cosford, J. Braid, & D. Broers-Freeman (Eds.), *What we know about health transition: The cultural, social and behavioural determinants of health* (Vol. 2, pp. 683–706). Canberra, Australia: Australian National University.

Popp, D., Laursen, B., Kerr, M., Stattin, H., & Burk, W. K. (2008). Modeling homophily over time with an actor-partner interdependence model. *Developmental Psychology, 44*, 1028–1039. doi:10.1037/0012-1649.44.4.1028

Porath, M. (2004). *The child as psychologist.* [Data set]. Unpublished data, Department of Educational and Counselling Psychology, and Special Education, University of British Columbia, Vancouver.

Porges, S. W. (2007). The polyvagal perspective. *Biological Psychology, 74*, 116–143. doi:10.1016/j.biopsycho.2006.06.009

Porges, S. W., Doussard-Roosevelt, J. A., & Maiti, A. K. (1994). Vagal tone and the physiological regulation of emotion. *Monographs of the Society for Research in Child Development, 59*(2-3, Serial No. 240), 167–186.

Porter, R. H., Makin, J. W., Davis, L. B., & Christensen, K. M. (1992). Breast-fed infants respond to olfactory cues from their own mother and unfamiliar lactating females. *Infant Behavior and Development, 15*, 85–93. doi:10.1016/0163-6383(92)90008-T

Posada, G., Carbonell, O. A., Alzate, G., & Plata, S. J. (2004). Through Colombian lenses: Ethnographic and conventional analyses of maternal care and their associations with secure base behavior. *Developmental Psychology, 40*, 508–518. doi:10.1037/0012-1649.40.4.508

Posner, M. I., Rothbart, M. K., & Sheese, B. E. (2007). Attention genes. *Developmental Science, 10*, 24–29.

Poston, D. L., Jr., & Falbo, T. (1990). Academic performance and personality traits of Chinese children: "Onlies" versus others. *American Journal of Sociology, 96*, 433–451.

Potter, D. (2010). Psychosocial well-being and the relationship between divorce and children's academic achievement. *Journal of Marriage and Family, 72*, 933–946. doi:10.1111/j.1741-3737.2010.00740.x

Poulin, F., Cillessen, A. H. N., Hubbard, J. A., Coie, J. D., Dodge, K. A., & Schwartz, D. (1997). Children's friends and behavioral similarity in two social contexts. *Social Development, 6*, 224–236. doi:10.1111/j.1467-9507.1997.tb00103.x

Poulin, F., Kiesner, J., Pedersen, S., & Dishion, T. J. (2011). A short-term longitudinal analysis of friendship selection on early adolescent substance use. *Journal of Adolescence, 34*, 249–256. doi:10.1016/j.adolescence.2010.05.006

Poulin, F., & Pedersen, S. (2007). Developmental changes in gender composition of friendship networks in adolescent girls and boys. *Developmental Psychology, 43*, 1484–1496. doi:10.1037/0012-1649.43.6.1484

Poulin-Dubois, D. (1999). Infants' distinction between animate and inanimate objects: The origins of naive psychology. In P. Rochat (Ed.), *Early social cognition: Understanding others in the first months of life* (pp. 257–280). Mahwah, NJ: Erlbaum.

Poulin-Dubois, D., Blaye, A., Coutya, J., & Bialystok, E. (2011). The effects of bilingualism on toddlers' executive functioning. *Journal of Experimental Child Psychology, 108*, 567–579. doi:10.1016/j.jecp.2010.10.009

Poulin-Dubois, D., Brooker, I., & Polonia, A. (2011). Infants prefer to imitate a reliable person. *Infant Behavior and Development, 34*, 303–309.

Poulin-Dubois, D., Graham, S., & Sippola, L. (1995). Early lexical development: The contribution of parental labelling and infants' categorization abilities. *Journal of Child Language, 22*, 325–343.

Poulin-Dubois, D., Lepage, A., & Ferland, D. (1996). Infants' concept of animacy. *Cognitive Development, 11*, 19–36. doi:10.1016/S0885-2014(96)90026-X

Poulin-Dubois, D., Serbin, L. A., Eichstedt, J. A., Sen, M. G., & Beissel, C. F. (2002). Men don't put on make-up: Toddlers' knowledge of the gender stereotyping of household activities. *Social Development, 11*, 166–181. doi:10.1111/1467-9507.00193

Powell, G. F., Brasel, J. A., & Blizzard, R. M. (1967). Emotional deprivation and growth retardation simulating idiopathic hypopituitarism. *New England Journal of Medicine, 276*, 1271–1278. doi:10.1056/NEJM196706082762301

Power, T. G. (2004). Stress and coping in childhood: The parents' role. *Parenting: Science and Practice, 4*, 271–317.

Powlishta, K. K. (1995). Intergroup processes in childhood: Social categorization and sex role development. *Developmental Psychology, 31*, 781–788. doi:10.1037/0012-1649.31.5.781

Powlishta, K. K., Serbin, L. A., & Moller, L. C. (1993). The stability of individual differences in gender typing: Implications for understanding gender segregation. *Sex Roles, 29*, 723–737. doi:10.1007/BF00289214

Pratt, M. W., Hunsberger, B., Pancer, S. M., & Alisat, S. (2003). A longitudinal analysis of personal values socialization: Correlates of a moral self-ideal in late adolescence. *Social Development, 12*, 563–585. doi:10.1111/1467-9507.00249

Pratt, M. W., Kerig, P., Cowan, P. A., & Cowan, C. P. (1988). Mothers and fathers teaching 3-year-olds: Authoritative parenting and adult scaffolding of young children's learning. *Developmental Psychology, 24*, 832–839.

Preissler, M. A., & Carey, S. (2004). Do both pictures and words function as symbols for 18- and 24-month-old children? *Journal of Cognition and Development, 5*, 185–212. doi:10.1207/s15327647jcd0502_2

Pressley, M., & Hilden, K. (2006). Cognitive strategies: Production deficiencies and successful strategy instruction everywhere. In W. Damon & R. M. Lerner (Series Eds.) & D. Kuhn & R. S. Siegler (Vol. Eds.), *Handbook of child psychology: Vol. 2. Cognition, perception, and language* (6th ed., pp. 511–556). Hoboken, NJ: Wiley.

Pressley, M., Levin, J. R., & McDaniel, M. A. (1987). Remembering versus inferring what a word means: Mnemonic and contextual approaches. In M. G. McKeown & M. E. Curtis (Eds.), *The nature of vocabulary acquisition* (pp. 107–127). Hillsdale, NJ: Erlbaum.

Preves, S. E. (2003). *Intersex and identity: The contested self.* New Brunswick, NJ: Rutgers University Press.

Prinstein, M. J., Brechwald, W. A., & Cohen, G. L. (2011). Susceptibility to peer influence: Using a performance-based measure to identify adolescent males at heightened risk for deviant peer socialization. *Developmental Psychology, 47,* 1167–1172.

Prinstein, M. J., & Cillessen, A. H. N. (2003). Forms and functions of adolescent peer aggression associated with high levels of peer status. *Merrill-Palmer Quarterly, 49,* 310–342. doi:10.2307/23096058

Prinstein, M. J., Rancourt, D., Guerry, J. D., & Browne, C. B. (2009). Peer reputations and psychological adjustment. In K. H. Rubin, W. M. Bukowski, & B. Laursen (Eds.), *Handbook of peer interactions, relationships, and groups* (pp. 548–567). New York, NY: Guilford Press.

Proulx, M. F., & Poulin, F. (2013). Stability and change in kindergartners' friendships: Examination of links with social functioning. *Social Development, 22,* 111–125. doi:10.1111/sode.12001

Pruett, M. K., Williams, T. Y., Insabella, G., & Little, T. D. (2003). Family and legal indicators of child adjustment to divorce among families with young children. *Journal of Family Psychology, 17,* 169–180. doi:10.1037/0893-3200.17.2.169

Public Health Agency of Canada. (2006). *Street youth in Canada: Findings from enhanced surveillance of Canadian street youth 1999-2003* (Catalogue No. HP5-15/2006). Retrieved from http://www.phac-aspc.gc.ca/std-mts/reports_06/pdf/street_youth_e.pdf

Public Health Agency of Canada. (2008). *Canadian perinatal health report, 2008 edition.* Available from http://www.publichealth.gc.ca/cphr/

Public Health Agency of Canada. (2009) *What mothers say: The Canadian maternity experiences survey.* Available from http://www.phac-aspc.gc.ca/rhs-ssg/survey-eng.php

Public Health Agency of Canada. (2010). *Canadian incidence study of reported child abuse and neglect—2008: Major findings.* Retrieved from http://www.phacaspc.gc.ca/cm-vee/csca-ecve/2008/cis-eci-04-eng.php

Public Health Agency of Canada. (2011). *The Chief Public Health Officer's report on the state of public health in Canada, 2011: Youth and young adults—Life in Transition.* Ottawa, ON: Author.

Puhl, R. M., & Schwartz, M. B. (2003). If you are good you can have a cookie: How memories of childhood food rules link to adult eating behaviors. *Eating Behaviors, 4,* 283–293. doi:10.1016/S1471-0153(03)00024-2

Punamäki, R.-L., Wallenius, M., Hölttö, H., Nygård, C.-H., & Rimpelä, A. (2009). The associations between information and communication technology (ICT) and peer and parent relations in early adolescence. *International Journal of Behavioral Development, 33,* 556–564. doi:10.1177/0165025409343828

Putallaz, M. (1983). Predicting children's sociometric status from their behavior. *Child Development, 54,* 1417–1426. doi:10.2307/1129804

Putnam, S. P., Gartstein, M. A., & Rothbart, M. K. (2006). Measurement of fine-grained aspects of toddler temperament: The Early Childhood Behavior Questionnaire. *Infant Behavior and Development, 29,* 386–401.

Puzzanchera, C. (2009, April). Juvenile arrests 2007. *Juvenile Justice Bulletin.* Retrieved from https://www.ncjrs.gov/pdffiles1/ojjdp/225344.pdf

Puzzanchera, C., Adams, B., & Hockenberry, S. (2012). *Juvenile court statistics 2009.* Pittsburgh, PA: National Center for Juvenile Justice.

Qin, D. B. (2009). Being "good" or being "popular": Gender and ethnic identity negotiations of Chinese immigrant adolescents. *Journal of Adolescent Research, 24,* 37–66. doi:10.1177/0743558408326912

Quiggle, N. L., Garber, J., Panak, W. F., & Dodge, K. A. (1992). Social information processing in aggressive and depressed children. *Child Development, 63,* 1305–1320. doi:10.2307/1131557

Quine, W. V. O. (1960). *Word and object.* Cambridge: Technology Press of the Massachusetts Institute of Technology.

Quinn, G. E., Shin, C. H., Maguire, M. G., & Stone, R. A. (1999, May 1). Myopia and ambient lighting at night. *Nature, 399,* 113–114.

Quinn, M., & Hennessy, E. (2010). Peer relationships across the preschool to school transition. *Early Education and Development, 21,* 825–842. doi:10.1080/10409280903329013

Quinn, P. C. (2005). Developmental constraints on the representation of spatial relation information: Evidence from preverbal infants. In L. Carlson & E. van der Zee (Eds.), *Functional features in language and space: Insights from perception, categorization, and development* (pp. 293–309). New York, NY: Oxford University Press.

Quinn, P. C., & Eimas, P. D. (1996). Perceptual organization and categorization in young infants. In C. Rovee-Collier & L. P. Lipsitt (Eds.), *Advances in infancy research* (Vol. 10, pp. 1–36). Westport, CT: Ablex.

Quinn, P. C., Yahr, J., Kuhn, A., Slater, A. M., & Pascalis, O. (2002). Representation of the gender of human faces by infants: A preference for female. *Perception, 31,* 1109–1121.

Radke-Yarrow, M., & Kochanska, G. (1990). Anger in young children. In N. L. Stein, B. Leventhal, & T. Trabasso (Eds.), *Psychological and biological approaches to emotion* (pp. 297–310). Hillsdale, NJ: Erlbaum.

Radke-Yarrow, M., & Zahn-Waxler, C. (1984). Roots, motives, and patterns in children's prosocial behavior. In E. Staub, D. Bar-Tal, J. Karylowski, & J. Reykowski (Eds.), *Development and maintenance of prosocial behavior: International perspectives on positive behavior* (pp. 81–99). New York, NY: Plenum Press.

Raevuori, A., Dick, D. M., Keski-Rahkonen, A., Pulkkinen, L., Rose, R. J., Rissanen, A., … Silventoinen, K. (2007). Genetic and environmental factors affecting self-esteem from age 14 to 17: A longitudinal study of Finnish twins. *Psychological Medicine, 37,* 1625–1633. doi:10.1017/S0033291707000840

Rafferty, Y., & Shinn, M. (1991). The impact of homelessness on children. *American Psychologist, 46,* 1170–1179. doi:10.1037/0003-066X.46.11.1170

Raghubar, K. P., Barnes, M. A., & Hecht, S. A. (2010). Working memory and mathematics: A review of developmental, individual difference, and cognitive approaches. *Learning and Individual Differences, 20,* 110–122. doi:10.1016/j.lindif.2009.10.005

Ragozin, A. S., Basham, R. B., Crnic, K. A., Greenberg, M. T., & Robinson, N. M. (1982). Effects of maternal age on parenting role. *Developmental Psychology, 18,* 627–634. doi:10.1037/0012-1649.18.4.627

Rai, R., & Regan, L. (2006, August 12). Recurrent miscarriage. *The Lancet, 368,* 601–611. doi:10.1016/S0140-6736(06)69204-0

Raikes, H., Pan, B. A., Luze, G., Tamis-LeMonda, C. S., Brooks-Gunn, J., Constantine, J., … Rodriguez, E. T. (2006). Mother-child bookreading in low-income families: Correlates and outcomes during the first three years of life. *Child Development, 77,* 924–953. doi:10.1111/j.1467-8624.2006.00911.x

Raikes, H. A., Robinson, J. L., Bradley, R. H., Raikes, H. H., & Ayoub, C. C. (2007). Developmental trends in self-regulation among low-income toddlers. *Social Development, 16,* 128–149.

Raikes, H. A., & Thompson, R. A. (2006). Family emotional climate, attachment security and young children's emotion knowledge in a high risk sample. *British Journal of Developmental Psychology, 24,* 89–104.

Raikes, H. A., & Thompson, R. A. (2008). Attachment security and parenting quality predict children's problem-solving, attributions, and loneliness with peers. *Attachment and Human Development, 10,* 319–344. doi: 10.1080/14616730802113620

Rakic, P. (1995). Corticogenesis in human and nonhuman primates. In M. S. Gazzaniga (Ed.), *The cognitive neurosciences* (pp. 127–145). Cambridge, MA: MIT Press.

Rakison, D. H., & Derringer, J. (2008). Do infants possess an evolved spider-detection mechanism? *Cognition, 107,* 381–393. doi:10.1016/j.cognition.2007.07.022

Rakison, D. H., & Lupyan, G. (2008). Developing object concepts in infancy: An associative learning perspective. *Monographs of the Society for Research in Child Development, 73*(1). doi:10.1111/j.1540-5834.2008.00454.x

Rakison, D. H., & Poulin-Dubois, D. (2001). Developmental origin of the animate-inanimate distinction. *Psychological Bulletin, 127,* 209–228.

Ramadoss, J., Lunde, E. R., Ouyang, N., Chen, W. J., & Cudd, T. A. (2008). Acid-sensitive channel inhibition prevents fetal alcohol spectrum disorders cerebellar Purkinje cell loss. *American Journal of Physiology: Regulatory, Integrative and Comparative Physiology, 295,* R596–603. doi: 10.1152/ajpregu.90321.2008

Ramani, G. B., & Siegler, R. S. (2008). Promoting broad and stable improvements in low-income children's numerical knowledge through playing number board games. *Child Development, 79,* 375–394. doi: 10.1111/j.1467-8624.2007.01131.x

Ramey, C. T., & Campbell, F. A. (1991). Poverty, early childhood education, and academic competence: The Abecedarian experiment. In A. C. Huston (Ed.), *Children in poverty: Child development and public policy* (pp. 190–221). Port Chester, NY: Cambridge University Press.

Ramey, C. T., Campbell, F. A., Burchinal, M., Skinner, M. L., Gardner, D. M., & Ramey, S. L. (2000). Persistent effects of early childhood education on high-risk children and their mothers. *Applied Developmental Science, 4,* 2–14.

Ramey, C. T., & Ramey, S. L. (2004). Early learning and school readiness: Can early intervention make a difference? *Merrill-Palmer Quarterly, 50,* 471–491.

Ramirez, G., & Beilock, S. L. (2011, January 14). Writing about testing worries boosts exam performance in the classroom. *Science, 331,* 211–213.

Ramirez, G., Gunderson, E. A., Levine, S. C., & Beilock, S. L. (2011). Spatial anxiety relates to spatial abilities as a function of working memory in children. *Quarterly Journal of Experimental Psychology, 65,* 474–487. doi: 10.1080/17470218.2011.616214

Ramsden, S., Richardson, F. M., Josse, G., Shakeshaft, C., Seghier, M. L., & Price, C. J. (2013). The influence of reading ability on subsequent changes in verbal IQ in the teenage years. *Developmental Cognitive Neuroscience, 6,* 30–39. doi: 10.1016/j.dcn.2013.06.001

Ramsden, S., Richardson, F. M., Josse, G., Thomas, M. S. C., Ellis, C., … Price, C. J. Verbal and non-verbal intelligence changes in the teenage brain? *Nature, 479,* 113–116. doi:10.1038/nature10514

Rao, N., & Stewart, S. M. (1999). Cultural influences on sharer and recipient behavior: Sharing in Chinese and Indian preschool children. *Journal of Cross-Cultural Psychology, 30,* 219–241. doi:10.1177/0022022199030002005

Rasbash, J., Jenkins, J., O'Connor, T. G., Tackett, J., & Reiss, D. (2011). A social relations model of observed family negativity and positivity using a genetically informative sample. *Journal of Personality and Social Psychology, 100,* 474–491. doi:10.1037/a0020931

Rasmussen, S. A. (2012). Human teratogens update 2011: Can we ensure safety during pregnancy? *Birth Defects Research Part A: Clinical and Molecular Teratology, 94,* 123–128. doi:10.1002/bdra.22887

Ratner, N., & Bruner, J. (1978). Games, social exchange and the acquisition of language. *Journal of Child Language, 5,* 391–401.

Rattan, A., Good, C., & Dweck, C. S. (2012). "It's ok—Not everyone can be good at math": Instructors with an entity theory comfort (and demotivate) students. *Journal of Experimental Social Psychology, 48,* 731–737. doi: 10.1016/j.jesp.2011.12.012

Rauer, A. J., Pettit, G. S., Lansford, J. E., Bates, J. E., & Dodge, K. A. (2013). Romantic relationship patterns in young adulthood and their developmental antecedents. *Developmental Psychology.* Advance online publication. doi:10.1037/a0031845

Raval, V. V., Goldberg, S., Atkinson, L., Benoit, D., Myhal, N., Poulton, L., & Zwiers, M. (2001). Maternal attachment, maternal responsiveness and infant attachment. *Infant Behavior & Development, 24,* 281–304. doi:10.1016/S0163-6383(01)00082-0

Raval, V. V., & Martini, T. S. (2009). Maternal socialization of children's anger, sadness, and physical pain in two communities in Gujarat, India. *International Journal of Behavioral Development, 33,* 215–229.

Raval, V. V., & Martini, T. S. (2011). "Making the child understand": Socialization of emotion in urban India. *Journal of Family Psychology, 25,* 847–856. doi:10.1037/a0025240

Raver, C. C., Jones, S. M., Li-Grining, C., Zhai, F., Bub, K., & Pressler, E. (2011). CSRP's Impact on low-income preschoolers' preacademic skills: Self-regulation as a mediating mechanism. *Child Development, 82,* 362–378. doi:10.1111/j.1467-8624.2010.01561.x

Raver, C. C., Jones, S. M., Li-Grining, C., Zhai, F., Metzger, M. W., & Solomon, B. (2009). Targeting children's behavior problems in preschool classrooms: A cluster-randomized controlled trial. *Journal of Consulting and Clinical Psychology, 77,* 302–316. doi:10.1037/a0015302

Rayner, K., Foorman, B. R., Perfetti, C. A., Pesetsky, D., & Seidenberg, M. S. (2001). How psychological science informs the teaching of reading. *Psychological Science in the Public Interest, 2,* 31–74.

Reardon, P., & Bushnell, E. W. (1988). Infants' sensitivity to arbitrary pairings of color and taste. *Infant Behavior and Development, 11,* 245–250. doi:10.1016/S0163-6383(88)80010-9

Recchia, H. E., & Howe, N. (2009). Associations between social understanding, sibling relationship quality, and siblings' conflict strategies and outcomes. *Child Development, 80,* 1564–1578. doi:10.1111/j.1467-8624.2009.01351.x

Reed, J. M., & Squire, L. R. (1998). Retrograde amnesia for facts and events: Findings from four new cases. *Journal of Neuroscience, 18,* 3943–3954.

Reese, E., & Fivush, R. (1993). Parental styles of talking about the past. *Developmental Psychology, 29,* 596–606.

Regan, P. C., & Joshi, A. (2003). Ideal partner preferences among adolescents. *Social Behavior and Personality: An International Journal, 31,* 13–20. doi:10.2224/sbp.2003.31.1.13

Reich, S. M., Subrahmanyam, K., & Espinoza, G. (2012). Friending, IMing, and hanging out face-to-face: Overlap in adolescents' online and offline social networks. *Developmental Psychology, 48,* 356–368. doi: 10.1037/a0026980

Reid, M. J., Webster-Stratton, C., & Hammond, M. (2007). Enhancing a classroom social competence and problem-solving curriculum by offering parent training to families of moderate- to high-risk elementary school children. *Journal of Clinical Child and Adolescent Psychology, 36,* 605–620. doi:10.1080/15374410701662741

Reijntjes, A., Thomaes, S., Kamphuis, J. H., Bushman, B. J., de Castro, B. O., & Telch, M. J. (2011). Explaining the paradoxical rejection-aggression link: The mediating effects of hostile intent attributions, anger, and decreases in state self-esteem on peer rejection-induced aggression in youth. *Personality and Social Psychology Bulletin, 37,* 955–963. doi:10.1177/0146167211410247

Reis, H. T., Lin, Y.-C., Bennett, M. E., & Nezlek, J. B. (1993). Change and consistency in social participation during early adulthood. *Developmental Psychology, 29,* 633–645. doi:10.1037/0012-1649.29.4.633

Reiss, D. (2010). Genetic thinking in the study of social relationships: Five points of entry. *Perspectives on Psychological Science, 5,* 502–515.

Reissland, N. (1985). The development of concepts of simultaneity in children's understanding of emotions. *Journal of Child Psychology and Psychiatry, 26,* 811–824.

Relier, J. P. (2001). Influence of maternal stress on fetal behavior and brain development. *Biology of the Neonate, 79,* 168–171. doi:10.1159/000047086

Ren, A., Qiu, X., Jin, L., Ma, J., Li, Z., Zhang, L., … Zhu, T. (2011). Association of selected persistent organic pollutants in the placenta with the risk of neural tube defects. *Proceedings of the National Academy of Sciences of the United States of America, 108,* 12770–12775. doi:10.1073/pnas.1105209108

Rende, R., & Plomin, R. (1995). Nature, nurture, and the development of psychopathology. In D. Cicchetti & D. J. Cohen (Eds.), *Developmental psychopathology: Vol. 1. Theory and methods* (pp. 291–314). New York, NY: Wiley.

Renken, B., Egeland, B., Marvinney, D., Mangelsdorf, S., & Sroufe, L. A. (1989). Early childhood antecedents of aggression and passive-withdrawal in early elementary school. *Journal of Personality, 57,* 257–281. doi:10.1111/j.1467-6494.1989.tb00483.x

Renold, E. (2001). 'Square-girls,' femininity and the negotiation of academic success in the primary school. *British Educational Research Journal, 27,* 577–588. doi:10.1080/01411920120095753

Renouf, A., Brendgen, M., Parent, S., Vitaro, F., David Zelazo, P., Boivin, M., … & Seguin, J. R. (2010). Relations between theory of mind and indirect and physical aggression in kindergarten: Evidence of the moderating role of prosocial behaviors. *Social Development, 19,* 535–555. doi:10.1111/j.1467-9507.2009.00552.x

Rescorla, L. A. (1980). Overextension in early language development. *Journal of Child Language, 7,* 321–335.

Rest, J. (1983). Morality. In P. H. Mussen (Series Ed.) & J. Flavell & E. Markman (Vol. Eds.), *Handbook of child psychology: Vol. 3. Cognitive development* (4th ed., pp. 556–629). New York, NY: Wiley.

Rest, J. R. (1979). *Development in judging moral issues.* Minneapolis: University of Minnesota Press.

Reynolds, A. J., Temple, J. A., Robertson, D. L., & Mann, E. A. (2001, May 9). Long-term effects of an early childhood intervention on educational achievement and juvenile arrest: A 15-year follow-up of low-income children in public schools. *Journal of the American Medical Association, 285,* 2339–2346.

Rhee, S. H., & Waldman, I. D. (2002). Genetic and environmental influences on antisocial behavior: A meta-analysis of twin and adoption studies. *Psychological Bulletin, 128,* 490–529. doi:10.1037/0033-2909.128.3.490

Rhee, S. H., Waldman, I. D., Hay, D. A., & Levy, F. (1999). Sex differences in genetic and environmental influences on DSM–III–R attention-deficit/hyperactivity disorder. *Journal of Abnormal Psychology, 108,* 24–41. doi:10.1037/0021-843X.108.1.24

Rheingold, H. L. (1982). Little children's participation in the work of adults, a nascent prosocial behavior. *Child Development, 53,* 114–125. doi:10.2307/1129643

Rheingold, H. L., & Cook, K. V. (1975). The contents of boys' and girls' rooms as an index of parents' behavior. *Child Development, 46,* 459–463. doi:10.2307/1128142

Rheingold, H. L., & Eckerman, C. O. (1970, April 3). The infant separates himself from his mother. *Science, 168,* 78–83.

Rhoades, K. A. (2008). Children's responses to interparental conflict: A meta-analysis of their associations with child adjustment. *Child Development, 79,* 1942–1956. doi:10.1111/j.1467-8624.2008.01235.x

Rhoades, K. A., Leve, L. D., Harold, G. T., Neiderhiser, J. M., Shaw, D. S., & Reiss, D. (2011). Longitudinal pathways from marital hostility to child anger during toddlerhood: Genetic susceptibility and indirect effects via harsh parenting. *Journal of Family Psychology, 25,* 282–291. doi:10.1037/a0022886

Ricard, M., & Allard, L. (1993). The reaction of 9- to 10-month-old infants to an unfamiliar animal. *Journal of Genetic Psychology, 154,* 5–16. doi:10.1080/00221325.1993.9914716

Rice, M. L. (2004). Growth models of developmental language disorders. In M. L. Rice & S. F. Warren (Eds.), *Developmental language disorders: From phenotypes to etiologies* (pp. 207–240). Mahwah, NJ: Erlbaum.

Rice, M. L., Huston, A. C., Truglio, R., & Wright, J. C. (1990). Words from "Sesame Street": Learning vocabulary while viewing. *Developmental Psychology, 26,* 421–428. doi:10.1037/0012-1649.26.3.421

Richards, M. H., Crowe, P. A., Larson, R., & Swarr, A. (1998). Developmental patterns and gender differences in the experience of peer companionship during adolescence. *Child Development, 69,* 154–163. doi:10.2307/1132077

Richman, C. L., Berry, C., Bittle, M., & Himan, M. (1988). Factors related to helping behavior in preschool-age children. *Journal of Applied Developmental Psychology, 9,* 151–165.

Rideout V. J., Foehr, U. G., Roberts, D. F. (2010). Generation M2: Media in the lives of 8–18 year-olds. Menlo Park, CA: Kaiser Family Foundation. Retrieved from http://www.kff.org/entmedia/upload/8010.pdf

Rideout, V. J., Vandewater, E. A., & Wartella, E. A. (2003). *Zero to six: Electronic media in the lives of infants, toddlers and preschoolers.* Retrieved from http://www.dcmp.org/caai/nadh169.pdf

Rieser, J. J., Garing, A. E., & Young, M. F. (1994). Imagery, action, and young children's spatial orientation: It's not being there that counts, it's what one has in mind. *Child Development, 65,* 1262–1278.

Riggs, N. R., Greenberg, M. T., Kusché, C. A., & Pentz, M. A. (2006). The mediational role of neurocognition in the behavioral outcomes of a social-emotional prevention program in elementary school students: Effects of the PATHS Curriculum. *Prevention Science, 7,* 91–102. doi:10.1007/s11121-005-0022-1

Riina, E. M., & McHale, S. M. (2012). The trajectory of coparenting satisfaction in African American families: The impact of sociocultural stressors and supports. *Journal of Family Psychology, 26,* 896–905.

Rimm-Kaufman, S. E., Curby, T. W., Grimm, K. J., Nathanson, L., & Brock, L. L. (2009). The contribution of children's self-regulation and classroom quality to children's adaptive behaviors in the kindergarten classroom. *Developmental Psychology, 45,* 958–972.

Rinaldi, C. M., & Howe, N. (2012). Mothers' and fathers' parenting styles and associations with toddlers' externalizing, internalizing, and adaptive behaviors. *Early Childhood Research Quarterly, 27*, 266–273. doi:10.1016/j.ecresq.2011.08.001

Riva Crugnola, C., Tambelli, R., Spinelli, M., Gazzotti, S., Caprin, C., & Albizzati, A. (2011). Attachment patterns and emotion regulation strategies in the second year. *Infant Behavior and Development, 34*, 136–151. doi:10.1016/j.infbeh.2010.11.002

Rizzolatti, G., & Craighero, L. (2004). The mirror-neuron system. *Annual Review of Neuroscience, 27*, 169–192. doi:10.1146/annurev.neuro.27.070203.144230

Roberts, B. W., & DelVecchio, W. F. (2000). The rank-order consistency of personality traits from childhood to old age: A quantitative review of longitudinal studies. *Psychological Bulletin, 126*, 3–25.

Roberts, B. W., Kuncel, N. R., Shiner, R., Caspi, A., & Goldberg, L. R. (2007). The power of personality: The comparative validity of personality traits, socioeconomic status, and cognitive ability for predicting important life outcomes. *Perspectives on Psychological Science, 2*, 313–345.

Roberts, K. C., Shields, M., de Groh, M., Aziz, A., & Gilbert, J. (2012). *Overweight and obesity in children and adolescents: Results from the 2009 to 2011 Canadian Health Measures Survey.* Health Reports [Statistics Canada catalogue no. 82-003-X], 23(3).

Robertson, D. L., Farmer, T. W., Fraser, M. W., Day, S. H., Duncan, T., Crowther, A., & Dadisman, K. A. (2010). Interpersonal competence configurations and peer relations in early elementary classrooms: Perceived popular and unpopular aggressive subtypes. *International Journal of Behavioral Development, 34*, 73–87. doi:10.1177/0165025409345074

Robertson, J., & Robertson, J. (Directors). (1971). *Young children in brief separation: Thomas, 2 years 4 months, in foster care for 10 days* [Motion picture]. England: Tavistock Institute of Human Relations.

Robertson, S. S. (1990). Temporal organization in fetal and newborn movement. In H. Bloch & B. Bertenthal (Eds.), *Sensory-motor organizations and development in infancy and early childhood* (pp. 105–122). Dordrecht, The Netherlands: Kluwer Academic.

Robin, D. J., Berthier, N. E., & Clifton, R. K. (1996). Infants' predictive reaching for moving objects in the dark. *Developmental Psychology, 32*, 824–835. doi:10.1037/0012-1649.32.5.824

Robinson, M., Mattes, E., Oddy, W. H., Pennell, C. E., van Eekelen, A., McLean, N. J., … Newnham, J. P. (2011). Prenatal stress and risk of behavioral morbidity from age 2 to 14 years: The influence of the number, type, and timing of stressful life events. *Development and Psychopathology, 23*, 507–520. doi:10.1017/S0954579411000241

Robinson, N. M., & Robinson, H. (1992). The use of standardized tests with young gifted children. In P. S. Klein & A. J. Tannenbaum (Eds.), *To be young and gifted* (pp. 141–170). Westport, CT: Ablex.

Robinson, P. (2009). *Parenting after separation and divorce: A profile of arrangements for spending time with and making decisions for children.* Retrieved from http://www.statcan.gc.ca/pub/85-002-x/2009004/article/10931-eng.htm#a6

Robnett, R. D., & Leaper, C. (2013). Friendship groups, personal motivation, and gender in relation to high school students' STEM career interest. *Journal of Research on Adolescence, 23*, 652-664.

Rochat, P. (1989). Object manipulation and exploration in 2- to 5-month-old infants. *Developmental Psychology, 25*, 871–884. doi:10.1037/0012-1649.25.6.871

Rochat, P., & Goubet, N. (1995). Development of sitting and reaching in 5- to 6-month-old infants. *Infant Behavior and Development, 18*, 53–68. doi:10.1016/0163-6383(95)90007-1

Rochat, P., & Morgan, R. (1995). Spatial determinants in the perception of self-produced leg movements in 3- to 5-month-old infants. *Developmental Psychology, 31*, 626–636. doi:10.1037/0012-1649.31.4.626

Rochat, P., & Striano, T. (2002). Who's in the mirror? Self–other discrimination in specular images by four- and nine-month-old infants. *Child Development, 73*, 35–46. doi:10.1111/1467-8624.00390

Roche, J., Petrunka, K., & Peters, R. DeV. (2008). *Investing in our future: Highlights of Better Beginnings, Better Futures research findings at grade 9.* Kingston, ON: Better Beginnings, Better Futures Research Coordination Unit.

Roche, K. M., Ghazarian, S. R., Little, T. D., & Leventhal, T. (2011). Understanding links between punitive parenting and adolescent adjustment: The relevance of context and reciprocal associations. *Journal of Research on Adolescence, 21*, 448–460. doi:10.1111/j.1532-7795.2010.00681.x

Rodgers, B., Power, C., & Hope, S. (1997). Parental divorce and adult psychological distress: Evidence from a national birth cohort: A research note. *Journal of Child Psychology and Psychiatry, 38*, 867–872. doi:10.1111/j.1469-7610.1997.tb01605.x

Rodkin, P. C., Farmer, T. W., Pearl, R., & Van Acker, R. (2000). Heterogeneity of popular boys: Antisocial and prosocial configurations. *Developmental Psychology, 36*, 14–24. doi:10.1037/0012-1649.36.1.14

Rodkin, P. C., Farmer, T. W., Pearl, R., & Van Acker, R. (2006). They're cool: Social status and peer group supports for aggressive boys and girls. *Social Development, 15*, 175–204. doi:10.1046/j.1467-9507.2006.00336.x

Rodriguez, M. L., Mischel, W., & Shoda, Y. (1989). Cognitive person variables in the delay of gratification of older children at risk. *Journal of Personality and Social Psychology, 57*, 358–367.

Roffwarg, H. P., Muzio, J. N., & Dement, W. C. (1966, April 29). Ontogenetic development of the human sleep-dream cycle. *Science, 152*, 604–619.

Rogers, F. (1996). *Dear Mister Rogers: Does it ever rain in your neighborhood? Letters to Mister Rogers.* New York, NY: Penguin Books.

Rogers, T. T., & McClelland, J. L. (2004). *Semantic cognition: A parallel distributed processing approach.* Cambridge, MA: MIT Press.

Rogoff, B. (2003). *The cultural nature of human development.* Oxford, England: Oxford University Press.

Rogosch, F. A., Cicchetti, D., & Aber, J. L. (1995). The role of child maltreatment in early deviations in cognitive and affective processing abilities and later peer relationship problems. *Development and Psychopathology, 7*, 591–609. doi:10.1017/S0954579400006738

Roisman, G. I., & Fraley, R. C. (2006). The limits of genetic influence: A behavior-genetic analysis of infant–caregiver relationship quality and temperament. *Child Development, 77*, 1656–1667. doi:10.1111/j.1467-8624.2006.00965.x

Roisman, G. I., Monahan, K. C., Campbell, S. B., Steinberg, L., & Cauffman, E. (2010). Is adolescence-onset antisocial behavior developmentally normative? *Development and Psychopathology, 22*, 295–311. doi:10.1017/S0954579410000076

Romano, E., Tremblay, R. E., Vitaro, F., Zoccolillo, M., & Pagani, L. (2001). Prevalence of psychiatric diagnoses and the role of perceived impairment: Findings from an adolescent community sample. *Journal of Child Psychology and Psychiatry, 42*, 451–461. doi:10.1111/1469-7610.00739

Rommetveit, R. (1985). Language acquisition as increasing linguistic structuring of experience and symbolic behavior control. In J. V. Wertsch (Ed.), *Culture, communication, and cognition: Vygotskian perspectives* (pp. 183–204). Cambridge, UK: Cambridge University Press.

Ronald, A., & Hoekstra, R. A. (2011). Autism spectrum disorders and autistic traits: A decade of new twin studies. *American Journal of Medical Genetics Part B: Neuropsychiatric Genetics, 156,* 255–274. doi:10.1002/ajmg.b.31159

Roopnarine, J. L., & Hossain, Z. (1992). Parent-child interactions in urban Indian families in New Delhi: Are they changing? In J. L. Roopnarine & D. B. Carter (Eds.), *Parent-child socialization in diverse cultures* (Vol. 5, pp. 1–16). Norwood, NJ: Ablex.

Roopnarine, J. L., Lu, M. W., & Ahmeduzzaman, M. (1989). Parental reports of early patterns of caregiving, play and discipline in India and Malaysia. *Early Child Development and Care, 50,* 109–120. doi:10.1080/0300443890500109

Rosch, E., Mervis, C. B., Gray, W. D., Johnson, D. M., & Boyes-Braem, P. (1976). Basic objects in natural categories. *Cognitive Psychology, 8,* 382–439. doi:10.1016/0010-0285(76)90013-X

Rose, A., & Montemayor, R. (1994). The relationship between gender role orientation and perceived self-competency in male and female adolescents. *Sex Roles, 31,* 579–595. doi:10.1007/BF01544281

Rose, A. J. (2002). Co-rumination in the friendships of girls and boys. *Child Development, 73,* 1830–1843.

Rose, A. J., Carlson, W., & Waller, E. M. (2007). Prospective associations of co-rumination with friendship and emotional adjustment: Considering the socioemotional trade-offs of co-rumination. *Developmental Psychology, 43,* 1019–1031. doi:10.1037/0012-1649.43.4.1019

Rose, A. J., & Rudolph, K. D. (2006). A review of sex differences in peer relationship processes: Potential trade-offs for the emotional and behavioral development of girls and boys. *Psychological Bulletin, 132,* 98–131. doi:10.1037/0033-2909.132.1.98

Rose, A. J., Swenson, L. P., & Carlson, W. (2004). Friendships of aggressive youth: Considering the influences of being disliked and of being perceived as popular. *Journal of Experimental Child Psychology, 88,* 25–45. doi:10.1016/j.jecp.2004.02.005

Rose, A. J., Swenson, L. P., & Waller, E. M. (2004). Overt and relational aggression and perceived popularity: Developmental differences in concurrent and prospective relations. *Developmental Psychology, 40,* 378–387. doi:10.1037/0012-1649.40.3.378

Rose, S. A., & Feldman, J. F. (1997). Memory and speed: Their role in the relation of infant information processing to later IQ. *Child Development, 68,* 630–641. doi:10.2307/1132115

Rose, S. A., Feldman, J. F., & Jankowski, J. J. (2011). Modeling a cascade of effects: The role of speed and executive functioning in preterm/full-term differences in academic achievement. *Developmental Science, 14,* 1161–1175. doi:10.1111/j.1467-7687.2011.01068.x

Roseberry, S., Richie, R., Hirsh-Pasek, K., Golinkoff, R. M., & Shipley, T. F. (2011). Babies catch a break: 7- to 9-month-olds track statistical probabilities in continuous dynamic events. *Psychological Science, 22,* 1422–1424. doi:10.1177/0956797611422074

Rosen, L. H., Underwood, M. K., & Beron, K. J. (2011). Peer victimization as a mediator of the relation between facial attractiveness and internalizing problems. *Merrill-Palmer Quarterly, 57,* 319–347.

Rosenberg, M. (1979). *Conceiving the self.* New York, NY: Basic Books.

Rosenfeld, A., & Wise, N. (2000). *The overscheduled child: Avoiding the hyper-parenting trap.* New York, NY: St. Martin's Griffin.

Rosengren, K. S., Gelman, S. A., Kalish, C. W., & McCormick, M. (1991). As time goes by: Children's early understanding of growth in animals. *Child Development, 62,* 1302–1320. doi:10.1111/j.1467-8624.1991.tb01607.x

Rosengren, K. S., & Hickling, A. K. (2000). Metamorphosis and magic: The development of children's thinking about possible events and plausible mechanisms. In K. S. Rosengren, C. N. Johnson, & P. L. Harris (Eds.), *Imagining the impossible: Magical, scientific, and religious thinking in children* (pp. 75–98). Cambridge, England: Cambridge University Press.

Rosenshine, B., & Meister, C. (1994). Reciprocal teaching: A review of the research. *Review of Educational Research, 64,* 479–530. doi:10.3102/00346543064004479

Rosenstein, D., & Oster, H. (1988). Differential facial responses to four basic tastes in newborns. *Child Development, 59,* 1555–1568. doi:10.2307/1130670

Ross, H. S., & Lollis, S. P. (1989). A social relations analysis of toddler peer relationships. *Child Development, 60,* 1082–1091.

Ross, N., Medin, D., Coley, J. D., & Atran, S. (2003). Cultural and experiential differences in the development of folk biological induction. *Cognitive Development, 18,* 25–47. doi:10.1016/S0885-2014(02)00142-9

Rotenberg, K. J., & Eisenberg, N. (1997). Developmental differences in the understanding of and reaction to others' inhibition of emotional expression. *Developmental Psychology, 33,* 526–537.

Roth-Hanania, R., Davidov, M., & Zahn-Waxler, C. (2011). Empathy development from 8 to 16 months: Early signs of concern for others. *Infant Behavior and Development, 34,* 447–458. doi:10.1016/j.infbeh.2011.04.007

Rothbart, M. K. (2012). *Becoming who we are: Temperament and personality in development.* New York, NY: Guilford Press.

Rothbart, M. K., & Bates, J. E. (1998). Temperament. In W. Damon (Series Ed.) & N. Eisenberg (Vol. Ed.), *Handbook of child psychology: Vol. 3. Social, emotional, and personality development* (5th ed., pp. 105–176). New York, NY: Wiley.

Rothbart, M. K., & Bates, J. E. (2006). Temperament. In W. Damon & R. M. Lerner (Series Eds.) & N. Eisenberg (Vol. Ed.), *Handbook of child psychology: Vol. 3. Social, emotional, and personality development* (6th ed., pp. 99–166). Hoboken, NJ: Wiley.

Rothbart, M. K., Derryberry, D., & Hershey, K. (2000). Stability of temperament in childhood: Laboratory infant assessment to parent report at seven years. In V. J. Molfese & D. L. Molfese (Eds.), *Temperament and personality development across the life span* (pp. 85–119). Mahwah, NJ: Erlbaum.

Rothbart, M. K., & Gartstein, M. A. (1998). The Infant Behavior Questionnaire (IBQ and IBQ-R). Retrieved from http://www.bowdoin.edu/~sputnam/rothbart-temperament-questionnaires/

Rothbart, M. K., Sheese, B. E., & Posner, M. I. (2007). Executive attention and effortful control: Linking temperament, brain networks, and genes. *Child Development Perspectives, 1,* 2–7. doi:10.1111/j.1750-8606.2007.00002.x

Rothbaum, F., Pott, M., Azuma, H., Miyake, K., & Weisz, J. (2000). The development of close relationships in Japan and the United States: Paths of symbiotic harmony and generative tension. *Child Development, 71,* 1121–1142.

Rotheram, M. J., & Phinney, J. S. (1987). Introduction: Definitions and perspectives in the study of children's ethnic socialization. In J. S. Phinney & M. J. Rotheram (Eds.), *Children's ethnic socialization: Pluralism and development* (pp. 10–28). Newbury Park, CA: Sage.

Rotheram-Borus, M. J., & Langabeer, K. A. (2001). Developmental trajectories of gay, lesbian, and bisexual youths. In A. R. D'Augelli & C. Patterson (Eds.), *Lesbian, gay, and bisexual identities and youth: Psychological perspectives* (pp. 97–128). New York, NY: Oxford University Press.

Rovee-Collier, C. (1997). Dissociations in infant memory: Rethinking the development of implicit and explicit memory. *Psychological Review, 104,* 467–498. doi:10.1037/0033-295X.104.3.467

Rovee-Collier, C. (1999). The development of infant memory. *Current Directions in Psychological Science, 8,* 80–85. doi:10.1111/1467-8721.00019

Rowe, D. C. (1994). *The limits of family influence: Genes, experience, and behavior.* New York, NY: Guilford Press.

Rowe, D. C., Jacobson, K. C., & Van den Oord, E. J. (1999). Genetic and environmental influences on vocabulary IQ: Parental education level as moderator. *Child Development, 70,* 1151–1162.

Rowe, M. L., & Goldin-Meadow, S. (2009, February 13). Differences in early gesture explain SES disparities in child vocabulary size at school entry. *Science, 323,* 951–953.

Rowe, M. L., Ozcaliskan, S., & Goldin-Meadow, S. (2008). Learning words by hand: Gesture's role in predicting vocabulary development. *First Language, 28,* 182–199. doi:10.1177/0142723707088310

Rowe, R., Costello, E. J., Angold, A., Copeland, W. E., & Maughan, B. (2010). Developmental pathways in oppositional defiant disorder and conduct disorder. *Journal of Abnormal Psychology, 119,* 726–738. doi:10.1037/a0020798

Rowley, S. J., Kurtz-Costes, B., Mistry, R., & Feagans, L. (2007). Social status as a predictor of race and gender stereotypes in late childhood and early adolescence. *Social Development, 16,* 150–168. doi:10.1111/j.1467-9507.2007.00376.x

Rubenstein, A. J., Kalakanis, L., & Langlois, J. H. (1999). Infant preferences for attractive faces: A cognitive explanation. *Developmental Psychology, 35,* 848–855. doi:10.1037/0012-1649.35.3.848

Rubin, K. H., Bukowski, W., & Parker, J. G. (1998). Peer interactions, relationships, and groups. In W. Damon (Series Ed.) & N. Eisenberg (Vol. Ed.), *Handbook of child psychology: Vol. 3. Social, emotional, and personality development* (5th ed., pp. 619–700). Hoboken, NJ: Wiley.

Rubin, K. H., Bukowski, W. M., & Parker, J. G. (2006). Peer interactions, relationships, and groups. In W. Damon & R. M. Lerner (Series Eds.) & N. Eisenberg (Vol. Ed.), *Handbook of child psychology: Vol. 3. Social, emotional, and personality development* (6th ed., pp. 571–645). Hoboken, NJ: Wiley.

Rubin, K. H., Coplan, R. J., & Bowker, J. C. (2009). Social withdrawal in childhood. *Annual Review of Psychology, 60,* 141–171. doi:10.1146/annurev.psych.60.110707.163642

Rubin, K. H., Fein, G. G., & Vandenberg, B. (1983). Play. In P. H. Mussen (Series Ed.) & E. M. Hetherington (Vol. Ed.), *Handbook of child psychology: Vol. 4. Socialization, personality, and social development* (4th ed., pp. 693–774). New York, NY: Wiley.

Rubin, K. H., Lynch, D., Coplan, R., Rose-Krasnor, L., & Booth, C. L. (1994). "Birds of a feather …": Behavioral concordances and preferential personal attraction in children. *Child Development, 65,* 1778–1785. doi:10.1111/j.1467-8624.1994.tb00848.x

Ruble, D. N., Grosovsky, E. H., Frey, K. S., & Cohen, R. (1992). Developmental changes in competence assessment. In A. K. Boggiano & T. S. Pittman (Eds.), *Achievement and motivation: A social-developmental perspective* (pp. 138–164). New York, NY: Cambridge University Press.

Ruble, D. N., Martin, C. L., & Berenbaum, S. A. (2006). Gender development. In W. Damon & R. M. Lerner (Series Eds.) & N. Eisenberg (Vol.

Ed.), *Handbook of child psychology: Vol. 3. Social, emotional, and personality development* (6th ed., pp. 858–932). Hoboken, NJ: Wiley.

Rudolph, K. D., & Clark, A. G. (2001). Conceptions of relationships in children with depressive and aggressive symptoms: Social-cognitive distortion or reality? *Journal of Abnormal Child Psychology, 29,* 41–56.

Rudolph, K. D., Dennig, M. D., & Weisz, J. R. (1995). Determinants and consequences of children's coping in the medical setting: Conceptualization, review, and critique. *Psychological Bulletin, 118,* 328–328.

Rudolph, K. D., & Flynn, M. (2007). Childhood adversity and youth depression: Influence of gender and pubertal status. *Development and Psychopathology, 19,* 497–521. doi:10.1017/S0954579407070241

Rudolph, K. D., Ladd, G. W., & Dinella, L. (2007). Gender differences in the interpersonal consequences of early-onset depressive symptoms. *Merrill-Palmer Quarterly, 53,* 461–488.

Rudolph, K. D., Lambert, S. F., Clark, A. G., & Kurlakowsky, K. D. (2001). Negotiating the transition to middle school: The role of self-regulatory processes. *Child Development, 72,* 929–946.

Rudolph, K. D., Lansford, J. E., Agoston, A. M., Sugimura, N., Schwartz, D., Dodge, K. A., … Bates, J. E. (2013). Peer victimization and social alienation: Predicting deviant peer affiliation in middle school. *Child Development.* Advance online publication. doi:10.1111/cdev.12112

Rueda, M. R., Posner, M. I., & Rothbart, M. K. (2011). Attentional control and self-regulation. In K. D. Vohs & R. F. Baumeister (Eds.), *Handbook of self-regulation: Research, theory, and applications* (2nd ed., pp. 284–299). New York, NY: Guilford Press.

Rueda, M. R., Rothbart, M. K., McCandliss, B. D., Saccomanno, L., & Posner, M. I. (2005). Training, maturation, and genetic influences on the development of executive attention. *Proceedings of the National Academy of Sciences of the United States of America, 102,* 14931–14936. doi:10.1073/pnas.0506897102

Rueter, M. A., & Conger, R. D. (1998). Reciprocal influences between parenting and adolescent problem-solving behavior. *Developmental Psychology, 34,* 1470–1482. doi:10.1037/0012-1649.34.6.1470

Ruff, H. A. (1986). Components of attention during infants' manipulative exploration. *Child Development, 57,* 105–114. doi:10.2307/1130642

Ruff, H. A., & Capozzoli, M. C. (2003). Development of attention and distractibility in the first 4 years of life. *Developmental Psychology, 39,* 877–890.

Ruffman, T., Slade, L., & Crowe, E. (2002). The relation between children's and mothers' mental state language and theory-of-mind understanding. *Child Development, 73,* 734–751. doi:10.1111/1467-8624.00435

Rumelhart, D. E., & McClelland, J. L. (1986). On learning the past tense of English verbs. In J. L. McClelland, D. E. Rumelhart, & PDP Research Group (Eds.), *Parallel distributed processing: Explorations in the microstructure of cognition: Vol. 2. Psychological and biological models* (pp. 170–215). Cambridge, MA: MIT Press.

Russell, A., & Finnie, V. (1990). Preschool children's social status and maternal instructions to assist group entry. *Developmental Psychology, 26,* 603–611. doi:10.1037/0012-1649.26.4.603

Russell, G., & Russell, A. (1987). Mother-child and father-child relationships in middle childhood. *Child Development, 58,* 1573–1585.

Russell, J. A., & Bullock, M. (1986). On the dimensions preschoolers use to interpret facial expressions of emotion. *Developmental Psychology, 22,* 97–102.

Russell, J. A., & Widen, S. C. (2002). A label superiority effect in children's categorization of facial expressions. *Social Development, 11,* 30–52.

Rutten, B. P., & Mill, J. (2009). Epigenetic mediation of environmental influences in major psychotic disorders. *Schizophrenia Bulletin, 35,* 1045–1056. doi:10.1093/schbul/sbp104

Rutter, M. (1979). Protective factors in children's responses to stress and disadvantage. In M. W. Kent & J. E. Rolf (Eds.), *Primary Prevention of Psychopathology: Vol. 3. Social competence in children* (pp. 49–74). Hanover, NH: University Press of New England.

Rutter, M., O'Connor, T. G., & The English and Romanian Adoptees (ERA) Study Team. (2004). Are there biological programming effects for psychological development? Findings from a study of Romanian adoptees. *Developmental Psychology, 40,* 81–94.

Rutter, M., Sonuga-Barke, E. J., Beckett, C., Castle, J., Kreppner, J., Kumsta, R., … Gunnar, M. R. (2010). Deprivation-specific psychological patterns: Effects of institutional deprivation. *Monographs of the Society for Research in Child Development, 75*(1, Serial No. 295), 1–252.

Ryan, C., Huebner, D., Diaz, R. M., & Sanchez, J. (2009). Family rejection as a predictor of negative health outcomes in white and Latino lesbian, gay, and bisexual young adults. *Pediatrics, 123,* 346–352. doi:10.1542/peds.2007-3524

Rymer, R. (1993). *Genie: An abused child's flight from silence.* New York, NY: HarperCollins.

Saarni, C. (1979). Children's understanding of display rules for expressive behavior. *Developmental Psychology, 15,* 424–429.

Saarni, C. (1984). An observational study of children's attempts to monitor their expressive behavior. *Child Development, 55,* 1504–1513.

Saarni, C., Campos, J. J., Camras, L. A., & Witherington, D. (2006). Emotional development: Action, communication, and understanding. In W. Damon & R. L. Lerner (Series Eds.) & N. Eisenberg (Vol. Ed.), *Handbook of child psychology: Vol. 3. Social, emotional, and personality development* (6th ed., pp. 226–299). Hoboken, NJ: Wiley.

Saarni, C., Mumme, D. L., & Campos, J. J. (1998). Emotional development: Action, communication, and understanding. In W. Damon (Series Ed.) & N. Eisenberg (Vol. Ed.), *Handbook of child psychology: Vol. 3. Social, emotional, and personality development* (5th ed., pp. 237–309). Hoboken, NJ: Wiley.

Sabbagh, M. A., & Shafman, D. (2009). How children block learning from ignorant speakers. *Cognition, 112,* 415–422.

Sabbagh, M. A., Xu, F., Carlson, S. M., Moses, L. J., & Lee, K. (2006). The development of executive functioning and theory of mind: A comparison of Chinese and U.S. preschoolers. *Psychological Science, 17,* 74–81. doi:10.1111/j.1467-9280.2005.01667.x

Sabongui, A. G., Bukowski, W. M., & Newcomb, A. F. (1998). The peer ecology of popularity: The network embeddedness of a child's friend predicts the child's subsequent popularity. In W. M. Bukowski & A. H. Cillessen (Eds.), *New Directions for Child and Adolescent Development: No. 80. Sociometry then and now: Building on 6 decades of measuring children's experiences with the peer group* (pp. 83–91). San Francisco, CA: Jossey-Bass.

Sackett, P. R., Borneman, M. J., & Connelly, B. S. (2008). High stakes testing in higher education and employment: Appraising the evidence for validity and fairness. *American Psychologist, 63,* 215–227. doi:10.1037/0003-066X.63.4.215

Sadato, N., Pascual-Leone, A., Grafman, J., Deiber, M. P., Ibañez, V., & Hallett, M. (1998). Neural networks for Braille reading by the blind. *Brain, 121,* 1213–1229. doi:10.1093/brain/121.7.1213

Saewyc, E. M. (2011). Research on adolescent sexual orientation: Development, health disparities, stigma, and resilience. *Journal of Research on Adolescence, 21,* 256–272. doi:10.1111/j.1532-7795.2010.00727.x

Saewyc, E., Poon, C., Wang, N., Homma, Y., Smith, A., & McCreary Centre Society. (2007). *Not yet equal: The health of lesbian, gay, & bisexual youth in BC.* Vancouver, BC: McCreary Centre Society.

Saffran, J., Hauser, M., Seibel, R., Kapfhamer, J., Tsao, F., & Cushman, F. (2008). Grammatical pattern learning by human infants and cotton-top tamarin monkeys. *Cognition, 107,* 479–500. doi:10.1016/j.cognition.2007.10.010

Saffran, J. R., Aslin, R. N., & Newport, E. L. (1996, December 13). Statistical learning by 8-month-old infants. *Science, 274,* 1926–1928.

Saffran, J. R., & Griepentrog, G. J. (2001). Absolute pitch in infant auditory learning: Evidence for developmental reorganization. *Developmental Psychology, 37,* 74–85. doi:10.1037/0012-1649.37.1.74

Saffran, J. R., Johnson, E. K., Aslin, R. N., & Newport, E. L. (1999). Statistical learning of tone sequences by human infants and adults. *Cognition, 70,* 27–52. doi:10.1016/S0010-0277(98)00075-4

Saffran, J. R., Loman, M. M., & Robertson, R. R. W. (2000). Infant memory for musical experiences. *Cognition, 77,* B15-B23. doi:10.1016/S0010-0277(00)00095-0

Saffran, J. R., Werker, J. F., & Werner, L. A. (2006). The infant's auditory world: Hearing, speech, and the beginnings of language. In W. Damon & R. M. Lerner (Series Eds.) & D. Kuhn & R. S. Siegler (Vol. Eds.), *Handbook of child psychology: Vol. 2. Cognition, perception, and language* (pp. 58–108). Hoboken, NJ: Wiley.

Sagi, A., Koren-Karie, N., Gini, M., Ziv, Y., & Joels, T. (2002). Shedding further light on the effects of various types and quality of early child care on infant–mother attachment relationship: The Haifa Study of Early Child Care. *Child Development, 73,* 1166–1186. doi:10.1111/1467-8624.00465

Sakai, T., Mikami, A., Tomonaga, M., Matsui, M., Suzuki, J., Hamada, Y., … Matsuzawa, T. (2011). Differential prefrontal white matter development in chimpanzees and humans. *Current Biology, 21,* 1397–1402.

Sale, A., Berardi, N., & Maffei, L. (2009). Enrich the environment to empower the brain. *Trends in Neurosciences, 32,* 233–239. doi:10.1016/j.tins.2008.12.004

Salihovic, S., Kerr, M., Özdemir, M., & Pakalniskiene, V. (2012). Directions of effects between adolescent psychopathic traits and parental behavior. *Journal of Abnormal Child Psychology, 40,* 957–969. doi:10.1007/s10802-012-9623-x

Sallquist, J., Eisenberg, N., Spinrad, T. L., Gaertner, B. M., Eggum, N. D., & Zhou, N. (2010). Mothers' and children's positive emotion: Relations and trajectories across four years. *Social Development, 19,* 799–821. doi:10.1111/j.1467-9507.2009.00565.x

Sallquist, J. V., Eisenberg, N., Spinrad, T. L., Reiser, M., Hofer, C., Zhou, Q., … Eggum, N. (2009). Positive and negative emotionality: Trajectories across six years and relations with social competence. *Emotion, 9,* 15–28. doi:10.1037/a0013970

Salmivalli, C., Kärnä, A., & Poskiparta, E. (2011). Counteracting bullying in Finland: The KiVa program and its effects on different forms of being bullied. *International Journal of Behavioral Development, 35,* 405–411. doi:10.1177/0165025411407457

Salmivalli, C., & Voeten, M. (2004). Connections between attitudes, group norms, and behaviour in bullying situations. *International Journal of Behavioral Development, 28,* 246–258. doi:10.1080/01650250344000488

Salthouse, T. A. (2009). Decomposing age correlations on neuropsychological and cognitive variables. *Journal of the International Neuropsychological Society, 15,* 650–661. doi:10.1017/S1355617709990385

Salvas, M.-C., Vitaro, F., Brendgen, M., Lacourse, É., Boivin, M., & Tremblay, R. E. (2011). Interplay between friends' aggression and friendship quality in the development of child aggression during the early school years. *Social Development, 20,* 645–663. doi:10.1111/j.1467-9507.2010.00592.x

Salvatore, J. E., Kuo, S. I.-C., Steele, R. D., Simpson, J. A., & Collins, W. A. (2011). Recovering from conflict in romantic relationships: A developmental perspective. *Psychological Science, 22,* 376–383. doi:10.1177/0956797610397055

Salzinger, S., Feldman, R. S., Ng-Mak, D. S., Mojica, E., & Stockhammer, T. F. (2001). The effect of physical abuse on children's social and affective status: A model of cognitive and behavioral processes explaining the association. *Development and Psychopathology, 13,* 805–825.

Sameroff, A., Seifer, R., Zax, M., & Barocas, R. (1987). Early indicators of developmental risk: Rochester Longitudinal Study. *Schizophrenia Bulletin, 13,* 383–394.

Sameroff, A. J. (1986). Environmental context of child development. *Journal of Pediatrics, 109,* 192–200.

Sameroff, A. J. (1998). Environmental risk factors in infancy. In J. G. Warhol (Ed.), *New perspectives in early emotional development* (pp. 159–171). Calverton, NY: Johnson & Johnson Pediatric Institute.

Sameroff, A. J., Seifer, R., Baldwin, A., & Baldwin, C. (1993). Stability of intelligence from preschool to adolescence: The influence of social and family risk factors. *Child Development, 64,* 80–97.

Sampa, A. (1997). Street children of Lusaka: "A case of the Zambia Red Cross Drop-in Centre." *Journal of Psychology in Africa (South of the Sahara, the Caribbean, and Afro-Latin America), 2,* 1–23.

Sampson, R. J., & Laub, J. H. (1994). Urban poverty and the family context of delinquency: A new look at structure and process in a classic study. *Child Development, 65,* 523–540. doi:10.1111/j.1467-8624.1994.tb00767.x

Samuelson, L. K. (2002). Statistical regularities in vocabulary guide language acquisition in connectionist models and 15–20-month-olds. *Developmental Psychology, 38,* 1016–1037.

Samuelson, L. K., & Horst, J. S. (2008). Confronting complexity: Insights from the details of behavior over multiple timescales. *Developmental Science, 11,* 209–215. doi:10.1111/j.1467-7687.2007.00667.x

Samuelson, L. K., & Smith, L. B. (2005). They call it like they see it: Spontaneous naming and attention to shape. *Developmental Science, 8,* 182–198. doi:10.1111/j.1467-7687.2005.00405.x

Samuelson, L. K., Smith, L. B., Perry, L. K., & Spencer, J. P. (2011). Grounding word learning in space. *PLoS ONE, 6*(12), e28095. doi:10.1371/journal.pone.0028095

Sandler, W., Meir, I., Padden, C., & Aronoff, M. (2005). The emergence of grammar: Systematic structure in a new language. *Proceedings of the National Academy of Sciences of the United States of America, 102,* 2661–2665. doi:10.1073/pnas.0405448102

Santos, R. G., Chartier, M. J., Whalen, J. C., Chateau, D., & Boyd, L. (2011). Effectiveness of school-based violence prevention for children and youth: A research report. *Healthcare Quarterly, 14,* 80–90. doi:10.12927/hcq.2011.22367

Saraswati, T. S., & Dutta, R. (1988). *Invisible boundaries, grooming for adult roles: A descriptive study of socialization in a poor rural and urban slum setting in Gujarat.* New Delhi, India: Northern Book Centre.

Saudino, K. J., & Eaton, W. O. (1991). Infant temperament and genetics: An objective twin study of motor activity level. *Child Development, 62,* 1167–1174.

Saudino, K. J., & Wang, M. (2012). Quantitative and molecular genetic studies of temperament. In M. R. Zentner & R. L. Shiner (Eds.), *Handbook of temperament* (pp. 315–346). New York, NY: Guilford Press.

Savage-Rumbaugh, E. S., Murphy, J., Sevcik, R. A., Brakke, K. E., Williams, S. L., & Rumbaugh, D. M. (1993). Language comprehension in ape and child. *Monographs of the Society for Research in Child Development, 58*(3–4, Serial No. 233).

Savin-Williams, R. C. (1989a). Coming out to parents and self-esteem among gay and lesbian youths. *Journal of Homosexuality, 18,* 1–35. doi:10.1300/j082v18n01_01

Savin-Williams, R. C. (1989b). Parental influences on the self-esteem of gay and lesbian youths: A reflected appraisals model. *Journal of Homosexuality, 17,* 93–109. doi:10.1300/j082v17n01_04

Savin-Williams, R. C. (1994). Verbal and physical abuse as stressors in the lives of lesbian, gay male, and bisexual youths: Associations with school problems, running away, substance abuse, prostitution, and suicide. *Journal of Consulting and Clinical Psychology, 62,* 261–269. doi:10.1037/0022-006X.62.2.261

Savin-Williams, R. C. (1996). Self-labeling and disclosure among gay, lesbian, and bisexual youths. In J. Laird & R. J. Green (Eds.), *Lesbians and gays in couples and families: A handbook for therapists* (pp. 153–182). San Francisco, CA: Jossey-Bass.

Savin-Williams, R. C. (1998a). *"… And then I became gay": Young men's stories.* New York, NY: Routledge.

Savin-Williams, R. C. (1998b). The disclosure to families of same-sex attractions by lesbian, gay, and bisexual youths. *Journal of Research on Adolescence, 8,* 49–68. doi:10.1207/s15327795jra0801_3

Savin-Williams, R. C. (2001). A critique of research on sexual-minority youths. *Journal of Adolescence, 24,* 5–13. doi:10.1006/jado.2000.0369

Savin-Williams, R. C. (2005). *The new gay teenager.* Cambridge, MA: Harvard University Press.

Savin-Williams, R. C. (2006). Who's gay? Does it matter? *Current Directions in Psychological Science, 15,* 40–44. doi:10.1111/j.0963-7214.2006.00403.x

Savin-Williams, R. C. (2008). Then and now: Recruitment, definition, diversity, and positive attributes of same-sex populations. *Developmental Psychology, 44,* 135–138. doi:10.1037/0012-1649.44.1.135

Savin-Williams, R. C., & Cohen, K. M. (2004). Homoerotic development during childhood and adolescence. *Child and Adolescent Psychiatric Clinics of North America, 13,* 529–549.

Savin-Williams, R. C., & Cohen, K. M. (2007). Development of same-sex attracted youth. In I. H. Meyer & M. E. Northridge (Eds.), *The health of sexual minorities: Public health perspectives on lesbian, gay, bisexual and transgender populations* (pp. 27–47). New York, NY: Springer.

Savin-Williams, R. C., & Diamond, L. M. (2000). Sexual identity trajectories among sexual-minority youths: Gender comparisons. *Archives of Sexual Behavior, 29,* 607–627. doi:10.1023/A:1002058505138

Savin-Williams, R. C., & Ream, G. L. (2003a). Sex variations in the disclosure to parents of same-sex attractions. *Journal of Family Psychology, 17,* 429–438. doi:10.1037/0893-3200.17.3.429

Savin-Williams, R. C., & Ream, G. L. (2003b). Suicide attempts among sexual-minority male youth. *Journal of Clinical Child and Adolescent Psychology, 32,* 509–522.

Savin-Williams, R. C., & Ream, G. L. (2007). Prevalence and stability of sexual orientation components during adolescence and young adulthood. *Archives of Sexual Behavior, 36*, 385–394. doi:10.1007/s10508-006-9088-5

Sawaya, A. L., Dallal, G., Solymos, G., de Sousa, M. H., Ventura, M. L., Roberts, S. B., & Sigulem, D. M. (1995). Obesity and malnutrition in a shantytown population in the city of São Paulo, Brazil. *Obesity Research, 3*(Suppl. 2), 107s–115s. doi:10.1002/j.1550-8528.1995.tb00453.x

Saxe, G. B., Guberman, S. R., & Gearhart, M. (1987). Social processes in early number development. *Monographs of the Society for Research in Child Development, 52*(2, Serial No. 216).

Saxe, R., & Powell, L. J. (2006). It's the thought that counts: Specific brain regions for one component of theory of mind. *Psychological Science, 17*, 692–699. doi:10.1111/j.1467-9280.2006.01768.x

Sayer, L. C. (2005). Gender, time and inequality: Trends in women's and men's paid work, unpaid work and free time. *Social Forces, 84*, 285–303. doi:10.1353/sof.2005.0126

Sayfan, L., & Lagattuta, K. H. (2009). Scaring the monster away: What children know about managing fears of real and imaginary creatures. *Child Development, 80*, 1756–1774.

Scaramella, L. V., Conger, R. D., Simons, R. L., & Whitbeck, L. B. (1998). Predicting risk for pregnancy by late adolescence: A social contextual perspective. *Developmental Psychology, 34*, 1233–1245. doi:10.1037/0012-1649.34.6.1233

Scaramella, L. V., Conger, R. D., Spoth, R., & Simons, R. L. (2002). Evaluation of a social contextual model of delinquency: A cross-study replication. *Child Development, 73*, 175–195. doi:10.1111/1467-8624.00399

Scaramella, L. V., Neppl, T. K., Ontai, L. L., & Conger, R. D. (2008). Consequences of socioeconomic disadvantage across three generations: Parenting behavior and child externalizing problems. *Journal of Family Psychology, 22*, 725–733. doi:10.1037/a0013190

Scarpa, A., Haden, S. C., & Tanaka, A. (2010). Being hot-tempered: Autonomic, emotional, and behavioral distinctions between childhood reactive and proactive aggression. *Biological Psychology, 84*, 488–496. doi:10.1016/j.biopsycho.2009.11.006

Scarr, S. (1992). Developmental theories for the 1990s: Development and individual differences. *Child Development, 63*, 1–19.

Scarr, S., & McCartney, K. (1983). How people make their own environments: A theory of genotype greater than environment effects. *Child Development, 54*, 424–435.

Scarr, S., & Salapatek, P. (1970). Patterns of fear development during infancy. *Merrill-Palmer Quarterly of Behavior and Development, 16*, 53–90.

Schaal, B., Marlier, L., & Soussignan, R. (2000). Human foetuses learn odours from their pregnant mother's diet. *Chemical Senses, 25*, 729–737. doi:10.1093/chemse/25.6.729

Schaal, B., Orgeur, P., & Rognon, C. (1995). Odor sensing in the human fetus: Anatomical, functional and chemo-ecological bases. In J.-P. Lecanuet, W. P. Fifer, N. A. Krasnegor, & W. P. Smotherman (Eds.), *Fetal development: A psychobiological perspective* (pp. 205–237). Hillsdale, NJ: Erlbuam.

Schaefer, D. R., Simpkins, S. D., Vest, A. E., & Price, C. D. (2011). The contribution of extracurricular activities to adolescent friendships: New insights through social network analysis. *Developmental Psychology, 47*, 1141–1152. doi:10.1037/a0024091

Schaeffer, C. M., Petras, H., Ialongo, N., Poduska, J., & Kellam, S. (2003). Modeling growth in boys' aggressive behavior across elementary school: Links to later criminal involvement, conduct disorder, and antisocial personality disorder. *Developmental Psychology, 39*, 1020–1035. doi:10.1037/0012-1649.39.6.1020

Schellenberg, E. G., & Trehub, S. E. (1996). Natural musical intervals: Evidence from infant listeners. *Psychological Science, 7*, 272–277. doi:10.2307/40062961

Schenck, C., Braver, S., Wolchik, S., Saenz, D., Cookston, J., & Fabricius, W. (2009). Relations between mattering to step- and non-residential fathers and adolescent mental health. *Fathering, 7*, 70–90. doi:10.3149/fth.0701.70

Schermerhorn, A. C., Chow, S. M., & Cummings, E. M. (2010). Developmental family processes and interparental conflict: Patterns of microlevel influences. *Developmental Psychology, 46*, 869–885. doi:10.1037/a0019662

Schermerhorn, A. C., D'Onofrio, B. M., Turkheimer, E., Ganiban, J. M., Spotts, E. L., Lichtenstein, P., … Neiderhiser, J. M. (2011). A genetically informed study of associations between family functioning and child psychosocial adjustment. *Developmental Psychology, 47*, 707–725. doi:10.1037/a0021362

Schieffelin, B. B., & Ochs, E. (Eds.). (1987). *Language socialization across cultures.* New York, NY: Cambridge University Press.

Schlaggar, B. L., & Church, J. A. (2009). Functional neuroimaging insights into the development of skilled reading. *Current Directions in Psychological Science, 18*, 21–26.

Schmidt, F. L., & Hunter, J. (2004). General mental ability in the world of work: Occupational attainment and job performance. *Journal of Personality and Social Psychology, 86*, 162–173. doi:10.1037/0022-3514.86.1.162

Schmidt, M. E., & Bagwell, C. L. (2007). The protective role of friendships in overtly and relationally victimized boys and girls. *Merrill-Palmer Quarterly, 53*, 439–460.

Schmidt, M. E., Pempek, T. A., Kirkorian, H. L., Lund, A. F., & Anderson, D. R. (2008). The effects of background television on the toy play behavior of very young children. *Child Development, 79*, 1137–1151.

Schneider, B. H., Atkinson, L., & Tardif, C. (2001). Child–parent attachment and children's peer relations: A quantitative review. *Developmental Psychology, 37*, 86–100. doi:10.1037/0012-1649.37.1.86

Schneider, B. H., Dixon, K., & Udvari, S. (2007). Closeness and competition in the inter-ethnic and co-ethnic friendships of early adolescents in Toronto and Montreal. *The Journal of Early Adolescence, 27*, 115–138. doi:10.1177/0022022100031002008

Schneider, B. H., Fonzi, A., Tomada, G., & Tani, F. (2000). A cross-national comparison of children's behavior with their friends in situations of potential conflict. *Journal of Cross-Cultural Psychology, 31*, 259–266. doi:10.1177/0022022100031002008

Schneider, W. (1998). Performance prediction in young children: Effects of skill, metacognition and wishful thinking. *Developmental Science, 1*, 291–297. doi:10.1111/1467-7687.00044

Schneider, W. (2011). Memory development in childhood. In U. Goswami (Ed.), *The Wiley-Blackwell handbook of childhood cognitive development* (2nd ed., pp. 347–376). Chichester, West Sussex, England: Wiley-Blackwell.

Schneider, W., Körkel, J., & Weinert, F. E. (1989). Domain-specific knowledge and memory performance: A comparison of high- and low-aptitude children. *Journal of Educational Psychology, 81*, 306–312.

Schniering, C. A., & Rapee, R. M. (2004). The relationship between automatic thoughts and negative emotions in children and adolescents: A test of the cognitive content-specificity hypothesis. *Journal of Abnormal Psychology, 113*, 464–470.

Schober-Peterson, D., & Johnson, C. J. (1991). Non-dialogue speech during preschool interactions. *Journal of Child Language, 18*, 153–170.

Shoda, Y., Mischel, W., & Peake, P. K. (1990). Predicting adolescent cognitive and self-regulatory competencies from preschool delay of gratification: Identifying diagnostic conditions. *Developmental Psychology, 26*, 978–986. doi: 10.1037/0012-1649.26.6.978

Schofield, T. J., Martin, M. J., Conger, K. J., Neppl, T. M., Donnellan, M. B., & Conger, R. D. (2011). Intergenerational transmission of adaptive functioning: A test of the interactionist model of SES and human development. *Child Development, 82*, 33–47. doi:10.1111/j.1467-8624.2010.01539.x

Scholl, B. J., & Leslie, A. M. (1999). Modularity, development and 'theory of mind.' *Mind and Language, 14*, 131–153. doi:10.1111/1468-0017.00106

Scholl, B. J., & Leslie, A. M. (2001). Minds, modules, and meta-analysis [Peer commentary on "Meta-analysis of theory-of-mind development: The truth about false belief" by H. M. Wellman, D. Cross, & J. Watson]. *Child Development, 72*, 696–701.

Scholte, R. H. J., Poelen, E. A. P., Willemsen, G., Boomsma, D. I., & Engels, R. C. M. E. (2008). Relative risks of adolescent and young adult alcohol use: The role of drinking fathers, mothers, siblings, and friends. *Addictive Behaviors, 33*, 1–14. doi:10.1016/j.addbeh.2007.04.015

Schonert-Reichl, K. A., Smith, V., Zaidman-Zait, A., & Hertzman, C. (2012). Promoting children's prosocial behaviors in school: Impact of the "Roots of Empathy" program on the social and emotional competence of school-aged children. *School Mental Health, 4*, 1–21. doi:10.1007/s12310-011-9064-7

Schoppe-Sullivan, S. J., Brown, G. L., Cannon, E. A., Mangelsdorf, S. C., & Sokolowski, M. S. (2008). Maternal gatekeeping, coparenting quality, and fathering behavior in families with infants. *Journal of Family Psychology, 22*, 389–398. doi:10.1037/0893-3200.22.3.389

Schuetze, P., Eiden, R. D., & Dombkowski, L. (2006). The association between cigarette smoking during pregnancy and maternal behavior during the neonatal period. *Infancy, 10*, 267–288. doi:10.1207/s15327078in1003_4

Schulenberg, J., Maggs, J. L., Dielman, T. E., Sharon, L. L., Kloska, D. D., Shope, J. T., & Laetz, V. B. (1999). On peer influences to get drunk: A panel study of young adolescents. *Merrill-Palmer Quarterly, 45*, 108–142. doi:10.2307/23093317

Schult, C. A., & Wellman, H. M. (1997). Explaining human movements and actions: Children's understanding of the limits of psychological explanation. *Cognition, 62*, 291–324.

Schultz, D., Izard, C. E., Ackerman, B. P., & Youngstrom, E. A. (2001). Emotion knowledge in economically disadvantaged children: Self-regulatory antecedents and relations to social difficulties and withdrawal. *Development and Psychopathology, 13*, 53–67.

Schulz, L. (2012). The origins of inquiry: Inductive inference and exploration in early childhood. *Trends in Cognitive Sciences, 16*, 382–389.

Schulz, L. E., & Sommerville, J. (2006). God does not play dice: Causal determinism and preschoolers' causal inferences. *Child Development, 77*, 427–442. doi:10.1111/j.1467-8624.2006.00880.x

Schutte, A. R., Spencer, J. P., & Schöner, G. (2003). Testing the dynamic field theory: Working memory for locations becomes more spatially precise over development. *Child Development, 74*, 1393–1417.

Schwartz, D., McFadyen-Ketchum, S., Dodge, K. A., Pettit, G. S., & Bates, J. E. (1999). Early behavior problems as a predictor of later peer group victimization: Moderators and mediators in the pathways of social risk. *Journal of Abnormal Child Psychology, 27*, 191–201. doi:10.1023/A:1021948206165

Schwartz, D., McFadyen-Ketchum, S. A., Dodge, K. A., Pettit, G. S., & Bates, J. E. (1998). Peer group victimization as a predictor of children's behavior problems at home and in school. *Development and Psychopathology, 10*, 87–99.

Schwartz, D., Tom, S. R., Chang, L., Xu, Y., Duong, M. T., & Kelly, B. M. (2010). Popularity and acceptance as distinct dimensions of social standing for Chinese children in Hong Kong. *Social Development, 19*, 681–697. doi:10.1111/j.1467-9507.2009.00558.x

Schwartz, O. S., Dudgeon, P., Sheeber, L. B., Yap, M. B., Simmons, J. G., & Allen, N. B. (2012). Parental behaviors during family interactions predict changes in depression and anxiety symptoms during adolescence. *Journal of Abnormal Child Psychology, 40*, 59–71. doi:10.1007/s10802-011-9542-2

Schwartz, P. D., Maynard, A. M., & Uzelac, S. M. (2008). Adolescent egocentrism: A contemporary view. *Adolescence, 43*, 441–448.

Schwartz, S., & Johnson, J. H. (1985). *Psychopathology of childhood: A clinical-experimental approach* (2nd ed.). New York, NY: Pergamon Press.

Schwartz, S. J., Mason, C. A., Pantin, H., & Szapocznik, J. (2009). Longitudinal relationships between family functioning and identity development in Hispanic adolescents: Continuity and change. *Journal of Early Adolescence, 29*, 177–211. doi:10.1177/0272431608317605

Schwartz-Mette, R. A., & Rose, A. J. (2012). Co-rumination mediates contagion of internalizing symptoms within youths' friendships. *Developmental Psychology, 48*, 1355–1365. doi:10.1037/a0027484

Schwarz, B., Mayer, B., Trommsdorff, G., Ben-Arieh, A., Friedlmeier, M., Lubiewska, K., … Peltzer, K. (2012). Does the importance of parent and peer relationships for adolescents' life satisfaction vary across cultures? *Journal of Early Adolescence, 32*, 55–80. doi:10.1177/0272431611419508

Seaton, E. K., Caldwell, C. H., Sellers, R. M., & Jackson, J. S. (2008). The prevalence of perceived discrimination among African American and Caribbean Black youth. *Developmental Psychology, 44*, 1288–1297. doi:10.1037/a0012747

Seaton, E. K., & Yip, T. (2009). School and neighborhood contexts, perceptions of racial discrimination, and psychological well-being among African American adolescents. *Journal of Youth and Adolescence, 38*, 153–163. doi:10.1007/s10964-008-9356-x

Seaton, E. K., Yip, T., & Sellers, R. M. (2009). A longitudinal examination of racial identity and racial discrimination among African American adolescents. *Child Development, 80*, 406–417. doi:10.1111/j.1467-8624.2009.01268.x

Sebanc, A. M., Kearns, K. T., Hernandez, M. D., & Galvin, K. B. (2007). Predicting having a best friend in young children: Individual characteristics and friendship features. *Journal of Genetic Psychology, 168*, 81–96. doi:10.3200/GNTP.168.1.81-96

Sebastian-Galles, N., Albareda-Castellot, B., Weikum, W. M., & Werker, J. F. (2012). A bilingual advantage in visual language discrimination in infancy. *Psychological Science, 23*, 994–999. doi:10.1177/0956797612436817

Seehagen, S., & Herbert, J. S. (2011). Infant imitation from televised peer and adult models. *Infancy, 16*, 113–136. doi:10.1111/j.1532-7078.2010.00045.x

Segal, N. L., McGuire, S. A., Havlena, J., Gill, P., & Hershberger, S. L. (2007). Intellectual similarity of virtual twin pairs: Developmental trends. *Personality and Individual Differences, 42*, 1209–1219. doi:10.1016/j.paid.2006.09.028

Seidman, E., Allen, L., Aber, J. L., Mitchell, C., & Feinman, J. (1994). The impact of school transitions in early adolescence on the self-system and perceived social context of poor urban youth. *Child Development, 65,* 507–522. doi:10.1111/j.1467-8624.1994.tb00766.x

Seifer, R., Sameroff, A. J., Barrett, L. C., & Krafchuk, E. (1994). Infant temperament measured by multiple observations and mother report. *Child Development, 65,* 1478–1490.

Seiffge-Krenke, I., Overbeek, G., & Vermulst, A. (2010). Parent–child relationship trajectories during adolescence: Longitudinal associations with romantic outcomes in emerging adulthood. *Journal of Adolescence, 33,* 159–171. doi:10.1016/j.adolescence.2009.04.001

Selfe, L. (1995). Nadia reconsidered. In C. Golomb (Ed.), *The development of artistically gifted children* (pp. 197–237). Hillsdale, NJ: Erlbaum.

Selfhout, M. H. W., Branje, S. J. T., Delsing, M., ter Bogt, T. F. M., & Meeus, W. H. J. (2009). Different types of Internet use, depression, and social anxiety: The role of perceived friendship quality. *Journal of Adolescence, 32,* 819–833. doi:10.1016/j.adolescence.2008.10.011

Selfhout, M. H. W., Branje, S. J. T., & Meeus, W. H. J. (2008). The development of delinquency and perceived friendship quality in adolescent best friendship dyads. *Journal of Abnormal Child Psychology, 36,* 471–485. doi:10.1007/s10802-007-9193-5

Seligman, M. E. P. (1975). *Helplessness: On depression, development, and death.* San Francisco, CA: Freeman.

Selman, R. L. (1980). *The growth of interpersonal understanding: Developmental and clinical analyses.* New York, NY: Academic Press.

Sénéchal, M., & LeFevre, J. (2002). Parental involvement in the development of children's reading skill: A five-year longitudinal study. *Child Development, 73,* 445–460. doi:10.1111/1467-8624.00417

Sénéchal, M., Ouellette, G., Pagan, S., & Lever, R. (2012). The role of invented spelling on learning to read in low-phoneme-awareness kindergartners: A randomized-control-trial study. *Reading and Writing, 25,* 917–934. doi:10.1007/s11145-011-9310-2

Senghas, A., & Coppola, M. (2001). Children creating language: How Nicaraguan sign language acquired a spatial grammar. *Psychological Science, 12,* 323–328.

Sentse, M., & Laird, R. D. (2010). Parent–child relationships and dyadic friendship experiences as predictors of behavior problems in early adolescence. *Journal of Clinical Child and Adolescent Psychology, 39,* 873–884. doi:10.1080/15374416.2010.517160

Serbin, L. A., & Karp, J. (2004). The intergenerational transfer of psychosocial risk: Mediators of vulnerability and resilience. *Annual Review of Psychology, 55,* 333–363. doi:10.1146/annurev.psych.54.101601.145228

Serbin, L. A., Peters, P. L., McAffer, V. J., & Schwartzman, A. E. (1991). Childhood aggression and withdrawal as predictors of adolescent pregnancy, early parenthood, and environmental risk for the next generation. *Canadian Journal of Behavioural Science, 23,* 318. doi:10.1037/h0079014

Serbin, L. A., Poulin-Dubois, D., Colburne, K. A., Sen, M. G., & Eichstedt, J. A. (2001). Gender stereotyping in infancy: Visual preferences for and knowledge of gender-stereotyped toys in the second year. *International Journal of Behavioral Development, 25,* 7–15. doi:10.1080/01650250042000078

Serbin, L. A., Poulin-Dubois, D., & Eichstedt, J. A. (2002). Infants' responses to gender-inconsistent events. *Infancy, 3,* 531–542. doi:10.1207/S15327078IN0304_07

Serbin, L. A., Powlishta, K. K., & Gulko, J. (1993). The development of sex typing in middle childhood. *Monographs of the Society for Research in Child Development, 58*(2, Serial No. 232), i–95. doi:10.2307/1166118

Serbin, L. A., Sprafkin, C., Elman, M., & Doyle, A. B. (1982). The early development of sex-differentiated patterns of social influence. *Canadian Journal of Behavioural Sciences, 14,* 350–363.

Serbin, L. A., Zelkowitz, P., Doyle, A.-B., Gold, D., & Wheaton, B. (1990). The socialization of sex-differentiated skills and academic performance: A mediational model. *Sex Roles, 23,* 613–628. doi:10.1007/BF00289251

Serrano, J. M., Iglesias, J., & Loeches, A. (1992). Visual discrimination and recognition of facial expressions of anger, fear, and surprise in 4-to 6-month-old infants. *Developmental Psychobiology, 25,* 411–425.

Sevy, A. B. G., Bortfeld, H., Huppert, T. J., Beauchamp, M. S., Tonini, R. E., & Oghalai, J. S. (2010). Neuroimaging with near-infrared spectroscopy demonstrates speech-evoked activity in the auditory cortex of deaf children following cochlear implantation. *Hearing Research, 270,* 39–47. doi:10.1016/j.heares.2010.09.010

Seyfarth, R. M., & Cheney, D. L. (1993). Meaning, reference, and intentionality in the natural vocalizations of monkeys. In H. L. Roitblat, L. M. Herman, & P. E. Nachtigall (Eds.), *Language and communication: Comparative perspectives* (pp. 195–220). Hillsdale, NJ: Erlbaum.

Shalev, R. S. (2007). Prevalence of developmental dyscalculia. In D. B. Berch & M. M. M. Mazzocco (Eds.), *Why is math so hard for some children? The nature and origins of mathematical learning difficulties and disabilities* (pp. 49–60). Baltimore, MD: Paul H. Brookes.

Shanahan, L., McHale, S. M., Crouter, A. C., & Osgood, D. W. (2007). Warmth with mothers and fathers from middle childhood to late adolescence: Within- and between-families comparisons. *Developmental Psychology, 43,* 551–563. doi:10.1037/0012-1649.43.3.551

Shanahan, L., McHale, S. M., Crouter, A. C., & Osgood, D. W. (2008). Linkages between parents' differential treatment, youth depressive symptoms, and sibling relationships. *Journal of Marriage and Family, 70,* 480–494. doi:10.1111/j.1741-3737.2008.00495.x

Shantz, C. U. (1987). Conflicts between children. *Child Development, 58,* 283–305. doi:10.2307/1130507

Shapiro, D. N., & Stewart, A. J. (2011). Parenting stress, perceived child regard, and depressive symptoms among stepmothers and biological mothers. *Family Relations, 60,* 533–544. doi:10.1111/j.1741-3729.2011.00665.x

Shapiro, L. R., & Hudson, J. A. (1991). Tell me a make-believe story: Coherence and cohesion in young children's picture-elicited narratives. *Developmental Psychology, 27,* 960–974.

Share, D. L. (2004). Knowing letter names and learning letter sounds: A causal connection. *Journal of Experimental Child Psychology, 88,* 213–233. doi:10.1016/j.jecp.2004.03.005

Shatz, M., & Gelman, R. (1973). The development of communication skills: Modifications in the speech of young children as a function of listener. *Monographs of the Society for Research in Child Development, 38*(5, Serial No. 152), 1–38.

Shaw, D. S., Criss, M. M., Schonberg, M. A., & Beck, J. E. (2004). The development of family hierarchies and their relation to children's conduct problems. *Development and Psychopathology, 16,* 483–500. doi:10.1017/S0954579404004638

Shaw, D. S., Gilliom, M., Ingoldsby, E. M., & Nagin, D. S. (2003). Trajectories leading to school-age conduct problems. *Developmental Psychology, 39,* 189–200. doi:10.1037/0012-1649.39.2.189

Shaywitz, B. A., Shaywitz, S. E., Pugh, K. R., Constable, R. T., Skudlarski, P., Fulbright, R. K., … Gore, J. C. (1995, February 16). Sex differences in the functional organization of the brain for language. *Nature, 373,* 607–609. doi:10.1038/373607a0

Shaywitz, S. E., Mody, M., & Shaywitz, B. A. (2006). Neural mechanisms in dyslexia. *Current Directions in Psychological Science, 15,* 278–281.

Sheehan, M. J., & Watson, M. W. (2008). Reciprocal influences between maternal discipline techniques and aggression in children and adolescents. *Aggressive Behavior, 34,* 245–255. doi:10.1002/ab.20241

Sheese, B. E., Voelker, P. M., Rothbart, M. K., & Posner, M. I. (2007). Parenting quality interacts with genetic variation in dopamine receptor D4 to influence temperament in early childhood. *Development and Psychopathology, 19,* 1039–1046. doi:10.1017/S0954579407000521

Shell, R., & Eisenberg, N. (1990). The role of peers' gender in children's naturally occurring interest in toys. *International Journal of Behavioral Development, 13,* 373–388. doi:10.1177/016502549001300309

Shepardson, D. P., & Pizzini, E. L. (1992). Gender bias in female elementary teachers' perceptions of the scientific ability of students. *Science Education, 76,* 147–153. doi:10.1002/sce.3730760204

Sheridan, C. J., Matuz, T., Draganova, R., Eswaran, H., & Preissl, H. (2010). Fetal magnetoencephalography—Achievements and challenges in the study of prenatal and early postnatal brain responses: A review. *Infant and Child Development, 19,* 80–93. doi:10.1002/icd.657

Shetty, P. (2006). Achieving the goal of halving global hunger by 2015. *Proceedings of the Nutrition Society, 65,* 7–18. doi:10.1079/PNS2005479

Shields M., Carroll, M. D., & Ogden C. L. (2011). *Adult obesity prevalence in Canada and the United States* (NCHS Data Brief, 56). Hyattsville, MD: National Center for Health Statistics.

Shields, M. (2006). *Overweight and obesity among children and youth.* Retrieved from http://www.statcan.gc.ca/pub/82-003-x/2005003/article/9277-eng.pdf

Shiller, V. M., Izard, C. E., & Hembree, E. A. (1986). Patterns of emotion expression during separation in the strange-situation procedure. *Developmental Psychology, 22,* 378–382. doi:10.1037/0012-1649.22.3.378

Shin, M. (2010). Peeking at the relationship world of infant friends and caregivers. *Journal of Early Childhood Research, 8,* 294–302. doi:10.1177/1476718x10366777

Shiner, R. L., Buss, K. A., McClowry, S. G., Putnam, S. P., Saudino, K. J., & Zentner, M. (2012). What is temperament now? Assessing progress in temperament research on the twenty-fifth anniversary of Goldsmith et al. *Child Development Perspectives, 6,* 436–444.

Shirtcliff, E. A., Granger, D. A., Booth, A., & Johnson, D. (2005). Low salivary cortisol levels and externalizing behavior problems in youth. *Development and Psychopathology, 17,* 167–184.

Shoal, G. D., Giancola, P. R., & Kirillova, G. P. (2003). Salivary cortisol, personality, and aggressive behavior in adolescent boys: A 5-year longitudinal study. *Journal of the American Academy of Child and Adolescent Psychiatry, 42,* 1101–1107. doi:10.1097/01.CHI.0000070246.24125.6D

Shoda, Y., Mischel, W., & Peake, P. K. (1990). Predicting adolescent cognitive and self–regulatory competencies from preschool delay of gratification: Identifying diagnostic conditions. *Developmental Psychology, 26,* 978–986. doi:10.1037/0012-1649.26.6.978

Shomaker, L. B., & Furman, W. (2009). Parent—adolescent relationship qualities, internal working models, and attachment styles as predictors of adolescents' interactions with friends. *Journal of Social and Personal Relationships, 26,* 579–603. doi:10.1177/0265407509354441

Short, J. F., Jr. (1996). Personal, gang, and community careers. In C. R. Huff (Ed.), *Gangs in America* (2nd ed., pp. 221–240). Thousand Oaks, CA: Sage.

Shrum, W., & Cheek, N. H., Jr. (1987). Social structure during the school years: Onset of the degrouping process. *American Sociological Review, 52,* 218–223. doi:10.2307/2095450

Shutts, K., Kinzler, K. D., McKee, C. B., & Spelke, E. S. (2009). Social information guides infants' selection of foods. *Journal of Cognition and Development, 10,* 1–17.

Shweder, R. A., Mahapatra, M., & Miller, J. G. (1987). Culture and moral development. In J. Kagan & S. Lamb (Eds.), *The emergence of morality in young children* (pp. 1–83). Chicago, IL: University of Chicago Press.

Siegel, L. S. (1993). The cognitive basis of dyslexia. In M. L. Howe & R. Pasnak (Eds.), *Emerging themes in cognitive development: Vol. 2. Competencies* (pp. 33–52). New York, NY: Springer-Verlag.

Siegler, R. S. (1976). The effects of simple necessity and sufficiency relationships on children's causal inferences. *Child Development, 47,* 1058–1063.

Siegler, R. S. (1986). Unities in strategy choices across domains. In M. Perlmutter (Ed.), *Minnesota Symposia on Child Psychology: Vol. 19. Perspectives on intellectual development* (pp. 1–48). Hillsdale, NJ: Erlbaum.

Siegler, R. S. (1987). The perils of averaging data over strategies: An example from children's addition. *Journal of Experimental Psychology: General, 116,* 250–264.

Siegler, R. S. (1988). Strategy choice procedures and the development of multiplication skill. *Journal of Experimental Psychology: General, 117,* 258–275.

Siegler, R. S. (1995). How does change occur: A microgenetic study of number conservation. *Cognitive Psychology, 28,* 225–273. doi:10.1006/cogp.1995.1006

Siegler, R. S. (1996). *Emerging minds: The process of change in children's thinking.* New York, NY: Oxford University Press.

Siegler, R. S. (2006). Microgenetic analyses of learning. In W. Damon & R. M. Lerner (Series Eds.) & D. Kuhn & R. Siegler (Vol. Eds.), *Handbook of child psychology: Vol. 2. Cognition, perception, and language* (6th ed., pp. 464–510). Hoboken, NJ: Wiley.

Siegler, R. S., & Booth, J. L. (2004). Development of numerical estimation in young children. *Child Development, 75,* 428–444. doi:10.1111/j.1467-8624.2004.00684.x

Siegler, R. S., & Chen, Z. (1998). Developmental differences in rule learning: A microgenetic analysis. *Cognitive Psychology, 36,* 273–310. doi:10.1006/cogp.1998.0686

Siegler, R. S., & Jenkins, E. (1989). *How children discover new strategies.* Hillsdale, NJ: Erlbaum.

Siegler, R. S., & Mu, Y. (2008). Chinese children excel on novel mathematics problems even before elementary school. *Psychological Science, 19,* 759–763.

Siegler, R. S., & Opfer, J. E. (2003). The development of numerical estimation evidence for multiple representations of numerical quantity. *Psychological Science, 14,* 237–250.

Siegler, R. S., & Pyke, A. A. (2013). Developmental and individual differences in understanding of fractions. *Developmental Psychology.* Advance online publication. doi:10.1037/a0031200

Siegler, R. S., & Ramani, G. B. (2009). Playing linear number board games—but not circular ones—improves low-income preschoolers' numerical understanding. *Journal of Educational Psychology, 101,* 545–560. doi:10.1037/a0014239

Siegler, R. S., Thompson, C. A., & Schneider, M. (2011). An integrated theory of whole number and fractions development. *Cognitive Psychology, 62,* 273–296. doi:10.1016/j.cogpsych.2011.03.001

Sigman, M. (1995). Nutrition and child development: More food for thought. *Current Directions in Psychological Science, 4,* 52–55. doi:10.1111/1467-8721.ep10771015

Sigman, M., & Ruskin, E. (1999). Continuity and change in the social competence of children with autism, Down syndrome, and developmental delays. *Monographs of the Society for Research in Child Development, 64*(1, Serial No. 256).

Signorella, M. L., Bigler, R. S., & Liben, L. S. (1997). A meta-analysis of children's memories for own-sex and other-sex information. *Journal of Applied Developmental Psychology, 18,* 429–445. doi:10.1016/S0193-3973(97)80009-3

Signorielli, N. (2001). Television's gender role images and contribution to stereotyping: Past, present, future. In D. G. Singer & J. L. Singer (Eds.), *Handbook of children and the media* (pp. 341–358). Thousand Oaks, CA: Sage.

Signorielli, N. (2012). Gender-role socialization in the twenty-first century. In V. Mayer (Ed.), *The international encyclopedia of media studie*s. doi:10.1002/9781444361506.wbiems116

Sijtsema, J. J., Veenstra, R., Lindenberg, S., & Salmivalli, C. (2009). Empirical test of bullies' status goals: Assessing direct goals, aggression, and prestige. *Aggressive Behavior, 35,* 57–67. doi:10.1002/ab.20282

Silk, J. S., Steinberg, L., & Morris, A. S. (2003). Adolescents' emotion regulation in daily life: Links to depressive symptoms and problem behavior. *Child Development, 74,* 1869–1880.

Silver, L. B. (1999). *Dr. Larry Silver's advice to parents on attention deficit hyperactivity disorder* (2nd ed.). New York, NY: Times Books.

Silverman, W. K., La Greca, A. M., & Wasserstein, S. (1995). What do children worry about? Worries and their relation to anxiety. *Child Development, 66,* 671–686.

Simion, F., Valenza, E., Macchi Cassia, V., Turati, C., & Umiltà, C. (2002). Newborns' preference for up–down asymmetrical configurations. *Developmental Science, 5,* 427–434. doi:10.1111/1467-7687.00237

Simon, T. J. (1997). Reconceptualizing the origins of number knowledge: A "non-numerical" account. *Cognitive Development, 12,* 349–372.

Simon, T. J., Hespos, S. J., & Rochat, P. (1995). Do infants understand simple arithmetic? A replication of Wynn (1992). *Cognitive Development, 10,* 253–269.

Simon, T. J., & Klahr, D. (1995). A computational theory of children's learning about number conservation. In T. J. Simon & G. S. Halford (Eds.), *Developing cognitive competence: New approaches to process modeling* (pp. 315–353). Hillsdale, NJ: Erlbaum.

Simon, T. J., & Rivera, S. M. (2007). Neuroanatomical approaches to the study of mathematical ability and disability. In D. B. Berch & M. M. M. Mazzocco (Eds.), *Why is math so hard for some children? The nature and origins of mathematical learning difficulties and disabilities* (pp. 283–305). Baltimore, MD: Paul H. Brookes.

Simon, V. A., Aikins, J. W., & Prinstein, M. J. (2008). Romantic partner selection and socialization during early adolescence. *Child Development, 79,* 1676–1692. doi:10.1111/j.1467-8624.2008.01218.x

Simons, R. L., & Associates (Ed.). (1996). *Understanding differences between divorced and intact families: Stress, interaction, and child outcome.* Thousand Oaks, CA: Sage.

Simons, R. L., & Johnson, C. (1996). Mother's parenting. In R. L. Simons & Associates (Eds.), *Understanding differences between divorced and intact families: Stress, interaction, and child outcome* (pp. 81–93). Thousand Oaks, CA: Sage.

Simons, R. L., Lei, M. K., Beach, S. R., Brody, G. H., Philibert, R. A., & Gibbons, F. X. (2011). Social environmental variation, plasticity genes, and aggression: Evidence for the differential susceptibility hypothesis. *American Sociological Review, 76,* 833–912. doi:10.1177/0003122411427580

Simons, R. L., Lei, M. K., Stewart, E. A., Brody, G. H., Beach, S. R., Philibert, R. A., & Gibbons, F. X. (2012). Social adversity, genetic variation, street code, and aggression: A genetically informed model of violent behavior. *Youth Violence and Juvenile Justice, 10,* 3–24. doi:10.1177/1541204011422087

Simpkins, S. D., Eccles, J. S., & Becnel, J. N. (2008). The mediational role of adolescents' friends in relations between activity breadth and adjustment. *Developmental Psychology, 44,* 1081–1094.

Simpson, E. L. (1974). Moral development research. *Human Development, 17,* 81–106.

Simpson, J. A., Collins, W. A., Tran, S., & Haydon, K. C. (2007). Attachment and the experience and expression of emotions in romantic relationships: A developmental perspective. *Journal of Personality and Social Psychology, 92,* 355–367. doi:10.1037/0022-3514.92.2.355

Sims, M., Hutchins, T., & Taylor, M. (1998). Gender segregation in young children's conflict behavior in child care settings. *Child Study Journal, 28,* 1–16.

Singer, L. T., Arendt, R., Minnes, S., Farkas, K., Salvator, A., Kirchner, H. L., & Kliegman, R. (2002, April 17). Cognitive and motor outcomes of cocaine-exposed infants. *Journal of the American Medical Association, 287,* 1952–1960.

Singh, L., Morgan, J. L., & Best, C. T. (2002). Infants' listening preferences: Baby talk or happy talk? *Infancy, 3,* 365–394. doi:10.1207/S15327078IN0303_5

Singh, L., Nestor, S., Parikh, C., & Yull, A. (2009). Influences of infant-directed speech on early word recognition. *Infancy, 14,* 654–666. doi:10.1080/15250000903263973

Singleton, J. L., & Newport, E. L. (2004). When learners surpass their models: The acquisition of American Sign Language from inconsistent input. *Cognitive Psychology, 49,* 370–407. doi:10.1016/j.cogpsych.2004.05.001

Sinopoli, K. J., Schachar, R., & Dennis, M. (2011). Reward improves cancellation and restraint inhibition across childhood and adolescence. *Developmental Psychology, 47,* 1479–1489. doi:10.1037/a0024440

Siqueland, E. R., & DeLucia, C. A. (1969, September 12). Visual reinforcement of nonnutritive sucking in human infants. *Science, 165,* 1144–1146.

Siqueland, E. R., & Lipsitt, L. P. (1966). Conditioned head-turning in human newborns. *Journal of Experimental Child Psychology, 3,* 356–376.

Skinner, B. F. (1953). *Science and human behavior.* New York, NY: Macmillan.

Skinner, B. F. (1957). *Verbal behavior.* New York, NY: Appleton-Century-Crofts.

Skinner, B. F. (1971). *Beyond freedom and dignity.* New York, NY: Knopf.

Skinner, E. A. (1985). Determinants of mother sensitive and contingent-responsive behavior: The role of childrearing beliefs and socioeconomic status. In I. E. Sigel (Ed.), *Parental belief systems: The psychological consequences for children* (pp. 51–82). Hillsdale, NJ: Erlbaum.

Skinner, E. A., Zimmer-Gembeck, M. J., & Connell, J. P. (1998). Individual differences and the development of perceived control. *Monographs of the Society for Research in Child Development, 63*(2–3, Serial No. 254).

Skoe, E. E. (1998). The ethic of care: Issues in moral development. In E. Skoe & A. von der Lippe (Eds.), *Personality development in adolescence:*

A cross national and life span perspective (pp. 143–171). New York, NY: Routledge.

Skoe, E. E., Hansen, K. L., Mørch, W. T., Bakke, I., Hoffmann, T., Larsen, B., & Aasheim, M. (1999). Care-based moral reasoning in Norwegian and Canadian early adolescents: A cross-national comparison. *The Journal of Early Adolescence, 19,* 280–291. doi:10.1177/0272431699019002007

Skwerer, D. P., & Tager-Flusberg, H. (2011). Williams syndrome: Overview and recent advances in research. In P. Howlin, T. Charman, & M. Ghaziuddin (Eds.), *The SAGE handbook of developmental disorders* (pp. 81–106). Newbury Park, CA: Sage.

Slaby, R. G., & Frey, K. S. (1975). Development of gender constancy and selective attention to same-sex models. *Child Development, 46,* 849–856. doi:10.2307/1128389

Slaby, R. G., & Guerra, N. G. (1988). Cognitive mediators of aggression in adolescent offenders: I. Assessment. *Developmental Psychology, 24,* 580–588. doi:10.1037/0012-1649.24.4.580

Slater, A., Bremner, G., Johnson, S. P., Sherwood, P., Hayes, R., & Brown, E. (2000). Newborn infants' preference for attractive faces: The role of internal and external facial features. *Infancy, 1,* 265–274. doi:10.1207/S15327078IN0102_8

Slater, A., Johnson, S. P., Brown, E., & Badenoch, M. (1996). Newborn infant's perception of partly occluded objects. *Infant Behavior and Development, 19,* 145–148. doi:10.1016/S0163-6383(96)90052-1

Slater, A., Mattock, A., & Brown, E. (1990). Size constancy at birth: Newborn infants' responses to retinal and real size. *Journal of Experimental Child Psychology, 49,* 314–322. doi:10.1016/0022-0965(90)90061-C

Slater, A., & Morison, V. (1985). Shape constancy and slant perception at birth. *Perception, 14,* 337–344. doi:10.1068/p140337

Slater, A., Morison, V., & Rose, D. (1984). New-born infants' perception of similarities and differences between two- and three-dimensional stimuli. *British Journal of Developmental Psychology, 2,* 287–294. doi:10.1111/j.2044-835X.1984.tb00936.x

Slater, A., Von der Schulenburg, C., Brown, E., Badenoch, M., Butterworth, G., Parsons, S., & Samuels, C. (1998). Newborn infants prefer attractive faces. *Infant Behavior and Development, 21,* 345–354. doi:10.1016/S0163-6383(98)90011-X

Slaughter, V., Jaakkola, R., & Carey, S. (1999). Constructing a coherent theory: Children's biological understanding of life and death. In M. Siegal & C. C. Peterson (Eds.), *Children's understanding of biology and health* (pp. 71–96). Cambridge, England: Cambridge University Press.

Slomkowski, C., Rende, R., Conger, K. J., Simons, R. L., & Conger, R. D. (2001). Sisters, brothers, and delinquency: Evaluating social influence during early and middle adolescence. *Child Development, 72,* 271–283. doi:10.1111/1467-8624.00278

Slough, N. M., McMahon, R. J., & The Conduct Problems Prevention Research Group. (2008). Preventing serious conduct problems in school-age youth: The Fast Track Program. *Cognitive and Behavioral Practice, 15,* 3–17. doi:10.1016/j.cbpra.2007.04.002

Sloutsky, V. M. (2010). From perceptual categories to concepts: What develops? *Cognitive Science, 34,* 1244–1286. doi:10.1111/j.1551-6709.2010.01129.x

Slutske, W. S., Moffitt, T. E., Poulton, R., & Caspi, A. (2012). Undercontrolled temperament at age 3 predicts disordered gambling at age 32: A longitudinal study of a complete birth cohort. *Psychological Science, 23,* 510–516.

Sluzenski, J., Newcombe, N. S., & Satlow, E. (2004). Knowing where things are in the second year of life: Implications for hippocampal development. *Journal of Cognitive Neuroscience, 16,* 1443–1451. doi:10.1162/0898929042304804

Smetana, J. G. (1988). Adolescents' and parents' conceptions of parental authority. *Child Development, 59,* 321–335. doi:10.2307/1130313

Smetana, J. G., & Asquith, P. (1994). Adolescents' and parents' conceptions of parental authority and personal autonomy. *Child Development, 65,* 1147–1162. doi:10.2307/1131311

Smetana, J. G., & Braeges, J. L. (1990). The development of toddlers' moral and conventional judgments. *Merrill-Palmer Quarterly, 36,* 329–346. doi:10.2307/23087284

Smider, N., Essex, M., Kalin, N., Buss, K., Klein, M., Davidson, R., & Goldsmith, H. (2002). Salivary cortisol as a predictor of socioemotional adjustment during kindergarten: A prospective study. *Child Development, 73,* 75–92.

Smiler, A. P., Frankel, L. B. W., & Savin-Williams, R. C. (2011). From kissing to coitus? Sex-of-partner differences in the sexual milestone achievement of young men. *Journal of Adolescence, 34,* 727-735. doi:10.1016/j.adolescence.2010.08.009

Smiley, P. A., & Dweck, C. S. (1994). Individual differences in achievement goals among young children. *Child Development, 65,* 1723–1743. doi:10.1111/j.1467-8624.1994.tb00845.x

Smith, A., & Schneider, B. H. (2000). The inter-ethnic friendships of adolescent students: A Canadian study. *International Journal of Intercultural Relations, 24,* 247–258. doi:10.1016/S0147-1767(99)00034-6

Smith, B. A., & Blass, E. M. (1996). Taste-mediated calming in premature, preterm, and full-term human infants. *Developmental Psychology, 32,* 1084–1089.

Smith, C. L., Calkins, S. D., Keane, S. P., Anastopoulos, A. D., & Shelton, T. L. (2004). Predicting stability and change in toddler behavior problems: Contributions of maternal behavior and child gender. *Developmental Psychology, 40,* 29–42. doi:10.1037/0012-1649.40.1.29

Smith, E. A., & Smith, S. A. (1994). Inuit sex-ratio variation: Population control, ethnographic error, or parental manipulation? *Current Anthropology, 35,* 594–625.

Smith, E. D., & Lillard, A. S. (2011). Play on: Retrospective reports of the persistence of pretend play into middle childhood. *Journal of Cognition and Development, 13,* 524–549. doi:10.1080/15248372.2011.608199

Smith, H. J., Sheikh, H. I., Dyson, M. W., Olino, T. M., Laptook, R. S., Durbin, C. E., … Klein, D. N. (2012). Parenting and child DRD4 genotype interact to predict children's early emerging effortful control. *Child Development, 83,* 1932–1944. doi:10.1111/j.1467-8624.2012.01818.x

Smith, L., & Yu, C. (2008). Infants rapidly learn word-referent mappings via cross-situational statistics. *Cognition, 106,* 1558–1568. doi:10.1016/j.cognition.2007.06.010

Smith, L. B. (2003). Learning to recognize objects. *Psychological Science, 14,* 244–250.

Smith, L. B. (2005). Action alters shape categories. *Cognitive Science, 29,* 665–679. doi:10.1207/s15516709cog0000_13

Smith, L. B., Jones, S. S., & Landau, B. (1992). Count nouns, adjectives, and perceptual properties in children's novel word interpretations. *Developmental Psychology, 28,* 273–286.

Smith, L. B., Thelen, E., Titzer, R., & McLin, D. (1999). Knowing in the context of acting: The task dynamics of the A-not-B error. *Psychological Review, 106,* 235–260.

Smith, L. M., LaGasse, L. L., Derauf, C., Grant, P., Shah, R., Arria, A., … Lester, B. M. (2006). The infant development, environment, and lifestyle study: Effects of prenatal methamphetamine exposure, polydrug exposure, and poverty on intrauterine growth. *Pediatrics, 118,* 1149–1156. doi:10.1542/peds.2005-2564

Smith, M., & Walden, T. (1999). Understanding feelings and coping with emotional situations: A comparison of maltreated and nonmaltreated preschoolers. *Social Development, 8,* 93–116. doi:10.1111/1467-9507.00082

Smith, R. L., & Rose, A. J. (2011). The "cost of caring" in youths' friendships: Considering associations among social perspective taking, co-rumination, and empathetic distress. *Developmental Psychology, 47,* 1792–1803. doi:10.1037/a0025309

Smith, W. E., & Smith, A. M. (1975). *Minamata.* New York, NY: Holt, Rinehart, and Winston.

Smotherman, W. P., & Robinson, S. R. (1987). Psychobiology of fetal experience in the rat. In N. A. Krasnegor, M. A. Hofer, W. P. Smotherman, & E. M. Blass (Eds.), *Perinatal development: A psychobiological perspective* (pp. 39–60). Orlando, FL: Academic Press.

Snarey, J. R. (1985). Cross-cultural universality of social-moral development: A critical review of Kohlbergian research. *Psychological Bulletin, 97,* 202–232. doi:10.1037/0033-2909.97.2.202

Snow, C. E. (1990). Building memories: The ontogeny of autobiography. In D. Cicchetti & M. Beeghly (Eds.), *The self in transition: Infancy to childhood* (pp. 213–242). Chicago, IL: University of Chicago Press.

Snow, C. E. (1999). Social perspectives on the emergence of language. In B. MacWhinney (Ed.), *The emergence of language* (pp. 257–276). Mahwah, NJ: Erlbaum.

Snyder, J., Brooker, M., Patrick, M. R., Snyder, A., Schrepferman, L., & Stoolmiller, M. (2003). Observed peer victimization during early elementary school: Continuity, growth, and relation to risk for child antisocial and depressive behavior. *Child Development, 74,* 1881–1898. doi:10.1046/j.1467-8624.2003.00644.x

Snyder, J., Cramer, A., Afrank, J., & Patterson, G. R. (2005). The contributions of ineffective discipline and parental hostile attributions of child misbehavior to the development of conduct problems at home and school. *Developmental Psychology, 41,* 30–41. doi:10.1037/0012-1649.41.1.30

Snyder, J., Reid, J., & Patterson, G. (2003). A social learning model of child and adolescent antisocial behavior. In B. B. Lahey, T. E. Moffitt, & A. Caspi (Eds.), *Causes of conduct disorder and juvenile delinquency* (pp. 27–48). New York, NY: Guilford Press.

Snyder, J., Schrepferman, L., McEachern, A., Barner, S., Johnson, K., & Provines, J. (2008). Peer deviancy training and peer coercion: Dual processes associated with early-onset conduct problems. *Child Development, 79,* 252–268. doi:10.1111/j.1467-8624.2007.01124.x

Snyder, J., Stoolmiller, M., Wilson, M., & Yamamoto, M. (2003). Child anger regulation, parental responses to children's anger displays, and early child antisocial behavior. *Social Development, 12,* 335–360.

Snyder, J. J., Schrepferman, L. P., Bullard, L., McEachern, A. D., & Patterson, G. R. (2012). Covert antisocial behavior, peer deviancy training, parenting processes, and sex differences in the development of antisocial behavior during childhood. *Development and Psychopathology, 24,* 1117–1138. doi:10.1017/S0954579412000570

Sobel, D. M., & Kirkham, N. Z. (2006). Blickets and babies: The development of causal reasoning in toddlers and infants. *Developmental Psychology, 42,* 1103–1115. doi:10.1037/0012-1649.42.6.1103

Soenens, B., Luyckx, K., Vansteenkiste, M., Luyten, P., Duriez, B., & Goossens, L. (2008). Maladaptive perfectionism as an intervening variable between psychological control and adolescent depressive symptoms: A three-wave longitudinal study. *Journal of Family Psychology, 22,* 465–474. doi:10.1037/0893-3200.22.3.465

Soken, N. H., & Pick, A. D. (1992). Intermodal perception of happy and angry expressive behaviors by seven-month-old infants. *Child Development, 63,* 787–795. doi:10.2307/1131233

Sokol, R. J., Delaney-Black, V., & Nordstrom, B. (2003, December 10). Fetal alcohol spectrum disorder. *Journal of the American Medical Association, 290,* 2996–2999. doi:10.1001/jama.290.22.2996

Solheim, E., Wichstrøm, L., Belsky, J., & Berg-Nielsen, T. S. (2013). Do time in child care and peer group exposure predict poor socioemotional adjustment in Norway? *Child Development.* Advance online publication. doi:10.1111/cdev.12071

Solmeyer, A. R., Killoren, S. E., McHale, S. M., & Updegraff, K. A. (2011). Coparenting around siblings' differential treatment in Mexican-origin families. *Journal of Family Psychology, 25,* 251–260. doi:10.1037/a0023201

Solomon, G. E., Johnson, S. C., Zaitchik, D., & Carey, S. (1996). Like father, like son: Young children's understanding of how and why offspring resemble their parents. *Child Development, 67,* 151–171.

Solomon, J., & George, C. (1999). The measurement of attachment security in infancy and childhood. In J. Cassidy & P. R. Shaver (Eds.), *Handbook of attachment: Theory, research, and clinical applications* (pp. 287–316). New York, NY: Guilford Press.

Solomon, J., George, C., & De Jong, A. (1995). Children classified as controlling at age six: Evidence of disorganized representational strategies and aggression at home and at school. *Development and Psychopathology, 7,* 447–463. doi:10.1017/S0954579400006623

Sommerville, J. A., & Crane, C. C. (2009). Ten-month-old infants use prior information to identify an actor's goal. *Developmental Science, 12,* 314–325. doi:10.1111/j.1467-7687.2008.00787.x

Sommerville, J. A., Woodward, A. L., & Needham, A. (2005). Action experience alters 3-month-old infants' perception of others' actions. *Cognition, 96,* B1-B11. doi:10.1016/j.cognition.2004.07.004

Song, C., Benin, M., & Glick, J. (2012). Dropping out of high school: The effects of family structure and family transitions. *Journal of Divorce and Remarriage, 53,* 18–33. doi:10.1080/10502556.2012.635964

Sophie, J. (1986). A critical examination of stage theories of lesbian identity development. *Journal of Homosexuality, 12,* 39–51. doi:10.1300/j082v12n02_03

Soska, K. C., Adolph, K. E., & Johnson, S. P. (2010). Systems in development: Motor skill acquisition facilitates three-dimensional object completion. *Developmental Psychology, 46,* 129–138. doi:10.1037/a0014618

Sowislo, J. F., & Orth, U. (2013). Does low self-esteem predict depression and anxiety? A meta-analysis of longitudinal studies. *Psychological Bulletin, 139,* 213–240. doi:10.1037/a0028931

Spearman, C. E. (1927). *The abilities of man, their nature and measurement.* New York, NY: Macmillan.

Spelke, E. S. (1976). Infants' intermodal perception of events. *Cognitive Psychology, 8,* 553–560.

Spelke, E. S. (1979). Perceiving bimodally specified events in infancy. *Developmental Psychology, 15,* 626–636. doi:10.1037/0012-1649.15.6.626

Spelke, E. S. (2000). Core knowledge. *American Psychologist, 55,* 1233–1243. doi:10.1037/0003-066X.55.11.1233

Spelke, E. S. (2003). What makes us smart? Core knowledge and natural language. In D. Gentner & S. Goldin-Meadow (Eds.), *Language in mind: Advances in the study of language and thought* (pp. 277–311). Cambridge, MA: MIT Press.

Spelke, E. S. (2011). Core systems and the growth of human knowledge: Natural geometry. In A. M. Battro, S. Dehaene, & W. J. Singer (Eds.), *The proceedings of the Working Group on Human Neuroplasticity and Education: Vol. 117. Human neuroplasticity and education* (pp. 73–99). Vatican City: Pontifical Academy of Sciences.

Spelke, E. S., & Cortelyou, A. (1981). Perceptual aspects of social knowing: Looking and listening in infancy. In M. E. Lamb & L. R. Sherrod (Eds.), *Infant social cognition: Empirical and theoretical considerations* (pp. 61–84). Hillsdale, NJ: Erlbaum.

Spelke, E. S., & Kinzler, K. D. (2007). Core knowledge. *Developmental Science, 10*, 89–96. doi:10.1111/j.1467-7687.2007.00569.x

Spelke, E. S., & Newport, E. L. (1998). Nativism, empiricism, and the development of knowledge. In W. Damon (Series Ed.) & R. M. Lerner (Vol. Ed.), *Handbook of child psychology: Vol. 1: Theoretical models of human development* (5th ed., pp. 275–340). Hoboken, NJ: Wiley.

Spelke, E. S., & Owsley, C. J. (1979). Intermodal exploration and knowledge in infancy. *Infant Behavior and Development, 2*, 13–27. doi:10.1016/S0163-6383(79)80004-1

Speltz, M. L., DeKlyen, M., Calderon, R., Greenberg, M. T., & Fisher, P. A. (1999). Neuropsychological characteristics and test behaviors of boys with early onset conduct problems. *Journal of Abnormal Psychology, 108*, 315–325. doi:10.1037/0021-843X.108.2.315

Spence, I., & Feng, J. (2010). Video games and spatial cognition. *Review of General Psychology, 14*, 92–104. doi:10.1037/a0019491

Spence, M. J., & Freeman, M. S. (1996). Newborn infants prefer the maternal low-pass filtered voice, but not the maternal whispered voice. *Infant Behavior and Development, 19*, 199–212. doi:10.1016/S0163-6383(96)90019-3

Spence, S. H., Sheffield, J. K., & Donovan, C. L. (2003). Preventing adolescent depression: An evaluation of the Problem Solving for Life Program. *Journal of Consulting and Clinical Psychology, 71*, 3–13.

Spencer, J. P., Clearfield, M., Corbetta, D., Ulrich, B., Buchanan, P., & Schöner, G. (2006). Moving toward a grand theory of development: In memory of Esther Thelen. *Child Development, 77*, 1521–1538. doi:10.1111/j.1467-8624.2006.00955.x

Spencer, J. P., Vereijken, B., Diedrich, F. J., & Thelen, E. (2000). Posture and the emergence of manual skills. *Developmental Science, 3*, 216–233. doi:10.1111/1467-7687.00115

Spencer, M. B., & Markstrom-Adams, C. (1990). Identity processes among racial and ethnic minority children in America. *Child Development, 61*, 290–310.

Spencer-Rodgers, J., Peng, K., Wang, L., & Hou, Y. (2004). Dialectical self-esteem and East-West differences in psychological well-being. *Personality and Social Psychology Bulletin, 30*, 1416–1432. doi:10.1177/0146167204264243

Spilich, G. J., Vesonder, G. T., Chiesi, H. L., & Voss, J. F. (1979). Text processing of domain-related information for individuals with high and low domain knowledge. *Journal of Verbal Learning and Verbal Behavior, 18*, 275–290. doi:10.1016/S0022-5371(79)90155-5

Spitz, R. A. (1945). Hospitalism: An inquiry into the genesis of psychiatric conditions in early childhood. *The Psychoanalytic Study of the Child, 1*, 53–74.

Spitz, R. A. (1946). Hospitalism: A follow-up report. *The Psychoanalytic Study of the Child, 2*, 113–117.

Spitz, R. A. (1949). The role of ecological factors in emotional development in infancy. *Child Development, 20*, 145–155.

Spivak, A. L., & Howes, C. (2011). Social and relational factors in early education and prosocial actions of children of diverse ethnocultural communities. *Merrill-Palmer Quarterly, 57*, 1–24.

Sprenger-Charolles, L. (2004). Linguistic processes in reading and spelling: The case of alphabetic writing systems: English, French, German and Spanish. In T. Nunes & P. Bryant (Eds.), *Handbook of children's literacy* (pp. 43–65). Dordrecht, The Netherlands: Kluwer.

Springer, K., & Keil, F. C. (1991). Early differentiation of causal mechanisms appropriate to biological and nonbiological kinds. *Child Development, 62*, 767–781. doi:10.1111/j.1467-8624.1991.tb01568.x

Springer, K., Ngyuen, T., & Samaniego, R. (1996). Early understanding of age- and environment-related noxiousness in biological kinds: Evidence for a naive theory. *Cognitive Development, 11*, 65–82. doi:10.1016/S0885-2014(96)90028-3

Srinivasan, M., & Carey, S. (2010). The long and the short of it: On the nature and origin of functional overlap between representations of space and time. *Cognition, 116*, 217–241. doi:10.1016/j.cognition.2010.05.005

Sroufe, L. A. (1979). Socioemotional development. In J. D. Osofsky (Ed.), *Handbook of infant development* (pp. 462–516). New York, NY: Wiley.

Sroufe, L. A. (1995). *Emotional development: The organization of emotional life in the early years.* Cambridge, England: Cambridge University Press.

Sroufe, L. A., Bennett, C., Englund, M., Urban, J., & Shulman, S. (1993). The significance of gender boundaries in preadolescence: Contemporary correlates and antecedents of boundary violation and maintenance. *Child Development, 64*, 455–466. doi:10.2307/1131262

Sroufe, L. A., Egeland, B., & Kreutzer, T. (1990). The fate of early experience following developmental change: Longitudinal approaches to individual adaptation in childhood. *Child Development, 61*, 1363–1373. doi:10.1111/j.1467-8624.1990.tb02867.x

Sroufe, L. A., & Waters, E. (1976). The ontogenesis of smiling and laughter: A perspective on the organization of development in infancy. *Psychological Review, 83*, 173–189.

St James-Roberts, I., Conroy, S., & Wilsher, C. (1998). Stability and outcome of persistent infant crying. *Infant Behavior and Development, 21*, 411–435. doi:10.1016/S0163-6383(98)90017-0

St James-Roberts, I., & Halil, T. (1991). Infant crying patterns in the first year: Normal community and clinical findings. *Journal of Child Psychology and Psychiatry and Allied Disciplines, 32*, 951–968.

Stack, D. M., & Arnold, S. L. (1998). Changes in mothers' touch and hand gestures influence infant behavior during face-to-face interchanges. *Infant Behavior and Development, 21*, 451–468. doi:10.1016/S0163-6383(98)90019-4

Stack, D. M., & Muir, D. W. (1990). Tactile stimulation as a component of social interchange: New interpretations for the still-face effect. *British Journal of Developmental Psychology, 8*, 131–145. doi:10.1111/j.2044-835X.1990.tb00828.x

Stack, D. M., & Muir, D. W. (1992). Adult tactile stimulation during face-to-face interactions modulates five-month-olds' affect and attention. *Child Development, 63*, 1509–1525. doi:10.1111/j.1467-8624.1992.tb01711.x

Stack, D. M., Muir, D. W., Sherriff, F., & Roman, J. (1989). Development of infant reaching in the dark to luminous objects and 'invisible sounds.' *Perception, 18*, 69–82.

Stams, G. J., Brugman, D., Deković, M., van Rosmalen, L., van der Laan, P., & Gibbs, J. C. (2006). The moral judgment of juvenile delinquents: A meta-analysis. *Journal of Abnormal Child Psychology, 34*, 692–708. doi:10.1007/s10802-006-9056-5

Stangor, C., & McMillan, D. (1992). Memory for expectancy-congruent and expectancy-incongruent information: A review of the social and social developmental literatures. *Psychological Bulletin, 111,* 42–61. doi:10.1037/0033-2909.111.1.42

Starkey, P. (1992). The early development of numerical reasoning. *Cognition, 43,* 93–126.

Statistics Canada. (2011a). *2011 census of Canada: Topic-based tabulations.* Available from http://www12.statcan.gc.ca/census-recensement/2011/dp-pd/tbt-tt/Rp-eng.cfm?lang=e&apath=3&detail=0&dim=0&fl=a&free=0&gc=0&gid=0&gk=0&grp=1&pid=102659&prid=0&ptype=101955&s=0&showall=0&sub=0&temporal=2011&theme=89&vid=0&vnamee=&vnamef=

Statistics Canada. (2011b). *Breastfeeding, 2009.* Retrieved from http://www.statcan.gc.ca/pub/82-625-x/2010002/article/11269-eng.htm

Statistics Canada. (2011c). *Family violence in Canada: A statistical profile* (Catalogue no. 85-224-X). Retrieved from http://www.statcan.gc.ca/pub/85-224x/85-224-x2010000-eng.pdf

Statistics Canada. (2012a). *2011 census of population: Linguistic characteristics of Canadians.* Retrieved from http://www.statcan.gc.ca/daily-quotidien/121024/dq121024a-eng.htm

Statistics Canada. (2012b). *Fifty years of families in Canada: 1961 to 2011—Families, households and marital status, 2011 census of population* (Catalogue no. 98-312X2011003). Retrieved from http://www12.statcan.gc.ca/census-recensement/2011/as-sa/98-312-x/98-312-x2011003_1-eng.pdf

Statistics Canada. (2012c). *Table 051-0002: Estimates of deaths, by sex and age group, Canada, provinces and territories annual (persons).* Available from http://www5.statcan.gc.ca/cansim/a26?lang=eng&retrLang=eng&id=0510002&paSer=&pattern=&stByVal=1&p1=1&p2=-1&tabMode=dataTable&csid=

Statistics Canada. (2013a). *2011 national household survey: Education in Canada—Attainment, field of and location of study.* Retrieved from http://www.statcan.gc.ca/daily-quotidien/130626/dq130626a-eng.pdf

Statistics Canada. (2013b). *Table 102-0504: Deaths and mortality rates, by age group and sex, Canada, provinces and territories* [Data file]. Available from http://www5.statcan.gc.ca/cansim/pick-choisir?lang=eng&p2=33&id=1020504

Statistics Canada. (2013c). *Table 105-0512: Health indicator profile, by Aboriginal identity, age group and sex, four year estimates, Canada, provinces and territories* [Data file]. Available from http://www5.statcan.gc.ca/cansim/pick-choisir?lang=eng&p2=33&id=1050512

Statistics Canada. (2013d). *Table 102-4503: Live births, by age of mother, Canada, provinces and territories, annual* [Data file]. Available from http://www5.statcan.gc.ca/cansim/a26?lang=eng&retrLang=eng&id=1024503&paSer=&pattern=&stByVal=1&p1=1&p2=-1&tabMode=dataTable&csid=lang=eng&retrLang=eng&id=1024503&paSer=&pattern=&stByVal=1&p1=1&p2=-1&tabMode=dataTable&csid=

Statistics Canada. (2013e). *Table 102-4509: Live births, by birth weight and sex, Canada, provinces and territories* [Data file]. Available from http://www5.statcan.gc.ca/cansim/pick-choisir?lang=eng&p2=33&id=1024509

Statistics Canada. (2013f). *Table 102-4511: Live births, birth weight indicators, by characteristics of the mother and child, Canada* [Data file]. Available from http://www5.statcan.gc.ca/cansim/pick-choisir?lang=eng&p2=33&id=1024511

Staub, E. (1979). *Positive social behavior and morality: Vol 2: Socialization and development.* New York: Academic Press.

Stecher, B. M., McCaffrey, D. F., & Bugliari, D. (2003, November 10). The relationship between exposure to class size reduction and student achievement in California. *Education Policy Analysis Archives, 11*(40). Retrieved June 2, 2005 from http://epaa.asu.edu/epaa/v11n40/.

Steeger, C. M., & Gondoli, D. M. (2013). Mother–adolescent conflict as a mediator between adolescent problem behaviors and maternal psychological control. *Developmental Psychology, 49,* 804–814. doi:10.1037/a0028599

Steele, H., Steele, M., & Croft, C. (2008). Early attachment predicts emotion recognition at 6 and 11 years old. *Attachment and Human Development, 10,* 379–393. doi:10.1080/14616730802461409

Steele, H., Steele, M., & Fonagy, P. (1996). Associations among attachment classifications of mothers, fathers, and their infants. *Child Development, 67,* 541–555.

Steenbeek, H., & van Geert, P. (2008). An empirical validation of a dynamic systems model of interaction: Do children of different sociometric statuses differ in their dyadic play? *Developmental Science, 11,* 253–281. doi:10.1111/j.1467-7687.2007.00655.x

Stein, N. L. (1988). The development of children's storytelling skill. In M. B. Franklin & S. S. Barten (Eds.), *Child language: A reader* (pp. 282–297). New York, NY: Oxford University Press.

Stein, Z., Susser, M., Saenger, G., & Marolla, F. (1975). *Famine and human development: The Dutch hunger winter of 1944–1945.* New York, NY: Oxford University Press.

Steinberg, L. (1987). Impact of puberty on family relations: Effects of pubertal status and pubertal timing. *Developmental Psychology, 23,* 451–460. doi:10.1037/0012-1649.23.3.451

Steinberg, L. (1988). Reciprocal relation between parent-child distance and pubertal maturation. *Developmental Psychology, 24,* 122–128. doi:10.1037/0012-1649.24.1.122

Steinberg, L. (1990). Autonomy, conflict, and harmony in the family relationship. In S. S. Feldman & G. R. Elliott (Eds.), *At the threshold: The developing adolescent* (pp. 255–276). Cambridge, MA: Harvard University Press.

Steinberg, L. (2010). A dual systems model of adolescent risk-taking. *Developmental Psychobiology, 52,* 216–224. doi:10.1002/dev.20445

Steinberg, L., Darling, N. E., & Fletcher, A. C. (1995). Authoritative parenting and adolescent adjustment: An ecological journey. In P. Moen, G. H. Elder, Jr., & K. Lüscher (Eds.), *Examining lives in context: Perspectives on the ecology of human development* (pp. 423–466). Washington, DC: American Psychological Association.

Steinberg, L., Lamborn, S. D., Darling, N., Mounts, N. S., & Dornbusch, S. M. (1994). Over-time changes in adjustment and competence among adolescents from authoritative, authoritarian, indulgent, and neglectful families. *Child Development, 65,* 754–770. doi:10.1111/j.1467-8624.1994.tb00781.x

Steinberg, L., & Morris, A. S. (2001). Adolescent development. *Journal of Cognitive Education and Psychology, 2,* 55–87.

Steinberg, L., Mounts, N. S., Lamborn, S. D., & Dornbusch, S. M. (1991). Authoritative parenting and adolescent adjustment across varied ecological niches. *Journal of Research on Adolescence, 1,* 19–36.

Steinberg, L., & Silverberg, S. B. (1986). The vicissitudes of autonomy in early adolescence. *Child Development, 57,* 841–851. doi:10.2307/1130361

Steiner, J. E. (1979). Human facial expressions in response to taste and smell stimulation. In H. W. Reese & L. P. Lipsitt (Eds.), *Advances in child development and behavior* (Vol. 13, pp. 257–295). New York, NY: Academic Press.

Steinmayr, R., & Spinath, B. (2009). What explains boys' stronger confidence in their intelligence? *Sex Roles, 61,* 736–749. doi:10.1007/s11199-009-9675-8

Stenberg, C. R., Campos, J. J., & Emde, R. N. (1983). The facial expression of anger in seven-month-old infants. *Child Development, 54*, 178–184.

Stern, D. N. (1985). *The interpersonal world of the infant: A view from psychoanalysis and developmental psychology.* New York, NY: Basic Books.

Sternberg, R. J. (1999). The theory of successful intelligence. *Review of General Psychology, 3*, 292–316. doi:10.1037/1089-2680.3.4.292

Sternberg, R. J. (2003). A broad view of intelligence: The theory of successful intelligence. *Consulting Psychology Journal: Practice and Research, 55*, 139–154. doi:10.1037/1061-4087.55.3.139

Sternberg, R. J. (2004). Culture and intelligence. *American Psychologist, 59*, 325–338.

Sternberg, R. J. (2008). g, g's, or Jeez: Which is the best model for developing abilities, competencies, and expertise? In P. C. Kyllonen, R. D. Roberts, & L. Stankov (Eds.), *Extending intelligence: Enhancement and new constructs* (pp. 225–266). New York, NY: Erlbaum.

Sterrett, E. M., Jones, D. J., McKee, L. G., & Kincaid, C. (2011). Supportive non-parental adults and adolescent psychosocial functioning: Using social support as a theoretical framework. *American Journal of Community Psychology, 48*, 284–295. doi:10.1007/s10464-011-9429-y

Stevens, T., Wang, K., Olivárez, A., Jr., & Hamman, D. (2007). Use of self-perspectives and their sources to predict the mathematics enrollment intentions of girls and boys. *Sex Roles, 56*, 351–363. doi:10.1007/s11199-006-9180-2

Stevenson, H. W. (1991). The development of prosocial behavior in large-scale collective societies: China and Japan. In R. A. Hinde & J. Groebel (Eds.), *Cooperation and prosocial behaviour* (pp. 89–105). Cambridge, England: Cambridge University Press.

Stevenson, H. W., Chen, C., & Lee, S.-y. (1993, January 1). Mathematics achievement of Chinese, Japanese, and American children: Ten years later. *Science, 259*, 53–58.

Stevenson, H. W., & Newman, R. S. (1986). Long-term prediction of achievement and attitudes in mathematics and reading. *Child Development, 57*, 646–659.

Stifter, C. A., Bono, M., & Spinrad, T. (2003). Parent characteristics and conceptualizations associated with the emergence of infant colic. *Journal of Reproductive and Infant Psychology, 21*, 309–322. doi:10.1080/02646830310001622123

Stifter, C. A., & Braungart, J. (1992). Infant colic: A transient condition with no apparent effects. *Journal of Applied Developmental Psychology, 13*, 447–462. doi:10.1016/0193-3973(92)90012-7

Stiles, J. (2008). *The fundamentals of brain development: Integrating nature and nurture.* Cambridge, MA: Harvard University Press.

Stipek, D. J., Gralinski, J. H., & Kopp, C. B. (1990). Self-concept development in the toddler years. *Developmental Psychology, 26*, 972–977. doi:10.1037/0012-1649.26.6.972

Stipek, D. J., Roberts, T. A., & Sanborn, M. E. (1984). Preschool-age children's performance expectations for themselves and another child as a function of the incentive value of success and the salience of past performance. *Child Development, 55*, 1983–1989.

Stocker, C. M., & Richmond, M. K. (2007). Longitudinal associations between hostility in adolescents' family relationships and friendships and hostility in their romantic relationships. *Journal of Family Psychology, 21*, 490–497.

Stocker, C. M., Richmond, M. K., Rhoades, G. K., & Kiang, L. (2007). Family emotional processes and adolescents' adjustment. *Social Development, 16*, 310–325.

Stoddart, T., & Turiel, E. (1985). Children's concepts of cross-gender activities. *Child Development, 56*, 1241–1252. doi:10.2307/1130239

Stone, L. B., Hankin, B. L., Gibb, B. E., & Abela, J. R. Z. (2011). Co-rumination predicts the onset of depressive disorders during adolescence. *Journal of Abnormal Psychology, 120*, 752–757. doi:10.1037/a0023384

Stone, L. J., & Church, J. (1957). *Childhood and adolescence: A psychology of the growing person.* New York, NY: Random House.

Stone, W. L., & Yoder, P. J. (2001). Predicting spoken language level in children with autism spectrum disorders. *Autism, 5*, 341–361.

Stouthamer-Loeber, M., Loeber, R., Wei, E., Farrington, D. P., & Wikström, P.-O. H. (2002). Risk and promotive effects in the explanation of persistent serious delinquency in boys. *Journal of Consulting and Clinical Psychology, 70*, 111–123. doi:10.1037/0022-006X.70.1.111

Stover, C. S., Connell, C. M., Leve, L. D., Neiderhiser, J. M., Shaw, D. S., Scaramella, L. V., ... Reiss, D. (2012). Fathering and mothering in the family system: Linking marital hostility and aggression in adopted toddlers. *Journal of Child Psychology and Psychiatry, 53*, 401–409. doi:10.1111/j.1469-7610.2011.02510.x

Strand-Brodd, K., Ewald, U., Grönqvist, H., Holmström, G., Strömberg, B., Grönqvist, E., ... Rosander, K. (2011). Development of smooth pursuit eye movements in very preterm infants: 1. General aspects. *Acta Paediatrica, 100*, 983–991. doi:10.1111/j.1651-2227.2011.02218.x

Strauch, B. (2003). *The primal teen: What the new discoveries about the teenage brain tell us about our kids.* New York, NY: Doubleday.

Strauss, R. S., & Pollack, H. A. (2003). Social marginalization of overweight children. *Archives of Pediatrics and Adolescent Medicine, 157*, 746–752. doi:10.1001/archpedi.157.8.746

Strayer, J. (1986). Children's attributions regarding the situational determinants of emotion in self and others. *Developmental Psychology, 22*, 649–654.

Streeter, L. A. (1976, January 1). Language perception of 2-month-old infants shows effects of both innate mechanisms and experience. *Nature, 259*, 39–41.

Streissguth, A. P. (2001). Recent advances in fetal alcohol syndrome and alcohol use in pregnancy. In Dharam Agarwal & H. K. Seitz (Eds.), *Alcohol in health and disease* (pp. 303–324). New York, NY: Marcel Dekker.

Streissguth, A. P., Bookstein, F. L., Barr, H. M., & Sampson, P. D. (1993). *The enduring effects of prenatal alcohol exposure on child development: Birth through seven years, a partial least squares solution.* Ann Arbor: University of Michigan Press.

Streri, A., & Spelke, E. S. (1988). Haptic perception of objects in infancy. *Cognitive Psychology, 20*, 1–23. doi:10.1016/0010-0285(88)90022-9

Striepens, N., Kendrick, K. M., Maier, W., & Hurlemann, R. (2011). Prosocial effects of oxytocin and clinical evidence for its therapeutic potential. *Frontiers in Neuroendocrinology, 32*, 426–450. doi:10.1016/j.yfrne.2011.07.001

Strohmeier, D., Kärnä, A., & Salmivalli, C. (2011). Intrapersonal and interpersonal risk factors for peer victimization in immigrant youth in Finland. *Developmental Psychology, 47*, 248–258. doi:10.1037/a0020785

Strohschein, L. (2005). Parental divorce and child mental health trajectories. *Journal of Marriage and Family, 67*, 1286–1300. doi:10.1111/j.1741-3737.2005.00217.x

Stroink, M. L., & Lalonde, R. N. (2009). Bicultural identity conflict in second-generation Asian Canadians. *The Journal of Social Psychology, 149*, 44–65. doi:10.3200/SOCP.149.1.44-65

Strough, J., & Berg, C. A. (2000). Goals as a mediator of gender differences in high-affiliation dyadic conversations. *Developmental Psychology, 36*, 117–125. doi:10.1037/0012-1649.36.1.117

Strough, J., & Covatto, A. M. (2002). Context and age differences in same- and other-gender peer preferences. *Social Development, 11*, 346–361. doi:10.1111/1467-9507.00204

Stuewig, J., Tangney, J. P., Heigel, C., Harty, L., & McCloskey, L. (2010). Shaming, blaming, and maiming: Functional links among the moral emotions, externalization of blame, and aggression. *Journal of Research in Personality, 44*, 91–102. doi:10.1016/j.jrp.2009.12.005

Stukas, A. A., Snyder, M., & Clary, E. G. (1999). The effects of "mandatory volunteerism" on intentions to volunteer. *Psychological Science, 10*, 59–64. doi:10.2307/40063378

Stukas, A. A., Switzer, G. E., Dew, M. A., Goycoolea, J. M., & Simmons, R. G. (1999). Parental helping models, gender, and service-learning. *Journal of Prevention and Intervention in the Community, 18*, 5–18. doi:10.1300/j005v18n01_02

Sturaro, C., van Lier, P. A. C., Cuijpers, P., & Koot, H. M. (2011). The role of peer relationships in the development of early school-age externalizing problems. *Child Development, 82*, 758–765. doi:10.1111/j.1467-8624.2010.01532.x

Sturge-Apple, M. L., Davies, P. T., & Cummings, E. M. (2006). Hostility and withdrawal in marital conflict: Effects on parental emotional unavailability and inconsistent discipline. *Journal of Family Psychology, 20*, 227–238. Retrieved from http://www.ncbi.nlm.nih.gov/pmc/articles/PMC3529153/

Sturge-Apple, M. L., Davies, P. T., Cicchetti, D., & Manning, L. G. (2012). Interparental violence, maternal emotional unavailability and children's cortisol functioning in family contexts. *Developmental Psychology, 48*, 237–249. doi:10.1037/a0025419

Subbotsky, E. (1994). Early rationality and magical thinking in preschoolers: Space and time. *British Journal of Developmental Psychology, 12*, 97–108. doi:10.1111/j.2044-835X.1994.tb00621.x

Subbotsky, E. (2005). The permanence of mental objects: Testing magical thinking on perceived and imaginary realities. *Developmental Psychology, 41*, 301–318. doi:10.1037/0012-1649.41.2.301

Subbotsky, E. V. (1993). *Foundations of the mind: Children's understanding of reality.* Cambridge, MA: Harvard University Press.

Subrahmanyam, K., Kraut, R., Greenfield, P., & Gross, E. (2001). New forms of electronic media: The impact of interactive games and the Internet on cognition, socialization, and behavior. In D. G. Singer & J. L. Singer (Eds.), *Handbook of children and the media* (pp. 73–99). Thousand Oaks, CA: Sage.

Suess, P. E., Porges, S. W., & Plude, D. J. (1994). Cardiac vagal tone and sustained attention in school-age children. *Psychophysiology, 31*, 17–22.

Sugimoto, T., Kobayashi, H., Nobuyoshi, N., Kiriyama, Y., Takeshita, H., Nakamura, T., & Hashiya, K. (2010). Preference for consonant music over dissonant music by an infant chimpanzee. *Primates, 51*, 7–12. doi:10.1007/s10329-009-0160-3

Sullivan, H. S. (1953). *The interpersonal theory of psychiatry* (H. S. Perry & M. L. Gawel, Eds.). New York, NY: Norton.

Sullivan, K., & Winner, E. (1993). Three-year-olds' understanding of mental states: The influence of trickery. *Journal of Experimental Child Psychology, 56*, 135–148. doi:10.1006/jecp.1993.1029

Sullivan, M. W., & Lewis, M. (2003). Contextual determinants of anger and other negative expressions in young infants. *Developmental Psychology, 39*, 693–705.

Sullivan, M. W., Lewis, M., & Alessandri, S. M. (1992). Cross-age stability in emotional expressions during learning and extinction. *Developmental Psychology, 28*, 58–63. doi:10.1037/0012-1649.28.1.58

Sulloway, F. J. (1996). *Born to rebel: Birth order, family dynamics, and creative lives.* New York, NY: Pantheon Books.

Sun, Y., & Li, Y. (2011). Effects of family structure type and stability on children's academic performance trajectories. *Journal of Marriage and Family, 73*, 541–556. doi:10.1111/j.1741-3737.2011.00825.x

Sundara, M., Polka, L., & Molnar, M. (2008). Development of coronal stop perception: Bilingual infants keep pace with their monolingual peers. *Cognition, 108*, 232–242. doi:10.1016/j.cognition.2007.12.013

Suomi, S. J., & Harlow, H. F. (1972). Social rehabilitation of isolate-reared monkeys. *Developmental Psychology, 6*, 487–496. doi:10.1037/h0032545

Super, C. M. (1976). Environmental effects on motor development: The case of "African infant precocity." *Developmental Medicine and Child Neurology, 18*, 561–567. doi:10.1111/j.1469-8749.1976.tb04202.x

Super, C. M., & Harkness, S. (1986). The developmental niche: A conceptualization at the interface of child and culture. *International Journal of Behavioral Development, 9*, 545–569. doi:10.1177/016502548600900409

Susman, E. J. (2006). Psychobiology of persistent antisocial behavior: Stress, early vulnerabilities and the attenuation hypothesis. *Neuroscience and Biobehavioral Reviews, 30*, 376–389. doi:10.1016/j.neubiorev.2005.08.002

Susman, E. J., Schmeelk, K. H., Ponirakis, A., & Gariepy, J. L. (2001). Maternal prenatal, postpartum, and concurrent stressors and temperament in 3-year-olds: A person and variable analysis. *Development and Psychopathology, 13*, 629–652.

Sutherland, K. E., Altenhofen, S., & Biringen, Z. (2012). Emotional availability during mother–child interactions in divorcing and intact married families. *Journal of Divorce and Remarriage, 53*, 126–141. doi:10.1080/10502556.2011.651974

Sutherland, S. L., & Friedman, O. (2012). Preschoolers acquire general knowledge by sharing in pretense. *Child Development, 83*, 1064–1071. doi:10.1111/j.1467-8624.2012.01748.x

Sutton, J. E., Joanisse, M. F., & Newcombe, N. S. (2010). Spinning in the scanner: Neural correlates of virtual reorientation. *Journal of Experimental Psychology: Learning, Memory, and Cognition, 36*, 1097–1107. doi:10.1037/a0019938

Suzuki, L. K., Davis, H. M., & Greenfield, P. M. (2008). Self-enhancement and self-effacement in reaction to praise and criticism: The case of multiethnic youth. *Ethos, 36*, 78–97. doi:10.1111/j.1548-1352.2008.00005.x

Svetlova, M., Nichols, S. R., & Brownell, C. A. (2010). Toddlers' prosocial behavior: From instrumental to empathic to altruistic helping. *Child Development, 81*, 1814-1827. Retrieved from http://www.ncbi.nlm.nih.gov/pmc/articles/PMC3088085/

Swahn, M. H., Simon, T. R., Arias, I., & Bossarte, R. M. (2008). Measuring sex differences in violence victimization and perpetration within date and same-sex peer relationships. *Journal of Interpersonal Violence, 23*, 1120–1138. doi:10.1177/0886260508314086

Swaim, R. C., Oetting, E. R., Thurman, P. J., Beauvais, F., & Edwards, R. W. (1993). American Indian adolescent drug use and socialization characteristics: A cross-cultural comparison. *Journal of Cross-Cultural Psychology, 24*, 53–70. doi:10.1177/0022022193241004

Swingley, D., & Aslin, R. N. (2000). Spoken word recognition and lexical representation in very young children. *Cognition, 76*, 147–166.

Szalacha, L. A., Erkut, S., García Coll, C., Alarcón, O., Fields, J. P., & Ceder, I. (2003). Discrimination and Puerto Rican children's and adolescents' mental health. *Cultural Diversity and Ethnic Minority Psychology, 9*, 141–155. doi:10.1037/1099-9809.9.2.141

Szatmari, P., Bryson, S. E., Boyle, M. H., Streiner, D. L., & Duku, E. (2003). Predictors of outcome among high functioning children with autism and Asperger syndrome. *Journal of Child Psychology and Psychiatry, 44,* 520–528. doi:10.1111/1469-7610.00141

Tager-Flusberg, H. (2007). Evaluating the theory-of-mind hypothesis of autism. *Current Directions in Psychological Science, 16,* 311–315. doi:10.1111/j.1467-8721.2007.00527.x

Tager-Flusberg, H., & Joseph, R. M. (2005). How language facilitates the acquisition of false-belief understanding in children with autism. In J. W. Astington & J. A. Baird (Eds.), *Why language matters for theory of mind* (pp. 298–318). New York, NY: Oxford University Press.

Taharally, L. C. (1991). Fantasy play, language and cognitive ability of four-year-old children in Guyana, South America. *Child Study Journal, 21,* 37–56.

Tajfel, H., & Turner, J. C. (1979). An integrative theory of intergroup conflict. In W. G. Austin & S. Worchel (Eds.), *The social psychology of intergroup relations* (pp. 33–47). Monterey, CA: Brooks/Cole.

Takahashi, K. (1986). Examining the strange-situation procedure with Japanese mothers and 12-month-old infants. *Developmental Psychology, 22,* 265–270. doi:10.1037/0012-1649.22.2.265

Tallal, P., & Fitch, R. H. (1993). Hormones and cerebral organization: Implications for the development and transmission of language and learning disabilities. In A. M. Galaburda (Ed.), *Dyslexia and development: Neurobiological aspects of extraordinary brains* (pp. 168–186). Cambridge, MA: Harvard University Press.

Tanaka, H., Black, J. M., Hulme, C., Stanley, L. M., Kesler, S. R., Whitfield-Gabrieli, S., … Hoeft, F. (2011). The brain basis of the phonological deficit in dyslexia is independent of IQ. *Psychological Science, 22,* 1442–1451.

Tandon, P. S., Zhou, C., & Christakis, D. A. (2012). Frequency of parent-supervised outdoor play of US preschool-aged children. *Archives of Pediatrics and Adolescent Medicine, 166,* 707–712. doi:10.1001/archpediatrics.2011.1835

Tangney, J. P., & Dearing, R. L. (2002). *Shame and guilt.* New York, NY: Guilford Press.

Tangney, J. P., Stuewig, J., & Mashek, D. J. (2007). Moral emotions and moral behavior. *Annual Review of Psychology, 58,* 345–372. doi:10.1146/annurev.psych.56.091103.070145

Tanner, J. M. (1961). *Education and physical growth: Implications of the study of children's growth for educational theory and practice.* London, England: University of London Press.

Tardif, T., Fletcher, P., Liang, W., Zhang, Z., Kaciroti, N., & Marchman, V. A. (2008). Baby's first 10 words. *Developmental Psychology, 44,* 929–938. doi:10.1037/0012-1649.44.4.929

Tarullo, A. R., Mliner, S., & Gunnar, M. R. (2011). Inhibition and exuberance in preschool classrooms: Associations with peer social experiences and changes in cortisol across the preschool year. *Developmental Psychology, 47,* 1374–1388. doi:10.1037/a0024093

Tasker, F., & Golombok, S. (1995). Adults raised as children in lesbian families. *American Journal of Orthopsychiatry, 65,* 203–215. doi:10.1037/h0079615

Taumoepeau, M., & Ruffman, T. (2006). Mother and infant talk about mental states relates to desire language and emotion understanding. *Child Development, 77,* 465–481.

Taumoepeau, M., & Ruffman, T. (2008). Stepping stones to others' minds: Maternal talk relates to child mental state language and emotion understanding at 15, 24, and 33 months. *Child Development, 79,* 284–302.

Taylor, J., Iacono, W. G., & McGue, M. (2000). Evidence for a genetic etiology of early-onset delinquency. *Journal of Abnormal Psychology, 109,* 634–643. doi:10.1037/0021-843X.109.4.634

Taylor, M. (1999). *Imaginary companions and the children who create them.* New York, NY: Oxford University Press.

Taylor, M., & Carlson, S. M. (1997). The relation between individual differences in fantasy and theory of mind. *Child Development, 68,* 436–455. doi:10.1111/j.1467-8624.1997.tb01950.x

Taylor, M., Carlson, S. M., Maring, B. L., Gerow, L., & Charley, C. M. (2004). The characteristics and correlates of fantasy in school-age children: Imaginary companions, impersonation, and social understanding. *Developmental Psychology, 40,* 1173–1187. doi:10.1037/0012-1649.40.6.1173

Taylor, M., & Mannering, A. M. (2007). Of Hobbes and Harvey: The imaginary companions created by children and adults. In A. Göncü & S. Gaskins (Eds.), *Play and development: Evolutionary, sociocultural, and functional perspectives* (pp. 227–246). New York, NY: Erlbaum.

Taylor, M. G. (1993). *Children's beliefs about the biological and social origins of gender differences* (Unpublished doctoral dissertation). University of Michigan, Ann Arbor.

Taylor, R. (2011). Kin support and parenting practices among low-income African American mothers: Moderating effects of mothers' psychological adjustment. *Journal of Black Psychology, 37,* 3–23. doi:10.1177/0095798410372623

Taylor, R. D., Seaton, E., & Dominguez, A. (2008). Kinship support, family relations, and psychological adjustment among low-income African American mothers and adolescents. *Journal of Research on Adolescence, 18,* 1–22. doi:10.1111/j.1532-7795.2008.00548.x

Teglas, E., Girotto, V., Gonzalez, M., & Bonatti, L. L. (2007). Intuitions of probabilities shape expectations about the future at 12 months and beyond. *Proceedings of the National Academy of Sciences of the United States of America, 104,* 19156–19159. doi:10.1073/pnas.0700271104

Teglas, E., Vul, E., Girotto, V., Gonzalez, M., Tenenbaum, J. B., & Bonatti, L. L. (2011, May 27). Pure reasoning in 12-month-old infants as probabilistic inference. *Science, 332,* 1054–1059.

Teinonen, T., Fellman, V., Näätänen, R., Alku, P., & Huotilainen, M. (2009). Statistical language learning in neonates revealed by event-related brain potentials. *BMC Neuroscience, 10,* 1–8. doi:10.1186/1471-2202-10-21

Tenenbaum, H. R., & Leaper, C. (2003). Parent-child conversations about science: The socialization of gender inequities? *Developmental Psychology, 39,* 34–47. doi:10.1037/0012-1649.39.1.34

Terrace, H. S., Petitto, L.-A., Sanders, R. J., & Bever, T. G. (1979, November 23). Can an ape create a sentence? *Science, 206,* 891–902.

Teunissen, H. A., Adelman, C. B., Prinstein, M. J., Spijkerman, R., Poelen, E. A. P., Engels, R. C. M. E., & Scholte, R. H. J. (2011). The interaction between pubertal timing and peer popularity for boys and girls: An integration of biological and interpersonal perspectives on adolescent depression. *Journal of Abnormal Child Psychology, 39,* 413–423.

Thanh, N. X., & Jonsson, E. (2010). Drinking alcohol during pregnancy: Evidence from Canadian community health survey 2007/2008. *Journal of Population Therapeutics and Clinical Pharmacology, 17*(2), e302-e307.

Thatcher, R. W. (1992). Cyclic cortical reorganization during early childhood. *Brain and Cognition, 20,* 24–50.

Thatcher, R. W. (1998). Normative EEG databases and EEG biofeedback. *Journal of Neurotherapy, 2,* 8–39. doi:10.1300/J184v02n04_02

Thelen, E. (1986). Treadmill-elicited stepping in seven-month-old infants. *Child Development, 57,* 1498–1506. doi:10.2307/1130427

Thelen, E. (1995). Motor development: A new synthesis. *American Psychologist, 50,* 79–95. doi:10.1037/0003-066X.50.2.79

Thelen, E. (2001). Dynamic mechanisms of change in early perceptual-motor development. In J. L. McClelland & R. Siegler (Eds.), *Mechanisms of cognitive development: Behavioral and neural perspectives* (pp. 161–184). Mahwah, NJ: Erlbaum.

Thelen, E., & Corbetta, D. (1994). Exploration and selection in the early acquisition of skill. *International Review of Neurobiology, 37,* 75–102.

Thelen, E., Corbetta, D., Kamm, K., Spencer, J. P., Schneider, K., & Zernicke, R. F. (1993). The transition to reaching: Mapping intention and intrinsic dynamics. *Child Development, 64,* 1058–1098.

Thelen, E., & Fisher, D. M. (1982). Newborn stepping: An explanation for a "disappearing" reflex. *Developmental Psychology, 18,* 760–775. doi:10.1037/0012-1649.18.5.760

Thelen, E., Fisher, D. M., & Ridley-Johnson, R. (1984). The relationship between physical growth and a newborn reflex. *Infant Behavior and Development, 7,* 479–493. doi:10.1016/S0163-6383(84)80007-7

Thelen, E., & Smith, L. B. (1998). Dynamic systems theories. In W. Damon (Series Ed.) & R. M. Lerner (Vol. Ed.), *Handbook of child psychology: Vol. 1. Theoretical models of human development* (5th ed., pp. 563–634). Hoboken, NJ: Wiley.

Thelen, E., & Smith, L. B. (2006). Dynamic systems theories. In W. Damon & R. M. Lerner (Series Eds.) & R. M. Lerner (Vol. Ed.), *Handbook of child psychology: Vol. 1. Theoretical models of human development* (6th ed., pp. 258–312). Hoboken, NJ: Wiley.

Thiessen, E. D., Hill, E. A., & Saffran, J. R. (2005). Infant-directed speech facilitates word segmentation. *Infancy, 7,* 53–71. doi:10.1207/s15327078in0701_5

Thiessen, E. D., & Saffran, J. R. (2003). When cues collide: Statistical and stress cues in infant word segmentation. *Developmental Psychology, 39,* 706–716.

Thinus-Blanc, C., & Gaunet, F. (1997). Representation of space in blind persons: Vision as a spatial sense? *Psychological Bulletin, 121,* 20–42.

Thomaes, S., Bushman, B. J., Stegge, H., & Olthof, T. (2008). Trumping shame by blasts of noise: Narcissism, self-esteem, shame, and aggression in young adolescents. *Child Development, 79,* 1792–1801. doi:10.1111/j.1467-8624.2008.01226.x

Thomas, A., & Chess, S. (1977). *Temperament and development.* New York, NY: Brunner/Mazel.

Thomas, A., Chess, S., & Birch, H. G. (1968). *Temperament and behavior disorders in children.* New York, NY: New York University Press.

Thomas, J. R., & French, K. E. (1985). Gender differences across age in motor performance: A meta-analysis. *Psychological Bulletin, 98,* 260–282. doi:10.1037/0033-2909.98.2.260

Thompson, E. M., & Morgan, E. M. (2008). "Mostly straight" young women: Variations in sexual behavior and identity development. *Developmental Psychology, 44,* 15–21. doi:10.1037/0012-1649.44.1.15

Thompson, R. A. (1998). Early sociopersonality development. In W. Damon (Series Ed.) & N. Eisenberg (Vol. Ed.), *Handbook of child psychology: Vol. 3. Social, emotional, and personality development* (5th ed., pp. 25–104). Hoboken, NJ: Wiley.

Thompson, R. A. (2006). The development of the person: Social understanding, relationships, conscience, self. In W. Damon & R. M. Lerner (Series Eds.) & N. Eisenberg (Vol. Ed.), *Handbook of child psychology: Vol. 3. Social, emotional, and personality development* (6th ed., pp. 24–98). Hoboken, NJ: Wiley.

Thompson, R. A. (2008). Early attachment and later development: Familiar questions, new answers. In J. Cassidy & P. R. Shaver (Eds.), *Handbook of attachment: Theory, research, and clinical applications* (2nd ed., pp. 348–365). New York, NY: Guilford Press.

Thompson, R. A. (2012). Whither the preconventional child? Toward a life-span moral development theory. *Child Development Perspectives, 6,* 423–429. doi:10.1111/j.1750-8606.2012.00245.x

Thompson, R. A., Lewis, M. D., & Calkins, S. D. (2008). Reassessing emotion regulation. *Child Development Perspectives, 2,* 124–131.

Thompson, R. A., & Newton, E. K. (2010). Emotion in early conscience. In W. F. Arsenio & E. A. Lemerise (Eds.), *Emotions, aggression, and morality in children: Bridging development and psychopathology* (pp. 13–31). Washington, DC: American Psychological Association.

Thompson, R. F. (2000). *The brain: A neuroscience primer* (3rd ed.). New York, NY: Worth.

Thompson, R. F., & Spencer, W. A. (1966). Habituation: A model phenomenon for the study of neuronal substrates of behavior. *Psychological Review, 73,* 16–43.

Thompson, T., Caruso, M., & Ellerbeck, K. (2003). Sex matters in autism and other developmental disabilities. *Journal of Learning Disabilities, 7,* 345–362. doi:10.1177/1469004703074003

Thompson, T. L., & Zerbinos, E. (1995). Gender roles in animated cartoons: Has the picture changed in 20 years? *Sex Roles, 32,* 651–673. doi:10.1007/BF01544217

Thornberry, T. P., Freeman-Gallant, A., Lizotte, A. J., Krohn, M. D., & Smith, C. A. (2003). Linked lives: The intergenerational transmission of antisocial behavior. *Journal of Abnormal Child Psychology, 31,* 171–184. doi:10.1023/A:1022574208366

Thornberry, T. P., Lizotte, A. J., Krohn, M. D., Farnworth, M., & Jang, S. J. (1994). Delinquent peers, beliefs, and delinquent behavior: A longitudinal test of interactional theory. *Criminology, 32,* 47–83. doi:10.1111/j.1745-9125.1994.tb01146.x

Thorne, B. (1986). Girls and boys together … but mostly apart: Gender arrangements in elementary schools. In W. W. Hartup & Z. Rubin (Eds.), *Relationships and development* (pp. 167–184). Hillsdale, NJ: Erlbaum.

Thorne, B. (1993). *Gender play: Girls and boys in school.* New Brunswick, NJ: Rutgers University Press.

Thorne, B., & Luria, Z. (1986). Sexuality and gender in children's daily worlds. *Social Problems, 33,* 176–190. doi:10.2307/800703

Thurstone, L. L. (1938). *Primary mental abilities.* Chicago, IL: The University of Chicago Press.

Tiedemann, J. (2000). Parents' gender stereotypes and teachers' beliefs as predictors of children's concept of their mathematical ability in elementary school. *Journal of Educational Psychology, 92,* 144–151. doi:10.1037/0022-0663.92.1.144

Tienari, P., Wahlberg, K.-E., & Wynne, L. C. (2006). Finnish adoption study of schizophrenia: Implications for family interventions. *Families, Systems, and Health, 24,* 442–451. doi:10.1037/1091-7527.24.4.442

Tietjen, A. M. (1986). Prosocial reasoning among children and adults in a Papua New Guinea society. *Developmental Psychology, 22,* 861–868. doi:10.1037/0012-1649.22.6.861

Tietjen, A. M. (2006). Cultural influences on peer relations: An ecological perspective. In X. Chen, D. C. French, & B. H. Schneider (Eds.), *Peer relationships in cultural context* (pp. 52–74). Cambridge, England: Cambridge University Press.

Tillman, K. H. (2008). "Non-traditional" siblings and the academic outcomes of adolescents. *Social Science Research, 37*, 88–108. doi:10.1016/j.ssresearch.2007.06.007

Tincoff, R., & Jusczyk, P. W. (1999). Some beginnings of word comprehension in 6-month-olds. *Psychological Science, 10*, 172–175. doi:10.1111/1467-9280.00127

Tisak, M. (1995). Domains of social reasoning and beyond. In R. Vasta (Ed.), *Annals of child development* (Vol. 11, pp. 95–130). London, England: Jessica Kingsley.

Tkachev, D., Mimmack, M. L., Ryan, M. M., Wayland, M., Freeman, T., Jones, P. B., ... Bahn, S. (2003, September 6). Oligodendrocyte dysfunction in schizophrenia and bipolar disorder. *The Lancet, 362*, 798–805. doi:10.1016/S0140-6736(03)14289-4

Tokunaga, R. S. (2010). Following you home from school: A critical review and synthesis of research on cyberbullying victimization. *Computers in Human Behavior, 26*, 277–287. doi:10.1016/j.chb.2009.11.014

Tolan, P. H., Gorman-Smith, D., & Henry, D. B. (2003). The developmental ecology of urban males' youth violence. *Developmental Psychology, 39*, 274–291. doi:10.1037/0012-1649.39.2.274

Tolchinsky, L. (2003). *The cradle of culture and what children know about writing and numbers before being taught.* Mahwah, NJ: Erlbaum.

Tom, S. R., Schwartz, D., Chang, L., Farver, J. A. M., & Xu, Y. (2010). Correlates of victimization in Hong Kong children's peer groups. *Journal of Applied Developmental Psychology, 31*, 27–37. doi:10.1016/j.appdev.2009.06.002

Tomada, G., & Schneider, B. H. (1997). Relational aggression, gender, and peer acceptance: Invariance across culture, stability over time, and concordance among informants. *Developmental Psychology, 33*, 601–609. doi:10.1037/0012-1649.33.4.601

Tomasello, M. (1987). Learning to use prepositions: A case study. *Journal of Child Language, 14*, 79–98. doi:10.1017/S0305000900012745

Tomasello, M. (1994). Can an ape understand a sentence? [Review of the monograph *Language comprehension in ape and child*, by E. S. Savage-Rumbaugh et al.]. *Language and Communication, 14*, 377–390.

Tomasello, M. (2001). Perceiving intentions and learning words in the second year of life. In M. Bowerman & S. C. Levinson (Eds.), *Language acquisition and conceptual development* (pp. 132–158). Cambridge, England: Cambridge University Press.

Tomasello, M. (2003). *Constructing a language: A usage-based theory of language acquisition.* Cambridge, MA: Harvard University Press.

Tomasello, M. (2008). *Origins of human communication.* Cambridge, MA: MIT Press.

Tomasello, M. (2009). *Why we cooperate.* Cambridge, MA: MIT Press.

Tomasello, M., & Barton, M. E. (1994). Learning words in non-ostensive contexts. *Developmental Psychology, 30*, 639–650. doi:10.1037/0012-1649.30.5.639

Tomasello, M., & Farrar, M. J. (1986). Joint attention and early language. *Child Development, 57*, 1454–1463.

Tomasello, M., Strosberg, R., & Akhtar, N. (1996). Eighteen-month-old children learn words in non-ostensive contexts. *Journal of Child Language, 23*, 157–176. doi:10.1017/S0305000900010138

Tomblin, J. B., Mainela-Arnold, E., & Zhang, X. (2007). Procedural learning in adolescents with and without specific language impairment. *Language Learning and Development, 3*, 269–293. doi:10.1080/15475440701377477

Tomkins, S. S., & Karon, B. P. (1962). *Affect, imagery, consciousness: Vol. 1. The positive affects.* New York, NY: Springer.

Tomlinson, H. B. (2009). Developmentally appropriate practice in the kindergarten year—Ages 5–6: An overview. In C. Copple & S. Bredekamp (Eds.), *Developmentally appropriate practice in early childhood programs serving children from birth through age 8* (3rd ed., pp. 187–216). Washington, DC: National Association for the Education of Young Children.

Tooley, G. A., Karakis, M., Stokes, M., & Ozanne-Smith, J. (2006). Generalising the Cinderella Effect to unintentional childhood fatalities. *Evolution and Human Behavior, 27*, 224–230.

Toomey, R. B., Ryan, C., Diaz, R. M., Card, N. A., & Russell, S. T. (2010). Gender-nonconforming lesbian, gay, bisexual, and transgender youth: School victimization and young adult psychosocial adjustment. *Developmental Psychology, 46*, 1580–1589. doi:10.1037/a0020705

Torassa, U. (2000, March 8). Leave it on: Study says night lighting won't harm children's eyesight. Retrieved from http://edition.cnn.com/2000/HEALTH/children/03/08/light.myopia.wmd/index.html

Tornello, S. L., Farr, R. H., & Patterson, C. J. (2011). Predictors of parenting stress among gay adoptive fathers in the United States. *Journal of Family Psychology, 25*, 591–600. doi:10.1037/a0024480

Toth, S. L., Rogosch, F. A., Manly, J. T., & Cicchetti, D. (2006). The efficacy of toddler-parent psychotherapy to reorganize attachment in the young offspring of mothers with major depressive disorder: A randomized preventive trial. *Journal of Consulting and Clinical Psychology, 74*, 1006–1016. doi:10.1037/0022-006X.74.6.1006

Totten, M. (2009, March). Aboriginal youth and violent gang involvement in Canada: Quality prevention strategies. *IPC Review, 3*, 135–156. Retrieved from http://sciencessociales.uottawa.ca/ipc/fra/documents/IPCR3Totten.pdf

Tottenham, N., Hare, T. A., Quinn, B. T., McCarry, T. W., Nurse, M., Gilhooly, T., ... Casey, B. J. (2010). Prolonged institutional rearing is associated with atypically large amygdala volume and difficulties in emotion regulation. *Developmental Science, 13*, 46–61. doi: 10.1111/j.1467-7687.2009.00852.x.

Tough, S., Tofflemire, K., Clarke, M., & Newburn-Cook, C. (2006). Do women change their drinking behaviors while trying to conceive? An opportunity for preconception counseling. *Clinical Medicine and Research, 4*(2), 97–105. doi:10.3121/cmr.4.2.97

Towe-Goodman, N. R., Stifter, C. A., Coccia, M. A., & Cox, M. J. (2011). Interparental aggression, attention skills, and early childhood behavior problems. *Development and Psychopathology, 23*, 563–576. doi: 10.1017/S0954579411000216

Tracy, J. L., & Randles, D. (2011). Four models of basic emotions: A review of Ekman and Cordaro, Izard, Levenson, and Panksepp and Watt. *Emotion Review, 3*, 397–405. doi:10.1177/1754073911410747

Trainor, L. J. (1996). Infant preferences for infant-directed versus noninfant-directed playsongs and lullabies. *Infant Behavior and Development, 19*, 83–92. doi:10.1016/S0163-6383(96)90046-6

Trainor, L. J., & Desjardins, R. N. (2002). Pitch characteristics of infant-directed speech affect infants' ability to discriminate vowels. *Psychonomic Bulletin and Review, 9*, 335–340. doi:10.3758/BF03196290

Trainor, L. J., & Heinmiller, B. M. (1998). The development of evaluative responses to music: Infants prefer to listen to consonance over dissonance. *Infant Behavior and Development, 21*, 77–88. doi:10.1016/S0163-6383(98)90055-8

Trainor, L. J., & Trehub, S. E. (1992). A comparison of infants' and adults' sensitivity to Western musical structure. *Journal of Experimental*

Psychology: Human Perception and Performance, 18, 394–402. doi:10.1037/0096-1523.18.2.394

Trainor, L. J., & Trehub, S. E. (1994). Key membership and implied harmony in Western tonal music: Developmental perspectives. *Perception and Psychophysics, 56*, 125–132.

Trainor, L. J., Wu, L., & Tsang, C. D. (2004). Long-term memory for music: Infants remember tempo and timbre. *Developmental Science, 7*, 289–296. doi:10.1111/j.1467-7687.2004.00348.x

Trehub, S. E., & Schellenberg, E. G. (1995). Music: Its relevance to infants. In R. Vasta (Ed.), *Annals of child development* (Vol. 11, pp. 1–24). London, England: Jessica Kingsley Publishers.

Trehub, S. E., Unyk, A. M., Kamenetsky, S. B., Hill, D. S., Trainor, L. J., Henderson, J. L., & Saraza, M. (1997). Mothers' and fathers' singing to infants. *Developmental Psychology, 33*, 500–507. doi:10.1037/0012-1649.33.3.500

Tremblay, R. E., Pihl, R. O., Vitaro, F., & Dobkin, P. L. (1994). Predicting early onset of male antisocial behavior from preschool behavior. *Archives of General Psychiatry, 51*, 732–739. doi:10.1001/archpsyc.1994.03950090064009

Trentacosta, C. J., Hyde, L. W., Shaw, D. S., Dishion, T. J., Gardner, F., & Wilson, M. (2008). The relations among cumulative risk, parenting, and behavior problems during early childhood. *Journal of Child Psychology and Psychiatry, 49*, 1211–1219. doi:10.1111/j.1469-7610.2008.01941.x

Trinder, L., Kellet, J., & Swift, L. (2008). The relationship between contact and child adjustment in high conflict cases after divorce or separation. *Child and Adolescent Mental Health, 13*, 181–187. doi:10.1111/j.1475-3588.2008.00484.x

Trivers, R. L. (1972). Parental investment and sexual selection, 1871–1971. In B. Campbell (Ed.), *Sexual selection and the descent of man* (pp. 136–179). Chicago, IL: Aldine.

Trivers, R. L. (1983). The evolution of cooperation. In D. Bridgeman (Ed.), *The nature of prosocial development* (pp. 95–112). New York, NY: Academic Press.

Trocmé, N., Lajoie, J., Fallon, B., & Felstiner, C. (2007). *Injuries and deaths of children at the hands of their parents* (CECW Information Sheet #57E). Toronto, ON: University of Toronto Faculty of Social Work.

Trommsdorff, G., Friedlmeier, W., & Mayer, B. (2007). Sympathy, distress, and prosocial behavior of preschool children in four cultures. *International Journal of Behavioral Development, 31*, 284–293. doi:10.1177/0165025407076441

Tronick, E. Z., Thomas, R. B., & Daltabuit, M. (1994). The Quechua manta pouch: A caretaking practice for buffering the Peruvian infant against the multiple stressors of high altitude. *Child Development, 65*, 1005–1013.

Trzesniewski, K. H., Donnellan, M. B., Moffitt, T. E., Robins, R. W., Poulton, R., & Caspi, A. (2006). Low self-esteem during adolescence predicts poor health, criminal behavior, and limited economic prospects during adulthood. *Developmental Psychology, 42*, 381–390. doi:10.1037/0012-1649.42.2.381

Trzesniewski, K. H., Kinal, M. P.-A., & Donnellan, M. B. (2010). Self-enhancement and self-protection in a developmental context. In M. D. Alicke & C. Sedikides (Eds.), *The handbook of self-enhancement and self-protection* (pp. 341–357). New York, NY: Guilford Press.

Tsao, F.-M., Liu, H.-M., & Kuhl, P. K. (2004). Speech perception in infancy predicts language development in the second year of life: A longitudinal study. *Child Development, 75*, 1067–1084. doi:10.1111/j.1467-8624.2004.00726.x

Ttofi, M. M., & Farrington, D. P. (2011). Effectiveness of school-based programs to reduce bullying: A systematic and meta-analytic review. *Journal of Experimental Criminology, 7*, 27–56. doi:10.1007/s11292-010-9109-1

Tucker-Drob, E. M., Rhemtulla, M., Harden, K. P., Turkheimer, E., & Fask, D. (2011). Emergence of a gene × socioeconomic status interaction on infant mental ability between 10 months and 2 years. *Psychological Science, 22*, 125–133. doi:10.1177/0956797610392926

Tully, L. A., Arseneault, L., Caspi, A., Moffitt, T. E., & Morgan, J. (2004). Does maternal warmth moderate the effects of birth weight on twins' attention-deficit/hyperactivity disorder (ADHD) symptoms and low IQ? *Journal of Consulting and Clinical Psychology, 72*, 218–226. doi:10.1037/0022-006X.72.2.218

Turcotte, M. (2011). *Women in Canada: A gender-based statistical report—Women and education* (Catalogue No. 89-503-X). Retrieved from http://www.statcan.gc.ca/pub/89-503-x/2010001/article/11542-eng.pdf

Turiel, E. (1987). Potential relations between the development of social reasoning and childhood aggression. In D. H. Crowell, I. M. Evans, & C. R. O'Donnell (Eds.), *Childhood aggression and violence: Sources of influence, prevention, and control* (pp. 95–114). New York, NY: Plenum Press.

Turiel, E. (1998). Moral development. In W. Damon (Series Ed.) & R. M. Lerner & N. Eisenberg (Vol. Eds.), *Handbook of child psychology: Vol. 3. Social, emotional, and personality development* (pp. 863–932). New York, NY: Wiley.

Turiel, E. (2006). The development of morality. In W. Damon & R. M. Lerner (Series Eds.) & N. Eisenberg (Vol. Ed.), *Handbook of child psychology: Vol. 3. Social, emotional, and personality development* (6th ed., pp. 789–857). Hoboken, NJ: Wiley.

Turiel, E. (2008). Thought about actions in social domains: Morality, social conventions, and social interactions. *Cognitive Development, 23*, 136–154. doi:10.1016/j.cogdev.2007.04.001

Turkheimer, E. (2000). Three laws of behavior genetics and what they mean. *Current Directions in Psychological Science, 9*, 160–164. doi:10.1111/1467-8721.00084

Turkheimer, E., Haley, A., Waldron, M., D'Onofrio, B., & Gottesman, I. I. (2003). Socioeconomic status modifies heritability of IQ in young children. *Psychological Science, 14*, 623–628.

Turley, R. N. L. (2003). When do neighborhoods matter? The role of race and neighborhood peers. *Social Science Research, 32*, 61–79.

Turnbull, C. M. (1972). *The mountain people.* New York, NY: Simon and Schuster.

Turner, C. M., & Barrett, P. M. (2003). Does age play a role in structure of anxiety and depression in children and youths? An investigation of the tripartite model in three age cohorts. *Journal of Consulting and Clinical Psychology, 71*, 826–833.

Turner, P. J., & Gervai, J. (1995). A multidimensional study of gender typing in preschool children and their parents: Personality, attitudes, preferences, behavior, and cultural differences. *Developmental Psychology, 31*, 759–772. doi:10.1037/0012-1649.31.5.759

Tuvblad, C., Raine, A., Zheng, M., & Baker, L. A. (2009). Genetic and environmental stability differs in reactive and proactive aggression. *Aggressive Behavior, 35*, 437–452. doi:10.1002/ab.20319

Twenge, J. M., & Nolen-Hoeksema, S. (2002). Age, gender, race, socioeconomic status, and birth cohort differences on the children's depression inventory: A meta-analysis. *Journal of Abnormal Psychology, 111*, 578–588.

Twyman, K., Saylor, C., Taylor, L. A., & Comeaux, C. (2010). Comparing children and adolescents engaged in cyberbullying to matched peers. *Cyberpsychology, Behavior and Social Networking, 13*, 195–199.

Tyler, K. A., & Bersani, B. E. (2008). A longitudinal study of early adolescent precursors to running away. *Journal of Early Adolescence, 28*, 230–251. doi:10.1177/0272431607313592

Tyler, K. A., Hagewen, K. J., & Melander, L. A. (2011). Risk factors for running away among a general population sample of males and females. *Youth and Society, 43*, 583–608. doi:10.1177/0044118x11400023

Tyler, K. A., Whitbeck, L. B., Hoyt, D. R., & Johnson, K. D. (2003). Self-mutilation and homeless youth: The role of family abuse, street experiences, and mental disorders. *Journal of Research on Adolescence, 13*, 457–474. doi:10.1046/j.1532-7795.2003.01304003.x

Tynes, B. M., Umaña-Taylor, A. J., Rose, C. A., Lin, J., & Anderson, C. J. (2012). Online racial discrimination and the protective function of ethnic identity and self-esteem for African American adolescents. *Developmental Psychology, 48*, 343-355. doi:10.1037/a0027032

Tyrka, A. R., Graber, J. A., & Brooks-Gunn, J. (2000). The development of disordered eating. In A. J. Sameroff, M. Lewis, & S. M. Miller (Eds.), *Handbook of developmental psychopathology* (pp. 607–624). New York, NY: Springer.

U.S. Census Bureau. (2011, November). *Child poverty in the United States 2009 and 2010: Selected race groups and Hispanic origin* (American Community Survey Briefs ACSBR/10-05). Washington, DC: Author.

U.S. Department of Health and Human Services, Administration for Children and Families, Administration on Children, Youth and Families, Children's Bureau. (2012). Child maltreatment 2011. Retrieved from http://www.acf.hhs.gov/programs/cb/resource/child-maltreatment-2011

Uller, C., Carey, S., Huntley-Fenner, G., & Klatt, L. (1999). What representations might underlie infant numerical knowledge? *Cognitive Development, 14*, 1–36.

Umaña-Taylor, A. J., Bhanot, R., & Shin, N. (2006). Ethnic identity formation during adolescence: The critical role of families. *Journal of Family Issues, 27*, 390–414. doi:10.1177/0192513x05282960

Umaña-Taylor, A. J., Gonzales-Backen, M. A., & Guimond, A. B. (2009). Latino adolescents' ethnic identity: Is there a developmental progression and does growth in ethnic identity predict growth in self-esteem? *Child Development, 80*, 391–405. doi:10.1111/j.1467-8624.2009.01267.x

Umana-Taylor, A. J., & Guimond, A. B. (2010). A longitudinal examination of parenting behaviors and perceived discrimination predicting Latino adolescents' ethnic identity. *Developmental Psychology, 46*, 636–650. doi:10.1037/a0019376

Underwood, B., & Moore, B. (1982). Perspective-taking and altruism. *Psychological Bulletin, 91*, 143–173. doi:10.1037/0033-2909.91.1.143

Underwood, M. K. (2003). *Social aggression among girls*. New York, NY: Guilford Press.

UNICEF. (2012). *The State of the World's Children 2012: Children in an urban world*. Retrieved from www.unicef.org/sowc2012/

Updegraff, K. A., Kim, J.-Y., Killoren, S. E., & Thayer, S. M. (2010). Mexican American parents' involvement in adolescents' peer relationships: Exploring the role of culture and adolescents' peer experiences. *Journal of Research on Adolescence, 20*, 65–87. doi:10.1111/j.1532-7795.2009.00625.x

Updegraff, K. A., McHale, S. M., & Crouter, A. C. (1996). Gender roles in marriage: What do they mean for girls' and boys' school achievement? *Journal of Youth and Adolescence, 25*, 73–88. doi:10.1007/BF01537381

Urberg, K. A., Değirmencioğlu, S. M., & Pilgrim, C. (1997). Close friend and group influence on adolescent cigarette smoking and alcohol use. *Developmental Psychology, 33*, 834–844.

Uttal, D. H., Liu, L. L., & DeLoache, J. S. (2006). Concreteness and symbolic development. In L. Balter & C. Tamis-LeMonda (Eds.), *Child psychology: A handbook of contemporary issues* (2nd ed., pp. 167–184). New York, NY: Psychology Press.

Vaillancourt, T., Brendgen, M., Boivin, M., & Tremblay, R. E. (2003). A longitudinal confirmatory factor analysis of indirect and physical aggression: Evidence of two factors over time? *Child Development, 74*, 1628–1638. doi:10.1046/j.1467-8624.2003.00628.x

Vaillancourt, T., & Hymel, S. (2006). Aggression and social status: The moderating roles of sex and peer-valued characteristics. *Aggressive Behavior, 32*, 396–408. doi:10.1002/ab.20138

Vaillant-Molina, M., & Bahrick, L. E. (2012). The role of intersensory redundancy in the emergence of social referencing in 5 1/2-month-old infants. *Developmental Psychology, 48*, 1–9. doi:10.1037/a0025263

Vainio, A. (2011). Religious conviction, morality and social convention among Finnish adolescents. *Journal of Moral Education, 40*, 73–87. doi:10.1080/03057240.2010.521390

Vaish, A., Carpenter, M., & Tomasello, M. (2009). Sympathy through affective perspective taking and its relation to prosocial behavior in toddlers. *Developmental Psychology, 45*, 534–543. doi:10.1037/a0014322

Vaish, A., Carpenter, M., & Tomasello, M. (2010). Young children selectively avoid helping people with harmful intentions. *Child Development, 81*, 1661–1669. doi:10.1111/j.1467-8624.2010.01500.x

Vaish, A., & Striano, T. (2004). Is visual reference necessary? Contributions of facial versus vocal cues in 12-month-olds' social referencing behavior. *Developmental Science, 7*, 261–269.

Valenza, E., & Bulf, H. (2007). The role of kinetic information in newborns' perception of illusory contours. *Developmental Science, 10*, 492–501. doi:10.1111/j.1467-7687.2007.00602.x

Valenzuela, M. (1997). Maternal sensitivity in a developing society: The context of urban poverty and infant chronic undernutrition. *Developmental Psychology, 33*, 845–855. doi:10.1037/0012-1649.33.5.845

Valeski, T. N., & Stipek, D. J. (2001). Young children's feelings about school. *Child Development, 72*, 1198–1213.

Valiente, C., Eisenberg, N., Fabes, R. A., Shepard, S. A., Cumberland, A., & Losoya, S. H. (2004). Prediction of children's empathy-related responding from their effortful control and parents' expressivity. *Developmental Psychology, 40*, 911–926.

Valkenburg, P. M., & Peter, J. (2007a). Online communication and adolescent well-being: Testing the stimulation versus the displacement hypothesis. *Journal of Computer-Mediated Communication, 12*, 1169–1182. doi:10.1111/j.1083-6101.2007.00368.x

Valkenburg, P. M., & Peter, J. (2007b). Preadolescents' and adolescents' online communication and their closeness to friends. *Developmental Psychology, 43*, 267–277. doi:10.1037/0012-1649.43.2.267

Valkenburg, P. M., & Peter, J. (2009a). Social consequences of the internet for adolescents: A decade of research. *Current Directions in Psychological Science, 18*, 1–5. doi:10.1111/j.1467-8721.2009.01595.x

Valkenburg, P. M., & Peter, J. (2009b). The effects of instant messaging on the quality of adolescents' existing friendships: A longitudinal study. *Journal of Communication, 59*, 79–97. doi:10.1111/j.1460-2466.2008.01405.x

Valkenburg, P. M., & Peter, J. (2011). Online communication among adolescents: An integrated model of its attraction, opportunities, and risks. *Journal of Adolescent Health, 48*, 121–127. doi:10.1016/j.jadohealth.2010.08.020

Vamvakoussi, X., & Vosniadou, S. (2010). How many decimals are there between two fractions? Aspects of secondary school students' understanding of rational numbers and their notation. *Cognition and Instruction, 28*, 181–209. doi:10.1080/07370001003676603

Van Beek, Y., Van Dolderen, M. S. M., & Demon Dubas, J. J. S. (2006). Gender-specific development of nonverbal behaviours and mild depression in adolescence. *Journal of Child Psychology and Psychiatry, 47*, 1272–1283. doi:10.1111/j.1469-7610.2006.01663.x

Van de Gaer, E., Pustjens, H., Van Damme, J., & De Munter, A. (2006). Tracking and the effects of school-related attitudes on the language achievement of boys and girls. *British Journal of Sociology of Education, 27*, 293–309. doi:10.1080/01425690600750478

van den Boom, D. C. (1994). The influence of temperament and mothering on attachment and exploration: An experimental manipulation of sensitive responsiveness among lower-class mothers with irritable infants. *Child Development, 65*, 1457–1477. doi:10.1111/j.1467-8624.1994.tb00829.x

van den Boom, D. C. (1995). Do first-year intervention effects endure? Follow-up during toddlerhood of a sample of Dutch irritable infants. *Child Development, 66*, 1798–1816. doi:10.1111/j.1467-8624.1995.tb00966.x

van den Boom, D. C., & Hoeksma, J. B. (1994). The effect of infant irritability on mother-infant interaction: A growth-curve analysis. *Developmental Psychology, 30*, 581–590.

van den Eijnden, R. J. J. M., Meerkerk, G.-J., Vermulst, A. A., Spijkerman, R., & Engels, R. C. M. E. (2008). Online communication, compulsive internet use, and psychosocial well-being among adolescents: A longitudinal study. *Developmental Psychology, 44*, 655–665. doi:10.1037/0012-1649.44.3.655

Van den Oord, E. J. C. G., Boomsma, D. I., & Verhulst, F. C. (2000). A study of genetic and environmental effects on the co-occurrence of problem behaviors in three-year-old-twins. *Journal of Abnormal Psychology, 109*, 360–372. doi:10.1037/0021-843X.109.3.360

Van Doesum, K. T., Riksen-Walraven, J. M., Hosman, C. M., & Hoefnagels, C. (2008). A randomized controlled trial of a home-visiting intervention aimed at preventing relationship problems in depressed mothers and their infants. *Child Development, 79*, 547–561. doi:10.1111/j.1467-8624.2008.01142.x

Van Doorn, M. D., Branje, S. J. T., & Meeus, W. H. J. (2008). Conflict resolution in parent-adolescent relationships and adolescent delinquency. *Journal of Early Adolescence, 28*, 503–527. doi:10.1177/0272431608317608

Van Doorn, M. D., Branje, S. J. T., & Meeus, W. H. J. (2011). Developmental changes in conflict resolution styles in parent–adolescent relationships: A four-wave longitudinal study. *Journal of Youth and Adolescence, 40*, 97–107. doi:10.1007/s10964-010-9516-7

Van Heugten, M., & Shi, R. (2009). French-learning toddlers use gender information on determiners during word recognition. *Developmental Science, 12*, 419–425. doi:10.1111/j.1467-7687.2008.00788.x

Van Houtte, M. (2004). Why boys achieve less at school than girls: The difference between boys' and girls' academic culture. *Educational Studies, 30*, 159–173. doi:10.1080/0305569032000159804

van IJzendoorn, M. H. (1995). Adult attachment representations, parental responsiveness, and infant attachment: A meta-analysis on the predictive validity of the Adult Attachment Interview. *Psychological Bulletin, 117*, 387–403.

van IJzendoorn, M. H., & Bakermans-Kranenburg, M. J. (2010). Invariance of adult attachment across gender, age, culture, and socioeconomic status? *Journal of Social and Personal Relationships, 27*, 200–208.

van IJzendoorn, M. H., & De Wolff, M. S. (1997). In search of the absent father—Meta-analyses of infant-father attachment: A rejoinder to our discussants. *Child Development, 68*, 604–609. doi:10.1111/j.1467-8624.1997.tb04223.x

van IJzendoorn, M. H., Juffer, F., & Duyvesteyn, M. G. C. (1995). Breaking the intergenerational cycle of insecure attachment: A review of the effects of attachment-based interventions on maternal sensitivity and infant security. *Journal of Child Psychology and Psychiatry, 36*, 225–248. doi:10.1111/j.1469-7610.1995.tb01822.x

van IJzendoorn, M. H., & Sagi, A. (1999). Cross-cultural patterns of attachment: Universal and contextual dimensions. In J. Cassidy & P. R. Shaver (Eds.), *Handbook of attachment: Theory, research, and clinical applications* (pp. 713–734). New York, NY: Guilford Press.

van IJzendoorn, M. H., & Sagi-Schwartz, A. (2008). Cross-cultural patterns of attachment: Universal and contextual dimensions. In J. Cassidy & P. R. Shaver (Eds.), *Handbook of attachment: Theory, research, and clinical applications* (2nd ed., pp. 880–905). New York, NY: Guilford Press.

van IJzendoorn, M. H., Schuengel, C., & Bakermans-Kranenburg, M. J. (1999). Disorganized attachment in early childhood: Meta-analysis of precursors, concomitants, and sequelae. *Development and Psychopathology, 11*, 225–249.

van IJzendoorn, M. H., Vereijken, C. M., Bakermans-Kranenburg, M. J., & Riksen-Walraven, J. M. (2004). Assessing attachment security with the Attachment Q Sort: Meta-analytic evidence for the validity of the observer AQS. *Child Development, 75*, 1188–1213. doi:10.1111/j.1467-8624.2004.00733.x

van Lier, P. A. C., van der Ende, J., Koot, H. M., & Verhulst, F. C. (2007). Which better predicts conduct problems? The relationship of trajectories of conduct problems with ODD and ADHD symptoms from childhood into adolescence. *Journal of Child Psychology and Psychiatry, 48*, 601–608. doi:10.1111/j.1469-7610.2006.01724.x

van Lier, P. A. C., Vitaro, F., Barker, E. D., Brendgen, M., Tremblay, R. E., & Boivin, M. (2012). Peer victimization, poor academic achievement, and the link between childhood externalizing and internalizing problems. *Child Development, 83*, 1775–1788. doi:10.1111/j.1467-8624.2012.01802.x

Van Loosbroek, E., & Smitsman, A. W. (1990). Visual perception of numerosity in infancy. *Developmental Psychology, 26*, 916–922.

Van Ryzin, M. J., & Dishion, T. J. (2012). The impact of a family-centered intervention on the ecology of adolescent antisocial behavior: Modeling developmental sequelae and trajectories during adolescence. *Development and Psychopathology, 24*, 1139–1155. doi:10.1017/S0954579412000582

van Wermeskerken, M., van der Kamp, J., Savelsbergh, G. J., & von Hofsten, C. (2013). Getting the closer object? An information-based dissociation between vision for perception and vision for movement in early infancy. *Developmental Science, 16*, 91–100. doi:10.1111/desc.12006

Van Zalk, M. H., Kerr, M., Branje, S. J., Stattin, H., & Meeus, W. H. (2010). It takes three: Selection, influence, and de-selection processes of depression in adolescent friendship networks. *Developmental Psychology, 46*, 927–938.

Van Zalk, N., Van Zalk, M., Kerr, M., & Stattin, H. (2011). Social anxiety as a basis for friendship selection and socialization in adolescents' social networks. *Journal of Personality, 79*, 499–525. doi:10.1111/j.1467-6494.2011.00682.x

Vandell, D. L. (2008). Baby sister/baby brother: Reactions to the birth of a sibling and patterns of early sibling relations. *Journal of Children in Contemporary Society, 19*, 13–37. doi:10.1300/j274v19n03_02

Vandell, D. L., Belsky, J., Burchinal, M., Steinberg, L., Vandergrift, N., & NICHD Early Child Care Research Network. (2010). Do effects of early child care extend to age 15 years? Results from the NICHD Study of Early Child Care and Youth Development. *Child Development, 81*, 737–756. doi:10.1111/j.1467-8624.2010.01431.x

Vanfossen, B., Brown, C. H., Kellam, S., Sokoloff, N., & Doering, S. (2010). Neighborhood context and the development of aggression in boys and girls. *Journal of Community Psychology, 38*, 329–349. doi:10.1002/jcop.20367

Vannatta, K., Gartstein, M. A., Zeller, M., & Noll, R. B. (2009). Peer acceptance and social behavior during childhood and adolescence: How important are appearance, athleticism, and academic competence? *International Journal of Behavioral Development, 33*, 303–311. doi:10.1177/0165025408101275

Vaquera, E., & Kao, G. (2008). Do you like me as much as I like you? Friendship reciprocity and its effects on school outcomes among adolescents. *Social Science Research, 37*, 55–72. doi:10.1016/j.ssresearch.2006.11.002

Varendi, H., Porter, R. H., & Winberg, J. (2002). The effect of labor on olfactory exposure learning within the first postnatal hour. *Behavioral Neuroscience, 116*, 206–211.

Vaughan, C. C. (1996). *How life begins: The science of life in the womb.* New York, NY: Times Books.

Vaughn, B. E., Vollenweider, M., Bost, K. K., Azria-Evans, M. R., & Snider, J. B. (2003). Negative interactions and social competence for preschool children in two samples: Reconsidering the interpretation of aggressive behavior for young children. *Merrill-Palmer Quarterly, 49*, 245–278.

Vellutino, F. R., & Scanlon, D. M. (1987). Phonological coding, phonological awareness, and reading ability: Evidence from a longitudinal and experimental study. *Merrill-Palmer Quarterly, 33*, 321–363.

Vellutino, F. R., Scanlon, D. M., & Spearing, D. (1995). Semantic and phonological coding in poor and normal readers. *Journal of Experimental Child Psychology, 59*, 76–123. doi:10.1006/jecp.1995.1004

Vera, E. M., & Quintana, S. M. (2004). Ethnic identity development in Chicana/o youth. In R. J. Velasquez, L. M. Arellano, & B. W. McNeill (Eds.), *The handbook of Chicana/o psychology and mental health* (pp. 43–59). Mahwah, NJ: Erlbaum.

Verma, S. (1999). Socialization for survival: Developmental issues among working street children in India. In M. Raffaelli & R. W. Larson (Eds.), *New Directions for Child and Adolescent Development: No. 85. Homeless and working youth around the world: Exploring developmental issues* (Vol. 1999, pp. 5–18). San Francisco, CA: Jossey-Bass.

Vernon, P. A., Wickett, J. C., Bazana, P. G., & Stelmack, R. M. (2012). The neuropsychology and psychophysiology of human intelligence. In R. J. Sternberg (Ed.), *Handbook of intelligence* (pp. 245–266). Cambridge, England: Cambridge University Press.

Véronneau, M.-H., Vitaro, F., Brendgen, M., Dishion, T. J., & Tremblay, R. E. (2010). Transactional analysis of the reciprocal links between peer experiences and academic achievement from middle childhood to early adolescence. *Developmental Psychology, 46*, 773–790. doi:10.1037/a0019816

Verschueren, K., Dossche, D., Marcoen, A., Mahieu, S., & Bakermans-Kranenburg, M. (2006). Attachment representations and discipline in mothers of young school children: An observation study. *Social Development, 15*, 659–675.

Verschueren, K., Marcoen, A., & Schoefs, V. (1996). The internal working model of the self, attachment, and competence in five-year-olds. *Child Development, 67*, 2493–2511. doi:10.1111/j.1467-8624.1996.tb01870.x

Vézina, M. (2012). *2011 general social survey: Overvew of families in Canada—Being a parent in a stepfamily: A profile.* Retrieved from http://www.statcan.gc.ca/pub/89-650-x/89-650-x2012002-eng.pdf

Viding, E., & McCrory, E. J. (2012). Genetic and neurocognitive contributions to the development of psychopathy. *Development and Psychopathology, 24*, 969–983.

Vikan, A., & Clausen, S. E. (1993). Freud, Piaget, or neither? Beliefs in controlling others by wishful thinking and magical behavior in young children. *Journal of Genetic Psychology, 154*, 297–314. doi:10.1080/00221325.1993.10532183

Vitaro, F., Barker, E. D., Boivin, M., Brendgen, M., & Tremblay, R. E. (2006). Do early difficult temperament and harsh parenting differentially predict reactive and proactive aggression? *Journal of Abnormal Child Psychology, 34*, 681–691. doi:10.1007/s10802-006-9055-6

Vitaro, F., Pedersen, S., & Brendgen, M. (2007). Children's disruptiveness, peer rejection, friends' deviancy, and delinquent behaviors: A process-oriented approach. *Development and Psychopathology, 19*, 433–453. doi:10.1017/S0954579407070216

Vohr, B. R., & Garcia Coll, C. T. (1988). Follow-up studies of high risk low-birthweight infants: Changing trends. In H. E. Fitzgerald, B. M. Lester, & M. H. Yogman (Eds.), *Theory and research in behavioral pediatrics* (Vol. 4, pp. 1–65). New York, NY: Plenum.

Volbrecht, M. M., Lemery-Chalfant, K., Aksan, N., Zahn-Waxler, C., & Goldsmith, H. H. (2007). Examining the familial link between positive affect and empathy development in the second year. *Journal of Genetic Psychology, 168*, 105–130. doi:10.3200/GNTP.168.2.105-130

Volkova, A., Trehub, S. E., & Schellenberg, E. G. (2006). Infants' memory for musical performances. *Developmental Science, 9*, 583–589. doi:10.1111/j.1467-7687.2006.00536.x

Volling, B. L., & Belsky, J. (1991). Multiple determinants of father involvement during infancy in dual-earner and single-earner families. *Journal of Marriage and the Family, 53*, 461–474.

Volling, B. L., & Feagans, L. V. (1995). Infant day care and children's social competence. *Infant Behavior and Development, 18*, 177–188. doi:10.1016/0163-6383(95)90047-0

Volling, B. L., Mahoney, A., & Rauer, A. J. (2009). Sanctification of parenting, moral socialization, and young children's conscience development. *Psychology of Religion and Spirituality, 1*, 53–68. doi:10.1037/a0014958

von der Lippe, A. L. (1999). The impact of maternal schooling and occupation on child-rearing attitudes and behaviours in low income neighbourhoods in Cairo, Egypt. *International Journal of Behavioral Development, 23*, 703–729. doi:10.1080/016502599383766

von Grünigen, R., Perren, S., Nägele, C., & Alsaker, F. D. (2010). Immigrant children's peer acceptance and victimization in kindergarten: The role of local language competence. *British Journal of Developmental Psychology, 28*, 679–697. doi:10.1348/026151009X470582

von Hofsten, C. (1979). Development of visually guided reaching: The approach phase. *Journal of Human Movement Studies, 5*, 160–178.

von Hofsten, C. (1982). Eye–hand coordination in the newborn. *Developmental Psychology, 18*, 450–461. doi:10.1037/0012-1649.18.3.450

von Hofsten, C. (1991). Structuring of early reaching movements: A longitudinal study. *Journal of Motor Behavior, 23*, 280–292. doi:10.1080/00222895.1991.9942039

von Hofsten, C. (2004). An action perspective on motor development. *Trends in Cognitive Sciences, 8*, 266–272. doi:10.1016/j.tics.2004.04.002

von Hofsten, C. (2007). Action in development. *Developmental Science, 10*, 54–60. doi:10.1111/j.1467-7687.2007.00564.x

von Hofsten, C., Dahlström, E., & Fredriksson, Y. (2005). 12-month-old infants' perception of attention direction in static video images. *Infancy, 8,* 217–231. doi:10.1207/s15327078in0803_2

von Hofsten, C., Vishton, P., Spelke, E. S., Feng, Q., & Rosander, K. (1998). Predictive action in infancy: Tracking and reaching for moving objects. *Cognition, 67,* 255–285. doi:10.1016/S0010-0277(98)00029-8

von Stumm, S., Hell, B., & Chamorro-Premuzic, T. (2011). The hungry mind: Intellectual curiosity is the third pillar of academic performance. *Perspectives on Psychological Science, 6,* 574–588.

Vondra, J. I., Shaw, D. S., Swearingen, L., Cohen, M., & Owens, E. B. (2001). Attachment stability and emotional and behavioral regulation from infancy to preschool age. *Development and Psychopathology, 13,* 13–33.

Voos, A. C., Pelphrey, K. A., Tirrell, J., Bolling, D. Z., Vander Wyk, B., Kaiser, M. D., ... Ventola, P. (2013). Neural mechanisms of improvements in social motivation after pivotal response treatment: Two case studies. *Journal of Autism and Developmental Disorders, 43,* 1–10. doi:10.1007/s10803-012-1683-9

Votruba-Drzal, E., Coley, R. L., & Chase-Lansdale, P. L. (2004). Child care and low-income children's development: Direct and moderated effects. *Child Development, 75,* 296–312. doi:10.1111/j.1467-8624.2004.00670.x

Vosniadou, S. (2010). Instructional considerations in the use of external representation: The distinction between perceptually based depictions and pictures that represent conceptual models. In L. Verschaffel, E. De Corte, T. de Jong, & J. Elen (Eds.), *Use of representations in reasoning and problem solving: Analysis and improvement.* Abingdon, Oxon, UK: Routledge.

Vouloumanos, A., Hauser, M. D., Werker, J. F., & Martin, A. (2010). The tuning of human neonates' preference for speech. *Child Development, 81,* 517–527. doi:10.1111/j.1467-8624.2009.01412.x

Vouloumanos, A., & Werker, J. F. (2009). Infants' learning of novel words in a stochastic environment. *Developmental Psychology, 45,* 1611–1617.

Voyer, D., Voyer, S., & Bryden, M. P. (1995). Magnitude of sex differences in spatial abilities: A meta-analysis and consideration of critical variables. *Psychological Bulletin, 117,* 250–270.

Vygotsky, L. S. (1962). *Thought and language* (E. Hanfmann & G. Vakar, Trans.). Cambridge, MA: MIT Press. (Original work published 1934)

Vygotsky, L. S. (1978). *Mind in society: The development of higher psychological processes* (M. Cole, V. John-Steiner, S. Scribner, & E. Souberman, Eds.). Cambridge, MA: Harvard University Press.

Wade, A., & Beran, T. (2011). Cyberbullying: The new era of bullying. *Canadian Journal of School Psychology, 26,* 44–61. doi:10.1177/0829573510396318

Wadsworth, S. J., Corley, R., Plomin, R., Hewitt, J. K., & De Fries, J. C. (2006). Genetic and environment influences on continuity and change in reading achievement in the Colorado adoption project. In A. C. Huston & M. N. Ripke (Eds.), *Developmental contexts in middle childhood: Bridges to adolescence and adulthood* (pp. 87–106). New York, NY: Cambridge University Press

Wagner, R. K., Torgesen, J. K., Rashotte, C. A., Hecht, S. A., Barker, T. A., Burgess, S. R., ... Garon, T. (1997). Changing relations between phonological processing abilities and word-level reading as children develop from beginning to skilled readers: A 5-year longitudinal study. *Developmental Psychology, 33,* 468–479.

Wai, J., Lubinski, D., Benbow, C. P., & Steiger, J. H. (2010). Accomplishment in science, technology, engineering, and mathematics (STEM) and its relation to STEM educational dose: A 25-year longitudinal study. *Journal of Educational Psychology, 102,* 860–871. doi:10.1037/a0019454

Wainright, J. L., & Patterson, C. J. (2006). Delinquency, victimization, and substance use among adolescents with female same-sex parents. *Journal of Family Psychology, 20,* 526–530. doi:10.1037/0893-3200.20.3.526

Wainright, J. L., & Patterson, C. J. (2008). Peer relations among adolescents with female same-sex parents. *Developmental Psychology, 44,* 117–126. doi:10.1037/0012-1649.44.1.117

Wainright, J. L., Russell, S. T., & Patterson, C. J. (2004). Psychosocial adjustment, school outcomes, and romantic relationships of adolescents with same-sex parents. *Child Development, 75,* 1886–1898. doi:10.1111/j.1467-8624.2004.00823.x

Wainryb, C., & Turiel, E. (1995). Diversity in social development: Between or within cultures? In M. Killen & D. Hart (Eds.), *Morality in everyday life: Developmental perspectives* (pp. 283–313). New York, NY: Cambridge University Press.

Wakefield, A. J., Murch, S. H., Anthony, A., Linnell, J., Casson, D. M., Malik, M., ... Walker-Smith, J. A. (1998, February 28). Ileal-lymphoid-nodular hyperplasia, non-specific colitis, and pervasive developmental disorder in children. *The Lancet, 351,* 637–641. doi:10.1016/S0140-6736(97)11096-0 (Retraction published February 6, 2010, *The Lancet, 375,* p. 445)

Wakeley, A., Rivera, S., & Langer, J. (2000). Can young infants add and subtract? *Child Development, 71,* 1525–1534.

Wakschlag, L. S., Gordon, R. A., Lahey, B. B., Loeber, R., Green, S. M., & Leventhal, B. L. (2000). Maternal age at first birth and boys' risk for conduct disorder. *Journal of Research on Adolescence, 10,* 417–441. doi:10.1207/SJRA1004_03

Waldman, I. D., Tackett, J. L., Van Hulle, C. A., Applegate, B., Pardini, D., Frick, P. J., & Lahey, B. B. (2011). Child and adolescent conduct disorder substantially shares genetic influences with three socioemotional dispositions. *Journal of Abnormal Psychology, 120,* 57–70. doi:10.1037/a0021351

Waldrip, A. M., Malcolm, K. T., & Jensen-Campbell, L. A. (2008). With a little help from your friends: The importance of high-quality friendships on early adolescent adjustment. *Social Development, 17,* 832–852. doi:10.1111/j.1467-9507.2008.00476.x

Walker, B. E., & Quarles, J. (1976). Palate development in mouse foetuses after tongue removal. *Archives of Oral Biology, 21,* 405–412.

Walker, C. M., Walker, L. B., & Ganea, P. A. (2013). The role of symbol-based experience in early learning and transfer from pictures: Evidence from Tanzania. *Developmental Psychology, 49,* 1315–1324. doi:10.1037/a0029483

Walker, K., Taylor, E., McElroy, A., Phillip, D.-A., & Wilson, M. N. (1995). Familial and ecological correlates of self-esteem in African American children. In M. N. Wilson (Ed.), *New Directions for Child and Adolescent Development: No. 68. African American family life: Its structural and ecological aspects* (Vol. 1995, pp. 23–34). San Francisco, CA: Jossey-Bass.

Walker, L. J. (1984). Sex differences in the development of moral reasoning: A critical review. *Child Development, 55,* 677–691. doi:10.2307/1130121

Walker, L. J. (1991). Sex differences in moral reasoning. In W. M. Kurtines & J. L. Gewirtz (Eds.), *Handbook of moral behavior and development: Vol. 2: Research* (pp. 333–364). Hillsdale, NJ: Erlbaum.

Walker, P., Bremner, J. G., Mason, U., Spring, J., Mattock, K., Slater, A., & Johnson, S. P. (2010). Preverbal infants' sensitivity to synaesthetic cross-modality correspondences. *Psychological Science, 21,* 21-25.

Walker, S. (2009). Sociometric stability and the behavioral correlates of peer acceptance in early childhood. *Journal of Genetic Psychology, 170*, 339–358. doi:10.1080/00221320903218364

Walker-Andrews, A. S. (1997). Infants' perception of expressive behaviors: Differentiation of multimodal information. *Psychological Bulletin, 121*, 437–456.

Walker-Andrews, A. S., & Dickson, L. R. (1997). Infants' understanding of affect. In S. Hala (Ed.), *The development of social cognition* (pp. 161–186). Hove, East Sussex, England: Psychology Press.

Wall, J. A., Power, T. G., & Arbona, C. (1993). Susceptibility to antisocial peer pressure and its relation to acculturation in Mexican-American adolescents. *Journal of Adolescent Research, 8*, 403–418. doi:10.1177/074355489384004

Wallerstein, J., & Lewis, J. M. (2007). Sibling outcomes and disparate parenting and stepparenting after divorce: Report from a 10-year longitudinal study. *Psychoanalytic Psychology, 24*, 445–458. doi:10.1037/0736-9735.24.3.445

Wallerstein, J. S., & Blakeslee, S. (1989). *Second chances: Men, women, and children a decade after divorce.* New York, NY: Ticknor & Fields.

Wallman, J. (1992). *Aping language.* Cambridge, England: Cambridge University Press.

Wang, D., Kato, N., Inaba, Y., Tango, T., Yoshida, Y., Kusaka, Y., … Zhang, Q. (2000). Physical and personality traits of preschool children in Fuzhou, China: Only child vs sibling. *Child: Care, Health and Development, 26*, 49–60. doi:10.1046/j.1365-2214.2000.00143.x

Wang, J.-L., Jackson, L. A., & Zhang, D.-J. (2011). The mediator role of self-disclosure and moderator roles of gender and social anxiety in the relationship between Chinese adolescents' online communication and their real-world social relationships. *Computers in Human Behavior, 27*, 2161–2168. doi:10.1016/j.chb.2011.06.010

Wang, M.-T., & Huguley, J. P. (2012). Parental racial socialization as a moderator of the effects of racial discrimination on educational success among African American adolescents. *Child Development, 83*, 1716–1731. doi:10.1111/j.1467-8624.2012.01808.x

Wang, Q. (2004). The emergence of cultural self-constructs: Autobiographical memory and self-description in European American and Chinese children. *Developmental Psychology, 40*, 3–15. doi:10.1037/0012-1649.40.1.3

Wang, Q. (2006). Earliest recollections of self and others in European American and Taiwanese young adults. *Psychological Science, 17*, 708–714. doi:10.1111/j.1467-9280.2006.01770.x

Wang, Q. (2007). "Remember when you got the big, big bulldozer?" Mother–child reminiscing over time and across cultures. *Social Cognition, 25*, 455–471. doi:10.1521/soco.2007.25.4.455

Wang, Q., & Fivush, R. (2005). Mother–child conversations of emotionally salient events: Exploring the functions of emotional reminiscing in European-American and Chinese families. *Social Development, 14*, 473–495.

Wang, X., Chen, C., Wang, L., Chen, D., Guang, W., & French, J. (2003). Conception, early pregnancy loss, and time to clinical pregnancy: A population-based prospective study. *Fertility and Sterility, 79*, 577–584.

Wang, Y., & Fong, V. L. (2009). Little emperors and the 4: 2: 1 generation: China's singletons. *Journal of the American Academy of Child and Adolescent Psychiatry, 48*, 1137–1139.

Ware, E. A., Uttal, D. H., Wetter, E. K., & DeLoache, J. S. (2006). Young children make scale errors when playing with dolls. *Developmental Science, 9*, 40–45. doi:10.1111/j.1467-7687.2005.00461.x

Warneken, F., Chen, F., & Tomasello, M. (2006). Cooperative activities in young children and chimpanzees. *Child Development, 77*, 640–663. doi:10.2307/3696552

Warneken, F., & Tomasello, M. (2006, March 3). Altruistic helping in human infants and young chimpanzees. *Science, 311*, 1301–1303.

Warneken, F., & Tomasello, M. (2008). Extrinsic rewards undermine altruistic tendencies in 20-month-olds. *Developmental Psychology, 44*, 1785–1788. doi:10.1037/a0013860

Waterman, A. S. (1999). Issues of identity formation revisited: United States and The Netherlands. *Developmental Review, 19*, 462–479. doi:10.1006/drev.1999.0488

Waters, E., & Cummings, E. M. (2000). A secure base from which to explore close relationships. *Child Development, 71*, 164–172. doi:10.1111/1467-8624.00130

Waters, E., Merrick, S., Treboux, D., Crowell, J., & Albersheim, L. (2000). Attachment security in infancy and early adulthood: A twenty-year longitudinal study. *Child Development, 71*, 684–689.

Waters, H. S. (1980). "Class news": A single-subject longitudinal study of prose production and schema formation during childhood. *Journal of Verbal Learning and Verbal Behavior, 19*, 152–167.

Waters, H. S. (1989, April). *Problem-solving at two: A year-long naturalistic study of two children.* Paper presented at the biennial meeting of the Society for Research in Child Development, Kansas City, MO.

Watson, J. B. (1924). *Behaviorism.* New York, NY: Norton.

Watson, J. B. (1928). *Psychological care of infant and child.* New York, NY: Norton.

Watson-Gegeo, K. A., & Gegeo, D. W. (1987). Calling-out and repeating routines in Kwara'ae children's language socialization. In B. B. Schieffelin & E. Ochs (Eds.), *Studies in the social and cultural foundations of language: No. 3. Language socialization across cultures* (pp. 17–50). New York, NY: Cambridge University Press.

Watt, H. M. G. (2006). The role of motivation in gendered educational and occupational trajectories related to maths. *Educational Research and Evaluation, 12*, 305–322. doi:10.1080/13803610600765562

Waxman, S. R. (1990). Linguistic biases and the establishment of conceptual hierarchies: Evidence from preschool children. *Cognitive Development, 5*, 123–150. doi:10.1016/0885-2014(90)90023-M

Waxman, S. R., & Hall, D. G. (1993). The development of a linkage between count nouns and object categories: Evidence from fifteen- to twenty-one-month-old infants. *Child Development, 64*, 1224–1241. doi:10.1111/j.1467-8624.1993.tb04197.x

Waxman, S. R., & Markow, D. B. (1995). Words as invitations to form categories: Evidence from 12- to 13-month-old infants. *Cognitive Psychology, 29*, 257–302. doi:10.1006/cogp.1995.1016

Waxman, S. R., & Markow, D. B. (1998). Object properties and object kind: Twenty-one-month-old infants' extension of novel adjectives. *Child Development, 69*, 1313–1329.

Waxman, S. R., & Senghas, A. (1992). Relations among word meanings in early lexical development. *Developmental Psychology, 28*, 862–873.

Way, N., & Greene, M. L. (2006). Trajectories of perceived friendship quality during adolescence: The patterns and contextual predictors. *Journal of Research on Adolescence, 16*, 293–320. doi:10.1111/j.1532-7795.2006.00133.x

Webster-Stratton, C. (1998). Preventing conduct problems in Head Start children: Strengthening parenting competencies. *Journal of Consulting and Clinical Psychology, 66*, 715–730. doi:10.1037/0022-006X.66.5.715

Webster-Stratton, C., Reid, M. J., & Stoolmiller, M. (2008). Preventing conduct problems and improving school readiness: Evaluation of the Incredible Years Teacher and Child Training Programs in high-risk schools. *Journal of Child Psychology and Psychiatry, 49*, 471–488. doi:10.1111/j.1469-7610.2007.01861.x

Weems, C. F., Taylor, L. K., Cannon, M. F., Marino, R. C., Romano, D. M., Scott, B. G., ... Triplett, V. (2010). Post traumatic stress, context, and the lingering effects of the Hurricane Katrina disaster among ethnic minority youth. *Journal of Abnormal Child Psychology, 38*, 49–56. doi:10.1007/s10802-009-9352-y

Wegner, D. M. (2002). *The illusion of conscious will.* Cambridge, MA: MIT Press.

Weinberg, M. K., & Tronick, E. Z. (1994). Beyond the face: An empirical study of infant affective configurations of facial, vocal, gestural, and regulatory behaviors. *Child Development, 65*, 1503–1515.

Weinburgh, M. (1995). Gender differences in student attitudes toward science: A meta-analysis of the literature from 1970 to 1991. *Journal of Research in Science Teaching, 32*, 387–398.

Weinstein, S. M., Mermelstein, R. J., Hankin, B. L., Hedeker, D., & Flay, B. R. (2007). Longitudinal patterns of daily affect and global mood during adolescence. *Journal of Research on Adolescence, 17*, 587–600. doi:10.1111/j.1532-7795.2007.00536.x

Weis, R., & Cerankosky, B. C. (2010). Effects of video-game ownership on young boys' academic and behavioral functioning: A randomized, controlled study. *Psychological Science, 21*, 463–470. doi:10.1177/0956797610362670

Weiss, B., Dodge, K. A., Bates, J. E., & Pettit, G. S. (1992). Some consequences of early harsh discipline: Child aggression and a maladaptive social information processing style. *Child Development, 63*, 1321–1335. doi:10.2307/1131558

Weisz, J. R., McCarty, C. A., & Valeri, S. M. (2006). Effects of psychotherapy for depression in children and adolescents: A meta-analysis. *Psychological Bulletin, 132*(1), 132–149. doi:10.1037/0033-2909.132.1.132

Weissman, M. D., & Kalish, C. W. (1999). The inheritance of desired characteristics: Children's view of the role of intention in parent–offspring resemblance. *Journal of Experimental Child Psychology, 73*, 245–265. doi:10.1006/jecp.1999.2505

Wellman, H. M. (2013). Universal social cognition: Childhood theory of mind. In M. R. Banaji & S. A. Gelman (Eds.), *Navigating the social world: What infants, children, and other species can teach us* (pp. 69–74). New York, NY: Oxford University Press.

Wellman, H. M., Cross, D., & Watson, J. (2001). Meta-analysis of theory-of-mind development: The truth about false belief. *Child Development, 72*, 655–684.

Wellman, H. M., & Gelman, S. A. (1998). Knowledge acquisition in foundational domains. In W. Damon (Series Ed.) & D. Kuhn & R. S. Siegler (Vol. Eds.), *Handbook of child psychology: Vol. 2. Cognition, perception, and language* (5th ed., pp. 523–573). Hoboken, NJ: Wiley.

Wellman, H. M., & Woolley, J. D. (1990). From simple desires to ordinary beliefs: The early development of everyday psychology. *Cognition, 35*, 245–275.

Wentzel, K. R. (2003). Sociometric status and adjustment in middle school: A longitudinal study. *Journal of Early Adolescence, 23*, 5–28. doi:10.1177/0272431602239128

Wentzel, K. R. (2009). Peers and academic functioning at school. In K. H. Rubin, W. M. Bukowski, & B. Laursen (Eds.), *Handbook of peer interactions, relationships, and groups* (pp. 531–547). New York, NY: Guilford Press.

Wentzel, K. R., & Asher, S. R. (1995). The academic lives of neglected, rejected, popular, and controversial children. *Child Development, 66*, 754–763. doi:10.2307/1131948

Wentzel, K. R., & Caldwell, K. (1997). Friendships, peer acceptance, and group membership: Relations to academic achievement in middle school. *Child Development, 68*, 1198–1209. doi:10.1111/j.1467-8624.1997.tb01994.x

Werebe, M. J. G., & Baudonniere, P.-M. (1991). Social pretend play among friends and familiar preschoolers. *International Journal of Behavioral Development, 14*, 411–428. doi:10.1177/016502549101400404

Werker, J. F. (1989, January-February). Becoming a native listener. *American Scientist, 77*, 54–59.

Werker, J. F., & Lalonde, C. E. (1988). Cross-language speech perception: Initial capabilities and developmental change. *Developmental Psychology, 24*, 672–683.

Werker, J. F., Pegg, J. E., & McLeod, P. J. (1994). A cross-language investigation of infant preference for infant-directed communication. *Infant Behavior and Development, 17*, 323–333. doi:10.1016/0163-6383(94)90012-4

Werker, J. F., & Tees, R. C. (1984). Cross-language speech perception: Evidence for perceptual reorganization during the first year of life. *Infant Behavior and Development, 7*, 49–63. doi:10.1016/S0163-6383(84)80022-3

Werner, E. E. (1989, April). Children of the Garden Island. *Scientific American, 260*(4), 106–108, 108D, 110–111.

Werner, N. E., & Crick, N. R. (2004). Maladaptive peer relationships and the development of relational and physical aggression during middle childhood. *Social Development, 13*, 495–514. doi:10.1111/j.1467-9507.2004.00280.x

Werner, N. E., & Hill, L. G. (2010). Individual and peer group normative beliefs about relational aggression. *Child Development, 81*, 826–836. doi:10.1111/j.1467-8624.2010.01436.x

West, M. J., & Rheingold, H. L. (1978). Infant stimulation of maternal instruction. *Infant Behavior and Development, 1*, 205–215. doi:10.1016/S0163-6383(78)80031-9

Westinghouse Learning Corporation. (1969). *The impact of Head Start: An evaluation of the effects of Head Start on children's cognitive and affective development.* Springfield, VA: Clearinghouse for Federal Scientific & Technical Information.

Weston, D., Ivins, B., Zuckerman, B., Jones, C., & Lopez, R. (1989). Drug exposed babies: Research and clinical issues. *Zero to Three, 9*, 1–7.

Whipple, N., Bernier, A., & Mageau, G. A. (2011). A dimensional approach to maternal attachment state of mind: Relations to maternal sensitivity and maternal autonomy support. *Developmental Psychology, 47*, 396–403. doi:10.1037/a0021310

White, B. L. (1985). *The first three years of life* (Rev. ed.). New York, NY: Prentice-Hall.

White, L. K., Lamm, C., Helfinstein, S. M., & Fox, N. A. (2012). Neurobiology and neurochemistry of temperament in children. In M. R. Zentner & R. L. Shiner (Eds.), *Handbook of temperament* (pp. 347–367). New York, NY: Guilford Press.

White, M. I., & LeVine, R. A. (1986). What is an *ii ko* (good child)? In H. W. Stevenson, H. Azuma, & K. Hakuta (Eds.), *Child development and education in Japan* (pp. 55–62). New York, NY: Freeman.

Whitehead, J. M. (1996). Sex stereotypes, gender identity and subject choice at A-level. *Educational Research, 38,* 147–160. doi:10.1080/0013188960380203

Whitehead, K. A., Ainsworth, A. T., Wittig, M. A., & Gadino, B. (2009). Implications of ethnic identity exploration and ethnic identity affirmation and belonging for intergroup attitudes among adolescents. *Journal of Research on Adolescence, 19,* 123–135. doi:10.1111/j.1532-7795.2009.00585.x

Whitehurst, G. J., & Lonigan, C. J. (1998). Child development and emergent literacy. *Child Development, 69,* 848–872.

Whitehurst, G. J., Zevenbergen, A. A., Crone, D. A., Schultz, M. D., Velting, O. N., & Fischel, J. E. (1999). Outcomes of an emergent literacy intervention from Head Start through second grade. *Journal of Educational Psychology, 91,* 261–272.

Whitesell, N. R., & Harter, S. (1996). The interpersonal context of emotion: Anger with close friends and classmates. *Child Development, 67,* 1345–1359.

Whiteside, M. F., & Becker, B. J. (2000). Parental factors and the young child's postdivorce adjustment: A meta-analysis with implications for parenting arrangements. *Journal of Family Psychology, 14,* 5–26. doi:10.1037/0893-3200.14.1.5

Whiteside-Mansell, L., Bradley, R. H., Owen, M. T., Randolph, S. M., & Cauce, A. M. (2003). Parenting and children's behavior at 36 months: Equivalence between African American and European American mother-child dyads. *Parenting: Science and Practice, 3,* 197–234. doi:10.1207/S15327922PAR0303_02

Whiting, B. B., & Edwards, C. P. (1988). *Children of different worlds: The formation of social behavior.* Cambridge, MA: Harvard University Press.

Whiting, B. B., & Whiting, J. W. (1975). *Children of six cultures: A psychocultural analysis.* Cambridge, MA: Harvard University Press.

Whitley, B. E. (1997). Gender differences in computer-related attitudes and behavior: A meta-analysis. Computers in *Human Behavior, 13,* 1–22. doi:10.1016/S0747-5632(96)00026-X

Whitney, M. P., & Thoman, E. B. (1994). Sleep in premature and full-term infants from 24-hour home recordings. *Infant Behavior and Development, 17,* 223–234. doi:10.1016/0163-6383(94)90001-9

Wichstrom, L. (1999). The emergence of gender difference in depressed mood during adolescence: The role of intensified gender socialization. *Developmental Psychology, 35,* 232–245.

Wickrama, K. A. S., Lorenz, F. O., Conger, R. D., Elder, G. H., Jr., Abraham, W. T., & Fang, S.-A. (2006). Changes in family financial circumstances and the physical health of married and recently divorced mothers. *Social Science and Medicine, 63,* 123–136. doi:10.1016/j.socscimed.2005.12.003

Widen, S. C., & Naab, P. (2012). Can an anger face also be scared? Malleability of facial expressions. *Emotion, 12,* 919–925.

Widen, S. C., & Russell, J. A. (2003). A closer look at preschoolers' freely produced labels for facial expressions. *Developmental Psychology, 39,* 114–127.

Widen, S. C., & Russell, J. A. (2010a). Children's scripts for social emotions: Causes and consequences are more central than are facial expressions. *British Journal of Developmental Psychology, 28,* 565–581.

Widen, S. C., & Russell, J. A. (2010b). Descriptive and prescriptive definitions of emotion. *Emotion Review, 2,* 377–378.

Wiesner, M., & Kim, H. K. (2006). Co-occurring delinquency and depressive symptoms of adolescent boys and girls: A dual trajectory modeling approach. *Developmental Psychology, 42,* 1220–1235. doi:10.1037/0012-1649.42.6.1220

Wigfield, A., Eccles, J. S., Schiefele, U., Rosser, R. W., & Davis-Kean, P. (2006). Development of achievement motivation. In W. Damon & R. M. Lerner (Series Eds.) & N. Eisenberg (Vol. Ed.), *Handbook of child psychology: Vol. 3. Social, emotional, and personality development* (6th ed., pp. 933–1002). Hoboken, NJ: Wiley.

Wigfield, A., Eccles, J. S., Yoon, K. S., Harold, R. D., Arbreton, A. J. A., Freedman-Doan, C., & Blumenfeld, P. C. (1997). Change in children's competence beliefs and subjective task values across the elementary school years: A 3-year study. *Journal of Educational Psychology, 89,* 451–469. doi:10.1037/0022-0663.89.3.451

Wiggers, M., & van Lieshout, C. F. (1985). Development of recognition of emotions: Children's reliance on situational and facial expressive cues. *Developmental Psychology, 21,* 338–349.

Wilgenbusch, T., & Merrell, K. W. (1999). Gender differences in self-concept among children and adolescents: A meta-analysis of multidimensional studies. *School Psychology Quarterly, 14,* 101–120. doi:10.1037/h0089000

Wilk, S. L., Desmarais, L. B., & Sackett, P. R. (1995). Gravitation of jobs commensurate with ability: Longitudinal and cross-sectional tests. *Journal of Applied Psychology, 80,* 79–85.

Williams, T. S., Connolly, J., Pepler, D., & Craig, W. (2003). Questioning and sexual minority adolescents: High school experiences of bullying, sexual harassment, and physical victimization. *Canadian Journal of Community Mental Health, 22*(2), 47–58.

Williams, T., Connolly, J., Pepler, D., & Craig, W. (2005). Peer victimization, social support, and psychosocial adjustment of sexual minority adolescents. *Journal of Youth and Adolescence, 34,* 471–482. doi:10.1007/s10964-005-7264-x

Willinger, M. (1995). SIDS prevention. *Pediatric Annals, 24,* 358–364.

Willis, C. (2009). *Teaching infants, toddlers, and twos with special needs.* Beltsville, MD: Gryphon House.

Wilson, E. O. (1975). *Sociobiology: The new synthesis.* Cambridge, MA: Belknap Press of Harvard University Press.

Wilson, M., & Brooks-Gunn, J. (2001). Health status and behaviors of unwed fathers. *Children and Youth Services Review, 23,* 377–401. doi:10.1016/S0190-7409(01)00138-4

Wilson, S. P., & Kipp, K. (1998). The development of efficient inhibition: Evidence from directed-forgetting tasks. *Developmental Review, 18,* 86–123. doi:10.1006/drev.1997.0445

Wilson, T. D. (2002). *Strangers to ourselves: Discovering the adaptive unconscious.* Cambridge, MA: Harvard University Press.

Wilson, T. D., & Dunn, E. W. (2004). Self-knowledge: Its limits, value, and potential for improvement. *Annual Review of Psychology, 55,* 493–518. doi:10.1146/annurev.psych.55.090902.141954

Wimmer, H., Mayringer, H., & Raberger, T. (1999). Reading and dual-task balancing: Evidence against the automatization deficit explanation of developmental dyslexia. Journal of Learning Disabilities, 32, 473–478.

Winner, E. (1996). *Gifted children: Myths and realities.* New York, NY: Basic Books.

Winsler, A., De Leon, J. R., Wallace, B. A., Carlton, M. P., & Willson-Quayle, A. (2003). Private speech in preschool children: Developmental stability and change, across-task consistency, and relations with classroom behaviour. *Journal of Child Language, 30,* 583–608.

Witherington, D. C., Campos, J. J., & Hertenstein, M. J. (2007). Principles of emotion and its development in infancy. In J. G. Bremner &

A. Fogel (Eds.), *Blackwell handbook of infant development* (pp. 427–464). Malden, MA: Blackwell.

Witherington, D. C., & Crichton, J. A. (2007). Frameworks for understanding emotions and their development: Functionalist and dynamic systems approaches. *Emotion, 7,* 628–637. doi:10.1037/1528-3542.7.3.628

Witkowska, E., & Gådin, K. G. (2005). Have you been sexually harassed in school? What female high school students regard as harassment. *International Journal of Adolescent Medicine and Health, 17,* 391–406. doi:10.1515/IJAMH.2005.17.4.391

Wittmann, B. C., Daw, N. D., Seymour, B., & Dolan, R. J. (2008). Striatal activity underlies novelty-based choice in humans. *Neuron, 58,* 967–973. doi:10.1016/j.neuron.2008.04.027

Witvliet, M., Brendgen, M., van Lier, P. A., Koot, H. M., & Vitaro, F. (2010). Early adolescent depressive symptoms: Prediction from clique isolation, loneliness, and perceived social acceptance. *Journal of Abnormal Child Psychology, 38,* 1045–1056. doi:10.1007/s10802-010-9426-x

Witvliet, M., Olthof, T., Hoeksma, J. B., Goossens, F. A., Smits, M. S. I., & Koot, H. M. (2010). Peer group affiliation of children: The role of perceived popularity, likeability, and behavioral similarity in bullying. *Social Development, 19,* 285–303. doi:10.1111/j.1467-9507.2009.00544.x

Wolfe, S. M., Toro, P. A., & McCaskill, P. A. (1999). A comparison of homeless and matched housed adolescents on family environment variables. *Journal of Research on Adolescence, 9,* 53–66. doi:10.1207/s15327795jra0901_3

Wolff, P. H. (1987). *The development of behavioral states and the expression of emotions in early infancy: New proposals for investigation.* Chicago, IL: University of Chicago Press.

Wolitzky-Taylor, K. B., Ruggiero, K. J., Danielson, C. K., Resnick, H. S., Hanson, R. F., Smith, D. W., … Kilpatrick, D. G. (2008). Prevalence and correlates of dating violence in a national sample of adolescents. *Journal of the American Academy of Child and Adolescent Psychiatry, 47,* 755–762. doi:10.1097/CHI.0b013e318172ef5f

Wolpert, L. (1991). *The triumph of the embryo.* Oxford, England: Oxford University Press.

Wood, C. C. (1976). Discriminability, response bias, and phoneme categories in discrimination of voice onset time. *Journal of the Acoustical Society of America, 60,* 1381–1389.

Wood, D. (1986). Aspects of teaching and learning. In M. Richards & P. Light (Eds.), *Children of social worlds: Development in a social context* (pp. 191–212). Cambridge, England: Polity Press.

Wood, D., Bruner, J. S., & Ross, G. (1976). The role of tutoring in problem solving. *Journal of Child Psychology and Psychiatry, and Allied Disciplines, 17,* 89–100.

Wood, J. N., & Spelke, E. S. (2005). Infants' enumeration of actions: Numerical discrimination and its signature limits. *Developmental Science, 8,* 173–181. doi:10.1111/j.1467-7687.2005.00404.x

Wood, W., & Eagly, A. H. (2002). A cross-cultural analysis of the behavior of women and men: Implications for the origins of sex differences. *Psychological Bulletin, 128,* 699–727. doi:10.1037/0033-2909.128.5.699

Woodhouse, S. S., Dykas, M. J., & Cassidy, J. (2012). Loneliness and peer relations in adolescence. *Social Development, 21,* 273–293. doi:10.1111/j.1467-9507.2011.00611.x

Woodward, A. L. (1998). Infants selectively encode the goal object of an actor's reach. *Cognition, 69,* 1–34. doi:10.1016/S0010-0277(98)00058-4

Woodward, A. L., & Hoyne, K. L. (1999). Infants' learning about words and sounds in relation to objects. *Child Development, 70,* 65–77.

Woodward, A. L., & Markman, E. M. (1998). Early word learning. In W. Damon (Series Ed.) & D. Kuhn & R. S. Siegler (Vol. Eds.), *Handbook of child psychology: Vol. 2. Cognition, perception, and language* (5th ed., pp. 371–420). Hoboken, NJ: Wiley.

Woodward, L. J., & Fergusson, D. M. (1999). Childhood peer relationship problems and psychosocial adjustment in late adolescence. *Journal of Abnormal Child Psychology, 27,* 87–104. doi:10.1023/A:1022618608802

Woolley, J. D. (1997). Thinking about fantasy: Are children fundamentally different thinkers and believers from adults? *Child Development, 68,* 991–1011. doi:10.1111/j.1467-8624.1997.tb01975.x

Woolley, J. D., & Phelps, K. E. (1994). Young children's practical reasoning about imagination. *British Journal of Developmental Psychology, 12,* 53–67. doi:10.1111/j.2044-835X.1994.tb00618.x

World Health Organization. *The WHO child growth standards* [Data file]. Available from http://www.who.int/childgrowth/standards/en/

Wortley, S., & Tanner, J. (2006). Immigration, social disadvantage and urban youth gangs: Results of a Toronto-area survey. *Canadian Journal of Urban Research, 15*(2), 18–37.

Wu, P., Robinson, C. C., Yang, C., Hart, C. H., Olsen, S. F., Porter, C. L., … Wu, X. (2002). Similarities and differences in mothers' parenting of preschoolers in China and the United States. *International Journal of Behavioral Development, 26,* 481–491. doi:10.1080/01650250143000436

Wynn, K. (1992, August 27). Addition and subtraction by human infants. *Nature, 358,* 749–750. doi:10.1038/358749a0

Wynn, K. (1995). Infants possess a system of numerical knowledge. *Current Directions in Psychological Science, 4,* 172–177.

Wynn, K. (2000). Findings of addition and subtraction in infants are robust and consistent: Reply to Wakeley, Rivera, and Langer. *Child Development, 71,* 1535–1536.

Wynn, K. (2008). Some innate foundations of social and moral cognition. In P. Carruthers, S. Laurence, & S. Stich (Eds.), *The innate mind: Foundations and the future* (pp. 330–347). Oxford, England: Oxford University Press.

Xie, H., Drabick, D. A. G., & Chen, D. (2011). Developmental trajectories of aggression from late childhood through adolescence: Similarities and differences across gender. *Aggressive Behavior, 37,* 387–404. doi:10.1002/ab.20404

Xu, F., & Arriaga, R. I. (2007). Number discrimination in 10-month-old infants. *British Journal of Developmental Psychology, 25,* 103–108.

Xu, F., & Denison, S. (2009). Statistical inference and sensitivity to sampling in 11-month-old infants. *Cognition, 112,* 97–104. doi:10.1016/j.cognition.2009.04.006

Xu, F., & Garcia, V. (2008). Intuitive statistics by 8-month-old infants. *Proceedings of the National Academy of Sciences of the United States of America, 105,* 5012–5015. doi:10.1073/pnas.0704450105

Xu, F., & Kushnir, T. (2013). Infants are rational constructivist learners. *Current Directions in Psychological Science, 22,* 28–32. doi:10.1177/0963721412469396

Xu, F., & Pinker, S. (1995). Weird past tense forms. *Journal of Child Language, 22,* 531–556.

Xu, F., & Spelke, E. S. (2000). Large number discrimination in 6-month-old infants. *Cognition, 74,* B1-B11.

Xu, L. M., Li, J. R., Huang, Y., Zhao, M., Tang, X., & Wei, L. (2012). AutismKB: An evidence-based knowledgebase of autism genetics. *Nucleic Acids Research, 40,* D1016–1022. doi:10.1093/nar/gkr1145

Xu, Y., Farver, J. A. M., Schwartz, D., & Chang, L. (2004). Social networks and aggressive behaviour in Chinese children. *International Journal of Behavioral Development, 28,* 401–410. doi:10.1080/01650250444000090

Xu, Y., Farver, J. A. M., & Zhang, Z. (2009). Temperament, harsh and indulgent parenting, and Chinese children's proactive and reactive aggression. *Child Development, 80,* 244–258. doi:10.1111/j.1467-8624.2008.01257.x

Xue, Y., & Meisels, S. J. (2004). Early literacy instruction and learning in kindergarten: Evidence from the Early Childhood Longitudinal Study—Kindergarten Class of 1998–1999. *American Educational Research Journal, 41,* 191–229.

Yamada, H. (2009). Japanese children's reasoning about conflicts with parents. *Social Development, 18,* 962–977. doi:10.1111/j.1467-9507.2008.00492.x

Yamagata, K. (1997). Representational activity during mother-child interaction: The scribbling stage of drawing. *British Journal of Developmental Psychology, 15,* 355–366. doi:10.1111/j.2044-835X.1997.tb00526.x

Yaman, A., Mesman, J., van IJzendoorn, M. H., & Bakermans-Kranenburg, M. J. (2010). Parenting and toddler aggression in second-generation immigrant families: The moderating role of child temperament. *Journal of Family Psychology, 24,* 208–211. doi:10.1037/a0019100

Yang, S.-J., Stewart, R., Kim, J.-M., Kim, S.-W., Shin, I.-S., Dewey, M., … Yoon, J.-S. (2013). Differences in predictors of traditional and cyber-bullying: A 2-year longitudinal study in Korean school children. *European Child and Adolescent Psychiatry, 22,* 309–318. doi:10.1007/s00787-012-0374-6

Yap, M. B., Allen, N. B., O'Shea, M., di Parsia, P., Simmons, J. G., & Sheeber, L. (2011). Early adolescents' temperament, emotion regulation during mother-child interactions, and depressive symptomatology. *Development and Psychopathology, 23,* 267–282. doi:10.1017/S0954579410000787

Yarrow, M. R., Scott, P. M., & Zahn-Waxler, C. Z. (1973). Learning concern for others. *Developmental Psychology, 8,* 240–260. doi:10.1037/h0034159

Yates, M., & Youniss, J. (1996). A developmental perspective on community service in adolescence. *Social Development, 5,* 85–111. doi:10.1111/j.1467-9507.1996.tb00073.x

Yau, J., & Smetana, J. G. (1996). Adolescent-parent conflict among Chinese adolescents in Hong Kong. *Child Development, 67,* 1262–1275. doi:10.1111/j.1467-8624.1996.tb01794.x

Yau, J., Smetana, J. G., & Metzger, A. (2009). Young Chinese children's authority concepts. *Social Development, 18,* 210–229. doi:10.1111/j.1467-9507.2008.00463.x

Ybarra, M. L., & Mitchell, K. J. (2007). Prevalence and frequency of internet harassment instigation: Implications for adolescent health. *Journal of Adolescent Health, 41,* 189–195. doi:10.1016/j.jadohealth.2007.03.005

Yeager, D. S., Miu, A. S., Powers, J., & Dweck, C. S. (2013). Implicit theories of personality and attributions of hostile intent: A meta-analysis, an experiment, and a longitudinal intervention. *Child Development, 84,* 1651–1667. doi:10.1111/cdev.12062

Yeates, K. O., & Selman, R. L. (1989). Social competence in the schools: Toward an integrative developmental model for intervention. *Developmental Review, 9,* 64–100. doi:10.1016/0273-2297(89)90024-5

Yonas, A. (1981). Infants' responses to optical information for collision. In R. Aslin, J. R. Alberts, & M. R. Petersen (Eds.), *Development of perception: Psychobiological perspectives: Vol. 2. The visual system* (pp. 313–334). New York, NY: Academic Press.

Yonas, A., Cleaves, W. T., & Pettersen, L. (1978). Development of sensitivity to pictorial depth. *Science, 200,* 77–79.

Yonas, A., Elieff, C. A., & Arterberry, M. E. (2002). Emergence of sensitivity to pictorial depth cues: Charting development in individual infants. *Infant Behavior and Development, 25,* 495–514. doi:10.1016/S0163-6383(02)00147-9

Young, C. B., Wu, S. S., & Menon, V. (2012). The neurodevelopmental basis of math anxiety. *Psychological Science, 23,* 492–501. doi:10.1177/0956797611429134

Young, L. D., Suomi, S. S., Harlow, H. F., & McKinney, W. T., Jr. (1973). Early stress and later response to separation in rhesus monkeys. *American Journal of Psychiatry, 130,* 400–405.

Young, S. K., Fox, N. A., & Zahn-Waxler, C. (1999). The relations between temperament and empathy in 2-year-olds. *Developmental Psychology, 35,* 1189–1197. doi:10.1037/0012-1649.35.5.1189

Youngblade, L. M., & Belsky, J. (1992). Parent-child antecedents of 5-year-olds' close friendships: A longitudinal analysis. *Developmental Psychology, 28,* 700–713. doi:10.1037/0012-1649.28.4.700

Youngblade, L. M., & Dunn, J. (1995). Individual differences in young children's pretend play with mother and sibling: Links to relationships and understanding of other people's feelings and beliefs. *Child Development, 66,* 1472–1492. doi:10.1111/j.1467-8624.1995.tb00946.x

Youniss, J. (1980). *Parents and peers in social development: A Sullivan-Piaget perspective.* Chicago, IL: University of Chicago Press.

Youniss, J., & Smollar, J. (1985). *Adolescent relations with mothers, fathers, and friends.* Chicago, IL: University of Chicago Press.

Yuan, S., & Fisher, C. (2009). "Really? She blicked the baby?": Two-year-olds learn combinatorial facts about verbs by listening. *Psychological Science, 20,* 619–626. doi:10.1111/j.1467-9280.2009.02341.x

Yuill, N., & Perner, J. (1988). Intentionality and knowledge in children's judgments of actor's responsibility and recipient's emotional reaction. *Developmental Psychology, 24,* 358–365. doi:10.1037/0012-1649.24.3.358

Zachrisson, H. D., Dearing, E., Lekhal, R., & Toppelberg, C. O. (2013). Little evidence that time in child care causes externalizing problems during early childhood in Norway. *Child Development, 84,* 1152–1170. doi:10.1111/cdev.12040

Zadnik, K., Jones, L. A., Irvin, B. C., Kleinstein, R. N., Manny, R. E., Shin, J. A., & Mutti, D. O. (2000, March 9). Myopia and ambient night-time lighting. *Nature, 404,* 143–144. doi:10.1038/35004661

Zahn-Waxler, C., Friedman, R. J., Cole, P. M., Mizuta, I., & Hiruma, N. (1996). Japanese and United States preschool children's responses to conflict and distress. *Child Development, 67,* 2462–2477.

Zahn-Waxler, C., Radke-Yarrow, M., & King, R. A. (1979). Child rearing and children's prosocial initiations toward victims of distress. *Child Development, 50,* 319–330. doi:10.2307/1129406

Zahn-Waxler, C., Radke-Yarrow, M., Wagner, E., & Chapman, M. (1992). Development of concern for others. *Developmental Psychology, 28,* 126–136. doi:10.1037/0012-1649.28.1.126

Zahn-Waxler, C., & Robinson, J. (1995). Empathy and guilt: Early origins of feelings of responsibility. In J. P. Tangney & K. W. Fischer (Eds.), *Self-conscious emotions: The psychology of shame, guilt, embarrassment, and pride* (pp. 143–173). New York, NY: Guilford Press.

Zakay, D. (1992). The role of attention in children's time perception. *Journal of Experimental Child Psychology, 54,* 355–371.

Zakay, D. (1993). The roles of non-temporal information processing load and temporal expectations in children's prospective time estimation. *Acta Psychologica, 84,* 271–280.

Zani, B. (1991). Male and female patterns in the discovery of sexuality during adolescence. *Journal of Adolescence, 14,* 163–178. doi:10.1016/0140-1971(91)90029-Q

Zarbatany, L., McDougall, P., & Hymel, S. (2000). Gender-differentiated experience in the peer culture: Links to intimacy in preadolescence. *Social Development, 9,* 62–79. doi:10.1111/1467-9507.00111

Zatorre, R. J., & Belin, P. (2001). Spectral and temporal processing in human auditory cortex. *Cerebral Cortex, 11,* 946–953.

Zatorre, R. J., Belin, P., & Penhune, V. B. (2002). Structure and function of auditory cortex: Music and speech. *Trends in Cognitive Sciences, 6,* 37–46.

Zatorre, R. J., Evans, A. C., Meyer, E., & Gjedde, A. (1992, May 8). Lateralization of phonetic and pitch discrimination in speech processing. *Science, 256,* 846–849.

Zelazo, P. D., Müller, U., Frye, D., & Marcovitch, S. (2003). The development of executive function in early childhood. *Monographs of the Society for Research in Child Development, 68*(3, Serial No. 274), 11–27.

Zelazo, P. D., Reznick, J. S., & Spinazzola, J. (1998). Representational flexibility and response control in a multistep multilocation search task. *Developmental Psychology, 34,* 203–214.

Zelazo, P. R., Zelazo, N. A., & Kolb, S. (1972, April 21). "Walking" in the newborn. *Science, 176,* 314–315.

Zeman, J., & Garber, J. (1996). Display rules for anger, sadness, and pain: It depends on who is watching. *Child Development, 67,* 957–973.

Zentner, M. R., & Kagan, J. (1996, September 5). Perception of music by infants [Letter to the editor]. Nature, 383, 29. doi:10.1038/383029a0

Zentner, M. R., & Kagan, J. (1998). Infants' perception of consonance and dissonance in music. *Infant Behavior and Development, 21,* 483–492. doi:10.1016/S0163-6383(98)90021-2

Zevalkink, J., Riksen-Walraven, J. M., & Van Lieshout, C. F. (1999). Attachment in the Indonesian caregiving context. *Social Development, 8,* 21–40.

Zevenbergen, A. A., & Whitehurst, G. J. (2003). Dialogic reading: A shared picture book reading intervention for preschoolers. In A. van Kleeck, S. A. Stahl, & E. B. Bauer (Eds.), *On reading books to children: Parents and teachers* (pp. 177–200). Mahwah, NJ: Erlbaum.

Zevin, J. D., Datta, H., & Skipper, J. I. (2012). Sensitive periods for language and recovery from stroke: Conceptual and practical parallels. *Developmental Psychobiology, 54,* 332–342. doi:10.1002/dev.20626

Zhai, F., Brooks-Gunn, J., & Waldfogel, J. (2011). Head Start and urban children's school readiness: A birth cohort study in 18 cities. *Developmental Psychology, 47,* 134–152. doi:10.1037/a0020784

Zhang, S. (1997). Investigation of behavior problem of only child in kindergarten children in a Beijing urban area. *International Medical Journal, 4,* 117–118.

Zhang, T.-Y., & Meaney, M. J. (2010). Epigenetics and the environmental regulation of the genome and its function. *Annual Review of Psychology, 61,* 439–466. doi:10.1146/annurev.psych.60.110707.163625

Zheng, W., & Shimmele, C. (2009). Divorce and repartnering. In M. Baker (Ed.), *Families: Changing trends in Canada.* Whitby, ON: McGraw-Hill Ryerson.

Zhou, Q., Eisenberg, N., Wang, Y., & Reiser, M. (2004). Chinese children's effortful control and dispositional anger/frustration: Relations to parenting styles and children's social functioning. *Developmental Psychology, 40,* 352–366. doi:10.1037/0012-1649.40.3.352

Zhou, Q., Wang, Y., Deng, X., Eisenberg, N., Wolchik, S. A., & Tein, J.-Y. (2008). Relations of parenting and temperament to Chinese children's experience of negative life events, coping efficacy, and externalizing problems. *Child Development, 79,* 493–513. doi:10.1111/j.1467-8624.2008.01139.x

Ziegler, J. C., Pech-Georgel, C., George, F., Alario, F.-X., & Lorenzi, C. (2005). Deficits in speech perception predict language learning impairment. *Proceedings of the National Academy of Sciences of the United States of America, 102,* 14110–14115. doi:10.1073/pnas.0504446102

Zimmer, E. Z., Chao, C. R., Guy, G. P., Marks, F., & Fifer, W. P. (1993). Vibroacoustic stimulation evokes human fetal micturition. *Obstetrics and Gynecology, 81,* 178–180.

Zimmer-Gembeck, M. J., Siebenbruner, J., & Collins, W. A. (2001). Diverse aspects of dating: Associations with psychosocial functioning from early to middle adolescence. *Journal of Adolescence, 24,* 313–336. doi:10.1006/jado.2001.0410

Zimmer-Gembeck, M. J., Siebenbruner, J., & Collins, W. A. (2004). A prospective study of intraindividual and peer influences on adolescents' heterosexual romantic and sexual behavior. *Archives of Sexual Behavior, 33,* 381–394. doi:10.1023/B:ASEB.0000028891.16654.2c

Zimmer-Gembeck, M. J., & Skinner, E. A. (2011). Review: The development of coping across childhood and adolescence: An integrative review and critique of research. *International Journal of Behavioral Development, 35,* 1–17. doi:10.1177/0165025410384923

Zimmerman, F. J., Christakis, D. A., & Meltzoff, A. N. (2007). Associations between media viewing and language development in children under age 2 years. *Journal of Pediatrics, 151,* 364–368. doi:10.1016/j.jpeds.2007.04.071

Zimmermann, P., Maier, M. A., Winter, M., & Grossmann, K. E. (2001). Attachment and adolescents' emotion regulation during a joint problem-solving task with a friend. *International Journal of Behavioral Development, 25,* 331–343.

Zlotnick, C., Kronstadt, D., & Klee, L. (1998). Foster care children and family homelessness. *American Journal of Public Health, 88,* 1368–1370. doi:10.2105/AJPH.88.9.1368

Zucker, K. J. (2006). Commentary on Langer and Martin's (2004) "How dresses can make you mentally ill: Examining gender identity disorder in children." *Child and Adolescent Social Work Journal, 23,* 533–555. doi:10.1007/s10560-006-0074-5

Zucker, K. J., & Bradley, S. J. (1995). Gender identity disorder and psychosexual problems in children and adolescents. New York, NY: Guilford Press.

Name Index

Note: Page references followed by an *f* indicate a figure; those followed by a *t* indicate a table; and those followed by an *n* indicate a source note.

Subject Index

Note: Page references followed by an *f* indicate a figure; those followed by a *t* indicate a table; those followed by an *n* indicate a note.